Lecture Notes in Artificial Intelligence 4027

Edited by J. G. Carbonell and J. Siekmann

Subseries of Lecture Notes in Computer Science

Henrik Legind Larsen   Gabriella Pasi
Daniel Ortiz-Arroyo   Troels Andreasen
Henning Christiansen (Eds.)

Flexible Query Answering Systems

7th International Conference, FQAS 2006
Milan, Italy, June 7-10, 2006
Proceedings

Volume Editors

Henrik Legind Larsen
Daniel Ortiz-Arroyo
Aalborg University Esbjerg Computer Science Department
Niels Bohrs Vej 8, 6700 Esbjerg, Denmark
E-mail: hll@sis-rc.org, do@cs.aaue.dk

Gabriella Pasi
Università degli Studi di Milano Bicocca
Via Bicocca degli Arcimboldi 8, 20126 Milano, Italy
E-mail: pasi@disco.unimib.it

Troels Andreasen
Henning Christiansen
Roskilde University, Computer Science Section
P.O. Box 260, 4000 Roskilde, Denmark
E-mail: {troels, henning}@ruc.dk

Library of Congress Control Number: 2006926504

CR Subject Classification (1998): I.2, H.3, H.2, H.4, H.5

LNCS Sublibrary: SL 7 – Artificial Intelligence

ISSN 0302-9743
ISBN-10 3-540-34638-4 Springer Berlin Heidelberg New York
ISBN-13 978-3-540-34638-8 Springer Berlin Heidelberg New York

Springer is a part of Springer Science+Business Media

springer.com

Printed in Germany

Typesetting: Camera-ready by author, data conversion by Scientific Publishing Services, Chennai, India
Printed on acid-free paper SPIN: 11766254 06/3142 5 4 3 2 1 0

Preface

This volume constitutes the proceedings of the 7th International Conference on Flexible Query Answering Systems, FQAS 2006, held in Milan, Italy, on June 7-10, 2006. FQAS 2006 is preceded by the 1994, 1996 and 1998 editions, held in Roskilde, Denmark. More recently, FQAS 2000 was held in Warsaw, Poland, and the 2002 and 2004 editions were held in Copenhagen, Denmark, and in Lyon, France, respectively.

FQAS is the premier conference concerned with the very important issue of providing users of information systems with flexible querying capabilities and with an easy and intuitive access to information. More specifically, the overall theme of the FQAS conferences is the modelling and design of innovative and flexible modalities for accessing information systems. The main objective is to achieve more expressive, informative, cooperative, and productive systems which facilitate retrieval from information repositories such as databases, libraries, heterogeneous archives, and the Web.

The usual information systems are typically equipped with standard query languages or access modalities which are often inadequate to express user needs as well as to effectively visualize the retrieved results. FQAS is a multidisciplinary conference that draws on several research areas, including information retrieval, database management, information filtering, knowledge representation, computational linguistics and natural language processing, artificial intelligence, soft computing, classical and non-classical logics, and human–computer interaction.

Several fields are covered by the papers included in the conference proceedings among which are information retrieval, database management, query-answering, knowledge discovery and mining techniques, semantic Web technologies spanning ontology and context modelling, user modelling and personalization.

These proceedings contain 60 original papers from various fields addressing key topics in FQAS. We wish to thank all contributors for their excellent papers and the referees, publisher, and sponsors for their efforts. We thank the organizers of the special sessions: Rita De Caluwe, Guy De Tré, Gabriella Kazai, Mounia Lalmas, Luis Iraola, Carolina Gallardo, and Jesús Cardeñosa. Special thanks also to the invited speakers: Stefano Ceri from Politecnico di Milano and Prabhakar Raghavan from Yahoo! Research. Finally, we extend our gratitude to the members of the International Advisory Board, the members of the International Program Committee, the additional reviewers, and the session chairs. All of them made the success of FQAS 2006 possible.

April 2006

Henrik Legind Larsen
Gabriella Pasi
Daniel Ortiz-Arroyo
Troels Andreasen
Henning Christiansen

Preface

This volume constitutes the proceedings of the 7th International Conference on Flexible Query Answering Systems, FQAS 2006, held in Milan, Italy, on June 7–10, 2006. FQAS 2006 is preceded by the 1994, 1996 and 1998 editions, held in Roskilde, Denmark, then the FQAS 2000 held in Warsaw, Poland, and the 2002 and 2004 editions were held in Copenhagen, Denmark, and in Lyon, France, respectively.

FQAS is the premier conference concerned with the very important issue of providing users of information systems with flexible querying capabilities, and with an easy and intuitive access to information. More specifically, the overall theme of the FQAS conferences is the modelling and design of innovative and flexible modalities for accessing information systems. The main objective is to achieve more expressive, informative, cooperative, and productive systems which facilitate retrieval of information from sources such as databases, libraries, heterogeneous archives, and the Web.

The usual information systems are typically equipped with standard query languages or access modalities which are often inadequate to express user needs as well as to effectively visualize the retrieved results. FQAS is a multidisciplinary conference drawing on several research areas, including information retrieval, database management, information filtering, knowledge representation, computational linguistics and natural language processing, artificial intelligence, soft computing, classical and non-classical logics, and human–computer interaction.

These fields are covered by the papers included in the conference proceedings among which several are [illegible] information retrieval, [illegible] query answering, [illegible] Web [illegible] ontologies, [illegible] query [illegible] modelling, user modelling, and personalization.

These proceedings consist of original papers from various fields addressing key topics in FQAS. We wish to thank all contributors for their excellent papers and the referees, publisher, and sponsors for their effort. We thank the organizers of the special sessions: Elsa [illegible], Guy De Tré, Gabriella Pasi, Montserrat [illegible], Luis Iraola, Carolina Gallardo, and Jesús Cardeñosa. Special thanks also to the invited speakers: Stefano Ceri from Politecnico di Milano and Prabhakar Raghavan from Yahoo! Research. Finally, we extend our gratitude to the members of the International Advisory Board, the members of the International Program Committee, the additional reviewers and the session chairs. All of them made the success of FQAS 2006 possible.

April 2006

Henrik Legind Larsen
Gabriella Pasi
Daniel Ortiz-Arroyo
Troels Andreasen
Henning Christiansen

Organization

FQAS 2006 was organized by the Department of Informatics, Systems and Communication (DISCo) of the Università degli Studi di Milano Bicocca, Italy, and by the Department of Computer Science, Aalborg University Esbjerg in collaboration with the Center for TeleInFrastruktur (CTIF), Aalborg University. The local organization was done in cooperation with AEIT (Federazione di Elettrotecnica, Elettronica, Automazione, Informatica e Telecomunicazioni).

Conference Committee

Co-chairs Henrik Legind Larsen (Aalborg University Esbjerg, Denmark)
Gabriella Pasi (Università degli Studi di Milano Bicocca, Italy)

Organization Committee

Carlo Batini, Università degli Studi di Milano Bicocca, Italy
Gloria Bordogna, CNR-IDPA, Italy
Stefano Ceri, Politecnico di Milano, Italy
Ernesto Damiani, Università degli Studi di Milano, Italy
Luciano D'Andrea, AEIT, Milano, Italy
Daniel Ortiz-Arroyo, Aalborg University Esbjerg, Denmark

Local Organization

Luciano D'Andrea, AEIT, Italy
Giuseppe Notaro, AEIT, Italy
Fabrizia Pellegrini, Università degli Studi di Milano Bicocca, Italy
Silvia Robaldo, Università degli Studi di Milano Bicocca, Italy
Robert Villa, CNR, Italy

Program Committee

Maristella Agosti, Italy
Gianni Amati, Italy
Troels Andreasen, Denmark
Francesca Arcelli, Italy
Elham Ashoori, UK
Djamal Benslimane, France
Catherine Berrut, France
Elisa Bertino, Italy

Gloria Bordogna, Italy
Bernadette Bouchon-Meunier, France
Mohand Boughanem, France
Jan Chomicki, USA
Henning Christiansen, Denmark
Davide Ciucci, Italy
Marco Colombetti, Italy
Fabio Crestani, UK
Juan Carlos Cubero, Spain
Ernesto Damiani, Italy
Agnieszka Dardzinska, Poland
Flavio De Paoli, Italy
Guy De Tré, Belgium
Alberto Del Bimbo, Italy
Marcin Detyniecki, France
Didier Dubois, France
Hans Dybkjær, Denmark
Ronald Fagin, USA
Juan Manuel Fernandez-Luna, Spain
Carolina Gallardo-Pérez, Spain
Alexander Gelbukh, Mexico
Mercedes Martínez González, Spain
Marco Gori, Italy
Enrique Herrera-Viedma, Spain
Luis Iraola, Spain
Hideo Joho, UK
Gareth Jones, UK
Francois-Xavier Josset, France
Jaap Kamps, Holland
Gabriella Kazai, UK
Etienne Kerre, Belgium
Werner Kiessling, Germany
Mounia Lalmas, UK
Lars Bo Larsen, Denmark
Anne Laurent, France
Vincenzo Loia, Italy
David Losada, Spain
Christophe Marsala, France
Maria Jose Martín-Bautista, Spain
Andrea Maurino, Italy
Riccardo Mazza, Switzerland
Enza Messina, Italy
Stefano Mizzaro, Italy
Manuel Montes-y-Gómez, Mexico
Ashley Morris, USA
Amihai Motro, USA
Noureddine Mouaddib, France
Jose Olivas, Spain
Daniel Ortiz-Arroyo, Denmark
Stefano Paraboschi, Italy
Jovan Pehcevski, Australia
Olivier Pivert, France
Olga Pons, Spain
Giuseppe Psaila, Italy
Zbigniew Ras, USA
Guillaume Raschia, France
Berthier Ribeiro-Neto, Chile
Elie Sanchez, France
Raimondo Schettini, Italy
Michel Scholl, France
Fabrizio Sebastiani, Italy
Andrzej Skowron, Poland
Nicolas Spyratos, France
Christopher Stokoe, UK
Umberto Straccia, Italy
Heiner Stuckenschmidt, Netherlands
Lynda Tamine, France
Letizia Tanca, Italy
Zahir Tari, Australia
Bernd Thomas, Germany
Vicenc Torra, Spain
Farouk Toumani, France
María Amparo Vila, Spain
Robert Villa, Italy
Luis Villaseñor-Pineda, Mexico
Peter Vojtas, Slovakia
Adnan Yazici, Turkey
Fabio Zanzotto, Italy

International Advisory Board

Troels Andreasen, Denmark
Patrick Bosc, France
Jesús Cardeñosa, Spain
Henning Christiansen, Denmark

Bruce Croft, USA
Rita De Caluwe, Belgium
Robert Demolombe, France
Jorgen Fischer Nilsson, Denmark
Norbert Fuhr, Germany
Christian S. Jensen, Denmark
Janusz Kacprzyk, Poland
Don Kraft, USA
Henrik Legind Larsen, Denmark
Amihai Motro, USA
Gabriella Pasi, Italy
Henri Prade, France
Keith van Rijsbergen, UK
Ronald R. Yager, USA
Slawomir Zadrozny, Poland

Sponsoring Institutions

AICA - Associazione Italiana per l'informatica ed il Calcolo Automatico
DISCo Università degli Studi di Milano Bicocca, Italy
Dipartimento di Tecnologie dell'Informazione - Università di Milano, Italy

Problems and Challenges in the Integration of Semantic Services

Stefano Ceri

Politecnico di Milano

About eight years ago, as a reaction to the technologist view on the essential aspects of information management community (performance, performance, performance), I claimed that there were three fundamental problems in future of information systems: semantics, semantics, semantics. The claim is becoming more and more accepted as time goes by: the current work on the semantic Web the most visible example. However, while the need for semantics grows, the hope for achieving large, internationally adopted, shared semantic knowledge seems to decrease. Rather, the effort is concentrated on building semantic islands, which can be separately proved as being internally consistent and self-sufficient for simple tasks. Then, the interaction among such isolated worlds becomes the real hard problem to solve.

In this talk, after giving some general background, I will focus on interoperability among semantic services, specifically focusing on search services. I will start from the observation that search services can become very strong in their specific semantic domain, e.g. give very good instruments for extracting knowledge from a given semantic island. However, they currently do not allow higher order search, i.e., the ability to either distribute a high level query to the right service, or to integrate results of the search into a single result. My classical example, also presented as a challenge at a recent workshop, is find an ethnical restaurant in a nice place close to Milano; the problem hinted by this example is that we may perhaps be able to find a geo-localization service understanding how close is a nice place from Milano or a trusted restaurant guide returning us a description of the food being served by restaurants together with their location. However, answering this query at the current state-of-the-art requires a strong involvement of a knowledgeable user, who should inspect the search services one at a time, feeding the results of one search as input to the next one, until he gets a reasonable answer. We will discuss how to approach this problem in a way that offers to users the impression of a higher-order search engine which performs some of the integration required by the query, thereby trying to build a bridge between semantic islands, and we will hint to other research efforts which show some common aspects with this approach.

The Changing Face of Web Search

Prabhakar Raghavan

Yahoo! Research

Web search has come to dominate our consciousness as a convenience we take for granted, as a medium for connecting advertisers and buyers, and as a fast-growing revenue source for the companies that provide this service. Following a brief overview of the state of the art and how we got there, this talk covers a spectrum of technical challenges arising in web search - ranging from spam detection to auction mechanisms.

Table of Contents

Flexibility in Database Management and Querying

Vagueness and Uncertainty in XML Querying and Retrieval

Special Session Organized by Gabriella Kazai, Mounia Lalmas, and Gabriella Pasi

Information Retrieval and Filtering

Knowledge and Data Extraction

Intelligent Information Extraction from Texts

Special Session Organized by Luis Iraola, Carolina Gallardo, and Jesus Cardeñosa

Knowledge Representation and Reasoning

Project-Join-Repair: An Approach to Consistent Query Answering Under Functional Dependencies

Jef Wijsen

Université de Mons-Hainaut, Mons, Belgium
jef.wijsen@umh.ac.be
http://staff.umh.ac.be/Wijsen.Jef/

Abstract. *Consistent query answering* is the term commonly used for the problem of answering queries on databases that violate certain integrity constraints. We address this problem for universal relations that are inconsistent with respect to a set of functional dependencies. In order to obtain more meaningful repairs, we apply a project-join dependency prior to repairing by tuple deletion. A positive result is that the additional project-join can yield tractability of consistent query answering.

1 Motivation

In the Internet age, data are ubiquitous and cannot be expected to be globally consistent. The database systems in which such data are stored and queried, should be capable of handling this *inconsistency* phenomenon. A way to deal with the problem is to rectify the database before proceeding to queries. Since there is usually no single best way to solve an inconsistency, we will generally end up with a set of possible *database repairs*. Such set of possible databases defines an *incomplete database*, a concept that has been studied for a long time [1]. When a query is asked on an incomplete database, the *certain query answer* is defined as the intersection of the answers to the query on every possible database. The motivation for intersecting query answers should be clear: although we do not know which database is the "right" one, we do know that it will (at least) return this certain answer. If the incomplete database is made up of repairs, the certain answer has also been called the *consistent answer*.

Repairing with respect to functional and key dependencies is commonly done by tuple deletion (inserting new tuples will not take away the inconsistency anyway). In this article, we propose a novel approach, termed "project-join-repair," for repairing a universal relation subject to a set of functional dependencies (fd's). We next motivate the approach by three examples.

Example 1. The first row in the following relation states that on January 7, twenty units of product P1 have been shipped to customer C1 called A. Jones. The constraints are $\mathsf{Cid} \rightarrow \mathsf{CName}$ (the same identifier cannot be used for different customers) and, since quantities are daily totals per product and client, $\{\mathsf{Date}, \mathsf{Pid}, \mathsf{Cid}\} \rightarrow \mathsf{Qty}$. The first fd is violated, because C1 appears with two

H.L. Larsen et al. (Eds.): FQAS 2006, LNAI 4027, pp. 1–12, 2006.

different names. We could repair this relation by deleting either the first or the second tuple. However, it may be more meaningful to assume that names are mistaken, and that "A. Johnson" should read "A. Jones," or *vice versa*.

I	Date	Pid	Qty	Cid	CName
	7 Jan	P1	20	C1	A. Jones
	8 Feb	P2	15	C1	A. Johnson

We propose a novel way to make the intended rectification. First, we apply the join dependency $\bowtie[\{\mathsf{Date},\mathsf{Pid},\mathsf{Qty},\mathsf{Cid}\},\{\mathsf{Cid},\mathsf{CName}\}]$, that is, we take the join of the projections on $\{\mathsf{Date},\mathsf{Pid},\mathsf{Qty},\mathsf{Cid}\}$ and $\{\mathsf{Cid},\mathsf{CName}\}$. This join dependency (jd) corresponds to a lossless-join decomposition in third normal form (3NF). The lossless-join property means that applying the jd will not insert new tuples into consistent relations. However, since one fd is violated in our example, the join contains two new tuples (followed by $*$).

$\pi_{\mathsf{Date},\mathsf{Pid},\mathsf{Qty},\mathsf{Cid}}(I)$	Date	Pid	Qty	Cid
	7 Jan	P1	20	C1
	8 Feb	P2	15	C1

$\pi_{\mathsf{Cid},\mathsf{CName}}(I)$	Cid	CName
	C1	A. Jones
	C1	A. Johnson

	Date	Pid	Qty	Cid	CName	
$\pi_{\mathsf{Date},\mathsf{Pid},\mathsf{Qty},\mathsf{Cid}}(I)$	7 Jan	P1	20	C1	A. Jones	
$\bowtie$	8 Feb	P2	15	C1	A. Johnson	
$\pi_{\mathsf{Cid},\mathsf{CName}}(I)$	7 Jan	P1	20	C1	A. Johnson	$(*)$
	8 Feb	P2	15	C1	A. Jones	$(*)$

Next, we take as repairs the maximal (under set inclusion) consistent subsets of the join relation. This gives us the two intended repairs:

J_1	Date	Pid	Qty	Cid	CName
	7 Jan	P1	20	C1	A. Jones
	8 Feb	P2	15	C1	A. Jones

J_2	Date	Pid	Qty	Cid	CName
	8 Feb	P2	15	C1	A. Johnson
	7 Jan	P1	20	C1	A. Johnson

Example 2. The following relation I is subject to the functional dependencies $\mathsf{Name} \rightarrow \{\mathsf{Birth},\mathsf{Sex},\mathsf{ZIP}\}$ and $\mathsf{ZIP} \rightarrow \mathsf{City}$. The latter fd is violated.

I	Name	Birth	Sex	ZIP	City
	An	1964	F	7000	Mons
	Ed	1962	M	7000	Bergen

Again, instead of deleting either tuple, it is reasonable to assume that Mons should be Bergen, or *vice versa*.[1] We can obtain this effect by first applying the jd $\bowtie[\{\mathsf{Name},\mathsf{Birth},\mathsf{Sex},\mathsf{ZIP}\},\{\mathsf{ZIP},\mathsf{City}\}]$ and then repair by tuple deletion. Here are the two repairs that result from this project-join-repair scenario:

J_1	Name	Birth	Sex	ZIP	City
	An	1964	F	7000	Mons
	Ed	1962	M	7000	Mons

J_2	Name	Birth	Sex	ZIP	City
	An	1964	F	7000	Bergen
	Ed	1962	M	7000	Bergen

Again, the intended rectifications have been made.

[1] Bergen is actually the Dutch name for the city of Mons situated in the French speaking part of Belgium.

Example 3. By varying the jd, we can fine-tune the effect of the repairing work.

I Name	Birth	Sex	ZIP	City
An	1964	F	7000	Mons
An	1952	F	8000	Namur

In the above relation, both An's birth year and ZIP code are inconsistent. If we apply our project-join-repair approach relative to the join dependency $\bowtie [\{\mathsf{Name}, \mathsf{Birth}, \mathsf{Sex}, \mathsf{ZIP}\}, \{\mathsf{ZIP}, \mathsf{City}\}]$, then An's birth year 1964 will remain tied to ZIP code 7000, and 1952 to 8000. However, the join dependency $\bowtie [\{\mathsf{Name}, \mathsf{Birth}, \mathsf{Sex}\}, \{\mathsf{Name}, \mathsf{ZIP}\}, \{\mathsf{ZIP}, \mathsf{City}\}]$ allows "uncoupling" birth years and ZIP codes. In this way, we find, among others, the following repair which combines An's birth date 1964 found in the first tuple with An's ZIP code 8000 found in the second tuple:

J Name	Birth	Sex	ZIP	City
An	1964	F	8000	Namur

This way of repairing may be meaningful in a situation where the first row about An comes from a data source that is precise on birth dates, while the second row comes from a data source that is precise on ZIP codes.

It is tempting to think that the effect of the project-join-repair approach could also be obtained by repairing the projections, instead of repairing the join relation. However, this is generally not true. The first tuple in the following relation means that An is living in Belgium, earns 10K, and pays 20% taxes. The constraints are $\mathsf{Name} \rightarrow \mathsf{Country}$, $\mathsf{Name} \rightarrow \mathsf{Income}$, and $\{\mathsf{Country}, \mathsf{Income}\} \rightarrow \mathsf{Tax}$. The latter functional dependency expresses that the tax rate depends on the country and the income. The projections corresponding to the join dependency $\bowtie [\{\mathsf{Name}, \mathsf{Country}\}, \{\mathsf{Name}, \mathsf{Income}\}, \{\mathsf{Country}, \mathsf{Income}, \mathsf{Tax}\}]$ are shown.

I Name	Country	Income	Tax
An	Belgium	10K	20%
An	France	12K	20%

$\pi_{\mathsf{Name},\mathsf{Country}}(I)$

Name	Country
An	Belgium
An	France

$\pi_{\mathsf{Name},\mathsf{Income}}(I)$

Name	Income
An	10K
An	12K

$\pi_{\mathsf{Country},\mathsf{Income},\mathsf{Tax}}(I)$

Country	Income	Tax
Belgium	10K	20%
France	12K	20%

Now consider what happens when we repair the three components by tuple deletion. If we retain $\{\mathsf{Name} : \text{An}, \mathsf{Country} : \text{Belgium}\}$ in the first component, and $\{\mathsf{Name} : \text{An}, \mathsf{Income} : \text{12K}\}$ in the second, then the joined tuple $\{\mathsf{Name} : \text{An}, \mathsf{Country} : \text{Belgium}, \mathsf{Income} : \text{12K}\}$ does not match any tuple in the third component. That is, the join of the repaired components can be empty. On the other hand, the project-join-repair approach will first join the three (unrepaired) components, which in this case happens to yield the original relation I. The result of the join will then be repaired by tuple deletion. No repair will be empty.

The remainder of the article is organized as follows. Section 2 defines the query class of *rooted rules*. Section 3 defines the problem we are interested in, namely the complexity of consistent query answering under the project-join-repair approach. Section 4 introduces acyclic sets of fd's and their properties. Section 5 presents the main result of the article, which is the tractability of consistent query answering under the project-join-repair approach in cases of practical interest. Section 6 contains a comparison with related work.

2 Rooted Rules

We will assume a single "universal" relation, which will be subject to decompositions.

Definition 1. *We assume a set of* variables *disjoint from a set of* constants. *A* symbol *is either a constant or a variable. A relation schema is a sequence* $\langle A_1, A_2, \ldots, A_n \rangle$ *of distinct* attributes. *The definitions to follow are relative to this relation schema.*

For tuples and relations, we will use both the named *and* unnamed *perspective [2], whichever is most convenient in the technical treatment. Under the unnamed perspective, a* tuple *is a sequence* $\langle s_1, \ldots, s_n \rangle$ *of symbols. If each* s_i *is a constant, then the tuple is called* ground. *Under the named perspective, this tuple is encoded by the mapping* $\{(A_1, s_1), \ldots, (A_n, s_n)\}$.

A relation *is a finite set of tuples. We will require that relations be* typed, *meaning that the same variable cannot appear in distinct columns. A relation is* ground *if all its tuples are ground.*

The construct of conjunctive query, also called rule, is defined as usual [2], with the minor difference that we assume a single relation and hence do not need distinguished relation symbols. We then proceed by defining the subclass of rooted rules.

Definition 2. *A* rule-based conjunctive query *(or simply* rule*)* q *is an expression of the form* $h \leftarrow B$ *where the rule* body B *is a (typed) relation and the rule* head h *is a tuple such that every variable that occurs in* h *also occurs in* B. *The* answer *to this rule* q *on a (not necessarily ground) relation* I, *denoted* $q(I)$, *is defined by* $q(I) = \{\theta(h) \mid \theta$ *is a substitution such that* $\theta(B) \subseteq I\}$. *A rule* $\langle\rangle \leftarrow B$, *with a head of zero arity, is called Boolean; the answer to such rule is either* $\{\langle\rangle\}$ *or* $\{\}$.

Free variables are defined as usual. To define the notion of free tuple, we assume that the relation schema under consideration has a unique key K. Then, a tuple in the body of a rule is called free if its key value is composed of constants and free variables only. A quasi-free variable is a variable that occurs only in free tuples.

Definition 3. *Assume relation schema* $\langle A_1, A_2, \ldots, A_n \rangle$ *with a unique key* $K \subseteq \{A_1, \ldots, A_n\}$. *Let* $q : h \leftarrow B$ *be a rule. A variable is called* free *if it occurs in* h*; otherwise it is* nonfree. *A tuple* $t \in B$ *is called free if for each* $A_i \in K$, $t(A_i)$ *is either a free variable or a constant. A nonfree variable is called* quasi-free *if it occurs only in free tuples.*

To gain some intuition, assume schema $\langle A_1, \ldots, A_n \rangle$ with key $K = \{A_1, \ldots, A_k\}$ ($k \leq n$). Let $\langle \underline{s_1, \ldots, s_k}, s_{k+1}, \ldots, s_n \rangle$ be a tuple in the rule body, where underlined symbols correspond to key attributes. Assume that one of $s_{k+1}, \ldots, s_n$ is a quasi-free variable, say z. Since quasi-free variables occur only in free tuples, each $s_1, \ldots, s_k$ must be a constant or a free variable. If θ is a valuation that maps the rule body into a relation that satisfies the key constraint, then the value $\theta(z)$ is fully determined by the value of θ on the free variables.

Finally, a rule is rooted if every variable that occurs more than once in it, is free or quasi-free.

Definition 4. *Assume relation schema $\langle A_1, A_2, \ldots, A_n \rangle$ with a unique key $K \subseteq \{A_1, \ldots, A_n\}$. A rule $q : h \leftarrow B$ is called* rooted *if every variable that occurs more than once in B, is either free or quasi-free.*

Two rooted rules relative to the relation schema $\langle \mathsf{Name}, \mathsf{Birth}, \mathsf{Sex}, \mathsf{ZIP}, \mathsf{City} \rangle$ of Example 2 are shown next, in which the underlined positions correspond to the key Name. Since all tuples in the rule bodies are free, all variables can have multiple occurrences.

- Get names of male persons living in An's city.

$$\langle x_n \rangle \leftarrow \langle \underline{x_n}, x_b, \mathrm{M}, x_z, x_c \rangle, \langle \underline{\mathrm{An}}, y_b, y_s, y_z, x_c \rangle$$

- For each male person, get names of same-aged female persons living in the same city.

$$\langle x_n, y_n \rangle \leftarrow \langle \underline{x_n}, x_b, \mathrm{M}, x_z, x_c \rangle, \langle \underline{y_n}, x_b, \mathrm{F}, y_z, x_c \rangle$$

  If we remove y_n from the rule head, then this rule is no longer rooted. Indeed, after removing y_n from the rule head, the last tuple is no longer free, hence x_b and x_c are no longer quasi-free and must not occur more than once.

3 Consistent Query Answering

We assume familiarity with the notions of *functional dependency* (fd) and *multivalued dependency* (mvd) [3, 2]. Join dependencies and keys are recalled next.

Definition 5. *Let $U = \{A_1, \ldots, A_n\}$, the set of attributes. A* join dependency *(jd) σ is an expression $\bowtie [X_1, \ldots, X_m]$ where $\bigcup_{i=1}^{m} X_i = U$. The result of* applying this jd *σ on relation I, denoted $\sigma(I)$, is defined by $\sigma(I) = \pi_{X_1}(I) \bowtie \pi_{X_2}(I) \ldots \bowtie \pi_{X_m}(I)$, where π and $\bowtie$ are the projection and join operators of the relational algebra. A ground relation I* satisfies *σ, denoted $I \models \sigma$, if $I = \sigma(I)$.*

If Σ is a set of fd's over U, then a key *of Σ is a minimal (under set inclusion) set $K \subseteq U$ such that $\Sigma \models K \rightarrow U$.*

The next definition introduces by-now-standard constructs of repair and consistent query answer. The motivation for intersecting query answers has been provided in the first paragraph of this article.

Definition 6. *Let Σ be a set of fd's and I a ground relation. A* repair *of I under Σ is a maximal (under set inclusion) relation $J \subseteq I$ such that $J \models \Sigma$. The* consistent query answer *to a rule q on I under Σ, denoted $q_\Sigma(I)$, is defined as follows:*

$$q_\Sigma(I) = \bigcap\{q(I) \mid I \text{ is a repair of } I \text{ under } \Sigma\} .$$

Given a set Σ of fd's and a rule q, consistent query answering is the complexity of (testing membership of) the set:

$$\mathsf{CQA}(\Sigma, q) = \{I \mid I \text{ is a ground relation and } q_\Sigma(I) = \{\}\} .^2$$

That is, on input I, decide whether I yields an empty consistent query answer. Note that the constraints and the query are fixed and the complexity is in the size of the input relation, known as "data complexity." We now introduce a novel related problem. Let Σ be a set of fd's and σ a jd such that $\Sigma \models \sigma$:

$$\mathsf{CQAJD}(\Sigma, \sigma, q) = \{I \mid I \text{ is a ground relation and } q_\Sigma(\sigma(I)) = \{\}\} .$$

Intuitively, we first repair by tuple insertion relative to the weaker constraint σ (weaker in the sense that $\Sigma \models \sigma$), which yields $\sigma(I)$. Next, we apply standard consistent query answering relative to Σ using tuple deletion. Clearly, if we choose σ to be the identity jd (that is, $\sigma = \bowtie [U]$), then $\mathsf{CQAJD}(\Sigma, \sigma, q) = \mathsf{CQA}(\Sigma, q)$. Also, $\mathsf{CQAJD}(\Sigma, \sigma, q)$ is in **NP** for any set Σ of fd's and rule q, because the jd σ can be applied in polynomial time and $\mathsf{CQA}(\Sigma, q)$ is in **NP** for fd's [4].

4 Acyclic Fd's and Preparatory Jd's

The main result of this paper will be the tractability of $\mathsf{CQAJD}(\Sigma, \sigma, q)$ under certain conditions for Σ and σ. These conditions, which are not too severe and allow many practical cases, are introduced next. First, we define acyclic sets of fd's. The definition is relative to a minimal cover of fd's, which is a reduced representative for a set of fd's. See [2, page 257] or [3, page 390].

Definition 7. *The* dependency graph *of a set Σ of fd's is defined as follows:*

- *the vertices are the dependencies of Σ;*
- *there is an oriented edge from the vertex $X \to A$ to the vertex $Y \to B$ if $A \in Y$.*

We call Σ acyclic *if it has a minimal cover whose dependency graph contains no cycle.*

For example, the set $\{AB \to C, C \to A\}$ is cyclic. The set $\{A \to B, C \to D, AD \to B, BC \to D\}$ has minimal cover $\{A \to B, C \to D\}$ and is acyclic.

[2] Note that our definition tests for emptiness of consistent query answers, whereas other authors have used the complement problem which tests for nonemptiness [4].

Theorem 1. *Every acyclic set Σ of fd's has a unique minimal cover and a unique key.*

Next, we define a restriction on jd's.

Definition 8. *Let Σ be set of fd's and σ a jd, both over the same set U of attributes. We say that σ is* repairing-preparing *for Σ, denoted $\Sigma \looparrowright \sigma$, if the following two conditions are satisfied:*

1. *$\Sigma \models \sigma$; and*
2. *for every $X \to Y \in \Sigma$, either $\Sigma \models X \to U$ or for every $A \in Y$, $\sigma \models X \twoheadrightarrow A$.*

Because of the first condition, if $\Sigma \looparrowright \sigma$, then for every relation I, $I \models \Sigma$ implies $\sigma(I) = I$. That is, applying the jd is the identity on consistent relations. The second condition, which may be less intuitive, ensures that applying the jd will distribute "erroneous" values over tuples. In Example 1, for example, the join relation satisfies $\mathsf{Cid} \twoheadrightarrow \mathsf{CName}$: both the 7 Jan and the 8 Feb shipments are joined to both names (A. Jones and A. Johnson). Clearly, $\Sigma \looparrowright \sigma$ can be decided using the chase technique [2].

Example 4. Assume $\{\mathsf{Name}, \mathsf{Birth}, \mathsf{Sex}, \mathsf{ZIP}, \mathsf{City}\}$ subject to the acyclic set $\Sigma = \{\mathsf{Name} \to \mathsf{Birth}, \mathsf{Name} \to \mathsf{Sex}, \mathsf{Name} \to \mathsf{ZIP}, \mathsf{ZIP} \to \mathsf{City}\}$. It can be verified that:

$$\Sigma \looparrowright \bowtie [\{\mathsf{Name}, \mathsf{Birth}, \mathsf{Sex}, \mathsf{ZIP}\}, \{\mathsf{ZIP}, \mathsf{City}\}]$$
$$\Sigma \looparrowright \bowtie [\{\mathsf{Name}, \mathsf{Birth}, \mathsf{Sex}\}, \{\mathsf{Name}, \mathsf{ZIP}\}, \{\mathsf{ZIP}, \mathsf{City}\}]$$

All jd's used in Section 1 are repairing-preparing.

Given Σ, a natural question is whether a jd σ that corresponds to a good decomposition in 3NF, will satisfy $\Sigma \looparrowright \sigma$. In response, we note that even for acyclic sets of fd's, the classical 3NF Synthesis algorithm (see Algorithm 11.2.13 in [2]) can yield a join dependency that is not repairing-preparing. For example, for $\Sigma = \{A \to C, B \to D, CD \to E\}$, the jd $\bowtie [AB, AC, BD, CDE]$ corresponds to the decomposition of $ABCDE$ given by this algorithm (decomposition in 3NF with a lossless join and preservation of dependencies). Since it can be verified that $\Sigma \not\models A \to ABCDE$ and $\sigma \not\models A \twoheadrightarrow C$, it follows $\Sigma \not\looparrowright \sigma$.

Finally, we note that the relation $\looparrowright$ does not depend on the representation chosen for Σ:

Proposition 1. *Let Σ and Σ' be sets of fd's, and σ a jd. If Σ and Σ' are equivalent and $\Sigma \looparrowright \sigma$, then $\Sigma' \looparrowright \sigma$.*

5 Tractability of CQAJD for Rooted Rules

We show that consistent query answering in the project-join-repair approach is tractable for rooted rules under certain restrictions for Σ and σ (Theorem 2). We then show that there are cases where repairing by mere tuple deletion is

I	Name	Birth	Sex	ZIP	City
	An	1964	F	7000	Mons
	An	1952	F	7000	Mons
	Ed	1970	M	7000	Bergen

$\rightarrow$

$\sigma(I)$	Name	Birth	Sex	ZIP	City
	An	1964	F	7000	Mons
	An	1964	F	7000	Bergen
	An	1952	F	7000	Mons
	An	1952	F	7000	Bergen
	Ed	1970	M	7000	Mons
	Ed	1970	M	7000	Bergen

$\swarrow$

H	Name	Birth	Sex	ZIP	City
	An	y	F	7000	z
	Ed	1970	M	7000	z

Fig. 1. Computing a relation H that returns consistent answers to rooted rules

intractable, but becomes tractable under project-join-repair. Finally, we show that moving beyond rooted rules leads to intractability.

The following lemma states the conditions under which project-join-repair preserves, in every repair, all key values of the original relation. We assume that each fd in a given set Σ of fd's is of the form $X \rightarrow A$, where A is a single attribute not in X.

Lemma 1. *Let Σ be an acyclic set of fd's such that no two fd's of Σ have the same right-hand side. Let σ be a jd such that $\Sigma \nrightarrow \sigma$. Let K be the unique key of Σ (uniqueness follows from Theorem 1). For every relation I, if J is a repair of $\sigma(I)$ under Σ, then $\pi_K(J) = \pi_K(I) = \pi_K(\sigma(I))$.*

The following Theorem 2 shows tractability of $\mathsf{CQAJD}(\Sigma, \sigma, q)$. Moreover, the theorem has a constructive proof, which provides an effective way for computing consistent query answers. Figure 1 shows the construction on a simple example. First, apply the jd $\sigma = \bowtie [\{\mathsf{Name}, \mathsf{Birth}, \mathsf{Sex}, \mathsf{ZIP}\}, \{\mathsf{ZIP}, \mathsf{City}\}]$, giving $\sigma(I)$. Next, the relation H contains one tuple for every distinct key value in $\sigma(I)$ (the key is Name). Variables are used to represent uncertain values. Initially, all variables are distinct. Next, since An and Ed share the same ZIP code, we know that they must live in the same city (because of the constraint $\mathsf{ZIP} \rightarrow \mathsf{City}$), hence the double occurrence of z. The construction is in polynomial time in the size of I. The proof of Theorem 2 shows that for every rooted rule q, the ground tuples in $q(H)$ coincide with the consistent answer $q_\Sigma(\sigma(I))$. Note incidentally that the rooted rule *"Get names of male persons living in An's city"* returns Ed because of the double occurrence of z. Note also that there is no need to materialize the repairs of $\sigma(I)$ under Σ.

Theorem 2. *Let Σ be an acyclic set of fd's such that no two fd's of Σ have the same right-hand side. Let K be the unique key of Σ. Let σ be a jd such that $\Sigma \nrightarrow \sigma$. Then, for every rooted rule q, $\mathsf{CQAJD}(\Sigma, \sigma, q)$ is in $\mathbf{P}$.*

In Section 1, we illustrated that the project-join-repair approach can give us more natural repairs in general. The following theorem states a very pleasant result: in addition to naturalness, we may gain tractability. The jd in this theorem corresponds to a standard 3NF decomposition.

Theorem 3. *Assume relation schema* $\langle A, B, C, D, E, F\rangle$. *Let* $\Sigma = \{A \rightarrow D, B \rightarrow E, C \rightarrow F\}$ *(the key is ABC) and* $\sigma = \bowtie [ABC, AD, BE, CF]$. *Let* $q : \langle\rangle \leftarrow \langle \underline{x}, \underline{y}, \underline{z}, 0, 0, 0\rangle$, *a rooted rule. Then,* $\Sigma \not\leftrightarrow \sigma$, *and* $\mathsf{CQAJD}(\Sigma, \sigma, q)$ *is in* **P**, *but* $\mathsf{CQA}(\Sigma, q)$ *is* **NP**-*complete.*

Proof. The **P** result follows from Theorem 2. **NP**-hardness of $\mathsf{CQA}(\Sigma, q)$ can be proved by a reduction from 3DM (three-dimensional matching).

Moving beyond rooted rules results in intractability.

Theorem 4. *Assume relation schema* $\langle A, B, C\rangle$. *Let* $\Sigma = \{A \rightarrow B, A \rightarrow C\}$ *(the key is A) and* $\sigma = \bowtie [AB, AC]$. *Let* $q : \langle\rangle \leftarrow \langle \underline{u}, y, 0\rangle, \langle \underline{w}, y, 1\rangle$, *a rule that is not rooted since y appears twice but is neither free nor quasi-free. Then,* $\Sigma \not\leftrightarrow \sigma$, *but* $\mathsf{CQAJD}(\Sigma, \sigma, q)$ *is* **NP**-*complete.*

Proof. See Theorem 3.3 in [4]. The relation in that proof satisfies σ.

6 Related Work

Main Contribution. We studied the problem of repairing a "universal" relation relative to a set of fd's. We illustrated by a number of examples that better repairs can be obtained by first applying a jd prior to repairing by tuple deletion. By varying the jd, attributes can be kept together or treated as being independent. As for the complexity, Theorem 3 shows that consistent query answering can be intractable under standard repairing by tuple deletion, but tractable under project-join-repair. This a pleasant result: increased naturalness and decreased complexity go hand in hand. Tractability was proved for the class of rooted rules. We next compare our contribution with existing work.

Join Graphs. An elegant approach to compute consistent query answers is query rewriting: a given query is rewritten such that the new query returns the consistent answer on any, possibly inconsistent, database. Obviously, if the rewritten query is wished to be first-order expressible [5, 6], then unless **P**=**NP**, this approach is limited to sets Σ of constraints and queries q for which $\mathsf{CQA}(\Sigma, q)$ is in **P**.

Fuxman and Miller [7] give an algorithm for first-order rewriting of a subclass of conjunctive queries under primary key constraints. They define the *join graph* of a rule as a graph whose vertices are the atoms in the body of the query. There is an oriented edge from $R(\underline{s_1, \ldots, s_k}, s_{k+1}, \ldots, s_n)$ to a distinct atom P if some $s_{k+1}, \ldots, s_n$ is a nonfree variable that also occurs in P. There is a self-loop on $R(\underline{s_1, \ldots, s_k}, s_{k+1}, \ldots, s_n)$ if some $s_{k+1}, \ldots, s_n$ is a nonfree variable that occurs twice in the atom. In this representation, the underlined coordinates constitute the primary key of the relation. Fuxman and Miller [7] give a query rewriting algorithm for queries with acyclic join graphs that contain no repeated relation symbols. Moreover, they require that every join of two atoms involves all key attributes of one of the atoms, a condition that was relaxed later on by Grieco et al. [8]. Our rooted rules are more general insofar as they can have cyclic join graphs and contain repeated relation symbols.

Example 5. Consider relation schema $\langle \mathsf{Name}, \mathsf{Birth}, \mathsf{Sex}, \mathsf{ZIP}, \mathsf{City} \rangle$. The following rooted rule gets, for each male person, the names of same-aged female persons living in the same city.

$$\langle x_n, y_n \rangle \leftarrow \langle \underline{x_n}, x_b, \mathrm{M}, x_z, x_c \rangle, \langle \underline{y_n}, x_b, \mathrm{F}, y_z, x_c \rangle$$

The join graph contains a cycle, because x_c is nonfree and occurs in two distinct atoms (likewise for x_b). Here is the query obtained by projecting the rule body on the components of the jd $\bowtie [\{\mathsf{Name}, \mathsf{Birth}, \mathsf{Sex}, \mathsf{ZIP}\}, \{\mathsf{ZIP}, \mathsf{City}\}]$. The relation symbols R_1 and R_2 are used for the first and second component respectively.

$$\langle x_n, y_n \rangle \leftarrow \begin{array}{l} R_1(\underline{x_n}, x_b, \mathrm{M}, x_z), R_2(\underline{x_z}, x_c), \\ R_1(\underline{y_n}, x_b, \mathrm{F}, y_z), R_2(\underline{y_z}, x_c) \end{array}$$

Each relation symbol occurs twice in the rule body, and the join graph contains two cycles, each of which connects atoms with the same relation symbol.

The following example shows that rooted rules can yield queries where the join between two atoms does involve only a subset of the key attributes.

Example 6. Consider relation schema $\langle \mathsf{Name}, \mathsf{Country}, \mathsf{Income}, \mathsf{Tax} \rangle$ and Σ with three fd's: $\mathsf{Name} \rightarrow \mathsf{Country}$, $\mathsf{Name} \rightarrow \mathsf{Income}$, and $\{\mathsf{Country}, \mathsf{Income}\} \rightarrow \mathsf{Tax}$. Let $\sigma = \bowtie [\{\mathsf{Name}, \mathsf{Country}\}, \{\mathsf{Name}, \mathsf{Income}\}, \{\mathsf{Country}, \mathsf{Income}, \mathsf{Tax}\}]$. It can be verified that $\Sigma \nrightarrow \sigma$. The following rooted rule gives the tax rate for each person:

$$\langle x_n, x_t \rangle \leftarrow R(\underline{x_n}, x_c, x_i, x_t)$$

Here is the decomposed query:

$$\langle x_n, x_t \rangle \leftarrow R_1(\underline{x_n}, x_c), R_2(\underline{x_n}, x_i), R_3(\underline{x_c}, \underline{x_i}, x_t)$$

Note that x_c in $R_1(\underline{x_n}, x_c)$ joins to the first attribute of the composite key in $R_3(\underline{x_c}, \underline{x_i}, x_t)$.

Defining Repairs. Consistent query answering gathered much attention since the seminal article by Arenas et al. [5], where repairs are defined in terms of the sets of inserted and deleted tuples. Note that for fd's, tuple insertions are useless for restoring consistency. Most approaches minimize sets of deleted and/or inserted tuples relative to set inclusion. Some authors also consider minimization with respect to cardinality [9, 10].

Recently, there has been a growing interest in repairing by value modification [11, 12, 13, 14]. Our project-join-repair approach can have the effect of value modifications, but is different from earlier proposals. Consider again the relation of Example 2.

I	Name	Birth	Sex	ZIP	City
	An	1964	F	7000	Mons
	Ed	1962	M	7000	Bergen

Our update-based repairing proposed in [15, 14] would come up with the four repairs shown next, where • is a placeholder for any ZIP code distinct from 7000. The project-join-repair approach will never introduce (placeholders for) new constants. However, as illustrated in Example 3, it yields J_1 and J_2 relative to the jd $\bowtie [\{\mathsf{Name}, \mathsf{Birth}, \mathsf{Sex}, \mathsf{ZIP}\}, \{\mathsf{ZIP}, \mathsf{City}\}]$. In general, it remains a subjective matter as to which repairing strategy yields the most intuitive repairs. However, we may opt for project-join-repair whenever this gives us tractability.

J_1	Name	Birth	Sex	ZIP	City
	An	1964	F	7000	Mons
	Ed	1962	M	7000	Mons

J_2	Name	Birth	Sex	ZIP	City
	An	1964	F	7000	Bergen
	Ed	1962	M	7000	Bergen

J_3	Name	Birth	Sex	ZIP	City
	An	1964	F	•	Mons
	Ed	1962	M	7000	Bergen

J_4	Name	Birth	Sex	ZIP	City
	An	1964	F	7000	Mons
	Ed	1962	M	•	Bergen

Computing Repairs and Consistent Query Answers. Several authors have investigated the use of logic solvers for database repairing [16, 9, 17]. They reduce database repairing and consistent query answering to the computation of models in some logical framework for which resolution methods exist. These articles focus more on expressiveness than on tractability. First-order query rewriting, discussed above, computes consistent query answers in polynomial time data complexity. The constructive proof of Theorem 2, illustrated by Fig. 1, could be termed "database rewriting," as the database is modified so as to return consistent answers to *any* rooted rule in polynomial time. In [18, 19], a practical implementation is presented for consistent query answering relative to denial constraints.

References

1. Imielinski, T., Lipski Jr., W.: Incomplete information in relational databases. J. ACM **31**(4) (1984) 761–791
2. Abiteboul, S., Hull, R., Vianu, V.: Foundations of Databases. Addison-Wesley (1995)
3. Ullman, J.D.: Principles of Database and Knowledge-Base Systems, Volume I. Computer Science Press (1988)
4. Chomicki, J., Marcinkowski, J.: Minimal-change integrity maintenance using tuple deletions. Information and Computation **197**(1-2) (2005) 90–121
5. Arenas, M., Bertossi, L.E., Chomicki, J.: Consistent query answers in inconsistent databases. In: Proc. 18th ACM Symp. on Principles of Database Systems, ACM Press (1999) 68–79
6. Celle, A., Bertossi, L.E.: Querying inconsistent databases: Algorithms and implementation. In: Proc. 1st Int. Conf. on Computational Logic (CL 2000). Volume 1861 of LNAI, Springer (2000) 942–956
7. Fuxman, A.D., Miller, R.J.: First-order rewriting for inconsistent databases. In: Proc. 10th Int. Conf. on Database Theory (ICDT 2005). Volume 3363 of LNCS, Springer (2005) 337–351

8. Grieco, L., Lembo, D., Rosati, R., Ruzzi, M.: Consistent query answering under key and exclusion dependencies: Algorithms and experiments. In: Proc. 14th ACM Int. Conf. on Information and Knowledge Management (CIKM '05), ACM (2005) 792–799
9. Arieli, O., Denecker, M., Nuffelen, B.V., Bruynooghe, M.: Database repair by signed formulae. In: Proc. 3rd Int. Symp. on Foundations of Information and Knowledge Systems (FoIKS '04). Volume 2942 of LNCS, Springer (2004) 14–30
10. Lin, J., Mendelzon, A.O.: Merging databases under constraints. Int. J. Cooperative Inf. Syst. **7**(1) (1998) 55–76
11. Bertossi, L.E., Bravo, L., Franconi, E., Lopatenko, A.: Complexity and approximation of fixing numerical attributes in databases under integrity constraints. In: 10th Int. Symposium Database Programming Languages (DBPL 2005). Volume 3774 of LNCS, Springer (2005) 262–278
12. Bohannon, P., Fan, W., Flaster, M., Rastogi, R.: A cost-based model and effective heuristic for repairing constraints by value modification. In: Proc. of the 24th ACM SIGMOD Int. Conf. on Management of Data, ACM Press (2005) 143–154
13. Flesca, S., Furfaro, F., Parisi, F.: Consistent query answers on numerical databases under aggregate constraints. In: 10th Int. Symposium Database Programming Languages (DBPL 2005). Volume 3774 of LNCS, Springer (2005) 279–294
14. Wijsen, J.: Database repairing using updates. ACM Trans. Database Syst. **30**(3) (2005) 722–768
15. Wijsen, J.: Condensed representation of database repairs for consistent query answering. In: Proc. 9th Int. Conf. on Database Theory (ICDT 2003). Volume 2572 of LNCS, Springer (2002) 378–393
16. Arenas, M., Bertossi, L.E., Chomicki, J.: Answer sets for consistent query answering in inconsistent databases. Theory and Practice of Logic Programming **3**(3-4) (2003) 393–424
17. Greco, G., Greco, S., Zumpano, E.: A logical framework for querying and repairing inconsistent databases. IEEE Trans. Knowledge and Data Eng. **25**(6) (2003) 1389–1408
18. Chomicki, J., Marcinkowski, J., Staworko, S.: Computing consistent query answers using conflict hypergraphs. In: Proc. 13th ACM Int. Conf. on Information and Knowledge Management (CIKM '04), ACM (2004) 417–426
19. Chomicki, J., Marcinkowski, J., Staworko, S.: Hippo: A system for computing consistent answers to a class of SQL queries. In: Proc. 9th Int. Conf. on Extending Database Technology (EDBT 2004). Volume 2992 of LNCS, Springer (2004) 841–844

Algebra-Based Identification of Tree Patterns in XQuery

Andrei Arion[1,2], Véronique Benzaken[2], Ioana Manolescu[1], Yannis Papakonstantinou[3], and Ravi Vijay[1,4]

[1] INRIA Futurs, Gemo group, France
firstname.lastname@inria.fr
[2] LRI, Univ. Paris 11, France
veronique.benzaken@lri.fr
[3] CSE Dept., UCSD, USA
yannis@cs.ucsd.edu
[4] IIT Bombay, India
ravivj@cse.iitb.ac.in

Abstract. Query processing performance in XML databases can be greatly enhanced by the usage of materialized views whose content has been stored in the database. This requires a method for identifying query subexpressions matching the views, a process known as view-based query rewriting. This process is quite complex for relational databases, and all the more daunting on XML databases.

Current XML materialized view proposals are based on tree patterns, since query navigation is conceptually close to such patterns. However, the existing algorithms for extracting tree patterns from XQuery do not detect patterns *across nested query blocks*. Thus, complex, useful tree pattern views may be missed by the rewriting algorithm. We present a novel tree pattern extraction algorithm from XQuery queries, able to identify larger patterns than previous methods. Our algorithm has been implemented in an XML database prototype [5].

1 Introduction

The XQuery language [23] is currently gaining adoption as the standard query language for XML. One performance-enhancing technique in XQuery processing is the usage of materialized views. The idea is to pre-compute and store in the database the result of some queries (commonly called *view definitions*), and when a user query arrives, to identify which parts of the query match one of the pre-computed views. The larger parts of the query one can match with a view, the more efficient query processing will be, since a bigger part of the query computation can be obtained directly from the materialized view.

Identifying useful views for a query requires reasoning about containment (e.g., is all the data in view v contained in the result of query q ?) and equivalence (e.g., is the join of views v_1 and v_2 equivalent to the query q ?). XML query ontainment and equivalence are well understood when views and queries are represented as *tree patterns*, containing tuples of elements satisfying specific

H.L. Larsen et al. (Eds.): FQAS 2006, LNAI 4027, pp. 13–25, 2006.

structural relationships [18, 19]. Moreover, popular XML indexing and fragmentation strategies also materialize tree patterns [10, 11, 13, 14]. Therefore, tree patterns are an interesting model for XML materialized views [3, 5, 6, 11, 12].

Our work is placed in the context of XQuery processing based on a persistent store. We make some simple assumptions on this context, briefly presented next.

Most persistent XML stores assign some *persistent identifiers* to XML elements. Such identifiers are often *structural*, that is, by comparing the identifiers id_1 and id_2 of two elements e_1 and e_2, one can decide whether some structural relationship exists between e_1 and e_2: for instance, whether e_1 is a child, parent, or sibling of e_2. The interest of structural identifiers is that establishing such relationships directly is much more efficient than navigating from e_1 to e_2 in the database to verify it. Numerous structural ID proposals have been made so far, see e.g. [2, 20]. *We assume persistent IDs are available in the store.* The IDs may, but do not need to, have structural properties.

Our second assumption is that a materialized view may store: (*i*) *node IDs* [10, 12, 14], (*ii*) node *values* (i.e., the text nodes directly under an element, or the value of an attribute) [10], and/or (*iii*) node *content*, that is, the full subtree rooted at an XML element (or a pointer to that subtree) [6]. This assumption provides for flexible view granularity.

To take advantage of tree pattern-shaped materialized views, one has to understand which views can be used for a query q. This process can be seen as a translating q to some *query patterns* $p_{q1}, \ldots, p_{qn}$, followed by a rewriting of every query pattern p_{qi} using the view patterns $p_{v1}, \ldots, p_{vm}$. The first step (query-to-pattern translation) is crucial. Intuitively, the bigger the query patterns, the bigger the view(s) that can be used to rewrite them, thus the less computations remain to be applied on top of the views.

The contribution of this paper is a provably correct algorithm identifying tree patterns in queries expressed in a large XQuery subset. The advantage of this method over existing ones [6, 9, 21] is that the patterns we identify are strictly larger than in previous works, and in particular may span over nested XQuery blocks, which was not the case in previous approaches. We ground our algorithm on an algebra, since (as we will show) the translation is quite complex due to XQuery complexity, and straightforward translation methods may loose the subtle semantic relationships between a pattern and a query.

Materialized views: advantages and drawbacks. A legitimate question is whether the cost of materializing and maintaining materialized views is justified by the advantages they provide ? It turns out that in XML persistent store, a tree-based approach is rarely (if ever !) sufficient to support complex querying. We survey XML storage and indexing strategies in [15]. Shredding schemes (aiming at loading XML documents in a set of relational tables) also offer an example of materialized XML views, recognized as such in [11, 16]. XML view maintenance in the presence of updates is a direction we are currently working on.

The paper is organized as follows. Section 2 motivates the need for pattern recognition in XQuery queries. Section 3 sets the formal background for the translation algorithm presented in Section 4.

2 Motivating Example

We illustrate the benefits of our tree pattern extraction approach on the sample XQuery query in Fig. 1, featuring three nested for-where-return blocks. An important XQuery feature to keep in mind is that when a return clause constructs new elements, if an expression found in the element constructor evaluates to $\emptyset$ (the empty result), an element must still be constructed, albeit with no content corresponding to that particular expression. For instance, in Fig. 1, if for some bindings of the variables $\$x$ and $\$y$, the expression $\$x//c$ yields an empty result, a res1 element will still be constructed, with no content corresponding to $\$x//c$ (but perhaps with some content produced by the nested for-where-return expression).

Next to the query, Fig. 1 depicts eleven possible corresponding query tree patterns. Each pattern is rooted at the $\top$ symbol, denoting the document root. Pattern edges may be labeled / for parent-child relationships, or // for ancestor-descendent relationships. Pattern nodes may be labeled with node names or with $*$ (any name). When a pattern node carries an ID symbol, the pattern is said to *contain the ID* of the XML nodes corresponding to the pattern node; similarly, if a pattern node is labeled $Cont$ (respectively, Val), the pattern is said to *contain the contents* (respectively, the value) of XML nodes corresponding to the pattern node. If a pattern node is annotated with a $Val = c$ predicate, for some constant c, then only XML nodes whose value satisfies that predicate (and the structural constraints on the node) will belong to the pattern.

We still need to explain the meaning of dashed pattern edges. These edges are *optional* in the following sense: an XML node matching the upper (parent/ancestor) node of a dashed edge may lack XML descendents matching the lower (child/descendent) node, yet that node may still belong to the pattern (if the edge was not optional, this would not be the case). If the lower node of a dashed edge was annotated with ID, Val or $Cont$, the pattern will contain some null ($\perp$) values to account for the missing children/descendents.

As previously mentioned, patterns play a dual role in our approach: view definitions, and query sub-expressions. Thus, each pattern $V_1, \ldots, V_{11}$ is a subexpression of the query at left, and (for our explanation) we also assume it is available as a materialized view. When a pattern is interpreted as a view, we say it stores various ID, $Cont$ and Val attributes; when it is interpreted as a query subexpression, we say it needs such attributes.

Let us now compare the ability of different algorithms to recognize the patterns in the query (thus, enable their usage for view-based query rewriting).

Several existing view-based XML query rewriting frameworks [6, 24] concentrate on XPath views, storing data for one pattern node only (since XPath queries have one return node), and lacking optional edges. Similar indexes are described in [10, 14]. In Fig. 1, the only XPath views are V_1-V_7, which represent the largest XPath patterns that one can derive from the query in Fig. 1; they store $Cont$ for all nodes which must be returned (such as the c, e and h nodes), and ID for all nodes whose values or content are not needed for the query, but which must be traversed by the query (such as the $a/*$, b, d nodes etc.) In this

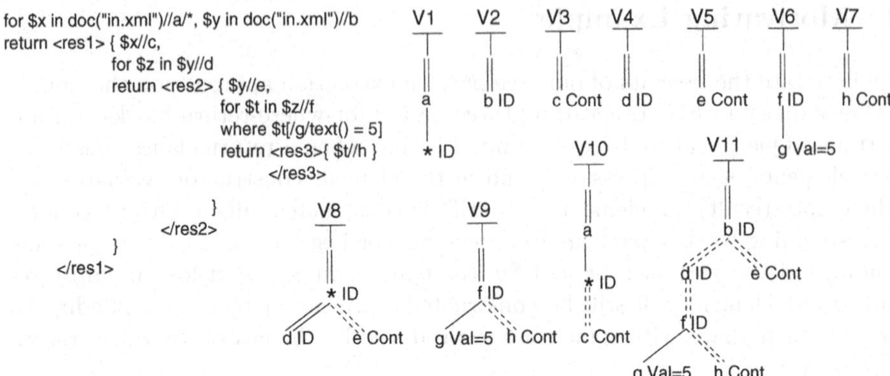

Fig. 1. Sample XQuery query and corresponding tree patterns/views

case, the only way to answer the query is to perform five joins and a cartesian product (the latter due to the fact that $\$x$ and $\$y$ are not connected in any way) to connect the data from V_1-V_7. This approach has some disadvantages. First, it needs an important amount of computations, and second, it may lead to reading from disk more data than needed (for instance, V_7 contains all h elements, while the query only needs those h elements under $//b//d//f$).

The algorithms of [9, 21] extract patterns storing information from several nodes, and having optional edges. However, these patterns are not allowed to span across nested for-where-return expressions. In Fig. 1, this approach would extract the patterns V_2, V_{10}, V_8 and V_9, thus the query can be rewritten by joining the corresponding views. This still requires three joins, and may lead to read data from many elements not useful to the query.

Our algorithm extracts from the query in Fig. 1 only two patterns: V_{10} and V_{11}. Based on these, we rewrite the query by a single join (more exactly, a cartesian product) of the corresponding V_{10} and V_{11} views, likely to be much less expensive than the other approaches.

Is a formal model required to describe pattern extraction ? The answer is yes, because one needs to model precisely (*i*) query semantics, typically using an algebra [7, 17, 22] and (*ii*) view semantics; in [4] we provided the full algebraic semantic of patterns such as those in Fig. 1. A formal model is needed, to ensure the patterns have exactly the same meaning as query subexpressions, or, when this is not the case, to compute *compensating actions* on the views. For instance, consider V_{11} in Fig. 1. Here, the d and the e nodes are optional descendents of the b nodes, and so they should be, according to the query. However, due to the query nesting, no e element should appear in the result, if its b ancestor does not have d descendents. This $d \to e$ dependency is not expressed by V_{11}, and is not expressible by any tree pattern, because such patterns only account for ancestor-descendent relationships. Thus, V_{11} is the best possible tree pattern view for the part of the query related to variable $\$y$, yet it is not exactly what we need. An (inexpensive) selection on V_{11}, on the condition $(d.ID \neq \bot) \vee (d.ID = \bot \wedge e.Cont = \bot)$, needs to be applied to adapt the view to the query.

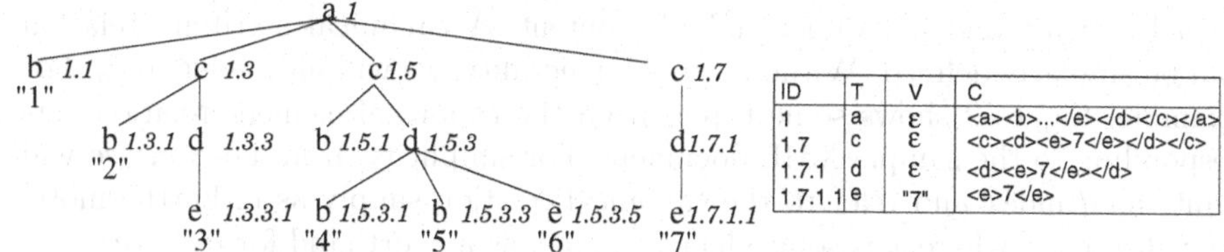

ID	T	V	C
1	a	ε	<a><b>...</e></d></c></a>
1.7	c	ε	<c><d><e>7</e></d></c>
1.7.1	d	ε	<d><e>7</e></d>
1.7.1.1	e	"7"	<e>7</e>

Fig. 2. Sample XML document and some tuples from its canonical relation

For simplicity, in this section, no nesting or grouping has been considered, neither in the patterns in Fig. 1, nor in the query rewriting strategies. However, given that XQuery does construct complex grouped results (e.g., all c descendents of the same $\$x$ must be output together in Fig. 1), pattern models considered in [4, 21], as well as our translation method, do take nesting into account.

3 Data Model, Algebra, and Query Language

3.1 Data Model

Let $\mathcal{A}$ be an infinite alphabet and $\mathcal{L}$, $\mathcal{I}$ be two disjoint subsets of $\mathcal{A}$. A special $\mathcal{A}$ constant ϵ denotes the empty string. We view an XML document as an unranked labeled ordered tree. Any node has a tag, corresponding to the element or attribute name, and may have a value. Attribute and element names range over $\mathcal{L}$, while values range over $\mathcal{A}$. The *value* of a node n belongs to $\mathcal{A}$ and is obtained by concatenating the text content of all children of n in document order; the result may be ϵ if the node does not have text children. The *content* of a node n is an $\mathcal{A}$ value, obtained by serializing the labels and values of all nodes from the tree rooted in n, in a top-down, left-to-right traversal. Nodes have unique *identities.* Let n_1, n_2 be two XML nodes. We denote the fact that n_1 is n_2's parent as $n_1 \prec n_2$, and the fact that n_1 is an ancestor of n_2 as $n_1 \prec\!\!\prec n_2$. We extend this notation to element IDs; $i_1 \prec i_2$ (resp. $i_1 \prec\!\!\prec i_2$) *iff* i_1 identifies n_1, i_2 identifies n_2 and $n_1 \prec n_2$ (resp. $n_1 \prec\!\!\prec n_2$).

We assume available an ID scheme I, that is, an injective function assigning to every node a value in $\mathcal{I}$. Figure 2 shows a simple XML document, where nodes are given structural ORDPATH identifiers [20].

We will rely on a nested relational model [1] as follows. The value of a tuple attribute is either a value from $\mathcal{A}$, or null ($\perp$), or a collection (set, list or bag) of homogeneous tuples. Notice the alternation between the tuple and the collection constructors. We use lowercase letters for relation names, and uppercase letters for attribute names, as in $r(A_1, A_2(A_{21}, A_{22}))$. Values are designated by lowercase letters. For instance, a tuple in $r(A_1, A_2(A_{21}, A_{22}))$ may have the value $t(x_1, [(x_3, \perp)\ (x_4, x_5)])$.

The basic ingredient of the algebraic expressions used in our translation method is a (virtual) relation capturing the data associated to an XML element. Given a document d, the *canonical element relation* $e_d(ID, T, V, C) \subseteq \mathcal{I} \times \mathcal{L} \times \mathcal{A} \times \mathcal{A}$ contains, for every element $n \in d$, a 4-tuple consisting of: the ID assigned to n by I; n's tag; n's value; and n's content. A canonical attribute relation can be similarly defined. Without loss of generality, we will only refer to e_d. For example, Figure 2 shows some tuples from the canonical element relation corresponding to the sample XML document. For simplicity, from now on, we will omit the d index and refer to the canonical relation simply as e. Furthermore, we will use e_x, where x is some element name, as a shorthand for $\sigma_{T=x}(e)$.

3.2 Logical Algebra

To every nested relation r, corresponds a Scan operator, also denoted r, returning the (possibly nested) corresponding tuples. Other standard operators are the cartesian product $\times$, the union $\cup$ and the set difference $\setminus$ (which do not eliminate duplicates).

We consider predicates of the form $A_i\ \theta\ c$ or $A_i\ \theta\ A_j$, where c is a constant. θ ranges over the comparators $\{=, \leq, \geq, <, >, \prec, \prec\!\!\prec\}$, and $\prec$, $\prec\!\!\prec$ only apply to $\mathcal{I}$ values.

Let *pred* be a predicate over atomic attributes from r, or r and s. Selections σ_{pred} have the usual semantics. A join $r \bowtie_{pred} s$ is defined as $\sigma_{pred}(r \times s)$. For convenience, we will also use outerjoins $⟕_{pred}$ and semijoins $\ltimes_{pred}$ (although strictly speaking they are redundant to the algebra). Another set of redundant, yet useful operators, are *nested joins*, denoted $\bowtie^n_{pred}$, and *nested outerjoins*, denoted $⟕^n_{pred}$, with the following semantics:

$$r ⟕^n_{pred} s = \{(t_1, \{t_2 \in s \mid pred(t_1, t_2)\}) \mid t_1 \in r\}$$
$$r \bowtie^n_{pred} s = \{(t_1, \{t_2 \in s \mid pred(t_1, t_2)\}\ ) \mid t_1 \in r, \{t_2 \in s \mid pred(t_1, t_2)\} \neq \emptyset\ \}$$

An interesting class of logical join operators (resp. nested joins, outerjoins, nested outerjoins, or semijoins) is obtained when the predicate's comparator is $\prec$ or $\prec\!\!\prec$, and the operand attributes are identifiers from $\mathcal{I}$. Such operators are called *structural joins*. Observe that we only refer to *logical structural joins*, independently of any physical implementation algorithm; different algorithms can be devised [2, 8].

Let $A_1, A_2, \ldots, A_k$ be some atomic r attributes. A projection $\pi_{A1,A2,\ldots,Ak}(r)$ by default does not eliminate duplicates. Duplicate-eliminating projections are singled out by a superscript, as in π^0. The group-by operator $\gamma_{A_1,A_2,\ldots,A_k}$, and unnest u_B, where B is a collection attribute, have the usual semantics [1].

We use the *map* meta-operator to define algebraic operators which apply *inside* nested tuples. Let *op* be a unary operator, $r.A_1.A_2.\ldots.A_{k-1}$ a collection attribute, and $r.A_1.A_2.\ldots.A_k$ an atomic attribute. Then, $map(op, r, A_1.A_2.\ldots.A_k)$ is a unary operator, and:

- If $k = 1$, $map(op, r, A_1.A_2.\ldots.A_k) = op(r)$.
- If $k > 1$, for every tuple $t \in r$:
  - If for every collection $r' \in t.A_1$, $map(op, r', A_2.\ldots.A_k) = \emptyset$, t is eliminated.
  - Otherwise, a tuple t' is returned, obtained from t by replacing every collection $r' \in r.A_1$ with $map(op, r', A_2.\ldots.A_k)$.

For instance, let $r(A_1(A_{11}, A_{12}), A_2)$ be a nested relation. Then, $map(\sigma_{=5}, r, A_1.A_{11})$ only returns those r tuples t for which *some* value in

$t.A_1.A_{11}$ is 5 (existential semantics), and reduces these tuples accordingly. *Map* applies similarly to π, γ and u. By a slight abuse of notation, we will refer to $map(op, r, A_1.A_2.\ldots.A_k)$ as $op_{A_1.A_2.\ldots.A_k}(r)$. For instance, the sample selection above will be denoted $\sigma_{A_1.A_{11}=5}(r)$.

Binary operators are similarly extended, via *map*, to nested tuples (details omitted).

The xml_{templ} operator wraps an input tuple into a single piece of XML text, by gluing together (some of) its attributes, and possibly adding tags, as specified by the tagging template *templ*. For every tuple t, whose data has already been grouped and structured, xml_{templ} thus outputs an $\mathcal{A}$ value which is the content of the newly created element. While this is slightly different from new node construction (as xml_{templ} does not create a new node identity), we use it here for simplicity and without loss of generality. Element construction operators closer to XQuery semantics [17, 22] could also be used.

3.3 Query Language

We consider a subset of XQuery, denoted $\mathcal{Q}$, obtained as follows.

(1) XPath$^{\{/,//,*,[\,]\}} \subset \mathcal{Q}$, that is, any core XPath [18] query over some document d is in $\mathcal{Q}$. We allow in such expressions the usage of the function *text()*, which on our data model returns the value of the node it is applied on. This represents a subset of XPath's absolute path expressions, whose navigation starts from the document root. Examples include $/a/b$ or $//c[//d/text() = 5]/e$. Navigation branches enclosed in [ ] may include complex paths and comparisons between a node and a constant $c \in \mathcal{A}$. Predicates connecting two nodes are not allowed; they may be expressed in XQuery for-where syntax (see below). **(2)** Let $\$x$ be a variable bound in the query context [23] to a list of XML nodes, and p be a core XPath expression. Then, $\$x\,p$ belongs to $\mathcal{Q}$, and represents the path expression p applied with $\$x$'s bindings list as initial context list. For instance, $\$x/a[c]$ returns the a children of $\$x$ bindings having a c child, while $\$x//b$ returns the b descendents of $\$x$ bindings. This class captures *relative* XPath expressions in the case where the context list is obtained from some variable bindings. We denote the set of expressions (1) and (2) above as $\mathcal{P}$, the set of path expressions. **(3)** For any two expressions e_1 and $e_2 \in \mathcal{Q}$, their concatenation, denoted e_1, e_2, also belongs to $\mathcal{Q}$. **(4)** If $t \in \mathcal{L}$ and $exp \in \mathcal{Q}$, element constructors of the form $\langle t\rangle\{exp\}\langle/t\rangle$ belong to $\mathcal{Q}$. **(5)** All expressions of the following form belong to $\mathcal{Q}$:

$$\boxed{xq}\quad \begin{array}{l} \text{for } \$x_1 \text{ in } p_1,\ \$x_2 \text{ in } p_2,\ \ldots,\ \$x_k \text{ in } p_k \\ \text{where } p_{k+1}\ \theta_1\ p_{k+2} \text{ and } \ldots \text{ and } p_{m-1}\ \theta_l\ p_m \\ \text{return } q(x_1, x_2, \ldots, x_k) \end{array}$$

where $p_1, p_2, \ldots, p_k, p_{k+1}, \ldots, p_m \in \mathcal{P}$, any p_i starts either from the root of some document d, or from a variable x_l introduced in the query before p_i, $\theta_1, \ldots, \theta_l$ are some comparators, and $q(x_1, \ldots, x_k) \in \mathcal{Q}$. Note that the return clause of a query may contain several other for-where-return queries, nested and/or concatenated and/or grouped inside constructed elements. The query in Figure 1 illustrates our supported fragment.

4 Pattern Extraction Algorithms

Our algorithm proceeds in two steps. First, $\mathcal{Q}$ queries are translated into expressions in the algebra previously described; Sections 4.1 and 4.2 explain this translation. Second, algebraic equivalence and decomposition rules are applied to identify, in the resulting expressions, subexpressions corresponding to tree patterns. The algebraic rules are quite straightforward. The ability to recognize pattern subexpressions is due to the formal algebraic pattern semantics provided in a previous work [4]. Section 4.3 illustrates it on our running example.

Queries are translated to algebraic expressions producing one $\mathcal{A}$ attribute, corresponding to the serialized query result. We describe query translation as a translation function $alg(q)$ for every $q \in \mathcal{Q}$. We will also use an auxiliary function $full$; intuitively, $full$ returns "larger" algebraic expressions, out of which alg is easily computed.

4.1 Algebraic Translation of Path Queries

For any $q \in \mathcal{P}$, let $ret(q)$ denote the return node of q. Let d be a document, and a an element name. Then:

$$full(d//*) \stackrel{\text{def}}{=} e, \text{ and } alg(d//*) \stackrel{\text{def}}{=} \pi_C(e)$$

$$full(d//a) \stackrel{\text{def}}{=} (e_a), \text{ and } alg(d//a) \stackrel{\text{def}}{=} \pi_C(e_a)$$

Translating $d/*$ and d/a requires care to separate just the root element from e:

$$full(d/*) \stackrel{\text{def}}{=} e_1 \setminus \pi_{e_3}(e_2 \bowtie_{e_2.ID \prec e_3.ID} e_3), \text{ and } alg(d/*) \stackrel{\text{def}}{=} \pi_C(full(d/*))$$

where e_1, e_2 and e_3 are three occurences of the e relation, $e_2.ID$ (respectively, $e_3.ID$) is the ID attribute in e_2 (respectively e_3), and the projection π_{e_3} retains only the attributes of e_3. The set difference computes the e tuple corresponding to the element that does not have a parent in e (thus, the root element). Similarly,

$$full(d/a) \stackrel{\text{def}}{=} e_a \setminus \pi_{e_3}(e_2 \bowtie_{e_2.ID \prec e_3.ID} e_3), \text{ and } alg(d/a) \stackrel{\text{def}}{=} \pi_C(full(d/a))$$

In general, for any $\mathcal{P}$ query q:

- If q ends in $text()$, then $alg(q) = \pi_{V_{last}}(\pi^0(full(q)))$, where V_{last} is the V attribute from the e_d relation corresponding to $ret(q)$. The inner projection π^0 eliminates possible duplicate nodes, in accordance with XPath semantics [23]. The outer projection ensures only the text value is retained.
- If q does not end in $text()$, then $alg(q) = \pi_{C_{last}}(\pi^0(full(q)))$, where C_{last} is the C attribute from the e_d relation corresponding to $ret(q)$.

Note that the resulting algebraic expressions return node *value* or *content*, while in general XPath queries may return *nodes*. Alternatively, node identifiers can be returned by setting, for node-selecting XPath queries, $alg(q) \stackrel{\text{def}}{=} \pi_{ID_{last}}(\pi^0(full(q)))$, where ID_{last} is the ID attribute from the e_d relation corresponding to $ret(q)$. Since XPath results frequently need to be returned in a serialized form, e.g., to be shown to a user, or sent in a Web service, we consider the C attribute is really returned, thus use $\pi_{C_{last}}$ in the translation.

We now focus on defining the $full$ algebraic function for path queries, keeping in mind how alg derives from $full$ for such queries. For any query $q \in \mathcal{P}$, we have:

$$full(q//a) \stackrel{\text{def}}{=} full(q) \bowtie_{e_q.ID \prec\!\!\prec e_a.ID} e_a$$

where $e_q.ID$ is the ID attribute in $full(q)$ corresponding to $ret(q)$, while $e_a.ID$ is the ID from the e_a relation at right in the above formula. When // is replaced with /, the translation involves $\prec$ instead of $\prec\!\!\prec$. We also have:

$$full(q[text() = c]) \stackrel{\text{def}}{=} \sigma_{V=c}(full(q))$$

If $q_1 \in \mathcal{P}$ and $q_2 \in \text{XPath}^{\{/,//,*,[]\}}$ is a relative path expression starting with a child navigation step, we have:

$$full(q_1[q_2]) \stackrel{\text{def}}{=} full(q_1) \ltimes_{e_1.ID \prec e_2.ID} full(//q_2)$$

where $e_1.ID$ is the ID corresponding to $ret(q_1)$, $//q_2$ is an absolute path expression obtained by adding a descendent navigation step, starting from the root, in front of q_2, and $e_2.ID$ corresponds to the first node of q_2. Here and from now on, we consider all relative path expressions start with a child step. If the first step is to a descendent, $\prec$ should be replaced with $\prec\!\!\prec$ in the translation.

Let $\$x$ be a variable bound to the result of query $q_{\$x}$, and q be a relative path expression starting with a child navigation step. Then:

$$full(\$x\ q) \stackrel{\text{def}}{=} full(q_{\$x}) \bowtie_{e_1.ID \prec e_2.ID} (full(q))$$

where $e_1.ID$ is the ID corresponding to $ret(q_{\$x})$, and $e_2.ID$ is the ID corresponding to the top node in $full(q)$.

Example. Consider the path expressions $p_{\$x} = //a/*$, $p_{\$y} = //b$, $p_{\$z} = \$y//d$ and $p_{\$t} = \$z//f$ (see Fig. 1). Applying the above rules, we obtain:

$$full(p_{\$x}) = e_a \bowtie_{e_a.ID \prec e.ID} e,\ \ full(p_{\$y}) = e_b$$
$$full(p_{\$z}) = full(p_{\$y}) \bowtie_{e_{\$y}.ID \prec\!\!\prec e_d.ID} e_d,$$
$$full(p_{\$t}) = full(p_{\$z}) \bowtie_{e_{\$z}.ID \prec\!\!\prec e_f.ID} e_f$$

Now consider the path expressions $p_1 = \$x//c$, $p_2 = \$y//e$, $p_3 = \$t[g/text() = 5]$ and $p_4 = \$t//h$, also extracted from the query in Fig. 1. We have:

$$full(p_1) = full(p_{\$x}) \bowtie_{e_{\$x}.ID \prec\!\!\prec e_c.ID} e_c,$$
$$full(p_2) = full(p_{\$y}) \bowtie_{e_{\$y}.ID \prec\!\!\prec e_e.ID} e_e,$$
$$full(p_3) = full(p_{\$t}) \ltimes_{e_{\$t}.ID \prec e_g.ID} \sigma_{V=5}(e_g),$$
$$full(p_4) = full(p_{\$t}) \bowtie_{e_{\$t}.ID \prec\!\!\prec e_h.ID} e_h$$

In the above, $e_{\$y}$, $e_{\$z}$ and $e_{\$t}$ are the e relations corresponding to the return nodes in the translations of $p_{\$x}$, $p_{\$y}$ and $p_{\$t}$. The alg expressions are easily obtained from $full$.

$\boxed{xq_1}$	for $\$x_1$ in p_1, $\$x_2$ in $\$x_1/p_2, \ldots, \$x_k$ in $\$x_1/p_k$ where $\$x_1/p_{k+1}\,\theta\,\$x_1/p_{k+2}$ and ... $\$x_1/p_{m-1}\,\theta\,\$x_1/p_m$ return $\$x_1/p_{m+1}, \$x_1/p_{m+2}, \ldots, \$x_1/p_n$

$$full(xq_1) \stackrel{\text{def}}{=}$$
$$\sigma_{A_{k+1}\,\theta\,A_{k+2},\ldots,A_{m-1}\,\theta\,A_m}(full(p_1) \bowtie_{ID_1 \prec ID_2} full(//p_2) \ldots \bowtie_{ID_1 \prec ID_k} full(//p_k)$$
$$\bowtie^n_{ID_1 \prec ID_{k+1}} full(//p_{k+1}) \bowtie^n_{ID_1 \prec ID_{k+2}} \cdots \bowtie^n_{ID_1 \prec ID_m} full(//p_m)$$
$$\bowtie^n_{ID_1 \prec ID_{m+1}} full(//p_{m+1}) \bowtie^n_{ID_1 \prec ID_{m+2}} \cdots \bowtie^n_{ID_1 \prec ID_n} full(//p_n))$$

$$alg(xq_1) \stackrel{\text{def}}{=} \pi_{A_{m+1},A_{m+2},\ldots,A_n}(full(xq_1))$$

Fig. 3. Generic XQuery query with simple return expression

4.2 Algebraic Translation of More Complex Queries

This section describes the translation of $\mathcal{Q}$ queries other than path expressions.

Concatenation. We have $alg(q_1, q_2) \stackrel{\text{def}}{=} alg(q_1) \parallel alg(q_2)$ and $full(q_1, q_2) \stackrel{\text{def}}{=} full(q_1) \parallel full(q_2)$, where , denotes query concatenation, and $\parallel$ concatenation of tuple lists.

Element constructors. Element constructor queries are translated by the following rule:

$$alg(\langle t\rangle\{q\}\langle/t\rangle) \stackrel{\text{def}}{=} xml(n(alg(q)), \langle t\rangle A_1 \langle/t\rangle)$$

where the nest operator n packs all tuples from $alg(q)$ in a single tuple with a single collection attribute named A_1. The second argument of the xml operator is a tagging template, indicating that values of the attribute named A_1 have to be packed in t elements. Furthermore, $full(\langle t\rangle\{q\}\langle/t\rangle) = n(full(q))$.

For-where-return expressions. The translation rules for such query expressions are outlined in Fig. 3 and Fig. 4. For simplicity, these rules use a single θ symbol for some arbitrary, potentially different, comparison operators.

(1) Simple return clauses. In the generic query xq_1 (Fig. 3), path expression p_1 is absolute, while all others are relative and start from a query variable $\$x_1$. Attribute ID_1 corresponds to $ret(p_1)$. The query returns some variables. Attribute ID_i is the attribute in $full(//p_i)$ corresponding to the top node of p_i, for every path expression p_i in $p_2, \ldots, p_m$. Attributes $A_{k+1}, A_{k+2}, \ldots, A_m$ are those returned by the algebraic translations of the relative path expressions of the where clause, more precisely, the attributes in $alg(//p_{k+1}), alg(//p_{k+2}), \ldots, alg(//p_m)$. Each A_{k+i} is V or C, depending on p_{k+i}. Note that once // is added in front of such a relative path expression, $//p_{k+i}$ is an absolute expression, thus translatable to the algebra. The child navigation step connecting $\$x_1$ and an expression p_{k+i} is captured by the join $\bowtie^n_{ID_1 \prec ID_i}$. As an effect of this nested structural join, A_i may be nested in σ's input, therefore, the selection has existential semantics (recall the *map*-based extension of σ to nested attributes from Section 3.2).

The xq_1 rule easily extends to queries where the for clause features several unrelated variables, the where clause contains predicates over one or two variables,

for $\$x$ in p_f where $pred(p_w(\$x))$ $\boxed{xq_2}$ return $fwr(\$x)$ $full(xq_2) \stackrel{\text{def}}{=} \sigma_{pred}(full(p_f) \bowtie^{n}_{ID_1 \prec ID_2} full(//p_w) \bowtie_{ID_1=ID_1} full(fwr(p_f))$ $alg(xq_2) \stackrel{\text{def}}{=} \pi_{fwr}(full(xq_2))$, respectively $xml_{templ(fwr)}(\pi_{fwr}(full(xq_2)))$
for $\$x$ in p_f where $pred(p_w(\$x))$ $\boxed{xq_3}$ return $\langle a \rangle$ { $fwr(\$x)$ } $\langle /a \rangle$ $full(xq_3) \stackrel{\text{def}}{=} \sigma_{pred}(full(p_f) \bowtie^{n}_{ID_1 \prec ID_2} full(//p_w) ⟕^{n}_{ID_1=ID_1} full(fwr(p_f))$ $alg(xq_3) \stackrel{\text{def}}{=} xml_{\langle a \rangle \cdot \langle /a \rangle}(\pi_{fwr}(full(xq_3)))$, resp. $xml_{\langle a \rangle templ(fwr) \langle /a \rangle}(\pi_{fwr}(full(xq_3)))$

Fig. 4. Generic XQuery queries with complex return clauses

and the return clause returns only variables. Each subquery corresponding to an independent variable in the for clause is then translated separatedly, and the resulting expressions are joined. From now on, without loss of generality, we will use one variable in each for clause; adding more variables depending on the first one leads to structural join subexpression in the style of $full(xq_1)$, while adding more unrelated variables leads to value joins as sketched above.

(2) Nested for-where-return queries. Such queries are illustrated by xq_2 and xq_3 in Fig. 4. Here, p_f is an absolute path expression, p_w a relative one, *pred* a simple comparison predicate, and fwr a (potentially complex, nested) for-where-return query.

(2.1) The outer query does not construct new elements. This is the case for xq_2 in Fig. 4. In $full(xq_2)$, ID_1 corresponds to $ret(p_f)$ and ID_2 to the top node in p_w. We add // in front of p_w to make it absolute. The query $fwr(p_f)$ is obtained from fwr by adding a new "for" variable $\$x'$ bound to p_f, and replacing $\$x$ by $\$x'$. Thus, $fwr(p_f)$ is decorrelated from (it does no longer depend on) $\$x$; the dependency is replaced by the join on ID_1. In $alg(xq_2)$, the projection π_{fwr} retains only the attributes from $alg(fwr(p_f))$. Two alternatives exist for $alg(xq_2)$, as shown in Fig. 4:

- If fwr does not construct new elements, the query (and its translation) recall xq_1.
- If fwr constructs new elements, the top operator in $alg(fwr(p_f))$ is $xml_{templ(fwr)}$, for some given tagging template $templ(fwr)$. In this case, $full(xq_2)$ is built using exactly the same template. Note how the XML constructor "sifts up" as the top algebraic operator in the translation, in this case, from $alg(fwr)$ to $alg(xq_2)$. All algebraic translations have at most one xml operator.

(2.2) The outer query constructs new elements. Query xq_3 in Fig. 4 encloses the results of some correlated query $fwr(\$x)$ in $\langle a \rangle$ elements. Therefore, in $full(xq_3)$ an outerjoin is used to ensure that xq_3 produces some output even for $\$x$ bindings for which $fwr(\$x)$ has an empty result. The outerjoin is nested, because all the results of $fwr(\$x)$ generated for a given $\$x$ must be included in a single $\langle a\rangle$ element. For $alg(xq_3)$, there are again two cases. If fwr does not construct new elements, and since xq_3 does, the tagging template is a simple $\langle a\rangle$ element. If fwr also constructs some elements, the xml operator in $alg(xq_3)$ builds a bigger tagging template, by enclosing $templ(fwr)$ in an $\langle a\rangle$ element.

The translation of more complex $\mathcal{Q}$ queries can be derived from the above rules.

Example. Let us translate the query q in Fig. 1 (also recall the path expressions at the end of Section 4.1, and their translations). We can write q as:

```
for $x in p$x, $y in p$y
return ⟨res1⟩{ p1,
            ⟨res2⟩{ p2, for $z in p$z where p3 return ⟨res3⟩{ p4 }⟨/res3⟩⟨/res2⟩ }
       ⟨/res1⟩
```

which can be furthermore abstracted into:

for $\$x$ in $p_{\$x}$, $\$y$ in $p_{\$y}$ return ⟨res1⟩{ p_1, ⟨res2⟩{ p_2, q_2 }⟨/res2⟩ } ⟨/res1⟩

where query q_2 is: for $\$z$ in $p_{\$z}$ where p_3 return ⟨res3⟩{ p_4 }⟨/res3⟩. Let us first translate q_2. Applying the xq_3 translation rule from Fig. 4, we obtain:

$$full(q_2) = full(p_{\$z}) \bowtie^{n}_{e_{\$z}.ID \prec e_3.ID} full(//p_3) \mathrel{\triangleright\!\!\!\sqsubset}^{n}_{e_{\$z}.ID = e_{\$z}.ID} full(p_{\$z}//p_4)$$

Applying the xq_3 rule again, twice, for q leads to:

$$(*)\ full(q) = full(p_{\$x}) \times full(p_{\$y}) \mathrel{\triangleright\!\!\!\sqsubset}^{n}_{e_{\$x}.ID = e_{\$x}.ID} full(p_1) \mathrel{\triangleright\!\!\!\sqsubset}^{n}_{e_{\$y}.ID = e_{\$y}.ID} full(p_2) \mathrel{\triangleright\!\!\!\sqsubset}^{n}_{e_{\$y}.ID = e_{\$y}.ID} full(q_2)$$

Finalizing q's translation, we have $alg(q) = xml_{templ}(full(q))$, where xml_{templ} is:

⟨res1⟩$e_1.C$⟨res2⟩$e_2.C$⟨ res3⟩$e_3.C$⟨/res3⟩⟨/res2⟩⟨/res1⟩

where $e_1.C$, $e_2.C$, $e_3.C$ are the C attributes corresponding to the path expressions p_1, p_2 and p_3 (those producing returned nodes). Observe that no data restructuring is needed in xml_{templ}, since the nested joins in $full(q)$ have grouped the data as the query required.

4.3 Isolating Patterns from Algebraic Expressions

Algebraic equivalence rules applied on (∗) bring $full(q)$ to the equivalent form:

$$\sigma_{(e_{\$z}.ID \neq \perp) \vee (e_{\$z}.ID = \perp \wedge e_2 = \perp)}(full(p_{\$x}) \mathrel{\triangleright\!\!\!\sqsubset}^{n}_{e_{\$x}.ID \lll e_c.ID} e_c \times full(p_{\$y}) \mathrel{\triangleright\!\!\!\sqsubset}^{n}_{e_{\$y}.ID \lll e_e.ID} e_e \mathrel{\triangleright\!\!\!\sqsubset}^{n}_{e_{\$y}.ID \lll e_d.ID} (e_d \mathrel{\triangleright\!\!\!\sqsubset}^{n}_{e_d.ID \lll e_f.ID} (e_f \bowtie^{n}_{e_f.ID \lll e_g.ID} \sigma_{V=5}(e_g) \mathrel{\triangleright\!\!\!\sqsubset}^{n}_{e_d.ID \lll e_h.ID} e_h)))$$

This rewriting has grouped together $full(p_{\$x})$ with the other subexpressions structurally related to $\$x$ (the join product before the $\times$). It has also grouped $full(p_{\$y})$ and the subexpressions structurally related to $\$y$ (the last two lines). It turns out that these correspond exactly to the algebraic semantics of patterns V_{10} and V_{11} in Figure 1. Thus:

$$alg(q) = xml_{templ}(\sigma_{(e_{\$z}.ID \neq \perp) \vee (e_{\$z}.ID = \perp \wedge e_2 = \perp)}(V_{10} \times V_{11}))$$

The σ is a by-product of transforming the equality joins in (∗) in structural joins.

References

1. S. Abiteboul, R. Hull, and V. Vianu. *Foundations of Databases.* Addison-Wesley, 1995.
2. S. Al-Khalifa, H.V. Jagadish, J.M. Patel, Y. Wu, N. Koudas, and D. Srivastava. Structural joins: A primitive for efficient XML query pattern matching. In *ICDE*, 2002.
3. S. Amer-Yahia and Y. Kotidis. Web-services architectures for efficient XML data exchange. In *ICDE*, 2004.
4. A. Arion, V. Benzaken, and I. Manolescu. XML Access Modules: Towards Physical Data Independence in XML Databases. XIME-P Workshop, 2005.
5. A. Arion, V. Benzaken, I. Manolescu, and R. Vijay. ULoad: Choosing the Right Store for your XML Application (demo). In *VLDB*, 2005.
6. K. Beyer, F. Ozcan, S. Saiprasad, and B. Van der Linden. DB2/XML: designing for evolution. In *SIGMOD*, 2005.
7. M. Brantner, S. Helmer, C.-C. Kanne, and G.Moerkotte. Full-Fledged Algebraic XPath Processing in Natix. In *ICDE*, 2005.
8. N. Bruno, N. Koudas, and D. Srivastava. Holistic twig joins: Optimal XML pattern matching. In *SIGMOD*, 2002.
9. Z. Chen, H.V. Jagadish, L. Lakshmanan, and S. Paparizos. From tree patterns to generalized tree patterns: On efficient evaluation of XQuery. In *VLDB*, 2003.
10. B. Cooper, N. Sample, M. Franklin, G. Hjaltason, and M. Shadmon. A fast index for semistructured data. In *VLDB*, 2001.
11. A. Deutsch and V. Tannen. MARS: A system for publishing XML from mixed and redundant storage. In *VLDB*, 2003.
12. H. V. Jagadish, S. Al-Khalifa, A. Chapman, L. Lakshmanan, A. Nierman, S. Paparizos, J. Patel, D. Srivastava, N. Wiwatwattana, Y. Wu, and C. Yu. Timber: A native XML database. *VLDB J.*, 11(4), 2002.
13. H. Jiang, H. Lu, W. Wang, and J. Xu. XParent: An efficient RDBMS-based XML database system. In *ICDE*, 2002.
14. R. Kaushik, P. Bohannon, J. Naughton, and H. Korth. Covering indexes for branching path queries. In *SIGMOD*, 2002.
15. I. Manolescu. XML query processing: storage and query model interplay. Tutorial at the EDBT summer school, available at www-rocq.inria.fr/~manolesc, 2004.
16. I. Manolescu, D. Florescu, and D. Kossmann. Answering XML queries over heterogeneous data sources. In *VLDB*, 2001.
17. I. Manolescu and Y. Papakonstantinou. An unified tuple-based algebra for XQuery. Available at www-rocq.inria.fr/~manolesc/PAPERS/algebra.pdf, 2005.
18. G. Miklau and D. Suciu. Containment and equivalence for an XPath fragment. In *PODS*, 2002.
19. F. Neven and T. Schwentick. XPath containment in the presence of disjunction, DTDs, and variables. In *ICDT*, 2003.
20. P. O'Neil, E. O'Neil, S. Pal, I. Cseri, G. Schaller, and N. Westbury. ORDPATHs: Insert-friendly XML node labels. In *SIGMOD*, 2004.
21. S. Paparizos, Y. Wu, L. Lakshmanan, and H. Jagadish. Tree logical classes for efficient evaluation of XQuery. In *SIGMOD*, 2004.
22. C. Ré, J. Siméon, and M. Fernandez. A complete and efficient algebraic compiler for XQuery. In *ICDE*, 2006.
23. XQuery 1.0. www.w3.org/TR/xquery.
24. W. Xu and M. Ozsoyoglu. Rewriting XPath queries using materialized views. In *VLDB*, 2005.

Approximate Querying of XML Fuzzy Data

Patrice Buche[1], Juliette Dibie-Barthélemy[1,2], and Fanny Wattez[1,2]

[1] Mét@risk MIA INRA
16, rue Claude Bernard,
F-75231 Paris Cedex 05
[2] UMR MIA INA P-G/INRA
16, rue Claude Bernard,
F-75231 Paris Cedex 05
{Patrice.Buche, Juliette.Dibie, Fanny.Wattez}@inapg.inra.fr

Abstract. The MIEL++ system integrates data expressed in two different formalisms: a relational database and an XML database. The XML database is filled with data semi-automatically retrieved from the Web, which have been semantically enriched according to the ontology used in the relational database. These data may be imprecise and represented as possibility distributions. The MIEL++ querying system scans the two databases simultaneously in a transparent way for the end-user. To scan the XML database, the MIEL query is translated into an XML tree query. In this paper, we propose to introduce flexibility into the query processing of the XML database, in order to take into account the imperfections due to the semantic enrichment of its data. This flexibility relies on fuzzy queries and query rewriting which consists in generating a set of approximate queries from an original query using three transformation techniques: deletion, renaming and insertion of query nodes.

1 Introduction

Numerous approaches have been proposed in the bibliography to introduce flexibility in the comparison between an XML tree query and XML data trees. The first one is based on the encoding of the XML data trees [6]. This method only permits the introduction of intermediate nodes in the tree query structure in order to carry out the comparison with the data trees. The second approach [1] is based on the rewriting of the XML tree query. It permits the introduction, renaming and deletion of nodes in the query. The third one [12] is a combination of the previous two: the data are encoded and the query is rewritten. It provides an accurate computation of the transformation cost between the query and the data. But, it is very difficult to use because it requires one to redefine the management of the index and data encoding in the XML Database Management System. In a fourth approach [2], fuzzy predicates are introduced into the query to express flexible selection conditions and to perform fuzzy subtree matching. But it does not take into account suppression and renaming of nodes. In this paper, we propose a new XML querying system. It combines the flexibility provided by the

H.L. Larsen et al. (Eds.): FQAS 2006, LNAI 4027, pp. 26–38, 2006.

use of fuzzy sets to represent the user's preferences in an XML query and the flexibility of XML query rewriting (including insertion, deletion and renaming of nodes) to perform an approximate comparison between an XML tree query and an XML data tree. Moreover, it supports XML imprecise data expressed as possibility distributions which is also an original contribution because few research has been done in modeling and querying imprecise XML data. To the best of our knowledge (see [10] for a recent synthesis), only imprecise data and probabilistic data modeling in XML have been proposed. Our querying system is fully compatible with XML querying standards since the final rewriting of the queries is performed in XQuery language (http://www.w3.org/XML/Query/).

This work is realised in the framework of a system development whose aim is to integrate heterogeneous data sources. Two approaches are generally considered to solve this problem: the data warehouse approach [14] in which data are transformed to be stored in one global schema and mediated architectures [15] where the data remain stored in the original sources, the mapping between the global integration schema and the schemas of original sources being carried out by wrappers. In our system, we propose data integration based on a *mediated architecture*. More precisely, we use a global schema to integrate data expressed in two different formalisms: a relational database and an XML database. This architecture, called MIEL++ [4], is close to a *Global as Views* approach, in which the global schema is defined in terms of the local schemas to be integrated, as in the TSIMMIS [13] system. An original aspect of our approach is that our XML database is comparable to a data warehouse, since it contains data, semi-automatically retrieved from the Web, which have been modified in order to be expressed in the same vocabulary and semantic relations as the ones used in the relational database [9]. These data, called SML data, may be imprecise [3] and represented as possibility distributions [17]. Moreover, in order to avoid empty answers, MIEL++ querying system proposes to the end-user to express selection criteria by means of fuzzy sets used as expression of preferences [3]. In [5], we have defined a wrapper which translates a MIEL query into an XML tree query to scan the XML database. We made the assumption that the XML data trees retrieved by the MIEL++ system have to fit exactly the structure of the XML tree query. This assumption does not permit the imperfections of the SML data to be taken into account. Therefore, we cannot make the assumption as in [11] that we know precisely the schema of the Web data sources we want to integrate. In this paper, we study the way of introducing more flexibility into the MIEL query processing of an XML database. This work is done in the framework of the development of a real data warehouse in an actual application domain: risk assessment in food safety.

In section 2, we briefly present firstly the fuzzy set framework that we use to represent imprecise data and preferences in the queries, secondly the MIEL query language and thirdly the way imprecise data are represented in an XML database. In section 3, we define a new wrapper which translates a MIEL query into a set of approximate XML queries. In section 4, we present the implementation and preliminary test results of this wrapper in a real application.

2 Backgrounds

2.1 Fuzzy Set Theory

In this article, we use the representation of fuzzy sets proposed in [16, 17].

Definition 1. A *fuzzy set* f on a definition domain $Dom(f)$ is defined by a membership function μ_f from $Dom(f)$ to $[0, 1]$ that associates the degree to which x belongs to f with each element x of $Dom(f)$.

The fuzzy set formalism can be used in two ways: (i) in the databases, in order to represent imprecise data expressed in terms of possibility distributions or (ii) in the queries, in order to represent fuzzy selection criteria which express the preferences of the end-user. A fuzzy set can be defined on a continuous or discrete definition domain (see Fig. 1). In order to answer queries in databases involving fuzzy sets, we must be able to compare fuzzy sets. Two scalar measures are classically used in the fuzzy set theory to evaluate the compatibility between an imprecise datum and end-user's preferences: a possibility degree of matching [17] and a necessity degree of matching [8]. In this paper, for simplicity reasons, we will only use the *possibility degree* of matching which is defined below.

Definition 2. Let f and g be two fuzzy sets defined on the same definition domain *Dom*, representing respectively a selection criterion and an imprecise datum, μ_f and μ_g being their membership functions. The *possibility degree of matching* between f and g is $\Pi(f, g) = sup_{x \in Dom}(min(\mu_f(x), \mu_g(x)))$. *The selection criterion is satisfied if and only if* $\Pi(f, g) > 0$.

2.2 The MIEL Query Language

In the MIEL++ system, the query processing is done through the MIEL query language. This query processing relies on the ontology of the databases, called *MIEL++ ontology*, which contains the vocabulary used by the end-users to express their queries. We first present the MIEL++ ontology and then, we introduce the MIEL query language by presenting the queries and their answers.

The MIEL++ ontology. The ontology is notably composed of: (1) a taxonomy of terms including the set of attributes which can be queried on by the

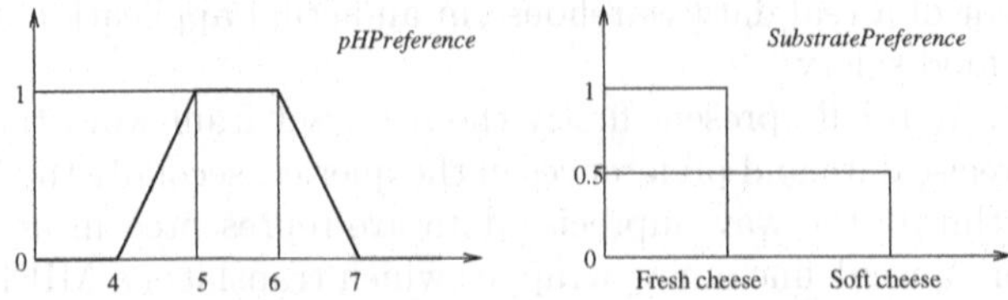

Fig. 1. An example of a continuous fuzzy set pHPreference noted [4,5,6,7] and a discrete fuzzy set SubstratePreference noted (1/Fresh cheese + 0.5/Soft cheese)

end-user, and their corresponding definition domains. Each attribute has a definition domain which can be numeric, "flat" symbolic (unordered constants) or hierarchized symbolic (constants partially ordered by the "kind-of" relation); (2) a relational schema, which corresponds to the schema of the relational database of the MIEL++ system. That relational schema is composed of a set of signatures of the possible relations between the terms of the taxonomy.

The queries. In the MIEL query language, a query is asked in a view, which is a pre-written query allowing the system to hide the complexity of the database schema. A view is characterized by its set of queryable attributes and by its actual definition. A query is then an instanciation of a given view by the end-user, by specifying, among the set of queryable attributes of the view, which are the selection attributes and their corresponding searched values, and which are the projection attributes of the query.

Definition 3. A *query* Q asked on a view V defined on n attributes $\{a_1, \ldots, a_n\}$ is defined by $Q = \{V, S, C\}$ where $S \subseteq \{a_1, \ldots, a_n\}$ represents the set of the projection attributes and where $C = \{c_1, \ldots, c_m\}$ is the set of conjunctive selection criteria. Each selection criterion c_i is restricted to an equality $< a_i = v_i >$ between an attribute $a_i \in \{a_1, \ldots, a_n\}$ and its searched value v_i which can be crisp or fuzzy and must be defined on a subset of the definition domain of a_i.

When the fuzzy value of a selection attribute has a hierarchized symbolic definition domain, the fuzzy set used to represent the fuzzy value can be defined on a subset of this definition domain. We consider that such a fuzzy set defines degrees implicitly on the whole definition domain of the selection attribute. In order to take those implicit degrees into account, the *fuzzy set closure* has been defined in [3]. Intuitively, the degrees are propagated to more specific values of the hierarchized symbolic domain. The fuzzy set closure is systematically used when a comparison involves two fuzzy sets (an expression of end-users' preferences and an imprecise datum) defined on a hierarchical definition domain.

The answers. An answer to a query Q must (1) satisfy all the selection criteria of Q in the meaning of definition 4 given below and (2) associate a constant value with each projection attribute of Q.

Definition 4. Let $< a = v >$ be a selection criterion and v' a value of the attribute a stored in the databases. The selection criterion $< a = v >$ is satisfied with the possibility degree $\Pi(cl(v), cl(v'))$ in the meaning of definition 2 where the *cl* function corresponds to the fuzzy set closure.

As the selection criteria of a query are conjunctive, we use the *min* operator to compute the adequation degree associated with the answer.

Definition 5. An *answer* to a query $Q = \{V, S, C\}$ is a set of tuples, each of the form $\{v_1, \ldots, v_l, ad_\Pi\}$, where $v_1, \ldots, v_l$ correspond to the crisp or fuzzy values associated with each projection attribute $a_i \in S$, where all the selection criteria $c_1, \ldots, c_m$ of Q are satisfied with the possibility degrees $\Pi_1, \ldots, \Pi_m$, and where ad_Π is the possibility degree of the answer to Q defined by: $ad_\Pi = min_{i=1}^{m}(\Pi_i)$.

2.3 The XML Database

The XML database has been built in the MIEL++ system in order to store information retrieved from the Web. It is a set of XML documents which may contain fuzzy values. We propose to model XML documents as fuzzy data trees [5, 4] which are data trees that allow fuzzy values to be represented. According to the definition of [7], a data tree is a triple (t, l, v) where t is a finite tree, l a labelling function that assigns a label to each node of t and v a partial value function that assigns a value to nodes of t. The couple (t, l) is called a labelled tree. The representation of fuzzy values relies on the fuzzy set formalism. For readability reasons in this paper, we only deal with discrete fuzzy sets. However, the contributions of this paper can easily be extended to continuous fuzzy sets.

Definition 6. A discrete fuzzy set f is represented by a data tree which is composed of a root labelled *DFS* and such that for each element x of $Dom(f)$, there exists a node labelled *ValF* that has two children labelled *Item* and *MD* (for Membership Degree) of respective values x and $\mu(x)$.

In a fuzzy data tree, the partial value function v can assign a crisp or a fuzzy value to a node, which is then called *crisp* or *fuzzy value node.*

Definition 7. A *fuzzy data tree* is a triple (t, l, v) where (t, l) is a labelled tree and v is a partial value function that assigns a value to the crisp and fuzzy value nodes of t. The value assigned to a crisp value node is an atomic value and the one assigned to a fuzzy value node is a data tree which conforms to definition 6.

A fuzzy data tree (t, l, v) is an *instance* [7] of a type tree (t_T, l_T) [1] if there exists a *strict type homomorphism* h from (t, l) to (t_T, l_T): (i) h preserves the root of t: $\text{root}(t_T) = h(\text{root}(t))$, (ii) h preserves the structure of t: whenever node m is a child of node n, $h(m)$ is a child of $h(n)$ and (iii) h preserves the labels of t: for each node n of t, $l(n){=}l_T(h(n))$.

Example 1. *Figure 2 gives two examples of fuzzy data trees representing two lines of a Web data table. The crisp value node* originalVal *represents the original value of a* Product *in the Web data table and the fuzzy value node* finalVal *is a discrete fuzzy set representing the terms of the MIEL++ taxonomy associated with the original value. See subsection 4.1 for more details.*

3 The Approximate Query Processing of the XML Base

The XML database is filled with data semi-automatically extracted from the Web. Its integration into the MIEL++ system is possible thanks to the semantic enrichment of its data according to the ontology (see subsection 4.1 for more details). This section presents the XML subsystem which realizes the query processing of the XML database by means of the MIEL query language. In order

[1] A type tree is a labelled tree such that no node has two children labelled the same.

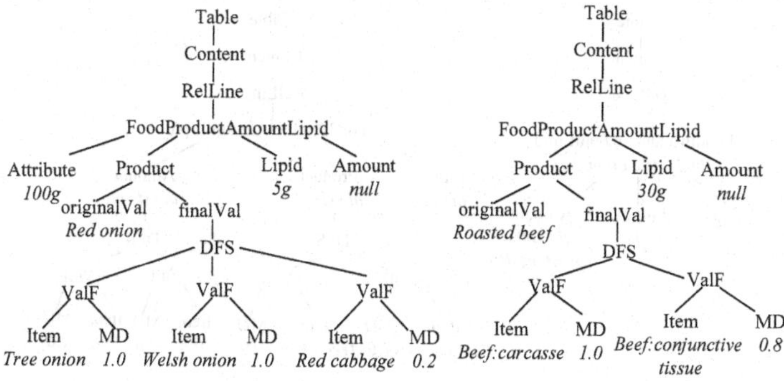

Fig. 2. Two fuzzy data trees

to take into account the imperfections coming from the semantic enrichment of the XML database, we propose to introduce flexibility into the query processing of the XML database using the following three techniques: deletion, renaming and insertion of query nodes. In this section, we define the notions of views, queries and answers of the MIEL query language in the XML subsystem.

3.1 The Views

The XML subsystem contains a set of views, which are built from the terms and the relations of the MIEL++ ontology and allow one to query the XML database. The information needed to perform approximate query processing is encoded at the view level. For each node of each view, except for the root of each view, we propose to define a deletion cost, renaming values and their costs.

Definition 8. A *view that conforms to a type tree* (t_T, l_T) is a 4-tuple $V{=}(t_V, l_V, w_V, c_V)$ where (t_V, l_V) is an instance of (t_T, l_T), w_V is a partial function that assigns the mark *ql* to crisp and fuzzy value nodes of t_V which are then queryable nodes, c_V is a partial function that assigns transformation information to each node and value node –except to the root– of t_V. The transformation information of a node n are represented by a couple of the form $(dc_n, \{(r_n^1, rc_n^1), \ldots, (r_n^p, rc_n^p)\})$ where dc_n is the deletion cost of the node n and $r_n^1, \ldots, r_n^p$ are the possible renamings of the node n with their corresponding costs $rc_n^1, \ldots, rc_n^p$.

Example 2. *The left side of figure 3 shows a view using the relation* FoodProductAmountLipid *involving three queryable attributes: the* product, *the* amount of the product *and the* quantity of lipid. *A deletion cost of* 1000 *(resp.* 100*) is associated with the node* FoodProductAmountLipid *(resp.* Amount*). A possible renaming in Relation (resp. Attribute) is associated with the node* FoodProductAmountLipid *(resp.* Amount*) with a renaming cost of* 50 *(resp.* 10*).*

3.2 The Queries

A query is built from a given view, where the end-user specifies: (i) among the set of queryable value nodes of the view, the selection and the projection value

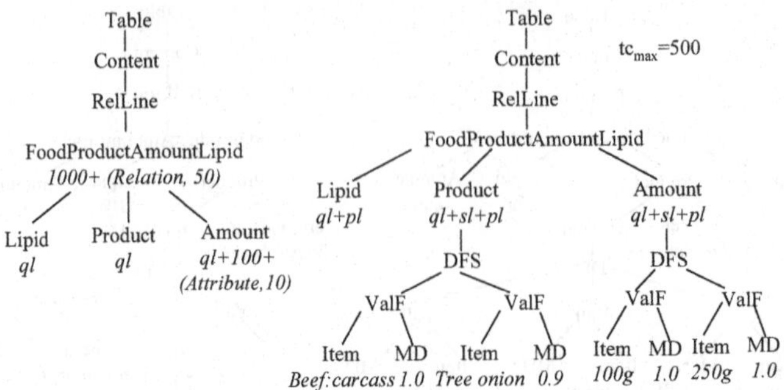

Fig. 3. An example of a view and a query defined on that view

nodes of the query and (ii) a transformation cost threshold which allows some transformations to be forbidden. The end-user can also modify the transformation information defined in the view.

Definition 9. A *query* that conforms to a type tree (t_T, l_T) is a 8-tuple Q=(t_Q, l_Q, w_Q, c_Q, tc_{max}, p_Q, s_Q, ws_Q) where:

- (t_Q, l_Q, w_Q, c_Q) is a view that conforms to (t_T, l_T);
- tc_{max} is the maximum acceptable transformation cost of the query;
- p_Q is a partial function that assigns the mark *pl* to the queryable value nodes of the view, which are considered as the *projection value nodes*;
- s_Q is a partial function that assigns the mark *sl* to the queryable value nodes of the view, which are considered as the *selection value nodes*, also called selection criteria;
- ws_Q is a partial value function that assigns a value to the selection value nodes of the query, such that the value assigned to a crisp value node is an atomic value and the value assigned to a fuzzy value node is a data tree with a root labelled DFS which conforms to definition 6.

As defined in definition 3, the value v of a selection criterion $< a = v >$, a being a value node of the query, must be defined on a subset of the definition domain of a. When this value is fuzzy, the fuzzy selection criterion which expresses the end-user's preferences is represented by a fuzzy set.

Example 3. *The query Q of figure 3 (right side) expresses that the end-user wants to obtain the product, the amount of product and the quantity of lipid from the view using the relation* FoodProductAmountLipid*. The fuzzy value assigned to the selection criterion* Product *can be interpreted as "the end-user wants Beef: carcass as a product, but he/she also accepts Tree onion with a lower interest". The associated maximum transformation cost* tc_{max} *is 500.*

3.3 The Approximate Queries

The search for approximate answers to an XML query Q is done in two steps. The first step consists in generating potential approximated queries from the query

Q by means of combinations of the following two transformation rules: (i) every node and value node of Q with a deletion cost can be deleted, (ii) every node and value node with renaming values and costs can be renamed. Each generated approximate query must have at least one projection value node and one selection value node, non necessarily distinct. In the second step, a transformation cost is computed with each potential approximate query generated as the sum of the deletion costs of the deleted nodes and the renaming costs of the renamed nodes from the query Q. Only the approximate queries with a transformation cost lower than the transformation cost threshold of the query Q are kept and will be executed to find the approximate answers to the query Q.

Definition 10. An approximate query generated from a query Q=(t_Q, l_Q, w_Q, c_Q, tc_{max}, p_Q, s_Q, ws_Q) is a 7-tuple A=(t_A, l_A, w_A, p_A, s_A, ws_A, tc_A) where:

- there exists a *weak structural homomorphism* h from the nodes of t_A into nodes of t_Q: (i) h preserves the root of t_A: root(t_A) = h(root(t_Q)) and (ii) h preserves the ancestor-descendant relationship of t_A: whenever node m is a descendant of node n, $h(m)$ is a descendant of $h(n)$;
- l_A is a labelling function that assigns to each node n in t_A either the label assigned by l_Q to the image node $h(n)$ in t_Q or a renaming value belonging to the transformation information $c_Q(h(n))$ of the image node $h(n)$ in t_Q;
- for every value node n of t_A such that $w_Q(h(n)) = ql$, we have $w_A(n) = ql$ and, for the other value nodes of t_A, w_A is not defined;
- for every value node n of t_A such that $p_Q(h(n)) = pl$, we have $p_A(n) = pl$ and, for the other value nodes of t_A, p_A is not defined. Moreover, there must exist at least one value node n in t_A such that $p_A(n) = pl$;
- for every value node n of t_A such that $s_Q(h(n)) = sl$, we have $s_A(n) = sl$ and, for the other value nodes of t_A, s_A is not defined. Moreover, there must exist at least one value node n in t_A such that $s_A(n) = sl$;
- for every value node n of t_A such that $ws_Q(h(n))$ is defined, we have $ws_A(n)$ = $ws_Q(h(n))$ and, for the other value nodes of t_A, ws_A is not defined;
- tc_A is the transformation cost of the query Q into the approximate query A: $tc_A = \sum_{i=1}^{l} dc_{n_d^i} + \sum_{i=1}^{q} rc_{n_r^i}$ where $c_Q(n)$=(dc_n, {(r_n^1, rc_n^1), ..., (r_n^p, rc_n^p)}) is the transformation information of a node n of t_Q (see definition 8), {n_d^1, ..., n_d^l} is the list of deleted nodes[2] of t_Q in t_A and {n_r^1, ..., n_r^q} is the list of renamed nodes[3] of t_Q in t_A. Moreover, tc_A must be lower or equal to the maximum acceptable transformation cost tc_{max} of the query.

Example 4. *Figure 4 gives two examples of approximate queries generated from the query Q of figure 3. The first approximate query (left side) has been generated by renaming the node* Amount *to* Attribute, *the second one (right side) by deleting the node* Amount.

[2] The list of nodes of t_Q such that n_d^i has no antecedent in t_A by h.

[3] The list of nodes of t_Q such that n_r^i has an antecedent in t_A by h and $l_Q(n_r^i) \neq l_A(h^{-1}(n_r^i))$.

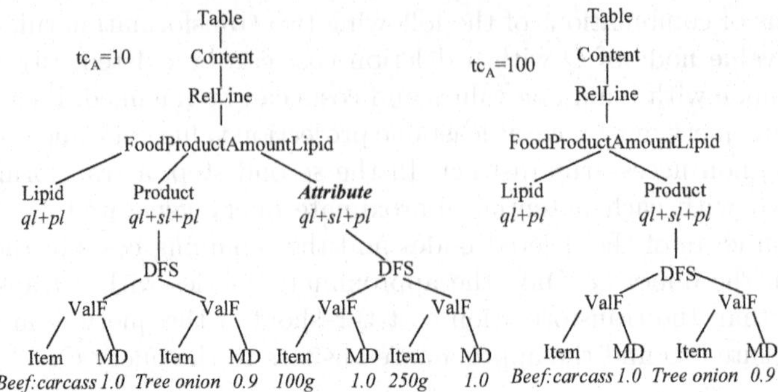

Fig. 4. Two examples of approximate queries generated from the query Q of figure 3

Remark 1. *Thanks to the representation of fuzzy values in a fuzzy data tree (see definition 7), there is no distinction between the deletion of a fuzzy value node and of a crisp value node: in both cases, the node and its value are deleted.*

3.4 The Answers

The approximate answer to an XML query Q is the union of the answers to the generated approximate queries from Q. While the generation of approximate queries from Q relies on the deletion and the renaming of nodes of Q, the computation of the answers to an approximate query A allows the insertion of nodes into A. An answer to an approximate query A (i) satisfies all the selection criteria of A in the meaning of definition 4 and (ii) associates a constant value with each projection value node of A. The search for the answers to an approximate query in an XML database is done through the valuation of the query on the fuzzy data trees of the database as defined below.

Definition 11. Let A=(t_A, l_A, w_A, p_A, s_A, ws_A, tc_A) be an approximate query generated from Q=(t_Q, l_Q, w_Q, c_Q, tc_{max}, p_Q, s_Q, ws_Q) which conforms to a type tree T=(t_T, l_T) and D=(t_D, l_D, v_D) be a fuzzy data tree instance of T. A *valuation* of A with respect to D is a mapping σ_D from t_A into t_D such that:

- σ_D is a *weak type homomorphism* from (t_A, l_A) into (t_D, l_D): σ_D is a weak structural homomorphism (see definition 10) and preserves the labels of t_A;
- σ_D satisfies each selection criterion n_s^i, $i \in [1, m]$, of A with the possibility degree $\Pi(ws_A(n_s^i), v_D(\sigma_D(n_s^i)))$.

The adequation degree of the fuzzy data tree D to the approximate query A through the valuation σ_D is $ad_{\Pi(D)} = min_{i \in [1,m]}(\Pi(ws_A(n_s^i), v_D(\sigma_D(n_s^i))))$.

An answer to an approximate query in the XML database is a set of tuples, where each tuple is composed of (i) a set of values given to each projection node, (ii) an adequation degree of the answer to the approximate query and (iii) a cost of transforming the initial query into the approximate query.

Definition 12. An *answer* to an approximate query A=(t_A, l_A, w_A, p_A, s_A, ws_A, tc_A) composed of m projection value nodes $n_p^1, \ldots, n_p^m$ in an XML database $\mathcal{W}$ is a set of tuples, each tuple being defined as follows: $\{ \cup_{i=1}^m v_D(\sigma_D(n_p^i)) \cup ad_{\Pi(D)} \cup tc_A \mid D$ is a fuzzy data tree of $\mathcal{W}$ and σ_D is a valuation of A w.r.t. $D\}$.

Example 5. *To facilitate result interpretation, answers are ordered first by ascending transformation cost (tc_A) and second by descending adequation degree ($ad_{\Pi(D)}$). The answer to the query Q of figure 3 according to the left approximate query of figure 4 in the fuzzy data trees of figure 2 is the following: {(Product.originalVal=Red onion, Product.finalVal=1.0/Tree onion+1.0/Welsh onion+0.2/Red cabbage, Attribute=100g, Lipid=5g, ad_Π=0.9, tc_A=10)}. The answer to the query Q of figure 3 according to the right approximate query of figure 4 in the fuzzy data trees of figure 2 is the following: {(Product.originalVal= Roasted Beef, Product.finalVal=1.0/Beef:carcass+0.8/Beef:conjunctive tissue, Lipid=30g, ad_Π=1.0, tc_A=100), (Product.originalVal=Red onion, Product. finalVal = 1.0/Tree onion+ 1.0/Welsh onion+ 0.2/Red cabbage, Lipid=5g, ad_Π =0.9, tc_A=100) }.*

Remark 2. *Note that when we compute the approximate answer to a query Q which is the union of the answers to the generated approximate queries from Q, we only keep tuples coming from distinct data trees of the XML database.*

4 Application

The approximate query processing detailed below has been applied to the XML database of the MIEL++ system. Subsection 4.1 briefly presents the SML process which permits this database to be filled. Subsection 4.2 presents the implementation of the approximate query processing and first experimental results.

4.1 The XML Database Filling

The XML database of the MIEL++ system is filled with data semi-automatically extracted from the Web. The search is focussed on pdf and html documents which contain data tables and concern the MIEL++ domain application. The Web data tables are extracted and translated into a generic XML representation of data table, called XTab. Those XTab documents are then transformed into SML (for Semantic Markup Language) documents, by a semantization process based on the MIEL++ ontology. Then it becomes possible to query the SML documents through the MIEL uniform query language. The SML process [9] achieves three kinds of semantic enrichment: (i) it associates terms of a Web data table with their corresponding terms in the MIEL++ taxonomy, (ii) when enough terms are identified in a given column of a Web data table, it becomes possible to identify the "title" of the column, otherwise the generic title *attribute* is associated with the column; (iii) it instanciates semantic relations of the ontology which appear in the Web table schema. That instanciation is done by comparing the previously identified columns with the signatures of the semantic relations of the ontology.

A semantic relation can be completely or partially represented in a Web table schema. Moreover, in [5], we propose a fuzzy semantic enrichment of the terms of a Web data table: each association between a term of a Web data table and a term belonging to the MIEL++ taxonomy is weighted by a possibility degree depending on their syntactic closeness. The SML documents thus contain fuzzy data: for a given term of a Web data table, its associated terms belonging to the taxonomy are represented by a discrete fuzzy set.

Example 6. *Figure 5 presents two examples of Web data tables and the corresponding tables obtained by semantic enrichment. In the left table, the first column has been identified as having the type* product *and the third one as having the type* lipid. *But the second one, which actually corresponds to the amount, has not been identified because the title of the column is an abbreviation (Qty). So it is associated with the generic type* attribute. *The semantic relations* FoodProductAmountLipid *of the MIEL++ ontology is only partially instanciated, because the attribute* Amount *is not in the Web table schema. The remaining column having the type* attribute *is added to the instanciation of the relation* FoodProductAmountLipid *in order to avoid bad interpretation of the data. The left fuzzy data tree of figure 2 corresponds to the third line of this Web data table. In the right table, the first column has been identified as having the type* product *and the second one as having the type* lipid. *Consequently, the relation* FoodProductAmountLipid *is only partially instanciated, because the attribute* Amount *is not in the Web table schema. The right fuzzy data tree of figure 2 corresponds to the second line of this Web data table.*

In example 5, the tuple of the first answer (tc_A=10) shows that the renaming of the node Amount *of the query Q to* Attribute *allows the value 100g to be retrieved even if the corresponding column (*Qty*) in the left Web data table of figure 5 has not been identified as an amount. The first tuple of the second answer shows that the deletion of the node* Amount *in the query Q allows pertinent information to*

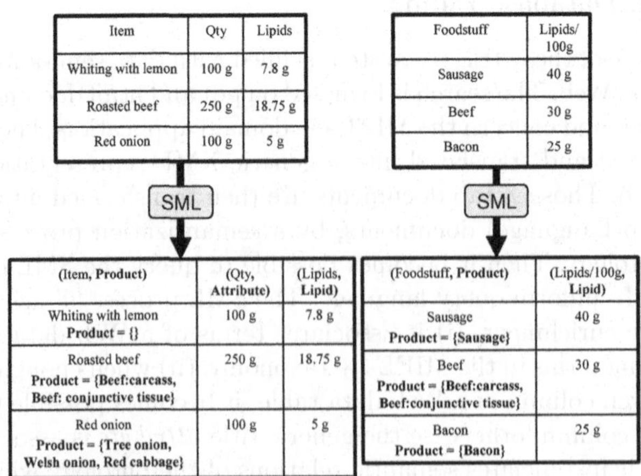

Item	Qty	Lipids
Whiting with lemon	100 g	7.8 g
Roasted beef	250 g	18.75 g
Red onion	100 g	5 g

Foodstuff	Lipids/ 100g
Sausage	40 g
Beef	30 g
Bacon	25 g

(Item, Product)	(Qty, Attribute)	(Lipids, Lipid)
Whiting with lemon **Product = {}**	100 g	7.8 g
Roasted beef **Product = {Beef:carcass, Beef: conjunctive tissue}**	250 g	18.75 g
Red onion **Product = {Tree onion, Welsh onion, Red cabbage}**	100 g	5 g

(Foodstuff, Product)	(Lipids/100g, Lipid)
Sausage **Product = {Sausage}**	40 g
Beef **Product = {Beef:carcass, Beef:conjunctive tissue}**	30 g
Bacon **Product = {Bacon}**	25 g

Fig. 5. Two examples of Web data tables and their associated semantic enrichment

be retrieved from the right Web data table of figure 5 even if the column amount has not been identified. In all the tuples of both answers, the insertion of the nodes originalVal *and* finalVal *into the query Q has been used.*

4.2 Implementation and Preliminary Tests

We have implemented a prototype of this querying system in Java using the Xquery processor Saxon (www.saxonica.com). Given an XML initial query, the program runs in the following three steps. In the first step, approximate queries are generated in XML documents from the initial query by means of deletion and renaming of nodes. In the second step, each distinct approximate query is translated into an XQuery query and executed in ascending order of its transformation cost. The result is built from the union of the answer to the initial query and the answers to the generated approximate queries, the duplicates being removed. Encouraging preliminary tests have been done on a database composed of 196 SML documents. Three different queries involving three different semantic relations have been tested. The first (resp. second and third) query contains 3 (resp. 2 and 2) selection and 3 (resp 3 and 2) projection attributes. Among the 93 results obtained, 66 are pertinent results obtained from the approximate queries, 4 of which being also obtained from the initial query.

5 Conclusion

In this paper, we propose a new XML querying system which harmoniously combines two kinds of complementary flexibility management. These two kinds of flexibility concern on the one hand the structure of the query tree and on the other hand the values stored in the data trees. Firstly, the calculation of a set of approximate queries from an initial one allowing insertion, renaming and deletion of nodes permits the retrieval of XML data trees whose structure is close to that of the initial query. Secondly, the expression of preferences in selection criteria of the query, by means of fuzzy sets, allows the end-user to enlarge the set of answers. Finally, this new querying system is able to manage imprecise data, represented by possibility distributions, stored in the XML database using fuzzy pattern matching techniques. In the very near future, we will realise experimentations of our approach in different application domains using different ontologies in order to evaluate the genericity of our approach. We will also study the way of introducing a "degree of uncertainty" in the partial instanciation of semantic relations of the ontology into a Web data table.

References

1. S. Amer-Yahia, S. Cho, and D. Srivastava, *Tree pattern relaxation*, EDBT, 2002.
2. D. Braga, A. Campi, E. Damiani, G. Pasi, and PL. Lanzi, *FXPath: Flexible querying of xml documents*, Proc. of EuroFuse 2002 (2002).

3. P. Buche, C. Dervin, O. Haemmerlé, and R. Thomopoulos, *Fuzzy querying of incomplete, imprecise and heterogeneously structured data in the relational model using ontologies and rules*, IEEE Trans. Fuzzy Systems **13** (2005), no. 3, 373–383.
4. P. Buche, J. Dibie-Barthélemy, O. Haemmerlé, and G. Hignette, *Fuzzy semantic tagging and flexible querying of xml documents extracted from the web*, Journal of Intelligent Information Systems **26** (2006), 25–40.
5. P. Buche, J. Dibie-Barthélemy, O. Haemmerlé, and M. Houhou, *Towards flexible querying of xml imprecise data in a data warehouse opened on the web*, FQAS 2004 (Lyon, France), LNAI #3055, Springer, June 2004, pp. 28–40.
6. E. Damiani and L. Tanca, *Blind queries to xml data*, DEXA'00, 2000, pp. 345–356.
7. C. Delobel, M. C. Rousset C. Reynaud, J.-P. Sirot, and D. Vodislav, *Semantic integration in xyleme: a uniform tree-based approach*, DKE. **44** (2003), no. 3, 267–298.
8. D. Dubois and H. Prade, *Possibility theory: an approach to computerized processing of uncertainty*, New York: Plenum Press, 1988.
9. H. Gagliardi, O. Haemmerlé, N. Pernelle, and F. Sais, *A semantic enrichment of data tables applied to food risk assessment*, DS'05, LNCS #3735, 2005, pp. 374–376.
10. Zongmin Ma, *Fuzzy database modeling with xml*, Springer., 2005.
11. Lucian Popa, Yannis Velegrakis, Renée J. Miller, Mauricio A. Hernández, and Ronald Fagin, *Translating web data.*, VLDB, 2002, pp. 598–609.
12. T. Schlieder, *Schema-driven evaluation of approximate tree-pattern queries*, Proceedings of EDBT, 2002.
13. Jeffrey D. Ullman, *Information integration using logical views.*, Theor. Comput. Sci. **239** (2000), no. 2, 189–210.
14. J. Widom, *Research problems in data warehousing*, Proceedings of the International Conference on Information and Knowledge Management, 1995.
15. G. Wiederhold, *Mediation in information systems*, ACM Computing Surveys **27** (1995), no. 2, 265–267.
16. L. Zadeh, *Fuzzy sets*, Information and control **8** (1965), 338–353.
17. ———, *Fuzzy sets as a basis for a theory of possibility*, Fuzzy Sets and Systems **1** (1978), 3–28.

Relaxation Paradigm in a Flexible Querying Context

Patrick Bosc, Allel HadjAli, and Olivier Pivert

IRISA/ENSSAT, Université de Rennes 1
6, rue de Kerampont – BP 80518, 22305 Lannion Cedex, France
{bosc, hadjali, pivert}@enssat.fr

Abstract. In this paper, we discuss an approach for relaxing a failing query in the context of flexible querying. The approach relies on the notion of proximity which is defined in a relative way. We show how such proximity allows for transforming a given predicate into an enlarged one. The resulting predicate is semantically not far from the original one and it is obtained by a simple fuzzy arithmetic operation. We show also how the search for a non-failing relaxed query over the lattice of relaxed queries can be improved by exploiting the notions of MFSs (*Minimal Failing Sub-queries*) and MGQs (*Maximally Generalized failing Queries*) of the original query.

1 Introduction

The rapid expansion of the Internet has made a variety of databases, including bibliographies, scientific databases, and travel reservation systems accessible to a large number of lay users. One of the common problems that users might be confronted with in their Web search is the *failing query problem*: users' queries return an empty set of answers. Users are frustrated by such kind of answers since they do not meet their expectations and interests. Their desire would be to find alternative answers that are related to the answers of the original queries. One technique that could enable for providing such answers is called *relaxation*. Query relaxation aims at expanding the scope of a query by relaxing the constraints involved in the query.

Let us note that manually relaxing failing queries is a tedious and time-consuming task. Since the late 80's, several automated approaches to query relaxation have been proposed [6]. The main goal of those approaches is to modify a failing user query into a relaxed query whose answer is non-empty, or at least to identify the cause of the failure. Some approaches are based on the concept of *false presupposition*. Recall that a *presupposition* of a statement is any statement entailed by the original. For instance, the statement "the king of France is bald" has as presupposition "there is a king of France" which is a *false* presupposition. Motro [10] has addressed the issue of empty answers by proposing a relaxation method which focuses on finding the false presuppositions of a failing query. Each generalization of the query is considered as a presupposition of the query. Query generalization is obtained by relaxing to a degree some of the conditions involved in the query. The system proposed can find all *Maximally Generalized failing Queries* (MGQs). Such responses have the potential to be too informative either to explain the failure or to help for turning the query into a non-failing one. A related approach has been proposed by Godfrey [7], who considers any sub-query (the query with some of its conditions eliminated) as a presupposition

H.L. Larsen et al. (Eds.): FQAS 2006, LNAI 4027, pp. 39 – 50, 2006.

of the query itself. The focus of this work is the search for *Minimal Failing Sub-queries* (MFSs) of a failing query. Such sub-queries are the smallest sub-queries that fail. They constitute a better response to failing database queries.

In the context of flexible queries (i.e., queries that contain gradual predicates), the empty answer problem could still arise. Namely, there is no available data in the database that *somewhat satisfies* the user query. Only few works have been done for dealing with this problem. They mainly aim at relaxing the fuzzy requirements involved in the failing user query. This can be done by applying a transformation to some or all conditions of that query. A flexible query relaxation approach has been proposed by Bosc *et al.* in [2][3]. It is based on a particular *tolerance relation* modeled by a *relative proximity* parameterized by a tolerance indicator. This notion of proximity is intended for defining a set of predicates that are close, semantically speaking, to a given predicate *P*. In this paper, we show how flexible conjunctive queries can be relaxed locally, i.e. the relaxation is performed only on some sub-queries of the failing query, using a tolerance-based transformation. On the other hand, we also show how the notions of MGQs and MFSs could be beneficial for relaxing such queries. In particular, we propose an efficient search technique for finding a non-failing query by exploiting the MFSs of the original query.

The paper is structured as follows. Section 2 recalls some relaxation approaches that have been proposed in the Boolean context. In section 3, we describe the problem of flexible query relaxation on the one hand, and propose a method to solve this problem on the other hand. Section 4 shows how the MFSs can be used for finding a non-failing query over the lattice of relaxed queries in an efficient way. Last, we briefly recall the main features of our proposal and conclude.

2 Boolean Query Relaxation

Let us first introduce the following basic notions. A conjunctive Boolean query Q is of the form $Q = A_1 \wedge \ldots \wedge A_N$, where each A_i is an atomic condition. Q' is a sub-query of Q iff $Q' = A_{s_1} \wedge \ldots \wedge A_{s_m}$, and $\{s_1, \ldots, s_m\} \subset \{1, \ldots, N\}$. Let us recall that with a Boolean query, an item from the database simply either matches or it does not. Moreover, if a sub-query fails, then the query itself must fail.

As mentioned in the Introduction, we can distinguish two main approaches that can be used to relax a conjunctive Boolean query when it fails to produce any answer:

- Motro's approach: It consists in transforming query conditions into more general conditions;
- Godfrey's approach: It aims at generalizing a query by removing some parts from the query.

Both of the two approaches are based on the notion of *false presuppositions.*

2.1 Motro's Approach

In [10], Motro has proposed an approach to deal with failing queries. This approach combines the notion of relaxing queries into more general queries and that of searching for false presupposition. The query generalizations are obtained by replacing some query conditions by more general ones. In particular, generalization can be performed by weakening mathematical conditions or removing non-mathematical conditions altogether. For instance, the condition *"salary ≥ 40 K€"* could be relaxed by considering the modified condition *"salary ≥ 39 K€"*. Let us consider the query Q_1 that retrieves the employees that satisfy the conditions: *age ≤ 30*, *gender = Female* and salary *≥ 40 k€*. The lattice of the generalizations of Q_1 is shown in Figure 1, where the notation *(x, y, z)* stands for a presupposition that there may be employees whose age is under *x*, whose sex is *y*, and whose yearly salary is at least *z*. The symbol * indicates any value (it cannot be generalized any further).

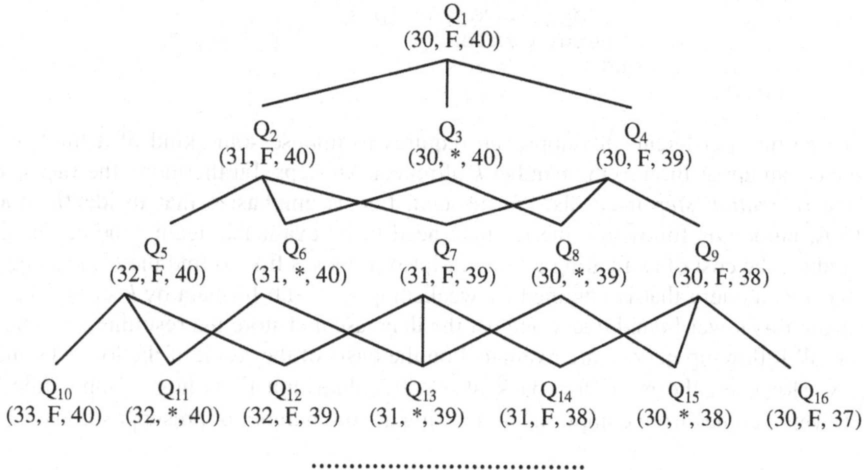

Fig. 1. Lattice of generalized queries

Let us note that a sub-query of a query is an *extreme generalization*: some of the conditions have been completely removed (they are vacuously true). Motro claims that often queries that result in null answers are based on *false presuppositions*. In such cases, instead to report the empty answer set, it is more cooperative to answer with information messages about the false presuppositions of the considered query. For extracting presuppositions from queries and verifying their correctness against the database, a tool called `SEAVE` has been proposed. Starting with the fact that the false presupposition that has no false presuppositions is the responsible of the failure of the query, `SEAVE` can return the set of all false presuppositions that are *significant* (presupposition such that every more general presupposition can produce some answers). Such presuppositions are also called *Maximally Generalized Failing Query* (MGQs). MGQs have the potential to be more informative and provide relaxation facilities to the user. They provide either an explanation for the failure or some assistance for turning the query into a non-failing query. A slightly modified `SEAVE` algorithm is sketched in Algorithm 1, where

- `test(p)` evaluates the presupposition *p* against the database: it returns *true* if *p* produces some answers, *false* if *p* fails.
- `mgp(p)` returns the set of immediate more general presuppositions of *p*. For instance, in Figure 1, if $p = Q_2$, then $mgp(p) = \{Q_5, Q_6, Q_7\}$.

Algorithm 1. A slightly modified version of SEAVE algorithm

```
boolean seave(p, var Mgq)
  begin
     if test(p) then return true
         else
           begin
             is_Mgq := true;
             Set := mgp(p);
             for q in Set do
               is_Mgq := is_Mgq and seave(q, Mgq);
             if is_Mgq then
               Mgq := Mgq ∪ {p};
             return false
           end;
  end;
```

To be more efficient, this approach requires to impose some kind of a limit, for instance, an upper limit to the number *k* of relaxation steps. Furthermore, the *step size of the relaxation step* must also be decided. Let us emphasize that to identify the MGQs, numerous follow-up queries may need to be evaluated against the database. To reduce the cost of evaluating a query, Motro proposes first to find the *lower bound query*, i.e., a query that is obtained by weakening each sub-formula by *k* steps. Then, evaluate this lower bound query against the database and store the resulting relations. Now, all follow-up queries are evaluated on the basis of the result of the lower bound query. However, the main drawback of SEAVE algorithm is its high computational cost, which comes from computing and testing a large number of presuppositions.

2.2 Godfrey's Approach

Godfrey [7] considers that any sub-query is a presupposition of the query itself. Let Q be a query composed of three atomic conditions, i.e. $Q = a(x) \wedge b(x) \wedge c(x)$. The lattice of sub-queries associated to Q is depicted in Figure 2 (each sub-query is marked with a number of answers that it produces).

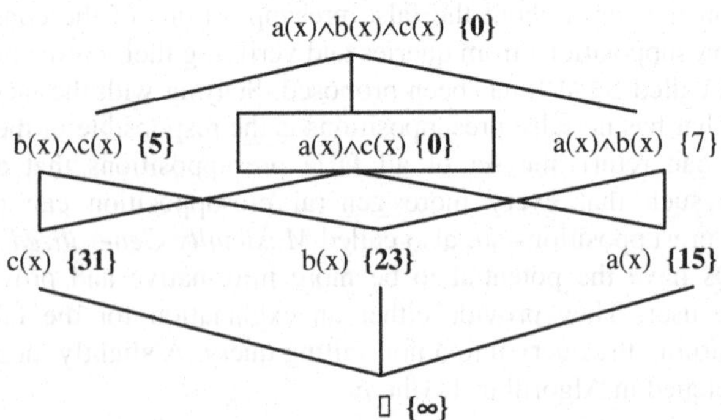

Fig. 2. Lattice of sub-queries (the symbol □ denotes an empty sub-query)

A query succeeds (that is, it results in some answers) if all its sub-queries succeed as well. When a query fails (that is, it results in no answers), it is worthwhile to identify presuppositions (sub-queries) that fail. It is a stronger statement to report the failure of the sub-query than to report the failure of the query itself. The focus of this work is the search for *Minimal Failing Sub-queries* (MFSs) of a failing query. Such sub-queries are the smallest sub-queries that fail.

Thus, the system reports not just the empty answer set but also the cause for the query failure by identifying one or more MFSs (note that an MFS is not unique, there may be many of them). An efficient algorithm is proposed in [7] to find an MFS of a query of *N* conjuncts, see Algorithm 2. This algorithm that proceeds depth-first and top-down, is polynomial and runs in *O(N)* time. The function `test(Q)` in Algorithm 2 consists in evaluating the query Q against the database such that: if the query fails, then `test` returns *true*. Otherwise, if the query has a non-empty answer set, `test` returns *false*.

Algorithm 2. Algorithm for finding an MFS in *N* steps [7]

```
boolean a_mfs_fast(Top, Mfs)
  begin
    if test(Top) then
            begin
              a_mfs_true(Top, Mfs, ∅);
              return true
            end
        else return false
  end;
a_mfs_true(Set, Mfs, Core)
 begin
  if Set = ∅ then Mfs := Core
    else
     begin
      choose Ele ∈ Set;
      if test((Set - Ele) ∪ Core) then
              a_mfs_true(Set - {Ele}, Mfs, Core)
        else a_mfs_true(Set - {Ele}, Mfs, Core ∪ {Ele})
     end;
  end;
```

The principle of this algorithm is based on the following observation: if a query $Q = \{e_1, e_2,..., e_N\}$ is evaluated *true* and the sub-query $(Q - \{e_i\})$ is evaluated *false* then any MFS of Q must contain the atom e_i. It has been shown that finding all MFSs of a query is intractable and is *NP-Complete* [7]. However, finding *k* MFSs, for any fixed *k*, can be done in polynomial time. The algorithm proposed has the following properties [8]:

- It never performs a redundant test: i) it never evaluates the same sub-query twice; ii) if a query was asked and evaluated empty, no super-query will then be asked; iii) if a query was asked and evaluated non-empty, no sub-query will then be asked.
- It exploits the decomposability of the relaxation search: all MFS of a failing sub-query are also MFS of the original query.

3 Flexible Query Relaxation

In this section, we first introduce the problem of query weakening in the fuzzy setting. Then, we describe a *proximity–based approach* for a single-predicate query.

3.1 Relaxation Problem

Flexible (or *fuzzy*) *queries* [1] are requests in which user's preferences can be expressed. The user does not specify crisp conditions, but soft ones whose satisfaction may be regarded as a matter of a *degree*. Then, he/she can distinguish between acceptable and non-acceptable answers in a more refined way than with a strictly Boolean filter. Towards this end, *vague predicates* are allowed in the requests; such predicates are represented by means of *fuzzy sets* [5] and model *gradual properties*. A typical example of a fuzzy query is: "retrieve the employees in a department which are *young* and *well-paid*". As a consequence, the elements in the result form a set of discriminated elements according to their global satisfaction of the conditions appearing in the user query.

Relaxing a failing fuzzy query consists in modifying the constraints involved in the query in order to obtain a less restrictive variant. Let Q be a fuzzy query of the form $P_1 \wedge \ldots \wedge P_N$ (where P_i is a fuzzy predicate), and assume that the set of answers to Q is empty. A natural way to relax Q, in order to obtain a non-empty set of answers, is to apply a *basic uniform transformation* to each predicate P_i. For instance, the predicate "*young*" could be transformed into the predicate "*more or less young*". This transformation process can be accomplished iteratively if necessary. Let us mention that some desirable properties are required for any transformation T when applied to a predicate P. In particular ($T(P)$ representing the modified predicate):

- (C_1): T is such that $\forall u \in$ domain(A), $\mu_{T(P)}(u) \geq \mu_P(u)$ where A is the attribute concerned by P;
- (C_2): T extends the support of the fuzzy predicate P, i.e. $S(P) = \{u \,/\, \mu_P(u) > 0\} \subset S(T(P)) = \{u \,/\, \mu_{T(P)}(u) > 0\}$ where $S(P)$ stands for the support of P;
- (C_3): T preserves the set of typical values of P, i.e. $C(P) = \{u \,/\, \mu_P(u) = 1\} = C(T(P)) = \{u \,/\, \mu_{T(P)}(u) = 1\}$ where $C(P)$ stands for the core of P.

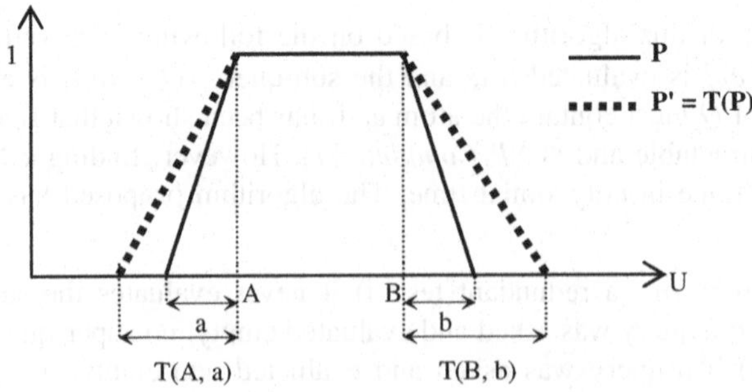

Fig. 3. Basic transformation

Then, if P is a fuzzy predicate represented by the trapezoidal membership function (*t.m.f.*) (A, B, a, b), the desired transformation T is such that $P' = T(P) = (A, B, T(A, a), T(B, b))$, where $[A, B]$ and $[A - T(A, a), B + T(B, b)]$ denote the core and the support of the modified predicate P' respectively. See Figure 3.

To be more efficient, a transformation T must still remain valid in the case of crisp predicates, i.e., predicates expressed in terms of *traditional intervals*. Besides, it is worthwhile that T allows for providing *semantic limits*. Namely, what is the maximum number of weakening steps such that the final modified query is *not too far*, semantically speaking, from the original user query. Such limits can offer a rational tool for *controlling the relaxation process*.

3.2 Proximity–Based Approach

Let us first recall the formal definition of the notion of a proximity relation.

3.2.1 Proximity Relation

Definition. A proximity relation is a fuzzy relation R on a scalar domain U, such that for $u, v \in U$,

(i) $\mu_R(u, u) = 1$ (reflexivity),
(ii) $\mu_R(u, v) = \mu_R(v, u)$ (symmetry).

The quantity $\mu_R(u, v)$ evaluates the proximity between elements u and v. In general, there are two ways for defining proximity on a scalar domain. We can evaluate to what extent $u - v$ is *close* to 0; this is the absolute comparative approach. Or, we may use relative orders of magnitude, i.e., we evaluate to what extent the ratio u/v is *close* to 1 or not. Our focus is on the latter interpretation. The reader can refer to [4] for the former definition of proximity and its use for the purpose of query weakening.

Relative Closeness. A *relative closeness* (*Cl*) has been extensively studied in [9]. It has been shown that the idea of relative closeness which expresses an approximate equality between two real numbers x and y, can be captured by the following relation:

$$\mu_{Cl}(x, y) = \mu_M(x/y),$$

where the characteristic function μ_M is that of a fuzzy number "*close to 1*", such that: i) $\mu_M(1) = 1$; ii) $\mu_M(t) = 0$ if $t \leq 0$ (assuming that two numbers which are close should have the same sign); iii) $\mu_M(t) = \mu_M(1/t)$ (this property implies that the support $S(M)$ is symmetric and is of the form $[1 - \varepsilon, 1/(1 - \varepsilon)]$ with ε is a real number).

M is called a *tolerance parameter*. In what follows, $Cl[M]$ denotes the closeness relation parameterized by the tolerance indicator M.

Semantic Properties of M. It has been demonstrated in [9] that the fuzzy number M which parameterizes closeness and negligibility relation (Ne) defined as $\mu_{Ne[M]}(x, y) = \mu_{Cl[M]}(x+y, y)$ *should be chosen such that its support* $S(M)$ *lies in the validity interval* $V = [(\sqrt{5} - 1)/2, (\sqrt{5} + 1)/2]$[1] *in order to ensure that the closeness relation be more restrictive than the relation "not negligible". This means that if the support of a*

[1] The following assumption holds: if x is close to y then neither is x negligible w.r.t. y, nor is y negligible w.r.t. x. Then, the interval V is the solution to the inequality $\mu_{Cl[M]}(x, y) \leq 1 - \max(\mu_{Ne[M]}(x, y), \mu_{Ne[M]}(y, x))$.

tolerance parameter associated with a closeness relation Cl is not included in V, then the relation Cl is not in agreement with the intuitive semantics underlying this notion.

3.2.2 Principle of the Approach

As pointed out in [2], a way to perform query weakening is to apply a tolerance relation to the fuzzy predicates involved in a query. A tolerance relation which is of interest in the context of query weakening can be conveniently modeled by the relation $Cl[M]$. Let $Q = P$ is a query involving one fuzzy predicate P. To relax this query we replace the predicate P by an enlarged fuzzy predicate P' defined as follows:

$$\forall u \in U,\ \mu_{P'}(u) = sup_{v \in U}\ min\ (\mu_P(v), \mu_{Cl[M]}(u, v)).$$

Using the extension principle, it is easy to check that $P' = P \otimes M$, where $\otimes$ is the product operation extended to fuzzy numbers, see [5]. Clearly, the relative closeness-based transformation leads to a modified predicate P' which gathers the elements of P and the elements outside P which are somewhat close to an element in P. Hence, this approach conveys a clear semantics.

Basic Transformation. In a formal way, the transformation T is such that

$$T(P) = P' = P \circ Cl[M] = P \otimes M,$$

where $\circ$ stands for the fuzzy composition operation [5]. Let $P = (A, B, a, b)$ and $M = (1, 1, \varepsilon, \varepsilon/(1 - \varepsilon))$ where ε stands for the *relative tolerance value* and lies in $[0, (3 - \sqrt{5})/2]$ (this interval results from the inclusion $S(M) \subseteq V$, see [9]). The predicate P' is such that $P' = (A, B, a + A{\cdot}\varepsilon, b + B{\cdot}\varepsilon/(1 - \varepsilon))$ using the above arithmetic formula. The desirable properties C_1 to C_3 are satisfied by P'. Namely, we have: i) $\forall u,\ \mu_{P'}(u) \geq \mu_P(u)$; ii) $S(P) \subset S(P')$; iii) $C(P) = C(P')$.

Now, according to Figure 3, the following equalities hold: $T(A, a) = a + A{\cdot}\varepsilon$ and $T(B, b) = b + B{\cdot}\varepsilon/(1 - \varepsilon)$. The quantity $A{\cdot}\varepsilon$ (respectively $B{\cdot}\varepsilon/(1 - \varepsilon)$)) represents the relaxation intensity in the left (respectively right) part of the membership function of P. Since $B{\cdot}\varepsilon/(1 - \varepsilon) > A{\cdot}\varepsilon$, then the relaxation is stronger in the left part than in the right part. This means that the weakening mechanism is of a *non-symmetrical* nature. Let us also emphasize that a *maximal relaxation*, denoted P^{max}, of a predicate P can be reached for the tolerance value $\varepsilon_{max} = (3 - \sqrt{5})/2 \cong 0.38$. Hence, $P^{max} = (A, B, a + A{\cdot}\varepsilon_{max}, b + B{\cdot}\varepsilon_{max}/(1 - \varepsilon_{max}))$.

In practice, if Q is a query containing a single predicate P (i.e., $Q = P$) and if the set of answers to Q is empty, then Q is relaxed by transforming it into $Q_1 = P \otimes M$. This transformation can be repeated n times until the answer to the revised question $Q_n = P \otimes M^n$ is not empty.

Controlling Relaxation. In order to ensure that the revised query Q_n is semantically close enough to the original one, the support of M^n should be included in the interval of validity V. In effect, the relation $Cl[M^n]$ is no longer a closeness relation semantically speaking when $S(M^n)$ does not lie in V, despite its appearance at the syntactic level. Then, the above iterative procedure will stop either when the answer is non-empty or when $S(M^n) \not\subset V$.

This weakening process can be formalized by algorithm 3.

Algorithm 3

```
let Q = P
let ε be a tolerance value          (* ε ∈ [0, (3 − √5)/2] *)
i := 0          (* i denotes the number of weakening steps *)
Q_i := Q
compute Σ_Qi     (* Σ_Qi represents the set of answers to Q_i *)
while (Σ_Qi = ∅ and S(M^(i+1)) ⊆ V) do
      begin
        | i := i+1
        | Q_i := P ⊗ M^i
        | compute Σ_Qi
      end
if Σ_Qi ≠ ∅ then return Σ_Qi endif.
```

4 Complex Fuzzy Queries Relaxation

A complex fuzzy query Q is of the form P_1 ***op*** P_2 ***op*** ... ***op*** P_N, where P_i is a fuzzy predicate and ***op*** stands for a connector which can express a *conjunction* (usually interpreted as a *'min'* in a fuzzy framework), a *disjunction*, etc... For the sake of simplicity and brevity, we only consider *conjunctive* queries of the form $P_1 \wedge P_2 \wedge \ldots \wedge P_N$. In practice, this is the kind of queries that is problematic since it suffices that one fuzzy predicate has an empty support so that the global answer is empty. Two strategies can be envisaged for the weakening procedure:

i) a *global* query modification which consists in applying uniformly the basic transformation to all the predicates in the query. Given a transformation T and a query $Q = P_1 \wedge \ldots \wedge P_N$, the set of revised queries related to Q resulting from applying T is $\{T^i(P_1)$ *and* $T^i(P_2)$ *and* ... $T^i(P_N)\}$, where $i > 0$ and T^i means that the transformation T is applied i times. This strategy is simple but conflicts somewhat with our aim, that is, to find the closest revised query.

ii) a *local* query modification which affects only some predicates (or sub-queries). Most of the time, only a part of the query is responsible for the empty answers. As a consequence, it is not necessary to modify all the predicates in the query to avoid this problem.

In the following, we only focus on this latter strategy of relaxation.

4.1 Local Strategy

In this case, the basic transformation applies only to sub-queries. Given a transformation T and a query $Q = P_1 \wedge \ldots \wedge P_N$, the set of modifications of Q by T is

$$\{T^{i_1}(P_1) \text{ and } T^{i_2}(P_2) \text{ and } \ldots\ T^{i_N}(P_N)\},$$

where $i_h \geq 0$ and T^{i_h} means that the transformation T is applied i_h times. Assume that all conditions involved in Q are of the same importance for the user and T has the same effect on all P_i. A total ordering ($\prec$) between the revised queries related to Q can be defined on the basis of the number of the applications of the transformation T.

Then, we have $Q' \prec Q''$ *if count(T in Q') < count(T in Q'')*. The total ordering induced by the transformation defines a lattice of modified queries. For instance, the lattice associated with the weakening of the query "$P_1 \wedge P_2$" is given in Figure 4.

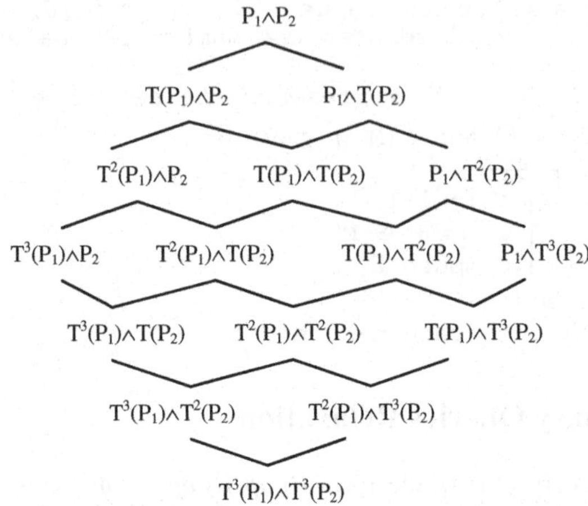

Fig. 4. A finite lattice of relaxed queries (reduce to three levels)

As can be seen, our relaxation technique consists in transforming a failing query into a more general query. This query generalization is obtained by replacing some query predicates by more general predicates. Therefore, our approach for relaxing flexible queries is similar to the one of Motro described in Section 2.1. The advantage of our approach is the fact that it leads to a *bounded lattice* of relaxed queries. Indeed, as mentioned in section 3.2.2 every predicate P_i can be maximally relaxed into P_i^{max}. Hence, the *maximal relaxation* of a query $Q = P_1 \wedge \ldots \wedge P_N$ is the modified query given by $Q^{max} = P_1^{max} \wedge \ldots \wedge P_N^{max}$. This lower bound query is inherent to the semantics underlying the relaxation mechanism proposed. It does not require any information from the user. Now, assume that each predicate in the query can be relaxed at least ω steps. Then, the number of steps to reach Q^{max} is $\omega \cdot N$ (see Figure 4).

4.2 Scanning the Lattice

In practice, there are three main issues that we must deal with when using a local strategy:

i) Define an intelligent way to exploit the lattice of weakened queries.
ii) Guarantee the property of equal relaxation for all fuzzy predicates.
iii) Study the user behavior with respect to the relaxation process, i.e., to what extent does the user have to intervene in this process?

Due to space limitation, we will not investigate the two latter issues. They have been discussed in [3][4]. In what follows, we only attempt to show how the scanning of the lattice can be done in an efficient way by exploiting the MFS of the failed original query. Let us first introduce the following results.

Let $Q = P_1 \wedge P_2 \wedge \ldots \wedge P_N$ be a failing query and $T(Q)$ a relaxed query of Q. Let also $mfs(Q) = \{P_{l_1} \wedge P_{l_2} \wedge \ldots \wedge P_{l_{m_1}}, \ldots, P_{l_1} \wedge P_{l_2} \wedge \ldots \wedge P_{l_{m_h}}\}$ be the set of MFSs of Q with $\{l_1, \ldots, l_{m_r}\} \subset \{1, \ldots, N\}$ for $r=1\ldots h$.

Proposition 1. If $T(Q) = Q - \{P_j\} \cup \{T(P_j)\}$ with $j \in \{l_1, \ldots, l_{m_r}\}$ and $1 \le r \le h$, then the MFSs of $T(Q)$ must be searched in $mfs(Q)$ by substituting $T(P_j)$ to P_j in each sub-query.

Proposition 2. If $T(Q) = Q - \{P_j\} \cup \{T(P_j)\}$ with $j \notin \{l_1, \ldots, l_{m_r}\}$ for $r = 1\ldots h$, then $mfs(Q)$ is also the set of MFSs of $T(Q)$.

Example. Assume that $Q = P_1 \wedge P_2 \wedge P_3 \wedge P_4$ and $mfs(Q) = \{P_1 \wedge P_3, P_1 \wedge P_4\}$. Then, If $T(Q) = T(P_1) \wedge P_2 \wedge P_3 \wedge P_4$, the MFSs of $T(Q)$ are searched in $\{T(P_1) \wedge P_3, T(P_1) \wedge P_4\}$.
If $T(Q) = P_1 \wedge T(P_2) \wedge P_3 \wedge P_4$, the MFSs of $T(Q)$ are the MFSs of Q.

From the two above propositions, it results that the set of MFSs of a relaxed query $T(Q)$ can be obtained from the MFSs associated to Q. Thus, in practice, it suffices to compute the set of MFSs of Q for deducing the MFSs of any relaxed query $T(Q)$. Let us note that Algorithm 2, designed for computing one MFS for a Boolean query, can easily be adapted in the case of flexible queries with no main changes.

Now assume that we have enumerated k MFSs of the query $Q = P_1 \wedge P_2 \wedge \ldots \wedge P_N$. As mentioned in section 2.2, this can be done in acceptable time (when k is not too large). Information about MFSs allows for providing an intelligent search technique over the lattice by avoiding evaluating some nodes. Indeed, the node in the lattice that preserves at least one MFS of its father-node (that is the node from which it is derived) does not have to be evaluated (since we are certain that it fails). This technique is sketched in Algorithm 4 where:

Algorithm 4

```
Let Q = P1 ∧ P2 ∧ ... ∧ PN ;
mfs(Q) = {Pl1∧Pl2∧...∧Plm1, ..., Pl1∧Pl2∧...∧Plmh};
found := false; i := 1;
while (i ≤ ω·N) and (not found) do
  begin
      Level = { Qi^1,···,Qi^ni }
      for req in Level do
         begin
           modif := true;
           for a_mfs in mfs(father(req)) do
              modif := modif ∧(a_mfs ∉ req)
           if modif then
             if evaluate(req) then
                   begin Level = ∅ and found := true end;
           if Level ≠ ∅ then compute mfs(req);
         end;
    i:=i+1;
 end.
```

- `Level` stands for the set of relaxed queries in level *i* of the lattice;
- `father(Q)` is the set of nodes from which *Q* can be derived, i.e., *Q* is an immediate relaxed variant of any query contained in `father(Q)`. For instance, in Figure 5, if $Q = T(P_1) \wedge T(P_2)$, then `father(Q)` $= \{T(P_1) \wedge P_2, P_1 \wedge T(P_2)\}$.
- `evaluate(Q)` is a function that evaluates *Q* against the database. It returns true if *Q* produces some answers, false otherwise.

As can be seen, to find the relaxed query with non-empty answers, several follow-up queries must be evaluated against the database. One way to substantially reduce the cost of this evaluation is: (i) to first evaluate the lower bound query Q^{max} and store the resulting items; (ii) then, each follow-up query will be evaluated on the basis of the result of Q^{max}.

5 Conclusion

We have presented a fuzzy set-based approach for handling query failure in a flexible context. The advantage of this approach is twofold. First, it provides rigorous semantic limits for controlling the relaxation process. Second, it operates only on the conditions involved in the initial user query without adding new conditions or performing any summarizing operation on the database. We have also shown how the information about the *MFSs* of the original failing query can be exploited to make more efficient the search over the lattice. One of our future works is to adapt the algorithm of searching for *MFSs* to work over extended lattice for finding the *MGQs* of a query (that are of major importance to help the user to find a non-failing query).

References

1. Bosc, P., Pivert O., "Some approaches for relational databases flexible querying". *J. of Intell. Inf. Syst.*, 1, pp. 323-354, 1992.
2. Bosc, O., HadjAli, A., Pivert, O., "Fuzzy closeness relation as a basis for weakening fuzzy relational queries," Proc. of 6th *Inter. Conf. FQAS*, Lyon, LNCS 3055, 2004, pp. 41-53.
3. Bosc, O., HadjAli, A., Pivert, O., "Towards a tolerance-based technique for cooperative answering of fuzzy queries against regular databases", Proc. of *the 7th Inter. Conf. CoopIS*, Cyprus, LNCS 3760, 2005, pp. 256-273.
4. Bosc, O., HadjAli, A., Pivert, O., "Weakening of fuzzy relational queries: An absolute proximity relation-based approach", *Submitted* to *Mathware & Soft Computing Journal.*
5. Dubois D., Prade H., Fundamentals of Fuzzy Sets. The Handbooks of Fuzzy Sets Series (Dubois D., Prade H., Eds), Vol. 3, Kluwer Academic Publishers, Netherlands, 2000.
6. Gaasterland, T., Godfrey, P., Minker, J., "An overview of cooperative answering", *Journal of Intelligent Information Systems*, 1(2), 1992, pp. 123-157.
7. Godfrey, P., "Minimization in cooperative response to failing database queries," *Inter. Journal of Cooperative Information Systems*, 6(2), pp. 95-149, 1997.
8. Godfrey, P., "Relaxation in Web Search: A new paradigm for search by Boolean queries", Personal Communication, March, 1998.
9. HadjAli A., Dubois D., Prade H., "Qualitative reasoning based on fuzzy relative orders of magnitude", *IEEE Transactions on Fuzzy Systems*, Vol. 11, No 1, pp. 9-23, 2003.
10. Motro A., "SEAVE: A mechanism for verifying user presuppositions in query systems", ACM Trans. on Off. Inf. Syst., 4(4), pp. 312-330, 1986.

A Functional Model for Data Analysis

Nicolas Spyratos*

Laboratoire de Recherche en Informatique,
Université de Paris-Sud,
91405 Orsay Cedex, France
spyratos@lri.fr

Abstract. We present a functional model for the analysis of large volumes of detailed transactional data, accumulated over time. In our model, the data schema is an acyclic graph with a single root, and data analysis queries are formulated using paths starting at the root. The root models the objects of an application and the remaining nodes model attributes of the objects. Our objective is to use this model as a simple interface for the analyst to formulate queries, and then map the queries to a commercially available system for the actual evaluation.

1 Introduction

In decision-support systems, in order to extract useful information from the data of an application, it is necessary to analyse large amounts of detailed transactional data, accumulated over time - typically over a period of several months. The data is usually stored in a so-called "data warehouse", and it is analysed along various dimensions and at various levels in each dimension [5, 10, 12].

A data warehouse functions just like a usual database, with the following important differences: (a) the data of a data warehouse is *not* production data but the result of integration of production data coming from various sources, (b) the data of a data warehouse is *historic* data, that is data accumulated over time, (c) access to the data warehouse by analysts is almost exclusively for reading and not for writing and (d) changes of data happen only at the sources, and such changes are propagated periodically to the data warehouse.

The end users of a data warehouse are mainly analysts and decision makers, who almost invariably ask for data aggregations such as "total sales by store", or "average sales by city and product category", and so on. In this context, the basic requirements by data analysts are (a) a data schema that is easy to understand and (b) a flexible and powerful query language in which to express complex data analysis tasks. The so called "dimensional schemas" and their associated "OLAP query languages" were introduced precisely to satisfy these requirements.

* Work conducted in part while the author was a visitor at the Meme Media Laboratory, University of Hokkaido, Sapporo, Japan.

H.L. Larsen et al. (Eds.): FQAS 2006, LNAI 4027, pp. 51–64, 2006.

This paper is focused on dimensional schemas and their OLAP query languages, as opposed to normalized relational schemas and their transaction processing languages.

Schema normalization was introduced in relational databases with the goal of increasing transaction throughput. Normalized schemas, however, rarely reflect the "business model" of the enterprise, that is the way the enterprise actually functions. Their main concern is to make database updating as efficient as possible, usually at the cost of rendering the schema virtually incomprehensible by the non specialist. Therefore normalized schemas are not suitable for data warehouses, as the analysts and decision makers of the enterprise are unable to "read" the schema and to formulate the queries necessary for their data analyses.

On-Line Analytic Processing, or OLAP for short, is the main activity carried out by analysts and decision makers [3, 4]. However, although several SQL extensions are available today for OLAP, there seems to be no agreement as to a simple conceptual model able to guide data analysis. The objective of this paper is to propose such a model.

The products offered today by data warehouse vendors are not satisfactory because (a) none offers a clear separation between the physical and the conceptual level, and (b) schema design is based either on methods deriving from relational schema normalization or on *ad hoc* methods intended to capture the concept of dimension in data. Consequently, several proposals have been made recently to remedy these deficiencies.

The proposal of the cube operator [7] is one of the early, significant contributions, followed by much work on finding efficient data cube algorithms [2, 9]. Relatively little work has gone into modelling, with early proposals based on multidimensional tables, called cubes, having parameters and measures [1, 11]. However, these works do not seem to provide a clear separation between schema and data. More recent works (e.g. in [8]) offer a clearer separation between structural aspects and content (see [17] for a survey).

However, a common characteristic of most of these models is that they somehow keep with the spirit of the relational model, as to the way they view a tuple in a table. Indeed, in all these models, implicitly or explicitly, a tuple (or a row in a table) is seen as a function associating each table attribute with a value from that attribute's domain; by contrast, in our model, it is each attribute that is seen as a function. Our approach is similar in spirit to the one of [6] although that work does not address OLAP issues.

Roughly speaking, in our model, the data schema is an acyclic graph with a single root, and a database is an assignment of finite functions, one to each arrow of the graph. The root of the graph is meant to model the objects of an application, while the remaining nodes model attributes of the objects. Data analysis queries (that we call OLAP queries) are formulated using paths starting at the root, and each query specifies three tasks to be performed on the objects: a classification of the objects into groups, following some criterion; a measurement of some property of objects in each group; a summarization of the measured properties in each group, with respect to some operation.

2 The Functional Algebra

In this section we introduce four elementary operations on (total) functions that we shall use in the evaluation of path expressions and OLAP queries later on.

Composition
Composition takes as input two functions, f and g, such that range(f) $\subseteq$ def(g), and returns a function g $\circ$ f: def(f) $\rightarrow$ range(g), defined by: (g $\circ$ f)(x)= g(f(x)) for all x in def(f).

Pairing
Pairing takes as input two functions f and g, such that def(f)= def(g), and returns a function f $\wedge$ g: def(f) $\rightarrow$ range(f) $\times$ range(g), defined by: (f $\wedge$ g)(x)= $\langle f(x), g(x) \rangle$, for all x in def(f). The pairing of more than two functions is defined in the obvious way. Intuitively, pairing is the tuple-forming operation.

Projection
This is the usual projection function over a Cartesian product. It is necessary in order to be able to reconstruct the arguments of a pairing, as expressed in the following proposition (whose proof follows easily from the definitions).

Proposition 1
Let $f : X \rightarrow Y$ and $g : X \rightarrow Z$ be two functions with common domain of definition, and let π_Y and π_Z denote the projection functions over the product $Y \times Z$. Then the following hold:

$$f = \pi_Y \circ (f \wedge g) \text{ and } g = \pi_Z \circ (f \wedge g)$$

In other words, the original functions f and g can be reconstructed by composing their pairing with the appropriate projection.

Restriction
It takes as argument a function $f : X \rightarrow Y$ and a set E, such that $E \subseteq X$, and returns a function $f/_E : E \rightarrow Y$, defined by: $(f/_E)(x) = f(x)$, for all x in E.

The four operations on functions just introduced form our *functional algebra.* It is important to note that this algebra has the closure property, that is the arguments and the result of each operation are functions. Well formed expressions of the functional algebra, their evaluation, and the evaluation of their inverses lie at the heart of the OLAP query language that we shall present later.

3 The Data Schema and the Data Base

In our model, the data schema is actually a directed acyclic graph (dag) satisfying certain properties, as stated in the following definition.

Definition 1. Data Schema
A *data schema*, or simply *schema*, is a finite, labelled dag, whose nodes and arrows satisfy the following conditions:

- *Condition 1* There is only one root
- *Condition 2* There is at least one path from the root to every other node
- *Condition 3* All arrow labels are distinct
- *Condition 4* Each node A is associated with a nonempty set of values, or *domain*, denoted as $dom(A)$

We recall that a directed acyclic graph always has one or more roots, a root being a node with no entering arrows. Condition 1 above requires that the graph have precisely one root. We shall label this root by O and we shall refer to it as the *origin*; it is meant to model the objects of an application.

Condition 2 requires that there be at least one path from the root to every other node. This condition makes sure that there are no isolated components in the schema (i.e. the graph is connected). We note that trees do satisfy conditions 1 and 2, therefore trees constitute the simplest form of schema in our model.

In a directed acyclic graph, it is possible to have "parallel" arrows (i.e. arrows with the same start node and the same end node). Such arrows can be distinguished only through their labels. This is the reason for having condition 3 above. In this respect, we shall use the notation $f : X \to Y$ to denote that f is the label of an arrow from node X to node Y; moreover, we shall call X the *source* of f and Y the *target* of f, that is $source(f) = X$ and $target(f) = Y$.

As we shall see shortly, each arrow $f : X \to Y$ will be interpreted as a total function from a set of X-values to a set of Y-values. Condition 4 makes sure that such values exist at every node.

Figure 1 shows an example of a schema that we shall use as our running example throughout the paper. This schema describes the data of a company that delivers products of various types to stores across the country. There is at most one delivery per store, per day. The data collected from delivery invoices is stored in a data warehouse and accumulated over long periods of time. Subsequently, they are analysed in order to discover tendencies in the movement of products. The knowledge extracted from the accumulated data is then used to improve the company operations.

The data that appears on an invoice consists of an invoice identifier, a date, the reference number of the store, and a sequence of products delivered during one visit; each product appearing on the invoice is characterized by a number (local to the voucher), followed by the product reference, and the number of units delivered from that product (the number of units is what we call Quantity in the schema). A pair composed of an invoice identifier and a product number on that invoice constitutes *one* object; and the origin of the schema shown in Figure 1 models the set of all such objects.

Each object is characterized by a Date, a Store, a Product, and a Quantity. These are the "primary" characteristics of the object. However, each of these characteristics determines one or more "secondary" characteristics of the

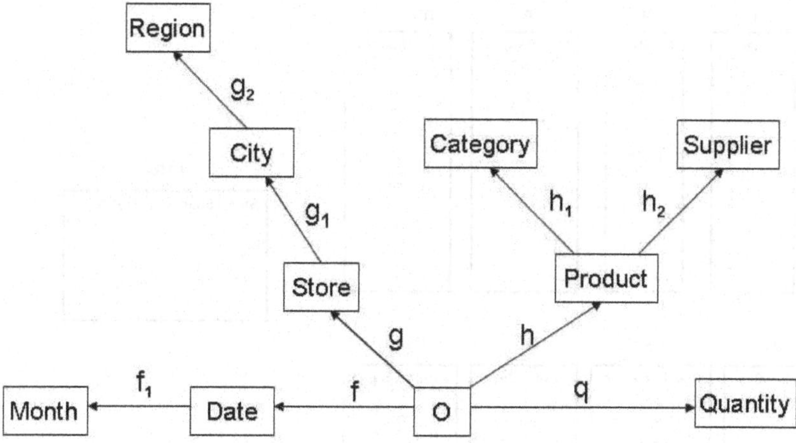

Fig. 1. Example of a data schema S

object. For example, Date determines Month; Store determines City, and City determines Region; finally, Product determines both, Category and Supplier. Although these secondary characteristics might not appear on the invoice, they can usually be inferred from the primary characteristics, and are useful for data analysis purposes (e.g. for aggregating the objects by region, by month and product, and so on). We shall refer to all the characteristics of the object (primary and secondary) as the *attributes* of the object.

Note that the schema of our running example is a tree, a choice made in order to simplify the presentation. However, it should be clear that what we will say in the remaining of this paper is valid for *all* forms of a schema, not just for tree schemas. In fact, non-tree schemas are important as they allow expressing multiple hierarchies among the attributes.

Having defined what a data schema is, we can now define the concept of a database.

Definition 2. Database
Let S be a schema. A *database* over S is a function δ that associates:

- each node A of S with a finite nonempty subset $\delta(A)$ of its domain
- each arrow $f : X \rightarrow Y$ of S with a total function $\delta(f) : \delta(X) \rightarrow \delta(Y)$.

Figure 2(a), shows a database δ over the schema S of our running example. In this figure, each arrow is associated with a binary table containing the function assigned to it by δ; for example, the arrow f : *Store* $\rightarrow$ *City* is associated with the binary table whose headings are Store and City.

Several remarks are in order here concerning the above definition of a database. Our first remark concerns notation. In the remainder of this paper, in order to simplify the presentation, we adopt the following abuse of notation: we use an arrow label such as f to denote both the arrow f and the function $\delta(f)$ assigned

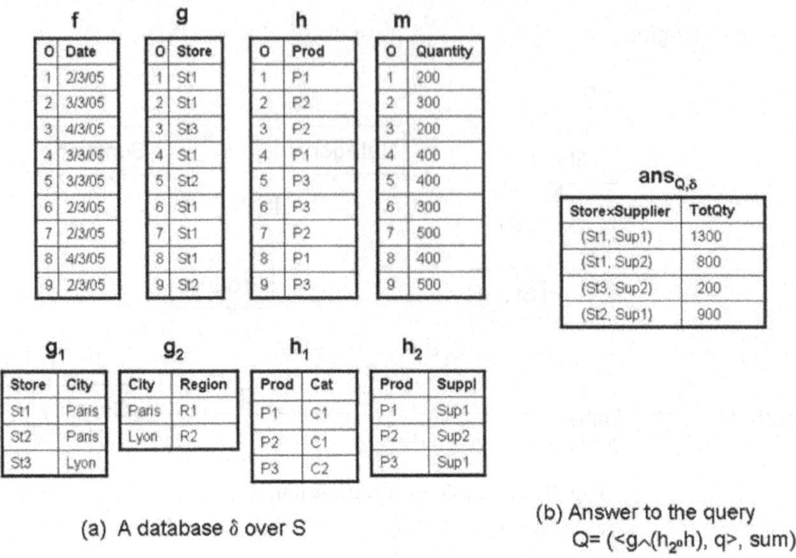

f

O	Date
1	2/3/05
2	3/3/05
3	4/3/05
4	3/3/05
5	3/3/05
6	2/3/05
7	2/3/05
8	4/3/05
9	2/3/05

g

O	Store
1	St1
2	St1
3	St3
4	St1
5	St2
6	St1
7	St1
8	St1
9	St2

h

O	Prod
1	P1
2	P2
3	P2
4	P1
5	P3
6	P3
7	P2
8	P1
9	P3

m

O	Quantity
1	200
2	300
3	200
4	400
5	400
6	300
7	500
8	400
9	500

g_1

Store	City
St1	Paris
St2	Paris
St3	Lyon

g_2

City	Region
Paris	R1
Lyon	R2

h_1

Prod	Cat
P1	C1
P2	C1
P3	C2

h_2

Prod	Suppl
P1	Sup1
P2	Sup2
P3	Sup1

(a) A database δ over S

$ans_{Q,\delta}$

Store×Supplier	TotQty
(St1, Sup1)	1300
(St1, Sup2)	800
(St3, Sup2)	200
(St2, Sup1)	900

(b) Answer to the query Q= (<g∧(h₂∘h), q>, sum)

Fig. 2. Example of database and OLAP query over S

to f by δ; similarly, we use an attribute label such as X to denote both the attribute X and the finite set $\delta(X)$ assigned to X by δ. This should create no confusion, as more often than not the context will resolve ambiguity. For example, when we write $def(f)$ it is clear that f stands for the function $\delta(f)$, as "def" denotes the domain of definition of a function; similarly, when we say "function f", it is clear again that f stands for the function $\delta(f)$ and not for the arrow f. We hope that this slight overloading of the meaning of symbols will facilitate reading.

Our second remark concerns the manner in which functions are assigned to arrows by the database δ. Each function f in a database can be given either extensionally, that is as a set of pairs $\langle x, f(x)\rangle$, or intentionally, that is by giving a formula or some other means for determining $f(x)$ from x. For example, the function $q : O \to Quantity$ can only be given extensionally, as there is no formula for determining the quantity of products to be delivered to a store; whereas the function $f_1 : Date \to Month$ will be given intentionally, as given a date one can compute the month: dd/mm/yy $\mapsto$ mm/yy. In fact, this is why $\delta(f_1)$ is not given in Figure 2(a).

Our third remark concerns the requirement that all functions assigned by the database δ to the arrows of S be total functions. This restriction could be relaxed, by endowing each attribute domain with a bottom element $\perp$ (meaning "undefined") and requiring that for any function $f : X \to Y$ we have (a) $f(\perp) =\perp$, that is "bottom can only map to bottom", and (b) if $x \notin def(f)$ then $f(x) =\perp$. Under these assumptions, the functions can again be considered as total functions. However, the resulting theory would be more involved and would certainly obscure some of the important points that we would like to bring forward concerning OLAP queries. Keep in mind, however, that the restriction that all functions assigned by δ be total functions entails the following property: for every pair of functions of the form $f : X \rightarrow Y$ and $g : Y \rightarrow Z$ we have $range(f) \subseteq def(g)$.

Our fourth and final remark concerns a particular way of looking at the functions of a database, namely as means for grouping objects together. Indeed, each function $f : X \rightarrow Y$ can be seen as grouping together the elements of X and "naming" each group using an element of Y. This is expressed by the inverse function f^{-1} which maps each y in the range of f to a nonempty subset of X as follows: $f^{-1}(y) = \{x \in X / f(x) = y\}$.

For example, consider the function $g_2 : City \rightarrow Region$ of our running example. The inverse g_2^{-1} maps each region r to the set of cities belonging to that region. As we shall see shortly, inverse functions play a crucial role in the evaluation of OLAP queries.

4 Path Expressions and OLAP Queries

Roughly speaking, a path expression over a schema S is a well formed expression whose operands are arrows from S and whose operators are those of the functional algebra. A path expression represents a generalized notion of arrow, and therefore a path expression has a source and a target. For example, referring to Figure 1, the expression $g \wedge (h_2 \circ h)$ is a path expression, whose source is O and whose target is $Store \times Supplier$. Below, we give a more formal definition of path expression, in which we use the following simplifying notation:

- for attributes A and B we write $A \subseteq B$ to denote that $dom(A) \subseteq dom(B)$
- for attributes $A_1, .., A_r$ we write $A_1 \times ... \times A_r$ to denote an attribute such that $dom(A_1 \times ... \times A_r) = dom(A_1) \times ... \times dom(A_r)$

Definition 3. Path Expression
Let S be a schema. A *path expression* e over S is defined by the following grammar, where "::=" stands for "can be", and p and q are path expressions:

e::= f, where f is an arrow of S; $source(e) = source(f)$ and $target(e) = target(f)$
$q \circ p$, where $target(p) = source(q)$; $source(e) = source(p)$ and target(e)=target(q)
$p \wedge q$, where $source(p) = source(q)$; $source(e) = source(p)$ and $target(e) = target(p) \times target(q)$
$p/_E$, where $E \subseteq source(p)$; $source(e) = E$ and $target(e) = target(p)$
$\pi_X(A_1 \times ... \times A_j)$, where $X = \{A_1, .., A_r\} \subseteq \{A_1), .., A_j)\}$; $source(e) = A_1 \times ... \times A_j$, $target(e) = A_1 \times ... \times A_r$

Here are some examples of path expressions over the schema S of Figure 1:

- $e_1 = f_1 \circ f$, with $source(e_1) = O$ and $target(e_1) = Month$
- $e_2 = f \wedge g$, with $source(e_2) = O$ and $target(e_2) = Date \times Store$
- $e_3 = ((g_2 \circ g_1 \circ g) \wedge (h_1 \circ h))$, with $source(e_3) = O$ and $target(e_3) = Region \times Category$

Now, the functions stored in a database represent information about some application being modelled. By combining these functions (using our functional algebra) we can derive new information about the application. Specifying what kind of new information we need is done using path expressions; and finding the actual information is done by evaluating these expressions.

Intuitively, given a path expression e over schema S, and a database δ over S, the evaluation of e proceeds as follows:

1. replace each arrow f of S appearing in e by the function $\delta(f)$;
2. perform the operations of the functional algebra (as indicated in the expression);
3. return the result

It is important to note that the evaluation of a path expression e always returns a function from the source of e to the target of e. More formally, we have the following definition.

Definition 4. The Evaluation of a Path Expression
Let S be a dimensional schema and e a path expression over S. Given a database δ over S, the *evaluation* of e with respect to δ, denoted $eval(e, \delta)$, is the function defined below, where p and q denote path expressions over S:

- if $e = f$, where f is an arrow of S, then $eval(e, \delta) = \delta(f)$;
- if $e = q \circ p$ then $eval(e, \delta) = eval(q, \delta) \circ eval(p, \delta)$;
- if $e = p \wedge q$ then $eval(e, \delta) = eval(p, \delta) \wedge eval(q, \delta)$;
- if $e = p/_E$ then $eval(e, \delta) = (eval(p, \delta))/dom(E)$
- if $e = \pi_X(A_1 \times ... \times A_j)$ then $eval(e, \delta) = \pi_X(\delta(A_1) \times ... \times \delta(A_j))$

A path expression of particular interest is obtained when we compose a path expression with a projection over the empty set. Indeed, if we apply the projection function $\pi_\emptyset$ on any nonempty Cartesian product $A_1 \times ... \times A_j$ the result is always the same, namely the *empty tuple*, denoted by λ. In other words, $\pi_\emptyset(A_1 \times ... \times A_j) = \{\lambda\}$, for any $A_1 \times ... \times A_j \neq \emptyset$. This particular path expression, is called the *constant path expression*, denoted by $\perp$. Clearly, the constant path expression evaluates to a constant function over any database and, as we shall see, it is useful in expressing OLAP queries of a special kind.

Path expressions are the basis for defining OLAP queries in our model. Roughly speaking, the purpose of an OLAP query is to perform a sequence of three tasks:

- *Grouping* (or *Classification*): group together the objects into mutually disjoint sets
- *Measuring*: in each group, for each object, measure some specified property of the object
- *Summarizing*: in each group, summarize the measured properties of the objects

Before giving formal definitions, let us illustrate these three tasks intuitively, using our running example. Suppose we want to evaluate the following query:

for each store-supplier pair, find the total quantity of products delivered

To do this, let us perform the three tasks described above, that is grouping, measuring, and summarizing.

Grouping. Two objects are put in the same group if they correspond to the same store-supplier pair. To check this condition, we need a function that takes as input an object and returns a store-supplier pair. Such a function can be obtained by evaluating a path expression with source O and with target $Store \times Supplier$. Referring to Figure 1, we can easily check that the only path expression having this property is the expression $u = (g \wedge (h_2 \circ h))$. Clearly, the inverse function u^{-1} associates each store-supplier pair to the set of all objects having that pair as image, and thus it groups the objects into the desired groups. (Note that, in presence of more than one such expression, a choice will have to be made by the user.) Concerning the actual calculations, we note that only the store-supplier pairs that belong to the range of u have nonempty inverses. Referring to Figure 1, we can easily check that the range of u contains four pairs: $\{(St1, Sup1), (St1, Sup2), (St3, Sup2) and (St2, Sup1)\}$; all other pairs of Store $\times$ Supplier have empty inverse images under u. The nonempty groups of objects obtained as inverse images of the pairs in the range of u are as follows:

$$u^{-1}((St1, Sup1)) = \{1, 4, 6, 8\}$$
$$u^{-1}((St1, Sup2)) = \{2, 7\}$$
$$u^{-1}((St3, Sup2)) = \{3\}$$
$$u^{-1}((St2, Sup1)) = \{5, 9\}$$

These four inverse images form a partition of O, and this partition is the result of the grouping.

Measurement. Within each group of objects, as computed in the previous step, and for each object in the group, we apply the function q in order to find the quantity of delivered products for that object:

$$\{1, 4, 6, 8\} \rightarrow \langle 200, 400, 300, 400\rangle$$
$$\{2, 7\} \rightarrow \langle 300, 500\rangle$$
$$\{3\} \rightarrow \langle 200\rangle$$
$$\{5, 9\} \rightarrow \langle 400, 500\rangle$$

Summarizing. For each group in the previous step, we sum up the quantities found, in order to obtain the total quantity of the group:

$$\langle 200, 400, 300, 400\rangle \rightarrow 1300$$
$$\langle 300, 500\rangle \rightarrow 800$$
$$\langle 200\rangle \rightarrow 200$$
$$\langle 400, 500\rangle \rightarrow 900$$

As we can see through the above three steps, each store-supplier pair (St, Sup) is associated to a group of objects $u^{-1}((St, Sup))$; and this group of objects, in turn, is associated to a total quantity of products delivered. This process is depicted below, where we summarize the results of the computations that took place:

$(St1, Sup1) \rightarrow \{1, 4, 6, 8\} \rightarrow 1300$
$(St1, Sup2) \rightarrow \{2, 7\} \rightarrow 800$
$(St3, Sup2) \rightarrow \{3\} \rightarrow 200$
$(St2, Sup1) \rightarrow \{5, 9\} \rightarrow 900$

The important thing to retain is that the above process defines a function from *Store* × *Supplier* to *Sales*. It is precisely this function that answers our original question, that is "for each store-supplier pair, find the total quantity of products delivered". This query and its answer are shown in Figure 2(b).

The above considerations lead to the following definition of OLAP query and its answer

Definition 7. OLAP query and its answer

- *OLAP Query*
  Let S be a schema. An OLAP Query over S is a (ordered) triple $Q = (u, v, op)$, satisfying the following conditions:
  - u and v are path expressions such that $source(u) = source(v) = O$
  - op is an operation over the target of v

  The expression u will be referred to as the *classifier* of Q and the expression v as the *measure* of Q.
- *Answer*
  Let δ be a database over S. The answer to Q with respect to δ is a function $ans_{Q,\delta}$: $target(u) \rightarrow target(v)$ defined by $ans_{Q,\delta}(y) = op(v(u^{-1}(y)))$, for all $y \in range(u)$.

Here are two more examples of queries, over the schema of our running example:

- $Q_1 = (f \wedge (h_1 \circ h), q, avg)$, asking for the average quantity by date and category
- $Q_2 = (f \wedge g, q, min)$, asking for the minimal quantity by date and store

It is important to note that the notions of "classifier" and "measure" in the above definition are *local* to a query. That is, the same path expression can be classifier in one query and measure in another. As an extreme example, consider the following two queries over the schema of our running example:

- $Q = (g, h, count)$, asking for the number of product references by store
- $Q' = (h, g, count)$, asking for the number of stores by product reference

An interesting class of OLAP queries is obtained when the classifier u is the constant expression (i.e. $u = \perp$) and v is any measure. Such queries have the form $Q = (\perp, v, op)$. As $\perp$ evaluates to a constant function over any database with nonempty set of objects, its inverse returns just one group, namely the set O of all objects. Hence the answer of Q associates the unique value λ in the range of u with $op(v(O))$. In our running example, the answer of the query $Q = (\perp, q, sum)$ will associate λ with 3200. Here, 3200 represents the total quantity delivered (i.e. for all dates, stores and products).

5 Optimization Issues

As we have seen in the previous section, the partition of O resulting from the grouping step, plays a crucial role in determining the answer. Given a query $Q = (u, v, op)$, the partition induced by the function u on the set of objects O is called the *support* of Q and it is denoted as s_Q. Query optimization consists in using the answer of an already evaluated query in order to evaluate the answer of a new query *without* passing over the data again; and the lattice of partitions of the set O is the formal tool to achieve such optimization.

Definition 8. The Lattice of Partitions
Let p, p' be two partitions of O. We say that p is *finer* than p', denoted $p \leq p'$, if for each group G in p there is a group G' in p' such that $G \subseteq G'$.

One can show that $\leq$ is a partial order over the set of all partitions of O (i.e. a reflexive, transitive and anti-symmetric binary relation over partitions). Under this ordering, the set of all partitions of O becomes a lattice in which the partition $\{O\}$ is the *top* (the coarsest partition) and the partition $\{\{o\}/o \in O\}$ is the *bottom* (the finest partition).

To see how this lattice can be used to achieve optimization, consider a query $Q = (u, v, op)$ which has already been evaluated. As we have explained earlier, if $y_1, .., y_k$ are the values in the range of u, then the support of Q is the following partition of O: $s_Q = \{u^{-1}(y_i)/i = 1, .., k\}$.

Based on the support, the answer to Q is expressed as follows: $ans_Q(y_i) = op(v(u^{-1}(y_i))), i = 1, .., k$.

Now, suppose that a new query $Q' = (u', v', op')$ comes in and we want to evaluate its answer. We claim that if $s_Q \leq s_{Q'}$ then the answer to Q' can be expressed in terms of the support of Q. This is based on a simple fact, which follows immediately from the definition of the partition ordering:

<u>*Fact*</u> : if $s_Q \leq s_{Q'}$ then each group G' in $s_{Q'}$ is the union of groups from s_Q.

As a result, if $G' = G_1 \cup \ldots \cup G_j$ then $op'(v'(G')) = op'(v'(G_1 \cup \ldots \cup G_j)) = op'(v'(G_1), \ldots, (v'(G_j))$.

As the support of Q has already been computed (and is available), we can apply v' and then op' "off-line" (i.e. *without* passing over the data again). Moreover, if $v = v'$ then we can reuse the measurements of Q as well. That is, if $v = v'$ then we have:

$$op'(v'(G_1), \ldots, (v'(G_j)) = op'(v(G_1), \ldots, (v(G_j))$$

Finally, if in addition $op = op'$ then we can reuse even the summarizations of Q, provided that the following property holds:

$$op(v(G_1), \ldots, v(G_j)) = op(op(v(G_1)), \ldots, op(v(G_j))$$

One can show that this property holds for most of the usual operations, namely "sum", "count", "max", and "min", but not for "avg". For example, $sum(2,4,6,8) = sum(sum(2,4),(sum(6,8))$, while $avg(2,4,6,8) \neq avg(avg(2,4), avg(6,8))$.

However, all the above results hold under the condition that $s_Q \leq s'_Q$ (see Fact above), so the question is: given two queries, Q and Q', can we decide whether $s_Q \leq s'_Q$?

To answer this question, we observe first that the classifier u of an OLAP query is essentially the pairing of a number of compositions. Therefore it is sufficient to answer the above question for two separate cases: when the classifier is a composition and when the classifer is a pairing. The following proposition provides the answers.

Proposition 2. Comparing Classifiers

- Grouping by Composition
  Let $Q = (u, v, op)$ and $Q' = (u', v', op')$ be two OLAP queries such $u = p$ and $u' = q' \circ p$, where p and q' are path expressions. Then $s_Q \leq s_{Q'}$.
- Grouping by Pairing
  Let $Q = (u, v, op)$ and $Q' = (u', v', op')$ be two OLAP queries such $u = p \wedge q$ and $u' = p$, where p and q are path expressions. Then $s_Q \leq s_{Q'}$.

In our running example, if $Q = (g, q, sum)$ and $Q' = (g_1 \circ g, q, sum)$, then $s_Q \leq s_{Q'}$, therefore the answer of Q' can be computed from that of Q. Similarly, if $Q = (g \wedge h, q, sum)$ and $Q' = (g, q, sum)$, then again $s_Q \leq s_{Q'}$, and the answer of Q' can be computed from that of Q.

The proof of the above proposition follows from properties of function inverses, as stated in the following proposition.

Proposition 3. Properties of Inverses

- *Composition*
  Let $f : X \rightarrow Y$ and $g : Y \rightarrow Z$ be two functions. Then for all $z \in range(g \circ f)$ we have: $(g \circ f)^{-1}(z) = \cup\{f^{-1}(y)/y \in g^{-1}(z))$ that is, a z-group under $g \circ f$ is the union of all y-groups under f, where y ranges over the z-group under g
- *Pairing*
  Let $f : X \rightarrow Y$ and $g : X \rightarrow Z$ be two functions. Then for all $(y, z) \in range(f \wedge g)$ we have: $(f \wedge g)^{-1}((y, z)) = f^{-1}(y) \cap g^{-1}(z)$

Lack of space does not allow further details on optimization. The interested reader is referred to the full paper.

6 Concluding Remarks

We have presented a functional model for data analysis, offering a clear separation between schema and data, as well as a functional algebra for data manipulation. We have also discussed some optimization issues, concerning the evaluation of OLAP queries.

Two important aspects of the model that are not treated in this paper are its expressive power and the computational complexity of OLAP queries. Regarding expressive power, we believe that one can gain useful insights by studying first how the operations of the relational algebra can be embedded in our functional algebra. As for computational complexity, the most appropriate context for its study seems to be the lattice of partitions of the set O. Work on computational complexity and optimization issues is ongoing, based on previous work by the author [15], and will be reported in a forthcoming paper [16].

Another generalization of the model concerns the existence of multiple business applications in the same enterprise. In our running example we have considered one such application, concerning delivery of products. A different business application (in the same enterprise) may concern investments; it will be modelled by a different schema with a different origin O', whose objects represent investment records. Although the two schemas may share some of their attributes, they will not be the same in general. Therefore the question arises how one does "joint" analysis in order to correlate results from both applications. Note that the need for two different schemas may arise even within the *same business application*, when one wants to consider the same data but from different perspectives (each perspective corresponding to a different set of dimensions). In relational terminology, this happens when the set of attributes in the fact table has two or more different keys.

Finally, one practical aspect concerning our model is its embedding into commercially available systems, and ongoing work considers its embedding into a relational system. In fact, a prototype is under development that uses our model as an interface for the definition of OLAP queries which are then passed on to a relational engine for the actual evaluation.

References

1. R. Agrawal, A. Gupta, and S. Sarawagi, S.: Modelling Multi-dimensional Databases. IBM Research Report, IBM Almaden Research Center (1995)
2. R. Agrawal et al.: On the computation of multidimensional aggregates. In Proceedings 22nd International Conference on Very Large Databases (1996)
3. Arbor Software Corporation, Sunnyvale, CA: Multi-dimensional Analysis: Converting Corporate Data into Strategic Information. White Paper (1993)
4. E.F. Codd: Providing OLAP (On-Line Analytical Processing) to User Analysts: an IT Mandate. Technical Report, E.F. Codd and Associates (1993)
5. C.J. Date: An introduction to database systems (8th edition). Addison-Wesley (2005)
6. R. Fagin et al.: Multi-structural databases PODS June 13-15, 2005, Baltimore, MD (2005)

7. J. Gray, A. Bosworth, A. Layman and H. Pirahesh: Data Cube: a relational aggregation operator generalizing group-by, crosstabs, and subtotals. Proceedings of ICDE'96(1996)
8. M. Gyssens, and L. Lakshmanan, L.: A foundation for Multidimensional databases. In Proceedings 22nd International Conference on Very Large Databases (1996)
9. V. Harinarayanan, A. Rajaraman, and J.D. Ullman: Implementing data cubes efficiently. SIGMOD Record, **25:2** (1996) 205–227
10. R. Kimball: The data warehouse toolkit. J. Wiley and Sons, Inc (1996)
11. C. Li and X.S. Wang: A data model for supporting on-line analytical processing. Proceedings Conference on Information and Knowledge Management (1996) 81–88
12. R. Ramakrishnan and J. Gehrke: Database Management Systems (third edition). McGraw-Hill (2002)
13. Red Brick Systems White Paper: Star schemes and star join technology. Red Brick Systems, Los Gatos, CA (1995)
14. N. Spyratos.: The Partition Model: A Functional Approach. INRIA Research Report **430** (1985)
15. N. Spyratos: The partition Model : A deductive database Model. ACM Transactions on Database Systems **12:1** (1987) 1–37
16. N. Spyratos: A Partition Model for Dimensional Data Analysis. LRI Research Report (2006)
17. P. Vassiliadis and T. Sellis: A survey of logical models for OLAP Databases. SIGMOD Record **28(4)** (1999) 64–69.

Materialization-Based Range and k-Nearest Neighbor Query Processing Algorithms*

Jae-Woo Chang and Yong-Ki Kim

Dept. of Computer Engineering, Chonbuk National Univ.,
Chonju, Chonbuk 561-756, South Korea
jwchang@chonbuk.ac.kr, ykkim@dblab.chonbuk.ac.kr

Abstract. Recently, the spatial network databases (SNDB) have been studied for emerging applications such as location-based services including mobile search and car navigation. In practice, objects, like cars and people with mobile phones, can usually move on an underlying network (road, railway, sidewalk, river, etc.), where the network distance is determined by the length of the practical shortest path connecting two objects. In this paper, we propose materialization-based query processing algorithms for typical spatial queries in SNDB, such as range search and k nearest neighbors (k-NN) search. By using a materialization-based technique with the shortest network distances of all the nodes on the network, the proposed query processing algorithms can reduce the computation time of the network distance as well as the number of disk I/Os required for accessing nodes. Thus, the proposed query processing algorithms improve the existing efficient k-NN (INE) and range search (RNE) algorithms proposed by Papadias et al. [1], respectively. It is shown that our range query processing algorithm achieves about up to one of magnitude better performance than RNE and our k-NN query processing algorithm achieves about up to 150% performance improvements over INE.

1 Introduction

In general, spatial databases has been well studied in the last two decades, resulting in the development of numerous spatial data models, query processing techniques, and index structures for spatial data [2]. Most of existing work considers Euclidean spaces, where the distance between two objects is determined by the ideal shortest path connecting them. However, in practice, objects, like cars and people with mobile phones, can usually move on an underlying network (road, railway, sidewalk, river, etc.), where the network distance is determined by the length of the practical shortest path connecting two objects on the network. For example, a gas station nearest to a given query q in Euclidean space may be more distant from q in a given network space than any other gas stations. Therefore, the network distance, rather than the Euclidean one, is an importance measure in spatial network databases. Recently, the

* This work is financially supported by the Ministry of Education and Human Resources Development (MOE), the Ministry of Commerce, Industry and Energy (MOCIE) and the Ministry of Labor (MOLAB) though the fostering project of the Lab of Excellency.

H.L. Larsen et al. (Eds.): FQAS 2006, LNAI 4027, pp. 65–74, 2006.

spatial network databases (SNDB) have been studied for emerging applications such as location-based services including mobile search and car navigation. [3]. Studies on SNDB can also be divided into three research categories, that is, data model, query processing techniques, and index structures. First, Speicys et al. [4] dealt with a computational data model for spatial network. Secondly, Jensen et al. [5] presented k-nearest neighbor (k-NN) query processing algorithms for SNDB. Thirdly, Papadias et al. [1] proposed query processing algorithms for range search, spatial joins, and closest pairs as well as k-NN. Finally, Pfoser and Jensen [6] designed a novel index structure for SNDB. In this paper, we propose materialization-based query processing algorithms for typical spatial queries in SNDB, such as range and k-NN queries. By using a materialization-based technique with the shortest network distances of all the nodes in the spatial network, the proposed query processing algorithms can reduce the computation time of the network distance of two nodes as well as the number of disk I/Os accesses for visiting the nodes. Thus, the proposed query processing algorithms can improve the existing efficient k-NN and range search algorithms proposed by Papadias et al. [1]. This paper is organized as follows. In Section 2, we introduce related work on query processing algorithms for SNDB. In Section 3, we present the architecture of underlying storage and index structures for SNDB. In Section 4 and 5, we propose materialization-based range and k-NN query processing algorithms, respectively. In Section 6, we provide the performance analysis of our k-NN and range query processing algorithms. Finally, we draw our conclusions and suggest future work in Section 7.

2 Related Work

In this section, we overview related work on query processing algorithms for spatial network databases (SNDB). First, Jensen et al. described a general framework for k-NN queries on moving objects in road networks [5]. The framework includes a data model and a set of concrete algorithms needed for dealing with k-NN queries. The data model captures road networks and data points with continuously changing locations. It encompasses two data representations. The detailed two-dimensional representation captures the geographical coordinates of the roads and moving objects. The more abstract graph representation captures the road and moving objects in a form that enables k-NN queries to be answered efficiently by using road distances instead of Euclidean distance. The algorithms for k-NN queries employ a client-server architecture that partitions the NN search. First, a preliminary best-first search for a nearest-neighbor candidate (NNC) set in a graph is performed on the server. Secondly, the maintenance of the query result is done on the client, which re-computes distances between data points in the NNC set and the query point, sorts the distances, and refreshes the NNC set periodically to avoid significant imprecision. Finally, the combination of NNC search with the maintenance of an active result provides the user with an up-to-date query result.

Next, Papadias et al. proposed a flexible architecture for SNDB by separating the network from the entity datasets [1]. That is, they employ a disk-based network representation that preserves connectivity and location, while spatial entities are indexed by respective spatial access methods for supporting Euclidean queries and dynamic updates. Using the architecture, they also developed two frameworks, i.e., Euclidean restriction and network expansion, for each of the most common spatial queries, i.e., nearest neighbors, range search, closest pairs, and distance joins. The proposed algorithms expand conventional query processing techniques by integrating connectivity and location information for efficient pruning of the search space. Specifically, the Euclidean restriction algorithms take advantages of the Euclidean low-bound property to prune the search space while the network expansion algorithms perform query processing directly in the network.

3 Storage and Index Structures for SNDB

Considering a road network, both network junctions and the starting/ending points of a road can be represented as nodes. The connectivity between two nodes can be represented as an edge. Each edge connecting node n_i and n_j includes a network distance $d_N(n_i, n_j)$ which equals the length of the shortest path from n_i to n_j in the network. Most of the existing work on index structures for SNDB focuses on storage structures representing spatial network, especially, storing both the nodes and the edges of the spatial network into a secondary storage. For a fast answer to users' spatial queries, however, it is necessary to efficiently index the spatial network itself as well as objects residing on the spatial network. The objects on the spatial network can be divided into two types according to their mobility, such as points of interest (POIs) and moving objects. To design our storage and index structures for SNDB, we make use of the following ideas. The first one is to differentiate the underlying network from POIs and moving objects. This separation has a couple of advantages. First, dynamic updates in each dataset can be handled independently. Secondly, new/existing datasets can be added to and removed from the system easily. The other one is to make a special treatment on storing and indexing moving objects' trajectories. Because moving objects are continuously moved on the spatial network, their trajectory information is generally large in size. To answer users' spatial query, the support for partial match retrieval on moving objects' trajectories is required. Based on the two main ideas, we design the architecture for storing and indexing spatial network data, point of interests (POIs), and moving objects in SNDB, as shown in Figure 1.

First of all, for the spatial network data, we design a spatial network file organization for maintaining both nodes and edges. For nodes, the node-node matrix file is used to store all the network distance d_N(ni, nj) between node ni and node nj and the node adjacent information file is used to maintain the connectivity between nodes. Both the node ID table and the hash table are used to gain fast accesses to the information of a specific node. For edges, the edge information file is used to store the edge information as well as to maintain POIs residing on an edge. The edge R-tree is used to locate edges rapidly for answering spatial queries. Secondly, we design a POI storage organization for POIs, like restaurants, hotels, and gas stations. The POI information file is used to store the information of POIs and its location in the underlying road network. The POI B+-tree is used to have fast accesses to the information of a specific POI. The edge R-tree is also used to find which edge a specific POI is covered by. Finally, for moving objects, such as cars, persons, motorcycles, etc., we design an object trajectory signature file to have fast accesses to the trajectories of a given moving objects. The architecture supports the following main primitive operations for dealing with SNDB. (i) find_edge(p) outputs a set of edges that covers a point p by performing a point location query on the network R-tree. If multiple edges cover p, the first one found is returned. This function is applied whenever a query is issued, so as to locate an edge which the query point is covered by. (ii) find_points(e) returns a set of POI points covered by the edge e. Specifically, it finds all the candidates points that fall on the MBR of e, and then eliminates the false hits using the edge information file. (iii) compute_ND(p1,p2) returns the network distance d_N(p1, p2) of two arbitrary points p1, p2 in the network. This can be achieved in a fast way by accessing the node-node matrix file incorporated into our architecture via the hash table.

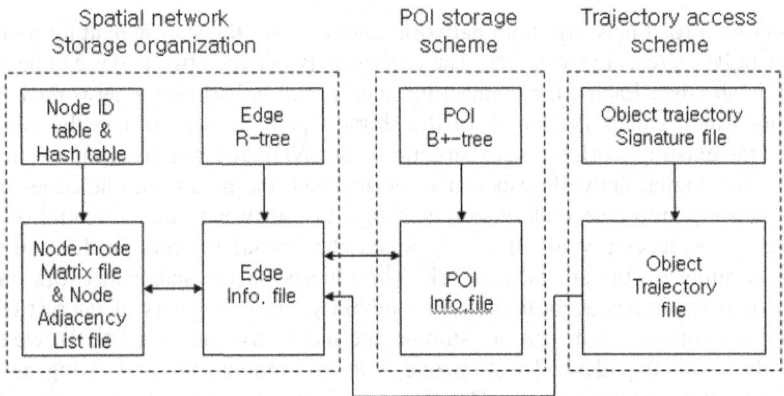

Fig. 1. Storage and index structures for SNDB

4 Materialization-Based Range Query Processing Algorithm

A range query processing algorithm for SNDB is quite different from the conventional ones proposed for the ideal Euclidean space [7] because objects can usually move only on the underlying network. For instance, suppose a query to find gas stations within 10Km from q in Figure 2. The results to satisfy the query in the Euclidean space are p1, p2, p3, and p4 while only p2 can satisfy the query in the network space. To design a range query processing algorithm in SNDB, it is possible to simply apply into the spatial network the conventional algorithms being proposed in Euclidean space [1]. But, the Euclidean restriction algorithm, called RER, generally requires a large number of disk I/O accesses to answer a range query in the underlying network. To remedy this problem, the network expansion algorithm, called RNE, was proposed [1], where it performs network expansion starting from an edge covering a query and determines if objects encountered are within a given range. However, both the RER and the RNE are inefficient where there are lots of roads, being represented as lines, and lots of intersections cross them, being represented as nodes, in spatial networks. This is because they require a lot of the computation time of network distance between a pair of nodes and the number of disk I/Os accesses for visiting nodes.

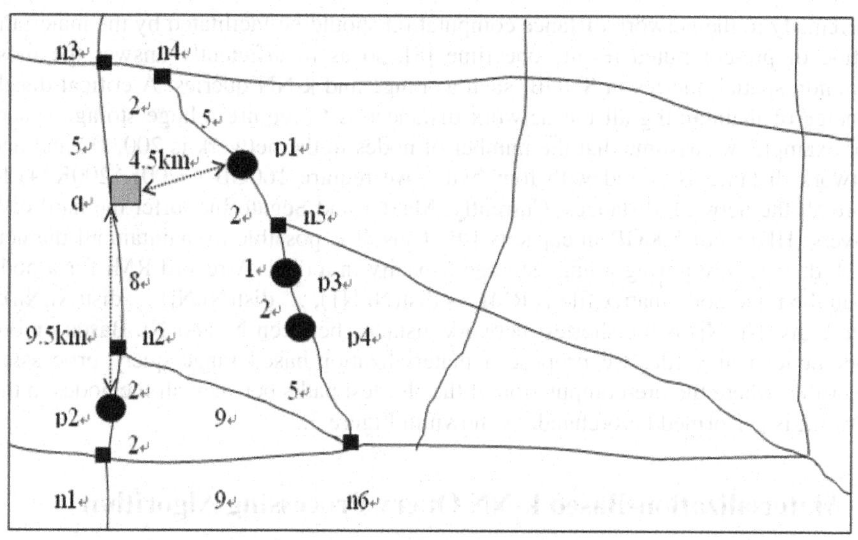

Fig. 2. Range search in Euclidean spaces and spatial networks

```
Algorithm Range(q,r) /* q is the query point and r is the network distance */
    Estimate D, the density of POIS in a circle made by r from q
    result = ∅
    if( D ≤ threshold_value ) {
            PE = Euclidean-range(q,e)
            for each point p in PE {
                dN(q,p) = compute_network_dist(q, e(ni,nj), p)
                if(d_N(q,p) ≤ r) result = result ∪ p  }
    } else {
        e(ni,nj) = find_edge(q)
        EN = expand-network(e(ni,nj)) // EN is a set of edges in the expanded network
        for each edge e(n,m) in EN {
            PS = set of POIs covered by e(n,m)
            for each p in PS {
                dN(q,p) = compute_network_dist(q, e(ni,nj), p)
                if(dN(q,p) ≤ r) result = result ∪ p  }
        } //end of for
    } //end of if else
End Range

Function compute_network_dist(q, e(ni,nj), p) /* q is a query point, p a target POI, and e(ni,nj) an edge covered by q */
    e(nk,nl) = find_edge(p)
    return dN(q,p)=min{dN(ni,nk)+dN(ni,q)+dN(nk,p),
                         dN(ni,nl)+dN(ni,q)+dN(nl,p),
                         dN(nj,nk)+dN(nj,q)+dN(nk,p),
                                  dN(nj,nl)+dN(nj,q)+dN(nl,p)}
End compute_network_dist
```

Fig. 3. Our materialization-based range query processing algorithm

To remedy it, the network distance computation should be facilitated by the materialization of pre-computed results one time [8], so as to efficiently answer the most common spatial queries in SNDB, such as range and k-NN queries. A critical disadvantage of maintaining all the network distances is to require a huge storage space. For example, we assume that the number of nodes in the network is 200,000 and one network distance is stored with four bytes, we require 160GB (=200K*200K*4) to store all the network distances. Currently, Maxter and Segate Inc. offer the hard disk drivers (HDDs) of 500GB in capacity [9]. Thus, it is possible to maintain all the network distances requiring a huge storage capacity in a disk. A record RMi for a node Ni in the node-node matrix file is RMi = <dist(Ni,N1), … dist(Ni,Nj) … dist(Ni,Nn)> where dist(Ni, Nj) is the shortest network distance between Ni and Nj. Based on our node-node matrix file, we propose a materialization-based range query processing algorithm where the pre-computation of the shortest paths between all the nodes in the network is performed beforehand, as shown in Figure 3.

5 Materialization-Based k-NN Query Processing Algorithm

In SNDB, a k-NN query processing algorithm for SNDN is quite different from the conventional ones which were proposed under the assumption that objects moves on the ideal Euclidean space [10]. As a result, the nearest neighbor of a query in the Euclidean space may be not the case in a spatial network. Figure 2 show an example of the case. That is, the nearest neighbor of q is p1 in the Euclidean space and the distance between q and p1 is 4.5Km. However, the nearest neighbor of q is p2, not p1, in the underlying network and the network distance is 10Km because there is no direct path between q and p1. To design a k-NN query processing algorithm in SNDB, it is possible to simply apply the conventional algorithms proposed for Euclidean space into the spatial network [1]. However, the Euclidean restriction algorithm, called IER, generally searches a large number of Euclidean nearest neighbors to find the network nearest neighbors, thus leading to a large number of disk I/O accesses to answer a k-NN query. To remedy this problem, the network expansion algorithm, called INE, was proposed [1]. The algorithm performs network expansion starting from a query and examines objects in the order that they are encountered until finding k-nearest neighbors. The algorithm computes the network distance of k-nearest neighbors from q and terminates when the network distance of the first node in a queue is grater than $d_{SN}(q, p)$. The IER and the INE have its own different approach to find nearest neighbors in a spatial network. That is, the IER first locates Euclidean nearest neighbors in a global manner and then compute their network distances from a query. On the contrary, the INE first locates an edge covering a query, and then expand the network starting from the edge, in a local manner. Thus, the IER performs well where lots of parallel roads intersect others in an orthogonal way, like Manhattan of New York City, while the latter algorithm performs well where roads are made avoiding obstacles, like a mountain area. Therefore, we need to consider the following for the effective integration of the two algorithms.

Consideration 1: To acquire the actual k-nearest neighbors of q efficiently in the underlying network, the initial set of near-optimal candidates for k nearest neighbors should be obtained.

Consideration 2: Once the initial set of near-optimal candidates for k nearest neighbors has obtained, the final k-nearest neighbors of q in the underlying network should be obtained using the initial set, as rapidly as possible.

```
Algorithm K-NN(q, k)   /* q is the query point */
1. Determine k', the number of initial Euclidean k-NNs and c',
the number of edge connection from q for acquiring initial can-
didates, depending on k.
2. e(ni,nj) = find_edge(q)
3. {p1,…,pk'} = Euclidean-NN(q,k')   // k' < k
4. for each pi
     dN(q,pi) = compute_network_dist(q, e(ni,nj), pi)
5. sort {p1,…,pk'} in ascending order of dN(q,pi)
6. Q = <(ni, dN(q,ni)), (nj, dN(q,nj))> // sorted by distance
7. En = expand_network(e(ni,nj), c', Q)// En is the set of edges
in a network being expanded by edge e(ni,nj) within c' connec-
tions from the edge. Q is updated through network expansion. //
8. SE = find-points(En) // SE is a set of POIs covered by En
9. {p1,…,pk} = the k network nearest neighbors by merging
{p1,…,pk'} and SE sorted in ascending order of their network
distance (pm,…pk may be Ø if the merged result contains just m-1
points with m ≤ k)
10. dmax = dN(q,pk) // if pk = Ø, dmax = ∞
11. for Pj which is originated from Euclidean-NN (q,k') {
12.   dN(q,pj) = compute_network_dist(q, e(ni,nj), pj)
13.   insert <nj, dN(q,pj)> into Q  }
14.   delele from Q the node n with the smallest dN(q,n)
15.   while(dN(q,n) < dmax) {
16.   for each non-visited adjacent node nj of n {
17.     Sp = find-point(e(nj,n))
18.     update {p1,…,pk} from {p1,…,pk} ∪ Sp
19.     dmax = dN(q,pk)
20.     dN(q,pj) = compute_network_dist(q, e(ni,nj), pj)
21.     insert <nj, dN(q,pj)> into Q  } // end of for each
22.   delele from Q the next node n with the smallest
dN(q,n)
23. } /* end of while
End K-NN
```

Fig. 4. Our materialization-based k-NN query processing algorithm

To satisfy the first consideration, we are required to build the initial set of candidates for k nearest neighbors by integrating the initial set construction part of the Euclidean restriction algorithm with that of the network expansion one. Because we obtain the initial set of candidates by combining a global initial set and a local initial set, it is possible to acquire an initial set of near-optimal candidates, regardless the characteristic of the underlying road network (Manhattan or a mountain area). To satisfy the second consideration, once obtaining an initial set of near-optimal candidates, we are required to find the final k-nearest neighbors using the network expansion algorithm. This is because we can obtain the final k-nearest neighbors in an efficient way by performing a local network search using the near-optimal candidates. That is, because a global search on the network has been performed to obtain the initial set of candidates, it is sufficient to perform only a local search on the network for the final k-nearest neighbors, thus enabling to achieve a good retrieval performance. In addition, because it takes much time to compute a network distance between two nodes during network expansion, it is required to makes use of our node-node matrix file. This makes it possible to obtain the shortest network distance between any specified node and one of nodes incident an edge covering a query in the fastest way, thus remarkably reducing the network distance computation time and the number of disk I/Os accesses for visiting nodes. We propose a materialization-based k-NN query processing algorithm to satisfy the above considerations, as shown in Figure 4.

6 Performance Analysis

For our experiment, we make use of a road network consisting of 170,000 nodes and 220,000 edges [11]. We also generate 10,846 points of interest (POIs) randomly on the road network by using RunTime21 algorithm [12]. We implement our range and k-NN query processing algorithms under Pentium-IV 2.0GHz CPU with 1GB main memory, running Window 2003.

For the materialization, we use 229G node-node matrix file. For performance analysis, we compare our rage query processing algorithm with RNE and our k-NN query processing algorithm with INE scheme because RNE and INE are considered as the most efficient query processing algorithm [1]. We measure a time for answering a range query whose radius r is between 10 and 200. Figure 5 shows the rage query processing times of RNE and our materialization-based range query processing algorithm (called OMR). The RNE and our OMR require about 0.24 and 0.17 seconds, respectively, when r = 10. In addition, the RNE and our OMR require about 2.25 and 0.24 seconds, respectively, when r = 100. It is shown that our OMR achieves about up to one of magnitude better performance than the RNE and the performance improvement of our OMR over the RNE is increased as the range r is increased. This is because our materialization-based OMR can reduce the network distance computation time and the number of disk I/Os required for accessing nodes by using our node-node matrix file.

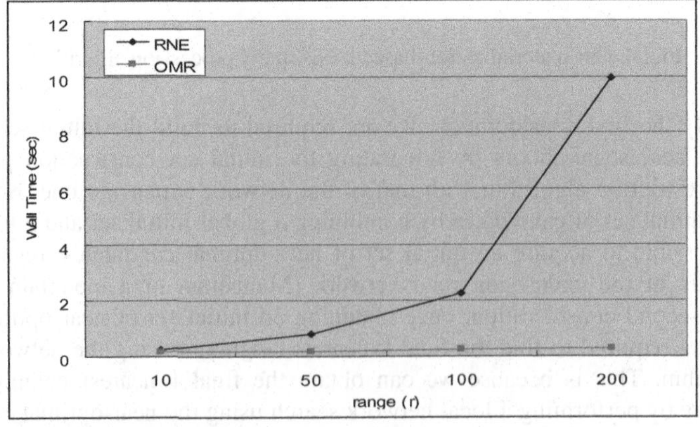

Fig. 5. Range query processing time

Figure 6 shows the k-NN query processing times of the INE and our materialization-based k-NN algorithm (called OMK). The INE and our OMK require about 0.059 and 0.058 seconds, respectively, when k = 1. In addition, the INE and our OMK require about 0.078 and 0.059 seconds, respectively, when k = 10. It is shown that the performance of OMK is nearly the same as that of INE when k=1 and the performance improvement of our OMR over the RNE is increased as k is increased. When k=100, our OMK achieves about up to 150% performance improvements over the INE since the INE and our OMK require about 0.098 and 0.069 seconds, respectively, This is because our materialization-based OMR can reduce the computation time of network distances between a pair of nodes met during network expansion and the number of disk I/Os required for accessing nodes by using our node-node matrix file.

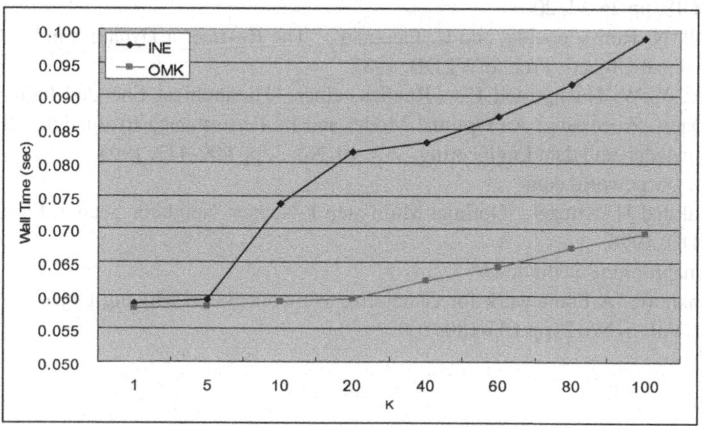

Fig. 6. k-NN query processing time

7 Conclusions and Future Work

In this paper, we designed efficient storage and index structures for spatial network databases (SNDB). Based on the structures, we proposed materialization-based range and k-NN query processing algorithms for SNDB. By using our node-node matrix file containing the shortest network distances of all the nodes in the spatial network, the proposed query processing algorithms can reduce the computation time of the network distances and the number of disk I/Os required for accessing the nodes It was shown that our range query processing algorithm achieved about up to one of magnitude better performance than the RNE and our k-NN query processing algorithm achieved about up to 150% performance improvements over INE. As future work, it is required to study on e-distance join and closest-pairs query processing algorithms for SNDB.

References

1. D. Papadias, J. Zhang, N. Mamoulis, and Y. Tao, "Query Processing in Spatial Network Databases" Proc. of VLDB, pp, 802-813, 2003.
2. S. Shekhar et al., "Spatial Databases – Accomplishments and Research Needs," IEEE Tran. on Knowledge and Data Engineering, Vol. 11, No. 1, pp 45-55, 1999.
3. J.-W. Chang, J.-H. Um, and W.-C. Lee, "An Efficient Trajectory Index Structure for Moving Objects in Location-Based Services," LNCS 3762, OMT Workshops, pp 1107-1116, 2005.
4. L. Speicys, C.S. Jensen, and A. Kligys, "Computational Data Modeling for Network-Constrained Moving Objects," Proc. of ACM GIS, pp 118-125, 2003.
5. C.S. Jensen, J. Kolář, T.B. Pedersen, and I. Timko, "Nearest Neighbor Queries in Road Networks," Proc. of ACM GIS, pp 1-8, 2003.
6. D. Pfoser and C.S. Jensen, "Indexing of Network Constrained Moving Objects," Proc. of ACM GIS, pp 25-32, 2003.
7. T. Seidl, N. Roussopoulos, and C. Faloutsos, "The R+-tree: a Dynamic Index for Multi-Dimensional Objects, Proc. of VLDB, 1987.
8. N. Jing, Y.-W. Huang, and E.A. Rundensteiner, "Hierarchical Encoded Path Views for Path Query Processing: An Optimal Model and Its Performance Evaluation," IEEE Tran. on Knowledge and data Engineering, Vol. 10, No. 3, pp 409-432, 1998.
9. http://www.pcworld.com
10. T. Seidl and H. Kriegel, "Optimal Multi-step k-Nearest Neighbor Search, Proc. of ACM SIGMOD, 1998.
11. www.maproom.psu.edu/dcw/
12. T. Brinkhoff, "A Framework for Generating Network-Based Moving Objects," GeoInformatica, Vol. 6, No. 2, pp 153-180, 2002.

Flexible Querying Using Structural and Event Based Multimodal Video Data Model

Hakan Öztarak[1] and Adnan Yazıcı[2]

[1] Aselsan Inc, P.O. Box 101, Yenimahalle, 06172, Ankara, Turkey
hoztarak@aselsan.com.tr
[2] Department of Computer Engineering, METU, 06531, Ankara, Turkey
yazici@ceng.metu.edu.tr

Abstract. Investments on multimedia technology enable us to store many more reflections of the real world in digital world as videos so that we carry a lot of information to the digital world directly. In order to store and efficiently query this information, a video database system (VDBS) is necessary. We propose a structural, event based and multimodal (SEBM) video data model which supports three different modalities that are visual, auditory and textual modalities for VDBSs and we can dissolve these three modalities within a single SEBM model. We answer the content-based, spatio-temporal and fuzzy queries of the user by using SEBM video data model more easily, since SEBM stores the video data as the way that user interprets the real world data. We follow divide and conquer technique when answering very complicated queries. We give the algorithms for querying on SEBM and try them on an implemented SEBM prototype system.

1 Introduction

Since multimodality of the video data comes from the nature of the video, it is one of the important research topics for the database community. Videos consist of visual, auditory and textual channels, which bring the concept of multimodality [1]. Modelling, storing and querying the multimodal data of a video is a problem, because users want to query these channels from stored data in VDBS efficiently and effectively. In [5], a **s**tructural and **e**vent **b**ased, **m**ultimodal (SEBM) video data model for VDBSs is proposed with querying facilities. SEBM video data model supports these three different modalities and we propose that we can dissolve them within a single SEBM video data model, which makes us find the answers of multimodal queries easily.

Definition of multimodality is given by Snoek et. al. as the capacity of an author of the video document to express a predefined semantic idea, by combining a layout with a specific content, using at least two information channels, [1]. Moreover they give the explanations of the modalities that we use in SEBM as:

- *Visual modality*: contains everything, either naturally or artificially created, that can be seen in the video document;

H.L. Larsen et al. (Eds.): FQAS 2006, LNAI 4027, pp. 75 – 86, 2006.

- *Auditory modality*: contains the speech, music, and environmental sounds that can be heard in the video document;
- *Textual modality*: contains textual resources that can be used to describe the content of the video document.

Nowadays researches are concentrating on efficient and effective ways of querying the multimodal data, which is integrated with temporal and spatial relationships. Modelling is as important as querying, because it is an intermediate step between data extraction and consumption. In general, researchers propose their querying algorithms with their data models. Snoek et. al. give the definition of multimodality and focus on similarities and differences between modalities in [1]. They work on multimodal queries in [18]. They propose a framework for multimodal video data storage, but only the semantic queries and some simple temporal queries are supported. They define collaborations between streams when extracting the semantic from the video. Oomoto et. al. don't work on multimodality but investigate the video object concept which is a base for spatio-temporal works [7]. Day et. al. extend the spatio-temporal semantic of video objects [17]. Ekin et. al. introduce object characteristics, and actors in visual events [4]. Köprülü et. al. propose a model that defines spatial and temporal relationships of the objects in visual domain which includes fuzziness, [3]. Durak in [2], extends the model proposed in [3]. She introduces a multimodal extension of the model and gives two different structures for visual, auditory and textual modalities. BilVideo is a good example for a VDBS, which considers spatio-temporal querying concepts, [8].

Main contributions of our work can be summarized as follows: In this study, we work on querying features of SEBM, which is based on human interpretation of video data. This interpretation is like telling what is happening in videos. If one can express information in digital world as human does in real world, then we think that all of the queries coming from a user can be handled more accurately and effectively. So we can bypass the problem of handling the models in different data structures and handle them separately as done in [2]. In SEBM, actor entities that are only defined for visual domains in [4] are modelled for multimodal domains. These entities give us the ability to express and query the structure of events in multimodal domains. Moreover object characteristics that involve a particular feature of an object or relation of an object with other objects are also introduced in SEBM for multimodal domains different than [7] which considers only visual domain. We propose some algorithms to query these stored relationships of video objects and events and follow divide and conquer approach in query processing to answer complex, nested, conjunctive, spatial, temporal, content-based and possibly fuzzy video queries. This approach gives us the ability to deal with much more complex and compound multimodal queries different than ones in [2] and [3]. We support these algorithms with an implemented querying prototype system that uses SEBM while modelling the data.

The rest of the paper is organized as follows: Section 2 presents how SEBM models the video data with exploring video segmentation, video entities and video actions. In Section 3, query processing on SEBM is investigated and content based, spatio-temporal, hierarchical and fuzzy queries are explored. Throughout the parts 2 and 3 the usage of SEBM is also explored. The last section provides conclusion with some future extensions of our model.

2 Modelling the SEBM Video Data Model

Single video is composed of sequential frames, which are individual images. Each frame has individual image properties like color or shape. Every image can contain objects, positioned on the image. However, when we arrange these images sequentially, we can see that these objects can be told to do something semantically and are part of some events. In [5], it is explained that human interprets the three modalities of the video data by using an event structure and we have developed our SEBM video data model by considering this fact. We position the video events at the core part of the SEBM video data model and propose that we can model every reality in videos by expressing them as video events or relating them with video events. SEBM is a kind of translation of human sentences, which s/he uses while interpreting the video data, to the video database model. We developed the SEBM video data model as a combination of five different sub-models. Fig.1 shows the hierarchical structure of these sub-models that we use while constructing the SEBM:

1. Video Sequence Sub-Model (segments the video according to the meaning as shown with the link-c)
2. Video Shot Sub-Model (segments the sequences according to low-level features of the them as shown with the link-d)
3. Video Object Sub-Model (stores the objects globally and access the spatio-temporal information of the objects through events, as shown with the link-a and f)
4. Video Object Characteristics Sub-Model (stores the objects features and their relationships, as shown with the link-b)
5. Video Event Sub-Model (stores the events under corresponding video segment with spatio-temporal information and associate their object structure, as shown with the link-e and f)

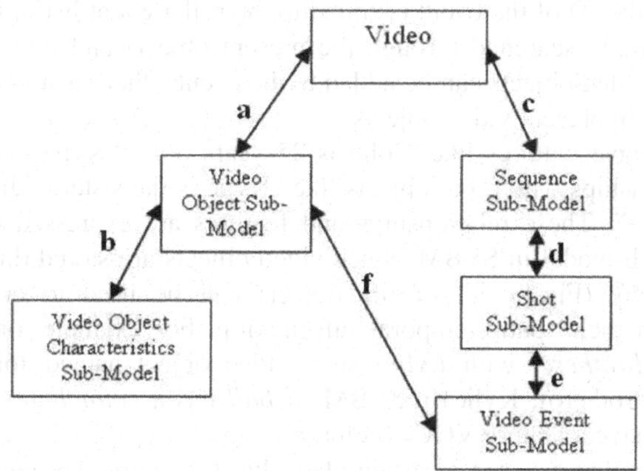

Fig. 1. Hierarchical Structure of SEBM Sub-Models

In [6], it is proposed that successful content-based video data management systems depend on three most important components: key-segments extraction, content descriptions and video retrieval. In our model, we firstly segment the whole video into meaningful intervals temporally according to the semantic; for example "party", "in house conversation" or "escape from prison". We call each of these meaningfully different segments as "scene" or "sequence". Zhang et. al. define video shot as a video sequence that consists of continuous video frames for one camera action and explain how camera changing or motions and special edit effects cause shot boundaries, [9]. By using this definition, we further temporally divide the sequences into smaller segments called "shots" according to the physical changing in parts, like colour. For example, if the camera or background changes at a particular point in a particular sequence, we split the sequence from that point. Since this splitting is done according to physical changing, automatization is much easier in that part than sequence segmentation. On the other hand, sequence segmentation requires much more artificial intelligence, since it is done according to the semantic. In our prototype system, while segmenting the video data, semi-automatic approach is used. Firstly, video is segmented according to the background changes automatically by using IBM MPEG-7 Annotation Tool, [10]. These segments are called shots and expressed in video shot sub-model. Then, these shots are manually grouped into sequences according to their semantics and expressed in video sequence sub-model. From shots, sequences are created. Every shot is a member of exactly one sequence. At the end of grouping, if the video has N number of shots and M number of sequence, N.M sequence-shot pairs are created. Video is a set of sequence-shot pairs.

Specific entities that are visible or tangible are called Video objects. Ekin et. al. call them as action units or interaction units, [4]. If we see or touch the entity in real world, we can declare it as a video object. For example; John, Kylie, t-shirt, hamburger etc. are video objects and expressed in video object sub-model. In SEBM, every video object has a list of roller event list which one can access the spatio-temporal information of the object directly through the object itself. This list is created automatically while creating the events. While objects are used to structure a particular event, the ID of the event is added to the roller event list of that object. The object is sequentially searched through the present objects and found in O(n) time. Since only the created objects can be added to the events, there is no possibility of not to find the object in present video objects.

Objects may have features like "John is 25 years old", "Kylie has blue eyes" or may have relationships with other objects like "Kylie is the sister of John", "John is a pilot of the plane". These relationships and features are expressed in video object characteristics sub-model in SEBM. Since video objects are stored directly under the video in hierarchy (Fig.1), all of the objects can be used to create a relation independent than their spatio-temporal information. For example, object *John* may have a relation *brotherof* with *Kylie*. So a video object named John will have a relation VOC={brotherof, Kylie}in SEBM. If *ball* has a *color blue*, then the object named *ball* will have a feature VOC={color, blue}.

Specific events that occur in a certain place during a particular interval of time are called video events. Video events stored under a particular shot of the video in SEBM and expressed in video event sub-model. As a result, particularly, every event belongs directly to some specific shot and indirectly to some specific sequence (Fig.1). Video events have event structure, which stores the subject, object, semantic place where the event occurs, accompanied object and directed object. For example in the sentence "John kills Kylie with a knife in the park", "John" is the subject, "Kylie" is the object, "Knife" is the accompanied object, "park" is the semantic place where the event occurs. Every event has start and end times labels, which is the temporal information for that event. Every event has visuality and auditorility flags that correspond their modality information. Moreover every event has keywords part to store extra information of an event or the words that can be heard in the auditory events. Keywords are free texts. If some audio event such as *John said "Hello"* must be declared, the word *hello* must be put in the keywords. The spatial information is stored in temporal and spatial region list (TSRL). The members of this list are minimum bounding rectangles (MBR) labelled by a specific time in a video. All the objects that belong to the event are positioned in defined MBRs. Textual information in the video is embedded into the model as making a new event named "isWritten" and putting the written text into the keyword field of the sub-model. The spatio-temporal information of the text is also included in the TSRL of the event.

3 Flexible Querying Using the SEBM Video Data Model

Semi-automatic extracted information from video(s) is stored in a video database and then queried and accessed, [5]. However, there are some issues while considering these processes. First of all, how the information is extracted and stored in a database? Then, when you store all information that you need about videos in a database, which types of queries are supported? How are these queries processed? Since there is no standard querying language or query models that you can use in video databases, querying the video database is a challenging problem. One possible solution is to develop a video data model that fits into the area of interest. We try to solve the problem of modelling the multimodal video data by using SEBM. Then we try to find the answers of the queries like; what is going on in the video, who are the people in the videos, what are the relations between them and what is happening when and where? In our developed prototype system, the database is queried about visual, auditory and textual contents. Spatio-temporal relations between events and objects are also queried. Moreover, hierarchical and conjunctive contents are also queried. Besides these, we handle the structural queries about objects and events. Fuzzy queries are also solved on SEBM prototype system.

3.1 Content Based Queries (Simple, Complex and Hierarchical)

Content Based Queries are about the content of the information that we extracted from the videos. With these queries, we can retrieve events, objects and their relationships in the video.

Definition 1 (Simple Content Based Queries). The content based queries, which are about only one of the SEBM sub-models. For example, "What information we store in a specific model entity (sequence, shot, object, characteristic or event)?" or "which model entity has the specific information that we supply, like name or timestamps (start or end points)?" can be two example queries. Since we have five different sub-model we also have five different SQs:

1. Queries about Video Sequence Sub-Model (SQ1)
2. Queries about Video Shot Sub-Model (SQ2)
3. Queries about Video Event Sub-Model (SQ3)
4. Queries about Video Object Sub-Model (SQ4)
5. Queries about Video Object Characteristics Sub-Model (SQ5)

Definition 2 (Complex Content Based Queries). The content based queries derived from simple queries and about the relationship information between sub-models. They are formatted by using the relationships between sub-models from simple queries as shown in Table.1.

Table 1. Complex Query Structures. Every complex query (CQ1-4) is constructed by using the relationships that are given in the column of formation structure. For example in order to query the relation between SQ2, SQ4 and SQ5, firstly the relation of (SQ2-CQ2) is used, and then CQ2 can be replaced by the structure of (SQ3-CQ1). The query becomes SQ2-SQ3-CQ1 and then CQ1 can be replaced by the structure of (SQ4-SQ5). The query becomes SQ2-SQ3-SQ4-SQ5. The result shows us that the relation should also consider the answer of SQ3, which is about video event sub-model. This complex query formation is shown in Fig.2.

Complex Query Type	Formation Structure	Example Queries
CQ1 Relations between objects and characteristics	SQ4 – SQ5	• Which kind of characteristics has the object named John? • Who is the brother of sister of John? • Who is the brother of the person seen in the event of eating between timestamps [3.0, 30.0]?
CQ2 Relations between events and objects, or events and characteristics	SQ3 – SQ4 SQ3 – SQ5 SQ3 – CQ1	• When does John give the book to the brother of Jimmy? • When is the text "Happy Birthday" seen on the screen? • When does John say "Hello" to the sister of Jimmy? • When does John crash to the chair where Jimmy sits?
CQ3 Relations between shots and events, objects or characteristics	SQ2 – SQ3 SQ2 – SQ4 SQ2 – SQ5 SQ2 – CQ2	• In which shot John gives the Hamburger to the sister of Jimmy?
CQ4 Relations between sequences and shot, event, object or characteristic	SQ1 – SQ2 SQ1 – SQ3 SQ1 – SQ4 SQ1 – SQ5 SQ1 – CQ3	• Which sequences have dinner shots? • In which sequence does John drive the car? • Give me the timestamps of the sequence where John fights with Kylie's brother.

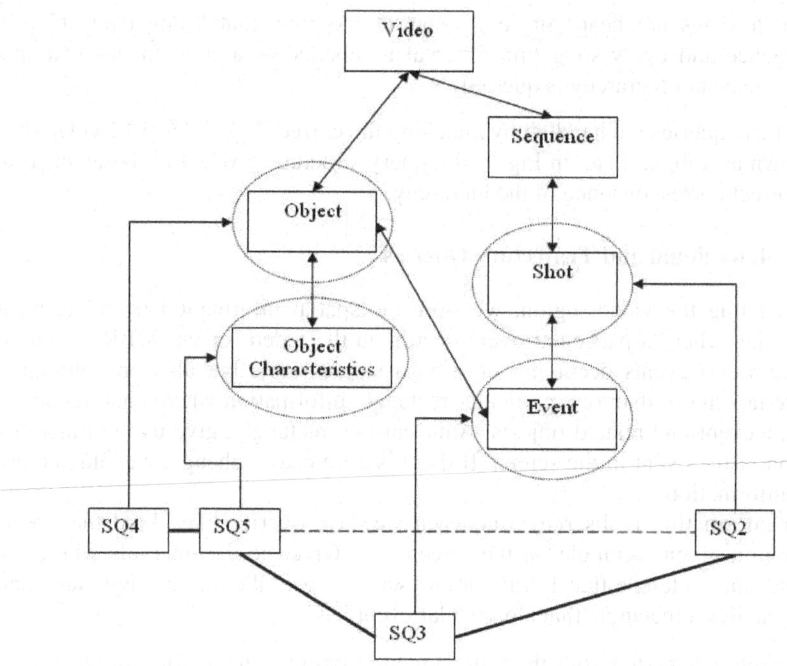

Fig. 2. Example Relation between CQs (formatted from SQs) and SEBM. (Video event sub-model is a bridge sub-model between Video shot sub-model and video object sub-model.)

These four types of CQs and five types of SQs can be used to compose much more complicated compound queries. Queries can be built to create conjunctive or disjunctive queries. For example, "When does John give Kylie's brother a hamburger while (and) Jimmy is saying hello?", "What are the sequences where the text "Happy birthday" appears on the screen or "strange noise" is heard at the background?". Since each of CQs is composed of SQs and possibly other CQs, the SQs are processed first and then the results of these SQs are merged to find the answer of CQs. That is, the divide and conquer technique is used. For example, assume that we have a query like "When does John give Kylie's brother a hamburger while (and) Jimmy is saying hello?" Firstly, we find Kylie's brother, Tom. Next, we find the intervals where John gives Tom a hamburger for example [t1,t2]. Next, we find when Jimmy says hello, for example [t3, t4]. Lastly, we merge (intersect) both intervals and find the common time interval [t5, t6], which is the result.

Video sequence-shot-event-object hierarchy is also queried in content-based queries and called as hierarchical queries. The hierarchy of video parts is shown in Fig.1. From the users point of view, either sequences or shots can be seen as big video parts containing small video parts i.e. events. Hierarchical queries are some kind of content-based queries but containing the hierarchy of video entities. For example:

- What is happening in the Party? (Assume "Party" is a sequence name and user wants to know which events take place in this sequence)

- Which songs are heard in song contest? (Assume that "song contest" is a sequence and every song time interval is labelled as a shot. In this example sequence-shot hierarchy is queried)

Hierarchical queries are handled by matching the correct links of SEBM video data model shown as a, b, c, d etc. in Fig.1 with query structure. Every link is searched to find the correct correspondence of the hierarchy.

3.3 Spatial, Regional and Trajectory Queries

While annotating the video region, we store the spatial information in video event sub-model, i.e. where a particular event occurs on the video screen. MBRs are used here. Since video events occur not only on a single frame but also on continuing frames, we take more than one particular rectangle information where each rectangle includes the event and related objects. Adjacent two rectangle, give us the trajectory information of the event in the screen. If there is a trajectory change, we add another rectangle information.

Region information is discrete. But when we have queries like "Find the events that occur in a given rectangle on the screen" or "Give me the intervals where the plane passes the rectangle that I draw on the screen", we take the rectangle area and look if it contains a rectangle that a particular event has.

SEBM prototype system runs the following algorithm for the regional queries.

1. For every event,
   a. For every region information of the event
      i. If the region that user enters while creating the query is equal to or contains the region of the event, add the event to the result list. For example in Fig.3, first region of the trajectory contains the region of the event

SEBM prototype system runs the following algorithm for the trajectory queries:

1. For every event,
   a. For every adjacent two region information of the event,
      i. If the first region that user enters while creating the query is equal to or contains the ith region of the event and the second region that user enters while creating the query is equal to or contains the $i+1^{th}$ region of the event as shown in Fig.3, add the event to the result list.

Spatial queries consists keywords for comparing two events TSRL information such as left, top, top-left or top-right. Other relations such as right or below can be thought as the inverse of left or top. Spatial relations consider the timestamps of TSRL information different than regional and trajectory queries, because the queried events must happen at the same time in the same video. Since the SEBM video data model stores the TSRL information not storing whole trajectory but only beginning, ending and direction changing locations, the whole trajectory of the events are created in run time of SEBM prototype system. Trajectory creation process considers time with width and height changing ratios through time. After trajectory creation process is done, the TSRL information consist not only beginning and ending locations but also intermediate locations.

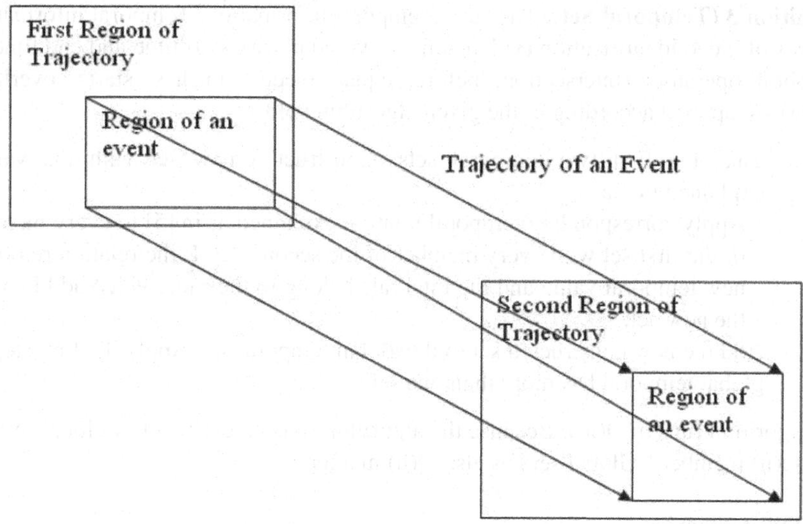

Fig. 3. Trajectory Query Relationship

SEBM prototype system runs the following algorithm for spatial queries:

1. For every two event,
   a. For every region of the first and second event that has same timestamp (or approximate timestamps)
      i. If the centers of regions provide the directional relations defined in [2] (left, right, top or bottom) then the timestamp is added to the result list.

3.4 Temporal Queries

Like spatial queries temporal queries are for querying the comparison. But they are for comparison of timestamps between two video entities. Durak uses temporal relationships as "before", "meets", "overlaps", "during", "starts", "finishes", "equal" which are defined formally by Allen in [19]. In order to make comparison between timestamps, some operations on intervals must be done, for instance union or intersection. Pradhan et. al. define these interval operations in [13]. For example (comparison keywords are written in italic):

Assume that the user wants to solve the following query:

- Find me the intervals when John says "Hello" to his brother before Kylie is seen on the screen and "Happy Birthday" is written on the board.

Query is divided into three sub-queries to solve them individually and after solving to combine the result by the user.

- Find me the intervals when John says "Hello" to his brother.
- Find me the intervals when Kylie is seen on the screen.
- Find me the intervals when "Happy Birthday" is written on the board.

Every query returns a temporal set as an answer.

Definition 3 (Temporal Set). The set of temporal information. Temporal information consists of video identification (video name or video place), start time and end time. Temporal operators (intersection, before, equal, meets, finishes, starts, overlaps, during) are applied according to the given algorithm below:

1. Take the first two temporal sets. Construct a new set with the values explained in 1.a.
   a. Apply corresponding temporal relation explained as in [5] to every member of the first set with every member of the second set. If the relation returns a new temporal value and the intervals belong to the same video add them to the new set.
2. Add the new constructed set to the global temporal set. Apply the first step, if global temporal has more than one set.

The algorithm runs in $O(n^2)$. Because the algorithm runs on every set of global set that have O(n) members. Global set has also O(n) members.

3.5 Fuzzy Queries

The nature of human interpretation of real world is not always discrete. Because there is always some unknown spatial information, the video data querying system should consider possible fuzzy queries. Fuzzy queries are constructed by giving some threshold value about the spatial relationship and they may involve some fuzzy conditions as explained in [3]. Threshold value may be given between 0.1 and 1.0 or by using some keywords such as "just", "slightly", etc.

For the fuzzy spatial relationships, Köprülü et. al. define membership functions by using membership values, [3]. The membership value of the relationship is calculated by using the angle between the line connecting the centres of MBRs and the x-axis. The membership functions are given in Table.2.

Table 2. Fuzzy Spatial Relationships

Relation	Angle	Membership Value
Top	arctan(x/y)	1-(angle/90)
Left	arctan(y/x)	angle/90
Top-Left	arctan(x/y)	1-(abs(angle-45)/45
Top-Right	arctan(y/x)	1-((angle-45)/45

Fuzzy queries are processed according to the given algorithm below:

1. For every two event,
   a. For every two region pair of the first and second event that has same timestamp (or approximate timestamps)
      i. If the centers of regions provide the directional relations given in part 3.3 and the threshold value is smaller than calculated membership value (using Table.2), then the timestamp is added to the result list.

For example:

- Show me the part of the video where the plane passes John just above his head. (Similar to spatial queries, the trajectory information of both plane and John is implicitly found as given in part 3.3. Then the positions of both video objects in a particular time are compared according to given membership value to find the solution by using Table.2)
- Show me the part of the video where the text "Happy Birthday" is seen around upper left corner of the screen with a threshold value 0.5. (Regional querying algorithm given in part 3.3 is applied here considering membership value by using Table.2)

3.6 Compound Queries

All content based, hierarchical, spatial, regional, trajectory, temporal or fuzzy queries may be joined to form more complex queries, which is called compound queries. Even compound queries can form more complex compound queries. This formation can be structured by using temporal and spatial relationships operators explained in previous parts. By solving and combining the partial answers of compound queries, the final answer can be formed. This approach is similar to that one we follow while solving the content based queries. For example:

- Show me the part of the video where John's brother who is the friend of the person seen at the upper left of the screen between 30th and 40th seconds is standing near the car on a chair *and* Kylie is walking through the door. (Complex Content based and trajectory queries are combined. Answers of both queries, which are temporal sets, are found and intersected)

Usage of SEBM gives us the ability to solve much more complex and nested queries different than [2 and 3]. We support this idea by implementing the SEBM prototype system, which uses XQuery [12] on Berkeley DB XML [11]. Since the user can form compound queries and answer them by using querying interface of SEBM prototype system, we have shown that SEBM can alter query intensity. SEBM prototype system shows the success of SEBM on compound querying rather than other systems like [14, 15 and 16].

4 Conclusion

The SEBM video data model makes it easy and effective to store the structural semantic information in a video database and then query the database. This video data model can be adapted to various domains, because it is based on understanding of the human about a particular video. Visual, auditory, and textual information in video are all considered in our model. Difficulties on modelling the structure of the video are overcame by using several sub-models. Very tightly coupled relations among these sub-models result in much more information embedded into the model than treating each independently. Query diversity is supported in our model. Content based, fuzzy, spatial and temporal queries are all supported. Automatization in annotation of the video is part of our implementation. In our prototype system, implemented with Java, XML is used to model the information in video and Berkeley XML DBMS is used to store and retrieve video information. Automatization in annotation of the video is part of our implementation. IBM MPEG-7 Annotation Tool is used for this purpose. For querying, XQuery facility of Berkeley XML DBMS is utilized. We plan to improve the fuzzy querying part by including the fuzzy relations and adding fuzzy features to the sub-models of SEBM.

References

[1] C. Snoek, M. Worring, "Multimodal Video Indexing: A review of the State of Art", Multimedia Tools and Applications, 25, pp: 5-35, 2005.

[2] N. Durak, "Semantic Video Modeling And Retrieval With Visual, Auditory, Textual Sources", Ms Thesis, METU, 2004.

[3] M. Köprülü, N.K. Çiçekli, A.Yazıcı, "Spatio-temporal querying in video databases". *Inf. Sci. 160(1-4),* pp.131-152, 2004.

[4] A. Ekin, M. Tekalp, and R. Mehrotra, "Integrated Semantic–Syntactic Video Modeling for Search and Browsing" in IEEE Transactions on Multimedia, VOL. 6, NO. 6, December 2004.

[5] H. Öztarak, "Structural and Event Based Multimodal Video Data Modelling", Ms Thesis, METU, 2005.

[6] D. Tjondronegoro, P. Chen, "Content-Based Indexing and Retrieval Using MPEG-7 and X-Query in Video Data Management Systems", World Wide Web: Internet and Web Information Systems, 5, 207–227, 2002.

[7] E. Oomoto and K. Tanaka, "OVID: Design and implementation of a video-object database system," IEEE Trans. Knowledge Data Eng.,vol.5, pp.629–643, Aug. 1993.

[8] Ö. Ulusoy, U. Güdükbay, M. Dönderler, Ş. Ediz and C. Alper, "BilVideo Database Management System", Proceedings of the 30th VLDB Conference, Toronto, Canada, 2004.

[9] Chengcui Zhang, Shu-Ching Chen, Mei-Ling Shyu, "PixSO: A System for Video Shot Detection", Proceedings of the Fourth IEEE Pacific-Rim Conference On Multimedia, pp. 1-5, December 15-18, 2003, Singapore.

[10] IBM MPEG-7 Annotation Tool Web site, www.alphaworks.com/tech/videoannex, Last date accessed: September, 2005.

[11] Berkeley DB XML Web Site, www.sleepycat.com Last date accessed: September, 2005.

[12] XQuery Web Site, www.w3.org/XML/Query, Last date accessed: September, 2005.

[13] Pradhan S., Tajima K., Tanaka K., "A Query Model to Synthesize Answer Intervals from Indexed Video Units", IEEE Trans. on Knowledge and Data Eng. Vol.13, No.5, pp. 824-838, Sept./Oct. 2001.

[14] S. Hammiche, S. Benbernou, M. Hacid, A. Vakali," Semantic Retrieval of Multimedia Data", MMDB'04, November 13, 2004, Washington, DC, USA.

[15] M.Lyu, E. Yau, S. Sze, "A Multilingual, Multimodal Digital Video Library System", JCDL'02, July 13-17, 2002, Portland, Oregon, USA.

[16] T. Kuo and A. Chen, "Content-Based Query Processing for Video Databases", IEEE Trans. on Multimedia. Vol.2, No.1, March 2000.

[17] Young F. Day, Serhan Dağtaş, Mitsutoshi Iino, Ashfaq Khokhar, Arif Ghafoor, "Object Oriented Conceptual Modeling of Video Data", Proc. Data Eng. (DE '95), pp. 401-408, 1995.

[18] C.G.M. Snoek, M. Worring, "Multimedia event based video indexing using time intervals" Technical Report 2003-01, Intelligent Sensory Information Systems Group, University of Amsterdam, August 2003.

[19] J. Allen, "Maintaining Knowledge about Temporal Intervals", Communications of ACM, 26 (11), pp. 832-843, 1983.

Reverse Nearest Neighbor Search in Peer-to-Peer Systems

Dehua Chen, Jingjing Zhou, and Jiajin Le

Col. of Computer Science, University of Donghua
P. O. Box 324, 200051, Shanghai, PRC
lydehua@mail.dhu.edu.cn
lejiajin@dhu.edu.cn

Abstract. Given a query point Q, a *Reverse Nearest Neighbor* (**RNN**) Query returns all points in the database having Q as their nearest neighbor. The problem of **RNN** query has received much attention in a centralized database. However, not so much work has been done on this topic in the context of Peer-to-Peer (P2P) systems. In this paper, we shall do pioneering work on supporting distributed **RNN** query in large distributed and dynamic P2P networks. Our proposed **RNN** query algorithms are based on a distributed multi-dimensional index structure, called *P2PRdNN*-tree, which is relying on a super-peer-based P2P overlay. The results of our performance evaluation with real spatial data sets show that our proposed algorithms are indeed practically feasible for answering distributed **RNN** query in P2P systems.

1 Introduction

The problem of *Reverse Nearest Neighbor* (RNN) Query [1,2,3,4,5,6,7,8,9,10] is to retrieve all data points in given multi-dimensional data sets whose Nearest Neighbor (NN) is a given query point. Although RNN is a complement of NN problem it is more complex than NN problem. The solutions from NN query cannot be directly applied to RNN query. This is because of the asymmetric relationship between NN/RNN: if a data point p is an RNN(q) (q is the nearest neighbor of p), it does not imply that p is the nearest neighbor NN(q) of q. The RNN problem has recently received considerable attention in the context of centralized database system due to its importance in a wide range of applications such as decision support system, profile-based marketing, document databases etc.

Nowadays, Peer-to-Peer (P2P) systems have become popular for sharing resources, information and services across a large number of autonomous peers in Internet. Especially, the applications of sharing multi-dimensional data (e.g. spatial data, documents, image files) in P2P systems are now being widely studied in the literatures [11,12,13,14,15,16,17]. However, most of these applications focus mainly on two types of queries: Range query and Nearest Neighbor (NN) query on the distributed data sets. And not so much effort is taken to support RNN search in such large distributed and ad-hoc environment. However, we believe that like its importance in the centralized database system, RNN query will become a practical

H.L. Larsen et al. (Eds.): FQAS 2006, LNAI 4027, pp. 87–96, 2006.

and important class of queries in P2P systems. Let us first consider an example in the P2P Geographic Information System (GIS) application. Suppose a large-scale chain supermarket is to open up a new supermarket at a location, the RNN query can be used to find the subset of existing supermarkets will be affected by the new supermarket, assuming people choose the nearest supermarket to consume. Another example is that when a new document is inserted into a P2P digital library, the RNN query can be used to ask the subset of authors of other documents who will find the new document interesting based on similarity to their documents. Therefore, this paper will investigate RNN search in distributed and dynamic P2P systems.

Like most of previous researches for RNN query in centralized database system, our proposed methods also build on tree-based multi-dimensional index structures (e.g. the R-tree family [18,19,20]). However, instead of maintaining a centralized multi-dimensional index in one centralized server, we propose a distributed multi-dimensional index, called P2PRdNN-tree, supported by a super-peer-based P2P overlay network. The P2PRdNN-tree structure enables efficient RNN search in large distributed environment. Like Rdnn-tree [2] proposed for centralized database context, our proposed distributed P2PRdNN-tree index structure stores extra information about nearest neighbor of data points in tree nodes. The extra information can efficiently reduce the search space and network communication

The remainder of this paper is organized as follows: Section 2 overviews the previous work. Section 3 presents our proposed super-peer-based P2P overlay and P2PRdNN-tree structure. Section 4 presents our proposed distributed RNN search algorithms. Section 5 provides experimental results and Section 6 summarizes our work.

2 Related Work

In Section 2.1, we shall briefly describe previous work on RNN query in centralized database systems. Section 2.2 overviews multi-dimensional data sharing in P2P systems.

2.1 RNN Search in Centralized Database Systems

Algorithms for processing RNN query in centralized databases can be classified into two categories depending on whether they require pre-computation or not.

The problem of RNN was first studied in [1]. The idea of the authors is to pre-compute, for each data point *d*, the distance *dnn* to its nearest neighbor NN(*d*). Thus, each data point is represented as a circle, whose center is the data point and whose radius is its *dnn*. Besides the R-tree that indexes the original data point, a separate R-tree is maintained which indexes the sets of such circles. The problem of finding RNN of a query point *Q* is then reduced to finding the circles that contain *Q*.

In order to avoid maintaining two separate R-trees, [2] combines the two indexes in the Rdnn-tree (R-tree containing Distance of Nearest Neighbors) index structure. Rdnn-tree differs from standard R-tree by storing extra information about NN of the data points for each tree node: for every leaf node, its record stores dnn, and for every non-leaf node, it record stores max_dnn (the maximum distance from every point in the sub-tree to its nearest neighbor). Therefore it requires prior computation of NN for each data point. The Rdnn-tree benefits RNN queries as follows. Let a non-leaf node be *N*, and let the query point be *Q*. If the distance between *Q* and the *MBR* (Minimal Bounding Rectangle) of *N* is bigger than *N*'s *max_dnn*, there is no need to search the sub-tree rooted by *N*. Inspired by the idea of Rdnn-tree, our proposed distributed multi-dimensional index structure also maintains extra information about the nearest neighbor in each tree node for assisting in efficient distributed RNN search.

There are several methods without relying on pre-computation. The approach of [3] divides the (2D) data space around the query point *Q* into six 60° regions, such that the only candidate of the RNN of *Q* in each region is exactly the NN of *Q*. So [3] finds the six NNs, and then check to see if each of them really considers *Q* as NN. [8] introduces another approach. Its idea is to find the NN (say o_1) of a query point *Q* first. Then consider the bisector of *Q* and o_1. All data points on the side of o_1 (except o_1 itself) can be pruned, since their distances to o_1 is no more than the distances to *Q*. Next, in the unpruned space, the NN to *Q* is found, and the space is further pruned. Finally, the unpruned space does not contain any data point. The only candidates of RNN are the identified NNs. The refinement step, which removes false positives, uses the previously pruned MBRs so that no tree node is visited twice throughout the algorithm.

Above we have reviewed the traditional monochromatic RNN query. There are other versions of RNN query have been proposed. [9][4] propose the solutions for *bichromatic* RNN queries where, given a set *Q* of queries, the goal is to find the points $d \in D$ that are closer to some $q \in Q$ than any other point of *Q*; [5] investigates *continuous* RNN queries on spatiotemporal data; [6] examines *stream* RNN queries where data arrive in the form of stream, and the goal is to report aggregate results over the RNNs of a set of query points.

2.2 Multi-dimensional Data Sharing in P2P Systems

The sharing of multi-dimensional data in P2P systems has become popular recently. CAN [21] can be regarded as the first P2P system supporting the sharing of multi-dimensional data since it has the same structure as the kd-tree[22] and grid-file[23]. pSearch [14], a P2P system based on CAN, is proposed for retrieving documents that are modeled as points in multi-dimensional space. [27] has proposed another system also based on CAN for supporting range query by including the ranges into hash functions. Most other systems such as [15] use space filling curves to map multi-dimensional data to one dimensional data. SkipIndex [16] is based on skip graph [28], which aims to support high dimensional similarity query. More recently, several distributed multi-dimensional index structures have been proposed in the literatures. [13] proposed an R-tree-based indexing structure for P2P systems in the context of sensor network. The proposed index structure in [13] is designed for optimize NN search. P2PR-tree [12] is another distributed multi-dimensional index structure based on R-tree. P2PR-tree is well designed for optimizing window query. [11] proposed VBI-tree, a new Peer-to-Peer framework based on a balanced tree structure overlay, which can support extensible centralized mapping methods and query processing based on a variety of multidimensional tree structures, including R-Tree, X-Tree [24], SSTree [25], and M-Tree [26].

3 P2PRdNN-Tree Structure

In this section, we first present a super-peer-based P2P overlay network and then propose P2PRdNN-tree implemented on top of such P2P overlay.

3.1 Super-Peer-Based Overlay

Peers in a P2P system may be organized by various network overlays. Considering the fact that peers in the network often vary widely in bandwidth and computing capacity, we organize peers into a super-peer-based P2P topology (shown as in Fig. 3.1).

In such super-peer-based P2P network infrastructure, a small subset of peers with relatively high stability and relatively high computing capacity are designated as super-peers. As we can see in the following sections, super-peers take over a lot of important responsibilities such as routing query and answer messages, initiating and maintaining local P2PRdNN-tree structure, distributing and executing of query plan. For simplicity, we connect super-peers with a main channel that acts as a broadcast routing mechanism and can be implemented in many different ways. Certainly, super-peers can also be arranged in more complex topology such as Hypercup [29].

Each peer storing and maintaining a set of multi-dimensional data points connects directly to one super-peer in the network. Peers can join and leave the system in any time and have relatively lower computing power.

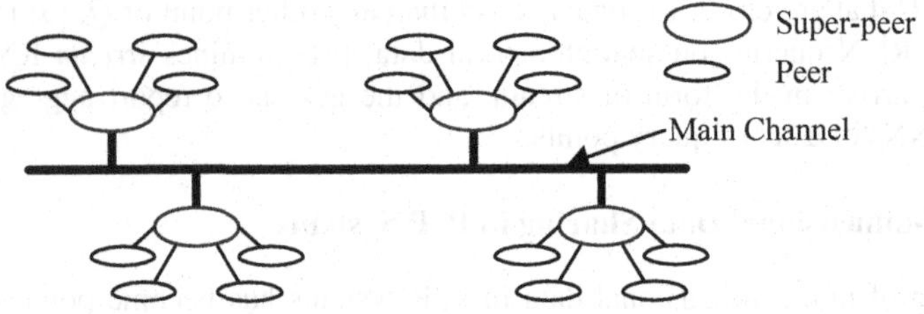

Fig. 3.1. Super-peer-based P2P overlay

3.2 P2PRdNN-Tree

In this section, we shall present the structure of P2PRdNN-tree based on our proposed super-peer-based P2P overlay in the above section.

Assume that each peer, say p, stores and manages a set D_p of n dimensional data points concerning a certain region of the n dimensional space. The region can be expressed in the form of the MBR_p that bounds the data points in D_p. We can also say that the peer p is responsible for the MBR_p. For each data point, say d, in the data set D_p, we compute the distance $L\_dnn_{Dp}(d)$ to its local nearest neighbor NN(d) in D_p. Please note that the local nearest neighbor of a point, defined here, may not be the real (global) nearest neighbor in all data sets available on the network. The real (global) nearest neighbor of a point may locate in other peer. This can be illustrated in Fig. 3.2. The real nearest neighbor b of data point d locates in peer B, and point a is the local nearest

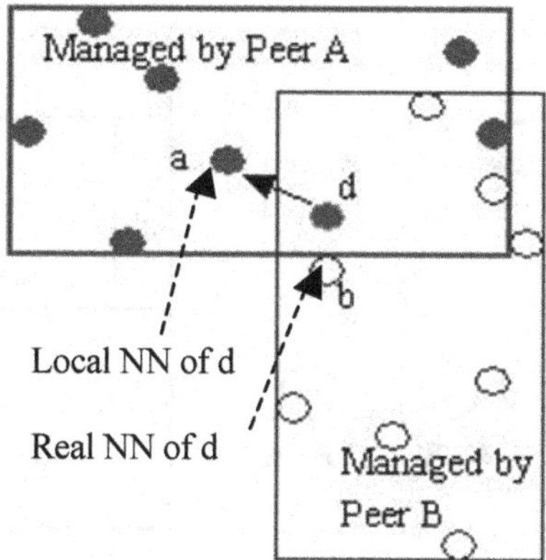

Fig. 3.2. The concept of Local nearest neighbor

neighbor of *d* in peer *A*. However, in order to avoid introducing extra network traffic, we do not compute here the distance between the point and its real nearest neighbor.

For each peer in the network, it should send its information to its corresponding super-peer. The information include the location of the peer (e.g. IP address and port), its responsible MBR and *max_dnn*=max{L_dnn_{Dp}(d)}. The super-peer shall initiate a P2PRdNN-tree structure based on the information from the peers connecting to it. We present the structure of P2PRdNN-tree in the following paragraphs.

In case of P2PRdNN-tree structure, each peer is assigned one leaf node of P2PRdNN-tree. Like the Rdnn-tree, the leaf node of P2PRdNN-tree contains entries of the form (*ptid*, L_*dnn*), where *ptid* refers to an *n* dimensional point and L_*dnn* is the distance from the point to its local nearest neighbor. The entries of a leaf node of tree are stored in the responsible peer.

As far as the super-peer is concerned, it does not hold the leaf level of P2PRdNN-tree. It maintains the non-leaf nodes of P2PRdNN-tree. Similar to Rdnn-tree, each non-leaf node of P2PRdNN-tree stores a set of entries of the form (*ptr*, *rect*, *max_dnn*). *ptr* is the address of a child node in the tree. If *ptr* points to a leaf node, the address refers to the location of the responsible peer and *rect* is the MBR of the leaf node. If *ptr* points to a non-leaf node, the *rect* is the MBR of all rectangles that are entries in the child node. *Max_dnn* is the maximum distance from every data point in the subtree to its nearest neighbor. For the root node of P2PRdNN-tree, it stores an additional entry of the form of (G_MBR, G_maxdnn), where G_MBR refers to the general MBR bounding all points managed by its connected peers, and G_maxdnn is the maximum max_dnn of all points in G_MBR.

Thus, for each super-peer and its directly-connecting peers, they maintain together a local P2PRdNN-tree indexing the data sets stored in the peers. Fig.3.3 shows a local P2PRdNN-tree structure. In the Fig.3.3 (b), Peer A ~H manage the data points of the regions a ~h respectively. In the local P2PRdNN-tree from Fig.3.3 (a), leaf nodes a ~h are managed by Peer A ~H respectively. The super-peer is responsible for maintaining other part of the tree (the non-leaf nodes i ~o).

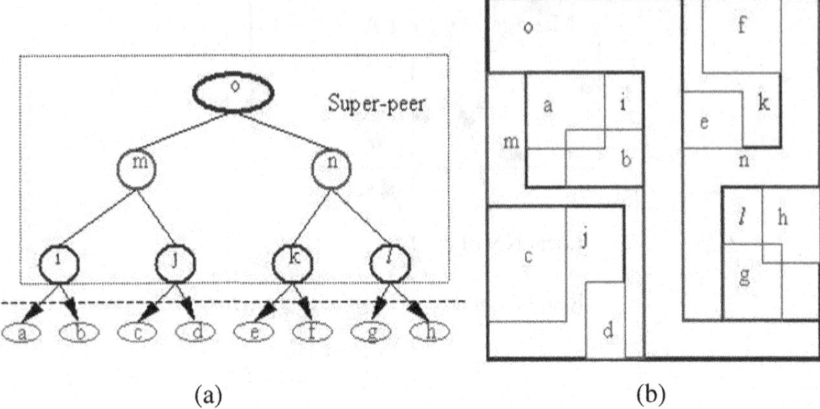

(a) (b)

Fig. 3.3. The P2PRdNN-tree index structure

4 RNN Search with P2PRdNN-Tree

In this section, we shall discuss how to process distributed RNN search based on the P2PRdNN-tree index structure presented in the above section.

Our distributed RNN search algorithm operates in two steps: (1) the filter step retrieves a candidate RNN set (discussed in section 4.1), and (2) the verification step eliminates false hits and reports the actual RNNs (discussed in section 4.2). The introduction of the second step has something to do with the definition of L_*dnn* presented in above section.

According to the distributed nature of the query and the P2P network, each step in the algorithm consists of three parts that are respectively executed by

(i) The super-peer initially receiving the query,
(ii) Other partitioning super-peers in the network,
(iii) And the local peers at each partitioning super-peer.

Let us now present the algorithm to answer a RNN query *Q* posed by peer *P* to super-peer *SP*, also called the initiating super-peer. The algorithm is entirely controlled by super-peer *SP*, which, whenever necessary, poses the requests to its connected peers and other super-peer in the network during the execution.

We shall study two steps in our proposed algorithm respectively as follows.

4. 1 Filter Step

When super-peer *SP* receives a RNN query *Q* from one of its connected peers. It first broadcasts via the main channel a query message in a form of (*Q*, Query_id) where *Q* indicates the query is a RNN query and Query_id is the unique identifier of the query. The Query_id prevents one super-peer or peer from receiving a query twice. Every super-peer (including *SP*) receiving the query message computes the distance Dist(*Q*, G_MBR) between *Q* and its G_MBR from the root node of its local P2PRdNN-tree. If Dist(*Q*, G_MBR) is greater than its corresponding G_maxdnn, we can conclude that any point in the G_MBR is not closer to *Q* than its nearest neighbor. In other words, there is no reverse nearest neighbor of *Q* in the G_MBR. Thus, we need not to search the peers connecting to this super-peer for reverse nearest neighbor. Then the super-peer discards the query message. Otherwise, the super-peer accepts the query and performs the filter algorithm (shown in Fig.4.1) by branch-and-bound traversing the local P2PRdNN-tree. For those super-peers accepting the query message, we call them query-partitioning super-peer (partitioning super-peer for short). Please note that the initiating super-peer may be partitioning super-peer.

Determining_candidates_of _RNN (Node *n*, Query *Q*)

If *n* is leaf node of P2PRdNN-tree, the partitioning super-peer sends a request to the peer who is responsible for the leaf node. And at the responsible peer, for each entries (*ptid*, L_*dnn*),

if Dist(*Q*, *ptid*)<L_*dnn*, outputs the data point referred by *ptid* as one of the candidate RNNs of *Q*, and sends the candidate to the initiating super-peer *SP*.

If *n* is non-leaf node of P2PRdNN-tree, then for each branch B=(*ptr*, *rect*, *max_dnn*),
if Dist(*Q*,*rect*)<*max_dnn*, call Determine_candidate_of_RNN (B.*ptr*,*Q*)

Fig. 4.1. The filter algorithm

4.2 Verification Step

When each candidate retrieved during the filter step arrives at the initiating super-peer *SP*, we need to verify whether the candidate is actual RNN of *Q*. For each candidate *c*, the initiating super-peer *SP* broadcasts via main channel a Range Query in the form of [*Q*(*c*,*r*), Query_id] where *Q*(*c*,*r*) refers to the query is a kind of circle range query with center point *c* and radiu *r*=Dist(*c*,*Q*), and Query_id is the unique identifier of the query.

Every super-peer (including *SP*) receiving the range query message checks whether its G_MBR covers or intersects the region of *Q*(*c*,*r*). If the result is false, then the super-peer discards the range query message. Otherwise, the super-peer accepts the range query and performs the verification algorithm by traversing the local P2PRdNN-tree using any existing range query algorithm on R-tree. Similarly, we call those super-peers accepting the query message as partitioning super-peer. The verification step terminates if all the partitioning super-peers report no points in the query region or if there is a partitioning super-peer reports points in the query region. If the former condition is satisfied, then the candidate *c* is an actual RNN of *Q* and is reported to the query peer by the initiating super-peer *SP*. Otherwise, the candidate *c* is discarded by *SP*.

5 Experiments

We conducted simulation experiments to evaluate the performance of our proposed algorithms. Our simulation environment comprised a 100-node computer cluster. In order to compare our work meaningfully against the centralized database context, we implement two different network topologies for organizing these machines: the first is Super-Peer (SP) based topology for P2P environment; the second is star topology for Client/Server (C/S) architecture. Our performance study was conducted using a real-world dataset known as *Tiger* data files.

For super-peer based topology, all simple peers have exactly one connection to a super-peer. The super-peers form their own P2P network. For the experiments described in this paper we use main channel to connect all super-peers. In our simulation experiments, we let each simple peer manage multiple leaf nodes of local P2PRdNN-tree. Each leaf node has more than 100000 spatial objects.

For star topology, all spatial objects are stored in one server to which all other peers connect. In the server, we index all objects by Rdnn-tree [2].

The simulation experiment results are shown in Fig.5.1. In the figure, the x-axis represents an inter-arrival rate of *n* RNN queries which implies *n* RNN queries were issued in the entire system every second. The y-axis represents the average completion time that indicates the average time taken for each query to return all answer from relevant peers. From the results in Fig.5.1, we find that as the inter-arrival rate of queries increases, the performance of C/S drops more quickly than SP. This occurs because in C/S *every* query has to be routed only to the centralized server. As a result, there are large job queues at the centralized server, thereby causing significantly increased waiting times at the server that ultimately causes severely the completion times to increase. In contrast, the decentralized nature of SP implies that query execution is performed in a distributed fashion, thereby ensuring the absence of any serious execution bottlenecks.

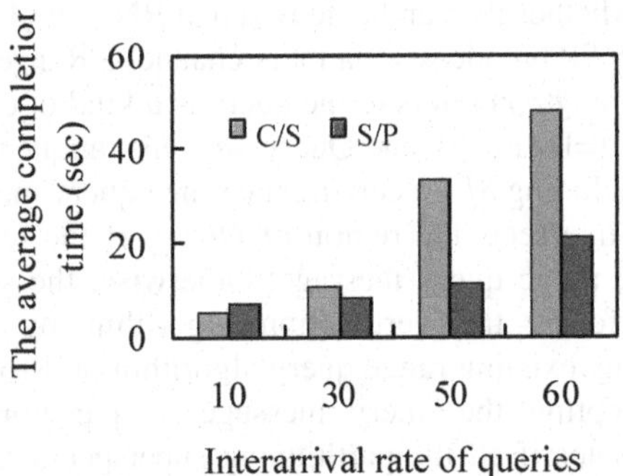

Fig. 5.1. The performance comparison between C/S and S/P

6 Conclusions and Future Work

In this paper, we have made the pioneering investigation on distributed Reverse Nearest Neighbor search in P2P systems. In our work, our proposed RNN search algorithms are based on the P2PRdNN-tree, a P2P version of Rdnn-tree, which is well-suited for RNN search in P2P environment. Meanwhile, our proposed P2PRdNN-tree also supports Range Query and Nearest Neighbor Query since it is also a variation of R-tree.

This paper does not discuss the issue of the update of our distributed P2PRdNN-tree when the evolutions of network and data take place. However, this issue is interesting and challenging. We plan to Study this issue in our future work.

This paper focuses on the traditional monochromatic RNN query in P2P systems. We also plan to investigate other RNN queries such as *bichromatic* RNN in distributed environment.

Our proposed solutions work well for low dimensional data. We wish to explore how to adjust our solutions for performing RNN search on high-dimensional data in P2P systems.

References

1. F. Korn and S. Muthukrishnan: Influence Sets Based on Reverse Nearest Neighbor Queries. In SIGMOD, 2000.
2. C. Yang and K. I. Lin: An Index Structure for Efficient Reverse Nearest Neighbor Queries. In ICDE, 2001.
3. I. Stanoi, D. Agrawal, and A. E. Abbadi: Reverse Nearest Neighbor Queries for Dynamic Databases. In SIGMOD Workshop on Research Issues in Data Mining and Knowledge Discovery, 2000.
4. I. Stanoi, M. Riedewald, D. Agrawal, and A. E. Abbadi: Discovery of Influence Sets in Frequently Updated Databases. In VLDB, 2001.
5. R. Benetis, C. S. Jensen, G. Karciauskas, and S. Saltenis: Nearest Neighbor and Reverse Nearest Neighbor Queries for Moving Objects. In IDEAS, 2002.
6. F. Korn, S. Muthukrishnan, and D. Srivastava: Reverse Nearest Neighbor Aggregates Over Data Streams. In VLDB,2002.
7. A. Singh, H. Ferhatosmanoglu, and A. S. Tosun: High Dimensional Reverse Nearest Neighbor Queries. In CIKM, 2003.
8. Y. Tao, D. Papadias, and X. Lian: Reverse kNN Search in Arbitrary Dimensionality. In VLDB, 2004.
9. T. Xia, D. Zhang, E. Kanoulas, and Y. Du: On Computing Top-t Most Inuential Spatial Sites. In VLDB, 2005.
10. M.Yiu and N. Mamoulis: Reverse Nearest Neighbors Search in Ad-hoc Subspaces. In ICDE, 2006.
11. H. V. Jagadish, B. C. Ooi, Q. H. Vu, R. Zhang, and A. Zhou: VBI-Tree: A Peer-to-Peer Framework for Supporting Multi-Dimensional Indexing Schemes. In ICDE, 2006.
12. A. Mondal, Yilifu, and M. Kitsuregawa: P2PR-tree: An R-tree-based Spatial Index for Peer-to-Peer Environments. In EDBT, 2004.
13. M. Demirbas and H. Ferhatosmanoglu: Peer-to-peer spatial queries in sensor networks. In P2P, 2003.
14. C. Tang, Z. Xu, and S. Dwarkadas: Peer-to-peer information retrieval using self-organizing semantic overlay networks. In SIGCOMM, 2003.
15. J. Lee, H. Lee, S. Kang, S. Choe, and J. Song: CISS: An efficient object clustering framework for DHT-based peer-to-peer applications. In DBISP2P, 2004.
16. C. Zhang, A. Krishnamurthy, and R. Y.Wang: Skipindex: Towards a scalable peer-to-peer index service for high dimensional data. Technical report, Princeton University, 2004.
17. Y. Shu, K.-L. Tan, and A. Zhou: Adapting the content native space for load balanced. In DBISP2P, 2004.

18. A. Guttman: R-trees: a dynamic index structure for spatial searching. In ACM SIGMOD International Conference on Management of Data, 1984.
19. N. Beckmann, H.-P. Kriegel, R. Schneider, and B. Seeger: The R*-Tree: an efficient and robust access method for points and rectangles. In ACM SIGMOD International Conference on Management of Data, 1990.
20. T. Sellis, N. Roussopoulos, and C. Faloutsos: The R+-tree: a dynamic index for multi-dimensional objects. In VLDB, 1987.
21. S. Ratnasamy, P. Francis, M. Handley, R. Karp, and S. Shenker: A scalable content-addressable network. In ACM Annual Conference of the Special Interest Group on Data Communication, 2001.
22. J. L. Bentley: Multidimensional binary search trees used for associative searching. Communications of the ACM, 18(9):509–517, Sep 1975.
23. K. Hinrichs and J. Nievergelt: The grid file: A data structure designed to support proximity queries on spatial objects. In Proceedings of the International Workshop on Graphtheoretic Concepts in Computer Science, 1983.
24. S. Berchtold, D. A. Keim, and H.-P. Kriegel: The X-tree: An index structure for high-dimensional data. In VLDB, 1996.
25. D. A. White and R. Jain: Similarity indexing with the SStree. In ICDE, 1996.
26. P. Ciaccia, M. Patella, and P. Zezula: M-tree: An efficient access method for similarity search in metric spaces. In VLDB, 1997.
27. O. D. Sahin, A. Gupta, D. Agrawal, and A. El Abbadi: A peer-to-peer framework for caching range queries. In ICDE, 2004.
28. J. Aspnes and G. Shah: Skip graphs. In Annual ACM-SIAM Symposium on Discrete Algorithms, 2003.
29. M. Schlosser, M. Sintek, S. Decker, and W. Nejdl: HyperCup-Hypercubes, Ontologies and efficient search on P2P networks. In International workshop on agents and peer-to-peer computing, 2002.

On Tuning OWA Operators in a Flexible Querying Interface

Sławomir Zadrożny[1] and Janusz Kacprzyk[2]

[1] Warsaw School of Information Technology,
ul. Newelska 6, 01-447 Warsaw, Poland
[2] Systems Research Institute PAS,
ul. Newelska 6, 01-447 Warsaw, Poland

Abstract. The use of the Yager's OWA operators within a flexible querying interface is discussed. The key issue is the adaptation of an OWA operator to the specifics of a user's query. Some well-known approaches to the manipulation of the weights vector are reconsidered and a new one is proposed that is simple and efficient.

1 Introduction

We consider a flexible querying interface supporting an extended version of SQL such as those proposed by Kacprzyk and Zadrożny [1, 2] and Bosc et al. [3]. Basically an extension of a traditional querying language is meant here to support *linguistic terms* in queries exemplified by fuzzy values such as "young" and fuzzy relations (fuzzy comparison operators) such as "much greater than" in the following SQL query:

```
SELECT *
FROM   employees
WHERE  (age IS young) AND                                        (1)
       (salary IS MUCH GREATER THAN 50000 USD)
```

Another class of relevant linguistic terms are *linguistic quantifiers* such as "most", "almost all" etc. In the extended query language advocated here they play the role of flexible aggregation operators. Kacprzyk and Ziółkowski [4], and then Kacprzyk, Ziółkowski and Zadrożny [5] proposed to use them to aggregate conditions in the WHERE clause of the SQL SELECT statement as, e.g. in

"*Most* of conditions among 'age IS *young*, salary IS *high*,...' are to be satisfied"

Bosc et al. (cf. e.g. [6]) proposed to use linguistic quantifiers with subqueries or against groups of rows as, e.g., in

```
SELECT   deptno
FROM     employees
GROUP BY deptno                                                  (2)
HAVING   most_of (young are well-paid)
```

H.L. Larsen et al. (Eds.): FQAS 2006, LNAI 4027, pp. 97–108, 2006.

Whatever the role a linguistic quantifier, it has to be somehow modelled, and a user has to be provided with some means for its definition and manipulation. Here we assume that the linguistic quantifiers are originally defined and interpreted in the sense of Zadeh. Then, during a query execution they are automatically re-interpreted in terms of Yager's OWA operators due to their high operability and intuitive appeal. Before the actual query execution the user may modify the OWA operators present in the query so as to better adjust them to his or her needs. We focus here on the guidelines that should be presented to the user in order to help him or her in an appropriate definition and manipulation of the OWA operator.

We will now briefly discuss linguistic quantifiers and Yager's OWA operators, well-known approaches to their tuning, show how they are used and manipulated in queries, and finally present an algorithm implemented in our FQUERY for Access package [1, 2].

2 Linguistic Quantifiers and the OWA Operators

Our starting point is Zadeh's calculus of linguistically quantified propositions [7] used to. It is a framework meant to model such expressions of natural language like

$$\text{“}\textit{Most}\text{ Swedes are }\textit{tall}\text{”} \tag{3}$$

where "Most" is an example of a linguistic quantifier. Other examples include "almost all", "much more than 50%" etc. We are here interested only in *relative* quantifiers such that: - their semantics refers to the proportion of elements possessing a certain property (in Example (3) it is the set of tall Swedes) among all the elements of the universe of discourse (in Example (3) it is the set of all Swedes);
and *nondecreasing* such that: - the larger such a proportion the higher the truth value of a proposition containing such a linguistic quantifier.

A linguistically quantified proposition exemplified by (3) might be formally written in a general form as

$$QxP(x) \tag{4}$$

where Q denotes a linguistic quantifier (e.g., *most*), $X = \{x\}$ is a universe of discourse (e.g., a set of Swedes), and $P(x)$ is a predicate corresponding to a certain property (e.g., of being *tall*).

The truth value of (4) is computed as follows. The relative quantifier Q is equated with a fuzzy set defined in $[0, 1]$. In particular, for a regular nondecreasing quantifier its μ_Q is assumed to be nondecreasing and normal, i.e.,

$$x \leq y \Rightarrow \mu_Q(x) \leq \mu_Q(y); \quad \mu_Q(0) = 0; \quad \mu_Q(1) = 1 \tag{5}$$

The particular $y \in [0, 1]$ correspond to proportions of elements possessing property P and $\mu_Q(y)$ assesses the degree to which a given proportion matches the semantics of Q. For example, Q = "most" might be given as:

$$\mu_Q(y) = \begin{cases} 1 & \text{for } y > 0.8 \\ 2y - 0.6 & \text{for } 0.3 \leq y \leq 0.8 \\ 0 & \text{for } y < 0.3 \end{cases} \tag{6}$$

The predicate P is modelled by an appropriate fuzzy set $P \in \mathcal{F}(X)$[1] characterized by its membership function μ_P.

Formally, the truth degree of (4) is computed using the following formula:

$$\text{Truth}(QxP(x)) = \mu_Q(\frac{1}{n}\sum_{i=1}^{n}\mu_P(x_i)) \tag{7}$$

where $r = \frac{1}{n}\sum_{i=1}^{n}\mu_P(x_i)$ and n is the cardinality of X.

The ordered weighted averaging operators (*OWA*) were introduced by Yager [8] and are defined as follows. Let $W \in [0,1]^m, W = [w_1, \ldots, w_m], \sum_{i=1}^{m} w_i = 1$ be a weight vector. Then the OWA operator of dimension m and weight vector W is a function $O_W : [0,1]^m \longrightarrow [0,1]$ such that:

$$O_W(a_1, \ldots, a_m) = W \circ B = \sum_{i=1}^{m} w_i b_i \tag{8}$$

where b_i is i-th largest element among a_i's and $B = [b_1, \ldots, b_m]$; $\circ$ denotes the scalar product.

The OWA operators generalize many widely used aggregation operators. In particular one obtains the maximum, minimum and average operators assuming $W = [1, 0, \ldots, 0, 0]$, $W = [0, 0, \ldots, 0, 1]$ and $W = [\frac{1}{m}, \frac{1}{m}, \ldots, \frac{1}{m}, \frac{1}{m}]$, respectively. We will denote these OWA operators as $O_{\max}, O_{\min}$ and O_{avg}, respectively.

Moreover, the OWA operators may be used to model linguistic quantifiers. Let us assume that Q is a regular non-decreasing linguistic quantifier in the sense of Zadeh (5). Then the weight vector of a corresponding OWA operator is defined due to Yager [8] as follows:

$$w_i = \mu_Q\left(\frac{i}{m}\right) - \mu_Q\left(\frac{i-1}{m}\right), \qquad i = 1, \ldots, m \tag{9}$$

Using this method for the linguistic quantifier in the sense of Zadeh given by (6) we obtain the OWA operator of dimension $m = 4$ with the following weight vector:

$$W = [0, 0.4, 0.5, 0.1] \tag{10}$$

Yager [8] introduced two measures characterizing the OWA operators: *ORness* and *dispersion*. The ORness of an OWA operator O_W of dimension m is denoted as ORness(O_W) and computed as follows:

$$\text{ORness}(O_W) = \frac{\sum_{i=1}^{m}(m-i)w_i}{m-1} \tag{11}$$

[1] We will denote a family of fuzzy sets defined in X as $\mathcal{F}(X)$.

In general ORness(O_W) $\in$ [0,1] and in particular:

$$\text{ORness}(O_{\min}) = 0, \quad \text{ORness}(O_{\max}) = 1 \quad \text{ORness}(O_{\text{avg}}) = 0.5$$

It is worth noticing that the value of the ORness measure of an OWA operator O_W may be interpreted as a result of applying this OWA operator to a specific argument vector, namely:

$$\text{ORness}(O_W) = O_W\left(\frac{m-1}{m-1}, \frac{m-2}{m-1}, \ldots, \frac{m-m}{m-1}\right) \tag{12}$$

The ORness is, in a sense, a measure of similarity of a given OWA operator to the "max" operator. Thus it may be used as a guideline in choosing or modifying an OWA operator. We will focus on that issue in Sections 3 and 5.

The measure of dispersion (entropy), disp(O_W), for an OWA operator O_W of dimension m is defined as follows:

$$\text{disp}(O_W) = -\sum_{\substack{i=1 \\ w_i \neq 0}}^{m} w_i \ln(w_i) \tag{13}$$

The closer the weights w_i are one to another (and, in consequence, closer to $1/m$), the higher the measure of dispersion is. The OWA operators with higher measures of dispersion take into account more arguments a_i being aggregated. The limit cases are again $O_{\min}$ and $O_{\max}$ that take into account one argument only: the smallest and the largest, respectively. Their dispersion measure is the lowest possible, equal to 0. The operator O_{avg} treats all arguments equally and has the highest possible measure of dispersion equal to $\ln(m)$.

3 Definition of the OWA Operators

The main problem addressed in this paper is how to define and manipulate the OWA operators. These problems are strictly related. The former has attracted much more attention. In the literature many approaches have been proposed. They may be briefly summarized as follows.

The weight vector W of an OWA operator O_W might be determined using:

1. experimental data: suppose a set of data $\{(a_1^j, \ldots, a_m^j, y^j)\}_{j=1,\ldots,n}$ is available; then assuming that $y_j = O_W(a_1^j, \ldots, a_m^j)\ \forall j$ the weights vector W best matching this assumption is sought for. Filev i Yager [9] formalized that problem as the search for the weights vector minimizing the sum of squared errors $\sum_{j=1}^{n}(y_j - \sum_{i=1}^{m} w_i b_i^j)^2$ Assuming a specific parametrized form of the weight vector $w_i = e^{\lambda_i}/\sum_{j=1}^{m} e^{\lambda_j}$, this optimization problem may be reduced to a constraint-free form (the previous forms requires the imposition of constraints securing that the weights are non-negative and summing up to 1.)

2. a linguistic quantifier in the sense of Zadeh: the OWA operator is meant to represent a given linguistic quantifier; thus its weights vector is computed using the formula (9).
3. a fixed value of certain characteristic features of the OWA operator: a weights vector W is sought so that to obtain this fixed value, possibly optimizing the value of another characteristic feature.

The first approach might be useful in the case of a flexible querying interface. However, it requires an extensive cooperation (interaction) with the user to collect a large amount of data. The second approach is fairly obvious and does not require additional comments. The third approach seems to be the most promising from the point of view of supporting both the definition and modification of an OWA operator.

O'Hagan [10] proposed to determine the weight vector W such that the OWA operator obtained has a fixed required value of the ORness measure and at the same time has the maximum possible value of the dispersion measure. The class of such operators is referred to as MEOWA (Maximum Entropy OWA) operators. Formally, they are determined by solving the following optimization problem:

$$disp(O_W) \longmapsto max \quad \text{subject to ORness}(O_W) = \alpha, \quad \sum_i^m w_i = 1, \quad w_i \geq 0 \;\; \forall i \tag{14}$$

where α is the required ORness measure value.

Filev and Yager [11] simplified this optimization problem using the Lagrange multipliers method. Then the problem boils down to finding the root of a polynomial of degree $m - 1$. Fuller and Majlender [12], assuming the same approach, proposed a simpler formulae for the weight vector W.

Fuller and Majlender considered also the variance of an OWA operator defined as:

$$\text{var}(O_W) = \sum_{i=1}^{m} \frac{(w_i - \frac{\sum_{i=1}^{m} w_i}{m})^2}{m} = \frac{1}{m}\sum_{i=1}^{m} w_i^2 - \frac{1}{m^2} \tag{15}$$

Then they proposed [13] a class of OWA operators analogous to MEOWA (14) where the variance instead of dispersion is maximized. Also in this case Fuller and Majlender developed analytical formulae for the weight vector W.

Filev and Yager also addressed the problem of determining the weights of an OWA operator with a required fixed value of the ORness measure. In [9] they proposed a simple approximate procedure for a certain class of OWA operators, referred to as *exponential OWA operators.*

The weights of the exponential OWA operators are defined as follows:

$$w_i = \alpha(1-\alpha)^{i-1}, \forall i \neq m; w_m = (1-\alpha)^{m-1} \tag{16}$$

where $\alpha \in [0,1]$ is a parameter that together with the dimension m fully characterizes an OWA operator.

For a fixed dimension m the value of the ORness measure of such an exponential OWA operator increases together with the value of α. Knowing this dependency it is possible to choose an appropriate value of α to obtain an OWA operator (16) having approximately a required level of the ORness measure.

Filev and Yager consider in [9] still another class of the OWA operators such that it is fairly easy to determine the weight vector W providing a required level of the ORness measure. The weights of these operators are all identical except for the first and the last one, i.e., w_1 and w_m. For such operators the ORness measure (11) may be expressed as follows [9]:

$$\text{ORness}(O_W) = 0.5 + 0.5(w_1 - w_m) \tag{17}$$

Thus in order to obtain a required ORness level, only w_1 and w_n satisfying (17) and $v_1, v_n \in [0, 1]$ have to be selected. The remaining weights are assumed to be identical, thus equal to:

$$w_i = \frac{1}{m-2}(1 - w_1 - w_m) \qquad 2 \leq i \leq m-1$$

Filev and Yager also proposed [9] a modified version of this method. Namely, the weights of an OWA operator of dimension m and of a required ORness measure value α are defined as:

$$w_i = \frac{1}{m}(1 - \mid \Delta \mid) \qquad 2 \leq i \leq m-1$$

$$\left.\begin{aligned} w_1 &= \tfrac{1}{m}(1 - \mid \Delta \mid) + \Delta \\ w_n &= \tfrac{1}{m}(1 - \mid \Delta \mid) \end{aligned}\right\} \text{if } \Delta > 0$$

$$\left.\begin{aligned} w_1 &= \tfrac{1}{m}(1 - \mid \Delta \mid) \\ w_n &= \tfrac{1}{m}(1 - \mid \Delta \mid) - \Delta \end{aligned}\right\} \text{if } \Delta \leq 0$$

where $\Delta \doteq 2(\alpha - 0.5)$.

It may be easily verified that such an OWA operator is a weighted average of the maximum (minimum) and the arithmetic average operators for $\Delta > 0$ ($\Delta \leq 0$). More precisely:

$$O_W = \Delta \max_i a_i + (1 - \Delta)\frac{\sum_{i=1}^m a_i}{m} \tag{18}$$

for $\Delta > 0$ and

$$O_W = \Omega \min_i a_i + (1 - \Omega)\frac{\sum_{i=1}^m a_i}{m} \tag{19}$$

for $\Delta \leq 0$; where $\Omega = -\Delta$.

Thus what is obtained is a class of OWA operators directly parametrized with the ORness measure value. The formulae (18)-(19) indicate, provide a clear interpretation for these operators in terms of the traditional aggregation operators of the maximum, minimum and arithmetic average.

Liu and Chen generalized the problem (14) replacing the requirement that the OWA operator O_W sought should have a specific value α of the ORness measure with the requirement that the O_W applied to a certain fixed argument $A = (a_1, \ldots, a_m)$ should yield the value α. Due to (12) the problem (14) is a special case of such a formulation for $A = (\frac{m-1}{m-1}, \ldots, \frac{m-m}{m-1})$. Liu and Chen proposed the solution to this generalized problem which again boils down to determining the roots of a certain polynomial.

4 Linguistic Quantifiers in Queries

As mentioned in the Introduction, the use of the linguistic quantifiers in various clauses of the SQL query might be conceived. Here we will focus on the way they are used in our FQUERY for Access package [1, 2], i.e., as operators aggregating conditions in the `WHERE` clause. Basically, the linguistic quantifiers are here defined according to Zadeh's calculus of linguistically quantified propositions, briefly recalled in the previous section. Such a representation has some advantages and primarily an easy scalability to a varying number of conditions to be aggregated. For example, having the linguistic quantifier "most" defined by (6) one may use it to interpret such a condition as:

$$\text{“}\textit{Most} \text{ of the predicates } \{P_i\}_{i=1,\ldots,n} \text{ are satisfied”} \tag{20}$$

for any number, n, of predicates. In the case when the linguistic quantifier "most" is explicitly represented by an OWA operator (e.g., such as (10)) of dimension m, it is directly applicable for the interpretation of (20) only for $n = m$. Thus we would have to define a separate OWA operator modelling the quantifier "most" for all conceivable numbers n of conditions to be aggregated in an expression of (20) type.

On the other hand, the OWA operators also have some advantages as a linguistic quantifier modelling tool. They offer a fine-grained control over the behavior of the modelled aggregation operator and provide for a more straightforward representation of classical operators. Thus in FQUERY for Access the linguistic quantifiers are firstly defined in the sense of Zadeh and later, during the query execution, they are interpreted and manipulated in terms of OWA operators.

FQUERY for Access maintains a dictionary of various linguistic terms defined by the user and available for the use in the queries. Among them are linguistic quantifiers in the sense of Zadeh. Each quantifier is identified with a piecewise-linear membership function and assigned a name. When inserting a quantifier into a query the user just picks up its name from the list of quantifiers available in the dictionary.

The linguistic quantifiers are used in a query to aggregate conditions like in (20). In case of such explicitly used quantifiers the user indicates if the original Zadeh interpretation should be applied or if the quantifier should be treated as the OWA operator defined by (9). Additionally, the system implicitly interpretes the AND and OR connectives used in the query as the minimum and maximum operators, respectively, that in turn are represented by the O_{min} and O_{max} OWA operators. It is assumed that the query condition is in the disjunctive normal form as it is usually the case of queries created using the Microsoft

Access querying interface. In order to easily identify the operators in a query it is assumed that the conjuncts of such a disjunctive normal form are ordered and numbered.

After starting the query execution the user has still an opportunity to adjust the vector of OWA operator weights to better match his or her understanding of the aggregation to be applied to the conditions in (20). Both explicitly and implicitly used OWA operators may be modified, and the form shown in Fig. 1 makes it possible

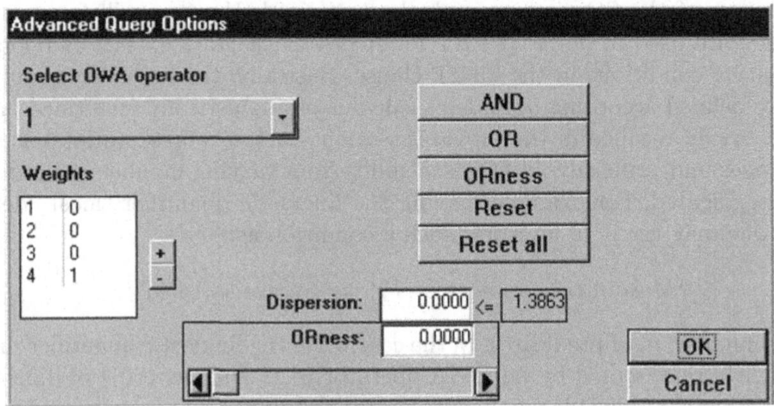

Fig. 1. FQUERY for Access form making possible modification of the OWA operators employed in a query

The list of OWA operators appearing in the executed query is shown in the upper left corner of this form. It comprises:

- all OWA operators explicitly used by the user in the query, Each operator is assigned a number indicating a conjunct number to which it applies. or the label "Global" in case of an operator concerning the whole query, i.e., corresponding to the disjunction of the conjuncts.
  For each OWA operator the name of the corresponding linguistic quantifier in the sense of Zadeh is also shown next to the conjunct number (this might be seen in Fig. 2).
- all implicit OWA operators, automatically inserted by FQUERY for Access and including:
  - a global one, corresponding to the disjunction connective - if a global linguistic quantifier has not been explicitly used by the user.
  - one OWA operator (O_{min} in particular) for each conjunct comprising more than one condition provided an explicit linguistic quantifier has not been used.

  An implicit OWA operator is assigned a number of the conjunct it applies to or the label "Global" – similarly to the explicit operators discussed above; however there is no name associated with it (cf. the column "Name" in Fig. 2).

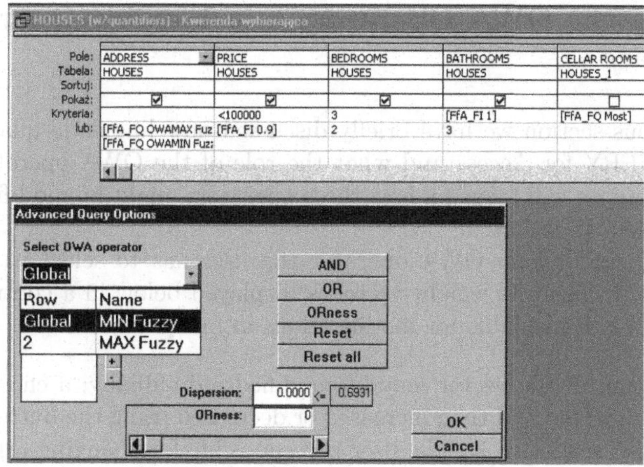

Fig. 2. FQUERY for Access form making possible modification of the OWA operators employed in a query with the list of the operators visible

Figure 1 corresponds to a query without explicitly used OWA operators and just one conjunct comprising four simple conditions. Due to that, on the list there is only one automatically inserted OWA operator taking place of the AND connective.

Figure 2 corresponds to a more complex query whose condition might be informally expressed in a way similar to (20) as follows:

"*All* (O_{min}) of the predicates:
{
Most of the predicates {(`price`<100000), (`bedrooms`=3)}
are satisfied,
Any (O_{max}) of the predicates {(`bedrooms`=2), (`bathrooms`=3)}
is satisfied
}
are satisfied"

where `price`, `bedrooms` and `bathrooms` correspond to attributes of a hypothetical real-estate database, characterizing a property (house) in terms of its price, the number of bedrooms and the number of bathrooms, respectively. Here the list contains two explicit operators. The first applies to the second conjunct and is the OWA version of the linguistic quantifier defined by the user under the name "Max Fuzzy" which is meant as a counterpart of the "max" operator (OR connective). The second operator plays the role of a global quantifier and is the OWA version of the linguistic quantifier defined by the user under the name "Min Fuzzy" which is meant as a counterpart of the "min" operator (AND connective). There is no implicit operator for the first conjunct as the user explicitly used for it a linguistic quantifier named "Most".

5 Tuning the OWA Operators in a Flexible Querying Interface

In the previous section we have briefly discussed how linguistic quantifiers are used in FQUERY for Access and what the role of the OWA operators in this respect is. Here we will focus on how these operators might be modified (tuned) before the query is executed.

In order to modify an OWA operator the user has to select it on the list shown in Fig. 1. Then its weight vector is displayed below in a control labelled "Weights" and it is available for modifications in many ways:

- each element of the vector may be modified individually; a chosen element has to be selected and then increased or decreased using the buttons labelled "+" and "-", respectively. The user is responsible for changing other weights too so that they sum up to 1; otherwise FQUERY for Access will not go to the next stage of query execution;
- pressing the button labelled "AND" (or "OR") sets the weights in such a way that the O_{min} (or O_{max}) operator are obtained;
- pressing the button "ORness" changes the weight vector in such a way that the ORness measure value of the resulting OWA operator is equal to the number entered in the formant labelled "ORness" located at the bottom of the form (cf. Fig. 1);
- pressing the button labelled "Reset" (or "Reset all") restores the weight vector of the selected operator (or of all listed OWA operators) to their original values.

The value of the ORness measure does not uniquely determine the OWA operator. Thus, any of the approaches to the tuning of the OWA operators discussed in the previous section are here applicable to set the weight vector. The difference of the setting considered here is that we start with a certain OWA operator and want to tune it in order to increase its ORness. However, an additional reasonable requirement might be such that the user wants to keep the changes as limited as possible or to preserve the consistency of the change in some other sense. For example, the user may look for an OWA operator more similar in its behaviour to the maximum operator but at the same time still "similar to the original OWA operator" being modified. In FQUERY for Access we have implemented a simple approximate algorithm that for an OWA operator O_W yields a new OWA operator O_V having a smaller/larger value of the ORness measure (as required by the user) and additionally preserving the consistency of the change in such a sense that:

$$O_V(a_1, \dots, a_m) \geq O_W(a_1, \dots, a_m) \quad \forall (a_1, \dots, a_m) \tag{21}$$

when an increase of the ORness is required, and

$$O_V(a_1, \dots, a_m) \leq O_W(a_1, \dots, a_m) \quad \forall (a_1, \dots, a_m) \tag{22}$$

when a decrease of the ORness is required. This seems to be consistent with expectations of the user requiring an increase/decrease of the ORness while is not in general guaranteed, i.e., there exist such pairs of the OWA operators O_W and O_V (cf., e.g., [14]) that: $\text{ORness}(O_W) > \text{ORness}(O_V)$ and at the same time there exists $A = (a_1, \ldots, a_m)$ such that $O_W(A) < O_V(A)$.

The algorithm used in FQUERY for Access consists of the following steps (here in the case when the increase of the ORness is required; in the opposite case the algorithm is analogous). Let $W = [w_1, \ldots, w_n]$ denote the weight vector of the OWA operator O_W, and z^0 denote the required increased value of the ORness measure ($z^0 \in (\text{ORness}(O_W), 1)$).

Then:

Step 1 $\Delta z := z^0 - \text{ORness}(O_W)$

Step 2 $k := \max_i\{i : w_i > 0\}$
$x := 2(n-1)\Delta z/k$

Step 3 if $x > w_k$ then $x := w_k$

Step 4 $w_k := w_k - x$
$w_i := w_i + x/(k-1) \qquad \forall i \in [1, k-1]$

Step 5 if $\text{ORness}(O_W) < z^0$ go to Step 1
STOP

The main idea is to reduce the element of the weight vector with the highest index by such a value x (thus highly contributing to the "ANDness" of the operator) that, when equally distributed among the remaining elements of the weight vector, yields an OWA operator with the ORness measure value equal or very close to the required one.

In Step 1 the required increase (Δ) of the ORness is computed. In Step 2 a positive element of the weight vector with the highest index is selected (of index k) and it is computed how much it should be reduced (x) to obtain a required value of the ORness measure. In Step 3 it is verified if the required reduction of the k-th element w_k of the weight vector (i.e., x) does not exceed its current value: if it is the case then the x is set equal to w_k (another iteration of the algorithm will be required). In Step 4 the weight vector is modified: w_k is reduced by x and the remaining elements of the vector W are increased by the same part of x, i.e., $x/(k-1)$. In Step 5 it is verified if the ORness measure value of the modified operator reaches the required level: if it is not the case, the next iteration starts from Step 1.

It is obvious that by construction of the algorithm the modified vector W verifies conditions required for the OWA operators, i.e., $W \in [0,1]^m$ and $\sum_{i=1}^{m} w_i = 1$ as well as has the required ORness measure value and satisfies (21), where W and V denote the original and modified weight vectors, respectively.

6 Concluding Remarks

We reconsidered the role of fuzzy linguistic quantifiers in flexible database queries, notably showing that Yager's OWA operators provide a flexible and efficient means of a fuzzy-quantifier-based aggregation. We discussed the tuning (selection of weights) of the OWA operators, and proposed an algorithm that is effective and efficient in the context of our FQUERY for Access package [1, 2].

References

1. Kacprzyk J., Zadrożny: The paradigm of computing with words in intelligent database querying. In Zadeh L.A., Kacprzyk J., eds.: Computing with Words in Information/Intelligent Systems. Part 1. Foundations. Part 2. Applications. Springer-Verlag, Heidelberg and New York (1999) 382–398
2. Kacprzyk J., Zadrożny S.: Computing with words in intelligent database querying: standalone and internet-based applications. Information Sciences (134) (2001) 71–109
3. Bosc P., Pivert O.: SQLf: A relational database language for fuzzy querying. IEEE Transactions on Fuzzy Systems **3**(1) (1995) 1–17
4. Kacprzyk J., Ziółkowski A.: Database queries with fuzzy linguistic quantifiers. IEEE Transactions on System, Man and Cybernetics (SMC-16) (1986) 474–479
5. Kacprzyk J., Zadrożny S., Ziółkowski A.: FQUERY III+: a "human consistent" database querying system based on fuzzy logic with linguistic quantifiers. Information Systems (6) (1989) 443–453
6. Bosc P., Prade H.: An introduction to the fuzzy set and possibility theory-based treatment of flexible queries and uncertain or imprecise databases. In: Uncertainty Management in Information Systems. Kluwer Academic Publishers, Boston (1996) 285–324
7. Zadeh L.A.: A computational approach to fuzzy quantifiers in natural languages. Computers and Mathematics with Applications **9** (1983) 149–184
8. Yager R.R.: On ordered weighted averaging aggregation operators in multi-criteria decision making. IEEE Transactions on Systems, Man and Cybernetics **18** (1988) 183–190
9. Filev D., Yager R.R.: On the issue of obtaining OWA operator weights. Fuzzy Sets and Systems **94** (1998) 157–169
10. O'Hagan M.: Aggregating template or rule antecedents in real-time expert systems with fuzzy set logic. In: Proceedings of the IEEE Asilomar Conference on Signals, Systems, Computers, Pacific Grove, USA (1988) 81–89
11. Filev D., Yager R.R.: Analytic properties of maximum entropy OWA operators. Information Sciences **85** (1995) 11–27
12. Fuller R., Majlender P.: An analytic approach for obtaining maximal entropy OWA operator weights. Fuzzy Sets and Systems **124**(1) (2001) 53–57
13. Fuller R., Majlender P.: On obtaining minimal variability OWA operator weights. Fuzzy Sets and Systems **136**(2) (2003) 203–215
14. Liu X., Chen L.: On the properties of parametric geometric owa operator. International Journal of Approximate Reasoning **35** (2004) 163–178

Towards a Flexible Visualization Tool for Dealing with Temporal Data

Guy de Tré[1], Nico Van de Weghe[2], Rita de Caluwe[1], and Philippe De Maeyer[2]

[1] Department of Telecommunications and Information Processing, Ghent University, Sint-Pietersnieuwstraat 41, B-9000 Gent, Belgium
[2] Geography Department, Ghent University, Krijgslaan 281 (S8), B-9000 Gent, Belgium
Guy.DeTre@telin.ugent.be

Abstract. Time plays an important role in our everyday's life. For a lot of observations we make and actions we perform, temporal information is relevant. The importance of time is reflected in the development of information systems such as (temporal) database systems and data warehouse systems, which have facilities to cope with temporal data and usually manage huge collections of historical data. It is a challenge to develop intuitive user interaction tools that allow users to fully explore these collections of temporal data. With this paper, we want to contribute to the development of such a tool. The presented approach is based on a visualization of time intervals as points in a two-dimensional space and on temporal reasoning based on this visualization. Flexibility is provided by allowing to cope with imperfections in both the modelling of time and the temporal reasoning.

Keywords: Time modelling, user interfaces, fuzzy set theory.

1 Introduction

The central role of temporality in many computer applications makes the representation, manipulation and visualization of temporal information highly relevant.

Related to database systems and data warehouse systems, several time models for the representation and manipulation of time have been proposed, each having its own applicability and limitations. Research on temporal models is in general motivated by the observation that most databases and data warehouses contain substantial amounts of temporal data, what makes that specific modelling and management techniques for temporal data are a requirement for an efficient exploitation of these data collections [7]. An interesting bibliographic overview of older work can be found in [13]. More recent work and state of the art are summarized in [12, 4]. There have also been some efforts to bring into line the resulting diversity of concepts and terminology [6].

Almost of equal importance, is research on the visualization of temporal data [9, 8, 10, 2]. As time is usually modelled using a one-dimensional time space, visualization of large amounts of temporal data tends to result in an overwhelming

H.L. Larsen et al. (Eds.): FQAS 2006, LNAI 4027, pp. 109–120, 2006.

image of (overlapping) intervals, which lacks clarity and does not provide the user with the insights and overviews that are necessary to fully explore the data. For the sake of illustration of the problem, consider for example the one-dimensional time lines used by historian to represent important dates and periods in history. Such time lines quickly tend to become overloaded with data when more facts are registered.

In this paper, we propose a flexible, alternative approach for the visualization of temporal data. The approach allows for a better human-computer interaction by providing users with a more compact visualization of the temporal data and the temporal relationships that exist between these data. By using the approach, the user should better understand the data and gain new insights, which on its turn should be supportive for the further exploration of the database or data warehouse. Moreover, the presented approach provides some flexibility and allows to deal with possible imperfections of the data (e.g., imprecision, incompleteness, or uncertainty), both at the level of the temporal data modelling and at the level of temporal reasoning. The presented approach is inspired by the work of Z. Kulpa [9, 10] in which a diagrammatic representation for interval arithmetic is presented. Flexibility is provided by applying fuzzy set theory [14].

The remainder of the paper is organized as follows. In Section 2, the basic framework of the visualization approach is described. Both the structural aspects and behavioral aspects are dealt with. The basic framework is generalized in Section 3 in order to be able to cope with imperfections of the data. In Section 4, an illustrative example demonstrating some of the potentials of the approach is presented. Finally, some conclusions are given in Section 5.

2 A Framework for Visualizing Temporal Data

2.1 Some Preliminaries

In this paper, it is implicitly assumed that time is modelled as being *discrete*, *linear* and *finite*. This means first of all that the restriction is accepted that time can only be observed using a limited precision, say Δ. This is not really a limitation, on condition that the precision is chosen sufficiently accurate. Indeed, this restriction results from the way observations and measurements are made and it conforms to the way data can be stored in computers. The discretization is necessary to circumvent the density problem (i.e., the fact that between any two distinct points, there always exists at least one other point). The need for non-linear structures with topologies such as branching time, parallel time, circular time etc. as suggested by some authors [11], is not supported in the model. Linearity implies a total order over the time points. Finally, our model is chosen to be finite in view of a computer representation. This implies that all values that exceed the determined upper and lower bound will be handled by introducing two special values ($-\infty$ and $+\infty$).

Observing time using a maximum precision Δ and with respect to a given origin t_0 involves a crisp discrete (countable) set of time points, given by:

$$T_{0,\Delta} = \{t_k \in T | t_k = t_0 + k\Delta, k \in \mathbb{Z}\}, \text{ where } \mathbb{Z} = \{0, 1, -1, 2, -2, \ldots\} \quad (1)$$

which is a proper subset of the set T, which represents the continuum of the physical time points. The discretization can be described as a surjective mapping from T on $T_{0,\Delta}$, which maps each $\tau \in T$ on the element $t_k \in T_{0,\Delta}$ that lies in the interval $\gamma_{0,k}$, $k \in \mathbb{Z}$, which is defined as:

$$[t_0 + k\Delta, t_0 + (k+1)\Delta[$$

or, alternatively:

$$[t_0 + (2k-1)\frac{\Delta}{2}, t_0 + (2k+1)\frac{\Delta}{2}[$$

The intervals $\gamma_{0,k}$ with Δ as length are usually called '*chronons*' in literature (cf. [6]). The introduction of chronons eliminates the necessity to make a distinction between points and intervals, because even a chronon, the smallest unit in the model, is essentially an interval.

2.2 Structural Aspects

Time is a very complex notion, which is used mostly rather intuitively within a context of physical phenomena and established conventions. Generally, temporal information can be subdivided in three categories.

1. *Durational information* is unrelated to a particular point in time and describes a duration: e.g. 5 days, 1h 35min.
2. *Positional temporal information* is related (directly or indirectly) to either the origin or the current time point (now): e.g. in the 18th century, yesterday.
3. *Repetitive temporal information* describes positional temporal information that repeats itself with a given period: e.g. every hour, monthly.

In this paper, only *time intervals* are dealt with. Time intervals allow to model positional temporal information [1] and are the basic building blocks of most time models supporting database and data warehouse systems. To handle durational and repetitive temporal information, other structures are necessary [3]. Such structures are not dealt with in this paper.

Visualizing time intervals. A time interval

$$[a, b]$$

is defined by a starting time point a and a length l, which defines the distance (number of chronons) from a to the ending time point b, i.e., $l = b - a$. A time point is equivalent to a time interval with $l = 0$ (or $b = a$). Note that the length of an interval is not the same as the duration of the interval: the length of a time point is 0, its duration is 1 chronon (Δ).

At the basis of the visualization approach is the visualization of intervals. Instead of representing time intervals on a one-dimensional time axis, time intervals are visualized as points in a two-dimensional space. This allows for a more compact representation. The two-dimensional space is defined by two orthogonal axes (cf. Figure 1):

- A horizontal axis $X = T_{position}$ that is used to represent positional information about the starting time points and ending time points of the time intervals and
- a vertical axis $Y = T_{length}$ that is used to represent length information about the time intervals.

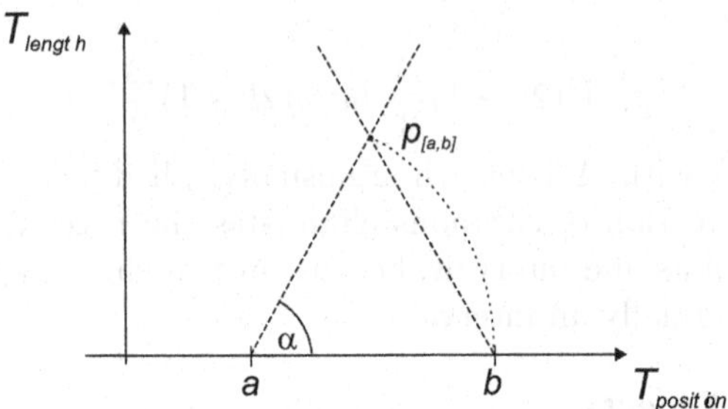

Fig. 1. Visualization of a time interval $[a, b]$

A time interval $[a, b]$ is visualized by a time point $p_{[a,b]}$, which position is obtained by rotating $[a, b]$ counterclockwise around a over a fixed angle α as depicted in Figure 1. This implies that the (x, y) coordinates of $p_{[a,b]}$ are given by:

$$x = a + d(a, b). \cos \alpha$$
$$y = d(a, b). \sin \alpha$$

where $d(a, b) = |b - a|$ is the distance between a and b, which corresponds to the length of the interval $[a, b]$. Because time points $a = [a, a]$ have a length 0, they are represented on the X-axis with coordinates $(a, 0)$.

For the sake of symmetry, the angle α will be chosen to be equal to 60° in the remainder of the paper (cf. Figure 1). In that case the (x, y) coordinates of $p_{[a,b]}$ become:

$$x = a + \frac{d(a, b)}{2}$$
$$y = d(a, b). \sin 60°$$

Special choices for α are:

- $\alpha = 0°$: in this case we obtain the classical one-dimensional representation of time where the X-axis represents the continuous time axis.
- $\alpha = 90°$: in this case the X-coordinate represents the real starting point of the interval ($x = a$), whereas the Y-coordinate represents the real length of the interval ($y = d(a, b)$).

Comparison with related work. The presented approach is related to the diagrammatic representation for interval arithmetic as presented by Z. Kulpa [9, 10], where $p_{[a,b]}$ is defined to be the top of the isosceles rectangle with basis $[a, b]$ and fixed basis angles $\alpha = 45°$. Furthermore, common aspects with the approach presented by G. Ligozat et al. [8, 2] are obtained when considering the special case where $\alpha = 90°$. The main advantage of the presented approach is due to its generality and its ability to work with different choices for the angle α. This supports the construction of more dynamical interfaces where the user can chose the angle that responds best to his/her needs.

2.3 Behavioral Aspects

In order to be useful, the compact representation of time should allow users to obtain efficient overviews and adequate insights in temporal data. Moreover the representation should support temporal reasoning in a rather intuitive way. Therefore it is a requirement that the thirteen possible relations between two time intervals, as defined by Allen in his interval-based temporal logic [1] also have an intuitive visual interpretation.

The thirteen Allen relations are depicted in Figure 2.

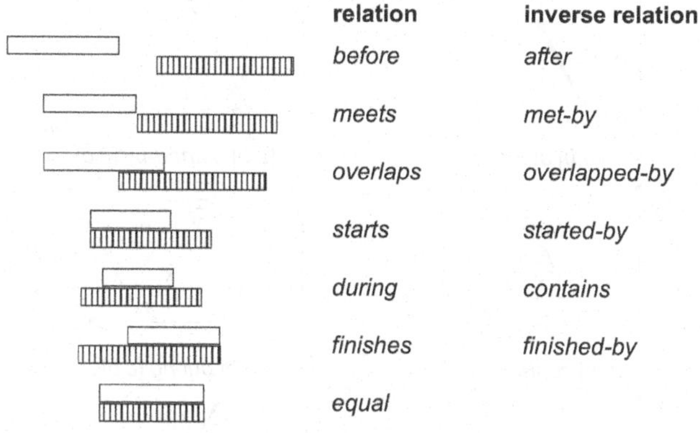

Fig. 2. The 13 Allen relations between two time intervals

Depending on the choice of the angle α, a number of Allen relationships can be visualized. In this paper, only the symmetrical case where $\alpha = 60°$ is described. The visualization of the 13 Allen relations is given in Figure 3. For each relation, the locations of the points $p_{[c,d]}$ that represent intervals $[c, d]$ that satisfy the relation are visualized (marked).

3 Generalizing the Framework: Coping with Imperfect Data

The visualization approach described in the previous section can be made more flexible by allowing imperfections at the levels of temporal data modelling and

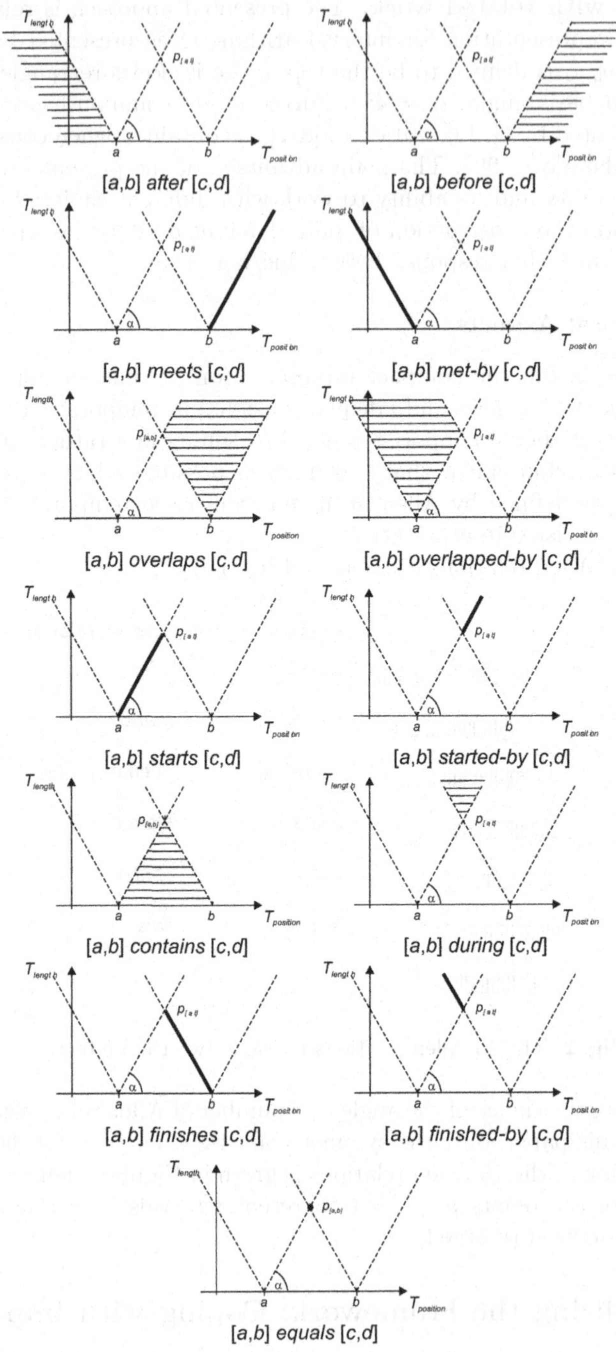

Fig. 3. Visualization of the 13 Allen relations

temporal reasoning. In order to cope with imperfections, fuzzy set theory is applied [14].

3.1 Structural Aspects

It might be the case that at least one of the start and end dates of a time interval is ill-known. If this is the case, the time interval is called a fuzzy time interval. Fuzzy time intervals can be modelled by a fuzzy set with a convex membership function, as illustrated at the left side of Figure 4. For more information about the interpretation and operations on fuzzy time intervals, we refer to [5].

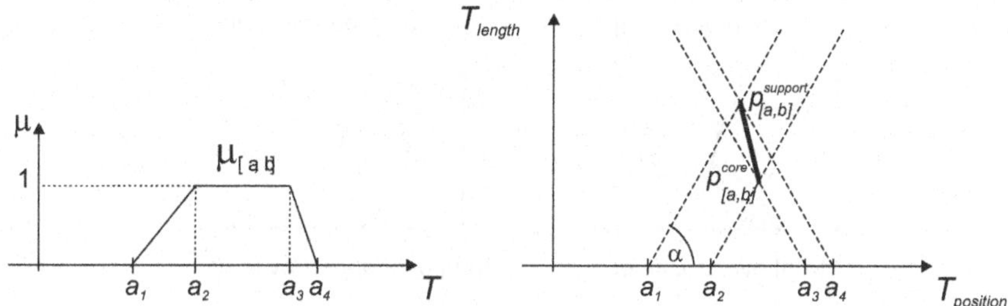

Fig. 4. Visualization of fuzzy time intervals

In general, any adequate convex membership function can be used for the modelling. In practice, normalized trapezoidal membership functions are frequently used as approximation, because these can be easily implemented. The normalized trapezoidal membership function $\mu_{[a,b]}$ of the fuzzy time interval $[a, b]$ is characterized by four time elements a_1, a_2, a_3 and a_4 of which a_1 and a_4 define the support of $[a, b]$ and a_2 and a_3 define the core of $[a, b]$. In the remainder of the paper the special case of fuzzy time intervals with normalized trapezoidal membership functions is studied.

A fuzzy time interval $[a, b]$ with normalized trapezoidal membership function $\mu_{[a,b]}$ is visualized by the line

$$[{p^{core}}_{[a,b]}, {p^{support}}_{[a,b]}]$$

which connects the points ${p^{core}}_{[a,b]}$ and ${p^{support}}_{[a,b]}$ that respectively represent the core

$$core([a, b]) = \{x|x \in T_{position} \wedge \mu_{[a,b]}(x) = 1\}$$

and support

$$support([a, b]) = \{x|x \in T_{position} \wedge \mu_{[a,b]}(x) > 0\}$$

of $[a, b]$ (cf. right side of Figure 4). Every other point of $[{p^{core}}_{[a,b]}, {p^{support}}_{[a,b]}]$ represents an α-cut

$$\{x|x \in T_{position} \wedge \mu_{[a,b]}(x) \geq \alpha\}$$

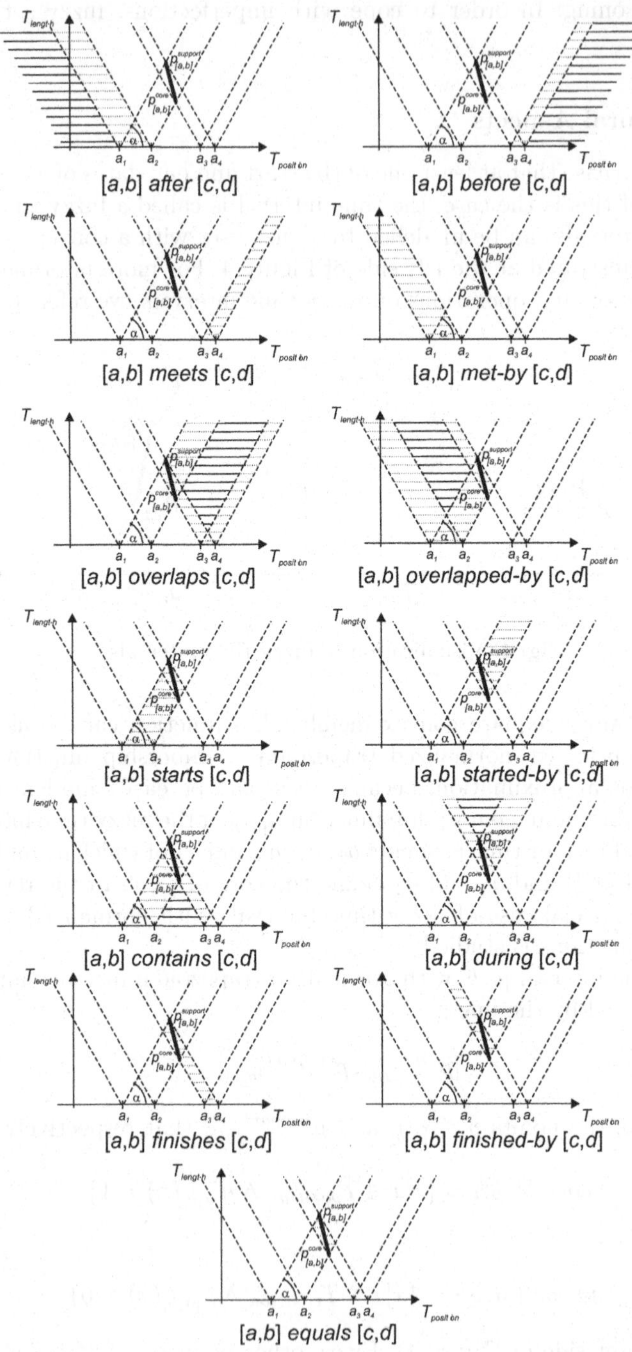

Fig. 5. Visualization of the 13 generalized Allen relations

or a strict α-cut

$$\{x | x \in T_{position} \wedge \mu_{[a,b]}(x) > \alpha\}$$

of $[a, b]$.

Because $core([a, b]) \subseteq support([a, b])$, the point $p^{core}{}_{[a,b]}$ must be located in the triangle determined by a_1, a_4 and $p^{support}{}_{[a,b]}$.

The special case of a crisp time interval $[a, b]$ is still visualized by a time point $p^{core}{}_{[a,b]} = p^{support}{}_{[a,b]}$, because in that case the $core([a, b]) = support([a, b])$.

3.2 Behavioral Aspects

In order to be supportive for temporal reasoning with ill-known time intervals, the thirteen Allen relations must be generalized for fuzzy time intervals and visualized in an intuitive way. The generalization of the Allen relations is dealt with in [5]. In that paper, it is also illustrated how the degree of certainty that an Allen relation holds for two given fuzzy time intervals $[a, b]$ and $[c, d]$ can be calculated. In this paper we focus on the visualization of the generalizations of the Allen relations. The generalized counterparts of the visualizations in Figure 3 are presented in Figure 5.

As can be observed in the visualizations of Figure 5, three kinds of areas can be distinguished:

- An area $\overline{A}$ where the relation does not hold (not marked),
- an area A where the relation holds (marked with full lines) and
- an area $\tilde{A}$ where the relation possibly holds (marked with dotted lines).

With respect to the location of the line $[p^{core}{}_{[c,d]}, p^{support}{}_{[c,d]}]$, which represents the fuzzy time interval $[c, d]$, the following situations can be distinguished:

- $[p^{core}{}_{[c,d]}, p^{support}{}_{[c,d]}]$ is completely located in $\overline{A}$: in this situation, the relation does not hold, for sure.
- $[p^{core}{}_{[c,d]}, p^{support}{}_{[c,d]}]$ is completely located in A: in this situation, the relations holds, for sure.
- $[p^{core}{}_{[c,d]}, p^{support}{}_{[c,d]}]$ (partly) overlaps $\tilde{A}$ or is located in $\tilde{A}$: in this situation, it is uncertain whether the relation holds or not. The degree of (un)certainty can be calculated as described in [5].

Beside these general situations, it is interesting to observe the following special cases:

- If the start date (resp. end date) is perfectly known, then the support and core intervals start (resp. end) at the same time point. In such cases, the straight lines $[a_1, p^{support}{}_{[a,b]}]$ and $[a_2, p^{core}{}_{[a,b]}]$ (resp. $[a_3, p^{core}{}_{[a,b]}]$ and $[a_4, p^{support}{}_{[a,b]}]$) coincide and $[p^{core}{}_{[a,b]}, p^{support}{}_{[a,b]}]$ is located on $[a_2, p^{core}{}_{[a,b]}]$ (resp. $[a_3, p^{core}{}_{[a,b]}]$), which is completely consistent with the description of Section 2.
- If the fuzzy interval is perfectly known, i.e. both the start date and the end date of the interval are perfectly known, then $p^{support}{}_{[a,b]}$ coincides $p^{core}{}_{[a,b]}$, which is again consistent with the perfectly known cases described in Section 2.

In these special cases, it can occur that $[p^{core}{}_{[c,d]}, p^{support}{}_{[c,d]}]$ is located in both A and $\overline{A}$, without crossing $\tilde{A}$. In such a situation it is uncertain whether the relation holds or not.

From the above cases, it should be clear that the presented approach is in fact a generalization of the approach that is described in Section 2.

4 An Illustrative Example

Consider the visualization of the reign periods of European leaders of states during the time period [1900 – 1910]. Furthermore, assume that some of these periods were ill-known to the person who entered them in the database. The full reign periods can be summarized in the following table:

Number	Country	Name	$support([a, b])$	$core([a, b])$
1	Belgium	Leopold II	[1865, 1908]	[1865, 1908]
2	Belgium	Albert I	[1908, 1934]	[1908, 1934]
3	France	Loubet	[1898, 1907]	[1899, 1906]
4	France	Fallières	[1906, 1913]	[1907, 1913]
5	Italy	Vittorio Emanuele III	[1899, 1944]	[1900, 1945]
6	Spain	Maria Cristina	[1885, 1902]	[1885, 1902]
7	Spain	Alfonso XIII	[1902, 1931]	[1903, 1930]
8	United Kingdom	Victoria	[1837, 1901]	[1837, 1901]
9	United Kingdom	Edward VII	[1901, 1910]	[1902, 1909]
10	United Kingdom	George V	[1910, 1935]	[1909, 1936]

If these time intervals are represented on a one dimensional time axis, it is difficult to obtain an overview and insight in the data because there is a lot of overlap between the intervals. Furthermore, if the visualization is further restricted to the time interval [1900, 1910], as is the case in this example, the visualization problem is even harder.

Using the presented approach, the same information, restricted to the time interval [1900, 1910], is visualized as shown in Figure 6 (a) —only the numbers are presented in the figure—. In the example there is no longer overlap between representations. To illustrate the visualization of the Allen relations, the relation 'overlapped-by' is shown for the record with number 3 ('Loubet'). All records, which representations are located in the area marked with full lines represent leaders of states whose reign period overlapped with the reign period of Loubet — within the restricted period of [1900, 1910]— (these are the records with number 7 and 9), for sure. Records, which representations are located in the area marked with dotted lines represent leaders whose reign period possibly overlapped with the reign period of Loubet —within the restricted period of [1900, 1910]— (record with number 4). All other records represent leaders whose reign period did not overlap with the reign period of Loubet, for sure.

Remark that on the basis of the full (unrestricted) temporal information in the table, the reign period of the records with number 1, 5, 6 and 8 also overlaps with the reign period of record 3. These records are, due to the restricted period of [1900, 1910], not retrieved by the 'overlapped-by' relation, but can be obtained by additionally considering the relations 'starts' and 'started-by'.

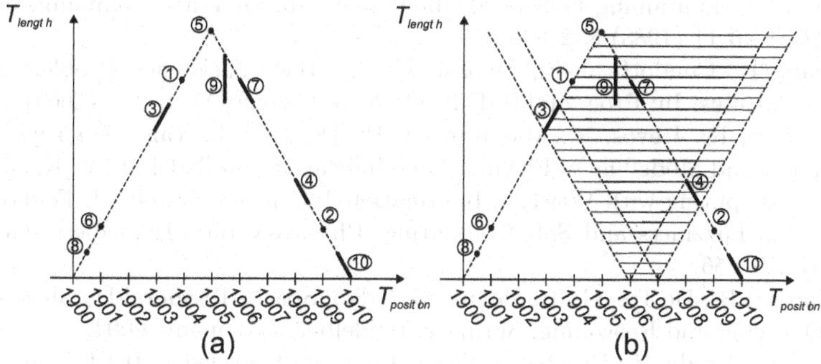

Fig. 6. Visualization of reign periods, restricted to the time period [1900, 1910]

5 Conclusions

In this paper, we have presented an approach to visualize fuzzy time intervals and the generalizations of the 13 Allen temporal relations. The approach is a generalization of a method for visualizing regular time intervals, that is closely related to the diagrammatic representation for interval arithmetic as presented by Z. Kulpa [9, 10], but has the advantage of providing the user with the ability to work with different choices for the angle α. This supports the construction of more dynamical interfaces where the user can chose the angle that responds best to his/her needs. As illustrated with the real world example, the presented approach allows for a better human-computer interaction by providing users with a more compact visualization of the temporal data and the temporal Allen relations that exists between these data. By using the approach, the user should better understand the data and gain new insights, which on its turn should be supportive for the further exploration of the database or data warehouse. By supporting fuzzy time intervals, the approach offers some flexibility and allows to deal with ill-known temporal data, both at the level of the data modelling and at the level of temporal reasoning.

In this paper it is assumed that fuzzy time intervals are modelled by convex fuzzy sets with a normalized trapezoidal membership function. Furthermore, for the sake of symmetry, a fixed angle α of 60° is used for the modelling. In general, more general convex membership functions can be used, as well as different choices for α are allowed. Future work will further explore the facilities of the model, including a study of its limitations when different choices for α are made, the modelling of operators like zooming, translations and stretching, the impact of granularities and the visualization of durational and repetitive temporal information. Another aspect to study is the incorporation of an efficient visualization technique for the representation of the degrees of uncertainty.

References

1. Allen, J.F.: Maintaining knowledge about temporal intervals. Communications of the ACM **26** 11 (1983) 832–843.
2. Balbiani, P., Condotta J.-F., Ligozat, G.: On the Consistency Problem for the INDU Calculus. In: Proc. of TIME-ICTL-2003, Caione, Australia, (2003) 1–11.
3. De Caluwe, R., Devos, F., Maesfranckx, P., De Tré, G., Van der Cruyssen, B.: Semantics and Modelling of Flexible Time Indications, in Zadeh, L.A., Kacprzyk J. (eds.), Computing with Words in Information/Intelligent Systems 1: Foundations, Studies in Fuzziness and Soft Computing, Physica-Verlag, Heidelberg, Germany (1999) 229–256.
4. De Caluwe, R., De Tré, G., Bordogna, G. (eds.): Spatio-Temporal Databases: Flexible Querying and Reasoning. Springer, Heidelberg, Germany, 2004.
5. Dubois, D., Prade, H.: Processing Fuzzy Temporal Knowledge. IEEE Transactions on Systems, Man and Cybernetics **19** 4 (1989) 729–744.
6. Jensen, C.S., et al.: A Consensus Glossary of Temporal Database Concepts. ACM SIGMOD Record **23** 1 (1994) 52–63.
7. Jensen, C.S., Snodgrass, R.T.: Temporal data management. IEEE Transactions on Knowledge and Data Engineering **11** 1 (1999) 36–44.
8. Ligozat, G.: Figures for Thought: Temporal Reasoning with Pictures. In: Proc. of AAAI'97 workshop on Spatial and Temporal Reasoning, Providence, Rhode Island, USA, (1997) 31–36.
9. Kulpa, Z.: Diagrammatic representation for a space of intervals. Machine Graphics and vision **6** 1 (1997) 5–24.
10. Kulpa, Z.: Diagrammatic representation for interval arithmetic. Linear Algebra and its Applications **324** (2001) 55–80.
11. McDermot, D.V.: A Temporal Logic for Reasoning about Processes and Plans. Cognitive Science **6** (1982) 101–155.
12. Roddick, J.F., Egenhofer, M.J., Hoel, E., Papadias, D., Salzberg, B.: Spatial, Temporal and Spatio-Temporal Databases – Hot Issues and Directions for PhD Research. ACM SIGMOD Record **33** 2 (2004) 126–131.
13. Tsotras, V.J., Kumar, A.: Temporal Database Bibliography Update. ACM SIGMOD Record **25** 1 (1996) 41–51.
14. Zadeh, L.A.: Fuzzy Sets. Information and Control **8** 3 (1965) 338–353.

XML-Structured Documents: Retrievable Units and Inheritance

Stephen Robertson[1], Wei Lu[2], and Andrew MacFarlane[3]

[1] Microsoft Research, 7 JJ Thomson Avenue,
Cambridge, UK and City University
ser@microsoft.com

[2] Center for Studies of Information Resources,
School of Information Management,
Wuhan University, China and City University
sa713@soi.city.ac.uk

[3] Centre for Interactive Systems Research,
Department of Information Science,
City University, London, UK
andym@soi.city.ac.uk

Abstract. We consider the retrieval of XML-structured documents, and of passages from such documents, defined as elements of the XML structure. These are considered from the point of view of passage retrieval, as a form of document retrieval. A retrievable unit (an element chosen as defining suitable passages for retrieval) is a textual document in its own right, but may inherit information from the other parts of the same document. Again, this inheritance is defined in terms of the XML structure. All retrievable units are mapped onto a common field structure, and the ranking function is a standard document retrieval function with a suitable field weighting. A small experiment to demonstrate the idea, using INEX data, is described.

1 Introduction

In this paper, we explore the translation of some current ideas in text and document retrieval to an environment with XML-structured documents. Specifically, we consider various parts of the document (defined as elements in the XML structure) as retrievable units in their own right, in a similar fashion to the retrieval of passages from unstructured documents. However, the XML provides us with the means to define *inheritance*, whereby an element can inherit information from other elements. The use of inherited information in a ranking function requires a good way to weight the information from different sources; this is provided by a form of field-weighting used in more conventional text-retrieval settings.

To illustrate some of these ideas we make use of the INEX document collections and experiments. However, we first set the scene with an overview of a number of facets of retrieval in the domain of text documents, which may be unstructured or have minimal explicit structure.

H.L. Larsen et al. (Eds.): FQAS 2006, LNAI 4027, pp. 121–132, 2006.

2 Background

'Unstructured' text documents have been the subject of retrieval systems and experiments for many years. From experiments on small collections of scientific abstracts in the 1960s, through mid-size collections of news and news-wire materials to huge collections of heterogeneous web pages today, we have very considerable experience and understanding of how to retrieve from such collections. Although there are very many variants and alternatives, the dominant approaches may be summarised as follows:

- Unstructured text queries;
- 'Bag-of-words' indexing of documents;
- Statistically-based scoring functions (to score each bag-of-words document against the current query);
- Ranked output

This is a broad characterisation – maybe a caricature – but does capture some of the important features of the experience and understanding.[1] In particular, the very cavalier 'bag-of-words' approach, which ignores many intuitions and understandings about language and meaning in other contexts, nevertheless has been remarkably successful for search. On the other hand, the necessity for good scoring functions is paramount.

That said, in the following sections we explore some of the variants and alternatives which modify this dominant view, in preparation for discussing our approach to XML-structured documents.

2.1 Passage Retrieval

The retrieval of (sub-document) passages has been an occasional interest within the document retrieval community for many years. One issue here has been that very few evaluation collections have relevance judgements at the passage level; however, passage retrieval has been tested as a method of doing document retrieval. Many of the problems and possibilities of using passage-level evidence, including all the ideas mentioned here, are discussed by Callan [1].

At the simplest level, passages may be defined more-or-less arbitrarily (for example in terms of fixed word-length windows on the text, or by means of relatively superficial parsing such as sentence or paragraph separation). Then each document is retrieved on the basis of the score of the best-matching passage within it, rather than on the basis of scoring the entire document. The model is effectively that the passage is the relevant part of the document, but since we have relevance judgements at document level only, we have to embed the task in a document retrieval one.

A variation on this theme is to mix the scores of the best-matching passage and the whole document. We might see this as based on the same model (the

[1] The notion that text itself is 'unstructured' is of course a gross over-simplification. However, we do not address the linguistic structure of text in the present paper.

passage is the relevant part), but with the additional assumption that the rest of the document also tells us something, provides some context, about the passage. Thus we evaluate the score of the passage, but allow it to *inherit* information from the document. This intuition informs the present paper.

2.2 Fields

One of the most obvious departures from the simplest bag-of-words model is the notion that some parts of the document/record are more informative than others. For a scientific paper, for example, we may guess that occurrences of words in the title or perhaps abstract are stronger indicators of the content of the paper than occurrences in the body text. We may operationalise this intuition by identifying a number of 'fields' or 'streams' in the documents – that is, a structure of fields that may be identified in or applied to every document in the collection. This is an important notion, whose value has been demonstrated both in formal experiments such as TREC (see e.g. [2]) and by the web search engines. In the latter case, the field structure must be applied to a very heterogeneous collection of documents. This implies a mapping of the features of each document type onto the common field structure. This mapping is typically a manual operation.[2]

The interaction of fields and bag-of-words scoring methods is not entirely trivial. A common approach has been to construct a separate bag-of-words for each field, derive separate scores for the query against each field, and then combine them (usually a weighted linear combination) into a single document score (see e.g. [4]). However, this approach conflicts with some characteristics of good bag-of-words scoring functions [5]. Instead, we need to construct a bag-of-words representation of the whole document which reflects the relative weights of the fields. Below, we use the BM25F method of doing this.

2.3 Inheritance Between and Within Documents

One of the techniques which has amply proved its value in the web context is the inheritance of anchor text. Web search engines typically place heavy reliance on this technique. The principle is that an HTML link between documents (the `<a href="..."> ... </a>` tag) encloses a piece of text in the source document which describes the destination document. The technique is to associate this piece of text with the destination document. Thus each document contains a single field which is the accumulation of all the anchor text from incoming links.

Experiments on web data [6] indicate that (despite the noise it may contain) this is an extremely valuable clue: anchor text is typically weighted highly, considerably higher than body text. Clearly, it depends on using a good form of field weighting.

A number of different approaches have been used at INEX to tackle the issue of inheritance within documents. Arvola et al [7] use a contextualisation function which uses the sum of BM25 weights divided by number of elements in which a weight is generated for a given term. Both Ogilvie and Callan [8] and

[2] See for example the mapping in [3].

Sigurbjornsson et al [9, 10] generate language models either for each element of the XML tree or a chosen subset of elements and use linear interpolation on the models to combine the evidence. Mass and Mandelbrod [11] create a different index for each element type, and use the vector space model, simply combining the scores of the cosine correlation function. They revised this method using linear interpolation on scores for each element in [12] to achieve improvements of average precision in the range 30%-50%.

2.4 Tuning

Any scoring function that contains free parameters must be tuned. For example, if we distinguish five fields, then we have four or five free field weights to choose (we may fix one of the fields at weight 1). Most basic bag-of-words scoring functions also contain their own free parameters.

The usual way to do this is to use some set of evaluation data (queries and relevance judgements) as a training set, and discover the combination of values of the free parameters that optimises some evaluation measure on this training set. There is a whole host of issues associated with this approach [13], which will not be further explored in the present paper.

Some researchers working with INEX data have tunable parameters in their models; in some cases, they have undertaken tuning experiments. Arvola et als [7] contextualisation function allows for each element to be weighted in different ways. A parameter can be associated with each element's language model in the linear interpolation method used in [8, 9, 10, 12]. Mass and Mandelbrod [12] tune the parameters for the vector space linear interpolation method to good effect (see section 2.3 above).

3 Passages and Inheritance in XML Documents

We assume that we have text documents with XML structure. That is, the content of the documents is (largely or entirely) text, quite possibly including relatively large blocks of undifferentiated text like paragraphs, but with some overall XML structure. Blobs of text are held within XML elements.

3.1 INEX Documents

We take the documents used in the INEX 2005 experiments to exemplify the idea; these are scientific papers and other contributions published in IEEE journals. They have XML structure that combines traditional structural elements (title, abstract, sections at various levels, bibliography etc.) with presentational matters (emphasis, font changes, mathematical material etc.). In fact structural and presentational matters are mixed with gay abandon: for example several different elements define 'paragraphs', either in particular presentation styles or with attributes which define the style.

The outline structure of an example INEX document is shown in Figure 1. In this outline, lower levels of the structure and all text have been removed; multiply-occurring elements have been reduced to one or two.

```
<article>
   <fno/>
   <doi/>
   <fm>
      <hdr> info about journal in which article appears </hdr>
      <tig> the title </tig>
      <au sequence="first"> 1st author name, affiliation </au>
      <au sequence="additional"> ditto for 2nd author </au>
      ...
      <abs> abstract as paragraphs of text </abs>
      <kwd> list of keywords </kwd>
   </fm>
   <bdy>
      <sec>
         <st> section title </st>
         <p> etc -- paragraphs of text;
                     bulleted lists; figures
      </sec>
      <sec>
         ...
         <ss1> (subsection)
            <st> subsection title </st>
            <p> etc -- paragraphs of text;
                        bulleted lists; figures
         </ss1>
         <ss1> ... </ss1>
      </sec>
      ...
   </bdy>
   <bm>
      <footnote id="T02001aff"> paragraphs etc. </footnote>
      <bib>
         <bibl>
            <h> header </h>
            <bb id="bibT02001"> bibliographic details </bb>
            <bb id="bibT02002"> ditto </bb>
            ...
         </bibl>
      </bib>
      <vt id="T0200a1"> author 1 details and picture </vt>
      <vt id="T0200a2"> ditto author 2 </vt>
      ...
   </bm>
</article>
```

Fig. 1. Outline of an example INEX document. Lower levels of the structure (including all presentation elements) and all text have been removed; many multiply occurring elements have been reduced in number; notes indicate the content of some elements in this example.

It seems likely that some structural elements would be very useful for part-document retrieval. We might reasonably define sections or some level of subsections as suitable units for retrieval; possibly also other elements such as bibliographic references or figures. However, it is equally clear that not all the XML elements are suitable for this purpose; consider the followin extreme example of a section title: `<st>C<scp>oncluding</scp> R<scp>emarks</scp></st>`. The `<scp>` tag represents a font (small capitals), and the enclosed text is a fragment of a word only, quite unsuitable as a retrievable unit.

Our choice is to make complete articles, sections, subsections at all levels and paragraphs into retrievable units. This is not to say that this choice is correct; it stresses the fact that this choice has to be made, and cannot simply be inferred from the XML structure. Retrievable units defined for our INEX 2005 experiments [14] included elements in the `<bm>` (back matter) tag and the abstract, but we might better consider these as ancillary matter, to be inherited as appropriate by other retrievable units, but not to be retrieved in their own right.

3.2 Inheritance

We have already discussed the notion of *fields* in a document. In this context, a very obvious field to consider is *title*. Complete articles have titles; sections and subsections also have or may have titles.

However, the interesting question arises concerning the relation between (say) the article title and the sections of the document. The article title describes the entire article, and therefore presumably also forms part of the description of each section or subsection within it. Similary, the main section title contributes to the description of the subsections.

Rather like the role of anchor text in web retrieval, we might reasonably assume that this information should be inherited appropriately. That is, if we consider a section as a retrievable unit, we should allow it to inherit information from outside itself that might be assumed to describe it. Thus sections should inherit article titles as well as their own; subsections should inherit both article and section titles. There may be other elements that should be inherited by the different levels: as indicated above, the abstract and bibliographic references are obvious examples.

The notion of inheritance may be compared to the mixing of whole-document score and passage score for passage retrieval; however, it is a more powerful and perhaps cleaner notion. It makes it quite clear that the passage (section, paragraph) is the retrievable unit; the role of the rest of the document is to tell us more *about the passage*. It also implies that if we are considering the passage for retrieval, we may choose to allow it to inherit selectively from the rest of the document, rather than simply inheriting its score.

3.3 Field Structure

Following the discussion above, we would like to regard each retrievable item as a kind of field-structured document. Given a field structure, we have good methods for scoring the unit against a query. One issue, as indicated above, is

Table 1. Retrievable elements mapped onto fields

	Field		
Retrievable element	Current title	Parent title(s)	Body text
article	article title	–	all text in article
section	section title (if present)	titles of article and all ancestor sections	all text in section
paragraph	–	ditto	all text in paragraph

(a dash indicates that the field is left empty)

that we need every retrievable item in the collection to be mapped onto *the same* field structure. Clearly, it is possible for a given field in a given item to be empty, but insofar as the different items will be competing against each other for retrieval, we need to ensure that items are balanced as far as possible.

In experiments for INEX 2005 [14], as an example of part of a mapping, we had a field for article title, for all retrievable elements. In other words, the article title was assumed to play the same role with respect to articles and to smaller units (sections and paragraphs). Section titles went to another field. Here we have reconsidered this mapping: a possible view is that a section title has the same relationship to the section in which it belongs as an article title has to the article. The relation of the article title to the section is different.

Another issue here is training. We need at the least a trainable weight for each separate field (possibly fixing one of them to 1). The more parameters, the more difficult training is and the more training data is needed. There is therefore good reason to start at least with a small number of fields.

Table 1 shows both the inheritance and field structure used in the present experiments. Again, it is not necessarily the best way to do it – it is offered as an example of how it might be done. Again, it is necessary to point out that this is a manually defined structure – we have no automatic methods of doing this.

4 Experiments

In this section, we describe a small experiment to illustrate some of the ideas presented above.

4.1 Data

The general XML structure of INEX documents has already been described. INEX 2005 provides both suitable test data (documents and topics) and a suitable methodology for trying out some of the above ideas. We use the CO (content only) topics. The data consists of 16819 articles, 40 topics and relevance judgements (see further below on the topics and judgements). Under our definition of retrievable unit (article, section, all levels of subsection and all types of paragraph), we identify 1529256 retrievable units in total.

We also need to perform some training in order to establish suitable values for the free parameters, particularly field weights. As is usual when training parameters, we would like to test the resulting trained algorithms on a different test set, to avoid overfitting. However, the set of topics for INEX 2005 CO is quite small (40 topics), and in fact only 29 of the 40 topics have relevance judgements. For these reasons we have abandoned the idea of a training-test split, and performed some training on the test set. Consequently, the results should be taken as indicative only. As a partial response to this problem, we have trained on one measure and evaluated on others, as discussed in section 4.3. Thus although it is likely that we have overfitted to some extent, accidental properties of the measures themselves will have been avoided. Note also that we are tuning only two parameters, which also reduces the danger of overfitting.

4.2 Ranking Function and Baselines

We use the BM25F (field-weighted extension of BM25) function mentioned above, as used in [5] (this reference also discusses the BM25 and BM25F parameters, which are therefore not further defined here). Essentially, BM25F combines information across fields at the term frequency level, and then combines information across terms. The BM25F parameters k_1 and b are taken as field-independent and fixed at $k_1 = 1.2$ and $b = 0.75$. BM25F also makes use of the average document length; in this context it would seem to make sense to interpret this as the average length of a retrievable unit, which will be much shorter than the average document. However, some preliminary experiments suggest that this does not work well; pending further investigation, we continue to use average document length.

We compare our present runs to the following:

- BM25 without field weights and without inheritance. For this we include the current title in with the section being retrieved – that is, we give the current title a weight of 1, the same as body text. Parent title is not included.
- Our INEX 2005 run (run 1). This was based on training of field weights at document level only. The field structures used in those experiments is slightly different from the present one.

4.3 Performance Measures

All evaluation for our experiments is done with the EVALJ package developed for INEX. The following is a brief account of some of the metrics defined for INEX 2005. Further information about the metrics is available from [16].

INEX defines normalized extended Cumulated Gain measures for particular rank positions i (nxCG[i]), and an average up to a rank position, MAnxCG[i]. There is also a measure called effort precision which may be averaged over recall levels (MAep). Also, in order to measure the ability of systems to retrieve specific relevant elements, the relevance judgements include exhaustivity and specificity components. These can be used in different ways, referred to as quantization levels.

In our experiment we have used MAnxCG[50] as the criterion for optimisation, on the grounds that we would like a ranking which is effective wherever the user stops searching. This optimisation is done separately on two quantization levels, quant(strict) and quant(gen). We then evaluate the results with nxCG[10], nxCG[25], nxCG[50], and MAep. All training and evaluation is done with the overlap=off option, which means that overlap is tolerated in the evaluation.

4.4 Tuning

Using the very simple set of fields and inheritance indicated above, and also using the above standard values for the BM25F parameters k_1 and b, we train by a simple grid search on a range of values of each parameter. The two parameters we train are the weight of the 'Current title' field wf(cur) and that of the 'Parent title' field wf(par) (the weight of the 'Body text' field is set to 1). Thus we train over a 2-dimensional grid. The granularity of the grid is significant. We first tune over a relatively coarse grid, to obtain an approximate optimum. We then fine-tune within a smaller range, to obtain a better approximation. The full range is 0–3000 (wf(cur)) and 0–100 (wf(par)).

A 3-dimensional plot of the performance surface over this grid (for the quant (gen) measure) is shown in Figure 2. It can be seen that the surface shows a peak at a very high weight for the current title, and a much lower one for the parent title, but both much higher than body text.

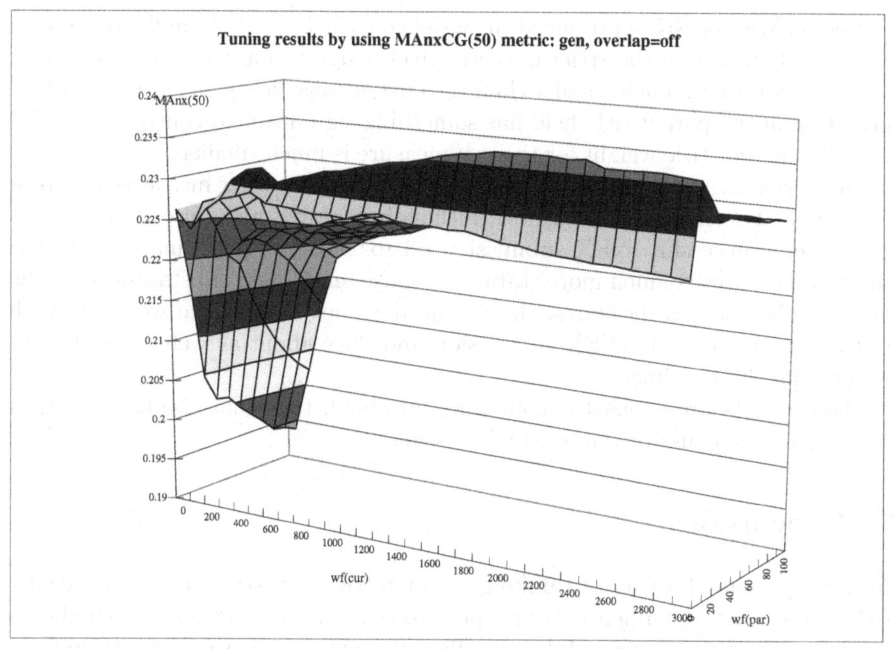

Fig. 2. Performance in the training set over a grid of values of the field weights (quant(gen))

Table 2. Field weights for the different runs

	wf(cur)	wf(par0)
Unweighted	1	0
City-INEX	2356	22
Tuned quant(strict)	1900	56
Tuned quant(gen)	2100	8

Table 3. Test results for different measures. Changes are relative to the baseline.

	nxCG(10)	change	nxCG(25)	change	nxCG(50)	change	MAep	change
quant(strict)								
Unweighted	0.0588	–	0.0808	–	0.1338	–	0.0343	–
City-INEX	0.0538	-9%	0.1174	+45%	0.1539	+15%	0.0267	-22%
Tuned	0.0973	+65%	0.1037	+28%	0.1643	+23%	0.0401	+17%
quant(gen)								
Unweighted	0.2126	–	0.2327	–	0.2306	–	0.0624	–
City-INEX	0.1875	-12%	0.1747	-25%	0.1800	-22%	0.0445	-29%
Tuned	0.2321	+9%	0.2407	+3%	0.2382	+3%	0.0610	-2%

4.5 Testing

Tuning on MAnxCG(50) produced the weightings in Table 2. As indicated above, the current tuning on the strict measure gives a significant weight to the parent title field (although much smaller than the current title field), suggesting that information in the parent title field has something significant to contribute to this task. The parent title weight for the gen measure is much smaller.

The performance of our tuned runs using the various other measures is shown in Table 3. For the strict measures, although we have not quite done as well as our very successful INEX submission on nxCG(25),[3] performance over the range of measures is much more stable; we consistently gain substantially on the baseline. For the gen measures, the tuning does not do quite so well, although it still outperforms our INEX submission and does about as well as or slightly better than the baseline.

These results are at least encouraging, although they must be taken with a pinch of salt, because of the overfitting issue.

5 Conclusions

We have presented a way of thinking about retrieval in structured (specifically XML-structured) documents. We propose to treat element retrieval as similar to document or passage retrieval, but to allow elements to inherit information from other elements. This can be done in the following way. First, the elements that

[3] Another City INEX submission did slightly better on nxCG(25) and significantly better on nxCG(50), but even less consistently overall.

are to be made retrievable must be selected. Next, a simple flat field-structure is defined, a single structure applicable to all retrievable elements. Next, a mapping is defined from the document elements to the field structure, for each type of retrievable element. This mapping defines the inheritance: that is, which elements will inherit information from other elements.

We may then use a standard document scoring-and-ranking function which is capable of differential weighting of fields. This is then likely to need tuning on a training set.

A small-scale experiment on INEX 2005 data has shown that this approach has some promise. First, it is possible to make a reasonable mapping of different elements onto a single flat field structure, and second, we have provided some experimental evidence that the inheritance idea is a useful one: in particular, it is useful for lower-level elements to inherit higher-level titles.

It is quite clear, however, that this test is a very partial one, and can be taken only as indicative in a small way. We expect in the future to conduct further and better-designed experiments to validate the ideas. These experiments should include much more detailed examination of the results, as well as being on a larger scale. Many questions remain, for example about how best both to choose inheritable elements and to map them onto a common field structure.

References

1. Callan, J.: Passage-level evidence in document retrieval. In Croft, W.B., van Rijsbergen, C.J., eds.: SIGIR '94: Proceedings of the 17th Annual International ACM SIGIR Conference on Research and Development in Information Retrieval, Springer-Verlag (1994) 302–310
2. Zaragoza, H., Craswell, N., Taylor, M., Saria, S., Robertson, S.: Microsoft Cambridge at TREC 2004: Web and HARD track. In Voorhees, E.M., Buckland, L.P., eds.: The Thirteenth Text REtrieval Conference, TREC 2004. NIST Special Publication 500-261, Gaithersburg, MD: NIST (2005) `http://trec.nist.gov/pubs/trec13/t13_proceedings.html`
3. Amitay, E., et al.: Juru at TREC 2003 – topic distillation using query-sensitive tuning and cohesiveness filtering. In Voorhees, E.M., Buckland, L.P., eds.: The Twelfth Text REtrieval Conference, TREC 2003. NIST Special Publication 500-255, Gaithersburg, MD: NIST (2004) 276–282 `http://trec.nist.gov/pubs/trec12/t12_proceedings.html`
4. Wilkinson, R.: Effective retrieval of structured documents. In Croft, W.B., van Rijsbergen, C.J., eds.: SIGIR '94: Proceedings of the 17th Annual International ACM SIGIR Conference on Research and Development in Information Retrieval, Springer-Verlag (1994) 311–317
5. Robertson, S., Zaragoza, H., Taylor, M.: Simple BM25 extension to multiple weighted fields. In Evans, D.A., Gravano, L., Hertzog, O., Zhai, C.X., Ronthaler, M., eds.: CIKM 2004: Proceedings of the 13th ACM Conference on Information and Knowledge Management, New York, ACM Press (2004) 42–49
6. Craswell, N., Hawking, D.: Overview of the TREC 2004 web track. In Voorhees, E.M., Buckland, L.P., eds.: The Thirteenth Text REtrieval Conference, TREC 2004. NIST Special Publication 500-261, Gaithersburg, MD: NIST (2005) 89–97 `http://trec.nist.gov/pubs/trec13/t13_proceedings.html`

7. Arvola, P., Junkkair, M., Kekalainen, J.: Generalized contextualisation method for XML information retrieval. In Herzog, O., Schek, H., Fuhr, N., Chowdhury, A., Teiken, W., eds.: CIKM 2005: Proceedings of the 14th ACM Conference on Information and Knowledge Management, New York, ACM Press (2005) 20–27
8. Ogilvie, P., Callan, J.: Hierarchical language models for XML component retrieval. In Fuhr, N., Malik, S., Lalmas, M., eds.: Advances in XML Information Retrieval: Third International Workshop of the Initative for the Evaluation of XML Retrieval, INEX 2004. LNCS 3493, Heidelberg, Springer (2005) 224–237
9. Sigurbjornsson, B., Kamps, J., de Rijke, M.: An element-based approach to XML retrieval. In Fuhr, N., Malik, S., Lalmas, M., eds.: INEX 2003: Second International Workshop of the Initative for the Evaluation of XML Retrieval, INEX (2004) 19–26
10. Sigurbjornsson, B., Kamps, J., de Rijke, M.: Mixture models, overlap, and structural hints in XML element retrieval. In Fuhr, N., Malik, S., Lalmas, M., eds.: Advances in XML Information Retrieval: Third International Workshop of the Initative for the Evaluation of XML Retrieval, INEX 2004. LNCS 3493, Heidelberg, Springer (2005) 104–109
11. Mass, Y., Mandelbrod, M.: Retrieving the most relevant XML components. In Fuhr, N., Malik, S., Lalmas, M., eds.: INEX 2003: Second International Workshop of the Initative for the Evaluation of XML Retrieval, INEX (2004) 53–58
12. Mass, Y., Mandelbrod, M.: Component ranking and automatic query refinement for XML retrieval. In Fuhr, N., Malik, S., Lalmas, M., eds.: Advances in XML Information Retrieval: Third International Workshop of the Initative for the Evaluation of XML Retrieval, INEX 2004. LNCS 3493, Heidelberg, Springer (2005) 134–140
13. Taylor, M., Zaragoza, H., Craswell, N., Robertson, S.: Optimisation methods for ranking functions with multiple parameters. Submitted for publication (2006)
14. Lu, W., Robertson, S., MacFarlane, A.: Field-weighted XML retrieval based on BM25. INEX 2005; Submitted for publication (2006)
15. INEX: INitiative for the evaluation of XML retrieval. `http://inex.is.informatik.uni-duisburg.de/2005/` (Visited 13 February 2006)
16. Kazai, G., Lalmas, M.: INEX 2005 evaluation metrics. `http://inex.is.informatik.uni-duisburg.de/2005/inex-2005-metricsv6.pdf` (2005) (Visited 22 February 2006).

Term Disambiguation in Natural Language Query for XML

Yunyao Li[1,*], Huahai Yang[2], and H.V. Jagadish[1,*]

[1] University of Michigan, Ann Arbor, MI 48109, USA
{yunyaol, jag}@umich.edu
[2] University at Albany, SUNY, Albany, NY 12222, USA
hyang@albany.edu

Abstract. Converting a natural language query sentence into a formal database query is a major challenge. We have constructed NaLIX, a natural language interface for querying XML data. Through our experience with NaLIX, we find that failures in natural language query understanding can often be dealt with as ambiguities in term meanings. These failures are typically the result of either the user's poor knowledge of the database schema or the system's lack of linguistic coverage. With automatic term expansion techniques and appropriate interactive feedback, we are able to resolve these ambiguities. In this paper, we describe our approach and present results demonstrating its effectiveness.

1 Introduction

Supporting arbitrary natural language queries is regarded by many as the ultimate goal for a database query interface. Numerous attempts have been made towards this goal. However, two major obstacles lie in the way: first, automatically understanding natural language (both syntactically and semantically) is still an open research problem itself; second, even if we had a perfect parser that could fully understand any arbitrary natural language query, translating this parsed natural language query into a correct formal query remains an issue since this translation requires mapping the user's intent into a specific database schema.

In [17, 18], we proposed a framework for building a generic interactive natural language query interface for an XML database. Our focus is on the second challenge—given a parsed natural language query (NLQ), how to translate it into a correct structured query against the database. The translation is done through mapping grammatical proximity of parsed tokens in a NLQ to proximity of corresponding elements in the result XQuery statement. Our ideas have been incorporated into a working software system called NaLIX[1]. In this system, we leverage existing natural language processing techniques by using a state-of-art natural language parser to obtain the semantic relationships between words in a given NLQ. However, the first challenge of understanding arbitrary natural language still remains. One solution to address the challenge is to provide training and enforce a controlled vocabulary. However, this requirement defeats our original purpose of building a natural language query interface for naive users.

* Supported in part by NSF IIS-0219513 and IIS-0438909, and NIH 1-U54-DA021519-01A1.

[1] NaLIX was demonstrated at SIGMOD 2005 and voted the Best Demo [17].

H.L. Larsen et al. (Eds.): FQAS 2006, LNAI 4027, pp. 133–146, 2006.

Through our experience with NaLIX, we find that several factors contribute to failures in natural language query understanding, and these failures can often be dealt with as ambiguities in term meaning. In this paper, we describe how we resolve these ambiguities with automatic term expansion techniques and appropriate interactive feedback facilities. In particular, we depict how we engage users, who are naturally more capable of natural language processing than any software, to help deal with uncertainty in mapping the user's intent to the result queries. We discuss the details of our approach in Sec. 3. We then evaluate the effectiveness of our term disambiguation techniques through a user study. The experimental results are presented in Sec. 4. In most cases, for a user query that initially could not be understood by the system, no more than three iterations appears to be sufficient for the user to reformulate it into an acceptable query. Previous studies [4, 23] show that even casual users frequently revise queries to meet their information needs. As such, our system can be considered to be very useful in practice. Examples illustrating our interactive term disambiguation approach are described in Section 5.

Finally, we discuss related work in Sec. 6 and conclude in Sec. 7. We begin with some necessary background material on our framework for building a generic natural language query interface for XML in Sec. 2.

2 From Natural Language Query to XQuery

Translating queries from natural language queries into corresponding XQuery expressions involves three main steps. The first step is token classification (Sec. 2.1), where terms in a parse tree output of a natural language parser are identified and classified according to their possible mapping to XQuery components. Next, this classified parse tree is validated based on a context-free grammar defined corresponding to XQuery (Sec. 2.2). A valid parse tree is then translated into an XQuery expression (Sec. 2.3). In this section, we briefly describe each of the three steps to provide necessary background information. More detailed discussion of these three key steps can be found in [18]. The software architecture of NaLIX has been described in [17].

2.1 Token Classification

To translate a natural language query into an XQuery expression, we first need to identify words/phrases in the original sentence that can be mapped into corresponding XQuery components. We call each such word/phrase a *token*, and one that does not match any XQuery component a *marker*. Tokens can further be divided into different

Table 1. Different Types of Tokens

Type of Token	Query Component	Description
Command Token(CMT)	Return Clause	Top main verb or wh-phrase [21] of parse tree, from an enum set of words and phrases
Order by Token(OBT)	Order By Clause	A phrase from an enum set of phrases
Function token(FT)	Function	A word or phrase from an enum set of adjectives and noun phrases
Operator Token(OT)	Operator	A phrase from an enum set of preposition phrases
Value Token(VT)	Value	A noun or noun phrase in quotation marks, a proper noun or noun phrase or a number
Name token(NT)	Basic Variable	A non-VT noun or noun phrase
Negation (NEG)	function not()	Adjective "not"
Quantifier Token(QT)	Quantifier	A word from an enum set of adjectives serving as determiners

Table 2. Different Types of Markers

Type of Marker	Semantic Contribution	Description
Connection Marker(CM)	Connect two related tokens	A preposition from an enumerated set, or non-token main verb
Modifier Marker(MM)	Distinguish two NTs	An adjectives as determiner or a numeral as predetermine or postdeterminer
Pronoun Marker(PM)	None due to parser's limitation	Pronouns
General Marker(GM)	None	Auxiliary verbs, articles

Table 3. Grammar Supported By NaLIX

1. Q → RETURN PREDICATE* ORDER_BY?
2. RETURN → CMT+(RNP|GVT|PREDICATE)
3. PREDICATE → QT?+((RNP$_1$|GVT$_1$)+GOT+(RNP$_2$|GVT$_2$)
4. |(GOT?+RNP+GVT)
5. |(GOT?+GVT+RNP)
6. |(GOT?+[NT]+GVT)
7. |RNP
8. ORDER_BY → OBT+RNP
9. RNP → NT |(QT+RNP)|(FT+RNP)|(RNP∧RNP)
10. GOT → OT|(NEG+OT)|(GOT∧GOT)
11. GVT → VT |(GVT∧GVT)
12. CM → (CM+CM)

Symbol "+" represents attachment relation between two tokens; "[]" indicates implicit token, as defined in Def. 11 of [18]

types as shown in Table 1 according to the type of components they match[2]. Enumerated sets of phrases (enum sets) are the real-world "knowledge base" for the system. In NaLIX, we have kept these small—each set has about a dozen elements. Markers can be divided into different types depending on their semantic contribution to the translation.

2.2 Parse Tree Validation

The grammar for natural language corresponding to the XQuery grammar supported by NaLIX is shown in Table 3 (ignoring all markers). We call a parse tree that satisfies the above grammar a *valid* parse tree. As can be seen, the linguistic capability of our system is directly restricted by the expressiveness of XQuery, since a natural language query that may be understood and thus meaningfully mapped into XQuery by NaLIX is one whose semantics is expressible in XQuery. Furthermore, for the purpose of query translation, only the semantics that can be expressed by XQuery need to be extracted and mapped into XQuery.

2.3 Translation into XQuery

A valid parse tree, obtained as described above, can then be translated into XQuery. XML documents are designed to be "human-legible and reasonably clear" [27]. Therefore, any reasonably designed XML document should reflect certain semantic structure isomorphous to human conceptual structure and hence expressible by human natural language. The major challenge for the translation is to utilize the structure of the natural

[2] When a noun/noun phrase matches certain XQuery keywords, special handling is required. Such special cases are not listed in the table and will not be discussed in the paper due to space limitation.

language constructions, as reflected in the parse tree, to generate appropriate structure in the XQuery expression. We address these issues in [18] through the introduction of the notions of *token attachment* and *token relationship* in natural language parse trees. We also propose the concept of *core token* as an effective mechanism to perform semantic grouping and hence determine both query nesting and structural relationships between result elements when mapping tokens to queries. Our previous experimental results show that in NaLIX a correctly parsed query is almost always translated into a structured query that correctly retrieves the desired answer (average precision = 95.1%, average recall = 97.6%).

3 Term Disambiguation

The mapping process from a natural language query to XQuery sometimes fails at token classification or parse tree validation stage. We observe that failures in this mapping process can always be dealt with as term ambiguities. Disambiguation of terms are thus necessary for properly mapping a user's intent into XQuery. In this section, we outline different types of failures we identified, and how they present themselves as term ambiguities. We then describe how we disambiguate the terms via automatic term expansion and interactive feedback.

3.1 Types of Failure

Parser failure. An obvious kind of failure in any natural language based system is one due to limited linguistic capability. In our system, a natural language query with correct grammar, though possible to be manually translated into XQuery, can still be found invalid at the validation step due to the incorrect parse tree generated by the parser. For example, for query "Display books published by addison-wesley after 1991," the parser we use generates a parse tree rooted by "published" as the main verb, and "display" as a noun underneath "books." This parse tree results in "published" being classified as unknown. A better parser may avoid such ambiguities, but such a solution is out of the scope of this paper.

Limited system vocabulary. A query sentence may contain terms that cannot be properly classified due to the restricted size of vocabulary that our system understands. For instance, it is impractical to exhaustively include all possible words for each type of token and marker in our system. As a result, there always exists the possibility that some words in a user query will not be properly classified. These words will be singled out in our system.

Inadvertent user error. Inadvertent user errors, such as typos, are unavoidable in any user interface. Such errors could cause failures in natural language query understanding, including unclassifiable terms and undesirable search results. Although some queries with typos can be successfully validated and translated, the results could be different from what the user desires, and are often found to be empty. For instance, the user may write "boks" instead of "books" in the query. Identifying such terms can help explain invalid queries and avoid frustrating users with unexpected results. Users may also write queries in incorrect grammar. These grammatically incorrect query sentences may result in certain words being labeled as untranslatable as well.

Limited user knowledge. Users often do not possess good knowledge of database schema. Although the requirement for users to have perfect knowledge of a XML document structure can be eliminated by using Schema-Free XQuery as our target language [16], users still need to specify query terms exactly matching element or attribute names in the database. Consequently, query sentences containing unmatched terms could result in misses, unless users are given the opportunities to choose a matching term.

Invalid query semantics. Any natural language system has to deal with situations where users simply do not intend to request an allowable system service. In our system, a user may write a natural language sentence that cannot be semantically expressed in XQuery. For example, some users typed "Hello world!" in an attempt to just see how the system will respond. Such a natural language query will of course be found to be invalid based on the grammar in Table 3, resulting in words such as "Hello" being marked as untranslatable.

3.2 Interactive Term Disambiguation

All five types of failures in natural language query translation can be dealt with as problems of term ambiguity, where the system cannot understand a term or find more than one possible interpretation of a term during the transformation into XQuery. Clever natural language understanding systems attempt to apply reasoning to interpret these terms, with limited success. Our approach is complementary: get the user to rephrase the query into terms that we can understand. By doing so, we shift some burden of semantic disambiguation from the system to the user, for whom such task is usually trivial. In return, the user obtains better access to information via precise querying.

A straightforward solution to seek the user's assistance is to simply return a notification whenever a failure happens and ask the user to rephrase. However, to reformulate a failed query without help from the system can be frustrating to the user. First of all, it is difficult for a user to recognize the actual reason causing the failures. For example, it is almost impossible for a casual user to realize that certain failures result from the system's limited vocabulary. Similarly, given the fact that an empty result is returned for a query, it is unlikely for the user to discover that it is caused by a mismatch between element name(s) in the query and the actual element name(s) in the XML document. In both cases, the user may simply conclude the system is completely useless as queries in perfect English fail every time. Furthermore, even if the user knows exactly what has caused the failures, to correct most failures is nontrivial. For instance, considerable effort will be required from the user to study the document schema in order to rephrase a query with mismatched element names.

From the above discussion, we can see that the difficulties in query reformulation without system feedback are largely due to the user's lack of (perfect) knowledge of the system and the XML document. Intuitively, query reformulation will be easier for the user if the system can provide the needed knowledge without demanding formal training. With this in mind, we designed the following interactive term disambiguation mechanism. First, unknown terms (beyond the system and document vocabulary

Table 4. Error Messages in NaLIX. (The error messages listed below do not include the highlighting of offending parts in the user sentence and the full informative feedback offered; objects in "⟨⟩" will be instantiated with actual terms at feedback generation time.)

Error 1	*The system cannot understand what ⟨UNKNOWN⟩ means. The closest term to ⟨UNKNOWN⟩ the system understands is ⟨KNOWN⟩. Please rewrite your query without using ⟨UNKNOWN⟩, or replace it with ⟨KNOWN⟩.*
Error 2	*The value "⟨VT⟩" cannot be found in the database.*
Error 3	*No element or attribute with the name "⟨NT⟩" can be found in the database.*
Error 4	*At least one noun phrase should be used.*
Error 5	*Please tell the system what you want to return from the database by using the following commands (list of ⟨CMT⟩).*
Error 6	*⟨FT⟩ must be followed by a common noun phrase.*
Error 7	*⟨CMT|OBT⟩ must be followed by a noun phrase (link to example usage of ⟨CMT|OBT⟩). Please specify what you want to return (if CMT) or order by (if OBT).*
Error 8	*CMT|OBT should not attach to a noun phrase. Please remove* $(RNP\|GVT)_1$.
Error 9	*The system does not understand what ⟨non-GOT|non-CM⟩ means. Please replace it with one of the following operators (a list of typical OTs with closest OT first) or connectors (a list of typical CMs with closest CM first).*
Error 10	*OBT should not be attached by a proper noun such as GVT.*
Error 11	*The system does not understand what ⟨GVT + RNP⟩ means. Please specify the relationship between ⟨GVT⟩ and ⟨RNP⟩ by using one of the following operators (a list of typical OTs with the closest OT first) or connectors (a list of typical CMs with the closest CM first).*
Error 12	*⟨GOT|CM⟩ must be followed by a noun phrase (example usage of ⟨GOT|CM⟩).*

Table 5. Warning Messages in NaLIX

Warning 1	*System may not be able to understand pronouns correctly. If you find the returned results surprising, try express your query without pronouns.*
Warning 2	*There is no element/attribute with the exact name ⟨NT⟩. You may choose one or more from the list (of matching elements/attribuates).*
Warning 3	*There are multiple elements/attributes with the value ⟨VT⟩. You may choose one from the list (of matching elements/attribuates).*
Warning 4	*We assume that ⟨NT⟩ elements/attributes is related with ⟨*`coretoken`*⟩. If this is not what you intended, you may choose one from the list (of matching elements/attribuates).*

boundary) and the exact terms violating the grammar in the parse tree are identified and reported in the feedback messages. The types of ambiguities caused by these terms are also reported. In addition, for each ambiguous term, appropriate terms that can be understood by the system are suggested to the user as possible replacement for the term. Finally, example usage of each suggested term is shown to the user. A complete list of error messages generated by our system is shown in Table 4.

The above feedback generation techniques work as three defensive lines against uncertainty in term disambiguation. Identification of term ambiguities is the first essential defensive line. It not only helps a user to get a better understanding of what has caused the query failure, but also narrows down the scope of reformulation needed for the user. Certain failures, such as those caused by typos, can easily be fixed based on the ambiguous terms identified. For others, the user may need to have relevant knowledge about the system or document vocabulary for term disambiguation. For such cases, our system uses term suggestion as the second defense line. Relevant terms in the system and document vocabulary are suggested based on their string similarity and function similarity (in the XQuery translation) to each ambiguous term. Obviously, not every term suggested can be used to replace the ambiguous term. The user is responsible for resolving the uncertainty issue associated with term suggestion by selecting suggested terms to replace the ambiguous term. Finally, when queries fail due to parser errors, incorrect grammar, or invalid query semantics, the exact terms causing the failures are difficult to pinpoint. The system is likely to wrongly identify term ambiguities and thus may generate less meaningful error messages and suggest irrelevant terms. For such cases, providing examples serves as the last line of defense. Examples supply helpful hints to the user with regard to the linguistic coverage of the system without specifying tedious rules. However, exactly how the information conveyed by the examples is used for term disambiguation is associated with greater uncertainty.

For some queries, the system successfully parses and translates the queries, yet may not be certain that it is able to correctly interpret the user's intent. These queries will be accepted by the system but with warnings. A complete list of warning messages is presented in Table 5.

3.3 Error Reporting

The failures of a natural language query may be attributed to multiple factors. For example, a query may contain multiple typos and mismatched element names. For such queries, multiple error messages will be generated and reported together, with the following exception. If an error message of category Error 1 is generated, then any error message of category Error 4 to 12 for the same query will not be reported to the user.

The above error reporting policy is based on the following observation: any parse tree containing unknown term(s) validates the grammar in Table 3. Therefore for the same query, error message(s) of both category Error 1 and category Error 4 to 12 are likely to be caused by the same unknown term(s). In such a case, an error message directly reporting the unknown term(s) provides more relevant information for query reformulation. Moreover, our study shows that users tend to deal with feedback message one at a time—withholding less meaningful error messages in the report is unlikely to have any negative impact over the reformulation.

3.4 Ontology-Based Term Expansion

A user may not be familiar with the specific attribute or element names contained in the XML document. For example, the document being queried uses *author*, while the user query says *writer*. In such a case, the Schema-Free XQuery translation of the query will not be able to generate correct results. We borrow term expansion techniques from information retrieval literature [2, 5, 22] to address such name-mismatch problems. When using term expansion techniques, one must deal with uncertainty associated with the added terms in the query representation. Such uncertainty is traditionally handled by introducing approximate scoring functions. However, terms added to the query may be weighted in a way that their importance in the query is different from the original concept expressed by the user. We avoid this issue by granting the user full control of the term expansion: warning messages are generated to alert the user whenever term expansion is employed; then the user may choose to use one or more of the terms added by the expansion in new queries. Uncertainty introduced by term expansion is thus explicitly revealed to the user and clarified by the user's response. Such an interactive term expansion process not only avoids the drawback of scoring functions, but also allows the user to gradually learn more about the XML database by revealing a part of the database each time. This approach is especially suitable for our system, since term expansion is limited to the terms used as attribute and element names in the XML document.

4 Experiment

We implemented NaLIX as a stand-alone interface to the Timber native XML database [1] that supports Schema-Free XQuery. We used Minipar [19] as our natural language parser. To evaluate our system, we conducted a user study with 18 untrained participants recruited from a university campus. Each participant worked on ten different search tasks adapted from the "XMP" set in the XQuery use cases [26]. Detailed discussion on the experimental set up and results on ease of use and retrieval performance of our system can be found in [18]. In this paper, we analyze the transcripts of system interaction with users to assess the effectiveness of our interactive term disambiguation approach.

Measurement. For each query initially rejected by the system, we recorded the number of iterations it took for a participant to reformulate the query into a system acceptable one or until time out (5 minutes for each search task). We also recorded the actual user input for each iteration in a query log. We then manually coded the query logs to determine how a user may have utilized the feedback messages in each reformulation process. The coding schema below were used:

- If the user changed a term that appears in the body of a feedback message in the next query input, we count the reformulation as being helped by the feedback message.
- If the user used a suggested term in the next query input, we count the term suggestion as being helpful.
- If the user rewrote the query in the same format as that of an example query contained in the feedback, then the example is regarded as useful.
- If we cannot attribute the user change(s) to any specific component of a feedback message, then the feedback is counted having failed to contribute to term disambiguation.

For example, one user initially wrote "List tiltes and editors." An error message "*tiltes* cannot be found in the database" was returned. The user then fixed the typo by changing "tiltes" into "titles" in the new query "List titles and editors," which was then accepted by the system. In this case, the disambiguation of term "tiltes" was considered as made with the assistance of the error message. Feedback message, suggested terms, and term usage examples are not exclusive from each other in assisting query reformulation. One or more of them may be utilized in a single iteration.

We consider the entire reformulation process as a whole when determining the types of helpful feedback. The reason is two-fold. First, we cannot determine the effectiveness of term disambiguation for a query until the reformulation is complete. Furthermore, users were often found to revise the query based on only one feedback at a time, even when multiple feedback messages were generated. Thus multiple iterations are needed

Table 6. Types of Aids Used in Query Reformulation

Body of Feedback Message	Suggested Term	Example	None
75.1%	22.4%	10.9%	7.3%

to disambiguate all the terms in one failed query, and they should be considered as parts of a whole reformulation process.

Results. We coded 166 query reformulation processes in total. The average number of iterations needed for participants to revise an invalid natural language query into a valid one was 2.55; the median number of iterations was 2.

The statistics on different types of aids utilized in the reformulations is listed in Table 6. As can be seen, the body of feedback messages provided helpful information for majority of the reformulation processes. Suggested terms and their example usage were found helpful for less than one quarter of the reformulations. Nevertheless, these two techniques are not thus less important. Both suggested terms and their example usage are most likely to be utilized when failures were caused by parser failure, grammar error, or incorrect query semantics. For such cases, there is no easy means to determine the actual factors resulting in the failure, because we depend on an outside parser to obtain dependency relation between words as approximation of their semantic relationships. In another word, it is unlikely for our system to generate insightful feedback messages for such failures. Even if we do have full access to the internals of a parser, we would still not be able to distinguish a parser failure from an incorrect query semantics. A user, however, has little difficulty in taking helpful hints from the identified problematic words, the suggested terms and their example usage to reformulate queries successfully. This is true even when the content of the error message is not entirely insightful.

5 Analysis and Discussion

In this section, three examples of iterations taken from our user study are presented. These illustrate how interactive term disambiguation helps to resolve different types of failures in natural language understanding.

Example 1 (Out of Vocabulary Boundary)

```
 User Input 0: Return list of all books with title and author
       Status: Rejected
Error Message: No element or attribute with the name ''list''
               can be found in the database.
 User Input 1: List all books by title and author
       Status: Accepted
```

In NaLIX, words/phrases in a given natural language query are classified based on small enumerate sets of phrases (Sec. 2.1) corresponding to XQuery components. A user may use terms outside of the system vocabulary. Some terms cannot be classified and are reported as unknown; others may be wrongly classified and result in error messages later on.

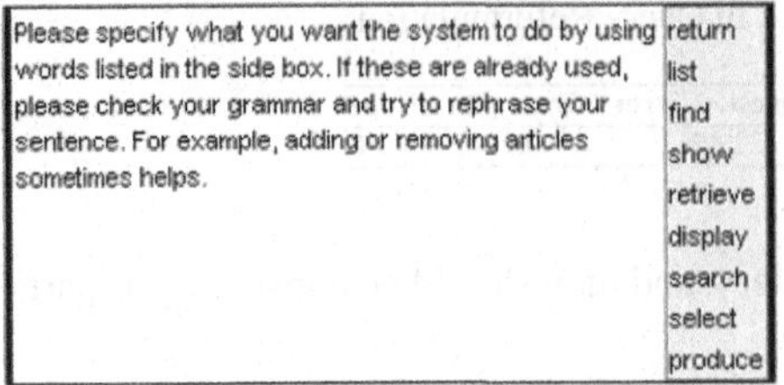

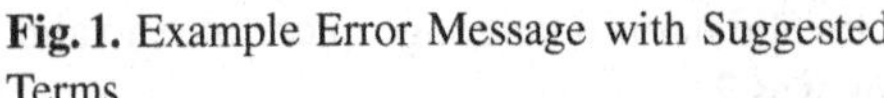
Fig. 1. Example Error Message with Suggested Terms

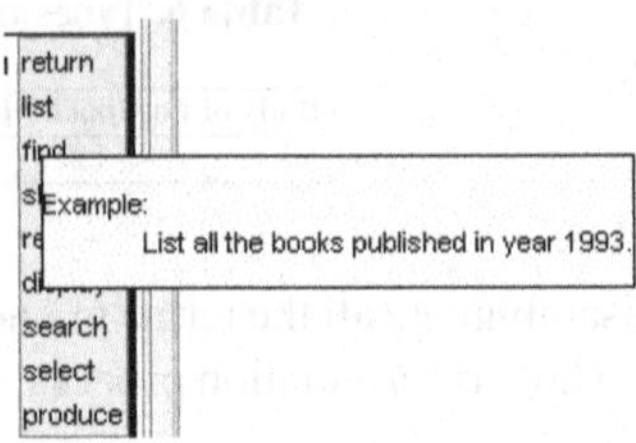

Fig. 2. Example Usage of a Suggested Terms

In this example, "list of" is beyond the boundary of system vocabulary. As a result, the token classification process wrongly identified "list" as a name token and "of" as a connection marker. NaLIX then reported failure when it tried to map "list" into a variable in XQuery, as no element or attribute with name "list" exists in the XML document of interest. The user recognized the term ambiguity from the feedback message generated and successfully disambiguated the term "list" by making minor changes to the original query. Specifically, the user removed "list of," implying that this phrase does not contribute to the query semantics, and replaced verb "return" with verb "list," implying that they are synonyms within the context of the query.

Example 2 (Parser Failure)

```
  User Input 0: Show titles and publishers
        Status: Rejected
 Error Message: As shown in Figure 1
  User Input 1: Display titles and publishers
        Status: Accepted
```

NaLIX relies on a natural language parser to obtain dependency relation between words. The parser we currently use is Minipar [19]. Like any other generic natural language parser, Minipar may produce an incorrect parse tree[3] for an arbitrary natural language sentence.

In this example, verb "show" was parsed as a noun and wrongly regarded as depending on "titles," rather than the other way around. It was thus identified as a name token, instead of a command token (corresponding to RETURN clause of XQuery). As a result, the arse tree validation process determined that a command token was lacking and reported so.

There is no easy way to resolve such parsing problems without building a better parser. Even generating a meaningful feedback message is extremely difficult: for instance, the feedback message for the above example is confusing, as the feedback message is generated based on a wrong parse tree. Therefore, we alert users the possible confusion, and include related terms and meaningful examples in the feedback to provide more information about the system's linguistic capability without requiring any formal training. As we can see from the above example, this feature is very helpful in

[3] Minipar achieves about 88% precision and 80% recall with respect to dependency relations with the SUSANNE Corpus[19].

practice. In this example, the feedback message generated based on the incorrect parse tree does not make much sense, as the user has already specified what to be returned in input 0. However, by replacing "show" with a suggested term "display," the user successfully revised the failed query into one that can be accepted by the system without changing the query semantics. We also observed that users sometimes took hints from the given examples by writing part of the query in the way shown in the examples, and thus successfully obtained a system-understandable query.

Like translation failures that result from parser failure, those caused by incorrect grammar (e.g., "What books have at least one author?") or invalid query semantics (e.g., "Return love.") also pose significant challenges to natural language query translation. It is often impossible to determine the actual reason for a failure solely on the basis of a parse tree. Therefore, the content of a generated error message usually is not helpful in term of pinpointing the exact problem. Nevertheless, users were found to be able to reformulate queries successfully in these cases with the help of identified problematic words, suggested terms, and examples.

Example 3 (Mixed Failures)

```
 User Input 0: List author's name and titles of all bkkos by
               that author.
       Status: Rejected
Error Message: 1. No element or attribute with the name
               ''name'' can be found in the database.
               2. No element or attribute with the name
               ''bkkos'' can be found in the database.
 User Input 1: List author's name and titles of all books by
               that author.
       Status: Rejected
Error Message: No element or attribute with the name ''name''
               can be found in the database.
 User Input 2: List author and titles of all books by that
               author.
       Status: Rejected
Error Message: As shown in Figure 1, 2
 User Input 3: List all the authors and titles of all books
               by each author
       Status: Accepted
```

Example 1 and 2 present cases where the failure of natural language query understanding can be contributed to a single factor. In practice, cases such as Example 3, where multiple factors result in a natural language query failure, are also common [4]. In the above example, the initial user input contains one typo "bkkos" and one mismatched name token "name." Our feedback messages reported both. Note, however, although the corresponding parse tree for this query was invalid, no related error message was reported following the policy described in Sec. 3.3.

[4] In our user study, nearly half of the iterations were caused by user error alone, about 10% by parser failure alone, and around 20% by a mixture of the two, with the remaining iterations caused by other factors.

The last iteration in the above example illustrates how a user can be helped for parser failures by example usage included in the feedback message. The user successfully reformulated input 2 into input 3 by adding "all the" before "authors" in similar way as the example usage shown for "list" (Figure 2).

From the above examples, we can see that in many cases, it is very difficult, if not impossible, to determine the exact reason for failures of natural language query understanding and to generate specific feedback messages. The same error "*list* is not found in the database" may be produced for failures caused by limited system vocabulary, where phrases such as "list of" cannot be properly translated into XQuery semantics, or by the user's poor knowledge of the document schema, where no object with the name "list" exists in the XML database. However, by handing the problem over to an interactive term disambiguation process, users can successfully reformulate queries with minimal efforts. In return, they can express richer query semantics, have more control over search results, and obtain results with better quality.

6 Related Work

In the information retrieval field, research efforts have long been made on natural language interfaces that take keyword search query as the target language [6, 8]. In recent years, keyword search interfaces to databases have begun to receive increasing attention [7, 10, 16, 12, 13], and have been considered a first step towards addressing the challenge of natural language querying. Our work builds upon this stream of research. However, our system is not a simple imitation of those in the information retrieval field in that it supports a richer query mechanism that allow us to convey much more complex semantic meanings than pure keyword search.

Extensive research has been done on developing natural language interfaces to databases (NLIDB), especially during the 1980's [3]. The architecture of our system bears most similarity to syntax-based NLIDBs, where the resulting parse tree of a user query is directly mapped into a database query. However, previous syntax-based NLIDBs, such as LUNAR [30], interface to application-specific database systems and depend on database query languages specially designed to facilitate the mapping from the parse tree to the database query [3]. Our system, in contrast, uses a generic query language, XQuery, as our target language. In addition, unlike previous systems such as the one reported in [25], our system does not rely on extensive domain-specific knowledge.

The idea of interactive NLIDBs has been discussed in some early NLIDB literature [3, 15]. Majority of these focus on generating cooperative responses using query results obtained from a database with respect to the user's task(s). In contrast, the focus of the interactive process in our system is purely query formulation—only one query is actually evaluated against the database. Several interactive query interfaces have been built to facilitate query formulation [14, 28]. These depend on domain-specific knowledge. Also, they assist the construction of structured queries rather than natural language queries.

Human computation refers to a paradigm of using human to assist computer in solving problems. The idea has been applied in areas such as imagine analysis, speech recognition, and natural language processing [9, 24, 29]. All these problems share one common characteristic—they appear to be difficult to computers to solve effectively, but are easy for humans. The natural language understanding problem in our system belongs to the same category. Our solution to this problem is interactive term disambiguation, where human assists to solve term ambiguities identified by the system. It can thus be considered as following a human computation approach as well.

NaLIX explicitly relies on query iterations to elicit user feedback. In the field of information retrieval, an alternative to manual feedback is to automatically infer feedback based on the user's interaction with the system (e.g. document browse pattern); such feedback can then be used to determine document relevance and to expand the original query to obtain more relevant results [11, 20, 31]. However, such an automatic feedback approach does not apply to NaLIX. First of all, explicit feedback requires much less user effort in our system - a user only need to read short feedback messages instead of long documents. More importantly, our system depends on explicit user feedback to resolve ambiguities in natural language understanding to generate precise database query. Unlike information retrieval queries, an incorrect database query will likely fail to produce any results that could be useful for enhancing the original query. Moreover, if we can infer proper information from query results and rewrite a structured query to get correct answer, we may have already solved the difficult natural language understanding problem.

7 Conclusion and Future Work

In this paper, we described term disambiguation in a natural language query interface for an XML database via automatic term expansion and interactive feedback. Starting from a failed natural language query, users reformulate a system understandable query with the help of feedback messages from the system. Uncertainty associated with term expansion, ambiguous term identification, term suggestion and term usage examples are explicitly revealed to the user in the feedback messages. The user then addressed such issues directly by query reformulation. Our user study demonstrates the effectiveness of our approach in handling failures in natural language query. The system as we have, although far from being able to pass Turing test, is already usable in practice.

In the future, we plan to investigate machine learning techniques to improve system linguistic coverage. We are also interested in integrating grammar checking techniques to deal with incorrect grammars. Additionally, we intend to redesign the user interface of our system for better usability. These techniques will all improve our interactive term disambiguation facility, and help users to formulate natural language queries that are a true expression of their information needs and are understandable by database systems.

References

1. Timber: http://www.eecs.umich.edu/db/timber/
2. WordNet: http://www.cogsci.princeton.edu/~wn/
3. I. Androutsopoulos et al. Natural language interfaces to databases - an introduction. *Journal of Language Engineering*, 1(1):29–81, 1995.

4. M. J. Bates. The design of browsing and berrypicking techniques for the on-line search interface. *Online Review*, 13(5):407–431, 1989.
5. A. Burton-Jones et al. A heuristic-based methodology for semantic augmentation of user queries on the Web. In *ICCM*, 2003.
6. J. Chu-carroll et al. A hybrid approach to natural language Web search. In *EMNLP*, 2002.
7. S. Cohen et al. XSEarch: A semantic search engine for XML. In *VLDB*, 2003.
8. S. V. Delden and F. Gomez. Retrieving NASA problem reports: a case study in natural language information retrieval. *Data & Knowledge Engineering*, 48(2):231–246, 2004.
9. J. A. Fails and D. R. Olsen. A design tool for camera-based interaction. In *CHI*, 2003.
10. L. Guo et al. XRANK: Ranked keyword search over XML documents. In *SIGMOD*, 2003.
11. W. Hill et al. Read wear and edit wear. In *CHI*, 1992.
12. V. Hristidis et al. Keyword proximity search on XML graphs. In *ICDE*, 2003.
13. A. Hulgeri et al. Keyword search in databases. *IEEE Data Engineering Bulletin*, 24:22–32, 2001.
14. E. Kapetanios and P. Groenewoud. Query construction through meaningful suggestions of terms. In *FQAS*, 2002.
15. D. Kupper et al. NAUDA: A cooperative natural language interface to relational databases. *SIGMOD Record*, 22(2):529–533, 1993.
16. Y. Li et al. Schema-Free XQuery. In *VLDB*, 2004.
17. Y. Li et al. Nalix: an interactive natural language interface for querying XML. In *SIGMOD*, 2005.
18. Y. Li et al. Constructing a generic natural language interface for an XML database. In *EDBT*, 2006.
19. D. Lin. Dependency-based evaluation of MINIPAR. In *Workshop on the Evaluation of Parsing Systems*, 1998.
20. M. Morita and Y. Shinoda. Information filtering based on user behavior analysis and best match text retrieval. In *SIGIR*, 1994.
21. R. Quirk et al. *A Comprehensive Grammar of the English Language*. Longman, London, 1985.
22. P. V. R. Navigli. An analysis of ontology-based query expansion strategies. In *Workshop on Adaptive Text Extraction and Mining*, 2003.
23. J. R. Remde et al. Superbook: an automatic tool for information exploration - hypertext? In *Hypertext*, pages 175–188. ACM Press, 1987.
24. B. C. Russell et al. Labelme: a database and web-based tool for image annotation. *MIT AI Lab Memo*, 2005.
25. D. Stallard. A terminological transformation for natural language question-answering systems. In *ANLP*, 1986.
26. The World Wide Web Consortium. XML Query Use Cases. W3C Working Draft. Available at http://www.w3.org/TR/xquery-use-cases/, 2003.
27. The World Wide Web Consortium. Extensible Markup Language (XML) 1.0 (Third Edition). W3C Recommendation. Available at http://www.w3.org/TR/REC-xml/, 2004.
28. A. Trigoni. Interactive query formulation in semistructured databases. In *FQAS*, 2002.
29. L. von Ahn and L. Dabbish. Labeling images with a computer game. In *CHI*, 2004.
30. W. Woods et al. *The Lunar Sciences Natural Language Information System: Final Report*. Bolt Beranek and Newman Inc., Cambridge, MA, 1972.
31. J. Xu and W. B. Croft. Query expansion using local and global document analysis. In *SIGIR*, 1996.

Using Structural Relationships for Focused XML Retrieval

Georgina Ramírez, Thijs Westerveld, and Arjen P. de Vries

Centre for Mathematics and Computer Science,
P.O. Box 94079, 1090 GB Amsterdam, The Netherlands
{georgina, thijs, arjen}@cwi.nl

Abstract. In *focused* XML retrieval, information retrieval systems have to find out which are the most appropriate retrieval units and return only these to the user, avoiding overlapping elements in the result lists. This paper studies structural relationships between elements and explains how they can be used to produce a better ranking for a focused task. We analise relevance judgements to find the most useful links between elements and show how a retrieval model can be adapted to incorporate this information. Experiments on the INEX 2005 test collection show that the structural relationships improve retrieval effectiveness considerably.

1 Introduction

Structured document retrieval systems use conventional information retrieval techniques to determine the order in which to best present results to the user, but, as opposed to traditional IR systems, they *also* choose the *retrieval unit*. Given an XML document collection, a structured document retrieval system could present to the user any of the marked up elements. The possible retrieval units vary widely in size and type; from small elements like italics and section titles, to large elements like document bodies, articles or even complete journals. It is the task of the system to decide which units are the most sensible to retrieve.

In *focused* XML retrieval (introduced at INEX 2005, see Section 2), this problem is even more apparent. The goal is to avoid returning overlapping elements in the result set, to make sure the user does not get to see the same information twice. For example, when both a paragraph and its containing section contain relevant information, a system is not allowed to return both elements. Instead, it should decide which of the two candidate results is the more useful. Thus, it should reason that when the section contains only one relevant paragraph, this paragraph may be more useful on its own than the section, while the user may prefer the full section if it contains multiple relevant paragraphs.

The typical approach to focused XML retrieval produces an initial ranking of all elements using an XML retrieval model, and then applies an algorithm to remove overlapping elements from the result set. Two main types of strategies have been proposed for overlap removal. The ones that use a simple method such as keeping the highest ranked element of each path and the ones that apply clever algorithms that take into account the relations in the tree hierarchy between the highly ranked elements.

H.L. Larsen et al. (Eds.): FQAS 2006, LNAI 4027, pp. 147–158, 2006.

This paper studies the effect of adapting the initial ranking before using the simple overlap removing technique. After introducing our laboratory setting, INEX (Section 2), and the overlap removal problem (Section 3), we analise relevance judgements to find useful dependencies (links) between elements in the XML tree and adapt the retrieval model to incorporate this information (Section 4). Section 5 demonstrates experimentally that this leads to better retrieval effectiveness. Finally, Section 6 summarises and discusses the main findings.

2 INEX and the Focused Retrieval Task

The *Initiative for the Evaluation of XML retrieval* (INEX) [2] is a benchmark for the evaluation of XML retrieval. The collection provided to the participants is a subset of IEEE Computer Society publications, consisting of 16.819 scientific articles from 24 different journals.

Topics and relevance judgements. The participants are responsible for creating a set of topics (queries) and for assessing the relevant XML elements for each of these topics. The relevance judgements are given by two different dimensions: exhaustivity (E) and specificity (S). The exhaustivity dimension reflects the degree to which an element covers a topic and the specificity dimension reflects how focused the element is on that topic. Thus, to assess an XML element, participants are asked to highlight the relevant parts of that elements (specificity) and to use a three-level scale $[0, 1, 2]$ to define how much of the topic that element covers (exhaustivity). For later usage in the evaluation metrics, the specificity dimension is automatically translated to a value in a continuous scale $[0 \ldots 1]$, by calculating the fraction of highlighted (relevant) information contained by that element. The combination of the two dimensions is used to quantify the relevance of the XML elements. Thus, a highly relevant element is one that is both, highly exhaustive and highly specific to the topic of request.

The focused task. INEX has defined various XML retrieval scenarios, each corresponding to a specific task. This paper addresses the **focused** task, where the goal is to find the *most* exhaustive and specific elements on a *path*. Once the element is identified and returned, none of the remaining elements in the path should be returned. In other words, the result list should not contain overlapping elements. We choose to evaluate our results for *content-oriented XML retrieval using content-only conditions* (CO). Content-only requests are free text queries that contain only content conditions (without structural constraints). The retrieval system may retrieve relevant XML elements of varying granularity.

The evaluation metrics. INEX 2005 has evaluated retrieval results using the *Extended Cumulated Gain* (XCG) metrics. We realise that these measures are not yet widely spread in the general IR community, but we prefer to report our results using these measures for comparison to other groups participating at INEX. Here, we briefly outline their main characteristics, and refer to [3] for a more detailed description. The XCG metrics are an extension of the cumulated gain (CG) metrics [5] that consider dependency between XML elements (e.g., overlap and near-misses). The XCG metrics include a user-oriented measure called normalised extended cumulated gain (nxCG) and a system-oriented measure called effort-precision/gain-recall (ep/gr). In comparison to the common IR evaluation measures, *nxCG* corresponds to a precision measure at a fixed cut-off, and *ep/gr* provides a summary measure related to mean average precision (MAP). To model different user preferences, two different quantisation functions are used. The *strict* one models a user who only wants to see highly relevant elements ($E = 2$, $S = 1$) and the *generalised* one allows different degrees of relevance.

3 Removing Overlap

In an XML retrieval setting, to identify the most appropriate elements to return to the user is not an easy problem. IR systems have the difficult task to find out which are the most exhaustive and specific elements in the tree, and return only these to the user, producing result lists without overlapping elements. Current retrieval systems produce an initial ranking of all elements with their 'standard' XML retrieval model, and then remove overlapping elements from the result set. A fairly trivial approach keeps just the highest ranked element, and removes the other elements from the result list (e.g. [10]). More advanced techniques (e.g., [1], [7], [8]) exploit the XML tree structure to decide which elements should be removed or pushed down the ranked list.

In the first approach, the information retrieval systems rely completely on the underlying retrieval models to produce the best ranking. Thus, the assumption is that the most appropriate element in a path has been assigned a higher score than the rest. This could indeed be the case, if the retrieval model would consider, when ranking, not only the estimated relevance of the XML element itself but also its *usefulness* compared to other elements in the same path. However, since most retrieval models rank elements independently, the highest scored element may not be the best one for a focused retrieval task. We argue that retrieval models should take into account the dependency between elements to produce a good ranking for focused XML retrieval.

As an example, consider the following baseline models:

1) A retrieval model ($base_{LM}$) based on simple statistical language models [9, 4]. The estimated probability of relevance for an XML element E_j is calculated as follows:

$$P_{LM}(E_j) = \prod_{i=1}^{n}(\lambda P(T_i|E_j) + (1-\lambda)P_{cf}(T_i)), \tag{1}$$

where:

$$P(T_i|E_j) = \frac{tf_{i,j}}{\sum_t tf_{t,j}} \text{ and } P_{cf}(T_i) = \frac{cf_i}{\sum_t cf_t},$$

2) The same retrieval model (LM) applying a length prior for length normalisation ($base_{LP}$). The probability of relevance is then estimated as:

$$P(E_j) = size(E_j)\ \ P_{LM}(E_j) \tag{2}$$

3) The same retrieval model (LM) but removing all the small elements (shorter than 30 terms) for length normalisation($base_{RM}$).

Using a $\lambda = 0.5$ and removing overlap with the simple algorithm of keeping the highest scored element in a path, we obtain the results shown in Table 1 for the three models described.

Table 1. Results for the different baselines runs in the focused task with strict (^{S}) and generalised (^{G}) quantisations

	nxCG[10]	**nxCG[25]**	**nxCG[50]**	**Maep**
$base^G_{LM}$	0.1621	0.1507	0.1557	0.0569
$base^G_{RM}$	**0.2189**	**0.2206**	**0.2100**	**0.0817**
$base^G_{LP}$	0.2128	0.1855	0.1855	0.0717
$base^S_{LM}$	**0.1016**	0.0855	**0.1207**	**0.0536**
$base^S_{RM}$	0.0610	**0.0974**	0.1176	0.0197
$base^S_{LP}$	0.0940	0.0910	0.1075	0.0503

In the generalised case, the length normalisation approaches help to improve the effectiveness of the system. This is because the original ranking contains many small elements that are ranked high but are not appropriate retrieval units. When applying length normalisation, other more lengthy units are pushed up the ranked list. These units tend to be more appropriate than the small ones, not only because longer elements contain more information but also due to the cumulative nature of the exhaustivity dimension. Since exhaustivity propagates up the tree, ancestors of a relevant element have an exhaustivity equal or greater than their descendants. These ancestors are relevant to some degree, even though their specificity may be low, i.e., even if they contain only a marginal portion of relevant text. Because far less large elements exist in a collection than small elements, researchers have found that it is worthwhile to return larger elements first [6], especially for INEX's *thorough* retrieval task (where systems are asked to identify all relevant elements, regardless their overlap). In the language modelling framework, this is achieved by introducing a length prior that rewards elements for their size.

In the focused task however, Table 1 shows that re-ranking the elements based on a length prior never results in the best retrieval results. This is explained by the contribution of the *specificity* dimension to the final relevance, which is captured best by the original language models. The elements pushed up the list by the length prior tend to be less specific, as they often cover more than one topic. In the generalised setting, where near-misses are allowed, removing the smallest elements is beneficial for retrieval effectiveness. In the strict case however, where near misses are not considered in the evaluation, the original ranking (without removing small elements) is the one that performs best. None of the three baseline models is satisfactory in all settings. Moreover, each of these models treat XML elements independently. We argue that in an XML retrieval setting, retrieval models should be aware of the structural relationships between elements in the tree structure. This is even more important when elements that are related through the tree hierarchy cannot all be presented to the user, as is the case in focused XML retrieval. In such a setting, the element's expected relevance of an element should depend on the expected relevance of its structurally related elements. If this structural information is already in the model, presenting a non-overlapping result list to the user becomes a presentation issue, performed by a simple post-filtering algorithm (which would work for any retrieval model). To achieve this goal, we analyse which are the relationships between retrieved elements and the most appropriate (highly relevant) elements and use this extra information to improve the initial ranking towards the task of focused retrieval.

4 Using Structural Relationships to Improve Focused Retrieval

For the reasons described in previous section, we want to extend the retrieval model in a way that the appropriate units are rewarded and therefore they get a higher score than the rest. For that, we analyse the INEX 2005 relevance assessments (version 7.0) to find out which are the relationships between retrieved elements and the most appropriate (highly relevant) elements. Once these relationships (links) are created, we use this extra information to reinforce the estimated relevance of (hopefully) the most appropriate units.

4.1 Discovering Links

To help the retrieval system to produce a proper ranking for the focused task, we need to learn what are the relationships between the retrieved XML elements in a baseline run and the elements identified in the INEX assessments as highly relevant for that topic. We consider that the most appropriate units to return to the user are those that are highly exhaustive ($E = 2$) and highly specific ($S >= 0.75$).

Our analysis is based on the top 1000 retrieved elements in a basic content-only run that uses a simple language modelling approach, which treats each element as a separate 'document' (described as $base_{LM}$ in Section 3). We study the occurrence of highly relevant elements in the direct vicinity of each retrieved element in the XML document. Since elements of different types (i.e., different tag names) are likely to show different patterns, we differentiate according to element type. In addition, we expect to observe different behaviour in front matter, body, and back matter. Figure 1 and 2 show results of an analysis of the ancestors of retrieved elements. The figure shows the probability for each level of finding the first highly relevant element when going up the tree from a retrieved element.[1] These graphs show for example that in the body part, retrieved `st` elements (section titles) are rarely relevant themselves, but their containing element, one level up, often is. The same holds for `fig` (figures)

[1] To avoid very dense graphs, we only show the most frequently retrieved element types; also the lines with very low probabilities are left out.

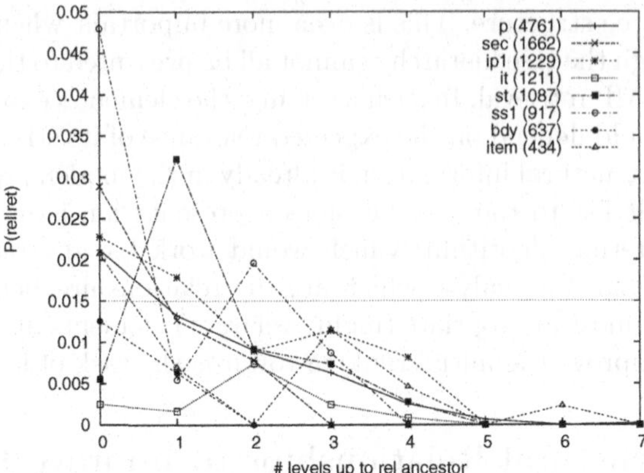

Fig. 1. Probability of finding the first highly relevant ancestor N levels up for the elements retrieved in the body

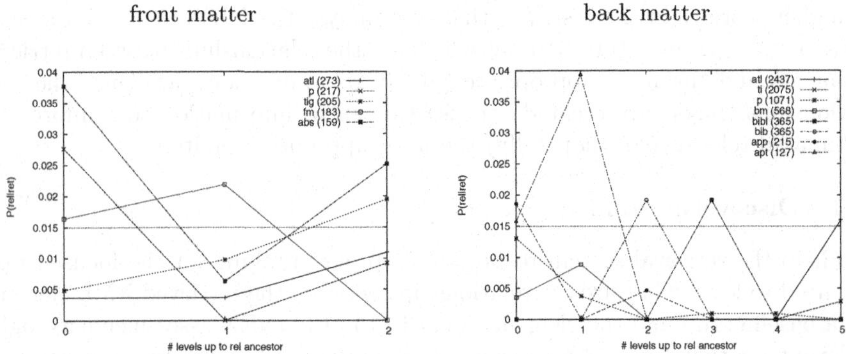

Fig. 2. Probability of finding the first highly relevant ancestor N levels up for elements retrieved in front matter and back matter

or `b` (bold) elements (not shown in the graph), while retrieved sections and subsections (`sec` and `ss1`) are mostly relevant themselves. For the retrieved elements in front and back matter (see Figure 2) it is generally needed to go more levels up to find the highly relevant elements, although elements such as `abs` (abstracts) and `p` (paragraphs) are mostly relevant themselves.

4.2 Using Links

To use the possible relationships between retrieved and highly relevant elements, we need to define a propagation method that uses this *link* information to reward highly relevant elements from the information of the retrieved ones. We propose the following approach:

For each of the element types, we create a link from that element type to the two levels where the probability of finding a highly relevant element is higher (the two highest peaks for each type in the graphs in Figure 1 and 2). For instance, in the body part of an article, a `st` (section title) will point to the containing element (level 1) but also to the parent of this element (level 2). In a similar way, a `ss1` (subsection) element will have a link to the element located two levels up in the tree structure and another one to itself (level 0).

Since to use the two highest peaks of a distribution does not mean that the probability they represent is high, we define two types of links: the *strong* ones, where the probability that the element pointed at is highly relevant exceeds a threshold, and the *weak* ones, where this probability (even being the highest for that element) is lower than the threshold. For the analysis and experiments of this first paper, we set this threshold to 0.015 (shown in all figures of Section 4.1). As an example, a subset of the INEX collection with the discovered relations is shown in Figure 3.

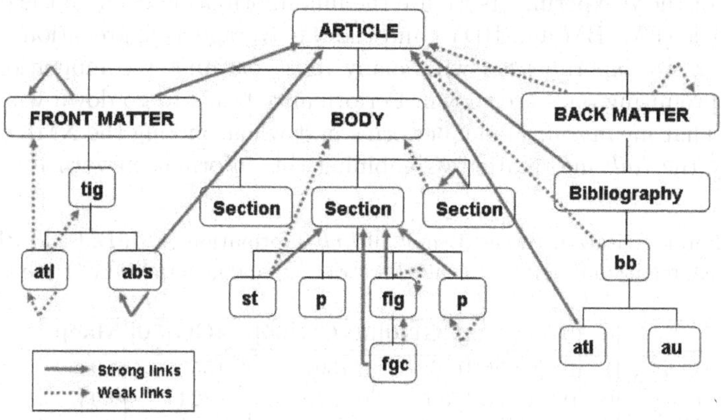

Fig. 3. Subset of article's structure with added links

Once the links and their types are defined, we need to define a model where the link information is used to propagate elements scores with the aim to reinforce the relevance of the most appropriate ones. We believe that the new score for any element in the XML document should be determined by a combination of the original score (estimated by the retrieval model) and the scores of the elements that point to it. Formally, we estimate the probability of relevance for an element in the following way:

$$P(E_j) = \alpha\ P_{LM}(E_j) + \beta\ aggr_{i \in sl(E_j)}(P_{LM}(i)) + \gamma\ aggr_{i \in wl(E_j)}(P_{LM}(i)), \quad (3)$$

where $P_{LM}(\cdot)$ is the score given to an element by the (baseline) language model; $sl(E_j)$ and $wl(E_j)$ are the sets of strong and weak links pointing to E_j; and *aggr* is an aggregation function that combines the scores of all the elements that point to E_j. Note that some of the links discovered are self references (e.g., Section to Section). This means that for these nodes, the original retrieval model score contributes to the final score in two ways, once as the original score, with weight α and once in an aggregate of strong or weak links with weight β or γ.

5 Experiments

To evaluate the performance of our approach, we experimented with: (1) The values for the parameters of our new model (Equation 3), (2) the usage of two different aggregation functions (average and max), and (3) the individual and combined contribution of the different divisions of an article: front matter (FM), back matter(BM) and body (BDY). For each of the experiments, we report results with the official INEX metrics: nxCG at three different cut-off points (10, 25 and 50) and MAep, the uninterpolated mean average effort-precision. Our baseline model is the one described in Section 3 as $base_{LM}$.

5.1 Parametrisation Values

The results of using different values for α, β, and γ in Equation 3 are shown in Table 2. For these experiments we use the link information from all the divisions of the article (FM, BM and BDY) and use the average as aggregation function.

Although we experimented with many more parameter combinations, only the most promising ones are shown. Performance tends to go down with higher α values. That means our model performs best when ranking the XML elements using only the *link* information. Combining this information with the original

Table 2. Parametrisation values. Use of all *link* information (FM, BM and BDY) and average as aggregation function. Results for strict (^{S}) and generalised (^{G}) quantisations.

	α	β	γ	**nxCG[10]**	**nxCG[25]**	**nxCG[50]**	**Maep**
$base^G_{LM}$	1	0	0	0.1621	0.1507	0.1557	0.0569
$run1^G$	0	0	1	0.1760	0.1370	0.1224	0.0375
$run2^G$	0	1	0	**0.2206**	**0.2213**	0.2235	**0.0798**
$run3^G$	0	0.9	0.1	0.2117	0.2170	0.2244	0.0783
$run4^G$	0	0.8	0.2	0.2106	0.2182	**0.2275**	0.0765
$run5^G$	0	0.7	0.3	0.2192	0.2182	0.2198	0.0746
$run6^G$	0	0.6	0.4	0.2100	0.1950	0.1998	0.0701
$run7^G$	0	0.5	0.5	0.2108	0.1926	0.2001	0.0690
$run8^G$	0.1	0.8	0.1	0.1980	0.1955	0.2055	0.0719
$run9^G$	0.1	0.7	0.2	0.2029	0.1909	0.1989	0.0700
$run10^G$	0.1	0.6	0.3	0.1999	0.1756	0.1837	0.0670
$base^S_{LM}$	1	0	0	0.1016	0.0885	0.1207	0.0536
$run1^S$	0	0	1	0.0577	0.0723	0.0796	0.0428
$run2^S$	0	1	0	**0.1154**	0.1561	**0.1696**	**0.0670**
$run3^S$	0	0.9	0.1	0.1077	**0.1577**	0.1585	0.0662
$run4^S$	0	0.8	0.2	0.0923	0.1500	0.1523	0.0563
$run5^S$	0	0.7	0.3	0.0962	0.1500	0.1515	0.0556
$run6^S$	0	0.6	0.4	0.0885	0.1207	0.1381	0.0544
$run7^S$	0	0.5	0.5	0.0846	0.1191	0.1396	0.0531
$run8^S$	0.1	0.8	0.1	0.1055	0.1570	0.1650	0.0597
$run9^S$	0.1	0.7	0.2	0.1093	0.1570	0.1650	0.0590
$run10^S$	0.1	0.6	0.3	0.1093	0.1292	0.1474	0.0582

scores of the elements hurts the performance in both quantisations. The results show that most of the parameter combinations outperform the baseline run. The run that performs better is the one that uses only the *strong* links information (run2). Note that this run already outperforms all the models described in Section 3. The most surprising result of these experiments is the big improvement obtained under the strict quantisation for nxCG at 25 and 50. That indicates that the use of the link information helps indeed in finding the most highly relevant elements.

5.2 Aggregation Functions

We experimented with two different aggregation functions: the average and the max. The average rewards the elements that have all of their inlinks relevant and punishes the ones that are pointed to also by irrelevant elements, while the max rewards the elements if they contain at least, one relevant element pointing to them, regardless of the other inlinks. We would expect that the average works well for links such as a paragraph to section, since, intuitively, a section is relevant if most of its paragraphs are. The max would work better for other types of links such as section title to section, where having only one of the inlinks relevant might already be a good indicator that the element is relevant. For these experiments we use the link information from the body part of the article (BDY) and several parametrization values. Results are shown in Table 3.

Table 3. Aggregation functions. Use of *link* information in the body part of the articles and MAX or AVG as aggregation functions. Evaluation with strict (^{S}) and generalised (^{G}) quantisations.

	α	β	γ	**nxCG[10]**		**nxCG[25]**		**nxCG[50]**		**Maep**	
				MAX	AVG	MAX	AVG	MAX	AVG	MAX	AVG
$run2^G$	0	1	0	0.2301	**0.2247**	0.2219	**0.2247**	0.2213	**0.2248**	**0.0805**	**0.0825**
$run4^G$	0	0.8	0.2	0.2350	0.2180	0.2246	0.2218	**0.2235**	0.2216	0.0801	0.0780
$run6^G$	0	0.6	0.4	**0.2404**	0.2059	**0.2267**	0.2076	0.2206	0.2093	0.0802	0.0746
$run9^G$	0.1	0.7	0.2	0.2138	0.2013	0.1964	0.1856	0.2078	0.1960	0.0720	0.0700
$run2^S$	0	1	0	**0.1173**	**0.1288**	0.1531	**0.1854**	0.1718	**0.1993**	**0.0761**	**0.0712**
$run4^S$	0	0.8	0.2	0.1000	0.0923	0.1469	0.1732	0.1676	0.1901	0.0680	0.0592
$run6^S$	0	0.6	0.4	0.0962	0.0846	0.1469	0.1716	0.1555	0.1884	0.0648	0.0587
$run9^S$	0.1	0.7	0.2	0.1170	0.1055	**0.1616**	0.1555	**0.1735**	0.1666	0.0694	0.0600

For most cases under the generalised quantisation the max operator outperforms the average. This means that the links pointing to an element are good indicators of relevance, regardless the number or relevance of other links pointing to that element. However, we can see that for nxCG at 25 and 50 under the strict quantisation, the average performs much better than the max. Which might indicate that the highly relevant elements are those that have many relevant links pointing to them.

5.3 Article's Divisions Contribution

We also analysed which of the divisions of an article contributes more to the gain of performance obtained by our approach. For that, we use the link information from each of the divisions independently and also combined. We use the max as aggregation function and two of the parametrisation value combinations. The results of these runs are shown in Table 4.

Table 4. Main article divisions: FM (front matter), BM (back matter) and BDY (body). Results using MAX as aggregation function. Evaluation with strict (^{S}) and generalised (^{G}) quantisations.

	Divisions used	α	β	γ	**nxCG[10]**	**nxCG[25]**	**nxCG[50]**	**Maep**
$base^G_{LM}$		1	0	0	0.1621	0.1507	0.1557	0.0569
$run2^G$	BM	0	1	0	0.0881	0.0662	0.0619	0.0150
$run2^G$	FM	0	1	0	0.1124	0.0826	0.0653	0.0197
$run2^G$	BDY	0	1	0	0.2301	0.2219	0.2213	0.0805
$run2^G$	BM+BDY	0	1	0	0.2123	0.1950	0.2018	0.0722
$run2^G$	FM+BDY	0	1	0	**0.2498**	**0.2413**	**0.2406**	**0.0898**
$run2^G$	BM+FM+BDY	0	1	0	0.2123	0.2003	0.2145	0.0745
$run4^G$	BM	0	0.8	0.2	0.1068	0.0760	0.0701	0.0177
$run4^G$	FM	1	0.8	0.2	0.0882	0.0713	0.0527	0.0144
$run4^G$	BDY	1	0.8	0.2	0.2350	0.2246	0.2235	0.0801
$run4^G$	BM+BDY	0	0.8	0.2	0.2229	0.1966	0.2003	0.0709
$run4^G$	FM+BDY	0	0.8	0.2	**0.2421**	**0.2366**	**0.2321**	**0.0835**
$run4^G$	BM+FM+BDY	0	0.8	0.2	0.2286	0.1981	0.2076	0.0724
$base^S_{LM}$		1	0	0	0.1016	0.0885	0.1207	0.0536
$run2^S$	BM	0	1	0	0.0000	0.0015	0.0010	0.0002
$run2^S$	FM	0	1	0	0.0170	0.0147	0.0303	0.0113
$run2^S$	BDY	0	1	0	0.1173	0.1531	0.1718	0.0761
$run2^S$	BM+BDY	0	1	0	0.1000	0.1268	0.1363	0.0649
$run2^S$	FM+BDY	0	1	0	**0.1327**	**0.1902**	**0.2134**	**0.0810**
$run2^S$	BM+FM+BDY	0	1	0	0.1077	0.1378	0.1566	0.0688
$run4^S$	BM	0	0.8	0.2	0.0077	0.0031	0.0026	0.0010
$run4^S$	FM	0	0.8	0.2	0.0115	0.0146	0.0180	0.0086
$run4^S$	BDY	0	0.8	0.2	0.1000	0.1469	0.1676	**0.0680**
$run4^S$	BM+BDY	0	0.8	0.2	0.0962	0.1191	0.1178	0.0613
$run4^S$	FM+BDY	0	0.8	0.2	**0.1038**	**0.1563**	**0.1743**	0.0674
$run4^S$	BM+FM+BDY	0	0.8	0.2	0.0962	0.1246	0.1271	0.0609

As expected, the only division that performs well on its own is the body part of the articles. To use only the links of the front and back matter hurts considerably the performance of the model. That is because with the parametrisation used, the original scores of the elements are cancelled out. Effectively, this means that elements without inlinks are removed from the result lists. When using a higher α the scores would be much better but probably not reaching the baseline model ones. For both runs and in both quantisations, the best combination is to use the front matter and the body divisions. This means that, while on its own body is the only effective document part, the links contained in the front matter are valuable. Either they point to relevant elements in the front matter itself (such as abstracts) or they help the retrieval model to give higher scores to the relevant articles. The back matter information hurts the performance of the system. A possible cause for this is that the information contained in the back matter should not be propagated up the tree but to the elements that refer to it. Further experimentation needs to be done to test this hypothesis.

6 Discussion

We presented an analysis of links between retrieved and relevant elements and used the findings to improve retrieval effectiveness in the focused retrieval task of INEX 2005. Our approach outperforms the baselines presented in all settings. Under the strict quantisation, this improvement is considerably big, indicating that the links discovered are very good pointers to highly relevant information. Perhaps our most striking finding is that the original score of an element is not a good indicator for the element's relevance. Ignoring that score and replacing it with a score based on the retrieval model scores of the elements that link to the element improves results significantly. Note that some of these links may be self links, which means that for some element types the original score *is* taken into account. We also showed that using the maximum score of all linked elements gives better results than taking an average. This indicates that a single good linked element can already indicates the merit of the element at hand. Furthermore, links from the document body turned out to be most valuable, but also front matter links contribute to the results. Back matter links are less valuable. Perhaps information from the back matter should be propagated to the elements that refer to it rather than up the tree, but this is subject to further study. Since, in the current paper, we performed the analysis and experiments in the same collection and topic set (INEX 2005), there is a big risk of overfitting. Still, we believe most of the links discovered are intuitive (e.g., section title to section or abstract to article) and therefore likely to be topic independent and recurring in other collections. If relevance assessments are not available, the discovered relationship information could be obtained from a person familiar with the XML structure of the collection (e.g. publisher) or probably by analysing clickthrough data. In any case, we showed that the structure in an XML tree can contain valuable information and therefore XML elements should not be treated independently.

References

1. Charles L. A. Clarke. Controlling Overlap in Content-Oriented XML Retrieval. In *Proceedings of the 28th Annual International ACM SIGIR Conference on Research and Development in Information Retrieval*, pages 314–321, New York, NY, USA, 2005. ACM Press.

2. Norbert Fuhr, Norbert Gövert, Gabriella Kazai, and Mounia Lalmas. INEX: INitiative for the Evaluation of XML Retrieval. In *Proceedings of the SIGIR 2002 Workshop on XML and Information Retrieval*, 2002.
3. Norbert Fuhr, Mounia Lalmas, Saadia Malik, and Gabriella Kazai, editors. *Advances in XML Information Retrieval. Fourth Workshop of the INitiative for the Evaluation of XML Retrieval (INEX 2005)*, volume 3977 of *Lecture Notes in Computer Science*. Springer-Verlag, 2006.
4. Djoerd Hiemstra. A Linguistically Motivated Probabilistic Model of Information Retrieval. In C. Nicolaou and C. Stephanidis, editors, *Proceedings of the Second European Conference on Research and Advanced Technology for Digital Libraries (ECDL)*, volume 513 of *Lecture Notes in Computer Science*, pages 569–584. Springer-Verlag, 1998.
5. Kalervo Järvelin and Jaana Kekäläinen. Cumulated gain-based evaluation of IR techniques. *ACM Trans. Inf. Syst.*, 20(4):422–446, 2002.
6. Jaap Kamps, Maarten de Rijke, and Börkur Sigurbjörnsson. Length Normalization in XML Retrieval. In *SIGIR '04: Proceedings of the 27th Annual International Conference on Research and Development in Information Retrieval*, pages 80–87. ACM Press, 2004.
7. Yosi Mass and Matan Mandelbrod. Experimenting Various User Models for XML Retrieval. In N. Fuhr, M. Lalmas, S. Malik, and G. Kazai, editors, *INEX 2005 Workshop Proceedings*, Dagstuhl, Germany, 2005.
8. Vojkan Mihajlović, Georgina Ramírez, Thijs Westerveld, Djoerd Hiemstra, Henk Ernst Blok, and Arjen P. de Vries. TIJAH Scratches INEX 2005: Vague Element Selection, Image Search, Overlap and Relevance Feedback. In N. Fuhr, M. Lalmas, S. Malik, and G. Kazai, editors, *INEX 2005 Workshop Proceedings*, Dagstuhl, Germany, 2005.
9. Jay M. Ponte and W. Bruce Croft. A Language Modeling Approach to Information Retrieval. In *SIGIR '98: Proceedings of the 21st Annual International ACM SIGIR Conference on Research and Development in Information Retrieval*, pages 275–281, New York, NY, USA, 1998. ACM Press.
10. Karen Sauvagnat, Lobna Hlaoua, and Mohand Boughanem. XFIRM at INEX 2005: ad-hoc, heterogenous and relevance feedback tracks. In N. Fuhr, M. Lalmas, S. Malik, and G. Kazai, editors, *INEX 2005 Workshop Proceedings*, Dagstuhl, Germany, 2005.

XML Fuzzy Ranking

Evangelos Kotsakis

Joint Research Center (CCR),TP267
Via Fermi 1, 21020 Ispra (VA), Italy
evangelos.kotsakis@jrc.it
http://www.jrc.it/

Abstract. This paper proposes a method of ranking XML documents with respect to an Information Retrieval query by means of fuzzy logic. The proposed method allows imprecise queries to be evaluated against an XML document collection and it provides a model of ranking XML documents. In addition the proposed method enables sophisticated ranking of documents by employing proximity measures and the concept of editing (Levenshtein) distance between terms or XML paths.

1 Introduction

Information Retrieval (IR) techniques have traditionally been applied to search large sets of textual data. The emerge of XML as a standard for data representation and exchange on the Internet poses new challenges to structured document retrieval. Integrating IR and XML search techniques could enable more sophisticated search on the structure as well as the content of the documents. Some of the recent XML-IR proposals [6, 8, 11, 4, 2] focus on indexing for improving the execution of simple IR-like queries. Other approaches [9, 15, 25] are based on soft computing techniques to model uncertainty. This paper is closer to the second approach and it uses fuzzy logic to rank the documents of an XML collection with respect an IR query. Ranking of structured documents is very important and may further boost the quality of the results. Ranking structured documents is mainly based on probabilistic models [24, 21, 11, 26] by mainly using the *idf* (inverse document frequency) and *tf*, within document frequency of terms.

Searching effectively large collections of XML documents requires a knowledge of the documents structure. For instance, using XQuery [5], it requires some knowledge on the XML schema (or DTD) [1, 3]. On the other hand searching XML documents from the Information Retrieval (IR) point of view requires little knowledge on the structure of the documents. Although knowledge on the XML schema could be desirable to reduce extensive search, it is not required. Another important aspect in retrieving XML documents is the relevance of the retrieved documents to the submitted query. In most cases, we are not interested in finding XML documents that exactly match the query but rather in XML documents, which are relevant to the query to some extent. Our tolerance to accept in the result set XML documents that do not precisely match the query is stemmed from the fact that the query itself is not precise. IR based queries cannot be precise mainly due to the lack of knowledge of the underlying document

H.L. Larsen et al. (Eds.): FQAS 2006, LNAI 4027, pp. 159–169, 2006.

collection structure and the inherent difficulty to formulate a query that precisely reflects what we are looking for. On the other hand, the relevance is by nature a *fuzzy concept*. So it seems that the employment of fuzzy logic for estimating the relevance of the documents to a given query is more expressive and promising.

Modeling vagueness in information retrieval has been addressed by several researchers [14, 15, 18, 25, 9] and recently in the area of XML documents through the INEX workshops [28, 7]. Weighted boolean models [14] have been proposed to handle constraints imposed by the query terms. Fuzzy set theory has been proposed [15, 16, 18, 25] for modeling flexible information retrieval systems. Models for integrating IR and database systems is presented in [12]. In the area of structured documents [25] fuzzy aggregations have been employed to facilitate retrieval. A survey on information retrieval techniques based on soft computing (mainly fuzzy sets and neural networks) is presented in [18]. In [9] the logical structure among objects have been employed to model structured documents in which the logical structure among objects is captured by means of knowledge augmentation. While in classical retrieval the quality is estimated by means of *idf* (inverse document frequency) and *tf* (within document term frequency), [27] proposes a third dimension called *accessibility* that captures the structure of the document. Vague queries and inexact data matching in databases is proposed in [22] and fuzzy Hamming distance that extends the Hamming concept for measuring dissimilarity between vector objects is proposed in [17].

This paper proposes a fuzzy logic based technique for ranking XML documents against a given query. The employment of fuzzy logic enables more sophisticated ranking by exploiting the imprecise formulation of the queries. To achieve this, a database is used for indexing purposes and for storing all the *facts* that constitute the XML document collection. Fuzzy measurements based on editing distance are used to handle uncertainty and imprecision. The rest of the paper is organized as follows: Section 2 discusses the IR query format. Fuzzy ranking is discussed in section 3. The realization of the database structure used to facilitate the ranking is presented in section 4. The fuzzy relevance of a document against to a subquery is discussed in the section 5. Some implementation notes are presented in the section 6 and the section 7 summarizes the contributions and concludes the paper.

2 Query Format

XML Querying mechanisms that facilitate Information Retrieval (IR) should allow the formulation of simple queries that require no knowledge of the underlying structure of the XML document collection. However, the query method should be also flexible enough to allow more complex queries that take into consideration the structure of the underlying documents. In addition the query mechanism should also allow the user to focus the search on particular XML elements that might be more interesting. So, element prioritization that reflects the importance of the element in context and in relation with other elements is equally important.

The proposed IR query model is relatively simple and it has been derived from Xpath [13] by adopting only the basic expressions for addressing parts of XML documents. Only few of the Xpath location paths and core function are supported. The objective is to keep the querying mechanism as simple as possible.

A query Q consists of one or more sub-queries q_i, each one being a simplified Xpath expression. The sub-queries can be connected with each other using ordinary conjunction and disjunction operators. Each sub-query is associated with a weight, which is called *relative importance*. The relative importance R is used as a tool that allows the user to express its preferences on particular sub-queries. This is a user defined quantity. Let n be the number of sub-queries that forms the query Q, then R and Q could be expressed as vectors.

$$Q = (q_1, q_2, \ldots, q_n)$$

$$R = (r_1, r_2, \ldots, r_n)$$

The relative importance R is defined such as

$$\sum_{i=0}^{n} r_i = 1$$

Each sub-query consists of two main components: the first one is for expressing the path and the second one for expressing a literal term found at the end of the path. For example the sub-query `/article/*/name[Kevin]` consists of the path expression `/article/*/name` and the literal term "Kevin", which is in fact part of the atomic value of the element "name". Special symbols such as * (matching any element) and // (descendent axis) could also be used to express a path.

Example 1. Consider the following XML file:

```
<article>
    <title> Knowledge-Based Automation Software</title>
    <author>
        <name> Kevin Smith</name>
        <affiliation> Member of IEEE</affiliation>
    </author>
    <abstract>
        This paper describes a knowledge-based approach to automate
        a software design method for concurrent systems. Production
        rules provide the mechanism for codifying a set of heuristics.
    </abstract>
</article>
```

A typical IR query and its associated "relative importance" vector could be formed as follows:

$$Q = \begin{pmatrix} q_1 : & //author/*[smith] \wedge \\ q_2 : & //abstract[knowledge] \wedge \\ q_3 : & /article/title[knowledge] \end{pmatrix}$$

$$R = (0.4, 0.2, 0.4)$$

The query Q above consists of three sub-queries q_1, q_2 and q_3 whose relative importance are 0.4, 0.2 and 0.4 respectively. The term *"knowledge"* found in the *"title"* element would yield a score twice as big as if it was found in the *"abstract"* element. This shows that the user is interested more about the term *knowledge* found in *title* rather in *abstract*. Using the relative importance vector, the user can focus the search on particular paths of the collection and retrieve those XML documents that are more relevant according to the user preferences.

3 Fuzzy Ranking

Suppose $D = (d_1, d_2, \ldots, d_m)$ is the vector representing the XML documents of the collection and $Q = (q_1, q_2, \ldots, q_n)$ is the vector representing the query. The problem is to find those XML documents that best satisfy the query or in other words they are relevant to the query. The relevance of the document d_i with respect to the sub-query q_j is measured by a rating, which is called *Degree of Satisfaction* DS_{ij}. The degree of satisfaction DS_i of the document d_i is defined by the following vector:

$$DS_i = (DS_{i1}, DS_{i2}, \ldots, DS_{in}) \tag{1}$$

Let $R = (r_1, r_2, \ldots, r_n)$ be the relative importance vector, then the relative degree of satisfaction DS_i^r of the document d_i is defined as

$$DS_i^r = (r_1 \cdot DS_{i1}, r_2 \cdot DS_{i2}, \ldots, r_n \cdot DS_{in}) \tag{2}$$

Which is in fact comprised of the performance of the document d_i on the n sub-queries taking into consideration the relative importance of the sub-query. Let $DS_{ij}^r = r_j \cdot DS_{ij}$ then the matrix in equation 3 gives the relative degree of satisfaction DS^r for the whole XML collection with respect to the query Q and the relative importance vector R.

$$DS^r = \begin{bmatrix} DS_{11}^r & DS_{12}^r & \ldots & DS_{1j}^r & \ldots & DS_{1n}^r \\ DS_{21}^r & DS_{22}^r & \ldots & DS_{2j}^r & \ldots & DS_{2n}^r \\ \vdots & \vdots & \ldots & \vdots & \ldots & \vdots \\ DS_{i1}^r & DS_{i2}^r & \ldots & DS_{ij}^r & \ldots & DS_{in}^r \\ \vdots & \vdots & \ldots & \vdots & \ldots & \vdots \\ DS_{m1}^r & DS_{m2}^r & \ldots & DS_{mj}^r & \ldots & DS_{mn}^r \end{bmatrix} \tag{3}$$

DS_{ij}^r is a real number within the interval $[0, 1]$ and represents the satisfaction of the document d_i with respect to the sub-query q_j. The estimation of DS_{ij} is discussed in section 5. This section explains how to rank the documents employing fuzzy logic by using the matrix in equation 3.

Suppose that the sub-queries $q_j, \forall j \in \{1 \dots n\}$ are connected with each other with disjunction, conjunction and negation operators. Each sub-query q_j may be seen as a fuzzy condition. In practice the definitions of the operators AND, OR and NOT may vary, but one popular definition is shown in Table 1.

Table 1. Fuzzy operators

Operator	Symbol	Definition
AND	$\wedge$	minimum value
OR	$\vee$	maximum value
NOT	$\neg$	negation (complement to 1)

Let w_i be the ranking weight of the document d_i with respect to the query Q, then w_i is given by the following tuple:

$$w_i = [DS_i^r, (Q, \vee, \wedge, \neg)] \tag{4}$$

Where DS_i^r is the document d_i relative satisfaction vector given by the equation 2 and $(Q, \vee, \wedge, \neg)$ is the query vector with the fuzzy connectors. The following example show how the value of w_i is calculated.

Example 2. Suppose we have three XML documents d_1, d_2 and d_3 and a query Q with three sub-queries q_1, q_2 and q_3, which are connected as $Q = q_1 \wedge (q_2 \vee q_3)$. Suppose also that the relative importance vector is $R = (0.31, 0.27, 0.42)$ and the degree of satisfaction DS matrix is given by

$$DS = \begin{bmatrix} 0.2 & 0.3 & 0.1 \\ 0.4 & 0.5 & 0.35 \\ 0.6 & 0.15 & 0.25 \end{bmatrix}$$

From the above, the relative degree of satisfaction DS^r is given by

$$DS^r = \begin{bmatrix} 0.31 \cdot 0.2 & 0.27 \cdot 0.3 & 0.42 \cdot 0.1 \\ 0.31 \cdot 0.4 & 0.27 \cdot 0.5 & 0.42 \cdot 0.35 \\ 0.31 \cdot 0.6 & 0.27 \cdot 0.15 & 0.42 \cdot 0.25 \end{bmatrix} = \begin{bmatrix} 0.0868 & 0.081 & 0.042 \\ 0.1736 & 0.135 & 0.147 \\ 0.2604 & 0.0405 & 0.105 \end{bmatrix}$$

By taking into account the definition in table 1, the ranking weights w_1, w_2 and w_3 of the documents d_1, d_2 and d_3 respectively are estimated as follows:

$$W = \begin{bmatrix} w_1 \\ w_2 \\ w_3 \end{bmatrix} = \begin{bmatrix} min(0.0868, max(0.081, 0.042)) \\ min(0.1736, max(0.135, 0.147)) \\ min(0.2604, max(0.0405, 0.105)) \end{bmatrix} = \begin{bmatrix} 0.081 \\ 0.147 \\ 0.105 \end{bmatrix}$$

Therefore, the highest ranked document to the query Q is document d_2, then it comes d_3 and d_1.

4 Database Structure

Before discussing the estimation of the Degree of Satisfaction DS_{ij}, it helps to understand how the XML documents have been stored in a relational database and how the XML facts (terms, paths, documents etc.) have been structured and the posting information is used to derive weights for both path expressions and literal terms.

The following entities are used to index an XML document collection:

$$paths\,(\underline{path\_id}, path\_name)$$
$$terms\,(\underline{term\_id}, term\_name, IDF)$$
$$docs\,(\underline{doc\_id}, doc\_name)$$

A *path_name* is a string of tags separated by slash (i.e. /article/author/name). The *"paths"* entity contains only those paths whose leafs are simple elements, that is, at the end of the path there is always a simple content elements (i.e. #PCDATA)

The *"terms"* entity contains every single term (excluding the stop words), which is not a tag, that is, it appears within the simple content of an element. An associated IDF (Inverse Document Frequency) value is also associated with each term of the XML document collection.

The *"docs"* entity contains information about each XML document of the collection. Relationships between the above three entities have been also defined in a way that reflects the structure of the XML document of the collection.

The above structure has been realized in a relational database. Figure 1 shows the schema of the database.

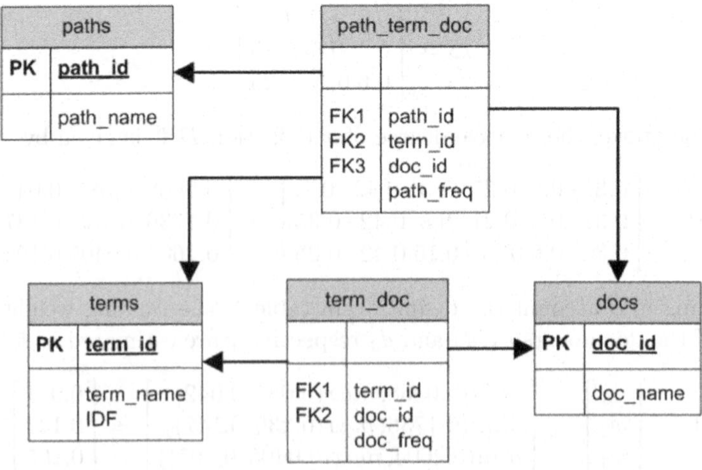

Fig. 1. Physical implementation of the database structure used to store an XML document collection

path_freq is the frequency of the term in the path and *doc_freq* is the frequency of the term in the XML document.

5 Degree of Satisfaction (DS)

The degree of satisfaction DS_{ij} represents the relevance of the document d_i with respect to the sub-query q_j. The sub-query q_j consists of two parts; the first one is the path expression $path(q_j)$ and the second one is the literal term expression $term(q_j)$ at the end of the path. The relevance of the document d_i to the sub-query q_j depends on the degree that q_j matches a path-term pair of d_i.

Suppose that the document d_i has k paths, $p_1, p_2, \dots p_k$ and l terms, $t_1, t_2, \dots, t_l$. By calculating the Levenshtein (or editing) distance between the $path(q_j)$ and each p_s for $s = 1 \dots k$, it yields a fuzzy number δ_{ij}

$$\delta_{ij} = \{\frac{v_1}{p_1}, \frac{v_2}{p_2}, \dots, \frac{v_k}{p_k}\}$$

The Levenshtein distance between paths is calculated by using the path tags as the editing granule. That is, */article/author* and */article/author/name* have Levenshtein distance equal to 1; it needs to delete one tag (i.e. "name") of the second to get the former. In case path expressions contain the descendant axis ("//") operator, the estimated distance is the minimum Levenshtein distance taken from all possible matches. For instance, in the XML document in the Example 1, the paths *//abstract* and *//name* match the paths */article/abstract* and */article/author/name* respectively whose distance is 3 (1 deletion and 2 insertions; substitution cost is double the insertion/deletion cost) and thus the distance between *//abstract* and *//name* is 3. In the case we had more than one matches, the minimum distance of all possible matches determines the distance between the paths. The value v_x for $x = 1 \dots k$ is the membership value and it is given by

$$v_x = e^{-x} \tag{5}$$

Where x is the Levenshtein distance between the $path(q_j)$ and p_x. The exponential function in equation 5 yields 1 (perfect match) when the Levenshtein distance $x = 0$. On the other hand when the distance gets larger, it tends to be zero. Figure 2 shows a graphical representation of the exponential membership function based on the editing distance.

The concept of editing distance is again applied to the comparison of the terms $t_1, t_2, \dots, t_l$ of the document d_i with $term(q_j)$, but in this case the editing granule is a single character rather a tag. The comparison yields a fuzzy number μ_{ij}, which is given by

$$\mu_{ij} = \{\frac{u_1}{t_1}, \frac{u_2}{t_2}, \dots, \frac{u_l}{t_l}\}$$

Again u_x is given by an exponential function in equation 5 where x is the editing distance between the term t_x and $term(q_j)$.

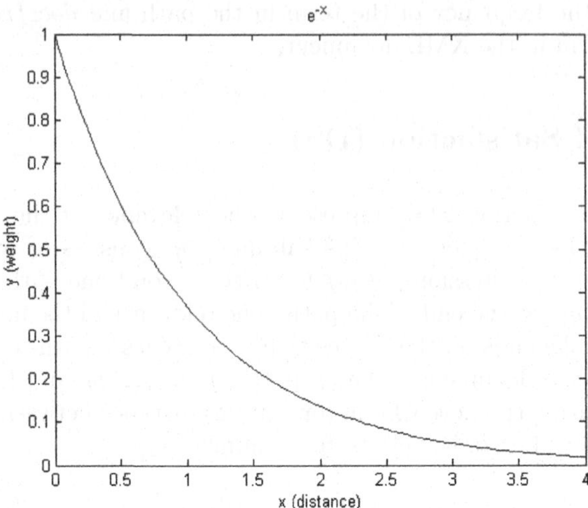

Fig. 2. $y = e^{-x}$ is the the fuzzy membership function representing the degree of *fuzzy* matching between two terms or paths given their Levenshtein distance x

Let M_i be the binary matrix i.e., a matrix each of whose elements is 0 or 1, that represents the binding of terms and paths in the document d_i. An element m_{xy} of the binary matrix is 1 when the path p_x contains the literal term t_y.

The degree of satisfaction DS_{ij} of the document d_i with respect to the sub-query q_j is given as

$$DS_{ij} = max\{m_{xy}min(v_x, u_y), \forall x, y \in d_i\} \tag{6}$$

Where $x = 1 \ldots k$ represents the paths in d_i and $y = 1 \ldots l$ represents the terms in d_i and m_{xy} is the corresponding entry of the binary matrix M_i. The above definition guarantees that if the sub-query q_j matches exactly a path-term pair of the document d_i the DS_{ij} is 1, otherwise if the matching is inexact, it will be a number within the interval $[0, 1]$.

Example 3. Suppose a document d has the following paths $p_1 = /article/author/name$, $p_2 = /article/title$ and the terms $t_1 = santos$, $t_2 = know$ and $t_3 = information$. A sub-query q could be $/article/author[santo]$ with $path(q) = /article/author$ and $term(q) = santo$. Let's assume that the binary matrix M is as follows:

$$M = \begin{bmatrix} 1 & 0 \\ 0 & 1 \\ 0 & 1 \end{bmatrix}$$

The matrix above shows that the term t_1 is under the path p_1, while the terms t_2 and t_3 are under the path p_2. Suppose that the cost of the Levenshtein editing operations are 1 for deletion and insertion and 2 for substitution, then δ and μ are as follows:

$$\delta = \{\frac{e^{-1}}{p_1}, \frac{e^{-2}}{p_2}\}$$

$$\mu = \{\frac{e^{-1}}{t_1}, \frac{e^{-5}}{t_2}, \frac{e^{-10}}{t_3}\}$$

The degree of satisfaction DS of the document d with respect to the sub-query q is given by

$$DS = max\{1 \cdot min(e^{-1}, e^{-1}), 1 \cdot min(e^{-2}, e^{-5}), 1 \cdot min(e^{-2}, e^{-10})\} = e^{-1}.$$

6 System Implementation

A prototype of the system has been developed using mainly open source software components. The database has been realized using the MySQL DBMS. All tools for processing the XML documents have been implemented in Perl [19]. For parsing the XML documents a module that is based on *Expat* [20] has been used. For manipulating the XML elements, the LibXML module has been utilized. LibXML supports a major standard for XML processing known as the Document Object Model (DOM) [23]. The web interface for submitting the queries has been realized using PHP [10]. For testing the system, the INEX 2002 [28, 7] XML document collection has been used.

7 Conclusions

This paper proposes a method of ranking XML documents, which is based on fuzzy logic. The advantages of the proposed method are the following:

- Allows the formulation of imprecise queries
- The use of fuzzy logic provides a quantitative tool for measuring the inexact matching between paths or other XML terms
- Easy to implement it
- The editing distance between paths provides an effective way to quantify the relevance of the paths according to their similarity against the query terms

Employing fuzzy logic seems to be a natural way to handle imprecision in evaluating XML-IR based queries. The combination of fuzzy measurements with probabilistic measurements may further improve the ranking quality.

References

1. Tim Bray, Jean Paoli, C. M. Sperberg-McQueen, Eve Maler and François Yergeau (eds): Extensible Markup Language (XML) 1.0 (Third Edition). W3C Recommendation, 04 February 2004. http://www.w3.org/TR/REC-xml/
2. Evangelos Kotsakis: XSD: A Hierarchical Access Method for Indexing XML Schemata. Knowledge and Information Systems **4**(2):168–201 (2002), Springer-Verlag.

3. David C. Fallside and Priscilla Walmsley (eds): XML Schema Part 0: Primer Second Edition. W3C Recommendation, 28 October 2004. http://www.w3.org/TR/xmlschema-0/
4. Holger Meyer, Ilvio Bruder, Andreas Heuer, Gunnar Weber: The Xircus Search Engine. Proceedings of the First Workshop of the INitiative for the Evaluation of XML Retrieval (INEX), Schloss Dagstuhl, Germany, December 9-11, 2002, pp. 119–124
5. Scott Boag, Don Chamberlin, Mary F. Fernández, Daniela Florescu, Jonathan Robie and Jérôme Siméon (eds): XQuery 1.0: An XML Query Language. W3C Candidate Recommendation, 3 November 2005. http://www.w3.org/TR/xquery/
6. Evangelos Kotsakis. Structured Information Retrieval in XML documents. In Proceedings of the seventeenth ACM Symposium on Applied Computing (SAC 2002), pp. 663–667, Madrid, Spain, March 10-14, 2002.
7. Initiative for the Evaluation of XML retrieval, INEX 2002, DELOS Network of Excellence for Digital Libraries, http://qmir.dcs.qmul.ac.uk/inex/index.html
8. Carlo Combi, Barbara Oliboni and Rosalba Rossato: Querying XML Documents by Using Association Rules, 16th International Workshop on Database and Expert Systems Applications (DEXA'05) (2005) pp. 1020–1024, Copenhagen, Denmark.
9. Mounia Lalmas, Thomas Rölleke: Four-Valued Knowledge Augmentation for Structured Document Retrieval. International Journal of Uncertainty, Fuzziness and Knowledge-Based Systems **11**(1): 67-86 (2003)
10. PHP Documentation Group: PHP-Hypertext Preprocessor, http://www.php.net/
11. Felix Weigel, Holger Meuss, Klaus U. Schulz and Francois Bry: Content and Structure in Indexing and Ranking XML, Proceedings of the 7th International Workshop on the Web and Databases (WebDB)(2004), Paris, France.
12. Norbert Fuhr: Models for Integrated Information Retrieval and Database Systems, IEEE Bulletin of the Technical Committe on Data Enginnering, Vol. 19 No. 1, March 1996 pp 3–13
13. James Clark and Steve DeRose (eds): XML Path Language (XPath) Version 1.0. W3C Recommendation, 16 November 1999. http://www.w3.org/TR/xpath
14. G. Pasi: A logical formulation of the Boolean model and of weighted Boolean models, Workshop on Logical and Uncertainty Models for Information Systems (LUMIS 99), University College London, 5-6 July 1999.
15. G. Bordogna, G. Pasi: Modeling Vagueness in Information Retrieval, in LNCS-1980 M. Agosti, F. Crestani and G. Pasi eds, "Lectures on Information Retrieval: Third European Summer-School, ESSIR 2000, Varenna, Italy, September 11-15, 2000, Springer Verlag, 2001.
16. Ronald R. Yager, Henrik Legind Larsen: Retrieving Information by Fuzzification of Queries. J. Intell. Inf. Syst. **2**(4): 421-441 (1993)
17. Abraham Bookstein, Shmuel Tomi Klein and Timo Raita: Fuzzy Hamming Distance: A New Dissimilarity Measure, In Lecture Notes in Computer Science Volume 2089 / 2001 A. Amir, G.M. Landau (Eds.): Combinatorial Pattern Matching: 12th Annual Symposium, CPM 2001 Jerusalem, Israel, July 1-4, 2001.
18. F. Crestani and G. Pasi: Soft Information Retrieval: Applications of Fuzzy Set Theory and Neural Networks, in Neuro-fuzzy tools and techniques, N.Kasabov Editor, Physica-Verlag , Springer-Verlag Group, 1999, pp. 287-313.
19. Larry Wall, Tom Christiansen and Jon Orwant: Programming Perl, 3rd Edition, July 2000, O'Reilly, ISBN: 0-596-00027-8
20. The Expat XML Parser, by James Clark http://expat.sourceforge.net/

21. Jens E. Wolff, Holger Flörke and Armin B. Cremers: XPRES: a Ranking Approach to Retrieval on Structured Documents. Technical Report JAI-TR-99-12, Institute of Computer Science III (1999)
22. Raquel Kolitski Stasiu, Carlos A. Heuser and Roberto da Silva: Estimating Recall and Precision for Vague Queries in Databases, In Lecture Notes in Computer Science Volume 3520, Oscar Pastor, Joo Falco e Cunha (eds: Advanced Information Systems Engineering: 17th International Conference, CAiSE 2005, Porto, Portugal, June 13-17, 2005, Springer Berlin
23. Document Object Model (DOM), http://www.w3.org/DOM/
24. Norbert Fuhr: A Probabilistic Framework for Vague Queries and Imprecise Information in Databases. Proceedings of VLDB 90, pp. 696-707, 1990.
25. Gabriella Kazai, Mounia Lalmas, Thomas Rölleke: A Model for the Representation and Focussed Retrieval of Structured Documents Based on Fuzzy Aggregation, String Processing and Information Retrieval (SPIRE) 2001: 123-135
26. Katsuya Masuda: A Ranking model of proximal and structural text retrieval based on region algebra. In Proceedings of the 41st Annual Meeting on Association for Computational Linguistics (ACL'03)- Volume 2, Pages: 50 – 57, Sapporo, Japan (2003)
27. Thomas Rölleke, Mounia Lalmas, Gabriella Kazai, Ian Ruthven, and Stefan Quicker: The Accessibility Dimension for Structured Document Retrieval, Lecture Notes in Computer Science Volume 2291/2002,Springer Berlin
28. Gabriella Kazai, Norbert Gövert, Mounia Lalmas, Norbert Fuhr: The INEX Evaluation Initiative, Lecture Notes in Computer Science Volume 2818/2003, Pages: 279 - 293, Springer Berlin

A Flexible News Filtering Model Exploiting a Hierarchical Fuzzy Categorization

Gloria Bordogna[1], Marco Pagani[1], Gabriella Pasi[2], and Robert Villa[2]

[1] CNR IDPA via Pasubio 5, 24044 Dalmine (BG) Italy
gloria.bordogna@idpa.cnr.it,
marco.pagani@idpa.cnr.it
[2] Università degli Studi di Milano Bicocca
Via Bicocca degli Arcimboldi 8, 20133 Milano, Italy
pasi@disco.unimib.it,
peng2@itc.cnr.it

Abstract. In this paper we present a novel news filtering model based on flexible and soft filtering criteria and exploiting a fuzzy hierarchical categorization of news. The filtering module is designed to provide news professionals and general users with an interactive and personalised tool for news gathering and delivery. It exploits content-based filtering criteria and category-based filtering techniques to deliver to the user a ranked list of either news or clusters of news. In fact, if the user prefers to have a synthetic view of the topics of recent news pushed by the stream, the system filters groups (clusters) of news having homogenous contents, identified automatically by the application of a fuzzy clustering algorithm that organizes the recent news into a fuzzy hierarchy. The filter can be trained explicitly by the user to learn his/her interests as well as implicitly by monitoring his/her interaction with the system. Several filtering criteria can be applied to select and rank news to the users based on the user's information preferences and presentation preferences. User preferences specify what information (the contents of interest) is relevant to the user, the sources that provide reliable information, and the period of time during which the information remains relevant. Each individual news or cluster of news homogeneous with respect to their content is selected based on a customizable multi criteria decision making approach and ranked based on a combination of criteria specified by the user in his/her presentation preferences.

1 Introduction

The huge amount of multimedia information available on the World Wide Web continues to stimulate the development of systems that support the easy access to information relevant to specific users' needs. These systems try to find a solution to the decision-making problem: how can the information items corresponding to the users' information preferences be identified [8]? Recommender systems and document filtering systems are information systems that work by directly pushing relevant information to user who does not have to formulate any explicit request, but solely based on a user profile representing user interests [2][9][19].

H.L. Larsen et al. (Eds.): FQAS 2006, LNAI 4027, pp. 170–184, 2006.

An important characteristic that must be ensured by a filtering system is flexibility intended as the ability of the system to customize its behaviour (selection and ranking criteria) to the personal interests and context of users.

In the present contribution we propose a novel news filtering model designed so as to meet flexibility at distinct levels:

- in modelling the capability to be both tolerant to the vagueness and uncertainty in judging the relevance of news to a specific user varying in time;
- in learning the changes of users' preferences over time;
- in "cataloguing" news into a flexible topical structure so as to give users a synthetic view of the main topics of interest dealt with in recent news.
- in presenting the filtered results to the user providing a way to customize the ranking criteria to the user, so as to provide full control on the results.

The result of such a filtering module is to push a ranked list of individual news and group of news, differentiated for distinct users, based on users profiles, and for a single user with respect to his/her information and presentation preferences varying over time.

In the following section we recall the main filtering models; in section 3 we illustrate the news filtering requirements and architectural specifications; in section 4 we present the architecture of the filtering module based on five main components; the fuzzy clustering algorithm designed to support news filtering is described in section 5, and the personalized filtering criteria are illustrated in section 6. The conclusions summarize the main characteristic of the proposed filtering approach.

2 Related Projects

A simple model of filtering that provides a convenient starting point was proposed by Belkin and Croft [2]. In this model the main components are the stream of incoming data, the user profiles, which represent the needs of the users of the filtering system, and a matching function that selects the items relevant to the users interest. The user can then evaluate the filtered results by explicitly activating a feedback to modify the user profile (the representation of user interests). This model does not define whether a profile corresponds to an individual user or a group or users. In most of the filtering works, a profile is assumed to correspond to an individual user (i.e. is a 'user profile'). Newer work has generally split feedback on the user interest into two types, implicit and explicit [1] [13]. Explicit feedback is where the user must explicitly indicate the relevance or utility of a document or group of documents, such as marking a document as relevant, or providing a rating for the document. Implicit feedback is where the actions of the user are recorded, and the view of the user is inferred from those actions. For example, some systems assume that the length of time a document is open will correspond to the interest the user has in the document (i.e. the longer a user reads a document, the more interesting that document will be to them).

A refinement of the filtering model by Belkin and Croft, is described by Oard and Marchionini [17] and depicted in Figure 1.

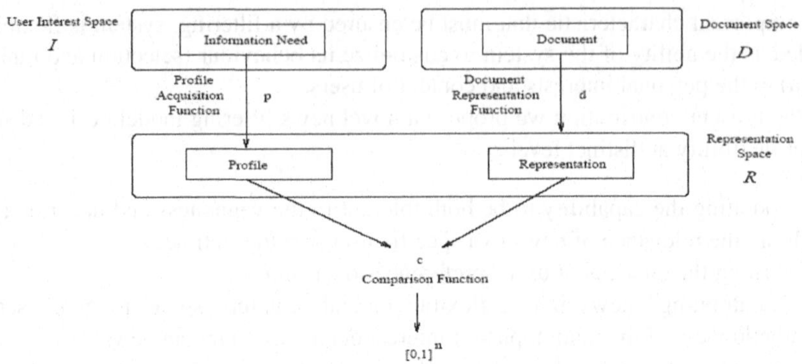

Fig. 1. Basic representation of a filtering model

In a very large number of filtering systems, documents and profiles are both represented by conventional IR style term vectors of weights (the significance degrees of the index terms in the documents and in the text describing the user's interests respectively), and the comparison is carried out with conventional measures such as the cosine similarity measure.

A common way of looking at text filtering is as a text retrieval problem, where the "query" is the profile, and the document stream is a continuously changing collection of documents. An alternative is to reverse this, and consider each new document as a query for the system, which should then retrieve the one or more profiles, which are most relevant to this document [9][10].

This way of seeing filtering is called *content-based* filtering. The heart of content-based filtering systems is a "matching function", which compares each new document with a user profile, and based on this matching determines the relevance or non-relevance of the document to the profile. Content-based filtering can therefore be seen as a type of document classification. Some classic content based filtering systems include SIFT and Okapi [24][3] [19].

Collaborative filtering is an alternative to content based filtering, which is based on the idea that similar people will use similar documents. Rather than using the content of the documents, it uses user ratings of documents. Based on these user ratings, the systems are able to compute the similarity between users based on their previous activity, and then recommend documents that have been used by one person, to other people who have similar needs. Collaborative filtering systems are also often called recommender systems for this reason. Classic collaborative filtering systems include GroupLens and the Amazon CF system [15]. Collaborative filtering techniques can recommend any type of document (either, texts, images in any format) since do not require the representation of their content [7]. The problem with their use is the start up of the system when no or very few user rating is available.

This is the reason that motivates the coupling of the two techniques in a single system [6]. One potential problem with these filtering systems is that all reasoning is done online, and this can result in an inefficient system when users expect quick responses. This time restriction becomes and obstacle to the improvement or extensions of the content-based filtering strategies. In order to improve both speed and effectiveness, current approaches to building filtering systems often try to perform some of the reasoning offline using clustering techniques [14][22][23]. Clustering can be adopted either to group users having potential similar interests, or to group the documents in topic categories, or even for both tasks. The clustering module is run off-line periodically so as to identify a reasonable number of documents' representatives (centroids) that can directly be matched with the user interests in the profiles thus reducing the number of the matching operations necessary to identify the interesting documents and achieving a speed up of the filtering task and an improvement of its effectiveness.

A novel approach in highly dynamic contexts where data change frequently, is called *category-based* filtering [21]. Category-based filtering can be seen mainly as an extension to existing filtering strategies in which user preferences reflect attitudes not towards single items, but categories of similar items. Its main characteristic is that selection of information is based on category ratings instead of single item ratings, in contrast to other content-based filtering strategies. To function, category-based filtering requires categorization of every item, either manually or by an automated process such as clustering. Selecting items based on category ratings instead of ratings of individual items is especially suited for domains where there is a constant flow of new information (e.g. news and adverts).

The filtering model that we propose integrates content-based filtering criteria with category-based filtering techniques so as to be much more flexible than traditional systems. In the next section the analysis of the user requirements and the design specifications of the filtering module are described.

3 The Filtering Requirements and Design Specifications

3.1 Requirement Analysis for the Filtering

The main objective of the proposed filtering system is to collect news from both newsfeeds and specialised archives in a personalised way and to push customized individual news and news stories (groups of news about the same topics) towards the user. From the users' requirements analysis the following primary needs for the filtering module have been identified [5].

User friendliness: the system must be easy for the journalists to use.
Freedom: the journalists need to control (and feel they have control) over the filtering criteria, i.e., the filtering criteria should be customisable and transparent to the user.
Narrowing the fields: journalists are scared of missing information, especially the system automatically filtering out potentially useful material; therefore the filtering criteria should not reject any potentially relevant news, but should tolerate degrees of under-satisfaction of the user's interests.
Full text indexing: filtering should be done based on the analysis of the full text of articles.
News lifecycle: the system should keep track of the filtered news over time, organising and grouping related news together, especially chronologically, and by news story, i.e. homogeneous topics. Further the novelty of a news with respect to the

ones already analysed should be evaluated since previously unseen news can have a greater relevance than already filtered ones.

Further, some wishes of the filtering module have also been identified:

"Comparison" functionality: Provide ways for journalists to find different views of the same subject or event. For example, a news can be viewed as part of several news stories depending on the focus on which we place the attention. Another example could be to have a method of finding the "source" or the latest news of a story, i.e., the first (last) news appearing on the stream about a topics.

3.2 Design Specifications for the Filtering Module

From the analysis of the users' requirements the following design specifications for the filtering module have been identified [5] .

A *user profile* is defined containing all data relating to a single user, split into the following rough categories [1].

Personal information, such as name, email etc of the user.

Information preferences intended as **what** information, from **where** (which information source) and **when** (the period of time in which the information remains of interest). The way in which **what**, i.e. the *user interest* or contents of interest to the user, is identified is based on both explicit specification of the user (explicit feedback through a set of keywords or a textual description) and implicit monitoring of the user-system interaction (implicit feedback exploiting accessed documents, documents printed, the time spent in reading a document as indications that the contents of those documents are of interest). The implementation of this learning capability of user interests responds to the need of a user *friendliness system*, not requiring too much burden to the user. The documents identified this way represent contents of interest to the user and are indexed by a full-text indexing procedure so as to satisfy the requirement *full text indexing*. The from **where** specification, i.e. the information sources of interest to monitor, are explicitly indicated by the user; further a trust score for each of them is both explicitly associated by the user himself or implicitly guessed by the system based on the frequency of interesting news originated by a source. Trust scores are conceived as indications of the potential reliability of the information sources to a specific user with respect to a given topical area, thus they influence the ranking of interesting news and not their selection, so as not to miss potentially relevant information generated by not trusted sources (which responds to the user requirement *Narrowing the fields*). Finally, the time in which the news arrives to the user, is compared to the **when** specification of the user, i.e., the period of time for which the news remains of interest to the user (to satisfy the *News lifecycle* requirement). Also this criterion influences the ranking and not the selection of news. An example of information preference specifying one single user interest, where and when preferences about it is reported in table 1.

Presentation preferences , i.e. how the information is to be displayed: several presentation modalities are possible:

- *single news* ranked based on a single or a nested combination of the following main criteria:
    1. *aboutness,* i.e. content similarity and completeness of the news with respect to the user interests,

2. *coverage*, i.e. content completeness with rest to user interest
3. news *timeliness* with respect to the **when** specification of the user ,
4. news *novelty*, intended as the amount of novel content in the news with respect to the contents of the already analysed news [25].
5. and finally to the *reliability* of the source (*trust score* of the information source and minimum acceptable trust value for the user interest).

- *clusters of news* (i.e., news stories) ranked based on one of the above criteria or a nested combination of the criteria and within each cluster based again on a specific criterion among the above, for example the degree of membership of the single news to the news story or chronologically ordered. Since a news can be associated with several news stories thus reflecting the ambiguity of the categorization, the application of a fuzzy clustering method to generate the news stories is most suited, and responds to the wish specified by the "*comparison*" functionality explained above.

Table 1. Example of user information preference

```
<user-interests>
  <interest name="TREC-R101">
     <!-- textual description of the user interest -->
     <description>
     Economic espionage What is being done to counter
     economic espionage internationally?  Documents
     which identify economic espionage cases and provide
     action(s) taken to reprimand offenders or terminate
     their behavior are relevant.  Economic espionage
     would encompass commercial, technical, industrial
     or corporate types of espionage. about military or
     political espionage would be irrelevant.
     </description>
     <!-- documents which are examples of the interest -->
     <example doc="1996091963261" score="1.0"/>
     <example doc="1996092782330" score="1.0"/>
     <!-- the trust scores -->
     <trust source="0" score="0.5"/>
     <trust source="1" score="0.6"/>
     <trust source="2" score="0.2"/>
     <!-- default trust value of any unknown source -->
     <default-trust value="0.5"/>
<!-- minimum trust value for the user interest -->
     <minimum-trust value="0.3"/>
     <!-- duration in seconds of relevance of user interest-->
     <time-window value="10000"/>
     <!—Max number of filtering results to maintain N value-->
     <filtering-results size="10"/>
  </interest>
</user-interests>
```

Since a user may be interested in numerous different subjects, the information and presentation preferences are split into a set of different user interests. Each interest is personal to the user to which it belongs, and plays an important part in the filtering module (which is intended not only to filter documents to users, but to the correct user interest).

4 Information Filtering Module Architecture

Based on the requirements analysis and design specifications discussed in the previous section, the Information Filtering module has been defined with the following architectural components as sketched in figure 2 [5][18].

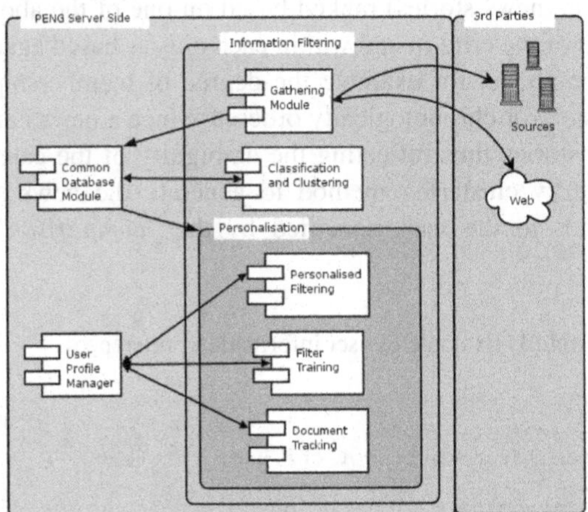

Fig. 2. Sketch of the filtering module architecture

A *gathering module* collects news from a range of information sources, those selected by the user and specified in his/her profile. This gathering may be passive (such as data arriving over a newsfeed) or active (such as from information scraped from web sites). Gathered material is tagged with the information source the data came from, the time it arrived, and other metadata, and is stored and indexed by the common database module.

A *common database module* in which all information pertaining the user profile, news gathered from the stream and users logs are stored. In the common database there are indexing functions of the open source Indri IRS that given a text, either a news d_i, or a textual description of a user interest u_i, can produce its representation as a vector of weights $[w_{i1}, \ldots, w_{iT}]$ in which T is the cardinality of the index space.

A *classification and clustering module* that performs a non-personalised and unsupervised categorisation of current news identifying clusters of topically similar news independent of user preferences and organized into a hierarchy. The identified fuzzy clusters are labelled by associating with them a string summarizing the main contents dealt with in the news highly belonging to the cluster. These fuzzy clusters are filtered to the user who has expressed the preference for such a kind of result presentation modality. This category-based filtering modality in which groups of similar news are filtered to the user allow to select news stories, aiding the user in categorising and understanding the news landscape at that time. This organization of filtering results may also allow easier access to topically relevant stories which nonetheless would not otherwise be classified as relevant to the user in a standard document oriented filtering algorithm.

The classification and clustering module operates periodically (at night), and generates a hierarchy of recently arrived news. During the day, the news pushed on the stream are classified with respect to the current hierarchy. The algorithm on which the fuzzy hierarchical clustering is based is described in the next section. The use of a fuzzy clustering algorithm is important [16], since many news stories may naturally be placed in more than one category. The clusters will again be stored as part of the common database manager, ready for the next stage of the process, the personalised filtering.

The *personalised filtering module* routes news or clusters to the relevant interests of each user (where each user may have multiple overlapping interests). The *matching function* applied by the filter is personalised to the user and performs the combined evaluation of each news with respect to five matching criteria:

- *aboutness,* i.e. the similarity of the news content with respect to user interest.
- *coverage* of the news content with respect to the user interesting contents, i.e., an estimation of the completeness of the news content with respect to the user interest.
- news *timeliness*, i.e., an estimation of the degree of satisfaction of the constraint imposed by the time window (duration of the relevance) on the time of arrival of the news.
- news *novelty,* the amount of new information contained into the news with respect to already seen news.
- *reliability* of news source, i.e. source *trust score*.

The personalisation affects the filter at distinct levels:

- at the level of selection of the news to be pushed to the user. This is done based on the content criteria (aboutness and coverage) with respect to the user interest specified in the *user information preferences*, i.e. **what** (user interests are to be filtered). If the user has specified that does not want duplicated news, the *novelty* criterion is also evaluated and used in combination with the previous ones to determine the selection.
- At the level of definition of the possible ranking criteria of the filtered news. These ranking criteria can be customized to the user and are specified in the *user information preferences*, **where** (reliability based on trust scores) and **when** (timeliness); these are explicitly indicated or implicitly guessed.
- Finally, at the level of specification of the desired presentation modality of the results in the *presentation preferences* where the desired grouping of the news is specified: for example, grouped by news stories and within a news story chronologically ranked so as to identify the source news of a story, or ordered by their membership to the group (fuzzy cluster) so as to identify the news more focused on a story.

The training of these personalised filters (one per user interest) is carried out by the *Filter Training module*. This takes relevance feedback from a user to train the filters to better identify relevant information for that user.

As far as the specific training of the user interest is concerned the *document training module* is the one in charge of managing both the explicit relevance information of the user, such as the user marking a document as relevant to a user interest, and the implicit information derived by the monitoring of user-system interaction (e.g. reading time as a gauge of the relevance of a document).

This above process, with the exception of the filter training, occurs continuously through the day, with or without user involvement. Filtering results, stored in each user profile, are kept up-to-date and ready for when a user logs onto the system. The three main filtering cycles are depicted in figure 3.

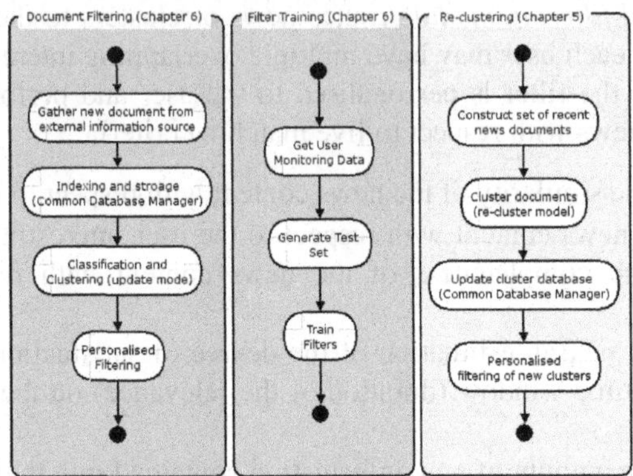

Fig. 3. The three main processing cycles of the Information Filtering Module

5 The Clustering Module

In the following we list the distinguished characteristics of the proposed unsupervised clustering algorithm to support category based news filtering. For a formal description of the algorithm and its evaluation experiments see [4].

The output of the proposed algorithm is a fuzzy hierarchy of the news given as input; this reflects the very nature of news, which may deal with multiple topics.

The algorithm computes a membership degree in [0,1] for each item (news) to each generated fuzzy cluster. This allows ranking the news within a cluster and thus easily supports flexible filtering strategies such as the selection of the top ranked news within a cluster of interest.

The generated fuzzy hierarchy represents the topics at different levels of granularity, from the most specific ones corresponding to the clusters of the lowest hierarchical level (the deepest level in the tree structure representing the hierarchy), to the most general ones, corresponding with the clusters of the top level. Since topics may overlap one another, the hierarchy is fuzzy allowing each cluster of a level to belong with distinct degrees to each cluster in the next upper level. To generate such a fuzzy hierarchy, we have defined a fuzzy agglomerative clustering algorithm based on the recursive application of the FCM algorithm [12]. The proposed algorithm works bottom up in building the levels of the fuzzy hierarchy. Once the centroids of the clusters in a level of the hierarchy are generated, the FCM is re-applied to group the newly identified centroids into new fuzzy clusters of the next upper level. In this way, each level contains fuzzy clusters that reflect topics homogeneous with respect to their specificity (or granularity), so that, in going up the hierarchy, more general topics are identified.

The clusters hierarchy can be easily and efficiently updated on-line when recent news arrive on the stream. This might possibly increase the number of the clusters already identified, and thus may require to compute the association of the old news to the new clusters. This has required the extension of the algorithm so as to perform an incremental clustering [23]. In order to guarantee an efficiency of updating we have assumed that the recent news do not change the already generated centroids of the pre-existing clusters. In fact, we assume that, when a given number of news on the stream is available (this number was estimated approximately equal to 5000 news, i.e. the number of news arriving on the stream a day in a real operative environment), the clustering algorithm is applied in "reset" modality (for example at night) to build a completely new fuzzy hierarchy of clusters. The evaluation experiments [4] estimated that the time needed to cluster 5000 news is around 1 hour 30' on a common PC with 1 GB Ram. In the interval of time between two subsequent runs of the clustering algorithm in reset modality (every day) an existing hierarchy is updated by running the algorithm in incremental modality, thus possibly adding new clusters each time a news is available from the streams. Thus, the news added through the incremental modality should not alter too much an existing hierarchy, allowing at the same time to achieve efficiency.

Besides these main characteristics of the proposed algorithm, more specific features have been considered. Since sparse vectors of weights represent news, in order to manage them in an efficient manner, the proposed algorithm adopts methods for dealing with sparse data optimizing the memory usage. This makes the algorithm suitable for dealing with large data sets. Since the optimal number of clusters to generate is unknown, the proposed algorithm automatically determines this number [4]. It is based on the analysis of the shape of the cumulative histogram curve of overlapping degrees between pairs of news vectors. Clearly, in climbing the hierarchy the number of clusters to detect decreases since the objective is to identify less clusters corresponding to more general topics. Finally, when the clusters are identified their labeling takes place with the aim of summarizing the main contents of the news highly member of the fuzzy cluster. A summarization technique is applied that first selects the M index terms with highest share among the news belonging to the top ranked lists of news of the cluster and then applies a further selection based on the discrimination power of the identified terms with respect to the other clusters. This last selection makes it possible to generate unique labels for the overlapping clusters.

6 The Personalized Filtering Matching Function

In this section we define the personalised filtering matching function. First we define the component matching functions of the single filtering criteria.

Aboutness: the news must be *similar* in some way to those that the user has already found interesting. A user interest is represented by a vector of all documents which have been rated as relevant by the named user interest by the user, u = $[w_1, w_2 \ldots w_T]$ there T is the size of the term vocabulary. Each w_i is given by the formula:

$$w_i = \frac{1}{|R|}\sum_{i \in R} w_{id}$$

which is the same as a Rocchio text classifier [20]. R is the set of documents judged as relevant by the user to the current interest (see table 1). In this case, since the filtering system is dependent on real time user feedback (via the training components) we assume that only positive evidence will be available.

The similarity matching function for comparing this centroid vector *c* to a news vector *d* is the cosine similarity:

$$Aboutness(d,c) = \frac{\sum_{i=1}^{T} w_{id} w_{ic}}{\sqrt{\sum_{i=1}^{T} w_{id}^2 \sum_{i=1}^{T} w_{ic}^2}}$$

In the cosine similarity measure, if either w_{id} or w_{ic} are zero in the numerator, that term of the sum will be zero (i.e. will not contribute to an increase in the similarity value). Due to the norm of vector *d* in the denominator an index term weight $w_{id} \neq 0$ contributes to decrease the *aboutness* degree even if w_{ic} in the user interest is null, then if the user does not mind about it. The *coverage* criterion allows balancing this undesired behaviour of the similarity definition.

Coverage: is important when compared with aboutness since it gives an idea of the completeness of a news with respect to the user interest (containment of the users interesting contents in the news contents). A simple *Coverage* measure between a user interest vector *c* and a news vector *d* is the fuzzy inclusion measure computed as [16] :

$$Coverage(c,d) = fuzzy\ inclusion(c,d) = \frac{\sum_{i=1}^{|T|} \min(w_{ic}, w_{id})}{\sum_{i=1}^{|T|} w_{ic}}$$

in which w_{id} and w_{ic} are the weights of vectors *d* and *c* respectively. This measure reaches the maximum of 1 when *c* is completely included in *d*. It is zero in case of no common index term, and assumes intermediate degrees that increase with the increase of the common indexes. It must be noticed that also the index term weight itself plays a role in that, to be completely included in *d*, all the index term weights of *c* must be smaller than the index term weights of *d*.

Novelty: if the document does not provide any new information to the user, then it is unlikely to be of use to the user. This may be especially important in the news field, where stories are bought and sold, and may appear at multiple times form multiple sources. The question of retrieval based on the novelty of a document has been addressed in the novelty track of TREC, and in the area of filtering, by the NewsJunkie system [25]. Based on the centroid *c* of user interests a simple way to gauge novelty is to take the vector difference between *c* of the known documents, and the vector *d* of the new document, i.e.:

$$novelty(d,c) = \sum_{i \in T} \begin{cases} w_{id} - w_{ic} & \textbf{if} \quad (w_{id} - w_{ic}) \geq 0 \\ 0 & \textbf{if} \quad (w_{id} - w_{ic}) < 0 \end{cases}$$

Notice that a user could be interested in receiving all the duplicates of a news from several news agencies so as to evaluate the "popularity " of a news. This is the reason that suggested us to leave this selection criterion optional.

Reliability: is likely to be important due to the need for accuracy in new articles. The minimum trust expected by the user, for all documents filtered to this user interest T_e. If this is set to a high value, the user expects only highly reliable documents (i.e. documents which can be trusted absolutely). If T_e value is low, then the reliability of a document is less important. By $T_a(d)$ we indicate the actual trust the user places in the source a of a document d, as supplied by the user in the definition of their in formation preferences (where). To allow the convenient comparison of these values, they can be assumed to be scaled between 0 and 1. Matching function of this criterion returns a value in [0,1], where 1 indicates that the news d is fully trusted and zero indicates that the news is not trusted at all and then should be ranked at the bottom of the filtered list of news.

$$Reliability(d) = \begin{cases} 11 & \textbf{if} \quad Ta(d) \geq T_e \\ \dfrac{T_a(d)}{T_e} & \textbf{otherwise} \end{cases}$$

Timeliness is important since news organisations are often judged by who gets a story out first, and being up-to-date is vital (news is better fresh). For timeliness, a single value t_{wi} may be set in the user information preferences indicating the "time window" with respect to the current time $t_{current}$ in which the user interest i remains relevant to the user, i.e. an estimate by the user of the duration of the relevance of a news about user interest i (ex for 3 days from now).
Its matching function is the following:

$$Timeliness\ (d) = \begin{cases} 1 & \textbf{if} \quad t_d < t_{wi} \\ \dfrac{\mathbf{t_{wi}}}{\mathbf{t_d}} & \textbf{otherwise} \end{cases}$$

where $t_d = t_{current} - t_{d\ arrival}$ with $t_{d\ arrival}$ being the time of arrival of the news d on the stream.

The personalized filtering process returning the list of news to the user is sketched in figure 4. This process takes in input either a news vector or a cluster vector (a centroid vector) and a single user interest in the user profile. The user through messages specifying the desired presentation modality controls the process.

First of all, the content of news or a cluster is evaluated against a user interest. A Retrieval Status Value (RSV) is computed as the maximum of the *aboutness* degree and the *coverage* degree. If the user in his/her presentation preference indicates to eliminate the duplicates and the news more or less similar to those already seen, the novelty score *n-score* is computed based on the evaluation of the *novelty* criterion. In

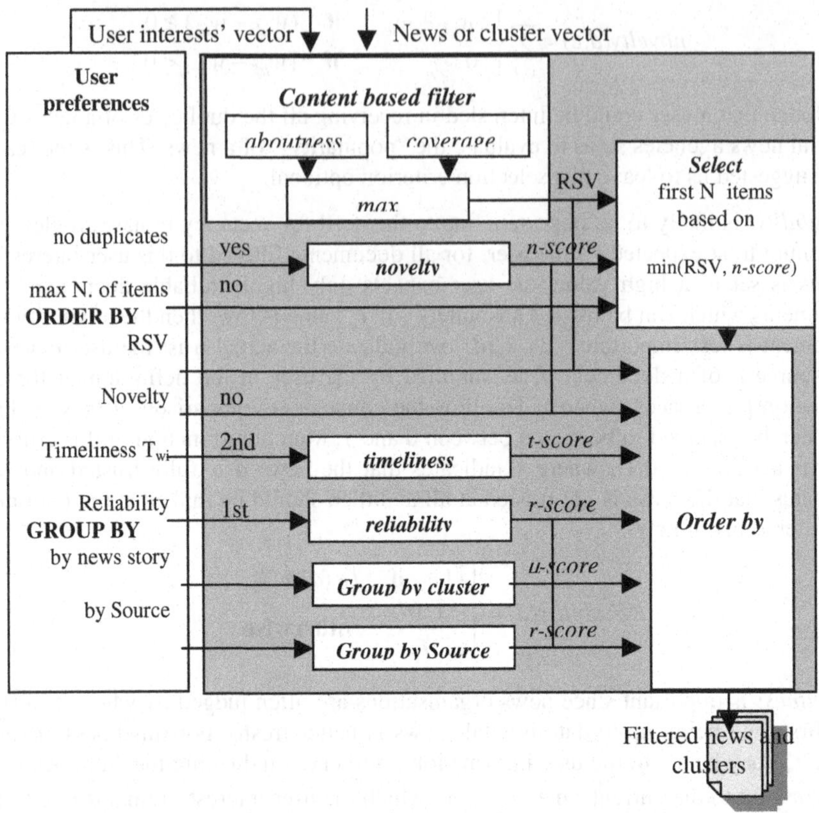

Fig. 4. Personalized Filtering process

this case the *minimum* between *n-score* and RSV is computed and used to rank the news, otherwise the ranking depends solely on RSV. This first ranking is used for selection purposes: the first N top ranked news and clusters are then filtered to the user. If no other presentation clause **order by** is specified, the news are presented in decreasing order of either RSV or min(RSV, *n-score*). In the case in which other **order by** options are specified, the selected news and clusters are presented organized according to the desired ranking criteria. When more order by options are set, a nested ranking list is provided to the user, for example, news first ranked by *reliability* score (*r-score*) and then by *timeliness* score (*t-score*) as depicted in the example in figure 4. Another presentation modality can be specified with the option **group by** (either news story or source trust score). When "**group by** news story" is specified the list of clusters filtered to the user interest are presented and ranked according to their RSV. Within each cluster the news can then be organized according to any combination of the other ranking criteria. For example, within each cluster news ordered by *membership* to the cluster (*μ–score*) and then by *timeliness* so as to identify the most focused news on the topics of the news story that was first broadcasted. This way the semantics of the ranking can be clearly understood by the user, who can have full control over it.

7 Conclusions

In this contribution we have illustrated a novel flexible news filtering model. The main characteristic of the filtering model is that it applies a combination of *content-based* filtering criteria, *category-based* filtering criteria, based on the application of a novel unsupervised hierarchical fuzzy clustering algorithm, and personalized *presentation preferences* criteria. The application of such criteria is customized to the user who can directly specify them in his user profile. In fact, the user profile besides specifying user interest contains also presentation preferences that can affect the ranking of the filtered results.

Acknowledgments

PENG "Personalised News content programminG Information" is a Specific Targeted Research Project (IST-004597) funded within the Sixth Program Framework of the European Research Area.

References

[1] Amato, G., Straccia, U., and Thanos, C. (2000) EUROgatherer: a Personalised Gathering and Delivery Service on the Web, in Proc. of the 4th SCI-2000.

[2] Belkin, Nicholas J. and Croft, W. Bruce (1992) Information filtering and Information Retrieval: Two sides of the same Coin?, in Communications of the ACM, 35 (12).

[3] Bell, Timothy A. H. and Moffat, Alistair (1996) The Design of a High Performance Information Filtering System, In SIGIR'96, Zurich, Switzerland.

[4] Bordogna G., Pagani M., Pasi G., Antoniolli L., Invernizzi F. (2006) An Incremental Hierarchical Fuzzy Clustering Algorithm Supporting News Filtering, in proc. IPMU 2006, Paris.

[5] Bordogna G., Pasi G., Pagani M., Villa R. "PENG Filtering model and Demos", PENG Deliverable 3.1, Nov. 2005.

[6] Claypool M., Gokhale A., Miranda T., Murnikov P., Netes D., Sartin M., (1999) Combining Content-based and Collaborative Filters in an Online Newspaper, in Proc. ACM SIGIR'99 Workshop on Recommender Systems-Implementation and Evaluation.

[7] Connor M., Herlocker J. (1999), Clustering for Collaborative Filtering, in Proc. of ACM SIGIR Workshop on Recommender Systems.

[8] Crestani F. and Pasi G., (2000) eds. "Soft Computing in Information Retrieval: Techniques and Applications." Physica-Verlag, Heidelberg.

[9] Foltz, P.W., and Dumais, S.T. (1992) Personalized information delivery: an analysis of information filtering methods, In Communications of the ACM 35, 12, 29-38

[10] Furnas, G. W., Landauer, T. K., Gomez, L. M. and Dumais, S. T. (1983) Statistical semantics: An analysis of the potential performance of keyword information systems. Bell Syst. Tech. J. 62, 6, 1753-1806.

[11] Gabrilovich, S. Dumais, and E. Horvitz (2004) Newsjunkie: Providing Personalized Newsfeeds via Analysis of Information Novelty, In WWW2004, New York

[12] Hathaway, R.J., Bezdek, J.C. and Hu Y. (2000) Generalized Fuzzy C-Means Clustering Strategies Using Lp Norm Distances, IEEE Trans. on Fuzzy Systems, 8(5), 576-582.

[13] Kilander F., A brief comparison of News filtering Software, http://www.glue.umd.edu/enee/medlab/filter/filter.html

[14] Kraft D., Chen J., Martin--Bautista M.J., Vila M.A.(2003), Textual Information Retrieval with User Profiles using Fuzzy Clustering and Inferencing, in Intelligent Exploration of the Web, Szczepaniak P., Segovia J., Kacprzyk J., Zadeh L.A. eds. Studies in Fuzziness and Soft Comp. Series, 111, Physica Verlag.

[15] Mackay, W.E., Malone, T.W., Crowston, K., Rao, R., Rosenblitt, D., Card, S.K. (1989) How do experienced information lens user use rules? In Proceedings of ACM CHI '89 Conference on Human Factors in Computing Systems (Austin, Tex. Apr. 30-May 4). ACM/SIGCHI, New York, 211-216.

[16] Miyamoto S. (1990), Fuzzy IR and clustering techniques, Kluwer.

[17] Oard, Douglas W. and Marchionini, Gary (1996) A Conceptual Framework for Text Filtering, technical report EE-TR-96-25 CAR-TR-830 CLIS-TR-96-02 CS-TR-3643, University of Maryland.

[18] Pasi G., Villa R. (2005), The PENG Project overview, in IDDI-05-DEXA Workshop, Copenhagen.

[19] Robertson, S. E., and Walker, S. (1999) Okapi/Keenbow at TREC-8, In NIST Special Publication 500-246: The Eighth Text REtrieval Conference (TREC 8).

[20] Salton G., and McGill M.J. (1984), Introduction to modern information retrieval. McGraw-Hill .

[21] Sollenborn, M., Funk P. (2002) Category-Based Filtering and User Stereotype Cases to Reduce the Latency Problem in Recommender Systems. In Proc. Of the 6th ECCBR2002, Springer Verlag Lecture Notes Series.

[22] Ungar, L.H., Foster, D.P.: (1998) Clustering Methods for Collaborative Filtering. Proceedings of the Workshop on Recommendation Systems, AAAI Press.

[23] Wai-chiu Wong, Ada Wai-chee Fu (2000), Incremental Document Clustering for Web Page Classification, in Proc. Int. Conf. IS2000, Aizu-Wakamatsu City, Japan.

[24] Yan, Tak W. and Garcia-Molina, Hector (1994) Index Structures for Information Filtering Under the Vector Space Model, in Proc. 10th IEEE Int. Conf. on Data Engineering, 337-347, Houston

[25] Zhang Y., Callan J., and Minka T. (2002) Novelty and Redundancy Detection in Adaptive Filtering, in Proc. of SIGIR'02, Tampere, Finland.

Query Phrase Suggestion from Topically Tagged Session Logs

Eric C. Jensen[1], Steven M. Beitzel[1], Abdur Chowdhury[2], and Ophir Frieder[1]

[1] Information Retrieval Laboratory, Illinois Institute of Technology,
10 W 31st St., Chicago, IL 60616, USA
{ej, steve, ophir}@ir.iit.edu

[2] America Online, Inc., 44100 Prentice Dr., Sterling, VA 20166, USA
Cabdur@aol.com

Abstract. Searchers' difficulty in formulating effective queries for their information needs is well known. Analysis of search session logs shows that users often pose short, vague queries and then struggle with revising them. Interactive query expansion (users selecting terms to add to their queries) dramatically improves effectiveness and satisfaction. Suggesting relevant candidate expansion terms based on the initial query enables users to satisfy their information needs faster. We find that suggesting query phrases other users have found it necessary to add for a given query (mined from session logs) dramatically improves the quality of suggestions over simply using cooccurrence. However, this exacerbates the sparseness problem faced when mining short queries that lack features. To mitigate this, we tag query phrases with higher level topical categories to mine more general rules, finding that this enables us to make suggestions for approximately 10% more queries while maintaining an acceptable false positive rate.

1 Introduction

Search system users typically pose short, vague queries and often revise them in an effort to find the desired, relevant results for their information need. Analysis of search session logs (containing the time-ordered queries submitted by a single user) has found that the average query is only 2.21 terms in length, but 33% of users reformulated their query at least once, with a mean of 2.84 queries per session [1]. Clearly, time and effort spent reformulating queries that yielded unsatisfactory results negatively impacts user satisfaction. This is exacerbated in environments such as a mobile interface where the interaction required to examine results and pose revised queries may be more tedious. Rather, a search interface capable of recognizing likely information needs for a vague query and suggesting relevant expansion terms to satisfy each of those needs is desirable.

It is clear that manual query refinement typically improves retrieval effectiveness. Kelly et al. shows a direct correlation between query length and effectiveness, finding that expanding queries using feedback from users via clarification forms significantly improved their performance over 45 TREC-style topics [2]. It is also well-documented that users are not often sure of the correct terms for

H.L. Larsen et al. (Eds.): FQAS 2006, LNAI 4027, pp. 185–196, 2006.

which to describe their information need [3]. As such, it is of interest to search services to be able to suggest additional terms and phrases to their users. For example, a vague query such as "tickets" might be quickly narrowed to satisfy a specific need by suggesting the terms "baseball," "concert," and "traffic." These suggestions serve as both clarifying aids to users, and a hint as to how the system interprets their queries as initially expressed. Studies have shown that users are more satisfied when they at least understand why a search system produced the given results [4]. Expansion suggestions help users to satisfy their information needs faster by reducing the interaction required to express them.

As with the search problem itself, term suggestion is complicated by the fact that typical, short queries on their own do not carry many features from which to determine relevant suggestions. The Zipfian nature of word frequencies is well known. The popularity of queries and query terms follows a similar distribution [5]. These studies have also shown that the population of queries is generally tail-heavy, with almost 50% of all queries occurring five times or less in a week. This preponderance of rare queries makes it difficult to base suggestions on the frequency of their term appearances and pure cooccurrence with query terms alone. If so many queries occur this rarely, the number of times users add the same expansion terms to those queries is an order of magnitude more rare. Nevertheless, this large number of previously unseen or very rarely seen queries must be addressed when doing suggestion. The intuition that these may be more descriptive and not need suggestions is not necessarily true, as there are many proper nouns, etc. that are rarely seen but nonetheless vague or ambiguous. For example, if a user searches for "fqas" it is likely to be a rare query. Any system that relies solely on exactly what other terms cooccur with "fqas" is not likely to be very helpful. This suggests that we must take a deeper look at the context in which phrases occur: the revisions other users have gone through in their sessions with similar queries.

The fundamental obstacle to mining session logs for suggestions is the increasing sparseness of the feature space as one moves from terms to queries to query revisions. As such, this paper has two main contributions. First, we mine suggestions from only phrases other users actually added for a given query. This dramatically improves the quality of suggestions over simply finding "related" cooccurring query terms. For example, the terms "baseball" and "game" frequently cooccur, but "game" is not a very useful term for narrowing the query "baseball" to a specific information need. "tickets", "scores," or "players" are more likely to get the user to the information they desire faster. Focusing on mining suggestions only from terms other users have actually used to "narrow" their query moves away from simple relatedness and focuses on actual likely user behavior. For example, a user might have a narrow session such as "new york baseball → yankees", meaning that they first searched for "new york baseball", and decided to narrow their scope by adding "yankees" later on in their session. We analyze these "narrow" sessions and use them to suggest terms for interactive query expansion. While this provides better suggestions, it does not address the previously mentioned issue of making suggestions for queries that are rare, but still in need of relevant suggestions. To mitigate this, we also map query terms to more abstract classes in order to mine patterns with any reasonable support frequency. We propose applying topical tags such as "MUSICIAN," "CITY," or "VIDEO_GAMES" to query phrases to achieve more general rules such as "US_LOCALITIES high → school". Because queries are short, however, traditional entity tagging is difficult to apply. Rather, we use manually-edited lists to identify topical tags. We evaluated these techniques using 44,918 sessions from a large AOL^{TM}search query log and manual evaluated over 7000 suggestions for 353 queries (the largest such manual evaluation we are aware of, available at http://ir.iit.edu/collections).

2 Prior Work

Leveraging users' reformulations depends on the ability to accurately partition a query log into user sessions. Murray, et al. examine how the method of session detection influences applications using those sessions, pointing out that defining sessions by a single timeout removes the possibility of studying meaningful time gaps between particular users' queries [7].

While term suggestion based on fixed vocabularies, or thesauri, are feasible in focused, relatively static environments [8], they are not scalable to large, dynamic environments such as the web. Several studies propose term suggestion based on query clustering. Wen et al. used direct clickthrough data as well as grouping of queries that return similar documents to perform a kind of query clustering, and showed that using this combined method outperforms both methods individually [9]. Baeza-Yates et al. cluster queries from a session log based on the terms in clicked documents and achieves 80% precision in their top three suggested queries for ten candidate queries from a Chilean query log [10] although again, no results using this clustering technique to aid in reformulation suggestion are provided.

Fonseca et al. found that when users manually expanded 153 queries with concepts mined from associated queries in a session log a 32-52% relative improvement in retrieval average precision was obtained [11]. Kawamae et al. defines a user behavior model quantifying the number of specializations, generalizations, etc. in a query log [12]. Jones and Fain quantify similar user behaviors from a log and find they can predict which query terms will be deleted in a session with 55.5% accuracy over 2000 queries [13]. These studies work to quantify the ways that users behave when they engage in query reformulation, but to our knowledge there have been no studies that make direct use of the actual terms added by users when attempting to narrow the scope of their queries. Huang et al. found that single terms suggested based on a cooccurrence matrix mined from Chinese query logs (in which phrases are less important than English ones) had much higher precision than those suggested based on retrieved documents over 100 queries [14]. Other studies focus on the more specific goal of suggesting terms to advertisers in a pay-per-performance search market. Gleich et al. used SVD to suggest terms from an advertising keyword database and achieved over 80% precision at up to 40% recall levels on the top 10,000 suggested terms for two queries [15].

Herlocker et al. reviews many metrics used to evaluate suggestion systems, dividing them into equivalence classes [16]. They also make the important distinction that this task must consider coverage over a representative sample of queries in addition to traditional precision. A proper evaluation requires "offline" evaluations on existing datasets in addition to live-user or "online" evaluations because it is often not feasible to manually evaluate enough queries for a successful online evaluation. If the sample of judged queries is too small, an online evaluation using the sample will not give a reliable measure of the true proportion of queries for which suggestions are being offered.

3 Methodology

Providing relevant suggestions for interactive query expansion depends on the ability to distinguish terms that focus the query on likely information needs from those that are simply related, and the ability to abstract rare queries and query terms to support suggestions for them. To address each of these issues, we propose two techniques. 1. Mining suggestions from other users' behavior in a query session log. 2. Tagging query phrases with topical categories to mine more general rules. As a baseline for the first technique, we use the simple cooccurrence of phrases in queries to make suggestions. Because they are non-exclusive, the gain in effectiveness when combining the second technique with the first is then measured rather than applying it to the poorer baseline.

All techniques use the same function for scoring candidate suggestions. There are many metrics for measuring the interestingness of cooccurrences or association rules. We initially chose frequency-weighted mutual information (FWMI) because of its simplicity and emphasis on the frequency of cooccurrences in addition to normalization by the probability of either term occurring independently [17]. However, we found, as they did, that a small number of very frequently occurring terms were scored too highly, producing irrelevant associations. We therefore weighted with the logarithm of the frequency instead (Equation 1) which performs much better for all techniques and is commonly done in information retrieval.

$$LFWMI(q, s) = \log_2(C(q \rightarrow s)) \log_2 \frac{P(q \rightarrow s)}{P(q)P(s)} \quad (1)$$

Equation 1 scores each candidate phrase for suggestion, s, with respect to a single query phrase, q. This would be sufficient if we treat each query as a single q, but to mine sufficient evidence to make suggestions for the large numbers of rare queries (as discussed in section 1), we must decompose each query Q into its component phrases q_i. In our experimentation, we limit phrases to term unigrams and bigrams, ignoring the position in which terms occur to further aggregate evidence. However, the cooccurrence counts from our training data enable us to intelligently chunk the query, so that when processing the query "new york state" we use the same mutual information metric to identify it as consisting of two phrases "new york" and "state" and not treat the unigrams "new" and "york" independently. After chunking the query, we average the mutual information for each candidate suggestion across the query's component phrases (Equation 2) to obtain the final score.

$$Score(Q, s) = \frac{\sum_{q_i \in Q} LFWMI(q_i, s)}{|Q|} \quad (2)$$

When mining the session log, we also decompose the sets of terms users add for a given query, so that we can combine evidence from sessions such as "new york → state college" and "new york → university state" to find that the unigram "state" is often added to queries containing the bigram "new york". When making suggestions, we do not suggest unigrams that also exist in bigram suggestions unless they are scored higher. Finally, we select a threshold minimum score required to make a suggestion, filtering out any suggestions below that threshold.

This same processing is done for all of our techniques. Only the definition of q_i and s varies. For the baseline cooccurrence technique, all unigram and bigram q_i are counted as candidate suggestions s for one another. At suggestion time, the same phrase based chunking and averaging above is applied. When using only those terms other users have actually applied to "narrow" their query, only the actual "narrow" unigrams and bigrams that are added in the subsequent query are counted as candidate suggestions s for the initial query phrases q_i. When topical tagging is applied, phrases are replaced with their tags and narrow terms are counted as candidate suggestions for unigrams and bigrams of the tagged query. For example, the session "new york state → college" would count "college" as a candidate suggestion for "US_STATE state" (a state name followed by the term "state") and for "US_STATE" alone. We combine suggestions from topical tagging and the terms alone by simply summing their scores if the same phrase is suggested by both, weighting the topically tagged scores at 20% of the literal ones because their generality makes them noisier.

4 Results

The definition of relevance in a phrase suggestion task is different from that in the information retrieval problem. Rather than assuming that the query represents a single information need and seeking to find documents relevant to that need, the suggestion task assumes a query could represent multiple information needs. A relevant suggestion, then, is one which would help to narrow the query into a particularly likely information need. We begin with a description of our session log and manual evaluation. Section 4.2 compares using only those phrases users actually add to narrow their queries versus a baseline of simply using cooccurring phrases. Section 4.3 goes on to combine suggestions based on topically tagging queries with those from the terms themselves.

4.1 Experimental Environment

We performed our experiments using session data from AOL™search query logs. A random sample of session data containing approximately five million queries from November 2004 through January 2005 was collected. The logs contain anonymous user ID's and the query terms that were used in the search. In total, there were 268,023 unique user ID's in the log, and approximately 28.4% of all queries were part of some kind of reformulation or revision (a similar finding to [1]). As discussed in section 2 there are many ways to define and determine session breaks. For the purposes of training and testing our techniques, we use only sequences of queries for which the same user inputs an initial query and then adds terms to that query without removing or changing any of the initial terms ("narrowing" their query). When the user makes multiple revisions of that type, we use only the terms in their initial and final query, with the assumption that if they succeeded in fulfilling their information need, it was with their final try. Obviously, suggestions should be useful for any initial query, but training and testing using cases where users delete some of their initial terms would complicate our evaluation. We trained our system using a random sample of 2/3 of the users in the log. The remaining 1/3 of the log was used for testing. It was comprised of 89,203 user ID's with 44,918 instances of pure "narrow" behavior.

Two evaluations are presented in parallel. The first is an "online" evaluation in which we had student assessors manually judge each suggestion as either relevant or not relevant for 353 distinct randomly sampled queries in the test 1/3 of the log. We pooled all suggestions from each of our techniques (21.5 per query on average) so that every suggestion evaluated was explicitly judged relevant or not relevant. On average, 17.8% of each pool (3.83 suggestions) were judged relevant. For 140 queries we had multiple assessors judge the same suggestions. Over these queries, 37% of the individual suggestion judgments disagreed. We had assessors rejudge that portion to form a single set of judgments for the rest of our evaluation. The second evaluation is an "offline" evaluation in which we treat only those terms the user actually added to a session (the "narrow" terms) as relevant and measure effectiveness over the entire test 1/3 of the log. Because this portion of the log contains all occurrences of queries, popular queries figure more heavily into the average performance than in the online evaluation which treats each query with equal weight. Also, the offline evaluation assumes only the actual phrase the user added is relevant. Therefore its associated error probabilities are very much inflated compared to the online one.

In both evaluations, we only examine the top five suggested phrases (ranked by score), with the intuition that suggesting a large number of phrases is not likely to be useful if the user must scroll through them to find an appropriate one. Different suggestion applications likely have different costs for retrieving irrelevant suggestions and missing relevant suggestions. Therefore, we apply filtering-style evaluation metrics, examining the probability of each of these two errors for varying thresholds on DET curves as is typically done in the Topic Detection and Tracking (TDT) conference [18]. To examine individual points (such as the optimal recall points in the tables below) we similarly combine the costs of these errors as is done at TDT (Equation 3) [19]. We estimate the probability of a suggestion being relevant for each query using the ratio of the number of relevant suggestions for that query to the maximum number of evaluated suggestions across all queries (65). This probably underestimates P(rel), disproportionately weighting P(miss). In our online evaluation, we set C_{miss} to be 10 times, and in the offline evaluation 20 times, that of C_{fa}, reflecting our focus on recall and correcting for the bias in P(rel).

$$Cost = C_{miss}P(miss)P(rel) + C_{fa}P(fa)(1 - P(rel)). \quad (3)$$

4.2 Session Narrows vs. Simple Cooccurrence

First, we examine the effectiveness of using phrases users actually added to their queries versus simply how many times phrases cooccurred in general. As can be seen by the online and offline evaluations in Figure 1 and Figure 2, using actual terms users added is much more effective. As is traditional with DET curves, these graphs are on log-log scales [18]. In the online evaluation, we see that at lower thresholds simple cooccurrence does not find more relevant suggestions, it just retrieves many bad ones. In the offline one, the miss rate continues to decrease as a larger number of rare queries are given suggestions. Some of the top associations found from other users "narrow" behavior are "blue book → kelly," "paul johnson → beheading" (because it was in the news at the time our log was collected), and "costumes → halloween."

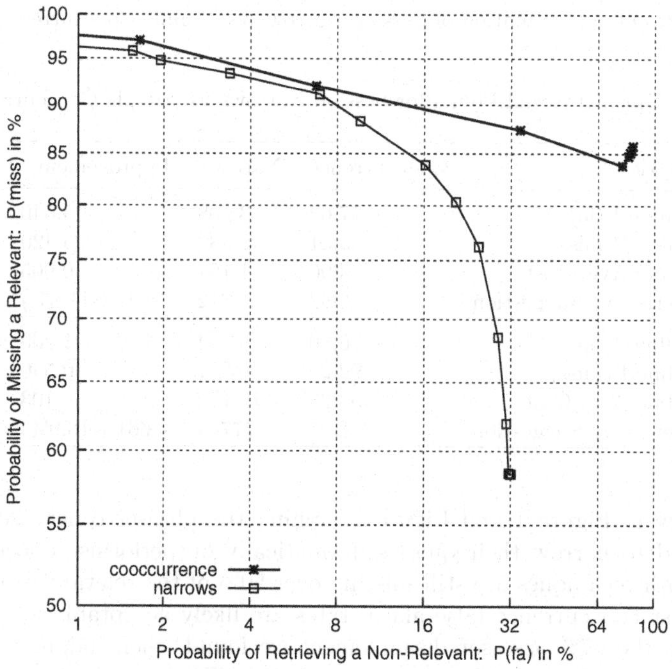

Fig. 1. Online Evaluation of Session Narrows vs. Simple Cooccurrence

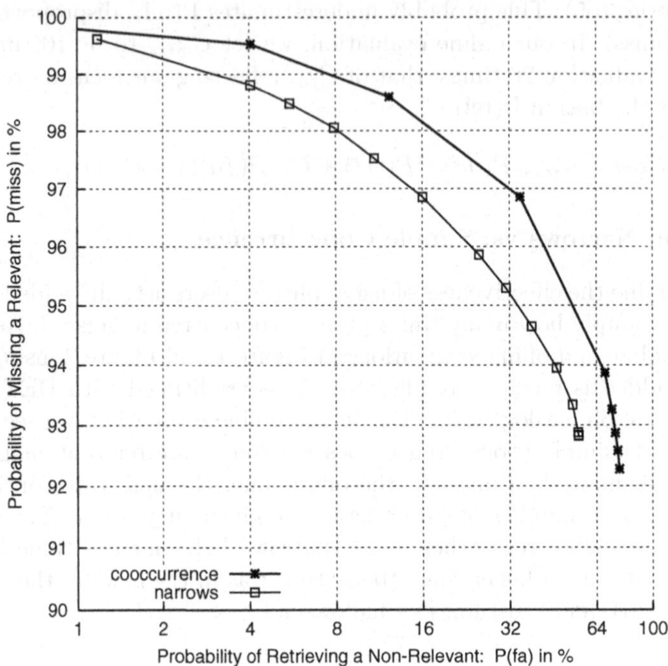

Fig. 2. Offline Evaluation of Session Narrows vs. Simple Cooccurrence

Table 1. Optimal Recall Points for Session Narrows vs. Simple Cooccurrence

Metric	Cooccurrence	Narrows	Improvement
Online P(fa)	77.62	32.08	45.540
Online P(miss)	83.81	58.39	25.420
Online Avg. Cost	2.096	1.191	0.905
Queries w/ Suggestion	353	312	-41 (-11.6%)
Offline P(fa)	76.80	55.54	21.260
Offline P(miss)	92.28	92.82	-0.540
Offline Avg. Cost	19.223	19.120	0.103
Queries w/ Suggestion	33425	27764	-5661 (-16.9%)

As we saw in Figure 1 and Figure 2, mining the phrases other users have actually used to narrow their queries dramatically outperforms cooccurrence. However, both techniques are still missing over 50% of the relevant results. All but the worst cooccurrence false alarm rates are likely acceptable as they are not far from the 37% assessor disagreement we found when judging. Table 1 contains the optimal recall points for each technique. While cooccurrence enables suggestions for more queries, it comes at a cost of 21% absolute increase in offline false alarms to gain 0.5% reduction in misses. Note that the number of queries with a suggestion for the offline evaluation is out of the 44,918 total in the 1/3 test portion of our log.

4.3 Session Narrows vs. Category Tagged Narrows

Next, we examine the performance of using the "narrow" terms users added for particular query terms versus that of also combining suggestions based on tagging the queries with topical categories. Topical tagging of query phrases is achieved using manually edited lists of phrases for 256 categories ranging in specificity and totalling 1.25 million phrases created by AOL^{TM}editors. Some of the top ranked narrows for topically tagged queries are "VIDEO_GAMES → xbox," "COUNTIES election → results" and "GARDEN high → school" (because GARDEN includes plant names such as redwood and laurel). The online and offline evaluations in Figure 3 and Figure 4 show that we can achieve substantially higher recall using the topical category tags. These graphs focus only on the high-recall (low probability of missing a relevant result) portion of the curves. The higher precision performance of topically tagging is equivalent to that of the terms alone. This is because we weight the suggestions from topical tagging at only 20% of those from the terms themselves when combining them, essentially placing the suggestions from topical tagging below any found

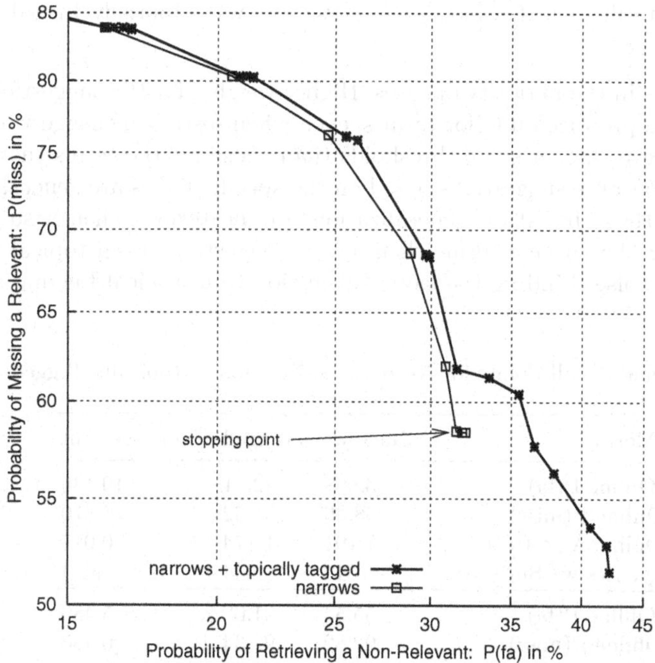

Fig. 3. Online Evaluation of Session Narrows vs. Narrows + Topically Tagged Narrows

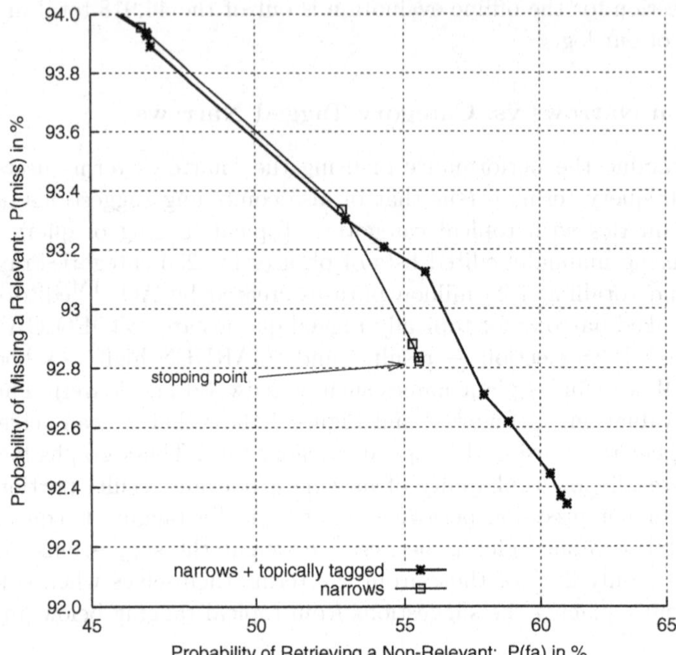

Fig. 4. Offline Evaluation of Session Narrows vs. Narrows + Topically Tagged Narrows

from the terms in the majority of cases. Higher weights for the suggestions from topical tagging produced inferior results, even when restricting suggestions from topical tagging to higher score thresholds than those for the terms themselves. This is likely because suggestions based on the specific terms are generally more reliable than those based on generalizations of the terms; when a suggestion is found using the specific terms themselves, suggestions from topical tagging can only add noise. Finding the same suggestion from topical tagging and the

Table 2. Optimal Recall Points for Narrows vs. Narrows + Topically Tagged Narrows

Metric	Narrows	Tagged	Improvement
Online P(fa)	32.08	42.21	-10.130
Online P(miss)	58.39	51.52	6.870
Online Avg. Cost	1.191	1.174	0.017
Queries w/ Suggestion	312	344	32 (10.3%)
Offline P(fa)	55.54	61.02	-5.480
Offline P(miss)	92.82	92.34	0.480
Offline Avg. Cost	19.120	19.079	0.041
Queries w/ Suggestion	27764	30402	2638 (9.5%)

terms themselves cannot be treated as multiple evidence of that suggestion being relevant.

Again, the benefit of using topical tagging is the ability to make relevant suggestions for a larger number of queries (to lower the probability of a miss). Whereas using only the phrases themselves cannot go below a "stopping point" of miss rate, no matter how low we set the threshold, topical tagging reaches nearly 7% below this in online miss rate, and reduces offline misses by nearly 0.5% with a cost of only approximately 5% increase in false alarms (as compared to 21% increase required for similar miss reduction when using cooccurrence). This stopping point for the phrases themselves is a direct result of the sparsity problem. No matter what quality of results are acceptable, there simply isn't evidence for making any suggestion for phrases that haven't been previously seen. Table 2 contains the optimal recall points for each technique. Using topical tagging we can increase recall while maintaining an acceptable false alarm rate.

5 Conclusion

It has been shown that searchers struggle in formulating the most effective queries for their information needs. Although it has also been documented that interactive query expansion by the user dramatically improves effectiveness, prior studies on making query reformulation suggestions using simple term cooccurrence have had only limited success. We have developed a technique for making suggestions that works by mining the terms other users actually added to a given initial query, improving the relevance of suggestions dramatically over simply using cooccurrence. We have also found that abstracting these queries with topical tags is effective in achieving substantially higher recall, allowing us to make suggestions for approximately 10% more queries while maintaining an acceptable false-positive rate. An obvious avenue for future work is to find a more principled way to combine evidence from each query phrase for a given association.

References

1. Spink, A., Jansen, B.J., Ozmutlu, H.C.: Use of query reformulation and relevance feedback by excite users. Internet Research: Electronic Networking Applications and Policy **10**(4) (2000) 317–328
2. Kelly, D., Dollu, V.D., Fu, X.: The loquacious user: A document-independent source of terms for query expansion. In: ACM Conference on Research and Development in Information Retrieval. (2005)
3. Belkin, N.J.: The human element: Helping people find what they don't know. Communications of the ACM **43**(8) (2000) 58–61
4. Hersh, W.: Trec 2002 interactive track report. In Voorhees, E.M., Buckland, L.P., eds.: Proceedings of the Eleventh Text Retrieval Conference (TREC 2002). Volume SP 500-251., NIST (2002)
5. Beitzel, S.M., Jensen, E.C., Chowdhury, A., Grossman, D., Frieder, O.: Hourly analysis of a very large topically categorized web query log. In: ACM SIGIR Conference on Research and Development in Information Retrieval. (2004) 321–328

6. Shen, X., Tan, B., Zhai, C.: Context sensitive information retrieval using implicit feedback. In: ACM Conference on Research and Development in Information Retrieval. (2005)
7. Murray, G.C., Lin, J., Chowdhury, A.: Characterizing web search user sessions with hierarchical agglomerative clustering. In: forthcoming. (2006)
8. Sihvonen, A., Vakkari, P.: Subject knowledge, thesaurus-assisted query expansion and search success. In: RIAO. (2004)
9. Wen, J.R., Zhang, H.J. Information Retrieval and Clustering. In: Query Clustering in the Web Context. Kluwer Academic Publishers (2003) 195–226
10. Baeza-Yates, R., Hurtado, C., Mendoza, M.: Query recommendation using query logs in search engines. In: International Workshop on Clustering Information over the Web. (2004)
11. Fonseca, B.M., Golgher, P., Pssas, B., Ribeiro-Neto, B., Ziviani, N.: Concept based interactive query expansion. In: ACM Conference on Information and Knowledge Management. (2005)
12. Kawamae, N., Takeya, M., Hanaki, M.: Semantic log analysis based on a user query behavior model. In: IEEE International Conference on Data Mining. (2003)
13. Jones, R., Fain, D.C.: Query word deletion prediction. In: ACM Conference on Research and Development in Information Retrieval. (2003)
14. Huang, C.K., Chien, L.F., Oyang, Y.J.: Relevant term suggestion in interactive web search based on contextual information in query session logs. Journal of the American Society of Information Science and Technology **54**(7) (2003) 638649
15. Gleich, D., Zhukov, L.: Svd based term suggestion and ranking system. In: IEEE International Conference on Data Mining. (2004)
16. Herlocker, J.L., Kostan, J.A., Terveen, L.G., Riedl, J.T.: Evaluating collaborative filtering recommender systems. ACM Transactions on Information Systems **22**(1) (2004) 553
17. Manning, C.D., Schutze, H.: Foundations of Statistical Natural Language Processing. MIT Press (1999)
18. Martin, A., Doddington, G., Kamm, T., Ordowski, M., Przybocki, M.: The det curve in assessment of detection task performance. In: Proceedings of the 5th ESCA Conference on Speech Communication and Technology (Eurospeech '97). (1997) 1895–1898
19. Manmatha, R., Feng, A., Allan, J.: A critical examination of tdt's cost function. In: Proceedings of the 25th annual international ACM SIGIR Conference on Research and Development in Information Retrieval. (2002) 403–404

Why Using Structural Hints in XML Retrieval?

Karen Sauvagnat, Mohand Boughanem, and Claude Chrisment

IRIT - SIG
{sauvagna, bougha, chrisment}@irit.fr
118 route de Narbonne, F-31062 Toulouse Cedex 4

Abstract. When querying XML collections, users cannot always express their need in a precise way. Systems should therefore support vagueness at both the content and structural level of queries. This paper present a relevance-oriented method for ranking XML components. The aim here is to evaluate whether structural hints help to better answer the user needs. We experiment (within the INEX framework) with users needs expressed in a flexible way (i.e with ou without structural hints). Results show that they clearly improve performance, even if they are expressed in an "artificial way". Relevance seems therefore to be closely linked to structure. Moreover, too complex structural hints do not lead to better results.

1 Introduction

The growing number of XML documents leads to the need for appropriate retrieval methods which are able to exploit the specific features of this type of documents. Hierarchical document structure can be used to return specific document components instead of whole documents to users. The main challenge in XML retrieval is therefore to retrieve the most exhaustive and specific information units.

These last years, many methods were proposed in the literature for finding relevant elements. They can be divided into two main sub-groups, depending on the way they consider the content of XML documents. On one hand, the ***data-oriented approaches*** use XML documents to exchange structured data (as for example whole databases). XML documents are seen as highly structured data marked up with XML tags. The database community was the first to propose solutions for the XML retrieval issue, using the data-oriented approach. Unfortunately, the proposed approaches typically expect binary answers to very specific queries. In the Xquery language for example, proposed by the W3C [3], SQL functionalities on tables (tuples collection) are extended to support similar operations on forests (trees collection), as XML documents can be seen as trees. An extension of XQuery with full-text search features is expected [23]. On the other hand, the ***document-oriented approaches*** consider that tags are used to describe the logical structure of documents, which are mainly composed of text. The IR community has adapted traditional IR approaches to address the user information needs in XML collection. Some of these methods are based on the vector space model [8], [16], [9], or on the probabilistic model, either using

H.L. Larsen et al. (Eds.): FQAS 2006, LNAI 4027, pp. 197–209, 2006.

a relevance propagation method [6] or using language models [18], [10]. Such methods have been evaluated since 2002 in the framework of the INEX (Initiative for the Evaluation of XML Retrieval) campaign. This initiative provides an opportunity for participants to evaluate their XML retrieval methods using uniform scoring procedures and a forum for participating organisations to compare their results.

One of the major issue discussed by INEX participants is the users model used when expressing queries. In classical IR, users often have difficulties to express their queries, because they do not know the collection or because they cannot express their information need in a precise way. XML documents emphasize the issue: if users want to express very specific queries, they should not only know the content of the collection, but also how it is structured. This can be a problem when collections contain heterogeneous documents (i.e. documents following different DTD): users cannot express all the possible structure constraints. They should consequently be able to express their need in a flexible way, either by giving some keywords, or by giving some structural hints about what they are looking for. Such hints should not be satisfied strictly, but should be considered as clues on which types of elements are most probably relevant for users. Systems dealing with such needs are therefore necessary [15].

The use of structural hints has already been explored during the INEX 2004 campaign. Results showed that structure was not really useful to improve performance [5]. However, Kamps et al. [11] showed that the use of structure in queries functions as a precision enhancing device, even if it does not lead to improved mean average precision scores. It is however difficult to draw conclusions on INEX 2004 results, since the pool used for the assessments was not only obtained with the content conditions of queries (most of the results in the pool were obtained using structure conditions of queries and bias the pool).

In this paper, we use a relevance-oriented method, based on relevance propagation, to evaluate whether the introduction of structure in queries composed of simple keyword terms (also called Content-only (CO) queries) can improve performance. *In other words, does a relevant structure exist for each information need ? Is relevance closely linked to structure ?*

The rest of the paper is organised as follows. Section 2 presents our baseline model, which uses a relevance propagation method. The INEX 2005 test suite and the associated metrics are described in section 3. At least, section 4 presents experiments we've done on the introduction of structure.

2 Baseline Model

The model we used is based on a generic data model that allows the processing of heterogeneous collection (collections that contain documents following different DTD). We consider that a structured document sd_i is a tree, composed of simple nodes n_{ij}, leaf nodes ln_{ij} and attributes a_{ij}. Leaf nodes ln_{ij} are content-bearer (i.e. they are text nodes) whereas other nodes only give indication on structure.

During query processing, relevance values are assigned to leaf nodes and relevance score of inner nodes are then computed dynamically.

2.1 Evaluation of Leaf Nodes Weights

The first step in query processing is to evaluate the relevance value of leaf nodes ln according to the query. Let $q = t_1, \ldots, t_n$ be a query composed of simple keyword terms (i.e. a CO query). Relevance values are computed using a similarity function $RSV(q, ln)$.

$$RSV_m(q, ln) = \sum_{i=1}^{n} w_i^q * w_i^{ln} \tag{1}$$

Where:

- w_i^q is the weight of term i in query q
- w_i^{ln} is the weight of term i in leaf node ln

According to previous experiments [21], we choose to use the following term weighting scheme, which aims at reflecting the importance of terms in leaf nodes, but also in whole documents:

$$w_i^q = tf_i^q \qquad w_i^{ln} = tf_i^{ln} * idf_i * ief_i \tag{2}$$

Where tf_i^q and tf_i^{ln} are respectively the frequency of term i in query q and leaf node ln, $idf_i = log(|D|/(|d_i| + 1)) + 1$, with $|D|$ the total number of documents in the collection, and $|d_i|$ the number of documents containing i, and ief_i is the inverse element frequency of term i, i.e. $log(|N|/|nf_i| + 1) + 1$, where $|nf_i|$ is the number of leaf nodes containing i and $|N|$ is the total number of leaf nodes in the collection.

Inner nodes relevance values are evaluated using one or more propagation functions, which depend on the searching task. These propagation functions are described in the following sections.

2.2 Relevance Propagation for Content-Only Queries

In our model, each node in the document tree is assigned a relevance value which is function of the relevance values of the leaf nodes it contains. Terms that occur close to the root of a given subtree seem to be more significant for the root element that ones at deeper levels of the subtrees. It seems therefore intuitive that the larger the distance of a node from its ancestor is, the less it contributes to the relevance of its ancestor. This is modeled in our propagation formula by the use of the $dist(n, ln_k)$ parameter, which is the distance between node n and leaf node ln_k in the document tree, i.e. the number of arcs that are necessary to join n and ln_k. Moreover, it is also intuitive that the more relevant leaf nodes a node has, the more relevant it is . We then introduce in the propagation function the $|L_n^r|$ parameter, which is the number of n descendant leaf nodes having a non-zero score. The relevance value r_n of a node n is finally computed according to the following formula:

$$r_n = |L_n^r| \sum_{k=1..N} \alpha^{dist(n, ln_k)-1} * RSV(q, ln_k) \tag{3}$$

where $\alpha \in]0..1]$, ln_k are leaf nodes being descendant of n and N is the total number of leaf nodes being descendant of n.

2.3 Relevance Propagation for Content-Only Queries with Structural Hints

Content Only queries with structural hints (also called CO+S queries) are queries containing structural constraints that should be interpreted as vague conditions. Such constraints can simply be constraints on the type of the returned elements (example 1), or content restrictions on the environment in which the requested element occurs (descendants or ancestors): we talk about hierarchical queries (example 2). Here are some examples of CO queries with structural hints (expressed in the XFIRM query language [20]):

- Example 1: *te: sec[electronic commerce e-commerce]* : user is looking for information about "electronic commerce e-commerce" that can be found in section elements (that are target elements(indicated with the terminal expression *te*))
- Example 2: *//article[business strategies]//te: sec[electronic commerce e-commerce]*: user is also looking for information about "electronic commerce e-commerce" which is probably in section elements of an article about "business strategies"

The evaluation of a CO+S query is carried out as follows :

1. Queries are decomposed into elementary sub-queries ESQ, which are of the form: $ESQ = tg[q]$, where tg is a tag name, i.e. a structure constraint, and $q = t_1, ..., t_n$ is a content constraint composed of simple keywords terms.
2. Relevance values are then evaluated between leaf nodes and the content conditions of elementary sub-queries
3. Relevance values are propagated in the document tree to answer to the structure conditions of elementary sub-queries
4. Original queries are evaluated thanks to upwards and downwards propagation of the relevance weights [20]

In step 3, the relevance value r_n of a node n to an elementary subquery $ESQ = tg[q]$ is computed according the following formula:

$$r_n = \begin{cases} \sum_{ln_k \in L_n} \alpha^{dist(n,ln_k)-1} * RSV(q, ln_k) \; if \; n \in construct(tg) \\ 0 \; else \end{cases} \quad (4)$$

where the result of the *construct*(tg) function is a set composed of nodes having tg as tag name, and $RSV(q, ln_k)$ is evaluated during step 2 with equation 1. The *construct*(tg) function uses a *Dictionary* Index, which provides for a given tag tg the tags that are considered as equivalent.

For processing CO+S queries, as structural conditions should be considered as vague conditions, we use a dictionary index composed of very extended equivalencies. For example, a section node (*sec*) can be considered as equivalent to both a paragraph (*p*) and a body (*bdy*) node (see Appendix for the dictionary index used on the INEX collection). This index is built manually.More details about CO+S queries processing can be found in [20].

2.4 Discussion

Many relevance propagation methods can be found in the literature [1] [2] [8] [7] [19]. Our approach differs from these previous works on two main points. The first point is that all leaf nodes are indexed, because we think that even the smallest leaf nodes can be relevant or can give information on the relevance of its ancestors. Advantages of such an approach are twofold: first, the index process can be done automatically, without any human intervention and the system will be so able to handle heterogeneous collections automatically; and secondly, even the most specific query concerning the document structure will be processed, since all the document structure is kept.

The second point is that the propagation is made step by step and takes into account the distance that separate nodes in the document tree.

Our aim here is not to present a new propagation method, but to evaluate whether the introduction of structure can improve overall performance of systems.

3 INEX 2005 Evaluation Campaign

3.1 Collection and Topics

We used the well-known INEX framework to evaluate the use of structural hints. The 2005 test collection completes the one used during the last years and is composed of more than 17000 documents with extensive XML markup, extracted from IEEE Computer Society journals published between 1995 and 2004.

Experiments presented here are related to the Content-Only (CO) task and the Content-Only+Structure (CO+S) task of the INEX 2005 campaign. The 2005 CO-CO+S tasks are composed of 29 topics and of the associated relevance judgments. An example of such topic can be found in table 1. We use the *title* part of topic for CO queries, and the *castitle* part for CO+S queries.

Only 19 topics have structural hints. In order to compared CO and CO+S tasks however, the 2 sets of queries we use need to have the same number of topics. We consequently use for each task two sets of queries, respectively called

Table 1. Example of CO-CO+S query

```
<inex_topic topic_id="202" query_type="CO+S">
<InitialTopicStatement> [...]</InitialTopicStatement>
<title> ontologies case study </title>
<castitle> //article[about(.,ontologies)]//sec[about(.,ontoologies case study)]</castitle>
<description> Case studues in the use of ontologies </description>
<narrative> I'm writing a report on the use of ontnnologies. I'm interested in knowing how ontologies are used to encode knowledge in real world scenarios. I'm particularly interested in knowing what sort of concepts and relations people use in their ontologies [...] </narrative>
</inex_topic>
```

full-set and *partial-set*. In the full set, all 29 topics are used. For CO+S task, when no *castitle* part is available, we create it in an artificial way, by adding *section* as structural constraint (*section* elements are elements that are the most often returned by systems [4]). In the partial set, only the 19 topics containing a *castitle* part are used. The partial set is used for the official submissions at the INEX 2005 CO+S task, whereas the full set is used for official submissions at the CO task.

Relevance judgments for each query are done by the participants. Two dimensions of relevance are used: exhaustivity (e) and specificity (s). Exhaustivity is measured using a 4-level scale: highly exhaustive (e=2), somewhat exhaustive (e=1), not exhaustive (e=0), too small (e=?). Specificity is measured on a continuous scale with values in [0,1], where s=1 represents a fully specific component (i.e. one that contains only relevant information).

During the assessments, structural conditions were ignored. Judges assessed the elements returned for CO+S queries as whether they satisfied the information need with respect to the content criterion only.

3.2 Metrics

Whatever the metrics used for evaluating systems, the two dimensions of relevance (exhaustivity and specificity) need to be quantised into a single relevance value. Quantisation functions for 2 user standpoints are used:

- a strict quantisation to evaluate whether a given retrieval approach is able of retrieving highly exhaustive and highly specific document components

$$f_{strict}(e,s) = \begin{cases} 1 \; if \; e = 2 \; and \; s = 1 \\ 0 \; otherwise \end{cases} \tag{5}$$

- a generalised quantisation has been used in order to credit document components according to their degree of relevance

$$f_{generalised}(e,s) = e * s \tag{6}$$

Official metrics are based on the extended cumulated gain (XCG) [14] [13]. The XCG metrics are a family of metrics that aim to consider the dependency of XML elements (e.g. overlap and near misses) within the evaluation. The XCG metrics include the user-oriented measures of normalised extended cumulated gain (nXCG) and the system-oriented effort-precision/gain-recall measures (ep/gr). The xCG metric accumulates the relevance scores of retrieved documents along a ranked list. Given a ranked list of document components, xCG, where the element IDs are replaced with their relevance scores, the cumulated gain at rank i, denoted as xCG[i], is computed as the sum of the relevance scores up to that rank:

$$xCG[i] = \sum_{j=1}^{i} xG[j] \tag{7}$$

For example, the ranking $xG_q =< 2, 1, 0, 1, 0, 0 >$ produces the cumulated gain vector of $xCG =< 2, 3, 3, 4, 4, 4 >$.

For each query, an ideal gain vector, xI, can be derived by filling the rank positions with the relevance scores of all documents in the recall-base in decreasing order of their degree of relevance. The corresponding cumulated ideal gain vector is referred to as xCI. By dividing the xCG vectors of the retrieval runs by their corresponding ideal xCI vectors, the normalised xCG ($nxCG$) measure is obtained:

$$nxCG[i] = \frac{xCG[i]}{xCI[i]} \tag{8}$$

For a given rank i, the value of $nxCG[i]$ reflects the relative gain the user accumulated up to that rank, compared to the gain he/she could have attained if the system would have produced the optimum best ranking. For any rank the normalised value of 1 represents ideal performance.

Analogue to the definition of $nxCG$, a precision-oriented XCG measure, effort-precision ep, is defined as:

$$ep(r) = \frac{e_{ideal}}{e_{run}} \tag{9}$$

where e_{ideal} is the rank position at which the cumulated gain of r is reached by the ideal curve and e_{run} is the rank position at which the cumulated gain of r is reached by the system run. A score of 1 reflects ideal performance, where the user need to spend the minimum necessary effort to reach a given level of gain.

Effort-precision, ep, is calculated at arbitrary gain-recall points, where gain-recall is calculated as the cumulated gain value divided by the total achievable cumulated gain:

$$gr[i] = \frac{xCG[i]}{xCI[n]} \tag{10}$$

where n is the total number of relevant documents.

The meaning of effort-precision at a given gain-recall value is the amount of relative effort (where effort is measured in terms of number of visited ranks) that the user is required to spend when scanning a systems result ranking compared to the effort an ideal ranking would take in order to reach a given level of gain relative to the total gain that can be obtained. See [13] for more details.

4 Experiments

We experiment with two search strategies, which correspond to different user needs: find all relevant information in the collection or find only the most relevant information:

- **find all highly exhaustive and specific elements** (*thorough strategy*). The nature of relevance in XML retrieval may imply overlapping elements (i.e. elements that are nested within each others) to be returned by systems. If a child element is relevant, so will be its parent, although to a greater or lesser extent. It is however a challenge to rank these elements appropriately, as systems that rank highly exhaustive and specific elements before less exhaustive and specific ones, will obtain a higher effectiveness performance.

– **find the most exhaustive and specific element in a path** (*focussed strategy*). No overlapping elements are allowed: for a given document, only elements that are not nested within each others can be returned.

It seems to us important to evaluate the use of structural hints on these two strategies, since they could lead to contradictory behaviors.

To answer to the thorough strategy, weighted sub-trees (equation 3 and 4) are simply ordered and returned by the system. In order to remove nodes overlap (focussed retrieval), we use the following strategy: for each relevant path, we keep the most relevant node in the path. The results set is then parsed again, to eliminate any possible overlap among results components.

4.1 Experiments with a Thorough Strategy

According to previous experiments, we use $\alpha = 0.1$ in equation 3 and $\alpha = 0.5$ in equation 4 (these values are optimal for the considering sub-tasks).

Figures 1 and 2 show the evolution of the nxCG metric, for both the full set and partial set of queries. Table 2 shows the results for the ep/gr-MAP metric.

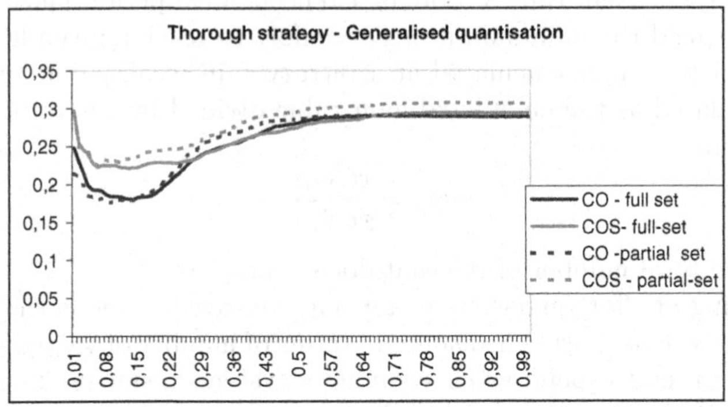

Fig. 1. nXCG evolution - Thorough strategy - Generalised quantisation

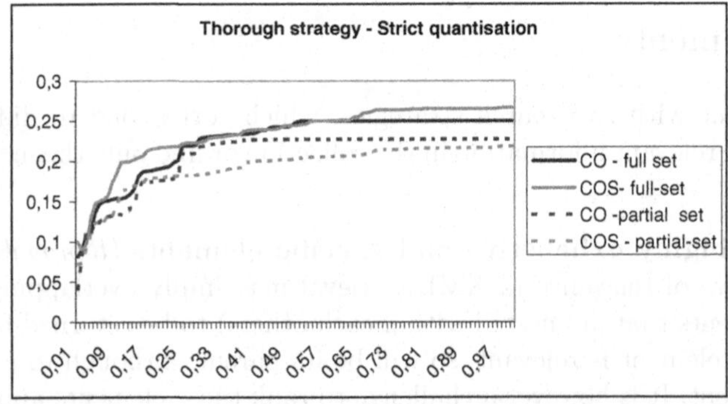

Fig. 2. nXCG evolution - Thorough strategy - Strict quantisation

Table 2. Comparison of CO/CO+S queries with MAP metric, Thorough strategy

		Generalised	Strict
Full-set	CO	0,0535	0,0234
	CO+S	0,0690	0,0240
	Gain	+29%	+3%
Partial-set	CO	0,0517	0,0158
	CO+S	0,0749	0,0163
	Gain	+45%	+3%

Results with CO+S queries are better for low levels of recall, and are comparable to those obtained for the CO strategy at other recall levels. However, if we considered average results (see table 2), the CO+S strategy is clearly preferable to the CO strategy.

If we now compare results for the full set and the partial set, we see that if we consider the generalised quantisation function, results are better with the partial set, whereas it is not the case when considering the strict quantisation function.

4.2 Experiments with a Focussed Strategy

For the focussed retrieval strategy, according to previous experiments, we use $\alpha = 0.1$ in equation 3 and $\alpha = 0.2$ in equation 4 (these values are optimal for the considering sub-tasks).

Figures 3 and 4 show the evolution of the nXCG metric, for both the full set and partial set of queries. Table 3 shows the results for the ep/gr-MAP metric.

At low levels of recall, results for the thorough strategy are comparable to results for the focussed strategy: CO+S queries allows to obtain better results than simple CO queries. However, we can observe reverse results for other recall levels. If we now consider average results, results obtained with CO+S queries outperformed again results obtained with CO queries.

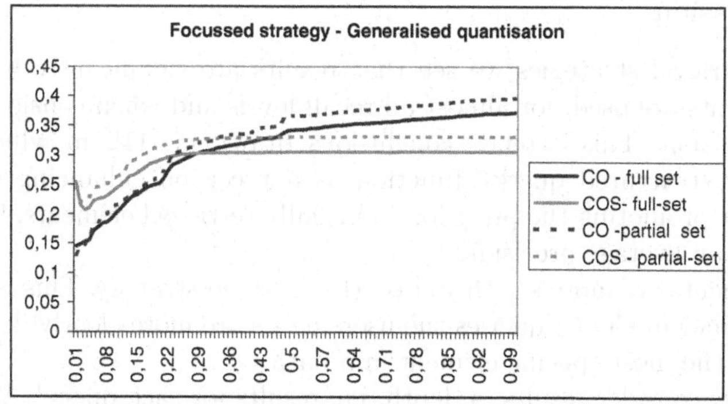

Fig. 3. nXCG evolution - Focussed strategy - Generalised quantisation

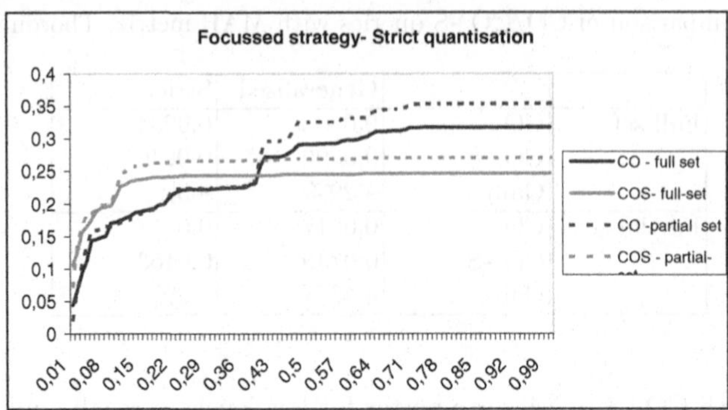

Fig. 4. nXCG evolution - Focussed strategy - Strict quantisation

Table 3. Comparison of CO/CO+S queries with MAP metric, Focussed strategy

		Generalised	Strict
Full set	CO	0,0538	0,0195
	CO+S	0,0782	0,0372
	Gain	+45%	+91%
Partial set	CO	0,0554	0,0167
	CO+S	0,0877	0,0353
	Gain	+58%	+111%

When comparing partial and full sets, we notice that results are in a general manner better for the partial set. This can be explained by the fact that the partial set only contains queries having a structural constraint defined by the user, whereas this constraints was artificially added for some queries in the full set. This is not surprising, since the user need is more clearly defined in queries of the partial set.

4.3 Discussion

For both retrieval strategies we see that results are significantly better when structural hints are used, for almost all recall levels and when considering mean average precision. This extends conclusions drawn in [11], in which authors showed that structured queries function as a precision enhancing device, i.e. are useful for promoting the precision in initially retrieved elements, but are not useful on mean average precision.

Improvements are more significant on the focussed strategy. This is not really surprising, since in CO+S queries the users needs are more clearly defined: they help finding the most specific element in a path.

Let us now consider results in depth, i.e. results for each query[1]. We see that CO+S queries improve results even for queries with an "artificial" structure con-

[1] Due to space limitation, results are not presented here.

straint, i.e. CO queries that do not have structural hints and for which we add the structural constraint (10 queries over 29). Queries for which no improvement is observed are queries having a too complex structure condition (i.e. having hierarchical conditions). This seems to show that only simple structural constraints are useful for improving overall performance, even if these constraints are artificial. In other words, it shows that relevant information seems to be located in some particular element types and that relevance is closely linked to structure. At last, we have to notice the relative high precision of our runs compared to INEX 2005 official submissions [5]. Most of our runs would have been ranked in the top ten for both quantisation functions. Best results are obtained for the CO-Focussed strategy: we would have been ranked first for generalised quantisation on nxCG[10], nXCG[25] and nXCG[50] metrics (official metrics at INEX 2005). We respectively obtain 0.2607, 0.2397 and 0.224, whereas best results were respectively 0.2181, 0.1918 and 0.1817, and were obtained by the University of Amsterdam with a language model-based method [22] and by IBM Haifa Research Lab [17] using the vector space model. We would also be in the top 5 for strict quantisation.

5 Conclusion

Content-oriented retrieval is one of the most challenging issue in XML retrieval, because queries do not contain indications on which type of elements should be returned to the user. In this paper, we present some experiments on the use of structural hints in queries (which allows the user to express queries in a more flexible way).

We can draw several conclusions from these experiments. First, the use of structural hints improve in a very significant way the system performance, both in average and at low levels of recall. This means that users have almost always an implicit structural need and that relevance is closely linked to structure. Moreover, structural hints have a higher impact for a focussed retrieval strategy than for a thorough retrieval strategy: they help the system to focus on the user information need. Third, the introduction of "artificial" structural hints also improve results: our system is consequently able to process queries in a flexible way. At last, no improvement is observed for structural queries having too complex structural conditions (i.e. hierarchical conditions): structure should consequently be only used as an indication of what type of elements should be retrieved.

In the future, we will apply these results for doing structured relevance feedback: as the use of structural hints improve significantly results, we will try to add them in CO queries when doing relevance feedback. The study of the type of relevant elements will allow us to better define the implicit need of the user and to express new queries with more relevant structural hints (than the artificial hints used in this article when none were available). Some preliminary work can be found in [12].

References

1. M. Abolhassani and N. Fuhr. Applying the divergence from randomness approach for content-only search in XML documents. In *Proceedings of ECIR 2004, Sunderland*, pages 409–419, 2004.
2. V. N. Anh and A. Moffat. Compression and an IR approach to XML retrieval. In *Proceedings of INEX 2002 Workshop, Dagstuhl, Germany*, 2002.
3. M. Fernandez, A. Malhotra, J. Marsh, M. Nagy, and N. Walsh. XQuery 1.0 and XPath 2.0 data model. Technical report, World Wide Web Consortium (W3C), W3C Working Draft, may 2003.
4. N. Fuhr, M. Lalmas, and S. Malik. INEX 2003 workshop proceedings, 2003.
5. N. Fuhr, M. Lalmas, S. Malik, and G. Kazai. INEX 2005 workshop pre-proceedings, 2005.
6. N. Fuhr, S. Malik, and M. Lalmas. Overview of the initiative for the evaluation of XML retrieval (INEX) 2003. In *Proceedings of INEX 2003 Workshop, Dagstuhl, Germany*, December 2003.
7. N. Gövert, M. Abolhassani, N. Fuhr, and K. Grossjohann. Content-oriented XML retrieval with hyrex. In *Proceedings of the first INEX Workshop, Dagstuhl, Germany*, 2002.
8. T. Grabs and H.-J. Scheck. Flexible information retrieval from xml with PowerDB XML. In *Proceedings in the First Annual Workshop for the Evaluation of XML Retrieval (INEX)*, pages 26–32, December 2002.
9. V. Kakade and P. Raghavan. Encoding XML in vector spaces. In *Proceedings of ECIR 2005, Saint Jacques de COmpostelle, Spain*, 2005.
10. J. Kamps, M. de Rijke, and B. Sigurbjornsson. Length normalization in XML retrieval. In *Proceedings of SIGIR 2004, Sheffield, England*, pages 80–87, 2004.
11. J. Kamps, M. Marx, M. de Rijke, and B. Sigurbjornsson. Structured queries in XML retrieval. In *Proceedings of CIKM 2005, Bremen, Germany*, 2005.
12. M. B. Karen Sauvagnat, Lobna Hlaoua. Xfirm at inex 2005: ad-hoc and relevance feedback tracks. In *INEX 2005 Workshop pre-proceedings, Dagstuhl, Germany*, november 2005.
13. G. Kazai and M. Lalmas. Inex 2005 evaluation metrics. In *Pre-proceedings of INEX 2005, Dagstuhl, Allemagne*, November 2005.
14. G. Kazai, M. Lalmas, and A. P. de Vries. The overlap problem in content-oriented XML retrieval evaluation. In *Proceedings of SIGIR 2004, Sheffield, England*, pages 72–79, July 2004.
15. M. Lalmas and T. Rölleke. Modelling vague content and structure querying in xml retrieval with a probabilistic object-relational framework. In *Proceedings of FQAS 2004, Lyon, France*, june 2004.
16. Y. Mass and M. Mandelbrod. Component ranking and automatic query refinement for XML retrieval. In *Proceedings of INEX 2004*, pages 134–140, 2004.
17. Y. Mass and M. Mandelbrod. Experimenting various user models for xml retrieval. In *Pre-Proceedings of INEX 2005, Dagstuhl, Germany*, 2005.
18. P. Ogilvie and J. Callan. Using language models for flat text queries in XML retrieval. In *Proceedings of INEX 2003 Workshop, Dagstuhl, Germany*, pages 12–18, December 2003.
19. T. Roelleke, M. Lalmas, G. Kazai, J. Ruthven, and S. Quicker. The accessibility dimension for structured document retrieval. In *Proceedings of ECIR 2002*, 2002.
20. K. Sauvagnat, M. Boughanem, and C. Chrisment. Answering content-and-structure-based queries on XML documents using relevance propagation . In *Information Systems - Special Issue SPIRE 2004* . Elsevier, 2006.

21. K. Sauvagnat, L. Hlaoua, and M. Boughanem. XML retrieval: what about using contextual relevance? In *ACM Symposium on Applied Ccomputing (SAC) - IAR (Information Access and Retrieval) , Dijon*, April 2006.
22. B. Sigurbjörnsson, J. Kamps, and M. de Rijke. The university of Amsterdam at INEX 2005: Adhoc track. In *Pre-Proceedings of INEX 2005 workshop, Dagstuhl, Germany*, november 2005.
23. W3C. XQuery and XPath full-text use cases. Technical report, World Wide Web Consortium (W3C), W3C working draft, february 2003.

A Dictionary Index

The first tag in each line is considered to be equivalent to the following tags.

Table 4. Dictionary index

p,ilrj,ip1,ip2,ip3,ip4,ip5,item-none,p1,p2,p3,sec,ss1,ss2,ss3,abs,bdy,article
ip1,p,ilrj,ip2,ip3,ip4,ip5,item-none,p1,p2,p3,sec,ss1,ss2,ss3,abs,bdy,article
sec,ss1,ss2,ss3,p,ilrj,ip1,ip2,ip3,ip4,ip5,item-none,p1,p2,p3,abs,bdy,article
dl,l1,l2,l3,l4,l5,l6,l7,l8,l9,la,lb,lc,ld,le,list,numeric-list,numeric-rbrace,bullet-list
h,h1,h1a,h2,h2a,h3,h4
abs,fm,article,p,ilrj,ip1,ip2,ip3,ip4,ip5,item-none,p1,p2,p3,sec,ss1,ss2,ss3,bdy
fm,article
bdy,article
bb,bm,bib,bibl,article
bib,bibl,article,bb,bm
atl,tig,st
st,atl,tig
snm,au
au,snm
vt,bm,article
fgc,fig,p,ilrj,ip1,ip2,ip3,ip4,ip5,item-none,p1,p2,p3,sec,ss1,ss2,ss3,abs,bdy,article
article,fm,bm,bdy,abs,p,ilrj,ip1,ip2,ip3,ip4,ip5,item-none,p1,p2,p3,sec,ss1,ss2,ss3

A Fuzzy Extension for the XPath Query Language

Alessandro Campi, Sam Guinea, and Paola Spoletini

Dipartimento di Elettronica e Informazione - Politecnico di Milano
Piazza L. da Vinci 32, I-20133 Milano, Italy
{campi, guinea, spoleti}@elet.polimi.it

Abstract. XML has become a widespread format for data exchange over the Internet. The current state of the art in querying XML data is represented by XPath and XQuery, both of which define binary predicates. In this paper, we advocate that binary selection can at times be restrictive due to very nature of XML, and to the uses that are made of it. We therefore suggest a querying framework, called FXPath, based on fuzzy logics. In particular, we propose the use of fuzzy predicates for the definition of more "vague" and softer queries. We also introduce a function called "deep-similar", which aims at substituting XPath's typical "deep-equal" function. Its goal is to provide a degree of similarity between two XML trees, assessing whether they are similar both structure-wise and content-wise. The approach is exemplified in the field of e-learning metadata.

1 Introduction

In the last few years XML has become one of the most important data formats for information exchange over the Internet. Ever since the advent of XML as a widespread data format, query languages have become of paramount importance. The principal proposals for querying XML documents have been XPath and XQuery. The first is a language that allows for the selection of XML nodes through the definition of "tree traversal" expressions. Although not a fully-fledged query language, it remains sufficiently expressive, and has become widely adopted within other XML query languages for expressing selection conditions. Its main advantage is the presence of a rich set of available built-in functions. XQuery, on the other hand, is W3C's current candidate for a fully-fledged query language for XML documents. It is capable of working on multiple XML documents, of joining results, and of transforming and creating XML structures. It builds upon XPath, which is used as the selection language, to obtain its goals. Both XPath and XQuery divide data into those which fully satisfy the selection conditions, and those which do not. However, binary conditions can be —in some scenarios— a limited approach to effective querying of XML data.

A few considerations can be made to justify this claim. First of all, even when XML schemas do exist, data producers do not always follow them precisely. Second, users often end up defining *blind* queries, either because they do not know the XML schema in detail, or because they do not know exactly what they are looking for. For example, they might be querying for some vague interest. Third, the same data can sometimes be described using different schemas. As it is often the case with semi-structured data, it is difficult to distinguish between the data itself and the structure containing it. There is an intrinsic overlap between data and structure and it is very common for "physically"

H.L. Larsen et al. (Eds.): FQAS 2006, LNAI 4027, pp. 210–221, 2006.

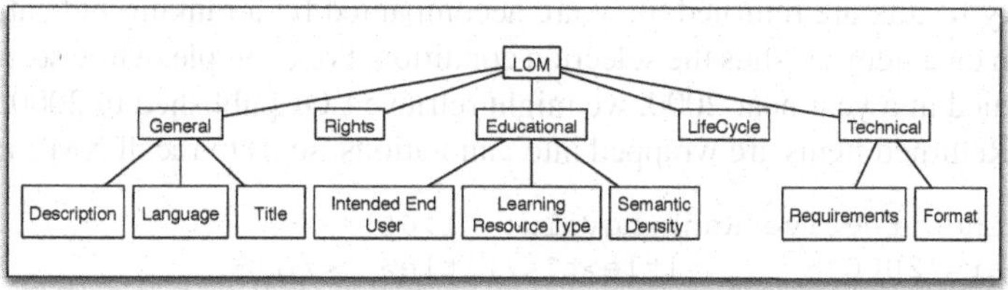

Fig. 1. A simplified representation of the structure of the LOM standard

near data to also be semantically related. It is easy to see how basing a binary query on such unsafe grounds can often lead to unnecessary silence.

For example, all these considerations are true in the field of e-learning metadata, which will constitute our explanatory context throughout this paper. In this field of research it is common to describe learning objects (LOs) using the LOM standard[1] and its XML representation. A simplified representation of the structure of these documents is shown in Figure 1. Within this context, we tackle the case in which a user is searching for a certain learning object across multiple and distributed repositories in which the same content may be stored with slightly different metadata.

In this paper, we propose a framework for querying XML data that goes beyond binary selection, and that allows the user to define more 'vague' and 'softer' selection criteria in order to obtain more results. To do so, we use concepts coming from the area of fuzzy logics. The main idea is that the selection should produce fuzzy sets, which differ from binary sets in the sense that it is possible to belong to them to different degrees. This is achieved through membership functions that consider the semantics behind the selection predicates (through domain specific ontologies or by calling WordNet), such as $Q : R[0,1]$, where $Q(x)$ indicates the degree to which the data x satisfies the concept Q. Concretely, we propose to extend the XPath query language to accommodate fuzzy selection. The choice has fallen on XPath since it presents a simpler starting point with respect to XQuery. Due to the considerations already stated and analised in [1], we define some extensions that constitute FXPath and fall into the following categories:

- Fuzzy Predicates: The user can express vague queries by exploiting fuzzy predicates, whose semantics can be based on structural relaxations or clarified through the use of domain specific ontologies.
- Fuzzy Tree Matching: Standard XPath provides a deep-equal function that can be used to assess whether two sequences contain items that are atomic values and are equal, or that are nodes of the same kind, with the same name, whose children are deep-equal. This can be restrictive, so we propose an extension named deep-similar to assess whether the sequences are similar both content-wise and structure-wise.

[1] This standard specifies the syntax and semantics of Learning Object Metadata, defined as the attributes required to describe a Learning Object. The Learning Object Metadata standards focuses on the minimal set of attributes needed to allow these Learning Objects to be managed, located, and evaluated. Relevant attributes of Learning Objects include object type, author, owner, terms of distribution, format and pedagogical attributes such as teaching or interaction style, grade level, mastery level, and prerequisites.

When query results are returned, they are accompanied by a ranking indicating "how much" each data item satisfies the selection condition. For example, while searching for LOs published in a year near 2000, we might retrieve LOs published in 2000, in 2001, 2002, etc. Returned items are wrapped into annotations, so as to recall XML tagging:

```
<!--RankingDirective RankingValue="1.0" -->
  <LO year="2000">    <title>t1</title>  </LO>
<!-- /RankingDirective -->
<!-- RankingDirective RankingValue=".8"-->
  <LO year="2001">    <title>t2</title>  </LO>
<!-- /RankingDirective -->
<!-- RankingDirective RankingValue=".65" -->
  <LO year="2002">    <title>t3</title>  </LO>
<!-- /RankingDirective -->
```

In this example it is possible to notice the presence of a ranking directive containing the ranking value —in the set $[0, 1]$— of each retrieved item. The closer it is to 1, the better the item satisfies the condition (i.e. to be published in a year near 2000).

The rest of this paper is structured as follows. Section 2 presents relevant and related work. Section 3 presents our approach for fuzzy predicates. Section 4 presents the concept of fuzzy tree matching and our implementation of the "deep-similar" function. Section 5 brings the two approaches together, and Section 6 concludes this paper.

2 Related Work

Fuzzy sets have been shown to be a convenient way to model flexible queries in [2]. Many attempts to extend SQL with fuzzy capabilities were undertaken in recent years. [3] describes SQLf, a language that extends SQL by introducing fuzzy predicates that are processed on crisp information. Fuzzy quantifiers allowing to define aggregated concepts have been proposed in [4] and [5].

The FSQL system [6], developed upon Oracle, represents imprecise information as possibility distributions stored in standard tables. Users write queries using FSQL, which are then translated into ordinary SQL queries that call functions provided by FSQL to compute the degrees of matching. Different approaches have been defined to compare fuzzy values. [7] proposes measures to evaluate (by considering similarity relations) how close two fuzzy representations are.

[8], based on possibility distribution and the semantic measure of fuzzy data, introduces an extended object-oriented database model to handle imperfect, as well as complex objects, in the real world. Some major notions in object-oriented databases such as objects, classes, objects-classes relationships, subclass/superclass, and multiple inheritances are extended in the fuzzy information environment.

In [9] the use of fuzzy querying in particular in the Internet is shown. This paper is an example of how fuzzy querying should be used in widely distributed data sources: it is shown how elements of fuzzy logic and linguistic quantifiers can be employed to attain human consistent and useful solutions.

[10] applies fuzzy set methods to multimedia databases which have a complex structure, and from which documents have to be retrieved and selected depending not only

on their contents, but also on the idea the user has of their appearance, through queries specified in terms of user criteria.

A stream of research on fuzzy pattern matching (FPM) started in the eighties, and was successfully used in flexible querying of fuzzy databases and in classification. Given a pattern representing a request expressed in terms of fuzzy sets, and a database containing imprecise or fuzzy attribute values, the FPM returns two matching degrees. An example of an advanced techniques based on FPM can be found in [11]. [12] proposes a counterpart of FPM, called "Qualitative Pattern Matching" (QPM), for estimating levels of matching between a request and data expressed with words. Given a request, QPM rank-orders the items which possibly, or which certainly match the requirements, according to the preferences of the user.

The problem of fuzzy similarity between graphs is studied in [13].

[14] presents FlexPath, an attempt to integrate database-style query languages such as XPath and XQuery and full-text search on textual content. FlexPath considers queries on structure as a template, and looks for answers that best match this template and the full-text search. To achieve this, FlexPath provides an elegant definition of relaxation on structure and defines primitive operators to span the space of relaxations. Query answering is now based on ranking potential answers on structural and full-text search conditions.

3 Fuzzy Predicates

Differently from classical binary logic semantics, fuzzy logics allow to describe reality using sets to which objects can belong to with a certain degree. Fuzzy sets, as introduced in [15], are described through a membership function $Q : X \rightarrow [0, 1]$, that assigns each object a membership degree for the considered set.

The main aspect of querying with vagueness is to analyze and choose the predicates that constitute the basic blocks for creating interrogations in the presence of uncertain data. Since the environment in which we apply fuzzy logics is XML, we can have vagueness at different levels in the interrogation: in PCDATA, in attributes, in tag-names, and in the information structure. The predicates we will analyze can be applied differently in all these contexts.

Definition 1. *The predicate* ***NEAR*** *defines the closeness among different elements and, depending on the type of element being treated, it can assume different meanings:*

1. *When the predicate NEAR is applied to a PCDATA value, the query selects nodes in which the PCDATA has a value close to the value expressed in the query. In this case the syntax is:*

```
"[{" "selection_node" ("NOT")? "NEAR" "compare_value }]"
```

2. *When the predicate NEAR is applied to an attribute value, the query selects nodes in which the attribute has a value close to the value expressed in the query. In this case the syntax is:*

```
"[{" "attribute_name" ("NOT")? "NEAR" "compare_value }]"
```

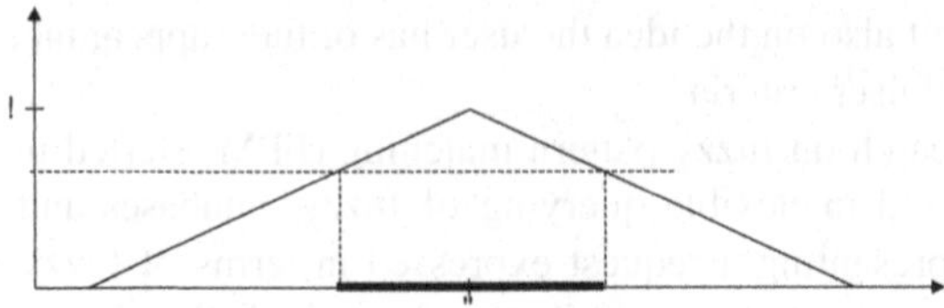

Fig. 2. An example of membership function and the concept of NEAR

3. *When the predicate NEAR is applied to a tag or to an attribute name, the query selects nodes with a name similar to the name expressed in the query, with the following syntax:*

```
"[{" ("NOT")? "NEAR" "node_name }]"
```

4. *When the predicate NEAR is inserted into the axis of a path expression, the selection tries to extract elements, attributes or text that are successors of the current node, giving a penalty which is proportional to the result's distance from the current node. The following syntax is used:*

```
"/{" ("NOT")? "NEAR::node_name"$
```

Let us now analyze how the predicate NEAR can be, in practice, applied to different fields and different data types. When the considered type is numeric, the query process is quite natural. We have defined a set of vocabularies tailored for different application domains. In these vocabularies we define a membership function and an $\alpha - cut$ that induces the concept of closeness for each particular type and field. Consider for example the following query:

```
\LOM[{\\duration NEAR PT1H}]
```

In this case, in terms of LOM duration, closeness can be naturally represented through a triangular membership function and what is NEAR is induced by an α−cut, with $\alpha = 0,6$ (see Figure 2).

The evaluation of textual information or strings is more complicated. In these cases we consider two different approaches: the first analyzes the linguistic similarity between two strings, while the other performs a semantic analysis between words. For the first problem we use the Levenshtein algorithm [16]. Given two strings S and T, it performs all the possible matchings among their characters, obtaining a matrix $|S| * |T|$ from which the distance between the two words is obtained. This approach can be useful when the same word appears in a tag written in a correct way and in an other misspelled, but in general it does not help us identify two words with the same meaning but different lexical roots. For analyzing the similarity from a semantics point of view it is necessary to integrate the system with a vocabulary that contains all possible synonyms. The vocabulary we use is called JWordNet[2]. In our querying process, we want to find both misspelled versions of a word x and words with the same meaning. That is why we use both evaluation methods, and consider the maximum value obtained.

[2] JWordNet is available at `http://wordnet.princeton.edu/`

The previous analysis of the use of the predicate NEAR for numeric and textual fields covers the first three meanings given in definition 1. Let us now analyze the fourth meaning, in which NEAR is applied within an axis.

```
\LOM[{\LOM\NEAR::duration}]
```

In this case, we search for a `duration` element placed near a `LOM` element. The degree of satisfaction of this predicate is a function of the number of steps needed to reach the `duration` element starting from the `LOM` one.

Besides the predicate NEAR we also introduce two other predicates:

- **APPROXIMATELY** allows to select —from a document— the elements with a given name that have a number of direct descendants close to the one indicated in the query. It is a derived predicate that can be substituted by a NEAR predicate applied to the result of the COUNT operator on the sons of a given node.
- **BESIDE**, applicable only to element names, is used to find the nodes that are close to the given node but not directly connected to it. The idea is to perform a horizontal search in the XML structure to find a given element's neighbors.

4 Deep-Similar

The *deep-similar* function is a fuzzy calculation of the distance between two XML trees based on the concept of Tree Edit Distance, a well-known approach for calculating how much it costs to transform one tree (the *source* tree) into another (the *destination* tree). Our novel contributions are that we consider structure, content, and the intrinsic overlap that can exist between the two. In particular, semantics are considered using Wordnet's system of hypernymys, as described in Section 3.

Another novel aspect of our approach is the introduction of a new Tree Edit Operation, called *Permute*. This new operation is added to the classic set of operations including *Insert*, *Delete*, and *Modify*. It is specifically introduced to tackle situations in which two nodes are present in both the source and the destination tree, but in a different order. This is an important aspect that cannot be ignored, since order often represents a important contribution to a tree's content. Moreover, we advocate that the costs of these operations cannot be given once and for all, but must depend on the nodes being treated.

Definition 2 (Deep-similar). *Given two XML trees T_1 and T_2, deep-similar(T_1, T_2) is the function that returns their degree of similarity as a value contained in the set [0,1]. This degree of similarity is given as 1 - (the cost of transforming T_1 into T_2 using Tree Edit Operations). Therefore, if two trees are completely different, their degree of similarity is 0; if they are exactly the same —both structure-wise and content-wise— their degree of similarity is 1.*

In order to transform the XML tree T_1 into T_2, the deep-similar function can use the following Tree Edit Operations:

Definition 3 (Insert). *Given an XML tree T, an XML node n, a location loc (defined through a path expression that selects a single node p in T), and an integer i, Insert(T, n, loc, i) transforms T into a new tree T' in which node n is added to the first level children nodes of p in position i.*

```
distribute-weight (Tree T, Weight w)
{
   wRoot = (f^x/m^y)
   annotate the root node with (w_root * w)
   for each first-level sub-tree s
   {
      w_subTree = b * L_S/L_T + (1-b) * l_S/l_T
      distribute-weight(s, (1-w_root)*w_subTree)
   }
}
```

Fig. 3. The *distribute-weight* algorithm

Definition 4 (Delete). *Given an XML tree T, and a location loc (defined through a path expression that selects a single node n in T), Delete(T, loc) transforms T into a new tree T' in which node n is removed.*

Definition 5 (Modify). *Given an XML tree T, a location loc (defined through a path expression that selects a single node n in T), and a new value v, Modify(t, loc, v) transforms T into a new tree T' in which the content of node n is replaced by v.*

Definition 6 (Permute). *Given an XML tree T, a location loc_1 (defined through a path expression that selects a single node n_1 in T), and a location loc_2 (defined through a path expression that selects a single node n_2 in T), Permute(T, loc_1, loc_2) transforms T into a new tree T' in which the locations of nodes n_1 and n_2 are exchanged.*

Before these operations can be applied to the source tree, two fundamental steps must be performed. The first consists in weighing the nodes within the two XML trees, in order to discover the importance they have within the trees. This will prove fundamental in calculating how much the edit operations cost. The second consists in matching the nodes in the source tree with those in the destination tree, and vice-versa. This step is paramount in discovering onto which nodes the different Tree Edit Operations must be performed. The costs of these Tree Edit Operations will be presented as soon as we complete a more in depth explanation of the two aforementioned steps.

4.1 Tree Node Weighing

Tree node weighing consists in associating a weight value —in the set [0,1]— to each and every node in an XML tree, by taking into consideration the structural properties it possesses due to its position within that very tree. The weighing algorithm we propose is devised to maintain a fundamental property, that the sum of the weights associated to all the nodes in a tree must be equal to 1.

In our framework, a function called *distribute-weight* is provided for this very reason. As seen in Figure 3, it is a recursive function that traverses the XML tree, annotating each node with an appropriate weight. It is recursive in order to mimic the intrinsic structural recursiveness present in XML trees, which are always built of one root-node and any number of sub-trees.

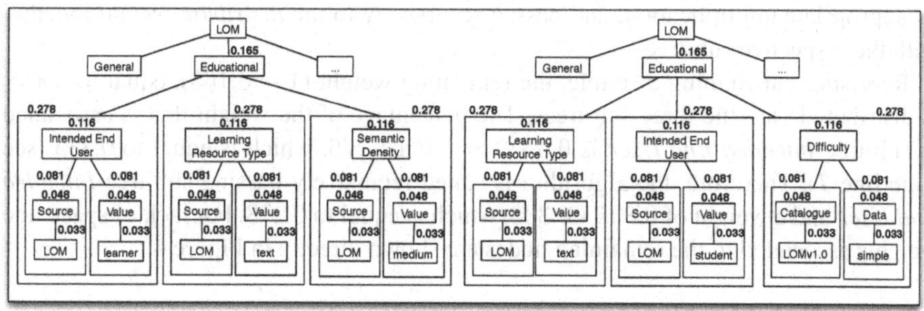

Fig. 4. The example

The algorithm is initially called passing it the entire tree to be weighed, and its total weight of 1. The first step is to decide how much of the total weight should be associated with the root-node (code line 3). Intuitively, the weight —and therefore the importance— of any given node is directly proportional to the number of first-level children nodes it possesses (variable f in code line 3) and inversely proportional to the total number of nodes in the tree (variable m in code line 3). The relationship is calibrated through the use of two constant exponents, x and y. After a great number of experiments in various contexts, the values 0.2246 and 0.7369 (respectively) have proven to give good results.

Regarding the example shown in Figure 4, we are interested in finding LOMs that possess similar educational metadata. The FXPath selection

```
\LOM{[deep-similar(Educational,\LOM[1]\educational] }
```

asks the system to provide just that. The Educational sub-tree from the left LOM is compared for similarity to the Educational sub-tree of the right LOM. Therefore, the algorithm is initially called passing it the sub-tree starting at node *Educational* and a weight of 1 to be distributed. The variable *wRoot* is calculated to be $3^{0.2246}/16^{0.7369}$, which is equal to 0.165.

The second step consists in deciding how to distribute the remaining weight onto the sub-trees. This cannot be done by simply looking at the number of nodes each of these sub-trees possesses. The importance —and therefore the weight— of a sub-tree depends both on the amount of "data" it contains (typically in its leaf nodes) and on the amount of "structure" it contains (typically in its intermediate nodes). These considerations are taken into account in code line 7, in which the variable L_s indicates the number of leaf nodes in sub-tree s, while the variable L_T indicates the number of leaf nodes in the tree T. On the other hand, the variable I_s indicates the number of intermediate nodes in sub-tree s, while the variable I_T indicates the number of intermediate nodes in the tree T. The balance between leaf and intermediate nodes is set through the use of the constant b. Our experiments have demonstrated that the algorithm is more effective if we balance the formula slightly in favor of the leaf nodes by setting b to 0.6. Code line 7, however, only gives the percentage of the remaining weight that should be associated to each sub-tree. The actual weight is calculated in code line 8 through an appropriate multiplication, and passed recursively to the *distribute-weight* together with the respective sub-tree.

Reprising our running example, the remaining weight (1 – 0.165), equal to 0.835, is distributed onto the three sub-trees. The percentage of the weight that is associated to sub-tree *Intended End User* is $0.6 * 2/6 + 0.4 * 2/6$, which is equal to 0.333 (see code line 7). Therefore, the algorithm is called recursively passing sub-tree *Intended End User* and a weight of $0.835 * 0.333$, which is equal to 0.278. For lack of space, the weights associated to the remaining nodes are shown directly in Figure 4.

4.2 Tree Node Matching

Tree Node Matching is the last step in determining which Tree Edit Operations must be performed to achieve the transformation. Its goal is to establish a matching between the nodes in the source and the destination trees. Whenever a match for a given a node *n* cannot be found in the other tree, it is matched to the *null* value.

In this step, we use an algorithm that takes into account more complex structural properties the nodes might have, and —for the first time— semantic similarity. It scores the *candidate nodes* by analyzing how "well" they match the *reference node*. The candidate node with the highest score is considered the reference node's match.

Regarding structural properties, the algorithm considers the following characteristics: *number of direct children, number of nodes in the sub-tree, depth of the sub-tree, distance from the expected position, position of the node with respect to its father, positions of the nodes in the sub-tree, same value for the first child node*, and *same value for the last node*. Each of these characteristics can give from a minimum of 1 point to a maximum of 5 points.

Regarding semantic similarity, the algorithm looks at the nodes' tag names. These are confronted using, once again, Wordnet's system of hypernymys (see Section 3). If the two terms are exactly the same, 1 point is given, if not their degree of similarity —a value in the set [0,1]— is considered.

4.3 Costs

Considerations presented in Sections 4.1 and 4.2 determine the costs the Tree Edit Operations have in our framework:

- The cost of the *Insert* edit operation corresponds to the weight the node being inserted has in the *destination* tree.
- The cost of the *Delete* edit operation corresponds to the weight the node being deleted from the *source* tree had.
- The cost of the *Modify* edit operation can be seen as the deletion of a node from the *source* tree, and its subsequent substitution by means of an insertion of a new node containing the new value. This operation does not modify the tree's structure, it only modifies its content. This is why it is necessary to consider the degree of similarity existing between the node's old term and its new one. The cost is therefore $k * w(n) * (1 - Sim(n, destinationNode))$, where *w(n)* is the weight the node being modified has in the *source* tree, the function Sim gives the degree of similarity between node n and the destination value, and *k* is a constant (0.9).

- The *Permute* edit operation does not modify the tree's structure. It only modifies the semantics that are intrinsically held in the order the nodes are placed in. Therefore, its cost is $h * [w(a) + w(b)]$, where *w(a)* is the weight of node *a*, *w(b)* is the weight of node *b*, and h is a constant value (0.36).

All the above cost-formulas are directly proportional to the weights of the nodes being treated. All of the operations, except *Permute*, can also be used directly on sub-trees as long as their total weights are used. A simple analysis shows that no cost can be higher than the weight of the nodes being treated, which means that the total cost cannot be higher than one, and that two trees' degree of similarity (*1- the cost of transforming* T_1 *into* T_2) must be a value in the set [0,1].

To conclude the running example (see Figure 4), the matchings, the needed tree edit operations, and their costs are presented in following table. The cost of the Modify operation in the third row is calculated as $0.9 * 0.033 * (1 - 0.769)$, while the cost of the Permute operation in row four is calculated as $0.36 * [0.278 + 0.278]$.

Source	*Destination*	*Operation*	*Cost*
null	Difficulty	Insert	0.278
Semantic Density	null	Delete	0.278
learner	student	Modify	0.006
Intended End User / Learning Resource Type	NA	Permute	0.2

The degree of similarity between the two Educational sub-trees can therefore be calculated as $1 - (0.278 + 0.278 + 0.006 + 0.2)$, which evaluates to 0.238. This means that the two LOMs have quite different Educational sub-trees.

If we had applied the same algorithm to the entire LOM trees, and had they differed only in their Educational sub-trees, a much higher degree of similarity would have been obtained.

5 Complex Queries Evaluation

Fuzzy predicates and fuzzy tree matching can be composed within a single query by combination through logical operators, that, in this context, are redefined to take into account the different semantics for predicates and sets. The following meanings for logical operators are used in this work:

- **NOT.** The negation preserves the meaning of complement, hence considered a fuzzy set A, with membership function Q, for each element a, if $a \in A$ implies $Q(a)$ then $a \notin A$ implies $1 - Q(a)$.
- **AND.** The conjunction of conditions can be considered in the following manner. Given n fuzzy sets $A_1, A_2, \ldots, A_n$ with membership functions $Q_1, Q_2, \ldots, Q_n$, and given the elements $a_1, a_2, \ldots, a_n$, if $I(a_1, a_2, \ldots, a_n)$ is the intersection of the conditions $(a_1 \in A_1), (a_2 \in A_2), \ldots, (a_n \in A_n)$ then $(a_1 \in A_1) AND (a_2 A_2) AND \ldots AND (a_n \in A_n)$ implies $I(a_1, a_2, \ldots, a_n)$ is $Q(a_1, a_2, , a_n)$ where $Q(a_1, a_2, \ldots, a_n) = min[Q_1(a_1), Q_2(a_2), \ldots, Q_n(a_n)]$. The chosen approach preserves the meaning of conjunction in a crisp sense. In

fact, once a threshold for the condition to hold has been fixed, it is necessary that all the conditions in the conjunction respect it. As in classical logic, for an AND condition to be true, all the conditions composing it have to be true.
- **OR.** The interpretation chosen for the union of conditions is symmetric with respect to conjunction. Given n fuzzy sets $A_1, A_2, \ldots, A_n$ with membership functions $Q_1, Q_2, \ldots, Q_n$, and given the elements $a_1, a_2, \ldots, a_n$, if $U(a_1, a_2, \ldots, a_n)$ is the union of the conditions $(a_1 \in A_1), (a_2 \in A_2), \ldots, (a_n \in A_n)$ then $(a_1 \in A_1) OR (a_2 A_2) OR \ldots OR (a_n \in A_n)$ implies $U(a_1, a_2, \ldots, a_n)$ is $Q(a_1, a_2, , a_n)$ where $Q(a_1, a_2, \ldots, a_n) = max[Q_1(a_1), Q_2(a_2), \ldots, Q_n(a_n)]$

Consider now a query combining the described fuzzy features:

```
\LOM{[deep-similar(educational,\LOM[1]\educational] AND
                                              \\duration NEAR PT1H }
```

The evaluation of such a query is the result of a four step process:

1. The query is transformed into a crisp one, capable of extracting data guaranteed to be a superset of the desired result. In the example we obtain `\LOM` which extracts all the LOMs, which are clearly a superset of the desired result.
2. Every fuzzy predicate p_i is evaluated w.r.t. each of the extracted data's items, and a degree of satisfaction is assigned through use of a variable v_i.
   In this example, we evaluate the deep-similar between the Educational sub-items, and to what degree the LOM's duration is NEAR to one hour (thanks to a devoted dictionary). For the first item of the result-set (the right-hand side LOM in Figure 4), the former evaluates to 0.238, and the latter to 0.67 (45 minutes against one hour).
3. An overall degree of satisfaction is obtained for each item in the result. This is done considering all the different predicates of the path expression in conjunction, in accordance to the crisp XPath semantics. In our example, we take the minor of the two degrees of satisfaction (0.238).
4. The items in the result are ordered according to the obtained degree of satisfaction.

The idea of considering all the different fuzzy predicates in conjunction can be too rigid in some contexts. An alternative approach can be to allow advanced users to explicitly bound each degree to a variable and to define a function to calculate the final degree of satisfaction. We define a `WITH RANKING` clause in order to combine the bound values in the final ranking. The following example shows a FXPath expression with two fuzzy conditions:

```
\LOM{[deep-similar(educational,\LOM[1]\educational] | v1 AND
                  \\duration NEAR PT1H | v2 WITH RANKING v1 * v2}
```

The ranking of the result set is obtained as the product of the values bound to $v1$ and $v2$. More complex `WITH RANKING` clauses could involve:

- linear combination of the values bound to the ranking variables:
  `WITH RANKING 0.4*v1 + 0.6*v2`
- normalized weighted average.

6 Conclusion

We have presented a framework for querying semi-structured XML data based on key aspects of fuzzy logics. Its main advantage is the minimization of the silent queries that can be caused by (1) data not following an appropriate schema faithfully, (2) the user providing a blind query in which he does not know the schema or exactly what he is looking for, and (3) data being presented with slightly diverse schemas. This is achieved through the use of fuzzy predicates, and fuzzy tree matching. Both rely on domain semantics for achieving their goal, and we currently propose WordNet for calculating semantic similarity. However, more precise domain specific ontologies could be used to obtain better results. Future work will, in fact, concentrate on further validating our approach using domain specific ontologies.

References

1. Braga, D., Campi, A., Damiani, E., Pasi, G., Lanzi, P.L.: FXPath: Flexible querying of xml documents. In: Proc. of EuroFuse. (2002)
2. Bosc, P., Lietard, L., Pivert, O.: Soft querying, a new feature for database management systems. In: DEXA. (1994) 631–640
3. Bosc, P., Lietard, L., Pivert, O.: Quantified statements in a flexible relational query language. In: SAC '95: Proceedings of the 1995 ACM symposium on Applied computing, New York, NY, USA, ACM Press (1995) 488–492
4. Kacprzyk, J., Ziolkowski, A.: Database queries with fuzzy linguistic quantifiers. IEEE Trans. Syst. Man Cybern. **16**(3) (1986) 474–479
5. Bosc, P., Pivert, O.: Fuzzy querying in conventional databases. (1992) 645–671
6. Galindo, J., Medina, J., Pons, O., Cubero, J.: A server for fuzzy sql queries. In: Proceedings of the Flexible Query Answering Systems. (1998)
7. Bosc, P., Pivert, O.: On representation-based querying of databases containing ill-known values. In: ISMIS '97: Proceedings of the 10th International Symposium on Foundations of Intelligent Systems, London, UK, Springer-Verlag (1997) 477–486
8. Ma, Z.M., Zhang, W.J., Ma, W.Y.: Extending object-oriented databases for fuzzy information modeling. Inf. Syst. **29**(5) (2004) 421–435
9. Kacprzyk, J., Zadrozny, S.: Internet as a challenge to fuzzy querying. (2003) 74–95
10. Dubois, D., Prade, H., Sèdes, F.: Fuzzy logic techniques in multimedia database querying: A preliminary investigation of the potentials. IEEE Transactions on Knowledge and Data Engineering **13**(3) (2001) 383–392
11. Mouchaweh, M.S.: Diagnosis in real time for evolutionary processes in using pattern recognition and possibility theory (invited paper). International Journal of Computational Cognition **2**(1) (2004) 79–112 ISSN 1542-5908.
12. Loiseau, Y., Prade, H., Boughanem, M.: Qualitative pattern matching with linguistic terms. AI Commun. **17**(1) (2004) 25–34
13. Blondel, V.D., Gajardo, A., Heymans, M., Senellart, P., Dooren, P.V.: A measure of similarity between graph vertices: applications to synonym extraction and Web searching. SIAM Review **46**(4) (2004) 647–666
14. Amer-Yahia, S., Lakshmanan, L.V.S., Pandit, S.: Flexpath: flexible structure and full-text querying for xml. In: SIGMOD '04: Proceedings of the 2004 ACM SIGMOD international conference on Management of data, New York, NY, USA, ACM Press (2004) 83–94
15. Zadeh, L.: Fuzzy sets. Information and Control. **8**(4) (1965) 338–353
16. Levenshtein: Binary codes capable of correcting deletions, insertions and reversals. Soviet Physics-Doklady **10** (1966) 707–710

Towards Flexible Information Retrieval Based on CP-Nets

Fatiha Boubekeur[1,2], Mohand Boughanem[1], and Lynda Tamine-Lechani[1]

[1] IRIT-SIG, Paul Sabatier University,
31062 Toulouse, France
[2] Mouloud Mammeri University,
15000 Tizi-Ouzou, Algeria
boubekeu@irit.fr, boughane@irit.fr,
tamine@irit.fr

Abstract. This paper describes a flexible information retrieval approach based on CP-Nets (Conditional Preferences Networks). The CP-Net formalism is used for both representing qualitative queries (expressing user preferences) and representing documents in order to carry out the retrieval process. Our contribution focuses on the difficult task of term weighting in the case of qualitative queries. In this context, we propose an accurate algorithm based on UCP-Net features to automatically weight Boolean queries. Furthermore, we also propose a flexible approach for query evaluation based on a flexible aggregation operator adapted to the CP-Net semantics.

1 Introduction

The main goal of an information retrieval system (IRS) is to find the information assumed to be relevant to a user query generally expressed by a set of keywords (terms) connected with Boolean operators. However, keywords-based queries don't allow expressing user preferences on the search criteria. Furthermore, the classical Boolean aggregation is too "crisp" defining strict matching mechanisms. The traditional IRS, too rigid, thus provide only partial results and sometimes even non-relevant ones. To tackle these problems, various works focused on the extension of the classical Boolean model, by introducing weights in the query [1], [7], [8], [12], [10], [11], in order to enable a fuzzy representation of the documents and a flexible query formulation. More precisely, the Boolean model extensions proposed make possible the expression of the user preferences within the query using flexible aggregation operators; these operators are also applied on documents in order to allow flexible indexing and consequently flexible query evaluation. However, assigning weights to query terms is not an easy task for a user, particularly when the query contains conditional preferences. We illustrate the problem we attempt to solve using the following example.

Information need: "*I am looking for housing in Paris or Lyon of studios or university room type. Knowing that I prefer to be in Paris rather than to be in Lyon, if I should go to Paris, I will prefer being into residence hall (RH) (we will treat residence hall as a single term), whereas if I should go to Lyon, a studio is more*

H.L. Larsen et al. (Eds.): FQAS 2006, LNAI 4027, pp. 222 – 231, 2006.

preferable to me than a room in residence hall. Moreover the Center town of Paris is more preferable to me than its suburbs; whereas if I must go to Lyon, I will rather prefer to reside in suburbs that in the center".

Such a query emphasizes conditional preferences. Taking into account the user preferences leads to the following query:

$$(Paris\ 0.9\ \wedge (RH\ 0.6\ \vee Studio\ 0.3)\ \wedge (Center\ 0.5\ \vee Suburbs\ 0.4))\ \vee$$
$$(Lyon\ 0.8\ \wedge (RH\ 0.5\ \vee Studio\ 0.8)\ \wedge (Center\ 0.7\ \vee Suburbs\ 0.8)).$$

In this representation, the weights of terms *R.H* and *Studio*, *Center* and *Suburbs*, are different when they are associated in *Paris* or *Lyon* respectively. This exactly expresses the conditional preferences of the user. The disjunctive normal form of this query is given by:

$$\begin{aligned}&(Paris\ 0.9 \wedge RH\ 0.6 \wedge Center\ 0.5) \vee (Paris\ 0.9 \wedge Studio\ 0.3 \wedge Center\ 0.5)\ \vee\\&(Paris\ 0.9 \wedge RH\ 0.6 \wedge Suburbs\ 0.4) \vee (Paris\ 0.9 \wedge Studio\ 0.3 \wedge Suburbs\ 0.4)\\&\vee (Lyon\ 0.8 \wedge RH\ 0.5 \wedge Center\ 0.7) \vee (Lyon\ 0.8 \wedge Studio\ 0.8 \wedge Center\ 0.7)\ \vee\\&(Lyon\ 0.8 \wedge RH\ 0.5 \wedge Suburbs\ 0.8) \vee (Lyon\ 0.8 \wedge Studio\ 0.8 \wedge Suburbs\ 0.8).\end{aligned} \quad (1)$$

Even thought this representation supports conditional preferences, nevertheless it poses problems. Indeed, assuming that each conjunctive sub-query of the whole query has a total importance weight, computed by aggregation of individual weights of its own terms (using *min* or *OWA* operators or simply by averaging for example), then we obtain: importance of *(Paris* $\wedge$ *Studio* $\wedge$ *Center)* is *0.56* whereas importance of *(Lyon* $\wedge$ *Studio* $\wedge$ *Center)* is *0.76* implying that the latest alternative is preferable than the preceding one. This is contradictory with the stated user preferences. Our weighting above is therefore incoherent.

This example outlines the impact of random or intuitive term weighting of a qualitative query on the semantic accuracy of the preferences it attempts to express. It illustrates the difficult task of query term weighting in a qualitative query. Other works in IR tackled this problem using more intuitive qualitative preferences, expressed with linguistic terms such: *important, very important*… [2], [3]. However, the problem of weighting terms belongs to the definition of both fuzzy concepts of importance and linguistic modifiers: *very, little*…

We propose, in this paper, a mixed approach for flexible IR which combines the expressivity property and the computation accuracy within a unified formalism: CP-Nets [4], [6]. More precisely, we propose to use the CP-Net formalism for two main reasons. The first one is to enable a graphical representation of flexible queries expressing user conditional preferences that can be automatically quantified using an accurate algorithm dedicated to UCP-Nets [5] valuation; such a quantification corresponds to the resolution of the problem of query term weighting presented above. The second reason is to allow a flexible query evaluation using a CP-Net document representation and a flexible matching mechanism based on the use of flexible aggregation operator adapted to the CP-Net semantics.

The paper is organized as follows: in section 2, we present the guiding principles of the CP-Nets and the UCP-Nets. The Section 3 describes our flexible information retrieval approach based on CP-Nets: we present namely our automatic CP-Nets weighting approach and our flexible CP-Net query evaluation method.

2 CP-Net Formalism

CP-Nets were introduced in 1999 [4] as graphical models for compact representation of qualitative preference relations. They exploit conditional preferential dependencies in the structuring of the user preferences under the *Ceteris-Paribus*[1] assumption. Preference relations in a CP-Net can also be quantified with utility values leading to a UCP-Net. We describe in this section the CP-Nets and UCP-Nets graphical models.

2.1 CP-Nets

A CP-Net is a Directed Acyclic Graph, or *DAG*, $G = (V, E)$, where V is a set of nodes $\{X_1, X_2, X_3 \ldots X_n\}$ that represent the preference variables and E a set of directed arcs expressing preferential dependencies between them. Each variable X_i takes values in the set $Dom(X_i) = \{xi_1, x_{i2}, x_{i3}, \ldots\}$. We note $Pa(X_i)$ the parent set of X_i in G. representing his predecessor in the graph. A set $\{X_i, Pa(X_i)\}$ defines a CP-Net family.

For each variable X_i of the CP-Net, is attached a conditional preference table ($CPT(X_i)$) specifying for each value of $Pa(X_i)$ a total preference order among $Dom(X_i)$ values. For a root node of the CP-Net, the *CPT* simply specifies an unconditional preference order on its values.

Figure 1 illustrates the CP-Net corresponding to the query (1). The variables of interest are V={*City, Housing, Place*} where *Dom(City)={Paris, Lyon}*, *Dom(Housing) = {RH, Studio}* and *Dom (Place) = {Center, Suburbs}*. In addition, *CPT(City)* specifies that *Paris* is unconditionally preferable to *Lyon* (*Paris* $\succ$[2] *Lyon*), whereas *CPT(Housing)* for example, specifies a preference order on *Housing* values, under the condition of the *City* node values (thus for example, if *Paris* then *RH* $\succ$ *Studio*).

We call an alternative of the CP-Net each element of the Cartesian product of all its nodes values fields. It is interpreted like a conjunction of its elements. For example, *(Paris, Studio, Center)* and *(Lyon, RH, Center)* are alternatives of the CP-Net presented in figure 1.

A CP-Net induces a complete preference graph built on the whole of its alternatives, ordered under the *Ceteris Paribus* assumption [4]:

$$\text{Let } x_1, x_2 \in Dom(X),\ x_1 \succ x_2 \text{ Ceteris Paribus if } \forall p \in Pa(X),\ \forall y \in V\text{-}\{X, Pa(X)\}: \\ x_1\, p\, y \succ x_2\, p\, y .$$

The preference graph induced by the CP-Net of Figure 1 is presented in Figure 2, in which a directed arrow from X_i node (alternative) to X_j node expresses that X_j is preferable to X_i *Ceteris Paribus*. Hence, the alternatives *(Paris, RH, Center)* and *(Lyon, RH, Center)* are comparable (since *Paris* $\succ$ *Lyon Ceteris Paribus*), whereas, the two alternatives *(Paris, RH, Suburbs)* and *(Paris, Studio, Center)* are not and thus cannot be ordered.

---

[1] All else being equal.

[2] Preference relation.

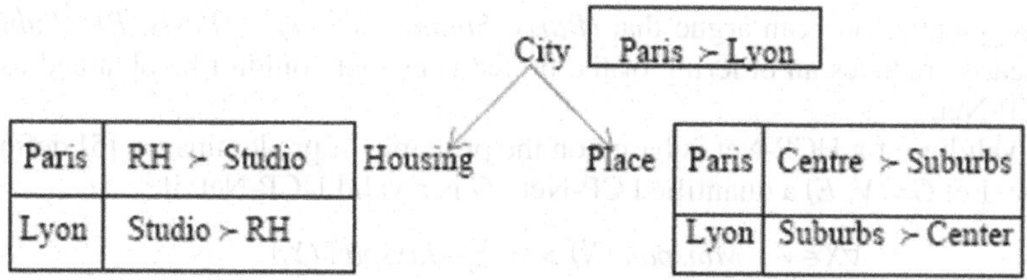

Fig. 1. CP-Net Representation of a Boolean query

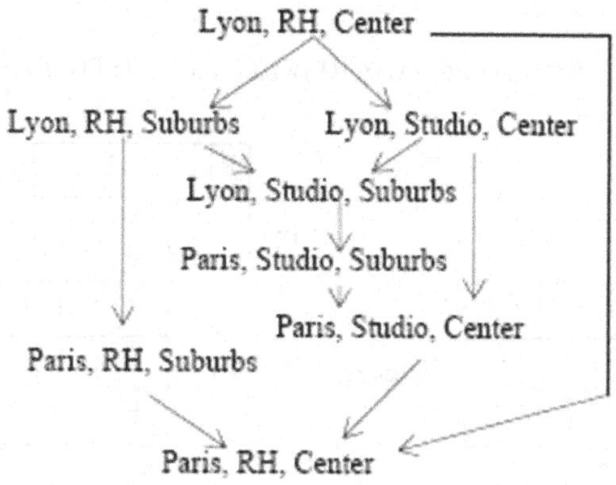

Fig. 2. A preference graph

2.2 UCP-Nets

A CP-Net doesn't allow comparison and ordering of all the possible alternatives. For this aim, one must quantify preferences. A UCP-Net [5] extends a CP-Net by quantifying the CP-Net nodes with conditional utility values (utility factors). A conditional utility factor $f_i(X_i, Pa(X_i))$ (we simply write $f_i(X_i)$), is a real value attached to each value X_i given an instantiation of its parents $Pa(X_i)$.

Therefore defining a UCP-Net amounts to define for each family $\{X_i, Pa(X_i)\}$ of the CP-Net, a utility factor $f_i(X_i)$. These factors are used to quantify the *CPTs* in the graph.

The utility factors are generalized additive independent (*GAI*) [5]. Formally, for a UCP-Net $G=(X, V)$ where $V=\{X_1,\ldots,X_n\}$, we compute the global utility of V denoted u(V) as follows:

$$u(V) = \Sigma_i f_i(X_i)\ . \quad (2)$$

In Figure 3, we present a UCP-Net that quantifies the CP-Net presented in Figure1.

For the UCP-Net of Figure 3, utility factors $f_1(City)$, $f_2(Housing, City)$ and $f_3(Place, City)$ being *GAI*, one has: $u(City, Housing, Place) = f_1(City) + f_2(Housing, City) + f_3(Place, City)$. This leads to the following: $u\ (Paris, Studio, Center) = 1.99$ and $u\ (Paris, RH, Suburbs) = 1.92$.

Consequently, one can argue that *(Paris, Studio, Center)* $\succ$ *(Paris, RH, Suburbs)*. This clearly traduces an ordering of the preferences that couldn't be obtained using a basic CP-Net.

The validity of a UCP-Net is based on the principle of predominance [5] defined as follows: Let $G=(V, E)$ a quantified CP-Net. G is a valid UCP-Net if :

$$\forall X \in V, \quad Minspan\,(X) >= \textstyle\sum_i Maxspan\,(Y_i)\,. \tag{3}$$

Where Yi is a descendant of X $(Y_i \in V \,/\, X = Pa(Y_i))$ and

$$Minspan(X) = min_{\,x_1,\, x_2\, \in Dom(X)}\,(min_{\,p \in Dom(Pa(X))}\,(|\, f_X(x_1, p) - f_X(x_2, p)|))\,.$$

$$Maxspan(X) = max_{x1,\, x2\, \in Dom(X)}\,(max_{\,p \in Dom(Pa(X))}\,(|\, f_X\,(x_1, p) - f_X(x_2, p)|)).$$

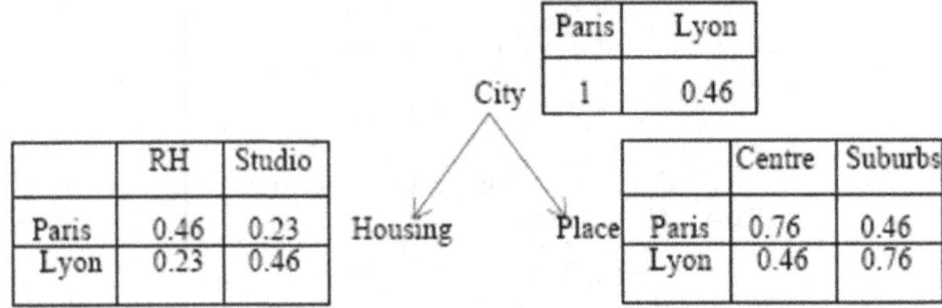

Fig. 3. An example of UCP-Net

3 Flexible Information Retrieval Based on CP-Nets

We describe in this section our flexible information retrieval approach based on CP-Nets. We show first of all how to use CP-Nets for expressing user qualitative queries, then we detail our approach for automatically weighting the related terms. We finally present our CP-Net semantics based flexible method for evaluating such preferential weighted queries.

3.1 Expressing Queries Using CP-Nets

The user preferences are expressed using concepts represented by variables. Each variable is defined on a domain of values (a value is therefore a query term). For each variable, the user must specify all of its preferential dependencies from which a CP-Net graph is built. The CP-Net query is then weighted by preference weights corresponding to utility factors. Our automatic weighting process is based on the predominance property stated above (section 2.2). We present it in the following:.

3.1.1 Weighting Queries Using UCP-Nets

Let $Q=(V,E)$ be a CP-Net query Q which expresses the qualitative conditional preferences of a user on n concepts (variables), X be a variable of Q, such as $|\,Dom(X)| = k$, and let $u(i)$ be the ith preference order on X's values (one assume $u(i)$ growing when i grows):

For any leaf node X, we generate the utilities simply as uniform preference orders over the set [0 1] as follows:

$$u(1) = 0 \text{ and } u(i) = u(i-1) + (1/(k-1)), \ \forall 1 < i <= k. \quad (4)$$

For any internal node X (X is not a leaf node), we compute $S = \sum_i Maxspan(B_i)$ where B_i represents the descendants of X. The predominance property (3) imposes that $Minspan(X) > = S$. Several values answer the condition correctly, the smallest one S is choosen, so that $Minspan(X) = S$. The utilities are computed as follows:

$$u(1) = 0 \text{ and } u(i) = u(i-1) + S, \ \forall 1 < i <= k. \quad (5)$$

We then easily compute: $Minspan(X) = |u(i+1) - u(i)|$ and $Maxspan(X) = |u(k) - u(1)|$.

The utility values obtained can be higher than 1 (particularly in the case of internal nodes), we propose a normalisation of the individual utility factors of the CP-Net and of the total utilities of each alternative as follows: For each CP-Net node X_j, let $Max_{X_j} = max_i(u(i))$ be the highest preference order on X_j values, then:

$$\forall X_j, \ \forall u(i), 1 \leq i \leq |Dom(X_j)|, \ u(i) = u(i) / \sum_j Max_{X_j}. \quad (6)$$

3.1.2 Illustration

Using the proposed method, the UCP-Net related to the query of Figure 1 is presented in Figure 4.

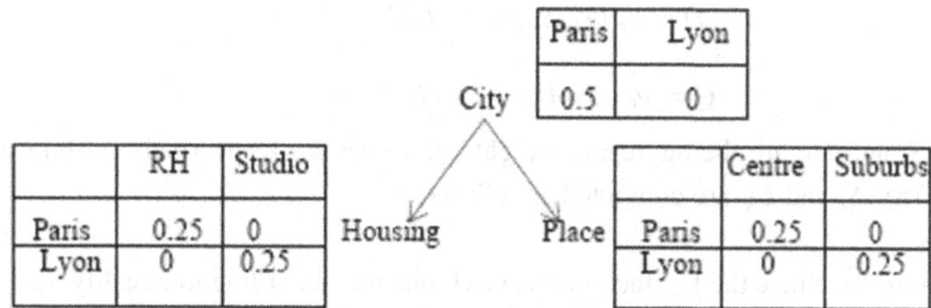

Paris	Lyon
0.5	0

	RH	Studio
Paris	0.25	0
Lyon	0	0.25

	Centre	Suburbs
Paris	0.25	0
Lyon	0	0.25

Fig. 4. A UCP-Net query

We thus obtain the following weighted Boolean query:

(Paris 0.5 ∧ (RH 0.25 ∨ Studio 0) ∧ (Center 0.25 ∨ Suburbs 0)) ∨ (Lyon 0 ∧ (RH 0 ∨ Studio 0.25) ∧ (Center 0 ∨ Suburbs 0.25)

From where: $u(Paris, Studio, Center) = 0.5$ and $u(Paris, RH, Suburbs) = 0.75$.

3.2 CP-Net Based Query Evaluation

Once the CP-Net query weighted, the retrieval process is launched during the first step on the whole of the nodes values of the CP-Net without taking account of weighting as a preliminary. The result is a list of probable relevant documents for the query. In the second step, an evaluation process based on semantics CP-Net ranks them by degree of relevance; for this aim, retrieved documents are first represented by CP-Nets, then an evaluation process is proposed to estimate the relevance status values of such CP-Net documents for the CP-Net query.

3.2.1 A Document as a CP-Net

Each assumed relevant document for a query $Q=(V,E)$ is represented by a CP-Net $D=(V, E')$. The corresponding topology is similar to the query CP-Net $Q=(V,E)$ but the CPTs are different. Indeed, the related CPTs quantify the importance of indexing terms in D as estimated within the terms weights based on a variant of *tf* idf*.

The document (respectively the query) is then interpreted as a disjunction of conjunctions, each one of them being built on the whole of the elements of the Cartesian product $Dom(X_1)* Dom(X_2)*\ldots* Dom(X_n))$ where X_i $(1 \le i \le n)$ are the CP-Net document (respectively query) nodes, that is to say:

$$D = \vee_{j_i} (\wedge_i (t_{i,j_i}, p_{i,j_i})) . \tag{7}$$

$$Q = \vee_{j_i} (\wedge_i (t_{i,j_i}, f_{i,j_i})) \tag{8}$$

Where $1 \le i \le n$, $1 \le j_i \le |Dom(X_i)|$, $t_{i,j_i} \in Dom(X_i)$, p_{i,j_i} is the weight of t_{i,j_i} in D (based on its occurrence frequency) and f_{i,j_i} is the weight of the term t_{i,j_i} (its utility) in Q being given a value of its parent.

Let us note $m = |Dom(X_1)| * |Dom(X_2)| *\ldots *|Dom(X_n)|$, by posing: $\wedge_i t_{i,j_i} = T_k$, with $1 \le k \le m$, the representations (7) and (8) are respectively brought to:

$$D = \vee_k (T_k, S_k) = \vee(T_k, S_k). \tag{9}$$

$$Q = \vee_k (T_k, U_k) = \vee(T_k, U_k). \tag{10}$$

Where S_k and U_k are the aggregate weights of values p_{i,j_i} respectively introduced in (7) and (8). S_k and U_k are computed as follows:

Computing U_k. Since the $f_{i,ji}$ factors are GAI, one has according to equality (2):

$$U_k = \Sigma_i f_{i,j_i} . \tag{11}$$

Computing S_k. We propose to compute the aggregated weight S_k, as weighted average of the p_{i,j_i} as follows: We first associate an importance of position G_X to nodes X of the CP-Net document according to their levels in the graph: if X is a leaf node: $G_X=1$; for any other node X such as B_l are the descendants of X and G_{B_l} their respective importance orders, one has:

$$G_X = max_l \, G_{B_l} + 1 . \tag{12}$$

The aggregate weight S_K introduced in (9) is then given by:

$$S_K = \Sigma_i p_{i,j_i} G_{X_i} / \Sigma_i G_{X_i} . \tag{13}$$

Where X_i is the node containing term (t_{i,j_i}) of D.

D_1 ((Paris, 0.7), (Lyon, 0.5), (RH, 0.2)) .

Fig. 5. Retrieved document

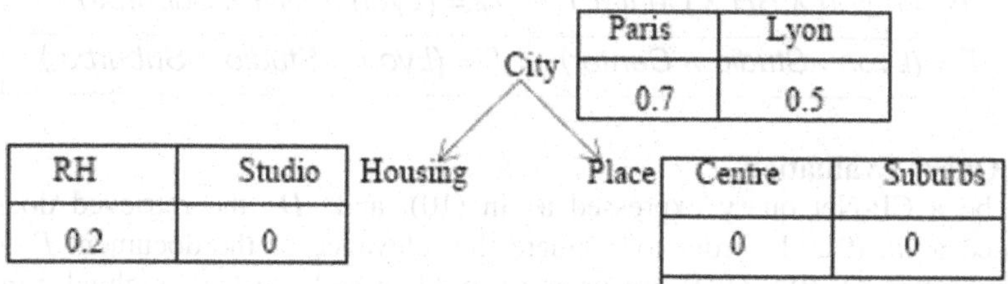

Fig. 6. D_1 as CP-Net

Thus for example, let us suppose that the retrieval process, launched initially on the whole terms of the weighted query of Figure 4, returns document D_1 presented in Figure 5, where each pair *(t, p)* respectively represents the term and its weight associated in the document. In Figure 6 we present the UCP-Net associated with documents D_1.

UCP-Net query introduced in Figure 4 and UCP-Net document introduced in Figure 6 are interpreted respectively using formulas (7) and (8), as follows:

$$Q = ((Paris,0.5) \wedge (RH,0.25) \wedge (Center,0.25)) \vee ((Paris,0.5) \wedge (RH,0.25) \wedge (Suburbs,0)) \vee ((Paris,0.5) \wedge (Studio,0) \wedge (Center,0.25)) \vee ((Paris,0.5) \wedge (Studio,0) \wedge (Suburbs,0)) \vee ((Lyon,0) \wedge (RH,0) \wedge (Center,0)) \vee ((Lyon,0) \wedge (RH,0) \wedge (Suburbs,0.25)) \vee ((Lyon,0) \wedge (Studio,0.25) \wedge (Center,0)) \vee ((Lyon,0) \wedge (Studio,0.25) \wedge (Suburb,0.25)) .$$

$$D_1 = ((Paris, 0.7) \wedge (RH, 0.2) \wedge (center, 0)) \vee ((Paris, 0.7) \wedge (RH, 0.2) \wedge (suburbs,0)) \vee ((Paris, 0.7) \wedge (Studio, 0) \wedge (center, 0)) \vee ((Paris, 0.7) \wedge (Studio, 0) \wedge (suburbs,0)) \vee ((Lyon, 0.5) \wedge (RH, 0.2) \wedge (center, 0)) \vee ((Lyon, 0.5) \wedge (RH, 0.2) \wedge (suburbs,0)) \vee (Lyon, 0.5) \wedge (Studio, 0) \wedge (center, 0)) \vee ((Lyon, 0.5) \wedge (Studio, 0) \wedge (suburbs,0)) .$$

Thus, the CP-Net query Q presented in figure 4 and the CP-Net document in Figure 6 are translated respectively according to formulas (9) and (10) into:

$$Q = (T_1, 1) \vee (T_2, 0.75) \vee (T_3, 0.75) \vee (T_4, 0.5) \vee (T_5, 0) \vee (T_6, 0.25) \vee (T_7, 0.25) \vee (T_8, 0.5) .$$

$$D_1 = (T_1, 0.4) \vee (T_2, 0.4) \vee (T_3, 0.35) \vee (T_4, 0.35) \vee (T_5, 0.3) \vee (T_6, 0.3) \vee (T_7, 0.25) \vee (T_8, 0.25) .$$

Where T_i, $1 \leq i \leq 8$ is given in Table 1, T_i's weight in Q (respectively in D_1) is computed using (11) (respectively (13)).

Table 1. Conjunctive sub-queries

T_1= (Paris∧ RH ∧ Center)	T_2 = (Paris ∧ RH ∧ Suburbs)
T_3= (Paris ∧ Studio ∧ Center)	T_4 = (Paris ∧ Studio ∧ Suburbs)
T_5 = (Lyon ∧ RH ∧ Center)	T_6 = (Lyon ∧ RH ∧ Suburbs)
T_7= (Lyon ∧Studio ∧ Center)	T_8= (Lyon ∧ Studio ∧ Suburbs)

3.2.2 Query Evaluation

Let Q be a CP-Net query expressed as in (10), and D the retrieved document expressed as in (9). In order to evaluate the relevance of the document D for the weighted query Q, $RSV(Q,D)$, we propose to adapt and use the weighted minimum operator [12], [9] as follows:

Let U_K be the importance weight of T_k in Q, $F(D, T_k) = S_K$, the weight of T_k in the document D, we note $RSV_{T_k}(F(D, T_k), U_k)$ the evaluation function of T_k for document D. The various weighted conjunctions (T_k, U_k) being bound by a disjunction, which gives:

$$RSV_{T_k}(F(D, T_k), U_k) = Min\ (S_k\ U_k). \tag{14}$$

$RSV(Q,d)$ is then obtained by aggregation of the whole of the weights of relevance computed in (14) as follows:

$$RSV(Q,D) = Max_K(Min\ (S_k, U_k)). \tag{15}$$

Using the Equalities (14) and (15), we compute the partial relevance of document D_1 for each sub-query T_k given in Table 1 and its total relevance for the disjunctive query Q as indicated in Table 2 below:

Table 2. Partial and total relevance of document D_1

	T_1	T_2	T_3	T_4	T_5	T_6	T_7	T_8	GRSV[3]
D_1	0.4	0.4	0.35	0.35	0	0.25	0.25	0.25	0.4

Document D_1 can thus be ordered either partially according to its partial relevance for each sub-query T_k, or globally according to its total relevance to query $Q = \vee T_k$.

4 Conclusion

We described in this paper a novel approach for flexible IR based on CP-Nets. The approach focuses on the representation of qualitative queries expressing user preferences. The formalism is graphic and qualitative what allows a natural and intuitive formulation and a simple and compact representation of the preferences. The qualitative formalism has a power of high expression but declines in computing

[3] Global RSV.

power. We proposed then to quantify it using utility values leading to a UCP-Net. The utilities, representing conditional importance weights of query terms, are computed automatically. The user is thus discharged from this tiresome and not less improbable task, and the generated weights are checked correct since based on theoretical bases of UCP-Nets. We also proposed a CP-Net based query evaluation. Our approach aims to represent retrieved document as CP-Net in order to estimate both its partial relevance and its total relevance to a given query by using of a flexible aggregation operator, the weighted minimum, which we adapted to CP-Nets semantics.

One interesting future work is the use of fuzzy concepts and linguistic terms in the user's need expression and their integration into the CP-Net semantics.

It would be either interesting to improve our approach by taking into account partial preference relations that could be expressed by the user.

References

1. Bordogna, G., Carrara, P., Pasi, G.: Query term weights as constraints in fuzzy information retrieval. Information Processing and Management, 27(1) (1991) 15-26.
2. Bordogna, G., Pasi, G.: A fuzzy linguistic approach generalizing Boolean information retrieval: a model and its evaluation. Journal of the American Society for Information Science, 44(2) (1993) 70-82.
3. Bordogna, G., Pasi, G.: Linguistic aggregation operators of selection criteria in fuzzy information retrieval. International Journal of Intelligent Systems, (10) (1995) 233-248.
4. Boutilier, C., Brafman, R., Hoos, H., Poole, D.: Reasoning with Conditional Ceteris Paribus Preference Statements. In Proc. of UAI, (1999) 71 –80.
5. Boutilier, C., Bacchus, F., Brafman, R.: UCP-networks: A directed graphical representation of conditional utilities. In Proc. of UAI, (2001) 56 –64.
6. Boutilier, C., Brafman, R., Domshlak, C., Hoos, H., Poole, D.: CP-Nets A tool for representing and reasoning about conditional ceteris paribus preference statements. Journal of Artificial Research Intelligence, (21) (2004) 135 –191.
7. Buell, D. A., Kraft, D. H.: A model for a weighted retrieval system. Journal of the American Society for Information Science, 32(3) (1981) 211-216,.
8. Crestani, F., Pasi, G.: Soft information retrieval: Applications of fuzzy Set Theory and Neural Networks. In "Neuro Fuzzy Techniques For Intelligent Information Systems ". N Kasabov and Robert Kozmz Editors, Physica –Verlag, Springer-Verlag Group, (1999) 287-313.
9. Dubois, D., Prade, H.: Weighted minimum and maximum operations in fuzzy set theory. Information Sciences, (39) (1986) 205-210.
10. Kraft, D. H., Buell, D.: Fuzzy sets and generalized Boolean retrieval systems. International Journal of Man-Machine Studies, 19(1) (1983) 45-56.
11. Pasi, G. :A logical formulation of the Boolean model and of weighted Boolean model. In Proceedings of the Workshop on Logical and Uncertainty Models for Information Systems, London, U.K (1999) 1 –11.
12. Yager, R.: A note on weighted queries in information retrieval systems. In Journal of American Society for Information Science, 38(1) (1987) 23-24.

Highly Heterogeneous XML Collections: How to Retrieve Precise Results?

Ismael Sanz[1], Marco Mesiti[2], Giovanna Guerrini[3], and Rafael Berlanga Llavori[1]

[1] Universitat Jaume I, Castellón, Spain
{berlanga, Ismael.Sanz}@uji.es
[2] Università di Milano, Italy
mesiti@dico.unimi.it
[3] Università di Genova, Italy
guerrini@disi.unige.it

Abstract. Highly heterogeneous XML collections are thematic collections exploiting different structures: the parent-child or ancestor-descendant relationships are not preserved and vocabulary discrepancies in the element names can occur. In this setting current approaches return answers with low precision. By means of similarity measures and semantic inverted indices we present an approach for improving the precision of query answers without compromising performance.

1 Introduction

Handling the heterogeneity of structure and/or content of XML documents for the retrieval of information is being widely investigated. Many approaches [1, 2, 9, 15] have been proposed to identify approximate answers to queries that allow structure and content condition relaxation. Answers are ranked according to quality and relevance scores and only the top-k better results are returned. Current approaches consider the presence of optional and repeatable elements, the lack of required elements and some forms of relaxation of the parent-child relationship among elements. However, they do not cope with all the forms of heterogeneity that can occur in practice due to structure and content heterogeneity. Suppose to have an heterogeneous collection of documents about books. In the collection information are organized either around authors (i.e., for each author the books he/she wrote) or around books themselves (i.e., for each book the list of its authors). Current approaches fail to find relevant solutions in this collection because they can relax structural constraints (i.e., `book/author` becomes `book//author`) but they are not able to invert the relationship (i.e., `book/author` cannot become `author//book`). In addition, few approaches [11, 13, 17] exploit an ontology or a string edit function for relaxing the exact tag name identification and thus allow the substitution of lexemes *author* and *book* with synonyms (e.g., *volume* and *composition* for book, *writer* and

H.L. Larsen et al. (Eds.): FQAS 2006, LNAI 4027, pp. 232–244, 2006.

creator for author) or with a similar string (e.g., *mybook* for book and *theAuthor* for author).

In this paper we deal with structural queries (named *patterns*) and we model them as graphs in which different kinds of constraints on the relationships among nodes (parent-child/ancestor-descendant/sibling) and on node tags (syntactic and semantic tag similarity) can be enforced or relaxed. The identification of the answers in the XML collection (*target*) is realized by the identification of *regions* in the target in which nodes are similar enough to the pattern, and similarity measures that evaluate and rank the obtained regions. This change of approach has the effect that the efficiency of traditional approaches is compromised, but the precision is increased. Since performance is very relevant, we introduce indexing structures for easily identifying regions. A semantic inverted index is built on the target whose entries are the stems of the tags in the target.

Ranked tree-matching approaches have been proposed for dealing with the NP complexity of the tree inclusion problems [7]. These approaches, instead of generating all (exponentially many) candidate subtrees, return a ranked list of "good enough" matches. In [14] query results are ranked according to a cost function through a dynamic programming algorithm, in [1] intermediate query results are filtered dynamically during evaluation through a data pruning algorithm, while `ATreeGrep` [16] is based on an exact matching algorithm, but a fixed number of "differences" in the result is allowed. Our approach returns as well a ranked list of "good enough" subtree matches, but it is highly flexible since it allows choosing the most appropriate structural similarity measure according to the application semantics. Moreover, our approach also includes approximate label matching, which allows dealing with heterogeneous tag vocabularies. Starting from the user query, approaches for structural and content scoring of XML documents [1, 2, 9, 15] generate query relaxations that preserve the ancestor-descendant relationships. These relaxations do not consider the actual presence of such a structure in the documents. In our approach, by exploiting the indexing structures, only the variations to the pattern that occur in the target are considered. Moreover, the ancestor-descendant relationships imposed by the query can be reversed. Work from the Information Retrieval (IR) area is also concerned with XML document retrieval [8], by representing them with known IR models. These approaches mainly focus on the textual content disregarding their structure. Our approach extends in different directions the work proposed in [11] where patterns are expressed as trees stating a preferred hierarchical structure for the answers to be retrieved. In this paper, by contrast, patterns are graphs in which different kinds of constraints on the relationships among nodes and on node tags can be expressed. Graph based flexible XML queries have been proposed in [4]. No ad-hoc structures for efficiently evaluating them is devised.

In the remainder, Section 2 introduces patterns, targets, and regions. Section 3 discusses similarity evaluation while region construction is presented in Section 4. Experiments are discussed in Section 5. Section 6 concludes.

2 Patterns, Targets, and Regions

We first define flexible queries, then the tree representation of XML document collections and finally the document portions that match a pattern.

Patterns as Labelled Graphs. When dealing with heterogeneous collections, users require to express their information requests through a wide range of approximate queries. In our approach, patterns are provided for the specification of approximate structural and tag conditions that documents or portions of them must cope with as much as possible. In the simplest form, a pattern is a set of labels for which a "preference" is specified on the hierarchical or sibling order in which such labels or similar labels should occur. Fig. 1(a) shows an example of this simplest form of pattern. Document portions that match such a pattern can contain elements with similar tags in a different order and bound by different descendant/sibling relationships. Some of the required elements can be missing.

Tighter constraints can be specified by setting stricter conditions on element names and on relationships among nodes. For example, Fig. 1(b) shows the pattern in Fig. 1(a) in which the `book` and `author` elements in the document portions should exactly be `book` and `author`, that is, synonyms are not allowed (plain ovals). As another example, Fig. 1(c) shows a combination of structural and tag constraints. The `author` element must be a child of the `book` element (plain arrow from `book to author`), `author` must be an ancestor of the `name` element (double line arrow) and right sibling of the `editor` element (double line arrow tagged `s`).

These are only few examples of the patterns that a user can create by specifying our constraints. Constraints are categorized as follows (a graphical representation is in Table 1): *(i) descendant constraints* $\mathcal{DC}$, described in Table 1:(1,2,3,4,5); *(ii) same level constraints* $\mathcal{LC}$, described in Table 1:(6,7,8,9,10); *(iii) tag constraints* $\mathcal{TC}$ described in Table 1:(11,12).

Definition 1. (Pattern). *A pattern $P = (V, E_D, E_S, C_{E_D}, C_{E_S}, C_V, label)$ is a directed graph where V is a set of nodes, label is the node labelling function, E_D and E_S are two sets of edges representing the descendant or same level relationship between pairs of nodes, respectively, C_{E_D}, C_{E_S}, and C_{E_S} are functions that associates with edges in E_D, edges in E_S, and nodes in V, respectively, a constraint in $\mathcal{DC}$, $\mathcal{SC}$, and $\mathcal{TC}$.*

Target and Its Semantic Inverted Index. The target is a collection of heterogeneous XML documents, conveniently represented as a labelled tree[1] whose root is labelled `db` and whose subelements are the documents in the collection. An example of target is shown in Fig. 2(a). The distance $Dist(u, v)$ between two nodes u, v in a tree is specified as the number of nodes traversed moving from u to v in the pre-order traversal. The *nearest common ancestor* $nca(u, v)$ between

[1] A *tree* $T = (V, E)$ is a structure s.t. $V = \mathcal{V}(T)$ is a finite set of *nodes*, $root(T) \in V$ is the tree root and E is a binary relation on V with the known restrictions on E that characterize a tree.

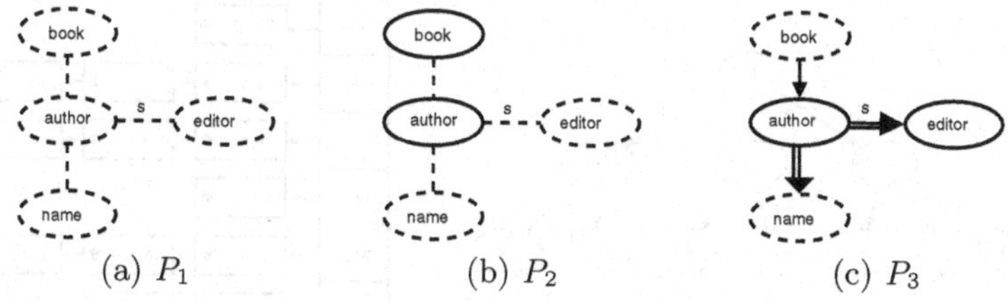

(a) P_1 (b) P_2 (c) P_3

Fig. 1. Pattern with (a) no constraints, (b) constraints on tags, (c) constraints on tags and structure

Table 1. Pattern constraints

#	Edge/Node repr.	Constraint description
1		$dc_1(u,v) = \texttt{true}$
2		$dc_2(u,v) = \texttt{true}$ if u is father of v or v is father of u
3		$dc_3(u,v) = \texttt{true}$ if u is father of v
4		$dc_4(u,v) = \texttt{true}$ if u is ancestor of v or v is ancestor of u
5		$dc_5(u,v) = \texttt{true}$ if u is ancestor of v
6		$sc_1(u,v) = \texttt{true}$
7		$sc_2(u,v) = \texttt{true}$ if u is sibling of v
8		$sc_3(u,v) = \texttt{true}$ if u is left (right) sibling of v
9		$sc_4(u,v) = \texttt{true}$ if u is in the same level of v
10		$sc_5(u,v) = \texttt{true}$ if u precedes (follows) v in the same level
11		$tc_1(v) = \texttt{true}$ if v is labelled by l or a label similar to l
12		$tc_2(v) = \texttt{true}$ if v is labelled exactly by l

two nodes u, v in a tree is the common ancestor of u and v whose distance to u (and to v) is smaller than the distance to u of any other common ancestor of u and v. Two labels are similar if they are identical, or synonyms relying on a given Thesaurus, or *syntactically similar* relying on a string edit function [18]. Let l_1, l_2 be two labels, $l_1 \simeq l_2$ iff: (1) $l_1 = l_2$ or (2) l_1 is a synonym of l_2, or (3) l_1 and l_2 are syntactically similar. Given a label l and a set of labels L, we introduce the operator *similarly belongs*, $\propto$: $l \propto L$ iff $\exists n \in L$ such that $l \simeq n$.

A semantic inverted index is coupled with the target. The index entries are the stems of the element tags occurring in the documents ordered according to

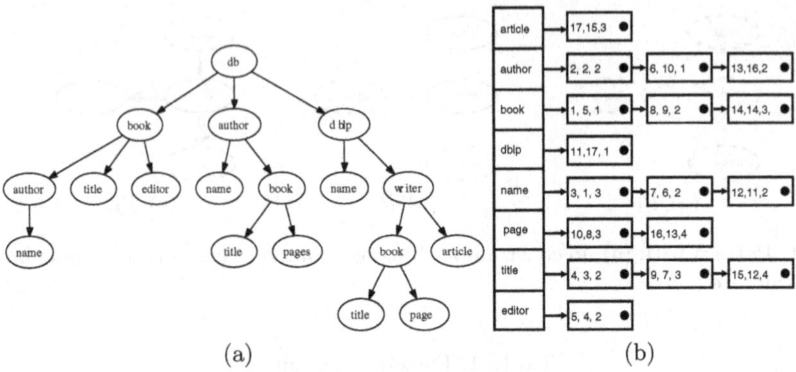

Fig. 2. (a) Tree representation of a collection of documents and (b) its inverted index

their pre-order traversal. Each entry contains the list of tags syntactically or semantically similar to the entry stem. For each node v, the list contains the 4-tuple $(pre(v), post(v), level(v), \mathcal{P}(v))$, representing the pre/post order ranking and level of v in the tree and its parent node. A node is identified by $pre(v)$. Fig. 2(b) depicts the inverted index for the target in Fig. 2(a). For the sake of graphical readability, the parent of each vertex is not represented (only a $\cdot$ is reported). We remark that the two elements `pages` and `page` belong to the same entry because they share the stem (`page`); elements `author` and `writer` belong to the same entry because they are semantically similar relying on WordNet.

Regions. Regions are the target portions containing an approximate match for the pattern. Different interpretations can be given to constraint violations that lead to different strategies for region construction.

Strategy 1: regions that do not meet one of the specified constraints should be eliminated. In this case, in the construction of regions when we detect that a constraint is violated the corresponding region should be pruned. This leads to reduce the number of regions to be checked.
Strategy 2: constraints in regions can be violated; violations, however, penalize the region in similarity evaluation. This approach requires considering constraints after having determined regions.

Choosing a strategy over another depends on the specific characteristics of the target application. In our approach we support both, and let the system designer decide which is most appropriate in each case. In what follows, we formalize the second strategy, since it is more flexible.

Regions in the collection that are similar to a pattern are identified in two steps. First, forgetting the constraints specified in the pattern and exploiting the target inverted index, we identify the subtrees, named *fragments*, of the target in which nodes with labels similar to those in P appear. Nodes in fragments are those nodes in the target with labels similar to those in the pattern. Two nodes u, v belong to the same fragment F for a pattern P, iff their labels as well as the label of their common ancestor *similarly belong* to the labels of the pattern.

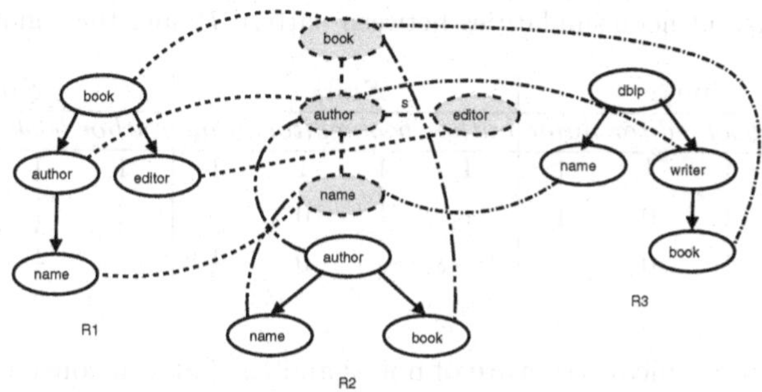

Fig. 3. Identification of different mappings

Definition 2. (Fragment). *A fragment F of a target $T = (V_T, E_T)$ for a pattern P is a subtree (V_F, E_F) of T for which the following properties hold:*

- *V_F is the maximal subset of V_T such that $root(T) \notin V_F$ and $\forall u, v \in V_F$, $label(u), label(v), label(nca(u, v)) \propto label(\mathcal{V}(P))$;*
- *For each $v \in V_F$, $nca(root(F), v) = root(F)$;*
- *$(u, v) \in E_F$ if u is an ancestor of v in T, and there is no node $w \in V_F$, $w \neq u, v$ such that w is in the path from u to v.*

Several fragments can be identified in a target. Fragments might be combined together when they are close and their combination can lead to a subtree more closely meeting the constraints expressed by the target. Regions are thus constructed by introducing (when required) a common unmatching ancestor.

Example 1. Consider as T the tree in the target in Fig. 2(a) whose label is `dblp`. Its left subtree contains the element `name`, whereas the right subtree contains the elements `writer` and `book`. T could have a higher similarity with the pattern tree in Fig. 1(a) than its left or right subtrees.

Definition 3. (Regions). *Let $F_P(T)$ be the set of fragments of a target T for a pattern P. The corresponding set of regions $R_P(T)$ is defined as follows.*

- *$F_P(T) \subseteq R_P(T)$;*
- *For each $F = (V_F, E_F) \in F_P(T)$ and for each $R = (V_R, E_R) \in R_P(T)$ such that $label(nca(root(F), root(R))) \neq$ `db`, $S = (V_S, E_S) \in R_P(T)$, where: $root(S) = nca(root(F), root(R))$, $V_S = V_F \cup V_R \cup \{root(S)\}$, $E_S = E_F \cup E_R \cup \{(root(S), root(F)), (root(S), root(R))\}$.*

Fig. 3 contains the three regions R_1, R_2, R_3 obtained for the pattern in Fig. 1(a). Regions R_1 and R_2 are simple fragments, whereas region R_3 is a combination of two fragments. We remark that the three regions present a different structure with respect to the one specified in the pattern.

3 Structural and Constraint Based Similarity Evaluation

In this section we first identify a mapping between the nodes in the pattern and the nodes in the region having similar labels. Then, by means of a similarity

Table 2. Different node similarities between pattern P_1 and the regions in Fig. 3

	Sim_M				Sim_L				Sim_D			
	author	*book*	*editor*	*name*	*author*	*book*	*editor*	*name*	*author*	*book*	*editor*	*name*
P_1/R_1	1	1	1	1	1	1	1	1	1	1	1	1
P_1/R_2	1	1	0	1	$\frac{1}{3}$	$\frac{1}{3}$	0	$\frac{1}{3}$	$\frac{1}{4}$	$\frac{1}{4}$	0	$\frac{1}{4}$
P_1/R_3	$1-\delta$	1	0	1	$1-\delta$	$\frac{1}{3}$	0	$\frac{1}{3}$	$\frac{3}{4}-\delta$	$\frac{1}{4}$	0	$\frac{1}{4}$

measure, the hierarchical structure of nodes and the pattern constraints are used to rank the resulting regions.

Mapping Between a Pattern and a Region. A mapping between a pattern and a region is a relationship among their elements that takes the tags used in the documents into account. Our definition relies on our second strategy and only require that the element labels are similar.

Definition 4. (Mapping M). *Let P be a pattern, and R a region subtree of a target T. A mapping M is a partial injective function between the nodes of P and those of R such that $\forall x_p \in \mathcal{V}(P), M(x_p) \neq \perp \Rightarrow label(x_p) \simeq label(M(x_p))$.*

The three patterns in Fig. 1 lead to an analogous mapping to the target in Fig. 2(a). The difference in score is determined by the following similarity measures.

Similarity Between Matching Nodes. Three approaches have been devised. In the first approach, the similarity depends on node labels and on the presence of tag constraints in the pattern. Similarity is 1 if labels are identical, whereas a pre-fixed penalty δ is applied if the tag constraint specified in the pattern is verified by the matching node in the region. If the tag constraint is not verified, similarity is 0. In the second approach, the match-based similarity is combined with the evaluation of the level at which x_p and $M(x_p)$ appear in the pattern and region structure, respectively. Whenever they appear in the same level, their similarity is equal to the similarity computed by the first approach. Otherwise, their similarity linearly decreases as the number of levels of difference increases. Since two nodes can be in the same level, but not in the same position, a third approach is introduced. Relying on the depth-first traversal of the pattern (where descendant edges are traversed before sibling edges) and the region, the similarity is computed by taking the distance of nodes x_p and $M(x_p)$ with respect to their roots into account. Thus, in this case, the similarity is the highest only when the two nodes are in the same position in the pattern/region.

Definition 5. (Similarity between Matching Nodes). *Let P be a pattern, R be a region in a target T, x_p a node of P, tc a tag constraint associated with x_p, and $x_r = M(x_p)$. Their similarity can be computed as follows:*

1. Match-based similarity:$Sim_M(x_p, x_r) = \begin{cases} 1 & \textit{if } label(x_p)=label(x_r) \\ 1-\delta & \textit{if } label(x_p)\simeq label(x_r),\ tc(x_r)=\texttt{true} \\ 0 & \textit{otherwise} \end{cases}$

2. Level-based similarity*: $Sim_L(x_p, x_r) = Sim_M(x_p, x_r) - \frac{|level_P(x_p) - level_R(x_r)|}{max(level(P), level(R))}$;*

3. Distance-based similarity*: $Sim_D(x_p, x_r) = Sim_M(x_p, x_r) - \frac{|d_P(x_p) - d_R(x_r)|}{max(d_P^{max}, d_R^{max})}$.*

In the last two cases the similarity is 0 if the obtained value is below 0.

Example 2. Table 2 reports the similarity of nodes of pattern P_1 in Fig. 1(a) with the corresponding nodes in the three regions, relying on the proposed similarity measures.

Similarity of a Region w.r.t. a Pattern. Once evaluated the similarity on the basis of the matching nodes and the tag constraints in the pattern, the constraints on the ancestor-descendant and sibling edges are considered as specified in the following definition. In order to obtain an evaluation of the mapping in the range [0,1] we first add to the evaluation of the nodes the number of edge constraints specified in the pattern that are met by the region. The obtained value is divided by the sum of the number of nodes in the pattern and the number of edge constraints specified in the pattern.

Definition 6. (Evaluation of a Mapping M). *Let M be a mapping between a pattern $P = (V, E_D, E_S, C_{E_D}, C_{E_S}, C_V, label)$ and a region $R = (V_R, E_R)$, and Sim one of the similarity measures of Definition 5. Let*

- *$MV = \sum_{x_p \in V : M(x_p) \neq \perp} Sim(x_p, M(x_p))$ be the evaluation of the mapping nodes between the two structures,*
- *$EC = \{(x_p, x_q) \in E_D \cup E_S | M(x_p) \neq \perp, M(x_q) \neq \perp\}$ be the set of edges in the pattern for which the nodes of the edges occur in the region,*
- *$VEC = \{(x_p, x_q) \in EC | Con \in C_{E_D} \cup C_{E_S},$ $Con((x_p, x_q))(M(x_p), M(x_q)) = true\}$[2] be the edges in C for which the corresponding constraints are verified.*

The evaluation of M is: $\mathcal{E}val(M) = \dfrac{MV + |VEC|}{|V| + |EC|}$

Once mappings have been evaluated, the similarity between a pattern and a region can be defined as the maximal evaluation so obtained.

Definition 7. (Similarity between a Pattern and a Region). *Let $\mathcal{M}$ be the set of mappings between a pattern P and a region R. Their similarity is defined as:*

$$Sim(P, R) = max_{M \in \mathcal{M}} \mathcal{E}val(M)$$

Example 3. Consider the situation described in Example 2. The similarities between the three patterns and the three regions computed according to the node similarity measures of Definition 5 are in Table 3.

[2] $Con((x_p, x_q))$ identifies a constraint c associated with the edge (x_p, x_q); c is applied to the corresponding edge in the region.

Table 3. Evaluation of similarity among patterns and regions

	P_1			P_2			P_3		
	Sim_M	Sim_L	Sim_D	Sim_M	Sim_L	Sim_D	Sim_M	Sim_L	Sim_D
R_1	1	1	1	1	1	1	1	1	1
R_2	$\frac{3}{4}$	$\frac{1}{4}$	$\frac{3}{16}$	$\frac{3}{4}$	$\frac{1}{4}$	$\frac{3}{16}$	$\frac{2}{3}$	$\frac{1}{3}$	$\frac{7}{24}$
R_3	$\frac{3-\delta}{4}$	$\frac{1-\delta}{4}$	$\frac{3-\delta}{16}$	$\frac{2}{4}$	$\frac{1}{6}$	$\frac{1}{8}$	$\frac{1}{3}$	$\frac{1}{9}$	$\frac{1}{12}$

4 Region Construction

There are two main challenges in region construction. First, only the information contained in the target index should be exploited and all the operations should be performed in linear time. Second, the evaluation of each pattern constraint should be computed in constant time. Region construction is realized in two steps: fragment construction and fragment merging. Fragment construction (detailed in the remainder of the section) is realized through the use of an index, named *pattern index*, that is computed on the fly on the basis of a pattern P and the semantic inverted index of a target T. Fragment merging (detailed in [12]) in a single region is performed when, relying on the adopted similarity function, the similarity of the pattern with the region is higher than the similarity with the individual fragments. In these evaluations the pattern constraints are considered and the following heuristic principle is exploited: only adjacent fragments can be merged since only in this case the regions can have an higher similarity than each single fragment.

Pattern Index. Given a pattern P, for every node v in P, all occurrences of nodes u in the target tree such that $label(v) \simeq label(u)$ are retrieved, and organized level by level in a *pattern index*. Each node in the pattern index is coupled with the following tuple ($\mathtt{TC}, \mathtt{DC}, \mathtt{SC}, \mathtt{VTC}, \mathtt{VDC}, \mathtt{VSC}$), where TC, DC, SC are sets that contain, respectively, the tag, descendent, and same level constraints specified for the matching node in the pattern (note that constraints on edges are reported in both nodes). Moreover, VTC, VDC, VSC are sets that will contain the verified constraints. In the creation of the pattern index the TC and VTC sets can be filled in, whereas the other constraints should be evaluated during fragment and region construction. The number of levels of the pattern index depends on the the levels in T in which nodes occur with labels similar to those in the pattern. For each level, nodes are ordered according to the pre-order rank. Fig. 4(a) contains the pattern index for the pattern in Fig. 1(c) evaluated on the target in Fig. 2(a). Tag constraints have been evaluated and those verified circled, whereas the violated ones have been overlined.

Identification of Fragments from the Pattern Index. Once the pattern index is generated, the fragments are obtained through a visit of the target structure. Moreover, for each node presenting a constraint, the constraint is checked. Each node v in the first level of the pattern index is the root of a fragment because, considering the way we construct the pattern index, no other

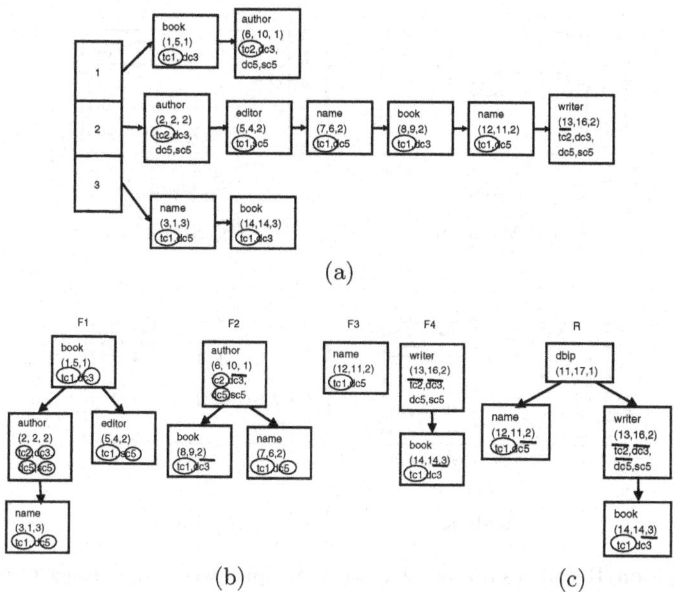

Fig. 4. (a) Pattern index, (b) fragments, and (c) a generated region

nodes can be the ancestor of v. Possible descendants of v can be identified in the underlying levels whereas sibling nodes can be adjacent in the same level. Given a generic level l of the pattern index, a node v can be a root of a fragment iff for none of the nodes u in previous levels, v is a descendant of u. If v is a descendant of a set of nodes U, v is considered the child of the node $u \in U$ such that $Dist(v, u)$ is minimal. Descendant and same level constraints can be evaluated when a node is attached to a fragment.

Our algorithm visits each node in the pattern index only once by marking in each level the nodes already included in a fragment. Its complexity is thus linearly proportional to the number of nodes in the pattern index. Fig. 4(b) illustrates fragments $F_1, \ldots, F_4$ obtained from the pattern index of Fig. 4(a). Fragments F_3 and F_4 are then merged in the region R in Figure 4(c).

5 Preliminary Experiments

To evaluate our approach we developed a prototype using the Berkeley DB library and tested the system with patterns expressed in the simplest form (that is, elements only bound by the ancestor-descendant relationship and tag similarity allowed). The performance was tested using synthetic collections with varying degrees of structural variations, ranging from 10^5 to 10^7 nodes and queries yielding result sets ranging between 7500 and 3×10^5 nodes; in every case the performance was shown to be linearly dependent on the size of the result set.

To evaluate the impact of constraint inclusion, as well as the different similarity measures for patterns and regions, we have tested our approach with the

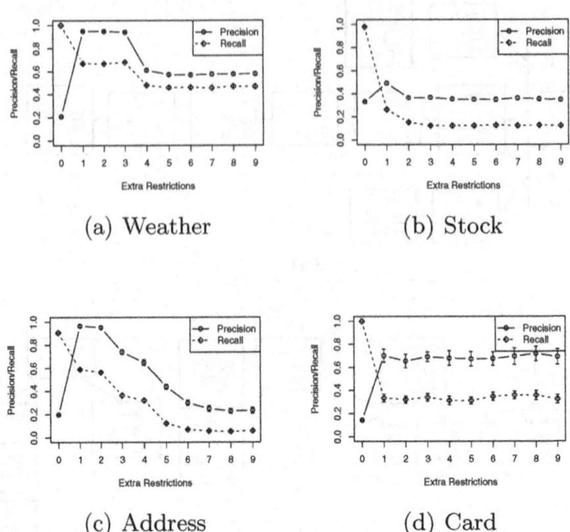

(a) Weather (b) Stock

(c) Address (d) Card

Fig. 5. Precision/Recall results for the selected topics wrt. the number of constraints included. The error bars are drawn at a 95% confidence level.

Table 4. Heterogeneity Measures for the selected ASSAM topics

Topic	*DIST*	*PCH*	*SIGN*	*SIBL*
Weather	1.0	100%	0%	93%
Stock	0.9	74%	11.6%	67%
Address	0.89	63%	0%	59%
Credit Card	0.5	75%	0%	59%

ASSAM dataset (`http://moguntia.ucd.ie/repository/datasets/`). This is a small collection (117 XML documents and 778 terms) that contains the conceptual schemas of a series of available public Web Services. These schemas present a high heterogeneity in both tag names and schema structures. For the evaluation, we have selected four topics from this dataset, namely: weather, stock index, address specifications and credit card information. For each topic, we assessed the sets of relevant results manually, for computing precision and recall values. For each topic we have generated a set of patterns randomly created by specifying a set of parameters (number of nodes, number of constraints, probability to identify regions for such a pattern).

To show the relevance of the proposed patterns in our context, we characterize each pattern with an estimate of the degree of heterogeneity of the result set. For all the parent/child relations (u, v) of the pattern generation tree, we calculate the global average distance ($DIST$) between u and v in all the database regions where they occur. We also calculate the percentage of these regions where (u, v) are actually parent/child relationships (PCH), and the percentage of regions where (u, v) inverts its direction ($SIGN$). For all the siblings relations (u, v) of the pattern generation tree, we calculate the percentage of fragments where they are actually siblings ($SIBL$). Table 4 shows the evaluation topics measures. Notice that some average distance ($DIST$) can be less than one. This is because some pairs of pattern labels can appear together in the same target tag (i.e. distance 0). Fig. 5 shows the impact of constraint inclusion in patterns when using the similarity function Sim_L. In the experiments we have measured the *precision* and *recall* considering the assigned target regions in the generation pattern tree. Notice that despite the heterogeneity degree of the selected patterns, we obtain good results for precision with respect to the case with 0 constraints. The exception is the topic "Address", which include very ambiguous terms that appear frequently in other topics (e.g. zip, street, etc.). This issue could be solved by using a more semantic-aware label distance measure.

6 Conclusions and Future Work

In this paper an approach for structure-based retrieval in highly heterogeneous XML collections has been devised. The peculiarity of the approach is that it does not rely on the document hierarchical organization. In order to deal with the high number of possible matchings, a semantic indexing structure and a similarity measure for pruning irrelevant results are exploited. Moreover, search patterns can contain constraints on element tags, descendant and sibling relationships. This allow the user to be aware of some (but not all) structural constraints in documents. Preliminary experimental results show the effectiveness of the proposed patterns to retrieve relevant document portions, though further research is required to define new similarity functions to handle the hardest cases.

As future work, we plan to include in our framework content conditions. In an heterogeneous environment like the one we focus on, content conditions can be specified both on the leaves and the internal nodes of the pattern. Moreover, we wish to consider the application of our techniques for the computation of approximate structural joins in highly heterogeneous XML collections and for subtree identification in heterogeneous XML Schemas collections.

References

1. Amer-Yahia, S., et al.: Tree Pattern Relaxation. EDBT. (2002) 496–513.
2. Amer-Yahia, S., et al.: Structure and Content Scoring for XML. VLDB. (2005).
3. Buneman, P., et al.: Adding Structure to Unstructured Data. ICDT. (1997).
4. Damiani, E., Tanca, L.: Blind Queries to XML Data. DEXA. (2000). 345–356.
5. Grust, T.: Accelerating XPath Location Steps. SIGMOD. (2002) 109–120.
6. Kanza, Y., Sagiv, Y.: Flexible Queries Over Semistructured Data. PODS. (2001).
7. Kilpeläinen, P.: Tree Matching Problems with Applications to Structured Text Databases. PhD thesis, University of Helsinki (1992).
8. Luk, R.W., et al.: A Survey in Indexing and Searching XML Documents. JASIS **53**:(2002)415–438.
9. Marian, A., et al.: Adaptive Processing of Top-k Queries in XML. ICDE. (2005).

10. Nierman, A., Jagadish, H.V.: Evaluating Structural Similarity in XML Documents. WebDB. (2002) 61–66.
11. Sanz, I., et al.: Approximate Subtree Identification in Heterogeneous XML Documents Collections. Xsym. LNCS(3671) (2005) 192-206.
12. Sanz, I., et al.: Highly Heterogeneous XML Collections: How to find "good" results?. TR University of Genova, 2006.
13. Schenkel, R., et al.: Ontology-Enabled XML Search. LNCS(2818),(2003)119-131.
14. Schlieder, T., Naumann, F.: Approximate Tree Embedding for Querying XML Data. In: ACM SIGIR Workshop on XML and IR. (2000).
15. Schlieder, T. Schema-Driven Evaluation of Approximate Tree Pattern Queries. EDBT. LNCS(2287). (2002) 514–532.
16. Shasha, D., et al.: ATreeGrep: Approximate Searching in Unordered Trees. In: 14th Conf. on Scientific and Statistical Database Management. (2002) 89–98.
17. Theobald, A., Weikum, G.: The Index-Based XXL Search Engine for Querying XML Data with Relevance Ranking. EDBT. LNCS(2287). (2002) 477-495.
18. Wagner, R.A., Fischer, M.J.: The String-to-string Correction Problem. J. of the ACM **21**:(1974)168–173.

Evaluation of System Measures for Incomplete Relevance Judgment in IR

Shengli Wu and Sally McClean

School of Computing and Mathematics, University of Ulster, UK
{s.wu1, si.mcclean}@ulster.ac.uk

Abstract. Incomplete relevance judgment has become a norm for the evaluation of some major information retrieval evaluation events such as TREC, but its effect on some system measures has not been well understood. In this paper, we evaluate four system measures, namely mean average precision, R-precision, normalized average precision over all documents, and normalized discount cumulative gain, under incomplete relevance judgment. Among them, the measure of normalized average precision over all documents is introduced, and both mean average precision and R-precision are generalized for graded relevance judgment. These four measures have a common characteristic: complete relevance judgment is required for the calculation of their accurate values. We empirically investigate these measures through extensive experimentation of TREC data and aim to find the effect of incomplete relevance judgment on them. From these experiments, we conclude that incomplete relevance judgment affects all these four measures' values significantly. When using the pooling method in TREC, the more incomplete the relevance judgment is, the higher the values of all these measures usually become. We also conclude that mean average precision is the most sensitive but least reliable measure, normalized discount cumulative gain and normalized average precision over all documents are the most reliable but least sensitive measures, while R-precision is in the middle.

1 Introduction

To evaluate the effectiveness of an information retrieval system, a test collection, which includes a set of documents, a set of topics, and a set of relevance judgments indicating which documents are relevant to which topics, is required. Among them, "relevance" is an equivocal concept [3, 11, 12] and relevance judgment is a task which demands huge human effort. In some situations such as to evaluate some searching services on the World Wide Web, complete relevance judgment is not possible. It is also not affordable when using some large document collections for the evaluation of information retrieval systems. For example, in the Text REtrieval Conferences (TREC) held by the National Institute of Standards and Technology of the USA, only partial relevance judgment is conducted due to the large number of documents (from 0.5 to several million) in the whole collection. A pooling method [8] has been used in TREC. For every query (topic) a document pool is formed from the

H.L. Larsen et al. (Eds.): FQAS 2006, LNAI 4027, pp. 245–256, 2006.

top 100 documents of all or a subset of all the runs submitted. Only those documents in the pool are judged by human judges and those documents which are not in the pool are not judged and are assumed to be irrelevant to the topic. Therefore, many relevant documents can be missed out in such processing [17]. "Partial relevance judgment" or "incomplete relevance judgment" are the terms used to refer to such situations.

The TREC's pooling method does not affect some measures such as precision at a given cut-off document level. However, in the evaluation of information retrieval systems, both precision and recall are important aspects and many measures concern both of them at the same time. In order to calculate accurate values for such measures, complete relevance judgment is required. Probably mean average precision (MAP) and R-precision are two such measures that are most often used recently. There have been some papers [1, 2, 5, 13] which investigate the reliability and sensitivity of MAP and R-precision.

In the context of TREC, Zobel [17] investigated the reliability of the pooling method. He found that in general the pooling method was reliable, but that recall was overestimated since it was likely that 30% ~ 50% of the relevant documents had not been found.

Buckley and Voorhees [5] conducted an experiment to investigate the stability of different measures when using different query formats. Results submitted to the TREC 8 query track were used. In their experiment, recall at 1000 document level had the least error rate, which was followed by precision at 1000 document level, R-precision, and mean average precision, while precision at 1, 10, and 30 document levels had the biggest error rates.

Voorhees and Buckley [14] also investigated the effect of topic size on retrieval results by taking account of the consistency of rankings when using two different sets of topics for the same group of retrieval systems. They found that the error rates incurred were larger than anticipated, therefore, researchers needed to be careful when concluding one method was better than another, especially if few topics were used. Their investigation also suggested that using precision at 10 document level incurred higher error rate than using MAP.

Concerning that fact that some existing evaluation measures (such as MAP, R-precision and precision at 10 document level) are not reliable for substantially incomplete relevance judgment, Buckley and Voorhees [6] introduced a new measure, which was related to the number of irrelevant documents occurring before a given number of relevant documents in a resultant list, to cope with such a situation.

Sanderson and Zobel [13] reran Voorhees and Buckley's experiment (Voorhees & Buckley, 2002) and had similar observations. But they argued that precision at 10 document level was as good as MAP if considering both the error rate of ranking and the human judgmental effort.

Järvelin and Kekäläinen [7] introduced cumulated gain-based evaluation measures. Among them, normalized discount cumulated gain (NDCG) concerns both precision and recall, which can be used as an alternative for MAP. Using cumulated gain-based evaluation measures, Kekäläinen [9] compared the effect of binary and graded relevance judgment on the rankings of information retrieval systems. She found that these measures correlated strongly under binary relevance judgment, but the correlation became less strong when emphasising highly relevant documents in graded relevance judgment.

However, the effect of incomplete relevance judgment on these measures is not well understood. It is interesting to evaluate these measures in such a condition. We include four measures (MAP, NAP, NDCG, and R-precision) in our investigation, since all of them concern precision and recall at the same time and therefore can be regarded as good system measures. Among them, normalized average precision over all documents (NAP) is introduced in this paper. In their original definitions, both MAP and R-precision can only be used under binary relevance judgment. Therefore, their definitions are generalized for graded relevance judgment in this paper. Both binary and graded relevance judgment are used. The rest of this paper is organized as follows: in Section 2 we discuss the four measures involved in our experiments. Then in Section 3, 4, and 5 we present the experimental results about different aspects of these four measures. Section 6 is the conclusion.

2 Four Measures

In this section we discuss the four measures used in this paper. MAP and R-precision have been used many times in TREC [15]. Both of them are defined under binary relevance judgment and have been used widely by researchers to evaluate their information retrieval systems and algorithms (e.g., in [4, 10, 16]). MAP uses the formula, $map = \frac{1}{total\_n} \sum_{i=1}^{total\_n} \frac{i}{p_i}$, to calculate scores. Here *total_n* is the total number of relevant documents in the whole collection for the information need and p_i is the ranking position of the i-th relevant documents in the resultant list. R-precision is defined as the percentage of relevant documents in the top *total_n* documents where *total_n* is the total number of relevant documents for the information need.

Now we generalize their definitions to make them suitable for graded relevance judgment. Suppose there are n relevance grades ranging from 1 to n (n means the most relevant state and 0 means the irrelevant state), then each document d_i can be assigned a grade $g(d_i)$ according to its degree of relevance to the given topic. One primary assumption we take for these documents in various grades is: a document in grade n is regarded as 100% relevant and 100% useful to users, and a document in grade i ($i<n$) is regarded as i/n% relevant and i/n% useful to users. One natural derivation is that one document in grade i is equal to i/n documents in grade n on usefulness. Based on such an assumption, we will define MAP and R-precision under graded relevance judgment. Suppose there are *total_n* documents whose grades are above 0 and $total\_n = |r_1| + |r_2| + \ldots + |r_n|$. Here $|r_i|$ denotes the number of documents in grade i.

Before we discuss how to generalize MAP and R-precision, let us introduce the concept of the best resultant list. For the given information need, a resultant list l is best if it satisfies the following two conditions:

- all the documents whose grades are above 0 appear in the list;
- for any document pair d_i and d_j, if d_i is ranked in front of d_j, then $g(d_i) \geq g(d_j)$.

Many resultant lists can be the best at the same time since more than one document can be in the same grade and the documents in the same grade can be arranged in different orders. For any pair of the best resultant lists l_1 and l_2, if d_j is a document in l_1, and d'_j is a document in l_2, and d_j is in the same ranking position in l_1 as d'_j in l_2, then d_j and d'_j must be in the same grade, or $g(d_j)=g(d'_j)$. Therefore, we can use $g\_best(d_j)$ to refer to the grade of the document in ranking position j in one of these best resultant lists. We may also sum up the grades of the documents in top $|r_n|$, top $(|r_n|+|r_{n-1}|)$, … , top $((|r_n|+|r_{n-1}|+\ldots+|r_1|)$ for any of the best resultant lists (these sums are the same for all the best resultant lists):

$$s\_best_n = \sum_{i=1}^{|r_n|} g(d_i),\ s\_best_{n-1} = \sum_{i=1}^{|r_n|+|r_{n-1}|} g(d_i),\ \ldots,\ s\_best = s\_best_1 = \sum_{i=1}^{|r_n|+|r_{n-1}|+\ldots+|r_1|} g(d_i)\ .$$

These sums will be used later in this paper.

One simple solution to calculate R-precision for a resultant list is to use the formula $r\_p = \frac{1}{s\_best}\sum_{j=1}^{total\_n} g(d_j)$. However, this formula does not distinguish the different positions of the documents if they are located in top *total_n*. It is the same effect for any document to occur in ranking position 1 or ranking position *total_n*. To avoid this drawback, we can use a more sophisticated formula. First we only consider the top $|r_n|$ documents and use $\frac{1}{s\_best_n}\sum_{j=1}^{|r_n|} g(d_j)$ to evaluate their precision, next we consider the top $|r_n|+|r_{n-1}|$ documents and use $\frac{1}{s\_best_{n-1}}\sum_{j=1}^{|r_n|+|r_{n-1}|} g(d_j)$ to evaluate their precision, continue this process until finally we consider all top *total_n* documents using $\frac{1}{s\_best}\sum_{j=1}^{|r_n|+|r_{n-1}|+\ldots+|r_1|} g(d_j)$. Combining all these, we have

$$r\_p = \frac{1}{n}\{\frac{1}{s\_best_n}\sum_{j=1}^{|r_n|} g(d_j) + \frac{1}{s\_best_{n-1}}\sum_{j=1}^{|r_n|+|r_{n-1}|} g(d_j) + \ldots + \frac{1}{s\_best}\sum_{j=1}^{|r_n|+|r_{n-1}|+\ldots+|r_1|} g(d_j)\} \qquad (1)$$

Please note that in the above Equation 1, each addend inside the braces can vary from 0 to 1. There are n addends. Therefore, the final value of r_p calculated is between 0 and 1 inclusive.

Next let us discuss MAP. MAP can be defined as $map = \frac{1}{s\_best}\{\sum_{i=1}^{total\_n} g(d_{p_i}) \cdot (\sum_{j=1}^{i} g(d_{p_j}))/p_i\}$. Here p_j is the ranking position of the j-th document whose grade is above 0, and $\sum_{j=1}^{i} g(d_{p_j})$ is the total sum of grades for documents up to rank p_i. Considering all these *total_n* documents in the whole collection whose grades are above 0, MAP needs to calculate the precision at all these document levels (p_1, p_2, …,

p_{total_n}). At any p_i, precision is calculated as $\sum_{j=1}^{i} g(d_{p_j})/p_i$, and then a weight of $g(d_{p_i})$ is applied. In this way the documents in higher grades have a bigger contribution to the final value of MAP.

Normalized average precision over all documents (NAP) is a new measure introduced in this paper. It can be defined as $nav = \frac{1}{nav\_best * t}\sum_{i=1}^{t}(\sum_{j=1}^{i} g(d_j))/i$. Here $(\sum_{j=1}^{i} g(d_j))/i$ is precision at document level i, $\frac{1}{t}\sum_{i=1}^{t}(\sum_{j=1}^{i} g(d_j))/i$ is average precision at all document levels, and *1/nap_best* is the normalization coefficient. *nap_best* is the NAP value for one of the best resultant lists.

NDCG was introduced in [7] by Järvelin & Kekäläinen graded relevance judgment. Each ranking position in a resultant document list is assigned a given weight. The top ranked documents are assigned the highest weights since they are the most convenient ones for users to read. A logarithmic function-based weighting schema was proposed in their paper, which needs to take a particular whole number b. The first b documents are assigned a weight of 1; then for any document ranked k which is greater than b, its weight is $w(k)=\log b/\log k$. Considering a resultant document list up to t documents, its discount cumulated gain (DCG) is $\sum_{i=1}^{t} w(i) * g(i)$, where $g(i)$ is the judged grade of the i-th document. DCG can be normalized using a normalization coefficient *dcg_best*, and *dcg_best* is the value of discount cumulated gain of the best resultant lists. Therefore, we have: $ndcg = \frac{1}{dcg\_best}\sum_{i=1}^{t} w(i) * g(i)$.

3 Effect of Incomplete Relevance Judgment on Measure Values

In this section we investigate how incomplete relevance judgment affects these measures on their values. Considering that the pooling method in TREC is a reasonable method for incomplete relevance judgment, we conduct an experiment to compare the values of these measures by using pools of different depths. In every year, a pool of 100 documents in depth was used in TREC to generate its *qrels* (relevance judgment file). Shallower pools of 10, 20,…, 90 documents in depth were used in this experiment to generate more *qrels*. For a resultant list and a measure, we calculate its value of the measure c_{100} using the 100 document *qrels*, then calculate its value of the measure c_i using the i document qerls (i = 10, 20, …., 90), an absolute difference can be calculated by $asb\_diff=|c_i-c_{100}|/c_{100}$. 9 groups of runs submitted to TREC (TREC 5-8: ad hoc track; TREC 9, 2001, and 2002: Web track; TREC 2003 and 2004: robust track) were used in the experiment. In some year, judged documents were divided into 2 categories: relevant and irrelevant; in some other years, judged documents were divided into 3 categories: relevant, highly relevant, and irrelevant. First we equally treat highly relevant documents and relevant documents, and just use a binary judgment for the evaluation of these runs. Figure 1 shows the difference of the four measure values when different *qrels* are used. Every data point in Figure 1 is the average of all the submitted runs in all 9 year groups. One general tendency for all four measures is: the shallower the pool is, the bigger the difference is. However, MAP is the worst considering the difference rate. When using a pool of 10 documents in depth, the difference rate for MAP is as big as 44%. In the same condition, it is about 32% for R-precision, about 30% for NAP, and 21% for NDCG_2 (2 was used as the base of its logarithmic function). For all four measures, it is generally true that the shallower the pool is, the bigger the value is.

Next we did the same experiment again but used different relevance judgments. This time we did not take an indiscriminate policy towards highly relevance documents. Instead, highly relevant documents were regarded as 100% relevant, relevant documents were regarded as 50% relevant. Submitted runs to TREC 9 (all 50 topics), 2001 (all 50 topics), and 2003 (the second half: topics 601-650) were used. The experimental result is shown in Figure 2. All the curves in Figure 2 and in Figure 1

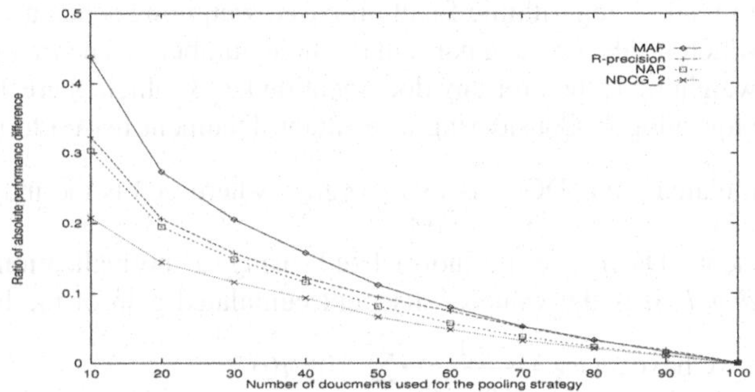

Fig. 1. Absolute differences of four measures when using pools of different depth (the pool of 100 documents in depth is served as baseline, binary relevance judgment)

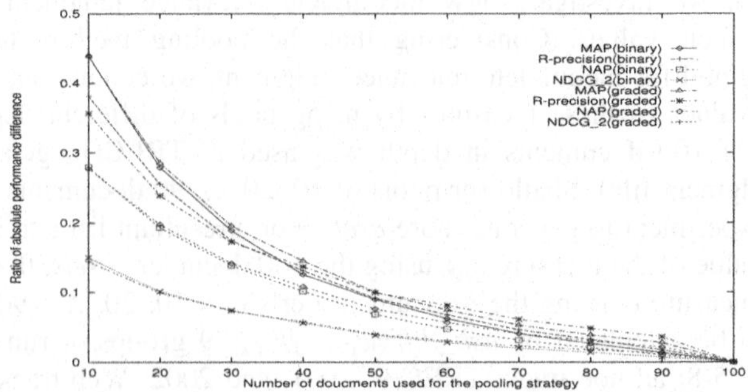

Fig. 2. Absolute difference of four measures when using pools of different depths (the pool of 100 documents in depth is served as baseline, three categories relevance judgment)

are very much alike; therefore, the same conclusion can be drawn here as with binary relevance judgments. However, Figures 1 and 2 can not be compared directly since the data set used for them are not identical. For a more reasonable comparison, the results of using both binary relevance judgment and graded relevance judgment with the same data set are presented in Figure 2. Comparing the corresponding curves for the same measure in Figure 2, we can observe that the curve of graded relevance judgments is always very close to its counterpart of binary relevance judgments.

4 Further Investigation About These Measure Values

Zobel [17] estimated that 30% ~ 50% of the relevant documents which might not be identified when using a pool of 100 documents. His estimation method was based on the 50 topics (251-300) in TREC 5. As an average, the estimated figure is reasonable. However, one topic can be very different from another as regards to the number of relevant documents. Some topics may have as few as 1 or 2 relevant documents, while some others may have over 100 relevant documents. In this section, we would go a step further to investigate the issue of missing relevant documents and the properties of the four measures across different topics under the pooling method.

For all 699 topics (one topic in TREC 2004 was dropped since it did not include any relevant document) in 9 year groups, we divided them into 11 groups according to the number of relevant documents identified for them. Group 1 (G_1) includes those topics with fewer than 10 relevant documents, group 2 (G_2) includes those topics with between 10 and 19 relevant documents, …, group 11 (G_{11}) includes those topics with 100 or more relevant documents. The number of topics in each group is as follows:

G1	G2	G3	G4	G5	G6	G7	G8	G9	G10	G11	Total
74	116	79	75	49	33	39	27	25	17	165	699

In this section, binary relevance judgment was used for the investigation. For every topic, we investigate the impact of the number of identified relevant documents for the topic on these four measures. Again, for those topic groups G_1 ~ G_{11} defined before in this section, we calculated the value differences of these measures using pools of different depths. Figure 3 shows the experimental result, in which each measure is drawn separately in (a), (b), (c), and (d). One common tendency for all these four measures is: the fewer the relevant documents are identified, the less difference the values of the same measure have with pools in different depths. For example, the curves of G_1 are always below all other curves, while the curves of G_{10} and G_{11} are above all other curves. Comparing all these curves of different measures, we can observe that bigger differences occur for the measure of MAP. For groups G_{10} and G_{11}, the value differences of MAP are 0.93 and 0.84 between a pool of 10 documents and a pool of 100 documents, while the figures for NAP are 0.60 and 0.51, the figures for R-precision are 0.48 and 0.52, and the figures for NDCG are 0.34 and 0.37. This experiment demonstrates that MAP is the most sensitive measure among these four measures.

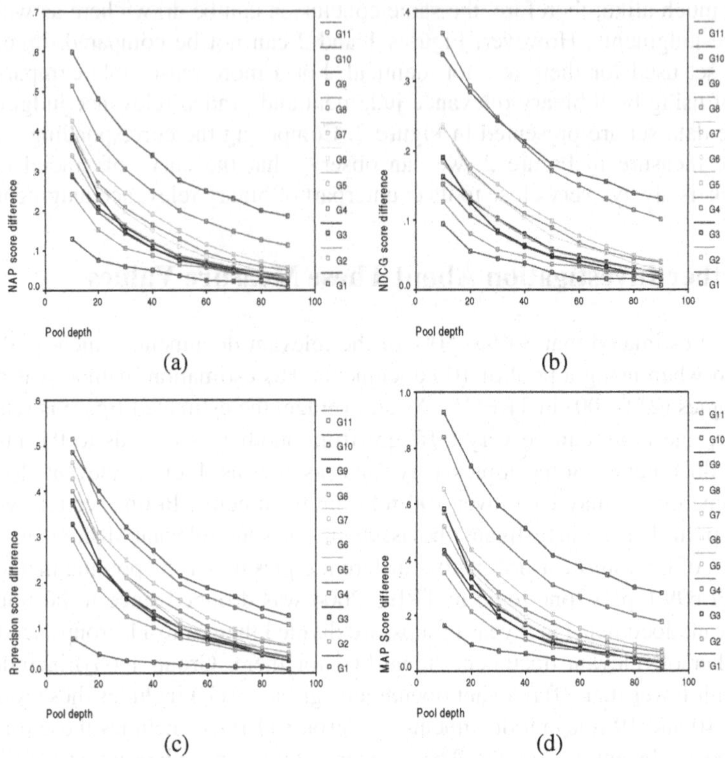

Fig. 3. Difference in performance values using pools of different depths

5 Error and Tie Rates of the Measures

In this section we present the result of an experiment whose methodology is similar to the one conducted by Buckley and Voorhees [5]. However, there are substantial differences between Buckley and Voorhees's experiment and our experiment here in this paper.

First, the experiment conducted by Buckley and Voorhees [5] only used the runs submitted to the TREC 8 query track. Here we use 9 groups of runs. Second, two measures (NAP and NDCG) are investigated in this paper that were not involved in Buckley and Voorhees's experiment. Third, graded relevance judgments are investigated in this paper but not in Buckley and Voorhees's investigation as well.

For a given measure, we evaluate all the results in a year group and obtain the average performance of them. Then we count how many pairs whose performance difference is above 5%. The tie rate is defined as the percentage of pairs whose performance difference is less than 5%. For those pairs whose performance difference is above 5%, we check if this is true for all the topics. Suppose we have two results *A* and *B* such that *A*'s average performance is better than *B*'s average performance by over 5% over all *l* topics. Then we consider these *l* topics one by one. If *A* is better than *B* by over 5% for *m* topics, and *B* is better than *A* by over 5% for *n* topics

($l \geq m+n$), then the error rate is $n/(\underline{m}+n)$, since for m times that the conclusion is consistent between a topic and the average of all the topics, and for n times that the conclusion is inconsistent between a topic and the average of all the topics.

Tables 1 and 2 show the error rates and the ties rates of the experiment, respectively. As in Section 3, 9 groups of runs in TREC were used. Binary relevance judgments and pools of different number of documents in depth were set up in the experiment. From Tables 1 and 2, we can observe NAP and NDCG_2 are close in both rates; both NAP and NDCG_2 have the lowest error rates but the highest tie rates; MAP has the highest error rates but the lowest tie rates; R-precision is in the middle in both tie rates and error rates. We can also observe that for all the measures, the values of error rates and tie rates are very close to each other when the pools are formed with different numbers of documents.

Table 1. Error rates of using different measures under binary relevance judgments (9 groups of runs in TREC)

Num. docs	MAP	R-precision	NAP	NDCG_2
10	0.2489	0.2087	0.1927	0.2014
20	0.2472	0.2123	0.1951	0.1985
30	0.2465	0.2140	0.1965	0.1974
40	0.2457	0.2147	0.1975	0.1970
50	0.2458	0.2157	0.1988	0.1975
60	0.2458	0.2158	0.1991	0.1977
70	0.2454	0.2159	0.1995	0.1978
80	0.2452	0.2160	0.1995	0.1979
90	0.2452	0.2157	0.1996	0.1980
100	0.2450	0.2157	0.1995	0.1980
Average	0.2461	0.2144	0.1978	0.1981

Table 2. Tie rates of using different measures under binary relevance judgment (9 groups of runs in TREC)

Num. docs	MAP	R-precision	NAP	NDCG_2
10	0.1001	0.1223	0.1613	0.1635
20	0.0966	0.1222	0.1522	0.1597
30	0.0954	0.1204	0.1484	0.1565
40	0.0936	0.1219	0.1460	0.1536
50	0.0940	0.1208	0.1440	0.1509
60	0.0932	0.1211	0.1434	0.1502
70	0.0937	0.1210	0.1419	0.1495
80	0.0937	0.1206	0.1417	0.1480
90	0.0931	0.1210	0.1408	0.1471
100	0.0927	0.1208	0.1409	0.1467
Average	0.0946	0.1212	0.1461	0.1526

The above experiment was repeated with graded relevance judgments. Three groups of runs in TREC (TREC 9, TREC 2001, and the second half of TREC 2003) were used. Table 3 and Table 4 show the results. These results are very much like the results in Tables 1 and 2. Please note that the results in Tables 1 & 3 and Tables 2 & 4 are not directly comparable, since the data set used are different. For a reasonable comparison, we calculate the average of error rates and tie rates using the same data set but binary relevance judgments (the last row of Table 3 and Table 4). Comparing the last two rows in Tables 3 and 4, we can observe that there is not much difference between them. We can conclude that the experimental results are consistent between binary relevance judgments and graded relevance judgments; on the other hand, graded relevance judgments can not help to reduce the error rates or tie rates compared with binary relevance judgments.

Actually, error rates can be regarded as a good indicator of reliability, while tie rates can be regarded as a good indicator of sensitivity, of the measure in question. For MAP, it has the highest error rates and the lowest tie rates among the four measures, which indicate that MAP is the most sensible, but the least reliable measure. On the other hand, NAP and NDCG have the lowest error rates but the highest tie rates, which indicate that both of them are the most two reliable, but the least two sensible measures. R-precision is not as sensitive as MAP, but is more sensitive than NAP and NDCG, and is not as reliable as NAP and NDCG, but is more reliable than MAP.

If we consider both tie rates and error rates at the same time and define a comprehensive measure (*com*) which sums them up. Then for both binary and graded relevance judgment, R-precision is the best with the lowest *com* value (0.3356 and 0.3522), MAP is in the second place (0.3407 and 0.3642), NAP is in the third place (0.3439 and 0.3711), and NGCG is the worst (0.3507 and 0.3792).

Table 3. Error rates of using different measures under graded relevance judgment (3 groups of runs in TREC)

Num. docs	MAP	R-precision	NAP	NDCG_2
10	0.2484	0.2085	0.1827	0.2028
20	0.2465	0.2136	0.1848	0.1986
30	0.2461	0.2137	0.1871	0.1971
40	0.2452	0.2141	0.1881	0.1972
50	0.2445	0.2146	0.1880	0.1963
60	0.2446	0.2149	0.1882	0.1963
70	0.2446	0.2156	0.1889	0.1960
80	0.2440	0.2152	0.1894	0.1959
90	0.2443	0.2161	0.1894	0.1961
100	0.2443	0.2159	0.1894	0.1959
Average	0.2453	0.2142	0.1877	0.1972
Ave (binary)	0.2433	0.2130	0.1878	0.1923

Table 4. Tie rates of using different measures under graded relevance judgment (3 groups of runs in TREC)

Num. docs	MAP	R-precision	NAP	NDCG_2
10	0.1158	0.1334	0.1939	0.1808
20	0.1167	0.1347	0.1886	0.1833
30	0.1165	0.1367	0.1861	0.1810
40	0.1184	0.1365	0.1821	0.1801
50	0.1198	0.1378	0.1822	0.1819
60	0.1196	0.1388	0.1822	0.1828
70	0.1194	0.1386	0.1812	0.1832
80	0.1215	0.1407	0.1798	0.1827
90	0.1208	0.1395	0.1789	0.1815
100	0.1209	0.1430	0.1789	0.1823
Average	0.1189	0.1380	0.1834	0.1820
Ave (binary)	0.1154	0.1433	0.1795	0.1848

6 Conclusions

In this paper we have investigated the properties of four measures namely mean average precision (MAP), R-precision, normalized average precision over all documents (NAP) and normalized discount cumulative gain (NDCG) when relevant judgment is incomplete. All these measures have one common characteristic: both precision and recall are implicit in their definitions. Therefore, they are good candidates for the evaluation of the effectiveness of information retrieval systems and algorithms.

9 groups of the submitted runs to TREC have been used in our experiments. Both binary relevance judgment and graded relevance judgment have been utilised. From these experimental results, we conclude that MAP is the most sensitive but least reliable measure, and both NAP and NDCG are the most reliable but least sensitive measure, while R-precision is in the middle. We believe that a good measure should be a good balance of these two somewhat contradictory properties: sensitivity and reliability. R-precision is the best to have a balance of them, MAP is in the second place, NAP is in the third place, and NDCG is the worst.

Among these four measures, normalized average precision (NAP) is introduced in this paper. It can be used for both binary relevance judgment and graded relevance judgment. Probably it is in a better position than NDCG to be justified since no parameter is required. In their original definitions, mean average precision and R-precision can only be used with binary relevance judgment, a generalized form of mean average precision and R-precision is provided in this paper.

Our experimental results also show that the values of all these four measures are very likely to be exaggerated when incomplete relevance judgment such as the pooling method is applied. Therefore, when explaining the results of such measures as mean average precision and R-precision which are used in TREC, care should be taken since their real values depend on the percentage of relevant documents which have been identified. From such a perspective, it is better to use reliable measures.

References

1. Aslam, J. A. and Yilmaz, E.: A geometric interpretation and analysis of R-precision. In *Proceedings of ACM CIKM'2005*, pages 664-671, Bremen, Germany, October-November.
2. Aslam, J. A. and Yilmaz, E. and Pavlu, V.: The maximum entropy method for analyzing retrieval measures. In *Proceedings of ACM SIGIR'2005*, pages 27-34, Salvador, Brazil.
3. Barry, C. L.: User-defined relevance criteria: an exploratory study. *Journal of the American Society for Information Science*, 45(3):149-159, 1994.
4. Bodoff, D. and Robertson, S.: A new united probabilistic model. *Journal of the American Society for Information Science and Technology*, 55(6):471-487, 2004.
5. Buckley, C. and Voorhees, E. M.: Evaluating evaluation measure stability. In *Proceedings of ACM SIGIR'2000*, pages 33-40, Athens, Greece.
6. Buckley, C. and Voorhees, E. M.: Retrieval evaluation with incomplete information. In *Proceedings of ACM SIGIR'2004*, pages 25-32, Sheffield, United Kingdom.
7. Järvelin, K. and Kekäläinen, J.: Cumulated gain-based evaluation of IR techniques. *ACM Transactions on Information Systems*, 20(4):442-446, 2002.
8. Sparck Jones, K. and van Rijisbergen, C.: Report on the need for and provision of an "ideal" information retrieval test collection. Technical report, British library research and development report 5266, Computer laboratory, University of Cambridge, Cambridge, UK, 1975.
9. Kekäläinen, J.: Binary and graded relevance in IR evaluations - comparison of the efforts on ranking of IR systems. *Information Processing & Management*, 41(5):1019-1033, 2005.
10. Lee, C. and Lee, G. G.: Probabilistic information retrieval model for a dependency structured indexing system. *Information Processing & Management*, 41(2):161-175, 2005.
11. Saracevic, T.: Relevance: A review of and a framework for thinking on the notion in information science. *Journal of the American Society for Information Science*, 26(6):321-343. 1975.
12. Schamber, L. and Eisenberg, M. B. and Nilan, M. S.: A re-examination of relevance: toward a dynamic, situational definition. *Information Processing & Management*, 26(6):755-776, 1990.
13. Sanderson, M. and Zobel, J.: Information retrieval system evaluation: Effort, sensitivity, and reliability. In *Proceedings of ACM SIGIR'2005*, pages 162-169, Salvador, Brazil.
14. Voorhees, E. M. and Buckley C.: The effect of topic set size on retrieval experiment error. In *Proceedings of ACM SIGIR'2002*, pages 316-323, Tampere, Finland.
15. Voorhees, E. M. and Harman, D.: Overview of the sixth text retrieval conference (trec-6). *Information Processing & Management*, 36(1):3-35:2000.
16. Xu, Y. and Benaroch, M.: Information retrieval with a hybrid automatic query expansion and data fusion procedure. *Information Retrieval*, 8(1):41-65, 2005.
17. Zobel, J.: How reliable are the results of large-scale information retrieval experiments. In *Proceedings of ACM SIGIR'1998*, pages 307-314, Melbourne, Australia.

A Hierarchical Document Clustering Environment Based on the Induced Bisecting k-Means

F. Archetti[1,2], P. Campanelli[1,2], E. Fersini[1], and E. Messina[1]

[1] DISCO, Università degli Studi di Milano Bicocca,
Via Bicocca degli Arcimboldi, 8
20126 Milano, Italy
{fersini, messina}@disco.unimib.it

[2] Consorzio Milano Ricerche, Via Cicognara 7,
20129 Milano, Italy
{archetti, campanelli}@milanoricerche.it

Abstract. The steady increase of information on WWW, digital library, portal, database and local intranet, gave rise to the development of several methods to help user in Information Retrieval, information organization and browsing. Clustering algorithms are of crucial importance when there are no labels associated to textual information or documents. The aim of clustering algorithms, in the text mining domain, is to group documents concerning with the same topic into the same cluster, producing a flat or hierarchical structure of clusters. In this paper we present a Knowledge Discovery System for document processing and clustering. The clustering algorithm implemented in this system, called Induced Bisecting k-Means, outperforms the Standard Bisecting k-Means and is particularly suitable for on line applications when computational efficiency is a crucial aspect.

1 Introduction

Document search results are often presented to user as a flat list of documents, ranked by their relevancies to a given query, and users have to examine all the titles and snippets of the documents in the list. This is a time consuming process because multiple topics can be mixed together. The need of improving the browsability of search engine results has increased the interest in different clustering approaches most of which based on vector space document models, also known as bag-of-words models [11]. As far as unsupervised classification algorithms are concerned, several approaches have been proposed [5][19] which play an important role in providing intuitive navigation and browsing mechanisms by organizing large amounts of information into a small number of meaningful clusters. An interesting clustering approach has been proposed in [18], which provides a mechanism to group those documents whose snippets share similar phrases, by using suffix trees. This approach is well suited for clustering web search; the only drawback is that the clustering is flat, while a hierarchical structure is usually more suitable for browsing on line search results, in particular when queries are about general topics possibly belonging to

H.L. Larsen et al. (Eds.): FQAS 2006, LNAI 4027, pp. 257 – 269, 2006.

different domains. Clustering algorithms that build meaningful hierarchies out of large document collections are ideal tools for their interactive visualization and exploration as they provide data-views that are consistent, predictable, and at different levels of granularity. The Scatter/Gather system [9], is an interactive environment which supports the browsing, of both summaries and contents, of all the texts in a collection. It uses a hierarchical agglomerative clustering algorithm, known as Buckshot [3], which is a combination of two approaches: k-Means and hierarchical agglomerative clustering (HAC). HAC works by considering each data point as a separate cluster and then combining them in new clusters. This continues until there are only *k* clusters and finally, the centroids of the clusters are used as the initial centroids for the k-Means algorithm. Another important clustering system for web search results is proposed in WebACE Project [6], which uses an algorithm, named Principal Direction Divisive Partitioning [1]. It constructs a binary tree hierarchy of clusters by encompassing the entire document collection, and recursively split clusters on the bases of a linear discriminant function derived from the principal direction, until a desired number of clusters are reached. Recently, commercial products as Vivisimo (http://vivisimo.com) and iBoogie (http://www.iboogie.com/) are available on the web. They are meta-search engines that add to the flat list of query result a hierarchical structure of document clusters. Another approach, for improving browsability of web documents, returned by a search engine, consists in classifying these entities with a model built on an existing taxonomy, such as Yahoo! (http://www.yahoo.com) or the Open Directory Project (http://www.dmoz.org). In order to build such taxonomy model Naïve Bayes based method can be applied: it performs a hierarchical classification and constructs distinct classifiers at the internal nodes of the taxonomy using all the document in its child node as training data [8]. The classification is then applied at every node until a leaf is reached.

In this paper, we propose a system for searching and clustering large corpus of documents by using an experimental approach for on line text processing and hierarchical clustering. The clustering algorithm we propose in this paper, called Induced Bisecting k-Means, is an extension of the Standard Bisecting k-Means [14][15] which makes it more stable with respect to noisy data and applicable to web search results. Preliminary experiments and evaluations are conducted to investigate its effectiveness. Results obtained seem to be promising both in terms of accuracy and computational time. The basic outline of this paper is as follows. Section 2 presents our methodological approach together with a brief description of the system architecture. In Section 3 the datasets and the performance measures used for the validation of our approach are described. In Section 4 a set of preliminary experimental results are presented and, finally, in Section 5 conclusions are derived.

2 System Model

We propose a Knowledge Discovery System able to satisfy the following requirements:

- *High Dimensionality*: it can process documents with thousands of relevant terms
- *Modular and Extensible*: the system is designed in a modular way, so that new functionalities could be easily added
- *Speed*: search and clustering features return relevant results in a few seconds

- *Non parametric:* user does not need to specify any input parameters, such as the desired number of clusters
- *Adaptability at different document formats*: in the web world, documents in plain-text format are diminishing, and in their place we increasingly find information presented in different physical formats, such as Microsoft Office document, HTML, XML, PDF format, etc…
- *Accuracy*: our clustering solution shows high intra-cluster similarity and low inter-cluster similarity, i.e., documents in the same cluster are very similar, but they are dissimilar to elements in other clusters.
- *Easy Browsing*: the hierarchical structure obtained with our approach is presented with a user interface, to provide document browsing.

In order to meet simultaneously all the requirements listed above, we had to extend and combine in an efficient way different methodologies of feature selection, information filtering and clustering. We give more details in the next sub-sections.

2.1 System Architecture

Our system is composed of the following modules:

1. Web Crawler and Freshness Manager
2. Indexing module
3. Searching and Data-Preparation
4. Clustering module
5. Presentation interface

The system is component-oriented designed around the inversion of control pattern and entirely written in Java; it offers document management and manipulation, adding functionalities of searching and clustering from unstructured text documents. Figure 1 illustrates a flow diagram relevant to the entire computational process.

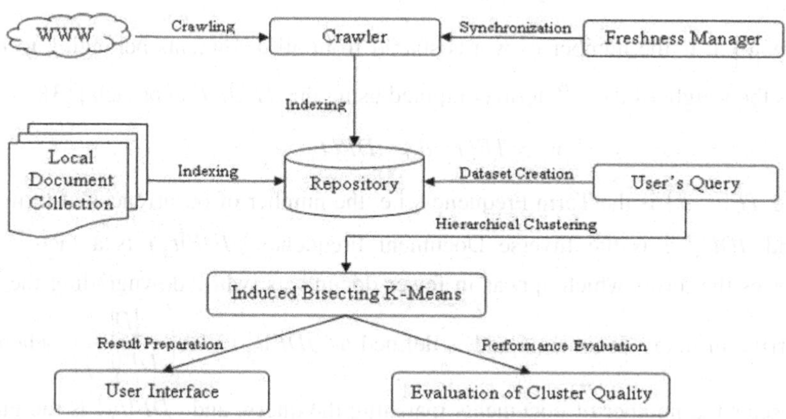

Fig. 1. Computational Process

2.2 Web Crawler and Freshness Manager

The Crawler, implemented as multithread process, retrieves web pages following their hyperlinks, and downloads relating documents on the local disk. In order to maintain locally stored pages "fresh" the crawler has to update its web pages periodically. We implemented a Freshness Manager in order to decide how often to refresh the page and maximize the "freshness" of downloaded pages. According to [2] a document is considered "fresh" when the local copy is equal to the real-world remote data. This component is able to estimate how often a page changes and to decide, through an optimization model, how often the pages need to be refreshed.

2.3 Indexing

The main functionality of this module is to organize documents into a highly efficient cross-reference lookup. Such indexing is based on inverted index structures. During the indexing phase, a pre-processing activity is performed in order to make page cases insensitive, remove stop words, acronyms, non-alphanumeric characters, html tags and apply stemming rules, using Porter's suffix stripping algorithm. This module, based on Lucene Library (http://lucene.apache.org/), is able to manage different document formats and it accommodates easily for user customization.

2.4 Searching and Data-Preparation

The searching function, provided by Lucene library, supports single and multiterm queries, phrase queries, wildcards, result ranking, and sorting. When a user submits a query about a topic of interest, this module retrieves matching documents. In order to prepare the input for the clustering module, the collection Q of returned documents is mapped into a matrix $M = [\, m_{ij} \,]$. Each row of M is represented by a document d, following the *Vector Space Model* [12]:

$$d = \left(w_1, w_2, \ldots w_{|V|}\right) \tag{1}$$

where $|V|$ it is the number of words shared from all documents belonging to Q and w_j is the weight of the jth term computed using the *TFxIDF* approach [13]:

$$w_j = TF(t_j, d) * IDF(t_j) \tag{2}$$

where $TF(t_j, d)$ is the Term Frequency, i.e. the number of occurrences of term t_j in *d*, and $IDF(t_j)$ is the Inverse Document Frequency. $IDF(t_j)$ is a factor which enhances the terms which appear in fewer documents, while downgrading the terms occurring in many documents and is defined as $IDF(t_j) = log\left(\frac{|D|}{DF(t_j)}\right)$, where $|D|$ represents the number of documents matching the query, and $DF(t_j)$ is the number of documents containing the jth term. The *TF* values are used to perform a feature selection procedure based on the *Term Frequency Variance (TFV)* index [4]:

$$q(t_j) = \sum_{i=1}^{n_1} f_i^2 - \frac{1}{n_1}\left[\sum_{i=1}^{n_1} f_i\right]^2 \tag{3}$$

where n_1 is the number of documents in Q containing t_j at least once. Now, let R be the set, with $|R| = r \times |V|$ and $r \leq 1$, containing the terms with highest quality, then only terms t_j having $q(t_j)$ greater than a given threshold parameter μ will be considered as columns of M, where $\mu = \min_{q(t_j) \in R} q(t_j)$. In our system we set $r = 0.05$.

This feature selection technique is suitable for the unsupervised requirement and requires lower computational cost compared to other feature selection techniques. Finally, in order to account for document of different lengths, each document vector is normalized so that it is of unit length.

2.5 Hierarchical Clustering

The approaches proposed in the literature for hierarchical clustering where mostly statistical with a computational complexity which is quadratic with respect to $|Q|$. A novel approach, Bisecting k-Means was proposed in [14][15], has a linear complexity and is relatively efficient and scalable.

It starts with a single cluster of all documents and works in the following way:

1. Pick a cluster S to split
2. Select two random seeds which are the initial centroids
3. Find 2 sub-clusters S_1 and S_2 using the basic k-Means algorithm.
4. Repeat step 2 and 3 for *ITER* times and take the split that produces the clustering with the highest Intra Cluster Similarity (ICS)

$$ICS_{S_k} = \frac{1}{|S_k|^2} \sum_{\substack{d \in S_k \\ d' \in S_k}} cos(d, d') \tag{4}$$

5. Repeat steps 1, 2 and 3 until the desired number of clusters is reached.

The major disadvantage of this algorithm is that it requires the a priori specification of K and *ITER* parameters. An incorrect estimation of K and *ITER* may lead to poor clustering accuracy. Moreover, the algorithm is sensitive to the noise which may affect the computation of cluster centroids. For any given cluster let N be the number of documents belonging to that cluster and R the set of their indices. In fact, the jth element of a cluster centroid is computed as:

$$c_j = \frac{1}{N} \sum_{r \in R} m_{rj} \tag{5}$$

where N represents the number of documents belonging to the cluster.

The centroid C may contain also the contribution of noisy terms contained in the documents which the pre-processing phase and feature selection phase have not been able to remove. To overcome these two problems we propose an extended version of the Standard Bisecting k-Means, named *Induced Bisecting k-Means*, whose main steps are described as follows:

1. Set the Intra Cluster Similarity (ICS) threshold parameter τ.
2. Build a distance matrix A, of dimension $|Q|x|Q|$, whose elements are given by the Euclidean distance between document

$$a_{ij} = \sqrt{\sum_{k=1}^{|V|} (m_{ik} - m_{jk})^2} \tag{6}$$

   where $i, j \in Q$.
3. Select, as centroids, the two documents i and j s.t. $a_{i,j} = \max_{l,m=\{1,\dots,|Q|\}} A_{lm}$.

The splitting is also different from the Standard Bisecting k-Means and is performed according to the following 3 steps:

4. Find 2 sub-clusters S_1 and S_2 using the basic k-Means algorithm.
5. Check the ICS of S_1 and S_2 as
   - If the ICS value of a cluster is smaller than τ, then reapply the divisive process to this set, starting form step 2.
   - If the ICS value of a cluster is over a given threshold, then stop.
6. The entire process will finish when there are no sub-clusters to divide.

The main differences of this algorithm with respect to the Standard Bisecting k-Means consist in:

- how the initial centroids are chosen: as centroids of the two child clusters we select the documents of the parent cluster having the greatest distance between them
- the cluster splitting rule: a cluster is split in two if its Intra Cluster Similarity is smaller than a threshold parameter τ. Therefore, the "optimal" number of cluster K is controlled by the parameter τ, the main advantages being that no input parameters *K* and *ITER* must be specified by the user.

Computational results seem to be very promising as it is shown in section 4.

2.6 Visualization

Our algorithm outputs a binary tree of documents, where each node represents a document collection about the same topic. This structure has been processed, in order to obtain a meaningful taxonomy, according to [7]. The new hierarchical structure is a tree-like structure presented by a simple GUI, where each internal node represents a higher-level concept that semantically includes all of its child concepts. Labels are assigned to each node of the taxonomy, by using the top *H* weighted values of the centroid vector and determine the terms which contribute to the top *H* terms. Other and more efficient way of choosing representative cluster labels can be implemented as reported in [7][16]. This will be one of the subjects of our future developments.

3 Datasets and Performance Evaluation

In this section we compare the Induced Bisecting k-Means, against the k-Means and Standard Bisecting k-Means algorithms. To evaluate clustering performance we used several benchmarks using all the terms of the dataset vocabulary, i.e. without *TFV* feature selection. More details are given in the next sub-sessions.

3.1 Datasets

The summary description of data sets used in this paper is shown in the table 1.

Table 1. Dataset description

	#classes	Average Class Size	#docs	#words
re0	13	115,7	1504	11465
re1	25	663	1657	3758
Wap	20	78	1560	8460
tr31	7	132,4	927	10128
tr45	10	69	690	8261

Datasets re0 and re1 are from Reuters-21587 test collection [10]. Dataset wap is from WebAce project [6]. Datasets tr31 and tr45 are from TREC-5 , TREC-6, and TREC-7 [17]. We collected documents that have relevance judgments and then selected documents that have just a single relevance judgment.

3.2 Evaluation of Cluster Quality

In order to evaluate the cluster quality, we used the widely adopted F-Measure. It combines the Precision and Recall measure which are computed as follows:

$$Recall(i,j)=\frac{n_{ij}}{n_i} \qquad Precision(i,j)=\frac{n_{ij}}{n_j} \tag{7}$$

where, n_j is the number of elements of cluster $j \in J$, n_i is the number of elements of class $i \in I$, and n_{ij} denotes the number of elements of class *i* in cluster *j*. The *F Measure* of cluster *j* and class *i* is given by:

$$F(i,j)=\frac{(2*Recall(i,j)*Precision(i,j))}{(Precision(i,j)+Recall(i,j))} \tag{8}$$

The overall quality of the clustering is given by a scalar F computed as:

$$F=\sum_i \frac{n_i}{n} \max_{j\in J}\{F(i,j)\} \tag{9}$$

As pointed out in section 2.6, both the Standard Bisecting k-Means and the Induced Bisecting k-Means generate binary trees that are subsequently transformed in a taxonomy. Then, there are two different ways of computing *F* which depend on the definition of *J*. In fact, given a binary tree, if we denote *E* as the set of all its nodes, and $L \subset E$ as the set of its leaf nodes, then the F-measure can be computed either setting $J = E$ or $J = L$.

4 Experimental Results

We ran the Induced Bisecting k-Means with different values of τ: 0.20, 0.10 and 0.05. Table 2-4 reports the F-measure computed using both *J=E* and *J=L*.

Table 2. Induced Bisecting k-Means performance with $\tau = 0.20$

τ = 0.20			
	J=E	J=L	# of cluster
re0	0.5895	0.3534	88
re1	0.6537	0.3867	124
wap	0.7706	0.3489	62
tr31	0.7282	0.4920	54
tr45	0.6214	0.2699	239

Table 3. Induced Bisecting k-Means performance with $\tau = 0.10$

τ = 0.10			
	J=E	J=L	# of cluster
re0	0.5076	0.3467	26
re1	0.6148	0.4480	39
wap	0.7648	0.5944	14
tr31	0.6644	0.6644	15
tr45	0.6174	0.3980	84

Table 4. Induced Bisecting k-Means performance with $\tau = 0.05$

τ = 0.05			
	J=E	J=L	# of cluster
re0	0.4472	0.4129	4
re1	0.5242	0.4973	12
wap	0.6552	0.6552	4
tr31	0.4840	0.4840	4
tr45	0.5547	0.5340	21

In order to compare our approach with the k-Means and the Standard Bisecting k-Means we set k equal to the number of clusters obtained by performing our approach.

Tables 5-9 show the F-measure obtained by running the k-Means algorithm on different datasets. Since the k-Means algorithm produces a flat clustering, we considered *J=L*.

Table 5.

Re0 with k=4	
	J=L
Run1	0.3373
Run2	0.3378
Run3	0.3537
Run4	0.3601
Run5	0.3579
Average	*0.3493*

Re0 with k=26	
	J=L
Run1	0.3279
Run2	0.3609
Run3	0.3294
Run4	0.3609
Run5	0.3803
Average	*0.3519*

Re0 with k=88	
	J=L
Run1	0.3576
Run2	0.3765
Run3	0.3221
Run4	0.3202
Run5	0.3191
Average	*0.3391*

Table 6.

Re1 with k=12	
	J=L
Run1	0.2422
Run2	0.2426
Run3	0.3353
Run4	0.2277
Run5	0.2589
Average	*0.2620*

Re1 with k=39	
	J=L
Run1	0.3298
Run2	0.3887
Run3	0.3376
Run4	0.2634
Run5	0.3130
Average	*0.3265*

Re1 with k=124	
	J=L
Run1	0.3157
Run2	0.2663
Run3	0.2823
Run4	0.3251
Run5	0.2614
Average	*0.2379*

Table 7.

Tr31 with k=4	
	J=L
Run1	0.3857
Run2	0.4135
Run3	0.4889
Run4	0.3859
Run5	0.3860
Average	*0.4120*

Tr31 with k=14	
	J=L
Run1	0.4140
Run2	0.3863
Run3	0.4751
Run4	0.4177
Run5	0.2774
Average	*0.3941*

Tr31 with k=62	
	J=L
Run1	0.4490
Run2	0.4711
Run3	0.3730
Run4	0.4059
Run5	0.3967
Average	*0.4120*

Table 8.

Tr45 with k=4	
	J=L
Run1	0.2356
Run2	0.3409
Run3	0.2533
Run4	0.2401
Run5	0.2856
Average	*0.2711*

Tr45 with k=15	
	J=L
Run1	0.2843
Run2	0.3504
Run3	0.2792
Run4	0.3215
Run5	0.2898
Average	*0.3050*

Tr45 with k=54	
	J=L
Run1	0.2750
Run2	0.2990
Run3	0.3651
Run4	0.2859
Run5	0.2867
Average	*0.3023*

Table 9.

Wap with k=21	
	J=L
Run1	0.3684
Run2	0.2498
Run3	0.3475
Run4	0.3343
Run5	0.3098
Average	*0.3219*

Wap with k=84	
	J=L
Run1	0.2220
Run2	0.1830
Run3	0.4130
Run4	0.3125
Run5	0.4314
Average	*0.3123*

Wap with k=239	
	J=L
Run1	0.2929
Run2	0.2939
Run3	0.2711
Run4	0.3004
Run5	0.2813
Average	*0.2879*

Tables 10-14 show the F-Measure obtained by running the Standard Bisecting k-Means, setting ITER=5 for every run, considering both *J=E* and *J=L*. For the wap dataset the F-Measure coefficient with K=129 are not available because the algorithm is not able to produce this number of clusters.

Table 10.

Re0 with k=4		
	J=E	J=L
Run1	0.3584	0.2760
Run2	0.4184	0.1186
Run3	0.3975	0.2954
Run4	0.4071	0.1519
Run5	0.3628	0.1149
Average	*0.3888*	*0.1930*

Re0 with k=26		
	J=E	J=L
Run1	0.5043	0.3166
Run2	0.5022	0.2852
Run3	0.5106	0.3044
Run4	0.4596	0.3553
Run5	0.4973	0.4062
Average	*0.4948*	*0.3335*

Re0 with k=88		
	J=E	J=L
Run1	0.5170	0.3947
Run2	0.5045	0.2859
Run3	0.4316	0.3563
Run4	0.5133	0.4184
Run5	0.4971	0.2913
Average	*0.4987*	*0.3493*

Table 11.

Re1 with k=12		
	J=E	J=L
Run1	0.2602	0.1946
Run2	0.2138	0.1413
Run3	0.2605	0.1929
Run4	0.2829	0.1552
Run5	0.3070	0.2808
Average	*0.2648*	*0.1929*

Re1 with k=39		
	J=E	J=L
Run1	0.3223	0.3211
Run2	0.3750	0.3121
Run3	0.2692	0.2092
Run4	0.4063	0.3166
Run5	0.3434	0.3360
Average	*0.3432*	*0.2990*

Re1 with k=124		
	J=E	J=L
Run1	0.3514	0.3514
Run2	0.3914	0.3693
Run3	0.3466	0.3145
Run4	0.4317	0.4156
Run5	0.4002	0.3981
Average	*0.3842*	*0.3697*

Table 12.

Tr31 with k=4		
	J=E	J=L
Run1	0.4172	0.1940
Run2	0.4839	0.1889
Run3	0.3870	0.1217
Run4	0.3845	0.1681
Run5	0.3872	0.2539
Average	*0.4119*	*0.1814*

Tr31 with k=14		
	J=E	J=L
Run1	0.5153	0.2958
Run2	0.6222	0.5467
Run3	0.3889	0.2276
Run4	0.4388	0.2020
Run5	0.5390	0.5315
Average	*0.5005*	*0.3607*

Tr31 with k=62		
	J=E	J=L
Run1	0.5447	0.4419
Run2	0.4850	0.4709
Run3	0.5244	0.4992
Run4	0.5112	0.4905
Run5	0.4933	0.3692
Average	*0.5117*	*0.4543*

Table 13.

Tr45 with k=4		
	J=E	J=L
Run1	0.3702	0.2093
Run2	0.3185	0.1682
Run3	0.3505	0.1023
Run4	0.2371	0.1682
Run5	0.2992	0.2814
Average	*0.3151*	*0.1858*

Tr45 with k=15		
	J=E	J=L
Run1	0.4069	0.3509
Run2	0.4485	0.3894
Run3	0.4347	0.3868
Run4	0.3646	0.3313
Run5	0.4216	0.3598
Average	*0.4152*	*0.3636*

Tr45 with k=54		
	J=E	J=L
Run1	0.3960	0.3256
Run2	0.4542	0.4353
Run3	0.4761	0.4173
Run4	0.3940	0.3820
Run5	0.4586	0.4215
Average	*0.4205*	*0.4104*

Table 14.

Wap with k=21		
	J=E	J=L
Run1	0.3895	0.2260
Run2	0.4126	0.2827
Run3	0.3626	0.2880
Run4	0.4618	0.3969
Run5	0.4444	0.3882
Average	*0.4141*	*0.3163*

Wap with k=84		
	J=E	J=L
Run1	0.4501	0.4251
Run2	0.3713	0.3110
Run3	0.4000	0.3972
Run4	0.5126	0.5037
Run5	0.3698	0.3212
Average	*0.4208*	*0.3916*

Finally, in Figures 2-4 it is possible to see the comparison among the results obtained by the different algorithms with *J*=*L*. Since both the k-Means and the Standard Bisecting k-Means set the centroids randomly, we considered the average F-measure obtained by 5 different runs. These results show that our approach

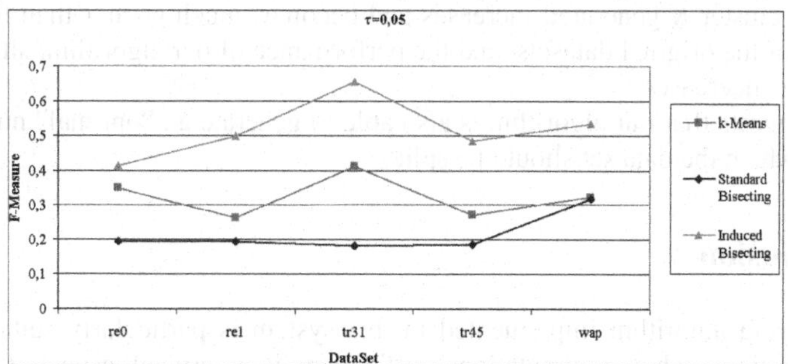

Fig. 2. Performance comparison with $\tau = 0.05$

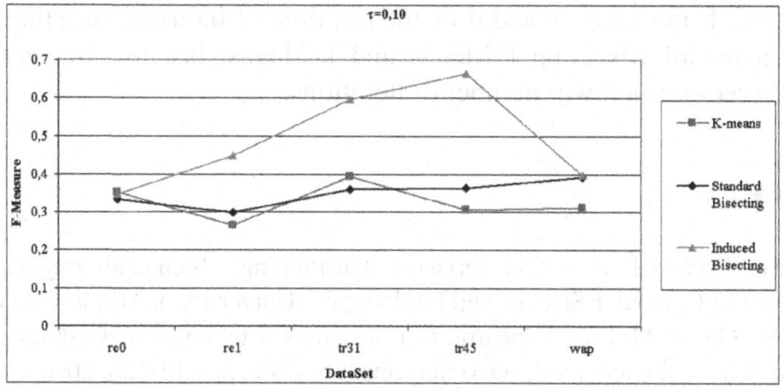

Fig. 3. Performance comparison with $\tau = 0.10$

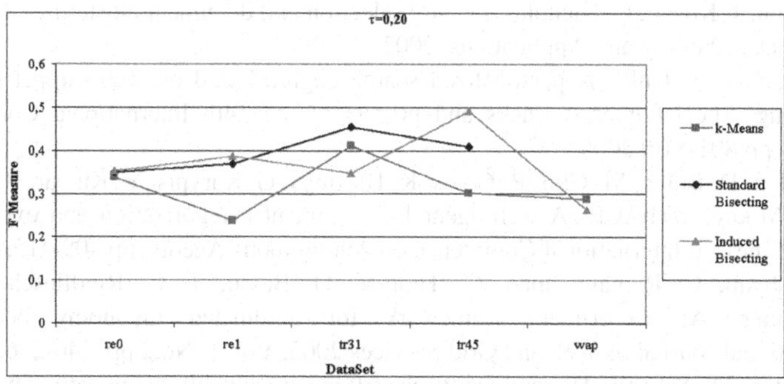

Fig. 4. Performance comparison with $\tau = 0.20$

outperforms both the k-Means and the Standard Bisecting k-Means. It is also interesting to note that by increasing the number K of clusters both k-Means and Bisecting k-Means give better performance while the F-Measure of our approach stretches to decrease by increasing K. Our approach gives better results for low values of τ equal to 0.10 and 0.05, that generate lower values of k that are closer to the number of classes in which the original datasets are split. While, when τ =0.20, the number of cluster K generated increases and becomes much greater than the number of classes of the original datasets, and the performance of our algorithm, although still competitive, decreases.

This suggests that our algorithm is also able to generate an "optimal" number K of cluster in which the data set should be split.

5 Conclusion

The clustering algorithm implemented in this system is particularly suitable for on line applications when computational efficiency is a crucial aspect. Our results indicate that Induced Bisecting k-Means is better than Standard Bisecting k-Means and k-Means both in terms of computational time and accuracy. More specifically, our approach produces significantly better clustering solutions quite consistently according to the F-measure. In addition, the run time of Induced Bisecting k-Means is lower than Standard Bisecting k-Means and k-Means, because it converges more quickly, i.e. it requires a lower number of iterations.

References

1. D. Boley, Principal Direction Divisive Partitioning, Technical Report TR-97-056, Department of Computer Science and Engineering, University of Minnesota, Minneapolis
2. J. Cho, H. Garcia-Molina, Synchronizing a database to improve freshness, In Proc. of ACM International Conference on Management of Data, pp 117-128, 2000
3. D. R. Cutting, J. O. Pedersen, D. Karger, and J. W. Tukey, Scatter/gather: A cluster-based approach to browsing large document collections, In Proc. of 15th Annual ACM-SIGIR, pp. 318-329, 1992
4. I. Dhillon, J. Kogan, C. Nicholas, Feature selection and document clustering, Book chapter in Text Data Mining and Applications, 2002
5. P. Ferragina, A. Gulli, A personalized search engine based on web-snippet hierarchical clustering, Special interest tracks and posters of the 14th International Conference on WWW, pp 801-810, 2005
6. E. H. Han, D. Boley, M. Gini, R. Gross, K. Hastings, G. Karypis, V. Kumar, B. Mobasher, and J. Moore, WebACE: A web agent for document categorization and exploration, In Proc. of the 2nd International Conference on Autonomous Agents, pp 408-415, 1998
7. V. Kashyap, C. Ramakrishnan, C. Thomas, D. Bassu, T. C. Rindflesch, A. Sheth, TaxaMiner: An experiment framework for automated taxonomy bootstrapping, International Journal of Web and Grid Services 2005, Vol. 1, No.2 pp. 240-266
8. D. Koller, M. Sahami, Hierarchically classifying documents using very few words, In Proc. of the 14th International Conference on Machine Learning, pp 170-178, 1997

9. P. Pirolli, P. Schank, M. Hearst, C. Diehl, Scatter/Gather Browsing Communicates the Topic Structure of a Very Large Text Collection, In Proc. of CHI, pp 213-220, 1996
10. Reuters-21578, http://www.daviddlewis.com/resources/testcollections/reuters21578/
11. G. Salton, M. J. McGill, Introduction to Modern Retrieval, McGraw-Hill Company, 1983
12. G. Salton, A. Wong, C. S. Yang, A vector space model for automatic indexing, Communications of ACM, vol. 18, Issue 11, pp 613-620, 1975
13. G. Salton, C. Buckley, Term weighting approaches in automatic text retrieval, Information Processing and Management, Vol. 24, Issue. 5, pp 513-523, 1988
14. M. Savaresi, D. L. Boley, On the performance of bisecting k-Means and PDDP, First SIAM International Conference on Data Mining , pp 1-14, 2001
15. M. Steinbach, G. Karypis, V. Kumar, A comparison of Document Clustering Techniques, In KDD Workshop on Text Mining, 2000
16. H. Toda, R. Kataoka, A search Result clustering Method using Informatively Named Entities, In Proc. of the 7th annual ACM International Workshop on Web information and data management, pp 81-86, 2005
17. TREC: Text Retrieval Conference, http://trec.nist.gov
18. O. Zamir, O. Etzioni, O. Madani, R. M. Karp, Fast and intuitive Clustering of Web document, In Proc. of KDD, pp 287-290, 1997
19. D. Zhang, Y. Dong. Semantic, Hierarchical, Online Clustering of Web Search Results. In Proc. of the 6th Asia Pacific Web Conference, 2004

Search Strategies for Finding Annotations and Annotated Documents: The FAST Service

Maristella Agosti and Nicola Ferro

Department of Information Engineering – University of Padua
Via Gradenigo, 6/b – 35131 Padova – Italy
{agosti, ferro}@dei.unipd.it

Abstract. This paper discusses two kinds of search strategies supported by the *Flexible Annotation Service Tool (FAST)*, an annotation service that can be used by different *Digital Library Management Systems (DLMSs)*. The first strategy concerns the search and retrieval of annotations, considered as stand-alone documents; while, the second one regards how to exploit annotations in order to search and retrieve annotated documents which are relevant for a user query. This paper describes the proposed search strategies in the light of the architectural design choices needed to support them.

1 Introduction

As observed by [10, p. 274], "the progress of the *Digital Library (DL)* field can be evaluated along several dimensions", one of which is called the *service dimension*, which "characterizes the complexity of processing that DLs and federations of DLs can manage on behalf of clients". In particular, we are interested in studying and developing a service able to add annotation capabilities on the documents managed by a *Digital Library Management System (DLMS)*, so that the service encapsulates all the complex processing needed to provide advanced annotation functionalities and can be easily "plugged" into different DLMSs.

We have designed and we are developing an annotation service for DLMSs, which is called *Flexible Annotation Service Tool (FAST)* [1, 2, 3, 4]. FAST offers basic annotation management functionalities and provides users with advanced search capabilities for retrieving both annotations and annotated documents on the basis of their annotations. This paper will introduce the search strategies supported by FAST in order to search for both annotations and annotated documents and it will describe the architecture of FAST with a particular focus on the architectural design choices which impact the search functionalities offered by the service.

The paper is organized as follows: Section 2 discusses the use of annotations in the context of DLMSs; Section 3 provides an overview of the FAST service; Section 4 describes the search strategies supported by FAST; Section 5 discusses the architecture of the system and its consequences on the offered search strategies; finally Section 6 draws some conclusions and provides an outlook of the future research work.

H.L. Larsen et al. (Eds.): FQAS 2006, LNAI 4027, pp. 270–281, 2006.

2 DLMSs and Annotations

DLMS are currently in a state of evolution: today they are simply places where information resources can be stored and made available, whereas for tomorrow they will become an integrated part of the way the user works. For example, instead of simply downloading a paper and then working on a printed version, a user will be able to work directly with the paper by means of the tools provided by the DLMS and share their work with colleagues. This way, the user's intellectual work and the information resources provided by the DLMS can be merged together in order to constitute a single working context. Thus, the DLMS is no longer perceived as something external to the intellectual production process and neither as a mere consulting tool, but instead as an intrinsic and active part of the intellectual production process [2].

Annotations are effective means in order to enable the paradigm of interaction between users and DLMSs envisioned above, since they are very well-established practices and widely used. Annotations are not only a way of explaining and enriching an information resource with personal observations, but also a means of transmitting and sharing ideas in order to improve collaborative work practices. Thus, annotations can be geared not only to the way of working of the individual and to a method of study, but also to a way of doing research, as it happens in the Humanities. Finally, annotations allow users to naturally merge and link personal contents with the information resources provided by the DLMS so that a common context that unifies all of these contents can be created.

With this last respect, documents managed by the DLMS and annotations constitute an hypertext [3, 4], since annotations allow the creation of new relationships among existing objects, by means of links that connect annotations together with existing objects. [9] points out that annotations are one of the activities that form the basis of any collaborative effort and for which hypermedia systems are ideally suited, while [12] considers annotations as a natural way of creating and growing hypertexts that connect information resources by actively engaging users. Moreover, DLMSs do not normally have a hypertext connecting information resources with each other; thus, annotations can turn out to be an effective way of associating a hypertext to a DLMS in order to enable an active and dynamic usage of information resources. This hypertext can span and cross the boundaries of the single DLMS, if users need to interact with the information resources managed by diverse DLMSs [2]. This latter possibility is quite innovative, because offers the means for interconnecting various DLMSs in a personalized way meaningful for the end-user and, as recognized also by [10], is a big challenge for next generation DLMSs.

In this evolving context, it becomes crucial to design and develop services able to provide annotation functionalities to many different DLMSs. Moreover, besides offering various annotation management facilities, these services should pay particular attention to offer support for integrating annotations into the information access and retrieval process. Indeed, the possibilities of collaboration and active involvement with digital resources uncovered by bringing annotations into DLMSs require that annotation are an integral part of the way in which users share, search, and retrieve information. Thus, we need to develop methods that allow us to search both for annotations themselves by taking into account their own features, and for annotated documents by exploiting the annotations linked to them. In the first case, the objective of our search are annotations and we need to develop techniques that exploit their peculiarities in order to effectively retrieve them. On the contrary, in the second case, we aim at searching annotated documents and annotations simply represent a means for retrieving better and more documents with respect to the case of a search without using annotations.

3 Overview of FAST

FAST is a flexible service designed to support both various architectural paradigms, such as *Peer-To-Peer (P2P)* or *Web Services (WS)* architectures, and a wide range of different DLMSs. The flexibility of FAST and its independence from any particular DLMS is a key feature to provide users with a uniform way of interaction with annotation functionalities, without the need of changing their annotative practices only because a user works with different DLMSs. In order to achieve the desired flexibly:

1. FAST is a stand-alone system, i.e. it is not part of any particular DLMS;
2. the core functionalities of the annotation service are separated from the functionalities needed to integrate it into different DLMSs;
3. the architecture is as modular as possible, so that different implementations of each component of FAST can be provided in order to add and/or modify its functionalities with the desired degree of granularity.

The choice of making FAST a stand-alone system is coherent with the approach adopted by different systems: for example, both Annotea [11, 13] and *Multimedia Annotation of Digital Content Over the Web (MADCOW)* [7] rely on stand-alone servers, that store and manage annotations separated from the annotated objects. On the other hand, the choice of separating the core functionalities of the annotation service, from the functionalities needed to integrate it into the different DLMSs is quite new. As a consequence of this architectural choice, it is worth pointing out that the FAST service knows everything about annotations, however it cannot do any assumption regarding the information resources provided by the DLMS, being that it needs to cooperate with different DLMSs. This situation is very different from what is commonly found today. For example, both Annotea and MADCOW are stand-alone systems but they are targeted to work with Web pages. Indeed, they assume that the annotated object has a structure compliant with *HyperText Markup Language (HTML)*, as an example, and that they can use *HyperText Transfer Protocol (HTTP)* to transport annotations. On the contrary, FAST cannot assume that it is dealing with either HTML documents or the HTTP protocol, but it has to avoid any constraints concerning both the annotated information resource and the available protocols. The only assumption about information resources that FAST can make is that each information resource is uniquely identified by a *handle*, which is a name assigned to an information resource in order to identify and facilitate the referencing to it, such as a *Uniform Resource Identifier (URI)* or a *Digital Object Identifier (DOI)*.

FAST models annotations according to the *Entity–Relationship (ER)* schema described in [1, 4, 5]: annotations are composite and complex multi-media objects, where each part of the annotation, called *sign of annotation*, has its own medium, e.g. text or audio, and a well-defined and explicit semantics, called *meaning of annotation*, according to an ontology of agreed meanings of annotation, e.g. comment, question, and so on. Annotations can annotate multiple parts of a given *Digital Object (DO)* and can relate this annotated DO to various other DOs, if needed. Furthermore, once it has been created, an annotation is considered as a first class DO, so that it can be annotated too. In this way, the model support users in creating not only sets of annotations concerning a DO, but also threads of annotations, i.e. annotations which reply to one another. These threads of annotations are the basis for actively involving users with the system and for enabling collaboration.

From a functional point of view, FAST provides annotation management functionalities, such as creation, storage, access, and so on. Furthermore, it supports collaboration among user by introducing scopes of annotation and groups of users: annotations can be private, shared or public; if an annotation is shared, different groups of users can share it with different permissions, e.g. one group can only read the annotation while another can also modify it. Note that the annotation management engine ensure that some validity constraints are complied with: for example, a private annotation cannot be annotated by a public annotation. In such cases there is a *scope conflict* – in the example, the author of the private annotation could see both the public and the private annotation, but another user could see only the public annotation which would be annotating something hidden to this user.

4 Search Strategies Supported by FAST

As introduced in Section 1, in order to effectively exploit annotations, we need to design and develop two complementar kinds of search strategy: the first kind of search strategy is concerned with the retrieval of annotations themselves and it is presented in Section 4.1; the second kind regards how to effectively exploit annotations when we search for annotated documents; this last strategy has been firstly discussed in [3] and its key points are briefly reported in Section 4.2.

Figure 1 shows the *Unified Modeling Language (UML)* class diagram of the interfaces that describe query capabilities supported by FAST. Note that we are defining the query capabilities of FAST in term of abstract interfaces, which control the general semantics of the query; on the other hand, we have a further degree of freedom given by the possible different implementations of each interface, which can vary the functionalities actually offered, still in the broad semantics prescribed by the corresponding interface. Finally, as we will discuss in

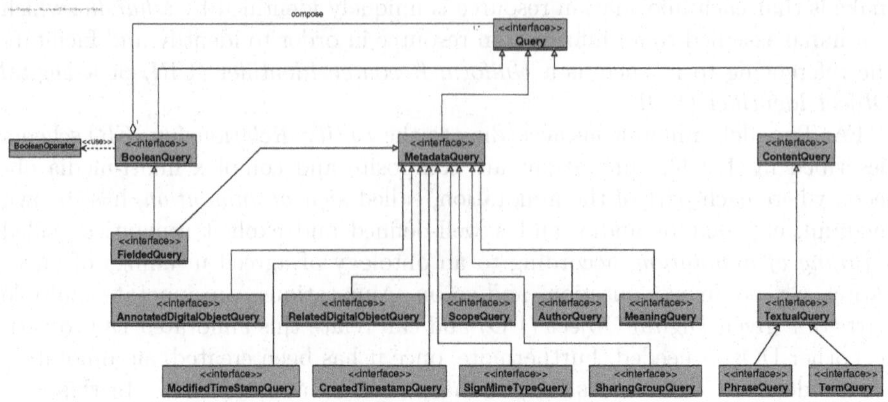

Fig. 1. UML class diagram of the query types supported by FAST

Section 5, different components of the FAST service are responsible for actually processing a query, according to its type and implementation.

4.1 Searching for Annotations

With respect to the first kind of search strategy, FAST offers three basic kinds of query: `MetadataQuery`, `ContentQuery`, and `BooleanQuery`.

The first query type, `MetadataQuery`, is intended for searching annotations on the basis of their metadata, such as for example the author of the annotation or the handle of the annotated DO. This kind of query is processed by using an *exact match* approach and annotations are retrieved in a *DataBase Management System (DBMS)* fashion. In order to actually carry out this kind of search, this interface is further specialised into a set of sub-interfaces that capture the different kinds of metadata available for an annotation. Thus, we have the following basic types of metadata query: the `AnnotatedDigitalObjectQuery` searches for all the annotations which are annotating a given DO; the `RelatedDigitalObjectQuery` has a similar purpose but for the DOs related by an annotation; the `ScopeQuery` selects annotations on the basis of their scope, i.e. private, shared, or public annotations; the `AuthorQuery` finds annotations with a given author; the `MeaningQuery` is intended for searching annotations with the specified meaning of annotation, e.g. for searching all the comments or all the counter-arguments; the `CreatedTimestampQuery` and the `ModifiedTimestampQuery` are used when we need annotations that have been, respectively, created or modified in a time stamp before, equal, or after the specified one; the `SignMimeTypeQuery` searches for annotations which contain a sign of annotation with the specified *Multipurpose Internet Mail Extensions (MIME)* type, e.g. for searching all the annotations containing a textual part or a graphical part; finally, the `SharingGroupQuery` looks annotations on the basis of the groups which are sharing them, as for example the annotations shared by a given group with read and write permission. Note that the MetadataQuery covers both the metadata that are sometimes called *structural metadata*, such as the AnnotatedDigitalObjectQuery or the MeaningQuery, and those metadata that are sometimes referred as *administrative metadata*, such as ScopeQuery or SharingGroupQuery.

The second query type, ContentQuery, is concerned with the search and retrieval of annotations on the basis of their actual content. Thus, this kind of search requires a *best match* approach and annotations are retrieved in an *Information Retrieval System (IRS)* fashion. Even if annotations are in general multi-media compound objects, at the moment, the only medium supported by FAST for search purposes is the text. Thus, the general ContentQuery is specialised by the TextualQuery which is focused on searching for annotations that contain signs of annotations with a textual MIME type; nevertheless the query hierarchy and the architecture of FAST, as we will see in Section 5, are designed for seamlessly supporting the introduction of new content queries for other kinds of medium, such as images or audio, by simply providing new sub-interfaces of ContentQuery. The TextualQuery is further specialised by two basic query types: the TermQuery that matches annotations against a given term, and PhraseQuery that matches annotations against a given phrase, that is a particular sequence of terms.

The third query type, BooleanQuery, represents a query that matches annotations against a combination of other queries by using the AND, OR, and NOT BooleanOperators. Thus, it is a compound query whose aim is to increase the expressive power of the basic queries described above. For example, we could search for annotations with the specified author and the given scope, or we may search for annotations containing one term but not another one. Note that, even if the class hierarchy is designed for supporting the case, the present prototype implementation of FAST does not allow mixed boolean queries, that are boolean queries combining metadata and content queries together.

A final kind of query is the FieldedQuery, which is not a new type of query but instead it is a convenience query type. It allows us to create the most commonly used boolean queries involving annotation's metadata by ensuring that some general query semantics is preserved. For example, by using MetadataQuery and BooleanOperator, it would be possibile to create a syntactically correct query that asks for private annotations that are shared by a given group; this would result in a "wrong" query with an empty result set, because by definition private annotations cannot be shared by any group. On the other hand, the contract specified by the FieldedQuery interface ensures that the constraints set on the scope of an annotation are coherent with other possibile constraints on its sharing groups, otherwise an appropriate exception is thrown.

4.2 Searching for Documents by Exploiting Annotation

When we plan to exploit annotations for searching annotated documents, we need to develop a search strategy which is able to effectively take into account the multiple sources of evidence which come from both documents and annotations,

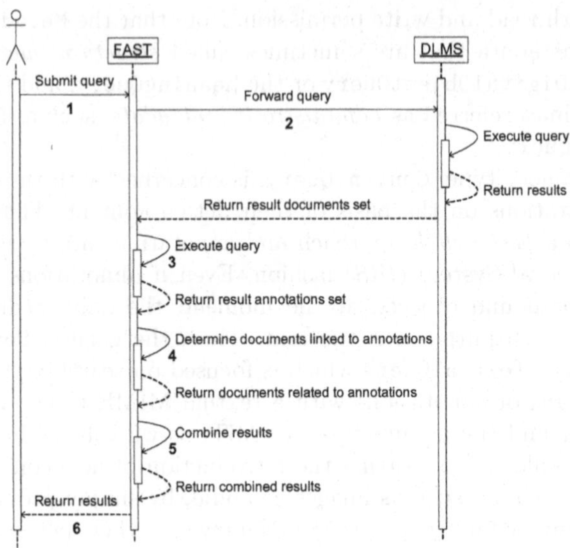

Fig. 2. UML sequence diagram of the search strategy for searching documents by exploiting annotations (from [3])

as proposed in [3]. In fact, the combining of these multiple sources of evidence can be exploited in order to improve the performances of an information management system. Our aim is to retrieve more documents that are relevant and to have them ranked in a way which is better than a system that does not makes use of annotations.

In order to carry out this search strategy, we need to deal with two kinds of DOs, that are documents and annotations. Let D be the *set of documents* and $d \in D$ is a generic document; let A be the *set of annotations* and $a \in A$ is a generic annotation; let $DO = D \cup A$ be the set of digital objects and $do \in DO$ is a generic digital object, which can be either a document or an annotation. Finally, let Q be the *set of user queries* and $q \in Q$ is a generic query. The UML sequence diagram of Figure 2 summarizes our search strategy:

1. the user submits a query $q \in Q$ to FAST;
2. FAST forwards the query to the DLMS, which searches for documents to retrieve for the query q.

   We call $R_{d,q} \subseteq D$ the result set returned by the DLMS, $s_{d,q} \in [0, 1]$ the similarity score of the document d with respect to the query q. According to our architecture, $R_{d,q}$ is completely defined and managed by the DLMS and FAST has no control over $R_{d,q}$. Thus, the DLMS has the function of providing $R_{d,q}$ and a similarity score $s_{d,q}$ for each document $d \in R_{d,q}$ to FAST;
3. FAST searches for annotations to retrieve for the query q, according to the search strategies described in Section 4.1.

We call $R_{a,q} \subseteq A$ the result set returned by FAST, $s_{a,q} \in [0,1]$ the similarity score of the annotation a with respect to the query q.According to our architecture, $R_{a,q}$ is completely defined and managed by FAST;

4. FAST determines the documents associated to the annotations contained in $R_{a,q}$, by using a *mapping function* $\mathrm{M} : A \to D$, that associates an annotation $a \in A$ to a document $d \in D$. To carry out the mapping function M, FAST exploits the hypertext existing between documents and annotations, introduced in Section 1, and follows the paths that link annotations to annotated documents.

   We call $R_{d,a} \subseteq D$ the set containing the documents associated to the annotations in $R_{a,q}$, i.e. $R_{d,a} = \mathrm{M}(R_{a,q})$; $s_{d,a} \in [0,1]$ is the similarity score of a document $d \in R_{d,a}$;
5. FAST combines the two sets $R_{d,q}$ and $R_{d,a}$ into one set $R_d = R_{d,q} \cup R_{d,a} \subseteq D$ in order to obtain only one list of retrieved documents. $s_d \in [0,1]$ is the similarity score of a document $d \in R_d$, obtained combining $s_{d,q}$ and $s_{d,a}$;
6. FAST returns the list of retrieved documents to the user.

We can point out some interesting characteristics of this search strategy. Firstly, in the fourth step FAST needs to employ both *Hypertext Information Retrieval (HIR)* [6] and data fusion techniques [8]: indeed, different paths in the hypertext allow FAST to associate annotations to documents, which are necessary to determine $R_{d,a}$ from $R_{a,q}$; furthermore, FAST has to exploit also data fusion techniques in order to compute the similarity score $s_{d,a}$ of a document d from the similarity scores $s_{a,q}$ of the annotations linked to d. Secondly, in the fifth step we need to combine the similarity scores $s_{d,q}$ computed by the DLMS with the similarity scores $s_{d,a}$ computed by FAST, which is a data fusion problem. Finally, the sequence diagram of Figure 2 highlights that we are dealing with a distributed search problem. For further details on this search strategy, please refer to [3].

With respect to the query class hierarchy shown in Figure 1, this search strategy involves mainly content queries, because we have no information about the documents managed by the DLMS and thus we remit to the DLMS the task of retrieving documents on the basis of their content. In line of principle, it would be possibile to take into consideration also some metadata query, especially on the annotation side of this search strategy, but this is left for future investigation.

5 Architecture of FAST

FAST adopts a three-layers architecture – the data, application and interface logic layers – and is designed at a high level of abstraction in terms of abstract *Application Program Interfaces (APIs)* using an *Object Oriented (OO)* approach. In this way, we can model the behaviour and the functioning of FAST without worrying about the actual implementation of each component. Different alternative implementations of each component could be provided, still keeping a coherent view of the whole architecture of the FAST service. We achieve this abstraction level by means of a set of interfaces, which define the behaviour of each component of FAST in abstract terms. Then, a set of abstract classes partially implement the interfaces in order to define the actual behaviour common to all of the implementations of each component. Finally, the actual implementation is left to the concrete classes, inherited from the abstract ones, that fit FAST into a given architecture. Java[1] is the programming language in use for developing FAST. Java ensures us great portability across different hardware and software platforms, thus providing us with a further level of flexibility.

The UML class diagram of figure 3 presents the main interfaces involved in the definition of the data and application logic layers, which are the ones responsible for the actual query processing. The user interface layer is not reported in figure 3 since issues concerning the visualization of query results are out of the scope of the present paper.

5.1 Data Logic Layer

The data logic layer manages the actual storage of the annotations and provides a persistence layer for storing and retrieving the objects which represent the annotation and which are used by the upper layers of the architecture.

`Datastore` is a façade for the following interfaces: `AnnotationDAO`, `UserDAO`, `GroupDAO`, `MeaningDAO`, and `LoggerDAO`, which define the operations needed to ensure the persistence of the different objects managed by the system. These interfaces are designed according to the *Data Access Object (DAO)* design pattern[2]. The DAO implements the access mechanism required to work with the underlying data source, e.g. it may offer access to a *Relational DBMS (RDBMS)* by using the *Java DataBase Connectivity (JDBC)*[3] technology. Besides ensuring the persistence of the differen objects managed by the system, the `Datastore` is responsible also for actually processing both metadata queries and boolean queries, composed by only metadata queries. We use the PostgreSQL[4] DBMS in order to perform the actual storage of the annotations, and a concrete class implementing the `Datastore` interface has been developed in order communicate with PostegreSQL by using JDBC.

The `Indexer` interface is responsible for the processing of content queries. In particular, in the prototype of FAST we have implemented a textual indexer based on the Lucene[5] library able to manage the different kinds of textual query. As introduced in Section 4.1, support for further kind of media can be easily added by proving additional implementations of the `Indexer` interface, specialised for the desired medium.

Finally, the `Datalogic` interface provides coherent access to the underlying components and forwards queries either to the `Datastore` or the the proper `Indexer`, according to whether they are metadata or content queries.

[1] `http://java.sun.com/`
[2] `http://java.sun.com/blueprints/corej2eepatterns/Patterns/`
[3] `http://java.sun.com/products/jdbc/`
[4] `http://www.postgresql.org/`
[5] `http://lucene.apache.org/`

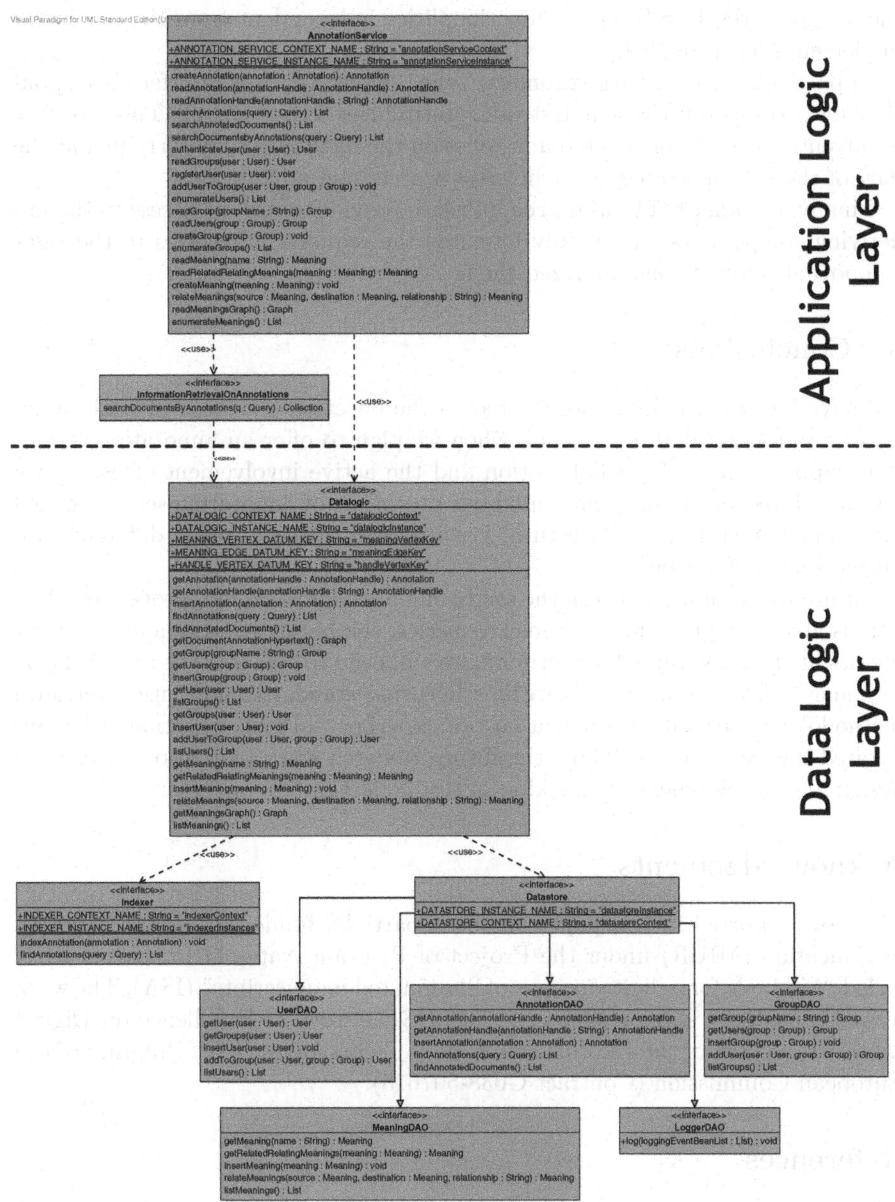

Fig. 3. UML class diagram of the data and application logic layers of FAST

5.2 Application Logic Layer

The application logic layer provides advanced functionalities that make use of annotations, such as for example the search strategy described in Section 4.2. As in the case of the data logic layer, we define a set of abstract API that make the access to the FAST service functionalities independent from the particular implementation provided.

In particular, the `InformationRetrievalOnAnnotations` interface is responsible for carrying out the search strategy introduced in Section 4.2. This interface is currently being implemented and relies on the `Datalogic` for carrying out the part of the search strategy that involves searches on annotations.

Finally, the `AnnotationService` interface provides coherent access to the underlying components and mainly forwards the requests it receives to the right component, after having analyzed them.

6 Conclusions

We have introduced the issues related to the effective searching of both annotations and annotated documents, when we plan to offer an annotation service that supports both the collaboration and the active involvement of users in a DLMS. Moreover, we have presented our prototype of annotation service, called FAST, introducing its architectural features with respect to the different supported search strategies.

Future research will concern the study of more complex query processing algorithms able to support mixed boolean queries, combining metatada and content queries at the same time. Furthermore, we will need to evaluate the retrieval performances of the proposed algorithms by using standard information retrieval methodologies. Finally, there is a lack of experimental test collections with annotated digital contents. Thus, the future research work may also concern the design and development of this kind of test collection.

Acknowledgements

The work reported in this paper has been partially funded by Italian Ministry of Education (MIUR) under the Project of Relevant National Interest (PRIN) called "Methods for a digital corpus of illuminated manuscripts" (ISA). The work was also partially supported by the DELOS Network of Excellence on Digital Libraries, as part of the Information Society Technologies (IST) Program of the European Commission (Contract G038-507618).

References

1. M. Agosti and N. Ferro. Annotations: Enriching a Digital Library. In T. Koch and I. T. Sølvberg, editors, *Proc. 7th European Conference on Research and Advanced Technology for Digital Libraries (ECDL 2003)*, pages 88–100. LNCS 2769, Springer, Heidelberg, Germany, 2003.
2. M. Agosti and N. Ferro. A System Architecture as a Support to a Flexible Annotation Service. In C. Türker, M. Agosti, and H.-J. Schek, editors, *Peer-to-Peer, Grid, and Service-Orientation in Digital Library Architectures: 6th Thematic Workshop of the EU Network of Excellence DELOS. Revised Selected Papers*, pages 147–166. LNCS 3664, Springer, Heidelberg, Germany, 2005.

3. M. Agosti and N. Ferro. Annotations as Context for Searching Documents. In F. Crestani and I. Ruthven, editors, *Proc. 5th International Conference on Conceptions of Library and Information Science – Context: nature, impact and role*, pages 155–170. LNCS 3507, Springer, Heidelberg, Germany, 2005.
4. M. Agosti, N. Ferro, I. Frommholz, and U. Thiel. Annotations in Digital Libraries and Collaboratories – Facets, Models and Usage. In R. Heery and L. Lyon, editors, *Proc. 8th European Conference on Research and Advanced Technology for Digital Libraries (ECDL 2004)*, pages 244–255. LNCS 3232, Springer, Heidelberg, Germany, 2004.
5. M. Agosti, N. Ferro, and N. Orio. Annotating Illuminated Manuscripts: an Effective Tool for Research and Education. In M. Marlino, T. Sumner, and F. Shipman, editors, *Proc. 5th ACM/IEEE-CS Joint Conference on Digital Libraries (JCDL 2005)*, pages 121–130. ACM Press, New York, USA, 2005.
6. M. Agosti and A. Smeaton, editors. *Information Retrieval and Hypertext*. Kluwer Academic Publishers, Norwell (MA), USA, 1996.
7. P. Bottoni, R. Civica, S. Levialdi, L. Orso, E. Panizzi, and R. Trinchese. MADCOW: a Multimedia Digital Annotation System. In M. F. Costabile, editor, *Proc. Working Conference on Advanced Visual Interfaces (AVI 2004)*, pages 55–62. ACM Press, New York, USA, 2004.
8. W. B. Croft. Combining Approaches to Information Retrieval. In W. B. Croft, editor, *Advances in Information Retrieval: Recent Research from the Center for Intelligent Information Retrieval*, pages 1–36. Kluwer Academic Publishers, Norwell (MA), USA, 2000.
9. F. G. Halasz. Reflections on NoteCards: Seven Issues for the Next Generation of Hypermedia Systems. *Communications of the ACM (CACM)*, 31(7):836–852, 1988.
10. Y. Ioannidis, D. Maier, S. Abiteboul, P. Buneman, S. Davidson, E. A. Fox, A. Halevy, C. Knoblock, F. Rabitti, H.-J. Schek, and G. Weikum. Digital library information-technology infrastructures. *International Journal on Digital Libraries*, 5(4):266–274, 2005.
11. J. Kahan and M.-R. Koivunen. Annotea: an open RDF infrastructure for shared Web annotations. In V. Y. Shen, N. Saito, M. R. Lyu, and M. E. Zurko, editors, *Proc. 10th International Conference on World Wide Web (WWW 2001)*, pages 623–632. ACM Press, New York, USA, 2001.
12. C. C. Marshall. Toward an Ecology of Hypertext Annotation. In R. Akscyn, editor, *Proc. 9th ACM Conference on Hypertext and Hypermedia (HT 1998): links, objects, time and space-structure in hypermedia systems*, pages 40–49. ACM Press, New York, USA, 1998.
13. W3C. Annotea Project. `http://www.w3.org/2001/Annotea/`, October 2005.

Assisted Query Formulation Using Normalised Word Vector and Dynamic Ontological Filtering

Heinz Dreher and Robert Williams

Curtin University of Technology, GPO Box U1987
Perth, Western Australia 6845
{Heinz.Dreher, Bob.Williams}@cbs.curtin.edu.au

Abstract. Information seekers using the usual search techniques and engines are delighted by the sheer power of the technology at their command – speed, quantity. Upon closer inspection of the results, and reflection upon the next stages of the information seeking knowledge work, users are typically overwhelmed, and frustrated. We propose a partial solution by focusing on the query formulation aspect of the information seeking problem. First we introduce our version of a semantic analysis algorithm, named Normalised Word Vector, and explain its application in assisted query formulation. Secondly we introduce our ideas of supporting query refinement via Dynamic Ontological Filtering.

1 Introduction

Information and Communications Technologies (ICT) pervade our society in which a growing proportion of the work is mental work (typically referred to as knowledge work) as opposed to physical work. The record of empowerment of physical workers through technology clearly shows the enormous benefit in terms of increased production, efficient and effective utilisation of resources, and greater safety for workers. Knowledge workers should expect to see similar gains in capacity, productivity, and in the quality of outputs, but progress in the empowerment of the knowledge worker needs a boost so that this promise and expectation can be realised. It is not so much a case of lack of vision:

> Neither the naked hand nor the understanding left to itself can effect much. It is by instruments and helps that the work is done, which are as much wanted for the understanding as for the hand. And as the instruments for the hand either give motion or guide it, so the instruments of the mind supply either suggestions for the understanding or cautions. [1].

More recently, by some three and a quarter centuries, Vannevar Bush [2] shared with us his vision of how research workers could be empowered with his MEMEX device. But despite the vision, and the tremendous advances in ICT, and their now pervasive nature, the knowledge worker is left languishing by and large. For example, whilst a literature search can now be conducted in a matter of days if not hours where only two decades ago it took weeks if not months, the researcher is confronted with millions upon millions of 'hits'.

H.L. Larsen et al. (Eds.): FQAS 2006, LNAI 4027, pp. 282 – 294, 2006.

Present methods of refinement of the result of a query or search are inadequate – there is far too much material which is potentially relevant. Additionally, users, don't really know what is relevant until some way through the discovery, learning, or knowledge acquisition process. Help is needed with the Query-formulation → Find → Re-formulation phases of knowledge work.

In this article we consider the query-formulation aspect of the general problem. There are two contributions we propose to integrate into search and find processes. Firstly, an adaptation of a semantic analysis algorithm named Normalised Word Vector (NWV) developed by Williams [7] for the MarkIT (www.essaygrading.com) Automated Essay Grading project [8] with the aim of accepting natural language query expressions. Secondly, we propose a dynamic ontological filter to be applied to the query in order to maximise search relevance. Categorizing the results returned by search engines and presenting the categories to the user through a special browser endowed with an ontology navigation scheme is expected to contribute to a refinement of the search query and hence improve relevance and thus information quality as required by the user.

2 Assisted Query Formulation – Empowering P to Refine Q

Imagine a human user P is interested in researching Yoga, and enters this as a search-term (Q) into Google which delivers circa 39 million results in one tenth of a second. This is impressive until P begins to use the returned results. P quickly determines that some strategy is needed to reduce the quantity and increase the relevance of the results, but to accomplish this P will need to refine Q, and proceeds using the traditional methods such as including Boolean operations, appending adjectives, enclosing search strings within quotes, and so on. P's focus has now been redirected from the concept "Yoga", as originally envisaged, to the science of search-term and query formulation. Actually, we all know that P did not have just "yoga' in mind, but some idiosyncratic aspect/s thereof. Surely we can better support P in the information seeking task pertaining to Yoga.

Consider the 7-Step process in Table 1, which we have termed Query-formulation → Find → Re-formulation (QFR).

Continuing our Yoga example from above, at Step 1) we have P composing a natural language query into the special browser.

Q = I would like to take an English language based Yoga-teacher course as soon as possible

(Google returns 900 odd results in about half a second, and if Q is enclosed in quotes, Google returns no matching documents, also quite speedily).

The NWV technology computes Normalised Concepts based on Q, which for example may be Language, Lifestyle, Time, Education. These constitute the 'core concepts' contained in Q - comprising Step 2). Varied forms of Q as expressed by various P would all yield the same Normalised Concepts thereby already greatly simplifying and focusing the subsequent document match and retrieval. At this point one may mention that the 'core concepts' could be readily translated into arbitrarily many natural languages, and depending on the respective thesaurus (or alternative) structures, similarly high quality results could be expected for those alternative language searches. Further, with such a simplified query form, it is possible to imagine a new FAQ database which efficiently supports Normalised Concept searching.

Step 3) of the QFR in Table 1 also categorizes the Normalised Concepts according to the currently activated ontological filter. At Step 4) our user P interacts with the content (Normalised Concepts) and with the structure (ontological view) of the idea behind the search query Q.

P repeats some steps until a much finer and accurate representation of the original Q is created. For example, P realised that Yoga courses everywhere in the world were not of interest, but rather, Yoga courses in Milano, Italy, or even more specifically in either San Giovanni or Corsico, respectively, on the north east and south west fringes of the Milano metropolis.

Now at Step 6), a truly proper representation of P's Q exists and is expected to result in a high quality outcome at Step 7).

Table 1. Query-formulation → Find → Re-formulation (QFR)

Step 1)	Person **P** has idea → constructs keywords or some text to explain the concept → call it **Q**.
Step 2)	Via a special browser, **Q** is 'acquired' by the NWV technology which makes computations based on some 'reference data' set. This is typically a thesaurus or alternative corpus obtained by some search-categorization process or by reference to a seed ontology - the Open Directory Project (www.dmoz.com) would be a suitable starting point.
Step 3)	A set of *Normalised Concepts* are returned in the context of the 'reference data' set and categorized by the reference to the current ontological view.
Step 4)	The special browser facilitates **P** to adjust (augment, amend, re-arrange, re-categorize, delete) **Q**, we now have **Q**i (i ranges from 1 for the first iteration to integer values such as 3 or 4, perhaps 7 at most).
Step 5)	Re-iterate through Steps 2) 3) and 4) until **P** is satisfied that **Q**n represents the true idea **P** had in mind for the search.
Step 6)	Submit **Q**n into ontological filter/disambiguation system to match the query/ontology/target data repository for the search.
Step 7)	Present results to **P** with options of re-iterating Step 6) after **P** refines/adjusts and/or repeats Step 5).

One might say that the technology helps watch over the P's and Q's. And this is properly as it should be, as compared with the user confronted with millions of documents returned in practically millionths of seconds – here the user is being supported by the technology rather than the technology dictating how/what the user should or can do. We would argue that our "Assisted Query Formulation using Normalised Word Vector and Dynamic Ontological Filtering" is truly empowering.

In the remainder of the paper we describe the two main components of our system: the Normalised Word Vector technology and the Dynamic Ontological Filtering, and give some examples of the technology at work.

3 The Normalised Word Vector Technology

NWV consists of two parts. First there is the thesaurus based vector representation which is explained via an example found in Tables 2, 3, and 4, and Fig. 1. Once the vector representations have been built, a document similarity measure may be calculated using geometrical constructs.

3.1 Thesaurus Based Vector Representation to Normalise Words in Documents

Vector algebra techniques are used to represent similarities in content between documents or natural language free text expressions. A thesaurus [5] is used to build this vector representation by 'normalising' the words in the documents by reducing all words to a thesaurus root word appropriate to the encompassing concept. The vector representation is then constructed from the enumeration of these concepts. In our work on automated essay grading [3], [8], we have shown the approach to perform satisfactorily; that is, as well as one would expect from humans. The following start-of-sentence fragments from successive sentences in three separate Document Texts are used to explain how this is accomplished.

Table 2. Document number and text

Document Number	Document Text
(1)	The tall girl… A large female
(2)	A major girl… A happy boy
(3)	The large girl… Some major holiday

Suppose a thesaurus exists with the following root Concept Numbers and Words:

Table 3. Concept number and words

Concept Number	Words
1.	the, a
2.	tall, large, major
3.	girl, female
4.	little
5.	happy
6.	boy
7.	some
8.	holiday

Three dimensional vector representations of the above document fragments on the first three Concept Numbers (1-3) can be constructed by counting the number of times a word belonging to that Concept Number appears in the document fragments. These vectors are given in Table 4.

Table 4. Document number and matching concepts

Document Number	Vector on first 3 concepts	Explanation
(1)	[2, 2, 2]	[The, a; tall, large; girl, female]
(2)	[2, 1, 1]	[A, a; major; girl]
(3)	[1, 2, 1]	[The; large, major; girl]

Fig. 1 presents these 3-dimensional vectors pictorially. Document Number (1) is the dotted line emerging from the origin at the bottom left and stretching to the upper right of the graph. Document Numbers (2) and (3) are to the left and right, respectively, of (1). Concepts 1, 2, and 3, are shown as orthogonal axes as a reference frame. The angles, Theta, are a measure of the separation between documents - Theta1 between (2) and (3) and Theta2 between (1) and (3).

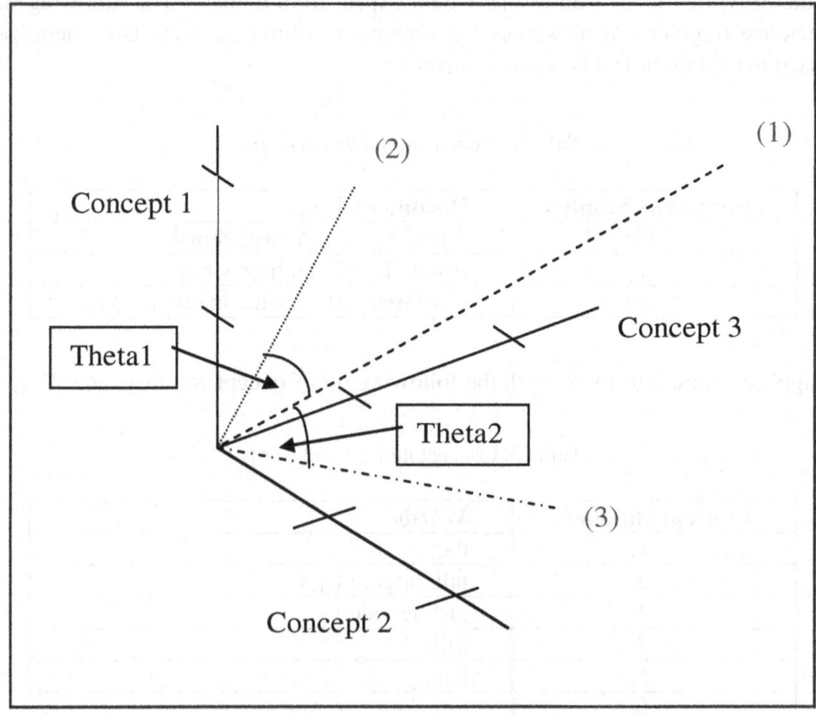

Fig. 1. Vector representation (broken lines) of documents

3.2 Document Similarity – Computing the Variable CosTheta

The closeness in terms of the semantics between documents (1) and (2), and (1) and (3) can be determined by looking at the closeness of their corresponding vectors. The angle between the vectors varies according to how 'close' the vectors are. A small angle indicates that the documents contain similar content; a large angle indicates that they do not have much common content. This measure of closeness can be quantified by looking at the cosines of Theta1 and Theta2. If documents (1) and (2) were identical, their vectors would be identical, and would be collinear, resulting in a cosine value of 1. If on the other hand, they were completely different, and therefore orthogonal, their cosines would be 0.

The variable named CosTheta used in the NWV algorithm is this cosine computed for the document (semantic content) being evaluated.

The Macquarie Thesaurus from The Macquarie Library Pty Ltd [5] is used to derive the normalised concepts. There are 812 concepts in this thesaurus, and all words in the documents are reduced to the appropriate within-context root concept. The vectors are constructed in this 812 dimensional space, and the vector theory carries over to these dimensions in exactly the same way – it is of course somewhat challenging to visualize the vectors in this 812D-hyperspace, as they cannot be represented graphically.

4 Applying NWV Technology to Query-Formulation

The reader can see that the scenario from an earlier section is readily supported by NWV technology. The documents referred to in Fig. 1 become the successive versions of **Q**, the query-formulation being constructed by the researcher **P**.

Next we consider a test of the NWV system of query-formulation based on expressions taken from essays written by year 10 Western Australian high school students on the topic of "The School Leaving Age". For example, suppose the user is interested in finding documents relating to the following content:

According to the Minister of Education, the legal age for students to leave school will be changed from 15 years of age to 17 in 2002.

Fig. 2. "The School Leaving Age" query formulation

The NWV system returned the following alternate natural language or textual query formulations by other 'researchers' together with a closeness representation. Four cases are presented in increasing order of 'semantic closeness' – 53%, 54%, 66% and 77%. In the figures below (see Legend), the "Master" corresponds to the Concepts derived from the text in Fig. 2 (blue, dark), and the "Target" corresponds to the text found in Figs. 3, 4, 5, and 6 (magenta or pink).

A comparison of the 'Master' dark blue coloured bar (left pair member) with the 'Target' light or magenta coloured bar (right pair member) affords a visual comparison of the semantic proximity by Concept. In the case of the Target text given in Fig. 3 above, which has 53% semantic commonality with the Master text given in Fig. 2, we can observe the numerous concept mismatches (“being”, “diagram”, “model”, “start”, “student”, and “ti…”). A similar mismatch, in relative terms, is observed in Fig. 4 below (note the change in vertical axis scale).

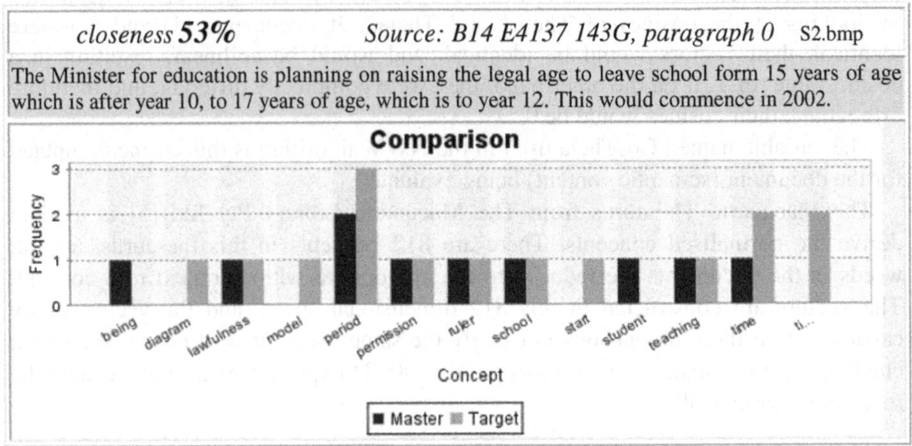

Fig. 3. 53% semantic proximity

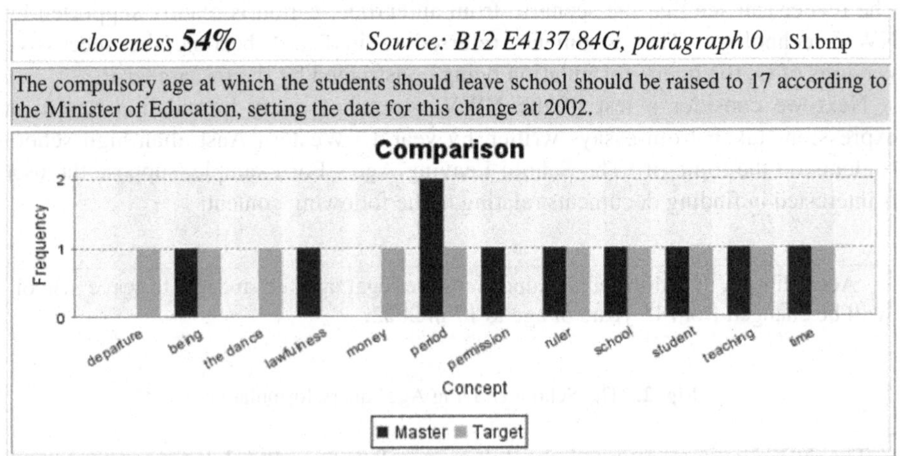

Fig. 4. 54% semantic proximity

The NWV technology is doing its job of representing the free text found in documents and documents fragments according to the conceptual structure found in the thesaurus. In this case we are using the Macquarie Thesaurus [5] but any structured corpus can be used. A visual representation is useful to the researcher **P** because the change in **Q** over the iterations can be modeled and interacted with to produce a superior future iterative version of **Q**.

In the last of the four cases of alternate query formulations, NWV returns a 77% degree of semantic closeness. Observe that there are only two mismatching concepts ("ruler", and "teaching") and that the frequency corresponds rather well also.

We are satisfied that NWV technology is supporting our purpose. Readers should take a moment or two to review the textual query formulations as given in these four figures and compare the meanings with that derived from the text in Fig. 2.

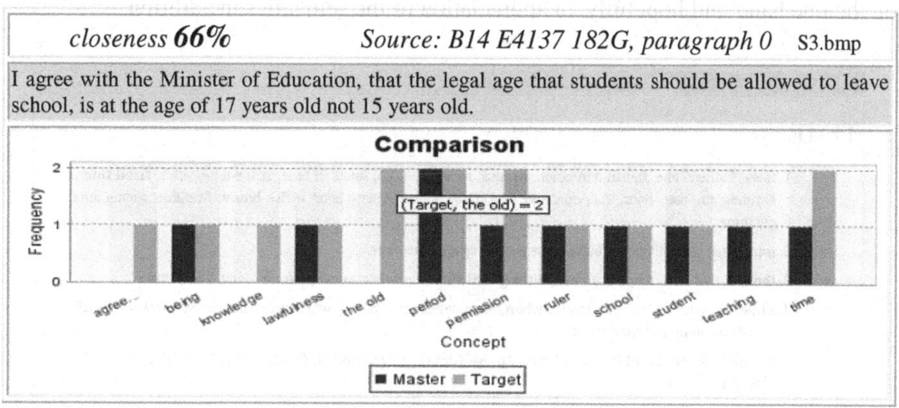

Fig. 5. 66% semantic proximity

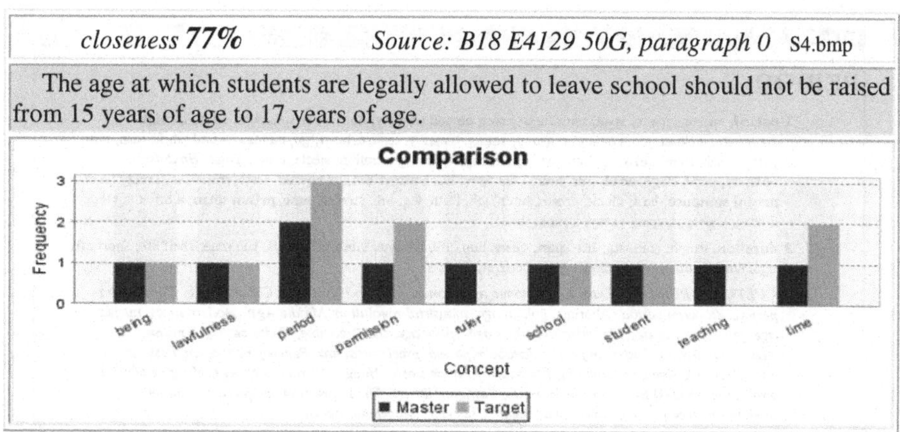

Fig. 6. 77% semantic proximity

The sequence depicted in Figs. 3 through 6 can be seen as a refinement of a query formulation with respect to a 'Master'. Of course this sequence has been artificially composed to emphasize the power of the NWV technology. Note how the Master and

Target concepts coincide as one progresses through the 53% match in Fig. 3 to the 77% match in Fig. 6.

Naturally, our explanation is incomplete without some further treatment of 'Concepts'.

We refer the reader to the following five Concept windows (Fig. 7 through Fig. 11) generated from the www.essaygrading.com site. They are the entries as produced by the Macquarie Thesaurus [5], the Concept Name in the window matching the Concept labels on the horizontal axes of the bar chart representations above. Inspection of the Concept window contents will permit an understanding of the complexity of the task on the one hand and hopefully an appreciation of the semantics in addition.

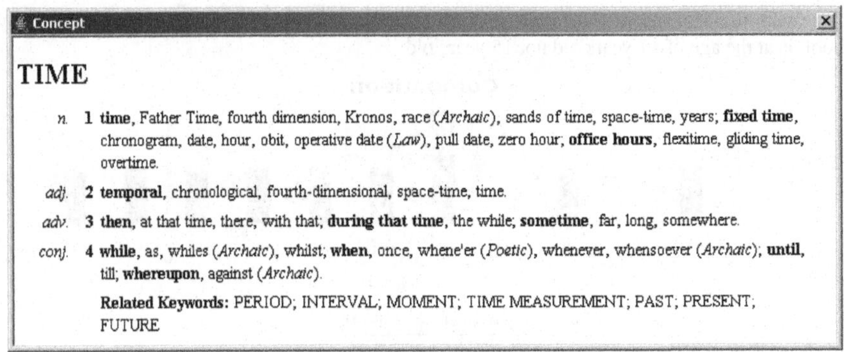

Concept

TIME

n. 1 **time**, Father Time, fourth dimension, Kronos, race (*Archaic*), sands of time, space-time, years; **fixed time**, chronogram, date, hour, obit, operative date (*Law*), pull date, zero hour; **office hours**, flexitime, gliding time, overtime.

adj. 2 **temporal**, chronological, fourth-dimensional, space-time, time.

adv. 3 **then**, at that time, there, with that; **during that time**, the while; **sometime**, far, long, somewhere.

conj. 4 **while**, as, whiles (*Archaic*), whilst; **when**, once, whene'er (*Poetic*), whenever, whensoever (*Archaic*); **until**, till; **whereupon**, against (*Archaic*).

Related Keywords: PERIOD; INTERVAL; MOMENT; TIME MEASUREMENT; PAST; PRESENT; FUTURE

Fig. 7. The concept TIME

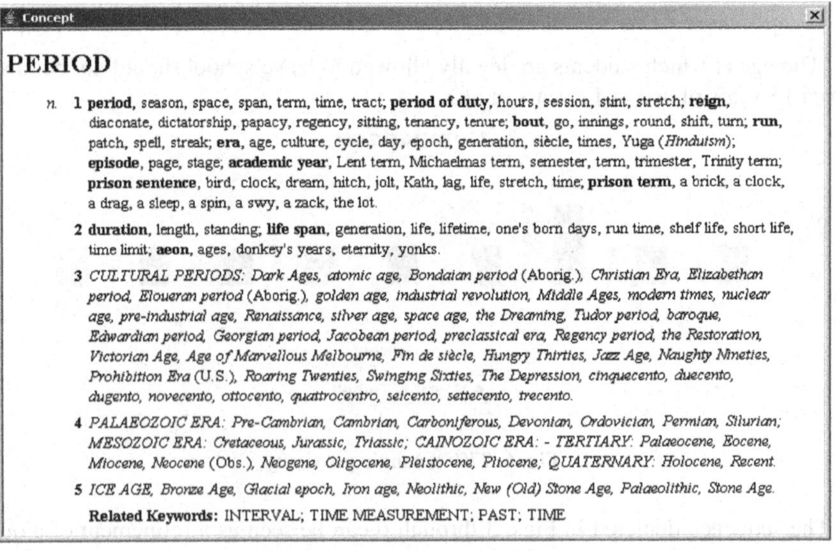

Concept

PERIOD

n. 1 **period**, season, space, span, term, time, tract; **period of duty**, hours, session, stint, stretch; **reign**, diaconate, dictatorship, papacy, regency, sitting, tenancy, tenure; **bout**, go, innings, round, shift, turn; **run**, patch, spell, streak; **era**, age, culture, cycle, day, epoch, generation, siècle, times, Yuga (*Hinduism*); **episode**, page, stage; **academic year**, Lent term, Michaelmas term, semester, term, trimester, Trinity term; **prison sentence**, bird, clock, dream, hitch, jolt, Kath, lag, life, stretch, time; **prison term**, a brick, a clock, a drag, a sleep, a spin, a swy, a zack, the lot.

2 **duration**, length, standing; **life span**, generation, life, lifetime, one's born days, run time, shelf life, short life, time limit; **aeon**, ages, donkey's years, eternity, yonks.

3 *CULTURAL PERIODS: Dark Ages, atomic age, Bondaian period* (Aborig.), *Christian Era, Elizabethan period, Eloueran period* (Aborig.), *golden age, industrial revolution, Middle Ages, modern times, nuclear age, pre-industrial age, Renaissance, silver age, space age, the Dreaming, Tudor period, baroque, Edwardian period, Georgian period, Jacobean period, preclassical era, Regency period, the Restoration, Victorian Age, Age of Marvellous Melbourne, Fin de siècle, Hungry Thirties, Jazz Age, Naughty Nineties, Prohibition Era* (U.S.), *Roaring Twenties, Swinging Sixties, The Depression, cinquecento, duecento, dugento, novecento, ottocento, quattrocentro, seicento, settecento, trecento.*

4 *PALAEOZOIC ERA: Pre-Cambrian, Cambrian, Carboniferous, Devonian, Ordovician, Permian, Silurian; MESOZOIC ERA: Cretaceous, Jurassic, Triassic; CAINOZOIC ERA: - TERTIARY: Palaeocene, Eocene, Miocene, Neocene* (Obs.), *Neogene, Oligocene, Pleistocene, Pliocene; QUATERNARY: Holocene, Recent.*

5 *ICE AGE, Bronze Age, Glacial epoch, Iron age, Neolithic, New (Old) Stone Age, Palaeolithic, Stone Age.*

Related Keywords: INTERVAL; TIME MEASUREMENT; PAST; TIME

Fig. 8. The concept PERIOD

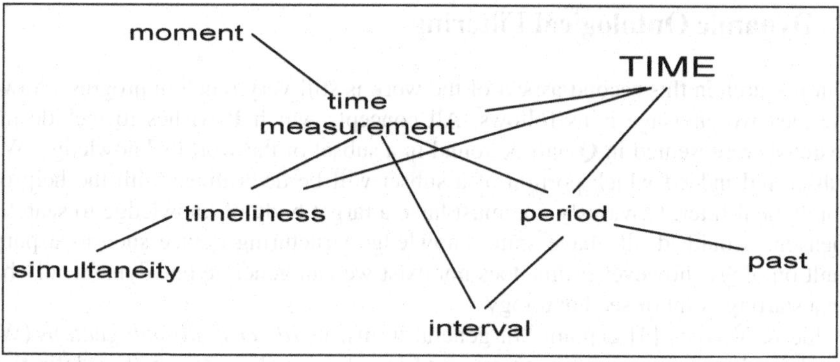

Fig. 9. The concept mapping for TIME and its relatives

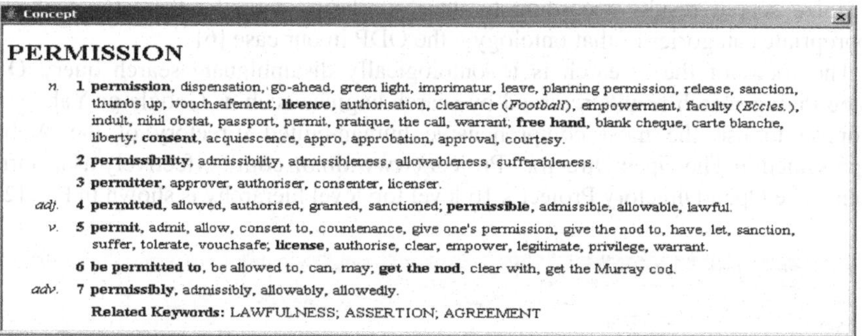

Fig. 10. The concept PERMISSION

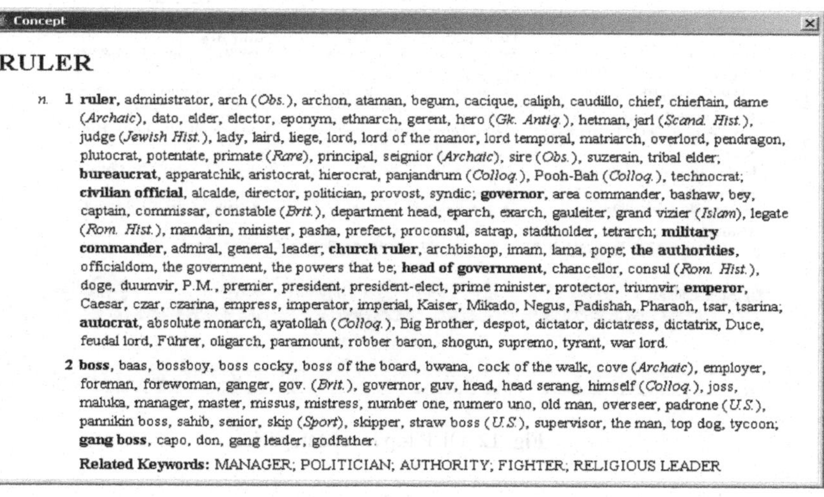

Fig. 11. The concept RULER

5 Dynamic Ontological Filtering

Our research in this second aspect of the work is still very much in progress, however the idea we envisage is as follows. All concepts which **P** wishes to include in the search as represented in **Q** will be found in a subset of the world's knowledge. Which subset and indeed which portion of a subset will be determined with the help of an ontological filter. Obviously one must have a target body of knowledge to search and then one would ideally have some knowledge structuring device such as a purpose built ontology, however if this does not exist we can generate one dynamically based on a starting point or seed ontology.

Ide & Veronis [4] explain "In general terms, *word sense disambiguation* (WSD) involves the association of a given word in a text or discourse with a definition or meaning (*sense*) which is distinguishable from other meanings potentially attributable to that word". Ontology based Query disambiguation or filtering will refine and re-organize search results according to their similarity with the thematic content of appropriate categories of that ontology – the ODP in our case [6].

The focus of the research is to ontologically disambiguate search query **Q** by categorizing search results returned by search engines such as Google or Yahoo. We propose to use the most comprehensive human-edited directory of the Web as represented in The Open Directory Project (www.dmoz.com), effectively as a starting point. The Open Directory Project's 16 level top level hierarchy is shown in Fig. 12.

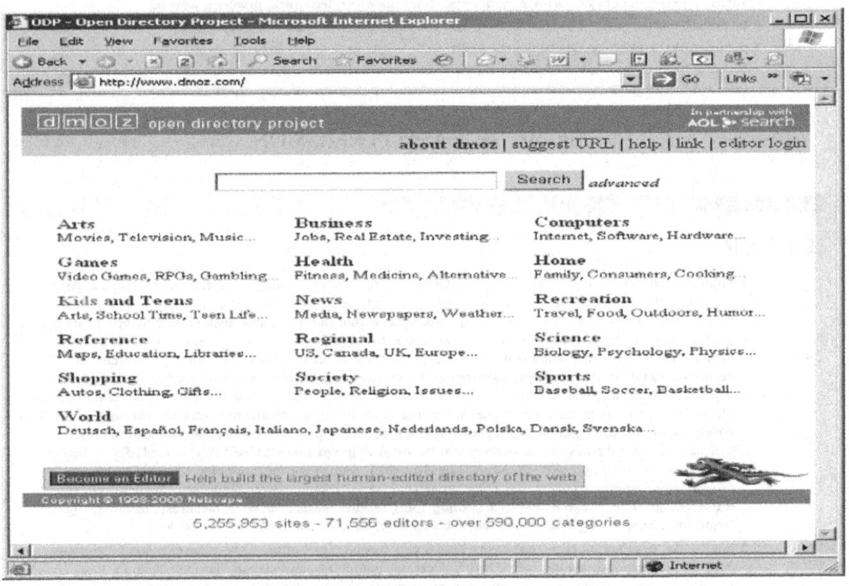

Fig. 12. ODP top level categories

A special browser is being developed which combines search engine results, the Open Directory Project (ODP) based ontology as a navigator, and search results categorization. Categories are formed based on the ODP as a predefined ontology and

NWV technology is to be employed to calculate the similarity between items retrieved by the search engine and concepts in the ODP. With the interaction of users, the proposed search-browser is expected to produce more relevant search results by excluding the irrelevant, and thereby improve the quality of information returned to the user.

The ODP structure is depicted in Fig. 13.

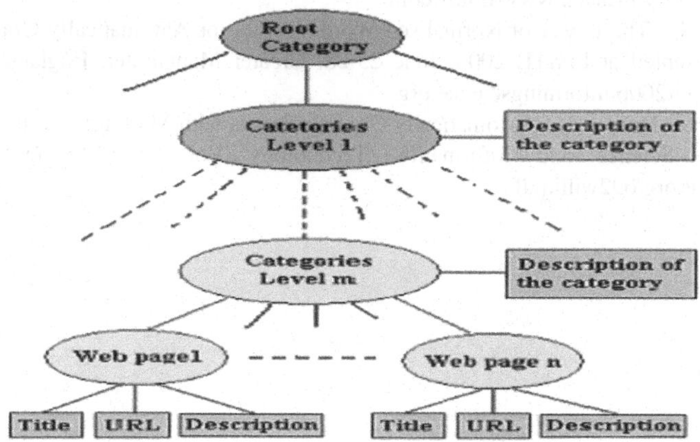

Fig. 13. Structure of the ODP

6 Summing Up

In the context of the Query-formulation → Find → Re-formulation phases of knowledge work, we set out to create some technology to provide "Assisted Query Formulation using Normalised Word Vector and Dynamic Ontological Filtering". We have introduced and explained the Normalised Word Vector technology and via our QFR scenario exemplified its operation. The second aspect of our work, the application of dynamic ontological filtering, is in progress.

Catering for user interaction at the initial stages of the Query-formulation → Find → Re-formulation phases of knowledge work to support the creation of a Query which is truly representative of the ideas the information seeker has in mind, and to categorise the search concepts according to a suitable ontology, is expected to produce in a higher precision of search results and accommodate a diversity of information seekers, with their diversity of information needs.

References

1. Bacon, Sir Francis: Novum Organum. In Advancement of Learning - Novum Organum - New Atlantis, William Benton, Encyclopaedia Britannica, Inc. 1952. Bk.1.Sect.2. (1620)
2. Bush, V.: As We May Think. Atlantic Monthly, 176(1) July. Boston, Massachusetts (1945) 101-108

3. Dreher, H.: Interactive On-line Formative Evaluation of Student Assignments. To be presented at InSITE 2006, June 25-28, Greater Manchester, England. Online Jan (2006) http://2006.informingscience.org
4. Ide, N., Veronis, J.: Word Sense Disambiguation: The State of Art. Computational Linguistics, Vol. 24, Mar. (1998) 1-40
5. Macquarie: 2006 www.macquariedictionary.com.au, http://www.wordgenius.com.au/wordgeniusthesaurus.html
6. Open Directory Project. www.dmoz.com
7. Williams, R.:. The Power of Normalised Word Vectors for Automatically Grading Essays. To be presented at InSITE 2006, June 25-28, Greater Manchester, England. Online Jan (2006) http://2006.informingscience.org
8. Williams, R., Dreher, H.: Automatically Grading Essays with Markit©. Journal of Issues in Informing Science and Information Technology Vol. 1, (2004).693-700 http://articles.iisit.org/092willi.pdf

Fuzzy Query Answering in Motor Racing Domain

Stefania Bandini, Paolo Mereghetti, and Paolo Radaelli

Dipartimento di Informatica, Sistemistica e Comunicazione
Università di Milano-Bicocca,
via Bicocca degli Arcimboldi 8,
20126 Milano, Italy
{bandini, mereghetti, radaelli}@disco.unimib.it

Abstract. Nuances in natural languages can be useful to effectively describe preferences and constraints over a complex and few formalized domain. In this paper we describe the architecture of a query answering system for the domain of motor racing which uses fuzzy logic and domain knowledge in order to carry out searches dealing with vague expression, either as search constraints or as relationship between entities attribute values.

1 Introduction

In this paper we describe a query answering system to retrieve data acquired in the construction of P-Race system [1]. P-Race is a CBR system developed to support the design of tyre treads for motor racing. It is aimed to represent and use the knowledge of compound designers and race engineers that have to decide which tyres to provide to each racing team.

In this perspective, the most important aspect of the domain are the geometric profile of the racing track and the nature of the track's asphalt (i.e. circuits with many bends and a rough type of asphalt wear tyres in a more relevant way that a circuit with few turns and smooth asphalt). Other relevant aspect of the domain are weather and track conditions, which are useful to select a slick or a rainy tyre type.

While precise data related to the relevant entities in the P-Race system is generally available, the knowledge that make use of those data (such as the description of the relationship between wheater conditions and tyre coumpounds) is not always formalized with a mathematical model, and usually is only described by using natural language. This lead to the impossibility to provide a precise outcome of the value of some high-level properties related to the system (for example, the degree of thermical stress induced in a type by a particular track). These imprecision make difficult, in turn, to understand what part of the data contained inside the database can be useful to solve a particular problem, or to determine with the adequate precision what are the constraints to give at the query answering system.

To avoid this problem, we formalized the ontological representation of the races domain, showing the relationship between the different properties of the concepts in the ontology (Fig. 1 shows a partial view of the P-Race ontology, with

H.L. Larsen et al. (Eds.): FQAS 2006, LNAI 4027, pp. 295–306, 2006.

some of the relevant concepts and properties). This allows a user to indicate the intended results of its query (i.e. "I want to find all races that cause a severe stress in the car's tyres"), delegating to the query answering system to figure out what are the database fields that contains values relevant to determine the stress level. Since, as noted above, a relevant part of the domain knowledge is not formalized, but is described with the natural language, we use fuzzy set theory to handle the meaning of vague and imprecise natural language expression. Our approach differs from fuzzy databases approach [2, 3, 4] because our formalization doesn't allow directly to express uncertain and vague attributes inside the database, but defines the concept of *quality* to model predicates allowing partial truth values, which can be used to formulate *soft constraints* [5] (i.e. constraints that can be fulfit only in a partial degree) over the entities in the domain.

Vague expressions can be used inside the system, to define relationships between concepts properties via a fuzzy rule-based system [6, 7], and it is useful because it allows to use natural language as a flexible query answering language [8]. Natural language queries, in turn, allow the users to formulate query that contains imprecise or vague constraint such as "a few chicanes" or "quite hot temperature". This approach gives the advantage to point on the value of qualitative knowledge, sited in the numerical representation of shared judgements based on qualitative descriptions.

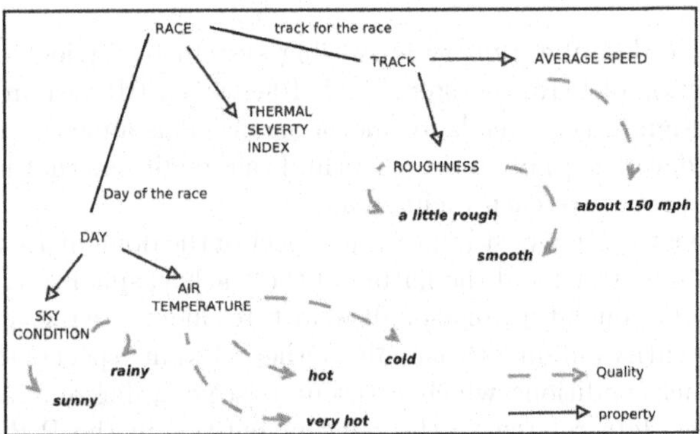

Fig. 1. A snippet of the P-Race domain representation

In the following, we describe the architecture of P-Race Query Answering system, an extension of P-Race that allows to make complex queries over the database used in the system.

2 P-Race Query Answering System Architecture

The proposed system is constituted by four main components. The query parser and semantic analyser convert user input, expressed in natural language, into a tree representation of the user requests. The query evaluation module evaluates the relevance of the instances present in the database according to this representation, and chooses what instances must be retrieved and what are to be discarded. The entity model hides the physical structure of the database, presenting to the rest of the system an abstract representation of the data contained in the P-Race database in terms of entities that own attributes and hold relationships within other entities. with this abstraction it's possible to enhance the data present in the database by introducing new attributes that are computed on the basis of the value of other attributes already present. A diagram of the system's architecture, which shows the data flow between the modules, is showed in Fig. 2

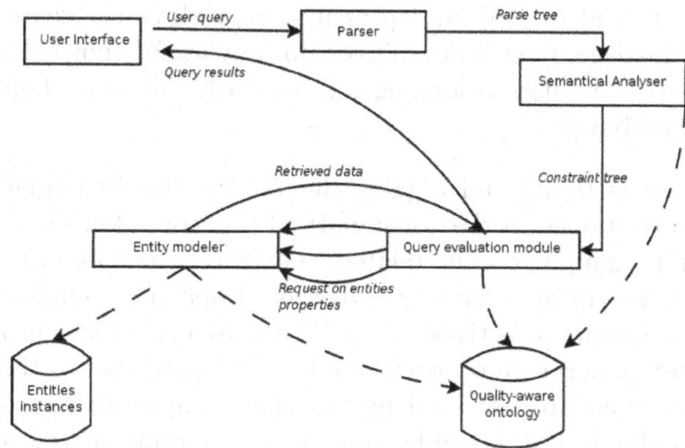

Fig. 2. The query answering system architecture

2.1 Chunk Parser

The parser goal is to analyse the user input sentence in order to extract the fragment of text that will be used to build the query. Moreover, the parser is in charge of building the parse tree that shows grammatical relationships inside those fragments. Each text fragment contains information related to the characteristics of the retrieved objects, which express the soft constraints to be applied to them. We call those information *qualities* of the entities to retrieve. For example, terms like "with a temperature of about 90°F" or "very smooth" are terms that relate to qualities. Each quality is related to a particular property of one of the entities in our domain ("a little rough" of Fig. 1, for example, is related to the roughness of a track).

In order to simplify the analysis process, a multi stage process has been designed (following Abney's ideas described in [9]).

First stage isolates and identifies the *chunks* present in the input sentence. Chunks are logical blocks which compose each sentence, usually spanning more than one syntagm [10, 11]. Three categories of chunks can be identified by our system: *goal* chunks are used to indicate what type of entity the user is interested to; *quality* chunks contain a single boundary the user posed on the data he want to retrieve; and *connective* chunks show how to bind different constraint chunks with each other.

Any syntagm sequence that isn't in one of those chunk is tagged as *garbage* and discarded in the further analysis.

For example, in the sentence *"I want to find all race tracks that are very fast and with few chicanes"* it is possible to isolate the following chunks:

- the goal chunk *race track* which describes the kind of entity to retrieve (as opposed,for example, to blend compounds)
- the quality chunks *very fast* and *with few chicanes*, that contains information about how to select the possible results to retrieve.
- the chunk *and* containing a connective.
- The chunk *I want to find all* represents the verb of the sentence but it is considered garbage, since it doesn't provide any useful knowledge about what kind of entities the user is looking for. Similarly, also the chunk *that are* is considered garbage.

The process of isolating and tagging the various chunks is mainly done using lexical-level contained in the vocabulary of the words known by the system. Know nouns, for example, can be related to entities which describe the domain (tracks, weather conditions, tyres, etc) or they properties (roughness, temperature, speed). Even some adjectives can be related to a particular property ("hot" is related to the temperature property, while "fast" is related to the speed property). These relationships are used by the chunk parser to figure out how to categorize each chunk. For example, goal chunks contains a term related to an entity, while quality chunks contains adverbs, adjectives and nouns that represent properties. This approach assumes the will be not ambiguity about the meaning of the terms that are related to each concept in the ontology.

2.2 Chunk Analysis

The second phase of the syntactic analysis has the goal of further investigating the structure of quality chunk, being quality chunks the ones that possess the richest internal structure. Its goal is to build a parse tree that shows the relationship between the syntagms that compose the chunk. This analysis is done with a context free parser, based upon unification grammar theories [12, 13]. In Fig. 3 there is a snapshot of some of the rules present in our grammar, expressed as feature structures [14], while Fig. 4 shows the feature structures associated to some of the terms composing the vocabulary.

A feature structure is composed by a set of named *features*, each one holding a value, that can be an atomic one or another feature structure. They are generally used to represent the properties that characterize a syntagm, since their recursiveness allows to efficiently represent parse trees. Unification rules work by finding a sequence feature structures that contains a selected set of features and values. When a sequence of syntagms verify the left hand side of rule, a new syntagm (represented as a new feature structure) is created. Rules using features structures can test or assert the equality of features' values by referring the values with the same index. For example, Rule 1 in Fig. 3 say that any sequence of a syntagm of category *Adj* followed by a *Property* syntagm will constitute a syntagm of category *Quality*. In order for the rule to hold, the second syntagm must have a feature called *RelProp*, whose value (referred in the rule as [3]) will be also the value of the *RelProp* feature in the syntagm that will be created by the rule. And the future parent syntagm will have, in its *Children* feature, a copy of the feature structures that represent the children syntagms. A detailed introduction to feature structures and unification-based formalism can be found in [13].

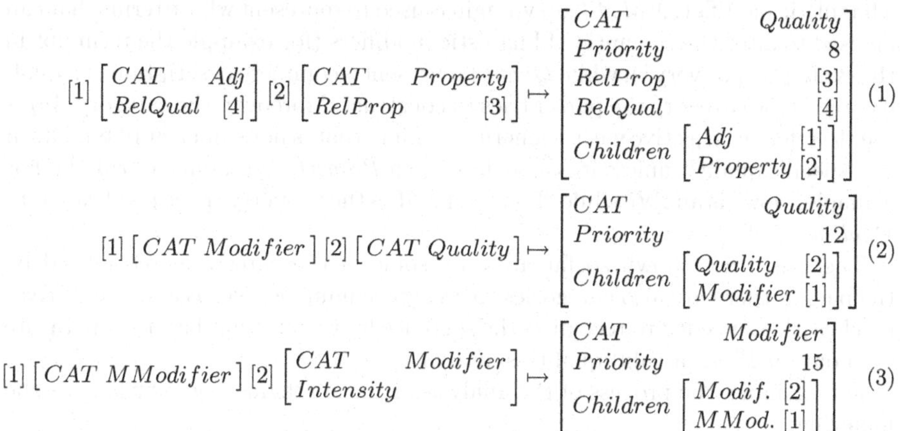

Fig. 3. Some rules used in the analysis of constraint chunk

Term	Features
extremely	CAT *Modifier*, Hedge-Type *Concentrator*, Intensity *3*, Priority *10*
fast	CAT *Quality*, QEV $f_{?,[speed],[high]}$, Priority *10*
high	CAT *Adj*, RelQual *high*, Priority *10*
hot	CAT *Quality*, QEV $f_{?,[temperature],[high]}$, Priority *10*
not	CAT *Negation*, Priority *10*
not	CAT *MModifier*, Formula $\lambda x.1 - \frac{1}{x}$, Priority *10*
very	CAT *Modifier*, Hedge-Type *Concentrator*, Intensity *2*, Priority *10*
very	CAT *MModifier*, Formula $\lambda x.2x$, Priority *10*

Fig. 4. Feature Structures associated to some of the vocabulary's words

Some of the features used in the rules have only a syntactic relevance (for example the feature *CAT* which represent the category of the syntagm, while *Children* is the features that contains the children syntagms of the current one), other contains also semantic level knowledge about the syntagm meaning (the feature *RelProp* indicates the noun of the property the syntagm is related to) and a third set of features are used to control the behavior of the parser. For example, the feature *Priority* is used to select the parse tree to prefer in case of ambiguity. When there is more than one applicable rule, the one selected is those whose composing syntagms have the better average priority value. Syntactic rules are intended to be independent of the applicative domain analysed, with the exception of some of the feature related to the semantic level. For example, the features that indicate what property or quality a term refers to are strictly related to the domain ontology.

To simplify the construction of a grammar, we adopted a semantic approach [15], defining syntagms for the concepts that are relevant in our domain representation (*entities*, *qualities* or *modifiers*) besides traditional linguistic syntagms such as noun or adjectives. Main categories recognized by our parser are the following: *Property* is a noun related to one of the properties of an entity, *Modifier* represents a linguistic modifier, *MModifier* syntagm is used to represent whose terms that can be used to alter the semantic of linguistic modifiers (for example the term not in the syntagm "not very"), while *Quality* represent a complete description of a quality, and is the category the parser tries to construct. Moreover, the category *Adj* is user to refer an adjective with a generic meaning, that is not sufficient to bind itself to a specific quality, unless it is associated to a *Property* syntagm (see rule 1). For exmaple, "low" is an *Adj*, while "fast" (related to the property speed) is of category *Quality*.

The categories shown so far are only some of the categories recognized by the parser: there are also categories to recognize numbers, verbs and connectives (such as those needed to recognize the sentence fragment "that has a temperature of about 79°F" as a valid quality syntagm.)

For example, the process of the analysis of the syntagm "not very fast" is the following:

1. The syntagm related to terminal symbols (i.e. words) are created. Even if there are only three words, 5 syntagms are built, because the words "not" and "very" can belong to two different syntagm categories, as it can be seen in Fig. 4.
2. The syntagm "not very" is created according to the rule 3 in Fig. 3
3. The syntagm "very fast" is created by rule 2
4. At this point, rule 2 can be applied in two different ways: combining the Negation "not" with the Quality "very fast" created in point 3, or by combining the Modifier "not very" (built in point 2) with the Quality "fast". The second case is selected, since the average priority the the components is 11 in the first case and 12.5 in the second one.

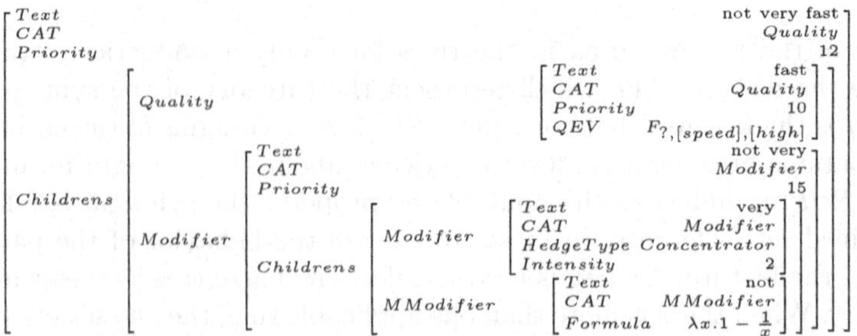

Fig. 5. The feature structure which represent the parse tree for the text "not very fast"

In Fig. 5 we show the feature structure representing the parse tree generated in the previous example. (In the example, the feature "text" indicate the text that constituites the syntagm).

2.3 Semantic Analyser

Semantic analysis module's goal is to translate the information provided by the parser (the list of relevant chunks, and the parse trees related to quality chunks) into a tree structure (called constraint tree) which formalize the request the user pones on the entities it want to retrieve. In the same way as the parser, semantic analysis is done in two stages: on the first one it uses quality chunks to obtain the function used to evaluate domain entities according to the meaning of each chunk, and in the second one builds a hierarchical representation of those functions, that takes care of the coordination between the user requests.

We use fuzzy set theory [16, 17] to formalize the semantic of the qualities syntagms which compose quality chunks. The task accomplished in the first stage of the semantic analysis if to assign the appropriate fuzzy-set F_q to each quality q expressed in the user query. The fuzzy set F_q will have as domain the set P of the possible values of the property the quality q is related to. For example, the fuzzy set related to the quality "not very fast" will be defined over the domain of the possible Speed values.

To describe formally the procedure used to find the correct fuzzy-set, we must define the concept of *quality evaluation function*

Definition 1. *Given an entity E and a quality q related to a property p of E, a* quality evaluation function *for q is a fuzzy-set $F_{E,p,q}$ whose membership function is $f_{E,p,q} : C \mapsto [0,1]$, $f_{E,p,q}(x) = f_q(E.p(x))$.*

In the definition, the expression $E.p(x)$ indicates the value of the property p for an instance x of the entity E. For example, the air temperature on January, 20th 2006 is indicated with the formula $Day.temperature(1/20/2006)$. Using a reference to the entity E in the query evaluation function allows to deal with two expression like "a hot day" or "a hot star".

To determine the correct quality evaluation function to build, each unification rule has an associated semantic rule. The semantic analyser execute a preorder scan in the parse tree, applying to each syntagm in the tree the semantic rule that correspond to the syntactic rule used to build the syntagm. Semantic rules work by reading, adding or modifying the features present into the syntagm. Since the feature structure of the parent syntagm contains inside the feature structure of their children, the results of the semantic analysis of child syntagms are available during the analysis of their parent.

For example, the sematic rules that are related to the syntactic rules defined in Fig. 3 are described below:

1. Rule 1 adds a feature named "QEV" whose value is $f_{?,[RelProp],[RelQual]}$, where $[RelQual]$ and $[RelProp]$ are substituted with the values of the features with the same name.

2. Rule 2 add a feature named "QEV" whose value will depend upon the value of the feature "QEV" in its *Quality* child and the features *Intensity* and *Hedge-Type* of its *Modifier* child (see below).
3. Rule 3 add the feature "Intensity" whose value is the evaluation on the formula $[MModifier.Formula]([Modifier.Intensity])$.

The feature named is used to build the quality evaluation function related to the quality owning the feature itself. The question mark in the formula will be replaced later in the process, using the value of the goal chunk to figure out what entity of the domain the user is interested to.

The meaning of rules 2 and 3 is related to the way we adopted to handle linguistic hedges. P-Race system understands four hedges [18, 7] categories: concentrators, dilatators, and contrast intensifiers described by Zadeh [19] and the *negatively* hedge described in [18] to represent the semantic of these hedges, we use the generalized families of function proposed in [18]. The intensity we associate to each modifier is used to determine the exact function to use when handling the modifier semantic. For example, concentrators function is $f^n(x)$, so the function for the concentrator "very" that has an intensity of 2 will be $f^2(x)$, while the intensity of extremely (intensity 3) will be $f^3(x)$.

A MModifier's effect is to change this value, in order to obtain a new linguistic hedge. For example, when used as a MModifier, "not" will alter the intensity of a modifier with the formula $1 - \frac{1}{n}$, where n is the original value of the intensity. With the rules described above, the semantic analysis of the syntagm represented in Fig. 5 is the following:

- According to rule 3, semantic analyser add the feature intensity of the child syntagm Modifier representing the text "not very". The feature value is $1 - \frac{1}{2} = \frac{1}{2}$.
- As per rule 2 creates the new feature QEV in the main syntagm, with the value $f^{\frac{1}{2}}_{?,speed,high}$.

In the next stage, the semantic analyser replaces the question mark contained in the QEV with the entity the user want to retrieve (that is obtained by analysing the goal chunk) and use the three values Entity, Property and Quality to figure out what membership function to use.

When the semantic analyser has found the quality evaluation function for each quality chunk, it builds a *constraint tree* which contain a structured representation of the soft constraints related to the search.

Definition 2. *A constraint tree can be recursively defined as follows:*

- *If $F_{E,p,q}$ is a quality evaluation function related to an entity E, then $F_{E,p,q}$ is a constraint tree. We say that such constraints tree is* valid *for E*
- *If $T_1, \ldots, T_n$ are n constraint trees valid for the same entity E, then $(\vee, T_1, \ldots, T_n)$ and $(\wedge, T_1, \ldots, T_n)$ are two constraint tree valid for E*
- *If T_1 and T_2 are two constraint tree valid for E, then $(\supset, T_1, T_2)$ is a constraint tree valid for E.*

Semantic analyser uses quality chunks as the future leaves of the constraint tree, and connective chunks as internal nodes. Priorities are defined between the different connectives, which are used to determine the hierarchical level of each connective when constructing the tree . For example, the three chunks "$chunk_1$ and $chunk_2$ or $chunk_3$" will be structured as $(\wedge,\ F_1\ (\vee\ F_2\ F_3))$, since "and" connective has a higher priority than "or", but a sequence "either F_1 and F_2 or F_3" will be parsed as $(\vee,\ (\wedge,\ F_1,\ F_2),\ F_3)$.

2.4 Query Evaluation Module

Query evaluation module is in charge to select what instances of the entities stored in the P-Race database are relevant to satisfy the requests of the user. Query evaluation module forwards its requests to the entity modeler module that handle the physical database access.

Query evaluation uses the constraint tree provided by the semantic analysis phase to figure out how to evaluate the possible results. For any constraint tree T valid for an entity E, we can define a function $Eval_T : E \mapsto [0, 1]$ that evaluates the relevance of an instance of E with respect to the soft constraints given inside the tree.

Definition 3. *$Eval_T$ is defined as follows:*

- *If T is in the form $F_{C,p,q}$ (i.e. is a quality evaluation function) and $x \in E$, then $Eval_T(x) = f_{C,p,q}(x)$*
- *If $T = (\vee, T_1, \ldots, T_n)$, then $Eval_T(x) = \bigoplus_i Eval_{T_i}(x)$ where $\oplus$ is a valid t-conorm chosen to handle the semantic of the disjunction connective.*
- *$T = (\wedge, T_1, \ldots, T_n)$ then $Eval_T(x) = \bigotimes_i Eval_{T_i}(x)$ where $\otimes$ is a valid t-norm chosen to handle the semantic of conjunction.*
- *If $T = (\supset, T_1, \ldots, T_n)$, then $Eval_T(e) = Eval_{T_1}(x) \rightarrow Eval_{T_2}(x)$, where $\rightarrow$ is the t-residuum chosen to handle implication semantic (see [20])*

Definition 3 is used to obtain a measure of the relevance of any object present in the database, and return to the user the most relevant entities (the exact number of retrieved entities is selectable).

In order to reduce computational load, query evaluation module doesn't evaluate all the instances stored inside the database, but tries to limit the valuation only to those entities that have some probability to lead to a relevance value higher than zero. To do so, it uses the definition of the qualities evaluation functions present in the database to extract rigid constraint about the properties of the entities to be retrieved. For example, when handling a constraint tree as $(\wedge, F_{Day,temperature,high}, F_{Day,WindSpeed,none})$, query evaluation module looks for the definition of the two quality evaluation function in order to determine the extension of their support. Supposing that all the temperatures lesser than 85°F and all wind speed higher than 1 mph will be outside the support of their respective fuzzy-sets, query evaluation module could ask for Days entities with $temperature \geqslant 85\ AND\ WindSpeed \leqslant 1$.

2.5 Entity Modeler

The Entity modeler is the module that is in charge to present an uniform way to access at the data stored in the database, allowing the rest of the system to query for entities and properties and mapping those requests to the appropriate database tables and fields. By hiding the physical structure of the database, it is possible to extend the knowledge contained in the ontology by adding new properties for the entities that aren't present in the original database. For this way, entity modeler distinguish between two kind of properties: simple and complex ones.

Simple properties we indicate all those properties whose values are know by the P-Race system and can be easily obtained. Usually the values for those properties are stored inside the DB, or it is possible to receive them from an external source (for example, information about weather condition can be queried to a on-line meteorological service). *Complex properties*, on the other hand, are properties whose values aren't immediately disposable to P-Race Query Answering System and must be computed or inferred in some way. The entity modeler takes care of carry out the computation of the property's values.

The most common type of complex properties is composed by the properties whose value is computable (or at least estimable) on the basis of other properties present in the ontology. For example, it is difficult to compute the global degree of stress that a track imposes to certain characteristic of a tyre (such as warming, adherence, inner or outer side wearing, etc). Such attributes are computed for each block (a segment of track with uniform characteristics, for example a chicane, a left turn, a straight track) and the global value is a weighed sum of the partial results. Another example could be to compute the average speed of a car by knowing the car's position in different time intervals. This gender of complex properties can be called *computable properties*. In order to be defines as computable, a complex property must posses a formula which allows us to evaluate its value.

When this formula is not known, it is sometime possible to obtain an approximate result by weighting the intensity of a series of other properties and qualities. Those properties and qualities influence the property we need to estimate, even if their exact relationship is unclear (and this make impossible to compute the property). Formally, this operation is done with the use of a fuzzy expert system [6, 7]. As demonstrated in [21], a fuzzy expert system can approximate an arbitrary continuous function, by looking at the partial membership of different properties in a system with respect to a series of fuzzy-sets. Within the definition we had given, we can say that a fuzzy expert system allows to evaluate the value of some property p on the basis of a series of qualities over the concepts that compose our domain.

The thermal severity index which is associated to a specific race, for example, is a focal attribute for determining the characteristic of the tyres to be used in a particular race, and its value can be approximated by looking at many other attributes such as asphalt characteristic, asphalt temperature, and weather conditions. The exact influence of many of those attributes cannot be determined precisely, and so it has been approximated by a fuzzy-set expert system. More details about the evaluation of the thermal severity index can be found in [1].

Entity modeler receives from the query evaluation the request of loading from the database instances of entities whose properties satisfy some constraint. It maps the constraint for simple properties into a SQL query, retrieve the object from the database and construct the corresponding entities. A this point it evaluates the constraint related to complex properties before to return the entities which satisfy the constraint to the query evaluation module.

3 Conclusions and Further Works

In this paper, we have presented a solution to perform complex database searches over a complex domain. We have introduced the *quality* concept to describe peculiar property of an object which is based upon one of its attributes and can be used to generate a soft constraint over the object itself. The constraint tree has been defined as a hierarchical indication of what qualities should be considered as significant in order to carry out the search. We also defined a parsing strategy which allows to express vague constraints using natural language expressiveness.

As future work, we will generalize the proposed solution in order to be applicable to other domains. One possible way to generalize the approach is to formalize the proposed entity modeling by adopting or extending a formal logic language which can handle vagueness (see [22, 23]).

Another enhancement we are deploying is the automatic generation of the fuzzy-sets. Our idea is to to generate automatically the fuzzy-set related to a particular property on the basis of the values of the instances of the property.

References

1. Bandini, S., Manzoni, S., Sartori, F.: Case memory management: Fuzzy-based knowledge acquisition and retrieval. In Baets, B.D., Fodor, J., Pasi, G., eds.: Proceedings of EUROFUSE 2002. (2002) 167–172
2. Yazici, A., George, R., Buckles, B.P., Petry, F.E.: A survey of coneptual and logical data models for uncertainty management. In Zadeh, L.A., Kacprzyk, J., eds.: Fuzzy Logic for the Management of Uncertainty. Wiley, New York (1992) 607–643
3. Bordogna, G., Pasi, G.: Modeling linguistic qualifiers of uncertainty in a fuzzy database. Int. J. Intell. Syst. **15**(11) (2000) 995–1014
4. Buckles, B.P., Perty, F.E.: A fzzy representation of data for relational databases. Fuzzy Sets and Systems **7** (1982) 31–43
5. de Givry, S., Zhang, W., eds.: Proceedings of the Seventh Interfational Workshop on Preferences and Soft Constraints (Soft2005). (2005)
6. Mamdani, E.H., Assilian, S.: Application of fuzzy logic to approximate reasoning using linguistic synthesis. IEEE Trans. on Computer Systems **C–26**(12) (1977) 1182–1191
7. Zadeh, L.A.: The concept of a linguistic variable and its application to approximate reasining — part i, ii and iii. Information Sciences **8–9** (1975) 199–251, 301–357, 43–80

8. Bordogna, G., Pasi, G.: Modeling vagueness in information retrieval. In Agosti, M., Crestani, F., Pasi, G., eds.: ESSIR. Volume 1980 of Lecture Notes in Computer Science., Springer (2000) 207–241
9. Abney, S.: Partial parsing via finite-state cascades. In: Workshop on Robust Parsing, 8th European Summer School in Logic, Language and Information, Prague, Czech Republic (1996) 8–15
10. Abney, S.: Parsing by chunks. In Berwick, R., Abney, S., Tenny, C., eds.: Principle-Based Parsing. Kluwer Academic Publishers (1991)
11. Osenova, P., Simov, K.: Between chunk ideology and full parsing needs. In: Proceedings of the Shallow Processing of Large Corpora (SProLaC 2003) Workshop, Lancaster, UK (2003)
12. Shieber, S.M., van Noord, G., Pereira, F.C.N., Moore, R.C.: Semantic head-driven generation. Computational Linguistics **16**(1) (1990) 30–42
13. Shieber, S.M.: An introduction to unification-based approaches to grammar. In: CSLI Lecture Notes. Volume 4. Chicago U. Press, Chicago (1986)
14. Johnson, M.: Features and formulae. Computational Linguistics **17**(2) (1991) 131–153
15. Hendrix, G., Sacerdoti, E., Sagalowicz, D., Slocum, J.: Developing a natural language interface to complex data. ACM Trasactions on Database Systems **3**(2) (1978) 105–147
16. Zadeh, L.A.: Fuzzy logic. IEEE Computer **21**(4) (1988) 83–93
17. Zadeh, L.A.: Fuzzy sets. Information. and Control **8** (1965) 338–353
18. Shi, H., Ward, R., Kharma, N.: Expanding the definitions of linguistic hedges. joint 9th IFSA World Congress and 20th NAFIPS International Conference (2001)
19. Zadeh, L.A.: A fuzzy-set-theoretic interpretation of linguistic hedges. Journal of Cybernetics **2**(3) (1972) 4–34
20. Klement, E.P., Mesiar, R., Pap, E.: Triangular Norms. Kluwer Academic, Dordrecht (2000)
21. Turunen, E.: Mathematics behind fuzzy logic. Physica. Varlag (1999)
22. H oldobler, S., Khang, T.D., St or, H.P.: A fuzzy description logic with hedges as concept modifiers. In Phuong, N.H., Nguyen, H.T., Ho, N.C., Santiprabhob, P., eds.: VJFuzzy'2002. InTech, Science and Technics Publishing House (2002) 25–34
23. Straccia, U.: Reasoning within fuzzy description logics. Journal of Artifical Intelligence Researches **14** (2001) 137–166

Using a Fuzzy Object-Relational Database for Colour Image Retrieval

Carlos D. Barranco[1], Juan M. Medina[2], Jesús Chamorro-Martínez[2], and José M. Soto-Hidalgo[2]

[1] Area of Computer Science, School of Engineering,
Pablo de Olavide University,
Utrera Rd. Km. 1, 41013 Seville, Spain
cdbargon@upo.es

[2] Department of Computer Science and Artificial Intelligence, University of Granada,
C/ Periodista Daniel Saucedo Aranda s/n, 18071 Granada, Spain
{medina, jesus, soto}@decsai.ugr.es

Abstract. The paper presents a fuzzy database management system, and a fuzzy method for dominant colour description of images, on which an image retrieval system is built. The paper shows the suitability of the fuzzy database management system for this kind of applications when the images are characterized by fuzzy data. The synergy of these two introduced components, improves traditional image retrieval systems in three aspects: natural and automatic image description, a natural and easy query language, and high performance in query resolution.

1 Introduction

Nowadays, large image collections offered to non expert users in near to real time environments (i.e. through web sites) are becoming more common. This kind of systems manage a huge amount of data, are concurrently accessed by many users, and require fast query resolution. In our opinion, three key issues are decisive in this kind of systems, natural and automatic image descriptors, a natural and easy query definition mechanism and high performance in query resolution. This paper proposes the usage of a combination of an automatic image description method and a Fuzzy Object-Relational Database Management System (FORDBMS) to solve these issues.

The initial approaches to image retrieval systems were based in textual descriptions of the images. Although it is an useful mechanism, the descriptions must be made by humans. Currently, image retrieval systems are based in automatic extracted image features, such as colour, texture and shape. Usually, these systems uses sample images or sketches to define queries, which can be inappropriate for non expert users.

In this paper we use a novel method for describing images based on its dominant colours [1]. This method takes advantage of fuzzy set theory for dealing with vagueness in colour descriptions. It describes the dominant colours of an image as fuzzy colours, and assign to each one a dominance degree. This fuzzy

H.L. Larsen et al. (Eds.): FQAS 2006, LNAI 4027, pp. 307–318, 2006.

approach lets define query conditions on the basis of linguistic terms, which seems to be more natural for non expert users.

The large amount of data requires a database management system (DBMS) to manage efficiently its storage and retrieval. The DBMS has to deal with the other two key issues: easy query definition and query processing performance.

To ensure high query processing performance, the employed DBMS must implement advanced query processing techniques, such as indexing and query optimization, and high availability, scalability and distribution degrees. Actual market leader DBMSs offer seamlessly all the previously required features. Despite of that, most actual DBMSs implements the relational data model, and some of them including object-relational features, which is not suitable to seamlessly manage fuzzy data required by the kind of image description algorithm considered in this paper.

On the other hand, a great research effort has been spend in making possible to store and manage fuzzy data in databases [2, 3, 4, 5, 6, 7]. Nevertheless, the existing fuzzy DBMSs (FDBMS) are research prototypes. These FDBMS, due to their early stage, are not able to ensure the previously required features for applications for the storage and retrieval of such large image databases.

In order to solve the drawbacks of both, actual DBMSs and the prototypical FDBMSs, we propose a Fuzzy Object-Relational model [8]. This model defines a group of types and operators to store, manage and query fuzzy data, which can be used to extend an Object-Relational DBMS (ORDBMS) to implement a FORDBMS. This extension consist in adding a group of user-defined types and operators to the ORDBMS taking advantage of its extension mechanisms. This approach combines the desired features of actual DBMSs and the ability of fuzzy data storage and handling of prototypical FDBMS. The resulting FORDBMS is very suitable for supporting flexible content based retrieval of images for the discussed type of systems.

This usage of extended datatypes and operators for including fuzzy data management in classical databases, matches with the SQL:1999 standard. This standard compliance lets express a fuzzy query in a fully SQL compliant sentence, which lets implement a SQL compatible fuzzy query definition language.

The rest of the paper is organized as follows. Section 2 introduces the mechanism for describing images based on its dominant colours. Section 3 describes the proposed FDBMS and depicts how it can be used to model the image descriptors. Section 4 describes the proposed operators for defining conditions used in image queries. Section 5 shows some query examples and their results. Finally, Section 6 highlight the concluding remarks and future works.

2 Dominant Fuzzy Colour Descriptor

To achieve a good performance in the retrieval process, efficient methods for describing images are needed. The current retrieval systems face this issue by means of features, such as colour, texture or shape [9]. In this context, dominant colours arise as a powerful tool for describing the representative colours in an image.

In this paper we propose to describe images by means of dominant fuzzy colours. Concretely, we face the colour description in two stages: firstly, a set of crisp dominant colours is extracted (sect. 2.1); then, each colour calculated in the previous stage is used to obtain the set of dominant fuzzy colours (sect. 2.2).

2.1 Dominant Colours

In this section a methodology to extract dominant crisp colours from images is presented using the HSI colour space. In this perceptual space, the hue component (H) represents the colour tone, saturation (S) is the amount of colour and the third component (I) is the amount of light. Let us remark that, although the red-green-blue (RGB) is the most used model to acquire digital images, it is well known that it is not adequate for colour image analysis. Furthermore, the colour components of this space do not have an intuitive interpretation according to the human perception of colour [9].

Dominant Crisp Colour Extraction. In the literature there are many crisp approaches to dominant colour extraction, for example those based on histogram analysis or clustering techniques. In this paper we will perform a clustering approach using the Batchelor&Wilking algorithm [10], where the number of clusters is unknown a priori. This method is initialized with one cluster consisting of all pixels and then an iterative split procedure is performed until a stopping criterion is met. This stopping criterion is based on a parameter $\theta \in [0,1]$ related to the maximum distance to be achieved between points within each cluster (in this paper we have fixed empirically $\theta = 0.3$). To measure the distance between points, the distance between HSI colours proposed in [11] will be used. As a result, we obtain a set of N clusters where the centroid of each cluster, calculated as the mean value, defines a dominant colour. In the following, the set of dominant colours will be noted as DCS, with

$$DCS = \{\mathbf{dc}_1, \mathbf{dc}_2, \ldots, \mathbf{dc}_N\} \ . \tag{1}$$

and $\mathbf{dc}_k = [h_k, s_k, i_k]$ being a dominant crisp colour represented in the HSI colour space.

Degree of Dominance. Intuitively, a colour is dominant to the extent it appears frequently in a given image. It seems natural to model the idea of frequent apparition by means of a fuzzy set over the percentages, i.e. a fuzzy subset of the real interval $[0,1]$. Hence, we define the fuzzy subset *Dominant* of colours as follows:

$$Dom(\mathbf{c}) = \begin{cases} 0 & fr(\mathbf{c}) \le u_1 \\ \frac{fr(\mathbf{c})-u_1}{u_2-u_1} & u_1 \le fr(\mathbf{c}) \le u_2 \\ 1 & fr(\mathbf{c}) \ge u_2 \end{cases} \ . \tag{2}$$

where $fr(c)$ is the percentage of pixels with colour $\mathbf{c}$ in the image under consideration, and u_1 and u_2 are two parameters such that $0 \le u_1 < u_2 \le 1$. We have empirically fixed them to be $u_1 = 0.05$ and $u_2 = 0.2$.

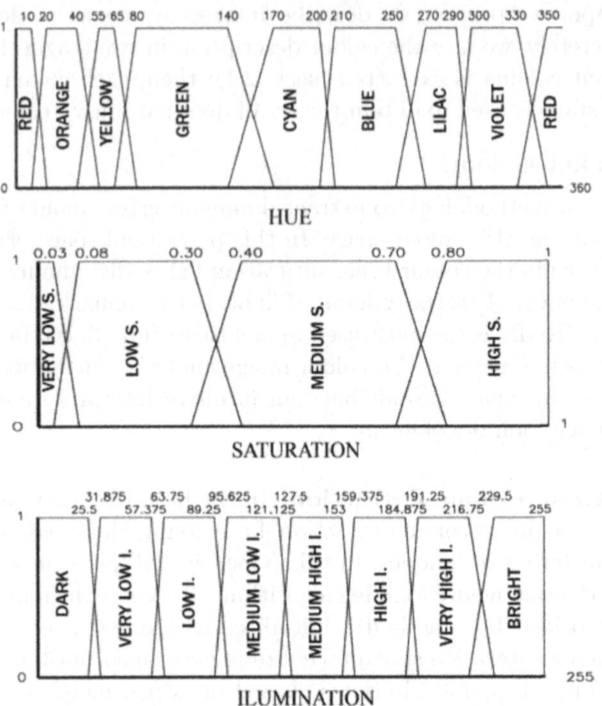

Fig. 1. Fuzzy HSI colour space

2.2 Dominant Fuzzy Colours

In this section, a set of dominant fuzzy colours is obtained taking as starting point the set of dominant crisp colours extracted in the previous one.

For this purpose, the fuzzy HSI colour space presented in [1] will be used. In this proposal, a fuzzy HSI colour $\widetilde{C}$ is defined as a linguistic label whose semantics is represented by a fuzzy subset of $[0, 2\pi] \times [0, 1] \times \{0, \ldots, 255\}$. Then, a fuzzy HSI colour space $\widetilde{HSI}$ is defined as a set of fuzzy HSI colours that define a partition of $[0, 2\pi] \times [0, 1] \times \{0, \ldots, 255\}$.

To define and represent a fuzzy HSI colour space, [1] propose to employ a fuzzy hue space, a fuzzy saturation space and a fuzzy intensity space, consisting of fuzzy hues, fuzzy saturations and fuzzy intensities, respectively (see Fig. 1). Then, a fuzzy HSI colour $\widetilde{C}$ can be defined and represented in practice by a triple $[\widetilde{C}_H, \widetilde{C}_S, \widetilde{C}_I]$, where $\widetilde{C}_H$, $\widetilde{C}_S$, and $\widetilde{C}_I$ are a fuzzy hue, a fuzzy saturation and a fuzzy intensity, respectively (see [1] for more details)

On the basis of the fuzzy HSI colour space defined in [1], we introduce the concept of dominant fuzzy colour in an image as follows:

Definition 1. *A dominant fuzzy colour is a fuzzy HSI colour that appears frequently in the image.*

As in the case of dominant crisp colours, this definition is imprecise in nature, i.e., "dominant" is an imprecise concept defined on the set of fuzzy colours.

Many approaches are possible to calculate how dominant a fuzzy colour is in an image. One possible approach is to calculate the frequency with which each fuzzy colour appears in the image, by using some fuzzy cardinality measure. This will be dealt with in future papers.

One alternative approach we adopt in this paper is to obtain the fuzzy subset of dominant fuzzy colours from the set of crisp dominant colours. We shall consider that a fuzzy colour is dominant to the extent that it matches a dominant crisp colour. This leads to the following definition:

Definition 2. *Let* $DCS = \{\mathbf{dc}_1, \ldots, \mathbf{dc}_N\}$ *be the set of dominant crisp colours where* $\mathbf{dc}_k = [h_k, s_k, i_k]$. *The fuzzy subset of dominant fuzzy colours for an image will be*

$$\widetilde{DCS} = \bigcup_{k \in \{1,\ldots,N\}} \widetilde{DCS}_k \ . \tag{3}$$

where

$$\widetilde{DCS}_k = \sum_{\widetilde{C} \in \widetilde{HSI}} \left(\widetilde{C}(\mathbf{dc}_k) \otimes Dom(\mathbf{dc}_k) \right) / \widetilde{C} \ . \tag{4}$$

with $\otimes$ *being a t-norm (we use the minimum in this paper) and where* $\widetilde{C}$ *is a fuzzy colour of the fuzzy HSI colour space* $\widetilde{HSI}$, *and the union is performed using the maximum.*

Hence, for each dominant crisp colour $\mathbf{dc}_k$, we obtain the possibility distribution given by equation (3), where the degree of dominance associated to each $\widetilde{C}$ is calculated as the minimum between the membership degree of $\mathbf{dc}_k$ to $\widetilde{C}$ and the dominant degree of $\mathbf{dc}_k$. If a fuzzy colour $\widetilde{C}$ is compatible with several dominant crisp colours, then different degree of dominance will be obtained for $\widetilde{C}$ corresponding to each crisp colour compatible with it; in this case, the maximum of these degrees will be selected as the final degree of dominance of $\widetilde{C}$ as (4) shows.

3 Fuzzy Object-Relational Database Management System

This section briefly introduces our FORDBMS datatypes to show its modeling capabilities. Afterwards, the usage of this capabilities to model image descriptors for an image retrieval system is detailed.

3.1 User-Defined Types for Fuzzy Data

A wide variety of fuzzy data can be handled and represented by our FORDBMS through its user-defined datatypes. The available datatypes for fuzzy data management are the following:

- Atomic fuzzy types (AFT): This type groups subtypes for representing fuzzy data as a possibility distribution defined on crisp domains.
  - Ordered AFT (OAFT): This type handles fuzzy data defined on ordered domains by means of trapezoidal possibility distributions.
  - Non ordered AFT (NOAFT): The type lets define possibility distributions on non ordered finite scalar domains with a similarity relation defined between the domain elements.
- Fuzzy collections (FC): This type groups subtypes for representing fuzzy sets of objects of a particular class. The elements can be fuzzy or crisp data.
  - Conjunctive FC (CFC): The semantics of the set is inclusive, the set represents every element within it.
  - Disjunctive FC (DFC): The semantics of the set is exclusive, the set can only represent one of its elements.
- Fuzzy objects (FO): This type is used to group user-defined datatypes whose attribute types, or some of them, are fuzzy types. Every attribute of the datatypes extending FO datatype is associated with a degree to measure its *importance* in the fuzzy object comparison algorithm.

3.2 Modeling the Flexible Dominant Colour Image Descriptor

The previously introduced method for image description generates a data set representing the dominant colours of an image. In an image retrieval system supported by a DBMS, a user-defined database datatype, for this data set, would ease storage, handling and querying these image descriptors. The datatypes for representing fuzzy data of our FORDBMS are a convenient base to build the image descriptor datatype because the image description data set includes fuzzy data representing flexible colour descriptions. Additionally, the FORDBMS operators for fuzzy data querying let the definition of flexible conditions on the image descriptor.

The datatype *DominantColorSet* models the proposed image description dataset. This datatype is modeled as show in Fig. 2. The classes in this figure follow a colour code where, the datatypes provided by our FORDBMS to represent fuzzy data have a dark grey background, a black background for the abstraction of the basic types of the host ORDBMS on which the FORDBMS is built, and a white background for the datatypes created to built de image descriptor datatype. Let us describe the definition of *DominantColorSet* datatype by a *bottom to top* approach.

The basic components of a fuzzy colour are the linguistics labels representing fuzzy hue, saturation and intensity values. These linguistics labels represents trapezoidal possibility distributions defined on crisp hue, saturation and intensity domains, as shown previously in Fig. 1. As all the underlying domains are ordered, an OAFT derived datatype could be defined for each HSI colour component. Hence, the datatypes *FHue*, *FSaturation* and *FIntensity* are defined for each colour component, representing the fuzzy hue ($\widetilde{H}$), saturation ($\widetilde{S}$) and intensity ($\widetilde{I}$) spaces respectively. On these datatypes the linguistic labels in Fig. 1 are defined, in order to use these linguistic labels as value for the datatypes.

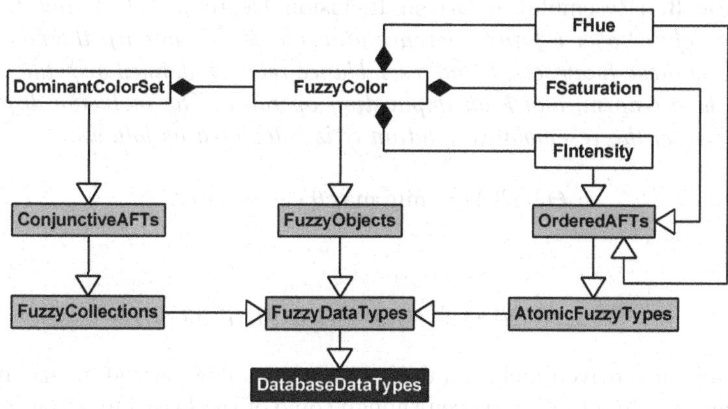

Fig. 2. UML diagram for DominantColorSet datatype

According to the previous definitions, a fuzzy colour is represented as a triple $[\widetilde{H}, \widetilde{S}, \widetilde{I}]$. In fact, a fuzzy colour can be viewed as a group of three linguistic labels, each one representing a value on fuzzy hue, saturation and intensity spaces respectively. In the database, a fuzzy colour is represented by the datatype *FuzzyColor*. This datatype is defined by composing three values of *FHue*, *FSaturation* and *FIntensity*, the same way that a fuzzy colour is defined previously. The *FuzzyColor* datatype is modeled as a FO derived datatype with three attributes of *FHue*, *Fsaturation* and *FIntensity* datatypes respectively.

Finally, the *DominantColorSet* datatype is defined. The data of this datatype represents a fuzzy subset of fuzzy colours $\widetilde{DCS}$. The membership degree of each fuzzy colour in the fuzzy set corresponds to its degree of dominance, which is calculated following (4). As $\widetilde{DCS}$ is a fuzzy set of complex elements, which are also fuzzy, the *DominantColorSet* datatype must be derived from FC. Taking into account the conjunctive semantics of $\widetilde{DCS}$, the *DominantColorSet* datatype is defined as a CFC derivative whose members are of *FuzzyColor* datatype.

4 Fuzzy Operators for Colour Based Image Retrieval

This section describes the most significant operators for the fuzzy datatypes described earlier. These operators will be used later for defining flexible selection conditions in image retrieval queries.

4.1 Fuzzy Inclusion Operator

The fuzzy inclusion operator, `FInclusion(A,B)`, returns the degree of which $A \subseteq B$, where A and B are instances of CFC. This degree is calculated in our approach by a adaptation of the *Resemblance Driven Inclusion Degree* introduced in [12]. This proposal is peculiar because it computes the inclusion degree of two fuzzy sets whose elements are also imprecise.

Definition 3. (Resemblance Driven Inclusion Degree). *Let A and B be two fuzzy sets defined over a finite reference universe $\mathcal{U}$, μ_A and μ_B the membership functions of these fuzzy sets, S the resemblance relation defined over the elements of $\mathcal{U}$, $\otimes$ be a t-norm, and I an implication operator. The inclusion degree of A in B driven by the resemblance relation S is calculated as follows:*

$$\Theta_S(B|A) = \min_{x \in \mathcal{U}} \max_{y \in \mathcal{U}} \theta_{A,B,S}(x,y) \ . \qquad (5)$$

where

$$\theta_{A,B,S}(x,y) = \otimes(I(\mu_A(x), \mu_B(y)), \mu_S(x,y)) \ . \qquad (6)$$

The resemblance driven inclusion degree does not allow partial inclusion, which means that $Theta_S(B|A) > 0$ even though some of the least important elements of A are not members of B. It can be very interesting for colour based retrieval for decrease the importance of less dominant colours with respect to very dominant colours. For this reason, we propose, inspired by [13], to modify (5) substituting the minimum aggregation by a weighted mean aggregation, whose weight values are the membership degrees in A of the elements of $\mathcal{U}$. This proposal allow partial inclusion, and takes into account the *importance* of each included element in terms of relative membership. The *Modified Resemblance Inclusion Degree* is defined in (7), where $|A| = \sum_{x \in \mathcal{U}} \mu_A(x)$.

$$\Theta_S(B|A) = \sum_{x \in \mathcal{U}} \frac{\mu_A(x)}{|A|} \cdot \max_{y \in \mathcal{U}} \theta_{A,B,S}(x,y) \ . \qquad (7)$$

The implementation of `FInclusion(A,B)`, used to calculate the results shown in this paper, takes the minimum as t-norm, and as implication operator the one defined in (8).

$$I(x,y) = \begin{cases} 1 & \text{if } x \leq y \\ y/x & \text{otherwise} \end{cases} \ . \qquad (8)$$

4.2 Fuzzy Equality Operator

The fuzzy equality operator, `FEQ(A,B)`, calculates the resemblance degree between two values of a fuzzy datatype. The way this calculus is done depends on the fuzzy datatype of the operands.

Fuzzy Equality Operator for Conjunctive Fuzzy Collections. If `A` and `B` are two instances of a CFC derived datatype, the resemblance degree is calculated according to the *Generalized Resemblance between Fuzzy Sets* proposed in [12]. This method is based on the *Resemblance Driven Inclusion Degree* by applying the concept of double inclusion, shown in (9).

$$A = B \text{ if, and only if, } (A \subseteq B) \wedge (B \subseteq A) \ . \qquad (9)$$

Definition 4. *(Generalized resemblance between fuzzy sets). Let A and B be two fuzzy sets defined over a finite reference universe $\mathcal{U}$, over which a resemblance relation S is defined, and $\otimes$ be a t-norm. The generalized resemblance degree between A and B restricted by $\otimes$ is calculated by means of the following formulation:*

$$\beth_{S,\otimes}(A,B) = \otimes(\Theta_S(B|A), \Theta_S(A|B)) \ . \tag{10}$$

The previous definition uses the modifications proposed in (7), therefore this operator aggregates the results of `FInclusion(A,B)` and `FInclusion(B,A)`. In order to increase the flexibility of the equality operator, a modification for (10) consisting in substituting the t-norm by a arithmetic mean aggregation is proposed. This modification makes the fuzzy equality operator to not penalize so much asymmetric inclusions degrees as minimum t-norm does, which leads to get more flexible comparisons.

Fuzzy Equality Operator for Fuzzy Colour Instances. When the operator `FEQ(A,B)` is applied on instances of a class derived from FO, in this paper on instances of the datatype *FuzzyColor*, the resemblance degree of these objects is calculated using the following method.

Definition 5. *(Object Resemblance Degree). Let o_1 and o_2 be two objects of the class C, $obj.a_i$ the value of the i-th attribute of the object obj, n the number of attributes defined in the class C, and FEQ the resemblance operator.*

$$OR(o_1, o_2) = \frac{1}{n} \sum_{i \in \mathcal{A}}^{n} FEQ(o1.a_i, o2.a_i) \ . \tag{11}$$

5 Retrieving Images by Dominant Colour Criteria

The previous set of fuzzy datatypes and operators makes our FORDBMS able to answer queries including conditions defined on the set of dominant colours which describes images in a database. The proposed approach to create a FORDBMS based on a commercial ORDBMS by extending it with user defined datatypes and operators, let to express these queries as SQL, following the latest standard.

A dominant colour based condition is, actually, a fuzzy condition defined on the fuzzy set of fuzzy colours which describes each image in a database. This kind of conditions are based on the usage of the previously defined *fuzzy inclusion operator* or the *fuzzy equality operator for CFC*. Through these operators, a condition requiring that a fuzzy set of fuzzy colours is included, or resembles to, the dominant colour descriptor of each image in a database can be defined.

Each user defined fuzzy colour for a condition can be defined by using the linguistic labels previously defined for each HSI colour component. This way, a query is defined with natural colour descriptors, which means an advantage in contrast to numerical definition. Additionally, this condition definition way makes possible to define different conditions on each HSI colour component, and to omit requirements for a colour component by using the linguistic label *unknown* defined by the membership function $\mu(a) = 1, \forall a \in D(A)$, where $D(A)$ is the underlying domain for the attribute A.

5.1 Query Examples

This section shows some query examples, based on the fuzzy inclusion and equality of fuzzy sets of dominant colours, and its results.

Dominant Colour Inclusion Query. An example of a condition using the fuzzy inclusion operator could be "*Retrieve all the images including the fuzzy colour bright very high saturated red*". This condition is defined using the fuzzy inclusion operator on the image descriptor and the user defined fuzzy set of dominant colours, which in the example includes only the fuzzy colour [*red, veryhighsat,bright*]. This query is expressed in SQL using the previously defined datatypes and operators as the following sentence:

```
SELECT image,cdeg(1) FROM images WHERE FCond( FInclusion(
  ColorDescriptor,
  DominantColorSet(1.0, FuzzyColor(
        FHue('red'),FSaturation('veryhighsat'),Intensity('bright')
        ) ) ) , 1 ) > 0 ORDER BY 2 DESC;
```

Figure 3 shows the results of the previous query and a more complex example of this type of queries applied on a database of 160 flag images. In this figure the first column shows the fuzzy colours which must be included in the resulting images, and for each fuzzy colour a sample crisp colour which fits it. The second column shows the query results ordered by relevance.

Another example of this kind of condition is the requirement "*Retrieve all the images including bright colours*". In this case, the inclusion operator must ensure to include the fuzzy colour [*unknown, unknown, bright*]. Note the usage of the label *unknown* to avoid to define the condition for the hue and saturation components. The previously defined query, applied on a database of about 700 colour images, obtains the results show in Fig. 4 which are ordered by relevance.

Dominant Colour Resemblance Query. Another interesting kind of queries is the one which includes a condition to retrieve the set of images of a database

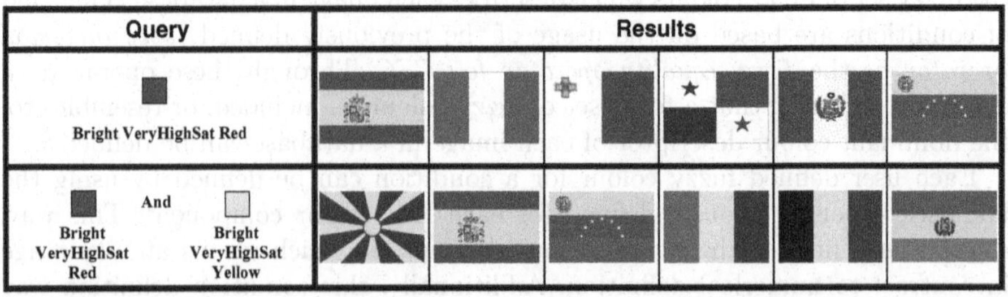

Query	Results
Bright VeryHighSat Red	
Bright VeryHighSat Red And Bright VeryHighSat Yellow	

Fig. 3. Colour inclusion query results using all the colour components

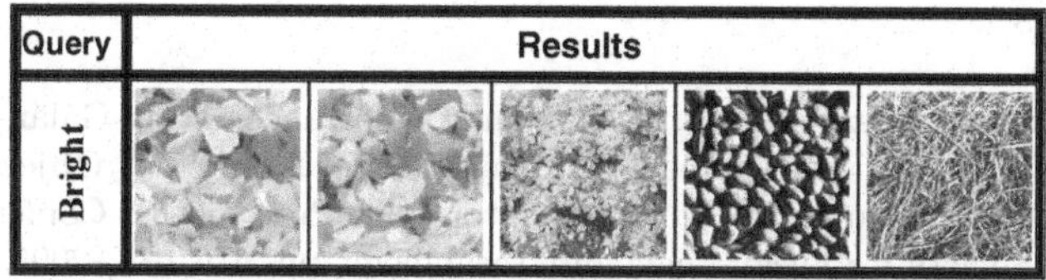

Fig. 4. Colour inclusion query results using only the intensity component

with a dominant colour pattern similar to the one associated with a sample image. This kind of conditions are defined by using the *fuzzy equality operator for CFC*, which computes the resemblance degree between the sets of dominant colours of an image in the database and the sample image. A sample query of this kind is:

```
SELECT a.image,cdeg(1) FROM images a, images b WHERE b.id=# AND
FCond( FEQ( a.ColorDescriptor, b.ColorDescriptor ),1 ) > 0
ORDER BY 2 DESC;
```

Several examples of this kind of queries, applied on a database with about 700 colour images, are shown in Fig. 5. In each example, the fist column shows the sample image, and the second column shows the set of images ordered by relevance with a dominant colour pattern similar to the image sample.

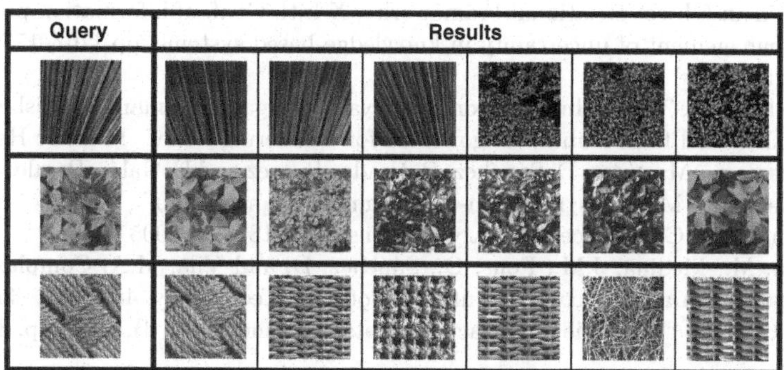

Fig. 5. Image resemblance query results

6 Concluding Remarks and Future Works

This paper has shown the suitability of a FORDBMS for flexible image retrieval systems. The synergy of a fuzzy approach for dominant colour description extraction, and the ability of the proposed FORDBMS to represent and handle complex fuzzy data, results in a powerful system for content based image retrieval.

Future works will focus on new methods for indexing fuzzy data in order to boost query processing performance. These indexing methods will be based on traditional indexing methods for an easy integration in the host ORDBMS.

References

1. J.Chamorro-Martínez and J.M. Medina and C. Barranco and E. Galán-Perales and J.M. Soto-Hidalgo, "An Approach to Image Retrieval on Fuzzy Object-Relational Database using Dominant Color Descriptors", in Proc. of 4th Conference of the European Society for Fuzzy Logic and Technology, pp. 676–684, 2005
2. R. De Caluwe, Fuzzy and Uncertain Object-Oriented Databases: Concepts and Models, Advances in Fuzzy Systems-Applications and Theory. Vol 13. World Scientific, 1997.
3. S. Fukami, M. Umano, M. Muzimoto, H. Tanaka, "Fuzzy Database Retrieval and Manipulation Language", IEICE Technical Reports, Vol. 78, N. 233, pp. 65–72, AL-78–85 (Automata and Language) 1979.
4. J. Galindo, J.M. Medina, O.Pons, J.C. Cubero, "A Server for Fuzzy SQL Queries", Flexible Query Answering Systems, eds. T. Andreasen, H. Christiansen and H.L. Larsen, Lecture Notes in Artificial Intelligence (LNAI) 1495, pp. 164–174. Ed. Springer, 1998.
5. H. Prade, C. Testemale, "Generalizing Database Relational Algebra for the Treatment of Incomplete or Uncertain Information and Vague Queries", Information Sciences Vol. 34, 1984, pp. 115–143.
6. M. Umano, "Freedom-O: A Fuzzy Database System", Fuzzy Information and Decision Processes. Gupta-Sanchez edit. North-Holand Pub. Comp. 1982.
7. M. Zemankova-Leech, A. Kandel, "Fuzzy Relational Databases – A Key to Expert Systems", Köln, Germany, TÜV Rheinland, 1984.
8. J.C. Cubero, N. Marín, J.M. Medina, O. Pons, M.A. Vila, "Fuzzy object Management in an Object-Relational Framework", X Intl. Conf. of information processing and management of uncertainty in knowledge-based systems, pp.1767–1774. 2004. Perugia (Italy).
9. A. Del Bimbo, "Visual Information Retrieval", Morgan Kaufmann Publishers, 2001
10. A.K. Jain and R.C. Dubes, "Algorithms for Clustering Data", Prentice Hall, 1988
11. J. Chamorro-Martínez, D. Sánchez, B. Prados-Suarez and E. Galán-Perales, "Fuzzy Connectivity Measures for Path-based Image Segmentation", in Proc. of IEEE International Conference on Fuzzy Systems, pp. 218–223, 2005
12. Marín, M., Medina, J.M., Pons, O., Sánchez, D. and Vila, M.A. Complex object comparison in a fuzzy context. Inf. and Software Technology, 45(7):431–444. 2003
13. J. A. Goguen, "The logic of inexact concepts", Synthese, 9(3–4), 1969, pp. 325–373.

Structural and Semantic Modeling of Audio for Content-Based Querying and Browsing

Mustafa Sert[1,2], Buyurman Baykal[3], and Adnan Yazıcı[4]

[1] Başkent University, Department of Computer Engineering, 06530 Ankara, Turkey
msert@baskent.edu.tr

[2] Gazi University, Faculty of Technical Education, Department of Electronics and Computer Education, 06500 Ankara, Turkey

[3] Middle East Technical University, Department of Electrical and Electronics Engineering, 06531 Ankara, Turkey
buyurman@metu.edu.tr

[4] Middle East Technical University, Department of Computer Engineering, 06531 Ankara, Turkey
yazici@ceng.metu.edu.tr

Abstract. A typical content-based audio management system deals with three aspects namely audio segmentation and classification, audio analysis, and content-based retrieval of audio. In this paper, we integrate the three aspects of content-based audio management into a single framework and propose an efficient method for flexible querying and browsing of auditory data. More specifically, we utilize two robust feature sets namely MPEG-7 Audio Spectrum Flatness (ASF) and Mel Frequency Cepstral Coefficients (MFCC) as the underlying features in order to improve the content-based retrieval accuracy, since both features have some advantages for distinct types of audio (e.g., music and speech). The proposed system provides a wide range of opportunities to query and browse an audio data by content, such as querying and browsing for a chorus section, sound effects, and query-by-example. In addition, the clients can express their queries in the form of *point*, *range*, and k-*nearest neighbor*, which are particularly significant in the multimedia domain.

1 Introduction

Traditional information retrieval (IR) systems provide access to data stored in the form of relational tables through forms-like interfaces. The clients specify their queries by filling the forms and supplying strict conditions on the attributes stored in the database. In the case of multimedia information retrieval (MIR), this approach can lead to unexpected results since the clients might not have prior knowledge about the structure of information stored in the database. A solution approach to this problem may be to allow the use of approximate queries through well-designed user interfaces. In order to enable such a capability, efficient storage and retrieval models should be designed and developed since multimedia content have complex structures. Various studies have emphasized

H.L. Larsen et al. (Eds.): FQAS 2006, LNAI 4027, pp. 319–330, 2006.

on image and video indexing and retrieval [1, 4, 5, 6]. Auditory data (e.g., music, speech, sound effects), on the other hand, has not been considered as much as the other media types. We can explore the existing research on content-based audio management in three categories: (1) segmentation and classification of audio data into predefined classes, such as speech, music, environmental sound, and silence; (2) content-based audio retrieval (CBAR); (3) audio analysis. Therefore, an audio content management system should support all of these issues.

In the first category, most of the audio segmentation methods deal with feature extraction. These studies [10, 11, 12] can be examined in three groups. One of them is a segmentation method which involves with the classification of audio data segments into predefined classes (e.g., music, speech, and environmental sound) [10]. The other group is to detect the abrupt changes in feature values of audio data[11]. The last one is another segmentation method which consists of relative silences or pauses in an audio data[12]. Our segmentation method relies on the second group, namely detecting abrupt changes in feature values, and advances it by realizing a structural similarity analysis technique.

In the CBAR category, a widely used approach is to extract a set of acoustic features for each sound and query item. One attempt based on this motivation is the work carried out by the Muscle Fish [7]. In this work, they made use of statistical values, which are obtained from the mean, variance, and autocorrelation parameters of five features namely loudness, pitch, brightness, bandwidth, and harmonicity. However, merely statistical values are not suitable for sounds that have multiple timbre [9]. One specific technique is used in [8], where the Mel Frequency Cepstral Coefficients (MFCC) are used as features, and sounds are characterized by templates that are obtained from a tree-based vector quantizer. However, this method fails to distinguish music and environmental sounds that have distinct timbres in general, since the MFCC does not represent the timbre of music, as well.

In the audio analysis category, the main aim is to obtain structural descriptions of auditory data for efficient indexing and retrieval. Audio analysis studies, such as semantic audio segmentation [13], music thumbnailing [2, 3, 13], music summarization [14, 19], and chorus detection [15, 20], although carrying different titles, all share the same goal of facilitating an efficient browsing and searching of audio files. Indeed, they are all built upon the identification of important audio excerpts that are adequate to represent the entire audio file. However, current studies have some drawbacks in terms of detecting all repetitive structures and recognition accuracy, and hence need some improvements.

In this paper, we integrate the three considered aspects of content-based audio management into a single framework and propose an efficient method for flexible querying and browsing of auditory data. More specifically, we utilize two robust feature sets namely MPEG-7 Audio Spectrum Flatness (ASF) [16] and MFCC as the underlying features, in order to improve the content-based retrieval accuracy, since both features have some advantages for distinct types of audio data (e.g., music and speech). The proposed system provides a wide range of opportunities to query and browse an audio content, such as querying and browsing for a chorus section, sound effects, and query-by-example. In addition, the clients can express their queries in the form of *point*, *range*, and *k-nearest neighbor*, which are particularly significant in the multimedia domain. The ability of querying and browsing for a chorus section is achieved by our previous work in [22], which describes the extraction of audio excerpts.

The paper is organized as follows. Section 2 briefly describes our approach to decomposition of audio excerpts through self-similarity analysis. In Section 3, we introduce content-based querying and browsing facilities of the proposed framework through the generated similarity matrix. Finally, the experimental results and the concluding remarks are presented in Section 4 and 5, respectively.

2 Decomposition of Audio Excerpts

The selection of feature sets for analysis and retrieval plays an essential role in the accuracy of results. Thus, we utilize the MPEG-7 ASF and the MFCC as the underlying feature sets. For brevity, we do not include the extraction process of these features. The interested readers can refer to [22, 16] for further details.

2.1 Structural Similarity Analysis

The proposed approach is based on the work in [18], and it is extended to improve the recognition accuracy by altering the underlying feature set, utilizing the *k-means* algorithm to cluster the detected chorus sections, and performing additional post processing techniques.

Constructing the Similarity Matrix. In order to detect the repetitive patterns within music or speech, our analysis begins with the calculation of similarities between the feature vectors of ASF and MFCC. If the result of comparisons between feature vectors lead to small distances, then it is represented with dark pixels in the matrix, otherwise it is represented with brighter pixels.

Let V_i and V_j be the feature vectors of frames i and j in the feature matrix for an audio data. Then the similarity is defined by the *Euclidean* norm as follows:

$$\sigma(V_i, V_j) = \sqrt{\sum_{k=1}^{m} (V_{i_k} - V_{j_k})^2} \qquad (i, j, m \in Z^+). \tag{1}$$

where $\sigma(V_i, V_j)$ denotes the similarity between frame i and j, whereas m represents the vector lengths. The resulting similarity matrix is a diagonally symmetric matrix with the dimension of $n \times n$, where n denotes the number of temporal frames ($30ms$ each) within a given audio file. Fig. 1 presents an example of the similarity matrix using a 2-D gray image plot in which each pixel represents the distance value as a gray level.

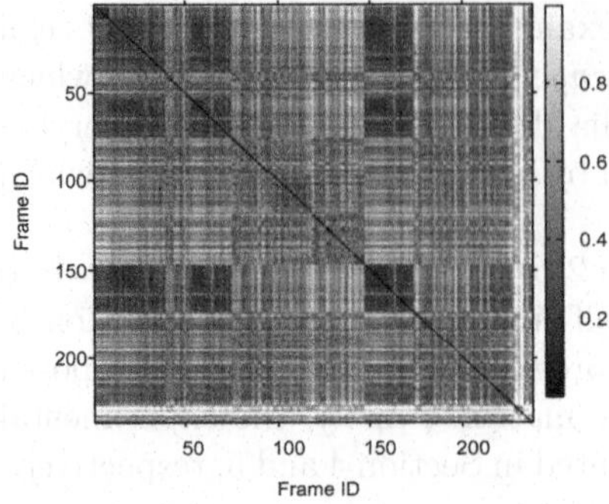

Fig. 1. Initial similarity matrix computed using the ASF feature from the song "Tahitian Moon" by Perry Farell

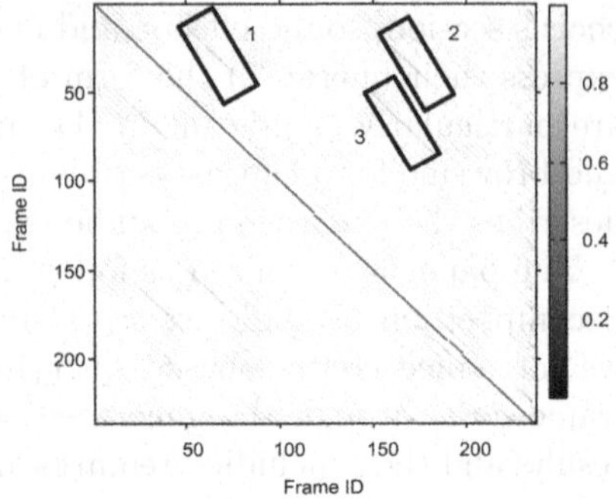

Fig. 2. The similarity matrix computed after the post processing for the song "Tahitian Moon" by Perry Farell

Post Processing. As depicted in Fig. 1, this form of the similarity matrix does not reveal the repetitive patterns, since many discrete values of the feature vectors are small and very close to each others even if they have significant differences between them. Therefore, we realize two consecutive approaches to reveal the differences between the feature vectors. The first one is to normalize the values of similarity matrix σ between 0 and 1 to obtain a uniform distribution (2) and the second one is to strengthen the diagonal stripes by performing a diagonal summation process over the matrix (3).

$$\overline{\sigma}_{x,y} = \frac{\sigma_{x,y} - \min(\sigma)}{\max(\sigma) - \min(\sigma)} \ . \tag{2}$$

$$\widehat{\sigma}_{x,y} = \sum_{i=1}^{k} \overline{\sigma}_{x+i,y+i} \ . \tag{3}$$

where $\widehat{\sigma}$ represents the resulting similarity matrix and k represents the strengthen order. Selection of the strengthen order is important, since it depends to the length of the sought pattern. Our experiments shown that strengthen order between 5 and 12 is suitable for detecting repetitive patterns in music and speech.

In order to prevent vertical and horizontal lines disturbing diagonal lines, we remove the horizontal and vertical lines from the similarity matrix. To this end, we implement an image processing technique by applying a kernel of size $b \times b$. Basically, a kernel is a small $2-D$ array (e.g., 3x3, 5x5, or 11x11) compared to original similarity matrix. In our experiments we use a kernel of size 11×11. The main diagonal elements of this kernel are filled by 10, whereas all other elements are -1. If this kernel is moved around the similarity matrix $\widehat{\sigma}$, it would respond more strongly to lines in the -45° direction with the following relation:

$$R = \sum_{i=1}^{b^2} \omega_i z_i \ . \tag{4}$$

where z_i is the distance value of the similarity matrix associated with kernel coefficient ω_i, R indicates the response of the kernel at any point, and b^2 is the total number of coefficients in the kernel. This results the matrix $\breve{\sigma}$ in Fig. 2.

2.2 Pattern Extraction

Above, similar regions within the matrix are becoming visible as diagonal stripes. The next step towards the matrix is to interpret and cluster the visible patterns.

Interpretation of Patterns. In Fig. 2, three repeated patterns are depicted for the song "Tahitian Moon" by *Perry Farell*. In the figure, the repeated patterns are manually annotated by rectangular shapes, in order to make clear the following descriptions. The diagonal line with label 1 represents the first repetition of the chorus section. The line with label 2 corresponds to the second repetition of the chorus section. The first occurrence of the chorus section is invisible due to the main diagonal. The line with label 3 represents the repetition of the chorus section 2. Thus, the chorus section with number 3 is not required in the pattern extraction process. The location of first chorus section is obtained by projecting the diagonal line with label 1 to the main diagonal and then to the time line. The idea behind this approach can be explained as follows. The reader should notice that, the pattern with label 1 is the first *repetition* of the sought chorus section. Therefore we should find the location of first *occurrence* of the chorus section. To this end, we project the beginning and ending indices of the first repetition into the main diagonal, since first occurrence of the pattern is defined by the self-similarity of some frames to themselves and invisible due to the main diagonal. The locations of other chorus sections are determined in a similar fashion. The projections of detected patterns are depicted in Fig. 3.

Clustering of Patterns. In some cases, one can encounter distinct repetitive patterns within a given audio piece. To the best of our knowledge, the longest pattern is perceived as the *most salient* in the similarity matrix. Hence, we choose the longest pattern as the summary to enable the expressive power of the summaries. This approach not only yields expressive summaries, it also eliminates the stop-words in speech, as well.

In general, given a similarity matrix, three steps are needed for salient object extraction. Firstly, we compute the lower and upper bounds of threshold, namely $lThr$ and $uThr$, by the direction of maximum rate of change of $\mathbf{S}$, where $\mathbf{S}$ is the sorted vector of the similarity matrix in ascending order. Since the similarity matrix is diagonally symmetric, we only sort the upper triangular of the matrix. The algorithm obtains the direction of maximum rate of change by computing first order derivative of $\mathbf{S}$ and denoted by $\nabla\mathbf{S}$. Consequently, we assign $lThr$ and $uThr$ to the first and second minimum values of $\nabla\mathbf{S}$, respectively. The flat area as depicted in Fig. 4 represents the pixel values of visible patterns, whereas the area, excluding the flat area, denotes the background. Therefore, we preserve the pixel values between the $lThr$ and $uThr$ while removing the rest.

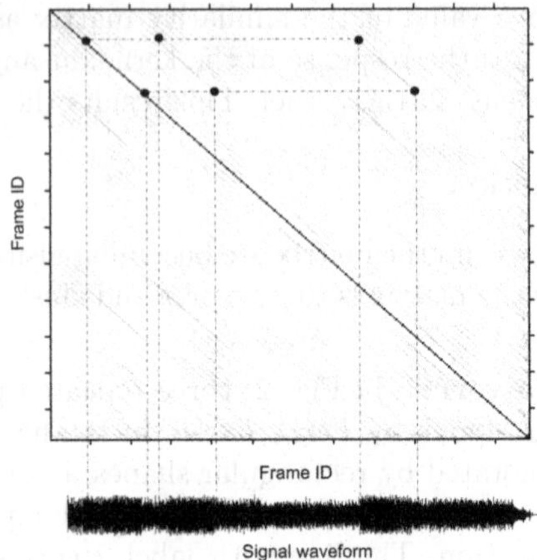

Fig. 3. Projections of the pattern locations for the song "Tahitian Moon" by Perry Farell

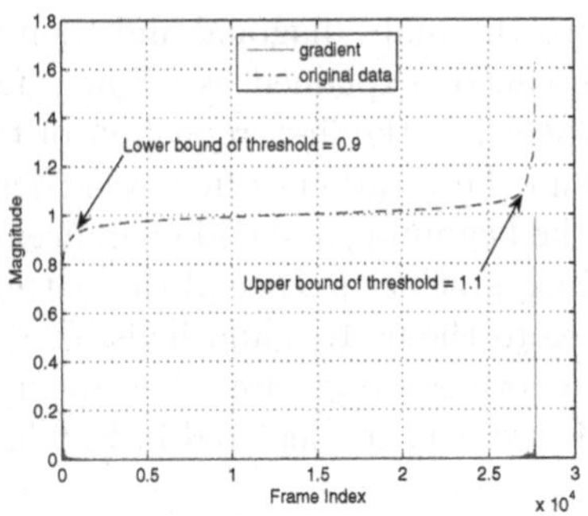

Fig. 4. Computing the thresholds for the song "Tahitian Moon" by Perry Farell

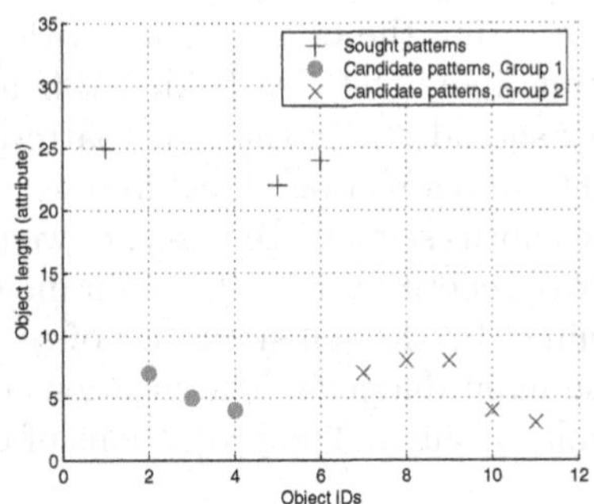

Fig. 5. Clustering example for the song "Tahitian Moon" by Perry Farell

The next step is to compute the lengths of all candidate patterns from the similarity matrix. We compute the lengths of each pattern by using the method that has been described in Fig. 3. The result of this step is a matrix and denoted by **A**. The first column of **A** represents the object (each diagonal line) IDs, and the second column denotes the object lengths as the attributes.

Since a similarity matrix may contain many diagonal lines in different sizes, and our aim is to extract the most representative ones, we need a method to group the similar (in terms of length) lines into the same cluster. Therefore, we make use of the *k-means* clustering algorithm [17] as follows: After defining the number of clusters *k*, we determine the initial centroid coordinate of matrix **A**, sequentially. For instance, if the number of cluster is three, then the first three elements of the matrix **A** is selected as the coordinate of the centroids. The grouping is then performed by minimizing the sum of squares of distances between the data and the corresponding cluster centroid. Knowing the members of each group, then we compute the new centroid of each group based on the new memberships. This process is continued in the same manner and terminated when there is no object that moves to a group. The result of clustering for the song "Tahitian Moon" by Perry Farell is depicted in Fig. 5.

3 Querying and Browsing

In the previous section we introduced a new method to extract and describe an audio content in terms of audio excerpt. We believe that, this type of information is suitable for audio indexing and thumbnailing, and CBAR applications can benefit much from the results of this analysis. Following sub-sections describe our approach to the CBAR by using the generated similarity matrix, as well as introducing various querying capabilities of the proposed framework. The framework is able to answer both structural and semantic queries. The semantic queries are enabled by the provided sound effect database. The clients can express their queries based on predefined keywords, such as gun-shot, explosion, animal sounds, and so forth. For instance, clients can express a semantic query in the form of "*find audio pieces that contains a gun-shot effect*".

3.1 Pattern Matching

In content-based retrieval of audio data, the query is an audio file and the result is a list of audio files ranked by their similarity. Therefore, we need a suitable method to search a query item within the database. Due to the problems reported in [21], the most suitable method deals with a set of extracted audio features that characterize the audio content. In this approach, a set of features, which are generally represented by vectors, are compared with each other. This is a pattern matching problem.

Our solution to this problem is to compute the cross-correlations of corresponding feature matrices. It provides a measure of the degree to which two sequences are similar. For given feature matrices $f(x, y)$ and $w(x, y)$, let $w(x, y)$ be the sought matrix of size JxK within the matrix $f(x, y)$ of size MxN. The cross-correlation between $f(x, y)$ and $w(x, y)$ is

$$c(x, y) = \sum_{m=0}^{J-1} \sum_{n=0}^{K-1} f(m, n) w(x + m, y + n) . \tag{5}$$

for $x = 0, 1, 2, ..., M - 1$, $y = 0, 1, 2, ..., N - 1$, and the summation is carried out over the region where w and f overlap. The maximum value(s) of c indicates the position(s), where w best matches f. Contrary to equation (1) in which V_i and V_j represent the feature vectors of two *distinct frames* within a given audio, in equation (5) the matrices represent the features of two *distinct audio pieces* and have a relation such that $J \leq M$ and $K \leq N$.

We present two different scenarios in order to demonstrate the results of pattern matching algorithm given in equation (5). For brevity, we do not illustrate the figures for both scenarios; instead we include the significant one in the paper.

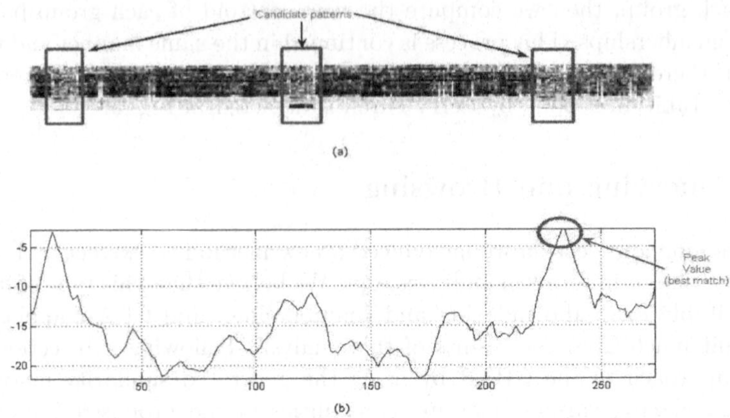

Fig. 6. Correlation result for the first scenario. (a) $2-D$ gray image plot of the feature vector; (b) corresponding correlation vector.

In the *first scenario*, we add three different sound effects, representing gun-shots, into the random locations of Vivaldi's The Four Seasons - Spring Concerto. In order to constitute a real-world scenario, the effects are added as a background sound. Afterwards, a gun-shot effect, which is distinct from the added ones, is defined as the query item. The kind of information obtained by the correlation is depicted in Fig. 6. In this figure, the $2-D$ gray image plot of the search space based on MPEG-7 ASF is illustrated in Fig. 6.a. The reader should note that, the ASF representation of the gun-shot effects, annotated with rectangles are readily visible in Fig. 6.a. The result of correlation is also depicted in Fig. 6.b. The peak of the correlation vector occurs where the search pattern is best correlated and is annotated in Fig. 6.b. This result conveys that, the proposed approach together with the MPEG-7 ASF justifies the expected results.

In the *second scenario*, we add two different sound effects, representing explosions, into the random locations of Vivaldi's The Four Seasons - Spring Concerto. In order to constitute a real-world scenario, again the explosion effects are added as a background sound. Afterwards, the explosion effect, which is the same with the second one, is defined as the query item. The results obtained from this scenario show that, the proposed approach together with the underlying feature set justifies the expected results.

The x-axis of Fig. 6.b represents the frame index of a match where the search pattern is best correlated. Thus, we make use of this information to locate the desired item. In addition, this information is also valuable for browsing and querying issues of the proposed framework, that is, we use the same information while realizing the k-*nearest* and *range* queries.

3.2 Point Queries

In point queries, a client query is represented by a feature vector, and the best match in the database is returned as the query result. This process is realized by

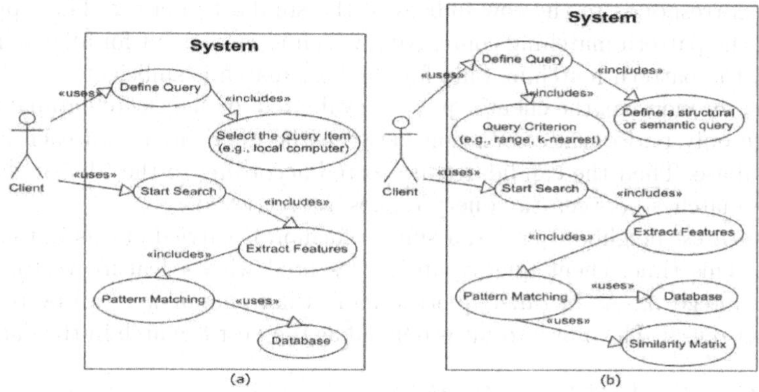

Fig. 7. UML use-case diagrams: (a) Point queries; (b) Range queries

computing the cross-correlations of corresponding feature vectors as described in the pattern matching section. More specifically, the client supplies an audio file to be queried, and selects either the MPEG-7 ASF or MFCC features, that will be used in comparisons. The UML use-case diagram, which demonstrates the interactions between the client and the system, is depicted in Fig. 7.a. In this type of queries, the system is able to answer all kind of queries in the form of "*find audio pieces similar to the one being supplied*" (query-by-example). In all cases, only one answer is returned to the client.

3.3 Range and K-Nearest Neighbor Queries

In range queries, a client query is represented by a feature vector and a similarity range. The UML use-case diagram, which demonstrates the interactions between the client and the system, is depicted in Fig. 7.b. The similarity range can be expressed either by a percentage value (e.g., $80\% - 90\%$) or a value between $0-1$. Contrary to point queries, more than one answer can be returned in this type of queries. Two cases of range queries are: (1) querying for a specific pattern within an audio; (2) querying for a specific pattern within the whole database.

In the first case, all the sequences that match for a given query range should be returned as the query answer. This property is particularly useful for browsing of an audio by content, and indexing video content using audio clues. We perform two consecutive steps in order to answer this type of queries. The first step is to compute the cross-correlation between the query item and the target audio based on the selected feature vector, and to return the frame index of the best match from the correlation vector. Since the main aim is to retrieve all candidates within the query range, the second step is to determine the locations of other candidates that satisfy the query condition. To this end, we benefit from the similarity matrix that is generated for each audio, since the (dis)similarities of each frame to all other frames for an audio are already stored in this matrix. Thus, we can simply obtain the other candidates by using the index value returned from the correlation, since the index value returned from the correlation process corresponds to the row indices of the similarity matrix. This approach reduces the pattern matching complexity, which is carried out for all candidates; instead, the pattern matching only for the best match is sufficient.

In the second case, the client's query is evaluated for the entire database. This time, we only perform a correlation between the query item and each item in the database. Then the candidates are sorted according to the (dis)similarities, and the matches between the query ranges are retrieved.

In k-*nearest* neighbor queries, a similar fashion is carried out as in the *range* queries. This time, client queries are represented with a feature vector and a positive integer k. As in range queries, more than one answer can be returned for a user query. The query result is defined as the best k-match in the database.

3.4 Querying by Chorus Sections

In Section 2, we described extraction of the expressive summaries in terms of chorus and key concept for music and speech, respectively. This type of information is particularly valuable in music industry, such as one can perform browsing or querying using the generated summaries. An additional use of this query can be the musical copyright management.

In chorus queries, a client query is an audio clip and performed as follows: Firstly, the query item supplied by the client is analyzed in order to generate the expressive summary for that item. Afterwards, we obtain a feature vector, which knows the location of its expressive summary for the query item. Secondly, we correlate this summary with the previously generated and stored summaries within the database. The reader should note that, the query is carried out between the generated summaries, thus reducing the search complexity. The final step is to populate and rank the query results according to their relevance.

4 Experimental Results

In our experiment, we create an audio database, which consists of approximately 4 hours and 28 minutes of songs (totally 64 songs), 32 minutes of speech clips, and 100 sound effects. The songs are mostly populated from the artist *The Beatles*.

All the songs are sampled at the rate of $44.1kHz$, stereo channel, and encoded by $16 - bit$ per sample. For evaluations, the output of the proposed approach is compared with a number of chorus sections obtained by manually annotating each audio clip. In the overall, our method correctly extracted and located 148 of 172 chorus sections, which results $148/172 = 86\%$ recall rate within the songs. When the MFCC is applied to our algorithm, it results 82% recall rate within the songs. As a result, the MPEG-7 ASF performs slightly better than the MFCC.

In the case of speech data, we prepared a scenario that deals with synthetic data due to the lack of sufficient annotated speech clips. In order to generate synthetic data that are suitable for our approach, we prepared three speech texts that include some words repeating themselves in regular frequencies. The first one is obtained from a news portal regarding with *South Asia Quake*, and the other two are selected from computer science lecture notes. These texts are then sampled at the rate of CD quality by talking to a microphone. In order to take into account the potential acoustics variations, this procedure is carried out for five male and female speakers. The evaluation for speech data is then performed in a similar fashion as music data. The method correctly extracts and locates 93 of 120 key concepts within the speech clips, which results $93/120 = 78\%$ recall rate for the database. Particularly, the recognition rate of the MFCC (87%) is slightly better than the recognition rate of the MPEG-7 ASF (78%), since some male and female speeches are better recognized by the MFCC than by the MPEG-7 ASF. This result can be described by the utilized frequency scale of both features. For speech data, the frequency scaling utilized by the MFCC (linear scale below $1kHz$ and logarithmic scale above $1kHz$) is more robust compared to MPEG-7 ASF, since voice signals have most of their energy below 1 kHz.

5 Conclusion

In this paper, we integrated the three considered aspects of content-based audio management into a single framework and proposed an efficient method for flexible querying and browsing of auditory data. The querying and browsing facilities are realized based on the audio excerpts and the generated similarity matrix. It is presented how audio excerpts and similarity matrix can be used in flexible querying of large audio databases consisting of music, speech, and sound effects. We make use of the MPEG-7 ASF and the MFCC feature sets in order to improve the content-based retrieval accuracy, since both features have some advantages over music and speech data. Experiments show that the MPEG-7 ASF is superior to the MFCC for musical audio, on the other hand, the MFCC performs better job than the MPEG-7 ASF for speech data.

Topics for future research include the integration of the proposed framework with a Web-based query interface and to explore possible enhancements in the feature and excerpt extraction processes.

Acknowledgment

The authors would like to thank Prof. Dr. İnan Güler for his valuable assistance and support.

References

1. Aigrain, P., Zhang, H., Petkovic, D.: Content-based Representation and Retrieval of Visual Media: A State-of-the-art Review. Multimedia Tools and Applications, 3(3):179-202 (1996)
2. Chai, W., Vercoe, B.: Music Thumbnailing via Structural Analysis. Proceedings of ACM Multimedia Conference, (2003)
3. Bartsch, M., Wakefield, G.: Audio Thumbnailing of Popular Music Using Croma-Based Representations. IEEE Transactions on Multimedia, 7(1):96-104 (2005)

4. Bach, J.R.: The Virage Image Search Engine: An Open Framework for Image Management. In Proceedings of SPIE'96, San Jose California (1996)
5. Niblack, W., Zhu, X., et al.: Updates to the QBIC System. In Proceedings of SPIE'98, San Jose California (1998)
6. Amato, G., Mainetto, G., Savino, P.: An Approach to a Content-Based Retrieval of Multimedia Data. Multimedia Tools and Applications, 7(1/2):9-36 (1998)
7. Wold, E., Blum, T., Keislar, D., et al.: Content-based Classification, Search, and Retrieval of Audio. IEEE Multimedia, 3(3):27-36 (1996)
8. Foote, J.: Content-based Retrieval of Music and Audio. In Proc. of SPIE'97, (1997)
9. Zhang, T., Jay Kuo, C.-C.: Content-based Classification and Retrieval of Audio. In Proceedings of SPIE'98, San Diego (1998)
10. Lu, L., Jiang, H., Zhang, H.: A Robust Audio Classification and Segmentation Method. In Proc. of the 9th ACM Int. Conf. on Multimedia, Ottawa Canada (2001)
11. Tzanetakis, G., Cook, P.: Multifeature Audio Segmentation for Browsing and Annotation. In IEEE WASPAA conference, New Paltz NY (1999)
12. Pfeiffer, S.: Pause Concepts for Audio Segmentation at Different Semantic Levels. In Proc. of the 9th ACM Int. Conf. on Multimedia, Ottawa Canada (2001)
13. Chai, W., Vercoe, B.: Structural Analysis of Musical Signals for Indexing and Thumbnailing. In Proceedings of the 3rd ACM/IEEE-CS joint Conference on Digital Libraries, Houston Texas (2003)
14. Cooper, M., Foote, J.: Summarizing Popular Music via Structural Similarity Analysis. In IEEE WASPAA conference, New Paltz NY (2003)
15. Goto, M.: A Chorus-Section Detecting Method for Musical Audio Signals. In IEEE Int. Conf. on Acoustics, Speech, and Signal Processing, Hong Kong China (2003)
16. MPEG-7.: Information Technology - Multimedia Content Description Interface - Part 4: Audio ISO/IEC JTC 1/SC 29/WG 11 (2000)
17. Lloyd, S.P.: Least Squares Quantization in PCM. IEEE Transaction on Information Theory, IT-2:129-137 (1982)
18. Wellhausen, J., Crysandt, H.: Temporal Audio Segmentation using MPEG-7 Descriptors. In Proceedings of SPIE, Santa Clara (CA) USA (2003)
19. Xu, C., Zhu, Y., and Tian, Q.: Automatic Music Summarization Based on Temporal, Spectral and Cepstral Features. Proceedings of IEEE ICME'02, (2002)
20. Lu, L., Wang, M., and Zhang, H.J.: Repeating Pattern Discovery and Structure Analysis from Acoustic Music Data (MIR' 04), New York USA (2004)
21. Lu, G.: Indexing and Retrieval of Audio: A Survey. Multimedia Tools and Applications, 15(3):269-290 (2001)
22. Sert, M., Baykal, B., Yazıcı, A.: Generating Expressive Summaries for Speech and Musical Audio using Self-similarity Clues. To appear in Proc. of IEEE ICME2006, Toronto, Ontario Canada (2006)

Similarity Between Multi-valued Thesaurus Attributes: Theory and Application in Multimedia Systems

Tom Matthé[1], Rita De Caluwe[1], Guy De Tré[1], Axel Hallez[1], Jörg Verstraete[1], Marc Leman[2], Olmo Cornelis[2], Dirk Moelants[2], and Jos Gansemans[3]

[1] Ghent University, Dept. of Telecommunications and Information Processing, Sint-Pietersnieuwstraat 41, B-9000 Gent, Belgium
{Tom.MATTHE, Rita.DECALUWE, Guy.DETRE, Axel.HALLEZ, Jorg.VERSTRAETE}@UGent.be

[2] Ghent University, Dept. of Musicology, Blandijnberg 2, B-9000 Gent, Belgium
{Marc.LEMAN, Olmo.CORNELIS, Dirk.MOELANTS}@UGent.be

[3] Royal Museum for Central Africa, Dept. of Ethnomusicology, Leuvensesteenweg 13, B-3080 Tervuren, Belgium
Jos.GANSEMANS@africamuseum.be

Abstract. In this paper, the theoretical aspects of calculating the similarity between sets, and its generalizations multisets, fuzzy sets and fuzzy multisets, is presented. Afterwards, this theory is applied to enhance the facilities for accessing a multimedia system, namely when searching for correspondence between multi-valued attributes, which are coupled with a thesaurus. Furthermore, to allow flexibility in this search, thesauri with similarities defined between the thesaurus terms are considered. As a possible application, the DEKKMMA project is introduced, a project about an audio archive of African music.

1 Introduction

Musical audio is an important multimedia type. It is also an important issue for archivists all over the world. The DEKKMMA-project[1], a cooperation between the Royal Museum for Central Africa and Ghent University, is an example of this. Mainly due to Belgium's colonial history, the Royal Museum for Central Africa near Brussels owns one of the largest and world wide most important collections of music recordings from Central Africa. Apart from conservation and sometimes restoration of the historical sources such as wax cylinders, sonofil wires and magnetic tapes, the museum wanted to preserve its rich musical audio collection and linked contextual information in a digital audio archive. The primary goal of the DEKKMMA-project is to digitize the museum collection and to set up a database

[1] The DEKKMMA-project is financed by the Belgian Federal Science Policy Office under project nr. 12/AE/212. The work presented in this paper is realized within the scope of this project.

H.L. Larsen et al. (Eds.): FQAS 2006, LNAI 4027, pp. 331–342, 2006.

system that allows to store both the digital sources and the contextual information. The secondary goal of the project is to open up the archive to a broad public in such a way that different groups of users, such as visitors, researchers, etc., can easily and efficiently find the information they are looking for.

This paper focusses on one aspect of accessing such a multimedia system, namely finding similarities between attributes of the meta-data[2] of different records in the database, such as the title of the piece, the geographical origin, the name of the musicians, instruments used ... This is an important aspect when searching for similarities between different records, e.g. when querying by 'example' to find the records *similar* to the 'example'.

The focus in this paper will lie on multi-valued attributes (single-valued attributes are special cases of this). As an illustration, consider the instrumental composition of the audio pieces in the archive. Users might be interested in searching for pieces with a similar instrumental composition to that of the piece they have found already.

To allow flexibility in the search, multi-valued attributes coupled with a thesaurus which stores also similarities between different thesaurus terms, will be considered.

In the following Section, the theoretical aspects of calculating the similarity between different types of sets (*regular* sets, multisets, fuzzy sets and fuzzy multisets) is presented. How to apply the theory when comparing multi-valued attributes is subsequently discussed in Section 3. Finally, in Section 4, some conclusions and plans for future work are stated.

2 Similarity in Set Theory

The similarity between two concepts A and B (notation: $sim(A, B)$) is the degree to which A corresponds to B. In general, a similarity relationship needs to satisfy following properties:

- **Reflexivity** $\forall x : sim(x, x) = 1$
- **Symmetry** $\forall x, y : sim(x, y) = sim(y, x)$
- **Transitivity** $\forall x, z : sim(x, z) \geq \sup_y \ \min(sim(x, y), sim(y, z))$

As similarity measure, the Jaccard similarity measure [4] is taken here. The proposal of usage of the fuzzy Jaccard coefficient as a measure of similarity for building fuzzy thesauri is due to Miyamoto [9, 12, 15] who first used it in the context of information retrieval and clustering.

The Jaccard similarity measure is defined as the number of elements shared by the two concepts, divided by the total number of unique elements in both concepts combined. In set theory this can be expressed as the ratio of the number of corresponding elements in A and B, to the total number of elements in A and B together. In this paper only discrete and finite sets will be considered.

[2] In the audiovisual world, meta-data is the contextual information about the music. In the database world, meta-data refers to information about the database and its schema.

The following subsections will successively discuss the similarity between sets, multisets, fuzzy sets and fuzzy multisets.

2.1 Sets

Let A and B be sets. The number of corresponding elements in A and B is the cardinality of the intersection of A and B, while the total number of elements in A and B is the cardinality of the union of A and B. This leads to the following formula for calculating the similarity between A and B ($|Z|$ denotes the cardinality of a set Z):

$$sim(A, B) = \frac{|A \cap B|}{|A \cup B|} \tag{1}$$

When defining sets by means of a characteristic function $f : X \to \{0, 1\}$ (notation: $A = \langle X, f \rangle$), where X is the domain or universe, the cardinality can be calculated as the sum, over all elements x in the domain X, of $f(x)$ ($|A| = \sum_x f(x)$).

Let $A = \langle X, f \rangle$ and $B = \langle X, g \rangle$ be sets in X, with respective characteristic functions f and g, then

$$\begin{aligned} A \cap B = \langle X, m \rangle \text{ with } \forall x \in X : \; m(x) &= \begin{cases} 1 & \text{if } f(x) = 1 \wedge g(x) = 1 \\ 0 & \text{otherwise} \end{cases} \\ &= \min(f(x), g(x)) \end{aligned} \tag{2}$$

and

$$\begin{aligned} A \cup B = \langle X, n \rangle \text{ with } \forall x \in X : \; n(x) &= \begin{cases} 1 & \text{if } f(x) = 1 \vee g(x) = 1 \\ 0 & \text{otherwise} \end{cases} \\ &= \max(f(x), g(x)) \end{aligned} \tag{3}$$

The similarity can then be calculated as:

$$sim(A, B) = \frac{|A \cap B|}{|A \cup B|} = \frac{\sum_x m(x)}{\sum_x n(x)} = \frac{\sum_x \min(f(x), g(x))}{\sum_x \max(f(x), g(x))} \tag{4}$$

Example
Figure 1 shows an example: let $A = \{a, b, c, d, e\}$ and $B = \{a, c, e, f\}$ be two sets.

Then: $A \cap B = \{a, c, e\}$, $A \cup B = \{a, b, c, d, e, f\}$ and $sim(A, B) = \frac{|A \cap B|}{|A \cup B|} = \frac{3}{6} = \frac{1}{2}$.

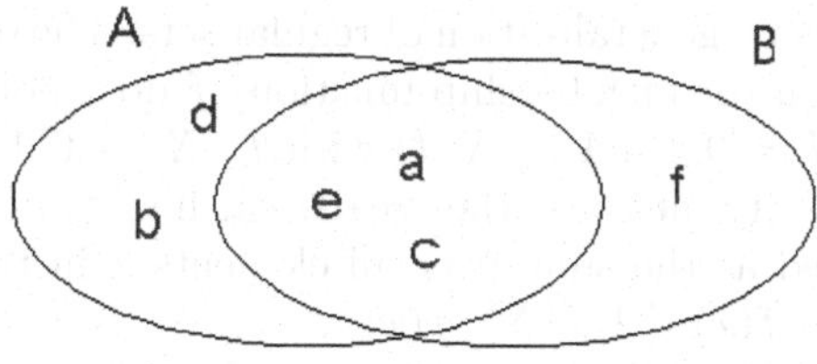

Fig. 1.

2.2 Multisets

Multisets (also called bags) are a generalization of regular sets [1, 2, 6, 9, 10, 17]. The difference is that the characteristic function f does not map to $\{0, 1\}$, but to $\mathbb{N}$, the set of the natural numbers ($A = \langle X, f\rangle$ with $f : X \to \mathbb{N}$ is a multiset). The cardinality of a multiset can still be calculated as the sum, over all elements x in the domain X, of its characteristic function $f(x)$ ($|A| = \sum_x f(x)$).

Let $A = \langle X, f\rangle$ and $B = \langle X, g\rangle$ be multisets in X, with respective characteristic functions f and g, then

$$A \cap B = \langle X, m\rangle \text{ with } \forall x \in X : \; m(x) = \min(f(x), g(x)) \tag{5}$$

and

$$A \cup B = \langle X, n\rangle \text{ with } \forall x \in X : \; n(x) = \max(f(x), g(x)) \tag{6}$$

The similarity can then be calculated as:

$$sim(A, B) = \frac{|A \cap B|}{|A \cup B|} = \frac{\sum_x m(x)}{\sum_x n(x)} = \frac{\sum_x \min(f(x), g(x))}{\sum_x \max(f(x), g(x))} \tag{7}$$

Example

Figure 2 shows an example: let $A = \{a, a, a, b, b, c, d, e\}$ and $B = \{a, a, c, c, e, f, f\}$ be two multisets.

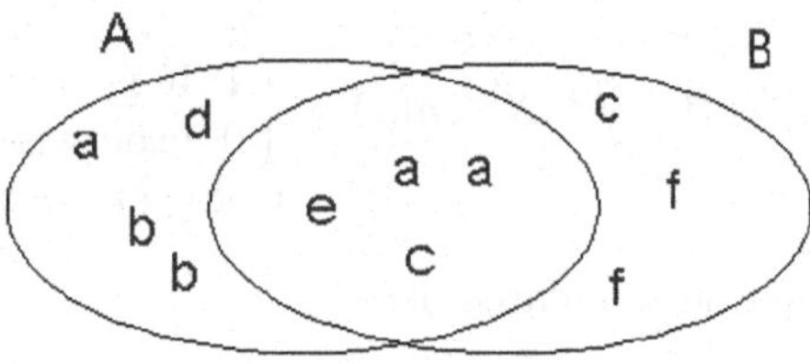

Fig. 2.

Then: $A \cap B = \{a, a, c, e\}$, $A \cup B = \{a, a, a, b, b, c, c, d, e, f, f\}$ and $sim(A, B) = \frac{|A \cap B|}{|A \cup B|} = \frac{4}{11}$.

2.3 Fuzzy Sets

Fuzzy sets [18] are also a generalization of regular sets. The difference is that the characteristic function (or membership function) f does not map to $\{0, 1\}$, but to the unit interval $I = [0, 1]$ ($A = \langle X, f\rangle$ with $f : X \to [0, 1]$ is a fuzzy set). For calculating the similarity measure, the "scalar cardinality" of a fuzzy set will be used, which is defined as the sum, over all elements x in the domain X, of its membership function $f(x)$ ($|A| = \sum_x f(x)$).

Let $A = \langle X, f\rangle$ and $B = \langle X, g\rangle$ be fuzzy sets in X, with respective characteristic functions f and g, then (using the standard intersect and union operators [18]):

$$A \cap B = \langle X, m \rangle \text{ with } \forall x \in X: \; m(x) = \min(f(x), g(x)) \tag{8}$$

and

$$A \cup B = \langle X, n \rangle \text{ with } \forall x \in X: \; n(x) = \max(f(x), g(x)) \tag{9}$$

The similarity can then be calculated as:

$$sim(A, B) = \frac{|A \cap B|}{|A \cup B|} = \frac{\sum_x m(x)}{\sum_x n(x)} = \frac{\sum_x \min(f(x), g(x))}{\sum_x \max(f(x), g(x))} \tag{10}$$

Example
Let $A = \{(a, 1), \; (b, 0.3), \; (c, 0.8), \; (d, 0.6), \; (e, 0.2)\}$ and
$B = \{(a, 0.7), \; (c, 1), \; (e, 0.4), \; (f, 0.9)\}$ be two fuzzy sets, then:
$A \cap B = \{(a, 0.7), \; (c, 0.8), \; (e, 0.2)\}$,
$A \cup B = \{(a, 1), \; (b, 0.3), \; (c, 1), \; (d, 0.6), \; (e, 0.4), \; (f, 0.9)\}$
and $sim(A, B) = \frac{|A \cap B|}{|A \cup B|} = \frac{1.7}{4.2}$.

2.4 Fuzzy Multisets

Fuzzy multisets [3, 7, 8, 9, 13, 14, 16, 17] are a combination of fuzzy sets and multisets. It are multisets in which the elements have a membership degree in the unit interval $I = [0, 1]$. $A = \langle X, f \rangle$ is a fuzzy multiset if the characteristic function f maps to the powerset of multisets over $I = [0, 1]$: $f : X \rightarrow \wp(\langle [0, 1], g \rangle)$, with $g : [0, 1] \rightarrow \mathbb{N}$.

For calculating the similarity measure, the "scalar cardinality" of a fuzzy multiset will be used, which is defined as the sum, over all elements x in the domain X, of the sum of the elements in the multiset $f(x)$ over $I = [0, 1]$ to which x is mapped: $|A| = \sum_x \sum_{i \in f(x)} i \cdot g(i)$, where $g(i)$ is the multiplicity of $i \in [0, 1]$ in the multiset $f(x)$ over $[0, 1]$.

Example
$A = \{(a, 1), \; (a, 0.8), \; (a, 0.3), \; (b, 0.9), \; (b, 0.1), \; (d, 0.7), \; (d, 0.7), \; (d, 0.4)\}$ is a fuzzy multiset over domain $X = \{a, b, c, d\}$, with $f(a) = \{1, \; 0.8, \; 0.3\}$, $f(b) = \{0.9, \; 0.1\}$, $f(c) = \emptyset$ and $f(d) = \{0.7, \; 0.7, \; 0.4\}$. Another notation is: $A = \{(a, [1, \; 0.8, \; 0.3]), \; (b, [0.9, \; 0.1]), \; (d, [0.7, \; 0.7, \; 0.4])\}$, with $[x, y, z]$ here as the representation of a multiset. The scalar cardinality is calculated as: $|A| = 1 + 0.8 + 0.3 + 0.9 + 0.1 + 0 + 0.7 \times 2 + 0.4 = 4.9$

Let $A = \langle X, f \rangle$ and $B = \langle X, g \rangle$ be fuzzy multisets in X, with respective characteristic functions f and g, as followed:

$$A = \{(x_1, [\mu_{11}, \ldots, \mu_{1l_1}]), \ldots, (x_n, [\mu_{n1}, \ldots, \mu_{nl_n}])\} \tag{11}$$

and

$$B = \{(x_1, [\mu'_{11}, \ldots, \mu'_{1l'_1}]), \ldots, (x_n, [\mu'_{n1}, \ldots, \mu'_{nl'_n}])\} \tag{12}$$

Now suppose that, $\forall i$, $[\mu^p_{i1}, \ldots, \mu^p_{il^p_i}]$ and $[\mu'^p_{i1}, \ldots, \mu'^p_{il'^p_i}]$ are permutations of $[\mu_{i1}, \ldots, \mu_{il_1}]$ and $[\mu'_{i1}, \ldots, \mu'_{il'_1}]$ respectively, which are in decreasing order, and which have all the same length l (if necessary extra $0's$ are added): $l^p_1 = \ldots = l^p_n = l'^p_1 = \ldots = l'^p_n = l$. Then (using the standard intersect and union operators):

$$A \cap B = \langle X, m \rangle \text{ with } \forall x_i \in X: \; m(x_i) = \{\mu^{\cap}_{i1}, \ldots, \mu^{\cap}_{il}\} \\ \text{where } \mu^{\cap}_{ij} = \min(\mu^p_{ij}, \mu'^p_{ij}) \tag{13}$$

and

$$A \cup B = \langle X, n \rangle \text{ with } \forall x_i \in X: \; n(x_i) = \{\mu^{\cup}_{i1}, \ldots, \mu^{\cup}_{il}\} \\ \text{where } \mu^{\cup}_{ij} = \max(\mu^p_{ij}, \mu'^p_{ij}) \tag{14}$$

The similarity can then be calculated as:

$$sim(A, B) = \frac{|A \cap B|}{|A \cup B|} = \frac{\sum_{i,j} \mu^{\cap}_{ij}}{\sum_{i,j} \mu^{\cup}_{ij}}. \tag{15}$$

Example

Let $A = \{(a, 0.3), (a, 1), (a, 0.5), (b, 0.9), (b, 0.1), (d, 0.4), (d, 0.7), (d, 0.7)\}$ and $B = \{(a, 0.6), (a, 0.7), (c, 1), (c, 0.3), (d, 0.4), (d, 0.5), (e, 0.9)\}$ be two fuzzy multisets. First they have to be rewritten as:

$A = \{ (a, 1), (a, 0.5), (a, 0.3), (b, 0.9), (b, 0.1), (b, 0), (c, 0), (c, 0), (c, 0), (d, 0.7), (d, 0.7), (d, 0.4), (e, 0), (e, 0), (e, 0)\}$,

$B = \{ (a, 0.7), (a, 0.6), (a, 0), (b, 0), (b, 0), (b, 0), (c, 1), (c, 0.3), (c, 0), (d, 0.5), (d, 0.4), (d, 0), (e, 0.9), (e, 0), (e, 0)\}$

and then:

$A \cap B = \{ (a, 0.7), (a, 0.5), (a, 0), (b, 0), (b, 0), (b, 0), (c, 0), (c, 0), (c, 0), (d, 0.5), (d, 0.4), (d, 0), (e, 0), (e, 0), (e, 0)\}$,

$A \cup B = \{ (a, 1), (a, 0.6), (a, 0.3), (b, 0.9), (b, 0.1), (b, 0), (c, 1), (c, 0.3), (c, 0), (d, 0.7), (d, 0.7), (d, 0.4), (e, 0.9), (e, 0), (e, 0)\}$

and $sim(A, B) = \frac{|A \cap B|}{|A \cup B|} = \frac{\sum_{i,j} \mu^{\cap}_{ij}}{\sum_{i,j} \mu^{\cup}_{ij}} = \frac{2.1}{6.9}$.

3 Similarity Between Multi-valued Thesaurus Attributes

In this section, the theoretical concepts presented in previous section are applied in the context of calculating the similarity between multi-valued thesaurus attributes. Consider for instance an audio archive. Typically, the meta-data stored in the audio archive consists of several thesaurus based attributes, like geographical information, instrument(s) used, genre, function, etc. It might be useful to users who are querying the archive to allow them to use 'query by *example*', e.g. when the user has an *example* record, which he or she likes, he or she might be very interested in finding similar records. An important aspect in finding similar records is finding similarities between the multi-valued (and, as a special case, single-valued) attributes of the meta-data, e.g. finding a similar instrumental composition.

The value of a multi-valued thesaurus attribute can be expressed as a set (or possibly a multiset) of thesaurus terms. For the moment, only crisp (multi)sets will be considered, and to be easily comparable, all thesaurus terms come from the same level in the thesaurus hierarchy. Therefor, in what follows, it is assumed that the thesauri have no hierarchies. The next subsections will look at different types of thesauri, from simple to more advanced, and how to calculate the similarity measure using these thesauri. As example of a multi-valued attribute, the instrumental composition of a record in an audio archive will be considered, which is a set or multiset of instruments used in the audio fragment.

3.1 Thesaurus as a List of Values

First take a look at the simplest form of a thesaurus, a crisp thesaurus with no synonyms or similarities between thesaurus terms. In fact, in this case the thesaurus is just a list of possible values for the coupled attribute, e.g. a list of possible instruments. The similarity, in e.g. instrumental composition, between two records can be easily calculated as the similarity between the respective sets (or multisets) of thesaurus terms representing the multi-valued attributes, as presented above.

Example
Let $A = \{x,\ u,\ v\}$ and $B = \{x,\ x,\ y,\ z\}$ be two multisets representing the instrumental composition of two records, then the similarity is $\frac{1}{6}$ ($A \cap B = \{x\}$, $A \cup B = \{x,\ x,\ u,\ v,\ y,\ z\}$).

3.2 Thesaurus with Synonyms

In a more advanced thesaurus, some terms can be defined as synonyms of other terms. E.g. in an instruments thesaurus the “Traverso” can be defined as a synonym for the “Transverse flute”. If this is the case, similarity between instrumentation of different records can not be directly calculated as the similarity between the respective (multi)sets, because although two terms are unequal, it is perfectly possible that they are synonyms of one another and should be considered as completely similar.

Therefor, when multi-valued attribute A is compared to multi-valued attribute B (coupled to the same thesaurus), and some of the values in the (multi)set representing A are synonyms of a value in the (multi)set representing B, either A (or B) has to be transformed in terms of the values of B (respectively A), taking into account the synonyms defined in the thesaurus. Only the values having a synonym in the other attribute have to be transformed. The other values can stay unaltered. After the transformation, the similarity can be calculated as the similarity measure between the respective multisets.

Example
Let $A = \{u\}$ and $B = \{x,\ y,\ z\}$ be two multisets (actually, in this case, they are regular sets) representing the instrumental composition of two records. First try

to transform A (take the multiset with lowest cardinality) in terms of instruments in B. If instrument u is not a synonym of any of the instruments in B (x, y, z), A does not need transformation and the similarity between the two records, regarding the instrumentation, can be calculated as the similarity between the (multi)sets A and B, which is $\frac{0}{4} = 0$ ($A \cap B = \emptyset$, $A \cup B = \{u, x, y, z\}$). However if instrument u is a synonym of one of the instruments in B (take x), A first has to be transformed into $A = \{x\}$, after which the similarity between the two records can be calculated as the similarity between the (multi)sets A and B, which is $\frac{1}{3}$ ($A \cap B = \{x\}$, $A \cup B = \{x, y, z\}$).

When transforming multiset A in terms of values in multiset B, the cardinality of the values in B have to be taken into account. When more than one value in multiset A is equal to or a synonym of the same value in multiset B (with cardinality c), only c of them can be regarded as equal and can be transformed. Following algorithm formalizes the transformation process.

Algorithm

Let A and B be two multi-valued attributes coupled with a thesaurus with synonyms, and A and B their respective multisets representing them. To calculate the similarity between A and B, first transform the multiset with lowest cardinality as followed (suppose A has the lowest cardinality):

1. Set $X = A$ as source and $Y = B$ as target multiset.
2. **Eliminate equals.** If u appears both in X and Y, with respective cardinalities c_u^X and c_u^Y, then delete u c_u times from both X and Y, with $c_u = \min(c_u^X, c_u^Y)$. Do this for every value appearing both in X and Y, then $X = X \setminus (X \cap Y)$ and $Y = Y \setminus (X \cap Y)$.
3. **Eliminate synonyms.** If u and v are synonyms and appear in X and Y respectively, with cardinalities c_u^X and c_v^Y, then replace u by v in multiset A, and this c times, with $c = \min(c_u^X, c_v^Y)$. Also delete u c times from X and v c times from Y.
   Repeat this step for all synonyms (still) appearing in X and Y.

Once A is transformed, the similarity between A and B can be calculated as the similarity measure between multisets A and B: $sim(A, B) = \frac{|A \cap B|}{|A \cup B|}$.

Example

Let $A = \{x, u, v\}$ and $B = \{x, x, y, z\}$ be two multisets representing the instrumentation of two records, and instruments u and v are synonyms of instrument x. Then A must be transformed to $A = \{x, x, v\}$ (v cannot be transformed to x because there are already 2 other synonyms (or equals) of x), and the similarity is $\frac{2}{5}$ ($A \cap B = \{x, x\}$, $A \cup B = \{x, x, v, y, z\}$).

3.3 Thesaurus with Similarities

Finally consider a thesaurus where not only synonyms can be defined, but also similarities in $[0, 1]$ between thesaurus terms. E.g. in an instruments thesaurus it might be possible to consider a "Recorder" as similar to a "Transverse flute" to a degree 0.6. In this case, when calculating the similarity between the instrumentation of two records, the similarities between the instruments in the thesaurus have to be taken into account. There are not only synonyms (similarity 1), but also *partial* synonyms (similarity in $]0,1[$).

Therefor, when a multi-valued attribute A is compared to another multi-valued attribute B (coupled to the same thesaurus), and some of the values in the (multi)set representing A are similar to a value in the (multi)set representing B, either A (or B) has to be transformed in terms of the values of B (respectively A), taking into account the similarities defined in the thesaurus. But this time, in contrast to the situation in previous subsection, the result of the transformation will be a fuzzy multiset.
When transforming, the cardinality has to remain unchanged. Therefor, when transforming u in terms of x (where u is similar to x with degree $s \in [0,1]$), the result will not be x/s but $\{(x,s),\ (u,1-s)\}$.

Finally the similarity can be calculated as the similarity measure between a fuzzy multiset and a multiset, which is a special case of calculating the similarity measure between two fuzzy multisets, which is explained above.

Example
Let $A = \{u\}$ and $B = \{x,\ y,\ z\}$ be two multisets (actually, in this case, they are regular sets) representing the instrumental composition of two records. First try to transform A (take the multiset with lowest cardinality) in terms of values in B. If instrument u is not similar to any of the instruments in B $(x,\ y,\ z)$, A does not need transformation and the similarity between the two records, regarding the instrumentation, can be calculated as the similarity between the (multi)sets A and B, which is $\frac{0}{4} = 0$ $(A \cap B = \emptyset,\ A \cup B = \{u,\ x,\ y,\ z\})$. However if instrument u is similar to one of the instruments in B (take x) with similarity degree s, A first has to be transformed into fuzzy (multi)set $A = \{(x,s),\ (u,1-s)\}$, after which the similarity between the two records can be calculated as the similarity between the fuzzy (multi)sets A and B, which is $\frac{s}{4-s}$ $(A \cap B = \{(x,s)\},\ A \cup B = \{(u,1-s),\ (x,1),\ (y,1),\ (z,1)\})$. Following algorithm formalizes the transformation process:

Algorithm
Let A and B be two multi-valued attributes coupled with a thesaurus with similarities, and A and B their respective multisets representing them. To calculate the similarity between A and B, first transform the multiset with lowest cardinality as followed (suppose A has the lowest cardinality):

1. Set $X = A$ as source and $Y = B$ as target multiset.
2. **Eliminate equals.** If u appears both in X and Y, with respective cardinalities c_u^X and c_u^Y, then delete u c_u times from both X and Y, with $c_u = \min(c_u^X, c_u^Y)$. Do this for every value appearing both in X and Y, then $X = X \setminus (X \cap Y)$ and $Y = Y \setminus (X \cap Y)$.

3. **Eliminate similarities.** Take the couple (u, v) with highest similarity degree s_{uv}, where u appears in X and v appears in Y, with respective cardinalities c_u^X and c_v^Y. Replace replace u by $\{(v, s_{uv}),\ (u, 1 - s_{uv})\}$ in fuzzy multiset A, and this c times, with $c = \min(c_u^X, c_v^Y)$. Also delete u c times from X and v c times from Y.
   Repeat this step until there are no more couples $(u, v) \in X \times Y$ with similarity degree $s_{uv} > 0$.

Once A is transformed, the similarity between A and B can be calculated as the similarity measure between fuzzy multisets A and B: $sim(A, B) = \frac{|A \cap B|}{|A \cup B|}$.

Example
Let $A = \{x,\ u,\ v,\ w\}$ and $B = \{x,\ x,\ y,\ y,\ z\}$ be two multisets representing the instrumentation of two records, and $s_{ux} = 0.8$, $s_{vx} = 0.6$ and $s_{wy} = 0.9$ are similarity degrees between instruments u and x, v and x and w and y respectively. Then the transformation process is as followed:

1. $X = A = \{x,\ u,\ v,\ w\}$ and $Y = B = \{x,\ x,\ y,\ y,\ z\}$.
2. **Eliminate equals.** $X = X \setminus (X \cap Y) = \{u,\ v,\ w\}$ and $Y = Y \setminus (X \cap Y) = \{x,\ y,\ y,\ z\}$.
3. **Eliminate similarities.** $s_{wy} > s_{ux} > s_{vx}$
   3.1 $s_{wy} = 0.9$
   $A = \{x,\ u,\ v,\ (y, 0.9),\ (w, 0.1)\}$
   $X = \{u,\ v\}$ and $Y = \{x,\ y,\ z\}$
   3.2 $s_{ux} = 0.8$
   $A = \{x,\ (x, 0.8),\ (u, 0.2),\ v,\ (y, 0.9),\ (w, 0.1)\}$
   $X = \{v\}$ and $Y = \{y,\ z\}$
   3.3 No more similarity couples can be found in $X \times Y$

Finally A is transformed to $A = \{x,\ (x, 0.8),\ (u, 0.2),\ v,\ (y, 0.9),\ (w, 0.1)\}$.
Then: $A \cap B = \{(x, 1),\ (x, 0.8), (y, 0.9)\}$
$A \cup B = \{(x, 1),\ (x, 1),\ (u, 0.2),\ (v, 1),\ (y, 1),\ (y, 1),\ (w, 0.1),\ (z, 1)\}$
and the similarity is $sim(A, B) = \frac{|A \cap B|}{|A \cup B|} = \frac{2.7}{6.3}$.

4 Application in DEKKMMA

As said above, the DEKKMMA project tries to open up an archive of music from Central Africa to a broad public. The goal is to enhance the users search facilities by developing a music information retrieval system aiming at making the audio archive accessible, not only on the basis of the meta-data, but also on the basis of audio content specifications (e.g. rhythm, melody, ...). Query by example could be very useful for different types of users: for museum visitors, e.g. while trying to find music that resembles something they already know; for researchers, e.g. for clustering; ...

Finding similarities between the (multi-valued) meta-data attributes will play an important part in realizing this. E.g. the instrumentation of the music is very important in African music, so when searching for similar audio fragments, a similar instrumentation will be important. But also other attributes could be used, like genre, function, style of playing, geographical origin, ... In the end, the user will be able to perform a search in the archive, based on the combination of the attributes that he/she selects. Possibly, preferences can be attached to them, indicating the relative importance of the respective attributes.

5 Conclusions and Future Work

This paper presented theoretical aspects of calculating the similarity between different types of sets: *regular* set, multisets, fuzzy sets and fuzzy multisets. Afterwards, this theory was applied to calculate the similarity degree between multi-valued attributes, coupled with a thesaurus. To allow flexibility, thesauri with similarities defined between the different thesaurus terms were considered. As an example, the instrumental composition of records in an audio archive was taken.

Future work involves the implementation within the DEKKMMA project, and the integration of the techniques shown here in a larger framework for music information retrieval [11]. Querying based on multiple attributes, with relative preferences attached to them, should be considered. However, searching for similarities between (multi-valued) attributes is only one aspect (of many) in a music information retrieval system. The goal is to combine the techniques presented here with other techniques for flexible querying and also with techniques for audio mining, which work on the information lying in the music itself (rhythm, melody, ...).

Other future work will be to consider fuzzy information in the database itself. In that case the starting point for calculating the similarity degree will not be multisets, but fuzzy multisets, and the algorithm needs to be adapted to that end.

Finally the techniques should be completed to also be able to handle thesauri with hierarchies, and also ontologies.

References

1. W.D. Blizzard, "The Development of Multiset Theory", *Modern Logic* **1** (1991) 319–352.
2. W.D. Blizzard, "Dedekind multiset and function shells", *Theoretical Computer Science* **110** (1993) 79–98.
3. P. Bosc, L. Liétard, O. Pivert, D. Rocacher, *Base de donnée - Gradualité et imprécision dans les bases de données: Ensembles flous, requêtes flexibles et interrogation de données mal connues*, Ellipses (2004).
4. P. Jaccard, "The distribution of the flora of the alpine zone", *New Phytologist* **11** (1912) 37–50.
5. G.J. Klir and B. Yuan, *Fuzzy Sets and Fuzzy Logic: Theory and Applications*, Prentice Hall, New Jersey, USA (1995).

6. D.E. Knuth, *The art of computer programming, Vol 2: Seminumerical Algorithms*, Addison-Wesley, Boston, MA (1981).
7. B. Li, W. Peizhang, L. Xihui, "Fuzzy bags with set-valued statistics", *Journal of Computational and Applied Mathematics* **15** (1988) 811–818.
8. B. Li B, "Fuzzy bags and applications". *Fuzzy Sets and Systems* **34** (1990) 61–71.
9. Z.-Q. Liu, S. Miyamoto (Eds.), *Soft computing and human-centered machines*, Springer, Tokyo (2000).
10. Z. Manna, R. Waldinger, *The logical basis for computer programming, Vol 1: Deductive reasoning*, Addison-Wesley, Boston, MA (1985).
11. T. Matthé, G. de Tré, A. Hallez, R. de Caluwe, M. Leman, O. Cornelis, D. Moelants, J. Gansemans, "A framework for flexible querying and mining of musical audio archives", *Proc. of First International Workshop on Integrating Data Mining, Database and Information Retrieval IDDI 2005, at DEXA 2005* (Copenhagen, Denmark, August 22, 2005) 1041–1054.
12. S. Miyamoto, *Fuzzy sets in information retrieval and cluster analysis*, Kluwer Academic Publishers, Dordrecht (1990).
13. S. Miyamoto, "Basic operations of fuzzy multisets". *Journal of Japanese Society of Fuzzy Theory Systems* **8** (1996) 639–645 [in Japanese].
14. S. Miyamoto, "Fuzzy Multisets and Their Generalizations". *Lecture Notes In Computer Science* **2235** (2000) 225–236.
15. S. Miyamoto, "Information clustering based on fuzzy multisets". *Information Processing and Management: an International Journal* **39** 2 (2003) 195–213.
16. A. Ramer, C-C. Wang, "Fuzzy multisets". *Proc. of 1996 Asian Fuzzy Systems Symposium* (Kenting, Taiwan, Dec 11-14, 1996) 429–434.
17. R.R. Yager, "On the theory of bags", *International Journal of General Systems* **13** (1986) 23–37.
18. L.A. Zadeh, "Fuzzy Sets", *Information and Control* **8** 3 (1965) 338–353.

Robust Query Processing for Personalized Information Access on the Semantic Web

Peter Dolog[1], Heiner Stuckenschmidt[2], and Holger Wache[3]

[1] L3S Research Center, Hannover, Germany
dolog@l3s.de
[2] Universität Mannheim, Germany
heiner.stuckenschmidt@uni-mannheim.de
[3] Vrije Universiteit Amsterdam, The Netherlands
holger@cs.vu.nl

Abstract. Research in Cooperative Query answering is triggered by the observation that users are often not able to correctly formulate queries to databases that return the intended result. Due to a lack of knowledge of the contents and the structure of a database, users will often only be able to provide very broad queries. Existing methods for automatically refining such queries based on user profiles often overshoot the target resulting in queries that do not return any answer. In this paper, we investigate methods for automatically relaxing such over-constraint queries based on domain knowledge and user preferences. We describe a framework for information access that combines query refinement and relaxation in order to provide robust, personalized access to heterogeneous RDF data as well as an implementation in terms of rewriting rules and explain its application in the context of e-learning systems.

1 Introduction

Research in Cooperative Query answering is triggered by the observation that users are often not able to correctly formulate queries to databases that return the intended result. This is even more the case for semantic web systems based on RDF for the following reasons:

- The data accessed often comes from different sources. The internal structure of these sources is not always known.
- The data is semi structured. Sources do not have to describe all aspects of the information resources.
- There is no fixed integrated schema. Each source can have its own schema, sources may make partial use of different available schemas.

With the increasing popularity of RDF as a representation language in domains such as medicine [17] or e-leaning [4] this problem becomes more pressing. If RDF query languages are to be used in a large scale we have to make sure that people will be able to formulate meaningful queries. If this is not the case, we have to find ways to still provide the user with the intended results. Cooperative query processing aims at supporting

H.L. Larsen et al. (Eds.): FQAS 2006, LNAI 4027, pp. 343–355, 2006.

the user by automatically modifying the query in order to better fit the real intention of the user. Based on the assumed kind of mismatch between the users intention and the formulated query there are different techniques used. We consider two basic mechanisms of cooperative query processing, *query refinement* and *query relaxation* which are briefly presented in the following.

1.1 Query Refinement and Relaxation

Due to a lack of knowledge of the contents and the structure of a database, users will often only be able to provide very broad queries, for example in terms of the type of the objects she wants to retrieve and maybe one or two properties. Taking an example from the domain of e-learning, the user might be able to specify that she is looking for a lecture on the Java Programming Language. Learning resources, however, are often annotated with a fair amount of metadata that specifies important information such as the assumed level of expertise and required previous knowledge. In order to select learning resources that are suited for the user, these additional properties have to be specified in the query as well. Dolog et al [4] show that this information can be included into a user query based on a user profile. They describe a method for automatically refining queries with information from the user profile thereby enabling a pre-selection of query answers.

A problem of the automatic refinement of queries lies in the fact that it often overshoots the target instead of too many results an automatically refined query often returns no result at all, because none of the resources exactly matches the users needs. A possible solution to this problem is to successively relax the constraints imposed in the refinement step. Different Techniques for relaxing queries have been proposed in the database area. Gaasterland et al [6] provide a unifying view on different relaxation techniques in terms of replacing subexpressions in the query. In previous work we described an approach for relaxing conjunctive queries over description logic knowledge bases by removing conjuncts from the query in a particular order [16, 18] .

1.2 Contributions

In this paper, we build upon existing work on query refinement for personalized information access and extend it in the following ways:

- We describe a framework for information access that combines query refinement and relaxation in order to provide robust, personalized access to heterogeneous RDF data.
- We propose an implementation of the framework in terms of conditional rewriting rules for RDF query patterns.
- We discuss the application of the framework in the context of an existing e-learning system.

2 Background

User queries to the open learning environment will consist of one or several keywords related to the topic the user wants to learn about. The result is a list of learning resources including information about the subject and the title of the resource as well as

```
SELECT * FROM
  {Resource} subject {Subject},
  {Resource} title {Title},
  {Resource} description {Description},
WHERE
  Subject Like "inference engines"
```

(a) Basic Query

```
SELECT * FROM
  {Resource} subject {Subject},
  {Resource} title {Title},
  {Resource} description {Description},
  {Resource} language {Language},
  {Resource} requires {} subject {Prerequisite},
  {User} hasPerformance {Performance},
  {Performance} learning_competency {Competence}
WHERE
  Subject Like "inference engines",
  Prerequisite = Competence,
  Language = de,
  User = user42
```

(b) Refined Query

Fig. 1. Rewriting-based Query Refinement

a description of the content. In order to produce this list, the user request is translated into a query an RDF query language that matches the metadata use to describe learning resources in the system. Figure 1(a) shows the query corresponding to a user request for "inference engines" in SeRQL[1] syntax .

In a second step, the general query shown in figure 1(a) is adapted to better reflect the learning preferences of the user. In this step, the query is refined by extending it with additional constraints that are derived from the user profile. This is done by extending the path expression in the FROM and by adding variable assignments in the WHERE part of the query. Typical additions to a query are a restriction of the language of resources to the preferred language of the user and a general constraint demanding that the user must have all competencies that are required for understanding the resource.

Figure 1(b) shows the result of refining the general query from figure 1(a) with language and competence constraints.

In practice it turns out that the approach of personalization by query refinement suffers from serious problems. In fact problems occur in both steps of the query formulation process. The first problem already occurs when the basic query is formulated. In our open learning repository, this query does not return any result despite the fact that there are 8 resources on the subject. The reason for this is that only about 10% of all resources are completely annotated with subject, title and description. Unfortunately, all 8 potential answers miss at least one of these properties and are therefore not returned as an answer. This problem can be reduced but *making predicates or triples optional in the query*.

Another problem lies in the fact, that the subject assigned to a course does not always correctly summarize the content. In our test data set for example, if the user provides the keyword "Lernen" (German for "learning") no resources are returned despite the fact that there are resources for instance about Bayesian learning and learning in case based reasoning. The problem is here that in the case of the first resource the term learning only occurs in the title, but not the subject. In the case of the second resource, the term only occurs in the description and is mentioned neither in the subject nor the title of the resource. This problem can be used by *replacing predicates in patterns by other ones* based on domain knowledge.

[1] http://www.openrdf.org/doc/sesame/users/ch06.html, We omit namespaces for the sake of readability

We can observe the similar problems in connection with the refinement of the general query based on the user profile as the competence of a user is often defined in terms of learning resources that were successfully mastered by the student. If the subject of previous courses do not exactly match the requirements for a new resource, thus source is excluded from the results even if the topics are very similar. A mechanism for *replacing values in patterns* in query restrictions should be provided to solve the problem by replacing required competence by a similar or more general one. A more general mechanism for approaching this kind of problem is to *replace values by variables and restrict the value of the variable using an appropriate predicate* in the WHERE part of the query.

Further Problems arise from the inflexible nature of the rewriting mechanism that instantiates variables with the preferred value and leaves no room for taking the second best choice if the available resources are for example not in the preferred language, the user does not have all but most of the required competencies or the competencies of the user are not the same but very similar to the required ones. We will come back to these examples when we discuss our solution to the problem.

3 Rewriting RDF Queries

We propose an approach for query rewriting based on Event-Condition-Action (ECA) rules (see e.g. [13]) to solve the problem of over-constraint queries. This rewriting relaxes the over-constraint query based on rules and in order defined by events and conditions. This has an advantage that we start with the strongest possible query that is supposed to return the "best" answers satisfying most of the conditions. If the returned result set is either empty or contains unsatisfactory results, the query is modified either by replacing or deleting parts of the query, or in other words relaxed. The relaxation should be a continuous step by step, (semi-)automatic process, to provide a user with possibility to interrupt further relaxations. Before we investigate concrete relaxation strategies in the context of our example domain, we first give a general definition of the framework for re-writing an RDF query.

Each resource is annotated with an RDF description which can be seen as a set of triples [8]. A query over these resources is formulated as triple patterns and a set of conditions that restrict the possible variables bindings in the patterns. Each triple pattern represents a set of triples. The corresponding abstract definition of a query focuses the essential features of queries over RDF; several concrete query languages are based on these ideas including SeRQL which we use in our examples in figure 1.

Definition 1 (RDF Query). *Let $\mathcal{T}$ be a set of terms, $\mathcal{V}$ a set of variables, $\mathcal{RN}$ a set of relation names, and $\mathcal{PN}$ a set of predicate names. The set of possible triple patterns $\mathcal{TR}$ is defined as $\mathcal{TR} \subseteq 2^{(\mathcal{T}\cup\mathcal{V})\times(\mathcal{RN}\cup\mathcal{V})\times(\mathcal{T}\cup\mathcal{V})}$. A query Q is defined as the tuple $\langle M_Q, O_Q P_Q\rangle$ with $M_Q, O_Q \in \mathcal{TR}$ and $P_Q \subseteq \mathcal{P}$ where M_Q is the set of mandatory pattern (patterns that have to be matched by the result, O_Q is a set of optional pattern (patterns that contribute to the result but do not necessarily have to match the result) and $\mathcal{P}$ is the set of predicates with name $\mathcal{PN}$, defined over $\mathcal{T}$, and $\mathcal{V}$.*

The triple patterns M_Q in a query Q determine those ground triples where a substitution τ exists (τ may also exist for a subset of patterns in O_Q). Formally a substitution τ is a list of pairs (X_i, T_i) where each pair tells which variable X_i has to be replaced by $T_i \in \mathcal{T} \cup \mathcal{V}$. Applied to a query, the substitution τ replaces variables in TR_Q with appropriate terms. If $\tau(M_Q)$ is equal to some ground triples then the substitution is valid. All valid substitutions for M_Q plus existing substitutions for O_Q constitute answers to the query. The predicates P_Q restrict these substitutions additionally because only those bindings are valid answers where the predicates, i.e. $\tau(P_Q)$, are also satisfied. The predicates define additional constraints for the selection of appropriate triples. Using this abstract definition, the query in figure 1(a) would be represented as

$$\begin{aligned} M_Q &= (\{(Resource, subject, Subject), \\ &\quad (Resource, title, Title) \\ &\quad (Resource, description, Description)\}, \\ O_Q &= \{\} \\ P_Q &= \{like(Subject, \text{“}inferenceengines\text{”})\} \end{aligned}$$

where $Resource, Subject, Title, Description \in \mathcal{V}$, as well as $subject, title, description, \text{“}inferenceengines\text{”} \in \mathcal{T}$ and $like \in \mathcal{PN}$. Alternatively, we could use variables as placeholders for the relations and assign the concrete relation names to them as conditions that use the equality predicate. The corresponding definition of the example query would be

$$\begin{aligned} M_Q &= \{(Resource, R1, Subject), \\ &\quad (Resource, R2, Title) \\ &\quad (Resource, R3, Description)\}, \\ O_Q &= \{\} \\ P_Q &= \{R1 = subject, R2 = title, R3 = description, \\ &\quad like(Subject, \text{“}inferenceengines\text{”})\} \end{aligned}$$

where $Resource, Subject, Title, Description, R1, R2, R3 \in \mathcal{V}$, $subject, title, description, \text{"}inferenceengines\text{”} \in \mathcal{T}$ and $like, = \in \mathcal{PN}$. This later representation can be seen as a normal form for queries that makes it easier to formulate re-writings in a general way. For sake of readability we will refer in the following to the original form instead of the normal form.

Based on the abstract definition of an RDF query, we can now define the notion of a rewriting rule and rewriting process as such. We define rewriting in terms of rewriting rules that take parts of a query, in particular triple patterns and conditions, as input and replace them by different elements.

In our work, we employ the principle of rewriting rules that are inspired by ECA-rules (event-condition-action rules) [3, 12] for continuous relaxation of user queries. A rewriting rule formally consists of three parts: a *pattern*, a *replacement* and some *conditions*. The pattern corresponds to the event, i.e. in our case an occurrence of particular triple patterns or predicates in a query. The replacement contains the terms which will substitute the matched pattern in a query; the replacement can be seen as the action in the ECA principle. Conditions constrain the rewriting and determine when particular rule can be fired because the rewriting rule can only be applied if the conditions are satisfied. These conditions can be used to define certain relaxation strategies. In particular, we will see later that conditions can be based on user preferences or background knowledge about the domain.

Definition 2 (Rewriting Rule). *A rewriting rule R is a 3-tuple $\langle PA, RE, CN\rangle$ where PA and RE are RDF queries according to Definition 1 and CN is a set of predicates.*

For conditions the same constructs as for queries are used where the possible results are also constrained by predicates. Patterns and replacements formally have the same structure like queries. They also consist of a set of triples and predicates. But patterns normally do not address complete queries but only a subpart of a query. Using this definition we can specify a rewriting rule that extends the simple query in figure 1(a) with the language preference of the user 42.

$$\begin{aligned} PA &= (\{(Resource, title, Subject)\}, \emptyset, \emptyset) \\ RE &= (\{(Resource, title, Subject), \\ &\quad (Resource, language, Language)\}, \emptyset, \\ &\quad \{Language = X\}) \\ CN &= \{languagePreference(User, X)\} \end{aligned}$$

where $languagePrefernce$ is a predicate which looks in his user profile for the language preference of $User$ who is in our case user 42.

While this example contained a rule for refining a query, we will see later that we can use the same mechanism for defining relaxations on a query.

In general a rewriting rules is applicable to all queries which contain the pattern at least as a part. The pattern does not have to cover the whole query. Normally it addresses some triples as well as some predicates in the query. In order to write more generic rewriting rules the pattern must be instantiated which is done by an substitution.

Definition 3 (Pattern Matching). *A pattern PA of a rewriting rule R is applicable to a query $Q = \langle M_Q, O_Q, P_Q\rangle$ if there are subsets $M'_Q \subseteq M_Q$, $O'_Q \subseteq O_Q$ and $P'_Q \subseteq P_Q$ and a substitution θ with $\langle M'_Q, O'_Q, P'_Q\rangle = \theta(PA)$.*

In contrast to term rewriting systems [1] the definition of a query as two sets of triples and predicates simplifies the pattern matching, i.e. the identification of the right subpart of the query for the pattern match. A subset of both sets has to be determined which must be syntactically equal to the instantiated pattern. Please note that due to set semantics, the triples and predicates in the pattern may be distributed over the query.

Now we will define how the new rewritten query is constructed with the help of the rewriting rule and pattern matching.

Definition 4 (Query Rewriting). *If a rewriting rule $R = \langle PA, RE, CN\rangle$*

- *is applicable to a query $Q = \langle M_Q, O_Q, P_Q\rangle$ with subsets $M'_Q \subseteq M_Q$, $O'_Q \subseteq O_Q$ and $P'_Q \subseteq P_Q$ substitution θ*
- *$\theta(CN)$ is satisfied,*

then the rewritten query $Q^R = \langle M_Q^R, O_Q^R, P_Q^R\rangle$ can be constructed with $M_Q^R = (M_Q \setminus M'_Q) \cup \theta(TR_{RE})$, $O_Q^R = (O_Q \setminus O'_Q) \cup \theta(TR_{RE})$ and $P_Q^R = (P_Q \setminus P'_Q) \cup \theta(P_{RE})$ with $RE = \langle TR_{RE}, P_{RE}\rangle$.

Informally spoken, if the pattern match a query and the conditions are satisfied then the matched pattern is substituted by the replacement.

Applied the above rewriting rule to the basic query we get the following refined rule:

$$\begin{aligned} M_Q &= (\{(Resource, subject, Subject), \\ &\quad (Resource, title, Title) \\ &\quad (Resource, description, Description), \\ &\quad (Resource, language, Language)\}, \\ O_Q &= \emptyset \\ P_Q &= \{like(Subject, \text{“}inferenceengines\text{”}), \\ &\quad \{Language = \text{“}de\text{”}\}) \end{aligned} \tag{1}$$

Please note that the language preference of user 42 is “de” which means German.

4 Domain-Dependent Relaxation

In general the rewriting is a very powerful approach in order to manipulate the over-constrained query. With replacing parts of a query we can realize four types of actions and or course arbitrary combinations of these actions:

- *Making Patterns optional* — this provides a query which considers a situation that some of the patterns do not have to appear in metadata. A query then gives also results where particular predicate relaxed to an optional predicate does not occur;
- *Replacing Value* — this provides a query where particular predicate value is replaced with another value or a variable. Taxonomies may be used to provide siblings, more general terms, and so on;
- *Replacing Patterns/Predicate* — this provides a query where particular triple resp. predicate in restrictions is replaced by another triple resp. predicate. A domain knowledge is employed for this purposes. For example, if a subject query is not satisfied, it may be replaced by title query with similarity measures;
- *Deleting Patterns/Predicate* — this provides a query where particular predicate is deleted from a query completely.

As such, these operations are independent of the application domain and the user preference.

The connection to the domain and the user can be made using a set of special predicates in the condition of the rewriting rules that link the manipulation to specific aspects of the domain and the user model. In the following, we discuss two specific predicates for including information about the domain and the user into the rewriting process.

Domain-preferred-over(X,Y). This predicate indicates that due to the special nature of the domain a certain relation or value is a better choice for retrieving exact results than another one. We can use this to relax queries by replacing a highly preferred value by a less preferred one that is more likely to deliver a result even if this result may be less exact.

User-preferred-over(X,Y). This predicate is defined in the context of a specific user and indicates that the user considers a certain relation more important or prefers a certain value over another one. We can use this predicate to relax queries by replacing highly preferred values by less preferred ones or for deciding which of the predicates in a query can be relaxed more easily, because the user considers it less important.

In order to make the relaxation smooth, we consider these predicate to be non-transitive. The concrete implementation depends on the chosen representation of the domain and the user profile. In the following, we show how domain and user specific relaxations can be specified using these predicates.

Domain Preferences. For example, in the learning environment a user searches a resource with a specific subject. But if there is no resource with that subject then we would like to relax the query that the subject term can also appear in the title of a resource description. This strategy can be derived from a domain preference stating that the "subject" relation has the highest priority as it can be assumed to most precisely reflect the content of a resource followed by the "title" and finally the "description" relation. For the actual relaxation process each of these relations is implemented by a rewriting rule like the following:

$$\begin{aligned} PA &= (\{(Resource, subject, Subject)\}, \emptyset, like(Subject, Value) \\ RE &= (\{(Resource, R, New)\}, \{(Resource, subject, Subject)\}, \\ &\quad \{like(New, Value)\}) \\ CN &= \{domain - preferred - over(subject, R)\} \end{aligned}$$

The triple `{Resource} subject {Subject}` looks for any resource `Resource` with subject `Subject`. The predicate *like* constrains the variable `Subject` to the user's term (`Value`), i.e. the subject the user is looking for. If a query contains such an triple and such an predicate then the rewriting rule is applicable.

The replacement part of the rule defines how the matched triple and predicate has to be replaced. The subject Pattern is replaced by the second triple `{Resource} R {New}`. The pattern about the subject of the resource is made optional because the reason that the original query did not produce any result might have been that the relevant resources did not have any subject.

The rewriting rule can be applied to the query in Figure 1b). The result is shown in Figure 2.

This rule can easily be generalized to a rule that applies to any kind of preferences between relations in query patterns. In this case the concrete relation subject has to be replaced by an appropriate variable. In this case, the rewriting process is completely controlled by the definition of preferences between relations and values.

User Preferences. Another kind of relaxation is the rewriting the over-constrained query according to the knowledge about the user. In the learning scenario the user

```
SELECT * FROM
  [{Resource} subject {Subject}],
  {Resource} title {New},
  {Resource} title {Title},
  {Resource} description {Description},
  {Resource} language {Language},
  {Resource} requires {} subject {Prerequisite},
  {User} hasPerformance {} learning_competency {Competence}
WHERE
  New Like "*inference engines*",
  Prerequisite = Competence,
  Language = de,
  User = user42
```

Fig. 2. Relaxed Query

```
SELECT * FROM
  [{Resource} subject {Subject}],
  {Resource} title {TMPTitle},
  {Resource} title {Title},
  {Resource} description {Description},
  {Resource} language {Language},
  {Resource} requires {} subject {Prerequisite},
  {User} hasPerformance {} learning_competency {Competence}
WHERE
  TMPTitle Like "*inference engines*",
  Prerequisite = Competence,
  Language = nl,
  User = user42
```

Fig. 3. Example of rewritten Query

might prefer learning resources in German but Dutch may also be okay. This knowledge is used to refine the query, i.e. looking for resources in German. However if there is no resources in German then the query can be relaxed according to user's second preference.

In contrast to the domain preferences mentioned in the last section that can be specified inside the application, these preferences can be different for each user. As a consequence we have to provide an interface where each user can specify his or her personal preferences that can then be stored in the user profile. A user interface for that is very simple, a slider is provided next to each item at a user interface for specifying an importance of the predicate for a user. The default slider positions are provided according to a default domain knowledge. Using our general environment model, these preferences can be used in the same way as domain preferences once they have been entered by the user. The use of the corresponding preference relations in the rewriting process is illustrated by the following example.

$$\begin{aligned} PA &= (\{(Resource, language, Language), \emptyset, \{Language = L1\}) \\ RE &= (\{(Resource, language, Language), \emptyset, \{Language = L2\})\} \\ CN &= \{user - preferred - over(L1, L2)\} \end{aligned}$$

The rule tries to relax user's first language preference to his second reference as stored in his profile. The value of the first preference is replaced by the value of the second preference. Assuming that user-preferred-over(de,nl) holds, the result of applying this rewriting to the query in figure 2(b) is the query shown in figure 3

The above rewriting rule can easily be generalized to a rewriting for any value preference. The condition then would be that the environment items of such preferences must not refer to the subject predicate `language` but only to the same predicate (which is represented as a variable). So a variable instead of the literal `language` in the condition yields into a general rewriting rule for value preferences.

5 Relaxation Strategies

As we have seen in the examples above, different modifications can be combined either in the same rewriting rules or by successive application of re-writing rules on the result of the previous one. In the example above the order in which the rules are applied does not matter as the changes are independent, we can easily see, however, that sets of re-writing rules do have have to be confluent. If we add a rule that remove the subject pattern, the language preference can still be changed independently from others, but we have to decide whether to remove the subject pattern or whether to ask for titles that contain the topic instead. Different techniques have been proposed to cope with this situation. We can distinguish the following general strategies:

User Interaction. As described in [11] possible re-writings and the resulting queries can be represented as a graph structure. This representation can be used to guide the user through the space of re-writings by presenting all possible rewriting and the corresponding answers to the user letting her decide which way to proceed.

Heuristic Search. On a more general level, the process of query refinement can be formulated as a heuristic search problem. The search space consists of all possible queries and re-writing rules are used to navigate in the search space. Different search strategies can be employed to determine the best sequence of re-write operations. Heuristics used range from the number of results, the degree of ambiguity of the query [14] or the effort needed to recompute the result of the new query from the result of the previous one [15]. A general problem of heuristic search approaches to relaxation strategies is the lack of an appropriate termination criterion that determines when the search has reached a goal state. This problem can be addressed by limiting the search depth and picking the solution with the best heuristic evaluation. Another possibility is to implement an interactive search paradigm where the system evaluates different alternatives using heuristic search and lets the user decide with of the sequences to use.

Divide and Conquer. In the context of relational databases, divide and conquer techniques have been investigated that process different possible relaxations in parallel and merge the results of these parallel evaluations. Promising approaches of this type are top-k methods [5, 7, 2] and skylining algorithms [10, 9]. Top-k needs a function which associates a ranking number with each answer. The k best answers)with respect to this function) across all possible relaxations are returned. Obviously, the function should operate independently from the relaxation in order to select answers from different relaxations. Skylining assume that the data is organized according to several independent dimensions. It tries to return the best answers according to each dimension. In this context the dimensions are the different possibilities of relaxations. Skylined relaxation returns the best answer from each possible relaxation.

6 Implementation

We have implemented and tested the relaxation approach described in this paper in a prototypical fashion. In particular, we defined a PROLOG based language for specifying and operationalizing re-writing rules. The corresponding languages operates on RDF queries specified in SeRQL, but can easily be adapted to any other RDF query language. We tested the rewriting approach on an existing e-learning data that can be accessed via the Sesame System. Currently, the relaxation approach is being integrated into the distributed e-learning system described in [4].

7 Conclusions and Further Work

In this paper, we have proposed a framework for query relaxation to provide personalized information access to resources on the semantic web. The framework is based on the event-condition-action (ECA) paradigm where events are matching patterns, conditions are based on ordering between concepts of common sense domain knowledge and user preferences, and actions are the replacements for relaxing a query. The relaxation is based on the term rewriting principles enhanced with conditions provided by the ECA paradigm. This integration is a contribution to the term rewriting domain. The relaxation is controlled by conditions from domain and user preference ontology. The order is given by importance of predicates and values in the ontology for environment preferences, user profile, and common sense domain knowledge. This makes the approach very well suitable for the access to metadata on the semantic web as the domain knowledge helps to overcome the fact of heterogeneity and differences in how the metadata are authored on the semantic web.

In our further work, we would like to concentrate on the algorithms for determining termination of relaxation. We have considered several strategies in this paper but it requires further studies to give a recommendation how to decide among them. We also would like to experiment with different user preference models and how they contribute to the relaxation process. Last but not least, user preference elicitation methods and techniques needs to be studied to get as accurate user preferences as possible to support personalized access to information on the semantic web.

Acknowledgments

This work is partly supported by KNOWLEDGEWEB (IST-2004-507482) and PROLEARN (IST-2004-507310), EU funded projects in the semantic web and technology-enhanced learning areas.

References

1. Franz Baader and Tobias Nipkow. *Term rewriting and all that.* Cambridge University Press, New York, NY, USA, 1998.
2. Nicolas Bruno, Luis Gravano, and Amélie Marian. Evaluating top-k queries over web-accessible databases. In *Proceedings of the 18th International Conference on Data EngineeringE*, pages 369–. IEEE Computer Society, 2002.
3. Stefano Ceri. A declarative approach to active databases. In Forouzan Golshani, editor, *ICDE*, pages 452–456. IEEE Computer Society, 1992.
4. Peter Dolog, Nicola Henze, Wolfgang Nejdl, and Michael Sintek. Personalization in distributed e-learning environments. In *Proc. of WWW2004 — The Thirteen International World Wide Web Conference*, New Yourk, May 2004. ACM Press.
5. Ronald Fagin, Amnon Lotem, and Moni Naor. Optimal aggregation algorithms for middleware. In *PODS '01: Proceedings of the twentieth ACM SIGMOD- SIGACT-SIGART symposium on Principles of database systems*, pages 102–113, New York, NY, USA, 2001. ACM Press.

6. Terry Gaasterland, Parke Godfrey, and Jack Minker. An overview of cooperative answering. *Journal of Intelligent Information Systems*, 1(2):123–157, 1992.
7. Ulrich Güntzer, Wolf-Tilo Balke, and Werner Kießling. Optimizing multi-feature queries for image databases. In Amr El Abbadi, Michael L. Brodie, Sharma Chakravarthy, Umeshwar Dayal, Nabil Kamel, Gunter Schlageter, and Kyu-Young Whang, editors, *VLDB 2000, Proceedings of 26th International Conference on Very Large Data Bases, September 10-14, 2000, Cairo, Egypt*, pages 419–428. Morgan Kaufmann, 2000.
8. Pat Hayes. Rdf semantics. Recommendation, W3C, 2004.
9. Werner Kießling and Gerhard Köstler. Preference sql - design, implementation, experiences. In *Proceedings of 28th International Conference on Very Large Data Bases (VLDB02)*, pages 990–1001, 2002.
10. M. Lacroix and Pierre Lavency. Preferences; putting more knowledge into queries. In Peter M. Stocker, William Kent, and Peter Hammersley, editors, *Proceedings of 13th International Conference on Very Large Data Bases (VLDB87)*, pages 217–225. Morgan Kaufmann, 1987.
11. A. Motro. Flexx: A tolerant and cooperative user interface to database. *IEEE Transactions on Knowledge and Data Engineering*, 2(2):231–245, 1990.
12. George Papamarkos, Alexandra Poulovassilis, and Peter T. Wood. Event-condition-action rule languages for the semantic web. In Isabel F. Cruz, Vipul Kashyap, Stefan Decker, and Rainer Eckstein, editors, *SWDB*, pages 309–327, 2003.
13. N. Paton. *Active Rules in Database Systems*. Springer, 1999.
14. Nenad Stojanovic. On analysing query ambiguity for query refinement: The librarian agent approach. In *Conceptual Modeling - ER 2003*, volume 2813 of *Lecture Notes in Computer Science*, pages 490 – 505. Springer-Verlag, 2003.
15. H. Stuckenschmidt. Similarity-based query caching. In *th Internationa Conference on Flexible Query Answering System FQAS*, Lecture Notes in Artificial Intelligence, Lyon, France, 2004. Springer Verlag.
16. H. Stuckenschmidt and F. van Harmelen. Approximating terminological queries. In *Proceedings of the Fifth International Conference on Flexible Query Answering Systems FQAS 2002*, Lecture Notes in Artificial Intelligence, Copenhagen, Denmark, 2002. Springer Verlag.
17. Heiner Stuckenschmidt, Anita de Waard, Ravinder Bhogal, Christiaan Fluit, Arjohn Kampman, Jan van Buel, Erik van Mulligen, Jeen Broekstra, Ian Crowlesmith, Frank van Harmelen, and Tony Scerri. Exploring large document repositories with rdf technology - the dope project. *IEEE Intelligent Systems*, 2004. to appear.
18. Holger Wache, Perry Groot, and Heiner Stuckenschmit. Scalable instance retrieval for the semantic web by approximation. In *Proceedings of the 6th International Conference on Web Information Systems Engineering (WISE'05)*, 2005.

Appendix

```
PATTERN
  {Resource} subject {Subject}
  WHERE
  Subject Like Value^^xsd:string,
REPLACE-BY
  [{Resource} subject {Subject}],
  {Resource} R {T}
  WHERE
  T Like NEW
WITH
  domain-preferred-over(subject,R)
  NEW = concat("*",concat(Value,"*"))
```

Fig. 4. Re-writing rule for replacing subject with title

```
 PATTERN
  {Resource} language {Language}
  WHERE
  Language = L1,
REPLACE-BY
  {Resource} language {Language}
  WHERE
  Language = L2,
WITH
  user-preferred-over(L1,L2)
```

Fig. 5. Specification of the Re-writing rule for langauge preferences

Navigating Multimodal Meeting Recordings with the Meeting Miner

Matt-Mouley Bouamrane and Saturnino Luz

Department of Computer Science
Trinity College Dublin, Ireland
{Matt.Bouamrane, Saturnino.Luz}@cs.tcd.ie

Abstract. We present Meeting Miner, a multimodal meeting browser for navigating recordings of online text and speech collaborative meetings. Meetings are recorded through a collaborative writing environment specially designed to capture participants activities. This information, usually lost in common recordings of multimodal meetings, offers novel possibilities for indexing, navigation and information retrieval in archived meetings. Meeting Miner uses temporal information from the logs of actions captured on self-contained information items (paragraphs of text) to uncover potential information links between these semantic data units. A novel space-based action navigation scheme is presented. Keywords and topic search as well as more advanced queries can be performed by the system. We illustrate the system navigation modalities with several browsing examples.

1 Introduction

As computers become ubiquitous tools for communication over the Internet, more and more applications are being designed and implemented which support online remote synchronous collaboration, including environments for collaborative writing, learning and design [1, 2, 3, 4]. Computer mediated communication offers users the possibility of recording online meetings thus freeing participants from distracting and time consuming tasks such as note taking and production of minutes. However, as the number of stored meetings grow, so does the complexity of extracting meaningful information from the recordings. Therefore, in order to be truly effective, a conferencing capture system needs to offer users efficient means of navigating the recordings. Accessing specific parts of time-based media (audio/video) is particularly challenging as they often contain information which can not be easily visualised or summarised. The work presented in this paper is placed within the context of a growing research interest in applications for visual mining of multimodal meeting data in order to support users' meeting browsing requirements. The paper is organised as follows: we review existing paradigms and systems for multimodal meeting browsing, we then describe the specificity of our own meeting recording environment — a collaborative writing architecture with an audio communication channel and structured activity logging of participants interactions — and finally, present Meeting Miner and illustrate the system navigation modalities with several browsing examples.

H.L. Larsen et al. (Eds.): FQAS 2006, LNAI 4027, pp. 356–367, 2006.

2 Related Work

Multimodal meeting browsing is an open research area as it seeks to resolve issues relating to multimedia search and retrieval, visualisation and integration of multiple modalities, cooperative computing and cooperation modelling. Existing systems include the Meeting Browser [5] in which automatic speech recognition (ASR) transcripts are used for meeting navigation and summarization. The SCAN (Spoken Content based Audio Navigation) system [6] uses acoustic and prosodic features for audio segmentation and a number of information retrieval techniques applied on ASR transcripts for speech recording indexing. In MeetingViewer [7], interaction events are timestamped and subsequently used as an activity index in the user interface. COMAP (Content MAPper) and HANMER (HANd held Meeting browsER) [8] use an inter media activity metric for significant meeting events ranking. A detailed description of meeting browsing techniques and applications can be found in [9].

3 Meeting Recording Environment

The meetings targeted by our prototype are non-collocated computer mediated *speech-and-text* meetings typically involving a small number of participants. Recordings were produced with RECOLED [10, 11] (REcording COLlaborative EDitor), a collaborative writing environment, with structured activity logging and designed to be used along with an audio communication channel (RTP-Real Time Protocol multicast). In this environment, the chosen granularity of the data units for capturing operation logs are the paragraphs of text. These are self-contained information items with persisting histories when the segments are moved or altered. After some pre-processing, the meeting recorder produces an archive consisting of: decoded audio files, a profile of user activity detailing the time of individual speech exchanges and an XML file containing the textual content of the shared document along with interaction metadata. Every time an editing operation is performed on the document, a corresponding timestamp is generated and associated with the paragraph in which the modification occurred


```
- &lt;segment id="4.1"&gt;
    <timestamp actionid="17" agent="2" action="NewLine_Insert" start="215" end="215"/>
    <timestamp actionid="19" agent="2" action="Insert" start="215" end="217"/>
    <timestamp actionid="20" agent="2" action="Delete" start="220" end="222"/>
    <timestamp actionid="21" agent="2" action="Insert" start="221" end="221"/>
    <timestamp actionid="22" agent="2" action="Insert" start="222" end="226"/>
    <timestamp actionid="24" agent="1" action="Insert" start="231" end="231"/>
    <timestamp actionid="57" agent="2" action="Insert" start="486" end="495"/>
    budget of 3000 from the student union
  &lt;/segment&gt;
```


Fig. 1. Paragraph timestamps

```
<action id="57" type="Insert" startT="486" endT="495" paragraphs="4.1,4.1.1" startOffset="15"> from the student union
<action id="58" type="Insert" startT="496" endT="498" paragraphs="4.1.1" startOffset="0"> maybe chga </action>
<action id="59" type="Delete" startT="498" endT="499" paragraphs="4.1.1" startOffset="8" endOffset="9"> ga </actio
<action id="60" type="Insert" startT="499" endT="502" paragraphs="4.1.1" startOffset="8"> arge people </action>
```


Fig. 2. Action timestamps

(Fig. 1). The timestamps contain the name of the agent who performed the operation, the start and end time of the operation, and the nature of the operation, such as *Edit*, *Insert*, *Point*, *Paste*, *Cut* and *Gesture* (telepointing and free hand drawing). A detailed description of the timestamping model designed to manage paragraph history in case of modifications to document structure can be found in [12]. A second set of action timestamps accurately describe the content of all operations performed (Fig. 2).

4 Temporal Information Retrieval Paradigms

4.1 Extended Overlap of Temporal Intervals

The current version of the Meeting Miner makes exclusive use of the temporal information detailed in the previous section for information visualisation and retrieval. We are currently experimenting with incorporating an ASR component in order to fine tune querying and topic segmentation. The initial speech segmentation is done by (i) speakers identity and (ii) silence detection. Due to the nature of the audio communication architecture during the meeting session, initially in RTP format, this information is simply inferred from the RTP source identifier and packet counts. Retrieval units in the Meeting Miner are then essentially defined through *extended* concurrency of participants' interactions and speech exchanges.

Extended concurrency [13] differs from strict interpretation of temporal interval *overlap* relationships [14] in that the former allows for a tolerance value (system or user defined) between temporal intervals. In a strict interpretation of temporal overlap, only the intervals I_1 and I_2 of Fig. 3 would be considered to overlap . With extended concurrency, two subsequent media intervals separated by a duration less than the tolerance value (I_2 and I_3) are also considered to be

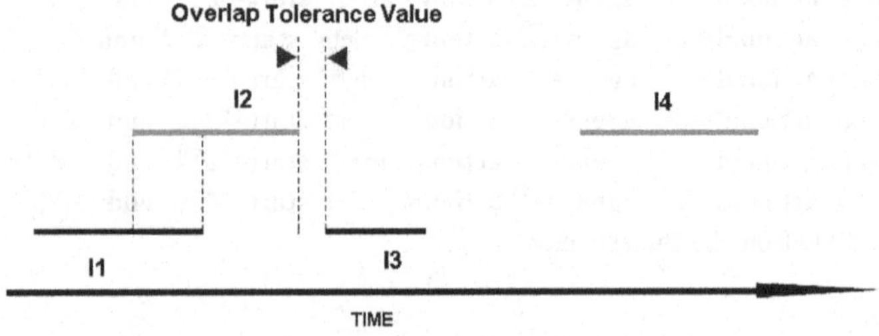

Fig. 3. Strict vs Extended Temporal Interval Overlap Relationships

overlapping. In remote meetings, participants tend not to start speaking immediately one after another, usually waiting a second or two in order to make sure that the other person has finished making his point. Similarly, there will usually be a delay of a few seconds between participants reaching a decision and subsequently typing the implications down. Thus, the idea behind using extended overlap as a basis for information retrieval is based on our observations that in accordance with the natural structure of discourse, media intervals in close time proximity are often semantically related. This can be viewed as the question-answer pair paradigm [5] where adjacent speech exchanges are more informative jointly than when considered on their own. A more detailed discussion on media stream interactions and implications for media intervals temporal segmentation can be found in [13].

4.2 Paragraph-Based Retrieval

Paragraph level history is designed to follow the creation and modifications of the semantic units of the document. Each paragraph is associated with a list of editing and gesturing actions as well as corresponding (concurrent) participants' audio exchanges. Thus, a user can inquire about the context of each individual text units by exploring a hierarchical tree structure called a paragraph's *temporal neighbourhood* [8], generated as follows: first combine all actions performed on a specific paragraph with all concurrent speech exchanges, then subsequently link all previously retrieved speech segments to concurrent actions performed on *other* paragraphs. The spread of the paragraph retrieval unit can be controlled by adjusting the overlap tolerance value mentioned in the previous section.

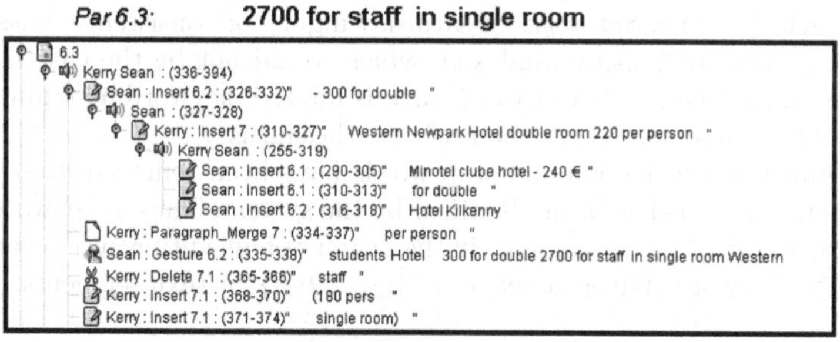

Fig. 4. A paragraph Temporal Neighbourhood

An overlap tolerance value set to zero ensures that information retrieved is directly related to a manipulation of a specific paragraph, thus ensuring good precision but possibly missing related peripheral information. Inversely, increasing the tolerance value may increase recall but at the expense of including irrelevant information. A detailed description of paragraph level retrieval and browsing can be found in [15]. Fig. 4 is an example of the visual representation of a paragraph's temporal neighbourhood produced by the Meeting Miner. The content of textual edits provides clues to surrounding audio segments. Speakers identities and segments duration information are provided besides the audio nodes. A user can listen to the actual speech by simply clicking on the corresponding node.

4.3 Keywords and Topic Search

In addition to paragraph-based temporal neighbourhood retrieval, the Meeting Miner offers other indexing and navigation modalities, such as keyword and topic searches. The Meeting Miner automatically identifies a set of potential keywords and the user can decide to view these in an alphabetical order, ranked by term frequency or simply by time of appearance. Keyword indexing is done by looking at the content of the action timestamps (Fig. 2). However, when typing, participants often make typographic or spelling mistakes, which will often be almost immediately corrected. This means that individual edits may contain single letters or a few letters (deleted or replaced) and mispelt words as shown in Fig. 5.

In order to identify meaningful words, one possible solution would be to check word tokens contained in the editing actions against a thesaurus through approximate string matching. We decided instead to use the set of words ($\mathcal{W}$) contained in the final textual outcome ($\mathcal{O}$) of the meeting as the possible vocabulary ($\mathcal{V}$). The motivations for this choice are the following: as $\mathcal{V}$ contains the set of all words in the meeting outcome (i) it is reasonable to assume it will contain all the most important words used during the meeting (ii) this ensures there can not be out-of-vocabulary items: as long as they are present in the final outcome, proper nouns such as names of people and places (i.e: *Kilkenny*), will also be indexed as keywords (iii) a by product of the previous rule is that if a participant uses abbreviations (i.e: *Sat night* for saturday night), or consistently misspell the same word, these will also be indexed, which would not be the case if using a thesaurus (iv) as the number of words in $\mathcal{V}$ is limited, keyword matching will be less computationally expensive than using a thesaurus.

Once punctuation, figures and stop words have been removed from $\mathcal{V}$, a set of potential keywords has been identified by the system. Thus, a keyword search returns the set of all audio segments in the vicinity of an editing action containing the specific keyword. Given a set $\mathcal{T} = \{t_1, ..., t_{|T|}\}$ of text segments, a set of

Raw Edit	Extracted Keywords
Weekend In	Weekend
Hotel KJI	Hotel
Kilkenny	Kilkenny
: Vist	
travel bu c	travel
m,	
by hired bus	hired bus
25 earch	
Sat Night	Sat Night

Fig. 5. Raw content of edits and extracted keywords

speech segments $\mathcal{S} = \{s_1, ..., s_{|\mathcal{S}|}\}$, and a specific keyword $\mathcal{K}w$, a keyword search returns a set of speech segments $\mathcal{KS}$ as shown below.

Definition 1. *A* keyword search *is a function* $\mathcal{KS} : \mathcal{V} \rightarrow 2^{\mathcal{S}}$

$$\mathcal{KS}(\mathcal{K}w) \;=\; \{s_i \mid (s_i \text{ overlaps } t_j) \wedge (\mathcal{K}w \in t_j)\}$$

Note that the retrieval method does not rely on speech recognition so it is not subject to traditional ASR shortcomings such as disfluencies in spontaneous, human-to-human dialogues, lack of word or sentence boundaries, poor recording conditions, crosstalk, inappropriate language models, out-of-vocabulary items and variations in speaking styles and pronunciations which means that for a certain percentage of people, some systems may have very low recognition rates [16]. Although this simple heuristic works surprisingly well in practice, there will be occasions when selected audio segments do not contain the relevant keyword. We are currently investigating the integration of a speech recognition component in the Meeting Miner in order to assign confidence measures to the audio segments associated with a specific keyword. For topic search, we simply define a topic as a conjunction of keywords searches:

Definition 2. *A* Topic search *is a function* $\mathcal{TS} : \mathcal{V} \rightarrow 2^{\mathcal{S}}$

$$\mathcal{TS}(\mathcal{K}w_1 \wedge ... \wedge \mathcal{K}w_j) = K\mathcal{S}(\mathcal{K}w_1) \cup ... \cup K\mathcal{S}(\mathcal{K}w_j)\}.$$

4.4 Action-Based Browsing

One can also consider a participant's space-based interactions as another media stream, sharing the time dimension with the audio stream. This can be exploited in two ways for meeting browsing. The first one consists in displaying the content of concurrent actions while playing the time-based media. In figure 6, listening to audio segment Au_1 would prompt the display of the text "*180 per person*". In other words, it consists in the synchronous play-back of multiple media streams as previously implemented in a number of multimodal browsers [7, 17, 18]. However, the time relationship between the media can also be exploited by visualising the space-based interactions as a navigation tool into the time-based media recording. Using a slide bar to navigate the timeline will display concurrent space-based actions, thus offering hints about the content of surrounding audio segments. In figure 6, the navigator will prompt the display of the message "*180 per person*", which suggest that surrounding speech exchanges deal with costs (*of a room*). The definite appeal of such a navigation method is that space-based actions will generally have strong associated semantics and are appropriate for quick visual scanning, thus potentially offering a powerful indexing method into the time-based media. Interactions are discrete, generally sparse enough so as not to overload a user with information, and tend to form natural semantic clusters over time (when a specific topic is discussed) allowing for discrimination and segmentation of topics within a meeting recording. This indexing method is also perfectly accurate in timing and content as it is not subject to recognition errors.

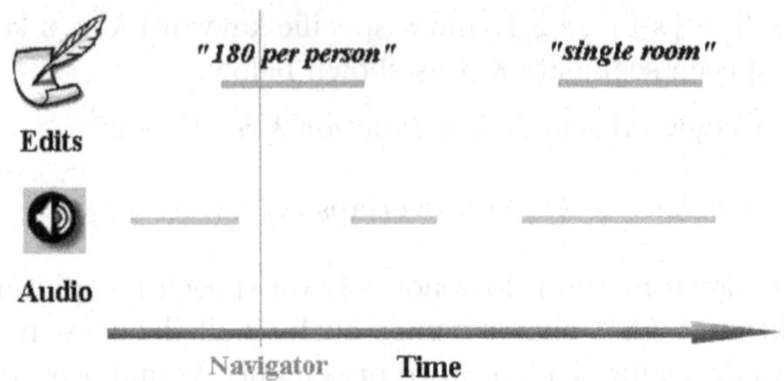

Fig. 6. Using the content of Edits as an audio navigation tool

5 The Meeting Miner

The Meeting Miner user interface is shown in Fig. 7. The main user interface components are described below:

Document View. displays the meeting final text document in the lower pane. Each paragraph in the document view is indexed for easy cross referencing. Participants' individual contributions can be highlighted according to a color code. When the paragraph-based view is selected, clicking on an individual paragraph will display the paragraph temporal neighbourhood.

Tool Bar. Enables the user to adjust system settings to best suit his preferences.

Upper panel. The upper pane can be one of two views, depending on how the user wishes to browse the meeting. In a paragraph-based retrieval, clicking on a specific paragraph will prompt the display of the tree-structured paragraph retrieval unit consisting of the content of editing nodes, and corresponding audio nodes, with the name of all the active participants within the duration of these temporal intervals (Fig. 4).

An alternative view is the topic view, or *contextual neighbourhood* view. When this mode is selected, regions where audio contributions are likely to be related to the topic selection (a set of keywords selected in the topic panel) are highlighted. Clicking on a particular interval will play the corresponding audio.

Keyword Indexer. Above the audio view showing speech according to speakers, it displays significant keywords in order to offer hints of audio content. These keywords are extracted from the text actions described in Fig 2.

Keyword Panel. Displays all the potential keywords from the text document identified by the system. The list of keywords can be displayed in alphabetical order, frequency ranking or simply time of appearance. The user can dynamically update the list (removing words under a certain frequency or only select keywords associated with a certain type of action, etc.)

Topic Panel. The user can dynamically choose a set of keywords. A subsequent topic search will highlight audio segments associated with these keywords.

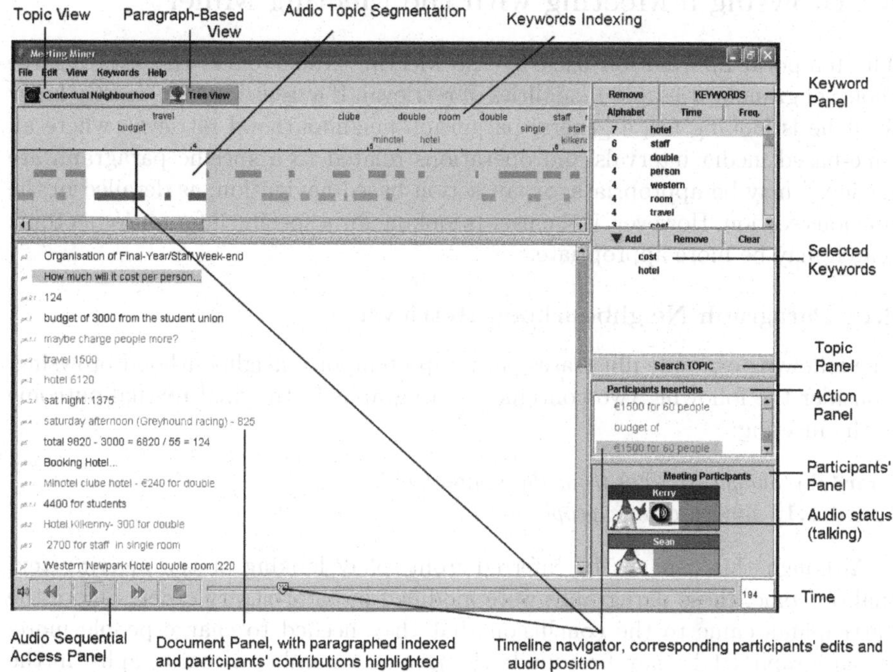

Fig. 7. MeetingMiner

The audio intervals selected by the topic search are segments in the neighbourhood of participants' edits which contain the keywords.

Action Panel. Used in conjunction with the timeline navigator (slider) bar, it displays the nature of concurrent participants' edits for action-based browsing.

Participants' Panel. Displays the names of the participants. Each participant is assigned a unique colour code which highlights on the interface the ownership of the various text and audio contributions. A little audio icon is also displayed to show participants current activities (speaking, idle, etc).

Audio Panel. rovides sequential and random access to the audio file. The browser's audio mode settings offers the user several navigation options such as skipping silences, or, if the topic mode is selected, jumping to the next topical segments. Similar functionalities were implemented in the SpeechSkimmer [19].

Timeline Navigator (slider). The navigator's purpose is twofold: first, it offers a reference point into the audio recording. It also offers random access to the audio file. While moving the slider, participants' concurrent actions are displayed in the Action Panel, so the user can decide to stop and listen to a specific section of the recording if he were to see an action of particular interest (as described in section 4.4).

6 Browsing a Meeting with the Meeting Miner

The temporal information used by the Meeting Miner offers the user a large choice of granularities and modalities of retrieval. If a user does not exactly know what he is looking for, a general paragraph neighbourhood retrieval, where all time-based media intervals and operations related to a specific paragraph are retrieved may be appropriate, or, an action-based navigation, as detailed in the previous section. However, if the user is looking for a specific information, a topic search may be more appropriate.

6.1 Paragraph Neighbourhood Retrieval

The following example illustrates paragraph temporal neighbourhood browsing. Consider the following two contiguous paragraphs in the final textual outcome of the meeting:

(par4.1) *budget of 3000 from the student union*
(par4.1.1) *maybe charge people more?*

Although this can not be inferred from solely looking at the meeting textual outcome, these paragraphs were modified in an arbitrary order. Before the participants came to the conclusion that they needed to charge people more, in paragraph 4.1.1, they first made changes to a number of paragraphs, in the following order :

(par12.2) *bus hire 1500 for 60 people*
(par4.2) *travel 1500*
(par6.1.1) *4400 for students 2700 for staff in single room*

The subjects participants discuss while these paragraphs are modified are as follow :

(Au1) *(par12.2,4.2) travel arrangements, cost of hiring a bus, existence of a budget*
(Au2) *(par6.1.1) hotel expenses*
(Au3) *(par4.1.1) need to charge people more*

In other words, only when the participants realised that the cost of travel and the hotel would exceed their initial budget (paragraph 4.1) did they make the suggestion that they will need to ask people to financially contribute to the trip (paragraph 4.1.1).

6.2 Action-Based Navigation

In action-based navigation, it is envisaged that the user will move the slider along the timeline until he sees an information of interest. In Fig. 7, the Action Panel highlights the fact that at this specific point in time, one of the participants typed the words: "*€1500 for 60 people*". If the user were to play the corresponding audio, this is what he would hear:

(participant 1). Ok, then we can get every body on the bus so I guess we should make every body go on the bus unless they really want to get there on their own (...) if we are going to need to hire a bus **for 60 people** anyway
(participant 2). That's true but what if they insist that they want to get there by their car
(participant 1). Well I guess we'll just have to let them go, I don't know
(participant 2). So we'll say then the bus is going to cost **€1500** for 45 people.

6.3 Keyword and Topic Searches

Keyword and topic searches will provide results similar to the previous example, except that the set of speech turns retrieved are not only punctual but spread over the entire meeting duration (whenever the keywords are typed or pointed at). The skip forward/backward functionalities of the Audio Panel can be used to bring the user to the next/previous set of audio segments which have been identified as being relevant to the search. To avoid jitters, segments in close time proximity are merged for smooth listening when the set of audio segments are played back. If a user were to find a specific set of audio segments to be particularly interesting, the audio functionalities provided by the Meeting Miner will enable him to explore surrounding segments.

6.4 Discussion

Meeting browser systems are notoriously hard to evaluate. Unlike in speech recognition and spoken document retrieval, where the TRECs 6-8 (Text REtrieval Conference) tracks [20] set forth precise evaluation tasks, with specific evaluation metrics on well defined corpus collections, the diversity of multimodal meeting collections and modalities chosen for browsing recordings makes defining evaluation metrics and systems' comparisons impractical. Therefore, systems have typically been evaluated by user testing. At the time of writing this paper, a usability study and evaluation of the Meeting Miner is ongoing.

7 Conclusion and Future Work

We have presented Meeting Miner, a multimodal mining tool which makes exclusive use of interaction temporal information captured with a purposely designed collaborative writing environment with structured activity logging. We have illustrated the system's browsing functionalities with several examples. We have developed a number of novel information retrieval techniques based on the specificity of the temporal information available from our meeting corpus. Paragraph temporal neighbourhood retrieval uncovers potential semantic links between non-contiguous text items which are not necessary obvious when solely looking at a meeting's outcome. Space-based actions navigation is also appropriate for quick visual scanning, as actions will generally have strong associated semantics and potentially offer a powerful indexing method into the time-based media. We have defined keyword and topic searches based on analysing the content of editing actions' content. The appeal of the indexing and navigation methods presented in this paper lie in the fact that space-based interactions are discrete, generally sparse enough so as not to overload a user with information, and tend to form natural semantic clusters over time (when a specific topic is discussed) allowing for discrimination and segmentation of topics within a meeting recording. These methods require no training, are computationally inexpensive and are not subject to recognition errors. Informal trials of the Meeting Miner have shown encouraging results while a full evaluation of the system is ongoing. We are currently experimenting with integrating an ASR component in the Meeting Miner in order to complete and fine tune the existing temporal mining architecture presented.

References

1. Rahman, S.M., Sarker, R., Bignall, B.: Application of multimedia technology in manufacturing: a review. Comput. Ind. **38**(1) (1999) 42–52
2. Jermann, P., Soller, A., Muehlenbrock, M.: From mirroring to guiding: A review of state of the art technology for supporting collaborative learning. In: Proceedings of the first European conference on computer-supported collaborative learning. (2001) 324–331
3. Bafoutsou, G., Mentzas, G.: Review and functional classification of collaborative systems. In: International Journal of Information Management. Volume 22. (2002) 281–305
4. van Leeuwen, J.: Computer support for collaborative work in the construction industry. Proceedings of the International Conference on Concurrent Engineering (2003) 599–606
5. Waibel, A., Bett, M., Metze, F., Ries, K., Schaaf, T., Schultz, T., Soltau, H., Yu, H., Zechner, K.: Advances in automatic meeting record creation and access. In: Proceedings of the International Conference on Acoustics, Speech and Signal Processing. (2001) 597–600
6. Whittaker, S., Hirschberg, J., Amento, B., Stark, L., Bacchiani, M., Isenhour, P., Stead, L., Zamchick, G., Rosenberg, A.: Scanmail: a voicemail interface that makes speech browsable, readable and searchable. In: Proceedings of the SIGCHI conference on Human factors in computing systems,CHI '02, New York, NY, US, ACM Press (2002) 275–282
7. Geyer, W., Richter, H., Abowd, G.D.: Making multimedia meeting records more meaningful. In: Proceedings of International Conference on Multimedia and Expo, ICME '03. Volume 2. (2003) 669–672
8. Luz, S., Masoodian, M.: A model for meeting content storage and retrieval. In: Proceedings of the 11th International Multimedia Modelling Conference, MMM'05, IEEE Press (2005) 392–398
9. Bouamrane, M.M., Luz, S.: Meeting browsing, state of the art review. to appear in special issue of User-Centered MultiMedia, Multimedia Systems Journal, Susan Boll and Gerd Utz Westermann eds., Springer (2006)
10. Bouamrane, M.M., King, D., Luz, S., Masoodian, M.: A framework for collaborative writing with recording and post-meeting retrieval capabilities. IEEE Distributed Systems Online (2004) Special issue on the 6th International Workshop on Collaborative Editing Systems.

11. Masoodian, M., Luz, S., Bouamrane, M.M., King, D.: Recoled: A group-aware collaborative text editor for capturing document history. In: Proceedings of WWW/Internet 2005. Volume 1., Lisbon (2005) 323–330
12. Bouamrane, M.M., Luz, S., Masoodian, M., King, D.: Supporting remote collaboration through structured activity logging. In Hai Zhuge, G.C.F., ed.: Proceedings of 4th International Conference in Grid and Cooperative Computing, GCC 2005, LNCS. Volume 3795 / 2005., Beijing, China, Springer-Verlag GmbH (2005) 1096–1107
13. Luz, S., Bouamrane, M.M.: Exploring the structure of media stream interactions for multimedia browsing. In Detyniecki, M., Jose, J.M., Nrnberger, A., Rijsbergen, C.J., eds.: Adaptive Multimedia Retrieval: User, Context, and Feedback: Third International Workshop, AMR 2005, Revised Selected Papers. Volume 3877 of Lecture Notes in Computes Science., Springer-Verlag (2006) 79–90
14. Allen, J.F.: Maintaining knowledge about temporal intervals. Communications of the ACM **11**(26) (1983) 832–843
15. Bouamrane, M.M., Luz, S., Masoodian, M.: History based visual mining of semi-structured audio and text. In: Proceedings of Multimedia Modelling, MMM06 Beijing, China, IEEE Press (2006) 360–363
16. Furui, S.: Automatic speech recognition and its application to information extraction. In: Proceedings of the 37th annual meeting of the Association for Computational Linguistics on Computational Linguistics, Morristown, NJ, US, Association for Computational Linguistics (1999) 11–20
17. Brotherton, J.A., Bhalodia, J.R., Abowd, G.D.: Automated capture, integration, and visualization of multiple media streams. In: Proceedings of the IEEE International Conference on Multimedia Computing and Systems, ICMCS '98, Washington, DC, US, IEEE Computer Society (1998) 54
18. Wellner, P., Flynn, M., Guillemot, M.: Browsing recorded meetings with FERRET. In Bengio, S., Bourlard, H., eds.: Proceedings of Machine Learning for Multimodal Interaction: First International Workshop, MLMI 2004. Volume 3361., Martigny, Switzerland, Springer-Verlag GmbH (2004) 12–21
19. Arons, B.: Speechskimmer: a system for interactively skimming recorded speech. In: ACM Transactions on Computer-Human Interaction. Volume 4,1., New York, NY, US, ACM Press (1997) 3–38
20. Garofolo, J.S., Voorhees, E.M., Auzanne, C.G., Stanford, V.M.: Spoken document retrieval: 1998 evaluation and investigation of new metrics. In: Proceedings of ESCA ETRW on Accessing Information in Spoken Audio., Cambridge (1999) 1–7

Personalized Web Recommendation Based on Path Clustering

Yijun Yu, Huaizhong Lin, Yimin Yu, and Chun Chen

Computer Institute, Zhejiang University, 310027 Hangzhou, China
yijunyu@mail.hz.zj.cn, linhz@zju.edu.cn,
billyuym@163.com, chenc@cs.zju.edu.cn

Abstract. Each user accesses a Website with certain interests. The interest can be manifested by the sequence of each Web user access. The access paths of all Web users can be clustered. The effectiveness and efficiency are two problems in clustering algorithms. This paper provides a clustering algorithm for personalized Web recommendation. It is path clustering based on competitive agglomeration (PCCA). The path similarity and the center of a cluster are defined for the proposed algorithm. The algorithm relies on competitive agglomeration to get best cluster numbers automatically. Recommending based on the algorithm doesn't disturb users and needn't any registration information. Experiments are performed to compare the proposed algorithm with two other algorithms and the results show that the improvement of recommending performance is significant.

1 Introduction

Currently World Wide Web is developing rapidly. The managers of Websites need good auto-subsidiary tool, which can adjust the configuration of Web page dynamically according to the user's interest. Thus they can improve service and develop peculiar electronic business to satisfy the demands of visitors much better. For the visitors, what they want is a characteristic Web page with much better service that can satisfy various demands and they also expect to receive an illumination from other users who have a similar access interest. From some points of view, visitors are also not very clear about these demands. Moreover, an important method to solve these two demands is to use Web Usage mining to recommend Web personalized Web page.

The term 'Web Usage Mining'[1] was introduced by Cooley et al., in 1997, in which they define Web usage mining as the 'automatic discovery of user access patterns from Web Servers'. Web Usage mining has gained much attention in the literature as a potential approach to fulfill the requirement of Web personalization[2]. Personalized Web recommendation is one form of Web personalization that could find important applications in e-business (such as google.com and Amazon.com) and e-learning sectors. Web pages are recommended to a user according to user interest that anticipates the user's needs. In this paper, we focus on the personalized Web recommendation of Web pages that are adapted according to user interest.

H.L. Larsen et al. (Eds.): FQAS 2006, LNAI 4027, pp. 368 – 377, 2006.

User access pattern is important in personalized Web recommendation system. The drawbacks of previous methods[3,4] are that not it ignores the facts that the available element will be close to zero with the increase of the user's access time and the number of clustering is given by people, which can not dynamically adjust according to personal access. Most of the research in personalized Web recommendation recently is collaborative filtering[5,6], which needs extra information to distinguish personal activities. However, this input may have some errors and may be outdated. Authors in Paper [7,8] use K-means clustering to recommend Web personalized page, which does not consider the relationship between the user's personality and the access path. The algorithm presented in this paper can overcome these drawbacks.

2 Path Clustering Based on Competitive Agglomeration

Path clustering based on competitive agglomeration (PCCA) is a partition algorithm, not a hierarchical clustering algorithm. The algorithm clusters according to path similarity, improves K-paths algorithm [9], and can get best cluster numbers automatically by competitive agglomeration method.

2.1 Definitions

We should consider that user access is sequence for Web page in clustering. Web users access Web page according to their interest, of course, their interest is different. So, the sequence can present user access interest.

Definition 1. The user access transaction t is defined as:

$$t=< l_1^t.url ,..., l_r^t.url >, \tag{1}$$

Here, L is the user's access log set, $l\in L$, $l_i^t.url$ is hyperlink address of the Web page.

For urls in current accessing Web page, people always have been more interested in url accessed earlier than url accessed later. It is obviously that there is relation between user interest and user access path. So, we define user interest as follow.

Definition 2. The user's interest is defined as:

$$\mathrm{I}(l_i^t.url)=m-i+1, \quad 1\leq i\leq m \tag{2}$$

Here, $l_i^t.url$ is hyperlink address of the Web page, m is the number of Web page in Website. It is obviously that there is relation as below.

$$\mathrm{I}(l_1^t.url)>\mathrm{I}(l_2^t.url)>\ldots> \mathrm{I}(l_i^t.url), \ 1\leq i\leq m$$

Definition 3. Given two user access transaction t and s, the similarity between them sim(t,s) is defined as:

$$\text{sim}(t,s)=\frac{\left|I(l_i^t.url)\cap I(l_i^s.url)\right|}{\left|I(l_i^t.url)\cup I(l_i^s.url)\right|},\ 1\le i\le m \tag{3}$$

Here, I(·)is the user's interest of accessing Web page.

Definition 4. Considering user access interest, the user access transaction t can be defined as:

$$t=<u_1^t, u_2^t, \ldots, u_i^t>,\ 1\le i\le m \tag{4}$$

Where, $u_i^t = \begin{cases} I(l_j^t.url) & if\ (l_j^t.url \in t) \\ 0 & otherwise \end{cases}$

Here, L is the user's access log set, $l\in L$, $l_i^t.url$ is hyperlink address of the Web page. We cluster the matrix of t.

Definition 5. Cluster center $C_{\text{center}}(c)$ is the longest public similarity path, which is the most typical path started from the starting point. The result set of the cluster is:

$$C=\{c_1, c_2, \ldots, c_k\},\qquad 1\le k\le n \tag{5}$$

For every cluster $c\in C$, the number of transaction t belonging to cluster c is n, therefore the definition of cluster centers is:

$$C_{\text{center}}(c)=<l_1'.url, l_2'.url, \ldots, l_k'.url>, \tag{6}$$

Where

$$l_k'.url = \arg_{l_k.url}(\max(count(l_k.url))), t\in c,\ l_k.url\in t, l_k.url \notin \{l_1'.url, \ldots, l_{k-1}'.url\}.$$

Here, count($l_k.url$)is the number of different $l_k.url$.

Given a user access transaction set T, every row is composed of user transaction, there are n transactions. The algorithm divides T into k clusters to make the total sum of the center similarity of the transaction the smallest. We can get the cluster center of the every cluster by formula (5). This process can be described as such mathematic problem:

$$\text{Minimize: } P(W,T,C)=\sum_{j=1}^{k}\sum_{i=1}^{n} w_{ij}\,\text{sim}(t, C_{\text{center}}(c_j))\ \square \tag{7}$$

Satisfy:

$$\sum_{j=1}^{k} w_{ij}=1, w_{ij}\ge 0, i=1,\ldots,n,\ j=1,\ldots,k. \tag{8}$$

Here, W is a division matrix of $n \times k$, C={ c_1 , c_2 ..., c_n }is the result set of the clustering, and sim(·,·) is the similarity of two paths defined in definition 3.

2.2 Competitive Agglomeration

The principle of the competitive agglomeration [10] is as follows. It divides the data set into many small clusters, as the algorithm is processing, the neighboring clusters will compete with each other. The cluster who loses the competition will become smaller until it vanishes, which makes the number of the clusters to be an optimized number. Because formula (7) is combined with competitive agglomeration, the objective function can be defined as:

$$P(W,T,C) = \sum_{j=1}^{k}\sum_{i=1}^{n} w_{ij}\,\text{sim}(t, C_{\text{center}}(c_j)) - \eta \sum_{j=1}^{k}\sum_{i=1}^{n} w_{ij} \tag{9}$$

Where:

$$\sum_{j=1}^{k} w_{ij} = 1, w_{ij} \geq 0, i \in \{1,...,N\}, j \in \{1,...,k\}.$$

The number of the cluster K in competitive agglomeration is refreshed dynamically in formula (9). The right side of the equation is used to control the scale of the cluster to get a compact cluster. When the number of cluster equals to the number of the transactions, which means every transaction becomes a cluster, the first item becomes minimal. The second item of the equals is the total sum of the number of the cluster base, which is used to control the number of the cluster. When all the transactions are put into one cluster and other clusters are empty, the second item becomes minimal. The combination of the two items and the selection of an appropriate η will minimize the similarity of the path, and put the data set into the cluster which has the smallest number. Lagrange coefficient is used in formula (9) to get the membership grade $w_{st}^{\min}$ [10], which can minimize the formula (9).

$$w_{st}^{\min} = w_{st}^{\text{KP}} + w_{st}^{\text{Bias}}, \tag{10}$$

Here, $w_{st}^{\min}$ is the minimization of membership grade; w_{st}^{KP} is the membership grade of the K-paths; w_{st}^{Bias} is the deviation of the membership grade.

$$w_{st}^{\text{KP}} = \frac{1}{\text{sim}(t, C_{\text{center}}(c_s))} / \left(\sum_{j=1}^{k} \frac{1}{\text{sim}(t, C_{\text{center}}(c_j))}\right), \tag{11}$$

$$w_{st}^{\text{Bias}} = \frac{\eta}{\text{sim}(t, C_{\text{center}}(c_j))}(N_s - \overline{N_t}), \tag{12}$$

N_s is the base of the cluster c_s in formula (12).

$$N_s = \sum_{m=1}^{N} w_{sj} \ , \tag{13}$$

$\overline{N_t}$ is defined as :

$$\overline{N_t} = (\sum_{j=1}^{k} \frac{1}{\text{sim}(t, C_{\text{center}}(c_j))} N_j) / (\sum_{j=1}^{k} \frac{1}{\text{sim}(t, C_{\text{center}}(c_j))}). \tag{14}$$

Formula (14) is a simple weighted average. The weight of the every cluster means how close all the transactions of that cluster are to the cluster center.

In formula (14), the first item of the right hand of w_{st}^{KP} has the same membership grade with the k-paths algorithm. They only consider the relative distance of the path similarity. The second item of the right hand is a deviation with a symbol. The cluster is positive when the base of the cluster is larger than the average base, therefore the membership grade will increase. On the contrary, the cluster is negative when the base of the cluster is smaller than the average base, therefore the membership grade will decrease. When the base of the cluster is below the threshold, the cluster will be discarded and the number of the clusters will be refreshed. As a result, the fake cluster will vanish gradually. Because the number of cluster is larger than the number really needed, every real cluster is divided into many small clusters. By the process of the algorithm, the second item expands every cluster, including data object as much as possible. In the mean time, the restriction in formula (11) makes the neighboring clusters compete with one another and only a small number of the clusters win in the competition while the others become smaller and smaller until they finally vanish.

In the process of competitive agglomeration, it is very important to choose appropriate η in formula (9), which shows that how important the second item on the right side is to the first item. In order to make the competitive agglomeration independent of the center similarity of the cluster, the value of η should have some relation with these two items:

$$\eta \propto \frac{\sum_{i=1}^{k}\sum_{j=1}^{n} w_{ij} \, \text{sim}(t, C_{\text{center}}(c_i))}{\sum_{i=1}^{k}\sum_{j=1}^{n} w_{ij}}, \tag{15}$$

Using the value of η in paper[10]:

$$\eta(k) = \omega(k) \frac{\sum_{i=1}^{k}\sum_{j=1}^{n} w_{ij} \, \text{sim}(t, C_{\text{center}}(c_i))}{\sum_{i=1}^{k}\sum_{j=1}^{n} w_{ij}}, \tag{16}$$

Here, η is a function with k iteration, ω is defined as follows[10]:

$$\omega(k) = \omega_0 e^{-k/\tau}. \tag{17}$$

Here, ω_0 is an initialization value, τ is a timed constant.

The new cluster algorithm can know the number of the clusters automatically. When we do search in personalized Web recommendation, the threshold we set at first is lager than the numbers of clusters really needed, using the competitive agglomeration to decrease the numbers of the cluster until getting an optimal number. Furthermore, we can put the noisy data into a noisy cluster to reduce the bad impact on the performance of the cluster and thus enhance the result of the cluster.

2.3 Problem Solving

Problem P can be solved by solving the following two sub-questions based on competitive agglomeration method.

In first sub-question, the fixed variable C is used and marked as $\overline{C}$.The question has been changed to $P(W,T,\overline{C})$, where the cluster center is fixed and the partition matrix is changed. The value of W is according to the similarity between the user's access transaction and the cluster center.

In second sub-question, the fixed variable W is used and marked as $\overline{W}$. The question has been changed to $P(\overline{W},T,C)$, where partition matrix is fixed and cluster center is changed. We can solve it by getting the cluster center defined in the formula (5).

So the PCCA algorithm to solve the problem P is as follows:

(1) Initialization:
    set n=0,
    given a initial value of C^0,
    get the value of W^0 through solving $P(W,T,C^0)$.
(2) Change the cluster center:
    set $\overline{W} = W^i$,
    get the value of C^i through solving $P(\overline{W},T,C)$.
    If $P(\overline{W},T,C^i)$)= $P(\overline{W},T,C^{i+1})$), then
        output $\overline{C} = C^{i+1}$, terminate the protocol;
    Else goto the third step.
(3) Designating a cluster:
    set $\overline{C} = C^{i+1}$,
    get the value of W^{i+1} through solving $P(W,T,\overline{C})$.
    If $P(W^i,T,\overline{C}) = P(W^{i+1},T,\overline{C})$, then
        output W^i and $\overline{C}$, terminate the protocol;
    Else i=i+1,
    goto the second step.

Both PCCA algorithm and K-paths algorithm are partition clusters. They usually terminate in a local optimal cluster. Because the function $P(\cdot,\cdot)$ is not prominent and it descends strictly, so after finite steps, the algorithm will terminate at a local minimal point. The time complexity of the algorithm that is the same as the K-paths algorithm's, is O(*Iknm*), *I* is the number of the iteration. PCCA algorithm pays much attention to the user's access interest and uses competitive agglomeration method. The latter experiment proves that the result of clustering can be improved significantly for personalized Web recommendation.

3 Recommendation Set

The recommendation set is composed of useful links based on the user navigation activities on the Website. Before the Web page is sent to the client, the recommendation link is added to the last demanding page of the sessions which the users will access. We use association rule method [11] to generate recommendation set in a cluster transaction. The confidence[12] of Web page is larger than the value of association Web page set. The Web page set is this cluster's recommendation set.

Definition 6. The support of accessing Web page *s* is defined as:

$$\text{support}(s)=\frac{\text{count}(s)}{\text{count}(C)}, \tag{18}$$

Here, *C* is a cluster, count(*s*) is the number of transaction containing Web page *s* in *C*, count(*C*) is the number of transactions in *C*.

Definition 7. The confidence of accessing Web page *s* is defined as:

$$\text{confidence}(s,s')=\frac{\text{support}(s\cap s')}{\text{support}(s)}, \tag{19}$$

Here, *s'* is a Web page. If confidence (*s,s'*) is larger than threshold θ which is a constant, then $s\rightarrow s'$ is an association rule. The recommendation set of *s* in *C* is composed by all *s'*.

4 Experiments

The data set used in this experiment is from the Website—"NASA". The NASA data set contains two months worth of all HTTP requests to the NASA Kennedy Space Center WWW server in Florida. The log was collected from 00:00:00 August 1,1995 through 23:59:59 August 31,1995. In that period there were 1,569,898 requests. There were a total of 18,688 unique IPs visiting pages, having a total of 171,529 effective sessions. A total of 15,429 unique pages were visited.

Doing experiment with PCCA algorithm, we have selected randomly some transactions (30,51,70,95,108) as starting cluster center in the experiment from the user's transaction data set. Let confidence threshold θ to 5, the comparison of run time between PCCA algorithm and K-path algorithm proposed by Wang[9] is shown as figure 1.

In this paper, the value of k is determined by experiment. The experiment result shows that the correct rate is good when k equal to 70, as figure 2 shows. When the value of k is too large or too small, the correct rate of recommendation will decrease. η is a function with k iteration. It is also an important variable of competitive agglomeration method.

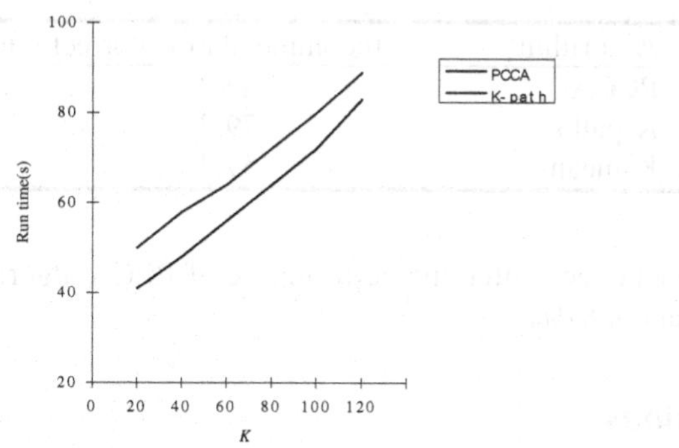

Fig. 1. The comparison of run time between PCCA algorithm and K-path algorithm

We should have an appropriate selection of the value of n. The value of n is very important to the cluster, so in order to have a good efficient algorithm, we choose a minor n that is less than 8 in our experiment[9]. Different experiments have been done according to different value of n, as the figure 3.

The experiment result shows that the algorithm has a better correct rate of recommendation when n=6. When the value of n is too large or too small, the correct rate of recommendation will decrease. We have tested the experiment result on some other different data sets, the result is consistent.

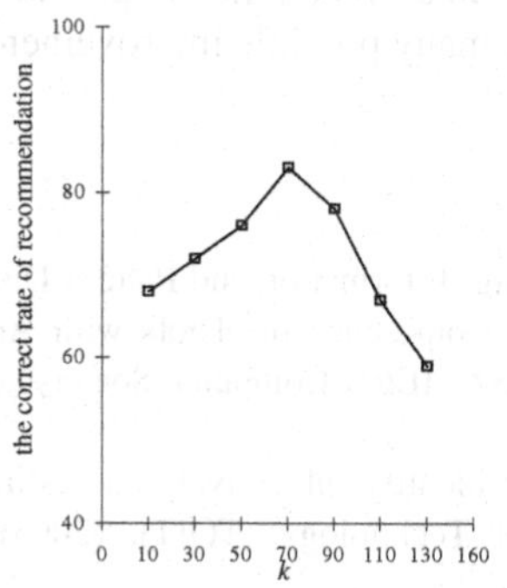

Fig. 2. Relation between K and recommendation correct rate

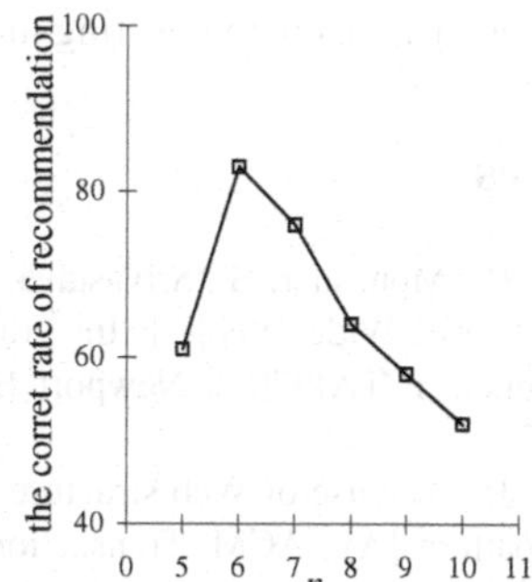

Fig. 3. Relation between n and recommendation correct rate

In table 1, a comparison is made by experiment among PCCA algorithm proposed in this paper, K-paths algorithm proposed by Wang[9] and K-means algorithm proposed by Mobasher[7,8](given the number of user's transaction is 20). Given the number of recommending Web page is 5, the value of n in PCCA algorithm and K-paths algorithm is 6 and the value of k in the K-means algorithm is $n/10$. Because the K-means algorithm can not judge whether the recommending Web page is good or not, so we select randomly 5 Web pages in the recommendation set.

Table 1. Comparison of recommendation correct rate

Algorithm	recommendation correct rate /□□□
PCCA	87.2
K-paths	79.7
K-means	57.3

The experiment shows that the performance of PCCA algorithm about correct rate is very good, about 87%.

5 Conclusions

At present, it is an interesting research for personalized Web recommendation. In this paper, we propose a new clustering algorithm. It is path clustering based on competitive agglomeration (PCCA). PCCA algorithm is effective and efficient. It has been proved by the experiment on the real data set. Based on competitive agglomeration method, the algorithm pays much attention to the user's access interest, so we needn't have user's registration information and user profiles, which can recommend without interrupting users. The algorithm avoids information deviations and outdated information as well. The algorithm has also solved the problem that the available elements will be close to zero with the increase of the users' visits and the numbers of the cluster is given by people beforehand which can not adjust dynamically by the user's access interest. The experiment results show that PCCA algorithm is effective and efficient to Web personalized recommending. Our future work will perform extensible testing and investigate many possible improvements.

References

1. Cooley, R., Mobasher, B., Srivastava, J.: Web Mining: Information and Pattern Discovery on the World Wide Web[A]. In: 9th International Conference on Tools with Artificial Intelligence, ICTAI97[C], Newport Beach, CA, USA, IEEE Computer Society, (1997): 558-567
2. Cooley, R.: The use of Web structure and content to identify subjectively interesting Web usage patterns[A]. ACM Transactions on Internet Technology (TOIT), (2003) ,3(2): 93-116
3. NASRAOUI, O., FRIGUI, H., KRISHNAPURAM, R.: Extracting Web user profiles using relational competitive fuzzy clustering [J]. International Journal on Artificial Intelligence Tools, 2000,9(4):509-526

4. MOBASHER, B., DAI, H., LUO, T.: Discovery and evaluation of aggregate usage profiles for Web personalization[J].Data Mining and Knowledge Discovery,2002,6(1):61-82
5. ENEMBRECK, F., BARTHES, J.A.: Agents for collaborative filtering [A]. Proc of Cooperative Information Agents VII, 7th International Workshop, CIA 2003 [C], Helsinki, Finland: Springer, (2003):184-191
6. BRIGGS, P., SMYTH, B.: On the use of collaborative filtering techniques for the prediction of Web search result rank [A]. Adaptive Hypermedia and Adaptive Web-Based Systems, 3rd International Conference, AH 2004 [C], Eindhoven, Netherlands: Springer,2004:380-383
7. MOBASHER, B., COOLEY, R., SRIVASTAVA, J., Automatic personalization based on Web usage mining[J]. Communications of the ACM, 2000,43(8): 142-151
8. HUANG Z., Extensions to the k-Means Algorithm for Clustering Large Data Sets with Categorical Values[J]. Data Mining and Knowledge Discovery, (1998),2(3): 283-304
9. WANG, S., GAO, W., LI, J.T.: Path clustering: discovering the knowledge in the Website [J]. Journal of Computer Research & Development,(2001),38(4): 482-486
10. FRIGUI, H., KRISHNAPURAM, R.: A robust clustering algorithm based on competitive agglomeration and soft rejection of outliers [A]. Conference on Computer Vision and Pattern Recognition (CVPR'96)[C], San Francisco, CA, USA:IEEE Computer Society, (1996):550-555
11. CHUN, J., OH, J., KWON, S.: Simulating the effectiveness of using association rules for recommendation systems [C]. AsiaSim04, Jeju Island, Korea: Springer, (2005):306-314
12. JI, G.L., SUN, Z.H.: An algorithm for mining optimized confidence quantitative association rules [J]. Journal of Southeast University (Natural Science Edition), (2001)□31(2):31-34

The Lookahead Principle for Preference Elicitation: Experimental Results

Paolo Viappiani[1], Boi Faltings[1], and Pearl Pu[2]

[1] Artificial Intelligence Laboratory (LIA)
[2] Human Computer Interaction Group(HCI)
Ecole Polytechnique Fédérale de Lausanne (EPFL)
1015 Lausanne, Switzerland
{paolo.viappiani, boi.faltings, pearl.pu}@epfl.ch

Abstract. Preference-based search is the problem of finding an item that matches best with a user's preferences. User studies show that example-based tools for preference-based search can achieve significantly higher accuracy when they are complemented with suggestions chosen to inform users about the available choices.

We discuss the problem of eliciting preferences in example-based tools and present the lookahead principle for generating suggestions. We compare two different implementations of this principle and we analyze logs of real user interactions to evaluate them.

1 Introduction

People increasingly rely on web applications to search products in online catalogs. It is common to let the user express preferences on attributes and then let a database system find the most preferred item according to these preferences. We call this task *preference-based search.*

The most common search facility is based on a form that is directly mapped to a database query and returns a list of the most suitable options. The user has the option to return to the initial page and change his preferences and then carry out a new search. This is the case for example when searching for flights on the most popular travel web sites[1][2]. Such tools are only as good as the query the user formulates. A study [3] has shown that among the users of such sites only 18% are satisfied with their final choice.

Database researchers have studied query systems that evaluate predicates with a continuous degree of validity and allow partial matches, as in fuzzy sql (`FSQL`) [2] and `Preference SQL` [8].

A key issue for preference-based search systems is how to acquire or learn preferences from the user.

One way to obtain the user model is to elicit it by a set of questions. However, it has been shown that this can lead to significant inaccuracies in the user model,

[1] `http://www.travelocity.com/`
[2] `http://www.expedia.com`

H.L. Larsen et al. (Eds.): FQAS 2006, LNAI 4027, pp. 378–389, 2006.

because users may not be able to give the correct answer at the time that they are asked by the elicitor [14]. In most cases, users do not know exactly what they are looking for: they might consider different trade-offs or they might even have conflicting desires about the features the item should have. Psychological studies [11] have shown that people construct their preferences while learning about the available products. Therefore preference-based search should also help users in formulating accurate preferences.

An alternative that often results in models of higher quality is to let users volunteer their preferences. For example, in [10] it has been shown that in a collaborative filtering system, letting users themselves propose items they want to rate yields better results than a strategy where the items are chosen to optimally elicit the preference model.

An interesting technique for letting users volunteer their preferences is an interaction where the system shows proposed options and lets users express their preferences as *critiques* stimulated by these examples. This technique is called *example* or *candidate* critiquing, and has been explored by several authors [5, 9, 18, 17].

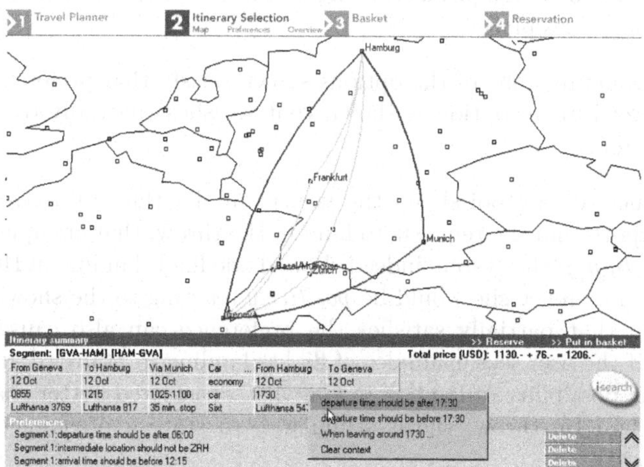

Fig. 1. Isy-travel is an example-critiquing tool for planning business-trips. Here the user is planning a one-day trip from Geneva to Hamburg. The preference model is shown at the bottom, and the user can state additional preferences by clicking on features of the shown example.

Figure 1 shows Isy-travel, a commercial tool for business travelers [12]. Here, the user is shown examples of options that fit the current preference model well. The idea is that an example either is the most preferred one, or there is some aspect in which it can be improved. Thus, on any of the examples, any attribute can be selected as a basis for critiquing. For instance, if the arrival time is too late, then this can be critiqued. The critique then becomes an additional preference in the model.

The advantage of such a system in the elicitation of preferences is that examples help users reason about their own preferences, revise them if they are inconsistent, have an idea of which preferences can be satisfied and make tradeoff decisions.

Example critiquing achieves higher decision accuracy when the displayed options are complemented with suggestions chosen to inform users about available choices [16]. The cognitive effort is comparable to simple interfaces such as a ranked list [15].

In this paper, we discuss the role of suggestions in stimulating preference expression in form of critiques. We present two alternative implementations of the *lookahead* principle on which the generation of suggestions is based and show the complexity of the computation. Finally we make an evaluation on some real user interaction logs.

2 Incremental Preference Model Acquisition

In example-critiquing, preferences are stated as reactions to displayed options. We can classify such critiques according to the context in which the statement of a preference takes place:

negative reaction none of the options shown satisfy that preference
positive reaction an option is shown that satisfies (partially or completely) the preference

For instance, if the tool shows the user examples that all arrive at London Stansted airport, and she requests to land in Heathrow, that critique would be a *negative reaction*. If the system indeed showed one flight landing in Heathrow, by stating that preference she would be *positively* reacting to the shown examples.

An option that partially satisfies the preference can also cause preference expression. If the user sees examples of flights landing in Stansted and Gatwick, by seeing the possibility of landing in Gatwick, considered better than Stansted but worse than Heathrow, she is stimulated to state a preference about the landing airports.

This simple distinction is quite fundamental in understanding the cognitive process of constructing preferences and designing the elicitation process. If certain preferences are missing from the current model of the user, the system provides examples that do not satisfy those unknown preferences. If the user is aware of all of her preferences, she can realize the necessity to state them to the system by posting what we have called a *negative reaction* critique. However our intuition is that this is not always the case, because the user might not know all the available options. Moreover, stating a preference costs some user effort (in our prototype, 2 selections and 2 clicks) and she would make that effort only if she perceives this as beneficial.

To use a metaphor, the process of example-critiquing is hill-climbing: the user states preferences as long as she perceives it as bringing to a better solution. However, the process might end in a local optimum; a situation in which the user can no longer see potential improvement. For example, a user looking for a notebook computer might start looking for a low price, and thus find that all models weigh about 3 kg. Since all of the presented models have about the same weight, he or she might never bother to look for lighter models. This influence of current examples prevents the user from refocussing the search in another direction; this is known as the *anchoring effect* [19].

For these reasons the displayed set consists of two parts:

- a **candidate** set of options that are optimal for the preference model, and
- a **suggested** set of options that are chosen to optimally stimulate the expression of preferences.

2.1 Suggestions: Diversity and Lookahead Principle

The importance of the diversity of the example shown was recognized by Linden, S. Hanks and N. Lesh [9] who explicitly generated examples that showed the extreme values of certain attributes, called *extreme examples*. However, an extreme example might often be an unreasonable choice: it could be a cheap flight that leaves in the early morning, a student accommodation where the student has to work for the family, an apartment extremely far from the city. Moreover, in problems with many attributes, there will be too many extreme or diverse examples to choose from, while we have to limit the display of examples to few of them.

We assume that the user is minimizing her own effort and will add preferences to the model only when she can expect them to have an impact on the solutions. This is the case when:

- she can see several options that differ in a possible preference, and
- these options are relevant, i.e. they could be reasonable choices, and
- these options are not already optimal, so a new preference is required to make them optimal.

In all other cases, stating an additional preference is likely to be irrelevant. When all options would lead to the same evaluation, or when the preference only has an effect on options that would not be eligible anyway, stating it would only be wasted effort. This leads us to the following *lookahead* principle as a basis for suggestion strategies:

> Suggestions should not be optimal under the current preference model, but should provide a high likelihood of optimality when an additional preference is added.

We stress that this is a heuristic principle based on assumptions about human behavior that we cannot formally prove. However in the last section we will provide empirical evidence of the correctness of this principle.

3 Theoretical Model

3.1 Modeling Items and Preferences

We assume that items are modeled by a fixed set of m attributes that each take values in associated domains. Domains can be *enumerated*, consisting of a set of discrete elements, or *numeric*. In this paper, we consider preferences on individual attributes, i.e. we do not consider conditional preferences. A preference r is an order relation of the values of an attribute a.

For a practical preference-based search tool, it is convenient to express preferences in a concise way. We consider total orders (each pair is comparable) and express them by a numerical cost function c, $d_k \rightarrow \Re^+$, that maps a domain value d_k of an attribute a_k to a real number. A preference always applies to the same attribute a_k; we use the notation $c_i(o)$ to express the cost that the function assigns to the value of option o for that attribute. Whenever o_1 is preferred to o_2 according to preference i, the first will have lower cost (for preference i) than the second: $c_i(o_1) < c_i(o_2)$.

An overall ranking of options can be obtained by combining the cost functions for all stated preferences. Some researchers [5] have proposed the use of machine learning algorithms for finding the best aggregate function for a particular user. In our systems, we combine them using a weighted sum, which corresponds well to standard multi-attribute utility theory [6]. Thus, if $\mathcal{R}_c = \{c_1, .., c_s\}$ is the set of the cost functions of all preferences that the user has stated, we compute the cost $C(o) = \sum_{c_i \in \mathcal{R}_c} w_i \cdot c_i(o)$. Option o_1 is preferred over option o_2 whenever it has a lower cost, i.e. $C(o_1) < C(o_2)$.

The user states preferences in a qualitative way (for example "the price should be less than 500 dollars"). We map these qualitative statements into parameterized functions that are standardized to fit average users. These are chosen with respect to the application domain.

Preference modeling for example-critiquing is discussed in more detail in [13]. In [7], the authors propose a similar model of preferences that allows prioritizing constraints and skyline queries.

3.2 Dominance Relation and Pareto Optimality

We model preferences by standardized functions that correctly reflect the preference order of individual attribute values but may be numerically inaccurate. When generating suggestions we would like to use a model that is not sensitive to this numerical error. We thus use the qualitative combination concepts of *dominance* and *Pareto optimality*:

An option o is **(Pareto) dominated by** another option $\bar{o}$ (equivalently we say that $\bar{o}$ dominates o) if

- $\bar{o}$ is not worse than o according to all preferences in the preference model: $\forall c_i \in R : c_i(\bar{o}) \leq c_i(o)$
- $\bar{o}$ is strictly better than o for at least one preference: $\exists c_j \in R : c_j(\bar{o}) < c_j(o)$

An option o is **Pareto-optimal** if it is not Pareto-dominated by any other option. The dominance relation is a partial order of the options that we will denote with the $\succ$ operator; Pareto-optimal options can also be seen as the set of maximal options with respect to the dominance relation.

The **dominating set** is the set of options that dominates a particular option.

3.3 Model-Based Suggestion Strategy

In [16] we proposed different strategies that use the concept of pareto optimality to implement the lookahead principle stated in the introduction: suggestions should not be optimal yet, but have a high likelihood of becoming optimal when an additional preference is added. We call them *model-based* suggestion strategies because they specifically choose examples to stimulate the expression of additional preferences based on the current preference *model*.

In our applications, users initially state only a subset R of their true preference model $\overline{R}$. When a preference is added, dominated options with respect to R can become Pareto-optimal. The lookahead principle can be formulated as follows: an ideal suggestion is an option that is Pareto-optimal with respect to the full preference model $\overline{R}$, but is dominated in R, the partial preference model.

The model based suggestions try to guess the chance that a (dominated) option has to become Pareto-optimal. This can happen when a new preference is added to the model and the option is strictly better than any dominating option with respect to this new preference.

Supposing that o_d dominates o, we use a heuristic estimation of the probability that a hidden preference on attribute a_i makes o better than o_d according to that preference, hence escaping the dominance relation. Such a heuristic considers the difference between the attribute values: the higher this difference, the more likely a new preference will make the option preferred. The reasoning is illustrated in Figure 2. The chances that a new preference will treat o_1 and o_2 differently depends on the difference between their values. Assuming that the shape of such a cost function is a step function with a sharp increase from 0 to 1 and the reference point falls at any point with equal probability, then the chance of breaking the dominance is directly proportional to this difference.

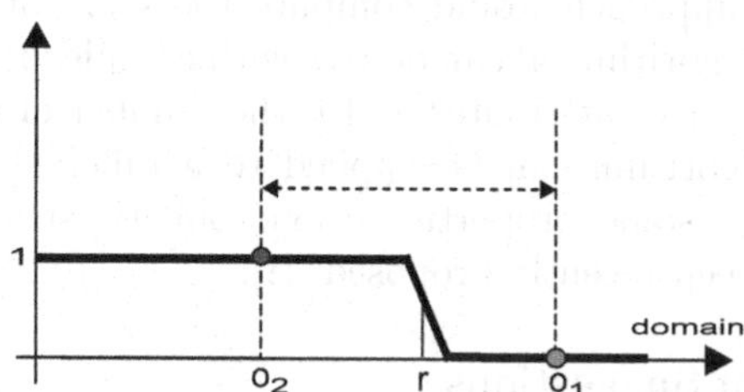

Fig. 2. For an ordered attribute, a new preference will prefer o_1 over o_2 if the reference value r falls between the values of the attribute, and the preference is of the right polarity

For attributes with enumerated domains, it is sufficient to check if the attributes takes different values. If so, there will be equal chances that one is preferred over the other. If the values are the same, the dominance relation cannot be broken by a preference on this attribute.

3.4 Utility Dominance

Other forms of dominance can be defined as extensions of Pareto-dominance such that if o Pareto-dominates o' then o also dominates o'. In particular, we might use the total ordering established by the combination function defined in the preference modeling formalism, such as a weighted sum. We call this *utility-domination*, and the utility-optimal option is the most preferred one.

An option can become utility-optimal only if it is strictly better than all options that currently utility-dominate it, although this is not a sufficient condition. The utility dominance method consists of checking the probability of breaking utility dominance. The advantage is that the dominating set is easily computed by simply checking the cost: once we have the ranking for the current preferences, the utility-dominating set will be composed by all the options with a higher ranking.

4 Algorithms

In this section we analyze the algorithms to compute the candidates and suggestion examples and their complexity.

4.1 Generation of Candidates

Preference-based search looks for the option that best satisfies a preference model, given an aggregate cost function that merge the individual preferences. The best options can be found by sorting the database items according to their cost. This is known as the *top-k query* [4]. The set of options retrieved $\{o_1, .., o_k\}$ is such that $C(o_1) \leq C(o_2) \leq .. \leq C(o_k)$ and for any other option $\bar{o}$ in the database $C(\bar{o}) \geq C(o_k)$.

While the trivial approach would compute the score of each option in the database, the *Fagin* algorithm [4] can do this with complexity $O(N^{(m-1)/m}k^{1/m})$ where m is the number of attributes and k the number of candidates we want to generate. This algorithm can be applied to a different aggregate function as long as it satisfies some properties (monotonicity, strictness). Even faster optimizations have been recently proposed [1].

4.2 Generation of Suggestions

The model-based strategy requires the analysis of the dominance relation as a preliminary phase, so that it is possible to associate a given option to its set of dominators (the options that dominate it). Pareto dominance or utility dominance can be used.

Algorithm 1. Model-based suggestions(int n)
δ heuristics based on the normalized differences

```
for all option ∈ OPTIONS do
  p(option) = 0
  for all a_i ∈ A_u = {attributes with no preferences} do
    p(option, a_i) = 1 //contribution for attribute a_i
    for all o_d ∈ O_D = {o_d ∈ O : o_d ≻ option} do
      //we iterate over the set of options that dominate o
      δ̄ ← δ_i(o, o_d)
      p(option, a_i) = update(p(option, a_i), δ̄)
  p(option) = 1 − ∏_i(1 − p(option, a_i))
suggList ← order options according p
return first n options in suggList;
```

We stress that the computation of the suggestions requires more effort than the Pareto or skyline queries (that do not return the dominating sets).

The algorithm for model-based suggestions is presented in Algorithm 1. *Update* is responsible for updating the value for the estimation of the probability $p(o, a_i)$ of becoming Pareto-optimal given that the missing preference is on a_i; its precise definition depends on the particular assumptions on the possible preferences.

In the *probabilistic* strategy, the update multiplies the current value by $w_i * \delta_i(o, o_d)$, where $\delta_i(o, o_d)$ is the heuristic estimation presented in the previous section (based on the normalized distance between the attribute values) calculated for attribute a_i and w_i is a weight representing the probability that there is a preference on that attribute. Intuitively, the more dominating options there are, the more $p(o, a_i)$ decreases.

In another model-based strategy, the *attribute* strategy, we assume that the preferences that the user can state are only of the kind `LessThan` or `GreaterThan` (the user cannot express preferences for a value in the middle). Therefore, for each attribute we check whether the current option has a value that is either smaller or bigger than any value of the dominating options: only in this case a preference can break all the dominance relations simultaneously. In this strategy, `update` will take the minimum of the absolute values of the $\bar{\delta}$, and returns 0 if they are of different signs.

Complexity. The main issue is that we do not simply need to find Pareto-optimal options but also need to know all the options that dominate a given one. Thus, most of the optimizations used by skyline queries cannot be used.

The analysis of the Pareto dominance relation makes a series of pairwise checks between the options of the catalog. Each one evaluates two options, say o_1 and o_2, to determine whether o_1 dominates o_2, o_2 dominates o_1, they are equally preferred for all the preferences, or they are not comparable (i.e. there is no dominance in either direction). This is done by considering iteratively each of the preferences and comparing o_1 and o_2 for at most m comparisons (as soon as two preferences give opposite order of o_1 and o_2, they are not comparable), where m is the number of preferences, so the complexity is $O(m)$. In the worst case we have to make $n(n-1)/2$ checks. So the complexity of the complete dominance analysis is $O(n^2m)$.

Our model based strategies have complexity $O(nmd)$, where m is the number of attributes and d is the number of dominating options. It is difficult to calculate an average value for d in function of n, because it depends on the data and correlation between attribute values. While generally the set of dominating options is much smaller than the set of options, in the worst case they can be a linear fraction of n. Sorting the options according to the resulting probability (to select the best n) costs $nlogn$ in term of complexity.

The overall complexity is $O(n^2)$: while this complexity was not a problem for our prototype, we expect it to be more problematic as the item collections grow. Approximations will be necessary for large databases.

If utility dominance is considered, the dominating set of an option is the set of all options with lower cost. However this simplification of the preliminary phase does not improve the overall complexity of the generation of suggestions. In fact we have to make, for each option, a comparison to its utility-dominators. These are 1 for the first option in the rank, 2 for the second, and n for the last. Again, we have a total complexity of $O(n^2)$.

5 Evaluation

In this section, we evaluate the lookahead principle through real user interactions. Previously [16] we conducted user studies to evaluate the decision accuracy of example critiquing with and without suggestions on a prototype for student accommodation search called *FlatFinder*. After picking their choices with different versions of the tool, users were asked to determine their best choice by carefully examining the entire database. The decision of the tool was deemed accurate whenever this choice agreed with the tool. We found that with the aid of suggestions, users state more preferences and, more importantly, achieve a much higher decision accuracy (up to 70%).

We then investigated more closely how people state preferences, using the logs from this user test and from more recent experiments. A total of 100 interaction logs were considered. 40 of these were interactions of users using the interface without suggestions (showing 6 candidate optimal examples) and the rest were interactions of users using the interface with suggestions (3 candidates and 3 suggestions shown at each cycle), calculated according to the two semantics (Pareto and utility dominance).

We expected to find an empirical confirmation of our lookahead principle for generating suggestions.

First, we counted the frequency of the different types of critiquing described before. As shown in Table 1, in most cases (79%) a preference is stated as a positive reaction to one of the displayed options. This supports our intuition: users are likely to state preferences when they see examples that show options that differ in a possible preference.

Table 1. In the majority of cases a preference is stated when the user sees an example that satisfies it (positive reaction to the displayed options)

Critiques	Frequency
Positive reactions	0.79
Negative reactions	0.21

Table 2. Summary of the user experiment comparing the interface with and without suggestions (average per user). The initial preferences are the ones stated in the initial cycle of the interaction, before having seen any example, while the final preferences are those in the last interaction cycle. The number of critiques on new attributes are a particular case of preference revision. Decision accuracy was evaluated by asking the subjects to carefully examine the entire database of offers to determine their target option, that was compared with the choice made with the search tool.

	Interface without suggestions	Interface with suggestions
interaction time (min.)	8:09	7:39
number of initial preferences	3.03	3.30
critiques (preference revisions)	5.96	6.49
critiques on new attributes	2.65	3.45
number of final preferences	4.90	5.70
decision accuracy	45%	75%

Table 3. Evaluation of the implementations of the lookahead strategy for each type of the interface: no suggestions, model-based suggestion implemented with Pareto dominance relation, model-based suggestions with utility dominance. The table shows the fraction of positive critiques that are either Pareto or utilitarian critiques. In most cases a critique is stated when there is a displayed example that becomes Pareto-optimal because of the addition of a preference.

	Fraction of positive critiques for each interface			
Critiques	No sugg.	Suggestions (Pareto)	Suggestions (Utility)	Overall
Pareto critiques	47%	60%	42%	49%
Utilitarian critiques	36%	33%	35%	35%

Surprisingly, there was no significant difference in the fraction of positive critiques between the users of the interface with suggestions and those of the interface without suggestions. However as shown in Table 2 the first group made more critiques on new attributes (3.45 vs 2.65) on average, and achieved higher decision accuracy (75% against 45%) meaning that the preferences acquired with the suggestions are more accurate.

Then, we looked more closely at the positive critiques to support the second part of our intuition, that the user states a preference when she sees options that can be a reasonable choice and a new preference is required to make them optimal. We checked how many times the user stated a preference that made one of the displayed options optimal, considering the two possible definition of dominance relation: Pareto dominance and Utility dominance. We call **Pareto** the critiques in which a Pareto-dominated option becomes Pareto-optimal; **Utilitarian** the critiques in which a Utility dominated option becomes Utility optimal.

In Table 3 we show the results for different kind of interactions: interface without suggestions, interface with suggestions computed with pareto-dominance and suggestions generated with utility-dominance. Overall, nearly half (49%) of the positive critiques are stated as Pareto critiques; the fraction increases up to 60% when suggestions are generated according to this principle. In all the circumstances, the frequency of Pareto critiques dominates that of utilitarian critiques. Therefore, Pareto optimality seems to be a reasonable way to implement the lookahead principle.

6 Conclusions

Preference-based search is a ubiquitous problem on the web. Tools based on examples can achieve higher decision accuracy than the traditional form filling approach. User studies show the importance of suggestions to make the users aware of possible choices and stimulate the preference expression.

We presented the lookahead principle that identifies good suggestions as items that have high likelihood of becoming optimal when other possible preferences are considered. By examining user behavior we found empirical evidence that suggestions are an important means to stimulate the user to refine the query. Most of the times (79%) users state preferences when they see examples that are perceived as improvement.

We discussed two possible implementations of the principle, one based on Pareto optimality and one based on a Utility ranking. The evaluation shows that the first seems to better represent the cognitive process of the user as it explains up to 60% of the cases.

References

1. W.-T. Balke and U. Güntzer. Multi-objective query processing for database systems. In M. A. Nascimento, M. T. Özsu, D. Kossmann, R. J. Miller, J. A. Blakeley, and K. B. Schiefer, editors, *VLDB*, pages 936–947. Morgan Kaufmann, 2004.
2. B. P. Buckles and F. E. Petry. Fuzzy databases in the new era. In *SAC*, pages 497–502, 1995.
3. M. S. D. W. Equity. Transportation e-commerce and the task of fulfilment, 2000.
4. R. Fagin. Fuzzy queries in multimedia database systems. In *PODS '98: Proceedings of the seventeenth ACM SIGACT-SIGMOD-SIGART symposium on Principles of database systems*, pages 1–10, New York, NY, USA, 1998. ACM Press.
5. S.-w. H. Hwanjo Yu and K. C.-C. Chang. Rankfp: A framework for supporting rank formulation and processing. In *ICDE 2005*, pages 514–515, 2005.
6. R. L. Keeney and H. Raiffa. *Decisions with Multiple Objectives: Preferences and Value Tradeoffs*. John Wiley and Sons, New York, 1976.

7. W. Kiesling. Foundations of preferences in database systems. In *VLDB 2002*, pages 311–322, 2002.
8. W. Kießling and G. Köstler. Preference sql - design, implementation, experiences. In *VLDB*, pages 990–1001, 2002.
9. G. Linden, S. Hanks, and N. Lesh. Interactive assessment of user preference models: The automated travel assistant. In *Proceedings, User Modeling '97*, 1997.
10. S. M. McNee, S. K. Lam, J. A. Konstan, and J. Riedl. Interfaces for eliciting new user preferences in recommender systems. In P. Brusilovsky, A. T. Corbett, and F. de Rosis, editors, *User Modeling 2003*, LNCS 2702, pages 178–187. Springer, 2003.
11. J. Payne, J. Bettman, and E. Johnson. *The Adaptive Decision Maker.* Cambridge University Press, 1993.
12. P. Pu and B. Faltings. Enriching buyers' experiences: the smartclient approach. In *SIGCHI conference on Human factors in computing systems*, pages 289–296. ACM Press New York, NY, USA, 2000.
13. P. Pu and B. Faltings. Decision tradeoff using example-critiquing and constraint programming. *Constraints: An International Journal*, 9(4), 2004.
14. P. Pu, B. Faltings, and M. Torrens. Effective interaction principles for online product search environments. In *Proceedings of the 3rd ACM/IEEE International Conference on Web Intelligence.* IEEE Press, September 2004.
15. P. Pu and P. Kumar. Evaluating example-based search tools. In *ACM Conference on Electronic Commerce (EC'04)*, 2004.
16. P. Pu, P. Viappiani, and B. Faltings. Increasing user decision accuracy using suggestions. In *CHI*, page to appear, April 2006.
17. H. Shimazu. Expertclerk: Navigating shoppers buying process with the combination of asking and proposing. In *Proceedings of the 17 International Joint Conference on Artificial Intelligence (IJCAI'01)*, volume 2, pages 1443–1448, 2001.
18. B. Smyth and L. McGinty. The power of suggestion. In *IJCAI*, pages 127–132, 2003.
19. A. Tversky. Judgement under uncertainity: Heuristics and biases, 1974.

Improving the User-System Interaction in a Web Multi-agent System Using Fuzzy Multi-granular Linguistic Information

E. Herrera-Viedma[1], C. Porcel[2], A.G. Lopez-Herrera[3], S. Alonso[1], and A. Zafra[1]

[1] Dept. of Computer Science and Artificial Intelligence, University of Granada
{viedma, salonso}@decsai.ugr.es
[2] Dept. of Computer Science, University of Cordoba
cporcel@uco.es
[3] Dept. of Computer Science, University of Jaen
agabriel@ujaen.es

Abstract. Nowadays, information gathering in Internet is a complex activity and Internet users need systems to assist them to obtain the information required. In an earlier studies [5, 6, 16] we presented different fuzzy linguistic multi-agent models for helping users in their information gathering processes on the Web. In this paper, we present a new fuzzy linguistic multi-agent model to access information on the Web that incorporates the use of fuzzy multi-granular linguistic modeling to improve its user-system interaction and be more user-friendly.

Keywords: Web, intelligent agents, fuzzy linguistic modelling.

1 Introduction

Information gathering on Internet is a very important, widely studied and hotly debated topic. One of the central problems in Internet is the growth of information to which Internet users are exposed. The exponential increase of Web sites and Web documents is contributing to that Internet users not being able to find the information they seek in a simple and timely manner. Users are in need of systems to help them cope with the large amount of information available on the Web [2, 18, 21, 22]. Examples of such systems include Web search engines, meta-search engines, multi-agent systems and information filtering systems [1].

A multi-agent system is one in which a number of agents cooperates and interact with each other in a distributed environment. On the Web the activity of a multi-agent system consists in to assist Internet users in information gathering processes by means of distributed intelligent agents in order to find the fittest information to their information needs. In a typical multi-agent system, the agents work together to achieve a global objective based on distributed data and control. Multi-agent systems have been widely used in Web applications [23, 25]. In the activity of a multi-agent system a basic aspect is an efficient communication among agents. The great variety of representations of the information in Internet

H.L. Larsen et al. (Eds.): FQAS 2006, LNAI 4027, pp. 390–403, 2006.

is the main obstacle to this communication, and the problem becomes more noticeable when users take part in the process. This reveals the need of more flexibility in the communication among agents and between agents and users [5, 29, 30]. To solve this problem we have applied satisfactorily the fuzzy linguistic approach [8, 9, 11, 31] in the development of different models of distributed multi-agent systems [5, 6, 16]. In these models the communication processes are improved by representing the information by means of linguistic labels. The drawback is that as the user queries as the relevance degrees of retrieved documents are assessed using the same linguistic label set with the same semantics. However, both concepts are different and have a different interpretation, and therefore, it seems reasonable and necessary to assess them with different linguistic label sets, i.e., by using multi-granular linguistic assessments [12, 15].

The aim of this paper is to present a new model of Web multi-agent system to access and retrieve information on the Web that incorporates in its activity the use of fuzzy multi-granular linguistic information to improve the user-system interaction. The communication among the agents of different levels and among the agents and users is carried out by using fuzzy multi-granular linguistic information, i.e., the different types of information that participate in the activity of the Web multi-agent system (query weights, user satisfaction degrees, relevance degrees, recommendations) are assessed with different uncertainty degrees, using several label sets with a different granularity of uncertainty. As in [16] we use the 2-tuple fuzzy linguistic representation [11] to model the linguistic information. To process the multi-granular linguistic information in the Web retrieval context we propose a method based on hierarchical linguistic contexts [12] as representation base of the multi-granular linguistic information. This new Web multi-agent model allows to represent the information in the retrieval processes with different levels of granularity. In such a way, the elements that participate in the retrieval processes are represented better and the user-system interaction is improved.

The rest of the paper is structured as follows. Section 2 reviews the fuzzy multi-granular linguistic modeling. Section 3 presents the new Web multi-agent model, and finally, some concluding remarks are pointed out.

2 Fuzzy Multi-granular Linguistic Modeling

In this section we present the fuzzy multi-granular linguistic modeling used to design the Web multi-agent model. So, we analyze the 2-tuple fuzzy linguistic approach [11], the concept of fuzzy multi-granular linguistic information and the fuzzy linguistic hierarchies [4] used in [12] to represent fuzzy multi-granular linguistic information.

2.1 The 2-Tuple Fuzzy Linguistic Approach

The 2-tuple fuzzy linguistic approach was introduced in [11] to overcome the problems of loss of information of other fuzzy linguistic approaches [8, 9, 10, 31].

Its main advantage is that the linguistic computational model based on linguistic 2-tuples can carry out processes of computing with words easier and without loss of information. To define it we have to establish the 2-tuple representation model and the 2-tuple computational model to represent and aggregate the linguistic information, respectively.

2.1.1 The 2-Tuple Representation Model

Let $S = \{s_0, ..., s_g\}$ be a linguistic term set with odd cardinality ($g + 1$ is the cardinality of S), where the mid term represents an assessment of approximately 0.5 and with the rest of the terms being placed symmetrically around it. We assume that the semantics of labels is given by means of triangular membership functions represented by a 3-tuple (a, b, c) and consider all terms distributed on a scale on which a total order is defined $s_i \leq s_j \Longleftrightarrow i \leq j$.

In this fuzzy linguistic context, if a symbolic method [8,9,10] aggregating linguistic information obtains a value $\beta \in [0, g]$, and $\beta \notin \{0, ..., g\}$, then an approximation function is used to express the result in S.

Definition 1. [11] *Let β be the result of an aggregation of the indexes of a set of labels assessed in a linguistic term set S, i.e., the result of a symbolic aggregation operation, $\beta \in [0, g]$. Let $i = round(\beta)$ ($round(\cdot)$ is the usual* round *operation) and $\alpha = \beta - i$ be two values, such that, $i \in [0, g]$ and $\alpha \in [-.5, .5)$ then α is called a Symbolic Translation.*

Roughly speaking, the symbolic translation of a linguistic term, s_i, is a numerical value assessed in $[-.5, .5)$ that supports the "difference of information" between a counting of information $\beta \in [0, g]$ obtained after a symbolic aggregation operation and the closest value in $\{0, ..., g\}$ that indicates the index of the closest linguistic term in S ($i = round(\beta)$).

The 2-tuple representation model is developed from the concept of symbolic translation by representing the linguistic information by means of 2-tuples (s_i, α_i), $s_i \in S$ and $\alpha_i \in [-.5, .5)$:

- s_i represents the linguistic label of the information, and
- α_i is a numerical value expressing the value of the translation from the original result β to the closest index label, i, in the linguistic term set ($s_i \in S$).

This model defines a set of transformation functions between numeric values and 2-tuples.

Definition 2. [11] *Let $S = \{s_0, ..., s_g\}$ be a linguistic term set and $\beta \in [0, g]$ a value representing the result of a symbolic aggregation operation, then the 2-tuple that expresses the equivalent information to β is obtained with the function $\Delta : [0, g] \longrightarrow S \times [-0.5, 0.5)$ such that*

$$\Delta(\beta) = (s_i, \alpha), \text{ with } \begin{cases} s_i & i = round(\beta) \\ \alpha = \beta - i & \alpha \in [-.5, .5) \end{cases}$$

where s_i has the closest index label to "β" and "α" is the value of the symbolic translation.

In [11] was demonstrated that for Δ there exists Δ^{-1} defined as $\Delta^{-1}(s_i, \alpha) = i+\alpha$, and that the conversion of a linguistic term into a linguistic 2-tuple consists of adding a symbolic translation value of 0: $s_i \in S \Longrightarrow (s_i, 0)$.

2.1.2 2-Tuple Computational Model

The 2-tuple computational model is defined by presenting the comparison of 2-tuples, a negation operator and aggregation operators of 2-tuples.

1. Comparison of 2-tuples. The comparison of linguistic information represented by 2-tuples is carried out according to an ordinary lexicographic order. Let (s_k, α_1) and (s_l, α_2) be two 2-tuples, with each one representing a counting of information:

- If $k < l$ then (s_k, α_1) is smaller than (s_l, α_2).
- If $k = l$ then
  1. if $\alpha_1 = \alpha_2$ then (s_k, α_1) and (s_l, α_2) represent the same information,
  2. if $\alpha_1 < \alpha_2$ then (s_k, α_1) is smaller than (s_l, α_2),
  3. if $\alpha_1 > \alpha_2$ then (s_k, α_1) is bigger than (s_l, α_2).

2. Negation operator of 2-tuples. $Neg((s_i, \alpha)) = \Delta(g - (\Delta^{-1}(s_i, \alpha)))$.
3. Aggregation operators of 2-tuples. The aggregation of information consists of obtaining a value that summarizes a set of values, therefore, the result of the aggregation of a set of 2-tuples must be a 2-tuple. In the literature we can find many aggregation operators which allow us to combine the information according to different criteria. Using functions Δ and Δ^{-1} that transform without loss of information numerical values into linguistic 2-tuples and viceversa, any of the existing aggregation operators can be easily extended for dealing with linguistic 2-tuples. Some examples are:

Definition 3. *Let $x = \{(r_1, \alpha_1), \ldots, (r_n, \alpha_n)\}$ be a set of linguistic 2-tuples, the 2-tuple arithmetic mean $\overline{x}^e$ is computed as,* $\overline{x}^e[(r_1, \alpha_1), \ldots, (r_n, \alpha_n)] =$
$\Delta(\sum_{i=1}^{n} \frac{1}{n}\Delta^{-1}(r_i, \alpha_i)) = \Delta(\frac{1}{n}\sum_{i=1}^{n} \beta_i)$.

Definition 4. *Let $x = \{(r_1, \alpha_1), \ldots, (r_n, \alpha_n)\}$ be a set of linguistic 2-tuples and $W = \{w_1, ..., w_n\}$ be their associated weights. The 2-tuple weighted average $\overline{x}^w$ is:* $\overline{x}^w[(r_1, \alpha_1), \ldots, (r_n, \alpha_n)] = \Delta(\frac{\sum_{i=1}^{n} \Delta^{-1}(r_i, \alpha_i) \cdot w_i}{\sum_{i=1}^{n} w_i}) = \Delta(\frac{\sum_{i=1}^{n} \beta_i \cdot w_i}{\sum_{i=1}^{n} w_i})$.

Definition 5. *Let $x = \{(r_1, \alpha_1), \ldots, (r_n, \alpha_n)\}$ be a set of linguistic 2-tuples and $W = \{(w_1, \alpha_1^w), ..., (w_n, \alpha_n^w)\}$ be their linguistic 2-tuple associated weights. The 2-tuple linguistic weighted average $\overline{x}_l^w$ is:* $\overline{x}_l^w[((r_1, \alpha_1), (w_1, \alpha_1^w))...((r_n, \alpha_n), (w_n, \alpha_n^w))] = \Delta(\frac{\sum_{i=1}^{n} \beta_i \cdot \beta_{W_i}}{\sum_{i=1}^{n} \beta_{W_i}})$*, with* $\beta_i = \Delta^{-1}(r_i, \alpha_i)$ *and* $\beta_{W_i} = \Delta^{-1}(w_i, \alpha_i^w)$.

2.2 Fuzzy Multi-granular Linguistic Information

In any fuzzy linguistic approach, an important parameter to determinate is the "granularity of uncertainty", i.e., the cardinality of the linguistic term set S used to express the linguistic information.

According to the uncertainty degree that an expert qualifying a phenomenon has on it, the linguistic term set chosen to provide his knowledge will have more or less terms. When different experts have different uncertainty degrees on the phenomenon, then several linguistic term sets with a different granularity of uncertainty are necessary (i.e. multi-granular linguistic information) [12, 15, 17]. In the latter case, we need tools for the management of fuzzy multi-granular linguistic information.

2.3 Fuzzy Linguistic Hierarchies

A *fuzzy linguistic hierarchy* is a set of levels, where each level is a linguistic term set with different granularity from the remaining of levels of the hierarchy [4]. Each level belonging to a linguistic hierarchy is denoted as $l(t,n(t))$, being t a number that indicates the level of the hierarchy and $n(t)$ the granularity of the linguistic term set of the level t.

Usually, fuzzy linguistic hierarchies deal with linguistic terms whose membership functions are triangular-shaped, symmetrical and uniformly distributed in [0,1]. In addition, the linguistic term sets have an odd value of granularity representing the central label the value of *indifference*.

The levels belonging to a fuzzy linguistic hierarchy are ordered according to their granularity, i.e., for two consecutive levels t and $t{+}1$, $n(t+1) > n(t)$. Therefore, each level $t+1$ provides a linguistic refinement of the previous level t.

A fuzzy linguistic hierarchy, LH, is defined as the union of all levels t: $LH = \bigcup_t l(t, n(t))$. To build LH we must keep in mind that the hierarchical order is given by the increase of the granularity of the linguistic term sets in each level. Let $S^{n(t)} = \{s_0^{n(t)}, ..., s_{n(t)-1}^{n(t)}\}$ be the linguistic term set defined in the level t with $n(t)$ terms, then the building of a fuzzy linguistic hierarchy must satisfy the following fuzzy linguistic hierarchy basic rules [12]:

1. To preserve all *former modal points* of the membership functions of each linguistic term from one level to the following one.
2. To make *smooth transactions between successive levels.* The aim is to build a new linguistic term set, $S^{n(t+1)}$. A new linguistic term will be added between each pair of terms belonging to the term set of the previous level t. To carry out this insertion, we shall reduce the support of the linguistic labels in order to keep place for the new one located in the middle of them.

Generically, we can say that the linguistic term set of level $t{+}1$, $S^{n(t+1)}$, is obtained from its predecessor level t, $S^{n(t)}$ as: $l(t, n(t)) \rightarrow l(t+1, 2 \cdot n(t) - 1)$.

Table 1. Fuzzy Linguistic Hierarchies

	Level 1	Level 2	Level 3
l(t,n(t))	l(1,3)	l(2,5)	l(3,9)
l(t,n(t))	l(1,7)	l(2,13)	

Table 1 shows the granularity needed in each linguistic term set of the level t depending on the value *n(t)* defined in the first level (3 and 7 respectively).

In [12] it was demonstrated that the fuzzy linguistic hierarchies are useful to represent and combine fuzzy multi-granular linguistic information without loss of information. To do this, a family of transformation functions between labels from different levels was defined:

Definition 6. *Let $LH = \bigcup_t l(t, n(t))$ be a fuzzy linguistic hierarchy whose linguistic term sets are denoted as $S^{n(t)} = \{s_0^{n(t)}, ..., s_{n(t)-1}^{n(t)}\}$. The transformation function between a 2-tuple that belongs to level t and another 2-tuple in level $t' \neq t$ is defined as:*

$$TF_{t'}^{t} : l(t, n(t)) \longrightarrow l(t', n(t'))$$

$$TF_{t'}^{t}(s_i^{n(t)}, \alpha^{n(t)}) = \Delta(\frac{\Delta^{-1}(s_i^{n(t)}, \alpha^{n(t)}) \cdot (n(t') - 1)}{n(t) - 1})$$

As it was pointed out in [12] this family of transformation functions is bijective.

3 A Web Multi-agent Model Based on Fuzzy Multi-granular Linguistic Information

In this Section we present a new fuzzy linguistic Web multi-agent model that improves the user-system interaction. It is developed from multi-agent model defined in [16] but using in its activity fuzzy multi-granular linguistic information.

As aforementioned, in multi-agent systems an important problem is the design of appropriate communication protocols among the agents, which is more noticeable when users take part in the process. We deal with this problem by using different fuzzy linguistic approaches [8, 9, 11, 31] as a way to introduce and handle flexible information by means of linguistic labels in the communication processes of some multi-agent models [5, 6, 16].

In [16] we presented a Web multi-agent model that combines in its activity the two more important existing filtering techniques, content-based filtering and collaborative filtering [26, 27]. In a search session a user provides his/her information needs by means of a linguistic multi-weighted query and an interest topic. Then, in a first phase the system develops the documentary retrieval using the user query, in a second phase it develops the documentary filtering using the user interest topic, and finally in a third phase it receives the user feedback, i.e., user recommendations on the accessed documents. In the complete retrieval process the linguistic information is represented using the same linguistic term set.

In this paper we present a new Web multi-agent model that could be considered as a refined system of that drawn in [16]. The refinement consists to carry out the communication among the agents of different levels and between users and agents by using different label sets, i.e. working with fuzzy multi-granular linguistic information, in order to allow a higher flexibility in the processes of communication of the system and in such a way, to improve the user-system interaction.

We consider that different assessments of retrieval activity must be assessed on different label sets, i.e., by using fuzzy multi-granular linguistic information. We assume that in the agent system the threshold weights and the relative importance weights associated with the terms of the user queries, the satisfaction degrees of weighted user queries, the relevance degree of the retrieved documents and the recommendations of the documents are expressed by means of linguistic values assessed in linguistic term sets with different granularity, S_1, S_2, S_3, S_4 and S_5 respectively. We use the linguistic term sets represented in fuzzy linguistic hierarchies to express linguistic information. For example, assuming the linguistic hierarchy shown in Table 1, the users can assess the threshold weights in the second level ($S_1 = S^5$), the relative importance weights associated with the terms in a queries in the first one ($S_2 = S^3$), the agents can assess the satisfaction degrees of a query in the second one ($S_3 = S^5$), the relevance degrees of the retrieved documents in the third one ($S_4 = S^9$), and the recommendations expressed by the users in the third one ($S_5 = S^9$).

The new Web multi-agent model presents a architecture with seven levels of activity as in [16] (see Figure 1) but all of them working with multi-granular linguistic information:

Level 1: *Internet user*, which expresses his/her information needs by means of a linguistic multi-weighted query. Each term of a user query can be weighted simultaneously by two linguistic weights. The first weight is associated with a classical threshold semantics and the second one with a relative importance semantics. Then, the user makes a query to look for those documents related to the terms $\{t_1, t_2, ..., t_m\}$, which are weighted by a linguistic degree of threshold $\{p_1^1, p_2^1, ..., p_m^1\}$ with $p_i^1 \in S_1$, and by a linguistic degree of relative importance $\{p_1^2, p_2^2, ..., p_m^2\}$ with $p_i^2 \in S_2$. All this information is given by the user to the *interface agent.*

Level 2: *Interface agent*(one for user), that communicates the user's weighted query to the task agents, and filters the retrieved documents from task agents in order to give to the users those that satisfy better their needs.

Level 3: *Collaborative filtering agent* (one for interface agent), that communicates the user multi-weighted query to the task agent, receives the more relevant documents chosen by the task agent, retrieves the recommendations on such documents from a collaborative recommendation system using only the recommendations of users with similar profiles to the user that introduce the query ($RC^{\mathcal{A}_i} = \{RC_1^{\mathcal{A}_i}, ..., RC_v^{\mathcal{A}_i}\}$ $RC_j^{\mathcal{A}_i} \in S_5 \times [-0.5, 0.5)$), filters the documents by recalculating their relevance using these recommendations, and communicates these documents together with their new relevance degrees to the interface agent. Later, it carries out the tasks to update in the collaborative recommendation system the recommendations on the documents used by the user, i.e., it invites user to provide a recommendation rc_y on each chosen document $d_y^U \in DU$ and this recommendation is stored in the collaborative recommendation system together with the recommendations provided by other users that used d_y^U.

Level 4: *Task agent* (one for interface agent, generally), that communicate the user's query to the information agents, and get those documents from every

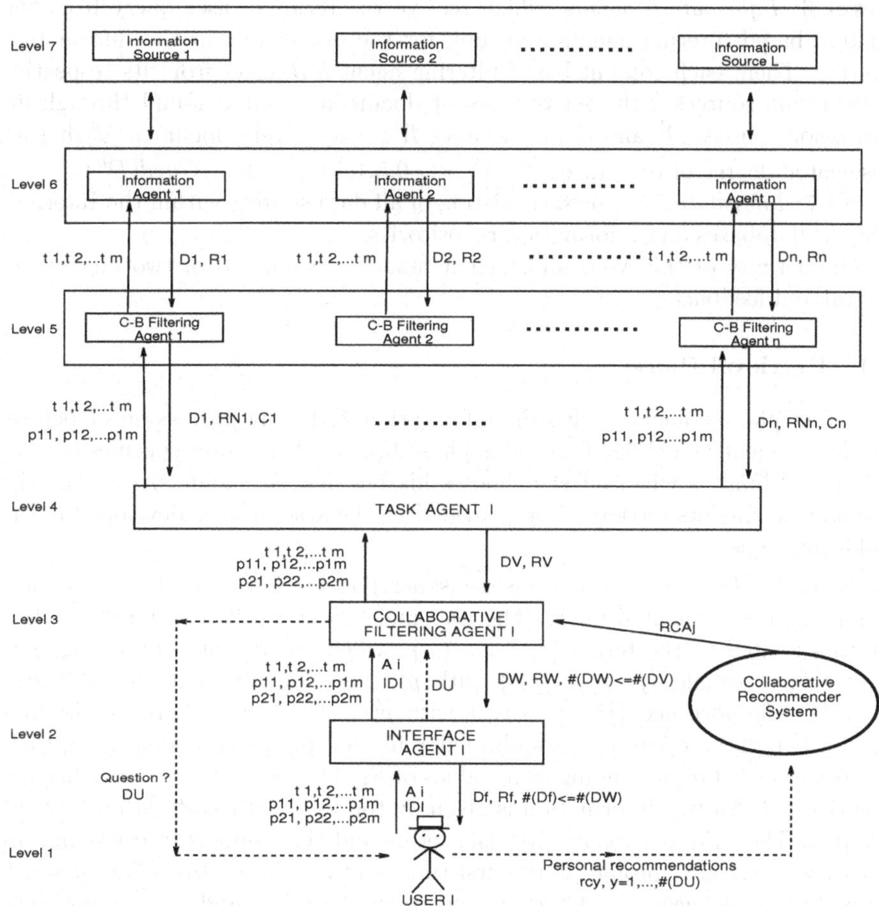

Fig. 1. Structure of a Multi-agent Model Based on Filtering Agents

information agent that fulfills better the query, fusing them and resolving the possible conflicts among the information agents.

Level 5: *Content-based filtering agent* (one for agent information). Each content-based filtering agent communicates the terms of user query to its respective information agent and filters the relevant documents provided by its information agent by recalculating their relevance using the threshold weights. Then, the task agent receives from every content-based filtering agent h a set of documents and their relevance (D^h, RN^h), where every document d_h^h has associated a linguistic degree of relevance expressed in linguistic 2-tuples $rn_j^h \in S_4 \times [-0.5, 0.5)$ $(j = 1, ..., Card(D^h))$. It also receives a set of linguistic degrees of satisfaction $C^h = \{c_1^h, c_2^h, ..., c_m^h\}$, $c_i^h \in S_3 \times [-0.5, 0.5)$ of this set of documents D^h with regard to every term of the query t_i.

Level 6: *Information agents*, which receive the terms of user query from the content-based filtering agents and look for the documents in the information sources. Then, each content-based filtering agent h receives from its respective information sources h the set of relevant documents that it found through information sources D^h and their relevance R^h, where every document d_j^h has an associated degree of relevance $r_j^h \in S_4 \times [-0.5, 0.5)$ $(j = 1, ..., Card(D^h))$.
Level 7: *Information sources*, consisting of all data sources within the Internet, such as databases and information repositories.

The activity of this Web multi-agent model is composed of two phases, retrieval and feedback.

3.1 Retrieval Phase

This first phase coincides with the information gathering process developed by the multi-agent model itself, i.e., this phase begins when a user specifies his/her query and finishes when he/she chooses his/her desired documents among the relevant documents retrieved and provided by the system. It is developed in the following steps:

Step 1: An *Internet user* expresses his/her information needs by means of a linguistic multi-weighted query. The user makes a query to look for those documents related to the terms $\{t_1, t_2, ..., t_m\}$, which are weighted by a linguistic degree of threshold $\{p_1^1, p_2^1, ..., p_m^1\}$ with $p_i^1 \in S_1$, and by a linguistic degree of relative importance $\{p_1^2, p_2^2, ..., p_m^2\}$ with $p_i^2 \in S_2$. Furthermore, in the first user-system interaction, user should define his/her profile $(\mathcal{P}_i)$ identifying their interests in each topic ranging from values of S_4. The user also expresses his/her identity $\mathcal{ID}$. All this information is given by the user to the *interface agent.*
Step 2: The *interface agent* gives the terms and their importance weights together with the user profile (in the first time) to the *collaborative filtering agent.*
Step 3: The *collaborative filtering agent* gives the terms and their importance weights to the *task agent.*
Step 4: The *task agent* communicates the terms of the query and their importance weights to all the *content-based filtering agents* to which it is connected.
Step 5: Each *content-based filtering agent h* makes the query to its respective *information agent h* and gives it the terms of the query $\{t_1, t_2, ..., t_m\}$.
Step 6: All the *information agents* that have received the query, look for the documents that better satisfies it in the *information sources.* Documents are represented in the *information sources* using an index term based representation as in Information Retrieval [1, 13, 14]. Then, there exists a finite set of index terms $T = \{t_1, ..., t_l\}$ used to represent the documents and each document d_j is represented as a fuzzy subset $d_j = \{(t_1, F(d_j, t_1)), ..., (t_l, F(d_j, t_l))\}, F(d_j, t_i) \in [0, 1]$, where F is any numerical indexing function that weights index terms according to their significance in describing the content of a document. $F(d_j, t_i) = 0$ implies that the document d_j is not at all about the concept(s) represented by index term t_i and $F(d_j, t_i) = 1$ implies that the document d_j is perfectly represented by the concept(s) indicated by t_i.

Step 7: Each *content-based filtering agent h* receives from its respective *information agent h* a set of documents and their relevances (D^h, R^h) ordered decreasingly by relevance. Every document d_j^h has an associated linguistic degree of relevance $r_j^h \in S_4 \times [-0.5, 0.5)$ which is calculated as

$$r_j^h = \overline{x}^e[\Delta(g \cdot F(d_j^h, t_1)), \ldots, \Delta(g \cdot F(d_j^h, t_m))] = \Delta(g \cdot \sum_{i=1}^{m} \frac{1}{m} F(d_j^h, t_i)),$$

being $g+1$ the cardinality of S_4. Each *content-based filtering agent h* filters documents received from its respective *information agent h* by recalculating their relevance by means of a linguistic matching function $e_h : (S_4 \times [-0.5, 0.5)) \times S_1 \rightarrow S_4 \times [-0.5, 0.5)$, which is defined to model the semantics of threshold weights associated with the query terms. This linguistic matching function requires a previous transformation of threshold weights expressed in labels of S_1 that must be transformed in labels of S_4, to make uniform the multi-granular linguistic information, we chose the linguistic term set used to express the relevance degrees. We use the transformation function viewed in Definition 6, $(TF_{t'}^t)$, to transform the linguistic labels in level S_1 (t) to labels in level S_4 (t'), and then we obtain new linguistic threshold weights $\{p_1^{1'}, p_2^{1'}, ..., p_m^{1'}\}$, $p_i^{1'} \in S_4$ for the terms $\{t_1, t_2, ..., t_m\}$. Then, each *content-based filtering agent h* calculates a new set of relevance degrees $RN^h = \{rn_j^h, j = 1, ..., card(D^h)\}$ characterizing the documents D^h, which is obtained as

$$rn_j^h = \overline{x}^e[e_h(\Delta(g \cdot F(d_j^h, t_1)), p_1^{1'}), ..., e_h(\Delta(g \cdot F(d_j^h, t_m)), p_m^{1'})] =$$

$$\Delta(\sum_{i=1}^{m} \frac{1}{m} \Delta^{-1}(e_h(\Delta(g \cdot F(d_j^h, t_i)), p_i^{1'}))).$$

Step 8: The *task agent* receives from every *content-based filtering agent* a set of documents and their new relevance (D^h, RN^h). It also receives a set of linguistic degrees of satisfaction $C^h = \{c_1^h, c_2^h, ..., c_m^h\}$, $c_i^h \in S_3 \times [-0.5, 0.5)$ of D^h with regard to every term of the query as

$$c_i^h = \overline{x}^e[e_h(\Delta(g \cdot F(d_1^h, t_i)), p_i^{1'}), ..., e_h(\Delta(g \cdot F(d_{card(D^h)}^h, t_i)), p_i^{1'})] =$$

$$\Delta(\sum_{j=1}^{card(D^h)} \frac{1}{card(D^h)} \Delta^{-1}(e_h(\Delta(g \cdot F(d_j^h, t_i)), p_i^{1'}))).$$

Then, the *task agent* selects the number of documents to be retrieved from each *content-based filtering agent h*. So, it applies the following three steps:
Step 8.1: The *task agent* orders D^h with respect to the new relevance RN.
Step 8.2: The *task agent* aggregates both linguistic information weights, the satisfactions of the terms of the query from every *information agent*, $(c_i^h, \alpha_i), c_i^h \in S_3$, and the importance weights that the user assigned to these terms, (p_i^2, α_i), $p_i^2 \in S_2$, using the aggregation process for fuzzy multi-granular linguistic information presented in [12], which is composed of two phases:

1. *Normalization Phase*: The linguistic term set used to express the relevance is chosen to make uniform the multi-granular linguistic information. Then, all the information are expressed in that linguistic term set by means of 2-tuples.
2. *Aggregation Phase*: Through a 2-tuple aggregation operator the information is aggregated. In this paper we use the 2-tuple linguistic weighted average operator, $\overline{x}_l^w$, for combining the satisfactions of the terms of the query and the importance weights.

Let $\{[(p_1^2, \alpha_1), (c_1^h, \alpha_1^w)], ..., [(p_m^2, \alpha_m), (c_m^h, \alpha_m^w)]\}$, $p_i^2 \in S_2$ *and* $c_i^h \in S_3$ be the set of pairs of importance and satisfaction to be aggregated by the task agent for every information agent h. Then, for combining them first the linguistic 2-tuples values $(p_i^2, \alpha_i), p_i^2 \in S_2$ and $(c_i^h, \alpha_i^w), c_i^h \in S_3$ are transformed in the linguistic term set used to express the relevance degrees, in this case S_4, obtaining their corresponding values $(p_i^{2'}, \alpha_i')$, $p_i^{2'} \in S_4$ and $(c_i^{h'}, \alpha_i^{w'})$, $c_i^{h'} \in S_4$. Once the fuzzy multi-granular information has been unified according to the 2-tuple linguistic weighted average operator definition, the aggregation of the pair associated with every term is obtained as $\lambda^h = \overline{x}_l^w([(p_1^{2'}, \alpha_1'), (c_1^{h'}, \alpha_1^{w'})], ..., [(p_m^{2'}, \alpha_m'), (c_m^{h'}, \alpha_m^{w'})])$.

Step 8.3: To gather the best documents from *content-based filtering agents*, the *task agent* selects a number of documents $k(D^h)$ from every *content-based filtering agent h* being proportional to its respective degree of satisfaction λ^h, $k(D^h) = round(\frac{\sum_{i=1}^n card(D^i)}{n} \cdot P_s^h)$, where $P_s^h = \frac{\Delta^{-1}(\lambda^h)}{\sum_{i=1}^n \Delta^{-1}(\lambda^h)}$ is the probability of selection of the documents from *content-based filtering agent h.*

Step 9: The *collaborative filtering agent* receives from the *task agent* a list of documents $DV = \{d_1^V, ..., d_v^V\}$ ordered with respect to their relevance RV, such that, i) $r_j^V \geq r_{j+1}^V$, ii) for a given document $d_j^V \in DV$ there exists a h such that $d_j^V \in D^h$ and $r_j^V \in RN^h$, and iii) $card(DV) = v \leq \sum_{i=1}^n k(D^i)$.

Then, *collaborative filtering agent* filters the documents provided by the *task agent* using the recommendations on such documents provided by other users with similar preferences (checking their profile) in previous searches. These recommendations are stored together with user profiles in a *collaborative recommender system.* This is done in the following steps:

Step 9.1: The *collaborative filtering agent* asks *collaborative recommender system* the recommendations existing on DV of that users with a similar profile to the active user ($\mathcal{P}_i$) and retrieves them, $RC^{\mathcal{P}_i} = \{RC_1^{\mathcal{P}_i}, ..., RC_v^{\mathcal{P}_i}\}$, $RC_j^{\mathcal{P}_i} \in S_5 \times [-0.5, 0.5)$.

Step 9.2: The *collaborative filtering agent* filters the documents by recalculating their relevance using these recommendations $RC^{\mathcal{P}_i}$. Then, for each document $d_j^V \in DV$ a new linguistic relevance degree r_j^{NV} is recalculated from r_j^V and $RC_j^{\mathcal{P}_i}$ by means of the 2-tuple weighted operator $\overline{x}^w$ given in Definition 4: $r_j^{NV} = \overline{x}^w(r_j^V, RC_j^{\mathcal{P}_i})$, using, for example, the weighting vector $W = [0.6, 0.4]$.

Step 10: The *interface agent* receives from the *collaborative filtering agent* a list of documents $DW = \{d_1^W, ..., d_w^W\}$ ordered with respect to their relevance RW, such that, i) $r_j^W \geq r_{j+1}^W$, ii) for a given document $d_j^W \in DW$ there exists a i such that $d_j^W = d_i^V$ and $r_j^W = r_i^{NV}$, and iii) $card(DW) = w \leq v = card(DV)$.

Then, the *interface agent* filters these documents in order to give to the user only those documents that fulfill better his/her needs, which we call D_f. For example, it can select a fixed number of documents K and to show the K best documents.

3.2 Feedback Phase

This second phase coincides with the updating process of collaborative recommendations on desired documents existing in the collaborative recommender system, i.e., this phase begins when the *interface agent* informs the documents chosen by the user to the *collaborative filtering agent* and finishes when the recommender system recalculates and updates the recommendations of the desired documents. In collaborative recommender systems the people collaborate to help one another to perform filtering by recording their reactions to documents they read [19, 27]. This feedback activity is developed in the following steps:

Step 1: The *interface agent* gives the user's identity $\mathcal{ID}$ (usually his/her e-mail) together with the set of documents $DU = \{d_1^U, ..., d_u^U\}$, $u \leq card(D_f)$ used by the user to the *collaborative filtering agent.*
Step 2: The *collaborative filtering agent* asks user his/her opinion or evaluation judgements about DU, for example by means of an e-mail.
Step 3: The *Internet user* communicates linguistic evaluation judgements to the *collaborative recommender system*, rc_y, $y = 1, ..., card(DU)$, $rc_y \in S_5$.
Step 4: The *collaborative recommender system* recalculates the linguistic recommendations of set of documents DU by aggregating again the opinions provided by other users together with those provided by the Internet user. This can be done using the 2-tuple aggregation operator $\overline{x}^e$ given in Definition 3. Then, given a chosen document $d_y^U \in DU$ that receives a recommendation or evaluation judgement rc_y from the Internet user, and supposing that in the collaborative recommender system there exists a set of stored linguistic recommendations $\{rc_1, ..., rc_M\}$, $rc_i \in S_5$ associated with d_y^U for the user profile $\mathcal{P}_i$, which were provided by M different users in previous searches, then a new value of recommendation of d_y^U is obtained as $RC_y^{\mathcal{P}_i} = \overline{x}^e[(rc_1, 0), ...(rc_M, 0), (rc_y, 0)]$.

4 Concluding Remarks

We have presented a new fuzzy linguistic Web multi-agent model where the communication processes carried out in the information gathering are modeled by means of the fuzzy multi-granular linguistic information. To do so, we have used the hierarchical linguistic contexts and the 2-tuple linguistic computational model. The use of the fuzzy multi-granular linguistic information allows a higher flexibility and expressiveness in the communication among the agents and between users and agents in the information gathering process and it does not decrease the precision of system in its results and the complexity of the processes is not increased.

Acknowledgments

This work has been partially supported by Research Project TIC2003-07977.

References

1. R. Baeza-Yates, B. Ribeiro-Neto, Modern information retrieval, Adisson, 1999.
2. G. Bordogna, G. Pasi, R.R. Yager. *Soft approaches to distributed information retrieval.* International Journal of Approximate Reasoning, 34 (2003) 105-120.
3. W. Brenner, R. Zarnekow and H. Witting, *Intelligent Software Agent, Foundations and Applications.* Springer-Verlag. Berlin Heidelberg (1998).
4. O. Cordón, F. Herrera and I. Zwir. *Linguistic modelling by hierarchical systems of linguistic rules.* IEEE Transactions on Fuzzy Systems, 10 (1) (2001) 2-20.
5. M. Delgado, F. Herrera, E. Herrera-Viedma, M.J. Martín-Bautista, M.A. Vila, Combining linguistic information in a distributed intelligent agent model for information gathering on the Internet, in P.P. Wang, Ed., *Computing with Words,* (John Wiley & Son, 2001) 251-276.
6. M. Delgado, F. Herrera, E. Herrera-Viedma, M.J. Martín-Bautista, L. Martínez, M.A. Vila. A communication model based on the 2-tuple fuzzy linguistic representation for a distributed intelligent agent system on Internet, *Soft Computing,* 6 (2002) 320-328.
7. J. Ferber, *Multi-Agent Systems: An Introduction to Distributed Artificial Intelligence.* Addison-Wesley Longman, New York (1999).
8. F. Herrera, E. Herrera-Viedma, J.L. Verdegay, A model of consensus in group decision making under linguistic assessments. *Fuzzy Sets and Systems,* 78 (1996) 73-87.
9. F. Herrera, E. Herrera-Viedma, J.L. Verdegay, Direct approach processes in group decision making using linguistic OWA operators, *Fuzzy Sets and Systems,* 79 (1996) 175-190.
10. F. Herrera, E. Herrera-Viedma, Aggregation operators for linguistic weighted information, *IEEE Trans. on Systems, Man and Cybernetics, Part A: Systems and Humans,* 27 (5) (1997) 646-656.
11. F. Herrera, L. Martínez, A 2-tuple fuzzy linguistic representation model for computing with words, *IEEE Transactions on Fuzzy Systems,* 8(6) (2000) 746-752.
12. F. Herrera, L. Martínez, A model based on linguistic 2-tuples for dealing with multigranularity hierarchical linguistic contexts in multiexpert decision-making, *IEEE Transactions on Systems, Man and Cybernetics. Part B: Cybernetics,* 31(2) (2001) 227-234.
13. E. Herrera-Viedma, Modeling the retrieval process of an information retrieval system using an ordinal fuzzy linguistic approach, *J. of the American Society for Information Science and Technology,* 52(6) (2001) 460-475.
14. E. Herrera-Viedma, An information retrieval system with ordinal linguistic weighted queries based on two weighting elements, *Int. J. of Uncertainty, Fuzziness and Knowledge-Based Systems* 9 (2001) 77-88.
15. E. Herrera-Viedma, O. Cordón, M. Luque, A.G. López, A.M. Muñoz, A Model of Fuzzy Linguistic IRS Based on Multi-Granular Linguistic Information, *International Journal of Approximate Reasoning,* 34(3) (2003) 221-239.
16. E. Herrera-Viedma, F. Herrera, L. Martínez, J.C. Herrera, A.G. López, Incorporating filtering techniques in a fuzzy linguistic multi-agent model for information gathering on the Web, *Fuzzy Sets and Systems,* 148 (1) (2004) 61-83.

17. E. Herrera-Viedma, F. Mata, L. Martínez, F. Chiclana, A consensus support system model for group decision-making problems with multi-granular linguistic preference relations, *IEEE Transactions on Fuzzy Systems* 13(5) (2005) 644-658.
18. E. Herrera-Viedma, G. Pasi, A.G. Lopez-Herrera, C. Porcel, Evaluating the information quality of Web sites: A methodology based on fuzzy computing with words, *Journal of the American Society for Information Science and Technology* 57(4) (2006) 538-549.
19. E. Herrera-Viedma, E. Peis, Evaluating the informative quality of documents in SGML-format using fuzzy linguistic techniques based on computing with words, *Information Processing & Management* 39(2) (2003) 195-213.
20. N. Jennings, K. Sycara, M. Wooldridge, A roadmap of agent research and development, *Autonomous Agents and Multi-Agents Systems*, 1 (1998) 7-38.
21. M. Kobayashi, K. Takeda, Information retrieval on the web, *ACM Computing Surveys*, 32(2) (2000) 144-173.
22. S. Lawrence, C. Giles, Searching the web: General and scientific information access, *IEEE Comm. Magazine*, 37 (1) (1998) 116-122.
23. H. Lieberman, Personal assistants for the Web: A MIT perspective. In M.Klusch(Ed.), *Intelligent Information Agents* (Springer-Verlag, 1999) 279-292.
24. P. Maes, Agents that reduce work and information overload, *Comm. of the ACM*, 37 (1994) 31-40.
25. A. Moukas, G. Zacharia, P. Maes, Amalthaea and Histos: Multiagent systems for WWW sites and representation recommendations, in M. Klusch(Ed.), *Intelligent Information Agents* (Springer-Verlag, 1999) 293-322.
26. A. Popescul, L.H. Ungar, D.M. Pennock, S. Lawrence, Probabilistic models for unified collaborative and content-based recommendation in sparce-data environments. In *Proceedings of the Seventeenth Conference on Uncertainty in Artificial Intelligence (UAI)*, San Francisco, (2001) 437-444.
27. P. Reisnick, H.R. Varian, Recommender Systems. Special issue of Comm. of the ACM, 40 (3) (1997).
28. K. Sycara, A. Pannu, M. Williamson, D. Zeng, Distributed intelligent agents, *IEEE Expert* (1996) 36-46.
29. R.R. Yager, Protocol for negotiations among multiple intelligent agents, in: J. Kacprzyk, H. Nurmi and M. Fedrizzi Eds., *Consensus Under Fuzziness* (Kluwer Academic Publishers, 1996) 165-174.
30. R.R. Yager, Intelligent agents for World Wide Web advertising decisions, *International J. of Intelligent Systems*, 12 (1997) 379-390.
31. L.A. Zadeh, The concept of a linguistic variable and its applications to approximate reasoning. Part I, *Information Sciences*, 8 (1975) 199-249, Part II, *Information Sciences*, 8 (1975) 301-357, Part III, *Information Sciences*, 9 (1975) 43-80.

Using Dynamic Fuzzy Ontologies to Understand Creative Environments

Silvia Calegari and Marco Loregian

Dipartimento di Informatica, Sistemistica e Comunicazione,
Università degli Studi di Milano Bicocca,
via Bicocca degli Arcimboldi 8,
20126 Milano, Italy
{calegari, loregian}@disco.unimib.it

Abstract. This paper presents a method to model knowledge in creative environments using dynamic fuzzy ontologies. Dynamic fuzzy ontologies are ontologies that evolve in time to adapt to the environment in which they are used, and whose taxonomies and relationships among concepts are enriched with fuzzy weights (i.e., numeric values between 0 and 1). Such cognitive artifacts can provide for higher user awareness in learning environments, as well as for greater creative stimulus for knowledge discovery. This paper gives the definitions of dynamic fuzzy ontologies, the details of how fuzzy values are dynamically assigned to concepts and relations, and presents an experimental evaluation of the proposed approach.

1 Introduction

ATELIER (Architecture and Technologies for Inspirational Learning Environments) is an EU-funded project that is part of the Disappearing Computer initiative[1]. The aim of the project is to build a digitally enhanced environment supporting creative learning processes in architecture and interaction design education. The ATELIER studio is a room in which students feel comfortable with technology and which they can fully configure to fit their needs [1]. Several technologies have already been adopted to build a complex system to support students, and make their work easier, so they can focus more on their actual tasks rather than on learning how to use the system. The ATELIER software infrastructure provides the means for devices and applications to communicate. It also includes a hyper-media database (HMDB) that is used to store all digital material collected by the students.

Students in creative learning environments work daily with very large amounts of documents created during group projects. It is important that they can easily find and access their own data, as well as those of others, and also that they have means to sort, annotate and browse such digital material. The contents that they create and collect (e.g., digital pictures, handmade sketches, notes,

[1] http://www.disappearing-computer.net

H.L. Larsen et al. (Eds.): FQAS 2006, LNAI 4027, pp. 404–415, 2006.

videos) can be analyzed in different ways and from different points of view since the same item can be given different meanings and relevance according to the *context* in which it is used.

Context can be defined as "the location, identity and state of people, groups and computational and physical objects" [2]. In ATELIER, an approach has been studied to provide students with contents that can enhance their learning experience by presenting surprising yet meaningful information. The approach relies on an ontology and exploits user profiles and system history, also considering the specific applications that students are using [3].

More precisely, to support students in creative practices an ontology-driven selection facility (including the metrics and an algorithm) has been developed to move from one document to another in a creative path without involving users in typing and explicit query writing. This research has been the starting point for the work presented in this paper, highlighting the need for a more flexible knowledge representation in the creative environment.

The main contribution of this paper is the description of how we shifted from a "classical" ontology [4] to a **dynamic fuzzy ontology**, where dynamic refers to the maintenance process [5] and scalability of the representation. We define the properties of such an artifact and describe the steps through which it has been built and evaluated.

A fuzzy ontology is an ontology whose instances are weighted according to their semantic representativeness of the class to which they belong. Instances of concepts have a *membership value* that is ranged between 0 and 1. Membership assumes a higher value for those instances that "better" represent the concept. Calegari and Ciucci presented a more complete introduction to fuzzy ontologies [6], from which the following definition (later complemented by Definition 2) is derived:

Definition 1. *A* ***fuzzy ontology*** *is an ontology extended with fuzzy values assigned through the functions*
$m : Instances \mapsto [0, 1]$
$v : Property\_values \mapsto [0, 1]$

Section 2 presents the metrics to assign the fuzzy values to a given ontology. The values can be updated at runtime, so that the ontology consistently represent the status of the system with respect to the domain of interest. The ontology evolves in time and can be considered a *dynamic* fuzzy ontology [5, 6].

The proposed approach is evaluated experimentally in Section 3, where some data are analyzed and an interactive tool developed for ATELIER is presented. Sections 4 and 5 present related work and concluding remarks.

2 Building the Fuzzy Ontology

In order to make an ontology dynamically adapt to the context in which it is used, i.e., to what students are doing with documents and applications, the ontology has to be updated according to actions taking place.

When a query is performed on the HMDB (e.g., to insert a new document or to search for other documents), the ontology has to be provided with additional information, according to a set of relevant factors. Among other factors [3], the following two have been assumed to be prominent in determining the metrics to compute this kind of information:

1. *User's expertise*: the more the user who is interacting with the system is expert with respect to a certain topic (i.e., the more he/she is prolific, therefore influent within the community), the more his/her actions will have an impact on the ontology [7].
2. *Correlations* between keywords used to describe documents: when concepts are used together in a query, a relationship between them is established (also known in literature as co-occurrence [8]).

A correlation in a fuzzy ontology can be formally defined in the following way:

Definition 2. *A* ***correlation*** *in a fuzzy ontology is a binary and symmetric relation between concepts, and it is provided with a fuzzy value:*
$corr : Instances \times Instances \mapsto [0, 1]$.

A correlation is binary, meaning that it describes the way in which **couples** of concepts are tied by a relationship, and symmetric, meaning that the order in which keywords are written in a query is not relevant. Richer semantic expressiveness can be achieved in queries when conceptual modifiers are used:

Definition 3. *A* ***conceptual modifier*** *in a query is a special word that is used to characterize how a keyword should be intended with respect to the others or with respect to the expected results. A positive β value is associated to each conceptual modifier in a given numeric interval. β is used as an exponent to modify the value of an existing membership or correlation.*

For example, the most common conceptual modifiers are *little, very, quite*, etc. Queries with conceptual modifiers are in the form: "*very(red)*", "*little(yellow green)*", "*little(pink) OR moderately(black white)*". Modifiers apply to all keywords in brackets, in order to form an independent query, but the composition of "modified" sub-queries is usually considered as a whole. According to existing literature [9] the following β mappings can be adopted:

Table 1. Beta values corresponding to the most common conceptual modifiers

Modifier	β
little	0.5
enough	0.6
moderately	0.8
quite	1.2
very	1.5
totally	2

Before entering into the details of the metrics to update fuzzy values in practice, values are assigned to *instances* of concepts and correlations. This detail is sometimes omitted for the sake of conciseness, and it can be done because only one instance is allowed for each concept (since concepts are only used for indexing and searching documents, and not to directly make reasoning on document instances) and for each correlation (i.e., each correlation is uniquely defined by the two concepts it ties).

2.1 How to Update the Membership Value of Individual Concepts

When a query involving a particular concept is performed, the first factor to be estimated is the expertise of the user who is interacting with the system. Expertise is computed as the ratio between the number of documents created by the person (and classified according to the specific concept) and those belonging to the same set but created by other people. This value (*exp*) is an estimation of the relative importance of the author with respect to the community of users who have created documents related to the concept.

$$exp_i = \frac{1 + \left|\{d \mid author(d) \wedge d \in Docs_i\}\right|}{1 + \left|\{Docs_i\}\right|} \quad (1)$$

When a concept is used for the first time in a query, it is added to the ontology and an instance of it is created having the membership (m) set equal to:

$$m_{(0)}(i) = exp_i \quad (2)$$

In practice m is set to 1, as it can be noted by resolving equation 1 when there is only one document indexed using keyword i and it is authored by the user himself. For other queries the updated value of m is set equal to:

$$m_{(n)}(i) = \frac{((m_{n-1}(i))^{\frac{1}{\beta_i}} + 1) \cdot exp_i}{Q_i + 1} \quad (3)$$

where the numerator is computed according to the current membership value, to the conceptual modifier used in the query, and according to user's expertise. The denominator is computed as follows, to normalize the final value of the ratio in the interval [0,1]:

$$Q_i = \frac{\left|\{q_i \in Queries_i\}\right|}{\left|\{Queries\}\right|} \quad (4)$$

where $\left|\{Queries\}\right|$ is the total number of queries performed in the system and $\left|\{q_i \in Queries_i\}\right|$ is the number of queries in which keyword i has been used.

2.2 How to Update the Value of Correlations

In a similar way, metrics to compute updated values for correlations—when performing a query—can be written. Expertise has to be evaluated with respect to couples of keywords (remember that we defined the correlation between concepts as a binary and symmetric relation).

$$exp_{i,j} = \frac{1 + \left|\{d \mid author(d) \wedge d \in Docs_{i,j}\}\right|}{1 + \left|\{Docs_{i,j}\}\right|} \tag{5}$$

When a correlation is created (at time n), its value is computed taking into account the current membership values of both the concepts to be correlated and the specific conceptual modifier:

$$corr_{(0)}(i,j) = ((m_n(i) + m_n(j))^{\frac{1}{\beta_{i,j}}} + 1) \cdot exp_{i,j} \tag{6}$$

In the following steps, also the existing value of $corr$ is taken into account:

$$corr_{(n)}(i,j) = min\{1, corr_{n-1}(i,j) + \frac{|((m_n(i) + m_n(j))^{\frac{1}{\beta_{i,j}}} + 1) \cdot exp_{i,j} - corr_{n-1}(i,j)|}{Q_{i,j} + 1}\} \tag{7}$$

where it is necessary to choose the minimum value between 1 and the new value computed for $corr_n$, to be certain that the value is in $[0, 1]$. In the formula above:

$$Q_{i,j} = \frac{\left|\{q_{i,j} \in Queries_{i,j}\}\right|}{\left|\{Queries\}\right|} \tag{8}$$

where $\left|\{Queries\}\right|$ is the total number of queries performed in the system and $\left|\{q_{i,j} \in Queries_{i,j}\}\right|$ is the number of queries in which both keyword i and keyword j have been used.

3 Evaluating the Fuzzy Ontology

In order to evaluate the effectiveness of the proposed approach, two strategies have been adopted. First, the impact of the fuzzy ontology on system users has been rapidly evaluated by developing a tool to interact with a graphical representation of the ontology. The tool is intended to show a "snapshot" of the environment (from a knowledge perspective), in order to be able to easily exploit the ontology and its correlations and to interact with the HMDB (see Section 3.2). The second evaluation (Section 3.1) is based on an experimental approach: the evolution of the ATELIER fuzzy ontology has been simulated by re-enacting the history of one of the projects lead during the life of the system. Document insertions in the HMDB, as well as search queries recorded during these experiments have been used to calculate the membership values of concepts and correlations. After this kind of training, more test queries have been used to evaluate the behavior of the fuzzy ontology in response to queries written using conceptual modifiers. The aim of this last test is to simulate the act of allowing students to use conceptual modifiers in queries to see how the fuzzy ontology adapts to the event.

3.1 Analysis of the Simulation

During the ATELIER project, the life of various student projects have been logged. All actions performed on the HMDB and on the ontology during these experiences have been saved on files that are now part of the project documentation. One of the logs, referring to a short experience at the Academy of Fine Arts in Vienna, has been used to simulate the introduction of a fuzzy ontology.

The HMDB had been filled with 485 documents, collected by six different students over two weeks. The same students had also performed 138 search queries on the HMDB during the life of the project, but the conceptual modifiers could not be used. These same operations have been used to compute the values of the fuzzy ontologies, according to the metrics described in the previous Section.

The ontology then counted 118 concepts, tied by 431 correlations. Fig. 1 shows the growth in size of the sets of concepts and correlations during the experiment. Quite obviously, the number of concepts grew more slowly than the number of correlations discovered among them, and they both tended to stabilize after a while.

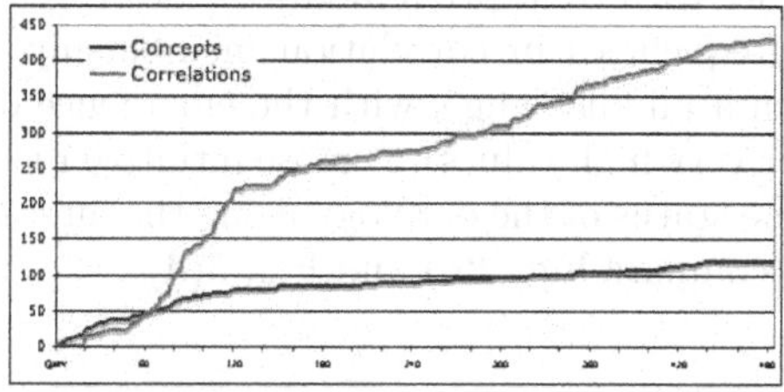

Fig. 1. Evolution of the ontology: increasing number of concepts and correlations

After this construction phase, the fuzzy ontology has been monitored to evaluate the impact of conceptual modifiers. 50 more queries *with conceptual modifiers* have been used as an input to retrieve inspirational documents from the HMDB.

The algorithm adopted in ATELIER before this work has not been designed to deal with modifiers, therefore some slight changes have been necessary. The inspirational extraction algorithm [3] can be briefly summarized as follows: when a query is sent to the application implementing the extraction mechanism, a query extension mechanism is adopted, based on correlations in the ontology. The original query is extended to also include concepts that are correlated with the starting ones. The query is then pruned by excluding keywords that cannot be related to the starting ones by a direct path in the taxonomy. Keywords kept in the enriched query are then weighted to establish their importance in the query, and information provided by conceptual modifiers can be used here:

$$k_i = \frac{\sum_{j=i,\, j\neq i}^{n} [corr(i,j)]^{\beta_{i,j}}}{l_i^2} \cdot [m(i)]^{\beta_i} \tag{9}$$

Documents having been indexed with at least one of the keywords in the query are then extracted from the HMDB and their distance from the query is computed as follows:

$$d(x,k) = \frac{\sum_{i=1}^{n} (w_{x,i} \cdot k_i)}{\sqrt{\sum_{i=1}^{n} w_{x,i}^2 \cdot \sum_{i=1}^{n} k_i^2}} \tag{10}$$

Relevance of the results is then computed, in order to express the ability of each document to fulfill the "inspirational expectations" of the user.

$$R(x) = d(x,k) \cdot match(x,k) \tag{11}$$

Where $match(x,k)$ is the percentage of the keyword set that the single document is able to cover. This experiment proved that the fuzzy ontology can be used to support the existing application, and it can also carry a noteworthy improvement in performance. With the earlier approach, system history must be evaluated for each query, and it cannot be properly stored. Fuzzy values and correlations embedded in the fuzzy ontology allow for a quicker execution of the computation.

The fuzzy values in the ontology have been compared before and after the execution of the queries with conceptual modifiers (see Fig. 2). After the queries, the distribution of frequencies in correlation membership values seems to be more homogeneous in a middle range, with the emergence of other cases at the extremes (very low or very high values). A more intuitive reading of Fig. 2 can be seen by comparing the status of the ontology using the interactive tool presented in the next Section (compare Fig. 3(c) and Fig. 3(d)).

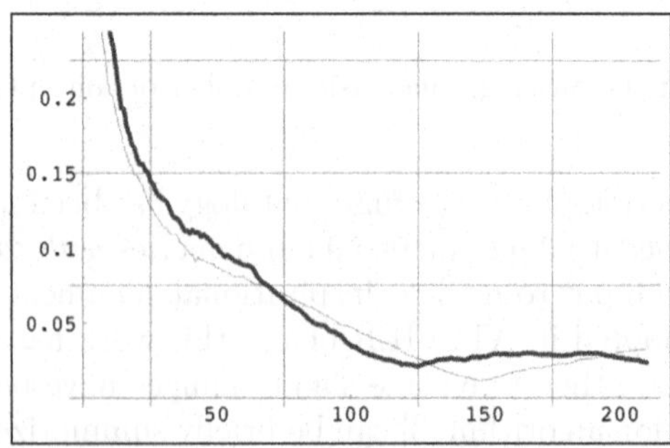

Fig. 2. Plot resulting from the spectra analysis of the frequencies with which correlation membership values are distributed before (thinner red line) and after (thicker blue line) executing 50 queries with conceptual modifiers

3.2 The Interactive Tool

The application developed to make users interact with the fuzzy ontology is a Java^{TM} component that has been integrated with the original ATELIER infrastructure. The purpose of the tool is to intuitively highlight the concepts and the correlations that are predominant in the current state of the system (according to the factors and metrics introduced in Section 2). Fig. 3 presents some screenshots of the tool.

Fig. 3(a) presents the status of the system at an early stage of students' work. Note that the relative importance of concepts is highlighted by circles with different radius: the higher the membership value of the instance of a concept, the

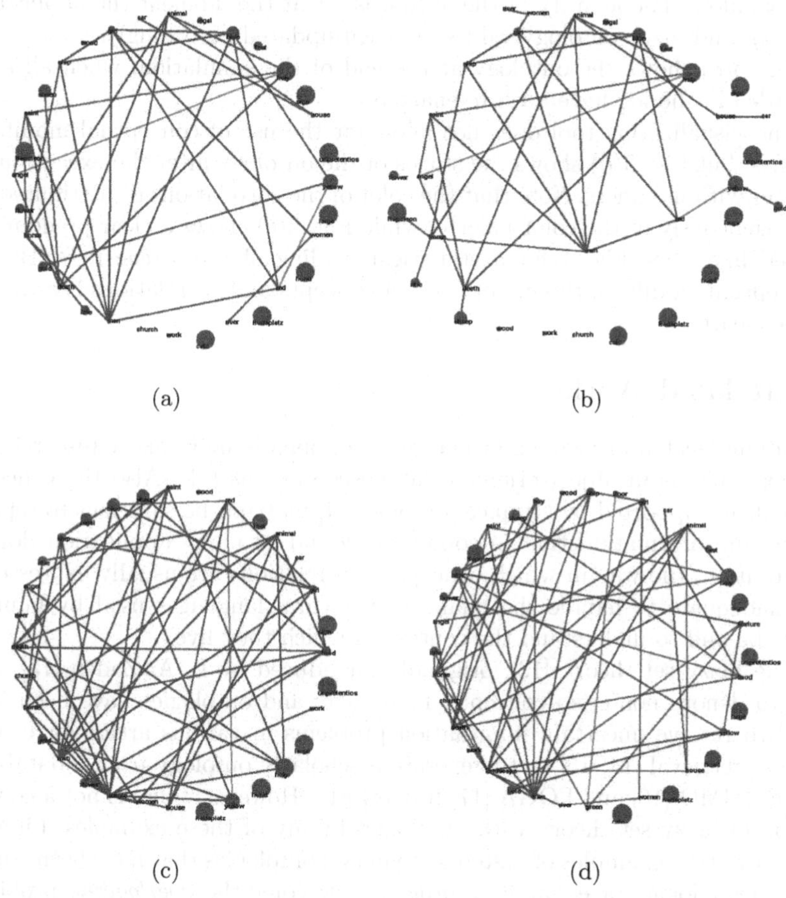

Fig. 3. A set of screenshots showing (a) an intermediate step of the simulated evolution of the system, based on the log of a previous experience. Step (b) shows how concepts can be re-arranged. Step (c) shows a later step of the evolution, at the end of the re-enactment of the log file. Step (d) shows the ontology after introducing the possibility of operating with conceptual modifiers.

bigger the circle. To improve graph readability, a different strategy (i.e., not size) has been adopted to represent correlations. Correlation values are mapped on a blue-to-red and transparent-to-opaque color palette. Strongest correlations are drawn with opaque red lines, while weakest ones are depicted as semi-transparent blue lines. Concepts are initially drawn on a circle. Concepts with a higher number of correlations are alternated with those having less. The number of lines entering the same circle (i.e., concept) is the third parameter to judge the relative importance of a concept in the ontology: i.e., the emission/reception (also referred as *popularity*) of each node in the graph representing the ontology [10].

Concepts can be dynamically re-arranged in the case where the presentation is unclear to the user, as in Fig. 3(b). Double-clicking on any concept or correlation is equal to submitting a query to the HMDB, to get all related documents in a new window. The identity of the author is set at the moment the application is started, and fuzzy ontology values are then updated accordingly.

Fig. 3(c) shows the ontology at the end of the simulation, when all actions recorded in the log have been re-enacted.

The visualization tool does not allow for the use of conceptual modifiers in queries, but Fig. 3(d) shows the status of the ontology after the execution of 50 queries with modifiers. Note that the color of the correlations is distributed more homogeneously in the color palette, while Fig. 3(c) shows a clear predominance of red lines. See Fig. 1 for a statistical reading of the screenshots. By using conceptual modifiers, the importance of concepts and correlations is established more clearly.

4 Related Work

Handling faceted or vague information is an open issue in many research areas, for example as in object-oriented databases systems [11]. Also the conceptual formalism supported by a typical ontology [4] may not be sufficient to represent uncertain information that is commonly found in many application domains. In addition, the way in which concepts and relations are usually expressed can be inadequate to handle the nuances of natural languages used by human to describe and to understand the context in which they live.

The fuzzy set theory [12], originally introduced by L. A. Zadeh [13], allows one to denote non-crisp concepts. Fuzzy sets and ontologies have been jointly used to resolve uncertain information problems in various areas, for example, in text retrieval [14, 15] or to generate a scholarly ontology from a database in the ESKIMO [16] and FOGA [17] frameworks. However, there is not a complete fusion of fuzzy set theory with ontologies in any of these examples. Literature presents other examples of systems relying on ontologies that have been enriched with fuzzy logic: for example in order to overcome the *overloading* problem in the retrieval of medical documents [18], and in Chinese news summarization [19].

The way in which this paper approaches the problem of constructing a meaningful representation of an environment from actions performed in a system is not novel: interesting points of contact can be found with Social Networks Analysis (SNA) [20] and sociometry.

Social Networks Analysis [10], also referred to as Network Theory, encompasses a set of methods to express the relationships existing within communities. Social networks are defined in terms of individuals and ties. Along with the criteria adopted to classify individuals is experience, measured by expertise [7, 21]. It is often computed adopting metrics based on *joint activities* (i.e., counting how many times an individual performed analogous tasks [22]). At a collaborative level, the (relative) strength of ties [23] can be measured according to several parameters, such as the flow of email messages [24] or of interactions between individuals. Metrics based on *joint cases* have been defined considering the frequency with which two individuals happen to work together [22].

The study of social or knowledge relationships often requires the introduction of relations that are more general than that introduced in Section 2. In particular, it might not be sufficient to define correlations as being binary and symmetric—as they usually happen to be n-ary and asymmetric. Groups and communities are generally composed of more than two people, and the "direction" of the relation is driven from the social or organizational role of the individuals involved.

From an applicative perspective, the metrics presented can be compared to methods of sociometry (or sociography) [22]. Sociometry refers to methods presenting data on interpersonal relationships in graph or matrix form, as in the tool of Section 3.2.

Also the experimental approach adopted in Section 3 is available in literature. Event logs have been used to draw maps of the social relations in organizations [22]. The process of extracting data from the history of a system (i.e., from its logs, containing information on time, actions and performers) to obtain general and abstract information on a system and on its users within an organization is generally known as process mining [25]. Different strategies for process mining have often been used in the field of workflow management systems [26], in order to understand the flow of information across work activities and to draw processes.

5 Concluding Remarks

This paper shows how fuzzy ontologies can be dynamically built and updated. Two notions are particularly relevant in this work: (*a*) that of instances representing a concept in various degrees and (*b*) that of the "strength" of the correlation between two concepts. By allowing richer descriptions of the domain, dynamic fuzzy ontologies can be exploited to provide users with a higher awareness of the knowledge that the system is retaining. Dynamic fuzzy ontologies can provide for a flexible support in work settings where innovation is essential (e.g., where new artifacts are designed and workers have to constantly deal with new ideas) and can also be fruitfully exploited at the interaction level, as shown by the tool presented in Section 3.2.

The approach has been evaluated experimentally by measuring how the steps of the proposed process have changed the test ontology, which had been created during a previous experience. Data have been collected that justify the claim that fuzzy ontologies fit the domain of interest better than "regular" ones.

While an integration of different search applications has already been achieved in ATELIER by employing a single interaction interface [27], still no experiment has been lead to provide for real interoperability among these same applications at a knowledge level. Dynamic fuzzy ontologies, thanks to their richness and flexibility, seem to be suitable instruments to pursue this kind of integration.

Further investigations of the topic are also being carried on with respect to dynamic distributed ontologies [28], i.e., the integration of different ontologies used within different environments. This work, along with the investigation of the field of social networks, could carry the work presented here to a much larger scale.

Acknowledgements

The work presented in this paper has been partially supported by the ATELIER project (IST-2001-33064).

References

[1] Binder, T., Michelis, G.D., Gervautz, M., Jacucci, G., Matkovic, K., Psik, T., Wagner, I.: Supporting configurability in a mixed-media environment for design students. Personal Ubiquitous Comput. **8** (2004) 310–325

[2] Abowd, G.D., Dey, A.K., Brown, P.J., Davies, N., Smith, M., Steggles, P.: Towards a better understanding of context and context-awareness. In: HUC '99, London, UK, Springer-Verlag (1999) 304–307

[3] Calegari, S., Loregian, M.: Ontologies help finding inspiration: a practical approach in multimedia information management. In: PAKM2004. Volume 3336 of LNCS., Springer-Verlag (2004) 307–318

[4] Gruber, T.R.: A translation approach to portable ontology specifications. Knowl. Acquis. **5** (1993) 199–220

[5] Loregian, M., Telaro, M.: Dynamic ontologies and cooperative learning. In: Supplements to Proceedings of COOP 2004. (2004) 73–80

[6] Calegari, S., Ciucci, D.: Integrating Fuzzy Logic in Ontologies. In: ICEIS 2006 (in print). (2006)

[7] Mockus, A., Herbsleb, J.D.: Expertise browser: a quantitative approach to identifying expertise. In: ICSE '02, ACM Press (2002) 503–512

[8] Raghavan, V.V., Wong, S.K.M.: A critical analysis of vector space model for information retrieval. Journal of the American Society for Information Science **37** (1986) 279–287

[9] Khang, T.D., Störr, H., Hölldobler, S.: A fuzzy description logic with hedges as concept modifiers. In: Third International Conference on Intelligent Technologies and Third Vietnam-Japan Symposium on Fuzzy Systems and Applications. (2002) 25–34

[10] Wasserman, S., Faust, K.: Social network analysis. Cambridge University Press, Cambridge (1994)

[11] Marín, N., Pons, O., Miranda, M.A.V.: A strategy for adding fuzzy types to an object-oriented database system. Int. J. Intell. Syst. **16** (2001) 863–880

[12] Klir, G., Yuan, B.: Fuzzy Sets and Fuzzy Logic: Theory and Applications. Prentice Hall (1995)

[13] Zadeh, L.A.: Fuzzy sets. Inform. and Control **8** (1965) 338–353
[14] Singh, S., Dey, L., Abulaish, M.: A Framework for Extending Fuzzy Description Logic to Ontology based Document Processing. In: AWIC 2004. Volume 3034 of LNAI., Springer-Verlag (2004) 95–104
[15] Abulaish, M., Dey, L.: Ontology Based Fuzzy Deductive System to Handle Imprecise Knowledge. In: InTech 2003. (2003) 271–278
[16] Matheus, C.: Using Ontology-based Rules for Situation Awareness and Information Fusion. In: W3C Workshop on Rule Languages for Interoperability. (2005)
[17] Quan, T., Hui, S., Cao, T.: FOGA: A Fuzzy Ontology Generation Framework for Scholarly Semantic Web. In: KDO-2004. (2004) 37–48
[18] Parry, D.: A fuzzy ontology for medical document retrieval. In: DMWI2004. (2004) 121–126
[19] Chang-Shing, L., Zhi-Wei, J., Lin-Kai, H.: A fuzzy ontology and its application to news summarization. IEEE Transactions on Systems, Man, and Cybernetics-Part B: Cybernetics **35** (2005) 859–880
[20] Monge, P., Contractor, N.: Theory of Communicatin Networks. Oxford University Press (2003)
[21] Richard Crowder, Gareth Hughes, W.H.: An agent based approach to finding expertise. In: PAKM2002. Volume 2569 of LNCS., Springer-Verlag (2002) 179–188
[22] van der Aalst, W.M.P., Reijers, H.A., Song, M.: Discovering Social Networks from Event Logs. Comp. Supported Coop. Work **14** (2005) 549–593
[23] Granovetter, M.: The strength of weak ties. American Journal of Sociology **78** (1973) 1360–1380
[24] Ogata, H., Yano, Y., Furugori, N., Jin, Q.: Computer supported social networking for augmenting cooperation. Comp. Supported Coop. Work **10** (2001) 189–209
[25] Agrawal, R., Gunopulos, D., Leymann, F.: Mining process models from workflow logs. In: EDBT '98. (1998) 469–483
[26] Cook, J.E., Wolf, A.L.: Discovering models of software processes from event-based data. ACM Trans. Softw. Eng. Methodol. **7** (1998) 215–249
[27] Loregian, M., Matković, K., Psik, T.: Seamless browsing of visual contents in shared learing environments. In: PerComW2006, IEEE Computer Society (2006) 235–239
[28] De Paoli, F., Loregian, M.: Context-aware Applications with Distributed Ontologies. CAiSE '06 Workshops (In print). (2006)

Dynamically Personalized Web Service System to Mobile Devices*

Sanggil Kang[1], Wonik Park[2], and Young-Kuk Kim[2]

[1] Department of Computer Science, The University of Suwon,
San 2-2, Wau-ri, Bongdam-eup, Hwaseong, Gyeonggi-do 445-743, South Korea
sgkang@suwon.ac.kr

[2] Department of Computer Engineering, Chungnam National Univeristy
220 Gung-dong, Yuseong-Gu, Daejeon 305-764, South Korea
{wonik78, ykim}@cnu.ac.kr

Abstract. We introduce a novel personalized web service system through mobile devices. By providing only users' preferred web pages or smaller readable sections, service elements, the problem of the limitation of resource of mobile devices can be solved. In this paper, the preferred service elements are obtained from the statistical preference transactions among web pages for each web site. In computing the preference, we consider the ratio of the length of each web page and users' staying time on it. Also, our system dynamically provides the personalized web service according to the different three cases such as the beginning stage, the positive feedback, and the negative feedback. In the experimental section, we demonstrate our personalized web service system and show how much the resource of mobile devices can be saved.

1 Introduction

Using web services has already become an essential part of our everyday life. Because of development and popularization of mobile devices characterized with mobility and ubiquity, the existing wire internet service is rapidly expanding to the wireless internet service through the mobile devices. In order to enable to provide web services to mobile devices, it is needed to transfer web pages to a suitable format. However, it is challenge because of the limitation of the monitor size of mobile devices and their resources. As a try to solve the problems, some researchers render a web page on a small display with various techniques such as four-way scrolling [1], web-clipping [2], and miniaturization of web pages [3, 4]. However, those techniques can not overcome the limitation of resources of mobile devices because all contents of a web site have to be delivered to users once the users request the web service.

In order to solve the problem, we provide a personalized web service according to users' preference of each web page. The preference of the web pages can be obtained

* This research was supported by the Ministry of Information and Communication, Korea, under the College Information Technology Research Center Support Program, grant number IITA-2005-C1090-0502-0016.

H.L. Larsen et al. (Eds.): FQAS 2006, LNAI 4027, pp. 416 – 426, 2006.

from the navigation history of users who visited the web site through computers. By providing only users' preferred web pages or smaller readable sections, the problem of the resource limitation can be solved to some extent. In this paper, we find the preferred web pages from the statistical preference transactions among web pages. In computing the preference, we consider the ratio of the length of each web page to users' staying time on it. Also, our system dynamically provides the personalized web service according to the different three cases such as the beginning stage, the positive feedback, and the negative feedback. In the experimental section, we demonstrate our personalized web service system and show how much the resource of mobile devices can be saved.

The remainder of this paper is organized as follows. Section 2 describes related works of various web content presentation techniques and personalization techniques. Section 3 defines fundamental terms related to our work. In Section 4, we describe our personalized web service system. Section 5 describes the architecture of our system. In Section 6, we show the experimental result of our system and its analysis. We then conclude our paper in Section 7.

2 Related Work

Many studies have been done about how to present web contents effectively on mobile devices in order to overcome the limitation of their monitor size. Researchers in Palm Inc. [2] made information in smaller chunks and compiled them into a compact format that can be decoded on the Palm VII. The Wireless Access Protocol's Markup Language (WMA) [5] replaces HTML to its own markup language to lay out each page for optimal viewing on small screen. The technique is effective, but it has to prepare the same information for both standard web browsers and PDAs. Another popular technique is to miniaturize standard Web pages by the ProxiWeb browser [4]. This technique is also effective, but it needs the large amount of necessary scrolling action.

Even though the techniques above can solve the problem on providing the standard web pages to the small mobile devices, they can not overcome the limitation of resources of mobile devices. In order to solve the problem, we provide the personalized web pages or smaller readable sections, called fragments.

Various personalization techniques can be classified into three possible categories such as the rule-based, inference method, and collaborative filtering. The rule-based recommendation is usually implemented by a predetermined rule, for instance, if - then rule. Kim et al. [6] proposed a marketing rule extraction technique for personalized recommendation on internet storefronts using tree induction method [7]. As one of representative rule-based techniques, Aggrawall et al. [8, 9] proposed a method to identify frequent item sets from the estimated frequency distribution using association-rule mining algorithm [10]. The inference method is the technique that a user's content consumption behavior is predicted based on the history of personal content consumption behaviors. Ciaramita et al. [11] presented a Bayesian network [12], the graphical representation of probabilistic relationship among variables which are encoded as nodes in the network, for verb selectional preference by combining the statistical and knowledge-based approaches. The architecture of the Bayesian network was determined by the lexical hierarchy of Wordnet [13]. Lee [14] designed an interface agent to predict a user's resource usage in the UNIX domain by the probabilistic estimation of behavioral patterns from the user behavior history. Collaborative filtering (CF) technique recommends a target user the preferred content of the group whose content consumption mind is similar to that of the user. Because of the mature of the technique, CF has been attractive for predicting various preference problems such as net-news [15, 16], e-commerce [17-19], digital libraries [20, 21], digital TV [22, 23], etc.

3 Definitions of Web Navigation Information and Page Segment

To provide the personalized web service to mobile devices, the web server of a web site needs to collect the log information of the visitors of the web site. Also, we have to segment each web site to smaller fragments such as the service page, the service region, and service element as seen in Fig. 1.

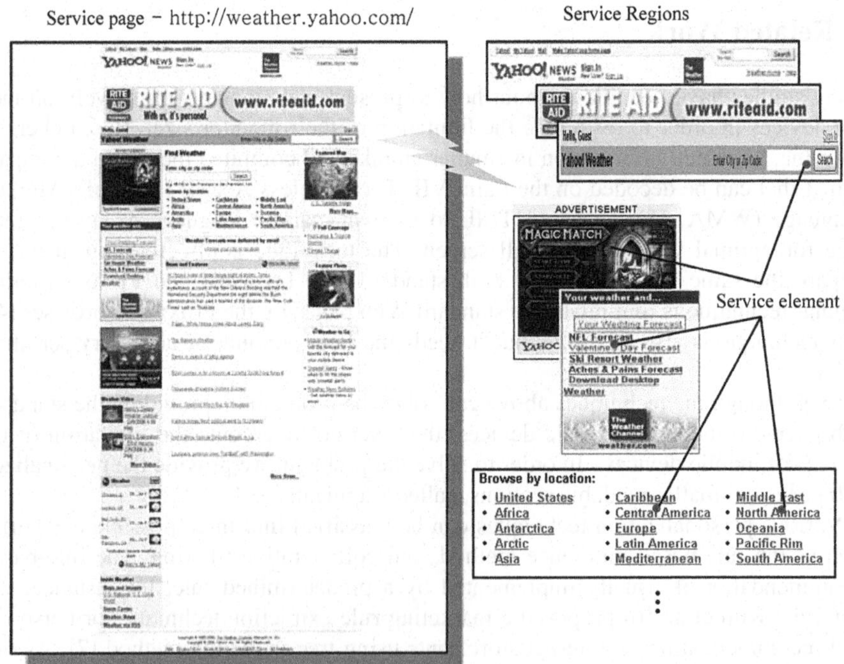

Fig. 1. An example of the page segment

From the collected visitors' log information, we can infer the preference of those segments using only the implicit log information which is users' web-page navigation behavior. The web-page navigation behavior is defined as a user's transactions among the segments during a session. The session means the period from visiting and leaving the web-site. Using the method explained in [24], the segments can be automatically obtained as follows: Each web fragment engine in a web server extracts <HTML><HEAD>~</HEAD><BODY> from the proxy server and generate a new page with basic frame. Then, in order to segment the new page into sections, we find the position of the <TABLE> tag and classify the content of the page.

4 Proposed Personalized Web Service System

4.1 Statistical Preference Transactions of Web-Pages

In general, a website is hierarchically structured with four levels such as the home page, service page, the service region, and the service element as seen in Fig. 2. According to website, the service page can be linked to the different number of service regions, which can also have different number of service elements. For the convenience, we denote the homepage, the service page, the service region, and the service element as level l=0, l=1, l=2, and l=3, respectively. Also, the entry of each level is described as node as in Fig. 2.

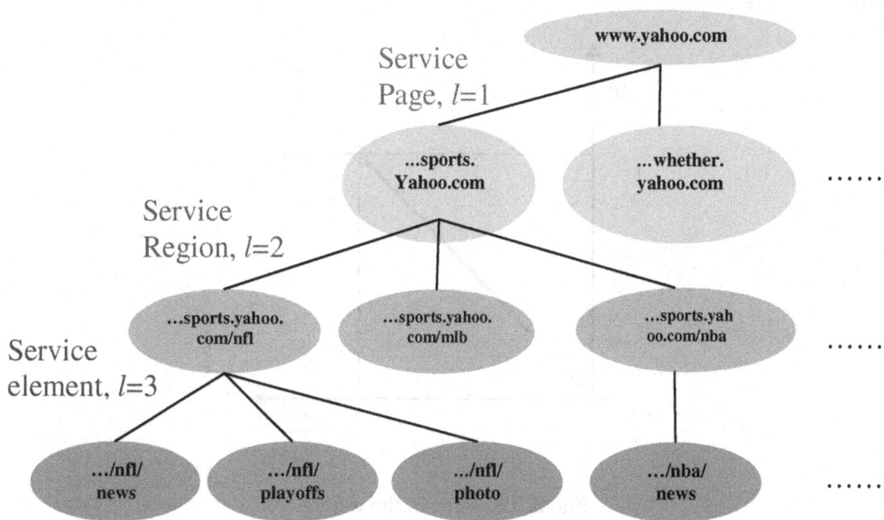

Fig. 2. The tree structure of a web site

Usually, the preference of each node is defined as the frequency of users‘ visiting from users' usage history collected in a web server. Thus, the more frequently visited is a node, the node is considered more preferred by users. Also, the transaction of visiting from a node at a level to another page at the next level is called preference transaction. The statistical preference transaction from a node at higher level to nodes at its lower level can be computed as follows:

$$p_{l,l+1}(i,j) = \frac{n_{l,l+1}(i,j)}{\sum_j n_{l,l+1}(i,j)} \qquad (1)$$

where, $p_{l,l+1}(i, j)$ is the statistical preference transaction from node i at level l to node j at level l+1 and $n_{l,l+1}(i, j)$ is the frequency of the transactions from node i at level l to node j at level l+1. In Equation (1), the frequency of visiting a node is the absolute count of visiting regardless of users' staying time on the node. However, the staying time can be a critical factor for estimating the preference of the node. For instance, if a user stays a node shortly, it can not be meant that the user is interested in the node. To compensate the problem, we need to count the frequency of the visiting in a relative manner, with taking into the consideration of the staying time. Also, the length of each node is various according to the amount of its contents. To take into the consideration, the staying time needs to be measured in a relative manner, too. In other words, the longer is the content in a node, users need the longer the staying time to read it. According to the ratio of staying time to the length of the content in a node, we provide the weight to the computation of the frequency. The weight can be computed as in Fig. 3.

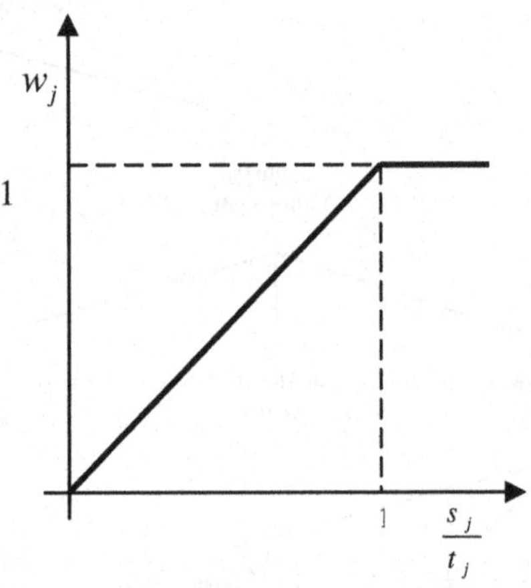

Fig. 3. The slope of the weight

The weight can also be expressed as Equation (2).

$$w_j = \begin{cases} \frac{s_j}{t_j}, & \text{for } s_j < t_j \\ 1, & \text{for } s_j \geq t_j \end{cases} \qquad (2)$$

where s_j is the staying time duration at node j and t_j is the standard reading time duration of node j estimated by expert or by transferring the length of content to the time length. The statistical preference transaction with the weight can be expressed as Equation (3).

$$p_{l,l+1}(i,j) = \frac{\overline{w}_j n_{l,l+1}(i,j)}{\sum_j \overline{w}_j n_{l,l+1}(i,j)} \quad (3)$$

where $\overline{w}_j$ is the average weight to the frequency $n_{l,l+1}(i,j)$ of the transaction node *i* at level *l* to node *j* at level *l*+1.

4.2 Dynamical Web Service Algorithm

From the values of the statistical preference transactions between node *i* at level *l* to *j* at level *l*+1 for ∀ *i*, *j*, we can provide the personalized service elements for three cases such as the beginning stage, the positive feedback, and the negative feedback. The beginning stage means the firstly provided element service for the service request by users. The positive feedback case means the case the user likes the previous served service element, while the negative feedback case is reverse of it.

For the beginning stage, we provide the service element with the highest preference at the lowest level 3 by chasing the link chained with the highest ranked preferred node at each level. The link can be expressed as $x_{0,1_{r1}} \rightarrow x_{1_{r1},2_{r1}} \rightarrow x_{2_{r1},3_{r1}}$ here, $x_{0,1_{r1}}$, $x_{1_{r1},2_{r1}}$, and $x_{2_{r1},3_{r1}}$ are the first ranked preferred service page at level 1, service region at level 2, and the first ranked preferred fragment at level 3, respectively. Therefore, fragment $x_{2_{r1},3_{r1}}$ is served.

For the positive feedback case, the next ranked service element of the previously served service element is served. For example, if the user likes the service of $x_{2_{r1},3_{r1}}$ and red it all content in $x_{2_{r1},3_{r1}}$ then $x_{2_{r1},3_{r2}}$, which is the second ranked preferred service element linked to the same service region, is served.

For the negative feedback case, the service moves to the next ranked service region of the previously served service region. Then, the first ranked preferred service element at the next ranked service region is served. For example, if the user does not like the service of $x_{2_{r1},3_{r1}}$ and did not read its contents then $x_{2_{r2},3_{r1}}$, which is the first ranked preferred fragment at the second ranked preferred service region, is served.

As explained above, our method can dynamically provide the personalized web service by adapting the various cases of users' feedback. In addition, our method can compensate the resource limitation of mobile devices because we do not need to provide too low ranked or no ranked service elements.

5 System Architecture

Fig. 4 shows the system architecture of personalized web service based on mobile gateway. The architecture is composed of main five modules such as Web Collection, Page Reconstruction, Page Reconstruction Cache, Recommendation, Document Conversion, and Protocol Confirmation.

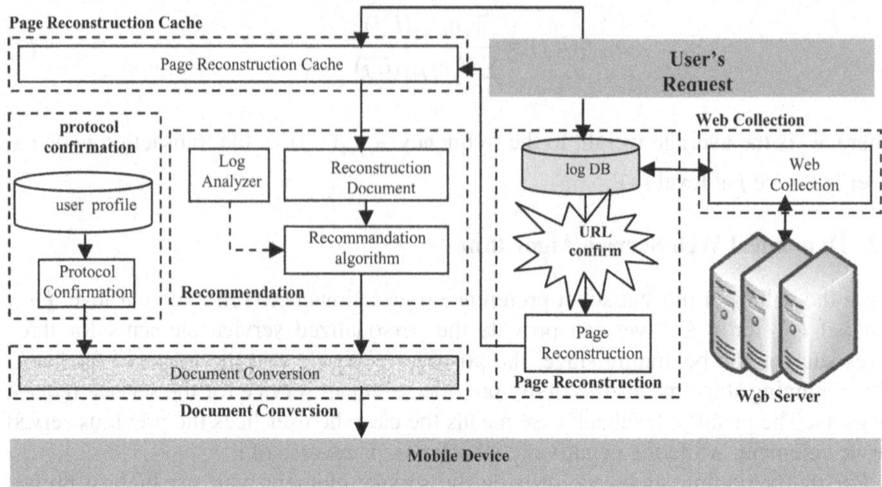

Fig. 4. The architecture of mobile gateway system

The Web Collection module collects the HTML of web-pages from web server. The Page Reconstruction module partitions the collected HTML into page fragments as explained in Section 3. The page fragments are stored in the Page Reconstruction Cache module for re-usage. The Recommendation module provides or recommends the users' preferred fragments from the fragments stored in the Page Reconstruction Cache as using our preference algorithm. The Document Conversion module converts the preferred fragments to the format suitable for the user's mobile device. In order to do document conversion, we need to know the information of the user's mobile device. It can be done by analyzing HTTP header of web-pages in the Protocol Confirmation module, as seen in Fig. 5. In the figure, the underlined commend line is the information of a user's mobile device.

```
RECV HEADER : GET http://plus.cnu.ac.kr/ HTTP/1.1
Host:plus.cnu.ac.kr
x-up-tpd-session-headers:User-Agent, Accept-Charset, Accept-Language, x-wap-prof
ile, Accept-Encoding, x-up-proxy-enable-trust, x-up-devcap-cc
User-Agent:OPWV-SDK/62 UP.Browser/6.2.2.1.208 (GUI) MMP/2.0
Accept-Charset:ks_c_5601
Accept-Language:ko
x-wap-profile:"http://developer.openwave.com/uaprof/OPWVSDK62.xml"
Accept-Encoding:deflate,gzip
x-up-proxy-enable-trust:1
x-up-devcap-cc:1
Accept:application/smil, application/vnd.phonecom.mmc-xml, application/vnd.uplan
et.bearer-choice, application/vnd.uplanet.bearer-choice-wbxml, application/vnd.w
ap.wmlc, application/vnd.wap.xhtml+xml, application/xhtml+xml, image/bmp, image/
gif, image/jpeg, image/png, image/vnd.wap.wbmp, image/x-up-wpng, multipart/mixed
, multipart/related, text/html, text/plain, text/vnd.sun.j2me.app-descriptor, te
xt/vnd.wap.wml, audio/x-wav, audio/wav, audio/imelody, audio/midi, audio/AMR, au
dio/AMR-WB, audio/mpeg, video/mpeg, text/x-pcs-gcd, application/x-pmd
```

Fig. 5. The information of HTTP header

6 Experiment

6.1 Experimental Environment

Fig. 6 shows the experimental environment of our personalized web service. We implemented our system by the TCP/IP socket network with the mobile gateway in the Linux environment. The access to simulator is enabled by binding a specific port. In order to allow the connections of multiple users to the gateway server at the same time, the POSIX pthread, which is the Linux standard thread, is used. In order to test our personalized web service, SDK 6.22 of WML browser produced by Openwave Corp. is used. Also, we made a sample web site by modifying yahoo.com. To allow users to connect to the sample pages in the sample web site, the apache was used in the gateway server.

To analyze users' log information, the Squid [25] is used. The Squid is very flexible for adapting it to a specific experimental environment, as an open source web proxy cache driven in Unix.

We collected the navigation information of the sample yahoo.com for 200 students enrolled in University of Suwon in Korea. The sample yahoo.com has 100 service elements. The navigation information had been collected from the log data recorded for 7 days.

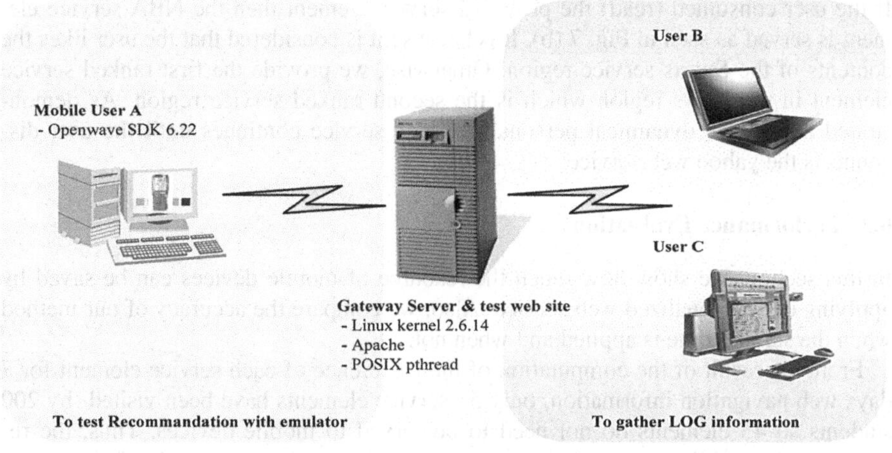

Fig. 6. The experimental environment

6.2 Demonstration of Our Method

In this section, we show the demonstration of our personalized web service according to the three different scenarios. Using the equations in Chapter 5, we computed the preference of each service region and the corresponding service elements. From the result, the order of preference of service regions was Sports, News, Shopping, etc. Under the Sports region, the order of the preference of service elements was NFL, NBA, Soccer, etc. Under the News region, the talk over jobs was the best preference.

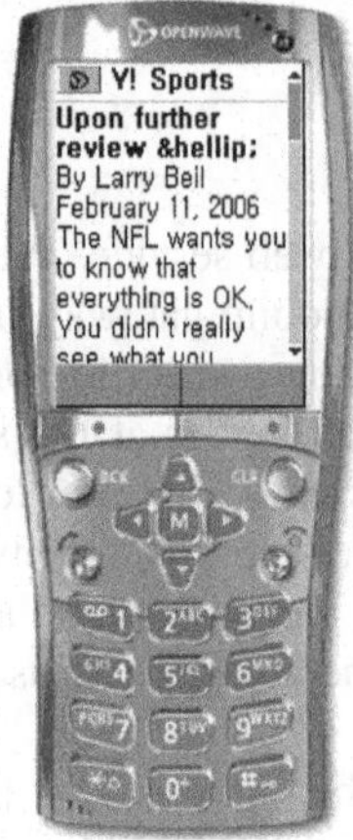

(a) The beginning stage

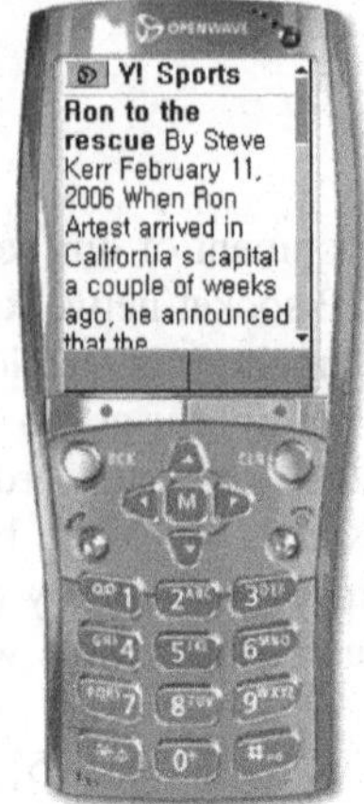

(b) The positive feedback stage

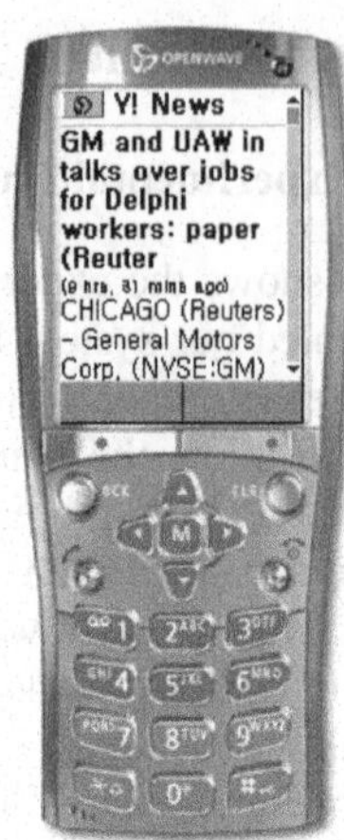

(c) The negative feedback stage

Fig. 7. The examples of dynamical web service for each case

As shown in Fig. 7(a), the content about NFL is provided when a user requests the yahoo web service, because the NFL service element was the first ranked preference. If the user consumed (read) the provided service element then the NBA service element is served as seen in Fig. 7 (b). It is because it is considered that the user likes the contents of the Sports service region. Otherwise, we provide the first ranked service element in the News region which is the second ranked service region. As demonstrated above, the dynamical personalized web service continues until the user disconnects the yahoo web service.

6.3 Performance Evaluation

In this section, we show how much the resource of mobile devices can be saved by applying our personalized web service. Also, we compare the accuracy of our method when the staying time is applied and when not.

From the result of the computation of the preference of each service element for 7 days web navigation information, only 57 service elements have been visited by 200 students so 43 elements do not need to be served to mobile devices. Thus, the resource of the mobile devices can be saved as much as the amount of 43 elements and can be utilized by any other services.

We also examined the accuracy of the personalized web service for both when the staying time is applied and not applied in computing the preference of each element. The 150 students are used for training our system out of 200 students and 50 students are used for testing the accuracy of our system. The accuracy evaluation was repeated by varying the collection period of the users' log information. As seen in Fig. 8, the accuracy is better when the staying time is applied than when not applied, regardless of the collection period. As seen in the figure, the accuracy increases as the collection period increases. However, the increase is very gentle from day 5.

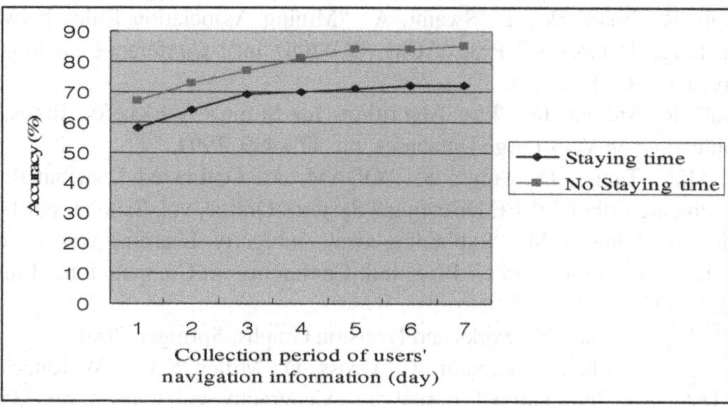

Fig. 8. The comparison of the performances for both the staying time is considered and not considered in computing the preference of the service elements.

7 Conclusion

In this paper, we proposed a novel personalized web service system through mobile devices. The experimental results in the previous section showed that the limitation of mobile devices can be compensated by utilizing our system. Also, it was shown that we can have better performance by considering the staying time for estimating the preference of each service element than not.

However, the 200 students might not be enough for verifying that our system is excellent. It is needed to collect more users' web navigation information. Also, we need to do further study for developing an automatic algorithm to segment various website into smaller segments suitable for being viewed on various types of mobile devices. It is because each mobile device can have different size of screen.

References

1. Jones, M., Marsden, G., Mohd-Nasir, N., Boone, K & Buchanan G, " Improving Web Interaction on Small Displays. Proc. WWW8. Vol 1, pp. 51-59, 1999.
2. Palm, Inc., Web Clipping Development. http://www.palmos.com/dev/tech/webclipping/.
3. Fox, A., Goldberg, I., Gribble, S.D., Lee, D.C, Polito, A.. & Brewer, E.A.: A Experience With Top Gun Wingman: A Proxy-Based Graphical Web Browser for the 3Com PalmPilot. Conference Repots of Middleware, 1998.
4. ProxiNet, Inc., ProxiWeb: http://www.proxinet.com/.
5. Buyukkokten, O., Garcia-Molina, H., Paepcke, A., & Winograd, T.: Power Brower: Efficient Web Browsing for PDAs. Proc. CHI'2000, pp. 430-437, 2000.
6. Kim, J.W., Lee, B.H., Shaw, M.J., Chang, H.L., Nelson, M.: Application of Decision-Tree Induction Techniques to Personalized Advertisements on Internet Storefronts," International Journal of Electronic Commerce, vol. 5, no. 3, pp. 45-62, 2001
7. Quinlan, J.R., Induction of Decision Trees, "Machine Learning," vol. 1, no. 1, pp. 81-106, 1986

8. Aggrawall, R., Imielinski, T., Swami, A., "Mining Association Rules between Sets of Items in Large Databases," Proc. ACM SIGMOD Int'l Conference on Management of Data, pp. 207-216 , 1994
9. Aggrawall, R., Srikant, R., "Fast Algorithms for Mining Association Rules," Proc. 20th Int'l Conference on Very Large Databases, pp. 478-499, 1994
10. Ashrafi, M.Z., Tanizr, D., Smith, K., "ODAM: An Optimized Distributed Association Rule Mining algorithm," IEEE Distributed Systems Online, vol. 3, no. 3, pp. 1-18, 2004
11. Ciaramita, M., Johnson, M., "Explaining away ambiguity: Learning verb selectional preference with Bayesian networks," Proc. Intl. Conference on Computational Linguistics, pp. 187-193, 2000
12. Jensen, F. V., Bayesian Networks and Decision Graphs, Springer, 2001.
13. Miller, G., Beckwith, R., Fellbaum, C., Gross, D., Miller, K.J., "Wordnet: An On-line Lexical Database," International Journal of Lexicography, vol. 3, no. 4, pp. 235-312, 1990
14. Lee, J.J., "Case-based plan recognition in computing domains," Proc. The Fifth International Conference on User Modeling, pp. 234-236, 1996
15. Resnick, P., Lacovou, N., Suchak, M., Bergstrom, P., Riedl, J., "GroupLens: An Open Architecture for Collaborative Filtering of Netnews," Internet Research Report, MIT Center for Coordination Science, 1994, http://www-sloan.mit.edu/ccs/1994wp.html
16. Maltz, D.A., "Distributing Information for Collaborative Filtering on Usenet net News," SM Thesis, Massachusetts Institute of Technology, Cambridge, MA, 1994
17. Schafer, J.B., Konstan, J., Riedl, J., "Recommender systems in e-commerce," ACM Conference on Electronic Commerce, pp. 158-166, 1999
18. Linden, G., Smith, B., York, J., "Amazon.com Recommendations: Item-To-Item Collaborative Filtering," IEEE Internet Computing, vol. 7, no. 1, pp. 76-80, 2003
19. Herlocker, J.L., Konstan, J.A., Terveen, L.G., Riedl, J.T., "Evaluating Collaborative Filtering Recommender Systems", ACM Transactions on Information Systems vol. 22, no. 1, pp. 5-53, 2004
20. Bollacker, K.D., Lawrence S., Giles, C.L., "A System for Automatic Personalized Tracking of Scientific Literature on the Web," Proc. ACM Conference on Digital Libraries, pp. 105-113, 1999
21. Torres, R., McNee, S.M., Abel, M., Konstan, J.A., Riedl, J., "Enhancing Digital Libraries with TechLens+", ACM/IEEE-CS Joint Conference on Digital Libraries, pp. 228-236, 2004
22. Cotter, P., Smyth, B., "Personalization Techniques for the Digital TV world," Proc. European Conference on Artificial Intelligence, pp. 701-705, 2000
23. Lee, W.P., Yang, T.H., "Personalizing Information Appliances: A Multi-agent Framework for TV Program Recommendations, " Expert Systems with Applications, vol. 25, no. 3, pp. 331-341, 2003
24. Jeon, Y., Hwang, E., "Automatically Customizing Service Pages on the Web for Mobile Devices," Lecture Notes in Computer Science, vol. 2822, pp. 53-65, 2003
25. Squid Web Proxy Cache- http://www.squid-cache.org/

Flexible Shape-Based Query Rewriting

Georges Chalhoub[1], Richard Chbeir[1], and Kokou Yetongnon[1]

[1] Computer Science Department, LE2I – Bourgogne University
BP 47870 21078 Dijon - France
gchalhoub@bdl.gov.lb
{rchbeir, Kokou}@u-bourgogne.fr

Abstract. A visual query is based on pictorial representation of conceptual entities and operations. One of the most important features used in visual queries is the shape. Despite its intuitive writing, a shape-based visual query usually suffers of a complexity processing related to two major parameters: 1-the imprecise user request, 2-shapes may undergo several types of transformation. Several methods are provided in the literature to assist the user during query writing. On one hand, relevance feedback technique is widely used to rewrite the initial user query. On the other hand, shape transformations are considered by current shape-based retrieval approaches without any user intervention. In this paper, we present a new cooperative approach based on the shape neighborhood concept allowing the user to rewrite a shape-based visual query according to his preferences with high flexibility in terms of including (or excluding) only some shape transformations and of result sorting.

1 Introduction

A visual language is based on pictorial representation of conceptual entities and operations through which users compose iconic or visual sentences [25]. Several visual features (such as icons, predefined shapes, primitive shapes, sample images, etc.) can be combined together using spatial, temporal and logical operators. Shape-based queries are widely used in visual languages due to their simplicity and intuitivity. Three main categories of shape-based visual languages are provided in the literature: Iconic-based [15, 17, 19], Sketch-based [18, 20], and Query By Image [21, 26]. Using these user-friendly languages, the user can easily visualize and graphically query the database. However, several limitations are identified and related to the use of each one of these methods. For instance, when using iconic-based languages, the query may encounter some ambiguities when the operators and objects number increases [19]. In sketch languages, the queries are user-talent dependent and may lead to several interpretations [19]. Query by image queries are very restrictive when the user does not have a sample image expressing his needs. To handle these limitations and make the retrieval process more cooperative, several techniques have been provided in the literature [7, 8].

Widely used in several search engines and for textual data, the query rewriting technique has been studied in several domains [12]. The relevance feedback is one of the query rewriting techniques [22, 23, 24]. It aims at providing users the opportunity

H.L. Larsen et al. (Eds.): FQAS 2006, LNAI 4027, pp. 427–440, 2006.

to evaluate search results by selecting relevant (or irrelevant) ones. The system can then iteratively rewrite the initial query in function of the selected sets given by the user after each step. However, most of current approaches do not allow the user to specify neither the degree of relevance (or irrelevance) of each result, nor the order of searching and/or displaying retrieval results. In essence, shape retrieval is a complex task due to several transformations (occlusion, articulation, rotation, translation, scaling, etc.) that a shape may undergo. When retrieving similar shapes, current techniques are able to consider only a set of domain-related transformations within a predefined execution order. Moreover, in order to keep the retrieval interfaces user friendly, they attempt, even when using relevance feedback techniques, to simplify the user intervention by limiting the input or feedback parameters which is very restrictive when formulating complex queries (which transformations to include or to exclude?, which sorting order?, etc.). In [12], an interesting rewriting approach has been provided for multimedia queries. The authors have defined a relaxation and a constraint functions to rewrite only textual-oriented queries using the user profile. In this paper, we extend their approach to shape features and define a formal language for shape rewriting. Here, the relaxation function allows considering all types of shape transformation (stretching, occlusion, rotation etc.), while the constraint function aims at:

1. Including and/or excluding shapes from the relaxation result,
2. Assigning an order to relaxation results according to the user requests.

This paper is organized as follows. First, we explain the motivation of this work. After, we give a snapshot of the related work. In section 4, we detail our rewriting method, and give some examples. Section 5 is devoted to present our implementation. Finally, we conclude and pin down some of our future directions.

2 Motivation

To explain the motivation of this work, let us consider the following example: A journalist takes using a digital camera some snapshots in front of the finish line of the 100, 200, and 400 meters men competitions in the 10th IAAF World Championships in Athletics. Afterwards, he stores the captured pictures in an image database (or repository) without any annotation. The journalist uses a retrieval tool that extracts from the stored images a set of corresponding shape representations as shown in figure 1. The tool provides a shape-based sketch and iconic-based image retrieval interface, with a relevance feedback technique to refine the user query. It uses global similarity measure between shapes (figure 2) allowing the user to express the similarity degree by giving a similarity threshold[1] $\varepsilon \in [0, 1]$.

To write his weekly report, the journalist wants to look for only Golden winners' shots taking at the final stage of the competition. He formulates his query Q by drawing a sample shape (imagining a typical one when wining a competition at the arrival stage) as follows:

Q: 

[1] Is related to the number of links to consider when computing the similarity.

The query results expected by the journalist must contain the following shapes:

- Shape D which is the initial query,
- Shape I and J representing an athlete raising two hands,
- Shape B representing an athlete raising only one hand.

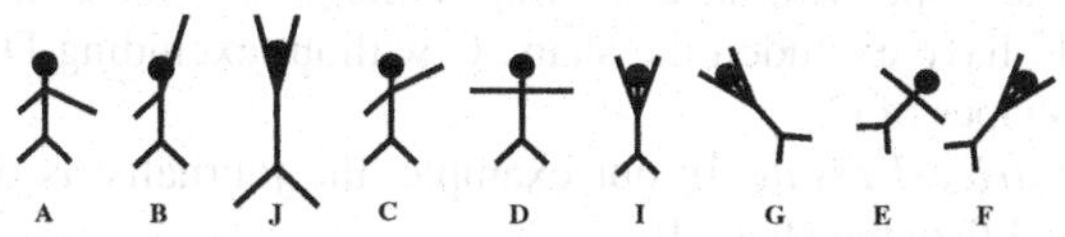

Fig. 1. A set of shapes representation in the database

In the following, we give a traditional technique scenario describing the steps followed by the journalist attempting to obtain the expected relevant results:

1. The journalist gives the initial query Q (shape D) using a threshold ε_1 (we assume here that the distance within ε_1, gives one neighborhood link when computing similar shapes).
2. The system formulates the query and returns the most similar or closest shapes (D, C, E and I) as appearing in figure 2
3. The journalist marks E and I as relevant shapes, and C as irrelevant one
4. The system rewrites the query by excluding similar shapes to C, and including similar ones to E and I. The new result contains
5. shape D and J (which are expected)
6. shape F and G (close to I) which are unexpected
7. The journalist may mark new irrelevant and relevant shapes until having shapes D, I and J.

The result may never contain shape B (eliminated when the journalist has eliminated C) and the silence rate, if best, would be of 1/(1+3)=0.25.

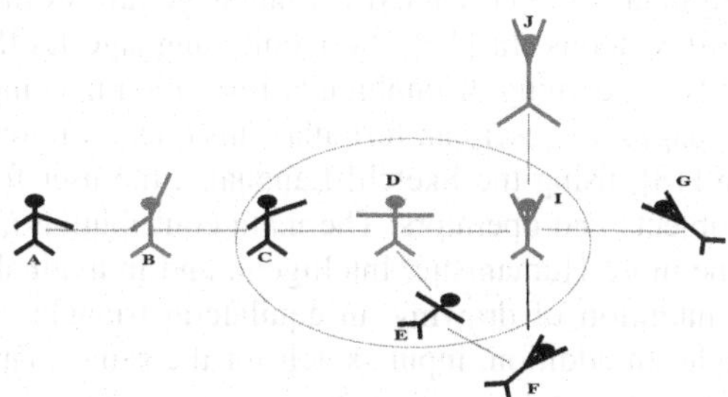

Fig. 2. Similarity links between shapes

In the above scenario, we attempted to show how most approaches using relevance feedback would usually work when cooperating with the end-user to retrieve expected results. However, we do believe that a shape-based visual query approach should be more flexible and provide:

- *Higher expressive similarity measure:* A shape may undergo several transformations. The user should be able to exclude all shapes resulting from one or more transformations. In our example, the journalist would have excluded the rotation transformation results and thus reduced the feedback interaction numbers.
- *Customized inclusion and exclusion parameters*: The user may want to exclude from the result a shape without excluding its neighborhoods. In our example, the journalist would have excluded the shape C without excluding D and B which are neighborhood shapes of C.
- *Customizable retrieval result:* In our example, the journalist is more interested in the shape D and I than the shape B.

3 Related Work

Widely used in several Information Retrieval Systems (IRS), query rewriting (or reformulation) techniques allow a system to cooperate with the user during the retrieval phase in order to better meet his requirements. Two main rewriting techniques categories are identified:

- *Query-oriented techniques*: considered as being a valuable tool to improve the performance of retrieval systems [3], they are used to obtain a new query by modifying the initial query on the basis of current user feedbacks. The relevance feedback[2] is one example of such used techniques.
- *User-oriented techniques*: rewrite the initial query according to predefined parameters stored in a user model or profile [16] without studying the current needs of the user. Rewriting parameters can be based on user IP address, language, country, etc.

Iconic languages allow the user to formulate queries using predefined icons representing domain-related objects and operators. In [15], the authors present a visual query language, MQuery, able to support multimedia data in addition to alphanumeric one. Using MQuery, the user formulates his query by dragging shape elements from the schema diagram to a query window and asks the system to insert, retrieve, delete, or update any matching data. In [17], CIGALES language allows the user to formulate queries using predefined icons. In [19], the iconic language LVIS, is presented and allows more flexibility concerning the ambiguity resolution in complex queries.

Using sketch languages, the user can formulate his query without the constraints of predefined icons. In [18], using the Sketch! Language, the user formulates his query by drawing spatial objects and operators. The main contribution in [20], is to make a user interface (UI) be more Humanistic, Intelligent, and individualized. For example, if the user has the intention of drawing an equilateral triangle, the UI corrects the inexact drawn triangle. In addition, input sketch for the same shape may be different from user to user.

Query By Image (QBI) technique allows the user to provide a set of query images (usually one image) similar to those stored in the corpus. It has been studied and integrated in several retrieval systems and DBMS. In [21], the authors describe a visual query language (VQL) among time series data. Here, the user interactively specifies a

[2] We will give more details about it in the following subsections.

search pattern, after what the system finds similar shapes and returns a ranked list of matched ones. Another interesting shape application on time series and life time data is presented in [26], where the authors defined the similarity transformation distance, in order to measure the similarity between a shape and its transformation within a given threshold.

In the literature, other studies aim at incorporating human perception subjectivity into the retrieval process and providing users the opportunity to evaluate retrieval results. In [22], a survey on relevance feedback in CBIR is presented. The central idea in classical methods of relevance feedback is query re-weighting. The re-weighting aims at enhancing the importance of those dimensions of a feature that helps in retrieving and reduces the importance of those that hinder this process. However, low-level features alone are not enough effective in representing users' feedbacks and in describing their intentions. For this reason, the authors present iFind, a web-based image retrieval system that combines keyword-based image search and query by image technique. In [23], the authors define a relevance feedback method that takes as input a query image and a list of images that have been marked as either relevant or irrelevant by the user. Another interesting work is addressed in [24], where the authors present three levels: the object, the physical features and the representation of each feature (for example color histogram and color moment for the color feature). To integrate relevance feedback, the authors add a set of similarity measures to each feature representation, and assign weights to each component in the three-layer object/query representation.

It goes without saying that all the above works are interesting and facilitate the query formulation using a visual interface and content-based retrieval with the possibility of the user relevance feedback. However, these techniques did not deal with the following issues:

- In relevance feedback techniques, the user can qualify the object as relevant or irrelevant. However, he has no choice to specify the degree of relevance or irrelevance which might be of great importance in shape-based retrieval because priorities would express the real word significance of each shape.
- During the retrieval process, shape matching is expressed according to shape similarity without considering each shape transformation. In some situations, this would increase the retrieval steps and silence rate.

4 Shape Based Query Rewriting

In this paper, we extend the textual-oriented rewriting approach presented in [12] by considering the shape feature and providing a flexible formal language for shape-based query rewriting. An initial user query Q is formally rewritten into Q^A as follows:

$$Rewriting(Q, \{R, T\}, \{C\}) \rightarrow Q^A$$

Where R is a shape transformation, T is a threshold, and C is a constraint set.

Our proposal is independent of the methods and algorithms used to represent or retrieve a shape. However, two main properties in the algorithms are required to rewrite the shape query using our approach:

- Uniqueness: the algorithm must associate to each shape only one representation (a graph, tree, etc.).
- Cost calculation: the algorithm must be able to calculate the cost of matching between two shapes representations.

In the following, we give a definition concerning the dissimilarity cost matching between two shapes[3]. After, we define the concept of shape neighbourhood. The cost and the neighbourhoods are defined with respect to each shape transformation. To classify neighbourhood elements, we affect to each one a weight expressing the closeness to the original shape. Based on these definitions, we explain our rewriting approach and study several current shape representation methods provided in the literature.

4.1 Definitions

Definition 1. Matching cost
A matching cost is calculated to measure the dissimilarity between one shape *A* and another shape *B* having undergone a transformation *R*. To represent a shape, two approaches are provided in the literature: curve-based [1,5,6] and graph-based approaches [9,10,11]. For instance, in graph-based approach [10], each shape is represented as a graph and the dissimilarity between two shapes is measured by calculating the matching cost of their corresponding graphs. The matching cost between two shape graphs A and B can be computed as follows:

- Contour matching: considering a_1, a_2 two nodes in the graph of A and b_1, b_2 their mapping nodes in the graph of B. The cost between edges (a_1, a_2) and (b_1, b_2) is calculated from the cost of comparing their correspondent contours. The calculation function returns the cost with respect to the curvatures at (a_1, a_2) and (b_1, b_2).
- Transformation matching: the structure of a graph may change due to the transformations like *stretching and occlusion.* A transformation cost is calculated for each transformation. For instance, the stretching transformation cost is calculated by comparing an edge of a shape graph with a path of the other shape graph. Graph matching operations can be done using the A*LIKE algorithm [16].

Formally, we note the cost of matching between two shapes A and B, $Cost_{Mt}(A,B)$ considering the contour matching $cost_c$ and the transformation R, $cost_R$ as follows:

$$Cost_{Mt}(A,B) = Cost_C(A,B) + Cost_R(A,B) \tag{1}$$

Definition 2. Shape Neighbourhood
The neighborhood of the shape A according to a transformation R and a threshold ε_R, is defined by the set $V_R(A, \varepsilon_R)$ as follows:

[3] The given cost definition is based on graph matching algorithms.

- The matching cost between an element (shape) B belonging to $V_R(A, \varepsilon_R)$ and the shape A is less than or equal to ε_R. In other words, B is considered as a transformation of the original shape A by the transformation R within a threshold ε_R.
- ε_R is a threshold defined with respect to the transformation R. We note that the domain of ε is related to the shape transformation. For instance, if the transformation R is a *shape rotation* then the domain of ε is the interval [0, 360]. For other transformations, the domain of ε is different. Thus, the value of ε should be normalized. This normalization can be done by a linear function for a given ε:

$$\varepsilon_R = f(\varepsilon) = \frac{\varepsilon - \min}{\max - \min + 1} \tag{2}$$

Where max and min are respectively the maximum and the minimum values of ε *in each domain.*

- The same function is applied to cost normalization.

We represent a formal definition of the neighborhood of a shape A as follows:

$$V_R(A,\varepsilon) = \{B \,/\, B \in R(A) \text{ and } \mathrm{Cost}_{\mathrm{Mt}}(A,B) \le \varepsilon_R)\} \tag{3}$$

Definition 3. Shape weighting

In the neighbourhood of a shape A, the elements have different *weights.* The weight of an element is defined according to its closeness to the original shape A. The elements in the neighbourhood are sorted according to their weights. To express the weight, we associate to each shape B a positive real value less than or equal to 1. The weight W_B is associated with a shape B as follows:

$$W_B = 1 - \mathrm{Cost}_{\mathrm{Mt}}(A,B) \tag{4}$$

You can observe, the weight of a shape B is less than the weight of the original shape A. This weight is useful in shape relaxation to classify the query result according to the closeness to the original shape.

4.2 Rewriting Process

Now, let us explain how we rewrite a shape–based visual query using our approach. The rewriting process based on two principal functions: Relax function F_R and Constraint function F_C. These two functions were defined to relax terms and relations in [12]. We extend their use as follows: The function F_R allows returning a set of relaxed shapes, and F_C controls the returned result of F_R. Shape rewriting can be formally defined as:

$$\texttt{Rewrite(shape element)} = \texttt{Rewrite}(\delta) = F_C(F_R(\delta)) = F_C(\delta') = \delta'_C \tag{5}$$

Definition 4. Shape element δ

The shape element δ is a triplet (**A, R, T**) where:

- **A**: is the original shape that the user wants to relax
- **R**: is the transformation function applied to **A**
- **T**: is the relaxation threshold of **A** in R. **T** ∈ [0, 1] and represents the maximum distance of a shape B ∈ V_R (**A**) to consider in the relaxation.

Definition 5. Relax function FR

We define $\mathbf{F_R}$ as the relaxation function to be applied on an element δ. It returns a sorted set δ' of couples (shape, weight) related to **A** in descending order. Each couple of δ' is a node (value and weight) selected from the neighbourhood of **A** with respect to the transformation **R**. The distance (weight difference) between **A** and a selected shape is less than or equal to **T**. $\mathbf{F_R}$ is formally formulated as follows:

$$\mathbf{F_R}: \delta = (\mathbf{A}, \mathbf{R}, \mathbf{T}) \rightarrow \mathbf{F_R}(\delta) = \delta' = \{(\mathbf{shape}, \mathbf{W}), \leq_W\} \qquad (6)$$

Definition 6. Constraint function F_C

Sometimes, the user desires to exclude (or include) some shapes from the result set δ'. To accomplish this, we define a constraint set **C** and a constraint function $\mathbf{F_C}$ as follows:

- C is a set of shapes. It is represented by a set of couples (δ'_P, W) where δ'_P is a subset of δ'. It contains both the set of shapes to be excluded (or included) from the result, and shapes whose weights are to be modified. δ'_p may contain one or several shapes.
- $\mathbf{F_C}$ is a function that applies C constraints to the result δ' as follows:

$$\mathbf{F_C}: (\delta', \mathbf{C}) \rightarrow \mathbf{F_C}(\delta', \mathbf{C}) = \delta'_c = \delta' - \{(\delta_p', \mathbf{W}') \text{ where } (\delta_p', \mathbf{W}) \in \mathbf{C} \text{ and } 0 \leq \mathbf{W} < 1\} \cup \{(\delta_p', \mathbf{W}) \text{ where } (\delta_p', \mathbf{W}) \in \mathbf{C} \text{ and } 0 < \mathbf{W} \leq 1\} \qquad (7)$$

In other words:

- If W = 1 then $\mathbf{F_C}$ includes the shapes of δ_p' to the relaxation result δ',
- If W = 0 then $\mathbf{F_C}$ excludes the shapes of δ_p' from relaxation result δ',
- If 0 < W < 1 then $\mathbf{F_C}$ modifies the weight of the shapes of δ_p' in the relaxation result (if Val exists in the result).

4.3 Discussion

In this section, we show how the query (re)writing of our motivation section example can be done using our approach. Consider now transformations (Occlusion, Rotation, and Stretching) when computing the similarity between shapes (figure 3) allowing the user to give a threshold $\varepsilon \in [0,1]$ for each transformation measure. Our approach is also applicable if only one similarity measure is used. To obtain expected results, the following steps are applied:

1. The journalist formulates the query Q and gives the following parameters:
   - exclude rotated shapes (ε_R=0)
   - include occluded shapes using ε_O
   - include stretched shapes using ε_S

2. The system formulates the query and returns the most similar or closest shapes (D, C, and I)
3. The journalist marks C as irrelevant (without excluding its neighborhood shapes), E and I as relevant result
4. The retuned most similar shapes: D, I, J, B.

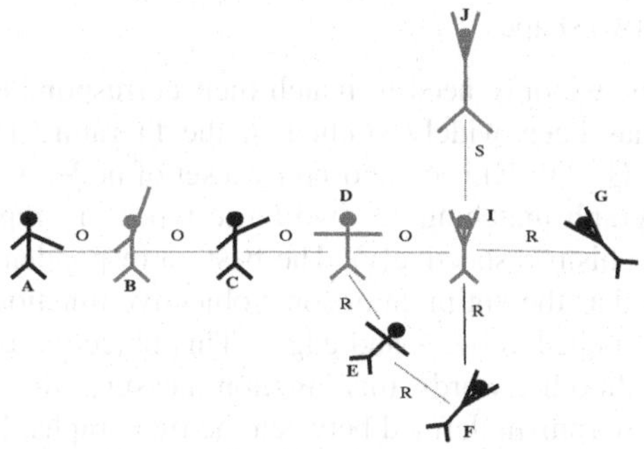

Fig. 3. Transformation links between shapes

The above scenario shows that our proposal is able to:

- Allow the user to specify results priorities. For instance, if the journalist is interested the most in shape D for all competitors then he associates to the stretching transformation the first priority. The highest priority results are shapes taller or shorter than D within a stretching threshold given by the user.
- Allow the user to exclude a shape, from the result, without excluding its neighborhood shapes. For instance, in step 3 of the above scenario, the journalist excludes shape C without excluding shapes B and D.
- Decrease the silence rate because of its higher expressive power.
- Decrease the user interventions during the search process.

5 Implementation

To validate our approach, we implemented a Java-based prototype able to provide to the user a shape-based retrieval interface dealing with several shape transformations such as *stretching, occlusion, articulation,* and *rotation.* As we mentioned before, curve-based approaches [1,5,6] and graph-based approaches [9,10,11] are provided in the literature to represent the shape. In our prototype, we adopted a graph-based method called ***shape-axis*** [9,10,11]. It consists of representing each shape by a unique axis tree for similarity computation. It has been chosen for various reasons:

- The shape-axis method can illustrate the skeleton of both the open and the closed curves as mentioned in [9], because its main goal is to determine the axis that describes the shape independently of the continuity or the discontinuity of the curve. The major handicap of the segmentation method, studied in [4], is the absence of considering an open curve to determine its unique skeleton representation. This can present a real problem when trying to treat such a contour.

- The *shape-axis* representation is sensitive to stretching; this can be solved by merging some correspondent nodes together. It presents also some sensitivity toward the occlusion that can be treated by cutting some unused nodes. These operations are used to minimize the similarity distance between two shapes. In [3], these operations are studied and the authors try to calculate the cost of similarity between two shapes.

To match two shapes, we only need to match their corresponding graphs. The graph matching problem has been widely studied in the literature [13, 14]. Basically, a graph representation **G= (V, E)** is composed by a set of nodes V and a set of edges E. **Exact** and **inexact** graph matching are two basic types of graph matching (isomorphism and homomorphism respectively). The best correspondence of a graph matching problem is defined as the optimum of some objective function which measures the similarity between matched vertices and edges. This objective function is also called *fitness function* [13]. In other words, this function measures the fitness of the isomorphism and the homomorphism defined between the two graphs. In shape axis method, the A*LIKE algorithm is used to match graphs of two different shapes, and calculated costs are used to measure the dissimilarity of the matched graphs.

In the following subsections, we briefly explain how the cost of two graphs matching is calculated in the case of stretching transformation[4], and show a running retrieval example using our prototype.

5.1 Neighborhood and Relaxation

Based on matching cost, the shape neighborhood is defined according to the stretching transformation allowing to apply relaxation and constraint functions used in our approach.

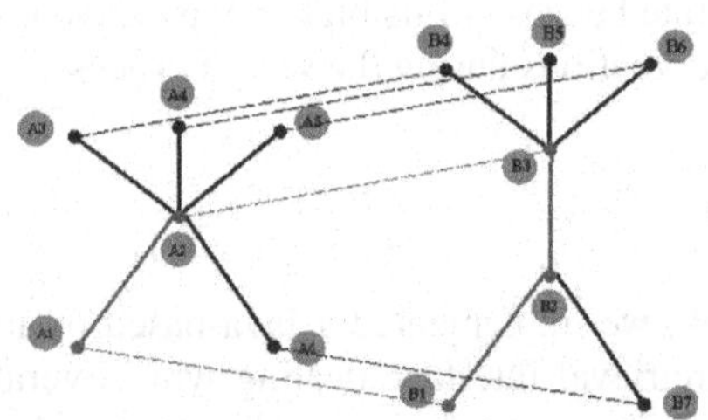

Fig. 4. The graph of representation of two different shapes

As mentioned and studied in [10], we specify for each shape a unique SA-tree. The SA-tree represents the axis of the shape. Stretching or articulating a shape causes some deformations, and consequently changes its appropriate shape representation, by adding additional bifurcations (internal segments connecting two nodes). Referring to figure 4, we observe the occurred changes that increase the complexity of calculating

[4] Other transformations are computed similarly.

the similarity between two inexact matching shapes due here to the added segment (bifurcation between the nodes [B2,B3]) on the articulated image (shape B).

The similarity between A and B can be identified by computing the correspondence (commonly called Edge-to-path correspondence) between them using a merging operation. In [10], the authors tried to find the total cost of correspondent segments CostS, and suggested to use a penalty cost for the merging operation. This cost is called CostM that computes the cost of the merged segment and its correspondent node. To compute the similarity between two shapes, the authors proposed to calculate the total cost representing the similarity cost of the compared parts of the two shapes. To calculate the cost between the edge (A2, A1) and the path (B1, [B2, B3]), we must take into account the cost of the correspondent edges (B2, B1), (A2, A1), with addition to the merging cost CostM as follows:

$$\text{Cost}[p(B_1,[B_2, B_3]),e(A_2, A_1)] = Cost_S(CT(B_2,B_1),CT(A_2, A_1))+Cost_M([B_2, B_3], A_2) \quad (8)$$

Where:

- **B:** is an image with additional segment on its representation (containing two bifurcation nodes).
- **A:** original image
- **[B_2, B_3]:** is the additional edge to be merged.

The correspondence in this case is edge-to-path correspondence, where the edge **e(A_2, A_1)** corresponds to the path **p(B_1, B_2, B_3)**.

The total cost of matching between A and B is represented as follows:

$$\text{Cost}_{Mt}(A, B) = \text{Cost}_S (A,B) + \text{Cost}_M(A, B) \quad (9)$$

In this way, we are able to define the *Stretching neighborhood* V_S of a shape A, using the set of shapes B where the matching cost Cost_S(A,B) and the merging cost Cost_M(A, B) are less than the value C_s given by the user. The neighborhood is formally defined as follows:

$$V_S(A, C_s) = \{B \,/\, (\text{Cost}_S(A,B)+\text{Cost}_M(A,B) \leq C_s) \quad (10)$$

V_S represents the neighborhood set that enables 2 parameters:

1. The original image A to be compared with the articulated image B
2. **C** is the threshold of the exact matching plus the cost the merging operation. C is defined by the user.

5.2 Prototype

Our java-based prototype uses a shape-based visual retrieval interface (Figure 5) composed of several zones:

1. **Zone 1:** used to formulate a visual query by selecting an existing image or by drawing a new one. This version of our prototype allows the users to only select SVG documents.
2. **Zone 2:** contains the corresponding graph of the shape given by the user. We use XML (eXtensible Markup Language) to represent the shape graph structure. Figure 6

shows an example of the XML file representing the shape axis of the initial shape given by the user.

3. **Zone 3:** allows the user to include or exclude one or more of the following transformations:
   - *Rotation* with a rotation threshold
   - *Occlusion* with segment and/or angle variations thresholds
   - *Articulation* with segment and/or angle variations thresholds
   - *Stretching* with segment variation threshold

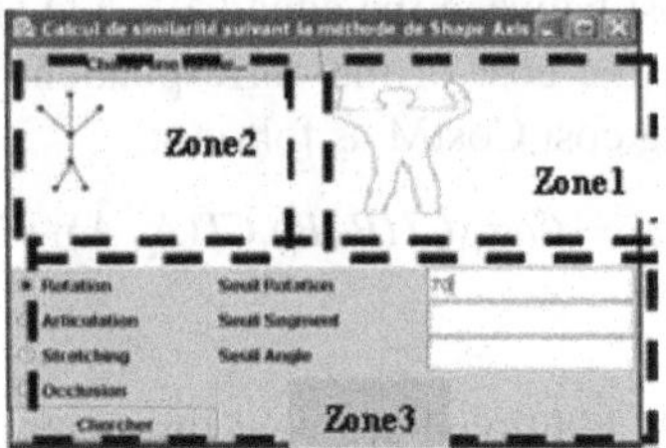

Fig. 5. Prototype retrieval interface

According to the input shape query and parameters given by the user, the prototype computes the shape neighbourhoods (one per transformation), and returns the result of rewriting process.

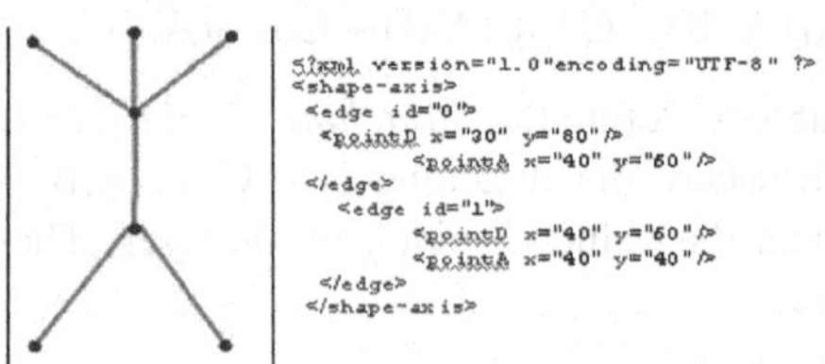

Fig. 6. The shape axis of the initial shape and its corresponding XML file

If we consider the running example in figure 5, figure 7a shows the visual query rewriting result after the unique rotation inclusion, with a given threshold of 70.

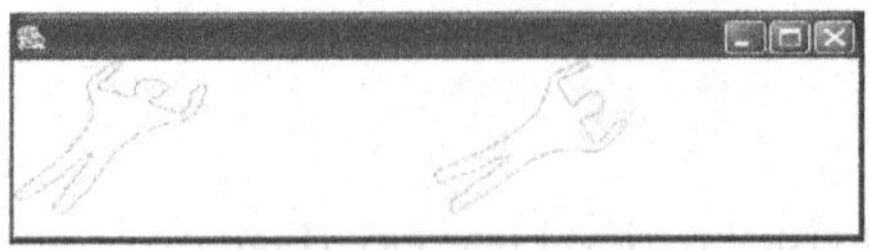
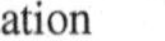

a- Results with only rotation

b- Results with only occlusion and stretching

Fig. 7. Prototype retrieval results

The user can also select several independent transformations with various corresponding thresholds. Figure 7b shows the query rewriting results, where the user includes occlusion and stretching transformations and excludes other transformations.

6 Conclusion

In this paper, we proposed a new visual shape-based query rewriting approach. It allows the user to have higher expressive power than traditional shape-based retrieval approaches. Customized inclusion and exclusion parameters are provided to the user when (re)formulating the query. In addition, the retrieval result shapes can be sorted according to the user preferences.

We are currently studying curve-based approaches provided in the literature and how we can integrate them into the prototype. We are also experimenting our prototype using a SVG database with about 600 documents. Our future work will address the integration of physical features like colour and texture into our rewriting approach.

References

1. Boaz J. Super, Improving Object Recognition Accuracy and Speed through Non-Uniform Sampling, Proc. of the SPIE Conference on Intelligent Robots and Computer SPIE Vol. 5267, pp. 228-239, 2003
2. Sundar, H., Silver, D., Gagvani, N. and Dickinson, S. Skeleton Based Shape Matching and Retrieval. Shape Modeling International, pp. 130-139, 2003
3. Long, H. and Leow, W. K. Perceptual consistency improves image retrieval performance , ACM SIGIR, pp. 434-435, 2001
4. Shah, J. Skeletons of 3D Shapes. 5th international conference on Scale Space and PDE methods in computer vision. 339-350 2005
5. Latecki, L. J., Lakaemper, R. and Wolter, D. Optimal Partial Shape Similarity. Image and vision computing, 227-236, 2005
6. Carlin, M. Measuring the Performance of Shape Similarity Retrieval Methods. SINTEF Electronics and cybernetics, vol.84 (1), pp. 44-61, Norway, 2001.
7. Gaasterland, T., Godfrey, P. and Minker, J. An overview of cooperative answering. Journal of Intelligent Information Systems, pp 123-157, 1992.
8. Gaasterland, T., Godfrey, P. and Minker, J. Relaxation as a platform of cooperative answering. Journal of Intelligent Information Systems, pp 293-321, 1992.
9. Tyng-Luh Liu. A Generalized Shape Axis Model for Planar Shapes. IPCR, pp. 3491-3495, 2000.
10. Liu, T., Geiger, D. Approximate Tree Matching and Shape Similarity. IEEE 17th International Conference on Computer Vision, pp 456-462, 1999.
11. Liu, T., Geiger, D. and Kohn R., Representation and Self-Similarity of Shapes. Int'l Conf. Computer Vision, Bombay, 1129-1138, 1998
12. Chalhoub G., Saad S., Chbeir R. and Yetongnon K., Adaptive data retrieval in multimedia DBMS, CSITeA_04 Cairo 2004
13. Bengoetxea, E., Inexact Graph Matching Using Estimation of Distribution Algorithms , Phd thesis Ecole Nationale Supérieure des Télécommunications (Paris) 2002
14. Bengoetxea, E., Graph Matching as a combinatorial Optimization Problem With Constraints, Ecole Nationale Supérieure des Télécommunications (Paris) 2002.
15. Dionisio, J., Cardenas, A. MQuery: A Visual Query Language for Multimedia, Timeline and Simulation Data, Journal of Visual Languages and Computing pp 377-401, 1996,
16. Google, http://www.google.com (Last visited 11/09/2005)
17. Aufaure, P., A High-Level Interface Language for GIS, Journal of Visual Languages and Computing, 6(2): 167-182, 1995.

18. Meyer, B., Beyond Icons: Towards New Metaphors for Visual Query Languages for Spatial Information Systems, Proceedings of the first International Workshop on Interfaces to Database Systems, pp 113-135, 1992.
19. Aufaure, M. , Bonhomme, C. , and Lbath, A. LVIS : Un Langage Visuel d'Interrogation de Bases de Données Spatiales , BDA'98, Tunisie, pp 527-545, 1998
20. Xiaogang X., Wenyin L., Xiangyu J., and Zhengxing S. Sketch-based user interface for creative tasks, In Proc. 5th Asia Pacific Conference on Computer Human Interaction HI2002), pp 560-570, 2002.
21. Haigh, K., Foslien, W., and Guralnik, V. Visual Query Language: Finding patterns in and relationships among time series data. Seventh Workshop on Mining Scientific and Engineering Datasets, 24 Apr 2004
22. Zhang, H., Chen, Z., Liu, W. Relevance Feedback in Content-Based Image Search. ww.research.microsoft.com
23. MacArthur, S. D., Brodley, C. E. and Shyu, C. Relevance Feedback Decision Trees in Content-Based Image Retrieval, in Proceedings of the IEEE Workshop on Content-Based Access of Image and Video Libraries, pp 68-72, June 2000.
24. Rui, Y., Huang, T., Ortega, M., and Mehrotra, S. Relevance feedback: A power tool for interactive content-based image retrieval, IEEE transactions on circuits and video technology pp 644-655, 1998
25. Chang, S., Costagliola, G., Pacini, G. and Tucci. M., Visual Language System for User Interfaces, IEEE Software, pages. 33-44, March 1995.
26. Goldin D. et al. Normalization of Life Science Data for Shape-based Similarity Querying, BECAT/CSE Technical Report TR-04-1, January 2004

On Semantically-Augmented XML-Based P2P Information Systems

Alfredo Cuzzocrea

Department of Electronics, Computer Science, and Systems
University of Calabria, Italy
cuzzocrea@si.deis.unical.it

Abstract. Knowledge representation and extraction techniques can be efficiently used to improve data modeling and IR functionalities of P2P Information Systems, which have recently attracted a lot of attention from industrial and academic researchers. These functionalities can be achieved by pushing semantics in both data and queries, and exploiting the derived expressiveness to improve file sharing primitives and lookup mechanisms made available from first-generation P2P systems. XML-based P2P Information Systems are a more specific and interesting instance of this class of systems, where the overall data domain is composed by very large, Internet-like distributed XML repositories from which users extract useful knowledge manly by means of IR methodologies implemented on the top of XML join queries. This paper focuses on several aspects of XML-based P2P Information Systems, raging from foundations and definitions to knowledge representation and extraction models and algorithms, along with their experimental evaluation. However, the results presented in this paper can also be adapted to deal with any kind of data format (e.g., HTML).

1 Introduction

During the last years, there was a growing interest for *P2P Information Systems* (P2P IS) [1,2], mainly because they fit a wide number of real-life IT applications. Digital libraries are only a significant instance of P2P IS, but it is very easy to foresee how large the impact of P2P IS on innovative and emerging IT scenarios, such as *e*-procurement and *e*-government, will be during the next years.

P2P networks are natively built on the top of a very large repository of data objects (e.g., files), which is intrinsically distributed, fragmented, and partitioned among *participant* peers. P2P Users are usually interested in (*i*) retrieving data objects containing information of interest, like video and audio files, and (*ii*) sharing information with other (participant) users/peers. From the *Information Retrieval* (IR) perspective, P2P users (*i*) typically submit short, loose queries by means of keywords derived from natural language-style questions (e.g., "*find all the music files containing Mozart's compositions*" is posed through the keywords "*compositions*" and "*Mozart*"), and (*ii*), due to resource-sharing purposes, are usually interested in retrieving as result a *set* of data objects rather than only one. Then, well-founded IR methodologies like ranking can be successfully applied on intermediate results (i.e., sets of data objects) to improve system capabilities thus achieving performances better than those of more

H.L. Larsen et al. (Eds.): FQAS 2006, LNAI 4027, pp. 441 – 457, 2006.

traditional database-like query schemes. Furthermore, the P2P IR mechanism is "self-alimenting" as intermediate results can be then re-used for sharing new information, or for setting and specializing new search/query activities. In other words, from the database perspective, P2P users typically adopt a semi-structured (data) model for querying data objects rather than a structured (data) model. On the other hand, efficiently accessing data in P2P systems, which is an aspect directly related with the above issues, is a relevant and still incompletely solved open research challenge [1].

Basically, P2P IS extend the traditional functionalities of P2P systems (i.e., file sharing primitives and simple lookup mechanisms based on partial- or exact-match of strings), by adding to the primitive of the latter useful (and more complex) knowledge representation and extraction techniques. Achieving the definition of new knowledge delivering paradigms over P2P networks is the main goal of this effort. In fact, the completely decentralized nature of P2P networks, which enable peers and data objects to come and go at will, allows us to *(i)* successfully exploit self-alimenting mechanisms of knowledge production, and *(ii)* take advantage from innovative knowledge representation and extraction models based on semantics, metadata management, probability etc.

Despite more or less advanced query strategies, all today P2P systems are devoted to cover their initial goals, and, as a consequence, there is a strength, effective demand for enriching P2P systems with functionalities that *(i)* are proper of the information systems, such as *Knowledge Discovery* (KD)- and IR-style data object querying, and *(ii)* cannot be supported by the actual data representation and query models of (traditional) P2P systems. Hence, P2P IS represent an attempt to support even complex processes like knowledge representation, discovering, and management over P2P networks. More properly, knowledge representation and management techniques mainly concern with the modeling of P2P IS, whereas knowledge discovering techniques (implemented via IR functionalities) mainly concern with the querying (i.e., knowledge extraction) of P2P IS.

All considering, we can claim that traditional P2P functionalities are inadequate for the innovative requirements of P2P IS, whereas P2P systems relying on XML repositories, whose management has reached a sufficient maturity by now, offer from a side all the typical functionalities supported by a P2P system, such as information sharing, dynamism, and scalability, and from another side native support for real-life IT application scenarios (as XML data are semi-structured by definition). Furthermore, by adopting XML as core data model, it is possible to meaningfully augment *semantics of data*, and supporting advanced KD- and IR-style functionalities. In fact, complex mining/reasoning models, like those based on graphs and trees, can be natively derived from the structure of XML data, which are intrinsically hierarchical, and used to infer knowledge via semantics, also adopting a large set of already-available algorithms and techniques coming from well-known, mature scientific disciplines like *Data Mining* (DM) and *Knowledge Discovery in Databases* (KDD).

As will be evident through the paper, even if our proposal is targeted at XML documents, it can be extended to deal with different kinds of document (e.g., HTML pages). Thus, in the rest of the paper, due to its popularity, we assume of dealing with XML documents as a relevant case of interest.

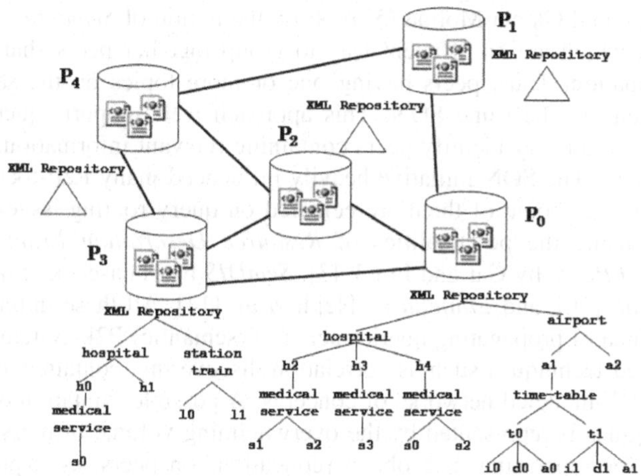

Fig. 1. The data layer of an XML-based P2P health information system

On the basis of these considerations, we address the application scenario drawn by P2P IS whose participant peers contain XML repositories in form of collection of XML documents that are grouped on the basis of a *context*, thus building clusters of resources that are tightly (semantically) related. We name such systems as *XML-based P2P Information Systems*. An instance of the addressed application scenario is depicted in Fig. 1, which shows the data layer of an XML-based P2P Health Information System. In such system, peers mainly contain information about hospitals and medical services in a certain urban area, and other related and useful information such as locations of airports and train stations, time-tables of public services, hotels and availabilities etc concerning with the same area. Users of such system are interested in retrieving (useful) knowledge by means of *XQuery*-formatted join queries over the (distributed) XML repositories.

Join queries are widely recognized as the most useful ones for users, mainly because knowledge is typically distributed on different data sources rather than being centralized in a unique data provider. More specially, with respect to the goals of our works, join queries over distributed XML repositories effectively represent an adequate solution for supporting advanced KD- and IR-style functionalities within XML-based P2P IS, being knowledge production, processing, and fruition intrinsically decentralized and distributed processes.

2 Related Work

Our proposal belongs to the so-called *Intelligent Query Routing Techniques* on P2P networks, whose main goal is to provide efficiency during the query evaluation on large and dynamic P2P networks via intelligent schemes. Some comprehensive overviews on these techniques can be found in the works of Tsoumakos and Roussopoulos [16] and Zeinalipour-Yazti *et al.* [17]. In this Section, we focus on approaches that are close to ours, and we remand to Sect. 8 for their experimental evaluation against our proposal.

First, Crespo and Garcia-Molina [5] propose the notion of *Semantics Overlay Networks* (SON), which are an efficient way to group together peers sharing the same schema information. Thus, peers having one or more topics on the same *thematic hierarchy* belong to the same SON. This approach well supports query routing as every peer p_i can quickly identify peers containing relevant information, by avoiding network flooding. The SON initiative heavily influenced many P2P-focused research projects; among all, some of them are centered on query routing issues in SON, by meaningfully using the potentialities of *Resource Description Framework* (RDF) constructs: *RDFPeers* by Cai and Frank [3], *SemDIS* by Halaschek *et al.* [9], *Piazza* by Halevy *et al.* [10], and *Edutella* by Nejdl *et al.* [14]. All these initiatives have in common the idea of propagating queries across a (semantic) P2P system by means of semantics-based techniques such as correlation discovering, containment etc, mainly working on RDF-modeled networks of concepts. A possible limitation of SON-based P2P IR techniques is represented by the overwhelming volume of messages that can be generated for supporting data object replications on peers, as required by SON design guidelines [5]. Thus, P2P applications running on the top of SON-based models for query routing can incur excessive overheads on network traffic.

An interesting solution to this problem has been proposed by Li et *al.* [12]: they suggest using *signatures on neighboring peers* for directing searches along selected *network paths*, and introduce some schemes to facilitate efficient searching of data objects. Signatures are a way of adding semantics to data, by building a bit vector *V*; *V* is generated according to the following two steps: (*i*) hashing the content of a data object into bit strings, said *BS*, and (*ii*) applying a bitwise operator OR on *BS*. The so-built bit strings are used at query time by performing a bitwise operation AND on the *search signature* (i.e., the signature of the term used as search key) and the *data signature* (i.e., the signature stored on the current peer). In [12], the authors show how some proposed flooding-based search algorithms allow the signatures of the neighboring peers to be efficiently exploited for enhancing search results, and, moreover, an extensive experimental section clearly confirms the effectiveness of their proposed technique in comparison with existing P2P content search methods [12].

The *Intelligent Search Mechanism* (ISM), proposed by Zeinalipour-Yazti *et al.* [18], represents instead a novel approach for supporting IR over P2P networks by (*i*) minimizing the number of messages sent among the peers, and (*ii*) minimizing the number of peers that are involved for each search request. To this end, ISM is composed by: (*i*) a *Profile Mechanism*, according to which each peer builds a "profile" for each of its neighboring peer; (*ii*) a *Query Similarity* function, which calculates the similarity queries to a new query; (*iii*) a *Relevance Rank*, which is a ranking technique for peers that takes as input the (neighboring) peer profiles, and produces as output a ranked list of (neighboring) peers used to bias the search towards the most relevant peers; and (*iv*) a *Search Mechanism*, which implements the ISM search policy. In [18], the authors show how ISM works well (*i*) when peers hold some specialized knowledge about the P2P environment, and (*ii*) over P2P networks having high degrees of query locality; in these particular conditions, ISM outperforms some previous work, such as the techniques *Breadth First Search* (BFS), which is employed in *Gnutella* [7], and *Random Breadth First Search* (RBFS), which is a modified version of BFS proposed by Kalogeraki et *al.* [11] where random extractions are used to select the "next" peers during search operations.

Finally, Lv *et al.* [13] present the *Random Walkers Algorithm* (RWA), according to which each peer forwards the query message (called, in this context, *walker*) to another of its neighboring peers at random. To improve performances and reduce query time, the original idea of using one walker only is extended to the usage of $k > 1$ walkers, which are consecutively sent from the sender peer.

3 Semantically-Augmented XML-Based P2P Information Systems: Foundations, Definitions, and a Reference Architecture

Regarding to the application scenarios for P2P IS discussed in Sect. 1, the most important research challenge is *pushing semantics in data and queries to support even complex knowledge representation and extraction processes, by improving query capabilities (and performances) of P2P IS, mainly performed in the vest of IR functionalities*. To this end, in this paper we propose a knowledge representation framework, enriched via semantics, for efficiently representing and processing knowledge in P2P IS. In our opinion, the traditional query model of P2P systems, based on routing queries towards peers containing the information of interest according to a given policy (e.g., random schemes), can be sensitively improved by building *semantically-related communities* of peers, called *Semantic Communities of Peers* (SCoP), which (*i*) store XML data about related concepts, and (*ii*) can be used to *drive* query execution, by avoiding resource-intensive network flooding (i.e., reducing the hop number during search operations). As we better motivate in Sect. 6, with respect to previous similar proposals, the most important innovation carried by SCoP is that SCoP are built *by taking into account the analysis of the (past) query results only*, without consider pre-fixed schemes (e.g., knowledge representation schemes imposed by the system author) or intensional (i.e., schema-based) models (e.g., [3,5,9,10,14]). From a theoretical point of view, this approach is just opposite to the so-called *Distributed Information Retrieval* (DIR) approach [4], which assumes that peers have a *global knowledge* of the system (e.g., some statistical knowledge about the content of *each* XML repository). In other words, our framework assumes that peers only have a *local knowledge* of the system, i.e. *knowledge about queries flooded through their neighboring peers*. As a consequence, the comparison of our proposed framework against proposals adhering to the class of DIR techniques is outside of the scope of this paper.

The described approach leads to the definition of the so-called *Semantically-Augmented XML-based P2P Information Systems* (P2P IS for short), which allow the traditional functionalities of P2P systems to be improved via semantics. While SCoP are the "way" of *representing* knowledge in our proposed framework, some *graph-based computational models* and relative algorithms realize the way of *processing and extracting* knowledge from very large XML repositories, thus improving the semantic expressiveness of the knowledge discovery phases. Formally, in our proposed framework, we define a P2P Information System P^+ as a triple $P^+ = \langle P, \Upsilon, S\rangle$, such that (*i*) P is a P2P system relying on a domain of distributed XML repositories D^{XML}, (*ii*) Υ is a set of predicates supporting knowledge extraction mechanisms from (XML) data in D^{XML} via IR methodologies, and (*iii*) S is a formal semantics used to optimize query executions in Υ processes. Furthermore, given a P2P IS P^+, we define a SCoP C on P^+ as a collection of peers in P^+ that contain semantically related (XML) data in D^{XML}, whose relationships are built on the basis of (past) query results analysis, by exploiting the local knowledge about the neighboring peers.

The knowledge representation framework for P2P IS we propose is characterized by a multi-layer architecture, mainly devoted to capture knowledge management and extraction tasks in such systems. Our architecture is thus composed by two mainly layers which, in turn, are composed by sub-components. This organization aims at maintaining the framework as more general and extensible as possible, in order to easily add further functionalities when available. The two main layers of the proposed framework are: (*i*) the *Knowledge Modeling Layer* (KML), which deals with the problem of modeling and representing the target P2P IS via knowledge representation and management techniques; (*ii*) the *Knowledge Discovering Layer* (KDL), concerning with query functionalities of P2P IS (i.e., knowledge extraction), which are those of main interest for P2P users/applications, and are widely recognized in the vest of IR techniques. In more detail, the KML interacts with the XML repositories forming the *Data Layer* of our reference architecture, whereas the KDL implements the knowledge representation-based models mentioned above, and supports KD- and IR-style advanced functionalities in peers located in the *P2P Layer* of our reference architecture.

4 Modeling XML Documents and Repositories Via Semantics

A basic component of the framework we propose is the XML data model, which deals with modeling both XML documents and repositories. In order to introduce it, we need to provide some fundamental definitions. First, we represent an XML document as a rooted, labeled tree, according to the widely-accepted model for XML data (e.g., W3C consortium). Secondly, we introduce the concept of *forest* as the underlying XML data model for any XML repository in a given P2P IS modeled according to our reference framework (see Sect. 3). As a consequence, we define a forest as a rooted, unordered collection of XML documents that is dynamically produced on a peer via popular publisher/subscriber mechanisms of modern IT applications, like B2C and B2B *e*-commerce systems.

A critical point of our data model concerns with how concepts related to an XML document are represented and managed. Given an XML document X, the concepts held by X are represented as an ordered list of *terms* $\ell(X) = \{t_0, t_1, \ldots, t_{n-1}\}$, which are derived from the document according to an arbitrary procedure. Without loss of generality, we assume that $\ell(X)$ does not contain duplicated items. We point out that our framework is orthogonal to the particular generating procedure, and any kind of solution can be applied to build the list (e.g., automatic or manual methods).

Following the approach above, we obtain a sort of *annotation of XML documents by concepts*, which allows us to augment the semantics of documents and improve the capability of processing them. It should be noted that the described mechanism is similar to what happens with the classical use of keyword metadata to describe documents, but targeted to capture semantics of them. The derived benefits are mainly evident in the query execution phase, as, for instance, we can know the kind of data contained in an XML document without accessing the entire document. But, above all, concepts are the basic entities for building SCoP over the target P2P IS, as we better describe in Sect. 6. We point out that semantic models more complex than lists, such as trees and graphs, and their variants, could be used in substitution of the former, thus achieving a greater semantic expressiveness in representing knowledge in form of related concepts. Nevertheless, we discard such models because of (*i*) they are computationally more "heavy" than lists, and, as a consequence, update procedures for our framework would be more resource-intensive and would reduce the scalability of the same framework, and (*ii*) since P2P IS users are usually interested in loose, incomplete query answers, lists efficiently fulfill this requirement with low computational overheads, yet preserving the scalability of the framework, which is a rigorous requirement for P2P systems and applications.

In a similar spirit of what done for P2P IS, we introduce the *semantically-augmented* "counterparts" for both the entities XML document and forest, i.e. the *semantically-augmented XML document* and the *semantically-augmented XML forest*, which are used to build and maintain SCoP. Formally, a semantically-augmented XML document X^* is a couple $X^* = \langle X, \ell(X)\rangle$, such that X is an XML document, and $\ell(X)$ is the ordered list of concepts held by X. Furthermore, a semantically-augmented XML forest F^* is a couple $F^* = \langle F, \ell(F)\rangle$, such that F is an XML forest, and $\ell(F)$ is the list of concepts held by F, obtained by merging, without duplicates, the concept lists $\ell(X_k)$ of all the XML documents X_k in F, i.e. $\ell(F) = \bigcup_k \ell(X_k)$.

It is a matter to derive that, given a set of XML documents $\mathfrak{R}$, the forest built on it, denoted by $F(\mathfrak{R})$, is computed in time $O(|\mathfrak{R}|)$, such that $|\mathfrak{R}|$ is the size of $\mathfrak{R}$. Secondly, given a set of XML documents $\mathfrak{R}$, and the forest $F(\mathfrak{R})$ built on it, the time complexity of building the concept list $\ell(F) \in F^*$ linearly depends on $O(|\mathfrak{R}|)$. It should be noted that both these nicely properties ensure that, in our framework, data update procedures require a linear (polynomial) time, thus avoiding to introduce computational overheads that could seriously mine the scalability of P2P IS.

5 Modeling and Evaluating Semantically-Augmented Queries

Just like we do with XML documents (see Sect. 4), we model queries as collections of terms representing the expressed (search) concepts. This approach quite resembles the *Latent Semantic Indexing* (LSI) proposal by Deerwester *et al.* [6], and presents some advantages that we describe next. Given a user query Q, the concepts expressed by Q are represented as an ordered list of terms $\varphi(Q) = \{u_0, u_1, \ldots, u_{m-1}\}$, and, formally, we name the couple $Q^* = \langle Q, \varphi(Q)\rangle$ as *semantically-augmented query*. Similarly to the list of terms of XML documents, without loss of generality, we assume that $\varphi(Q)$ does not contain duplicated items. Furthermore, like documents, lists of terms can be extracted from various classes of queries, e.g. XML queries.

We evaluate a semantically-augmented query Q^* against a semantically-augmented XML document X^* by simply applying the *matching criterion* between terms (i.e., concepts). In other words, we assume that the evaluation of Q^* against X^* produces a non-null answer if there exists at least a term u_j in $\varphi(Q)$ that matches with a term t_i in $\ell(X)$, otherwise the evaluation fails. This is formally modeled by the following function *semEvalDoc*:

$$semEvalDoc(Q^*, X^*) = \begin{cases} TRUE & \ell(X) \cap \varphi(Q) \neq \varnothing \\ FALSE & \ell(X) \cap \varphi(Q) = \varnothing \end{cases} \quad (1)$$

The function *semEvalDoc* is easily generalized for capturing the case in which a query Q is evaluated against an XML repository instead of an XML document. In this case, the matching of the terms in $\varphi(Q)$ is checked against the list of terms $\ell(F)$ of the XML forest F^* representing the target repository, as modeled by the following function *semEvalRep*:

$$semEvalRep(Q^*, F^*) = \begin{cases} TRUE & \ell(F) \cap \varphi(Q) \neq \varnothing \\ FALSE & \ell(F) \cap \varphi(Q) = \varnothing \end{cases} \quad (2)$$

Now we highlight some advantages of the approach we use to model queries. First, the usage of list of terms for both XML documents and repositories (see Sect. 4) allows us to evaluate queries against the two kinds of data source in the same way, by providing facilities at the formal modeling level as well as the implementation level (and, as a consequence, mitigating scalability issues). Secondly, regarding the efficiency of our query evaluation scheme, it should be noted that the computational cost needed for evaluating queries against both XML documents and repositories is bounded by the logarithm (time) complexity. In more detail, given a semantically-augmented XML document X^*, and a semantically-augmented query Q^*, Q^* is evaluated against X^* in time $O(|\varphi(Q)| \cdot \log|\ell(X)|)$. Furthermore, given a semantically-augmented XML forest F^*, and a semantically-augmented query Q^*, Q^* is evaluated against F^* in time $O(|\varphi(Q)| \cdot \log|\ell(F)|)$.

6 Knowledge Representation Model

The basic component of our knowledge representation model is the *Semantic Relationship Matrix* (SRM), which supports SCoP definition and management. Given a peer p_i of a P2P IS P^+, and the set of its neighboring peers $\Psi(p_i)$, the SRM defined on p_i, denoted by $M(p_i)$, is a two-dimensional matrix such that rows represent the neighboring peers $p_j \in \Psi(p_i)$ of p_i, and columns represent the set of *neighboring concepts* $\Omega(p_i)$ of p_i obtained by merging, without duplicates, the concepts held in the neighboring peers, i.e. $\Omega(p_i) = \bigcup_{j=0}^{|\Psi(p_i)|-1} \ell(F_j)$, being $\ell(F_j)$ the XML forest modeling the repository stored in p_j. It should be noted that $\Omega(p_i)$ models the local knowledge in our framework.

Each entry of $M(p_i)$, denoted by $M_i[p_h][t_k]$, contains the object NULL if the concept t_k is not held by the neighboring peer p_h or there is not any (semantic) relationship among concepts held in p_i and concepts held in p_h; otherwise, it contains an object $m_{h,k} = \langle s_{h,k}, w_{h,k} \rangle$ such that $s_{h,k}$ is a percentage value, and $w_{h,k}$ is the list of the last N queries, being N a framework parameter that is empirically fixed. In more detail, $s_{h,k}$ represents the percentage number of queries successfully completed by flooding the P2P network from p_i towards p_h in searching for XML data holding the concept t_k, with respect to the total number of queries posed to p_i and searching for the concept t_k.

We assume that a query Q is successfully completed if the user, after having look-upped on the P2P network the location of the XML data belonging to the result of Q, denoted by $D^{XML}(Q)$, then accesses or downloads them. In a similar spirit, $w_{h,k}$ represents the list of the last N queries posed to p_i and which were routed towards p_h in searching for XML data holding the concept t_k. It should be noted that, in order to compute $s_{h,k}$, we take into account the successfully completed queries only, whereas $w_{h,k}$ is computed by also considering queries that were not successfully completed, but routed towards p_h.

We highlight that usually SRMs are sparse matrices (due to the typical nature and topology of P2P networks), so that we can adopt efficient techniques and algorithms for representing and processing them. Furthermore, it should be noted that we propose a very simple relationship description model (i.e., based on the existence of the direct relationship, without any inferred or derived relationship) instead of more complex models known in literature. This because of, as stated in Sect. 3, our main goal is building SCoP by considering the analysis of query results with respect to the neighboring peers only (thus, exploiting the local knowledge), without any pre-fixed scheme or intensional model. The most important benefit deriving from this approach is that our SCoP-based framework can be maintained very efficiently as SRMs are built incrementally, when queries are posed to peers, thus avoiding to introduce excessive computational overheads. Furthermore, storing the list of the last N queries allows us to efficiently support SCoP maintenance operations, since, in consequence of a framework update U, we only need to handle the involved-by-U queries and peers, without recursively propagating updates to other peers (the reader should keep in mind that this is another benefit coming from the usage of the local knowledge). As a consequence, we obtain that, given a peer p_i in a P2P IS P^+, the SRM $M(p_i)$ is incrementally built and maintained in time $O(1)$.

Now we focus the attention on the spatial complexity of SRMs, which is an important aspect to be considered in our framework. Since SRMs are usually sparse, given a peer p_i in a P2P IS P^+, such that (*i*) $Z = |\Psi(p_i)|$ is the number of its neighboring peers, (*ii*) $T = |\Omega(p_i)|$ is the number of its neighboring concepts, and (*iii*) Z_{eff} and T_{eff} are the number of neighboring peers and the number of concepts for which the corresponding entry $M(p_i)$ is not null respectively, the SRM $M(p_i)$ is $O(Z_{eff} \times T_{eff}) << O(Z \times T)$ in size (i.e., there exists a very efficient way of representing SRMs).

To adequately support our knowledge extraction models and algorithms, which are presented in Sect. 7, we need to introduce the definition of the so-called *RDF Schema Graph* (RSG), which is another component of our knowledge representation model. Given a peer p_i of a P2P IS P^+, the RSG defined on p_i, denoted by $R(p_i)$, is used to represent relationships among the neighboring concepts $\Omega(p_i)$ of p_i, by making use of the RDF. At query time, $R(p_i)$ allows us to discover relationships among (search) concepts, according to the guidelines we present in Sect. 7. The usage of RDF makes our proposed framework able to encapsulate and take advantage from some well-known RDF properties, which we briefly summarize next. First, RDF allows us to successfully represent networks of related classes/concepts, and efficiently supports the definition of predicates on these relationships. Secondly, RDF views can be easily derived starting from RDF schemas by using well-known declarative languages for processing RDF-based knowledge, such as *RDF Query Language* (RQL) and *RDF View Language* (RVL). Furthermore, the namespace mechanism supported by RDF naturally marries the definition of SCoP on a PSP IS, and can be efficiently used to improve the expressiveness in the knowledge representation task, as, for instance, we could define *hierarchies of SCoP* by significantly enhancing semantic capabilities and functionalities of P2P IS. Finally, it is easy to note that, like SRMs, RSGs can also be represented and managed very efficiently.

7 Knowledge Extraction Model

In order to efficiently support the knowledge extraction task in our framework, we introduce a graph-based computational model founding on the so-called *Semantic Relationship Graph* (SRG). Given a peer p_i of a P2P IS P^+, the SRG defined on p_i, denoted by $G(p_i)$, is used to extract knowledge from p_i. In more detail, given a query Q, according to our knowledge extraction strategy, we dynamically build, for each peer p_i involved by search operations of Q, the SRG $G(p_i)$ starting from the SRM $M(p_i)$ and the RSG $R(p_i)$, and use it to bias the search towards relevant peers. SRG is a labeled graph, where each label on an arc a between two peers p_i and p_j is an object $l_{i,j} = \langle C_j, \vartheta_{i,j} \rangle$, such that (*i*) C_j is the concept retrieved by accessing p_j from p_i, and (*ii*) $\vartheta_{i,j}$ is a weight used to model the relevance and the goodness of biasing the search along a (furthermore, $\vartheta_{i,j}$ supports our cost-based algorithm for extracting (useful) knowledge from XML repositories (see Sect. 7.1)). It should be noted that this approach allows us to achieve the important benefit of having a graph-based model for

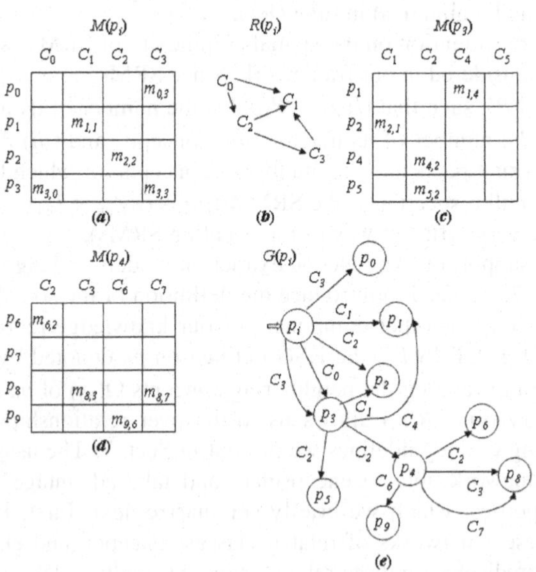

Fig. 2. Building a 3-degree SRG $G(p_i)$

reasoning on knowledge held in peers, thus improving the expressiveness and the possibilities of the knowledge extraction phase. From a computational point of view, we highlight that the proposed approach does not introduce excessive computational overheads, as the SRG is built on the top of the neighboring peers so that the numbers of nodes and arcs in SRG are, typically, bounded. As a consequence, SRG can be dynamically materialized in main memory, and, thus, good performances are usually obtained.

Given a peer p_i belonging to a P2P IS P^+, the SRG $G(p_i)$ represents semantic relationships among concepts (*i*) held in the neighboring peers of p_i (i.e., the set $\Psi(p_i)$), and (*ii*) that can be "reached" starting from p_i. In more detail, $G(p_i)$ is dynamically built starting from the SRM $M(p_i)$ and the RSG $R(p_i)$ by *mining* both the entities, i.e. by discovering (*i*), from $M(p_i)$, *direct relationships* among the concepts held in $\Psi(p_i)$, and (*ii*), from $R(p_i)$, *indirect relationships* among the concepts held in $\Psi(p_i)$. In some sense, $G(p_i)$ *extends* the knowledge kept in the two entities (i.e., the SRM $M(p_i)$ and the RSG $R(p_i)$) by realizing an *instance of this knowledge* during the query execution task. For these reasons, in our framework, we distinguish between the so-called *static knowledge*, i.e. the knowledge kept in the entities SRM and the RSG, and the so-called *dynamic knowledge*, i.e. the knowledge kept in the entity SRG. The former describes knowledge represented *by* topological/semantic properties of the underlying P2P network. The latter describes knowledge that can be inferred *from* topological/semantic properties of the underlying P2P network.

Since the set $\Omega(p_i)$ is built by merging the concept sets held in the set $\Psi(p_i)$ (see Sect. 6), we obtain that, in general, a same concept C_i can be reached starting from a given peer p_i according to the following possibilities: (*i*) via a direct (semantic) path from p_i to $p_j \in \Psi(p_i)$, denoted by δ-*path(i,j)*, or, alternatively, (*ii*) via an indirect (semantic) path from p_i to a peer p_j that, *in general*, could not belong to $\Psi(p_i)$, denoted by σ-*path(i,j)*. δ- and σ-paths are discovered from p_i by mining the entities SRM $M(p_i)$ and the RSG $R(p_i)$. In more detail, δ-paths are directly extracted from $M(p_i)$. On the contrary, to discover the σ-paths, we adopt a Δ-*step propagation strategy*, such that Δ is an empirically set framework parameter. Given a search concept C_i and a *current* peer p_i (i.e., the peer that is currently processed by our search algorithm), our strategy determines *how the corresponding search space* $S(C_i)$ *(i.e., the space of all the neighboring concepts) must be browsed.* The "result" of this relationship discovery task starting from p_i is "materialized" into the SRG $G(p_i)$. Particularly, we name the obtained mining structure as Δ-*degree SRG.*

The Δ-degree SRG $G(p_i)$ building process is as follows. Starting from p_i, we first derive all the relationships modeled by $M(p_i)$, thus adding an arc $\langle p_i,p_j\rangle$ for each peer p_j having a non-null entry in $M(p_i)$ (see Sect. 6). Then, for each of the so-determined peer p_j, we access the SRM $M(p_j)$ and we add a new arc $\langle p_j,p_w\rangle$ for each peer p_w having a non-null entry in $M(p_j)$ in correspondence of concepts C_i modeled in the RSG $R(p_i)$. In turn, we iterate this process for other Δ-1 times (i.e., until the max depth from p_i to the actual p_w in the SRG $G(p_i)$ is Δ). To give an example, consider Fig. 2, where the construction of the SRG $G(p_i)$ for the peer p_i using a 3-step propagation strategy is shown.

Now, we focus our attention on how to compute the weights $\vartheta_{i,j} \in l_{i,j}$ of the SRG (note that the concepts $C_j \in l_{i,j}$ are computed by mining the SRM and RSG, as described above), after that nodes and arcs of the SRG are determined according to the previous building process. Given two peers p_i and p_j, we compute the weight $\vartheta_{i,j}$ for the arc $\langle p_i,p_j\rangle$ of $G(p_i)$ as follows:

$$\vartheta_{i,j} = \frac{\Gamma(\delta - path(i,j))}{\sum_{k=i}^{j-1} \Gamma(\sigma - path(k,k+1))} \tag{3}$$

where $\Gamma(\delta\text{-}path(i,j))$ is defined as follows:

$$\Gamma(\delta - path(i,j)) = s_{i,j} \in M(p_i) \tag{4}$$

and $\Gamma(\sigma\text{-}path(i,j))$ as follows:

$$\Gamma(\sigma - path(i,j)) = \sum_{k=i}^{j-1} \Gamma(\delta - path(k,k+1)) \tag{5}$$

and $\Gamma(\bullet)$ is a function costing a given path in $G(p_i)$.

7.1 A Cost-Based Algorithm for Extracting Knowledge from P2P IS

Selecting the "next" peer p_j to be processed starting from the "current" peer p_i in searching for XML data holding the concept C_j is the fundamental step of our cost-based knowledge extraction algorithm. We remark that our goal is to reduce the hop number during search operations, while at the same time extract useful knowledge. To this end, we devise a cost-based algorithm that tries to minimize the σ-paths from the current peer p_i to the next peer p_j in the SRG, which is thus used as formal computational model.

In the more general case, starting from a peer p_i, we have a *set* of σ-paths that can be followed for accessing the XML data of interest (from Sect. 7, note that δ-paths are particular instances of σ-paths). We denote the set of possible paths σ-paths in $G(p_i)$ that originate from p_i as follows:

$$\Phi(p_i) = \{\sigma_0, \sigma_1, \ldots, \sigma_{|\Phi(p_i)|-1}\} \tag{6}$$

The *best* σ-path σ* belonging to $\Phi(p_i)$ is the one definitively used to extract the XML data of interest, and it is obtained by minimizing the following cost function modeling the sum of all the weights $\vartheta_{i,j}$ belonging to σ*:

$$\Im(i,j) = \sum_{k=i}^{j-1} \vartheta_{i,j} : (i,j) \in \sigma^* \tag{7}$$

The algorithm `extractXMLData`, which codifies this strategy, takes as input (*i*) the peer p_i on which it is activated, (*ii*) the concept of interest list *queryList*, which implements the list of terms $\varphi(Q)$ in our query model (see Sect. 5) and contains the concepts for which the related XML data must be retrieved, and (*iii*) the input parameter Δ (see Sect. 7), and returns as output the XML data of interest holding the concepts belonging to *queryList*. The way of presenting the final result is a non-trivial engagement in highly dynamic environments such as P2P networks. The (possible) solution we use in the algorithm `extractXMLData` consists in presenting the retrieved data as an *XML view* over the distributed XML repositories.

8 Experimental Study

In order to conduct a fine and accurate experimental validation of our proposed knowledge representation-based framework, we devised an experimental framework for supporting IR over P2P IS. In such a framework, we implemented a Java-based P2P environment simulator where peers and XML repositories, capturing the P2P Layer and the Data Layer of our reference architecture respectively (see Sect. 3), are represented.

One of the first problems we addressed in modeling our experiments was about how to distribute peers over the network: regarding to this aspect, we chose a network topology such that peers are uniformly distributed over the network. This choice was driven by the literature evidence claiming that several previous works focused on similar experimental methodologies (e.g., [12,13]) have shown that this configuration is the "best-in-laboratory" one. For what concerns with the data support of our P2P environment simulator, we employed a modified version of the popular synthetic XML data set generator *XMark* [15], where an ad-hoc built thesaurus, called *ContentThesaurus*, replaces the original XMark Shakespeare's literature with context-oriented contents (remember our characterization of "context" for P2P IS presented in Sect. 1). Furthermore, in such a data support solution, concepts expressed by contents stored in *ContentThesaurus* are materialized within another specific thesaurus, called *ConceptThesaurus*, according to our XML data model for documents and repositories described in Sect. 4. Besides, a very simple cluster-based indexing data structure is in charge of maintaining the pointers between contents in *ContentThesaurus* and related concepts in *ConceptThesaurus*. Among other well-understood and accepted advantages [15], adopting XMark inside our experimental framework allows us to generate synthetic XML repositories having different structure and size, thus making our experiments more close to scenarios drawn by real-life IT applications. For what concerns with populating the (virtual) P2P environment (i.e., distributing the XML repositories across the peers in the network), we adopted the solution of doing this according to an input, customizable distribution, in a similar way to what done with the modeling of the network topology. To this end, we exploited the Uniform (similarly to the previous case) and Zipf distributions because of, as widely established, they meaningfully represent the two opposite situations where, in the first case, data are uniformly distributed over the P2P network, and, in the second case, data are non-uniformly distributed over the P2P network, and asymmetric data loads are present. In addition, in our experimental framework, queries were simply modeled by means of uniform extractions over *ConceptThesaurus*, thus obtaining random lists of concepts that ensure an unbiased experimental evaluation.

In our experimental setting, the hardware infrastructure was composed by 10 workstations interconnected with a 10/100 LAN, each of them equipped with a processor *AMD Athlon XP 2600+* at 2.133 GHz and 1 GB RAM, and running *SUSE Linux 9.1*. On the top of our Java-based P2P environment simulator, we deployed 200 peers, each of them running like a single peer on a single host, thanks to the multi-threading programming environment offered by the Java platform. The data layer of our experimental setting was obtained by producing synthetic contents and concepts concerning with an *e*-tourism P2P IS where XML repositories contain related data from which useful knowledge such as information for reaching the tourist places, locations of hotels and restaurants and related services, information on historical/archeological sites, information on gastronomic tours, information on events and movies etc can be extracted. By exploiting our modified version of the XML data set generator XMark, we obtained several (synthetic) XML repositories having various structure (in particular, the maximum depth and the maximum width of the XML documents ranged in the intervals [5, 15] and [50, 650] respectively) and size (in particular, the size of the XML documents ranged in the interval [1, 45] MB). To model the data loads of the P2P network, we used the Uniform distribution defined over the range [0, 199], and the Zipf distribution with characteristic parameter z equal to 0.5. Synthetic queries were generated by means of uniform extractions over *ConceptThesaurus*, by making use of concepts coming from the tourism context like as "destination", "holiday", "social event" etc.

As comparison techniques, we chose the following ones: Gnutella [7], RWA [13], ISM [18], and the neighborhood signature technique [12] (particularly, in this case we use the PN-A scheme). Furthermore, we set the TTL parameter equal to 5. The goal of our experimental study is probing the quality of the IR support of our proposed framework against state-of-the-art techniques.

In our experiments, we considered the following metrics: (*i*) the *Average Message Number* (AMN), which measures the average number of messages used to retrieve documents of interest; (*ii*) the *Average Hop Number* (AHN), which measures the average number of hops needed to retrieve documents of interest; (*iii*) the *Recall Rate* (RR), which is the fraction of retrieved documents with respect to the collection of all the documents involved by a given search task. It should be noted that AMN and AHN mainly test the efficiency of the techniques, whereas RR is used to investigate on the accuracy of the techniques. All such metrics were produced with respect to the *Number of Queries* (NoQ) used to retrieve documents of interest. The latter parameter influences, from a side, the quality of the search results as, in general, the higher is the number of queries employed in the search task, the higher is the quality of the retrieved results; from another side, such as parameter is also a way for evaluating the scalability of the investigated techniques, as, in general, the higher is the number of queries employed in the search task, the higher are the computational overheads introduced in the P2P network, as a high volume of query (routing) messages is needed.

Fig. 3 shows the results of our experimental study for both Uniform and Zipfian data loads. Before to discuss the experimental results, we highlight that, overall, we obtain better performances for Uniform data loads rather than for the Zipfian ones, as expected. In fact, Uniform data loads avoid generating, at query time, unreachable P2P network segments, whereas Zipfian data loads may cause this problem, as data can be asymmetrically located in specific segments of the P2P network. All considering, from the analysis of such results, it follows that ISM and the approach we propose (named as "Sem" in Fig. 3) present the best behavior. In more detail, as regards the AMN-based metrics, ISM outperforms our approach. This is due to the fact that,

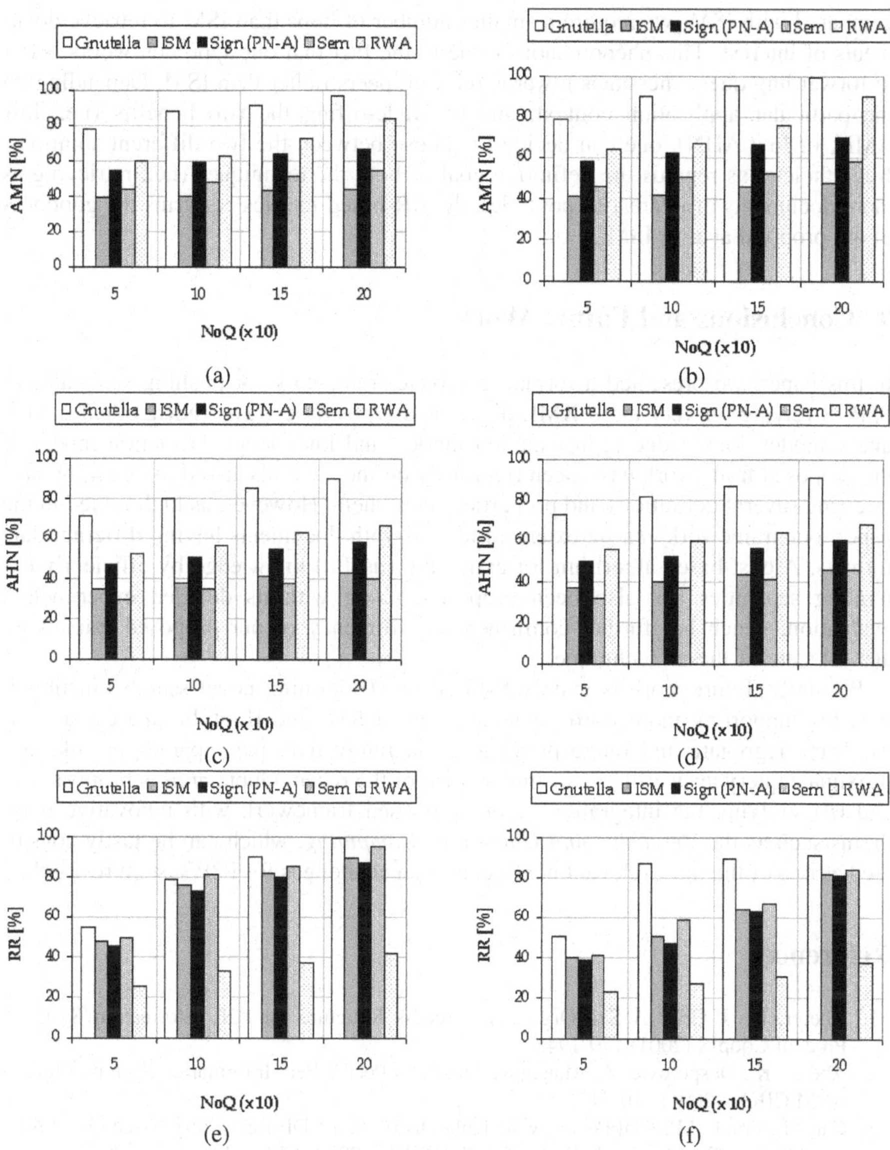

Fig. 3. Experimental results: AMN w.r.t. NoQ for Uniform data loads (*a*); AMN w.r.t. NoQ for Zipfian data loads (*b*); AHN w.r.t. NoQ for Uniform data loads (*c*); AHN w.r.t. NoQ for Zipfian data loads (*d*); RR w.r.t. NoQ for Uniform data loads (*e*); RR w.r.t. NoQ for Zipfian data loads (*f*)

in the average case, our proposed approach requires a quite higher computational cost in terms of query messages to retrieve documents of interest rather than ISM. Contrarily, as regards the AHN-based metrics, our approach outperforms ISM; in other words, even if our approach introduces a little computational overhead when compared with ISM, we require a smaller number of hops than ISM to retrieve documents of interest. This phenomenon is due to the fact that our approach works better in forwarding query messages towards relevant peers rather than ISM. Depending on the particular application context, and by trade-offing the two benefits (i.e., low AMN, or low AHN), one can decide to choose between the two different solutions. Nevertheless, as regards the definitive goal of both the techniques (i.e., retrieving as more documents of interest as possible), the RR-based metrics confirms the goodness of our proposal against ISM.

9 Conclusions and Future Work

In this paper, we presented a formal, complete framework for pushing semantics in P2P IS relying on very large XML distributed repositories. The (XML) data model, query model, knowledge representation model, and knowledge extraction model of the proposed framework have been rigorously defined and discussed in detail, by also inferring several definitions and properties about them. However, as highlighted in the paper, our framework can be extended to deal with documents having different data formats. A cost-based algorithm for extracting (useful) knowledge by efficiently exploiting semantics has also been proposed, along with its detailed experimental evaluation, which has further confirmed the efficiency of our proposed framework against state-of-the-art techniques.

Presently, future work is mainly focused on (*i*) defining novel search functionalities for supporting more useful content-oriented KD- and IR-style queries, such as Boolean, aggregate and range predicates, via innovative query paradigms like approximate query answering, in a similar spirit of the recent Gupta *et al.*'s proposal [8], and (*ii*) studying the integration of our proposed framework with innovative paradigms such as the *Pervasive and Ubiquitous Computing*, which can be justly considered as one of the most relevant next-generation challenges for P2P system research.

References

1. Aberer, K.: P-Grid: A Self-Organizing Access Structure for P2P Information Systems. Proc. of CoopIS (2001) 179-194.
2. Aberer, K., Despotovic, Z.: Managing Trust in a Peer-2-Peer Information System. Proc. of ACM CIKM (2001) 310-317.
3. Cai, M., Frank, M.: RDFPeers: A Scalable Distributed RDF Repository based on a Structured Peer-to-Peer Network. Proc. of ACM WWW (2004) 650-657.
4. Callan, J.: Distributed Information Retrieval. Advances in Information Retrieval, Kluwer Academic Publishers (2000) 127-150.
5. Crespo, A., Garcia-Molina, H.: Semantic Overlay Networks for P2P Systems. Stanford Technical Report, Computer Science Department, Stanford University (2003).
6. Deerwester, S., Dumais, S.T., Furnas, G.W., Landauer, T.K., Harshman, R.: Indexing by Latent Semantic Analysis. Journal of the American Society for Information Science, Vol. 41, No. 6 (1999) 391-407.
7. The Gnutella File Sharing System. Web pages available at http://gnutella.wego.com.

8. Gupta, A., Agrawal, D., El Abbadi, A.: Approximate Range Selection Queries in Peer-to-Peer Systems. Proc. CIDIR (2003) online edition available at http://www-db.cs.wisc.edu/cidr/cidr2003/program/p13.pdf.
9. Halaschek, C., Aleman-Meza, B., Arpinar, I.B., Sheth, A.P.: Discovering and Ranking Semantic Associations over a Large RDF Metabase. Proc. of VLDB (2004) 1317-1320.
10. Halevy, A.Y., Ives, Z.G., Mork, P., Tatarinov, I.: Piazza: Data Management Infrastructure for Semantic Web Applications. Proc. of ACM WWW (2003) 556-567.
11. Kalogeraki, V., Gunopulos, D., Zeinalipour-Yazti, D.: A Local Search Mechanism for Peer-to-Peer Networks. Proc. of ACM CIKM (2002) 300-307.
12. Li, M., Lee, W.-C., Sivasubramaniam, A.: Neighborhood Signatures for Searching P2P Networks. Proc. of IEEE IDEAS (2003) 149-159.
13. Lv, Q., Cao, P., Cohen, E., Li, K., Shenker, S.: Search and Replication in Unstructured Peer-to-Peer Networks. Proc. of ACM ICS (2002) 84-95.
14. Nejdl, W., Wolpers, M., Siberski, W., Schmitz, C., Schlosser, M., Brunkhorst, I., Loser, A.: Super-Peer-based Routing and Clustering Strategies for RDF-based P2P Networks. Proc. of the ACM WWW (2003) 536-543.
15. Schmidt, A., Waas, F., Kersten, M., Carey, M., Manolescu, I., Busse, R.: XMark: A Benchmark for XML Data Management. Proc. of VLDB (2002) 974-985.
16. Tsoumakos, D., Roussopoulos, N.: A Comparison of Peer-to-Peer Search Methods. Proc. of ACM WebDB (2003) 61-66.
17. Zeinalipour-Yazti, D., Kalogeraki, V., Gunopulos, D.: Information Retrieval Techniques for Peer-to-Peer Networks. IEEE CiSE Magazine, Special Issue on Web Engineering, IEEE Publications, Vol. 30, No. 4 (2004) 12-20.
18. Zeinalipour-Yazti, D., Kalogeraki, V., Gunopulos, D.: Exploiting Locality for Scalable Information Retrieval in Peer-to-Peer Systems. Information Systems, Elsevier Science, Vol. 30, No. 4 (2005) 277-298.

Optimal Associative Neighbor Mining Using Attributes for Ubiquitous Recommendation Systems

Kyung-Yong Jung[1], Hee-Joung Hwang[2], and Un-Gu Kang[2]

[1] School of Computer Information Engineering, Sangji University, Korea
kyjung@sangji.ac.kr
[2] Department of Information Technology Engineering,
Gachon University of Medicine and Science, Korea

Abstract. Ubiquitous recommendation systems predict new items of interest for a user, based on predictive relationship discovered between the user and other participants in Ubiquitous Commerce. In this paper, optimal associative neighbor mining, using attributes, for the purpose of improving accuracy and performance in ubiquitous recommendation systems, is proposed. This optimal associative neighbor mining selects the associative users that have similar preferences by extracting the attributes that most affect preferences. The associative user pattern comprising 3-*AU*s (groups of associative users composed of 3-users), is grouped through the ARHP algorithm. The approach is empirically evaluated, for comparison with the nearest-neighbor model and k-means clustering, using the MovieLens datasets. This method can solve the large-scale dataset problem without deteriorating accuracy quality.

1 Introduction

Nowadays, most personalized ubiquitous recommendation systems in ubiquitous commerce utilize collaborative filtering systems, in order to recommend increasingly appropriate items, which are based on the ratings of other users who have similar preference. Ubiquitous commerce that is connected to the existing e-commerce is developed. So it is interesting to provide the personalized item services suitable to the requirements and the activities of the users in ubiquitous space based on the electronic and physical space [14]. The Grouplens for Usenet news [10] was the first collaborative filtering system to deal with massive data sets. Grouplens addressed this large item set characteristic, by creating a separate item partition for each Usenet discussion group [2]. Collaborative filtering systems recommend information through building a user profile from various preferences for specific items, and comparing these preferences with other users, for the same items. The similarity of preferences between a specific user and other users is computed from the correlation coefficient. Predicting preference for a certain item is based on other users' preference for that item, and the similarity between each other. In reflecting human opinions, collaborative filtering has several advantages: filtering items that are not easily analyzed by automated processes, filtering items based on quality, and filtering serendipitous items. However, collaborative filtering does not use attributes of items in any way. In this paper, optimal associative neighbor mining using the attributes, for

H.L. Larsen et al. (Eds.): FQAS 2006, LNAI 4027, pp. 458 – 469, 2006.

the purpose of improving accuracy and performance in ubiquitous recommendation systems, is presented. The term attribute is used for representing a primary attribute that influences the preference for the item.

The rest of this paper is organized as follows. Section 2 describes briefly the nearest-neighbor model, k-means clustering, and the threshold-neighbor model. Section 3 and Section 4 illustrate the proposed the optimal associative neighbor mining using the attributes in detail. In Section 5, the experimental results are presented. The conclusions are given in Section 6.

2 Neighbor Selections for Ubiquitous Recommendation Systems

Ubiquitous recommendation systems predict new items of interest for a user, based on the predictive relationship discovered between the user and other participants. In U-Commerce environment, to support personalization services, a system should recognize preferred items through the preference analysis such as personal profile or case of personal commerce. Based on this, ubiquitous systems recommend the items that are expected for the users to prefer according to the situation, so it can help commerce easily. Most successful research and commercial ubiquitous recommendation systems using collaborative filtering, are based on nearest-neighbor model [2], k-means clustering [1], and threshold-neighbor model [13].

2.1 Nearest-Neighbor Model

The nearest-neighbor model selects the nearest neighbors who have similar preference to the user by computing the similarities based on the preference. It only uses the neighbors who have higher correlation with the users than others. Collaborative filtering systems based on the nearest-neighbor method, works in three simple phases. First, users of the collaborative filtering system rate items that they have previously experienced. Second, the collaborative filtering system matches users with other participants of the system, having similar rating patterns. This is usually achieved through statistical correlation. The matches are selected, becoming known as neighbors of the user. Third, items that the neighbors have experienced and rated highly, but which the user has not yet experienced and rated highly, will be recommended to the user, ranked based on the neighbors to the user [2]. Collaborative filtering system should even consider some users who may give bad influences on prediction quality. It has been shown in several investigations that the ubiquitous recommendation system with the nearest neighbor model has better quality of prediction than the traditional collaborative filtering [13].

2.2 K-Means Clustering

The K-means clustering algorithm [1,12] has been shown to be effective in producing good cluster results for many practical applications and in non-hierarchical clustering methods. This algorithm initially takes the number of elements in the population equal to the final required number of clusters. The final required number of clusters is chosen, such that the points are mutually farthest apart. Next, each element in the population is examined and assigned to one of the clusters, depending on the minimum distance. The center position is recalculated as an element is added to the cluster, and this process continues until all the elements are grouped into the final required number of clusters. However, the K-means clustering algorithm requires time proportional to the product of number of patterns and number of clusters per iteration. This is very computationally expensive, especially for large datasets [10].

2.3 Threshold-Neighbor Model

The threshold-neighbor model selects the neighbors who belong to a certain range with respect to the similarities of the preferences. Contrary to the nearest-neighbor model, the number of neighbors selected by this method varies, because it selects neighbors according to a certain threshold. In the ubiquitous recommendation systems with the threshold-neighbor model, the positive neighbors whose correlations to the users are greater than equal to threshold are selected as the neighbors. However, it is also negative neighbors whose correlations to the users are less than and equal to threshold, because they could contribute toward the better neighbor selection for the users as they provide negative opinions to the users. It is obvious that selecting only negative neighbors results in worse prediction qualities than the case in which only positive neighbors are selected [13].

3 Optimal Associative Neighbor Mining

Optimal associative neighbor mining is used through data mining to perform ubiquitous recommendation systems. This is also used to promote the accuracy and performance, by reducing a high dimensional feature space using the Apriori algorithm. The accuracy of optimal associative neighbor mining depends on the number of users for composing associative users. We show how the numbers of users for composing associative users at the Apriori algorithm are selected efficiently.

3.1 Representation for Associative User

The commonly used 'bag-of-users' user representation scheme, is adopted, in which the structure of the user profile and the order of the users in the database [10] is ignored. In this paper, an effective user selection method based on optimal associative user mining, is proposed. The 'bag-of-users' as a 'bag-of-associative users' including several users instead of just a single user, is represented. The feature vectors represent the associative users observed after the preprocessing of the MovieLens datasets [9].

The Associative User (*AU*)_List is defined as: $AU = \{(U_{1r}: u_{11}\&u_{12}\ldots\&u_{1(r-1)} \rightarrow u_{1r}), (U_{2r}: u_{21}\&u_{22}..\&u_{2(r-1)} \rightarrow w_{2r}),..,(U_{kr}: u_{k1}\&u_{k2}..\&u_{k(r-)} \rightarrow u_{kr}),..,(U_{pr}: u_{p1}\&u_{p2}\ldots\&u_{p(r-1)} \rightarrow u_{pr})\}$. Here, each user in $(u_{k1}\&u_{k2}\ldots\&u_{k(r-1)} \rightarrow u_{kr})$ represents one of the associative users. "p" in *AU* represents the number of associative users in the database. "r" in *AU* represents the number of users in associative users. "&" in the pairs of users means that the pairs of users have a high degree of semantic relatedness. "$u_{k1}\&u_{k2}\ldots\&u_{k(r-1)}$" is an antecedent of the associative user, $(u_{k1}\&u_{k2}\ldots\&u_{k(r-1)} \rightarrow u_{kr})$ and "u_{kr}" is a consequent of the associative user, $(u_{k1}\&u_{k2}\ldots\&u_{k(r-1)} \rightarrow u_{kr})$. This user representation is used to select the features for the associative user mining process.

3.2 Selection for Associative User Mining

The Apriori algorithm can mine association rules using the data mining technique. The process of mining association rules between users consists of two stages. In the first stage, compositions having transaction support in excess of minimum support are found, in order to constitute a list of frequent users. In the second stage, the list of frequent users is used to create association rules from the database. As for all frequent users (L), find subset instead of all empty sets of frequent users. As for each subset (A), if the ratio of support (L) to support (A) is not less than minimum confidence, the rule of A→(L-A) type is displayed. The support of this rule is support (L) [3].

In order to constitute the bag of associative users, confidence and support should be decided. Equation (1), used to determine the level of confidence, can be obtained as follows. Equation (1) is the result of dividing the number of transactions including all users of u_1 and u_2 by the number of transactions including only the users of u_1.

$$Confidence(u_1 \rightarrow u_2) = Pr(u_2 | u_1) \quad (1)$$

Equation (2), used to determine the support, represents the frequency of each associative user among all the user sets. Equation (2) is the result of dividing the number of transactions including all items of u_1 and u_2 by the total number of transactions within the database.

$$Support(u_1 \rightarrow u_2) = Pr(u_2 \cup u_1) \quad (2)$$

In order to extract the most appropriate associative user, the confidence should be fixed at not less than 85 and the support should be not more than 25 [5,6]. Table 1 reconfigures items to evaluate the preference of user transactions. The transaction number means the items to evaluate the preference, and the extracted user is to organize the candidate user set and the frequency user set. According to this method of feature selection, the user $\{AU_i\}$ can be described in Equation (3).

$$\{AU_i\}=\{AU_{1r}, AU_{2r}, AU_{kr}, AU_{pr}\},\ i=1,2,\ldots,m \quad (3)$$

Table 1. The user transaction for associative user mining

Transaction No.	The extracted users
1	u_1, u_2, u_3, u_4
2	$u_1, u_2, u_3, u_5, u_6, u_7, u_8, u_{12}$
3	$u_9, u_3, u_2, u_{10}, u_5, u_{11}$
4	$u_3, u_{13}, u_{14}, u_{15}, u_{16}, u_{17}$
5	u_3, u_{13}, u_{18}
6	$u_3, u_{13}, u_{15}, u_{19}, u_{20}$
7	u_{21}, u_{22}
8	u_{23}, u_{24}, u_{25}

Table 2 presents the steps used for extracting the associative users using the Apriori Algorithm. L_3 Frequent 3-userset is extracted $\{u_1, u_2, u_3\}$, $\{u_2, u_3, u_5\}$, $\{u_2, u_5, u_{15}\}$, $\{u_3, u_{13}, u_{15}\}$ according to the Apriori Algorithm.

Table 2. The steps used for extracting the association users using the Apriori Algorithm

C_1 Candidate 1-userset	$u_{1(2)},u_{2(3)},u_{3(6)},u_{4(1)},u_{5(2)},u_{6(1)},u_{7(1)},u_{8(1)},u_{9(1)},u_{10(1)},u_{11(1)},u_{12(1)},u_{13(1)},$ $u_{14(1)},u_{15(2)},u_{16(1)},u_{17(1)},u_{18(1)},u_{19(1)},u_{20(1)},u_{21(1)},u_{22(1)},u_{23(1)},u_{24(1)},u_{25(1)}$
L_1 Frequent 1-userset	$u_{1(2)},u_{2(3)},u_{3(6)},u_{5(2)},u_{13(3)},u_{15(2)}$
C_2 Candidate 2-userset	$(u_1,u_2)_{(2)},(u_1,u_3)_{(2)},(u_1,u_5)_{(1)},(u_1,u_{13})_{(0)},(u_1,u_{15})_{(0)},(u_2,u_3)_{(3)},(u_2,u_5)_{(2)},$ $(u_2,u_{13})_{(0)},(u_2,u_{15})_{(0)},(u_3,u_5)_{(2)},(u_3,u_{13})_{(3)},(u_3,u_{15})_{(2)},(u_5,u_{13})_{(0)},(u_5,u_{15})_{(0)},$ $(u_{13},u_{15})_{(2)}$
L_2 Frequent 2-userset	$(u_1,u_2)_{(2)},(u_1,u_3)_{(2)},(u_2,u_3)_{(3)},(u_2,u_5)_{(2)},(u_3,u_5)_{(2)},(u_3,u_{13})_{(3)},(u_3,u_{15})_{(2)},$ $(u_{13},u_{15})_{(2)}$
C_3 Candidate 3-userset	$(u_1,u_2,u_3)_{(2)},(u_1,u_2,u_5)_{(0)},(u_1,u_2,u_{13})_{(0)},(u_1,u_2,u_{15})_{(0)},(u_2,u_3,u_{15})_{(0)},$ $(u_1,u_3,u_{13})_{(0)},(u_1,u_3,u_{15})_{(0)},(u_2,u_3,u_5)_{(2)},(u_2,u_3,u_{13})_{(0)},(u_1,u_3,u_5)_{(1)},$ $(u_2,u_5,u_{15})_{(2)},(u_2,u_5,u_{13})_{(0)},(u_3,u_5,u_{13})_{(0)},(u_3,u_5,u_{15})_{(0)},(u_3,u_{13},u_{15})_{(2)},$ $(u_{13},u_{15},u_1)_{(0)},(u_{13},u_{15},u_2)_{(1)},(u_{13},u_{15},u_3)_{(0)},(u_{13},u_{15},u_5)_{(0)}$
L_3 Frequent 3-userset	$(u_1,u_2,u_3)_{(2)}$, $(u_2,u_3,u_5)_{(2)}$, $(u_2,u_5,u_{15})_{(2)}$, $(u_3,u_{13},u_{15})_{(2)}$

3.3 Associative User Pattern Generation

The associative user pattern representation includes not just 2-associative users but as many as 5 associative users present in the database. At a confidence level of 85 and a support level of 25 in the Apriori algorithm, some characteristic user combinations, can be captured, where the number of users increases. The process of generating the pattern is performed in the *n* database retrieval step, where *n*-associative users are generated in the last pass. An illustration of this is the accumulated number of associative user patterns during the process of generating the pattern for 20,864 users in Figure 1(a). Let *AU* denote an associative user involved in the generation of the associative user using the Apriori algorithm.

In Figure 1, the number of associative user patterns generated using 2-*AU*s can be seen to be larger than that in the other cases (149,894 for 2-*AU*s vs. 12,936 for 3-*AU*s vs. 3,822 for 4-*AU*s vs. 191 for 5-*AU*s). Figure 1(a) presents the result of clustering process performed using the new features that were generated. In order to evaluate the performance of the clustering process in each case (2-*AU*s, 3-*AU*s, 4-*AU*s, 5-*AU*s), the ARHP algorithm is used on 20,864 users. In the case where the ARHP algorithm using *AU* clusters a user behavior into all of the classes except for the genre class, this is considered to be incorrect clustering. The accuracy of the clustering process is the rate of user behavior correctly classified for 20,864 users. In Figure 1(b), time (sec) represents the response time of the associative user clustering process. As the graph demonstrates, the 2-*AU*s case exhibits very poor performance. However, the accuracy of the clustering process 2-*AU*s is higher than using that 4-*AU*s, but lower than that using 3-*AU*s. The clustering process using 3-*AU*s is much more accurate than the other cases. In addition, the 3-*AU*s case exhibits relatively good performance. The 4-*AU*s case exhibits very good performance. However, the accuracy of the clustering process using 4-*AU*s is far lower than the cases. Therefore, in this case, it is appropriate to use the 3-associative users format for the pattern selection of associative user clustering.

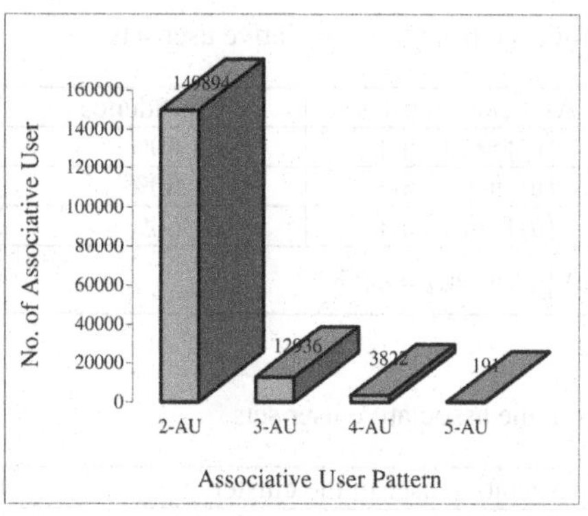

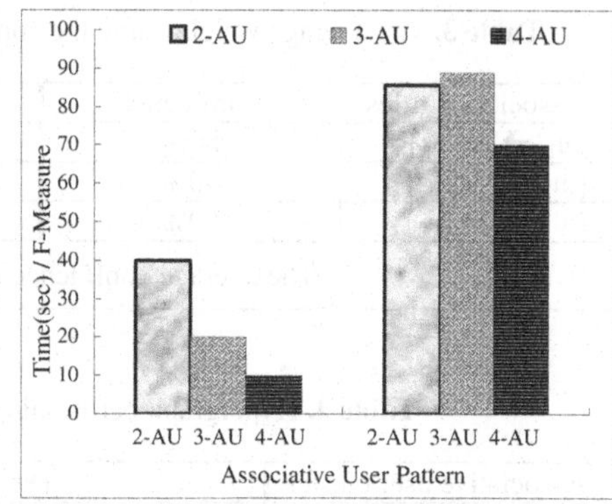

(a) Generating associative user pattern (b) Result of clustering process

Fig. 1. The generating associative user pattern and the result of clustering process

3.4 Clustering of Associative Users Using ARHP Algorithm

The Association Rule Hypergraph Partitioning algorithm (ARHP) is used for clustering related items using association rules and hypergraph partitioning [3,7]. Formally, a hypergraph H={*V*, *E*} consists of a set of vertices (*V*) constituted with users and a set of hyperedges (*E*) denoting frequent usersets, where each hyperedge is a subset of the vertex set, V. A hypergraph is an extension of a graph in the sense that each hypergraph can connect more than two vertices.

In this paper, the vertex set corresponds to the distinct users in the MovieLens dataset [9] and the hyperedges correspond to the most frequent *k*-usersets. The weight of the Hypergraph Partitioning process is used as the confidence of the association rule when using the Apriori algorithm. The frequent *k*-usersets derived from the association rules are used to group users into a hypergraph edge, and the hypergraph partitioning algorithm is used to find clusters. For example, if $\{u_1, u_2, u_3\}$ is a frequent 3-userset, then the hypergraph contains a hyperedge that connects u_1, u_2, and u_3. The weight of a hypergraph is determined by the functioning confidences of all the association rules involving all of the users in the hypergraph. The cluster that the transaction belongs to is determined by calculating the score of each cluster based on the users in the transaction and the users in the clusters. A simple score function might be the ratio $|T \cap C_i|/|C_i|$, where T is the transaction and C_i is a cluster of users. A transaction belongs to the cluster that has the highest score with respect to the transaction. Table 3 presents the average weight using the confidence from the associative user sets $\{u_1, u_2, u_3\}$. The average confidence 80% is weight for a hypergraph partitioning.

Table 4 presents the result of the hypergraph partitioning using the ARHP algorithm in the associative user sets. Table 4 consists of 3 associative user clusters about 25 users given Table 1.

Table 3. The average weight using the confidence from the associative user sets

Association rules	Confidence	Association rules	Confidence
$\{u_1\}\rightarrow\{u_2, u_3\}$	80%	$\{u_2\}\rightarrow\{u_1, u_3\}$	40%
$\{u_1, u_2\}\rightarrow\{u_3\}$	40%	$\{u_2, u_3\}\rightarrow\{u_1\}$	80%
$\{u_1, u_3\}\rightarrow\{u_2\}$	60%	$\{u_3\}\rightarrow\{u_1, u_2\}$	60%
The average confidence of $\{u_1, u_2, u_3\}$ = 80%			

Table 4. Hypergraph partitioning in the associative user sets

Associative user cluster	The associative user in the cluster
1	$\{u_{13}, u_{14}, u_{15}, u_{16}, u_{17}, u_{18}, u_{19}, u_{20}, u_{22}, u_{23}\}$
2	$\{u_2, u_3, u_4, u_5, u_9, u_{10}, u_{11}\}$
3	$\{u_1, u_6, u_7, u_8, u_{12}, u_{21}, u_{24}, u_{25}\}$

4 Optimal Associative Neighbor Mining Using Attributes

Optimal associative neighbor mining using attributes is used to select the nearest neighbors, who have similar preferences to the active user, by extracting the attributes that most affect preferences. The difference between the current collaborative filtering and collaborative filtering using the attributes involves whether all the neighbors are used. That is, collaborative filtering involves the selection of all other users who have similar tastes or opposite tastes to the active user by means of the *Pearson* correlation coefficient [12]. These users' preferences are used in predicting the preference of a target item for the active user. However, collaborative filtering using the attributes only involves users that have similar tastes, in order to select a user that has higher correlation coefficient than the active user. The correlation is generally computed with the *Pearson* correlation coefficient.

4.1 Extraction of the Associative User's Attributes

To overcome that collaborative filtering does not use the attributes of items at all, such that item attribution provides more efficient filtering, collaborative filtering using the attributes is used, through the extraction of the user's attributes. The attributes of the movie are taken to be the genre [5]. In general, this means that user preferences for movies are mainly affected by their genre. The representative attributes are defined to be the primary factors that influence the preference for a particular item. Table 5 presents the algorithm used to determine the attributes of an associative user. The extraction of the user's attributes uses items rating user preferences. For the purpose of extracting the representative genre, in this paper, the ratings of the user's preference are summed for each genre of the item. The attribute with the maximal summation is considered to be the representative attribute. The collaborative filtering using the attributes is used in order to compose the training set, restricted to each attributes and used to predict when the correct neighbors are found.

Table 5. Extraction of the associative user's attributes

```
Algorithm. Extraction of the associative user's attributes
   Input: The items which an associative user evaluates the preference → Score of Item[k]
   Output: The associative user's attributes → MainGenreID
GenreSum[Num_Genre] ← 0
GenreCount[Num_Genre] ← 0
for k is items that user rated do // k is the item which the user evaluates
   for c is the genre of Item[k] do // c is the genre of the item k
      GenreSum[c] ← GenreSum[c] + Score of Item[k]
      GenreCount[c]++
   endfor
endfor
for j=1 to Num_Genre do
   MainGenreID ← Max(MainGenreID, GenreSum[j]/GenreCount[j])
endfor // Extraction of the attributes
Extraction-Attributes[MainGenreID] ← Add UserID
return
```

4.2 Collaborative Filtering Using Attributes

Another collaborative filtering method is presented, that uses the age, gender and zip code, in order to improve the accuracy of the prediction. The rating of the user's preferences depends on the user's environment. Therefore, in this paper, the users are grouped by age, gender and zip code, in order to take the relationship between age and gender, in addition to geographical factors, into consideration.

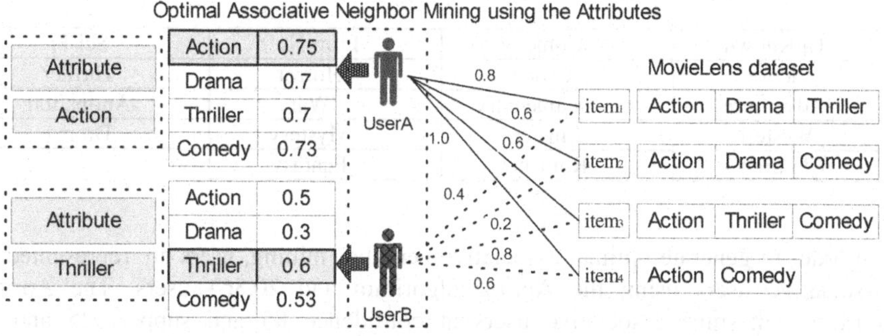

Fig. 2. Procedure to extract the attributes of an associative user

For each age, gender and zip code grouping, derived from all of the user profiles, an active user, whose profile is composed of the average of the group preferences for each attribute, is created. The users' ages are split into 8 age groups (1-14, 15-19, 20-24, 25-29, 30-39, 40-49, 50-59 and 60-69) and zip codes are divided into 7 US regions (Mid-Atlantic, Midwest, Northeast, Rockies, South, Southeast, and West). The predicted preference is obtained, along with the attributes, age, gender, and zip code grouping.

Figure 2 presents the procedure used to extract the attributes of the associative users. The associative users evaluate the preference of items with the genre different from each other. User A and User B are the users in the optimal associative neighbor mining described in Section 3. The attribute of User A is the action, and the attribute of User B is the thriller. The users evaluated the preference on the same items, but different results appear the attribute of the user. This is because the degree of user preference, according to the viewpoint, is different.

5 Evaluation

There are three methods in neighbor selection based on the Nearest-Neighbor Model (NNM), K-Means Clustering (KMC), and the Threshold-Neighbor Model (TNM). NNM and KMC method among those methods represent improved neighbor selection accuracy significantly. So, in order to evaluate the performance of the Optimal Associative Neighbor Mining using the attributes (OANM), neighbor selection methods for the ubiquitous recommendation systems are compared with NNM and KMC.

Experiments are performed on a subset of movie rating data, collected from the MovieLens dataset of the GroupLens Research Center [9]. The dataset consists of preferences for 1,612 movies rated by 20,864 users explicitly. The user preferences are represented as numeric values for 1 to 5 at interval of 1, that is, 1, 2, 3, 4, and 5. In the MovieLens dataset, one of the valuable attributes of an item is genre of a movie. There are nineteen different genres as shown in Table 6.

Table 6. The genre attributes of a movie

UnKnown	Comedy	Film-Noir	Sci-Fi
Action	Crime	Horror	Thriller
Adventure	Documentary	War	Animation
Western	Musical	Mystery	Drama
Children's	Romance	Fantasy	

In order to generate optimal associative neighbor mining, users are represented as 3-associative users using the Apriori algorithm and 20,864 users. The Apriori algorithm can mine associative users at confidence 85 and support 25 and 3-association rule. As an experimental result, 167,729 numbers of the associative user pattern and the confidence are created in the user transaction. In addition, 3-AUs represents comparatively good speedup. It is relevant to use the 3-associative users format in pattern selection for the associative user pattern. The associative user pattern is grouped according to the genre, using the ARHP Algorithm.

In addition to the above, it is important to evaluate recall and precision in conjunction, because it is easy to optimize either one separately. In order to quantify this with a single measurement, the F-measure in Equation (4) is used, which is a weighted combination of recall and precision widely used in Information Retrieval and Psychology [4].

$$F\_measure = \frac{(\beta^2+1)\times P\times R}{\beta^2\times P+R} \quad R=\frac{x}{x+z}100\% \quad P=\frac{x}{x+y}100\% \tag{4}$$

R and P in Equation (4) represent the recall and precision. "x" is the number of users, which appear in both classes. "y" is the number of users, which appear in classes categorized by the first method but not in the class categorized by second method. "z" is the number of users, which appears in the class categorized by the second method but not in the class categorized by the first method. The larger F-measure is, the better the classification performance is. Here, â represents the relative weight of recall for precision. For â=1.0, the weight of recall and precision is the same. The larger â is, than 1.0, the larger the relative weight of recall for precision is. In this experiment, the results of F-measure for â=1.0 and changing â from 0.7 to 2.0.

Figure 3 summarizes the performance of the three methods. In Figure 3(a), it is seen that OANM is more accurate than the other methods (average 89.12 for OANM vs. 76.36 for KMC vs. 84.62 for NNM). In Figure 3(b), both OANM, as well as

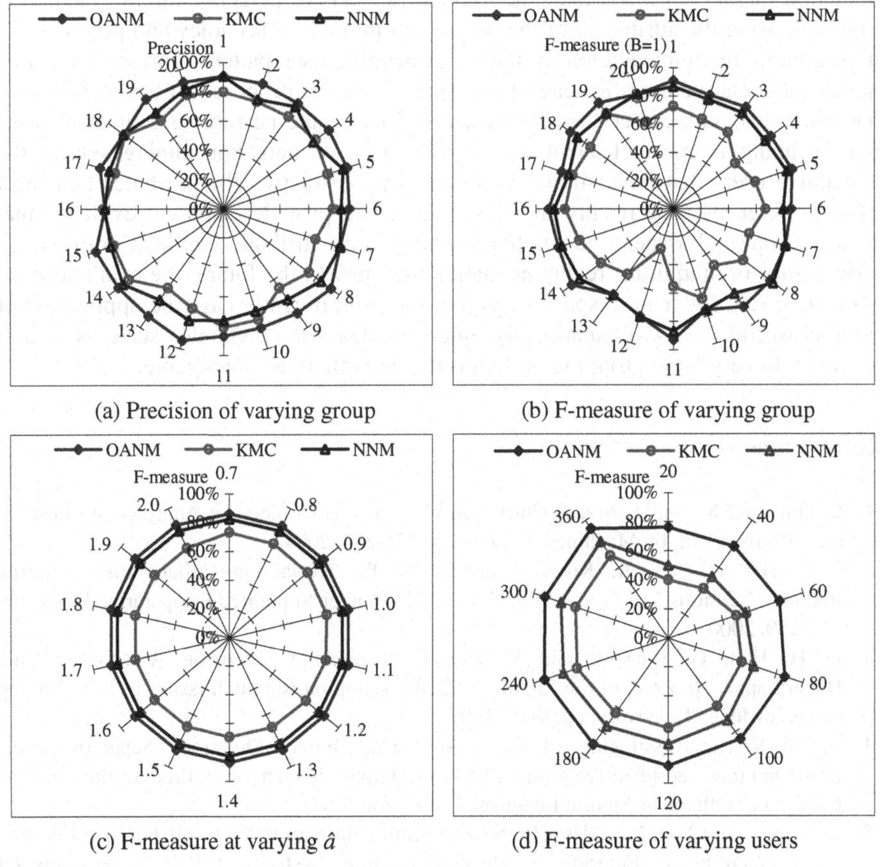

(a) Precision of varying group

(b) F-measure of varying group

(c) F-measure at varying *â*

(d) F-measure of varying users

Fig. 3. Performance of the OANM method compared to KMC method and NNM method

NNM, can be seen to have a significant advantage in recall (average 89.96 for OANM vs. 88.43 for NNM) but KMC is low in recall (average 61.35 for KMC). In addition, OANM has a substantial advantage over KMC. In Figure 3(c), varying with change for with â, from 0.7 to 2.0, it can be seen that all methods have similar performance in recall and precision. In Figure 3(d), it can be seen that OANM has higher performance than other methods (average 89.12 for OANM vs. 59.33 for KMC vs. 65.55 for NNM).

These results are encouraging and provide empirical evidence that the use of OANM can lead to improved performance of ubiquitous recommendation systems.

6 Conclusion

It is very crucial for ubiquitous recommendation systems to have a capability of making accurate prediction by retrieving and analyzing of various preferences for specific items. Collaborative filtering is widely used for ubiquitous recommendation systems. Hence various efforts to overcome its drawbacks have been made to improve prediction quality. In this paper, the optimal associative neighbor mining method is proposed, using the attributes for the purpose of improving accuracy and performance in ubiquitous recommendation systems. Associative user pattern representation that includes associative users instead of just single users, is proposed. It has been shown that when associative users are composed of 3-users, the performance of associative user grouping is most efficient. Optimal associative neighbor mining selects the associative users that have similar preferences by extracting the attributes that most affect preferences. The results are encouraging and provide empirical evidence that the use of optimal associative neighbor mining using attributes can lead to improved performance in ubiquitous recommendation systems. In the future, the availability of associative rule for feature space reduction may significantly ease the application of more powerful and computationally intensive learning methods, such as neural networks, to very large grouping problems that are otherwise intractable.

References

1. C. Ding and X. He, "K-Means Clustering via Principal Component Analysis," In Proc. of the 21th Int. Conf. on Machine Learning, pp. 225-232, 2004.
2. J. L. Herlocker, J. A. Konstan, and J. Riedl, "Explaining Collaborative Filtering Recommendations." In Proc. of the Conf. on Computer Supported Cooperative Work, pp. 241-250, 2000.
3. E. H. Han, G. Karypis, and V. Kumar, "Clustering based on Association Rule Hypergraphs," In Proc. of the SIGMOD'97 Workshop on Research Issues in Data Mining and Knowledge Discovery, pp. 9-13, 1997.
4. H. Yu, V. Hatzivassiloglou, "Towards Answering Opinion Questions: Separating Facts from Opinions and Identifying the Polarity of Opinion Sentences, In Proc. of the Conf. on Empirical Methods in Natural Language Processing, 2003.
5. K. Y. Jung and J. H. Lee, “User Preference Mining through Hybrid Collaborative Filtering and Content-based Filtering in Recommendation System," IEICE Transaction on Information and Systems, Vol. E87-D, No. 12, pp. 2781-2790, 2004.

6. S. J. Ko and J. H. Lee, "Optimization of Association Word Knowledge Base through Genetic Algorithm," In Proc. of the 4th Int. Conf. on Data Warehousing and Knowledge Discovery, LNCS 2454, pp. 212-221, 2002.
7. G. Karypis, "Evaluation of Item-Based Top-N Recommendation Algorithms," Technical Report CS-TR-00-46, Computer Science Dept., University of Minnesota, 2000.
8. J. Wang, A. P. de Vries, and M. J.T. Reinders, "A User-Item Relevance Model for Log-based Collaborative Filtering," In Proc. of the European Conf. on Information Retrieval, LNCS 3936, pp. 37-48, 2006.
9. MovieLens Collaborative Filtering Data Set, http://www.cs.umn.edu/research/GroupLens/, Grouplens Research Project, 2000.
10. T. Michael, *Maching Learning*, McGraq-Hill, pp. 154-200, 1997.
11. R. Torres, S.M. McNee, M. Abel, J.A. Konstan, and J. Riedl, "Enhancing Digital Libraries with TechLens+," In Proc. of the 4th ACM/IEEE Joint Conf. on Digital Libraries, pp. 228-237, 2004.
12. J. L. Herlocker, J. A. Konstan, L. G. Terveen, and J. T. Riedl, "Evaluating Collaborative Filtering Recommender Systems," ACM Transactions on Information Systems (TOIS) archive, Vol. 22, No. 1, pp. 5-53, 2004.
13. T. H. Kim and S. B. Yang, "Using Attribute to Improve Prediction Quality in Collaborative Filtering," In Proc. of the 5th Int. Conf. on E-Commerce and Web Technologies, LNCS 3182, pp. 1-10, 2004.
14. J. H. Hwang, M. S. Gu, and K. H. Ryu, "Context-Based Recommendation Service in Ubiquitous Commerce," In Proc. of the Int. Conf. on Computational Science and Its Applications, LNCS 3481, pp. 966-976, 2005.

Mining Interest Navigation Patterns Based on Hybrid Markov Model

Yijun Yu, Huaizhong Lin, Yimin Yu, and Chun Chen

Computer Institute, Zhejiang University, 310027 Hangzhou, China
yijunyu@mail.hz.zj.cn, linhz@zju.edu.cn, billyuym@163.com, chenc@cs.zju.edu.cn

Abstract. Each user accesses a Website with certain interest. The interest is associated with his navigation patterns. The interest navigation patterns represent different interest of the users. In this paper, hybrid Markov model is proposed for interest navigation pattern discovery. The novel model is better in prediction overlay rate and prediction correct rate than traditional Markov models. User group interest is also defined in this paper. The probability of user group interest navigation from one page to another is computed by navigation path characteristics and time characteristics. Compared with the previous ones, the results of the experiment show that the performance is improved efficiently by the hybrid Markov model.

1 Introduction

When a user accesses a Website, he has some interest and different users have different interest when they access the Website through different paths. The different interest of the users is associated with interest navigation patterns. So, mining navigation pattern can reflect the users' access interest.

There are many efforts toward mining various patterns from Web logs, such as "Footprints" [1], "WUM" [2], etc. "Footprints" takes an optimizing approach. Its idea is that visitors to a Website leave their "Footprints" behind. Over time, "Paths" accumulate in the most heavily traveled areas. New visitors to the site can use these well worn paths as indicators of the most interesting pages to access. "WUM" improves this approach. It defines the g-sequences in order to mine the navigation patterns and gives a mining language MINT. Chen et al[3] map the log data into relational tables and employ the standard data mining approaches to discover the user navigation patterns. Borges and Levene [4] apply hypertext probabilistic grammar to discover the user navigation patterns and propose the use of entropy as an estimator of the statistical properties of the grammar.

All these approaches ignore the facts that users are actually interested in only a certain part of every Web page and the characteristics of every access Web page can reflect interest intensity of Web page content. They only discover the navigation patterns according to the users' access sequence.

In this paper, we define user group and user group interest intensity. Based on these definitions, we present hybrid Markov model for interest navigation patterns.

H.L. Larsen et al. (Eds.): FQAS 2006, LNAI 4027, pp. 470–478, 2006.

The novel model can help the designer of the Website understand the users' interest better and improve the design of the Website. At the same time, the model can help users to understand their access behaviors and access content better.

2 Definitions

2.1 Keyword of User Access Page

When users access Website, there are some basic facts, such as: Every user accesses Website by different paths, every Web page in Website includes one keyword at least and these keywords can be used as representation of pages' contents. The Web pages the user access should be those that users are interested because users have intentions when they access a Website.

The user access keyword represented as *k* set indicates the contents of a Web page and they are a simple description of the contents of a Web page. A Web page may include several keywords. The contents of Web page can be represented by the Web page's keywords. In order to indicate user's access interest, we give the definition as follows:

Definition 1. The transaction of the user access keyword: The user access transaction is composed of Web pages that the user accesses. Every Web page is represented by a group of keywords. As every url comprises of several keyword σ and every keyword is represented by *K* set, the user access keyword transaction is defined as follows:

$$t_k(u_i,url_s) = < k_1, k_2, \ldots\ldots, k_j > \tag{1}$$

Here, $\boldsymbol{u}$ is the user's set, u_i is the user who accesses Web page currently, url_s is currently accessed Web page, k_j is currently accessed keyword.

The support to the user access keyword is the access number of certain keyword k_j in a user access keyword transaction through url_s, defined as $\text{support}(u_i,url_s,k_j)$.

The user access time length is composed of four parts. There are page loading time, page sending time, user view time and user request time. As the log time is recorded by seconds, page loading time and page sending time are close to zero, the time length is composed of user viewing time and page sending time. For a Website, page sending time should be less than time window *C*—a constant, which is mostly several seconds. As for pages that users are interested, time length is longer than *C* value.

Definition 2. The time length of user access keyword: the user will access longer time in the page if he is interested in one concept, suppose a url_s's access time length as $\text{L}(u_i,url_s)$, if the page has *f* keywords $k_1, k_2, \ldots\ldots, k_f$, the time length of the user accesses keyword k_j is :

$$\text{length}(u_i,url_s,k_j) = \begin{cases} \dfrac{\text{L}(u_i,url_s)}{f} & \text{if } k_j \text{ in } url_s; \\ 0 & \text{if } k_j \text{ not in } url_s. \end{cases} \tag{2}$$

Here u is users' set, u_i is the current user, url_s is currently accessed Web page and k_j is currently accessed keyword.

Definition 3. The total time length that user accesses keywords: in user access keyword transaction $t_k(u_i,url_s)$, the total time length of u_i's access keyword k_j is:

$$\text{sum}(u_i,url_s,k_j)=\begin{cases}\sum_{s=start}^{end}\text{length}(u_i,url_s,k_j) & \text{if } url_s \text{ in } t_k(u_i,url_s);\\ 0 & \text{if } url_s \text{ not in } t_k(u_i,url_s).\end{cases} \tag{3}$$

Here u is the user's set, u_i is the current user, url_s is currently accessed Web page, k_j is currently accessed keyword.

2.2 Interest Intensity of User Group

One user belongs to one special cluster in user cluster method. User and user cluster is one-to-one. In this paper, the concept of user group is proposed. One user belongs to several user groups and one user group includes several users. Based on above definitions, we define user group as follows:

Definition 4. User group is a group of users who have similar access interest.

$$U^G=<u_1,u_2,\ldots\ldots,u_i> \tag{4}$$

Users always select those interesting pages, so we propose a concept— the interest intensity of user group. It can reflect the proportion between the actual intensity and the intensity expected.

The support to user group access keyword is the access number of certain keyword k_j in a user group access keyword transaction through url_s, defined as $\text{Support}(U_i^G,url_s,k_j)$.

Definition 5. The time length of user group access keywords: user group will access longer time in the page if they are interested in a concept. Suppose a url_s access time length as $\text{L}(U_i^G,url_s)$ and if the page has f keywords $k_1,k_2,\ldots\ldots,k_f$, the time length of the user group access keyword k_j is :

$$\text{length}(U_i^G,url_s,k_j)=\begin{cases}\dfrac{\text{L}(U_i^G,url_s)}{f} & \text{if } k_j \text{ in } url_s;\\ 0 & \text{if } k_j \text{ not in } url_s.\end{cases} \tag{5}$$

Here U_i^G is user group who accesses Web page currently, url_s is currently accessed Web page and k_j is currently accessed keyword.

Definition 6. The total time length of user group access keywords: in user group access keyword transaction $t_k(U_i^G,url_s)$, the total time length of U_i^G 's access k_j is :

$$\mathrm{sum}(U_i^G, url_s, k_j) = \begin{cases} \sum_{s=start}^{end} \mathrm{length}(U_i^G, url_s, k_j) & \text{if } url_s \text{ in } t_k(U_i^G, url_s); \\ 0 & \text{if } url_s \text{ not in } t_k(U_i^G, url_s). \end{cases} \quad (6)$$

Here U_i^G is the user group who accesses Web page currently, url_s is currently accessed Web page and k_j is currently accessed keyword.

Definition 7. The interest intensity of the user group: if the interest of user group in url_s is intensified, the user group interest distribution of all keywords in the page can be obtained. It is the interest intensity the user group:

$$\mathrm{P}(k_j \mid (url_s, U_i^G)) = \frac{\sum_{i=1}^{N} (\mathrm{sum}(U_i^G, url_s, k_j) \cdot \mathrm{support}(U_i^G, url_s, k_j))}{\sum_{i=1}^{N} \sum_{m=1}^{M} (\mathrm{sum}(U_i^G, url_s, k_m) \cdot \mathrm{support}(U_i^G, url_s, k_j))} \quad (7)$$

Here U_i^G is the user group who accesses Web page currently, url_s is currently accessed Web page and k_j is currently accessed keyword.

3 Mining Interest Navigation Patterns

3.1 Markov Model

Markov model [5], widely used for statistics and machine learning, is used for prediction model research. Mogul [6] used Markov model of level N to improve Web cache's prefetching performance. Sarukkai [7] used Markov model to predict the next Web page to be accessed. Prolli [8] tested Markov models of different levels to improve the prediction performance of Web accessing. Traditional Markov model is based on the user's present page-browsing sequence and historical accessing record to predict the next Web page to be accessed.

Markov models of different levels are explained as follows:

Markov model of level 0 is unconditional page access probability. It can be obtained by computing page access probability during a certain period of time.

Markov model of level 1 is page to page transition probability.

Markov model of level K computes the transition probability of user access prior k(from 1 to n-1) pages to the n page.

In many applications, Markov models of low level can't accurately find the page that users will access. Because these models didn't consider user access history, they can't distinguish different users' behavior patterns [9] very well. It is partial to use Markov models of high level for better prediction results. But Markov models of high level have some deficiencies: the state-space complexity is too high, the prediction overlay rate [8] is too low. Because the state numbers of Markov models of high level permute and combine with data sequences changing, the state numbers of these models increase by index with model levels increasing, which obviously influences the prediction performance of Markov models and the functions of the system because of memory restricting [6]. In addition, Markov models of high level often lack matching sequence in prediction, which leads to low prediction overlay rate, etc.

3.2 Hybrid Markov Model

The overlay rate decreases with levels increasing in traditional Markov model. The Markov model of high level has a big problem except above deficiencies. It is that prediction overlay rate is too low to overlay too many Web pages. So, we propose a new Markov mode—hybrid Markov model (HMM). The Hybrid Markov Model combines Markov Models of different levels for prediction. It overcomes the problems that the state-space complexity of Markov models of low level is too high and the prediction overlay rate of Markov model of high level is too low.

Algorithm: building hybrid Markov model(HMM) M :

1. Initialize parameter, let prediction overlay rate's threshold to equal to θ , discrete.
2. Build Markov model of high level M_k .
3. Compute prediction overlay rate α .
4. If prediction overlay rate α is lower than θ , or k>1,k= k-1,go to 2.
5. Or, over.

We can build hybrid Markov model from above algorithm. The Markov model of high level M_k can be defined as follows:

1. a set of states Q, with specified initial and final states q_0 and q_E .
2. a set of transitions between states, every element is $q_1,\ldots q_{k-1} \rightarrow q_k$.
3. a discrete vocabulary of output symbols: $\Sigma = \sigma_1, \sigma_2, \ldots, \sigma_k$.

By starting from the initial state, transiting to a new state, emitting an output symbol, transiting to another state, emitting another symbol, and so on, it ends when a transition is made in the final state. The model generates an output symbol string: $X = x_1, x_2, \ldots, x_k$. Every transition exists a transition probability $\mathrm{P}(q_1,\ldots q_{k-1} \rightarrow q_k)$. It emits a special probability of an output symbol $P(X| \; q_k)$ in a state q_k .The probability of a string X being emitted by a Markov model of high level M_k is computed as a sum over all possible paths by:

$$\mathrm{P}(X \mid M_k) = \sum_{q_0,\ldots,q_e \in Q}^{E} \prod_{k=1}^{l+1} \mathrm{P}(q_1,\ldots q_{k-1} \rightarrow q_k)\mathrm{P}(x_k \mid q_k) \tag{8}$$

Here $\mathrm{P}(x_k \mid q_k)$=$\mathrm{P}(k_j \mid (url_s, UG_i))$ is defined based on definition 7.

$$\mathrm{P}(q_1,\ldots,q_{k-1} \rightarrow q_k) = \frac{\mathrm{count}(q_k)}{\mathrm{count}(q_1,\ldots,q_{k-1} \rightarrow q_k)} \tag{9}$$

Here, $\text{count}(q_1,...q_{k-1} \rightarrow q_k)$ is the number of transactions appearing simultaneously in neighboring areas in transaction set *T*. $\text{count}(q_k)$ is transaction number which contain q_k in transaction set.

If *k*=2, HMM is Markov model of level 1 M_1 and defined as follows:

1. a set of states *Q*, with specified initial and final state q_0 and q_E.
2. a set of transitions between states, every element is $q_{k-1} \rightarrow q_k$.
3. a discrete vocabulary of output symbols: $\Sigma = \sigma_1, \sigma_2, ..., \sigma_k$.

By starting from the initial state, transiting to a new state, emitting an output symbol, transiting to another state, emitting another symbol, and so on, it ends when a transition is made in the final state. The model generates an output symbol string: $X = x_1, x_2, ..., x_k$. Every transition exists a transition probability $\text{P}(q_{k-1} \rightarrow q_k)$. It emits a special probability of an output symbol-$P(X| q_k)$. The probability of a string *X* being emitted by Markov model of level 1 M_1 is computed as a sum over all possible paths by:

$$\text{P}(X \mid M_1) = \sum_{q_0,...,q_e \in Q} \prod_{k=1}^{l+1} \text{P}(q_{k-1} \rightarrow q_k)\text{P}(x_k \mid q_k) \tag{10}$$

Here, $\text{P}(x_k \mid q_k)=\text{P}(k_j \mid (url_s, UG_i))$ is defined based on definition 7.

$$\text{P}(q_{k-1} \rightarrow q_k) = \frac{\text{count}(q_k)}{\text{count}(q_{k-1} \rightarrow q_k)} \tag{11}$$

Here, $\text{count}(q_{k-1} \rightarrow q_k)$ is the number of transactions appearing simultaneously in the neighboring areas in transaction set *T*. $\text{count}(q_k)$ is transaction number which contain q_k in transaction set.

3.3 Mining Interest Navigation Patterns Based on Hybrid Markov Model

The interest distribution is defined by different keywords according to user access time length. Some path patterns related to one keyword are expected. In these path patterns, the probability is large for accessing the keyword, and the probability is small for accessing other keywords. The time that users access the keywords is very long and the access time is long in these path patterns. These path patterns are navigation pattern for the keyword interest of user group.

Navigation pattern based on user group interest using hybrid Markov model is defined as follows:

For user group, there is a symbol set $\Sigma = k_1, k_2, ..., k_k$.

(url_s, U_i^G) and (url_p, U_j^G) are neighbors in Website, there are transition probability $P((url_s, U_i^G) \rightarrow (url_p, U_j^G))$.

According to the interest intensity of the user group, there is a probability distribution $P(k_1 \mid (url_1, U_1^G)), ..., P(k_j \mid (url_s, U_i^G))$ of user group interest for keyword set $\Sigma = k_1, k_2, ..., k_k$ in every Web page node ($k_j \mid (url_s, U_i^G)$). It is interest probability of state node in hybrid Markov model, and defined based on definition 4.

There exists interest rule $R(\sigma|M, S_k)$ for accessing sequence S_k : S_k = (($k_1 \mid (url_1, U_1^G)$),……, ($k_j \mid (url_s, U_i^G)$)) and user group interest σ in hybrid Markov model.

There exists the set R of interest rules $R(\sigma|M, S_k)$ .The associate rules in set R can help the designer comprehending user access. The associate rule $R(\sigma|M, S_k)$ combines access numbers and access time for better reflecting user group access interest.

4 Experiments

In this section, we present our experimental results that test the performance of hybrid Markov model. We compare hybrid Markov model's performance with that of the traditional Markov models.

Our experiments draw on data collected from two Websites: NASA and MSN. The NASA data set contains two months worth of all HTTP requests to the NASA Kennedy Space Center WWW server in Florida. The log was collected from 00:00:00 August 1, 1995 through 23:59:59 August 31, 1995. In that period there were 1,569,898 requests. There were a total of 18,688 unique IPs access pages, having a total of 171,529 effective sessions. A total of 15,429 unique pages were accessed. The MSN.com log is obtained from the server log of msn.com, with all the identities of users stripped away. It consists of data collected from Jan 27,1999 to Mar 26,1999 with a total of 417,783 user requests. This log contains 722 unique IP's requesting 14,048 unique pages. The MSN.com log is unique in that some requests are from groups of users submitted by Proxies or ISP's. Therefore the length of some sessions was long. For example, the long sessions ranged from 8,384 consecutive visits to 166,073 visits.

The prediction overlay rate and the prediction correct rate are used as the evaluation criterion of the experiment. The prediction overlay rate is defined as the ratio of model's predictive page numbers and user actual access page numbers. The prediction correct rate is defined as the ratio of model's predictive page value and the value of the user's actual access page.

Firstly, we compare hybrid Markov model of level 6 with traditional Markov model of level 1-6 in prediction overlay rate. Because hybrid Markov model considers prediction situation of different levels, prediction overlay rate is larger than threshold. It is a corresponding prediction value for every user access. The prediction overlay rate descends with the increase of level of traditional Markov models, as figure 1 shows.

Second, we compare hybrid Markov model of level 6 with traditional Markov models of level 1-6 with prediction correct rate. The results are showed in figure 2. The prediction correct rate of hybrid Markov model is higher than the prediction correct rate of traditional Markov models.

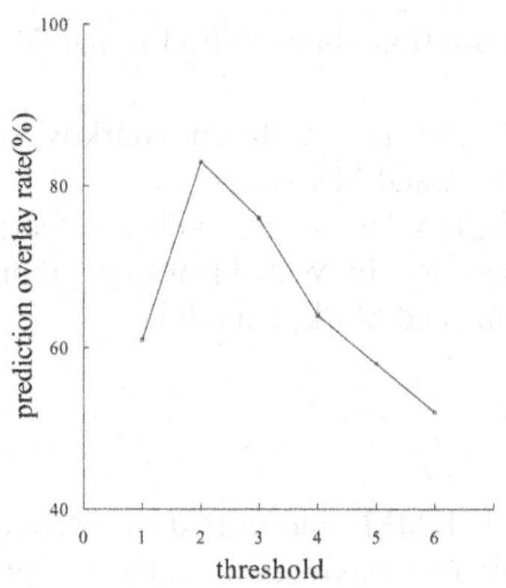

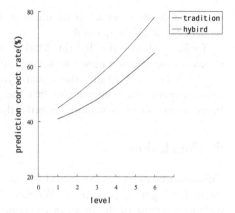

Fig. 1. Comparison about prediction overlay rate

Fig. 2. Comparison about prediction correct rate

Third, the building time of hybrid Markov model and traditional Markov models is compared, as figure 3 shows. The building time of hybrid Markov model increases by linear with level increasing, but the building time of tradition Markov model increases by index with level increasing. The building time of hybrid Markov model is fewer than the building time of traditional Markov models. The hybrid Markov model has better expansion.

Finally, the prediction time of hybrid Markov model and traditional Markov models is compared, as figure 4 shows. The experiment shows that the prediction time

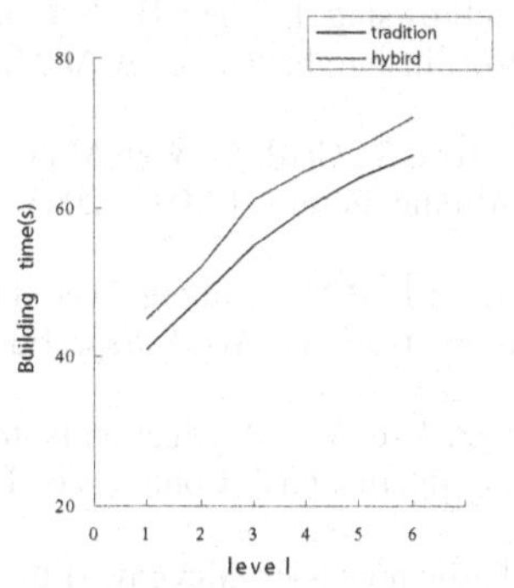

Fig. 3. Comparison in building time

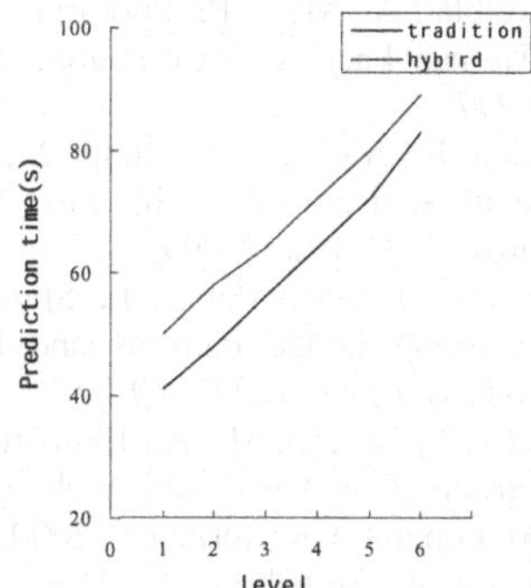

Fig. 4. Comparison in prediction time

Table 1. Comparison about recommendation correct rate

Markov model	NASA /%	MSN /%
Hybrid	82.2	78.2
High level	77.1	69.3
Low level	47.5	41.8

of hybrid Markov model is as much as the prediction time of traditional Markov models. So, it can be ignored.

Table 1 shows the hybrid Markov model and the tradition Markov model efficiency comparison between two data sets: NASA and MSN.

The experiment results show that hybrid Markov model has better effect. The above experiment results prove that the performance in Web browsing prediction based on hybrid Markov model is better than traditional Markov models.

5 Conclusions

This research proposes the hybrid Markov model (HMM) and uses it to discover the interest navigation patterns in Website. The interest navigation patterns represent different interest of the users in the content of the Website. The experiment results prove that the novel model is efficient for prediction. It shows that our model is better in prediction overlay rate and prediction correct rate than traditional Markov models. The HMM overcomes the problems that the state-space complexity of Markov models of low level is too high and the prediction overlay rate of Markov model of high level is too low. The experiment results also show that building the HMM doesn't need many time and the transition probability and the interest access probability are easily computed. We plan to perform extensible testing and investigate many possible improvements.

References

1. Wexelblat, A., Maes, P.: Footprints:History-rich Web browsing. In: the CHI 99 Conference on Human Factors in Computing Systems (CHI'99), Pittsburgh, PA, USA:ACM, (1999) 270-277
2. Bettina, B., Andreas, H., Dunja, M., Maarten, V.S., Myra, S., Gerd, S.: Web Mining: From Web to Semantic Web. In: First European Web Mining Forum, EMWF 2003, Cavtat-Dubrovnik, Croatia, (2003)
3. Zaiane, O.R., Srivastava, J., Spiliopoulou, M., Masand. B.M.: Mining Web Data for Discovering Usage Patterns and Profiles, In: 4th International Workshop, Edmonton, Canada: Springer, (2002) 19-29
4. Borges, J., Levene, M.: An Heuristic to Capture Longer User Web Navigation Patterns, In: Electronic Commerce and Web Technologies, First International Conference, EC-Web 2000, London, UK, Springer, (2000) 155-164
5. Papoulis, A.: Probability, random variables, and stochastic processes. McGraw Hill, 1991.
6. Mogul, J.C., Chan, Y., Kelly, T.: Design, Implementation and Evaluation of Duplicate Transfer Detection in HTTP. NSDI (2004) 43-56
7. Sarukkai, R.: Link prediction and path analysis using Markov chains. Computer Networks, 33(1-6),(2000) 377-386
8. Borges, J., Levene. M.: Generating Dynamic Higher-Order Markov Models in Web Usage Mining. In: Knowledge Discovery in Databases: PKDD 2005, 9th European Conference on Principles and Practice of Knowledge Discovery in Databases, Porto, Portugal, Springer,(2005) 34-45
9. Pirolli, P., Fu, W.: SNIF-ACT: A Model of Information Foraging on the World Wide Web. In: 9th International Conference(User Modeling 2003), UM 2003, Johnstown, PA, USA, Springer,(2003) 45-54

Partition-Based Approach to Processing Batches of Frequent Itemset Queries

Przemyslaw Grudzinski, Marek Wojciechowski, and Maciej Zakrzewicz

Poznan University of Technology
Institute of Computing Science
ul. Piotrowo 2, 60-965 Poznan, Poland
{marek, mzakrz}@cs.put.poznan.pl

Abstract. We consider the problem of optimizing processing of batches of frequent itemset queries. The problem is a particular case of multiple-query optimization, where the goal is to minimize the total execution time of the set of queries. We propose an algorithm that is a combination of the Mine Merge method, previously proposed for processing of batches of frequent itemset queries, and the Partition algorithm for memory-based frequent itemset mining. The experiments show that the novel approach outperforms the original Mine Merge and sequential processing in majority of cases.

1 Introduction

Discovery of frequent itemsets [1] is a very important data mining problem with numerous practical applications. Informally, frequent itemsets are subsets frequently occurring in a collection of sets of items. Frequent itemsets are typically used to generate association rules. However, since generation of rules is a rather straightforward task, the focus of researchers has been mostly on optimizing the frequent itemset discovery step.

Frequent itemset mining (and in general, frequent pattern mining) is often regarded as advanced querying where a user specifies the source dataset, the minimum support threshold, and optionally pattern constraints within a given constraint model [9]. A significant amount of research on efficient processing of frequent itemset queries has been done in recent years, focusing mainly on constraint handling and reusing results of previous queries [5][7][12][13].

Recently, a new problem of optimizing processing of batches of frequent itemset queries has been considered [19][20]. The problem was motivated by data mining systems working in a batch mode or periodically refreshed data warehouses, but is also relevant in the context of multi-user, interactive data mining environments. It is a particular case of multiple-query optimization [18], well-studied in database systems. The goal is to find an optimal global execution plan, exploiting similarities between the queries.

So far, two methods of processing batches of frequent itemset queries have been proposed: Mine Merge [19] and Common Counting [20]. Both methods exploit the overlapping between queries' datasets to reduce the overall processing time. Unfortunately, both methods have serious limitations, which is the motivation for further research on the topic.

H.L. Larsen et al. (Eds.): FQAS 2006, LNAI 4027, pp. 479 – 488, 2006.

Common Counting consists in concurrent executing of a frequent itemset mining algorithm for the queries, and integrating dataset scans performed by the queries. Common Counting was designed to work with Apriori [3], in case of which it needs to maintain candidate hash-trees of several queries in main memory. If not all the hash-trees fit into memory, the queries have to be scheduled into phases, which degrades Common Counting's performance. Application of Common Counting to newer pattern-growth mining algorithms [8] is problematic as these algorithms store a compressed form of the database in main memory, which may be infeasible for more than one query at the same time, even for today's machines.

The idea of Mine Merge is to transform the original batch of overlapping queries into the set of intermediate non-overlapping queries operating on dataset partitions, whose boundaries are defined by the overlapping between the original queries. After executing the intermediate queries, the answers to original queries are generated using the method proposed in [17] for memory-based partitioning. Mine Merge is not bound to a particular mining algorithm and its memory requirements are not greater that those of the basic mining algorithm applied to intermediate queries. The disadvantage of Mine Merge is that it requires significant overlapping between the queries in order to compensate the extra database scan needed to consolidate the results from intermediate queries.

In this paper we propose a novel method for processing batches of frequent itemset queries, called PMM+ (Partition Mine Merge Improved), which combines disk-based partitioning of Mine Merge with memory-based partitioning of the well-known Partition algorithm from [17]. The advantage of the new method is that it requires exactly two scans of the union of source datasets of the queries forming a batch.

The paper is organized as follows. In Section 2 we review related work. Section 3 contains basic definitions regarding frequent itemset queries and reviews the Mine Merge method for processing of batches of frequent itemset queries. The motivations underlying PMM+ and the new method itself are presented in Section 4. In Section 5 we present and discuss results of experiments conducted to evaluate performance of PMM+. Section 6 contains conclusions.

2 Related Work

Multiple-query optimization has been extensively studied in the context of database systems (see [18] for an overview). The idea was to identify common subexpressions and construct a global execution plan minimizing the overall processing time by executing the common subexpressions only once for the set of queries [4][10][15]. Data mining queries could also benefit from this general strategy, however, due to their different nature they require novel multiple-query processing methods.

To the best of our knowledge, the only two multiple-query processing methods for data mining queries are Mine Merge [19] and Common Counting [20], mentioned above. Recently, the need for multiple-query optimization has been postulated in the somewhat related research area of inductive logic programming, where a technique based on similar ideas as Common Counting has been proposed, consisting in combining similar queries into query packs [6].

As an introduction to multiple data mining query optimization, we can regard techniques of reusing intermediate or final results of previous queries to answer a new query. Methods falling into that category that have been studied in the context of frequent itemset discovery are: incremental mining [7], caching intermediate query results [14], and reusing materialized complete [5][12][13] or condensed [11] results of previous queries provided that syntactic differences between the queries satisfy certain conditions.

Dividing the dataset into partitions fitting into main memory in order to find locally frequent itemsets using only in-memory operations, and then integrating the partial results to find globally frequent itemsets was first considered in [17], where the Partition algorithm was proposed. The most important contribution of [17] was the proof that given the dataset divided into the set of non-overlapping partitions, an itemset can be globally frequent only if it is locally frequent in at least one of the partitions. Partition used a variation of Apriori for in-memory frequent itemset mining, and its advantage over the original Apriori was that it performed exactly two database scans: one to read the partitions and one to verify which of the locally frequent itemsets are globally frequent.

In [16] another memory-based partitioning algorithm H-Mine was proposed for frequent itemset mining, outperforming Partition thanks to: (1) replacing Apriori for in-memory mining with a newly developed efficient pattern-growth algorithm H-Mine(Mem), and (2) applying some optimizations in the consolidation step.

3 Background

3.1 Basic Definitions and Problem Statement

Frequent Itemset Query. A frequent itemset query is a tuple $dmq = (R, a, \Sigma, \Phi, \beta)$, where R is a relation, a is a set-valued attribute of R, Σ is a condition involving the attributes of R, Φ is a condition involving discovered itemsets, and β is the minimum support threshold. The result of dmq is a set of itemsets discovered in $\pi_a \sigma_\Sigma R$, satisfying Φ, and having support $\geq \beta$ (π and σ denote relational projection and selection operations respectively).

Example. Given the database relation $R_1(a_1, a_2)$, where a_2 is a set-valued attribute and a_1 is of integer type. The frequent itemset query $dmq_1 = (R_1, "a_2", "a_1>5", "|itemset|<4", 3\%)$ describes the problem of discovering frequent itemsets in the set-valued attribute a_2 of the relation R_1. The frequent itemsets with support of at least 3% and length less than 4 are discovered in the collection of records having $a_1>5$.

Elementary Data Selection Predicates. The set $S=\{s_1, s_2, ..., s_k\}$ of data selection predicates over the relation R is a set of elementary data selection predicates for a set of frequent itemset queries $DMQ = \{dmq_1, dmq_2, ..., dmq_n\}$ if for all u,v we have $\sigma_{su}R \cap \sigma_{sv}R = \emptyset$ and for each dmq_i there exist integers $a, b, ..., m$ such that $\sigma_\Sigma R = \sigma_{sa}R \cup \sigma_{sb}R \cup .. \cup \sigma_{sm}R$.

Example. Given the relation $R_1=(attr_1, attr_2)$ and three data mining queries: $dmq_1=(R_1, "attr_2", "5 <attr_1<20", \emptyset, 3)$, $dmq_2=(R_1, "attr_2", "0<attr_1<15", \emptyset, 5)$, $dmq_3=(R_1, "attr_2", "5<attr_1<15 \text{ or } 30<attr_1<40", \emptyset, 4)$. The set of elementary data selection predicates is then $S=\{s_1="0<attr_1<5", s_2="5<attr_1<15", s_3="15<attr_1<20", s_4="30<attr_1<40"\}$.

Problem Statement. Given a set of frequent itemset queries $DMQ = \{dmq_1, dmq_2, ..., dmq_n\}$, the problem of *multiple query optimization* of *DMQ* consists in generating such an algorithm to execute *DMQ* which minimizes the overall processing time.

3.2 Mine Merge

Similarly to Partition, Mine Merge employs the property that for a database divided into a set of disjoint partitions, an itemset which is frequent in a whole database, must also be frequent in at least one partition of it. The difference is that Partition uses memory-based partitions, determined by the amount of available main-memory, while Mine Merge operates on disk-based partitions, which are the consequence of overlapping between queries' datasets.

```
/* Generate intermediate data mining queries IDMQ = {idmq1, idmq2, ...} */
  IDMQ ←∅
  for each sj∈S do begin
    Q ← {dmqi∈DMQ | σsjR⊆σΣiR }
    intermediate_β ← min{βi | dmqi=(R, a, si, Φi, βi)∈Q}
    intermediate_Φ ←Φ1∨Φ2∨... ∨Φ|Q|, ∀i=1..|Q|, dmqi=(R, a, si, Φi, βi)∈Q
    IDMQ ← IDMQ ∪ idmqj=(R, a, sj, intermediate_Φ, intermediate_β)
  end
/* Execute intermediate data mining queries */
  for each idmqi ∈ IDMQ do
    IFi ← execute(idmqi)
/* Generate results for original queries DMQ = {dmq1, dmq2, ...} */
  for each dmqi∈ DMQ do
    C^i ← {c|c∈ ∪k IFk , σskR⊆σΣiR, c.count ≥ βi, c satisfies Φi}
  for each sj∈S do begin
    CC ← { C^i | σsjR⊆σΣiR };      /* select the candidates to count now */
    if CC≠∅ then count(CC, σsjR);
  end
  for (i=1; i<=n; i++) do
    Answer^i ← {c ∈ C^i | c.count ≥ βi}  /* generate responses */
```

Fig. 1. Mine Merge method

Mine Merge first generates a set of *intermediate data mining queries*, in which each data mining query is based on a single elementary selection predicate only. The intermediate data mining queries are derived from those original data mining queries that are sharing a given elementary selection predicate. The minimum support thresholds and selection conditions on itemsets for the intermediate queries are chosen so that their results are guaranteed to include all locally frequent itemsets for all the original queries that refer to the database partition corresponding to a given intermediate query.

Next, the intermediate data mining queries are executed sequentially using any frequent itemset mining algorithm (Apriori, Partition, etc.) and then their results are merged to form global candidates for the original data mining queries. Finally, a database scan is performed to count the global candidate supports and to answer the original data mining queries. The pseudocode of the Mine Merge algorithm is shown in Fig. 1.

4 PMM+: Combining Disk-Based and Memory-Based Dataset Partitioning

The problem of the basic Mine Merge algorithm is that it requires significant overlapping between the queries in order to compensate for the extra database scan needed to consolidate the results from intermediate queries. To avoid this problem we

```
/* Generate intermediate data mining queries IDMQ = {idmq_1, idmq_2, ...}
 * MEM_SIZE is the memory buffer size for reading database partitions
 */
  IDMQ ← ∅
  PDMQ ← ∅
  for each s_j∈S do begin
    Q ← {dmq_i∈DMQ | σ_sj R ⊆ σ_Σ R }
    intermediate_β ← min{β_i | dmq_i=(R, a, s_i, Φ_i, β_i)∈Q}
    intermediate_Φ ← Φ_1 ∨ Φ_2 ∨ ... ∨ Φ_|Q|, ∀i=1..|Q|, dmq_i=(R, a, s_i, Φ_i, β_i)∈Q
    IDMQ ← IDMQ ∪ idmq_j=(R, a, s_j, intermediate_Φ, intermediate_β)
  end
/* Partition intermediate data mining queries to fit their σ_si R in memory */
  for each idmq_i ∈ IDMQ do
    PDMQ ← PDMQ ∪ partition(idmq_i, MEM_SIZE)
/* Execute partitioned data mining queries */
  for each pdmq_i ∈ PDMQ do begin
    read_in_partition(σ_si R);
    PF_i ← execute(pdmq_i);
  end
/* Generate results for original queries DMQ = {dmq_1, dmq_2, ...} */
  for each dmq_i∈ DMQ do
    C^i ← {c|c∈ ∪_k PF_k , σ_sk R ⊆ σ_Σ R, c.count ≥ β_i, c satisfies Φ_i}
  for each s_j∈S do begin
      CC ← { C^i | σ_sj R ⊆ σ_Σ R };      /* select the candidates to count now */
      if CC≠∅ then count(CC, σ_sj R);
  end
  for (i=1; i<=n; i++) do
     Answer^i ← {c ∈ C^i | c.count ≥ β_i}  /* generate responses */
```

Fig. 2. PMM+ method

introduce a new method called Partition Mine Merge Improved (PMM+), which additionally partitions the intermediate queries in such a way that the data they operate on can completely fit in memory. Therefore, only a single database scan is needed to execute all the intermediate queries. After the partitioned intermediate queries have been executed, another database scan is performed to generate final results for the original data mining queries. In this way, PMM+ can execute a batch of data mining queries by reading the database only two times.

The pseudocode of the Partition Mine Merge Improved algorithm is shown in Fig. 2. The actual partitioning of the intermediate data mining queries (*partition()* function) can be performed either statically, with help of database query optimizer, or dynamically, while reading the database. Partitioning of the intermediate data mining queries must guarantee that their source data - $\sigma_{si}R$ – can completely fit in memory. Only then a query will be able to discover all the frequent itemsets by using fast in-memory scans.

Partition Mine Merge Improved introduces some overhead caused by discovering locally-frequent itemsets, which are then eliminated in the final scan phase. We expect this overhead to be slightly bigger compared to the basic Mine Merge because the intermediate data mining queries operate on smaller database fragments.

5 Experimental Results

To evaluate performance of the improved batch processing method for frequent itemset queries, we performed a series of experiments using a synthetic dataset generated with GEN [2] as the database. The dataset contained 100000 transactions built from 1000 different items. All the tested batches of queries operated on this dataset. We varied the number of queries in a batch, the level of overlapping between queries' datasets, the minimum support thresholds, and the variance of dataset sizes of the queries forming a batch. The experiments were conducted on a PC with AMD Athlon 1800+ processor and 256 MB of RAM, running Windows XP. The data resided in a flat file on disk, the algorithms were implemented in C++.

We implemented PMM+ with Apriori for in-memory frequent itemset mining. In all the tests, we compared its execution time with: (1) SEQA – sequential processing using Apriori, (2) SEQP – sequential processing using Partition, (3) AMM – Mine Merge using Apriori, and (4) PMM – Mine Merge using Partition. For the methods involving in-memory mining (SEQP, PMM, and PMM+) the amount of main memory reserved for that purpose was always 10000 of the average transaction size[1].

To evaluate performance of PMM+ in various circumstances, we used 14 different batches of queries, differing in the number of queries (two or three), dataset sizes, dataset overlapping, and minimum support thresholds. The execution times for the 14 test query batches of PMM+ and four reference methods are presented in Table 1.

[1] For the ease of implementation, we actually expressed the memory limit as 10000 transactions.

Table 1. Execution times of five methods of processing batches of frequent itemset queries for 14 test query batches

Case	Queries			Execution times [in seconds]				
	from	to	minsup	SEQA	SEQP	AMM	PMM	PMM+
1	1	70000	0,01	53	25	36	19	13
	20001	100000	0,01					
	30001	60000	0,01					
2a	1	70000	0,02	24	14	28	18	12
	50001	100000	0,01					
2b	1	70000	0,015	22	13	24	17	11
	50001	100000	0,015					
3a	1	70000	0,01	44	21	36	20	14
	20001	100000	0,01					
3b	1	70000	0,02	20	16	20	16	10
	20001	100000	0,02					
4a	1	70000	0,02	15	12	20	16	10
	60001	100000	0,02					
4b	1	70000	0,05	8	10	13	14	9
	60001	100000	0,05					
5	1	70000	0,01	26	16	29	18	12
	30001	100000	0,05					
6a	1	100000	0,01	35	16	36	20	14
	10001	30000	0,01					
6b	1	100000	0,05	13	12	19	16	10
	10001	30000	0,01					
7a	1	100000	0,10	10	9	16	14	10
	10001	20000	0,01					
7b	1	100000	0,05	11	10	16	15	11
	10001	20000	0,01					
7c	1	100000	0,03	16	11	21	16	11
	10001	20000	0,01					
7d	1	100000	0,01	32	15	36	19	14
	10000	20000	0,01					

The experiments show that PMM+ is the best from all the tested methods in majority of cases. In particular, PMM+ outperformed PMM and AMM for all tested batches. The average execution time of PMM+ was by 48% shorter than the average execution time of AMM (the original Mine Merge method) and by 32% shorter than the average execution time of PMM.

The only cases in which PMM+ lost to sequential processing (by 10% in the worst case) were 4b, 7a, and 7b. In case 4b the overlapping between the queries was very small and the support threshold very high (5%). As a result, there were only 2 Apriori iterations for each query, and sequential Apriori finished first. In cases 7a and 7b there were significant differences in dataset sizes and support thresholds of the queries. As a consequence, one of the queries completed very quickly, not leaving much space for I/O cost reduction with such a small part of the database shared between the queries.

In the next series of experiments we thoroughly evaluated the impact of the overlapping between the queries and the minimum support threshold on the performance of PMM+. This time we tested only batches of two queries operating on the datasets of equal size of 50000 transactions. We changed the overlapping between the queries (expressed as the percentage of transactions shared by the queries) from 0% to 100%, repeating the experiments for the minimum support thresholds of 1%, 3%, and 5%. Figures 3, 4, and 5 present execution times measured for PMM+ and four reference algorithms.

The experiments show that the processing time of PMM+ reduces linearly as the overlapping between queries' datasets increases. More importantly, the usability of PMM+ (i.e., its advantage over sequential processing) has improved significantly

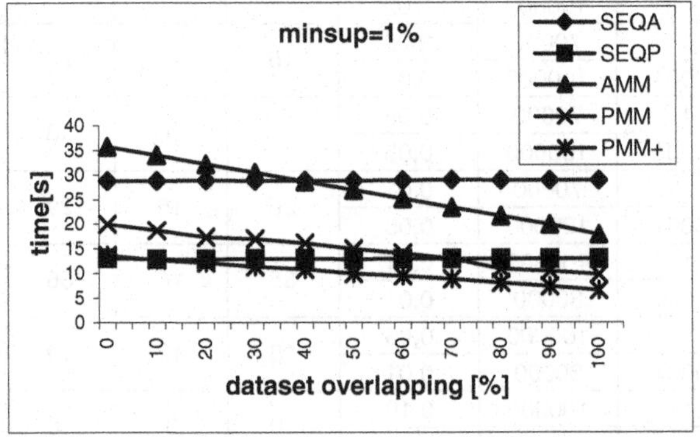

Fig. 3. Execution times for different levels of overlapping between two queries (minsup = 1%)

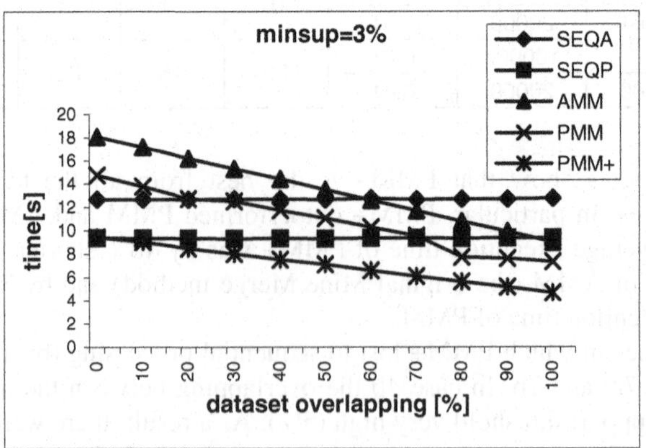

Fig. 4. Execution times for different levels of overlapping between two queries (minsup = 3%)

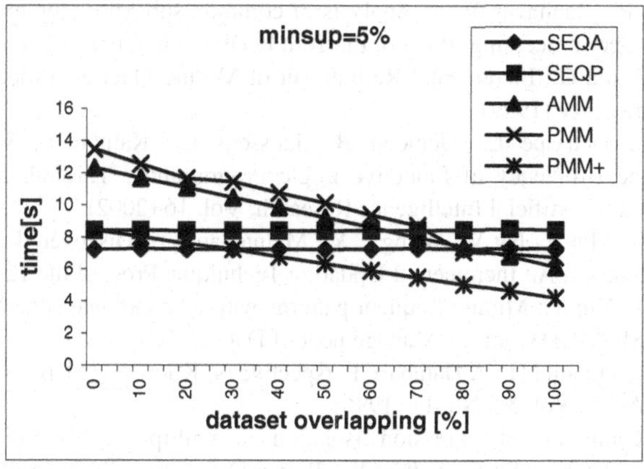

Fig. 5. Execution times for different levels of overlapping between two queries (minsup = 5%)

compared to the original Mine Merge. To outperform SEQA, AMM required at least 50% of overlapping for the supports of 1% and 3%, and 80% for the support of 5%. PMM+ was the most efficient of the tested methods if any overlapping between the queries occurred for the supports of 1% and 3%. PMM+ lost to SEQA only for the support of 5% and dataset overlapping less than 30%. This can be explained by the fact that for the support of 5% Apriori needed only 2 iterations to execute each of the queries. Nevertheless, even for such a high minimum support threshold, PMM+ was the most efficient method already starting with the dataset overlapping of 30%.

6 Conclusions

In this paper we considered the problem of optimizing batches of frequent itemset queries. We presented a novel batch processing technique, improving the previously proposed Mine Merge method. The new technique, called PMM+, combines disk-based dataset partitioning of Mine Merge with memory-based partitioning of the Partition frequent itemset mining algorithm. PMM+ minimizes I/O costs by performing exactly two scans over the union of datasets of frequent itemset queries forming a batch. The experiments show that PMM+ always performs better than the original Mine Merge and outperforms sequential processing in majority of cases.

References

1. Agrawal R., Imielinski T., Swami A: Mining Association Rules Between Sets of Items in Large Databases. Proc. of the 1993 ACM SIGMOD Conf. on Management of Data (1993)
2. Agrawal R., Mehta M., Shafer J., Srikant R., Arning A., Bollinger T.: The Quest Data Mining System. Proc. of the 2nd Int'l Conference on Knowledge Discovery in Databases and Data Mining (1996)
3. Agrawal R., Srikant R.: Fast Algorithms for Mining Association Rules. Proc. of the 20th Int'l Conf. on Very Large Data Bases (1994)

4. Alsabbagh J.R., Raghavan V.V.: Analysis of common subexpression exploitation models in multiple-query processing. Proc. of the 10th ICDE Conference (1994)
5. Baralis E., Psaila G.: Incremental Refinement of Mining Queries. Proceedings of the 1st DaWaK Conference (1999)
6. Blockeel H., Dehaspe L., Demoen B., Janssens G., Ramon J., Vandecasteele H.: Improving the Efficiency of Inductive Logic Programming Through the Use of Query Packs, Journal of Artificial Intelligence Research, Vol. 16 (2002)
7. Cheung D.W., Han J., Ng V., Wong C.Y.: Maintenance of Discovered Association Rules in Large Databases: An Incremental Updating Technique. Proc. of the 12th ICDE (1996)
8. Han J., Pei J., Yin Y.: Mining frequent patterns without candidate generation. Proc. of the 2000 ACM SIGMOD Conf. on Management of Data (2000)
9. Imielinski T., Mannila H.: A Database Perspective on Knowledge Discovery. Communications of the ACM, Vol. 39, No. 11 (1996)
10. Jarke M.: Common subexpression isolation in multiple query optimization. Query Processing in Database Systems, Kim W., Reiner D.S. (Eds.), Springer (1985)
11. Jeudy B., Boulicaut J-F.: Using condensed representations for interactive association rule mining. Proceedings of the 6th European Conference on Principles and Practice of Knowledge Discovery in Databases (2002)
12. Meo R.: Optimization of a Language for Data Mining. Proc. of the ACM Symposium on Applied Computing - Data Mining Track (2003)
13. Morzy T., Wojciechowski M., Zakrzewicz M.: Materialized Data Mining Views. Proceedings of the 4th PKDD Conference (2000)
14. Nag B., Deshpande P.M., DeWitt D.J.: Using a Knowledge Cache for Interactive Discovery of Association Rules. Proc. of the 5th KDD Conference (1999)
15. Roy P., Seshadri S., Sundarshan S., Bhobe S.: Efficient and Extensible Algorithms for Multi Query Optimization. ACM SIGMOD Intl. Conference on Management of Data (2000)
16. Pei J., Han J., Lu H., Nishio S., Tang S., Yang D.: H-Mine: Hyper-Structure Mining of Frequent Patterns in Large Databases (2001)
17. Savasere A., Omiecinski E., Navathe S.: An Efficient Algorithm for Mining Association Rules in Large Databases. Proc. 21th Int'l Conf. Very Large Data Bases (1995)
18. Sellis T.: Multiple-query optimization. ACM Transactions on Database Systems, Vol. 13, No. 1 (1988)
19. Wojciechowski M., Zakrzewicz M.: Evaluation of the Mine Merge Method for Data Mining Query Processing. Proc. of the 8th ADBIS Conference (2004)
20. Wojciechowski M., Zakrzewicz M.: On Multiple Query Optimization in Data Mining. Proc. of the 9th Pacific-Asia Conference on Knowledge Discovery and Data Mining (2005)

Cooperative Discovery of Interesting Action Rules

Agnieszka Dardzińska[1] and Zbigniew W. Raś[2,3]

[1] Bialystok Technical Univ., Mathematics Dept., 15-351 Bialystok, Poland
[2] Univ. of North Carolina, Computer Science Dept., Charlotte, NC 28223, USA
[3] Polish-Japanese Institute of Information Technology, Intelligent Systems Dept., ul. Koszykowa 86, 02-008 Warsaw, Poland

Abstract. Action rules introduced in [12] and extended further to e-action rules [21] have been investigated in [22], [13], [20]. They assume that attributes in a database are divided into two groups: stable and flexible. In general, an action rule can be constructed from two rules extracted earlier from the same database. Furthermore, we assume that these two rules describe two different decision classes and our goal is to re-classify objects from one of these classes into the other one. Flexible attributes are essential in achieving that goal since they provide a tool for making hints to a user what changes within some values of flexible attributes are needed for a given set of objects to re-classify them into a new decision class. There are two aspects of interestingness of rules that have been studied in data mining literature, objective and subjective measures [8], [1], [14], [15], [23]. In this paper we focus on a cost of an action rule which was introduced in [22] as an objective measure. An action rule was called interesting if its cost is below and support higher than some user-defined threshold values. We assume that our attributes are hierarchical and we focus on solving the failing problem of interesting action rules discovery. Our process is cooperative and it has some similarities with cooperative answering of queries presented in [3], [5], [6].

1 Introduction

There are two aspects of interestingness of rules that have been studied in data mining literature, objective and subjective measures [8], [1], [14], [15]. Objective measures are data-driven and domain-independent. Generally, they evaluate rules based on their quality and similarity between them. Subjective measures, including unexpectedness, novelty, and actionability, are user-driven and domain-dependent. A rule is actionable if user can do an action to his/her advantage based on this rule [8]. A formal definition of an action rule, constructed from certain pairs of classification rules, has been proposed in [12] and investigated further in [21], [22], [13], [20]. Interventions introduced in [7] are similar to action rules. The idea behind either action rules or interventions is to construct special kind of rules showing what changes in values of attributes,

H.L. Larsen et al. (Eds.): FQAS 2006, LNAI 4027, pp. 489–497, 2006.

for a given object, are needed in order to re-classify this object the way user wants. Assuming, for instance, that objects are customers, this re-classification may mean that a consumer not interested in a certain product, now may buy it, and therefore may shift into a group of more profitable customers.

The notion of a cost of an action rule was introduced in [22] as an objective measure. An action rule is called interesting if its cost is below some user-defined threshold value. For a given user, the cost associated with changes of values within one of his features is usually different than the cost associated with changes of values within his another feature. A heuristic strategy for replacing the initially extracted action rule by a composition of new action rules, dynamically built, was proposed in the paper by [22]. This composition of rules uniquely defines a new action rule and it is built with a goal to lower the cost of reclassifying objects supported by the initial action rule. However, in some cases the process of interesting action rules discovery may fail.

We assume, in this paper, that attributes are hierarchical and we show that failing problem of discovering interesting action rules can be treated in a similar way to the failing problem of database queries [3], [5], [6].

2 Information System and Action Rules

An information system is used for representing knowledge. Its definition, given here, is due to Pawlak [9].

By an information system we mean a triple $S = (U, A, V)$, where:

- U is a nonempty, finite set called the universe,
- A is a nonempty, finite set of attributes i.e. $a : U \longrightarrow V_a$ is a function for $a \in A$,
- $V = \bigcup\{V_a : a \in A\}$, where V_a is a set of values of the attribute $a \in A$.

Elements of U are called objects. In this paper, they are often seen as customers. Attributes are interpreted as features, offers made by a bank, characteristic conditions etc.

By a decision table we mean any information system where the set of attributes is partitioned into conditions and decisions. Additionally, we assume that the set of conditions is partitioned into stable and flexible. For simplicity reason, we assume that there is only one decision attribute. Date of birth is an example of a stable attribute. Interest rate on any customer account is an example of a flexible attribute (dependable on bank). We adopt the following definition of a decision table:

By a decision table we mean an information system of the form $S = (U, A_{St} \cup A_{Fl} \cup \{d\}, V)$, where $d \notin A_{St} \cup A_{Fl}$ is a distinguished attribute called decision. The elements of A_{St} are called stable conditions, whereas the elements of A_{Fl} are called flexible conditions.

As an example of a decision table we take $S = (\{x_1, x_2, x_3, x_4, x_5, x_6, x_7, x_8, x_9\}, \{a, c\} \cup \{b\} \cup \{d\}, V)$ represented by Table 1. The set $\{a, c\}$ lists stable

Table 1. Decision System

	a	b	c	d
x_1	2	1	2	L
x_2	2	1	2	L
x_3	1	1	0	H
x_4	1	1	0	H
x_5	2	3	2	H
x_6	2	3	2	H
x_7	2	1	1	L
x_8	2	1	1	L
x_9	2	2	1	L
x_{10}	2	3	0	L
x_{11}	1	1	2	H
x_{12}	1	1	1	H

attributes, b is a flexible attribute and d is a decision attribute. Also, we assume that H denotes a *high* profit and L denotes a *low* one.

In order to induce rules in which the THEN part consists of the decision attribute d and the IF part consists of attributes belonging to $A_{St} \cup A_{Fl}$, we can use *LERS* for rules extraction [2].

In order to efficiently extract such rules, when the number of attributes is large, we use sub-tables $(U, B \cup \{d\}, V)$ of S where B is a d-reduct (see [9]) in S. The set B is called d-reduct in S if there is no proper subset C of B such that d depends on C. The concept of d-reduct in S was introduced to induce rules from S describing values of the attribute d depending on minimal subsets of $A_{St} \cup A_{Fl}$.

By $L(r)$ we mean all attributes listed in the IF part of a rule r. For example, if $r_1 = [(a_1, 2) \wedge (a_2, 1) \wedge (a_3, 4) \longrightarrow (d, 8)]$ is a rule then $L(r_1) = \{a_1, a_2, a_3\}$.

By $d(r_1)$ we denote the decision value of that rule. In our example $d(r_1) = 8$. Similarly, if $a \in A_{St} \cup A_{Fl}$, then by $a(r_1)$ we mean the value of a in the classification part of r_1. For instance, in our example, $a_1(r_1) = 2$, $a_2(r_1) = 1$.

From Table 1, we can extract the following five rules which support is greater or equal to 2:

$$(b, 3) \wedge (c, 2) \longrightarrow (d, H),\ (a, 1) \wedge (b, 1) \longrightarrow (d, L),$$
$$(a, 1) \wedge (c, 1) \longrightarrow (d, L),\ (b, 1) \wedge (c, 0) \longrightarrow (d, H),$$
$$(a, 1) \longrightarrow (d, H)$$

Now, let us assume that $(a, v \longrightarrow w)$ denotes the fact that the value v of attribute a is changed to w. Similarly, $(a, \longrightarrow w)$ denotes the fact that the current value of attribute a is changed to w. The term $(a, v \longrightarrow w)(x)$ means that the property (a, v) of object x is changed to (a, w). Similarly, $(a, \longrightarrow w)(x)$ denotes the fact that the current value of attribute a for the object x is changed to w.

Let $S = (U, A_{St} \cup A_{Fl} \cup \{d\}, V)$ is a decision table and classification rules r_1, r_2 are extracted from S. The notion of e-action rule constructed from r_1, r_2 (see [21]) is recalled in the section below. First, we assume that:

- $B = A_{St} \cap L(r_1) \cap L(r_2)$,
- $u_i = e_i(r_2)$, where $\{e_1, e_2, ..., e_q\} = [A_{St} \cap [L(r_2) - L(r_1)]]$ and $1 \leq i \leq q$,
- $t_i = c_i(r_2)$, where $\{c_1, c_2, ..., c_r\} = [A_{Fl} \cap [L(r_2) - L(r_1)]]$ and $1 \leq i \leq r$,
- $v_i = b_i(r_1)$ and $w_i = b_i(r_2)$, where $\{b_1, b_2, ..., b_p\} = [A_{Fl} \cap L(r_1) \cap L(r_2)]$ and $1 \leq i \leq p$.

Additionally, the following two constraints are placed on rules r_1, r_2:

- $d(r_1) = k_1$, $d(r_2) = k_2$ and $k_1 \leq k_2$, (k_2 is a higher level class than k_1),
- $(\forall a \in B)[a(r_1) = a(r_2)]$,

By (r_1, r_2)-e-action rule on $x \in U$ we mean the expression r:

$$[\prod\{(a, a(r_1)) : a \in B\} \wedge (e_1, u_1) \wedge (e_2, u_2) \wedge ... \wedge (e_q, u_q) \wedge (b_1, v_1 \longrightarrow w_1) \wedge (b_2, v_2 \longrightarrow w_2) \wedge ... \wedge (b_p, v_p \longrightarrow w_p) \wedge (c_1, \longrightarrow t_1) \wedge (c_2, \longrightarrow t_2) \wedge ... \wedge (c_r, \longrightarrow t_r)](x) \Longrightarrow [(d, k_1 \longrightarrow k_2)](x)$$

The term " $\Longrightarrow$ " means *"it is expected that"*.

Object $x \in U$ supports (r_1, r_2)-e-action rule r in $S = (U, A_{St} \cup A_{Fl} \cup \{d\}, V)$, if x supports rule r_1, there is an object y supporting rule r_2, and the following conditions are satisfied:

- $(\forall i \leq p)[b_i(x) = v_i] \wedge d(x) = k_1$
- $(\forall i \leq p)[b_i(y) = w_i] \wedge d(y) = k_2$
- $(\forall j \leq q)[e_j(x) = e_j(y) = u_j]$
- $(\forall a \in B)[a(x) = a(r_1)]$

By the support of (r_1, r_2)-e-action rule r in S, denoted by $Sup_S(r)$, we mean the set of all objects in U supporting r in S.

By the confidence of (r_1, r_2)-e-action rule r in S, denoted by $Conf_S(r)$, we mean

$$[Sup_S(r)/Sup_S(L(r))] \times [Conf(r_2)]$$

To find the confidence of (r_1, r_2)-e-action rule in S, we divide the number of objects supporting (r_1, r_2)-e-action rule in S by the number of objects supporting left hand side of (r_1, r_2)-e-action rule times the confidence of the classification rule r_2 in S.

Finally, (r_1, r_2)-e-action rule is an action rule [12], if its structure is reduced to:

$$[(b_1, v_1 \longrightarrow w_1) \wedge (b_2, v_2 \longrightarrow w_2) \wedge ... \wedge (b_p, v_p \longrightarrow w_p)](x) \Longrightarrow [(d, k_1 \longrightarrow k_2)](x)$$

Also, we say that r is e-action rule in S, if there are classification rules r_1, r_2 extracted from S such that r is (r_1, r_2)-e-action rule in S.

3 Cost and Feasibility of Action Rules

Assume now that $S = (U, A_{St} \cup A_{Fl} \cup \{d\}, V)$ is a decision system, $b \in A_{Fl}$, and $b_1, b_2 \in V_b$ are its two values. By $\rho_{(S,x)}(b_1, b_2)$ we mean a number from $(0, +\infty]$ which describes the cost needed to re-classify a qualifying object $x \in U$ from b_1 to b_2. Object $x \in U$ qualifies for a change from b_1 to b_2, if $b(x) = b_1$. If the above change is not feasible in practice, then we write $\rho_{(S,x)}(b_1, b_2) = +\infty$. For instance, a user may have no clue how to relocate x, assuming that x is a person, from one place to another place. In such a case we would write $\rho_{(S,x)}(b_1, b_2) = +\infty$. The value of $\rho_{(S,x)}(b_1, b_2)$ close to *zero* is interpreted that it is quite trivial to re-classify x from b_1 to b_2 whereas any large value means that this re-classification is practically very difficult to achieve.

If $\rho_{(S,x)}(b_1, b_2) < \rho_{(S,x)}(b_3, b_4)$, then we say that the change of values from b_1 to b_2 is *more feasible* for x than the change from b_3 to b_4.

By $\rho_S(b_1, b_2)$, we mean the average cost of $\rho_{(S,x)}(b_1, b_2)$, for all qualifying objects $x \in U$. We assume here that values $\rho_S(b_1, b_2)$ are provided by experts. They are treated as atomic expressions and used to introduce the formal notion of the feasibility and the cost of action rules and e-action rules in S.

So, let us assume that $r = [\prod\{(a, a(r_1)) : a \in B\} \wedge (e_1, u_1) \wedge (e_2, u_2) \wedge ... \wedge (e_q, u_q) \wedge (b_1, v_1 \to w_1) \wedge (b_2, v_2 \to w_2) \wedge \wedge (b_p, v_p \to w_p)](x) \Rightarrow (d, k_1 \to k_2)(x)$ is a (r_1, r_2)-e-action rule in S. By the *cost* of r denoted by *cost*(r) we mean the value $\sum\{\rho_S(v_k, w_k) : 1 \le k \le p\}$. We say that r is *feasible*, if *cost*$(r) < \rho_S(k_1, k_2)$.

It means that for any feasible e-action rule r, the cost of the conditional part of r is lower than the cost of its decision part and clearly *cost*$(r) < +\infty$.

We say that e-action rule r is interesting, if its cost is below and its support is above some user defined threshold values.

Assume now that d is a decision attribute in S, $k_1, k_2 \in V_d$, and the user would like to re-classify objects in S from the group k_1 to the group k_2. To achieve that, he may look for an appropriate action rule, possibly of the lowest cost value, to get a hint which attribute values have to be changed. To be more precise, let us assume that $R_S[(d, k_1 \to k_2)]$ denotes the set of all e-action rules in S having the term $(d, k_1 \to k_2)$ on their decision site. Now, among all e-action rules in $R_S[(d, k_1 \to k_2)]$ he may identify a rule which has the lowest cost value. But the rule he gets may not be interesting one (because its cost is still too high). Let us notice that the cost of e-action rule

$$r = [\prod\{(a, a(r_1)) : a \in B\} \wedge (e_1, u_1) \wedge (e_2, u_2) \wedge ... \wedge (e_q, u_q) \wedge (b_1, v_1 \to w_1) \wedge (b_2, v_2 \to w_2) \wedge ... \wedge (b_p, v_p \to w_p)](x) \Rightarrow (d, k_1 \to k_2)(x)$$

might be high only because of the high cost of one of its sub-terms in the conditional part of that rule.

Let us assume that $(b_j, v_j \to w_j)$ is that term. One option to handle this is to look for e-action rule r_1 in $R_S[(b_j, v_j \to w_j)]$ which has the smallest cost value and next take the concatenation of rules r, r_1 [22]. If the cost of the resulting rule is still too high and assuming that the decision attribute is hierarchical and k_3 is a parent of k_2, we may try to re-classify objects from k_1 to k_3. If the generalized e-action rule is interesting, we should check the lowest cost and support of the re-classification from k_1 to a child of k_3 which is the nearest to k_2.

Now, we recall the definition of concatenation of two rules. Let us assume the following scenario. The action rule $r = [(b_1, v_1 \rightarrow w_1) \wedge (b_2, v_2 \rightarrow w_2) \wedge ... \wedge (b_p, v_p \rightarrow w_p)](x) \Rightarrow (d, k_1 \rightarrow k_2)(x)$, extracted from the information system S, is not interesting because at least one of its terms, let us say $(b_j, v_j \rightarrow w_j)$ where $1 \leq j \leq p$, has too high cost $\rho_{S_i}(v_j, w_j)$ assign to it.

In this case we look for a new feasible action rule $r_1 = [(b_{j1}, v_{j1} \rightarrow w_{j1}) \wedge (b_{j2}, v_{j2} \rightarrow w_{j2}) \wedge ... \wedge (b_{jq}, v_{jq} \rightarrow w_{jq})](y) \Rightarrow (b_j, v_j \rightarrow w_j)(y)$ which concatenated with r will decrease the cost value of desired reclassification.

By the concatenation of action rule r_1 with action rule r we mean a new feasible action rule $r_1 \circ r$ of the form:

$[(b_1, v_1 \rightarrow w_1) \wedge ... \wedge [(b_{j1}, v_{j1} \rightarrow w_{j1}) \wedge (b_{j2}, v_{j2} \rightarrow w_{j2}) \wedge ... \wedge (b_{jq}, v_{jq} \rightarrow w_{jq})] \wedge ... \wedge (b_p, v_p \rightarrow w_p)](x) \Rightarrow (d, k_1 \rightarrow k_2)(x)$
where x is an object in U.

The strategy of handling failing discovery of interesting action rules based on concatenation of action rules has one serious drawback. Each concatenation is decreasing the confidence of the resulting rule. If its confidence in S gets too low, then such action rule is no longer interesting to the user. The cooperative strategy, presented in this paper, gives an alternate approach to interesting action rules discovery.

4 Cooperative Discovery of Interesting Action Rules

Now, we present a simple example to illustrate the problem and outline the cooperative strategy of discovering interesting action rules. Let us assume that attributes a, e are stable in $S = (U, A \cup \{d\}, V)$, attributes b, c, d are flexible in S, and additionally the decision attribute d is hierarchical. Its structure, in Lisp-like notation, is given below:

$d[d_1[d_{[1,1]}, d_{[1,2]}], d_2[d_{[2,1]}, d_{[2,2]}], d_3[d_{[3,1]}, d_{[3,2]}]]$.

The system S is represented by Table 2.

We wish to reclassify objects x_3, x_4 in S, from the class described by value $d_{[1,1]}$ to the class described by $d_{[3,1]}$. The following two classification rules can be extracted from S:

$r_1 = [(a, a_1) \wedge (b, b_1) \wedge (c, c_1) \rightarrow (d, d_{[1,1]})]$,
$r_2 = [(e, e_2) \wedge (b, b_2) \wedge (c, c_2) \rightarrow (d, d_{[3,1]})]$.

From the rules r_1, r_2, the following e-action rule is constructed:

$r = [(a, a_1) \wedge (e, e_2) \wedge (c, c_1 \rightarrow c_2) \wedge (b, b_1 \rightarrow b_2)](x) \Rightarrow$
$(d, d_{[1,1]} \rightarrow d_{[3,1]})(x)$.

Rule r is supported by object x_4. Now, assume that the cost of reclassification $(c, c_1 \rightarrow c_2)$ is too high and this is the only fact which makes r not interesting

Table 2. Decision System S

X	a	b	c	e	d
x_1	a_2	b_1	c_1	e_1	$d_{[1,2]}$
x_2	a_2	b_1	c_1	e_2	$d_{[1,2]}$
x_3	a_1	b_1	c_1	e_1	$d_{[1,1]}$
x_4	a_1	b_1	c_1	e_2	$d_{[1,1]}$
x_5	a_1	b_2	c_2	e_2	$d_{[3,1]}$
x_6	a_2	b_2	c_1	e_2	$d_{[3,2]}$
x_7	a_1	b_2	c_1	e_2	$d_{[3,2]}$
x_8	a_1	b_1	c_2	e_2	$d_{[2,1]}$
x_9	a_1	b_2	c_2	e_1	$d_{[2,1]}$

for the user. In this case, we generalize $d_{[3,1]}$ to d_3. A new classification rule $r_3 = [[(b, b_2) \wedge (e, e_2)] \rightarrow (d, d_3)]$ can be extracted from S. It is supported by objects $\{x_5, x_6, x_7\}$. The classification rule r_2 was supported only by x_5. From r_1, r_3, a new e-action rule $r = [(a, a_1) \wedge (e, e_2) \wedge (b, b_1 \rightarrow b_2)](x) \Rightarrow (d, d_{[1,1]} \rightarrow d_3)(x)$ can be constructed. Since it does not refer to the attribute c and no new attributes are involved, the new e-action rule can be classified as interesting for the user. It is supported by object x_4 and its confidence is 100%. We can easily check that, in this particular example, its specification $r = [(a, a_1) \wedge (e, e_2) \wedge (b, b_1 \rightarrow b_2)](x) \Rightarrow [(d, d_{[1,1]} \rightarrow d_{[3,2]})](x)$ has the same support and confidence as the previous e-action rule and the same is classified as interesting for the user.

Now, let us assume that $r = [[(b_1, v_1 \longrightarrow w_1) \wedge (b_2, v_2 \longrightarrow w_2) \wedge ... \wedge (b_p, v_p \longrightarrow w_p)] \Longrightarrow (d, z_1 \longrightarrow z_2)]$ is an action rule which cost is above some user specified threshold value. Rule r is produced from two classification rules r_1, r_2, where:

$$r_1 = [(b_1, v_1) \wedge (b_2, v_2) \wedge ... \wedge (b_p, v_p)] \Longrightarrow (d, z_1),$$
$$r_2 = [(b_1, w_1) \wedge (b_2, w_2) \wedge ... \wedge (b_p, w_p)] \Longrightarrow (d, z_2).$$

We also assume that attribute d is hierarchical and by $h(z_2)$ we denote its value which is a parent of z_2 in the tree representing the domain of d.

Now, we construct a new classification rule $G_d(r_2)$ by generalizing the decision value z_2 in r_2 to $h(z_2)$. In the next step, we check if by dropping any of the terms (b_i, w_i) listed in $L(G_d(r_2))$ we get a new rule $r_2^{'}$ which has the confidence above some user defined threshold value. If this is the case, then we drop that term in r_2 and produce a new action rule from r_1, $r_2^{'}$ and check its cost. If the cost is still too high we continue the process. If the cost is below the threshold value we stop the process.

In general, e-action rules show what changes within some values of flexible attributes are needed for a given set of objects to re-classify them from their current class d_1 into a new decision class d_2. If a discovered e-action rule has too high cost, we can try to replace class d_2 by its generalization. If attribute d is hierarchical and the notion of a distance between its values is given, then d_2 after its generalization can be specialized to the value d_3 which is the closest to d_2. Also, generalizations usually increase the support of rules involved.

5 Conclusion

For mining interesting e-action rules, we assume that user provides three threshold values: maximum cost λ_1 , minimum support λ_2, and minimum confidence λ_3. They are called interesting if their cost is lower than λ_1, support is higher than λ_2, and confidence is also higher than λ_3. Discovered e-action rules which satisfy the threshold requirement for confidence and support usually have too high cost. The strategy proposed in [22] shows how to decrease the cost of e-action rules by concatenating them with rules which are cheaper. But, the concatenation of two e-action rules has support usually lower than the support of the rules involved. So, we can easily fall down below the threshold λ_2. If this strategy does not work, then the cooperative process proposed in this paper may still produce interesting e-action rules which are satisfactory for a user.

References

1. Adomavicius, G., Tuzhilin, A. (1997) Discovery of actionable patterns in databases: the action hierarchy approach, in *Proceedings of KDD97 Conference*, Newport Beach, CA, AAAI Press.
2. Chmielewski M. R., Grzymala-Busse J. W., Peterson N. W., Than S., (1993), The Rule Induction System LERS - a version for personal computers in *Foundations of Computing and Decision Sciences*, Vol. 18, No. 3-4, Institute of Computing Science, Technical University of Poznan, Poland, 181-212
3. Chu, W., Yang, H., Chiang, K., Minock, M., Chow, G., Larson, C. (1996) Cobase: A scalable and extensible cooperative information system, in *Journal of Intelligent Information Systems*, Vol. 6, No. 2/3, 223-259
4. Fensel, D., (1998), *Ontologies: a silver bullet for knowledge management and electronic commerce*, Springer-Verlag
5. Gaasterland, T. (1997) Cooperative answering through controlled query relaxation, in *IEEE Expert*, Vol. 12, No. 5, 48-59
6. Godfrey, P. (1993) Minimization in cooperative response to failing database queries, in *International Journal of Cooperative Information Systems*, Vol. 6, No. 2, 95-149
7. Greco S, Matarazzo B, Pappalardo N, Slowinski R (2005) Measuring expected effects of interventions based on decision rules, Special Issue on Knowledge Discovery, (Ed. Z.W. Raś), *Journal of Experimental and Theoretical Artificial Intelligence*, Taylor and Francis, Vol. 17, No. 1-2, 103-118
8. Liu, B., Hsu, W., Chen, S. (1997) Using general impressions to analyze discovered classification rules, in *Proceedings of KDD97 Conference*, Newport Beach, CA, AAAI Press
9. Pawlak Z., (1985), *Rough Ssets and decision tables*, in Lecture Notesin Computer Science 208, Springer-Verlag, 186-196.

10. Pawlak, Z., (1991), *Rough Sets: Theoretical aspects of reasoning about data*, Kluwer Academic Publisher.
11. Raś, Z., Dardzińska, A., (2002) Handling semantic inconsistencies in query answering based on distributed knowledge mining, in *Foundations of Intelligent Systems*, Proceedings of ISMIS'02 Symposium, LNCS/LNAI, No. 2366, Springer-Verlag, 66-74
12. Raś, Z., Wieczorkowska, A., (2000), Action Rules: how to increase profit of a company, in *Principles of Data Mining and Knowledge Discovery*, (Eds. D.A. Zighed, J. Komorowski, J. Zytkow), Proceedings of PKDD'00, Lyon, France, LNCS/LNAI, No. 1910, Springer-Verlag, 587-592
13. Raś, Z.W., Tzacheva, A., Tsay, L.-S., (2005) Action rules, in *Encyclopedia of Data Warehousing and Mining*, (Ed. J. Wang), Idea Group Inc., 1-5
14. Silberschatz, A., Tuzhilin, A., (1995) On subjective measures of interestingness in knowledge discovery, in *Proceedings of KDD'95 Conference*, AAAI Press.
15. Silberschatz, A., Tuzhilin, A., (1996) What makes patterns interesting in knowledge discovery systems, in *IEEE Transactions on Knowledge and Data Engineering*, Vol. 5, No. 6
16. Raś, Z., Gupta, S., (2002) Global action rules in distributed knowledge systems, in *Fundamenta Informaticae Journal*, IOS Press, Vol. 51, No. 1-2, 175-184
17. Skowron A., Grzymala-Busse J., (1991) From the Rough Set Theory to the Evidence Theory, in *ICS Research Reports*, 8/91, Warsaw University of Technology, October
18. Sowa, J.F., (2000) Ontology, Metadata and Semiotics, in *Conceptual Structures: Logical, Linguistic, and Computational Issues*, B. Ganter, G.W. Mineau (Eds), LNAI 1867, Springer-Verlag, 55-81
19. Suzuki, E., Kodratoff, Y., (1998) Discovery of surprising exception rules based on intensity of implication, in *Proc. of the Second Pacific-Asia Conference on Knowledge Discovery and Data mining (PAKDD)*
20. Tsay, L.-S., Raś, Z.W., Dardzińska, A. (2005) Mining E-Action Rules", in *Mining Complex Data*, Proceedings of 2005 IEEE ICDM Workshop in Houston, Texas, Published by Math. Dept., Saint Mary's Univ., Nova Scotia, Canada, 85-90
21. Tsay, L.-S., Raś, Z.W., (2005) Action rules discovery: System DEAR2, method and experiments, in *Special Issue on Knowledge Discovery*, Journal of Experimental and Theoretical Artificial Intelligence, Taylor and Francis, Vol. 17, No. 1-2, 119-128
22. Tzacheva, A., Raś, Z.W., (2005) Action rules mining, in *Special Issue on Knowledge Discovery*, International Journal of Intelligent Systems, Wiley, Vol. 20, No. 7, 719-736
23. Zbidi, N., Faiz, S., Limam, M.,(2006) On mining summaries by objective measures of interestingness, in Machine Learning, Springer, Vol. 62, No. 3, 175-198

Multi-module Image Classification System*

Wonil Kim[1], Sangyoon Oh[2,**], Sanggil Kang[3], and Dongkyun Kim[1]

[1] College of Electronics and Information Engineering at Sejong University, Seoul, Korea
wikim@sejong.ac.kr, kdk0909@paran.com
[2] Computer Science Department at Indiana University, Bloomington, IN, U.S.A.
ohsangy@cs.indiana.edu
[3] Department of Computer Science, The University of Suwon, Gyeonggi-do, Korea
sgkang@suwon.ac.kr

Abstract. In this paper, we propose an image classification system employing multiple modules. The proposed system hierarchically categorizes given sports images into one of the predefined sports classes, eight in this experiment. The image first categorized into one of the two classes in the global module. The corresponding local module is selected accordingly, and then used in the local classification step. By employing multiple modules, the system can specialize each local module properly for the given class feature. The simulation results show that the proposed system successfully classifies images with the correct rate of over 70%.

1 Introduction

The fast developing digital multimedia technology enables us to access much more information through the Internet and TV than any time before. The information is easily accessible, but it brings another side: how we store and manage these rich digital videos and images so that we can collect the proper information whenever and wherever we want. Because of recent hundreds of TV sports news programs broadcasted from all over the world, TV viewers need to choose the most interesting news and watch its highlight channel. Also, in order to manage a digital library for sports videos and images, we need an automatic image classification system.

The main purpose of this paper this paper is applying MPEG-7 to sports images for feature extraction and classification system. By analyzing MPEG-7 descriptors, we create a prototype system that can be used for sports image classification techniques under visual environments, and introduce an effective methodology of image classification via experiments. Our approach we present in this paper employs multi-module neural networks for the sports image classification system. The input value for the neural network is one of the values of visual features extracted by MPEG-7 descriptors.

In the next section, we discuss several related methods of the image classification including neural network and feature extraction using MPEG-7 descriptors. Then, we propose a Multi-Module Image Classification System in Section 3 and then discuss some simulation environments and results in Section 4. We conclude in Section 5.

* This paper is supported by Seoul R&BD Program.
** Author for correspondence : +1-812-856-0751.

H.L. Larsen et al. (Eds.): FQAS 2006, LNAI 4027, pp. 498 – 506, 2006.

2 Related Works

2.1 Multi-module Approach

Given a complicated input-output mapping problem, it is hard to design a single network structure and solve the problem with this architecture. It usually takes a long time to train a monolithic network and may not produce a good generalization result. Since the mapping may be realized by a local method which captures the underlying local structure [1], there has been considerable research [2, 3, 4, 5, and 6] designed to take advantage of a modular network architecture. In this paradigm, each module is assigned to a specific (local) area and focuses only on its special area. Learning is more efficient when a neural network is organized in this way.

A neural network is said to be modular if the computation performed by the network can be decomposed into two or more modules that operate on distinct inputs without communicating with each other [7]. The outputs of the module are mediated by an integrating unit that may not feed information back to the modules. In particular, the integrating unit decides how the outputs of the modules should be combined to form the final output of the system, and decides which modules should learn which training patterns. Modular networks utilize the principle of divide and conquer, which permits us to solve a complex computational task by dividing it into simpler subtasks and then combining their individual solutions [8].

The use of a local method offers the advantage of fast learning and therefore requires relatively few training iterations to learn the task. Alternatively, an approximation may be realized using a global method that captures the underlying global structure of mapping. The use of global methods offers the potential advantages of smaller storage requirement and better generalization performance. The use of a modular approach may also be justified on neurobiological grounds. Modularity appears to be an important principle in the architecture of vertebrate nervous systems, and there is much that can be gained from the study of learning in modular networks in different parts of the nervous system.

2.2 Image Classification

Image classification is the core process of digital image analysis. It is used in many areas like remote sensing and image retrieval. Remote sensing is the acquisition of meaningful information from an object by a recording device that is not in physical or intimate contact with the object. For example, image classification is applied to a data interpretation process of remotely acquired digital image by a Geographic Information System (GIS).

The image retrieval also uses image classification. A user requests an image by query and it returns an image (or a set of ordered images) from its image database by matching features, like color histogram and textual measures, of a query image with those of the database images. Image classification is also used to create image databases and adding images to it for the image retrieval system. The system extracts semantic description from images and putting them into semantically meaningful categories. We focus our related work survey on this kind of systems.

For content-based image retrieval systems, one of the classic classification problems is city images vs. landscapes. Gorkani and Picard [9] separate urban images and rural images using a multiscale steerable pyramid to find dominant orientations in four by four subblocks of image. They classify the image as a city scene if enough subblocks have vertical orientation tendency.

Vailaya et al. [10] also use city vs. landscape images to show how the high level classification problem (urban images vs. rural images and indoor vs. outdoor images) can be solved from low-level features geared toward the particular classes. They have developed a procedure to measure qualitatively the saliency of a low-level visual feature towards a classification problem based on the plot of the intra-class and inter-class distance distributions. They determine that the edge direction-based features have the most discriminative power for the classification problem.

Indoor-outdoor problem studied by Szummer and Picard is a variant scene classification problem. Their paper [11] shows the performance improvement by computing features on subblocks, classifying these subblocks, and combining results in stacks. Features in the study include histograms in the Ohta color space [1], multiresolution, simultaneous autoregressive model parameters, and coefficients of a shift-invariant DCT. For combining the results of subblocks, they compare the classification performance of the usage of a simple classifier, k-nearest neighbors, and that of other sophisticated classifiers, like neural networks and mixture of expert classifiers. In their test set results, the simple nearest neighbor classifier performs better.

Texture like a texture orientation used in Ref [9] is one of popular low-level features of images used for pattern retrieval. The paper presents a proposal that uses the Gabor wavelet features for texture analysis and provides a comprehensive experimental evaluation. Manjunath and Ma [13] indicate the analysis using Gabor wavelet features are more accurate in pattern retrieval than analyses using three other multiscale texture features: pyramid-structured wavelet transform (PWT), tree-structured wavelet transform (TWT), and multi-resolution simultaneous autoregressive model (MR-SAR) features by comparing them.

Another popular feature used to retrieve images from digital image libraries or multimedia databases is color histograms. It is the efficient and insensitive method, but course characteristics as well. So images, which have totally different appearances can have similar histograms. Pass and Zabih [14] propose a *Histogram refinement* technique for comparing images using additional constraints. The technique includes of splitting the pixels in a given bucket into several classes, based upon local property. The pixels in the same class can be compared with others in the same bucket.

3 The Proposed Two-Level Multi-module Image Classification System

In general, the accuracy of the sports image classification depends on the number of sports classes when a single neural network classifier (NNC) is used. As the number of classes increases, there is high possible that the accuracy of the classification decreases. Especially, it happens to have seriously bad performance for a few classes due to he black-box style learning of the neural network. To improve the accuracy of those classes, we propose the two-level multi-module image classification system as shown in Fig. 1. In the figure, the neural network classifier at level 1 identifies one of groups of sports image classes using the input features extracted from the MPEG-7

Color Layout descriptor. The input features are parsed to numerical values, which are suitable for neural network implementation and normalized to the 0-1 range. By normalizing the input features, it can avoid that input features with big number scale dominant the output of the NNC over input features with small number scale.

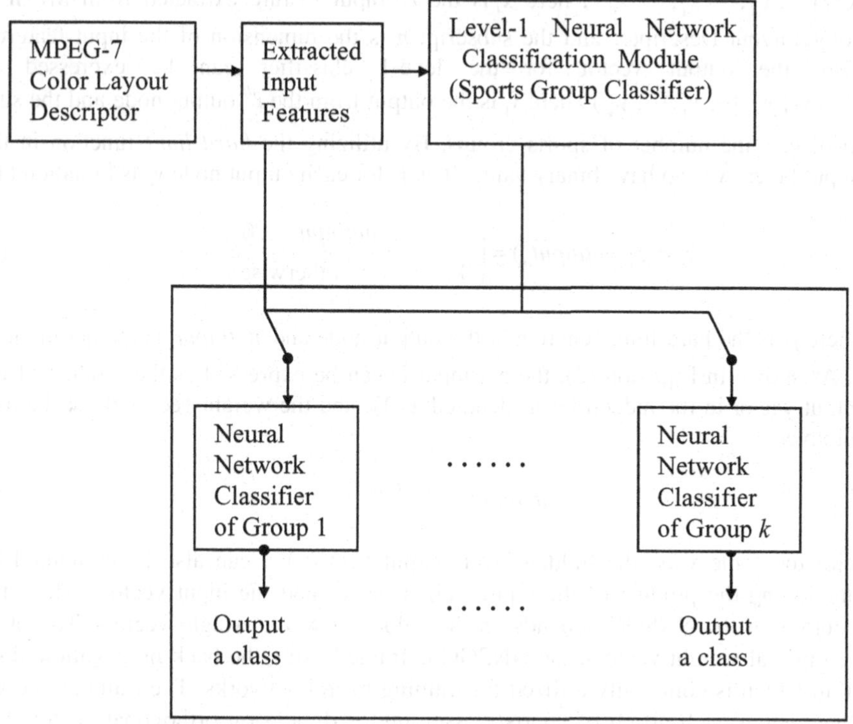

Fig. 1. Two-level multi-module sports image classification system

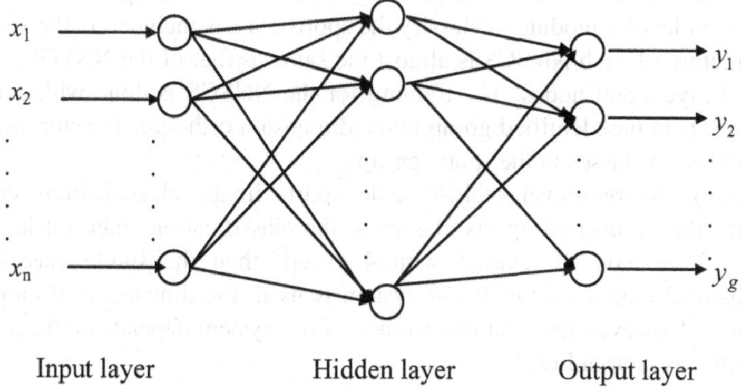

Fig. 2. An example of three layered NNSGC

Using the normalized input features and the groups of sports classes, we can model a neural network sports group classifier (NNSGC). Fig. 2 shows an example of the NNSGC with three layers, i.e., one input layer, one hidden layer, and one output layer.

Let us denote the input feature vector obtained from the MPEG-7 descriptor as $X=(x_1, x_2, \cdots, x_i, \cdots, x_n)$, here x_i is the ith input feature extracted from MPGE-7 Color Layout Descriptor and the subscript n is the dimension of the input features. Also, the output vector for the leve-1 classifier can be expressed as $Y=(y_1, y_2, \cdots, y_i, \cdots, y_g)$, here y_i is the output from the ith output node and the subscript g is the number of sports groups. By utilizing the *hard limit* function in the output layer, we can have binary value, 0 or 1, for each output node y_i as Equation (1).

$$y_i = f_o(netinput_o) = \begin{pmatrix} 1, & netinput_o \geq 0 \\ 0, & \text{otherwise} \end{pmatrix} \tag{1}$$

where f_o is the hard limit function at the output node and $netinput_o$ is the net input of f_o. As shown in Equation (2), the net input is can be expressed as the product of the output vector in the hidden layer, denoted as Y_h, and the weight vector W_o at the output layer.

$$netinput_o = W_o^{\,T} Y_h \tag{2}$$

With the same way, the hidden layer output vector, Y_h, can also be computed by functioning the product of the input weight vector and the input vector. Thus, the accuracy of the NNSGC depends on the values of whole weight vectors. To obtain the optimal weight vectors, the NNSGC is trained using the back-propagation algorithm which is commonly utilized for training neural networks. The training is done after coding each group of sports classes into g dimension orthogonal vector. For example, if we have two groups of sports classes then each group is coded to (1, 0) or (0, 1).

If the output of NNSGC is group j then the same input features as used in the NNSGC are fed into the corresponding neural network sports class classifier (NNSCS) j at level-2 module to classify the sports classes included in the sports group j. The structure of each NNSCS is almost the same as that of the NNSGC, except the number of layers and nodes. The training for the NNSCS is done with coding each class of sports in the identified group into c dimension orthogonal vector, here c is the number of sports classes in the sports group j.

By using the two-level multi-module sports image classification system, we can reduce the number of sports classes at the classification stage (at level-2). For example, if we have 16 classes with 4 groups then the single classifier needs 16-dimensional output vector. If our system is used, the dimension of output vector reduces to 4. However, the overall accuracy of our system depends on the accuracy of the NNSGC, as seen in Fig. 1.

4 Experiment

4.1 Experimental Environment

We implemented the two-level multi-module sports image classification system using 8 sports image data such as Taekwondo, Field & Track, Ice Hocky, Horse Riding, Skiing, Swimming, Golf, and Tennis. As explained in the previous section, we extracted 12 input features from query images using four MPEG-7 descriptors of Color Layout. The images were classified into two groups according to the characteristics of input features; one group includes Taekwondo, Field & Track, Ice Hocky, Horse Riding and the other group is the rest of classes. Also, 800 samples of were collected, 100 samples per class. For training the NNSGC at level-1 and the NNSCS at level-2, 80 samples per class are used, while 20 samples per class for test. The training and testing images are exclusive. We structured the three-layered NNC for each module. The hyperbolic tangent sigmoid function and hard limit function was used in the hidden layer and in the output layer, respectively. For training the NNC, we chose the back-propagation algorithm because of its training ability. In order to optimal weight vectors, large number of iterations (500,000 in this experiment) is selected.

4.2 Experimental Results

In this section, we compared the performances of the two-level multi-module sports image classification system and the single classification system for test samples. The tables from 1 to 3 show the performance of each module in our system.

Table 1 shows the performance of the level-1 module for identifying sports group. From the table, the accuracy of identifying each group is not perfect but acceptable, 90.79 % for the group 1 and 89.33 % for the group 2.

Table 2 and 3 show the accuracies of the first and the second module at level 2, respectively. From Table 2 and 3, the thing we should not overlook is that the values in the tables are the accuracies with assumption of the perfect identification at level 1. The overall accuracies can be obtained by the product of the accuracy of the identification of each group in Table 1 and the accuracies of the classes included in the group as seen in Table 2 and 3.

Table 1. The accuracies of the level-1 module for identifying sports group (%)

	Sports Group1(Taekwondo, Field & Track, Ice Hockey, Horse Riding)	Sports Group2 (Skiing, Swimming, Golf, Tennis)
Sports Group1 (Taekwondo, Field & Track, Ice Hockey, Horse Riding)	**90.79**	9.21
Sports Group2 (Skiing, Swimming, Golf, Tennis)	10.67	**89.33**

Table 2. The accuracies of the first level-2 module for classifying the classes in group 1 (%)

	Taekwondo	Field & Track	Ice Hockey	Horse Riding
Taekwondo	**88.89**	0.00	5.56	5.56
Field & Track	0.00	**72.22**	11.11	16.67
Ice Hockey	5.56	5.56	**77.78**	11.11
Horse Riding	0.00	0.00	0.00	**100.00**

Table 3. The accuracies of the second level-2 module for classifying the classes in group 2 (%)

	Skiing	Swimming	Golf	Tennis
Skiing	**90.91**	0.00	0.00	9.09
Swimming	4.55	**81.82**	4.55	9.09
Golf	4.55	4.55	**86.36**	4.55
Tennis	9.52	4.76	14.29	**71.43**

Table 4 shows the comparison between the overall accuracies of our system and those of the single classification system. From the table, it is shown that our system is effective for improving the performance of a couple of classes with bad performance when the single classification system is used. For example, the accuracies of Swimming and Tennis are 66.67% and 44.44 %, respectively when the single classification system is used. By utilizing our system, their accuracies are improved to 73.09% and

Table 4. The comparison of overall accuracies of our system and single classification system (%)

<table>
<tr><th colspan="2"></th><th>Taek-wondo</th><th>Field & Track</th><th>Ice Hockey</th><th>Horse Riding</th><th>Skiing</th><th>Swim-ming</th><th>Golf</th><th>Tennis</th></tr>
<tr><td rowspan="2">Taek-wondo</td><td>S</td><td>77.78</td><td>11.11</td><td>5.56</td><td>0.00</td><td>0.00</td><td>0.00</td><td>0.00</td><td>5.56</td></tr>
<tr><td>M</td><td>80.69</td><td>0.00</td><td>5.05</td><td>5.05</td><td colspan="4">9.21</td></tr>
<tr><td rowspan="2">Field & Track</td><td>S</td><td>0.00</td><td>66.67</td><td>5.56</td><td>16.67</td><td>0.00</td><td>0.00</td><td>0.00</td><td>11.11</td></tr>
<tr><td>M</td><td>0.00</td><td>65.57</td><td>10.09</td><td>15.13</td><td colspan="4">9.21</td></tr>
<tr><td rowspan="2">Ice Hockey</td><td>S</td><td>0.00</td><td>11.11</td><td>72.22</td><td>0.00</td><td>5.56</td><td>5.56</td><td>0.00</td><td>5.56</td></tr>
<tr><td>M</td><td>5.05</td><td>5.05</td><td>70.61</td><td>10.08</td><td colspan="4">9.21</td></tr>
<tr><td rowspan="2">Horse Riding</td><td>S</td><td>0.00</td><td>0.00</td><td>5.56</td><td>83.33</td><td>0.00</td><td>11.11</td><td>0.00</td><td>0.00</td></tr>
<tr><td>M</td><td>0.00</td><td>0.00</td><td>0.00</td><td>90.79</td><td colspan="4">9.21</td></tr>
<tr><td rowspan="2">Skiing</td><td>S</td><td>0.00</td><td>0.00</td><td>5.56</td><td>5.56</td><td>83.33</td><td>5.56</td><td>0.00</td><td>5.56</td></tr>
<tr><td>M</td><td colspan="4">10.67</td><td>81.21</td><td>0.00</td><td>0.00</td><td>8.12</td></tr>
<tr><td rowspan="2">Swim-ming</td><td>S</td><td>5.56</td><td>5.56</td><td>5.56</td><td>0.00</td><td>11.11</td><td>66.67</td><td>0.00</td><td>0.00</td></tr>
<tr><td>M</td><td colspan="4">10.67</td><td>4.06</td><td>73.09</td><td>4.06</td><td>8.12</td></tr>
<tr><td rowspan="2">Golf</td><td>S</td><td>16.67</td><td>5.56</td><td>0.00</td><td>5.56</td><td>0.00</td><td>0.00</td><td>72.22</td><td>0.00</td></tr>
<tr><td>M</td><td colspan="4">10.67</td><td>4.06</td><td>4.06</td><td>77.15</td><td>4.06</td></tr>
<tr><td rowspan="2">Tennis</td><td>S</td><td>11.11</td><td>11.11</td><td>0.00</td><td>5.56</td><td>16.67</td><td>11.11</td><td>0.00</td><td>44.44</td></tr>
<tr><td>M</td><td colspan="4">10.67</td><td>8.50</td><td>4.25</td><td>12.77</td><td>63.81</td></tr>
</table>

63.8%, respectively. However, it is shown that there is no big difference on the performances for the classes with acceptable performance for the single classification system. From the result, it can be said that our system can be effective for improving the classification performance of the sports classes with bad performance in the single classification system.

5 Conclusion

This paper proposed the two-level multi-module image classification system for classifying sports images using the input features extracted from the MPEG-7 Color Layout descriptor. As seen in the experimental section, our system can outperform the single classification system for the sports classes with bad performance in the single classification system. In addition, our system does not degrade the performance of the other classes with the acceptable performance in the single classification system. In the future work, different MPEG-7 descriptors will be applied for the classification task. Also, the different combinations of modules and levels are simulated for performance improvement.

References

1. R.A. Jacobs, M.I. Jordan, and A.G. Barto: Task decomposition through competition in a modular connectionist architecture: The what and where vision task, Cognitive Science, 15:219--250, 1991.
2. A. Waibel, H. Sawai, and K. Shikano: Modulraity and scaling in large phonemic neural networks. IEEE Transaction on Acoustics, Speech and Signal Processing, 37:1888-1897, 1989
3. D.L. Reilly, C. Scofield, C. Elbaum, and L.N. Copper: Learning system architectures composed of multiple learning modules. In IEEE Int'l Conf. Neural Networks, p.p. 495-503, 1989
4. R.A. Jacobs and M.I. Jordan: Hierarchical mixtures of experts and the EM algorithm. Neural Computation, 6:181-214, 1994
5. F.J. Smieja: Multiple network systems Minos modules: Task division and module discrimination, Proc. Of the 8th AISB conference on Artificial Intelligence, Leeds, April 1991
6. L.Y. Pratt and C. A. Kamm: Improving phoneme classification neural network through problem decomposition. In IEEE Int'l Joint Conf. Neural Networks, p.p. 821-826, 1991
7. D.N. Osherson, S. Weinstein, and M. Stoli: Modular learning, Computational Neuroscience, p.p. 369-377, 1990
8. S. Haykins, Neural Networks: A comprehensive Foundation. IEEE Press, Macmillan, NY, 1994
9. M. Gorkani and R. W. Picard, "Textual orientation for sorting photos at a glance," In Proceedings of International Conference on Pattern recognition, pp. 459-464, Jerusalem, Israel, October 1994
10. A. Vailaya, A. Jain, and H. J. Zhang, "On image classification: city images vs. landscapes," In Proceedings of IEEE Workshop on Content – Based Access of Image and Video Libraries, December 1998

11. M. Szummer and R. W. Picard, "Indoor-outdoor image classification," In Proceedings of IEEE International Workshop on Content – Based Access of Image and Video Libraries, Bombay India, December 1998
12. Y-I Ohta, T. Kanade, and T. Sakai, "Color information for region segmentation," Computer Graphics and Image Processing, vol. 13, No. 3, pp. 222-241, July 1980.
13. B. S. Manjunath and W. Y. Ma, "Texture features for browsing and retrieval of image data," IEEE Transactions on Pattern Analysis and Machine Intelligence," vol. 18, no. 8, August 1996.
14. G. pass and R. Zabih, "Histogram refinement for content-based image retrieval," In Proceedings of the 3rd IEEE Workshop on Applications of Computer Vision, Sarasota, Florida, USA, December 1996.

UNL as a Text Content Representation Language for Information Extraction*

Jesús Cardeñosa, Carolina Gallardo, and Luis Iraola

Dpto. Inteligencia Artificial Universidad Politécnica de Madrid
{carde, carolina, luis}@opera.dia.fi.upm.es

Abstract. This paper describes a new approach for describing contents through the use of interlinguas in order to facilitate the extraction of specific pieces of information. The authors highlight the different dimensions of a document and how these dimensions define the capacities of their respective contents to be found in the scalable process of finding information. A specific interlingua, UNL, will be described. This approach is illustrated both with rich examples of the followed model and with actual applications, that includes the description of some running projects based on the interlingual representation of contents.

Keywords: Textual contents representation, Interlinguas, UNL.

1 Textual Contents Representation

Information extraction and retrieval greatly benefits from intelligent text content representations. Most of the techniques employed for representing the knowledge contained in documents rely on some kind of linguistic analysis: the bottom line is that a content representation can be more easily achieved if we start from a representation of the linguistic meaning.

The overabundance of information accessible electronically and the standards currently employed for publishing it in the web force us to consider the semantic content as one of the many **dimensions** a document has, so a more holistic view of documents can be thought of if we consider as dimensions the distinctive sets of features that disjointly characterize a document. A plain text representation (one with no format or mark-up) may be viewed as not having any of these features. Layout, formatting and hyper-linking constitute a first dimension of the document. This first dimension may provide cues about specific information pieces contained in a document and can facilitate searching and extraction tasks. Thus, **format,** as it is typically encoded using HTML, can be considered as a first document dimension.

The recent emergence of the semantic web is the result of the application of new mark-up standards that are progressively enriching the document with what can be considered as a new, second dimension of a document: its **structure**. Specific information pieces can be extracted provided that they have been previously marked with

* This paper has been sponsored by the Spanish Research Council through the project PATRILEX-HUM2005-0726.

H.L. Larsen et al. (Eds.): FQAS 2006, LNAI 4027, pp. 507 – 518, 2006.

some meaningful tags. The most commonly used mark-up standard is XML. When employed in text processing applications, it allows any degree of analysis and consequently the information so tagged can be easily extracted by any XML-aware application.

Undoubtedly, XML has revolutionized the way we process textual contents, providing us with powerful and flexible mark-up languages for expressing document structure. However, finding specific information pieces requires a previous analysis of the document that contains it, and for that human intervention is still required. Question answering is in this respect quite different from information retrieval; a deeper analysis of the document is needed and this requires a new, extra dimension present in a document (the third one): its semantic **content**. This new dimension demands a powerful formalism for content representation and also suitable for deduction and inference, both required in question answering tasks. The general solution to this problem, currently unsolved, could take as its basis, in a credible and reliable way, the idea of content representation by means of an interlingua accompanied by a knowledge base that could support the tasks of finding and inferring information. This paper will describe an interlingua able to support these representational and deductive requisites.

2 Interlinguas as Textual Content Representation

The issue of representing (and extracting) the knowledge contained in texts written in a natural language dates back to pioneering works in knowledge representation in the AI field [1], [2], which will be referred to as "conceptual representations". A Conceptual Representation can be defined as a data-structure that represents the meaning of natural language expressions in an unequivocal way. Early conceptual representations can be characterized as very precise, domain dependent formalisms oriented towards inference but quite restricted in their expressivity. Thus Artificial Intelligence sought other ways for representing linguistically expressed knowledge while overcoming the narrowness of earlier conceptual representations, which resulted in the Interlinguas.

Interlinguas are mainly defined by the following characteristics:

- They deal with the representation of meaning, the most abstract and the deepest level of linguistic analysis. The interlingual approach attempts to find a meaning representation common to many (ideally to all) natural languages.
- An interlingua is another language and its vocabulary (usually concepts or semantic primitives), syntax (thematic and functional relations, formalism) and semantics (a subjacent ontology or knowledge base) need prior specification.

These facts support the idea of using an interlingua for representing the knowledge expressed in natural language, and thus becoming a candidate for the third semantic dimension of the representation of textual contents.

However, there are some obstacles in the design and further use of an interlingua, so that it has been proved almost unfeasible to find a suitable way to represent word meanings that is at the same time a) able to accommodate a wide variety of natural languages, b) easy to grasp and use, c) precise and unambiguous and d) expressive enough to capture the subtleties of word meanings expressed in natural languages.

These obstacles have influenced the evolution of interlinguas. Traditionally, interlinguas have been associated to the field of Machine Translation. Classical interlinguas, like ATLAS [3] or PIVOT [4] were designed as general domain main representational systems for a large number of natural languages. It could be said that general purpose interlingua-based MT systems failed, or at least did not meet its expectations.

Interlingua-based MT evolved into the so-called Knowledge Based Machine Translation. The KANT interlingua [5] and the Text Meaning Representations of the Mikrokosmos system [6] are included under this label. These interlinguas highlight the knowledge representation dimension of the interlingua as well as the linguistic aspects, adopting an ontological and frame-based approach for the definition of the concepts. The burden of such an intense and detailed knowledge-based conceptual modeling can only be afforded in specific domains and for a limited number of language pairs.

In spite of the difficulty of the design of "universal" interlinguas and the expensive creation of proper interlingual lexical resources, interlinguas can be useful and theoretical attractive. One of the pillars of most interlinguas (thematic or semantic role labeling) is considered to be of great utility in the areas of information retrieval and extraction, as shown in [7], [8]. This approach leaves aside the problem of the definition of the semantics and the vocabulary of the interlingua.

There also exist current enterprises which attempts to define complete interlinguas for the support of multilinguality, like the IAMTC interlingua [9] or UNL [10]. The IAMTC interlingua resorts to a progressive definition of the interlingua as long as it is needed. However IAMTC presents a major drawback: it uses a subjacent ontology (OMEGA v3), which makes the expansion of the interlingua dependent on the expansion of a general-domain ontology.

On the other hand, UNL –while provided of an autonomous vocabulary, syntax and semantics- does not required an subjacent ontology (and in the ten years of development, we do not feel it is needed) and its lexical resources are not as time-consuming as creating an ontology. UNL is an interlingua that, on the one hand, produces a representation of the document's content that removes away the details of the source language (so qualifying as a language independent representation) while on the other keeps enough linguistic information for making feasible text generation in a multilingual environment. This new approach finds equilibrium between a deep conceptual representation of meaning and the inclusion of some linguistic (language dependent) features that increase the expressivity of the interlingua. UNL will be presented in the next section.

3 The Universal Networking Language (UNL)

During the nineties, the University of the United Nations developed the Universal Networking Language (UNL), a language for the representation of contents in a language independent way, with the purpose of overcoming the linguistic barrier in Internet. It was only after years of intensive research and great efforts when the set of concepts and relations allowing the representation of any text written in any natural language was defined. This language has been proven tractable by computer systems, since it can be automatically transformed into any natural language by means of linguistic generation processes, just following its specifications [11].

The UNL is composed of three main elements: universal words, relations and attributes. Formally, a UNL expression can be view as a semantic net, whose nodes are the Universal words, linked by arcs labelled with the UNL relations. Universal Words are modified by the so-called attributes.The specifications of the language formally define the set of relations, concepts and attributes.

3.1 Universal Words

They constitute the vocabulary of the language, i.e., they can be considered the lexical items of UNL. To be able to express any concept occurring in a natural language, the UNL proposes the use of English words modified by a series of semantic restrictions that eliminate the lexical ambiguity present in natural languages. When there is no English word suitable for expressing a particular concept, the UNL allows the use of words coming from other languages. Whatever the source, universal words usually require semantic restrictions for describing precisely the sense or meaning of the base word. In this way, UNL gets an expressive richness from the natural languages but without their ambiguity. For example, the verb "land" in English has several senses and different predicate frames. Corresponding UWs for one sense of this verb would be:

The plane landed at the Geneva airport.

land(icl>do, plt>surface, agt>thing, plc>thing)

This UW corresponds to the definition "To alight upon or strike a surface". The proposed semantic restrictions stand for:

- **icl>do:** (where *icl* stands for *included*) establishes the type of action that "lands" belongs to, that is, actions initiated by an agent.
- **plt>surface:** (where *plt* stands for *place to*) expresses an inherent part of the verb meaning, namely that the final direction of the motion expressed by "land" is onto a surface.
- **agt>thing, plc>thing:** (where *agt* stands for *agent* and *plc* stands for *place*) establish the obligatory semantic participants of the predicate "land".

Although this method is far from perfect, it shows some advantages:

1. There is a consensual and "normalized" way to define UWs and how they should be interpreted. Thus, the meaning of stand-alone UWs can be easily grasped.
2. It is devoid of the ambiguity inherent to natural language vocabularies.
3. It may constitute the pivot to connect the vocabularies of natural languages.

The complete set of UWs composes the **UNL dictionary**. The UNL dictionary is complemented with local bilingual dictionaries, connecting UWs with headword (or lemmas) from natural languages. Local dictionaries are formed by pairs of the form:

<Headword, UW>

Being Headword any word from a given natural language and UW the corresponding representation of its sense in UNL. The following is a pair linking a Spanish headword with its UW:

<aterrizar, land(icl>do, plt>surface, agt>thing, plc>thing)>

The UNL dictionary constitutes a common lexical resource to all the natural languages currently represented in the project, so that words senses of different natural languages become linked via their UWs.

3.2 Relations

The second ingredient of UNL is a set of conceptual relations. Relations form a closed set defined in the specifications of the interlingua that characterise a set of semantic notions applicable to most of the existing natural languages. For instance, the notion of initiator or cause of an event (its agent) is considered one of such notions since it is found in most natural languages.

The current specification of UNL includes 41 conceptual relations. They are best presented grouping them into conceptually related families:

- **Causal relations:** including *condition*, *purpose*, or *reason*.
- **Temporal relations:** including *instant*, *period*, *sequence*, *co-occurrence*, *initial time* or *final time*.
- **Locative relations:** including *physical place, origin, destination, virtual place, intermediate place* and *affected place.*
- **Logical relations:** these are *conjunction, disjunction, attribution, equivalence* and *name.*
- **Numeric relations:** these are *quantity, basis, proportion and range.*
- **Circumstantial relations:** *method, instrument* and *manner*.
- **Argument relations**: *agent, object, goal* and *source*.
- **Secondary argument relations:** *co-agent, co-object, co-attribution, beneficiary,* and *partner.*
- **Nominal relations:** *possession, modification, destination, origin* and *meronymy (part of).*
- **Ontological relations:** *included in,* a hypernym of a UW and *equal to*, a synomyn of a UW.

Selecting the appropriate conceptual relation plus adequate universal words allows UNL to express the propositional content of any sentence.

3.3 Attributes

Contextual information is expressed in UNL by means of *attributes labels*. These attributes include notions such as information depending on the speaker, contextual information affecting both to the participants and to the predicate of the sentence, pragmatic notions, and typographical and orthographical conventions. Attribute labels are attached to UWs and have the following syntax:

.@<name of the attribute>

The UNL code takes the form of a directed hyper-graph. *Universal Words* constitute the nodes of the graph, while arcs are labelled with *conceptual relations*. In addition to simple nodes, hyper-nodes are also allowed as origin or destination of arcs and consist on UNL graphs themselves. The graphical representation of the UNL graph corresponding to the sentence “The boy eats potatoes in the kitchen” is graphically shown in figure 1.

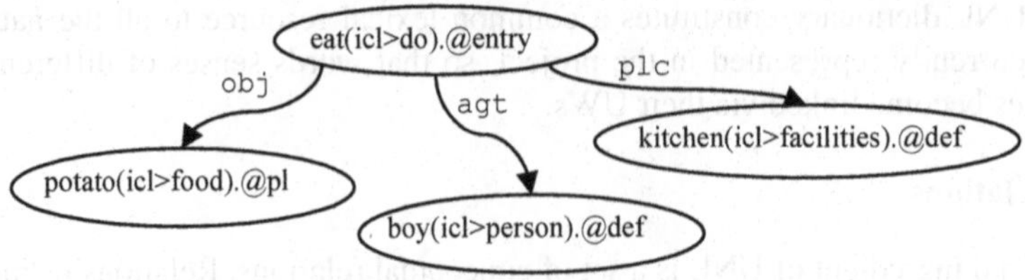

Fig. 1. Graphical Representation of UNL expression

Where @def means an entity or concept with definite and known reference; @pl means plurality and @entry designate the head of the sentence. Any UNL graph is canonically presented in textual form as a set of arcs. The textual representation of the UNL graph in figure 1 is as follows:

```
agt(eat(icl>do).@entry,boy(icl>person).@def)
plc(eat(icl>do).@entry,kitchen(icl>facilities).@def)
obj(eat(icl>do).@entry,potato(icl>food).@pl)
```

4 UNL for Text Content Representation

UNL can serve as a text content representation formalism in generic domains. When there is need for representing knowledge in a domain-independent way, researchers turn back to natural language in order to obtain the "semantic atoms" knowledge can be expressed in (such as in Wordnet [12], the Generalized Upper Model [13] or even CyC[1]). UNL follows this approach, providing an interlingual analysis of natural language semantics. UNL can be backed as a firm content representation language because of the following reasons:

1. The set of semantic relations between concepts is already standardized. Some relation groups such as the logical, temporal, spatial and causative relations have been widely employed in semantic analysis and in knowledge representation.
2. The set of attributes that modify concepts and relations is fixed and well-defined, guaranteeing a precise definition of contextual information. Thus, UNL provides mechanisms to clear-cut propositional from contextual meaning.
3. The semantic atoms (universal words) are not concepts but word senses, mainly extracted from the English lexicon for convenience reasons and organized according to hierarchical relations, like those present in Wordnet.
4. UNL syntax and semantics are formally defined.

But to really serve as a language for content representation, UNL must support deduction mechanisms. We will explore UNL deductive capabilities by examining how specific queries can be answered using UNL representations. The following text[2] contains information on Madrid's Spanish Theatre:

[1] http://www.cyc.com

[2] This fragment is an abridged translation of a general description of the building found at http://www.munimadrid.es/Principal/monograficos/TeatroEsp/teatro.htm

```
Between 1887 and 1894, the architect Mister Román Guerrero led the
refurbishment of the building housing the Spanish Theatre.
```

Its UNL graphical representation is that of figure 2. The semantic relations employed are:

- agt: agent, the initiator of an action.
- aoj: attribution, a property that is an attribute of a thing
- mod: modification, a concept that modifies another concept
- nam: name, an instance (typically expressed as a proper name) of a concept.
- obj: object, the entity primarily affected by an action.

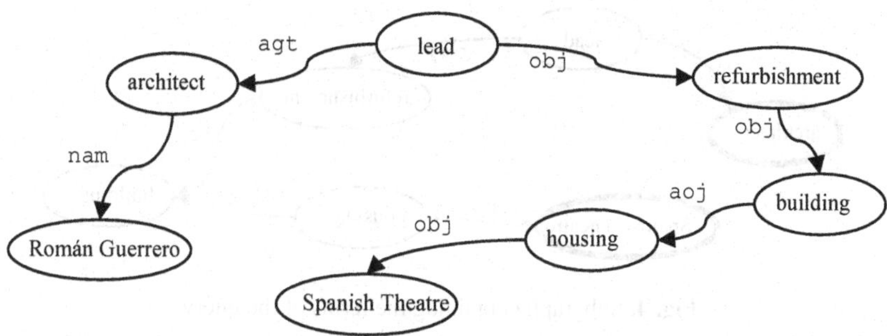

Fig. 2. Graphical representation of text

If we pose a direct query to a question answering system including this graph, the deduction process simply requires a matching procedure for semantic nets. Let's illustrate this procedure with the following query:

Who is the architect of the Spanish Theatre?

This question is converted into its UNL form by means of natural language analyzing modules. Wh- questions typically request specific pieces of information. When this query is transformed into UNL, "who" turns into the target node to be searched (that is, the unknown node), and the noun phrase "architect of the Spanish Theatre" turns into the binary relation:

mod(architect, "Spanish Theatre")

Where "mod" simply establishes a modifying relation between two concepts. As for the unknown node "who", linguistic analysis indicates that the user is asking for the name of a person (the entity described as architect in the question), and therefore the missing relation in the query is *nam,* and the complete UNL representation of the query becomes:

nam(architect, ?)
mod(architect, "Spanish Theatre")

The UNL graph for this query is shown in figure 3.

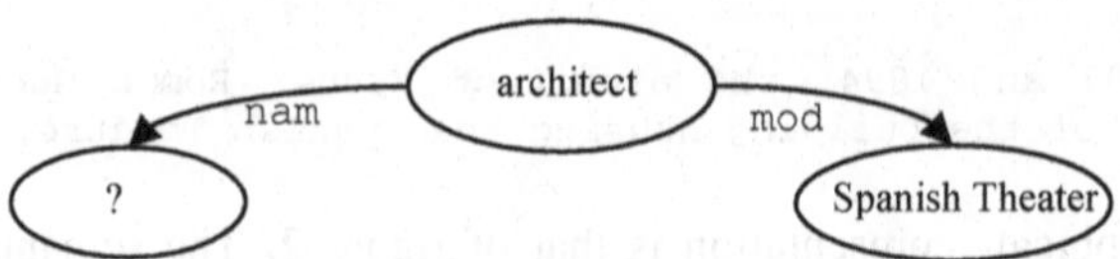

Fig. 3. Initial graph for the query

Looking at the UNL representation of figure 2, we can check that "architect" is not directly linked to "Spanish Theatre"; between these two nodes there is a sub-graph composed of the nodes "lead", "refurbishment", "building", "housing" and finally "Spanish Theater" (as shown in figure 4).

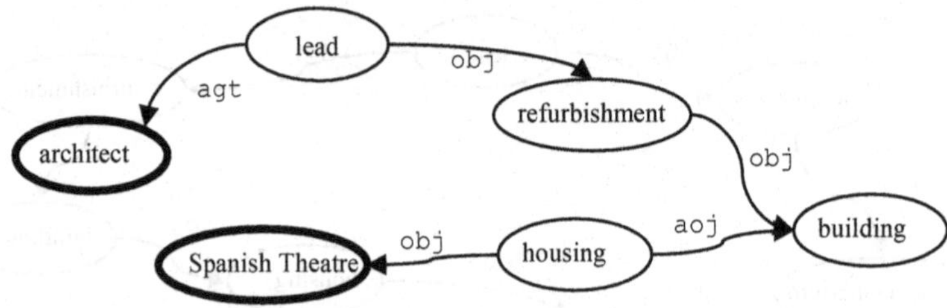

Fig. 4. Subgraph containing the terms of the query

Although there is no direct semantic connection between "architect" and "Spanish Theatre", there exists a path connecting both nodes. So, to a certain extent, it makes sense to talk about "an architect related in someway to the Spanish Theater". And the fact that there is a *nam* relation pending from the node "architect" strengthens the hypothesis that the unknown node (the target of our query) is "Román Guerrero".

Obviously, the fact that there is not a direct link between "architect", "Spanish Theatre" and "Román Guerrero" is a potential source of imprecision. Generally speaking, imprecision arises when the concepts and relations of the query can not be directly mapped to those present in a piece of information accessible to the system. In our example, the information employed for answering the query states that "Román Guerrero" was not the architect of the "Spanish Theatre", though he leaded a later refurbishment. This kind of imprecision has not either a clear or an easy solution. Complex inference mechanisms are required, based on the knowledge contained in the semantic net and also on the linguistic information extracted from the query. So far, search models combining linguistic and semantic knowledge have not been developed. One of the reasons for this insufficiency may lie in the fact that it has not been proposed a text content representation formalism which, based on an interlingua, is also suitable to be manipulated by semantic networks algorithms.

A second problem to be taken into account is uncertainty, and there is not a clear model for uncertainty resolution associated to the inferences performed in this type of representation either. Besides, there is no agreement on how to build a knowledge base from representations based on linguistic knowledge. Imprecision and uncertainty in UNL representations are currently a matter of research and experimentation and they must be regarded as a necessary counterpart of the expressive richness of the interlingua, specially when employed for text content representation in a generic domain. When used within a specific domain for representing knowledge expressed in a consistent and unambiguous way, UNL is capable of providing precise answers. However, the true potential of the interlingual approach shows when dealing with texts and queries expressed in natural language. One outstanding author on the concepts of uncertainty and imprecision, Zadeh in [14] has another definition of these terms, not completely equivalent to our definition. We present imprecision and uncertainty as fundamental and intrinsic problems of knowledge representations coming from natural language sources, whereas for Zadeh imprecision and uncertainty justifies the use of fuzzy logic based representations and inference.

Although searching on UNL graphs can yield precise answers, these also depend on the linguistic structure used when phrasing the query. Common phenomena like synonymy may obscure the result. For example, given the query:

What is the name of the architect of the edifice?

And a document fragment stating that:

John Smith, the designer of the edifice, ...

The query would not produce a satisfactory answer, given that the UW "designer" would not match the UW "architect", although our common sense tells us that the designer of an edifice probably qualifies as its architect. These kind of problems have a direct solution using UNL. Indirect inferences can be made with varying difficulty degree. If an original query does not produce any results, surrogate queries can be generated using the synonyms and hypernyms stored in the UNL knowledge base. The searching and matching mechanisms also allow for some degree of flexibility: part-of and is-a inferences can be made, close semantic relations (e.g. instrument and method, purpose and goal) can be replaced one for the other. All these strategies must of course be carefully adjusted as they implement a trade off between coverage (recall) and reliability (precision) in any information system.

5 Some Practical Applications: UNL in Practice

After presenting the building stones of the interlingua, its deductive capabilities, and its potential as contents representation, we will now turn our attention to its practical application in real scenarios: AgroExplorer and Patrilex.

5.1 AgroExplorer: A Query Answering System

AgroExplorer [15] is a language independent search engine with multilingual information access facilities that directly searches into UNL documents, developed at the Indian Institute of Technology, Bombay, in which one of the authors of this paper was directly involved in the development of the Spanish modules. Queries are transformed into UNL, so that the search engine only deals with UNL representations and it is therefore completely language independent. AgroExplorer also exploits the multilingual capabilities of UNL when rendering queries results. As long as language generators are available, answers can be generated into different natural languages.

The system is composed of a focused crawler, a search module, available enconverters[3] and language generators. The focused crawler gathers texts about agriculture from the Internet. Once a corpus on agriculture is gathered, the texts are tidied up from any HTML tag. The raw text extracted from the HTML pages is passed to the available enconverters to get the UNL representation of these texts.

When a query is posed by the user, it is directly translated into UNL (by means of enconverters, again), and is passed to the search module which performs a graph-based search on the documents according to the UNL expression of the query. The search module constitutes the nucleus of the system. This module is in charge of searching the documents that are relevant to a given query and to assign a relevance score on the retrieved documents.

The relevance of a page or document should be a combination of two rates: the global page relevance rank and the query specific page rank. However at this moment, only the query specific page rank is used. Due to the limited size of the current UNL document base, algorithms to rank web pages taking into account hyperlinks structure are not used.

The query specific page rank is used to score the relevance of the retrieved documents. There are two types of matching algorithms: complete matching (the easiest one) and partial matching. Matching is performed over an indexed version of the UNL documents. UNL documents are indexed on the edges of the UNL graphs so that an edge of a UNL graph is a tuple of the form:

$$r(UW_1, UW_2)$$

where *r* is the relation label and UW_1 and UW_2 are universal words.

For each edge present in a UNL corpus, a document identifier and the sentence number are also stored (d, s). Complete matching consists thus on finding all (d, s) pairs that contain all the tuples of the query by taking intersection of sets of (d,s) for each tuple of the query. However, complete matching poses more problems than it solves, so the system supports partial or approximate matching.

The search module also supports partial or approximate matching. In this case, the relevance of a given sentence in a document *r(s)* is mathematically as follows:

$$r(s) = \alpha \frac{n}{N} + (1-\alpha)\frac{l}{L} \tag{1}$$

Where, *n* is number of relation edges (of the query) found in the sentence. N is the total number of relation edges in the query. *l* is the number of *common links in the sentence and the query graph* and L is the total number of links between all UWs in the query; and α is an empirical constant.

The output of the Search Module is a set of UNL documents that are then generated into any of the available languages.

A complete description of this system can be found in [15] where the architecture, modules and search algorithm are fully described.

---

3 Within the UNL system, enconverters are the software modules in charge of translating natural language texts into their UNL representation.

5.2 PATRILEX and EXCOM

Patrilex[4] is a new project the authors are working on (it started on January, 2006) whose main objective is the definition of powerful search engines based on contents representation and models of inference with multilingual capabilities. The multiligualization of classical search engines, like those based on keywords, will pass through the use of an interlingual representation of concepts. In this case, contents are written in their original languages and we only use interlingual dictionaries where a concept is represented in a unique way and associated to different languages in a very precise manner. Table 1 shows how equivalent terms in different languages are linked by means of the Universal Word. This is other use of the interlingual approach.

Table 1. Linking different languages by means of the interlingual representation of concepts

Universal Word	Spanish	English	French	Italian
achieve(icl>do)	conseguir	achieve	réaliser	conseguire

In other project we have just started, EXCOM[5], we will explore the capacities of UNL to represent knowledge so that specific pieces of information can be searched for. It will be further improved with the creation of knowledge bases and methodologies to validate the inferred knowledge. EXCOM develops the approach presented in this paper.

6 Conclusions

Apart from multilingual generation applications, UNL is currently being employed as document representation formalism in tasks such as information extraction, and integration with other linguistic ontologies. UNL should not be seen either as just another interlingua neither as just another knowledge representation formalism. Its goal is to serve as an intermediate *knowledge* representation that can exploited by different knowledge intensive tasks.

UNL is a formalism worth to be considered particularly in those scenarios where:

1. Multilingual acquisition and dissemination of textual information is required,
2. Deep text understanding is required for providing advanced services such as question answering, summarization, knowledge management, knowledge-based decision support, language independent document repositories, etc. For all these tasks, a domain and task dependent knowledge base is needed and building it from UNL representations presents distinct advantages over other approaches.

These practical approaches of UNL demonstrate the capacity of interlinguas in general and UNL in particular to represent textual contents in varied and useful applications.

---

[4] PATRILEX number (HUM2005-07260) is a project sponsored by the Spanish Research Council.

[5] EXCOM (R05/11070) is sponsored by Universidad Politécnica de Madrid and the Autonomous Community of Madrid.

References

1. Quillian M.R.: Semantic Memory. M.Minsky (ed.): Semantic Information Processing. MIT press (1968)
2. Schank, R.C.: Conceptual Dependency: A Theory of Natural Language Understanding, Cognitive Psychology, vol 3 (1972) 532-631
3. Uchida, H.: ATLAS-II: A machine translation system using conceptual structure as an Interlingua. Proceedings of the Second Machine Translation Summit, Tokyo (1989)
4. Muraki, K.: PIVOT: Two-phase machine translation system. Proceedings of the Second Machine Translation Summit, Tokyo (1989)
5. Nyberg, E. H., and Mitamura, T.: The KANT system: fast, accurate, high-quality translation in practical domains. Proceedings of the 14th International Conference on Computational Linguistics COLING '92, vol. 4. Nantes, France (1992) 1254-1258
6. Beale, S., Nirenburg, S., and Mahesh, G.: Semantic Analysis in the Mikrokosmos Machine Translation Project. Proceedings of the Second Symposium on Natural Language Processing SNLP-95. Bangkok, Thailand (1995)
7. Litkowski, K.: Senseval-3 task: Automatic labeling of semantic roles. Proceedings of Senseval-3: The Third International Workshop on the Evaluation of Systems for the Semantic Analysis of Text. Association for Computational Linguistics for the Semantic Analysis of Text, Barcelona, Spain (2004) 9-12
8. Carreras, X., and Màrquez, L.: Introduction to the CoNLL-2004 Shared Task: Semantic Role Labeling. Proceedings of Eight Conference on Natural Language Learning, CoNLL-2004. Boston, MA, USA (2004) 89-97
9. Reeder, F, Dorr, B., Farwell, D., Habash, N. , Helmreich, S., Hovy, E. H., Levin, L., Mitamura, L., Miller, K., Rambow, O., Siddharthan, A.: Interlingual Annotation for MT Development. Proc. 6th Conference of the Association for Machine Translation in the Americas, AMTA Washington, DC, USA (2004) 236-245
10. Boguslavsky, I., Cardeñosa, J., Gallardo, C., and Iraola, L.: The UNL Initiative: An Overview. Lecture Notes in Computer Science, vol 3406 (2005) 377 – 387
11. Uchida, H.: The Universal Networking Language Specifications, v3.3 (2004) Available at http://www.undl.org
12. Fellbaum, C., (ed): WordNet: An Electronic Lexical Database. Language, Speech, and Communication Series, MIT Press (1998)
13. Bateman, J.A, Henschel, R., and Rinaldi, F.: The Generalized Upper Model 2.0. (1995). Available at http:// www.darmstadt.gmd.de/publish/komet/gen-um/newUM.html.
14. Zadeh, L. A note on web intelligence, world knowledge and fuzzy logic. Data and Knowledge Engineering, vol 50 (2004) 191-304
15. Bhattacharyya, P. et. al,: Agro-Explorer: A meaning based multilingual search engine. vailable at: http://www.projects.mlasia.iitb.ac. in/docs/agro_icdl.htm.

Information Theoretic Approach to Information Extraction

Giambattista Amati

Fondazione Ugo Bordoni
Rome Italy

Abstract. We use the hypergeometric distribution to extract relevant information from documents. The hypergeometric distribution gives the probability estimate of observing a given term frequency with respect to a prior. The lower the probability the higher the amount of information is carried by the term. Given a subset of documents, the information items are weighted by using the inversely related function of of the hypergeometric distribution. We here provide an exemplifying introduction to a topic-driven information extraction from a document collection based on the hypergeometric distribution.

1 Introduction

Information extraction is a wide concept denoting the art of extracting tokens, items or any other form of *relevant* textual information from a document collection. The basis of information extraction is the notion of relevant item with respect to the information need or task. Extracted information can be conceived either as a self-contained, or distilled text that carrying most of the information content that is however sufficient to explain, answer or complete the information need or task in a minimal, or compact or structured form. For example data extracted from documents may be regarded as attribute values for record fields to be filled into a relational database, like for example the undirected graphical models of the conditional random fields [11, 18]. A primary goal of information extraction is to locate a minimal set containing most of the candidate items for extracting information from the data. Once that the relevant information is extracted, it is further possible to classify and insert candidate items into predefined relations, categories or other structured textual information. This paper deals with the problem of circumscribing relevant information conditioned to an information need or task employing a very low cost of computational time and space. We indeed introduce a topic-biased selection of relevant items for information extraction. This selection problem is similar to the construction of automatic query expansion, and it can be indeed adapted to many different information retrieval and extraction tasks.

The items extracted with our technique torn out of their topic contexts might be without a self-contained meaning. We treat the extracted items as atomic elements or basic constituents to be used to single out other relevant pieces of text, whether they are attribute values, or phrases, paragraphs and sections. These pieces of text have the highest *information content* with respect to the background knowledge (for example a topic **q**), and if they are not used directly for filling field records of a relational database, then they can be used to weight and extract larger pieces of information.

H.L. Larsen et al. (Eds.): FQAS 2006, LNAI 4027, pp. 519–529, 2006.

To perform information extraction, we first define what in probability theory is called the population of the background knowledge $\mathbf{q}$. To define the topic population, we gather relevant documents into a single document set $\mathcal{P}_\mathbf{q}$. *This document set is automatically obtained as the set of pseudo-relevant documents, that is the set of the topmost retrieved documents given the query* $\mathbf{q}$. Then we use the pooling set $\mathcal{P}_\mathbf{q}$ to sample frequencies of terms. Thus, for each term of the population we compute the probability $\text{Prob}(\mathbf{f}|\mathbf{p}, \mathcal{P}_\mathbf{q})$ of the observed term frequency $\mathbf{f}$ in the pool $\mathcal{P}_\mathbf{q}$ with respect to the prior probability $\mathbf{p}$ of the term, where Prob is the hypergeometric distribution [1]. The *information content* of the item $\mathbf{t}$ conditioned to the background knowledge $\mathbf{q}$ is defined as the inverse relation of the probability:

$$\text{Inf}(\mathbf{t}|\mathbf{q}) = -\log \text{Prob}(\mathbf{f}|\mathbf{p}, \mathcal{P}_\mathbf{q})$$

We finally weight and select all terms $\mathbf{t}$ with the highest $\text{Inf}(\mathbf{t}|\mathbf{q})$. This selection procedure is actually very efficient, because $\text{Inf}(\mathbf{t}|\mathbf{q})$ only requires few accesses to small portions of the direct file of the collection. The compressed direct file of the collection occupies the same space of the compressed inverted file and decompression time of the loaded parts is irrelevant, because file access and processing concern only few documents per query.

Note that Prob is a second-order probability: it is the probability of obtaining a probability $\mathbf{f}$ given a prior $\mathbf{p}$. Therefore, we do not maximise the likelihood $\text{Prob}(\mathbf{f}|\mathbf{p}, \mathcal{P}_\mathbf{q})$ to extract a probability value for $\mathbf{p}$ as in the maximum likelihood estimator (MLE), but we directly use the probability Prob as an estimator of information content of the term $\mathbf{t}$.

To exemplify our methodology we now use three topics as examples. The collection is from disks 4 and 5 of TREC minus the CR collection and consists of about 2 Gbytes of data, with 528,107 documents. The three examples are non-informational topics of TREC. Instead these three topics require a list of values or names to be associated to the query.

We use two parameters to measure the specificity of the returned answer: the number of documents of the pool $\mathcal{P}_\mathbf{q}$, which is 8, and the minimal number of documents of the pool containing the term. If a term belongs at least to one document of $\mathcal{P}_\mathbf{q}$, then we call the term to be of *level 1 of generality*. It is of *level 2* if it belongs at least to 2 documents, and so on. As soon as the level n of generality increases the high informative terms become more general, being frequent but in several different documents of the pool. The level of generality of a term in the pool is a very important indicator of the semantic role of the term in the documents. If a term is in the level 1 but not in the level 2, then it is high probable that the term is an attribute value of some record field. On the contrary, as soon as the level of generality of the term is high, then the informative term might be used as a relation or a concept in a relation database. The examples below will illustrate this issue.

Example 1. Nobel prize winners. Among the first 37 new retrieved terms at level 1 we have 8 Nobel prize winners (they are in italics) out of 11 proper names (words that are not in dictionary[1]): prize (0.4953), nobel (0.1577), winner (0.1245),*MacRobert*

[1] We also provide an automatic method able to detect correct proper names without using dictionary or other natural language analysis in Section 4.

(0.1133), award (0.1005), science (0.0795), case (0.0743), *MacCready* (0.0735), innovation (0.0708), technology (0.0674), chemistry (0.0646), physics (0.0558), Kremer (0.0538), *Banting* (0.0512), book (0.0447), academy (0.0436), microjector (0.0426), creative (0.0406), success (0.0401), *Charpak* (0.0397), academy (0.0386), *Cech* (0.0358), discovery (0.0322), scientific (0.0306), inventor (0.0302), Orteig (0.0294), atom (0.0287), engine (0.0284), won (0.0278),*Draper* (0.0277),*Dehmelt* (0.0264), laureate (0.0262), insulin (0.0259), glory (0.0253), medicine (0.0253), universe (0.0250), praemium (0.0250), scanner (0.0249), *Ramsey* (0.0249), Prestel (0.0241).

The required information is the set of terms that are at level 1 and not at level 2, that is: *MacRobert, case, MacCready, Kremer, Banting, microjector, creative, Charpak, Cech, Orteig, Orteig, Draper, Dehmelt, insulin , praemium, scanner, Ramsey* and *Prestel.*

The terms that are at level 2 but not at level 3, are: *innovation, book, success, inventor, atom, engine, laurate, glory* and *universe.*

The most general terms, level 3, thus are: *nobel, prize, winner, award, science, technology, chemistry, physics, academy, discovery* and *medicine.*

Example 2. Let us classify the possible adverse effects experienced from the repeated use of aspirin. This is the description of a TREC topic, topic 338 "Risk of aspirin".

We submitted this topic to the 2GB TREC collection. We extracted the following single keywords items at level 2 of details:

	aspirin 0.835		
1:	ibuprofen 0.241	2:	kidney 0.216
3:	stroke 0.177	4:	heart 0.112
5:	physician 0.120	6:	doctor 0.107
7:	blood 0.106	8:	risk 0.100
9:	tablet 0.094	10:	medical 0.094
11:	drug 0.093	12:	clot 0.082
13:	study 0.080	14:	dose 0.076
15:	pain 0.076	16:	medicine 0.074
17:	patient 0.074	18:	disease 0.073
19:	pregnancy 0.062	20:	pregnant 0.059
21:	migraine 0.058	22:	attack 0.058
23:	warning 0.057	24:	take 0.055
25:	prevent 0.054	26:	label 0.053
27:	research 0.052	28:	fda 0.051
29:	journal 0.050	30:	counter 0.047
31:	inflammation 0.047	32:	women 0.047
33:	relieve 0.045	34:	painkiller 0.042
35:	men 0.042	36:	effect 0.041
37:	health 0.041	38:	prostaglandin 0.041
39:	bleeding 0.039		

Additional terms at level 1 that are not in the level 2 (the most specific terms) are: *Advil* (0.190), *ticlopidine* (0.085), *caffeine* (0.080), *Warfarin* (0.064), *Henrich* (0.063).

Terms that are at level 1 but not at level 2 or 3 are: *ibuprofen, kidney, pregnancy, pregnant, migraine, fda, painkiller, prostaglandin.*

The automatic technique for sentence extraction is explained in Section 4.

Before explaining the algorithm, however we want to explain why we have discovered some informative terms in the above list. Since we are not expert on the topic, we have submitted the query 338 "Risk of aspirin" to a WEB search engine, and we have manually extracted all relevant information from two of the topmost ranked documents retrieved on the WEB. All words and their relative tokens shown below in italics are those we have have automatically extracted from the TREC collection.

> *Aspirin* can help *prevent* a *heart attack* or *clot*-related *stroke* by lowering the *clotting* action of the *blood*'s platelets. But the same properties that make *aspirin* work in stopping *blood* from *clotting* may also cause unwanted side *effects*, such as stomach *bleeding*, *bleeding* in the brain, *kidney* failure, and other kinds of *strokes*. There may be a benefit to daily *aspirin* use if you have some kind of *heart desease* or *blood* vessel *disease*, or if you have evidence of poor *blood* flow to the brain. But only a *doctor* can tell you whether the *risks* of long-term *aspirin* use may be greater than the benefits.

To understand why we have those extracted words, we have also selected from the WEB by a search engine the first sentences reporting those single keywords. To do this we submitted the original query together with each extracted keyword.

For example, when we run the query with "ibuprofen" on the WEB, we have discovered that there is a risk of prescribing this anti-inflammatory medicine together with aspirin for patients suffering of cardiovascular diseases.

> A new *study* published in the December 20, 2001 issue of the New England *Journal* of *Medicine* has found that *ibuprofen* blocks the *heart*-protecting *effects* of *aspirin*.

Taking caffeine however is beneficial:

> This *study* therefore demonstrated that the addition of *caffeine* to *aspirin*, in a *dose* commonly employed in over-the-*counter drugs*, has significant beneficial consequences with respect to mood and performance.

The term warfarin appears because:

> Over a two-year period, we found no difference between *aspirin* and *warfarin* in the *prevention* of recurrent ischemic *stroke* or death or in the rate of major hemorrhage. Consequently, we regard both *warfarin* and *aspirin* as reasonable therapeutic alternatives.

Therefore the query "Risk of aspirin" has located items that indicates either an effective risk or a reduction risk effects of the use of aspirin. Nonetheless, among the 40 keywords extracted we find out that the first three highest ranked keywords (ibuprofen, kidney and strokes) show where the required information is located. These terms indeed are the *most informative terms* in the collection conditioned to the query "Risk of aspirin".

Example 3. The query is topic 380 *Obesity medical treatment*. Basically, the answer is a low calorie diet or a limited prescription of some medications or subsidiaries treatment, such as very low calorie diet. The most informative terms extracted from the TREC collections at level 1 are:

obesity 0.3694			
1:	diet: 0.5183	2:	calories: 0.2971
3:	weight: 0.2344	4:	Callaway: 0.2024
5:	fat: 0.1754	6:	cholesterol: 0.1513
7:	Wadden: 0.1356	8:	Optifast: 0.1174
9:	physician: 0.1094	10:	overweight: 0.1076
11:	medical: 0.1031	12:	patient: 0.0998
13:	VLCD: 0.0885	14:	loss: 0.0814
15:	heart: 0.0774	16:	treatment: 0.0766
17:	protein: 0.0737	18:	drug: 0.0720
19:	blood: 0.0690	20:	dieter: 0.0688
21:	food: 0.0668	22:	dietitian: 0.0664
23:	nutrition: 0.0661	24:	diabetes: 0.0653
25:	health: 0.0639	26:	low: 0.0634
27:	liquid: 0.0591	28:	program: 0.0571
29:	eat: 0.0565	30:	lose: 0.0559
31:	heat: 0.0549	32:	drink: 0.0545
33:	doctor: 0.0539	34:	insulin: 0.0525
35:	monitor: 0.0515	36 :	children: 0.0514
37:	disease: 0.0490	38:	intake: 0.0488
39:	symptom: 0.0469		

Terms that are al level 1 but not at level 2 or 3 are: *Callaway*, *Wadden*, *Optifast*, *physician*, *VLCD*, *dietitian*.

As in previous example before extracting automatically the most informative sentences biased by the topic we want explain why some informative terms appear in the above list. We ran the query on the WEB and we found that Dr. *Wadden* says the following:

> Pharmacotherapy is recommended for individuals with a BMI $\geq$ 30 kg/m2 in the presence of two or more *obesity*-related comorbidities (e.g., coronary *heart disease*, type 2 *diabetes*, or sleep apnea) and who cannot *lose weight* satisfactorily with more conservative approaches.

In one of the WEB document we saw that Wayne *Callaway* is an endocrinologist criticising VLCD:

> Very *Low Calorie Liquid Diet* (*VLCD*) should be reserved for very *obese* individuals who need to *lose weight* rapidly for *health* reasons and should only be used under strict *medical* supervision. The use of *VLCD* should be considered only after the failure of determined attempts to *lose weight* with conventional *diets*.

Finally, Optifast is a commercial product for VLCD. The term “heat” is because one WEB document reports:

Obesity has been found to be a risk factor for *heat* injury and *heat* disorders.

Again, many terms found on the WEB are also found in the TREC collection and indicates where relevant information is located (apart from sibutramine and orlistat that were not indexed in TREC).

These examples show that extracting single keywords from documents can be further assembled and used to locate relevant information within documents for different tasks, such as disambiguating, answering queries or accomplishing pre-classification tasks. Therefore a good technique for extracting highly informative words in information extraction is a necessary preliminary task.

2 Related Work

The literature on automatic query expansion and its strictly related subjects, such as relevance feedback, is huge [9, 14, 6, 13, 16, 8, 5, 7, 17, 19, 10, 20, 12].The basic and most effective strategy for performing query expansion is *local feedback*, also known as *pseudofeedback*.The term local feedback was introduced by Attar and Fraenkel [2] to denote the process of formulating a newimproved search based on clustering terms from the documents returned in a previous search. Clustering terms can be computationally expensive because of the size of term-by-term matrices which have to be built with a global statistical analysis. The local feedback technique is able to select a set of terms from the topmost retrieved documents in a first ranking pass. After this phase, the selected terms are added to the original query with a weight. Rocchio's methodology[15] is the most popular algorithm used to compute the weights of the terms in the expanded query.

In this paper we follow Divergence From Randomness approach to information extraction. It can be seen as a generalization of the approach used by Carpineto and Romano in [4, 3] which applied the Kullback-Leibler divergence [4].

3 Information Weights

Sampling is the experiment of extracting tokens from a set $\mathbf{V}$ of outcomes (the vocabulary or the index). The population of the terms is the set of all tokens of the collection. Each ball (token) of a term has a prior probability $\mathrm{Prob}(\mathtt{t})$ to be drawn. The set of topmost retrieved documents are regarded as a sample of the population of the query $\mathbf{q}$. In the information theoretic approach the information content function is inversely related to the probability of extracting a number $\mathbf{f}$ (term frequency) of tokens of the term out of $\mathbf{L}_{\mathcal{P}_\mathbf{q}}$ trials (sample size) and assuming as prior $\mathrm{Prob}(\mathtt{t})$.

3.1 Retrieved Documents as a Sample of the Query

The document sample set can be seen as a finite binary sequence of Bernoulli trials whose outcome can be either *a success*, that is an occurrence of the term, or *a failure*, that is an occurrence of a different term. To be more precise, we also assume that the finite binary sequence is *random*, that is any trial is statistically independent from its preceding trials. In a Bernoulli process the probability of a given sequence is

$$\mathrm{Prob}(\mathbf{f}|\mathbf{d},\mathbf{p}) = \mathbf{p}^{\mathbf{f}} \cdot (1-\mathbf{p})^{\mathbf{L}_{\mathcal{P}_\mathbf{q}}-\mathbf{f}}$$

where $\mathbf{p}$ is the prior probability of occurrence of the term and $\mathbf{L}_{\mathcal{P}_\mathbf{q}}$ is the size of the document sample.

There are $\binom{\mathbf{L}_{\mathcal{P}_\mathbf{q}}}{\mathbf{f}}$ of *exchangeable sequences* (in IR they are also called *a bag of words*), therefore the probability is given by the binomial

$$\mathrm{Prob}(\mathbf{f}|\mathbf{d},\mathbf{p}) = \binom{\mathbf{L}_{\mathcal{P}_\mathbf{q}}}{\mathbf{f}} \mathbf{p}^{\mathbf{f}} \cdot (1-\mathbf{p})^{\mathbf{L}_{\mathcal{P}_\mathbf{q}}-\mathbf{f}} \tag{1}$$

The likelihood $\mathrm{Prob}(\mathbf{f}|\mathbf{d},\mathbf{p})$ is maximised when $\mathbf{p}$ is the *maximum likelihood estimate MLE* of the term in the sample:

$$\hat{\mathbf{p}} = \frac{\mathbf{f}}{\mathbf{L}_{\mathcal{P}_\mathbf{q}}} \ (\mathrm{MLE}) \tag{2}$$

If the prior $\mathbf{p}$ is unknown, then the MLE is a good estimate for $\mathbf{p}$. However we know that the prior probability of occurrence of the term $\mathbf{t}$ is the relative term-frequency in the collection:

$$\mathrm{Prob}(\mathbf{t}) = \frac{\mathbf{F}}{\mathbf{L}} \tag{3}$$

Let us then substitute $\mathrm{Prob}(\mathbf{t})$ for $\mathbf{p}$ in Equation 1:

$$\mathrm{Prob}(\mathbf{f}|\mathbf{d}) = \binom{\mathbf{L}_{\mathcal{P}_\mathbf{q}}}{\mathbf{f}} \mathrm{Prob}(\mathbf{t})^{\mathbf{f}} \, (1-\mathrm{Prob}(\mathbf{t}))^{\mathbf{L}_{\mathcal{P}_\mathbf{q}}-\mathbf{f}} \tag{4}$$

and define a measure of divergence of the probabilities $\hat{\mathbf{p}}$ and $\mathrm{Prob}(\mathbf{t})$.

Equation 4 is maximised when the MLE is equal to $\mathrm{Prob}(\mathbf{t})$, and in such a case the term distributes randomly. MLE is equal to $\mathrm{Prob}(\mathbf{t})$ when the term is non informative term. On the contrary, Equation 4 is minimised when the two probabilities $\hat{\mathbf{p}}$ and $\mathrm{Prob}(\mathbf{t})$ diverge. Divergence occurs when the terms are informative. In other words the probability of Equation 4 is *inversely* related to a measure of informativeness of the term:

$$\mathrm{Inf}(\mathbf{t}|\mathbf{q}) = -\log_2 \mathrm{Prob}(\mathbf{f}|\mathrm{Prob}(\mathbf{t}))$$

Equation 4 derives also from the hypergeometric model. In a population of $\mathbf{L}$ balls there are $\mathbf{F}$ red balls. What is the probability that in a sample of cardinality $\mathbf{L}_{\mathcal{P}_\mathbf{q}}$ there is exactly a number $\mathbf{f}$ of red balls? There are $\binom{\mathbf{F}}{\mathbf{f}}$ ways to choose a red ball, and there are $\binom{\mathbf{L}-\mathbf{F}}{\mathbf{L}_{\mathcal{P}_\mathbf{q}}-\mathbf{f}}$ to choose a ball of different colour. All possible configurations are $\binom{\mathbf{L}}{\mathbf{L}_{\mathcal{P}_\mathbf{q}}}$. Therefore the probability is

$$\text{Prob}(\mathbf{f}|\mathbf{d}) = \frac{\binom{\mathbf{F}}{\mathbf{f}} \cdot \binom{\mathbf{L}-\mathbf{F}}{\mathbf{L}_{\mathcal{P}_\mathbf{q}}-\mathbf{f}}}{\binom{\mathbf{L}}{\mathbf{L}_{\mathcal{P}_\mathbf{q}}}} \tag{5}$$

The probability distribution of Equation 5 is called the *hypergeometric distribution*. An equivalent formula can be obtained by swapping $\mathbf{L}_{\mathcal{P}_\mathbf{q}}$ with $\mathbf{F}$:

$$\text{Prob}(\mathbf{f}|\mathbf{d}) = \frac{\binom{\mathbf{L}_{\mathcal{P}_\mathbf{q}}}{\mathbf{f}} \cdot \binom{\mathbf{L}-\mathbf{L}_{\mathcal{P}_\mathbf{q}}}{\mathbf{F}-\mathbf{f}}}{\binom{\mathbf{L}}{\mathbf{F}}}$$

A limit theorem for the hypergeometric distribution is the binomial distribution of Equation 4

$$\mathcal{B}(\mathbf{L}_{\mathcal{P}_\mathbf{q}}, \mathbf{f}, \text{Prob}(\mathbf{t})) = \binom{\mathbf{L}_{\mathcal{P}_\mathbf{q}}}{\mathbf{f}} \text{Prob}(\mathbf{t})^{\mathbf{f}} \left(1 - \text{Prob}(\mathbf{t})\right)^{\mathbf{L}_{\mathcal{P}_\mathbf{q}}-\mathbf{f}}$$

is obtained as a limiting form of the hypergeometric distribution when the population $\mathbf{L}$ is very large and the size of the sample is very small, that is when both $\frac{\mathbf{L}_{\mathcal{P}_\mathbf{q}}}{\mathbf{L}} \sim 0$ and $\frac{\mathbf{F}}{\mathbf{L}} \sim 0$. Thus, we derive Equation 4 from the hypergeometric distribution:

$$\begin{aligned} \text{Inf}(\mathbf{t}|\mathbf{q}) &= -\log_2 \text{Prob}(\mathbf{f}|\mathbf{d}, \mathbf{p} = \text{Prob}(\mathbf{t})) = -\log_2 \mathcal{B}(\mathbf{L}_{\mathcal{P}_\mathbf{q}}, \mathbf{f}, \text{Prob}(\mathbf{t})) \\ &= -\log_2 \left[\binom{\mathbf{L}_{\mathcal{P}_\mathbf{q}}}{\mathbf{f}} \text{Prob}(\mathbf{t})^{\mathbf{f}} \left(1 - \text{Prob}(\mathbf{t})\right)^{\mathbf{L}_{\mathcal{P}_\mathbf{q}}-\mathbf{f}} \right] \end{aligned}$$

We need to simplify relation 4 to have a workable model of information extraction. We use the Equation introduce in [1]:

$$\text{Inf}(\mathbf{t}|\mathbf{q}) \sim \mathbf{f} \cdot \log_2 \left(\frac{\hat{\mathbf{p}}}{\text{Prob}(\mathbf{t})} \right) + 0.5 \log_2 \left(2\pi \cdot \mathbf{f} \cdot (1 - \hat{\mathbf{p}}) \right).$$

4 Information Extraction with the Hypergeometric Distribution

We have shown that the hypergeometric distribution is used to express a divergence measure between two frequencies, the prior from the observed frequency. The hypergeometric distribution detects biased terms in the sample of documents satisfying a given topic. Now, we describe how to extract sentences. We first extract the highest informative terms conditioned by the topic, then we weight phrases and sentences by summing up the weights of all these highest informative terms.

For example, if we consider the topic "Risk of aspirin" and the first document retrieved from the TREC collection, we can rank the most informative sentences from this document containing 31 sentences. Sentences can be long or short, and long sentences contain in general more information. However, short sentences even if are less informative can contain more average information. Therefore, instead of using the absolute value of information content as sum of the single contributions of the extracted terms occurring in sentences, we may use the information content averaged with the number of non-functional words of the sentence[2]. The two topmost sentences are:

> There is no suggestion that regular aspirin will do much for those already at low risk of heart attack or stroke.
> (Average amount of information = 0.142)
>
> Aspirin can damage the kidney and perhaps the liver,which is why paracetamol is the preferred pain-reliever for the under-12s.
> (Average amount of information = 0.137)

Similarly, in the example of "Obesity Medical treatment", the first retrieved document of the TREC collection contains 99 sentences. The first two top ranked sentences by average information content are:

> Sentence 76: Both the manufacturers of very low calorie diets and their critics agree that the diets can be dangerous if they are not monitored by a physician.
> (Average inforrmation content =0.156)
>
> Sentence 40: Wadden also says the diets are less successful among those with moderate weight problems.(Average inforrmation content =0.148)
>
> Sentence 27: Diets are called protein sparing because they are designed to allow the dieter to lose fat instead of protein .(Average inforrmation content =0.141)

Information extraction analysis can be refined combining multiple sources of evidence as follows:

- Average information content is a form of expectation of information content over a probability measure $\mathbf{p}$. The *expectation* of information content is

$$E(\operatorname{Inf}(x|\mathbf{q})) = \sum_{\mathbf{t}\in x} \operatorname{Inf}(\mathbf{t}|\mathbf{q}) \cdot \mathbf{p}(\mathbf{t})$$

  over a probability measure $\mathbf{p}$. The prior $\mathbf{p}(\mathbf{t})$ can be defined according to a set of patterns (name, noun, etc.). For example the term "prize" occurs in 5241 documents with frequency 7636, while MacRobert occurs in 4 documents with frequency 12. If we define $\mathbf{p}(\mathbf{t})$ inversely proportional to document frequency we get "prize" with the expectation proportional to 49.909, and the term MacRobert with the expectation proportional to 14958.631. Similarly, the value "Prestel" for the named entity of Nobel prize winners, that is last in the ranked list of the most informative terms, has expectation proportional to 909.098, whilst the last word of the dictionary in the ranked list (scanner) has the expectation proportional to 44.576. Therefore all proper names of Nobel prize winners are among the first items of the list of answers to the topic.

[2] Functional words usually are the words contained in the stop list, or that occur randomly in documents.

- Bayes' theorem or the total probability theorem, can be used to extend expectation to of mutually exclusive groups c_i of patterns.
  Expectation can be extended to new parameters or categories as follows:

$$E(\,\mathrm{Inf}(\mathbf{t}|\mathbf{q})) = \sum_{\mathbf{t}}\sum_{c_i} \mathrm{Inf}(\mathbf{t}|\mathbf{q}) \cdot \mathbf{p}(\mathbf{t}|c_i)\mathbf{p}(c_i)$$

  For example, in the example of "Nobel prize winners" we may define c_1 as the *named entity* category and c_2 a dictionary term. $\mathbf{p}(\mathbf{t}|c_i)$ can be assigned according to the fact whether the term is in a dictionary or not, and $\mathbf{p}(c_i)$ is the marginal probability of the category c_i. In our example we may set the prior $\mathbf{p}(\mathbf{t}|c_1) > \mathbf{p}(\mathbf{t}|c_2)$.

5 Conclusions

We have shown how to extract relevant information from a large document collection conducted at retrieval time. Terms having the highest expectation of information content are used as constituents or basic elements to locate the position of relevant text. Given a topic, that is a background knowledge, highly informative terms can be filtered and classified into successive layers of generality. A level of generality simply is the document frequency of a term in the set of retrieved documents. We have exemplified the information extraction technique at a great level of detail with three examples. In the most simple task which consists in associating a set of proper names to unique entities, the information-theoretic technique is able to detect correct proper names without using dictionary or natural language analysis. For other non- informational tasks, the information-theoretic technique is able to locate the distilled information that contains explanations to a given topic.

References

1. AMATI, G. Frequentist and Bayesian approach to Information Retrieval. In *Proceedings of the 28th European Conference on IR Research (ECIR 2005)* (2006), vol. 3936 of *Lecture Notes in Computer Science*, Springer, pp. 13–24.
2. ATTAR, R., AND FRAENKEL, A. S. Local feedback in full-text retrieval systems. *Journal of the ACM (JACM) 24*, 3 (1977), 397–417.
3. CAI, D., VAN RIJSBERGEN, C. J., AND JOSE, J. M. Automatic query expansion based on divergence. In *Proceedings of the Tenth International Conference on Information and Knowledge Management (CIKM-01)* (New York, Nov. 5–10 2001), H. Paques, L. Liu, and D. Grossman, Eds., ACM Press, pp. 419–426.
4. CARPINETO, C., DE MORI, R., ROMANO, G., AND BIGI, B. An information theoretic approach to automatic query expansion. *ACM Transactions on Information Systems 19*, 1 (2001), 1–27.
5. CROFT, W. Relevance feedback and inference networks. In *Proceedings of the 16th Annual International ACM SIGIR Conference* (1993), pp. 2–11.
6. CROFT, W., AND HARPER, D. Using probabilistic models of document retrieval without relevance information. *Journal of Documentation 35* (1979), 285–295.

7. HAINES, D., AND CROFT, W. B. Relevance feedback and inference networks. In *Proceedings of the 16th annual international ACM SIGIR conference on Research and development in information retrieval* (1993), ACM Press, pp. 2–11.
8. HARMAN, D. Relevance feedback revisited. In *Proceedings of ACM SIGIR* (Copenhagen, Denmark, June 1992), pp. 1–10.
9. IDE, E. New experiments in relevance feedback. In *The SMART Retrieval System*, Salton, Ed. Prentice-Hall, 1971, pp. 337–354.
10. KWOK, K. L. A new method of weighting query terms for ad-hoc retrieval. In *Proceedings of the 19th annual international ACM SIGIR conference on Research and development in information retrieval* (1996), ACM Press, pp. 187–195.
11. LAFFERTY, J., MCCALLUM, A., AND PEREIRA, F. Conditional Random Fields: Probabilistic models for segmenting and labeling sequence data. In *ICML* (2001), C. E. Brodley and A. P. Danyluk, Eds., Morgan Kaufmann, pp. 282–289.
12. LAFFERTY, J., AND ZHAI, C. Document Language Models, Query Models, and Risk Minimization for Information Retrieval. In *Proceedings of ACM SIGIR* (New Orleans, Louisiana, USA, September 9-12 2001), ACM Press, New York, NY, USA, pp. 111–119.
13. ROBERTSON, S. On relevance weight estimation and query expansion. *Journal of Documentation 42*, 3 (1986), 288–297.
14. ROBERTSON, S. E., AND SPARCK-JONES, K. Relevance weighting of search terms. *Journal of the American Society for Information Science 27* (1976), 129–146.
15. ROCCHIO, J. Relevance feedback in information retrieval. In *The SMART Retrieval System*, Salton, Ed. Prentice-Hall, 1971, pp. 313–323.
16. SALTON, G., AND BUCKLEY, C. Improving Retrieval Performance by Relevance Feedback. *Journal of the American Society for Information Science 41*, 4 (1990), 182–188.
17. VOORHEES, E. M. Query expansion using lexical-semantic relations. In *Proceedings of the 17th annual international ACM SIGIR conference on Research and development in information retrieval* (1994), Springer-Verlag New York, Inc., pp. 61–69.
18. WELLNER, B., MCCALLUM, A., PENG, F., AND HAY, M. An integrated, conditional model of information extraction and coreference with application to citation matching. In *Conference on Uncertainty in Artificial Intelligence (UAI)* (2004).
19. XU, J., AND CROFT, W. Query expansion using local and global document analysis. In *Proceedings of ACM SIGIR* (Zurich, Switzerland, Aug. 1996), pp. 4–11.
20. XU, J., AND CROFT, W. B. Improving the effectiveness of information retrieval with local context analysis. *ACM Transactions on Information Systems (TOIS) 18*, 1 (2000), 79–112.

Data Stream Synopsis Using SaintEtiQ*

Quang-Khai Pham, Noureddine Mouaddib, and Guillaume Raschia

LINA - Polytech'Nantes
ATLAS-GRIM Group
2, rue de la Houssinire, BP 92208
44 322 Nantes cedex 03, France
{Quang-Khai.Pham, Noureddine.Mouaddib, Guillaume.Raschia}@univ-nantes.fr

Abstract. In this paper, a novel approach for building synopses is proposed by using a service and message-oriented architecture. The SAINTETIQ summarization system initially designed for very large stored databases, by its intrinsic features, is capable of dealing with the requirements inherent to the data stream environment. Its incremental maintenance of the output summaries and its scalability allows it to be a serious challenger to existing techniques. The resulting summaries present on the one hand the incoming data in a less precise form but is still on the other hand very informative on the actual content. We expose a novel way of exploiting this semantically rich information for query answering with an approach mid-way between blunt query answering and mid-way between data mining.

1 Introduction

Emerging applications are generating and exploiting data in the form of *data streams.* Such information, as opposed to the traditional way of managing information, is by essence on-line, potentially unlimited and unbounded. Interesting domains of application include network traffic surveillance and administration, financial analysis, sensor data feeds or web applications. The constraints of these application are related to their need for timely answers for decision making purposes. For example, when a broker has to decide whether to buy or sell stocks according to the evolution of different indexes, he needs a final answer within seconds or tens of seconds. When considering the streams, each one corresponding to the real-time evolution of a stock market index, generated by all the stock markets, it is virtually impossible to store the transiting data. Thus, we pinpoint the need for adapted structures for managing this versatile data.

While the data stream domain is relatively new, as opposed to the traditional database paradigm, synopses remain relatively unformalized. Gibbons and Matias define in [6] those, for a class of queries Q, as a function$f(n)$ that provides *(exact or approximate) answers to queries from Q that uses* $O(f(n))$ *space for a data set of size n, where* $f(n) = O(n^{\epsilon})$ *for some constant* $\epsilon < 1$. The evaluation criteria proposed are thus (i)the coverage of $f(n)$, (ii)the answer quality, (iii)the

* This work supported by the ACI APMD and SemWeb.

H.L. Larsen et al. (Eds.): FQAS 2006, LNAI 4027, pp. 530–540, 2006.

footprint, (iv)the query time and (v)the computation/update time (the reader is invited to refer to [6] for further details). We retain criteria (i), (ii), (iii) and (v) as a basis to evaluate and position our system comparatively to existing approaches. The challenge that then rises is to find a compromise optimizing these opposing criteria.

Motivating example. A certain number of present applications and needs motivate our research in this direction.

As an example, it is well-known that the only way for car industries to make profit is to reduce their costs. An option is to introduce more and more on-board electronics to replace previously hydraulic and pneumatic systems. Thus, Bosch is working on *motronic* (motorised + electronic) brakes that would be completely independent and would communicate via a wireless connection to a central on-board system. These are monitored in real-time through the sensor feeds they send to the server. Considering the limits of these on-board electronics, it is impracticable to store the data and necessary to provide timely answers.

Formulation of the problem. Recent applications are providing and using more and more input feeds in the form of data streams either structured or not. Due to the host system physical limitations(hard drive access times, computing capabilities, etc...) and the timely answers required, it is not realistic to try to deal with these new inputs with the existing techniques that have been developed for the traditional stored databases and/or data warehouses. On the other hand, even though timely answers are required by such applications, 100% exact answers may not be necessary.

Thus, the main problem for managing and exploiting data streams can partially be answered by providing data structures, called *synopses*, and algorithms to construct and maintain them, in a time and space cost-efficient fashion. These are part of the major criteria retained but these solutions also need to propose answers adapted to the requirements of the application considered, such as the class of queries addressed, and guarantee to a certain extent the quality of the answers provided.

Roadmap. The rest of the paper is organized as follows. First, an overview of the existing techniques and of their performances in designing synopses for data streams is presented in section 2. Then, we will discuss the SAINTETIQ approach for building summaries and the novel decision making-oriented paradigm that we propose for exploiting SAINTETIQ summaries in a data stream environment through section 3. Our perspectives and short & long term work will be introduced in section 4. Finally we will conclude this paper in section 5.

2 Related Work

Recent works on data streams have mostly focused on designing synopses, algorithms and/or (adapting) techniques from the traditional database domain for estimating one dimensional data values.

The most basic approach proposed relied on sampling the data stream. This statistical technique used in the stored database context keeps track of a subset of the data values. In a data stream environment, the performances would be appreciable in terms of space and time processing. However, the unknown size of the data set is a critical issue, thus making the approach poorly applicable.

Pretty similar to the sampling approach, load shedding was notably proposed by Babcock & al. in [4]. The idea was to drop sections of unprocessed data from the incoming stream in a two step process: (i)target sampling rates for the queries then (ii)execute the load shedding operation in the most efficient manner possible. This technique suffers from the same issue as the sampling approach; the unknown size of the data set remains a dead end.

Sliding windows focus mainly on recent data. Babcock & al.[3] define a random sample on a window of size n over the stream within which only k items are stored in memory. The authors achieve at best $O(k\ log(n))$ memory usage for their *priority-sample* algorithm developed for timestamp-based windows. The main drawback of this method, even though semantically easy to understand, is giving poor results on queries implying *older* data items.

Other researches have focused on providing methods coping with queries related to frequency moments F_n(see [2] for a more complete definition). The idea is to compute/approximate F_0 the number of distinct values in the sequence, F_1 the length of the sequence, F_2 the self-join size (or Gini's index of homogeneity) or F_∞ the most frequent item's multiplicity. Manku and Motwani proposed in [12] a probabilistic *Sticky Sampling Algorithm* for answering iceberg-like queries[11] (frequency counts exceeding user-defined thresholds). The algorithm computes ϵ-deficient synopses over data streams of singleton items. It was designed to sweep over the data stream and update concise samples[6] which are (item, count) pairs. Cormode and Muthukrishnan[5] proposed on their side an algorithm, based on a divide and conquer process using a dyadic range sum oracle, capable of providing the *k hottest* items for dynamic datasets.

A classic paradigm is representing synopses with histograms. The idea is to capture the data distribution at best with the objective of minimizing the errors while reconstructing the data values. The main approaches include V-Optimal, Equi-Width and End-biased histograms. V-Optimal histograms approximate the distribution of a set a data values $u_1, ..., u_n$ with a function $\hat{u}$ that minimizes the sum of squared error $\Sigma_i(u_i - \hat{u}(i))^2$ (or L^2). One of the most efficient sketching algorithms was proposed by Gilbert & al.[7] where the authors achieved to bound the sketch constructing time and footprint by $poly(B, log(N), log||A||, 1/\epsilon)$ where A is a vector(*buffer* in the case of data streams) of length N and B the number of *buckets* in the histogram. The main drawback of this sketching approach comes from the metric used (L^2) which is not adapted for representing isolated data values.

Equi-Width histograms as reminded by Poosala & al.[14] are meant to partition the data value space into β approximately equal *buckets* by generating quantiles or splitters. Greenwald and Khanna[8] presented a deterministic algorithm capable of computing quantiles in a single-pass and achieving $O(\frac{1}{\epsilon}log(\epsilon N))$

space while guaranteeing ϵN precision. The main weakness of such a method comes from atypical individual data that may be clustered in a same *bucket*.

Manku and Motwani[12] presented randomized and deterministic algorithms for computing *iceberg* queries[11] by using End-Biased histograms. Iceberg queries are computed aggregate functions over an attribute or a set of attributes to find aggregate values above user-defined threshold. The proposed algorithm achieve $O(\frac{1}{\epsilon}\ log(\epsilon N))$ space, where N is the length of the stream and guarantee that any element is undercounted by at most ϵN and that the reported count is not worse than ϵN from the actual count.

The last family of sketching techniques uses Haar wavelets as a decomposition function. An error tree compound of the wavelet coefficients is then computed [10]. Considering 8 data items, 8 wavelet coefficients are computed. These coefficients are enough to rebuild the original information. Given a chosen number of coefficients, let's say α, and an error measure m (L^2, maximum absolute error, maximum relative error, etc), research has been focused on selecting the α-best coefficients of the error tree that optimize the error measure m. In the latest work known, Karras and Mamoulis[9] propose one-pass algorithms adapted to the data stream environment (with an incremental construction of the error tree from a data stream) that minimises the maximum-error metrics. They achieve in terms of space complexity at best $O(N)$ and in terms of time complexity their algorithms converge to $O(N\ log^2(N))$ for the maximum absolute error metric and to $O(N\ log^3(N))$ for the maximum relative error metric.

In a Synthetic word. We have presented here a brief overview of existing techniques that answer the problem as we have formulated. Table 1 synthesizes, to our best, these techniques by positioning them according to Gibbons' criteria introduced earlier.

Approach	Coverage	Non–Coverage	Answer Quality	Footprint	Comp. & Update time	Observations
Sampling	Any request	Performs poorly on joins	Approximative & no guarantees	Potentially important	Rapid	Errors due to data distribution (high standard deviation)
Load Shedding	Any request	Performs poorly on joins	Approximative & no guarantees	Potentially important	Rapid	Errors due to data distribution (high standard deviation)
Sliding Windows	Requests on recent data	Requests on historical data	Good on recent data & Poorly on historical data	O(k Log N)	Rapid	
V–Optimal H.	Estimations in query optimizers, Frequent moments	The others	1/e but not adapted for isolated data (L^2 metric used)	Poly(B,Log N,1/e)	Poly(B,Log N,1/e)	
Equi–Width H.	Estimations in query optimizers, Frequent moments	The others	Not worse than eN but relatively poor for data distribution with high standard deviation	O(1/e Log eN)		
End–Biased H.	Aggregation & Iceberg queries	The others	Not worse than eN	O(1/e Log eN)		
Wavelets	Aggregation queries	The others	User defined	Converges to O(N)	Converges to O(N Log^2N) or O(N Log^3 N)	

Fig. 1. Summary of existing approaches

The most important remark that can be done concerns the domain of application of the different approaches. Most of them focus on providing data structures and algorithms capable of rebuilding (approximately) singleton data values and ensuring maximum control over the error rate.

Our Contribution. We propose to adapt a highly efficient on-line service-oriented summarization service capable of constructing a linguistic summary of very large tables and/or views called SAINTETIQ [1]. SAINTETIQ's summarization system takes a database in any form (tables, views, streams) as input and produces a reduced version of this input through both a rewriting and a generalization process. The resulting table provides tuples with less precision than the original but yet are very informative of the actual content of the database.

Definition 1 (SaintEtiQ Summary). *Let be a first normal form relation $R(A_1, \ldots, A_n)$ in the relational database model. The* SAINTETIQ *summarization system constructs a new relation $R^*(A_1, \ldots, A_n)$, in which tuples z are summaries and attribute values are linguistic labels describing a set of tuples R_z, sub-table of R. Thus, the* SAINTETIQ *system identifies statements of the form "Q tuples of R are (a_1^1 or a_1^2 ... or $a_1^{m_1}$) and ... and (a_2^1 ... or $a_n^{m_n}$)".*

SAINTETIQ was originally designed for summarizing very large databases. It was thus designed as a service-oriented (as a plugable webservice) scalable system with a linear time complexity ($O(n)$, with n the number of tuples to summarize) for the construction and maintenance of the summaries. SAINTETIQ computes and incrementally maintains a hierarchically arranged set of summaries, from the root (the most generic summary) to the leaves (the most specific ones). The reader is invited to refer to [15] for more thorough details. Therefore, we can sum up our contribution in three points.

The first one would be proposing a general framework adaptable to the data stream environment. We ensure a linear time complexity algorithm coupled with a user-definable space usage. Furthermore, the precision of our approach is driven by space usage. Incidentally, we comply with the criteria we have selected from Gibbon's definition. Therefore, we give here a truly interesting compromise by fixing the time complexity factor to an acceptable level and leaving the answer quality and space complexity to the user's need.

The second point is the proposal of a framework capable of dealing with multidimensional data in a user-understandable fashion, which is, to our knowledge, one of its unique features when compared to the existing techniques available for the data stream environment.

Finally but not the least, we propose a novel way of using the synopses built upon the content of the data streams in a datamining-fashioned way through the very informative summaries obtained via SAINTETIQ.

In the following section of this paper, we are going to present the SAINTETIQ process and will position it with more details according to Gibbons' criteria. Finally, we will introduce a novel vision on how data streams can be exploited in their overall form through SAINTETIQ summaries.

3 A SaintEtiQ Approach for Data Streams

3.1 The SaintEtiQ Model

The traditional SAINTETIQ summarization model takes database records as input and gives some kind of knowledge as output. The process is divided into two main steps: the first one consists in rewriting the input *raw* data and the second one is the learning or summarization step.

However, in order to cope with the data stream environment, it is necessary to add a preliminary step: *the data stream bufferization.* Therefore, the SAINTETIQ summarization model for data streams (SEQS MODS) becomes a 3 step process as shown in figure 2.

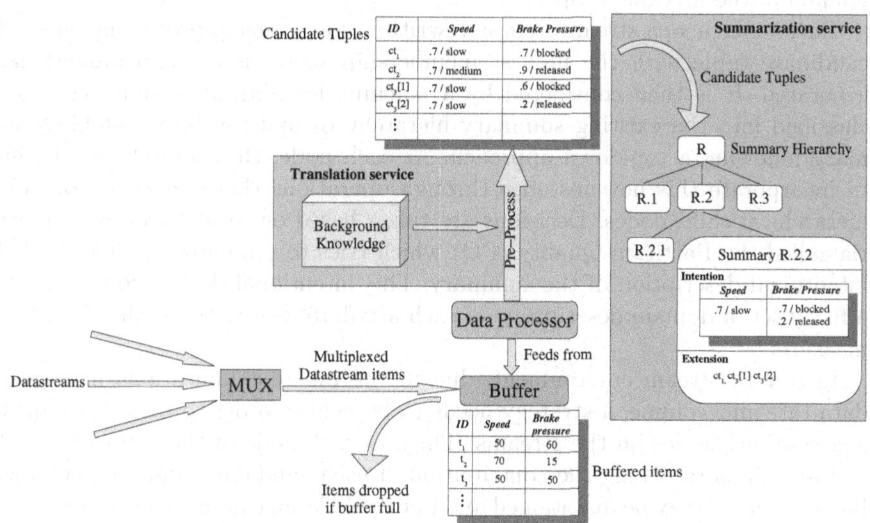

Fig. 2. SEQS MODS 3 step process for brake feeds

The primary stage is focused on receiving the (possibly) multiple streams. Thus, at the input of the system we introduce a multiplexer black-box. Its only purpose is to multiplex the input data into a single stream that will feed a buffer of user-defined size. At this stage of the process, there are many possible scenarii for feeding the buffer. The naive approach is to feed it until it is full then discard the items that do not fit until some space it released. More advanced techniques including *intelligent* sampling or load shedding (this then refers to related work) can be envisaged here. This step is generically illustrated by algorithm 1.

Once the buffer has input data, the *Data Processor*'s job is to retrieve single (or batches of) items and send those to the translation service for the rewriting task.

The rewriting step allows the system to rewrite the input stream items in order to be processed by the mining algorithm. This translation step gives birth to candidate tuples, which are different representations of a single stream item,

Algorithm 1. Data stream bufferization process

```
while (Data stream has input items) or (process not terminated by user) do
    Receive data from data stream s into sdata
    Apply policy for inserting sdata into buffer
    %% It can be load shedding, sampling or simply first-come, first-served %%
end while
```

in accordance with a Background Knowledge(BK). BK is made up of fuzzy partitions defined over attribute domains. Each class of a partition is also labelled with a linguistic descriptor which is provided by the user or a domain expert. For example, the fuzzy label "Slow" could belong to a partition built over the domain of the attribute "Speed".

Thus, once a *raw* stream item is rewritten, for reducing processing time, the candidate tuple with the highest membership scores is selected among those generated. It is then considered by a machine learning algorithm and is first classified into the existing summary hierarchy to find the best matching summary following a top-down approach. At each node, the hierarchy is modified to incorporate this new instance through operations that can create or delete hierarchical child nodes. Decisions are taken based on local optimization criteria called the Partition Quality (PQ) which tries to minimize the length of the intentional description of the summary. This intentional description is made of a fuzzy set of domain descriptors on each attribute associated with a possibility measure.

In a data stream environment, due to the inherent limitations in terms of data rate and volume, a strategy needs to be held in order to be able to answer aggregation queries on the streams. Thus, in each node of the hierarchy, tables or histograms recording the contribution of each candidate tuple to each fuzzy linguistic label may be maintained and updated. As an example, a summary node compound of the attributes `(Speed, Brake Pressure, Temperature)` may be associated with table 1.

Table 1. Attribute contribution table

Too fast	Released	Cool
5	4	6

The result is a set of summaries which each describe a subset of the data stream items coupled with quantitative information recorded in histograms. These summaries are hierarchically organized so that the root summary describes the overall data stream, and the leaf summaries describe a very precise subset of the stream. This part of the process is presented in the generic algorithm 2.

The scalability issues are inherent to the data stream paradigm; thus, SAINTETIQ is intrinsicly able to cope with the memory consumption and the time complexity factors in order to handle massive datasets. SAINTETIQ process time

Algorithm 2. SEQS MODS process

while Input data streams have items **do**
  Read data stream input from *buffer* into *sdata*
  Rewrite *sdata* in the translation service
  Retrieve cooked data into *cookedSData*
  Classify *cookedSData* in summary hierarchy through the summarization service
end while

complexity was designed to be linear ($0(n)$ with n the number of candidate tuples). In terms of space cost, it is obvious that the more precise the BK, the more voluminous the summaries will be. Let us denote S the average size in kilo-bytes of a summary or cooked data. In the average-case assumption, there are $\sum_{k=0}^{d} B^k = (B^{d+1} - 1)/(B - 1)$ nodes in a B-arity tree with d, the average depth of the hierarchy. Thus, the average space requirement is given by: $c_m = S \cdot \frac{B^{d+1}-1}{B-1}$. Based on real tests, $S = 3kB$ gives a rough estimation of the space required for each summary. However, the system was built in a way that it is possible to maintain only parts of the hierarchy in main memory and store the less accessed ones on disk.

Having said this, we are now able to position SaintEtiQ according to Gibbons' criteria.

Coverage. When constructing the output hierarchy it is currently possible to maintain a table/histogram of the contribution of each data stream item to each fuzzy linguistic label. This quantitative information is the key for answering aggregate, frequent moment or iceberg queries and potentially any other type of request, thus allowing the system to position itself on the same tracks as the previously presented techniques. However, if we consider joins, our systems is restricted to providing size estimations of the different attributes involved in the join, as it does not keep references to the stream items.

Answer Quality. As said earlier, the precision of the summaries evolve with the precision of the BK provided. The more accurate the BK, the more precise the summaries and as a result the more voluminous they are. It then becomes obvious that the quality of the answers provided depends mostly on the compromise on the quality of the input BK.

Let's take again the example of join queries. On the one hand, in the extreme case where the BK is very roughly defined, a large number of tuples may be selected for the cartesian product operation. Therefore, the selectivity power of the summary is very poor as many tuples will not participate in the cartesian product. On the other hand, if the data distribution can be estimated accurately on certain attributes, the tuples selected for the join operation are probabilistically better chosen, which means that most selected tuples will participate in the operation; thus the selectivity power of the summary, and the underlying histograms, may be dramatically increased.

This example pinpoints how important the definition of the BK influences the quality of the answers provided by the SaintEtiQ summaries. Therefore, an interesting axis of work may be oriented towards dynamically tuning the BK according to the distribution of the dataset, to the evaluation of the current performances and to the user's needs for a more data-oriented approach.

Footprint. As the computation and update time of a summary were designed to be linear, the footprint of the summaries is a major factor on which compromises must be done. Detailed BKs induce high memory consumption.

However, each node of the hierarchy was designed as an autonomous agent that can be serialized as a small binary stream. A *cache manager* can discard or resurrect *older* summaries to/from the disk providing disk accesses are acceptable for the system. Therefore, the footprint of the summaries is also a tunable factor according to the user's needs in terms of memory capabilities/savings.

Computation & Update time. The SAINTETIQ process was designed to be linear, $O(n)$, where n is the number of candidate tuples.

3.2 Novel Field of Application for Data Stream Synopses

The summaries resulting from processing multidimensional input data through SAINTETIQ convey semantically richer information than any other *traditional* data stream synopsis. This unique feature allows us to open the path to advanced applications such as identifying the topology of a group within the data stream. Thus, SAINTETIQ synopses are potentially geared towards a data mining-oriented usage. It seems interesting to associate decision making actions with (candidate tuple) pattern matching rules.

Let us take a different and maybe more challenging toy example, this time in the financial analysis environment. Suppose a broker needs to advice a customer for the investment into company A(CA). What he'll like to do is to sell both stocks of CA and other stocks to his customer. However, the latter would only buy if there are relative *guarantees* on the profitability of the transaction. Thus, imagine the following scenario: Company B (CB) wants to perform a takeover bid on CA - but CA is against. Therefore, in order to delay and/or avoid this operation, CA starts a takeover on Company C(CC). Incoming feeds would be in the form `(actor, target, price, number of stocks)`.

When processing these input stream *items*, as CA invests massively into CC, many candidate tuples in the form `(actor, target, cheap, plenty)` may be generated. An agent specially designed could then detect this tendency of the market. Speculatively speaking, stocks of CC are then susceptible to become more valuable in the short term. Thus, when considering this example, SEQS MODS summaries become very handful. The broker, within the first transactions, may be able to identify the tendency, which is those massive acquisitions of CC by CA at a *cheap* price (relatively to the probable future short-term value). He can then advice his customer to quickly invest with *high confidence* into CC stocks. Identifying these kind of topology is obviously a crucial parameter for his decision making job.

This toy example highlights the many possibilities offered in terms of application by SAINTETIQ summaries. They provide a rich background for advanced techniques, including mining or profiling, on data streams.

4 Perspectives and Future Work

Up till now, we be have based our talk on the experience and results that we have acquired in a traditionally stored database background. What we can at least guarantee with our current experiments on the current prototype is our ability to manage data streams with data rates at least equal to the system's current input capacity on stored databases. For the time being, our work is focused on optimizing the prototype so as to squeeze out the time consuming tasks entirely related to the stored database domain. Many optimization works, especially the implementation of the heuristics(see [15]), the cache management or the distribution of the process are currently on track. Once these are integrated into the system, we believe the summarization task will be dramatically sped up.

The second axis for our future work is to determine in the resulting summary hierarchy whether it is more interesting to keep the whole hierarchy structure or prune of it. Actually, as said earlier, the root of the hierarchy is the most general synopsis and the leaves are the most specific ones. It may not be interesting to conserve the root nor all of the leaves. Our attention is then directed towards finding a compromise between what needs to be kept and what doesn't. Obviously, this has an important impact on the summary maintaining process and the hence the performance of the overall architecture. This domain needs more thorough investigation.

Finally, we expect to take advantage of all the experience acquired here to adapt and optimize existing distributed architectures such as the WS-CatalogNet [13] or support applications as *"Advance Resource Reservation"*[16].

5 Conclusion

In this paper, we presented the integration of an on-line linguistic summarization process into a data stream environment. This is facilitated by the intrinsic feature of the SAINTETIQ system. By the system's advantages such as being an on-line service, as its scalability, as its reduced and controlled footprint and linear time complexity, SAINTETIQ is by essence ready for dealing with high data rate and voluminous data streams.

The summaries obtained through the process are furthermore semantically rich enough to open a new field of application on data streams. We are now able, through the same process, to summarize and mine the streams. It is now possible in a Decision Making paradigm to exploit the resulting summaries to explore and find profiles for example either in financial analysis or network surveillance and administration.

Immediate work is focused on optimizing and distributing the process for better performances in terms of stream processing.

At a medium term, we will investigate the way SAINTETIQ summaries may be pruned in order to improve the summarization process.

At last, further developments include the use of summaries to help query E-Community E-Catalogs or use their structure for data source selectivity which are domains potentially exposed to the data stream model. It would be, for instance, promising to implement such a service on an application level on mobile routers(MR) as described in [16] in order to help the MRs to optimize their network traffic.

References

1. SAINTETIQ. `http://www.simulation.fr/seq`.
2. B. Babcock, S. Babu, M. Datar, R. Motwani, and J. Widom. Models and issues in data stream systems. In *Proc. of ACM Symposium on Principles of Database Systems 2002*.
3. B. Babcock, M. Datar, and R. Motwani. Sampling from a moving window over streaming data. *2002 Annual ACM-SIAM Symposium on Discrete Algorithms (SODA 2002)*, 2002.
4. B. Babcock, M. Datar, and R. Motwani. Load shedding techniques for data stream systems. *20th International Conference on Data Engineering ICDE 2004*, 2004.
5. G. Cormode and S. Muthukrishnan. What's hot and what's not: Tracking most frequent items dynamically. In *Proc. of ACM Principles of Database Systems (PODS 2003)*, pages 296–306, 2003.
6. P. B. Gibbons and Y. Matias. Synopsis data structures for massive data sets. *DIMACS Series in Discrete Mathematics and Theoretical Computer Science*, 1998.
7. A. C. Gilbert, S. Guha, P. Indyk, Y. Kotidis, S. Muthukrishnan, and M. J. Strauss. Fast, small-space algorithms for approximate histogram maintenance. *STOC'02*, 2002.
8. M. Greenwald and S. Khanna. Space-efficient online computation of quantile summaries. *ACM SIGMOD 2001*, 2001.
9. P. Karras and N. Mamoulis. One-pass wavelet synopses for maximum-error metrics. In *Proc. of 31st VLDB Conference 2005*, 2005.
10. Y. Matias, J. S. Vitter, and M. Wang. Wavelet-based histograms for selectivity estimation. In *Proc. of the 1998 ACM SIGMOD International Conference on Management of Data (SIGMOD 1998)*, pages 448–459, June 1998.
11. R. Motwani, M. Fang, N. Shivakumar, H. Garcia-Molina, and J. D. Ullman. Computing iceberg queries efficiently. In *Proc. of the 24th VLDB Conference 1998*, pages 299–310, 1998.
12. R. Motwani and G. S. Manku. Approximate frequency counts over data streams. In *Proc. of the 28th VLDB Conference 2002*, 2002.
13. H.-Y. Paik, B. Benatallah, K. Baïna, F. Toumani, C. Rey, A. Rutkowska, and B. Harianto. Ws-catalognet: An infrastructure for creating, peering, and querying e-catalog communities. In *Proc. of the 30th VLDB Conference 2004*, 2004.
14. V. Poosala, Y. E. Ioannisdis, P. J. Haas, and E. J. Shekita. Improved histograms for selectivity estimation of range predicates. *22nd VLDB Conference 1996*, 1996.
15. R. Saint-Paul, G. Raschia, and N. Mouaddib. General purpose dataset summarization. *31st VLDB Conference 2005*, 2005.
16. A. Sun, M. Hassan, M. B. I. Hassan, P. Pham, and B. Benatallah. Fast and scalable access to advance resource reservation data in future mobile networks. *IEEE ICC*, 2006.

Face Detection Using Sketch Operators and Vertical Symmetry

Hyun Joo So[1], Mi Hye Kim[1], Yun Su Chung[2], and Nam Chul Kim[1]

[1] Laboratory for Visual Communications, School of Electrical Engineering and Computer Science,
Kyungpook National University, Daegu, 702-701 Korea
{ufo24, rlaalgp77}@vcl.knu.ac.kr, nckim@ee.knu.ac.kr
http://vcl.knu.ac.kr

[2] Biometric Chipset Technology Research Team, Electronics and Telecommunications Research Institute, Daejeon, 305-700, Korea
yoonsu@etri.re.kr

Abstract. In this paper, we propose an algorithm for detecting a face in a target image using sketch operators and vertical facial symmetry (VFS). The former are operators which effectively reflect perceptual characteristics of human visual system to compute sketchiness of pixels and the latter means the bilateral symmetry which a face shows about its central longitudinal axis. In the proposed algorithm, horizontal and vertical sketch images are first obtained from a target image by using a directional BDIP (block difference inverse probabilities) operator which is modified from the BDIP operator. The pair of sketch images is next transformed into a generalized symmetry magnitude (GSM) image by the generalized symmetry transform (GST). From the GSM image, face candidates are then extracted which are quadrangular regions enclosing the triangles that satisfy eyes-mouth triangle (EMT) conditions and VFS. The sketch image for each candidate is obtained by the BDIP operator and classified into a face or nonface by the Bayesian classifier. Among the face candidates classified into faces, one with the largest VFS becomes the output where the EMT gives the location of two eyes and a mouth of a target face. If the procedure detects no face, then it is executed again after illumination compensation on the target image. Experimental results for 1,000 320x240 target images of various backgrounds and circumstances show that the proposed method yields about 97% detection rate and takes a time less than 0.25 second per target image.

1 Introduction

Face detection is to automatically search out the locations of human faces in target images, which precedes image processing such as face retrieval, facial coding, face tracking, and face recognition. It is generally composed of face candidate detection and face-nonface classification [1]. The former may contain low-level analysis and face-like constellation analysis, and the latter feature enhancement, dimension reduction, and face-nonface discrimination. In low-level analysis, pixels which are closely related to significant information such as edge, generalized

H.L. Larsen et al. (Eds.): FQAS 2006, LNAI 4027, pp. 541–551, 2006.

symmetry (GS) [2], skin color, and motion are more emphasized or extracted from a target image. In face-like constellation analysis, using the output image by low-level analysis, face candidates are located which satisfy geometric relations of a face and its components such as eyes and a mouth, for example, eyes-mouth triangle (EMT) conditions [3]. As an input feature, each candidate may then enter a face-nonface discriminator directly, or through feature enhancement or even through dimension reduction using techniques such as principle component analysis (PCA) [4]. In conventional feature enhancement tools, there are horizontal and vertical Sobel operators [5], horizontal and $\pm\pi/4$ directional gradient operators [6], wavelet filters [7], and the combination of Harr wavelet, horizontal projection, and vertical projection [4]. In face-nonface discrimination, each raw or enhanced face candidate is decided to be a face or a nonface by a classifier such as Bayesian discriminator [4], support vector machine [8], Fisher linear discrimination [9], and neural network approach [10].

One can find many face detection algorithms which use gradient operators for lowlevel analysis or feature enhancement [2], [4]-[7]. However, most of gradient operators are oriented to edge extraction and sensitive to local change of illumination. On the other hand, the BDIP (block difference inverse probabilities) operator [11], which is recently known to yield excellent performance in content-based image retrieval, extracts not only edges but also valleys well that are perceptually more important features and is robust to local change of illumination. It also emphasizes more dark features than bright ones so as to output sketch-like images, which is consistent with the characteristics of human visual system. Since human eyes must be one of the best face detection systems, the BDIP operator is thus expected to be so helpful for face detection. In addition, it is a well-known common sense that a face is bilaterally symmetric about its central longitudinal axis, which has been used in many works such as facial component extraction from a face image [12], face authentication with 3D face images [13], and pose compensation for 3D face recognition [14]. Along with EMT conditions, the use of such VFS in face detection is expected to promote the detection performance greatly.

We propose a face detection algorithm using BDIP operators and VFS. In lowlevel analysis, a target image is converted into horizontal and vertical sketch images by a directional BDIP operator, which is modified from the BDIP operator, and then the pair of the sketch images produces a generalized symmetry magnitude (GSM) image by using the generalized symmetry transform (GST) [2]. In face-like constellation analysis, EMTs which satisfy EMT conditions and VFS are constructed from the GSM image and the quadrangular region enclosing the EMTs become face candidates. In face-nonface classification, the candidates which pass through the BDIP operator for feature enhancement and PCA for dimension reduction are decided to be faces or nonfaces by the Bayesian classifier. Among face candidates decided as faces, one with the largest VFS results in a detected face. If the detection procedure declares no face, it is executed again after illumination compensation on the target image.

2 Proposed Detection Method

2.1 Overview

The proposed method consists of face candidate detection and face-nonface classification as shown in Fig. 1. The input is a gray image with a frontal-view face revealing both eyes and a mouth. The former contains low-level analysis with directional BDIP operation and GST and face-like constellation analysis with EMT extraction and VSM (vertical symmetry magnitude) calculation. The latter has feature enhancement with BDIP operation, dimension reduction with PCA, and face-nonface discrimination with Bayesian classification. If the detection procedure finds no face, then it is executed again after illumination compensation is performed on the target image. If no face is declared in the second trial, the detection turns out to fail.

A target image is first converted into a vertical sketch image and a horizontal sketch image by a directional BDIP operator which will be described in Sect. 2.2, and the sketch images are then transformed to a GSM image by the GST. The GST originally measures the GSM for each pixel by summing the contribution of all the pairs of neighbor pixels, whose midpoints are the pixel, to its GSM. The contribution of each pair is defined as the multiplication of its two gradient magnitudes weighted by the functions of its two gradient phases and the distance between the paired pixels. For the computation of gradient magnitude and phase in the GST, we however choose the directional BDIP operator instead of conventional directional gradient operators.

Next, EMTs which fulfill EMT conditions for the geometry for eyes and a mouth [3] are extracted from the GSM image as follows. GSM regions are first segmented which have high GSMs, some of them are removed if their sizes are too small or large or their shapes are too narrow or broad, and the centroids of the remaining regions are computed. Then, the centroids are paired as candidates of eye centroids, among which the distances between paired pixels are too near or far are eliminated. Finally, each EMT is completed from each of the remaining pairs and the third centroid corresponding to a candidate of mouth centroid. The estimation of the third centroid will be described in Sect. 2.3.

Subsequently, only EMTs which satisfy VFS can be ones for face candidates. The VFS for each EMT is measured by VSM, which will be described in Sect. 2.3. The quadrangular regions enclosing the remaining EMTs with VFS become face candidates. The rotation compensation of each candidate is performed by affine

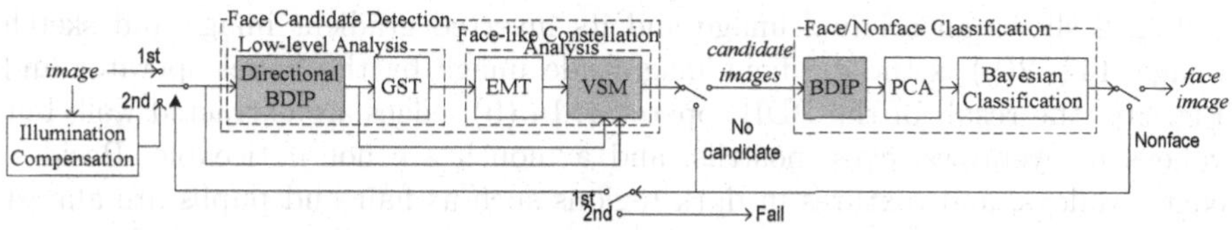

Fig. 1. Block diagram of the proposed face detection method

transform, and each compensated candidate is normalized in size by bilinear interpolation or decimation.

In face-nonface classification, a sketch image for each candidate is first obtained by the BDIP operator. Some significant principal components are then selected from each sketch image by PCA, which become an input feature of the Bayesian classifier. Each candidate with the principal components is finally classified into a face or a nonface according to the Bayes decision rule on a posteriori probabilities which are computed from the conditional probability of the face class and that of the nonface class, respectively. Each conditional probability density function is modeled as a multivariate normal distribution with the parameters obtained by training data, which is estimated by using the sketch image and its selected significant principal components. If a retrial is needed, the illumination of the target image is compensated by an image enhancement technique based on an advanced illumination-reflectance model [15].

2.2 Sketch Operator

The sketch operator which outputs a sketch-like image may be described by

$$\frac{|\overline{\nabla I_p}|}{\overline{I}_p} \tag{1}$$

where I_p denotes the intensity at a pixel p, $\overline{I}_p$ the local representative of neighbors of p, and $|\overline{\nabla I_p}|$ the magnitude of local representative gradient. Mean, median, and maximum can be listed as an operation which gives a local representative. As a result, a sketch operator emphasizes gradients in dark regions more than those in bright ones and is robust to local contrast or local change of illumination due to the normalization by the local representative.

BDIP. The BDIP operation is a sketch operator where the nominator is the magnitude of averaged nonlinear gradient in the window and the denominator is the maximum in the window, which is written as

$$BDIP(p) = \frac{\frac{1}{|W_p|}\sum_{q\in W_p}\left(\max_{r\in W_p} I_r - I_q\right)}{\max_{r\in W_p} I_r} \tag{2}$$

where W_p denotes the set of neighbors of p and $|W_p|$ its size. Through the normalization with the local maximum, the BDIP operator emphasizes gradients in dark regions more than in bright regions, which is consistent with the characteristics of human visual system known as Weber's law [16].

Fig. 2 shows an original image and its inverted gradient image and sketch image. Fig. 2(b) is the gradient magnitude image by the Sobel operator and Fig. 2(c) the result of the BDIP operator. In (b), edges are extracted well, but valleys in eyebrows, eyes, nostrils, and a mouth are not noticeable. Besides, edges, valleys, and textures in dark regions such as hair and pupils are almost never exposed. In (c), edges and valleys are extracted well, ones in dark regions are more enhanced, and textures in eyebrows and lips are enhanced as well.

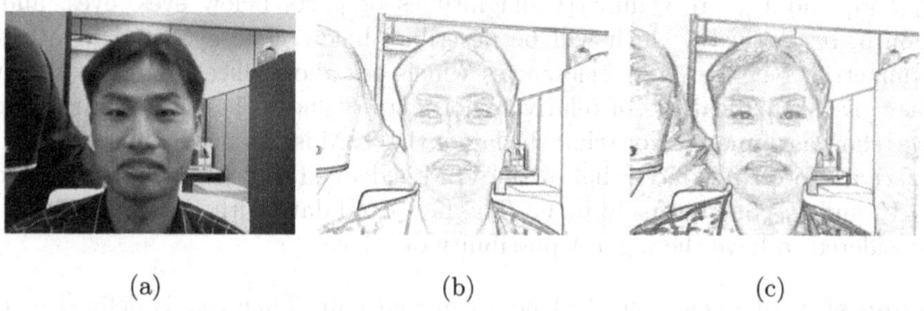

(a) (b) (c)

Fig. 2. (a) original image, (b) Sobel gradient image, and (c) BDIP image

Directional BDIP. Like directional Gradient operators such as the Sobel operator, we can modify the BDIP operator so as to have the directionality. Letting a pixel have the coordinate (x_p, y_p), a directional BDIP operator is defined as

$$\mathbf{s}_p = \left(\frac{\max\limits_{q \in W_p^{X+}} I_q - \frac{1}{|W_p^{X-}|} \sum\limits_{q \in W_p^{X-}} I_q}{\max\limits_{q \in W_p} I_q}, \frac{\max\limits_{q \in W_p^{Y+}} I_q - \frac{1}{|W_p^{Y-}|} \sum\limits_{q \in W_p^{Y-}} I_q}{\max\limits_{q \in W_p} I_q} \right) \quad (3)$$

where W_p^{X+}, W_p^{X-}, W_p^{Y+}, and W_p^{Y-} are subwindows as shown in Fig. 3. W_p^{X+} and W_p^{X-} are the forward and backward subwindow for the horizontal gradient of a center pixel, which are defined as $W_p^{X+} = \{q : x_q > x_p, \quad q \in W_p\}$ and $W_p^{X-} = \{q : x_q < x_p, \quad q \in W_p\}$ and W_p^{Y+} and W_p^{Y-} those for its vertical gradient defined similarly.

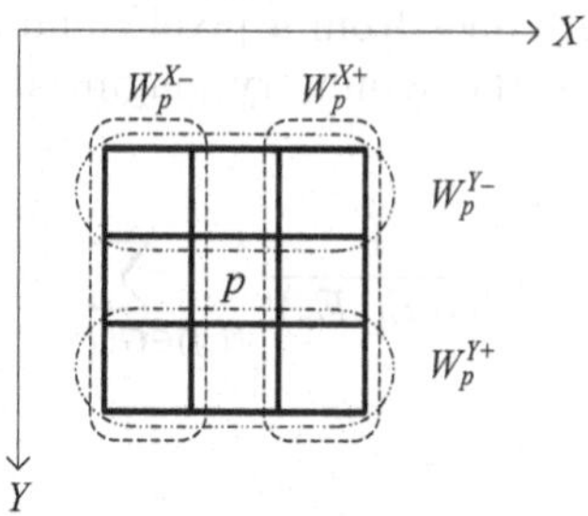

Fig. 3. Subwindows for a directional BDIP operator in a 3 × 3 window

2.3 VSM

The VSM for an EMT is defined as

$$V(l, r, m) = \frac{V_e(l, r) V_m}{V_b(l, r)} \quad (4)$$

where (l, r, m) denotes a triplet of vertices of the EMT which corresponds to a candidate triplet of centroids of a left eye, right eye, and mouth. $V_b(l, r)$,

$V_e(l,r)$, and V_m are symmetry magnitudes of parts below eyes, eyes, and a mouth, respectively, which will be described below. The eyes and mouth are symmetric, but the parts below eyes which are above cheeks are not because they give sketch features of relatively noisy, low values. That is, the parts below eyes show asymmetry. Note that the larger the VSM is, the more the possibility of a face is. To verify a face reliably, the VSM is defined to be directly proportional to V_e and V_m but inversely to V_b. The face candidate with the largest VSM is considered to have the highest possibility of a face.

Symmetry of eyes. Let (l,r) be a centroid pair. Then, β_{lr} is defined as the angle of the line $\overline{lr}$ passing l and r to the horizontal line. ϕ_l and ϕ_r are defined as the orientations of regions centered at l and r, respectively. Fig. 4 shows the symmetry for the pair of eyes segmented ideally in a face tilted by β_{lr} when both l and r are truly eye centroids. In the figure, the shade regions represent the eye regions. Since both of the two eyes are nearly perpendicular to the central longitudinal, the orientations are expected to be alike. Thus, an EMT should be removed if it possesses the pair of centroids of diverged orientations. As for the remaining EMTs, which are possible to form faces, the symmetry magnitudes of eyes are measured as follows.

Let E_l and E_r be left and right eye candidate regions centered on l and r, respectively. Then, $G(E_l, E_r)$ is defined as the set of pairs of pixels from E_l and E_r which have almost vertical symmetry about the longitudinal line passing the mid point between l and r of the latitudinal line $\overline{lr}$. That is,

$$G(E_l, E_r) = \{(i,j) : \beta_{ij} \approx \beta_{lr},\ d_i \approx d_j,\ i \in E_l,\ j \in E_r\} \tag{5}$$

where β_{ij} is the angle of the line $\overline{ij}$ passing pixels i and j to the horizontal line. The distances d_i and d_j are ones from a pixel i and a pixel j to the longitudinal line, respectively. Then, the symmetry magnitude is defined as the average contribution of pixel pairs:

$$V_E(l,r) = \frac{1}{|G(E_l, E_r)|} \sum_{(i,j) \in G(E_l, E_r)} v(i,j) \tag{6}$$

with

$$v(i,j) = \|\mathbf{s}_i\| \cdot \|\mathbf{s}_j\| \cdot [1 + h(i) \sin \psi_i] \cdot [1 + h(j) \sin \psi_j] \cdot [1 - \cos(\psi_i + \psi_j)], \tag{7}$$

$$\psi_i = \angle \mathbf{s}_i - \beta_{lr}, \tag{8}$$

and

$$h(i) = \begin{cases} -1, & y_i < (x_i - x_l) \tan \beta_{lr} + y_l \\ 1, & y_i > (x_i - x_l) \tan \beta_{lr} + y_l \end{cases} \tag{9}$$

where $\|\mathbf{s}_i\|$ and $\|\mathbf{s}_j\|$ are the magnitudes of the directional BDIP at pixels i and j, respectively. The phases ψ_i and ψ_j are ones of the directional BDIP compensated by a face tilt β_{lr}. The function h means whether the locations of a pixel pair are lower or higher than the line $\overline{lr}$. Generally, the intensity of an eye tends to decrease from the top to the center and increase from the center to the bottom, which are reflected by the sine terms in Eq. (6). When a pixel is located in the above part, the terms have the form of (1-sine) by Eq. (9) which is maximal at $-\pi/2$, which weights the intensity to be decreased. As shown in Fig. 4, the sum of phases, $\psi_i + \psi_j$, must be π or $-\pi$ when the pixels are vertically symmetric, which is reflected by the cosine term in Eq. (6).

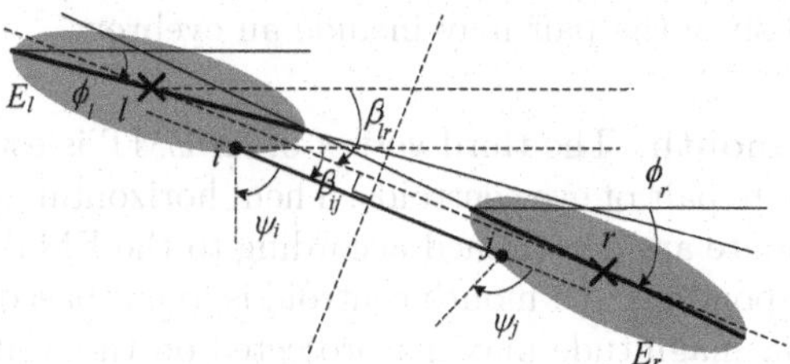

Fig. 4. Symmetry for the pair of eyes segmented ideally in case of a face tilted by β_{lr}

Symmetry of parts below eyes. Let B_l and B_r be parts below regions with paired centroids of l and r, respectively. Then, their vertical symmetry is defined as

$$V_b(l,r) = \frac{1}{|G(B_l, B_r)|} \sum_{(i,j)\in G(B_l,B_r)} \|\mathbf{s}_i\| \cdot \|\mathbf{s}_j\| \tag{10}$$

where $G(B_l, B_r)$ is the set given by substituting B_l and B_r for E_l and E_r in Eq. 5, respectively. Fig. 5 shows B_l and B_r. Fig. 5(a) shows that l and r are located in eyes. B_l and B_r are above cheek, and so their intensities vary smoothly.

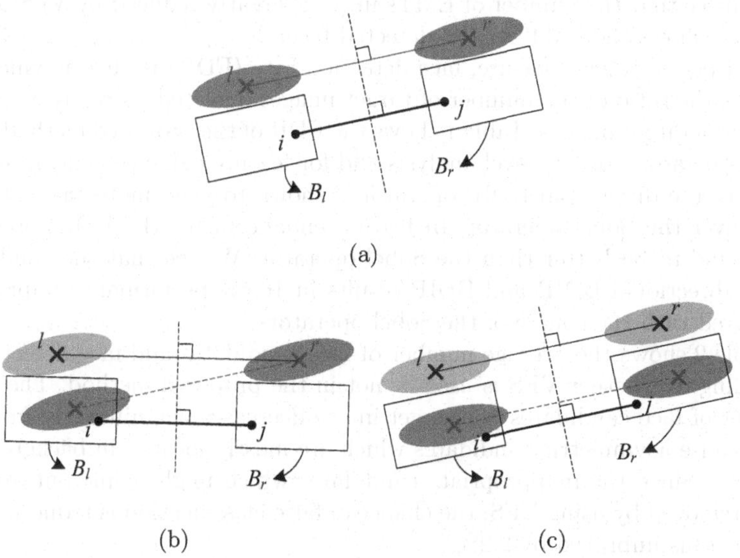

Fig. 5. Centroid pair (l, r) in (a) eyes, (b) an eye and an eyebrow, and (c) eyebrows

Since their sketch features are low and relatively noisy, they are not symmetry. Fig. 5(b) shows B_l and B_r when either of l and r is located in an eye and the other in an eyebrow. These B_l and B_r are not symmetric, and one of them gives significant sketch features. When both l and r are in eyebrows as shown in Fig. 5(c), B_l and B_r have symmetry because they are eyes. Consequently, the symmetry magnitudes in (b) and (c) are larger than that in (a). When a pair (l_1, r_1) has another pair (l_2, r_2) below it and $V_b(l_1, r_1) > V_b(l_2, r_2)$, the pair (l_1, r_1) is removed since the pair may include an eyebrow.

Symmetry of a mouth. The third vertex of an EMT is estimated as follows. Consider a candidate pair of eye centroids. Then, horizontal and vertical bounds for a mouth candidate are determined according to the EMT condition [3]. The third vertex corresponding to a mouth centroid is found based on the latitudinal positions of the GS magnitude maxima projected on the latitudinal axis which are left and right to the longitudinal line within the bounds. The symmetry of a mouth is calculated within the bounds by the GST.

3 Experimental Results

To evaluate the performance of the proposed detection method, 1,000 320×240 target images of various backgrounds and circumstances are used. Fig. 6 shows the intermediate results of our method for the target image in Fig. 2(a). Fig. 6(a) and (b) are a vertical sketch image and a horizontal sketch, respectively, which are displayed with a positive bias. Fig. 6(c) is the GSM image which is shown inverted. Fig. 6(d) shows the extracted EMTs and (e) EMTs for face candidates. We can see that the number of EMTs in (e) is greatly reduced by VFS over (d). Fig. 6(f) shows the EMT for the detected face.

As a performance measure, face detection rate (FDR) is chosen which is defined as the ratio of the number of target images detected correctly to the total number of target images. Table 1 shows the FDR of the proposed method according to operators for low-level analysis and for feature enhancement. In low-level analysis, the directional BDIP operator is shown to yield more than 11% FDR gains over the Sobel operator. In feature enhancement, the BDIP operator is also found to be better than the Sobel operator. We see that the combination of the directional BDIP and BDIP results in 16.6% performance improvement compared with the couple of the Sobel operators.

Table 2 shows the average number of face candidates and face detection rate according to whether VFS is used or not in the proposed method. The average number of face candidates per target image decreases magnificently from 10 to 1.4 because asymmetric candidates which are mostly located in background are removed. Since the inappropriate candidates which might come out are previously removed by using VFS, the chance of false classification is reduced and the FDR is thus improved by 2.2%.

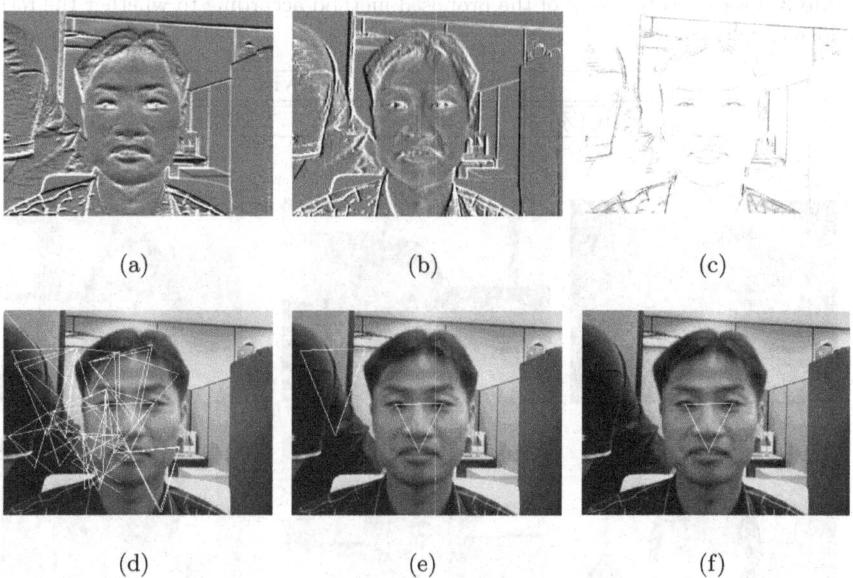

Fig. 6. (a) vertical sketch image, (b) horizontal sketch image, (c) GSM image, (d) extracted EMTs, (e) EMTs for face candidates, and (f) EMT for the detected face

Table 1. Face detection rate of the proposed method according to operators for low-level analysis and for feature enhancement

feature enhancement \ low-level analysis	Sobel	directional BDIP
Sobel	80.4	96.3
BDIP	85.7	97.0

Table 2. The average number of face candidates and face detection rate according to whether VFS is used or not in the proposed method

	Without VFS	With VFS
average number of candidates	10.0	1.4
FDR (%)	94.8	97.0

Table 3 shows the face detection rate of the proposed method according to whether the retrial is done or not. In this table, we see that the proposed method without retrial yields 95.1% FDR and the retrial after illumination compensation gives about 2% FDR improvement. It takes a time less than 0.25 second per target image when implemented with a Pentium IV 3.4 GHz processor and MS Visual C++ 6.0. Fig. 7 shows the EMTs for the faces detected in target images, which tells us that the proposed method detects faces well.

Table 3. Face detection rate of the proposed method according to whether the retrial is done or not

	Without retrial	With retrial
FDR (%)	95.1	97.0

Fig. 7. EMTs for faces detected by the proposed method

The proposed algorithm was tested mainly for target images each with a single face. It however may be expected to yield good performance even for target images with multiple faces which are not so tiny. Nevertheless, it is found that faces wearing dark glasses or ones with thick frames, or faces with beards may be major causes of failure.

4 Conclusions

We have proposed a face detection method using BDIP operators and VFS. Face candidates are extracted from the sequence of the directional BDIP operation, GST, EMT extraction, and VSM calculation. The candidates through the BDIP operator and PCA are then classified into faces or nonfaces by the Bayesian classifier. In the declaration of no face, the whole procedure is executed again after illumination compensation. Experimental results for target images showed that the directional BDIP operator for low-level analysis and the BDIP operator for feature enhancement produced great performance improvement over the couple of the Sobel operators. The introduction of VFS measured by VSM to face detection yielded a small improvement but reduced the time required for face detection because of much smaller number of candidates. It was finally shown that the proposed method yielded excellent face detection rate.

References

1. Hielmås, E.: Face Detection: A Survey, Computer Vision and Image Understanding, Vol. 83, **3** (2001) 236–274
2. Reisfeld, D., Wolfson, H., Yeshurun, Y.: Context Free Attentional Operators: The Generalized Symmetry Transform, Int. J. of Computer Vision, Vol. 14, **3** (1995) 119–130
3. Maio, D., Maltoni, D.: Real-time Face Location on Gray-Scale Static Images, Pattern Recognition, Vol. 33, **9** (2000) 1525–1539
4. Liu, C.: A Bayesian Discriminating Features Method For Face Detection, IEEE Trans. on PAMI, Vol. 25, **6** (2003) 725–740
5. Li, Y., Gong, S., Sherrah, J., Liddell, H.: Support Vector Machine Based Multi-View Face Detection and Recognition, Image and Vision Computing, Vol. 22, **5** (2004) 413–427
6. Huang, L.L., Shimizu, A., Hagihara, Y., Kobatake, H.: Gradient Feature Extraction for Classification-Based Face Detection, Pattern Recognition, Vol. 36, **11** (2003) 2501–2511
7. Gundimada, S., Asari, V.: Face Detection Technique Based on Rotation Invariant Wavelet Features, Int. Conf. on Information Technology: Coding and Computing, Vol. 2 (2004) 157–158
8. Osuna, E., Freund, R., Girosi, F.: Training Support Vector Machines: an Application to Face Detection, Proc. IEEE Conf on. Computer Vision and Pattern Recognition (1997) 130–136
9. Feng, Y.J., Shi, P.F.: Face Detection Based on Kernel Fisher Discriminant Analysis, Proc. IEEE Int. Conf. on Automatic Face and Gesture Recognition (2004) 381–384
10. Garcia, C., Delakis, M.: Convolutional Face Finder: a Neural Architecture for Fast and Robust Face Detection, IEEE Trans. on PAMI, Vol. 26, **11** (2004) 1408–1423
11. Chun, Y.D., Seo, S.Y., Kim, N.C.: Image Retrieval Using BDIP and BVLC Moments, IEEE Trans. on CSVT, Vol. 13, **9** (2003) 951–957
12. Katahara, S., Aoki, M.: Face Parts Extraction Windows Based on Bilateral Symmetry of Gradient Direction, Proc. Int. Conf. Computer Analysis of Image Patterns (1999) 489–497
13. Tsalakanidou, F., Malassiotis, S., Strintzis, M.G.: Exploitation of 3D Images for Face Authentication Under Pose and Illumination Variations, IEEE Int. Symposium on 3D Data Processing, Visualization and Transmission (2004) 50–57
14. Malassiotis, S., Strintzis, M.G.: Pose and Illumination Compensation for 3D Face Recognition, Proc. IEEE ICIP, Vol. 1 (2004) 91–94
15. Kimmel, R., Elad, M., Shaked, D., Keshet, R., Sobel, I.: A Variational Framework for Retinex, Int. J. Computer Vision, Vol. 52, **1** (2003) 7–23
16. Gonzalez, R.C., Woods, R.E.: Digital Image Processing, Addison Wesley, 1993

Discrimination-Based Criteria for the Evaluation of Classifiers

Thanh Ha Dang[1,2], Christophe Marsala[1], Bernadette Bouchon-Meunier[1], and Alain Boucher[2]

[1] Université Pierre et Marie Curie - Paris6, CNRS UMR 7606, DAPA, LIP6 8, rue du Capitaine Scott, Paris, F-75015, France

[2] Institut de la Francophonie pour l'Informatique, Equipe MSI, Bât D, 42 rue Ta Quang Buu, Hanoi, Vietnam

Abstract. Evaluating the performance of classifiers is a difficult task in machine learning. Many criteria have been proposed and used in such a process. Each criterion measures some facets of classifiers. However, none is good enough for all cases. In this communication, we justify the use of discrimination measures for evaluating classifiers. The justification is mainly based on a hierarchical model for discrimination measures, which was introduced and used in the induction of decision trees.

1 Introduction

Machine learning techniques become increasingly popular in both academic and industrial domains. In classification problems, the use of such techniques often involves the assessment of how good is a classifier in relation with a dataset. The standard practice is to take a collection of examples in the domain of interest, select randomly a subset of these examples as training set and apply machine learning algorithms to it for obtaining a classifier, which is also named classification model or model for short. Then this one is used to classify the remaining test cases. The performance of classifiers is usually evaluated by the classification results in the test sets.

Most of measures of evaluation are designed with the hypothesis that all examples are equally important and that datasets are distributed in a balanced manner by their classes. In the classical case, each example in the test set is classified in a class. But in the more general ones, probabilistic classification, possibilistic classification and fuzzy classification for instances, several classes may be assigned to an example.

A confusion matrix contains information about actual and predicted classifications done by a classification model. Performance of such model is commonly evaluated using the data in the matrix. Most of measures evaluate the relation between the predicted classes and the actual classes of examples on a test set and do not pay enough attention to the characterization of classification problems. For examples: accuracy, error rate, true/false positive rate, true/false negative rate, sensitivity, specificity, etc. So there is a bias on classification results concerned with the characterization of problems, in particular the distribution of

H.L. Larsen et al. (Eds.): FQAS 2006, LNAI 4027, pp. 552–563, 2006.

examples as showed by many authors [7, 12]. Sometimes, the classes have very unequal frequency. For instances, in e-commerce: 99% of visitors do not buy anything and only 1% of them buy something; in security, 99.99% of people are not terrorists; etc. The situation is similar with multiple classes. A majority class classifier can have a very high accuracy: 99% in the e-commerce situation, 99.99% in the security problem, but it should be useless.

In the last decade, the ROC curves have been widely used in the machine learning community [2, 6]. An attractive property of the ROC curves is the insensitivity to the class distribution. In many cases, such as rule sets, classifiers produce only a class decision for each example. The use of such a discrete classifier on a test set produces a single confusion matrix. From the matrix, only one point in ROC space is determined. In such cases, classifiers should be converted to generate scores from each example rather than just a class. Moreover, ROC analysis is not convenient for the choice of classifiers. For concluding that a classifier is better than another, the first one should be better than the second one over the whole performance space [11] i.e. it has a higher true positive rate and a lower false positive rate. Several information-based measures [3, 7, 8] which will be recalled in the next section, have been proposed for a similar purpose. They usually try to exclude the effect of prior class probabilities as with the ROC analysis.

In classification process, it can be pointed out two partitions of the test set. The first one is natural: examples are partitioned by their classes. The second one is the partition raised by a classifier. In this paper, we propose to consider the adequation between these two partitions. This allows an evaluation of the discrimination power of classification models with regard to the classes and a comparaison of classifiers. The initial idea was introduced for the induction of decision trees process [13] which helps to select the most adequate attribute for partitioning a learning set. The selected attribute is the most discriminated one with regard to the classes.

The paper is organized as follows. In Section 2, several criteria for classifier evaluation, in particular the information-based criteria are presented and formalized with a common formalism. In Section 3, a hierarchical model for measures of discrimination in inductive learning is recalled. In Section 4, the discrimination-based criteria are introduced based on the hierarchical model. In Section 5, several properties of the proposed criteria are presented. In Section 6, a set of experiments is done to illustrate and validate the use of these criteria. In the last section, a conclusion is done and future work is proposed.

2 Criteria for Classifier Evaluation

There are many criteria of performance for a classification model. We cite here a list of some usual criteria : accuracy, error rate, true/false positive rate, true/false negative rate, sensitivity, specificity, positive/negative predictive value, fallout, precision/recall, F measure, ROC convex hull, area under the ROC curve, calibration error, mean cross-entropy, root mean squared error, expected cost, explicit cost, etc. In several cases, the interpretability and the sensitivity based on a geometric analysis [1] of the model are considered.

In the next of this section, several information-based criteria for classifier evaluation are presented and formalized with a common formalism. Most of these measures are proposed for the probabilistic classification and they take the classical classification (target is one class and the classifier assigns one class to an example) as a particular one. They usually evaluate the coherence between the predicted probabilistic distribution by the classification model and the target probabilistic distribution for each example then aggregate them for the whole dataset.

Let $\xi_T = \{e_1, e_2, ..., e_N\}$ be a test set of examples. Suppose that an example e belongs to class c_e from a set of classes $\mathcal{C} = \{c_1, c_2, .., c_n\}$. Class c_e is the target class (also named the natural class or the real class) of classification process. In the more general case, each example is associated to a probabilistic distribution $(p_{c_1}(e), p_{c_2}(e), .., p_{c_n}(e))$, in which $p_{c_i}(e)$ is the probability that the example belongs to class c_i. This is the target of classifiers. The probabilistic distribution for the classical case is in the form $(0, .., 1, ..0)$, where 1 corresponds to class c_e.

Suppose that in the prior, the probability that an example e belongs to class c of $\mathcal{C}$ is $p_e(c)$. So the prior probabilistic distribution is $(p_e(c_1), p_e(c_2), .., p_e(c_n))$. This probabilitic distribution may be estimated from the frequency of each class in dataset.

Suppose that the posterior probability that an example e is classified in class c is $p'_e(c)$. This probability is returned by the classifier. So the posterior probabilistic distribution is $(p'_e(c_1), p'_e(c_2), .., p'_e(c_n))$. It is also called the predicted probabilistic distribution.

The cross-entropy error is described [3] for the case of two classes 0 et 1. It measures how close predicted values are to target values. In the simple case, with each example e we have either $p_0(e) = 1$ and $p_1(e) = 0$, or $p_0(e) = 0$ and $p_1(e) = 1$. It assumes that the predicted values are probabilities $p'_e(1)$ on the interval [0,1] that indicate the probability that the example is in class 1. Obviously, if $p_0(e) = 1$ and $p_1(e) = 0$ i.e. the example belongs to class 0, for the classification result, a small probability $p'_e(1)$ that the example belongs to class 1 is preferred. Otherwise the big $p'_e(1)$ is is preferred. The cross-entropy, that should be minimized, for an example e is defined as [1] :

$$\text{cross-entropy}(e) = -p_1(e)\log p'_e(1) - (1 - p_1(e))\log(1 - p'_e(1)) \tag{1}$$

The cross-entropy for a test set is defined as the sum of the cross-entropy for each example that belongs to the set. To make cross-entropy independent of dataset size, mean cross-entropy is defined by the sum of the cross-entropy for each example divided by the total number of examples in the test set.

The directed divergence i.e. Kullback-Leibler measure is also used in the domain. It measures the Kullback-Leibler distance between the predicted probabilistic distribution and the target probabilistic distribution of an example.

[1] In this paper, $\log x$ should be understand as $\log_2 x$.

$$d_{KL}((p_{c_1}(e), .., p_{c_n}(e)), (p'_e(c_1), .., p'_e(c_n))) = \sum_{i=1}^{n} p_{c_i}(e) \log \frac{p_{c_i}(e)}{p'_e(c_i)} \quad (2)$$

In the case of two classes and $(p_{c_1}(e), p_{c_2}(e), .., p_{c_n}(e))$ takes only one among two distributions (1,0) and (0,1), the directed divergence reduces to the cross-entropy mentioned previously because:

$$\begin{aligned} \text{cross-entropy}(e) &= -(p_1(e) \log p'_e(1) + (1 - p_1(e)) \log(1 - p'_e(1))) \\ &= -(p_e(1) \log p'_e(1) + p_e(0) \log p'_e(0)) \\ &= p_e(1) \log \frac{p_e(1)}{p'_e(1)} + p_e(0) \log \frac{p_e(0)}{p'_e(0)} \end{aligned} \quad (3)$$

with the convention: $0 \log 0 = 0$.

A disadvantage of the above measures is that their values are infinity when an example is completely bad classified, for instance the target distribution is (1,0) and the predicted distribution is (0,1). Moreover, they do not take into account the prior probabilistic distribution.

An information reward measure is proposed in [8]. It is applied in the case where each example e belongs to only one class c_e. In the binominal classification, for each example the information reward is defined as: $reward(e) = 1 + \log p'(c_e)$. It is 1 bit if the classification is correct ($p'(c_e) = 1$) and 0 bit for the complete ignorance in the classification task ($p'(c_e) = 0.5$) and it is negative if $p'(c_e) < 0.5$. Like the Kullback-Leibler distance, the information reward does not take into account the characterization of the problems, in particular the distribution of examples by their classes.

Unlike the previous measures, I. Kononenko and I. Bratko [7] proposed a measure that explicitly takes prior probabilities of classes into account. This interesting property is maintained in the discrimination-based measures which are introduced in the next sections. I. Kononenko and I. Bratko suggested to calculate the amount of information gained or lost in the classification of each example and then in the classification of the whole dataset. In prior, the amount of information necessary for confirming that e is in class c is: $-\log p_e(c)$ bits . Analogously, the amount of information necessary to correctly decide that e does not belong to class c is: $-\log(1 - p_e(c))$ bits. In posterior, if $p'_e(c_e) \geq p_e(c_e)$ then the probability of class c_e changes in the good direction, the gain of information in this case is: $-\log p_e(c_e) + \log p'_e(c_e)$ bits. If $p'_e(c_e) < p_e(c_e)$ then the probability of class c_e changes in the bad direction, the loss of information in this case is: $-\log(1 - p_e(c_e)) + \log(1 - p'_e(c_e))$ bits. The information score is the difference between the quantity of gained information and the quantity of lost information over all examples of the test set. It can be normalized by dividing by the number of examples in the test set.

3 Hierarchical Model for Measures of Discrimination

Let ξ be a training set. Suppose that each example e in ξ is described by means of a set of values for K attributes in a set $\mathcal{A} = \{A_1, A_2, .., A_K\}$ and belongs to a class from a set of classes $\mathcal{C}$. Each attribute A_j takes its value in the set $\{v_1, v_2, .., v_{m_{A_j}}\}$ where the values v_i can be either symbolic, numerical. In inductive learning, a decision tree is build to point out the relation between the values of attributes and the classes in $\mathcal{C}$. That enables us to obtain a class from any forthcoming description of an example.

A decision tree corresponds to a ranking of the attributes according to their influence related to the classes. The nodes of such a tree correspond to testing the value of an attribute, the vertices correspond to a given value, and the leaves are associated with a class. The main method to construct a decision tree is the so-called Top Down Induction method. The tree is constructed from its root to its leaves by successive partitioning of the training set into subsets. Each partition is done thanks to the values of a selected attribute and leads to the definition of a node of the tree labelled by this attribute. The selected attribute is the one that has the most discrimination power with regard to the classes. A measure of discrimination helps the choice by estimating the information brought out by an attribute. For instance, in the ID3 algorithm [13] the Shannon entropy [16] is used to measure the quantity of information. A leaf is constructed from a set that contains only examples with the same class.

In the induction of decision trees, the measure used to select the best attribute must fulfill a several properties. Such a measure is called a measure of discrimination. The hierarchical model of measures of discrimination has been proposed to validate a given function as a good measure of discrimination for a decision trees construction process [10]. A number of measures have been validated by this model [5]: Rényi entropy, Daróczy entropy, etc.

This hierarchical model, named $\mathcal{FGH}$-model is based on the definition of three levels $\mathcal{F}, \mathcal{G}, \mathcal{H}$ of functions. The functions in each level are aggregated to construct a measure of discrimination. The $\mathcal{F}$-level of functions is concerned by measuring the inclusion between the set of examples with class c_j and the set of examples with the value v_i for attribute A. The $\mathcal{G}$-level of functions is concerned by aggregating functions from the $\mathcal{F}$-level to measure the information brought out by a value v_i related to the whole set of classes $\mathcal{C}$. The $\mathcal{H}$-level of functions is concerned by aggregating functions from the $\mathcal{G}$-level to measure the discrimination power of attribute A related to $\mathcal{C}$. At each level, a set of properties required for the function is given.

Given a set X. Let $F[X]$ be the set of all subsets of X and $\mathbb{P}[X]$ be the set of all partitions of X.

Definition 1. ($\mathcal{F}$-function). *An $\mathcal{F}$-function is a function $F : F[X] \times F[X] \rightarrow \mathbb{R}^+$ such that:*

1. *$F(U, V)$ is minimum when $U \subseteq V$.*
2. *$F(U, V)$ is maximum when $U \cap V = \emptyset$.*
3. *$F(U, V)$ is strictly decreasing with $U \cap V$ i.e. $U \cap V_1 \subset U \cap V_2$ implies $F(U, V_1) > F(U, V_2)$.*

Given an $\mathcal{F}$-function F and a sequence of continuous functions $g_k : \mathbb{R}^k \longrightarrow \mathbb{R}^+$, $k \in \mathbb{N}$.

Definition 2. ($\mathcal{G}$-function). *An $\mathcal{G}$-function is a function G: $F[X]\times I\!P[X] \rightarrow I\!R^+$ such that:*

$$G(U, V) = g_n(F(U, V_1), F(U, V_2), .., F(U, V_n)) \tag{4}$$

where $V = \{V_1, V_2, .., V_n\}$ a partition of X and :

1. *$G(U, V)$ is minimum when there exists V_j $(1 \leq j \leq n)$ such that $U \subseteq V_j$.*
2. *$G(U, V)$ is maximum when $F(U, V_1) = F(U, V_2) = .. = F(U, V_n)$.*

Given an $\mathcal{G}$-function G and a sequence of continuous functions h_k :$\mathbb{R}^{+k} \longrightarrow \mathbb{R}^+$, $k \in \mathbb{N}$.

Definition 3. ($\mathcal{H}$-function). *An $\mathcal{H}$-function is a function H: $I\!P[X]\times I\!P[X] \rightarrow I\!R^+$ such that:*

$$H(U, V) = h_m(G(U_1, V), G(U_2, V), .., G(U_m, V)) \tag{5}$$

where $U = \{U_1, U_2, .., U_m\}$ a partition of X.

In inductive learning, the definition of $\mathcal{H}$-function can be applied to: X is a learning set, V is a partition of the set of examples according to classes, U is also a partition of the set of examples according to values of an attribute, U_i is the set of examples such that the value of attribute A is v_i. A $\mathcal{H}$- function measures the discriminating power of attribute A with regard to all classes. For more details on this model, see [10, 14].

4 Discrimination-Based Criteria

Inductive learning is a process to induce knowledge from cases or examples. Learning algorithms try to extract as must as possible the information in the dataset for constructing a classifier and use it to classify a set of new examples. The classifier should discriminate all examples by their classes. So it raises a partition of the set of examples. We propose to evaluate the discrimination power of the classifier by analysing the adequation between the partition generated by the classifier and the partition with regard to the real classes of examples i.e. the natural partition. Like the information-based criterion proposed by I. Kononenko and I. Bratko [7], the discrimination-based criteria take into account the difference between the information given by the classifier (posterior) and the available information on the test set (prior). But we consider directly the probabilistic distribution on the whole examples instead of the one for each individual.

We denote ξ_{Tc} the set of all examples in ξ_T belonging to class c and $\xi_{Tc'}$ the set of all examples in ξ_T classified in class c. So the proposed method evaluates the adequation between two partitions $\{\xi_{Tc_1}, \xi_{Tc_2}, .., \xi_{Tc_n}\}$ and $\{\xi_{Tc'_1}, \xi_{Tc'_2}, .., \xi_{Tc'_n}\}$.

Suppose that a classifier M is induced from ξ and it classifies all examples from a test set ξ_T. The classifier M labels each example e in ξ_T with a class in $\mathcal{C}$.

Table 1. Classification results by two classifiers: M_1 and M_2

Example	Real class	A_1	A_2	...	A_K	f_{M_1}	f_{M_2}
e_1	c_{e_1}	v_{11}	v_{12}	...	v_{1K}	c_{11}	c_{12}
e_2	c_{e_2}	v_{21}	v_{22}	...	v_{2K}	c_{21}	c_{22}
...	...	...	...	...	...	...	...
e_N	c_{e_N}	v_{N1}	v_{N1}	...	v_{NK}	c_{N1}	c_{N2}

Thus, from M we can introduce a new attribute f_M: for each example of ξ_T, the attribute takes the label assigned by M to the example as its value (Table 1).

As mentioned in the previous section, a measure validated by the hierarchical model can estimate the discrimination power of an attribute, in particular the new attribute f_M. Thus, it can measure the discrimination power of the classifier M. The measurement of the discrimination power of M consists also in 3 levels.

$\mathcal{F}$-level: The $\mathcal{F}$-level is concerned by measuring the adequation between the set of examples with class c_j and the set of examples classified in class c_i that we denote: $F(\xi_{Tc_j}, \xi_{Tc'_i})$. It takes its minimum value when the set of examples classified in class c_i is a subset of the set of examples with class c_j, and its maximum value when any example of class c_j is classified in class c_i.

$\mathcal{G}$-level: The $\mathcal{G}$-level is concerned by aggregating functions from the $\mathcal{F}$-level to measure the information brought out by classifying the examples in class c_i. It is noted $G(\{\xi_{Tc_1}, \xi_{Tc_2}, .., \xi_{Tc_n}\}, \xi_{Tc'_i})$. It takes its minimum value when there exists a class c_j that the set of examples classified in class c_i is a subset of the set of examples with class c_j (for example, in the case of ideal classifier). G takes its maximum value when the adequations of the set of examples classified in class c_i and each set of examples of the same class are identical. $\mathcal{H}$-level: The $\mathcal{H}$-level is concerned by aggregating functions from the $\mathcal{G}$-level to measure the discrimination power of the model M related to the whole classes in $\mathcal{C}$. It is noted $H(\{\xi_{Tc_1}, \xi_{Tc_2}, .., \xi_{Tc_n}\}, \{\xi_{Tc'_1}, \xi_{Tc'_2}, .., \xi_{Tc'_n}\})$.

This function measures the inadequation between the two partitions by the classifier and by the classes of examples. In other words, it measures how good the partition according to classifier M is. The smaller H the more two partitions are adequate. So a small value for H is preferred. When $H = 0$, the two partitions are the same.

It has been shown [9] that Shannon entropy [16], a very usual information measure, is a particular discrimination measure validated by the hierarchical model. In the next, we establish an evaluation criterion with the Shannon entropy for illustrating.

$\mathcal{F}$-level:

$$F(\xi_{Tc_j}, \xi_{Tc'_i}) = -\log \frac{|\xi_{Tc_j} \cap \xi_{Tc'_i}|}{|\xi_{Tc'_i}|} = -\log p(c_j|c'_i) \qquad (6)$$

where $p(c_j|c'_i)$ is the probability that an example classified in class c_i is in class c_j and $|.|$ is the cardinality of a set.

$\mathcal{G}$-level:

$$\begin{aligned} G(\{\xi_{Tc_1}, \xi_{Tc_2}, .., \xi_{Tc_n}\}, \xi_{Tc'_i}) &= \sum_{j=1}^{n} \frac{|\xi_{Tc_j} \cap \xi_{Tc'_i}|}{|\xi_{Tc'_i}|} F(\xi_{Tc_j}, \xi_{Tc'_i}) \\ &= -\sum_{j=1}^{n} \frac{|\xi_{Tc_j} \cap \xi_{Tc'_i}|}{|\xi_{Tc'_i}|} \log \frac{|\xi_{Tc_j} \cap \xi_{Tc'_i}|}{|\xi_{Tc'_i}|} \\ &= -\sum_{j=1}^{n} p(c_j|c'_i) \log p(c_j|c'_i) \\ &= I(\xi_{Tc'_i}) \end{aligned} \tag{7}$$

It is the entropy of the subset of examples classified in class c_i with regard to their real classes.

$\mathcal{H}$-level:

$$\begin{aligned} H(\{\xi_{Tc_1}, .., \xi_{Tc_n}\}, \{\xi_{Tc'_1}, .., \xi_{Tc'_n}\}) &= \sum_{i=1}^{n} \frac{|\xi_{Tc'_i}|}{|\xi_T|} G(\{\xi_{Tc_1}, .., \xi_{Tc_n}\}, \xi_{Tc'_i}) \\ &= \sum_{i=1}^{n} p(c'_i) I(\xi_{Tc'_i}) = I(\xi_T|M) \end{aligned} \tag{8}$$

where $p(c'_i)$ is the probability that an example is classified in class c_i and $I(\xi_T|M)$ is the entropy of the test set conditioned by classifier M.

We denote: $I(\xi_T)$ the entropy of the test set ξ_T :

$$I(\xi_T) = I(p_1, p_2, .., p_n) = -\sum_{i=1}^{n} p(c_i) \log p(c_i) \tag{9}$$

where $p(c_i)$ is the probability that an example of ξ_T is in class c_i.

The following formula allows us to measure the information bring out by classifier M:

$$\Delta I(M, \xi_T) = I(\xi_T) - I(\xi_T|M) \tag{10}$$

We have : $0 \leq \Delta I(M, \xi_T) \leq I(\xi_T)$.

In learning process, the algorithms try to learn as much as possible about the dataset. The information obtained in such a process enable the induction of the classifier. So the classifier can be considered as an information-holder. Therefore, the above formula measures how much information of the test set is hold in the classifier. In other words, it measures the part of necessary information for describing the test set gained by the learning process on the learning set. It expresses also the difference between the average uncertainty of the sets issued by the classifier from the whole test set and the uncertainty of the whole test set.

The ratio of information gain is defined as follows:

$$\tau(M, \xi_T) = \frac{\Delta I(M, \xi_T)}{I(\xi_T)} \tag{11}$$

We have : $0\% \leq \tau(M, \xi_T) \leq 100\%$.

$\tau(M, \xi_T)$ measures the ratio of information of the test set hold in the classifier. Of course, the grand ratio and the important information gain are preferred.

5 Additional Properties of the Discrimination-Based Criteria

The discrimination-based criteria evaluate the adequation between the natural partition of examples and the one raised by the classification model. They eliminate the bias on the examples distribution by their classes. It could be useful as criteria in addition to other existing ones. However, they just evaluate the discrimination capacity of the classifier but does not evaluate how correct the classification is. If we consider that a classification process is a successive performance of a process for discriminating the examples in a number of partitions and then a process for labelling each partition, the discrimination-based criteria evaluate the first one. Even in the case where the class assignment is bad (so accuracy is low) whereas the discrimination capacity is good, the classification model is not totally useless.

As argued in the previous section, if the classification model is perfect i.e. the good classification rate is 100% then model is also perfect by means of discrimination measure and $\tau(M, \xi_T) = 100\%$.

In the case of one class classifier that classifies all examples in only one class, the two partitions are completely inadequate and $\tau(M, \xi_T) = 0\%$.

In the case that each partition raised by the classification model has the same proportion of each class as the test set, we have: $\tau(M, \xi_T) = 0\%$.

As $\tau(M, \xi_T)$ is a normalized value, it can be an useful index when comparing the performance of a classification model across different datasets or comparing the performance of different classification model across the same dataset.

6 Some Experimental Results

A set of experiments has been conducted with several artificial datasets and datasets from the UCI repository of machine learning [15] to illustrate and validate the discrimination-based criteria. The *DTGen* software (Decision Tree Generator Software) [17, 4] has been used. The following results are obtained by running the ID3 algorithm for the construction of decision tree with the datasets. Each dataset is divided in two subsets which have similar numbers of examples in each class. One is used as the learning set in the training phase and another is used as the test set. This process is repeated several times then the average results are deduced. The criterion used is the one based on the Shannon entropy.

Let us consider the following confusion matrices (Table 2) for three artificial datasets. Each one contains 2 classes but has different distributions by their classes. The classification accuracy for the three datasets are identical: 80%. However, the classifier for the second dataset classifies all examples in the majority class, it does not give any useful information. So the information gain

Table 2. Confusion matrices for three artificial datasets

	Dataset 1		Dataset 2		Dataset 3	
	Positive	Negative	Positive	Negative	Positive	Negative
Positive	40	10	40	10	0	20
Negative	10	40	10	40	0	80

Table 3. Classification results for artificial datasets

	Dataset 1	Dataset 2	Dataset 3
Accuracy	80.0	80.0	80.0
Dataset entropy (bit)	1	0.72	0.88
Conditional entropy (bit)	0.72	0.72	0.69
Information gain (bit)	0.28	0.0	0.19
$\tau(\%)$	28	0	21.7

Table 4. UCI datasets description

	Pima Indian	Ecoli	Balance	Wavefo- rm	Glass	Iris	Ionosph- ere
Number of examples	768	336	625	300	214	150	351
Number of attributes	8	7	4	21	10	4	24
Number of classes	2	8	3	3	6	3	2
Class distribution	65.1% + 34.9%	42.6% + 22.9% + 15.5% + ...	46.8% + 46.8% + 7.4%	3 $\times$ 33.3%	35.5% + 32.7% + 13.5% + ...	3 $\times$ 33.3%	64.2% + 35.8%
% majority class	61.5	42.6	46.8	33.3	35.5	33.3	64.2

Table 5. Classification results for UCI datasets

	Pima Indian	Ecoli	Balance	Wavefo- rm	Glass	Iris	Ionosph- ere
Accuracy	69.37	78.24	76.52	66.61	65.11	96.0	87.21
Dataset entropy (bit)	0.93	2.18	1.31	1.58	2.14	1.58	0.94
Conditional entropy (bit)	0.85	0.99	0.79	1.25	1.38	0.22	0.55
Information gain (bit)	0.08	1.19	0.52	0.33	0.76	1.36	0.39
$\tau(\%)$	8.32	54.75	39.58	21.02	35.50	86.27	41.49

ratio in this case is 0%. The first dataset is more heterogeneous than the third one. It means that is more difficult to discriminate the examples. With the same classification accuracy, the classifier perform on the first dataset is more deserved than the one perform on the third dataset. The indicators related to the discrimination power validate this hypothesis.

Table 5 shows the results obtained by performing the experiments on several UCI datasets which are described in Table 4. In the Pima Indians diabetes dataset, the information gain ratio is small because the contribution of the classifier for discriminate the examples is relatively small, it does not make any significative difference to the one class classifier. The classification accuracies for the Ecoli dataset and for the Balance scale dataset are similar but the information gain ratio for the first one is clearly better. Because the Ecoli dataset is more complex than the Balance scale dataset (8 classes vs. 3 classes, 2.18 bits vs. 1.31 bits in the information measure), the classifier should work better in the Ecoli dataset for obtaining the close accuracy. There are the same situations between the Waveform dataset and the Glass Identification dataset and between the Iris plant dataset and the Ionosphere dataset.

7 Conclusion and Future Work

In this paper, the discrimination-based criteria have been proposed by considering the adequation between the partitions of the set of examples by their real classes and by the classifier. The criteria give us an additional index for evaluating a classification model. These criteria are designed based on the hierarchical model for discrimination measures. A set of experiments have been done to illustrate and validate the criteria.

In the future, the discrimination-based criteria should be extended for the more general case such as fuzzy classification or probability classification. It may be interesting to take into account the importance of examples.

As a classifier M can be regarded as a special attribute f_M, it suggests a possibility of aggregation of several classification models to obtain the more powerful one. Suppose that M_1, M_2, .., M_s are induced from the learning set. These classification models generate a set of attributes $\{f_{M_1}, f_{M_2}, .., f_{M_s}\}$ of the learning set. From the set of these attributes, a decision tree may be induced. An empirical validation of such a aggregation process should be done.

References

1. I. Alvarez. Explaining the result of a decision tree to the end-user. In *Proceedings of the 16th Eureopean Conference on Artificial Intelligence, ECAI'2004*, pages 411–415, 2004.
2. A. P. Bradley. The use of the area under the roc curve in the evaluation of machine learning algorithms. *Pattern Recognition*, 30(7):1145–1159, 1997.
3. R. Caruana, T. Joachims, and L. Backstrom. KDD-Cup 2004: results and analysis. *SIGKDD Explorations*, 6(2):95–108, 2004.
4. T. H. Dang. Entropies et leurs applications en apprentissage inductif *(rapport de pré-soutenance)*. Technical report, Université Paris 6, France, 2005.
5. T. H. Dang, B. Bouchon-Meunier, and C. Marsala. Measures of information for inductive learning. In *Proc. of Information Processing and Management of Uncertainty in Knownledge-Based Systems, IPMU'04*, pages 1495–1502, Perugia - Italy, July 2004.

6. T. Fawcett. Roc graphs: Notes and practical considerations for researchers. *Machine Learning*, (1-2), 2004.
7. I. Kononenko and I. Bratko. Information-based evaluation criterion for classifier's performance. *Machine Learning*, 6:67–80, 1991.
8. K. B. Korb, L. R. Hope, and M. J. Hughes. The evaluation of predictive learners: Some theoretical and empirical results. In *EMCL '01: Proceedings of the 12th European Conference on Machine Learning*, pages 276–287, London, UK, 2001. Springer-Verlag.
9. C. Marsala. *Apprentissage inductif en présence de données imprécises: construction et utilisation d'arbres de décision flous.* PhD thesis, Université Paris 6, France, 1998.
10. C. Marsala, B. Bouchon-Meunier, and A. Ramer. Hierarchical model for discrimination measures. In *Proc. of the eight IFSA'99 World Congres*, pages 339–343, Taipei - Taiwan, August 1999.
11. F. J. Provost and T. Fawcett. Analysis and visualization of classifier performance: Comparison under imprecise class and cost distributions. In *Knowledge Discovery and Data Mining*, pages 43–48, 1997.
12. F. J. Provost, T. Fawcett, and R. Kohavi. The case against accuracy estimation for comparing induction algorithms. In *ICML '98: Proceedings of the Fifteenth International Conference on Machine Learning*, pages 445–453, San Francisco, CA, USA, 1998. Morgan Kaufmann Publishers Inc.
13. J. Quinlan. Induction of decision trees. *Machine Learning*, 1(1):81–106, 1986.
14. A. Ramer, B. Bouchon-Meunier, and C. Marsala. An alytical structure of hierarchical discrimination. In *Proc. of the IEEE Int. Conf. on Fuzzy Systems, FUZZ-IEEE*, pages 1050–1053, Seoul - Korea, August 1999.
15. C. B. S. Hettich and C. Merz. UCI repository of machine learning databases, 1998.
16. C. Shannon. A mathematical theory of communication. *Bell System Technical Journal*, 27:379–423 and 623–656, July and October 1948.
17. F. Stermann and N. Longuet. Document technique de DTGen, rapport de stage de fin d'étude, DESS IA. Technical report, Laboratoire d'Informatique de Paris 6, Avril 2003.

A Hybrid Approach for Relation Extraction Aimed at the Semantic Web

Lucia Specia and Enrico Motta

Knowledge Media Institute & Centre for Research in Computing
The Open University - Walton Hall, MK7 6AA, Milton Keynes, UK
{L.Specia, E.Motta}@open.ac.uk

Abstract. We present an approach for relation extraction from texts aimed to enrich the semantic annotations produced by a semantic web portal. The approach exploits linguistic and empirical strategies, by means of a pipeline method involving processes such as a parser, part-of-speech tagger, named entity recognition system, pattern-based classification and word sense disambiguation models, and resources such as an ontology, knowledge base and lexical databases. With the use of knowledge intensive strategies to process the input data and corpus-based techniques to deal both with unpredicted cases and ambiguity problems, we expect to accurately discover most of the relevant relations for known and new entities, in an automated way.

1 Introduction

Relation Extraction (RE) consists of the identification of the semantic relations between pairs of terms in unstructured or semi-structured natural language documents. Semantic relations are useful for several applications, including the acquisition of terminological data, construction and extension of lexical resources and ontologies, question answering, information retrieval, semantic web annotation, etc.

In this paper we focus on the application of relation extraction to semantically annotate knowledge coming from raw text, as part of a framework aiming to automatically acquire high quality semantic metadata for the Semantic Web. One of the applications developed within this framework is the *KMi Semantic Web Portal*[1] [6], which analyzes data from texts, databases, and knowledge bases, in order to extract semantic knowledge from all of them in an integrated way, also verifying the quality of this knowledge, according to a domain ontology. The extracted knowledge is formalized into OCML and OWL representations[2].

Currently, the knowledge extracted by the semantic web portal from texts comprises mainly occurrences of entities (instances) that already exist in the knowledge base, and their properties also available in that knowledge base or in databases. It also includes occurrences of new entities, as given by a named entity recognition system, according to the possible types of entities in the domain ontology. Thus, already

[1] http://semanticweb.kmi.open.ac.uk:8080/ksw/index.html

[2] Examples of annotations produced by the KMi Semantic Web Portal for newsletters texts are available in http://plainmoor.open.ac.uk:8080/ksw/pages/news.jsp.

H.L. Larsen et al. (Eds.): FQAS 2006, LNAI 4027, pp. 564 – 576, 2006.

existent entities are semantically annotated with their properties provided by the knowledge base and databases. However, new knowledge about entities (especially relational) is not taken into account. Moreover, little is done with new entities, which are annotated only with their types.

In that context, the relation extraction approach presented here aims to identify the semantic relations between entities in the input texts. These include already existent relations between the entities in the knowledge base, new relations predicted as possible by the domain ontology, or completely new (unpredicted) relations. Additionally, new entities are identified in a more comprehensive way, and their relations are also extracted. As a consequence, extra knowledge about (existing and new) entities can be acquired, yielding a richer representation of the input data, and helping to solve problems that arise when mapping this unstructured data into a semantic representation, such as ambiguities. By identifying new entities in the text and recognizing their types, the approach could also be applied to ontology population. Moreover, since it extracts new relations between entities, it could be used as a first step for ontology learning.

The relation extraction approach makes use of a domain ontology, a knowledge base, and lexical databases, along with knowledge-based and empirical resources and strategies for linguistic processing. These include a lemmatizer, syntactic parser, part-of-speech tagger, named entity recognition system, and pattern matching and word sense disambiguation models. The input data used in the experiments with our approach consists of English texts from the Knowledge Media Institute (KMi)[3] newsletters. We believe that by integrating corpus and knowledge-based techniques and using rich linguistic processing strategies in a completely automated and unsupervised fashion, the approach can achieve more effective results than the previous work, in terms of both accuracy and coverage.

In the remaining of this paper we first describe some cognate work on relation extraction, particularly those exploring empirical methods, for various applications (Section 2). We then present our approach, showing its architecture and describing each of its main components (Section 3). Finally, we discuss next steps (Section 4).

2 Related Work

Several approaches have been proposed for the extraction of relations from unstructured sources. Recently, they have focused on the use of supervised or unsupervised corpus-based techniques in order to automate the task. A very common approach is based on pattern matching, with patterns composed by subject-verb-object (SVO) tuples. Interesting work has been done on the unsupervised automatic definition of patterns from a small number of seed patterns. These are used as a starting point to bootstrap the pattern learning process, by means of semantic similarity measures [20, 16].

Most of the approaches for relation extraction rely on the mapping of syntactic dependencies, such as SVO, onto semantic relations, using either pattern matching or other strategies, such as probabilistic parsing for trees augmented with annotations for entities and relations [11], or clustering of semantically similar syntactic dependencies, according to their selectional restrictions [5].

[3] http://kmi.open.ac.uk/

In corpus-based approaches, many variations are found concerning the machine learning techniques used to produce classifiers to judge relation as relevant or non-relevant. [14], e.g., uses probabilistic classifiers with constraints induced between relations and entities, such as selectional restrictions. Based on instances represented by a pair of entities and their position in a shallow parse tree, [17] uses support vector machines and voted perceptron as algorithms with a specialized kernel model. Also using kernel methods and support vector machines, [18] combines clues from different levels of syntactic information and applies composite kernels to integrate and extend the individual kernels.

The framework proposed by [6], still under development, similarly to our work aims at the automation of semantic annotations according to ontologies. Several supervised algorithms can be used on the training data represented through a canonical graph-based data model. The framework includes a shallow linguistic processing step, in which corpora are analyzed and a representation is produced according to the data model, and a classification step, where classifiers run on the datasets produced by the linguistic processing step.

Many relation extraction approaches have been also proposed focusing on the particular task of ontology development [10, 13, 15, 1]. These approaches aim to learn non-taxonomic relations between concepts, instead of lexical entries, addressed by traditional approaches within Information Extraction. However, in essence, they employ similar techniques, derived from text mining, to extract relations.

In the next section we describe our approach, which merges features that have shown to be effective in several of the previous works, in order to achieve more comprehensive and accurate results, aiming particularly at the generation of semantic annotation for the Semantic Web.

3 A Hybrid Approach for Relation Extraction

The proposed approach for relation extraction is illustrated in Fig. 1. It employs knowledge-based and (supervised and unsupervised) corpus-based techniques. The core strategy consists of mapping linguistic components with some syntactic relationship (a linguistic triple) into their corresponding semantic components. This includes mapping not only the relations, but also the linguistic terms linked by those relations. The identification of the linguistic triples involves a series of linguistic processing steps. The mapping between terms and concepts is guided by a domain ontology and a named entity recognition system. The identification of the relations relies on the knowledge available in the domain ontology and in a lexical database, and on pattern-based classification and sense disambiguation models.

The main goal of this approach is to provide rich semantic annotations that can be used, for example, by a semantic web portal. Since the resultant annotations include already existent and new entities and relations, there are other possible uses of our approach, including:

1) Ontology population: we map terms into new instances of concepts of an ontology and identify the relations between them, according to the possible relations in that ontology.

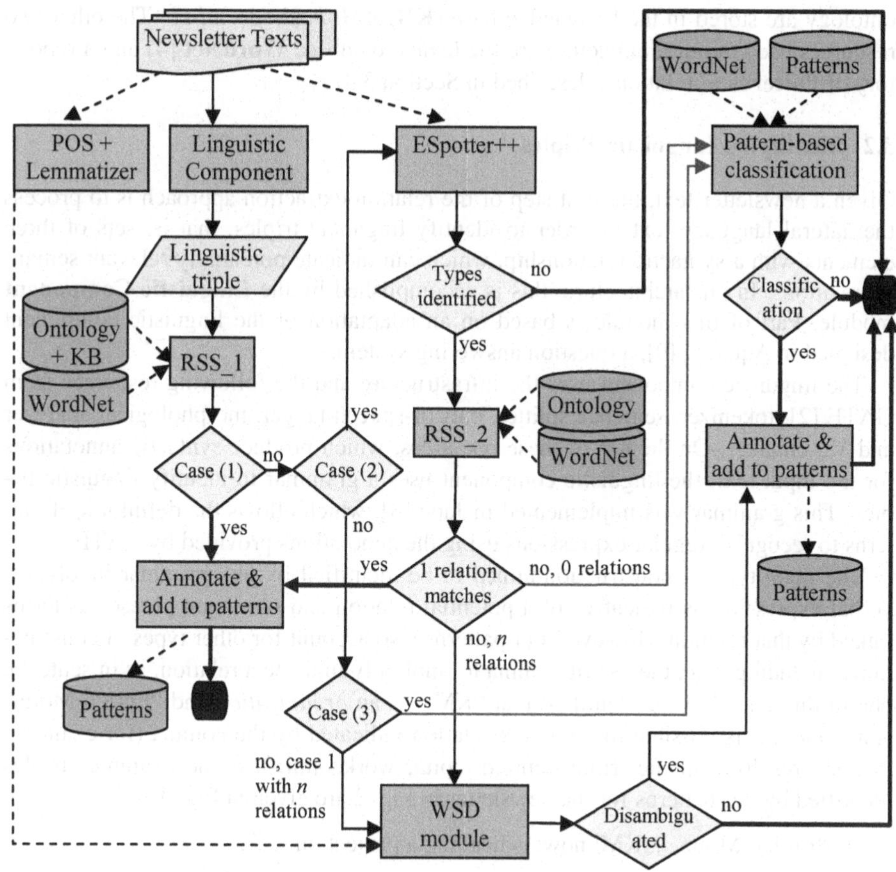

Fig. 1. Architecture of the proposed approach

2) Ontology learning: we identify new relations between existent concepts, which can be used as a first step to extend an existent ontology. Certainly, a subsequent step to lift relations between instances to an adequate level of abstraction would be necessary (e.g., [10]).

3.1 Context and Resources

The input to our experiments consists of electronic **Newsletter Texts** (KMi Planet[4]). These are short texts describing news of several natures related to KMi members: projects, publications, events, awards, etc. The domain **Ontology** used is the *KMi-basic-portal-ontology*. This was designed based on the AKT reference ontology[5] to include concepts relevant to the KMi domain. The instantiations of concepts in this

[4] http://news.kmi.open.ac.uk/kmiplanet/

[5] http://kmi.open.ac.uk/projects/akt/ref-onto/

ontology are stored in the knowledge base (**KB**) *KMi-basic-portal-kb*. The other two resources used in our architecture are the lexical database **WordNet** [4] and a repository of **Patterns** of relations, described in Section 3.4.

3.2 Identifying Linguistic Triples

Given a newsletter text, the first step of the relation extraction approach is to process the natural language text in order to identify linguistic triples, that is, sets of three elements with a syntactic relationship, which can indicate potentially relevant semantic relations. In our architecture, this is accomplished by the **Linguistic Component** module. Part of this module is based on an adaptation of the linguistic component designed in Aqualog [9], a question answering system.

The linguistic component uses the infrastructure and the following resources from GATE [2]: tokenizer, sentence splitter, part-of-speech tagger, morphological analyzer and VP chunker. On the top of these resources, which produce syntactic annotations for the input text, the linguistic component uses a grammar to identify linguistic triples. This grammar was implemented in Jape [3], which allows the definition of patterns to recognize regular expressions using the annotations provided by GATE.

The main type of construction aimed to be identified by our grammar involves a verbal expression as indicative of a potential relation and two noun phrases as terms linked by that relation. However, our patterns also account for other types of constructions, including, e.g., the use of comma to implicitly indicate a relation, as in sentence (1). In this case, having identified that "KMi" is an *organization* and "Enrico Motta" is a *person*, it is possible to guess the relation indicated by the comma (for example, "work", resulting in the triple <enrico-motta, work, kmi>). Some examples triples identified by our patterns for the newsletter in Fig. 2 are given in Fig. 3.

(1) "Enrico Motta, at KMi now, is heading a project on ….".

Nobel Summit on ICT and public services

Peter Scott attended the Public Services Summit in Stockholm, during Nobel Week 2005. The theme this year was Responsive Citizen Centered Public Services. The event was hosted by the City of Stockholm and Cisco Systems Thursday 8 December - Sunday 11 December 2005.

The Nobel Week Summit provides an unusual venue to explore the possibilities of the Internet with top global decision-makers in education, healthcare and government and to honor the achievements of the 2005 Nobel Peace Prize Laureate.

Fig. 2. Example of newsletter

<peter-scott,attend,public-services-summit>
<public-services-summit,located,stockholm>
<theme,is,responsive-citizen-centered-public-services>
<city-of-stockholm-and-cisco-systems,host,event>
<the-nobel-week-summit,provide,unusual-venue>
<unusual-venue,explore,the-possibilities-of-the-internet>

Fig. 3. Examples of linguistic triples for the newsletter in Fig. 2

Although we were concerned about making the Jape patterns as comprehensive as possible, they are based on shallow syntactic information only, and therefore they are not able to capture certain potentially relevant triples. To overcome this limitation, we employ a parser as a complementary resource to produce linguistic triples. We use Minipar (Lin, 1993), which produces functional relations for the components in a sentence, including subject and object relations with respect to a verb. This allows capturing some implicit relations, such as indirect objects and long distance dependence relations, which could not be identified by the Jape patterns. Fig. 4 shows some tuples extracted for the text in Fig. 2.

```
subject[peter_scott]+verb[attend]+verb_mod[during_nobel_week_2005]+
object[public_services_summit]+object_mod[in_stockholm]

subject[theme]+verb[be]+object[responsive]

subject[city]+subj_mod[of_stockholm]+verb[host]+object[event]
```

Fig. 4. Examples of tuples extracted from Minipar's dependency trees

Minipar's representation is converted into a triple format, repeating the verb when it is related to more than one subject or object. Thus, the intermediate representation provided both by GATE plus the Jape grammar and by Minipar consists of triples of the type: <noun_phrase, verbal_expression, noun_phrase>.

3.3 Identifying Ontological Entities and Relations

Given a linguistic triple, the next step is to verify whether the verbal expression in that triple conveys a relevant semantic relationship between entities (given by the terms) potentially belonging to an ontology. This is the most important phase of our approach and is represented by a series of modules in our architecture in Fig. 1. As first step we try to map the linguistic triple into an ontology triple, by using an adaptation of the Relation Similarity Service (RSS) also developed in Aqualog [9].

RSS tries to make sense of the linguistic triple by looking at the structure of the domain ontology and the information stored in the KB. In order to map a linguistic triple into an ontology triple, besides looking for an exact matching between the components of the two triples, RSS considers partial matchings by using a set of resources in order to account for minor lexical or conceptual discrepancies between these two elements. These resources include metrics for string similarity matching, synonym relations given by WordNet, and a lexicon of previous mappings between the two types of triples.

RSS was originally designed to be used in an interactive fashion by a question answering system. Therefore, the user is expected to point out the appropriate mapping when there is no matching between the linguistic and ontology triples. The user is also expected to disambiguate among several options of mappings. In order to achieve a fully automated annotation process we use other modules to map linguistic triples into ontology triples even if there is no matching according to RSS (Section 3.4) or if there is ambiguity (Section 3.5).

Different strategies are employed to identify matchings for terms and relations, as explained in Sections 3.3.1 and 3.3.2. The application of these strategies to map the linguistic triples into existent or new instances and relations is described in Section 3.3.3.

3.3.1 Mapping Terms

To map terms into entities, the following attempts are accomplished (in the given order):

1) Search the KB for an exact matching of the term with any instance.

2) Apply string similarity metrics[6] to calculate the similarity between the given term and each instance of the KB. A hybrid scheme combining three metrics is used: jaro-Winkler, jlevelDistance a wlevelDistance. It checks different combinations of threshold values for the metrics. The elements in our linguistic triples are lemmatized in order to avoid problems which could be incorrectly handled by the string similarity metrics (e.g., past tense).

   2.1) If there is more that one possible matching, check whether any of them is a substring of the term. For example, the instance name for "Enrico Motta" is a substring of the term "Motta", and thus it should be preferred to any other instance.

For example, the similarity values returned for the term "vanessa" with instances potentially relevant for the mapping are given in Fig. 5. The combination of thresholds specified for the metrics is met for the instance "Vanessa Lopez", and thus the mapping is (correctly) accomplished. If there is still more than one possible mapping for a term in the linguistic triple, we assume there is not enough evidence to map that term, and the triple is discarded.

```
jaroDistance for "vanessa" and "vanessa-lopez" = 0.8461538461538461wlevel for "vanessa" and "vanessa-lopez" = 1.0jWinklerDistance for "vanessa" and "vanessa-lopez" = 0.9076923076923077
```

Fig. 5. String similarity measures for the term "vanessa" and the instance "Vanessa Lopez"

3.3.2 Mapping Relations

In order to map the verbal expression into a conceptual relation, we assume that the terms of the triple have already been mapped either into instances of classes in the KB by RSS, or into potential new instances, by a named entity recognition system, as we explain will later in Section 3.3.3. The following attempts are then made for the verb-relation mapping:

1) Search the KB for an exact matching of the verbal expression with any existent relation for the instances under consideration or any possible relation between the classes (and superclasses) of the instances under consideration.

2) Apply the string similarity metrics to calculate the similarity between the given verbal expression and the possible relations between instances (or their classes) corresponding to the terms in the linguistic triple.

[6] Available in http://sourceforge.net/projects/simmetrics/.

3) Search for similar mappings for the types/classes of entities under consideration in a lexicon of mappings previously accomplished according to users' choices in Aqualog[7]. This lexicon contains ontology triples along with the given verbal expression which was mapped to the conceptual relation, as illustrated in Table 1. The use of this lexicon represents a simplified form of pattern matching in which only exact matching is considered.

Table 1. Examples of lexicon patterns

given_relation	class_1	conceptual relation	class_2
works	project	has-project-member	person
cite	project	has-publication	publication

4) Search for synonyms of the given verbal expression in WordNet, in order to verify if there is a synonym that matches (complete or partially, using string similarity metrics) any existent relation for the instances under consideration, or any possible relation between the classes (or superclasses) of those instances (likewise in step 1).

If there is no possible mapping for the term, the pattern-based classification model is triggered (Section 3.4). Conversely, if there is more than one possible mapping, the disambiguation model is called (Section 3.5).

3.3.3 RSS for Existing / New Instances, and Existent / Predicted Relations

In our architecture, RSS is represented by modules **RSS_1** and **RSS_2**. **RSS_1** first checks if the terms in the linguistic triple are instances of a KB (cf. described in Section 3.3.1). If the terms can be mapped to instances, it checks whether the relation given in the triple matches any already existent relation between for those instances, or, alternatively, if that relation matches any of the possible relations for the classes (and superclasses) of the two instances in the domain ontology (cf. Section 3.3.2). Three situations may arise from this attempt to map the linguistic triple into an ontology triple (Cases (1), (2), and (3) in Fig. 1):

Case (1) complete matching with instances of the KB and a relation of the KB or ontology, with possibly more than one valid conceptual relation being identified:

$$\langle \text{instance}_1, (\text{conceptual\_relation})^{+}, \text{instance}_2 \rangle.$$

Case (2) no matching or partial matching with instances of the ontology (the relation is not analyzed (*na*) when there is not a matching for instances):

$$\langle \text{instance}_1, na, ? \rangle \quad \text{or} \quad \langle ?, na, \text{instance}_2 \rangle \quad \text{or} \quad \langle ?, na, ? \rangle$$

Case (3) matching with instances of the KB, but no matching with a relation of the KB or ontology:

$$\langle \text{instance}_1, ?, \text{instance}_2 \rangle$$

If the matching attempt results in Case (1) with only one conceptual relation, then the triple can be formalized into a semantic annotation. This yields the annotation of an

7 http://plainmoor.open.ac.uk:8080/aqualog/index.html

already existent relation for two instances of the KB, as well as a new relation for two instances of the KB, although this relation was already predicted in the ontology as possible between the classes of those instances. The generalization of the produced triple for classes/types of entities, i.e., <class, conceptual_relation, class>, is added to the repository of **Patterns**.

On the other hand, if there is more than one possible conceptual relation in case (1), the system tries to find the correct one by means of a sense disambiguation model, described in Section 3.5. Conversely, if there is no matching for the relation (Case (3)), the system tries an alternative strategy: the pattern-based classification model (Section 3.4). Finally, if there is no complete matching of the terms with instances of the KB (Case (2)), it means that the entities can be new to the KB.

In order to check if the terms in the linguistic triple express new entities, the system first identifies to what classes of the ontology they belong. This is accomplished by means of ESpotter++, and extension of the named entity recognition system ESpotter [19].

ESpotter is based on a mixture of lexicon (gazetteers) and patterns. We extended ESpotter by including new entities (extracted from other gazetteers), a few relevant new types of entities, and a small set of efficient patterns. In Espotter++ all types of entities correspond to generic classes of our domain ontology. These types include: person, organization, event, publication, location, project, research-area, technology, date, etc.

In our architecture, if ESpotter++ is not able to identify the types of the entities, the process is aborted and no annotation is produced. This may be either because the terms do not have any conceptual mapping (for example "it"), or because the conceptual mapping is not part of our domain ontology. Otherwise, if ESpotter++ succeeds, we use the RSS again (RSS_2) in order to verify whether the verbal expression encompasses a semantic relation. Since at least one of the two entities is recognized by Espotter++, and therefore at least one entity is new, it is only possible to check if the relation matches one of the possible relations between the classes of the recognized entities (cf. Section 3.3.2).

If the matching attempt results in only one conceptual relation, then the triple will be formalized into a semantic annotation. This represents the annotation of a new (although predicted) relation and two or at least one new entity/instance. The produced triple of the type <class, conceptual_relation, class> is added to the repository of Patterns.

Again, if there are multiple valid conceptual relations, the system tries to find the correct one by means of a disambiguation model (Section 3.5). Conversely, if it there is no matching for the relation, the pattern-based classification model is triggered (Section 3.4).

3.4 Identifying New Relations – The Pattern Matching Model

The process described in Section 3.3 for the identification of relations accounts only for the relations already predicted as possible in the domain ontology. However, we are also interested in the additional information that can be provided by the text, in the form of new types of relations for known or new entities. In order to discover these relations, we employ a pattern matching strategy to identify relevant relations between types of terms.

The pattern matching strategy has proved to be an efficient way to extract semantic relations, but in general has the drawback of requiring the possible relations to be previously defined. In order to overcome this limitation, we employ a Pattern-based classification model that can identify similar patterns based on a very small initial number of patterns.

We consider patterns of relations between types of entities, instead of the entities themselves, since we believe that it would be impossible to accurately judge the similarity for the kinds of entities we are addressing (names of people, locations, etc). Thus, our patterns consist of triples of the type <class, conceptual_relation, class>, which are contrasted against a given triple using the classes already provided by the linguistic component or by ESpotter++ in order to classify relations in that triple as relevant or non-relevant.

The pattern-based classification model is based on the approach presented in [16]. It is an unsupervised corpus-based module which takes as examples a small set of relevant SVO patterns, called seed patterns, and uses a WordNet-based semantic similarity measure to compare the pattern to be classified against the relevant ones. Our initial seed patterns (see examples in Table 2) mixes patterns extracted from the lexicon generated by Aqualog's users (cf. Section 3.3.2) and a small number of manually defined relevant patterns. This set of patterns is expected to be enriched with new patterns as our system annotates relevant relations, since the system adds new triples to the initial set of patterns.

Table 2. Examples of seed patterns

class_1	conceptual relation	class_2
project	has-project-member	person
project	has-publication	publication
person	develop	technology
person	attend	event

Likewise [16], we use a semantic similarity metric based on the information content of the words in WordNet hierarchy, derived from corpus probabilities. It scores the similarity between two patterns by computing the similarity for each pair of words in those patterns. A threshold of 0.90 for this score was used here to classify two patterns as similar. In that case, a new annotation is produced for the input triple and it is added to the set of patterns.

It is important to notice that, although WordNet is also used in the RSS modules, in that case only synonyms are checked, while here the similarity metric explores deeper information in WordNet, considering the meaning (senses) of the words. It is also important to distinguish the semantic similarity metrics employed here from the string metrics used in RSS. String similarity metrics simply try to capture minor variations on the strings representing terms/relations, they do not account for the meaning of those strings.

3.5 Disambiguating Relations

The ambiguity arising when more than one possible relation exists for a pair of entities is a problem neglected in most of the current work on relation extraction. In our architecture, when the RSS finds more than one possible relation, we try to choose one relation by using the word sense disambiguation (**WSD**) system SenseLearner [12].

SenseLearner is minimally supervised WSD system to disambiguate all open class words in any given text, after being trained on a small data set, according to global models for word categories. The current distribution includes two default models for verbs, which were trained on a corpus containing 200,000 content words of journalistic texts manually tagged with their WordNet senses. Since SenseLeaner requires a corpus tagged with senses in order to be trained to specific domains and there is not such a corpus for our domain, we use one of the default training models, which accounts for the most common uses of the verbs. This is a contextual model that relies on the first word before and after the verb, and its POS tags. To disambiguate new cases, it requires only that these cases are annotated with the POS tags of the words. The use of lemmas of the words instead of the words yields better results, since the models were generated for lemmas. In our architecture, the POS and lemma annotations are produced by the component **POS + Lemmatizer**.

Since the WSD module disambiguates among WordNet senses, it is employed only after the use of the WordNet subcomponent by RSS. This subcomponent finds all the synonyms for the verb in a linguistic triple and checks which of them matches existent or possible relations for the terms in that triple. In some cases, however, there is a matching for more than one synonym. In WordNet, synonyms usually represent different uses of the verb. Therefore, the WSD module is used to identify in which sense the verb is being used in the sentence, allowing the system to choose one among the possible matchings.

For example, given the linguistic triple <enrico_motta, head, kmi>, RSS is able to identify that "enrico_motta" is a person, and that "kmi" is an organization. However, it cannot find an exact or partial matching (using string metrics), or even a matching given by the user lexicon. After getting the synonyms for "head" in WordNet, RSS verifies that two of them match possible relations in the ontology between a person and an organization: "direct" and "lead". In this case, the WSD module correctly disambiguates the sense of "head" in the input sentence from which the linguistic triple was produced as "direct".

3.6 Annotating Relevant Relations

To formalize the relations extracted, we use the representation specified for the KMi Semantic Web Portal, in order to make it straightforward to integrate this knowledge to the one produced by the portal. The representation of the entity "Enrico Motta" and of all the relations involving this entity from the news text in Fig. 6, e.g., is given in Fig. 7.

In this case, "Enrico-Motta" is an instance of kmi-academic-staff-member, a subclass of person in the domain ontology. The mapped relation "works-in" "knowledge-media-institute" already existed in the KB. The new relations pointed out by our approach are the ones referring to the award received from the "European Commission" (an organization, here), for three projects: "NeOn", "XMEDIA", and "OK".

KMi awarded £4M for Semantic Web Research

Professor Enrico Motta and Dr John Domingue of the Knowledge Media Institute have received a set of record-breaking awards totalling £4m from the European Commission's Framework 6 Information Society Technologies (IST) programme. This is the largest ever combined award obtained by KMi associated with a single funding programme. The awards include three Integrated Projects (IPs) and three Specific Targeted Research Projects (STREPs) and they consolidate KMi's position as one of the leading international research centers in semantic technologies. Specifically Professor Motta has been awarded:

a.. £1.55M for the project NeOn: Lifecycle Support for Networked Ontologies
b.. £565K for XMEDIA: Knowledge Sharing and Reuse across Media and
c.. £391K for OK: Openknowledge - Open, coordinated knowledge sharing architecture. ...

Fig. 6. Example of newsletter

```
(def-instance Enrico-Motta kmi-academic-staff-member
 ((works-in knowledge-media-institute)
  (award-from european-commission)
  (award-for NeOn)
  (award-for XMEDIA)
  (award-for OK)))
```

Fig. 7. Semantic annotations produced for the news in Fig. 6

4 Conclusions and Future Work

We presented a hybrid approach for the extraction of semantic relations from text. It was designed mainly to enrich the annotations produced by a semantic web portal, but can be used for other domains and applications, such as ontology population and development. Currently we are concluding the integration of the several modules composing our architecture. We will then carry experiments with our corpus of newsletters in order to evaluate the approach. Subsequently, we will incorporate the architecture to the semantic web portal and accomplish an extrinsic evaluation in the context of that application. Since the approach uses deep linguistic processing and corpus-based strategies not requiring any manual annotation, we expect it will accurately discover most of the relevant relations in the text.

References

1. Ciaramita, M., Gangemi, A., Ratsch, E., Saric, J., Rojas, I. Unsupervised learning of semantic relations between concepts of a molecular biology ontology. 19th IJCAI (2005) 659-664
2. Cunningham, H., Maynard, D., Bontcheva, K., and Tablan, V. GATE: A Framework and Graphical Development Environment for Robust NLP Tools and Applications. 40th ACL Meeting, Philadelphia (2002)
3. Cunningham, H., Maynard, D., and Tablan, V. JAPE: a Java Annotation Patterns Engine. Tech. Report CS--00--10, University of Sheffield, Department of Computer Science (2000)

4. Fellbaum, C. D. (ed). Wordnet: An Electronic Lexical Database. The MIT Press (1998)
5. Gamallo, P., Gonzalez, M., Agustini, A., Lopes, G., de Lima, V.S. Mapping syntactic dependencies onto semantic relations. ECAI Workshop on Machine Learning and Natural Language Processing for Ontology Engineering, Lyon, France (2002)
6. Iria, J. and Ciravegna, F. Relation Extraction for Mining the Semantic Web. Dagstuhl Seminar on Machine Learning for the Semantic Web, Dagstuhl, Germany (2005)
7. Lei, Y., Sabou, M., Lopez, V., Zhu, J., Uren, V., and Motta, E. An infrastructure for Acquiring High Quality Semantic Metadata. To appear in the 3rd ESWC, Budva, Montenegro (2006)
8. Lin, D. Principle based parsing without overgeneration. 31st ACL, Columbus (1993) 112-120
9. Lopez, V., Pasin, M., and Motta, E. AquaLog: An Ontology-portable Question Answering System for the Semantic Web. ESWC 2005, Creete, Grece (2005)
10. Maedche, A., Staab, S. Ontology learning for the semantic web. IEEE Intelligent Systems 16 (2001) 72-79
11. Miller, S., Fox, H., Ramshaw, L.A. and Weischedel, R.M. A novel use of statistical parsing to extract information from text. 6th ANLP-NAACL, Seattle (2000) 226-233
12. Mihalcea, R. and Csomai, A. SenseLearner: Word Sense Disambiguation for All Words in Unrestricted Text. 43rd ACL Meeting, Ann Arbor (2005)
13. Reinberger, M.L., Spyns, P. Discovering knowledge in texts for the learning of DOGMA inspired ontologies. ECAI 2004 Workshop on Ontology Learning and Population, Valencia (2004) 19-24
14. Roth, D., Yih, W. T. Probabilistic reasoning for entity & relation recognition. 19th COLING, Taipei, Taiwan (2002) 1-7
15. Schutz, A. and Buitelaar, P. RelExt: A Tool for Relation Extraction from Text in Ontology Extension. 4th ISWC (2005) 593-606
16. Stevenson, M. An Unsupervised WordNet-based Algorithm for Relation Extraction. 4th LREC Workshop Beyond Named Entity: Semantic Labeling for NLP Tasks, Lisbon (2004).
17. Zelenko, D., Aone, C., and Richardella, A. Kernel Methods for Relation Extraction. Journal of Machine Learning Research (2003). 3:1083-1106.
18. Zhao, S., Grishman, R. Extracting Relations with Integrated Information Using Kernel Methods. 43d ACL Meeting, Ann Arbor (2005)
19. Zhu, J., Uren, V., and Motta, E. ESpotter: Adaptive Named Entity Recognition for Web Browsing. 3rd Conference on Professional Knowledge Management, Kaiserslautern (2005) 518-529
20. Yangarber, R., Grishman, R., Tapanainen, P. Unsupervised Discovery of Scenario-Level Patterns for Information Extraction. 6th ANLP (2000) 282-289

An XML Framework for a Basque Question Answering System

Olatz Ansa, Xabier Arregi, Arantxa Otegi, and Andoni Valverde

IXA Group
University of the Basque Country
{olatz.ansa, xabier.arregi}@ehu.es,
{jibotusa, a.valverde}@si.ehu.es

Abstract. This paper presents a general platform for a Basque monolingual question answering (QA) system. It focuses on the architecture of the platform, paying special attention to: 1) the integration of the development and evaluation environments, and 2) the systematic use of XML declarative files to control the execution of the modules and the communication between them. Moreover, a first pilot experiment is discussed.

1 Introduction

Question answering systems tackle the task of finding a precise and concrete answer for a natural language question on a document collection.

These systems use information retrieval (IR) and natural language processing (NLP) techniques to understand the question and generate the answer properly. This task involves, on the one hand, the use and adaptation of IR and NLP resources, techniques and tools, and, on the other hand, allows the evaluation of such tools in a real application.

When dealing with the Basque QA system, we do not conceive the development and evaluation tasks as independent processes. On contrary, the idea is that the architecture of the general platform must support both the gradual development and the layered evaluation of the system. The objective is that the application of alternative techniques or the use of new resources and tools to be easily valuable. At the same time, the evaluation environment must make possible the extraction of qualitative and quantitative data to give feedback to the system, in order to facilitate the future improvement.

The current version of the question answering system takes Basque questions as input, and the corpus on which the answers are searched is written in Basque too. It incorporates tools and resources developed in IXA[1] group, like the morphosyntactic analyzer, the lemmatizer, and the named entity recognizer and classifier.

This paper focuses on the general architecture of the platform, which has two main components: the QA system itself and the evaluation environment.

[1] http://ixa.si.ehu.es

H.L. Larsen et al. (Eds.): FQAS 2006, LNAI 4027, pp. 577–588, 2006.

The remainder of the paper is organized as follows. Section two is devoted to introduce the general architecture of the platform. In section three we describe the QA system. Then, in section four evaluation issues are discussed. Finally, section five contains some conclusions and suggestions for future research.

2 General Platform: The XML Configuration File

The QA platform integrates the QA system and the evaluation environment. Both components are autonomous but are governed by one configuration file. The two components access to the testing database of questions and answers, where they find the information required for running and evaluating the system.

The current version of the QA system receives as input a set of Basque questions and returns as output an ordered list of answers for each of the questions. The answers are extracted from a Basque newspaper corpus.

The evaluation environment deals with the answers returned by the system and with the answers captured manually, which have been previously stored in the testing database. It assists in the task of deciding which of the automatically obtained answers are correct. This environment supports the management of the results in order to value the performance, obtain statistics, and detect the aspects to be improved. The evaluation process also allows the enrichment of the testing database by adding new correct answers and/or answer-containing passages when they have been automatically detected in the corpus.

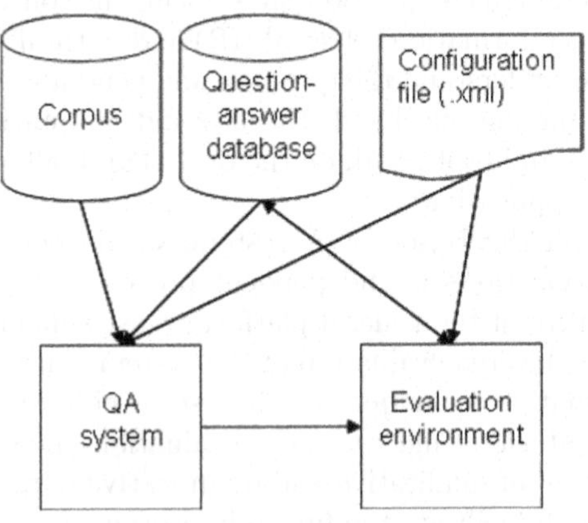

Fig. 1. The system general architecture

A XML configuration file governs the running of these components. The configuration file is a declarative document where all the features involved in a run are described. The set of features is divided into two categories:

1. General requirements. It includes specifications such as the corpus to be used, the processing model of the corpus, the location of the list of questions

to be answered, the description of the type of questions, and the metrics and conditions for the evaluation.
2. Descriptors of the QA process itself. This subset of features represents the characteristics of the answering process. Mainly, it determines which modules act during the answering process, describes them and specifies the parameters of each module. In that way, the process is controlled by means of the configuration file, and different processing options, techniques, and resources can be easily activated/deactivated and adapted. These descriptors constitute the documentation support of the system.

```
<?xml version="1.0" encoding="UTF-8"?>
<!DOCTYPE qa SYSTEM "qa.dtd">  <!--  Configuration of the QA platform -->
<qa>
      <corpus name="Euskaldunon Egunkaria" location="..." years="2000"
       size="..." type="newspaper">
          <processing level="medium">
              <tagger applied="yes">
                  <used-tool description="MORFEUS3.3.9" soap-service=""/>
              </tagger>
              <lemmatiser applied="yes">
                  <used-tool description="EUSLEM3.3.9" soap-service=""/>
              </lemmatiser>
              <wsd applied="no"/>
              <clustering applied="no"/>
              ...
          </processing>
      </corpus>
      <questions number="" type="factoid" subtype="who-is" difficulty="low"
       location="..."/>
      <evaluation layers-number="3">
          <global-measure name="Mean Reciprocal Rank"> ... </global-measure>
      </evaluation>
      <qasystem>
          <run name="question-answering" version="1.0" state="active">
              <process name="question-processing" state="active">
                  <process name="detecting-answer type" state="active">
                      <parameters number="">
                          <parameter name=""></parameter>
                      </parameters>
                  </process>
                  <process name="extracting-search-terms" state="active">
                      <parameters number="">
                          <parameter name=""></parameter>
                      </parameters>
                  </process>
                  ...
              </process>
              <process name="passage-retrieving" active="yes">
                  <used-tool description="swish-e" soap-service=""/>
                  ...
              </process>
              ...
          </run>
      </qasystem>
</qa>
```

The <qa> tag in the above example expresses the configuration of the QA platform. The corpus, questions and evaluation elements refer to general requirements, as they are not properly related to the QA system specifications. In the described configuration the corpus processing level is medium, the questions belong to the "who-is" factoid type, and the evaluation is carried out in a layered manner. The QA system integrates several processes that are hierarchically organized. For instance, the `detecting-answer type` process is included in the `question-processing` more general one. Each of the processes is described by its attributes along with the parameters that are used in the run. The `<used-tool>` tag refers to the employment of a specific tool, which usually is implemented as a SOAP service.

3 The QA System

The principles of versatility and adaptability have guided the development of the system. The system is based on web services, integrated using SOAP communication protocol. Some tools previously developed in the IXA group are reused as autonomous web services, and the QA system becomes a client that calls these services when it needs them. This distributed model allows to parameterize the linguistic tools, and to adjust the behaviour of the system during the development and testing phases.

The communication between the web services is done using XML documents. This model has been adopted by other systems (Tomás et al. 2005, Hiyakumoto 2004). Each service receives the input data in XML documents, and consults the general configuration file for specific information about execution parameters.

3.1 Modular Architecture

The current version has three main modules, as it is very common in the question answering systems:

Question analysis: the main goal of this module is to analyze the question and to generate the information needed for the next tasks. Concretely, a set of search terms are extracted for the passage retrieval module, and the expected answer type along with some lexical and syntactic information is passed to the answer extraction module.

The question analysis uses a set of general purpose tools like the morphological analyzer, *Morfeus* (Alegria et al., 2002), and the Name Entity recognizer and classifier, *Eihera* (Alegria et al., 2004).

All nouns, verbs, adjectives and abbreviations of the question constitute the set of search terms. They are lemmatized and arranged in descending order by their *Inverse Document Frequency* (IDF) value in the corpora.

Optionally, the search terms can be expanded using synonymy, hyponymy and hypernymy information. To do this, the system uses a service which consults the lexical-semantic database BasqueWN[2].

[2] It is the Basque version of EuroWordNet. This resource is integrated in the Multilingual Central Repository (MCR), which is a multilingual lexical database developed in the Meaning project (Atserias, 2004).

For identifying the expected answer type, a set of rules has been defined after the examination of a Basque question set.

All information obtained by this module is represented in a XML file. An example follows:

```
<question_analysis phase="search term expansion">
  <search_term frm="taldeko">
    <lex lem="talde" pos="IZE" case="" priority="original" idf="0.554914539" enti=""/>
    ...
    <lex lem="jendetza" pos="IZE" case="" priority="syns" idf="" enti=""/>
  </search_term>
  <search_term frm="nagusia">
    <lex lem="nagusi" pos="IZE" case="ABS" priority="original" idf="0.661616092" enti=""/>
    <lex lem="buru" pos="IZE" case="ABS" priority="syns" idf="" enti="" />
    ...
    <lex lem="adin-nagusitasun" pos="IZE" case="ABS" priority="syns" idf="" enti=""/>
  </search_term>
  <search_term frm="kantari">
    <lex lem="kantari" pos="IZE" case="" priority="original" idf="1.974341383" enti=""/>
    <lex lem="abeslari" pos="IZE" case="" priority="syns" idf="" enti="" />
  </search_term>
  <search_term frm="Oskorri">
   <lex lem="oskorri" pos="IZE" case="" priority="original" idf="2.8087944" enti="ENTI_ORG"/>
  </search_term>
  <term frm="Nor">
    <lex lem="nor" pos="IOR" case="ABS" priority="original" idf="" enti="" />
  </term>
  <term frm="da">
    <lex lem="izan" pos="ADT" case="" priority="original" idf="" enti="" />
  </term>
  <term frm="?">
    <lex lem="" pos="" case="" priority="original" idf="" enti="" />
  </term>
  <expected_answer_type>PERSON</expected_answer_type>
</question_analysis>
```

The <question_analysis> tag represents the results of the question analysis process. The question terms selected for the passage retrieval module are marked as search_term elements, and the rest of the question tokens are marked as term elements. For each term, whether search term or not, we represent its lemma (<lem> tag), the part-of-speech (<pos> tag), the level of priority according to the use of expansion techniques, the IDF value, and the class of the named-entity that it represents, if any. Moreover, the expected answer type is given.

Passage retrieval: the retrieval unit is the passage and not the entire document. The corpus is indexed by lemma using swish-e[3] search engine. The corpus is batch-processed: all words are lemmatized, and complex lexical units and entities are marked.

This module takes as input the search terms selected by the question analysis module and produces a set of queries. These queries are created using relaxation techniques (Bilotti, 2004), and are executed until one of them retrieves a passage.

An XML document is created with references to all retrieved documents and all the queries processed until a non-empty document collection is obtained.

---

[3] http://swish-e.org

```
<?xml version="1.0" encoding="UTF-8" ?>
<document_retrieval>
<swish_query query="(talde OR aldra OR sail OR saldo OR samalda OR ekipo OR unitate OR
                lagunarte OR multzo OR abeltalde OR artalde OR jendetza OR nahaspila)
                AND (nagusi OR ugazaba OR buru OR buruzagi OR agintzaile OR maisu OR
                jabe OR jaun OR jauntxo OR patroi OR ugazabandre OR adin-nagusitasun
                OR adinaro) AND (kantari OR abeslari) AND (oskorri)">

 <doc path="/egunkaria/2000/XML+p_code+s_code/m05/d2000062/p0004400.xml#4#15356"RANK="1000"/>
 <doc path="/egunkaria/2000/XML+p_code+s_code/m02/d2000033/p0004100.xml#1#6591" RANK="574"/>
</swish_query>
</document_retrieval>
```

As the above example shows, the texttt<swish_query> tag represents the query that will be sent to the information retrieval module. Each query is identified by a texttt<swish_query> tag, whether they return documents or not. The returned documents are tagged with texttt<doc>, where the `rank` attribute expresses the reliability.

Answer extraction: two tasks are performed in sequence: Candidate Extraction and Answer Selection. The candidate extraction consists of extracting all the candidate answers from the highest scoring passages. The answer selection consists of choosing the best five answers.

– Candidate Extraction. The process is carried out on the set of passages obtained in the previous step. First, all candidate answers are detected from each retrieved passage and a set of windows are defined around them. The selected window for each candidate answer is the smaller one which has all the query terms, or taxonomically related terms, in. Then, the candidate answer score is computed like this:

$$score_{CA} = \frac{\sum_{i=1}^{n} w_i}{n} \tag{1}$$

where n is the window size and w_i is the i word weight. w_i is 1 for search terms, 0.8 for the synonyms of the search terms, 0.5 for hyponyms and hypernyms, and 0.3 for other question terms.

An XML document is created with all candidate answers. Here is an example:

```
<?xml version="1.0" encoding="UTF-8" ?>
<candidate_answer_windows>
   <p doc="/egunkaria/2000/XML+p_code+s_code/m05/d2000062/p0004400.xml#4#15356">
      <candidate_token id="19" id_MW="19" lemma="Natxo_de_Felipe" window_size="40"
       weight="0.1049999999999">
        <token id="13" lemma="talde" pos="IZEARR" enti="" idf="0.55491453967"
         type="query_term" weight="1.0"/>
        <token id="14" lemma="lortu" pos="ADI" enti="" idf="" type="" weight="0"/>
         ...
        <token id="53" lemma="buru" pos="IZEARR" enti="" idf="" type="syns"
         weight="0.8"/>
      </candidate_token>
   </P>
   <p doc="/egunkaria/2000/XML+p_code+s_code/m02/d2000033/p0004100.xml#1#6591">
      <candidate_token id="8" id_MW="8" lemma="Santo_Tomas" window_size="57"
       weight="0.0526315789473">
        <token id="8" lemma="Santo" pos="IZEIZB" enti="" idf="" type="" weight="0"/>
        ...
```

```
          <token id="65" lemma="nagusi" pos="ADJIZO" enti="" idf="0.66161609254"
           type="query_term" weight="1.0"/>
        </candidate_token>
        <candidate_token id="26" id_MW="24" lemma="Natxo" window_size="41"
         weight="0.0731707317073">
          <token id="24" lemma="talde" pos="IZEARR" enti="" idf="0.55491453967"
           type="query_term" weight="1.0"/>
          ...
          <token id="65" lemma="nagusi" pos="ADJIZO" enti="" idf="0.66161609254"
           type="query_term" weight="1.0"/>
        </candidate_token>
      </p>
      ...
    </candidate_answer_windows>
```

The <candidate_answer_windows> tag represents the results of the candidate extraction task. <p> tag indicates the document where the candidate answers (<candidate_token> tag) are extracted from.

For each candidate_token we represent the lemma, the window size and the obtained weight. The context associated to each candidate_token is represented by means of the window tokens (<token> tag).

– Answer Selection. In order to select the best answers from the set of candidates, the same answers that appear in different passages must be combined. We try to map as identical those answers that refer to the same entity. The formula used to compute the final score of each answer is as follows:

$$final\_score_{CA} = \frac{\sum_{i=1}^{p} w_i}{N} \quad (2)$$

where p is the number of identical answers and N is the number of candidate answers.

An XML document is created with the system final answers. In the example, this is the list of the best five answers:

```
<?xml version="1.0" encoding="UTF-8" ?>
<answer_weighted>
   <ans lemma="Natxo De Felipe" weight="%2.2399201" />
   <ans lemma="Abesti" weight="%2.2222223" />
   <ans lemma="Felipe" weight="%1.75" />
   <ans lemma="Natxo" weight="%1.2195121" />
   <ans lemma="Santo Tomas" weight="%0.877193" />
</answer_weighted>
```

The <answer_weighted> element contains the list of ordered answers. The weight attribute of each answer (<ans> tag) indicates the confidence score of the system.

4 Evaluation

As we already pointed in section 2, the platform integrates an evaluation component, which supports the testing and assists in the improvement process.

The evaluation environment manages two information inputs. On the one hand, it receives an automatically obtained list of answers, and on the other hand, it manages the information stored in a question-answer database. A graphical user interface shows the correspondences between the expected and the obtained results.

This environment assists in the task of deciding the correctness of the results. Up to date no automatic techniques are applied to decide whether the system results are correct or not, so all the decisions are made by hand. The results are valued in a layered manner, dealing separately with the results of the different phases of the whole process. Basically, four different levels are distinguished according to the modules of the system: results of the question analysis, passages retrieved from the corpus, whole list of the candidate answers and ordered list of the selected answers.

The evaluation of a run enables to obtain comparable statistics and to extract considerations on the performance of the system. It also enables to see how suitable the used NLP tools are in the QA task.

4.1 Design and Creation of the Question-Answer Database

The creation of a question-answer collection is a must in order to carry out the evaluation of the system. We adopted two premises in the design of such a question-answer database: 1) Questions must be formulated in Basque, and the answers must be contained in a Basque corpus, and 2) the form and complexity of the questions and answers must be comparable with other internationally acknowledged question-answer collections, like the TREC or CLEF collections.

Our starting point to gather the questions was a set of 400 questions randomly selected from different TREC editions. These questions were then translated to Basque. But we realised that the majority of these questions have no answers in our corpus, so they were not appropriate for us. For this reason, in a second phase all the questions were *localized*. That means that they were rewritten taking into account two conditions: a) they must have answers in our corpus (exceptionally a few of them might not have any answer), and b) they must preserve the syntactic structure of the original question, the expected answer type, and the degree of difficulty.

Let us illustrate with an example. One of the randomly selected questions was number 642 from TREC9 edition: *Who's the lead singer of the Led Zeppelin band?*. This question was translated into Basque: *Nor da Led Zeppelin taldeko kantari nagusia?*. The translated question has no answer in the Basque corpus, so we need to localize it so that the corpus contains answer(s) for the question. In the example, changing the name of the band, and putting Oskorri (a Basque music band) instead of Led Zeppelin, the requirement is satisfied. The localized question is: *Nor da Oskorri taldeko kantari nagusia? (Whos the lead singer of the Oskorri band?)*.

Each localized question was stored along with the following information: TREC original English question, TREC edition, translated question, expected answer type of the original question, expected answer type of the localized question, answer(s) for the localized question, and document-identifiers where the answers were found.

The set of the expected answer types we use is the following: PERSON, ORGANIZATION, LOCATION, NUMERIC, TIME, PROPERTY, DEFINITION, MANNER and OTHER. The NUMERIC type is specialised in NUMERIC-MEASURE-DISTANCE and NUMERIC-MEASURE-DURATION. The TIME type is specialised in TIME-DATE.

A total of 396 questions were translated and localized. Most of them, 327, are of factoid type. Table 1 shows the number and percentage of questions for each interrogative pronoun.

Table 1. Question distribution according to their interrogative pronouns

Interrogative pronoun	Number of questions	Percentage
What	200	50.51%
When	45	11.36%
How	55	13.89%
Where	23	5.81%
Who	47	11.87%
Others	26	6.57%
Total	396	100%

4.2 An Example of a Layered Assessment of a Question

Taking the previous example as illustrative, we will explain the four evaluation layers.

At the first level, we evaluate if the selected search terms and the expected answer type are correct or not. The expected answer type could be evaluated automatically, as for each question the expected answer type is stored in the question-answer database. On contrary the evaluation of the selected search terms must be done by hand and is related to the passage retrieval module.

In the previous example, the system returns PERSON as expected answer type and the selected search terms are: *Oskorri, talde (band), kantari (singer), nagusi (lead)*. In this case the expected answer type is correct and all relevant question terms have been selected.

The second level analyze if the passages that contain the answer have been retrieved. At this level, the quality of the selected search terms and the quality of the expansion techniques are measured.

In the example, only a passage containing the selected search terms is retrieved, but it does not contain the answer. The passages with the correct answer have not been selected because the terms of the question do not coincide exactly with the terms of documents.

The use of lexical expansion could be valid to retrieve those passages that contain the answer. In the above example, we use BasqueWN for lexical expansion and obtain *abeslari*, which is a synonym of *kantari (singer)*, and in this way the document containing the answer is selected.

At this level, the question-answer database is enriched with new passages that contain the answer.

At the third layer, the candidate answers extracted from the selected passages are tested. That is, we see whether the correct answer is in the set of candidate answers. In the current version, the candidate answers selection module is closely dependent on the named entity recognizer and classifier, so this tool is indirectly evaluated.

At the fourth level, the correct answer precision is evaluated. We estimate the suitability of the criterion used for ranking the answer.

In the example the system responses correctly that the lead singer of the *Oskorri* band is *Natxo de Felipe.*

4.3 Discussion

By means of the first pilot experience we aim to assess the suitability of the evaluation environment.

The test has been carried out on 38 questions that follow the *"who-is"* and *"where-is"* patterns. The results have been evaluated manually according to the TREC guidelines.

For this pilot test we have used the corpus of the Basque newspaper Euskaldunon Egunkaria corresponding to the years 2000, 2001 and 2002. In our experiments we are using two versions of this corpus. The reduced version corresponds to the year 2000 and all the correct answers are contained in it. The size of the reduced corpus is of 9 million words and the whole version has 23 million words.

We will present and comment the obtained results (table 2), and will point out the main causes of the performance loss:

1. Passage retrieval: for all the questions the system retrieves any passage as can be seen in the first row. The point here is the quality of the retrieved passages, which will be evaluated in the next phase.
2. Candidate answers selection from passages. The number of questions with correct answers recovered from the passages is calculated here (see row 2). For the 65.79% of the questions we have obtained some candidate correct answer in the reduce corpus and 71.05% in the whole corpus.

   We realised that the named entity recognizer is the core of this task, so its behaviour determines the system performance. It is necessary a syntactic treatment in order to find the answer to some questions.
3. Answer selection. We calculate the number of questions that have the correct answer among the selected ones (see row 3). Among the questions with some candidate answer, the 88% have the correct one in the reduced corpus and 85.18% in the whole corpus.

   We would like to remark that, although all the questions have answer in the reduced corpus, the system performance does not decrease when the experiment is carried out over the whole corpus.

Finally, in order to have a general view of the system performance and to compare with other systems, the *"Mean Reciprocal Rank (MRR)"* is computed (see row 4).

Table 2. Evaluation of the pilot test

	Reduced corpus	Whole corpus
QRP	38	38
QRCA	25	27
QSCA	22	23
MRR	0.476	0.466

QRP: questions with retrieval passages
QRCA: questions with some correct answers retrieved in the candidate answers
QSCA: questions with correct answer selected

In the light of these results, it seems to be a critical point the extraction of candidate answers for questions. At the moment, for 34.21% of the questions the system does not get a correct candidate answer in the proposed list. This is due to:

1. The quality of the retrieved passages. In order to improve this quality lexical-semantic information could be used as has been said in section 4.2.
2. The extraction of answers from the candidate passages. New methods must be explored to extract more candidate answers from passages.

5 Conclusions and Future Work

We have presented an environment to manage the development and the evaluation of a Basque QA system. The environment is based on the integration of two components: the QA system itself, and the evaluation system.

We want to emphasize here the importance of taking into account the evaluation needs when designing a QA system. We adopted a distributed architecture, where different autonomous web services are integrated by means of the SOAP protocol. This organization allows running and evaluating each service separately. Each run is guided by a declarative XML configuration file, which describes all the execution options and parameters. Changing the configuration file enables to adapt the functionality of the different modules.

We try to exploit the adaptability of the system in the evaluation process. A database of questions and answers is the basis upon which the evaluation is carried out. 396 questions are stored in the database. We chose randomly the set of original questions from the TREC collection, translated them into Basque, and localized them so that the newspaper corpus contains the answers of the questions. In the localization process we preserve the structure of the original question. That means that the difficulty degree of both the original and the localized questions is quite similar. The evaluation environment let us to update and enrich the questions database.

The first pilot experiment shows that the evaluation environment is appropriate not only for the question answering task, but also for evaluating the performance of the NLP tools in this context.

With an eye to the future, once the general platform is consolidated, we aim to improve the QA system by applying more advanced techniques and exploiting other resources. We are involved in a testing phase, where we expect that the described platform will be helpful.

It is worthwhile to point that the Basque resources and tools are not so numerous. This limited context suggests the need of adopting multilingual strategies. At a longer term, the intensive use of multilingual resources (as the Multilingual Central Repository) and cross-lingual techniques are envisaged.

Acknowledgments

This work was partially funded by the Basque Government, SAIOTEK project (S-PE03UN14).

References

Agirre E., Ansa O., Arregi X., Artola X., Daz de Ilarraza A., Lersundi M.: A Conceptual Schema for a Basque Lexical-Semantic Framework. Complex (2003) Budapest, Hungary

Alegria I., Aranzabe M., Ezeiza A., Ezeiza N., Urizar R.: Robustness and customisation in an analyser/lemmatiser for Basque. LREC (2002)

Alegria I., Arregi O., Balza I., Ezeiza N., Fernandez I., Urizar R.: Design and Development of a Named Entity Recognizer for an Agglutinative Language. IJCNLP (2004)

Atserias J., Villarejo L., Rigau G., Agirre E., Carroll J., Magnini B., Vossen P.: The MEANING Multilingual Central Repository. Proc. of the 2nd Global WordNet Conference (2004) Brno, Czech Republic

Bilotti M.: Query Expansion Techniques for Question Answering. Master's thesis, Massachusetts institute of technology (2004)

Hiyakumoto L. S.: Planning in the JAVELIN QA System. CMU-CS-04-132 (2004)

Lersundi M.: Ezagutza-base lexikala eraikitzeko Euskal Hiztegiko definizioen azterketa sintaktiko-semantikoa. Hitzen arteko erlazio lexiko-semantikoak: definizio-patroiak, eratorpena eta postposizioak. PhD thesis (2005), UPV/EHU

Tomás D., Vicedo J.L., Saiz M., Izquierdo R.: Building an XML framework for Question Answering. CLEF (2005) Vienna, Austria

Ontology-Based Application Server to the Execution of Imperative Natural Language Requests

Flávia Linhalis and Dilvan de Abreu Moreira

University of São Paulo, Institute of Mathematics and Science Computing - ICMC
P.O. Box 688, São Carlos, Brazil
{flavia, dilvan}@icmc.usp.br

Abstract. This paper is about using ontologies to help the execution of imperative requests expressed in natural language. In order to achieve this goal, we developed the prototype of an Ontology-Based Application Server to the execution of Natural Language requests (NL-OBAS). The NL-OBAS provides services to allow users to describe requests in several natural languages and uses software components to execute them. One of the advantages of our approach is that natural language is first converted to an interlingua, UNL (Universal Networking Language). The interlingua allows the use of different human languages to express the requests (other systems are restricted to English). The semantics of the interlingua, enhanced by ontologies, is used to retrieve the appropriated software components to compose a dynamic service to execute the requests expressed in natural language.

1 Introduction

It is a fact that the Web has become the main interface for the exchange of information between government, institutions, small businesses and big companies computer systems and common people. An evidence of this is the growing use of application servers, like Jboss, WebSephere and Zope. Application servers provide support for Web application development by comprising functionalities of conventional middleware such as transaction monitors or object brokers, but they also incorporate technologies for Web access [1]. The goal of an application server is to transparently handle, in a Web environment, aspects like concurrency, naming, security, database connectivity (and so on) for distributed component based software. In a simplified and generalized view, we can say that an application server can facilitate the development of applications by providing transparency to the programmers. They also serve as a bridge between the users Internet browsers and the services offered by government and industry.

Application servers try to manage various issues (transactions, session management, user rights etc.) in an application independent way. This is achieved by software configured with the help of administration tools and corresponding configuration files. Though this constitutes a very flexible way of developing and administrating a distributed application, configuration files do not provide a

H.L. Larsen et al. (Eds.): FQAS 2006, LNAI 4027, pp. 589–600, 2006.

high-level of abstraction. The reason is that they lack a coherent formal model. Thus, it is very hard to find information that depends on the integration of several descriptions. For example, managing component dependencies, versions, and licenses is a typical problem in an ever-growing repository of programming libraries and components [1].

Oberle et al. [1] try to remedy these problems by applying Semantic Web technology, i.e. ontologies and inference engines, in the application server itself. In an Ontology-based Application Server (OBAS), an ontology can join together so far separated aspects of the server like security, component dependencies, version or deployment information. This should help the programmers in their complex tasks during the development of a program.

The architecture proposed and partially implemented by Oberle et al. [1] is suitable to enterprise applications because it includes, for example, transaction manager and security services. However, it is important to emphasize that an OBAS is characterized by the presence of an ontology to integrate the services of an application server, but not necessarily enterprise capabilities should be provided.

We can say that OBAS technology is the future for today's application servers. And, in the same way that current application servers now occupy a key position in the development of Web applications, in the future, OBASs, with their semantic centric approach, will have the same role in the development of Semantic Web applications.

The Web was a revolution making digital information available to anyone with a browser and an Internet connection. But, what is the next step for the Web? What if it could help to break down or at least to drastically lower the language barrier for the Internet? The Universal Networking Language (UNL) project [2] has exactly this goal. The Internet community is still segregated by language boundaries. Theoretically, this seems to be the only major obstacle standing in the way of international and interpersonal communication in the information society [3].

The UNU/IAS (Institute of Advanced Studies of the United Nations University) initiated the UNL project aiming to solve this problem. Started in 1996, the project embraces several universities and research institutions from Brazil, China, Egypt, France, Germany, India, Indonesia, Italy, Japan, Jordan, Latvia, Mongolia, Russia, Spain and Thailand. In the following years more groups are expected to join [3].

The project proposes an interlingua, entitled Universal Networking Language (UNL)[4]. UNL has sufficient expressive power to represent relevant information conveyed by natural languages. For each natural language, two systems should be developed: a DeConverter capable of translating texts from UNL to the target natural language, and an EnConverter which has to convert natural language texts into UNL. A DeConverter and EnConverter for each language form a Language Server residing somewhere in the Internet. All language servers will be connected to allow any Internet user to deconvert an UNL document found on the web into his/her native language, as well as to produce UNL representations of the texts he/she wishes to make available to the whole Internet community [3].

In this paper, we join the two ideas above: 1) to use UNL to break the language limits and 2) to use an OBAS to transparently help and to semantically enrich the dynamic composition and execution of services. We propose an Ontology-Based Application Server to execute Natural Language requests (NL-OBAS). In order to achieve this goal, the NL-OBAS performs a semantic mapping between UNL relations and software components using ontologies. With a NL-OBAS we could allow non-programmers to write simple programs (mainly requests) for servers, using their native language.

In the context of this work, Applications Servers refer to a software layer that transparently hides the dynamic composition of a service and joins together or searches for suitable software components to compose that service. An ontology is useful to integrate the services of the application server and help the composition of a dynamic service, using proper software components, to execute natural language requests.

This paper is organized as follows: section 2 discusses the advantages in developing an OBAS to execute imperative natural language requests expressed in several natural languages (NL-OBAS) and presents the NL-OBAS architecture. Section 3 describes each module of the NL-OBAS architecture and their relationships with practical examples using an implemented prototype in the course management domain. Section 4 discusses some related works. Section 5 concludes the paper with some remarks on future work.

2 An OBAS to Execute Natural Language Requests (NL-OBAS)

Several systems, developed throughout the last twenty-five years, have pursued the goal of describing user intentions in restricted natural language and have them executed by computers [5, 6, 7, 8]. Despite the intuitive appeal of natural languages, it has been argued that a language like English has too many ambiguities to be useful for communicating with computers. The UNL (Universal Networking Language) project aims to embody, in the cyber world, the functions of natural languages used in human communication. But, different from natural languages, UNL expressions can be unambiguous. Using UNL, people can express knowledge conveyed in several natural languages (English, French, Spanish, Portuguese, and so on). It also enables computers to intercommunicate, thus providing people with a linguistic infrastructure for distributing, receiving and understanding multilingual information [2].

Our goal is to be able to execute requests described in several restricted natural languages. In order to do this, requests are first converted into UNL. The UNL representation is used to extract relevant semantic information from the sentences that will be necessary to retrieve and execute software components. In this paper, requests refer to intentions described in a high level of semantic abstraction and related to a specific domain. For example, considering the domain of course management, valid requests could be:

(a) "Add student John Smith to the Hypermedia course."
(b) "Send an e-mail to the students of the Operating Systems course saying that the test will be on December 14th."

In order to achieve our goal, we developed a prototype of an Ontology-Based Application Server to execute imperative Natural Language requests described in several natural languages (NL-OBAS). The NL-OBAS translates the requests into UNL and uses ontologies to identify what components should be loaded to execute the requests. Its architecture is illustrated in Figure 1. Other projects with this purpose were not found in the literature, as discussed in section 4.

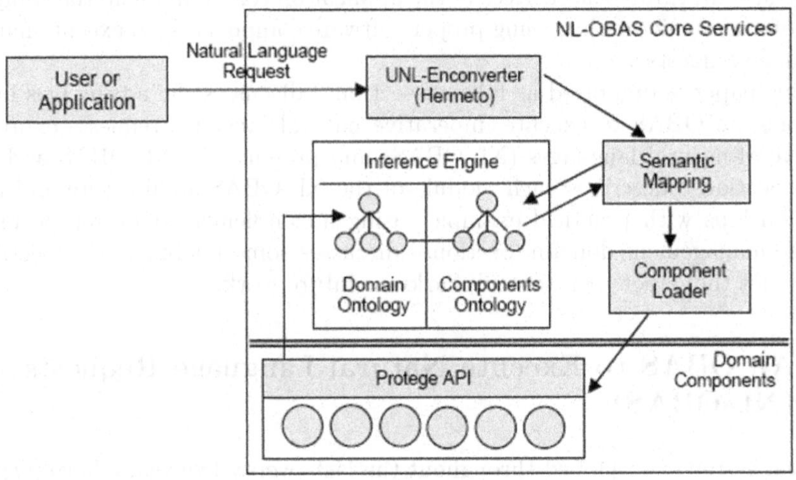

Fig. 1. Architecture of the NL-OBAS

The NL-OBAS architecture provides a service to convert natural language requests into UNL (UNL-Enconverter). The architecture also provides a Semantic Mapping Service, that uses an ontology to extract relevant information about the domain components and semantic information from the UNL representation of the request. The Component Loader service dynamically loads specific software components and executes methods to fulfill the natural language request. The NL-OBAS software components are related to a specific domain. These components are described in the Component Ontology (section 3.2) and the application domain is described in the Domain Ontology (section 3.3). The components can query and modify the Domain Ontology.

This NL-OBAS architecture is not suitable to run enterprise applications yet, because it does not include key enterprise level services, for example Transaction Manager, Naming and Security services.

For a better understanding about the functionality of the NL-OBAS services, it is necessary to provide a brief background about the UNL (Universal Networking Language) interlingua and project. Section 2.1 provides this background and, in section 3, a more detailed explanation about the services of the NL-OBAS architecture is given.

2.1 The UNL Project

As stated in the Introduction, the UNL (Universal Networking Language) Project proposes an interlingua with sufficient expressive power to represent relevant information conveyed by natural languages. For each natural language, two systems should be developed: a "Deconverter" capable of translating texts from UNL to this natural language, and an "Enconverter" that converts natural language texts into UNL. The enconverting and deconverting processes use a dictionary and grammar rules for each natural language.

UNL represents sentences using three elements [2]:

- Universal Words (UWs): Each UW relates to a concept and is represented as an English word that can be optionally supplied with semantic information to restrict its meaning. The following are examples of UWs: book, book(icl¿publication), book(icl¿reserve). In the two last examples, the meaning of book is restricted by other UWs (publication and reserve). The restrictions allow representing UWs as disambiguated English words.
- Relation Labels (RLs): RLs express semantic relations between UWs. There are today 45 RLs defined. The RLs are represented as a pair relation_label (UW1, UW2). For example:
  - agt (run, car): agt relation defines a thing that initiates an action. In our example “car” initiates the action “run”. It means that “car runs”.
  - obj (move, table): This relation defines a thing in focus that is directly affected by an event or state. In our example, it means the “table moved”.
- Atribute Labels (ALs): ALs express additional information about UWs, such as verb tense, intention, emphasis, etc. ALs are represented as UW.@atrib1. @atrib2...@atribn. For example: obj(eat.@past, apple.@pl). The AL @past indicates past and @pl indicates plural.

We do not intend to describe the UNL language here in details. A full specification of UNL can be found at http://www.undl.org.

3 Description of the NL-OBAS

In this section, a detailed explanation about NL-OBAS architecture (Figure 1) is given. We demonstrate its functionality with a prototype implementation for the course management domain. For a better understanding, we describe practical examples throughout this section using the developed prototype.

3.1 The UNL-Enconverter Service (Hermeto)

The UNL-Enconverter service receives natural language text as input and converts it into UNL. This conversion is performed by Hermeto system.

Hermeto is a standalone environment for fully automatic syntactic and semantic natural language analysis [9]. It can be used to convert any natural language into UNL. It receives as input a dictionary and a grammar that should be parameterized for each language, in a way very similar to the one required by the UNL Center Enconverter (EnCo) program [2]. However, Hermeto's environment is more user friendly than the one provided by EnCo. More information about Hermeto can be found in Martins et al [9].

Using Hermeto edition facilities we developed an English grammar and dictionary to the course management domain. Hermeto uses both to convert a natural language request into UNL. Currently, the input requests must be imperative sentences (however, the system can be extended to other sentence types).

Dictionaries and grammars could be defined to several natural languages. The requests expressed in any natural language should be converted to the same UNL representation. So, users could communicate with the service using their native language.

3.2 The Component Ontology

Figure 2 presents the Component Ontology classes, attributes and relationships. It was developed using Protégé tool [10] and it is represented in OWL (Ontology Web Language) [11]. The Component Ontology has to be instantiated in accordance with the syntactic and semantic characteristics of the components in the Domain Components Layer of the NL-OBAS. The remaining of this section is about particularities of some classes of this ontology.

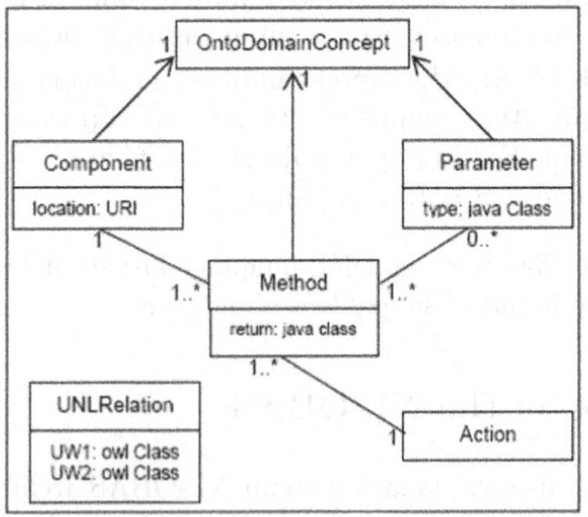

Fig. 2. Component Ontology

The instances of the *OntoDomainConcept* class correspond to concepts of the application domain that are also concepts represented as classes in the Domain Ontology (section 3.3). Each *Component* class instance corresponds to the representation of an application domain software component that can be related to one or more concepts (represented as instances) of the OntoDomainConcept class. For example, considering the web course management domain, "Student", "Teacher" and "Course" are concepts and belong to the OntoDomainConcept class. An instance of the Component class, like TeacherComponent, represents a component that is responsible for the execution of actions related to the "Teacher" concept.

The *Method* class instances correspond to the methods of each component. The *Parameter* class instances correspond to the arguments of each method. And finally, the *Action* class instances correspond to imperative verbs. Each verb (action) is related to one or more methods, and each method is related to one verb.

The *UNLRelation* class relates UNL relations to information about components. As stated in section 2.1, UNL relations (Relation Labels) express semantic relations between UWs and are represented as a pair relation_label(UW1, UW2). The aim of the UNLRelation class is to indicate the mapping between a particular relation label and the components, methods, arguments and actions. This class has instances representing all UNL relations being used in the imperative sentences related to the application domain.

Before defining the UNLRelation instances, it is necessary to observe what semantic information can be extracted from the UNL relations that are relevant to the UWs-Components mapping. Figure 3 illustrates the main UNL relations of the domain as instances of the UNLRelation class.

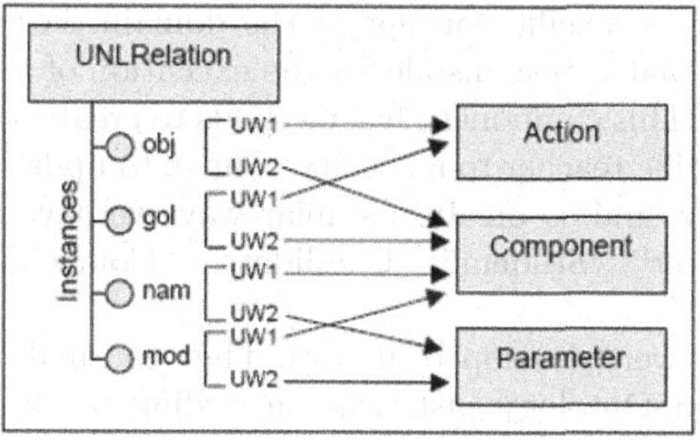

Fig. 3. UNLRelation class and its instances showing the UNL-Components Mapping

As shown in Figure 3, UW1 of the *obj* relation is always related to an action (it means that the value of UW1 can be any instance of the Action class in the Component Ontology). UW2 is related to a concept that should have one software component related to it. Similarly, for the *nam* relation, UW1 is always related to a concept and UW2 is always a parameter. In the same way, UWs of each relation can be related with the Component, Parameter or Action classes of the Component Ontology.

3.3 The Domain Ontology

The natural language requests are related to a specific domain that is represented in the Domain Ontology. We defined and instantiated the Domain Ontology with

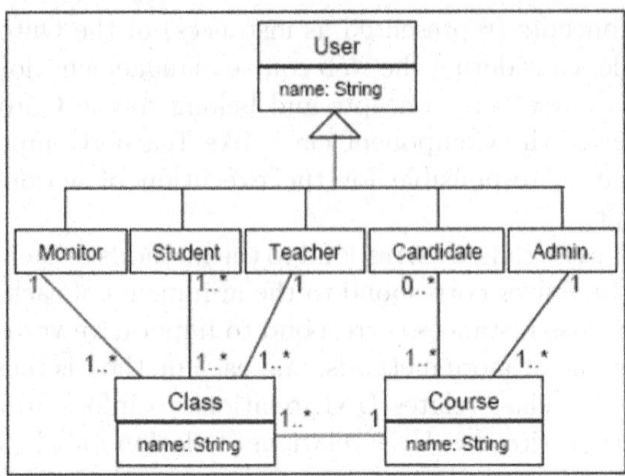

Fig. 4. Course Management Domain Ontology

relationships between the concepts of the course management domain (Figure 4). Just as the Component Ontology, the Domain Ontology was also developed using the Protégé tool [10] and it is represented in OWL [11].

3.4 The Domain Components Layer

We developed a set of components related to the course management domain, each one related to a specific concept of the domain. For example, we developed a component that is responsible for the execution of actions related to the "Teacher" concept. This component has methods to create, delete and list teachers, to assign a specific teacher to a specific course, to update information about a particular teacher, and so on. In a similar way, we have components related to the concepts "User", "Student", "Candidate", "Course", "Class", "Monitor" and "Administrator".

The components were developed in Java. They can make simple queries and modify the Domain Ontology instances, according to the user requests (see Figure 1). They can also perform external actions, such as send e-mails.

3.5 The Semantic Mapping Service

The Semantic Mapping Service performs a semantic mapping between UNL relations and the software components. Its goal is to identify what components, methods and arguments will be required to execute the request. In order to achieve this goal, the service uses the Component Ontology (section 3.2). A practical example of the steps performed before running the Semantic Mapping Service is given below.

Consider the examples of imperative natural language requests of Figure 5(a). They can serve as input to the UNL-Enconverter service. For example, considering the request number 2 of Figure 5(a) (Delete administrator Mary from course Java.), the UNL-Enconverter service generates the UNL representation shown in Figure 5(b).

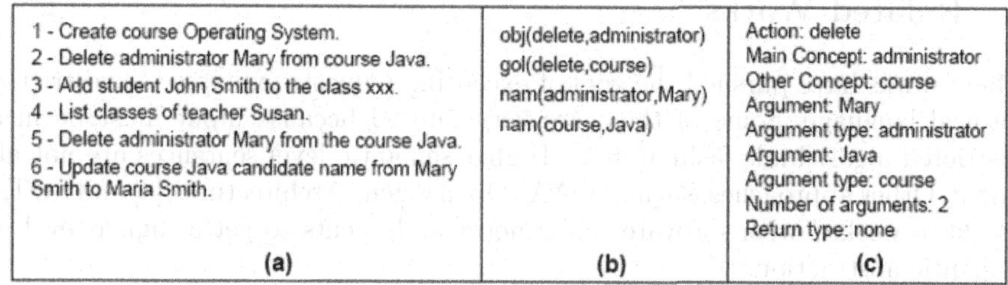

1 - Create course Operating System.
2 - Delete administrator Mary from course Java.
3 - Add student John Smith to the class xxx.
4 - List classes of teacher Susan.
5 - Delete administrator Mary from the course Java.
6 - Update course Java candidate name from Mary Smith to Maria Smith.
(a)
obj(delete,administrator)
gol(delete,course)
nam(administrator,Mary)
nam(course,Java)
(b)
Action: delete
Main Concept: administrator
Other Concept: course
Argument: Mary
Argument type: administrator
Argument: Java
Argument type: course
Number of arguments: 2
Return type: none
(c)

Fig. 5. (a) Requests examples, (b) UNL representation of request number 2, (c) relevant information extracted from the UNL representation of request number 2

The UNL representation (Figure 5b), serves as input to the Semantic Mapping Service. It separates the tokens and classify them using information from the Component Ontology, specially related to UNLRelation class instances, as shown in Figure 3. For the UNL representation shown in Figure 5(b), the Semantic Mapping Service identifies the relevant information shown in Figure 5(c). Using this information, the service uses the Component Ontology to discover which methods are related to the action "delete" and belong to the component associated to the "administrator" concept. Still using the Component Ontology, it retrieves data about the number of arguments, argument types and return type of each identified method. According to the information extracted from the UNL sentence (Figure 5c), the method that satisfies the request receives two arguments ("Mary" and "Java"), its argument types are "administrator" and "course" and it has no return type. This information is used to analyze the available methods and to conclude which one is the most suitable to execute the request. Finally, the Component Loader Service is called.

3.6 The Component Loader Service

The Semantic Mapping Service identifies, among the application domain components, which components, methods and arguments will be required to execute the UNL request. This information serves as input to the Component Loader that loads and executes the required components and methods.

Considering the request of the given example (Figure 5a, sentence number 2), the method called to execute the request will modify an instance of the Domain Ontology (the administrator will be deleted from the Java course). This ontology was developed using the Protégé tool [10], hence the components access it through the Protégé API. This API can be used directly by external applications to access Protégé knowledge bases without running the Protégé tool.

Currently, the NL-OBAS prototype works only with components written using the Java language (using Java Reflection to activate them), but it could be extended to work with components written in other programming languages.

4 Related Works

Many works have pursued the goal of executing requests expressed in restricted natural language. Some of them are very limited because input must be in a restricted algorithmic fashion [5, 7]. Higher semantic level sentences are not allowed. Other approaches, such as OAA (Open Agent Architecture) [6] and SOTA [8], have worked with software components and agents to get a higher level of semantic abstraction.

OAA [6] is a framework for constructing agent-based systems that makes it possible for software services to be provided through the cooperative efforts of distributed collections of agents. OAA provides an interface that accepts English sentences as input that are converted to ICL (Interagent Communication Language), a Prolog-based language. ICL is used, by the agents, to communicate with each other and to register their capabilities with a facilitator agent. The facilitator is responsible for matching ICL requests to choose the most suitable agents to execute these requests. Different from our approach, OAA does not use an explicit ontology and do not allow requests to be expressed in several natural languages.

SOTA [8] is an office task automation framework that uses web services, ontologies, and software agents to create an integrated service platform that provides user-centric support for automating intranet office tasks. SOTA can take plain English text sentences as input and serve users with a single and integrate user-interface form to access web services, thus avoiding the need to access each distributed service manually. SOTA performs its tasks in three phases: first it parses user input sentences to identify possible web services using an ontology, next it prepares most of the input data fields the services requires, and, finally, it combines related services to compose a single task flow. One of the major differentials of our approach is that the natural language requests are first converted to the UNL interlingua [2, 4], to allow users to express requests in several natural languages.

The CoSMoS (Component Service Model with Semantics) system [12] works with dynamic service composition using components. The authors propose a model that applies semantic graphs, ontologies and object-oriented model to compose dynamic services using semantic information from the components. But different from our approach, it does not use natural language to write the requests.

Sugumaran and Storey [13] use a semantic-based approach to component retrieval. Their work makes use of domain models containing the objectives, processes, actions, actors, and, an ontology of domain terms, their definitions, and relationships with other domain-specific terms. A reuse repository was developed containing the components relevant for the creation of new applications, along with their attributes and methods. Using natural language, a user can specify the requirements of a component he/she wishes to use. The natural language query is mapped into a SQL-like language. The domain ontology is used to refine and enhance the query, which is decomposed into processes and actions (methods). The decomposed query is then compared with the components capacities in the repository. The percentage of actions supported by a particular component or object indicates how relevant it is to that requirement. One of the differentials of our work is that, after searching for the suitable component, we also execute the request expressed in natural language.

References to works that use the semantics of an interlingua, enhanced by ontologies, to dynamically compose component-based services to execute requests, expressed in several natural languages, have not been found in the literature.

5 Conclusions and Future Work

This paper described the architecture and the development of an Ontology-Based Application Server prototype to execute imperative natural Language Requests (NL-OBAS). Our prototype provides basic services to receive restricted natural language requests, convert them into an interlingua (UNL - Universal Networking Language) and dynamically compose a service to execute the request. In order to achieve this goal, our prototype performs a semantic mapping between UNL relations and software components using ontologies. The advantage of using an interlingua, such as UNL, to describe natural language requests is that it can represent requests derived from different languages (English, Spanish, Portuguese, French, and so on) in a no ambiguous way.

The NL-OBAS architecture can be used in different application domains; it is just necessary to write the appropriate software components, define the dictionary and grammar rules (that will be used by the UNL-Enconverter service), create instances of the Component Ontology and define the Domain Ontology.

The dynamic service composition, currently performed by the prototype, is limited by the number of imperative verbs (actions) in a sentence. Each imperative verb can activate only one component. The improvement of this issue is one of our future works.

As another future work, we plan to extend the NL-OBAS architecture to support enterprise applications by providing services such as security and transaction management. It may be achieved by integrating it as a service in a J2EE application server, such as Jboss, and reusing its enterprise capabilities.

Acknowledgments

We would like to thank the Interinstitutional Center for Computational Linguistics (NILC), in São Carlos, Brazil, for making the Hermeto system available to our research. We also thank National Council for Scientific and Technological Development (CNPq), for partially funding this research.

References

1. Oberle, D., Eberhart, A., Staab, S. and Volz R. Developing and Managing Software Components in an Ontology-based Application Server. Proceedings of the 5th ACM/IFIP/USENIX international conference on Middleware, 2004, pp. 459-477.
2. UNL Center. The Universal Networking Language (UNL) Specifications. Version 2005. June 2005. http://www.undl.org/unlsys/unl/unl2005/.

3. Boguslavsky, I. et al. Creating a Universal Networking Language Module within an Advanced NLP System. Proceedings of the ACM International Conference on Computational Linguisitics, 2000, pp. 83-89.
4. Ushida, H. and Zhu, M. The Universal Networking Language beyond Machine Translation. International Symposium on Language and Cyberspace, Seoul (South Korea), 2001.
5. Ballard, B. A and Bierman, A. W. Programming in Natural Language: NLC as a Prototype. Proceedings of the ACM Annual Computer Science Conference (SCS79), ACM Press, 1979, pp. 228-237.
6. Cheyer, A and Martin, D. The Open Agent Architecture. Journal of Autonomous Agents and Multi-Agent Systems, v.4, n.1, 2001, pp.143-148.
7. Price, D., Riloff, E., Zachary, J. and Harvey, B. NaturalJava: A Natural Language Interface for Programming in Java. Proceedings of the 5th ACM International Conference on Intelligent User Interfaces (IUI05), ACM Press, 2000, pp. 207-211.
8. Tsai, T. M., Yu, H. K., Shih, H. T., Liao, P.Y., Yanh, R. D. and Chou, S. T. Ontology-Mediated Integration of Intranet Web Services. IEEE Computer, v. 36, n. 10, 2003, pp. 63-71.
9. Martins, R. T., Hasegawa, R. and Nunes, M. G. V. HERMETO: A NL Analysis Environment. Proceedings of 2nd Workshop da Tecnologia da Informação e da Linguagem Humana (TIL'04), Brazil, 2004, pp. 64-71.
10. Noy, N. F., Sintek, M., Decker, S., Crubezy, M., Fergerson, R. W. and Musen, M. A. Creating Semantic Web Contents with Protégé-2000. IEEE Intelligent Systems, v.16 n.2, 2001, pp. 60-71.
11. McGuinness, D. L. and van Harmelen, F. Web Ontology Language Overview. W3C Recommendation, February 2004. http://www.w3.org/TR/owl-features/.
12. Fujii, K. and Suda, T. Component Service Model with Semantics (CoSMoS): A New Component Model for Dynamic Service Composition. Proceedings of the International Symposium on Applications and the Internet Workshops (SAINTW04), IEEE Computer Society, 2004, pp. 348-354.
13. Sugumaran, V. and Storey, V. C. A Semantic-Based Approach to Component Retrieval. ACM SIGMIS Database, v. 34, n. 3, 2003, pp. 8-24.

Annotating Documents by Their Intended Meaning to Make Them Self Explaining: An Essential Progress for the Semantic Web

Hervé Blanchon and Christian Boitet

Laboratoire CLIPS BP 53
38041 Grenoble Cedex 9, France
{herve.blanchon, Christian.boitet}@imag.fr

Abstract. A Self-Explaining Document (SED) is a document enriched with annotations keeping track of all possible interpretations with respect to a given grammar and dictionary, as well as disambiguating choices. If disambiguation is complete and has been done by the author himself, a SED conveys "the author's intention". The availability of SEDs might considerably reduce misunderstanding between authors and readers, and perhaps lead to the assignment of a "meaning certification level" to any part of a document. We present ways to integrate these annotations into an arbitrary XML document (SED-XML), and to make them visible and usable to readers for accessing the "true content" of a document. We also show that, under several constraints, a SED, once translated into a target language L, might be transformed into an SED in L with no human interaction. Hence, the SED structure might be used in multilingual as well as in monolingual contexts, without addition of human work.

1 Introduction

We first proposed the concept of Self-Explaining Document in [5] as an answer to some question raised while experimenting with a new incarnation of the interactive translation paradigm, the DBMT approach (Dialogue-Based Machine Translation) in the LIDIA project [6]. We observed (again) that translation introduces ambiguities which are not present in the source text. Traduttore, traditore… For example, the two French words "remplacer" (replace by a new thing) and "replacer" (put back into place) were both translated by "replace" in English. It also happened that all disambiguated analyses of a sentence produce the same translation, as ambiguous as the original. One example was the translation from French into Russian of the famous sentence «the man sees the girl in the park with a telescope».

This raised an objection to DBMT: what is the use of disambiguating the source text if ambiguities reappear in the translation(s), or even worse if new ones are created? Would it not be better to try and produce translations which preserve the ambiguities, and dispense with Interactive Disambiguation (ID) altogether?

Unfortunately, the experience of human translation shows that ambiguities can be exactly preserved only in some cases, and that to do it purposefully is quite difficult and often leads to unnatural ways of expression in the translation. It is also quite clear

H.L. Larsen et al. (Eds.): FQAS 2006, LNAI 4027, pp. 601 – 612, 2006.

that the "transferable" ambiguities vary with the target language. Finally, although some texts may be intentionally ambiguous, especially in poetry and politics, we take it that the vast majority of ambiguities are not intentional, but are due to the intrinsic nature of natural languages. Of course, some authors write more clearly than others, but all authors write unambiguously in any programming language, unambiguous by construction, and ambiguously in any natural language, ambiguous by nature!

This motivated the idea of Self-Explaining Documents: if the source and target documents are accompanied by their (unambiguous) linguistic structure, with the indications of potentially ambiguous parts, and if the reader in the target language may obtain a clarification of unclear parts in a user-friendly way, the objection disappears. As human users are notably not very sensitive to ambiguities, however, we should find a way to warn the reader that the target text is ambiguous.

2 DBMT: A Context for SED Production

After having worked in the direction of "suboptimization" for 15 years [10], we turned to high quality Dialogue-Based Machine Translation. DBMT is a new paradigm derived from that of Interactive MT (IMT) and geared to various translation situations where other approaches, such as the Linguistic-Based (LBMT) and the Knowledge-Based (KBMT) approaches, are not adequate.

In DBMT, although the linguistic knowledge sources are still crucial, and extralinguistic knowledge might be used if available, emphasis is on indirect pre-editing through negotiation and clarification dialogues with the author in order to get high quality translations without revision.

Authors are distinguished from "spontaneous" writers or speakers by the fact that they want to produce a "clean" final message and may be willing to enter into such dialogues. The crucial difference with usual IMT is that interactive disambiguation is not performed during an analysis or transfer process, but on a "multiple" data structure factorizing all possible analysis results. Hence, the author is not "slave of the system", but decides if and when s/he wants to enter the disambiguation dialogue.

The first situation considered (in 1990) was the production of multilingual technical documentation in the form of HyperCard[1] documents. A page of such a document is a card. A card may contain different kinds of objects such as graphics, buttons and textual fields. The linguistic MT lingware was based on multilevel transfer with interlingual acceptions, properties and relations implemented in ARIANE-G5.

The first mockup, LIDIA-1 [6], demonstrates the idea on a HyperCard stack presenting short ambiguous French sentences in several disambiguating contexts. This document is translated into three documents, German, Russian and English. Although this mockup does not implement all features of the general design — a complete implementation would have called for considerably more human resources than were available — it demonstrates the potential of the approach.

[1] HyperCard is a Macintosh-based (MacOS-7 to MacOS-9) environment for the production of hypertextual documents called "stacks".

2.1 LIDIA-1 Through an Example

The author can trigger the most frequent functions through the LIDIA-1 palette. Its first line contains the LIDIA tools (process the selected object, show the treatment progress, show the annotations, and show the reverse translation). The second line contains browsing tools.

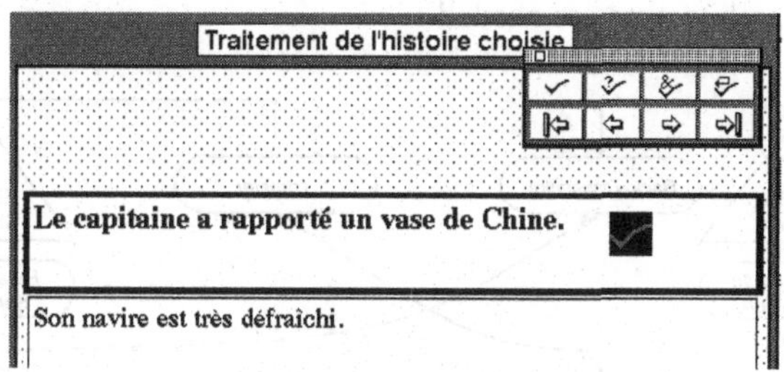

Fig. 1. Selection of a field to be translated[2]

After analysis, a button (**? !!** - **Fig. 2**) appears above the object to be translated if its content is ambiguous.

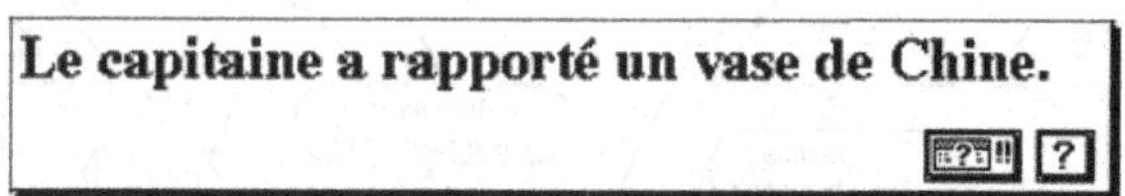

Fig. 2. Pending disambiguation questions[2]

When the author decides to disambiguate the object's content, s/he clicks on the button. Pending questions are then asked (**Fig. 3** & **Fig. 4**).

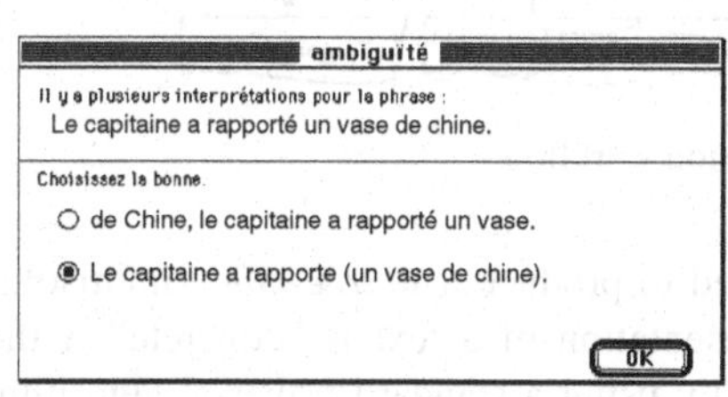

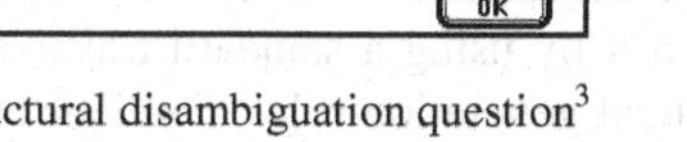

Fig. 3. Structural disambiguation question[3]

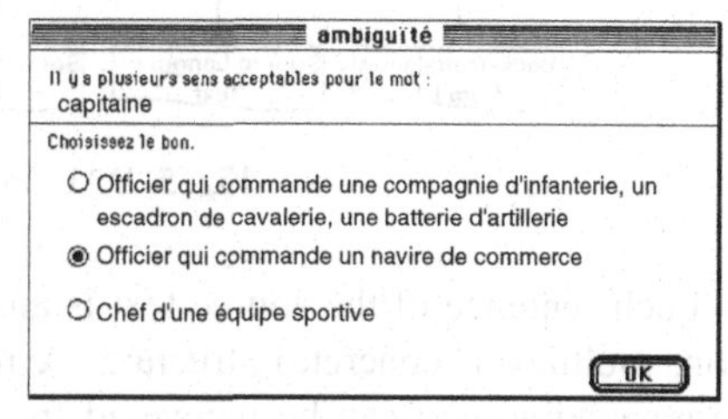

Fig. 4. Word sense question[4]

Finally, the system produces the corresponding "exact" translation. For our example sentence, we will get two different translations in German if we disambiguate according to two different contexts: (1) "Der *Hauptmann* hat eine Vase aus

[2] The captain brought back a vase (form/of) China.

[3] "From China, the captain brought back a vase" *vs.* "The captain brought a Chinese vase".

[4] Sense-1: army captain; Sense-2: boat captain; Sense-3: sports team captain.

China mitgebracht. Die Vase ist englisch.", and (2) "Der *Kapitän* hat eine chinesische Vase mitgebracht. Sein Boot ist sehr verblaßt."

2.2 SED Production in the DBMT Framework

Let us now explain how a SED can be produced. For this, some details about the LIDIA lingware architecture are needed.

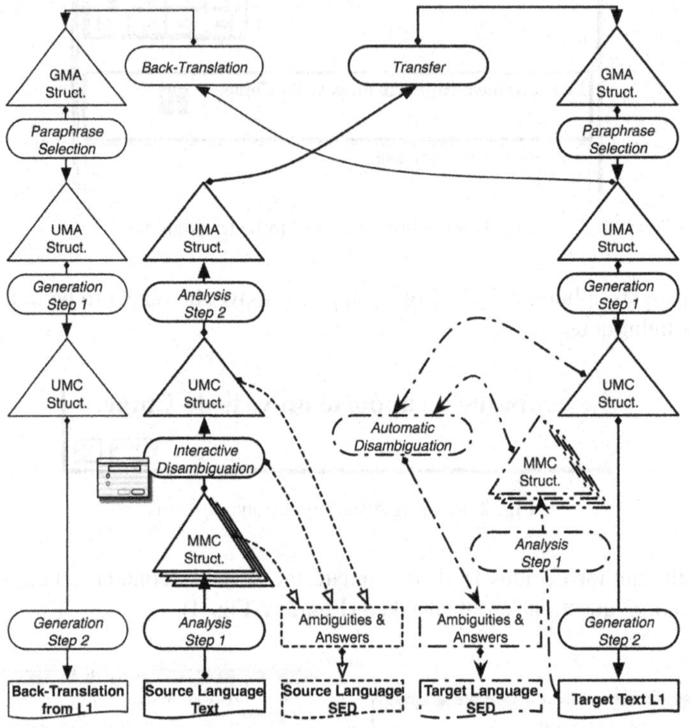

Fig. 5. DAE production workflow

Each sentence of the source text is analyzed to produce a *source-mmc* (multisolution, multilevel, concrete) structure. A representation of a text is "concrete" if the corresponding text can be recovered from it by using a standard traversal algorithm and simple morphological and graphematical generation rules. Familiar examples are textbook constituent structures and dependency structures (with left-to-right traversal of the leaves or infix traversal of all nodes). Otherwise, we say that the representation is "abstract". Note that the information contained in both kinds of structures (on labels and other more or less complex annotations) may be of the same linguistic "depth": there may be "deep" concrete structures and "surface" abstract structures, in this sense, although the opposite is of course more frequent.

This *source-mmc* structure is then used to produce a disambiguation question tree. Once the author has answered the questions, the system gets the non-ambiguous *source-umc* (unisolution, multilevel, concrete) structure chosen by the author.

This *source-umc* structure is abstracted into a *source-uma* (unisolution, multilevel, abstract) structure. In an abstract structure, some lexical information can be "featurized", and order would be normalized. Abstract representations of utterances are far superior to concrete representations as input and output structures of transfers in semantic transfer MT or as "lexical-conceptual structures" [7] in interlingual MT, especially between distant languages. But their relation to the corresponding utterances is not as clear, a natural consequence of abstraction.

A lexical and structural transfer component produces a *target-gma* (generating, multilevel, abstract) structure. In *gma* structures, non-interlingual linguistic levels are underspecified. If present, they are used only as reflections of corresponding surface levels in the source language, and are recomputed in the first generation phase, called "paraphrase choice".

The paraphrase selection step produces a *target-uma* structure. This structure is equivalent to the structure that would be obtained after analysis and disambiguation of the target text to be produced. The translation process ends with the syntactic and morphological generation phases.

In order to produce a SED, it suffices to keep the data structures used by the ID phase, namely: the *mmc* structure, the question tree, and the disambiguating path in it. **Fig. 5** gives a functional diagram of the workflow we just described.

2.3 LIDIA-1 Distributed Software Architecture

In the LIDIA-1 architecture, the coordination server, the redaction server, the communication server and the disambiguation server were AppleScript applets. They communicated through AppleEvent messages to coordinate their work. The coordination server scheduled the whole translation process for each translation unit. The author's workstation communicated with the translation server under the SMTP protocol.

3 SED Production within LIDIA-2

LIDIA-2 is a new Java front end for DBMT services developed since 2002. LIDIA-2 produces XML documents, from which SEDS are produced.

3.1 LIDIA-2: New Software Architecture and Environment

The LIDIA-1 implementation was tightly linked with Macintosh operating system before OS-X. The manipulated data were also very poor in terms of content (no memory of the intermediate processes is kept) and their representation (plain text files).

In LIDIA-2, all DBMT services are made available on Internet through a portable interface written in Java. We use a distributed components architecture experimented within the C-STAR [3] and NESPOLE! [8] projects of speech-to-speech translation. The basic idea is to let all the components interact through a communication server (ComSwitch), to which they are attached by a Telnet connection.

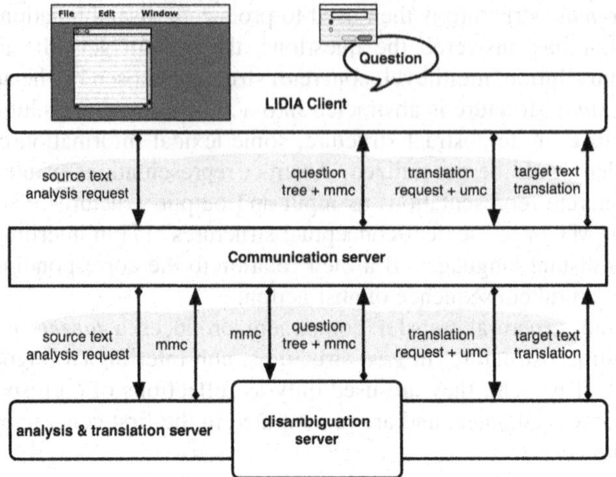

Fig. 6. LIDIA-2 architecture

LIDIA-2 appears as a text editor enhanced with DBMT functionalities. When the author has customized his environment, s/he can create a new document or open an existing one. The upper part of a document window displays its textual content, and the lower part displays information about the documents status.

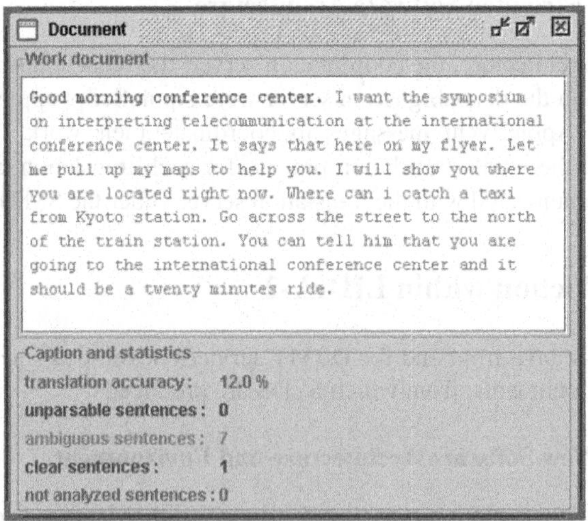

Fig. 7. Document window (after analysis step 1)

We use the ID module developed for English [2, 4]. Integration was immediate within our new architecture.

After the author has requested the analysis (**Fig. 7**), the ambiguous sentences are displayed in brown, and the unambiguous ones in green. In our example, only the first sentence is unambiguous sentence. When the author double-clicks an ambiguous sentence, the disambiguation questions tree prepared is traversed down.

For the sentence "I want the symposium on interpreting telecommunications at the international conference center", the root question (**Fig. 8**) is first asked. The Status part shows that this is the first question, and that at most, one question can follow. The author may Suspend or Reinitialize the session, or go back to the Previous question. When s/he has answered a question, s/he proceed to the Next one. When every question are answered, the author closes the session. At that point, for demonstration purposes, the sentences may be translated in French using a translation database.

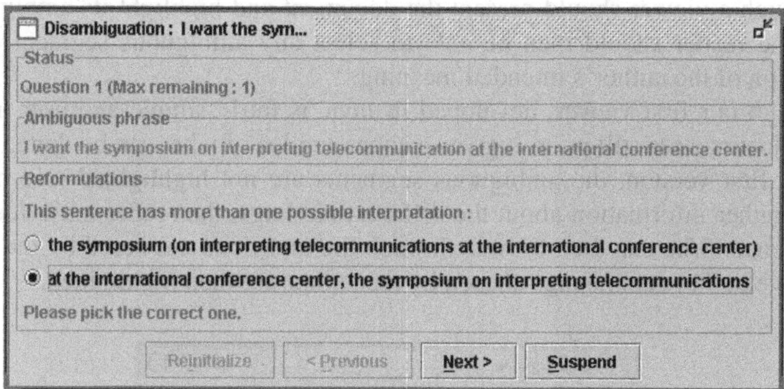

Fig. 8. Root question of the selected sentence

3.2 The LIDIA-2 Document

The XML document produced by LIDIA-2 is manipulated through the DOM API. When the author opens a document, its syntax is checked with the SAX API. The document contains a header, and its actual content. The header consists of a title and information about the author. The content is a set of paragraphs made of sentences.

```
<phrase source="ENG" stamp="51054803544695">
  <original><![CDATA[ I will show you where you are located right
now.]]></original>
  <question>
    <reformulation choix="NON"><![CDATA[I will show you (where you are located
right now).]]>
      <analyse><![CDATA[…]]></analyse>
    </reformulation>
    <reformulation choix="OUI"><![CDATA[right now, I will show you where you
are located.]]>
      <analyse><![CDATA[…]]></analyse>
    </reformulation>
  </question>
  <traduction cible="FRA"><![CDATA[Je vais tout de suite vous montrer où vous
êtes.]]></traduction>
</phrase>
```

Fig. 9. A LIDIA-2 document excerpt

Each sentence has a source language and a unique transaction identifier that allows the environment to keep track of the ongoing treatments for each sentence. The original content of the sentence, the answered question tree, and the produced translations are also represented. As far as the question tree is concerned, it stores the answer path through the different question items and the *umc* structure with its solution number associated with each terminal question.

3.3 Producing and Visualizing a DAE

After disambiguation, a source SED can be filtered out from the LIDIA-2 document. Sentences and answered disambiguation trees without the *umc* structures are kept.

As we want a SED to be a portable document, we developed a specialized viewer. Ideally, such a viewer should present the document and highlight its ambiguous segments. The reader should then be able to select any ambiguous segment and get a presentation of the author's intended meaning.

Although our first viewer, developed in Java, is fairly simple and user interaction with the document is still poor, it gives a concrete idea of what can be done.

In this first version, the ambiguous segments are not highlighted (see below): in order to gather information about the different readings, the reader must double-click on a sentence. S/he can then browse through the questions answered by the author of the document. The rephrasings chosen by the author are then highlighted.

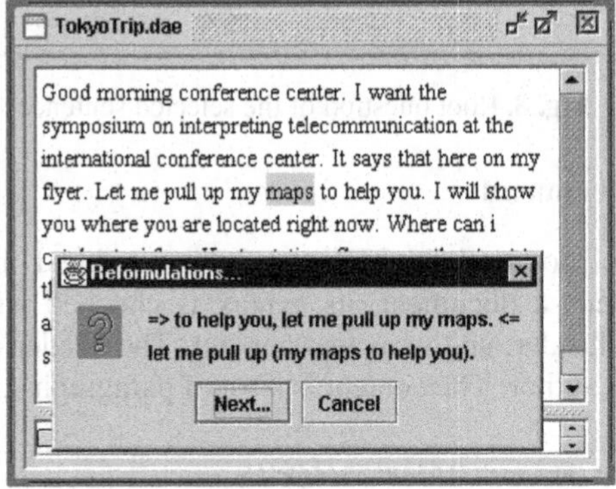

Fig. 10. Showing the author's chosen rephrasings

3.4 Outcome and Short Term Perspectives

Our first short-term goal is to make the ARIANE-G5 HTL modules for LIDIA available through the same ComSwitch as the disambiguation module. That would add new possibilities of experimentation. Going further on showing the ambiguities would require several changes in the disambiguation module itself.

The first version of the LIDIA-2 XML document structure is fairly simple, and all the information is not fully "XML-ized". For example, the *mmc* structure and the question tree use a Lisp-like representation requiring a specific module, although a DOM-based module would be more efficient and portable.

The question tree is XML-ized within the LIDIA-2 interface. It would be better to let the disambiguation module do it instead of producing a bracketed linear structure from a tree object.

Ariane-G5 does not handle XML-like data structure yet. We may implement a filter going back and forth between XML and ARIANE-G5 data structures. Such a component could be added transparently within the ComSwitch-based architecture.

4 Long Term Perspectives

The proposals we discuss now will impact on the HLT modules and/or the disambiguation module. They are thus long term goals.

4.1 Ambiguity Support and SED

4.1.1 Ambiguity as a Formal Object

In order to formalize the notion of ambiguity, let us take an example. Consider the utterance: **(1)** `Do you know where the international telephone services are located?`

The underlined fragment has an ambiguity of attachment, because it has two different "skeleton" [1] representations: `[international telephone] services / international [telephone services].`

As a title, this sequence presents the same ambiguity. However, it is not enough to consider it in isolation. Take for example: **(2)** `The international telephone services many countries`. The ambiguity has disappeared!

It is indeed frequent that an ambiguity relative to a fragment appears, disappears and reappears as one broadens its context in an utterance. For example, in **(3)** `The international telephone services many countries have established are very reliable`, the ambiguity has reappeared.

An *ambiguity occurrence*, or simply *ambiguity*, **A** of multiplicity n (n≥2) relative to a representation system R, may be formally defined as:

A = (U, F, <S_1, S_2, ..., S_m>, <f_1, f_2, ... , f_n>), where m≥n and:

- **U** is a complete utterance, called the *context* of the ambiguity **A**.
- **F** is a fragment of **U**, usually, but not necessarily connex, called the **support** of the ambiguity **A**.
- S_1, S_2, ..., S_m are proper representations of **U** in **R**, and f_1, f_2, ... , f_n are subparts of them representing F.
- Minimality condition:

For any fragment **F'** of **U** strictly contained in **F**, if f'_1, f'_2, ... , f'_n are respective parts of f_1, f_2, ... , f_n corresponding to **F'**, then there is at least one pair f'_i, f'_j (i≠j) such that $f'_i = f'_j$.

The kind of the ambiguity **A** depends on the difference between the s_i. It is defined in the framework of each **R**.

Fig. 11. Formal definition of ambiguity

From the examples above, we see that, in order to define properly what an ambiguity is, we must consider a fragment *within an utterance,* and clarify the idea that this fragment is the smallest (within the utterance) where the ambiguity can be observed.

A fragment **F** presents an ambiguity **A** of multiplicity n (n≥2) in an utterance **U** if it has n different proper representations which are all part of m (m≥n) proper representations of **U**.

F is an ambiguity support if it is minimal relative to that ambiguity. This means that any strictly smaller fragment **F'** of **U** will have strictly less than n associated sub-representations (at least two of the representations of **V** are equal with respect to **F'**).

In example (1) above, then, the fragment "the international telephone services", together with the two skeleton representations "the [international telephone] services / the international [telephone services]" is not minimal, because it and its two representations can be reduced to the subfragment "international telephone services" and its two representations (which are minimal).

4.1.2 Ambiguity Detection in the Current ID Process

The disambiguation methodology is based on the manipulation of tree structures. A kind of ambiguity is described with a set of patterns called an *ambiguity descriptor* (**Fig. 12**). A pattern contains variables and describes a tree structure with constraints on its geometry and labelling. Once an *ambiguity descriptor* has been recognized, a question is prepared.

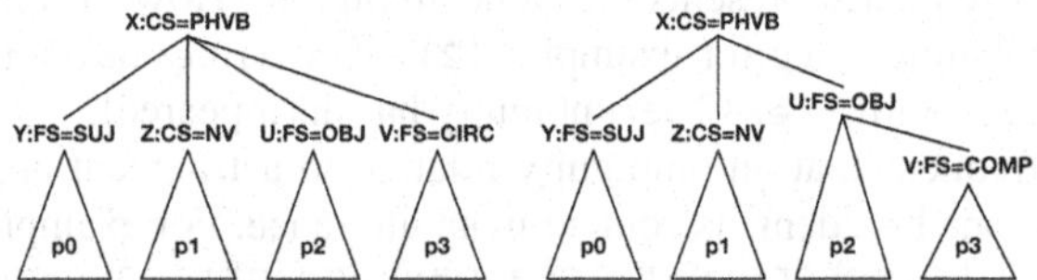

Fig. 12. An ambiguity detection beam

A question item is associated with each pattern of the beam and is produced through the manipulation, with a set of basic operators, of the values given to the variables instantiated during the recognition of the beam. The method associated with the left pattern in **Fig. 12** produces the following string: Text(**p2**), Text(**p0**) Text(**p1**) Text(**p2**). The method associated with the right pattern, produces the following string: Text(**p0**) Text(**p1**) Bracket(Text(**p2**), Text(**p3**)).

4.1.3 Towards a Better ID Preparation Process

In the current version of the French and English ID modules, within an *ambiguity descriptor*, the patterns are designed to capture the ambiguity support and some context. This context is used to produce a better labelling of the dialogue items.

For a SED, it seems to be very important to have a precise localization of the ambiguities that enable a precise highlighting of every ambiguity. It means that the ID preparation process should be able to provide the ambiguity support. They are two approaches to reach this goal.

In the first approach, the *ambiguity descriptor* patterns are not changed and the ambiguity support is associated with each *descriptor*. The support can be described in terms of the variables available in the patterns of the *descriptor*.

The second approach would change deeply the disambiguation preparation process. The new idea here is to let the patterns describe an ambiguity using only the ambiguity support. On the other hand, the rephrasing mechanism will have to pick up, in the *mmc* structure, the parts of the input text that have to be used to produce the dialogue items. It will also necessitate an embedded XML encoding of the ambiguity support allowing the GUI to clearly mark them.

4.2 Incomplete Disambiguation and Meaning Certification Levels

In the context of real applications, many ambiguities will arise, concerning word sense, attachment, argument structure, etc. Thus, there is a chance that for each sentence the question tree will be quite big, and the writer will not be willing to answer all questions, but only the most crucial ones.

Suppose that a sentence of length **N** has $\mathbf{k^N}$ interpretations and that the *ambiguity descriptors* are of average size **b. (k/b).N** questions in average would totally disambiguate the sentence. If, for example, **(k/b)=1/2**, there would be about 120 questions for a page of 240 words. Although answering them all may take 10 minutes or less[5] if we allow 5 seconds for each answer, the author may want to spend less time on ID.

In order to satisfy that need, answering all the questions in a question tree has not to be mandatory for the generation module to produce a translation. In other words, given an *mmc* structure, some disambiguation answers and maybe some user preferences or profile, the HLT modules have to be able to make a choice (using heuristics) and produce a unique translation, or to produce a factorized and linguistically "felicitous" representation for all remaining interpretations.

From the degree of completeness of the disambiguation of a sentence, and from the cruciality of the remaining ambiguities, it is certainly possible to compute a "meaning certification level" and associate it to the sentence. Meaning certification level can then be computed for paragraph, sections, etc., up to the whole documents, and more generally any part of it.

4.3 Target Language SED

In section 2.4, we have discussed why it would be very interesting to produce SEDs in target languages. Reaching such a goal is very demanding as far as the HLT module development is concerned because we need or each target language an "all path" analyzer which is an inverse of the generator. We intend to cooperate with other groups abroad to prototype that part.

5 Conclusion

The concept of SED appeared, and perhaps could only appear, in the context of our research on DBMT. That explains why, although it clearly opens many fascinating new possibilities in the use of numerical documents, no other researchers seem to work (yet!) on that concept.

However, we consider our research to be directly quite related to the larger and booming area of numerical documents and of the "semantic web" [11]. Starting from our first SED prototype, based on the new LIDIA-2 architecture, and primitive SED

[5] This has to be compared with the usual figures given by professional translators: 1 hour for each first draft translation, 20 minutes for the postedition in each target language.

viewer, we now plan to contribute to the subfield of active documents [9] by building a more sophisticated GUI embedded in *a la* Thot[6]-like.environment.

References

1. Black, E., Garside, R. and Leech, G.: Statistically-Driven Grammars of English: the IBM/Lancaster Approach. Rodopi. Amsterdam (1993)
2. Blanchon, H. An Interactive Disambiguation Module for English Natural Language Utterances. NLPRS'95. Seoul, Korea, vol. **2/2**: 550-555 (1995)
3. Blanchon, H. and Boitet, C.: Speech Translation for French within the C-STAR II Consortium and Future Perspectives. ICSLP 2000. Beijing, China, vol. **4/4**: 412-417 (2000)
4. Blanchon, H. and Fais, L.: Asking Users About What They Mean: Two Experiments & Results. HCI'97. San Francisco, California, vol. **2/2**: pp. 609-912 (1997)
5. Boitet, C.: Dialogue-Based MT and self explaining documents as an alternative to MAHT and MT of controlled language. Machine Translation Ten Years On. Cranfield, England (1994)
6. Boitet, C. and Blanchon, H.: Multilingual Dialogue-Based MT for monolingual authors: the LIDIA project and a first mockup. Machine Translation, vol. **9**(2): 99-132 (1995)
7. Levin, L. and Nirenburg, S. (1994) The Correct Place of Lexical Semantics in Interlingua. COLING-94. Kyoto, Japan, vol. **1/2**: pp. 349-355 (1994)
8. Metze, F., Mc Donough, J., Soltau, H., Waibel, A., Lavie, A., Burger, S., Langley, C., Levin, L., Schultz, T., Pianesi, F., Cattoni, R., Lazzari, G., Mana, N., Pianta, E., Besacier, L., Blanchon, H., Vaufreydaz, D. and Taddei, L.: The NESPOLE! Speech-to-Speech Translation System. HLT 2002. San Diego, California, USA (2002)
9. Quint, V. and Vatton, I.: Making structured documents active. Electronic Publishing Origination, Dissemination, and Design. vol. **7**(2): pp. 55-74 (1994)
10. Vauquois, B. and Boitet, C.: Automated Translation at Grenoble University. Computational Linguistics, vol. **11**(1): 28-36 (1985)
11. W3C (2001) Semantic Web. http://www.w3.org/2001/sw/.

[6] cf. http://opera.inrialpes.fr/Thot.en.html

Enhancing Short Text Retrieval in Databases

N. Marín, M.J. Martín-Bautista, M. Prados, and M.A. Vila

Intelligent Databases and Information Systems Research Group
`http://idbis.ugr.es`
Dept. of Computer Science and Artificial Intelligence
University of Granada, 18071 - Granada (Spain)
`{nicm, mbautis, prados, vila}@decsai.ugr.es`

Abstract. In this paper, we present a mechanism to deal with short text structures in relational databases. Text fields are transformed into a special knowledge representation named AP-structure based on the Apriori algorithm of the mining area. Once the abstract data type is obtained, the text fields can be summarized, mined, and queried in a easy way. The operations to query these fields are the main aim of this paper.

Keywords: Semantic querying, short texts, AP-sets, frequent itemsets, knowledge structure.

1 Introduction

Textual fields are not easy to treat in databases when a discovery process is carried out. The only operations over these fields are the classical ones in databases for text attributes such as to ask for the content of the field, or search for the fields containing a certain word or pattern. However, the lack of a reference domain for these fields make difficult operations such as semantic querying, mining, data warehousing, etc..

One possible solution to this problem is to give a structure to text fields. Although traditional Information Retrieval allow us to index these fields, a semantical structure should underly them. For this purpose, we propose an intermediate structure called AP-set [6] based on the frequent itemsets obtained by the Apriori algorithm of the mining area [2]. These sets are obtained as follows: all combinations of items in a transactional database are generated and only those having a support above a threshold called minsupport are considered and called frequent itemsets [1].

From the AP-set, abstract data types (ADT) can be established to facilitate its management. With this knowledge representation, different querying operations can be defined.

In the following section, we define the AP-set and the AP-structure concepts, as well as some operations to manage them regarding querying issues. An experimental example with a medical database is shown in Section 3. The problem of dealing with this new structure, in the context of an Object Relational Database

H.L. Larsen et al. (Eds.): FQAS 2006, LNAI 4027, pp. 613–624, 2006.

System (ORDBMS) is discussed in Section 4. Section 5 offers some query models to the new database, as well as some examples of these for our medical database. Finally, some conclusions and future work can be found in Section 6.

2 Definitions of the Knowledge Representation Structures

In this section we will formalize the ideas presented above by defining the mathematical structures which will be the basis for the formal representation of data. Firstly, we will establish the definition and properties of the sets of subsets which have the Apriori property [2], that we have called AP-Sets. Next, we will give the formal definition and properties of the underlying structure in the texts which is that of a set of AP-Sets.

In this paper we are concerned with querying problems, therefore we have only included here those theoretical questions which refer to this point. Other operations between sets and AP-Structures and between AP-Structures, as well as its properties, have been established in [6].

2.1 AP-Set Definition and Properties

Definition 1. AP-Set
Let $X = \{x_1 ... x_n\}$ be any referential and $\mathcal{R} \subseteq \mathcal{P}(X)$ (parts of the referential). We will say that $\mathcal{R}$ is an AP-Set if, and only if:

1. $\forall Z \in \mathcal{R} \Rightarrow \mathcal{P}(Z) \subseteq \mathcal{R}$
2. $\exists Y \in \mathcal{R}$ *such that* :
   (a) $card(Y) = max_{Z \in \mathcal{R}}(card(Z))$ *and* $\neg \exists Y' \in \mathcal{R} | card(Y') = card(Y)$
   (b) $\forall Z \in \mathcal{R}; Z \subseteq Y$

In the case of a text application, the referential would be terms and their frequencies.

The set Y of maximal cardinal characterizes the AP-Set and it will be called *spanning set of* $\mathcal{R}$. We will denote $\mathcal{R} = g(Y)$, that is $g(Y)$ will be the AP-Set with spanning set Y.

We will call *Level of* $g(Y)$ to the cardinal of Y. Obviously, AP-Sets of level equal to 1 are the elements of X and we will consider the empty set $\emptyset$ as the AP-Set of zero level. It should be remarked that the definition 1 implies that any AP-Set $g(Y)$ is in fact the reticulum of $\mathcal{P}(Y)$.

Definition 2. AP-Set Inclusion
Let $\mathcal{R} = g(R)$ and $\mathcal{S} = g(S)$ be two AP-Sets with the same referential:

$$\mathcal{R} \subseteq \mathcal{S} \Leftrightarrow R \subseteq S$$

Definition 3. Induced sub-AP-Set
Let $\mathcal{R} = g(R)$ and $Y \subseteq X$ be. We will say $\mathcal{S}$ is the sub-AP-Set induced by Y *iff:*

$$\mathcal{S} = g(R \bigcap Y)$$

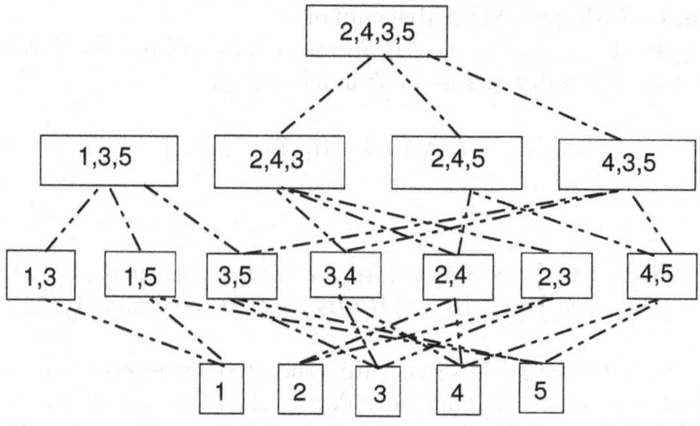

Fig. 1. AP-Structure reticulum

2.2 AP-Structure Definition and Properties

Once we have established the AP-Set concept, we will use it to define the information structures which appear when frequent itemsets are computed. It should be considered that such structures are obtained in an incremental way: initially, itemsets with cardinal equal to 1 are generated, next these ones are combined to obtain those of cardinal equal 2, and the process continues until itemsets of maximal cardinal are obtained, with a fixed minimal support. Therefore the final structure is that of a set of AP-Sets, which formally is defined as follows.

Definition 4. AP-Structure
Let $X = \{x_1 ... x_n\}$ be any referential and $S = \{A, B, ...\} \subseteq \mathcal{P}(X)$ such that:

$$\forall A, B \in S\,;\; A \nsubseteq B\,,\; B \nsubseteq A$$

We will call AP-Structure of spanning S, $\mathcal{T} = g(A, B, ...)$, *to the set of AP-Sets whose spanning sets are $A, B, ...$.*

It should be remarked that that any AP-Structure is a reticulum of subsets whose upper extremes are their spanning sets.

Figure 1 shows an example of the reticulum underlying in $g(\{1,3,5\}, \{2,4,3,5\})$.

Now we will give some definition and properties of these new structures.

Definition 5. *Let $\mathcal{T}_1$ and $\mathcal{T}_2$ be two AP-Structures with the same referential:*

$$\mathcal{T}_1 \subseteq \mathcal{T}_2 \Leftrightarrow \forall \mathcal{R} \text{ AP-Set of } \mathcal{T}_1\,,\; \exists \mathcal{S} \text{ AP-Set of } \mathcal{T}_2 \text{ such that } \mathcal{R} \subseteq \mathcal{S}$$

It should be remarked that the inclusion of AP-Sets corresponds to definition 2.

Definition 6. Induced AP-Substructure
Let $\mathcal{T} = g(A_1, A_2, ..., A_n)$ *be an AP-Structure with referential* X *and* $Y \subseteq X$. *We will define* AP-Substructure of $\mathcal{T}$ induced by Y*:*

$$\mathcal{T}' = \mathcal{T} \bigwedge Y = g(B_1, B_2, ..., B_m)$$

where

$$\forall B_i \in \{B_1, ..., B_m\} \Rightarrow \exists A_j \in \{A_1, A_2, ..., A_n\} \text{ such that } B_i = A_j \bigcap Y$$
$$\forall A_j \in \{A_1, ..., A_n\} \Rightarrow \exists B_i \in \{B_1, B_2, ..., B_m\} \text{ such that } A_j \bigcap Y \subseteq B_i$$

It is clear that $\mathcal{T}'$ is the AP-Structure generated by intersections of Y with the spanning sets of $\mathcal{T}$, without considering those intersections which are in contradiction with the AP-Structure minimal definition. The induced AP-Superstructure can also be defined in an analogous way [6].

The following example clarifies these ideas.

Example 1. From $X = \{1, 2, ..., 9\}$, $\mathcal{T} = g(\{1, 2, 3\}, \{2, 3, 4\}, \{4, 5\}, \{6\})$, and $Y = \{2, 3, 4, 5\}$, we have $\mathcal{T} \bigwedge Y = g(\{2, 3, 4\}, \{4, 5\})$.

It should be remarked that the set $\{2, 3\}$ is not included in $\mathcal{T} \bigwedge Y$, whereas this set belongs to the intersection of Y and the $\mathcal{T}$ spanning sets.

2.3 Matching Sets with AP-Structures

Now we will establish the basis for querying in a database where the AP-Structure appears as data type. The main idea is that users will express their requirements as term-sets while attribute values in the database will be AP-Structures. Therefore some kind of matching has to be given. To do it, two different alternatives can be considered.

Definition 7. Strong Matching
Let $\mathcal{T} = g(A_1, A_2, ..., A_n)$ *be an AP-Structure with referential* X *and* $Y \subseteq X$. *We define the* strong matching between Y and $\mathcal{T}$ *as a logical operation:*

$$Y \bigodot \mathcal{T} = \begin{cases} \textit{true if } \exists A_i \in \{A_1, A_2, ..., A_n\} \\ \qquad\qquad /Y \subseteq A_i \\ \textit{false} \quad \textit{otherwise} \end{cases}$$

Definition 8. Weak Matching
Let $\mathcal{T} = g(A_1, A_2, ..., A_n)$ *be an AP-Structure with referential* X *and* $Y \subseteq X$. *We define the* weak matching between Y and $\mathcal{T}$ *as a logical operation:*

$$Y \bigoplus \mathcal{T} = \begin{cases} \textit{true if } \exists A_i \in \{A_1, A_2, ..., A_n\} \\ \qquad\qquad /Y \bigcap A_i \neq \emptyset \\ \textit{false} \quad \textit{otherwise} \end{cases}$$

These definitions can be complemented by giving some measures or indices which quantify these matchings. The idea is to consider that the matching of a long set of terms will have an index greater than other with less terms, additionally if some term set match with more than one spanning set will have an index greater than that of the other one which only match with one set. Obviously two matching indices can be established, but both of them have similar definitions.

Definition 9. Strong (Weak) Matching Index
Let $\mathcal{T} = g(A_1, A_2, ..., A_n)$ *be an AP-Structure with referential* X *and* $Y \subseteq X$. *We define the* strong(weak) matching index between Y and $\mathcal{T}$ *as follows:*

$\forall A_i \in \{A_1, A_2, ..., A_n\}$ *we denote* $m_i(Y) = card(Y \bigcap A_i)/card(A_i)$, $S = \{i \in \{1, ..., n\} | Y \subseteq A_i\}$, $W = \{i \in \{1, ..., n\} | Y \bigcap A_i \neq \emptyset\}$.

Then we define the strong and weak matching indices between Y and $\mathcal{T}$ *as follows:*

$$\textbf{Strong index} = S(Y|\mathcal{T}) = \sum_{i \in S} m_i(Y)/n$$

$$\textbf{Weak index} = W(Y|\mathcal{T}) = \sum_{i \in W} m_i(Y)/n$$

Obviously:

$$\forall Y \text{ and } \mathcal{T}\ ,\ S(Y|\mathcal{T}) \in [0,1]\ ,\ W(Y|\mathcal{T}) \in [0,1] \text{ and } W(Y|\mathcal{T}) \geq S(Y|\mathcal{T}).$$

2.4 From Short Text Data to AP-Structures: Obtaining and Managing Structured Representations

As we commented in the introduction, the aim of this approach is to obtain a structured representation that keeps, in some sense, the meaning of the textual fields. For this purpose, it is necessary to find a non static representation, but a mathematical model with operations over the data, that is, to be an Abstract Data Type (ADT). In this way, we can implement the structure in a Object Relational Data Base System (ORDBMS), as well as its operations, in order to allow database queries.

A mechanism to obtain the AP-Sets to form an AP-Set structure from the original data was presented in [6]. The tasks are:

1. To obtain a data dictionary consisting in a list of the terms removing stop-words [9].
2. To transform the data into a transactional database, where the attributes are the different terms of the data dictionary, and each tuple corresponds to a record.
3. To obtain the frequent itemsets of the transactional database following an Apriori like algorithm [2].
4. The maximal itemsets form the reticular structure, that is, the AP-Sets, following the Apriori property.

It should be remarked that the AP-structure obtained by this procedure *almost* covers the whole information that the database has in the corresponding short text attribute. So, we can consider this one as the active domain of this attribute. Let us denote $\mathcal{D}$ this domain.

Obviously, each short text attribute value in a tuple should also be viewed as an AP-Structure that can be obtained as follows:

Let A be a short text attribute in the database, for each tuple t of the database, let Y_t be the term set obtained from $t[A]$ by removing stop words. Then, the AP-Structure corresponding to the A value of t is given by:

$$\mathcal{T} = Y_t \bigwedge \mathcal{D}$$

Therefore, the inclusion of the restriction operation in the ADT definition will allows us to get the representation, as AP-Structure, of each sort text value. This makes unnecessary to have explicitly recorded such representation for each attribute value.

The querying to the database can be performed from different point of views.

A The user could ask for the whole information included in the database, using the whole AP-Structure $\mathcal{D}$

B The user can give an initial list of terms to query without any knowledge about the vocabulary of the AP-structure. In this case he/she could firstly ask to the general active domain $\mathcal{D}$, looking for the term sets which match with its initial list.

  The matching taking into account in the query can be strong or weak based on the coincidence between the terms used in the query by the user and the terms stored in the AP-Structure. If these terms are included completely in the vocabulary of the AP-Structure, a strong matching will be carried out. Otherwise, a weak matching is performed, and the user can be helped with suggestions of new terms or similar terms which are included in the AP-Structure vocabulary.

C The user can give a list of terms asking directly to de database. In this case, the matching procedure is carried out against each AP-Substructure attribute value, and strong and weak matching indices have to be computed for each tuple. In this case, some kind of threshold should be included in the query, in order to avoid too huge answers.

3 Experimental Example

To carry out this experiment, textual fields from a medical database from the University Clinic Hospital San Cecilio of Granada have been considered. From 2072 records, we have extracted only the textual field of diagnostic. This field has short text as values (from one up to fifteen terms). Figure 2 presents an example of original text from some of these records.

Patient	Symptoms	...	Diagnostic
46735	Headache		Occipital sebaceous cyst
57856	Nuisances		Epidermal cyst
95465	Leg intensive pain		Subcapital fracture of femur
⋮	⋮	⋮	⋮

Fig. 2. Example of textual records from a medical database

Following the process described in Section 2.4, we obtain a dictionary of words from the set of records removing stop-words. Once we have transformed these records into a transactional database using the dictionary, we are ready to extract the itemsets following any Apriori like algorithm. Some of these itemsets are shown in Figure 3, where the support is defined as the frequency of the itemset in the transactional database.

Field 1	Field 2	Field 3	...	Support
right	fracture			4.26
right	femur			1.826
back	sebaceous	cyst		1.304
back	cyst			1.304
right	femur	fracture		1.173
femur	left			1.043
femur	fracture	left		1.043
⋮	⋮			⋮

Fig. 3. Example of itemsets and support

The itemsets form the AP-Set in the form of an inclusion reticular structure. An example of such structure is shown in Figure 4. The related AP-Sets form an AP-Structure.

All the AP-Structure reticula from the database form the super AP-structure which represents the ADT. The AP-Structures are the basis to query the database as is explained in the following section.

4 AP-Structure Representation in an Object Relational Database

According to the ideas presented in the previous sections, we will try to increase the question answering power of our database by means of the use of term-sets and AP-Structures for short text attribute representation. Table 1 summarizes this use.

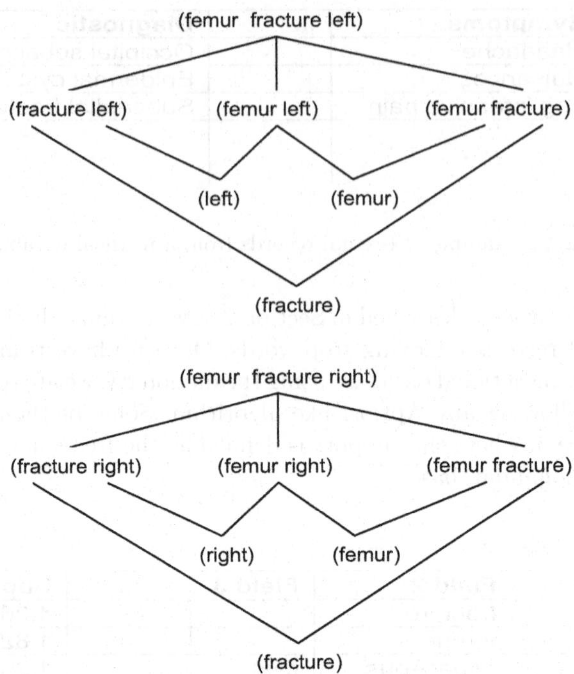

Fig. 4. Example of AP-Structure

4.1 Metadata Representation

We will need to store the appropriate AP-Structure for every short text attribute in a relation, in order to support the intended enhanced retrieval capability. Therefore, our database will have some additional metadata associated to each table, as figure 5 depicts.

Figure 6 represents the relationships between data and metadata. As can be observed, each short text attribute in a relation will need:

- The capability of perceive its different values as term sets and AP-Structures.
- The storage of the AP-Structure which represents its active domain.

To accomplish the first requirement, we can simply implement an extension of any conventional string type so that we can manage short texts as term sets (with the capability of interact with AP-Structures). For the sake of efficiency, we can also add an additional column to the relation so that the corresponding term sets can be stored for each tuple.

Table 1. Short text attributes extended representation

Element	Extended Representation
Attribute values	Term-Sets
Active attribute domain	AP-Structure

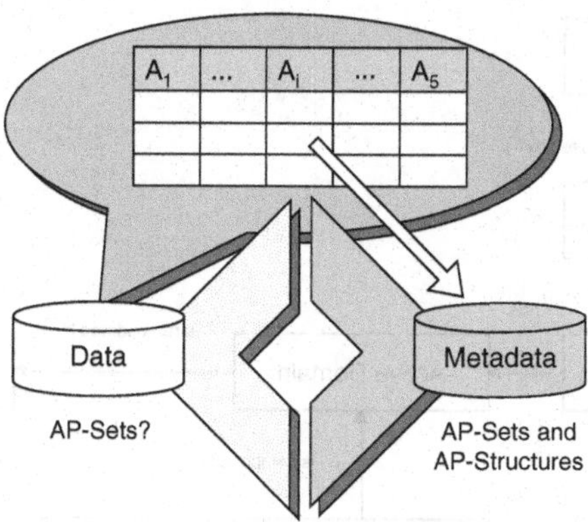

Fig. 5. Support for relation with short text attributes

To support the storage of the AP-Structures which represent active domains, we need an additional catalog relation, namely, `AD-Description`. Each tuple of this new relation must be able to indicate:

- The name of the short text attribute
- The name of the original relation
- The AP-Structure which represents the active domain

Let us now focus on the representation of term-sets, AP-Sets, and AP-Structures.

4.2 Representing AP-Sets and AP-Structures

As we have commented before, the computation of AP-Sets from short texts can be made by means of the use of any Apriori-like algorithm[2] together with some of the well-known mechanisms for removing stop words [9] in the text such as articles, pronouns, prepositions and so on.

The powerful modeling capabilities of Object Relational Database Management Systems ease the development and use of AP-Sets and AP-Structures in conventional databases. Both AP-Sets and AP-Structures are directed graphs, which can be stored with two different detail levels:

- Representing only the spanning set for the AP-Set and the collection of spanning sets for the AP-Structure.
- Representing the whole graphs.

Let us analyze these two alternatives:

- The first alternative is easier to implement and does not hardly increase the storage necessities of our database. As object-relational database systems provide different mechanisms to develop set-like attribute values, the

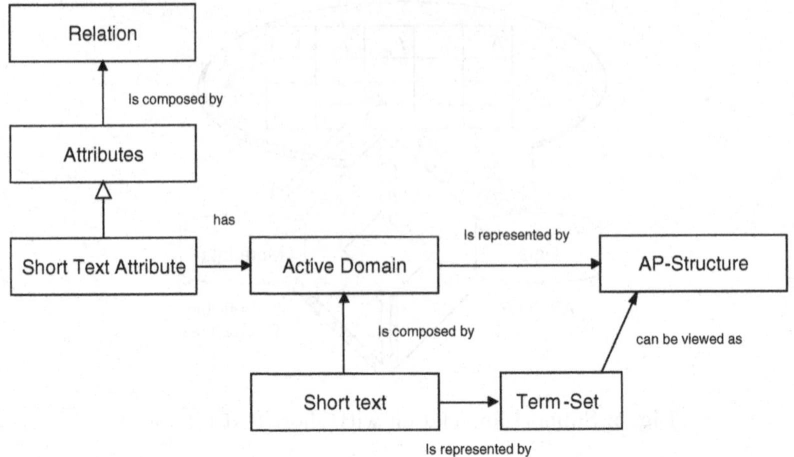

Fig. 6. Data and metadata relationships

representation of an AP-Set and an AP-Structure as a spanning set and a collection of spanning sets (respectively) is straightforward.

With this first alternative, AP-Structures can be represented creating a new user defined type as a collection of AP-Sets and with a set of operations which implement the behavior we have presented in previous sections.

– The second alternative demands much more additional storage space, but permits us to represent additional information which completes the AP-Structure description: if we represent it as graphs, we can also store the support values related to each node in the graph which can be very useful later in the query process.

  In order to minimize the representation of the graph we can use the ideas presented in [3], so that we do not have to represent the whole description of each node but only the variation with respect to the previous node.

  Taking into account these ideas, we can implement a new user defined type in order to support the graph, for example, using an adjacency list model [4]. Once again, object-relational capabilities make this implementation possible and ease to use.

5 Querying the System

According to the paragraph 2.4 there are two main ways to querying to the system:

– The first one asks for information about the terms used in the database and the way they are associated in structures. In this case the user knows nothing about the recorded data and query to the whole AP-Structure which is the active domain (points A and B in the paragraph 2.4).

– The second one corresponds to the point C of 2.4 and assumes that the user has some previous knowledge about the terms recorded in the database.

In the following paragraphs some examples of these queries are offered. They have been formulated in an SQL3- based language and using the experimental example showed in 3. In the following the metadata relation will be called `AP_description`, the data relation will be `emergency`, and the short text attribute will be `diagnostic`.

In this context, we can state the following example queries:

– Concerning metadata:
  - Queries asking for the list of spanning sets of a given ap-structure:

```
SELECT apstr.spanning()
FROM AP_description apstr
WHERE apstr.relation_name()='emergency'
  and apstr.attribute_name()='diagnostic';
```

    In our previous example the answer of this query would be:

```
(fracture, femur, left)
(fracture, femur, right)
```

  - Queries which look for a list of matching term subsets:

```
SELECT apstr.match('left','wound')
FROM AP-description apstr
WHERE apstr.relation_name()='emergency'
  and apstr.attribute_name()='diagnostic';
```

    In our previous example the answer would be:

```
- Weak matching (index 1/6)
- Matching maximal set (fracture, femur, left)
```

  - Queries which try to obtain a list of suggested data queries, in order to be used in a query on the data relation.

```
SELECT apstr.suggest('fracture','wound','femur')
FROM AP-description apstr
WHERE apstr.relation_name()='emergency'
  and apstr.attribute_name()='diagnostic';
```

    In our previous example the answer would be:

```
- Weak matching (index 1/2)
- Suggestion (fracture, femur)
```

– Concerning conventional data:
  A possible query to the database could be the one obtained in the above paragraph:

```
SELECT * FROM emergency
WHERE diagnostic.strong_match('fracture','femur')>0.5;
```

6 Conclusions and Future Work

The approach presented in the paper give us a way to handle textual fields in databases (Relational, OR, etc.). With a minimal preprocessing of the text and the obtaining of the frequent itemsets, a structure following the Apriori property can be constructed. The definition of mathematical operations to deal with this structure allows us to represent it as an ADT of any Object Relational database. From these initials results, the following problems will be addressed in the future:

- The complete development of the mathematical model and the query process, by carrying out more experiment.
- The study of the suitability of combining, aggregating, or summarizing different structures in the same database, or even to join different databases with textual fields.
- The attempt to include more information in the AP-structure by considering support valuation inside the definition.

References

1. R. Agrawal, T. Imielinski, A. Swami (1993). Mining Association rules between set of items in large databases. In *Proceedings of ACM SIGMOD Conference*, May, 1993, Washington DC, USA.
2. R. Agrawal, R. Srikant (1994). Fast Algorithms for mining Association rules. In *Proceedings of VLDB*, Sept, 1994, Santiago, Chile.
3. F. Berzal, J.C. Cubero, N. Marín, J.M. Serrano (2001). TBAR: An efficient method for association rule mining in relational databases. *Data and Knowledge Engineering*, Volume 37, Number 1, pp. 47-64.
4. J. Celko (2005). *SQL for smarties. Advanced SQL Programming.* Morgan Kaufmann.
5. C. Justicia, M.J. Martín-Bautista, D. Sánchez, M.A. Vila (2005). Text Mining: Intermediate Forms for Knowledge Representation. In *Proceedings of the conference Eusflat'2005*, pages 1082-1087, Barcelona, Spain, September 2005.
6. M.J. Martín-Bautista, M. Prados, M.A. Vila, S. Martínez-Folgoso (2006). A knowledge representation for short texts based on frequent itemsets. To appear in Proceedings of the 11th Conference of Information Processing and Management of Uncertainty (IPMU), Paris, July 2006.
7. R. Mack, M. Hehenberger (2002). Text-based knowledge discovery: search and mining of life-sciences documents. *Drug Discovery Today*, volume 7, number 11 (Suppl.)
8. M. Prados, C. Peña, B. Prados-Suárez, M.A. Vila (2006). Generation and use of one ontology for intelligent information retrieval from electronic health medical record. In *8th International Conference on Enterprise Information Systems*, May 2006, Cyprus (to appear).
9. G. Salton, M.J. McGill (1983). *Introduction to Modern Information Retrieval.* McGraw-Hill.

Evaluating the Effectiveness of a Knowledge Representation Based on Ontology in Ontoweb System

Tania C.D. Bueno[2], Sonali Bedin[1], Fabricia Cancellier[2], and Hugo C. Hoeschl[1]

[1] Instituto de Governo Eletrônico, Inteligência Jurídica e Sistemas – IJURIS,
Rua Lauro Linhares, 728 – sala 105 – Trindade - 88036-0002 - Florianópolis – SC – Brasil
{hugo, sonali}@ijuris.org,
http://www.ijuris.org

[2] WBSA Sistemas Inteligentes SA, Parque Tecnológico Alfa, Centro de
Tecnologia IlhaSoft, SC 401 Km 1 - Módulo 10 - Térreo B - João Paulo -
88030-000 - Florianópolis, SC – Brasil
{tania, fabricia}@wbsa.com.br
http://www.wbsa.com.br

Abstract. In the past few years, several studies have emphasized the use of ontologies as an alternative to information organization. The notion of ontology has become popular in fields such as intelligent information integration, information retrieval on the Internet, and knowledge management. Different groups use different approaches to develop and verify de effectiveness of ontologies [1] [2] [3]. This diversity can be a factor that makes it difficult the formularization of formal methodologies of evaluation. This paper seeks to provide a way to identify the effectiveness of the knowledge representation based on ontology that was developed trough Knowledge Based System tools. The reason for that is because all processing and storage of gathered information and knowledge base organization is done using this structure. Our evaluation is based on case studies in the Ontoweb system [4], involving real world ontology for money laundry domain. Our results indicate that modification of ontology structure can effectively reveal faults, as long as they adversely affect the program state.

1 Introduction

The application testing is an important stage of the system development process. These tests intend the verification of all the functionalities of the tool, inferring that the results are the ones expected when the system was conceived. However, it is particularly difficult to engage in ontology evaluation where the entire system design assumes a high degree of interaction between user and system, and makes explicit allowance for clarification and recovery. This is the case of KMAI - an intelligent knowledge management platform [5].

The unique approach towards the formal evaluation of ontologies is OntoClean [6], as it analyses the intentional content of concepts. Although it is well documented in numerous publications, and its importance is widely acknowledged, it is still used rather infrequently due to the high costs for applying OntoClean, especially on

H.L. Larsen et al. (Eds.): FQAS 2006, LNAI 4027, pp. 625–633, 2006.

tagging concepts with the correct meta-properties. Open response tests, especially those making use of nonsense words, require an extensive training of the listeners. However, additionally to the word and phoneme scores, possible confusions between phonemes are obtained. This allows for diagnostic analysis. Redundant material (sentences, rhyme tests) suffers from ceiling effects (100% score at poor-to-fair conditions) while tests based on nonsense words may discriminate between good and excellent conditions.

In earlier works, we used a methodology called Mind Engineering [7] to identify and organize ontologies using a collaborative web tool called Knowledge Engineering Suite (see item 2.2). This tool is a module of a KMAI Platform. Mind Engineering allows building a knowledge base, improving the construction of the ontology of the domain and the automatic representation of cases in knowledge-based systems, either in the legal area or any other knowledge management domain [8]. The methodology of test it is focused in the verification of the expected result of the system when of the use of the ontologies for the recovery of the information. The tests are affected from the terms that are part of the domain ontologies created for a specific application.

Despite the fact that testing provides a proof of correctness for only those test cases that pass, it remains popular due in part to its low, incremental cost. Our evaluation is based on two case studies involving real world applications based on ontology. Our results indicate that specification based assertions can effectively reveal faults, as long as they adversely affect the program state.

Therefore our paper is organized as follows. In section 2 we present the KMAI System and Knowledge Engineering structure. In section 3 we describe the participation of the ontology structure in the KMAI System and aspects of ontology application. In turn these aspects will be applied in our recall measures. In section 4 we will introduce ontology evaluation process. Section 5 will develop recall measures for ontology in the Ontoweb system. We end with a brief conclusion and with future work.

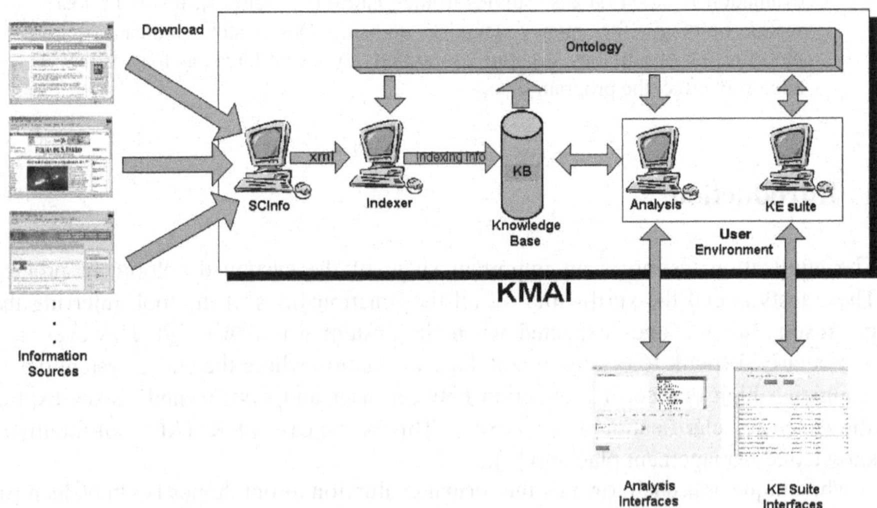

Fig. 1. The participation of the ontology structure in the Kmai System

2 Kmai System and Knowledge Engineering Suite

2.1 Kmai System

The Kmai System embraces the whole cycle of strategic information production, from the collection to the recovery for the user. Part of visualization of the system is in figure 1. It begins in the election of the digital sources to be monitored (Knowledge Engineering), separating structured data of those non-structured (about 90%) and submitting them to differentiated treatments. Data obtaining is made through Collection Agents connected to collections, each one representing a source of information, which can be from specific websites to documents storage directories (textual documents, spreadsheets, e-mails and reports in general) digitally existent in the organization.

The vision of the storage structure is physical, containing the items collected in pastes organized by domains. The collections are converted for a common pattern that allows communication with structured databases. The chosen format was XML (Extensible Markup Language). Text Mining is destined to extract concepts, statistics and important words of a group of documents to minimally structure them.

In that phase, three types of information are extracted: metadata (common document information, such as title and author), indexes (terms that describe the content of the document) and concepts (terms that describe the context of the document). This concepts are based on the ontologies defined in the Knowledge Engineering Suite (see item 2.2). Therefore, the cycle of the information production is completely assisted in a digital and intelligent way.

The retrieval process is cyclical, as the user describes the subject to be searched and the system shows, organized by the degree of similarity with the described subject, the related information, enabling the increasing of more specific information referring to the present elements on the searched subject, for instance, periods of time or information sources.

2.2 Knowledge Engineering Suite

This Module of Kmai System allows the building of the relationship tree, always considering the similarity between all the terms filed and the ones already existing on the base. These relationships allow the system to expand the search context. The organization of the tree allows the dynamic definition of the weights of the indicative expressions according to the query of the user. The fields with all available relationships are presented. They are the following: -synonyms; -related terms; "this is a type of"; "it belongs to this type"; "this is a part of"; "it is part of this". The editor presents the existing relationships and allows including them. Each relationship has a weight related to the defined indicative expression in the query by the user.

3 The Process of Ontology Construction

The ontologies structure is the heart of Ontoweb System. The reason for that is because all processing and storage of gathered information and knowledge base organization is done using this structure. It also plays an important role in the quality of the results presented to the user.

The participation of the ontology structure in the Kmai System occurs in three moments (see figure 1). At the first moment, the system extracts information from different previously selected sources. Each one of these documents is indexed based in the ontologies defined by the specialists and knowledge engineers during the knowledge engineering process. It means that the system will mark the documents with all indicative expressions found in the text, storing them in an organized way in the knowledge base. Thus, it is possible to make a pre-classification of the cases in the base according to what was defined in the knowledge organization promoted by the ontologies.

In a second moment, the ontologies are important in the analysis interface available to the user. The process begins at the moment in which the user types the input text for the search. At this point, the indicative expressions defined by the user that coincide with the ones presented in the ontology are identified. These expressions identified in the entry case determine the stream of relations that will be used by the system. It means that there is a dynamic relation between the way the user enters the indicative expression in the analysis interface and the way the relations in the Knowledge Engineering Suite are defined for this expression.

The first versions of the Knowledge Engineering Suite worked with key expressions, an approach that resulted in some rigidity in the ontology organization. The weight of the information that was typed by the user in the search text was not considered. In this new approach, the importance of the indicative expressions to be considered is defined by the user. The system gives priority to the expressions and search for the corresponding derivations for each case, according to the knowledge base. A priori, there is no hierarchy in the organization of the ontology in knowledge base. The weight of the relations will be based only in what is required by the search, where the context intended by the user is defined.

The third moment where the ontology takes part is in the Knowledge Engineering Suite, available in the system and integrated in its architecture. Through the Knowledge Engineering Suite the user is able to update the knowledge base with new expressions. At each new update in the ontology, the system re-indexes all the texts stored in the knowledge base, so the users may use this new ontology organization to search for documents previously indexed. It allows the verification of old documents that are related to a context that is important at the present moment. This way, it is possible to define a dateline about a subject, locating its start point.

It is important to highlight that this structure of contextualized ontologies allows automatic information indexing by the system and a knowledge acquisition that gives more qualitative answers in the retrieval process.

4 Ontology Evaluation

In the Ontoweb System the terms are organized in sub-domains, obeying criteria of relevance in the domain. The retrieval process is based on similarity between the number of terms, ontology and relationships presented in the text. These relationships are based on relevancy of the connection (synonyms – 0,99; related terms – 0,75;

"this is a type of"- 0,30; "it belongs to this type"- 0,30; "this is a part of"- 0,30; "it is part of this"- 0,30), see item 2.2.

In this perspective, the recall test identify if the ontology relationships improve de quality of the results in Ontoweb System. Thus, the ontology is inserted in the analysis for evaluation in two ways: textually, in the analyzer search where the document is presented orderly based on the similarity of the ontology and ontology relationships, or still in form of graphs that allow the evaluation the quantity of documents where that ontology and its relationships appear.

The process of test and evaluation of the ontologies define the effectives of relationships considering the amount of documents retrieved.

The first test is performed by the Knowledge Engineer during the ontology construction phase. First of all the relations of synonymous are created, for instance: money laundering is synonymous of dirty money and laundering operations. After that, the search function of the system is performed to verify the number of documents found and then the engineer starts to create "type of" and "part of" relations (e. g., combating money laundering, Offshore Financial Centers, Global Programme Against Money Laundering). To check if the relation falls within the context, a small increase in the number of documents retrieved has to be observed. Otherwise, if the number of documents retrieved is higher than 70% of the documents retrieved through the synonymous, then the relation will be considered not adequate; in the aforementioned example, "Offshore Financial Centers" is an expression too wide for the term "money laundering". The last relations to be inserted are the related terms (e.g. crime against the financial system, ideal financial heaven, organized crime) with weight 0.75. In this case, if the relation brings a search result above 150% of the documents retrieved by the first step, the term should be considered as inadequate for that set of relationships. In the example given, the expression "organized crime" presented a search result higher than 150% and the engineer should create a separate relation for that term with synonymous and other relations, if the term is considered important for the domain he is working on.

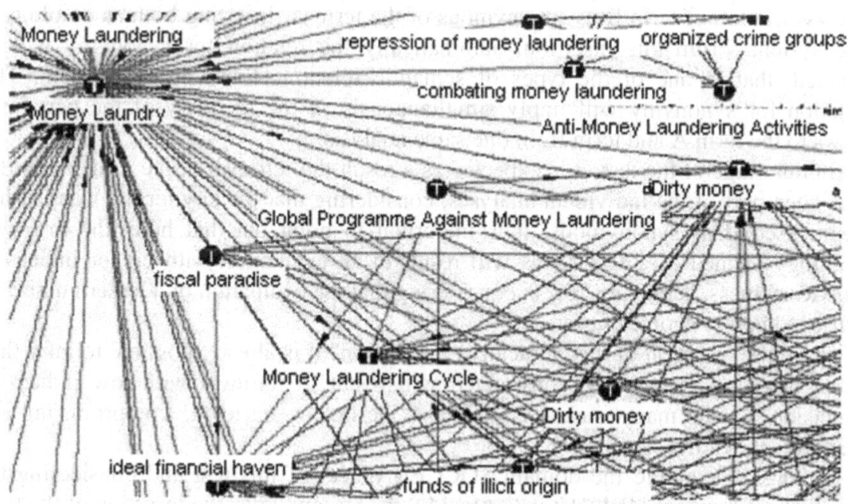

Fig. 2. Part of Money Laundry Ontology

Thus, after the definition of the search domain, the process is developed in some stages, as the following description. As an example, we will call the "indicative expression" A and B in the description of the process: a. Previous analysis of the A terms; b. Analysis of B terms; c. Elaboration of the relation of the terms A the B; d. Representation of error.

4.1 Previous Analysis of the A Terms

Initially it must be carried out a previous analysis of the "indicative expression" pertinent to this domain, aiming at verifying if they are excellent and if the retrieval represents a considerable number of news.

It is important to remark that, previously, the system must contain registered sources and knowledge base news of a minimum period the thirty days. These key-terms can be part of the ontology target of the analysis, and does not compromise the expected final results.

The analysis of the representation of these words will be made initially in the first page of retrieval of the system, where there shall be news in which these words are contemplated.

4.2 Analysis of B Terms

In this stage, the same analysis previously accomplished will contemplate other words, chosen at random or that they are part of the ontologies, as previously said. Here also the objective is the recovery of news, being that, different of the notice of the first test.

4.3 Elaboration of the Relation of the Terms A the B

After the individual evaluation of the terms A the B, with register of the gotten results, it takes the construction of the relation. This construction is accomplished by the association of term B as synonymous of the term A, inserting both as ontology in the system. From this insertion, automatically the relation for synonymy will be created, that is one of the types of semantic relations found in the system. This relation for synonymy will imply simultaneously in the recovery of the pertaining news to the term A and term B, in one same analysis.

In this stage of the test, it is expected as a result the retrieval of the same news that had been part of the individual analyses, considering that the key-terms A and B had been inserted as synonymous. It is important to point out that here, the test with ontology formed of a few terms will result in an evaluation with bigger indices of trustworthiness, achieving 100%, considering that the evaluation of a lesser number of retrieved news becomes faster.

From the insertion of the "indicative expression" it is already possible to infer that, if an ontology is not well constructed will result in retrieval with low indices of precision or, in many cases, completely inefficient retrieval, compromising the performance of the system.

Taking as example the domain SOCCER object of this test and considering the insertion of the term "Pelé", it is verified by the system, after the insertion of the term and normalizes the grammatical accent. Thus, for the domain SOCCER, "skin" will be related to the term. In this case, when the analysis of the system will retrieve news about skin, endocrinology, allergies, however, and some about "Pelé football player", it is considered that the presented error is not of the system, but an error of ontology construction. When the ontology was not constructed in the correct form to represent the expected knowledge, we proceed to its elimination of the "indicative expression" and initiate the construction of new "indicative expression" and its relationships, for a new stage of tests.

4.4 Representation of Error

The following stage of tests is related the representation of error, considering that the ontology correctly is constructed, already identified and corrected errors of relationship. The test consists of the construction of the relationship of the ontology constructed to a term that does not represent relation with the ontology.
For example, we take the indicative expression "money laundry (lavagem de dinheiro)" (see fig. 2), this expression is related to money laundry ontology in the ontoweb system. In this way, the system recovered 4.516 documents, in the period of two years, from one source *Agência Brasil.*

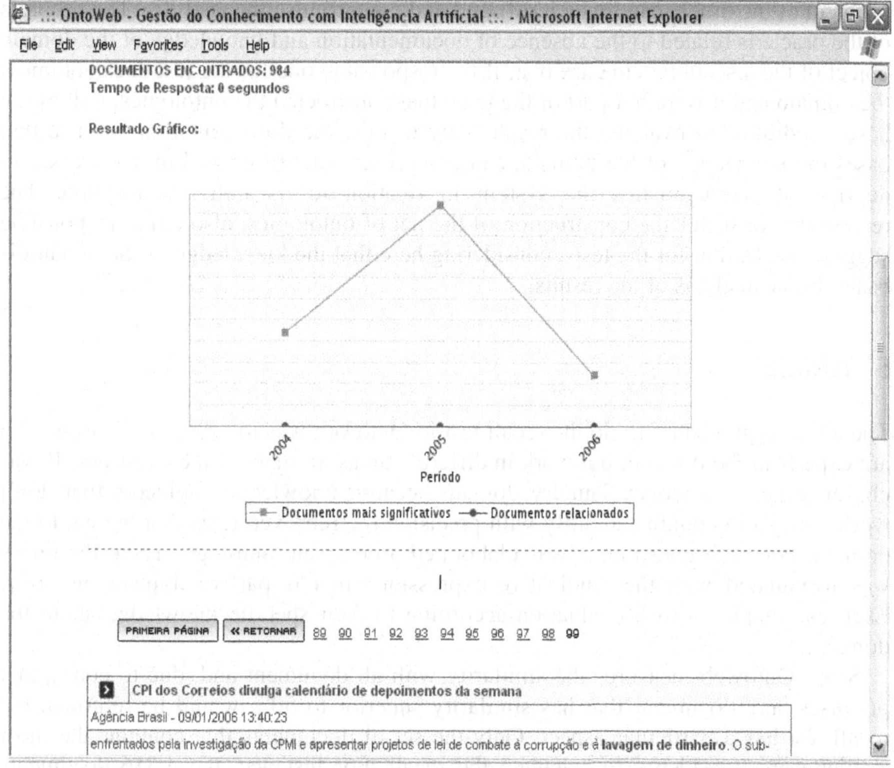

Fig. 3. The Result of Money Laundry ontology in the Ontoweb System

It was observed that documents with low similarity were retrieved due to the terms "bank secrecy" and "kidnapping". When testing the term "bank secrecy" the result was within the context of money laundering; however, other terms like "kidnapping" were totally out of the subject. The term "bank secrecy" retrieved 984 documents, for the same two-year period, and the documents with low similarity contained the term "money laundering" (see Figure 3). When testing the term "kidnapping", 1,422 documents were retrieved, with the most similar not referring to the "money laundering" crime; only the fifth, the sixth and the seventh documents connected "kidnapping" to "money laundering"
As another example, we define the term "soccer play" synonym of the term "Fabricia" (see item 2.2). Following, the user will proceed the search on soccer and will recoup as resulted, in bigger similarity, notice that consist information on "Fabricia". However, they do not have real relation with soccer, or soccer play. The system automatically makes this relation of synonymous and presents as resulted, the relations of "soccer" and the relations of "Fabricia". The recovery, considering this relation, will go to demonstrate if the system is functioning correctly. Another possible verification is related to the result, or either, the verification if the gotten results are the waited result.

It fits to stand out that when of the evaluation of the result, an external factor call problem of the oracle can make it difficult and compromise the analysis. The problem of the oracle is related to the absence of documentation and knowledge of the domain object of the test. In this in case that, if the responsible one for the test does not know the domain and it were not part of the team that constructed the ontologies, it does not have conditions to evaluate the result. Ally to this, the documentation absence that bases the knowledge of the domain, can compromise the result and in many cases to deprive of characteristics the system in relation to its initial conception. The responsible team for the construction of the net of ontologies, also either responsible suggests itself, that for the tests, considering here that the knowledge of the domain is basic for the analysis of the results.

5 Results

The adopted procedure to do the recall test in Ontoweb was to invite some users who are experts in the domain, but work in different areas, to make some questions. It was chosen experts in money laundry domain because knowledge engineers that don't work with them couldn't identify with precision the retrieved texts that belong to the domain. For each question, it was elaborated a complete ontology. Then, the query was formulated with the "indicative expression" that is part of domain ontology. Each user made an own evaluation according to their specific knowledge about the domain.

Since Ontoweb measures the similarity with all document and, due to conceptual premises, any document that has similarity superior to 50% would be returned, the recall test has a particular aspect. Only the set of documents that contains the most similar were considered to calculate the recall. For instance, the 4.516 documents returned by the query "money laundry" are all pertinent to the context, because all the documents has more than 50% of similarity. However, to verify the relevance of each indicative expression that composes the money laundry ontology. We use the process described in item 3.4 and observe when the expression was changed, a significant variation in the graph happens, superior to the existing document number about the subject in the knowledge base. With this, it was possible to identify the expressions less significant and those most ambiguous ones.

6 Future Work

We must instead develop a specification from the available documentation. The specification must then be validated as correct by domain experts. Once a formal specification has been obtained or created, the next task is to convert it into assertions. To ease this task, it is better to write the specification using a formal language and structure that matches that of the software.

Acknowledgments

Our thanks to researches and developers of WBSA who helped us in the Ontoweb system evaluation.

References

1. Duineveld, A. J. et al, 1999. WonderTools? A comparative study of ontological engineering tools. Twelfth Workshop on Knowledge Acquisition, Modeling and Management.Voyager Inn, Banff, Alberta, Canada.
2. Eriksson, H. et al, 1999. Automatic Generation of Ontology Editors. Twelfth Workshop on Knowledge Acquisition, Modeling and Management.Voyager Inn, Banff, Alberta, Canada.
3. Benjamins, V.R., 1998. The ontological engineering initiative (KA)2, Formal Ontology in Information systems. IOS Press, Amsterdam.
4. Ontoweb. Available at: http://www.wbsa.com.br Access on: 02 janeiro 2006.
5. Ribeiro, Marcelo Stopanovski. KMAI, da RC²D à PCE. Gestão do conhecimento com inteligência artificial, da representação do conhecimento contextualizado dinamicamente à pesquisa contextual estruturada. [2004]. Dissertação (Mestrado em Engenharia de Produção) – Universidade Federal de Santa Catarina, Florianópolis, 2003.
6. Völker, Joahnna, Vrandečić, Denny and Sure, York. Automatic Evaluation of Ontologies (AEON). Lecture Notes in Computer Science. Springer-Verlag GmbH. Vol. 3729/2005. Pag. 716 – 731.
7. Bueno, Tania C. D. et al, 2005. Knowledge Engineering Suite: A Tool to Create Ontologies for Automatic Knowledge Representation in Knowledge-Based Systems. Lecture Notes in Computer Science. Springer-Verlag GmbH. Volume 3591/2005. Page: 249.
8. Hoeschl, Hugo. C. et al, 2003. Structured Contextual Search For The Un Security Council. Proceedings of the fifth International Conference On Enterprise Information Systems. Anger, France, v.2. p.100 – 107.6. Bueno, Tânia C. D. et al, 1999. JurisConsulto: Retrieval in Jurisprudencial Text Bases using Juridical Terminology. Proceedings of the Seventh International Conference On Artificial Intelligence And Law. ACM, New York.
9. Faatz, Andreas, Steinmetz, Ralf. Ontology Enrichment Evaluation. Lecture Notes in Computer Science. Springer-Verlag. Vol. 3257/2004. Pag. 497 – 498.

Using Knowledge Representation Languages for Video Annotation and Retrieval

M. Bertini, G. D'Amico, A. Del Bimbo, and C. Torniai

D.S.I. - Università di Firenze - Italy
{bertini, damico, delbimbo, torniai}@dsi.unifi.it

Abstract. Effective usage of multimedia digital libraries has to deal with the problem of building efficient content annotation and retrieval tools. In particular in video domain, different techniques for manual and automatic annotation and retrieval have been proposed. Despite the existence of well-defined and extensive standards for video content description, such as MPEG-7, these languages are not explicitly designed for automatic annotation and retrieval purpose. Usage of linguistic ontologies for video annotation and retrieval is a common practice to classify video elements by establishing relationships between video contents and linguistic terms that specify domain concepts at different abstraction levels. The main issue related to the use of description languages such as MPEG-7 or linguistic ontologies is due to the fact that linguistic terms are appropriate to distinguish event and object categories but they are inadequate when they must describe specific or complex patterns of events or video entities. In this paper we propose the usage of knowledge representation languages to define ontologies enriched with visual information that can be used effectively for video annotation and retrieval. Difference between content description languages and knowledge representation languages are shown, the advantages of using enriched ontologies both for the annotation and the retrieval process are presented in terms of enhanced user experience in browsing and querying video digital libraries.

1 Introduction and Previous Work

An ontology is a formal and explicit specification of a domain knowledge, typically represented using linguistic terms: it consists of concepts, concept properties, and relationships between concepts.

Several standard description languages for the expression of concepts and relationships in domain ontologies have been defined in the last years: Resource Description Framework Schema (RDFS), Web Ontology Language (OWL) and, for multimedia, the XML Schema in MPEG-7. Using these languages metadata can be fitted to specific domains and purposes, yet still remaining interoperable and capable of being processed by standard tools and search systems.

Ontologies can effectively be used to perform semantic annotation of multimedia content. For video annotation this can be done either manually, associating the terms of the ontology to the individual elements of the video, or automatically, by exploiting results and developments in pattern recognition and image/video analysis. In this latter case, the terms of the ontology are put in correspondence with appropriate knowledge models that encode the spatio-temporal combination of low and mid level features.

H.L. Larsen et al. (Eds.): FQAS 2006, LNAI 4027, pp. 634–646, 2006.

Once these models are checked, video entities are annotated with the concepts of the ontology; in this way, for example in the soccer video domain, it is possible to classify highlight events in different classes, like *shot on goal*, *counter attack*, *corner kick*, etc.

Examples of automatic semantic annotation systems have been presented recently, many of them in the application domain of sports video. Regarding the analysis of soccer videos we can cite [1] where MPEG motion vectors, playfield shape and players position have been used with Hidden Markov Models to detect soccer highlights. In [2] Finite State Machines have been employed to detect the principal soccer highlights, such as shot on goal, placed kick, forward launch and turnover, from a few visual cues. Yu et al. [3] have used the ball trajectory in order to detect the main actions like touching and passing and compute ball possession statistics for each team; a Kalman filter is used to check whether a detected trajectory can be recognized as a ball trajectory.

In all these systems model based event classification is not associated with any formal ontology-based representation of the domain. Domain specific linguistic ontology with multilingual lexicons, and possibility of cross document merging has instead been presented in [4]. In this paper, the annotation engine makes use of reasoning algorithms to automatically create a semantic annotation of soccer video sources. In [5], a hierarchy of ontologies has been defined for the representation of the results of video segmentation. Concepts are expressed in keywords and are mapped in an *object ontology*, a *shot ontology* and a *semantic ontology*.

The possibility of extending linguistic ontologies with multimedia ontologies, has been suggested in [6] to support video understanding. Differently from our contribution, the authors suggest to use *modal keywords*, i.e. keywords that represent perceptual concepts in several categories, such as visual, aural, etc. A method is presented to automatically classify keywords from speech recognition, queries or related text into these categories. Multimedia ontologies are constructed manually in [7]: text information available in videos and visual features are extracted and manually assigned to concepts, properties, or relationships in the ontology. In [8] new methods for extracting semantic knowledge from annotated images is presented. Perceptual knowledge is discovered grouping images into clusters based on their visual and text features and semantic knowledge is extracted by disambiguating the senses of words in annotations using WordNet and image clusters. In [9] a Visual Descriptors Ontology and a Multimedia Structure Ontology, based on MPEG-7 Visual Descriptors and MPEG-7 MDS respectively, are used together with domain ontology in order to support content annotation. Visual prototypes instances are manually linked to the domain ontology. An approach to semantic video object detection is presented in [10]. Semantic concepts for a given domain are defined in an RDF(S) ontology together with qualitative attributes (e.g. color homogeneity), low-level features (e.g. model components distribution), object spatial relations and multimedia processing methods (e.g. color clustering) and rules in F-logic are used for detection on video objects.

Despite of the difficulty of including pattern specifications into linguistic ontologies, classification at the pattern description level can be mandatory, in many real operating contexts. Events that share the same patterns can be represented by *visual concepts*, instead of linguistic concepts, that capture the essence of the event spatio-temporal development. In this case high level concepts expressed through linguistic terms, and pattern specifications represented instead through visual concepts, can be both organized into new extended ontologies. In the following we will refer to them as *pictorially enriched ontologies*.

The basic idea behind pictorially enriched ontologies is that the concepts and categories defined in a traditional ontology are not rich enough to fully describe the diversity of all the visual events, and of their patterns, that normally are grouped in a same class and cannot support video annotation up to the level of detail of pattern specification. To a broader extent the idea of pictorially enriched ontologies can be extended to *multimedia enriched ontologies* where concepts that cannot be expressed in linguistic terms are represented by prototypes of different media like video, audio, etc.

This paper presents pictorially enriched ontologies, discusses a solution for their implementation for the soccer video domain and proposes a method to perform automatic soccer video annotation using these extended ontologies. The PE ontology creation process assigns multimedia objects to concepts and integrates the semantics described by the linguistic terms, while reasoning on the ontology adds a higher level of semantic annotation using the concepts relations, and allows to perform complex queries based on visual concepts and patterns of actions. The advantage of pictorially enriched ontologies is twofold:

- visual concepts allow to associate automatically occurrences of events or entities to higher level concepts by checking their proximity to visual concepts that are hierarchically linked to higher level semantics
- the unification in the same ontology both of specific domain concepts and their multimedia low and mid level descriptions allows the development of more user friendly interfaces for contend-based browsing and retrieval, using visual concepts and concepts relations.

The paper is organized as follows: an analysis of different ontologies standard languages is provided in Sect. 2. Creation of a pictorially enriched ontology for the representation of highlight patterns of soccer videos and the visual features extraction process are discussed in Sect. 3. Two algorithms that use the enriched ontology to perform automatic annotation are briefly presented in Sect. 4. In Sect. 5 is shown how the proposed ontology structure and ontology-based reasoning add a more refined annotation to the videos, allowing the retrieval of video content by mean of complex queries on the ontology. In Sect. 6 we discuss the preliminary results of the proposed system applied to soccer videos annotation. Finally, in Sect. 7 we provide conclusions and some future works.

2 Ontologies Standards

There are many differences between description languages based on XML (XML-Schema and MPEG-7) and knowledge representation languages (RDFS and OWL): both language categories can represent ontologies but with different capabilities of expressiveness and functionalities. MPEG-7 is a standard that has been built to define entities and their properties wrt the specific domain of multimedia content while RDFS and OWL are languages that can define an ontology in terms of concepts and their relationships regardless of the domain of interest. The advantages of using MPEG-7 in multimedia domain is due to the fact that it has been designed to fully describe multimedia document structure, but at the same time it reflects the "structural" lack of semantic expressiveness of XML. In fact XML can state only few relations and most of them are not explicitly semantic since XML Schema can only define syntactic structure for a specific document: typically in an XML document only taxonomy relations are stated and most of them imply other high level semantic relation that are not directly expressed.

Knowledge representation languages extend the capability and the expressiveness of XML. RDFS can define an ontology in terms of concepts, properties and relationships of concepts without any restriction. OWL adds to RDFS the capability to refine concept definition and class restrictions. Both of them are flexible and extensible because they are not standard for a specific domain but they have been designed as general-purpose languages for domain independent knowledge description. Moreover knowledge representation languages can support usage of inference engines that can enrich the knowledge of a domain with the inferred knowledge. Due to these intrinsic characteristics MPEG-7 and RDFS/OWL can have different scope of utilization in multimedia domain. MPEG-7, as a standard provides all the necessary definition for structural description of multimedia content in particular for low-level descriptors such as color and edge histograms, texture descriptors, motion parameters, etc., but on the other hand it cannot be extended and can hardly include, for instance, high semantic structured description of video content.

Low-level descriptors can be very useful for description purpose, similarity assessment and annotation in simple domains but for effective semantic annotation of complex video content both low and mid level features have to be taken into account. It is possible to create new MPEG-7 Description Schemas, and also Descriptors, using the MPEG-7 Description Definition Language (DDL), but it has to be noted that this language, based on a variation of XML Schema, is not a modeling language, but is rather to be used to express the results of modeling. RDFS and OWL can easily be used to represent any kind of domain so they are suitable for describing both the structure of a multimedia content as well as its content in a structured semantic way. It is possible to include in a single RDF or OWL document a domain ontology referring to, for instance, the soccer domain and a multimedia ontology describing the structure of video in terms of segments, regions, etc.

There are several advantages in using ontologies specific standards as RDF and OWL instead of MPEG-7:

- it is easier to add mid-level audio-visual descriptors that are related to the domain that is being annotated.
- it is possible to express easily complex semantic entities and their relations;
- it is possible to use reasoning tools to add high-level annotation or perform queries related to semantic content, rather than low level audio-visual descriptors;

It has to be noted that the possibility to translate MPEG-7 into an ontology language such as RDF and OWL has been exploited to overcome the lack of formal semantics of the MPEG-7 standard that could extend the traditional text descriptions into machine understandable ones. The first attempt that aimed to bridge the gap between the MPEG-7 standard and the ontology standards has been presented in [11] and [12]. In these works the first translation of the MPEG-7 MDS into RDFS has been shown. The resulting ontology has been also converted into DAML+OIL, and is now available in OWL. The ontology, expressed using OWL Full, covers the upper part of the Multimedia Description Schema (MDS) part of the MPEG-7 standard. It consists of about 60 classes and 40 properties. A methodology and a software implementation for the interoperability of MPEG-7 MDS and OWL has been presented in [13] and [14], developing from the previous work, and using OWL DL.

Another MPEG-7 Ontology is the one provided by the DMAG group at the Pompeu Fabra University[1]. This MPEG-7 ontology has been produced fully automatically from the MPEG-7 standard in order to give it a formal semantics. It is an OWL Full ontology, and aims to cover the whole standard and is thus the most complete one. It contains 2372 classes and 975 properties.

3 Pictorially Enriched Ontologies

As an example of pictorially enriched ontology we refer for the sake of clarity to Fig. 1, in which the linguistic and visual parts of the ontology are shown. The linguistic part is composed by the video and clip classes, the actions class and its highlights subclasses and an object class with its related subclasses describing different objects within the clips. In this example only placed kick, shot on goal and forward launch are shown.

The visual part is created adding to the linguistic part of the ontology the visual concepts as specializations of the linguistic concepts that describe the highlights. Visual concepts in the visual part are *abstractions* of video elements and can be of different types:

- *sequence* (the clip at the center of the cluster);
- *keyframes* (the key frame of the clip at the center of the cluster);
- *regions* (parts of the keyframe e.g. representing players);
- *visual features* (e.g. trajectories, motion fields, computed from image data ...).

Pictorially enriched ontologies are expressed using the OWL standard so that they can be shared and used in a search engine to perform content based retrieval from video databases or to provide video summaries.

The creation process of the pictorially enriched ontology is performed by selecting a representative set of sequences containing highlights described in the linguistic ontology, extracting the visual features and performing an unsupervised clustering. The clustering process, based on visual features, generates clusters of sequences representing specific pattern of the same highlight that are regarded as specialization of the highlight. Visual concepts for each highlight specialization are automatically obtained as the centers of these clusters.

Extraction of visual features is performed on MPEG videos, using both the compressed and uncompressed domain data. The MPEG motion vectors, that are used to

[1] http://dmag.upf.edu/ontologies/mpeg7ontos

calculate indexes of camera motion direction and intensity are extracted from the P and B frames. All the other visual features are extracted from the decompressed MPEG frames. In particular these features are the playfield shape, playfield lines and players blobs. From all these low-level features some higher level features are derived. In particular the playfield zone framed is recognized using naive Bayes classifiers that use particular shapes of the playfield region, the position of the playfield corner, the mid-field line position and the orientation of the playfield lines; twelve different playfield zones that cover all the playfield are recognized. A thorough description of this process can be found in our previous work [2]. Combining the recognized playfield zone with the estimation of the number of players of each blob, and the blob position, the number of players in the upper and lower part of the playfield are obtained.

The visual features used to describe visual concepts within the pictorially enriched ontology and to perform the annotation of unknown sequences are: *i)* the playfield area, *ii)* the number of players in the upper part of the playfield, *iii)* the number of players in the lower part of the playfield, *iv)* the motion intensity, *v)* the motion direction, *vi)* motion acceleration.

The first step of the pictorially enriched ontology creation is to define for each clip a feature vector V containing 6 distinct components. Each component is a vector U that contains the sequence of values of each visual feature. The length of feature vectors U may be different in different clips, depending on the duration and content of the clips. Vectors U are quantized, and smoothed to eliminate possible outliers. Then the clustering process groups the clips of the representative set according to their visual features. We have employed the fuzzy c-means (FCM) clustering algorithm to take into account the fact that a clip could belong to a cluster, still being similar to clips of different clusters. The maximum number of clusters for each highlight has been heuristically set to 10. The distance between two different clips has been computed as the sum of all the normalized Needleman-Wunch edit distances between the U components of the

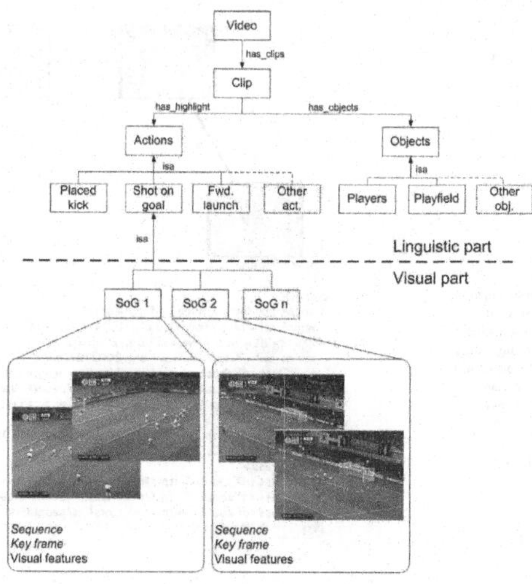

Fig. 1. Pictorially enriched ontology (partial view)

feature vector V of the clips, to take into account the differences in the duration and the temporal changes of the features values. Performance evaluation of the generation of pictorially enriched ontology has been analyzed in our previous work [15]. The PE Ontology contains both soccer domain description and video domain description. They are related by the "visual" extension of the ontology through the exploitation of mid-level features assigned to each clip. In Fig. 2 the browsing interface of a PE Ontology is shown. It has to be noted that the user is able not only to browse with a single interface concepts related both to soccer and video domain but he can easily have at a glance the visual specifications of the linguistic concepts. When the user wants to see the different visual specifications of the linguistic concept "Shot on Goal", he can simply select the concept and the interface provides the clips that represent that concept. Moreover a cluster view of similar visual concepts related to a linguistic concept is provided.

4 Automatic Video Annotation Using Enriched Ontologies

To annotate the content of a video, in terms of highlights, two problems have to be solved: the detection of the part of the video where the highlight is, and the recognition of the highlight. The pictorially enriched ontology created with the process described in Sect. 3 can be used effectively to perform automatic video annotation with higher level concepts that describe what is occurring in the video clips. This is done by selecting clips that are to be annotated in the video, and checking the similarity of the clip content with the visual prototypes included in the ontology. If similarity is assessed with a

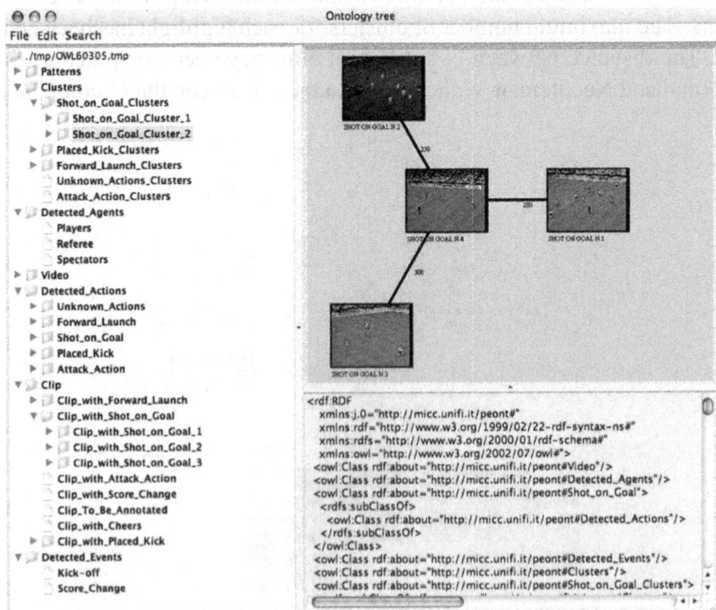

Fig. 2. A visualization of clips cluster for visual concept "Shot on Goal" within the PE Ontology Browser

particular visual concept then also higher level concepts in the ontology hierarchy, that are linked to the visual concept, are associated with the clip, resulting in a more complete annotation of the video content. The proposed annotation process is composed of two algorithms; a detailed description is provided in [16]. The first one selects the clips that are to be annotated from video sequences, such as shots or scenes automatically recognized or such as manual selections of clips, checking if they could contain some highlights; it is designed to be faster than performing an exhaustive analysis of all the clips that may be obtained within a sequence, partitioning it in sub-sequences. The second algorithm performs the annotation of the clips selected by the first algorithm.

The clip annotation algorithm is composed of two steps. In the first one an initial classification is performed evaluating the distance between visual prototypes and each clip. A clip is classified as an highlight type if its distance from a visual prototype is lesser than a computed threshold. In this step a special class (*Unknown action*) is created within the ontology, to hold all the clips that could not be classified by the algorithm. After each clip processing a FCM clustering is performed to re-evaluate the visual prototypes of the highlight. The second step analyzes each clip classified as *Unknown action*. A clip is classified as an highlight type if enough clips of that highlight type have a distance from the clip that is lesser than a computed threshold. If a clip is classified as an highlight type then FCM clustering is performed to re-evaluate the visual prototypes of this highlight.

At the end of the second step of the algorithm it is possible that some clips are still classified as types of *Unknown action*. These clips can be classified at later stage when other clips add more knowledge to the ontology, defining more visual prototypes or refining the clip classification according to the existing prototypes. The FCM clustering of clips annotated as *Unknown action* is performed to ease the manual annotation, allowing a user to annotate a whole cluster of clips. Among the clips that are classified as *Unknown action* there may be clips that do not contain an highlight, but that were selected by Alg. 1 as candidates to contain an highlight.

5 Querying the Ontology

Once videos are classified and annotated using the PE ontology it is possible to refine annotation by mean of reasoning on the ontology. In order to do this we have identified some "patterns" in the soccer video sequences in terms of series of detected actions and events. Analyzing the broadcasted video sequences we can notice, for instance, that if an attack action leads to a scored goal, cheers from spectators and superimposed text with score change are shown after the goal. We can identify a "pattern" for scored goal that contains possible combinations of detected actions and events and define a formal description of this pattern within the ontology by mean of conditions on class properties.

For instance the subclass *Video with scored goal*, which identify a sequence containing a scored goal, can be defined as *Video* that contains:

- Forward Launch Action followed by Shot on Goal Action followed by Cheers Event followed by Score Change Event or

- Placed Kick Action followed by Cheers Event followed by Score Change Event or
- Shot on Goal Action followed by Cheers Event followed by Score Change Event.

The reasoner evaluates the inferred types of each instance of the *Clip* and *Video* classes classifying them as a type of the proper subclass according to the detected actions or pattern they contain. For example a clip is classified as *Clip with Attack Action* by the reasoner if the *has highlight* property is related to subclass *Attack Action* of the *Detected Action* class. A video sequence is classified as *Video with scored goal* by the reasoner if the ordered sequence of clips contained corresponds to the pattern expressed by the *Patterns* class conditions.

The inferred type computation performed by the reasoner results in an enhanced annotation of video sequences and clips and allow to retrieve content performing complex queries on the ontology.

The PE Ontology structure and the visual prototype definition together with the enhanced annotation generated by the inference engine allow the user to easily perform semantic queries in order to retrieve video contents. For instance is possible to retrieve a video sequence asking for all the sequences that contain at least one placed kick, or for all the sequences that end with a forward launch or all the sequences with a scored goal that start with an attack action. Moreover, visual prototypes defined in the ontology can be used to refine retrieval using visual concepts. The system can retrieve all the video containing user-defined sequences of highlights and on each of them conditions of similarity to specific visual concept can be imposed. For the query user interface implementation we have used RACER [17] as description logic (DL) reasoner and nRQL [18] as query language.

A simple query interface that allows retrieval of video sequences composed by different video highlights, i.e. allowing retrieval of user defined patterns of actions has been integrated with the ontology browsing interface. Complexity of native nRQL query expression is transparent since the query interface is expressed in natural language (Fig. 3) and dynamically translates the user requests to formal nRQL queries.

6 Experimental Results

The proposed algorithms that perform automatic annotation, shown in Sect. 4, have been tested on MPEG-2 soccer videos from World Championship 2002, European Championship 2000 and 2004, recorded at 25 frame per second and with the resolution of 720×576 (PAL standard).

A set of representative sequences for three of the most important soccer highlights, namely shot on goal, placed kicks and forward launch, have been selected in order to create the pictorially enriched ontology. In particular 68 clips were manually annotated and selected (35 shots on goal, 16 forward launches and 17 placed kicks). The ontology creation process has been performed using this training set, obtaining 5 visual prototypes for shot on goal, 4 for forward launch and 3 for placed kick. Using this pictorially enriched ontology we have performed automatic video annotation on a different set of 242 clips that were automatically selected (85 shots on goal, 42 forward launches, 43 placed kicks and 72 that did not contain any highlight), using the process described

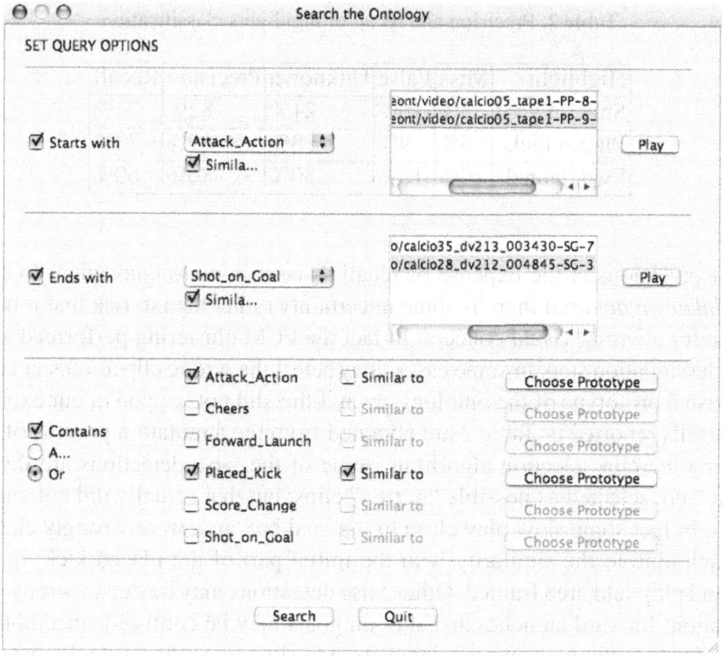

Fig. 3. PE Ontology query interface: the user is querying a sequence that starts with a attack action an finishes with a shot on goal. It is required that both actions are visually similar to a certain video clip. Moreover the video should contain any type of attack action or a placed kick visually similar to a model required by the user.

Table 1. Precision and recall of highlights/no highlights detection in video clips

	Precision	Recall
Action	100%	59%
No action	85%	100%

in Sect. 4. Table 1 reports precision and recall figures for the clip selection algorithm (Alg. 1), using the second test set. Table 2 reports precision and recall figures of Alg. 2 for the clips that were selected by Alg. 1 as candidates to contain highlights.

The goal of the clip selection algorithm is to detect all the clips that could contain possible highlights. To this end the conditions used to select a clip are loose enough to avoid misses of "Action" clips, while maintaining a relatively high precision figure of "No action" clips, as shown in Table 1. It has to be noted that at the end of this algorithm no clip has been annotated and inserted in the ontology, yet.

In the second table we have reported the percentage of clips that remained classified as *Unknown action* instead of reporting it in the Miss column because this kind of error may be corrected at a later stage, when more clips are fed to the system as described in Sect. 4. Anyway the figure of the clips classified as *Unknown action* has been taken into account to evaluate the recall performance. The algorithm aims to obtain the highest

Table 2. Precision and recall of highlights classification

Highlight	Miss	False	Unknown	Precision	Recall
Shot on goal	5%	16%	21%	82%	74%
Placed kick	9%	9%	18%	89%	73%
Fwd. launch	10%	10%	30%	86%	60%

values of precisions at the expense of recall since it is more convenient to classify a clip as *Unknown action* if there is some uncertainty rather then to risk that it becomes a prototype for a wrong visual concept. In fact the FCM clustering performed at the end of each classification step, in some cases, may select the wrong clip as cluster center and then as visual prototype of the ontology, even if this did not happen in our experiments.

The results reported in Table 2 are obtained from the annotation process of the clips selected by the clip selection algorithm; some of the false detections are then due to clips that were selected as possible "Action" clips, but that actually did not contain any highlight. In fact some slow play close to the goal box area were wrongly classified as placed kick, due to the similarity with the initial part of the placed kick, in terms of motion and playfield area framed. Other false detections may be due to wrong highlight classification: forward launches and shot on goals may be confused since both actions have similar behaviour in motion intensity and direction. Placed kicks have usually higher length then shot on goals, due to an initial part containing almost no motion where the players get prepared for the kick. In some cases the broadcasted video that we used in the experiments does not include this part of the placed kick, and thus they have a behaviour in terms of playfield area, motion and length that is very similar to that of shots on goal. Inspection of the clusters composed by clips annotated as *Unknown action* reported similar precision values of the annotated clips, thus a user may confidently annotate an entire cluster manually, simply inspecting the visual prototype.

7 Conclusions

The novelty of this paper is the presentation of pictorially enriched ontologies based both on linguistic and visual concepts and the implementation of two algorithms that perform automatic annotation of soccer video based on these extended ontologies.

With the proposed method annotation is performed automatically associating occurrences of events or entities to higher level concepts by checking their proximity to visual concepts that are hierarchically linked to higher level semantics, and applying reasoning to the ontology it is possible to exploit the domain knowledge and perform higher-level semantic annotation.

Differences between MPEG-7 and RDF/OWL have been presented and advantages of usage of knowledge description languages in automatic video annotation have been shown. Proper definition of specific domain ontologies, together with video and clip ontology describing low and mid level features, can improve the annotation process and provide user friendly visualization and query interfaces for video content browsing and retrieval.

Experimental results have been presented for typical soccer highlights in terms of precision and recall, showing that with pictorially enriched ontologies it is possible to perform automatic clips annotation up to the level of detail of pattern specification.

Our future work will deal with the improvement of the visual features set, the metrics and distances used in the ontology creation and in the annotation process, the improvement of the proposed interfaces for browsing and querying the pictorially enriched ontologies.

Acknowledgment. This work is partially supported by the Information Society Technologies (IST) Program of the European Commission as part of the DELOS Network of Excellence on Digital Libraries (Contract G038-507618).

References

1. Leonardi, R., Migliorati, P.: Semantic indexing of multimedia documents. IEEE Multimedia **9**(2) (2002) 44–51
2. Assfalg, J., Bertini, M., Colombo, C., Bimbo, A.D., Nunziati, W.: Semantic annotation of soccer videos: automatic highlights identification. Computer Vision and Image Understanding **92**(2-3) (2003) 285–305
3. X.Yu, Xu, C., Leung, H., Tian, Q., Tang, Q., Wan, K.W.: Trajectory-based ball detection and tracking with applications to semantic analysis of broadcast soccer video. In: ACM Multimedia 2003. Volume 3., Berkeley, CA (USA) (2003) 11–20
4. Reidsma, D., Kuper, J., Declerck, T., Saggion, H., Cunningham, H.: Cross document ontology based information extraction for multimedia retrieval. In: Supplementary proc. of the ICCS03, Dresden (2003)
5. Mezaris, V., Kompatsiaris, I., Boulgouris, N., Strintzis, M.: Real-time compressed-domain spatiotemporal segmentation and ontologies for video indexing and retrieval. IEEE Transactions on Circuits and Systems for Video Technology **14**(5) (2004) 606–621
6. Jaimes, A., Tseng, B., Smith, J.: Modal keywords, ontologies, and reasoning for video understanding. In: Int'l Conference on Image and Video Retrieval (CIVR 2003). (2003)
7. Jaimes, A., Smith, J.: Semi-automatic, data-driven construction of multimedia ontologies. In: Proc. of IEEE Int'l Conference on Multimedia & Expo. (2003)
8. Benitez, A., Chang, S.F.: Automatic multimedia knowledge discovery, summarization and evaluation. IEEE Transactions on Multimedia, Submitted (2003)
9. Strintzis, J., Bloehdorn, S., Handschuh, S., Staab, S., Simou, N., Tzouvaras, V., Petridis, K., Kompatsiaris, I., Avrithis, Y.: Knowledge representation for semantic multimedia content analysis and reasoning. In: European Workshop on the Integration of Knowledge, Semantics and Digital Media Technology. (2004)
10. Dasiopoulou, S., Mezaris, V., Kompatsiaris, I., Papastathis, V.K., Strintzis, M.G.: Knowledge-assisted semantic video object detection. IEEE Transactions on Circuits and Systems for Video Technology **15**(10) (2005) 1210–1224
11. Hunter, J.: Adding multimedia to the semantic web: Building an MPEG-7 ontology. In: The First Semantic Web Working Symposium, SWWS01, Stanford University, California, USA (2001)
12. Hunter, J.: An RDF schema/DAML+OIL representation of MPEG-7 semantics. Technical Report MPEG Document: ISO/IEC JTC1/SC29/WG11 W7807, ISO/IEC (2001)
13. Tsinaraki, C., Polydoros, P., Christodoulakis, S.: Interoperability support for ontology-based video retrieval applications. In: Proc. Image and Video Retrieval: Third International Conference, CIVR 2004, Image and Video Retrieval: Third International Conference, CIVR 2004, Lecture Notes in Computer Science 3115 Springer (2004)

14. Tsinaraki, C., Polydoros, P., Christodoulakis, S.: Interoperability of OWL with the MPEG-7 MDS. Technical report, Technical University of Crete / Laboratory of Distributed Multimedia Information Systems and Applications (TUC/MUSIC) (2004)
15. Bertini, M., Cucchiara, R., Del Bimbo, A., Torniai, C.: Video annotation with pictorially enriched ontologies. In: Proc. of IEEE Int'l Conference on Multimedia & Expo. (2005)
16. Bertini, M., Del Bimbo, A., Torniai, C.: Enhanced ontologies for video annotation and retrieval. In: Proceedings of ACM MIR. (2005)
17. Haarslev, V., Möller, R.: Description of the racer system and its applications. In: Proceedings International Workshop on Description Logics (DL-2001), Stanford, USA, 1.-3. August. (2001) 131–141
18. Haarslev, V., Möller, R., Wessel, M.: Querying the semantic web with racer + nrql. In: Proceedings of the KI-2004 International Workshop on Applications of Description Logics (ADL'04), Ulm, Germany, September 24. (2004)

Question Answering with Imperfect Temporal Information

Steven Schockaert[1], David Ahn[2], Martine De Cock[1], and Etienne E. Kerre[1]

[1] Department of Applied Mathematics and Computer Science
Ghent University, Krijgslaan 281 (S9), B-9000 Gent, Belgium
{Steven.Schockaert, Martine.DeCock, Etienne.Kerre}@UGent.be
[2] ISLA, University of Amsterdam
Kruislaan 403, 1098 SJ Amsterdam, The Netherlands
ahn@science.uva.nl

Abstract. A temporal question answering system must be able to deduce which qualitative temporal relation holds between two events, a reasoning task that is complicated by the fact that historical events tend to have a gradual beginning and ending. In this paper, we introduce an algebra of temporal relations that is well–suited to represent the qualitative temporal information we have at our disposal. We provide a practical algorithm for deducing new temporal knowledge, and show how this can be used to answer questions that require several pieces of qualitative and quantitative temporal information to be combined. Finally, we propose a heuristic technique to cope with inconsistencies that may arise when integrating qualitative and quantitative information.

1 Introduction

Question answering systems (QA–systems) are information retrieval systems that differ from traditional search engines in two ways: users can express their information need as natural language questions, and the result of the system is an answer to a question instead of a ranked list of possibly relevant documents.

In this paper we focus on (complex) temporal questions, such as *Which battles were fought in Belgium between D-Day and the unconditional surrender of Germany.* Not only are temporal questions interesting in their own right, a thorough understanding of temporal question answering is also indispensable to answer, for example, definition questions about events or even about persons. Furthermore, we believe that a temporal QA–system can provide a first step towards causal question answering, as for example an event B can only be a consequence of A, if A happened before B.

Temporal question answering [1, 5, 8] offers a lot of interesting challenges. For some events we may be able to extract an accurate time span from, for example, the web. For other events, however, we will only be able to find qualitative temporal information (e.g., A happened before B, A happened during B,...); hence, qualitative temporal reasoning is sometimes necessary to determine if an event is relevant for a particular question. Moreover, this qualitative temporal information may conflict with some of the time spans we have at our disposal.

H.L. Larsen et al. (Eds.): FQAS 2006, LNAI 4027, pp. 647–658, 2006.

Temporal reasoning is further complicated by the fact that many historical events are vague, i.e., their time span cannot be accurately captured by an interval with well–defined boundaries. This vagueness can be due to the fact that an event is characterized by a gradual beginning or ending (e.g., the Cold War, the Great Depression, ...). Another important cause for vagueness is that many large–scale historical events are in fact ill–defined aggregations of small–scale events. For example, World War II is a name that has been coined to refer to a number of battles and military operations around the first half of the 1940s. Some of these battles and military operations are clearly a part of World War II (e.g., the battle of the Bulge in 1944), while for others it may be hard to say whether or not this holds (e.g., the Japanese invasion of China in 1937).

In order to support efficient temporal question answering, we have (automatically) constructed a large knowledge base consisting of tens of thousands of events [1]. For some of these events, we have been able to extract an accurate time span, while for other events we only have qualitative temporal information at our disposal. To cope with vague events, we represent time spans of events as fuzzy sets, and model qualitative temporal relations using fuzzy relations. However, many temporal questions require reasoning to obtain an answer, i.e., several pieces of information, possibly coming from different sources, may have to be combined. Although there already exist some approaches to qualitative temporal reasoning that effectively deal with possibilistic uncertainty (e.g., [3, 4]), to our knowledge, the problem of qualitative temporal reasoning with vague events has not yet been considered.

In the next section, we explain how temporal information extracted from Wikipedia[1] and from the web is represented in the temporal relation algebra underlying the knowledge base of our system. It encompasses grounded events, i.e., dated events from Wikipedia and events for which we were able to construct a reliable (fuzzy) time interval, as well as ungrounded events for which we have only qualitative information at our disposal. In Section 3 we present an algebraic closure algorithm to derive new knowledge from the qualitative information in our initial knowledge base. At this point, because of space and time requirements, the available quantitative information about the grounded events is used only for inconsistency repairing. Finally, in Section 4 we explain how at question answering time both the initial and the newly derived qualitative information, as well as the quantitative information in our knowledge base are used to provide the answer.

2 Representing Temporal Information

To efficiently support temporal question answering, we have constructed (automatically) a large knowledge base by extracting relevant information from Wikipedia and from the web in general. Wikipedia is a freely available, online encyclopedia with broad coverage. It contains large lists of dated events which are relatively easy to extract. Moreover, the information in Wikipedia is much

[1] `http://www.wikipedia.org`

more reliable than information on the web in general. However, for some events, only a starting date, an ending date, or an underspecified date is given. Furthermore, for most large–scale events, no structured temporal information is given at all in Wikipedia. We cope with this lack of information by searching the web for beginning dates and ending dates using a simple pattern–based approach. If there is sufficient agreement among different web pages about the beginning and ending date of an event, we represent the time span of this event as an interval; if not, we use the techniques described in [11] to construct a suitable fuzzy set, which we call a fuzzy (time) interval in this context.

To increase the coverage of our knowledge base, we again make use of a pattern–based approach. For example, to find events that happened during an event e, we may send the query "happened during e" to Google[2]. The search results returned by Google are then analysed to find noun phrases that match this pattern. Finally, heuristics are used to decide if such a noun phrase constitutes a good, umambiguous description of a unique event. For some events, it is not possible to find any starting dates or ending dates on the web. Using these patterns, we can link these events to other events in the knowledge base, using chains of before and during relations. The construction and expansion of the knowledge base is discussed in more detail in a separate paper [1].

In this section, we discuss how the temporal information in our knowledge base can be represented. After providing the necessary background on fuzzy set theory, we show how the definitions of Allen's qualitative temporal relations [2] can be generalized to cope with fuzzy time intervals, allowing to effectively calculate which qualitative temporal relations hold between two grounded events, and to what degree. Next, we show how qualitative, as well as underspecified temporal information, can be represented in this framework. Finally, we introduce an algebra of temporal relations, which will serve as the basis for qualitative reasoning in Section 3.

2.1 Grounded Events

In defining a traditional set in a universe U we draw a sharp boundary between those objects of U that satisfy a certain property and those objects that do not. Therefore, classical sets are sometimes referred to as crisp sets in this context. Natural language, on the other hand, is pervaded with ill–defined concepts and properties for which such a sharp boundary may be difficult, if not impossible, to define. Fuzzy set theory [12] provides an alternative where this boundary between objects that satisfy a given property and objects that do not can be gradual. Formally, a fuzzy set A in a universe U is a mapping from U to the unit interval $[0, 1]$. For u in U, $A(u)$ is called the membership degree of u in A, where $A(u) = 1$ means u fully belongs to A and $A(u) = 0$ means u does not belong to A at all. If $A(u) = 1$ for some u in U, A is called normalised. A fuzzy relation in U is defined as a fuzzy set in $U \times U$.

In this paper, normalised fuzzy sets in $\mathbb{R}$ are used to represent the time span of vague events such as the Cold War, or the Great Depression. To adequately

[2] `http://www.google.com`

generalize the notion of a closed interval, we require that these fuzzy sets be convex and upper semicontinuous. Recall that a fuzzy set A is convex and upper semicontinuous iff for each α in $]0,1]$, the α–level set $\{x|A(x) \geq \alpha\}$ is a closed interval.

Note that, for crisp intervals $E_1 = [p^-, p^+]$ and $E_2 = [q^-, q^+]$, the following equivalence holds:

$$p^- \leq q^- \Leftrightarrow (\forall y \in \mathbb{R})(y \in E_2 \Rightarrow (\exists x \in \mathbb{R})(x \in E_1 \wedge x \leq y)) \tag{1}$$

To express that the beginning of a fuzzy interval E_1 is before the beginning of a fuzzy interval E_2, we generalize the expression in the right hand side of (1). In particular, to generalize the logical conjunction and implication to the unit interval $[0,1]$, we use the Łukasiewicz t–norm T_W and Łukasiewicz implicator I_W, defined by:

$$T_W(a,b) = \max(0, a+b-1)$$
$$I_W(a,b) = \min(1, 1-a+b)$$

for all a and b in $[0,1]$. It can be shown that this choice of fuzzy logic connectives leads to a generalization that satisfies many important properties [10]. To generalize the universal and existential quantification, the infimum and supremum are used. Finally to generalize the ordering relation $\leq$, we use the fuzzy relation $L^{\preccurlyeq}$ in $\mathbb{R}$ defined by $L^{\preccurlyeq}(x,y) = 1$ if $x \leq y$ and $L^{\preccurlyeq}(x,y) = 0$ otherwise[3]. Thus, we obtain the following formulation of $bb^{\preccurlyeq}(E_1, E_2)$, the degree to which the beginning of the fuzzy interval E_1 is before the beginning of the fuzzy interval E_2 [9]:

$$bb^{\preccurlyeq}(E_1,E_2) = \inf_{y \in \mathbb{R}} I_W(E_2(y), \sup_{x \in \mathbb{R}} T_W(E_1(x), L^{\preccurlyeq}(x,y))) \tag{2}$$

In the same way, we can express the degree $ee^{\preccurlyeq}(E_1, E_2)$ to which the end of E_1 is before the end of E_2, the degree $eb^{\preccurlyeq}(E_1, E_2)$ to which the end of E_1 is before the beginning of E_2, and the degree $be^{\preccurlyeq}(E_1, E_2)$ to which the beginning of E_1 is before the end of E_2 [9]:

$$ee^{\preccurlyeq}(E_1,E_2) = \inf_{x \in \mathbb{R}} I_W(E_1(x), \sup_{y \in \mathbb{R}} T_W(E_2(y), L^{\preccurlyeq}(x,y))) \tag{3}$$

$$eb^{\preccurlyeq}(E_1,E_2) = \inf_{x \in \mathbb{R}} I_W(E_1(x), \inf_{y \in \mathbb{R}} I_W(E_2(y), L^{\preccurlyeq}(x,y))) \tag{4}$$

$$be^{\preccurlyeq}(E_1,E_2) = \sup_{x \in \mathbb{R}} T_W(E_1(x), \sup_{y \in \mathbb{R}} T_W(E_2(y), L^{\preccurlyeq}(x,y))) \tag{5}$$

Note that $be^{\preccurlyeq}$, $bb^{\preccurlyeq}$, $ee^{\preccurlyeq}$ and $eb^{\preccurlyeq}$ are fuzzy relations in the universe of fuzzy time intervals. These fuzzy relations generalize some of the constraints between boundary points that are used in Allen's algebra [2] to define qualitative relations between crisp intervals.

---

[3] In [9], a more general approach is taken, where $L^{\preccurlyeq}(x,y)$ may express the degree to which x is before or at *approximately* the same time as y. This is useful to model imprecise qualitative relations such as "E_1 took place *more or less* during E_2".

2.2 Qualitative Relations

A lot of temporal information on the web is qualitative by nature, stating for example that event e_1 happened before e_2. Even if we have no groundings for those events, i.e., even if we can not run formulas (2)–(5), we know that the ending of e_1 is before the beginning of e_2. Hence, we can interpret this as $eb^{\preccurlyeq}(e_1, e_2) = 1$, where, for convenience, we use e_1 and e_2 both to refer to the events and to the unknown fuzzy intervals corresponding to their time spans[4]. In the same way, the fact that e_1 happened during e_2 can be interpreted as $bb^{\preccurlyeq}(e_2, e_1) = 1 \wedge ee^{\preccurlyeq}(e_1, e_2) = 1$. As another example, if e_1 and e_2 represent the life spans of two persons, $be^{\preccurlyeq}(e_1, e_2) = 1 \wedge be^{\preccurlyeq}(e_2, e_1) = 1$ expresses the fact that these persons were contemporaries.

In a similar way, we can represent underspecified information. Assume, for example, that we only know that event e began in September, 1939. In this case, e is added to the knowledge base as an ungrounded event, and a new event e' which is grounded with a fuzzy interval representing September 1939 (which will correspond to a crisp interval in this case) is also added to the knowledge base. The knowledge that e began in September 1939 can now be expressed as $bb^{\preccurlyeq}(e', e) = 1 \wedge be^{\preccurlyeq}(e, e') = 1$.

Finally, note that while we interpret, for example, "e_1 happened before e_2" as $eb^{\preccurlyeq}(e_1, e_2) = 1$, this might be too strong in some cases, i.e., it may only be that $eb^{\preccurlyeq}(e_1, e_2) \geq \delta$ (with $\delta \in]0, 1[$) holds. To make our knowledge base as informative as possible, we always use the strongest interpretations that do not lead to inconsistencies. In Section 3.2 we discuss how these initial interpretations can be weakened when the knowledge base is inconsistent.

2.3 An Algebra of Temporal Relations

We represent temporal relations as quadruples $[\alpha, \beta, \gamma, \delta]$, where $\alpha, \beta, \gamma, \delta \in [0, 1]$, with the following interpretation:

$$\begin{aligned} &e_1[\alpha, \beta, \gamma, \delta]e_2 \\ &\Leftrightarrow be^{\preccurlyeq}(e_1, e_2) \geq \alpha \wedge bb^{\preccurlyeq}(e_1, e_2) \geq \beta \wedge ee^{\preccurlyeq}(e_1, e_2) \geq \gamma \wedge eb^{\preccurlyeq}(e_1, e_2) \geq \delta \end{aligned}$$

i.e., temporal relations are defined as crisp relations expressing a lower bound for the fuzzy relations $be^{\preccurlyeq}$, $bb^{\preccurlyeq}$, $ee^{\preccurlyeq}$ and $eb^{\preccurlyeq}$. In the following, let $\mathcal{R}$ be the set of all temporal relations, i.e., $\mathcal{R} = \{[\alpha, \beta, \gamma, \delta] | \alpha, \beta, \gamma, \delta \in [0, 1]\}$. Our qualitative knowledge about the temporal relationship of two events e_1 and e_2 can then be completely described by a statement of the form:

$$e_1[\alpha_1, \beta_1, \gamma_1, \delta_1]e_2 \wedge e_2[\alpha_2, \beta_2, \gamma_2, \delta_2]e_1$$

[4] Allen [2] differentiates between on one hand "e_1 happened strictly before e_2", i.e., the ending of e_1 is strictly before the beginning of e_2, and on the other hand "e_1 meets e_2", i.e., the ending of e_1 coincides with the beginning of e_2. Due to the high ambiguity of natural language, such a fine–grained distinction is not useful in the context of our question answering system.

Intersection, union, equivalence, inclusion, and strict inclusion of temporal relations are defined in the usual way, i.e., for two crisp relations R_1 and R_2 in the universe of all fuzzy time intervals $\mathcal{F}$, we have:

$$(\forall(e_1, e_2) \in \mathcal{F}^2)(e_1(R_1 \cap R_2)e_2 \Leftrightarrow e_1R_1e_2 \wedge e_1R_2e_2)$$
$$(\forall(e_1, e_2) \in \mathcal{F}^2)(e_1(R_1 \cup R_2)e_2 \Leftrightarrow e_1R_1e_2 \vee e_1R_2e_2)$$
$$R_1 = R_2 \Leftrightarrow (\forall(e_1, e_2) \in \mathcal{F}^2)(e_1R_1e_2 \Leftrightarrow e_1R_2e_2)$$
$$R_1 \subseteq R_2 \Leftrightarrow R_1 \cap R_2 = R_1$$
$$R_1 \subset R_2 \Leftrightarrow R_1 \subseteq R_2 \wedge R_2 \not\subseteq R_1$$

If $R_1 \subseteq R_2$, we say that R_1 is a stronger relation than R_2.

Lemma 1. *If E_1 and E_2 are fuzzy time intervals, it holds that:*

$$eb^{\preccurlyeq}(E_1, E_2) \leq bb^{\preccurlyeq}(E_1, E_2) \leq be^{\preccurlyeq}(E_1, E_2) \tag{6}$$
$$eb^{\preccurlyeq}(E_1, E_2) \leq ee^{\preccurlyeq}(E_1, E_2) \leq be^{\preccurlyeq}(E_1, E_2) \tag{7}$$

This lemma shows that the four components of a temporal relation are not independent of each other. For example, if we know that $e_1[0.3, 0.5, 0.1, 0.2]e_2$ holds, we also know that $e_1[0.5, 0.5, 0.1, 0.2]e_2$ and $e_1[0.5, 0.5, 0.2, 0.2]e_2$ must hold. In other words, $[0.3, 0.5, 0.1, 0.2]$, $[0.5, 0.5, 0.1, 0.2]$, and $[0.5, 0.5, 0.2, 0.2]$ denote the same temporal relation.

Lemma 2. *If E_1 and E_2 are fuzzy time intervals, it holds that:*

$$be^{\preccurlyeq}(E_1, E_2) = 1 \vee eb^{\preccurlyeq}(E_1, E_2) = 0$$

Hence, we also have that $[0.3, 0.5, 0.1, 0.2]$, and $[1, 0.5, 0.1, 0.2]$ denote the same temporal relation. Therefore, we introduce an operator *norm* that transforms a temporal relation into a canonical form:

$$norm([\alpha, \beta, \gamma, \delta]) = \begin{cases} [1, \max(\beta, \delta), \max(\gamma, \delta), \delta] & \text{if } \delta > 0 \\ [\max(\alpha, \beta, \gamma), \beta, \gamma, 0] & \text{otherwise} \end{cases}$$

If $norm(R) = R$, then R is called normalised. Obviously $norm(R)$ is normalised for every temporal relation R. We can prove the following proposition.

Proposition 1. *If $R = [\alpha, \beta, \gamma, \delta]$ is a normalised temporal relation, there always exist fuzzy intervals A and B such that:*

$$be^{\preccurlyeq}(A, B) = \alpha \wedge bb^{\preccurlyeq}(A, B) = \beta \wedge ee^{\preccurlyeq}(A, B) = \gamma \wedge eb^{\preccurlyeq}(A, B) = \delta$$

Corollary 1. *Let $R_1 = [\alpha_1, \beta_1, \gamma_1, \delta_1]$ and $R_2 = [\alpha_2, \beta_2, \gamma_2, \delta_2]$ be normalised temporal relations. It holds that:*

$$R_1 = R_2 \Leftrightarrow \alpha_1 = \alpha_2 \wedge \beta_1 = \beta_2 \wedge \gamma_1 = \gamma_2 \wedge \delta_1 = \delta_2$$

This corollary expresses that the operator *norm* indeed transforms temporal relations into a canonical form; hence, our normalization operator is well–defined. It is easy to see that if $R_1 = [\alpha_1, \beta_1, \gamma_1, \delta_1]$ and $R_2 = [\alpha_2, \beta_2, \gamma_2, \delta_2]$, it holds that:

$$R_1 \cap R_2 = [\max(\alpha_1, \alpha_2), \max(\beta_1, \beta_2), \max(\gamma_1, \gamma_2), \max(\delta_1, \delta_2)] \tag{8}$$

Moreover, if R_1 and R_2 are normalised, we have that:

$$R_1 \subseteq R_2 \Leftrightarrow \alpha_1 \geq \alpha_2 \wedge \beta_1 \geq \beta_2 \wedge \gamma_1 \geq \gamma_2 \wedge \delta_1 \geq \delta_2 \tag{9}$$

3 Reasoning with Imperfect Temporal Information

3.1 Deduction Algorithm

The composition of R_1 and R_2 is defined as:

$$e_1(R_1 \circ R_2)e_2 \Leftrightarrow (\exists e \in \mathcal{F})(e_1 R_1 e \wedge e R_2 e_2) \tag{10}$$

i.e., $R_1 \circ R_2$ is the strongest relation that is assured to hold between e_1 and e_2 using only the knowledge that $e_1 R_1 e$ and $e R_2 e_2$ for some fuzzy time interval e. As in many algebras for qualitative temporal or spatial reasoning, our algebra is not closed under composition. Therefore, we use the notion of weak composition [7], which is defined for relations R_1 and R_2 as the strongest relation $R_1 \diamond R_2$ in $\mathcal{R}$ that contains $R_1 \circ R_2$, i.e.:

$$R_1 \circ R_2 \subseteq R_1 \diamond R_2 \wedge (\forall R \in \mathcal{R})(R_1 \circ R_2 \subseteq R \Rightarrow R_1 \diamond R_2 \subseteq R) \tag{11}$$

i.e., $R_1 \diamond R_2$ is the strongest relation in $\mathcal{R}$ that is assured to hold between e_1 and e_2 using only the knowledge that $e_1 R_1 e$ and $e R_2 e_2$ for some fuzzy time interval e. Intuitively, the weak composition operator can be seen as an optimal operator for propagating temporal knowledge in a particular algebra. Unfortunately, (11) does not tell us how to compute the weak composition of two relations in practice. The following important proposition gives us a practical characterization of weak composition of temporal relations.

Proposition 2. *Let $R_1 = [\alpha_1, \beta_1, \gamma_1, \delta_1]$ and $R_2 = [\alpha_2, \beta_2, \gamma_2, \delta_2]$ be normalised temporal relations. It holds that:*

$$\begin{aligned} R_1 \diamond R_2 = [\alpha', \\ & \max(T_W(\beta_1, \beta_2), \min(\alpha_1 + T_W(\delta_2, \gamma_1), \delta_2, \beta_1 + T_W(\delta_2, \alpha_1))), \\ & \max(T_W(\gamma_1, \gamma_2), \min(\alpha_2 + T_W(\delta_1, \beta_2), \delta_1, \gamma_2 + T_W(\delta_1, \alpha_2))), \\ & \max(T_W(\delta_1, \beta_2), T_W(\gamma_1, \delta_2), \min(\delta_1, \delta_2))] \end{aligned}$$

where

$$\alpha' = \begin{cases} \max(T_W(\beta_1, \alpha_2), T_W(\alpha_1, \gamma_2)) & \textit{if } T_W(\alpha_1, \delta_2) = 0 \textit{ and } T_W(\delta_1, \alpha_2) = 0 \\ \min(\alpha_1, \alpha_2) & \textit{otherwise} \end{cases}$$

Let the qualitative temporal information we have at our disposal be represented as temporal relations $R_{ij} = [\alpha_{ij}, \beta_{ij}, \gamma_{ij}, \delta_{ij}]$ such that $e_i R_{ij} e_j$ holds for all $1 \leq i, j \leq n$, $i \neq j$. We apply the weak composition to derive as much new information as possible from the qualitative information in our knowledge base, which was initially gathered as described in Section 2.2.

Example 1. Let the temporal relations between e_1, e_2 and e_3 be given by $R_{12} = [0.8, 0.5, 0.3, 0]$, $R_{23} = [1, 0.6, 0.9, 0]$, and $R_{13} = [0.6, 0.3, 0.3, 0]$. Using Proposition 2 we can deduce that also $R_{12} \diamond R_{23} = [0.7, 0.1, 0.2, 0]$ holds between e_1 and e_3. Thus we obtain that R_{13} should be replaced by the stronger temporal relation $[0.6, 0.3, 0.3, 0] \cap [0.7, 0.1, 0.2, 0] = [0.7, 0.3, 0.3, 0]$.

To deduce stronger temporal relations in the way of Example 1, we use Algorithm 1, which is similar in spirit to Allen's path–consistency algorithm [2]. It can be shown that this algorithm has a worst–case complexity of $O(n^4)$. We stress once more that only temporal relations based on qualitative information gathered as described in Section 2.2 serve as input to Algorithm 1. Hence, newly derived temporal relations are also based solely on qualitative information. However, we do check if these new relations are consistent with the known groundings, i.e., with the available quantitative information, and only in this case they are used in further deductions.

It can be shown that the set of qualitative temporal relations in our knowledge base is always consistent, i.e., for every event e_i we can always find a fuzzy interval E_i such that all the relations R_{jk} are satisfied ($1 \leq j, k \leq n$). In other words, inconsistencies can only arise when at least some of the events are grounded. In the following discussion, let $\mathcal{E}$ be the set of events and $\mathcal{G}$ the set of grounded events in our knowledge base ($\mathcal{G} \subseteq \mathcal{E}$). If, for example, $e_1 \in \mathcal{G}$ and $e_2 \in \mathcal{G}$ then we know the exact degree $be^{\preccurlyeq}(E_1, E_2)$ to which the beginning of e_1 is before the end of e_2. On the other hand, suppose that we have deduced, using the available qualitative information, that α_{12} is a lower bound for this degree. Hence, if $be^{\preccurlyeq}(E_1, E_2) < \alpha_{12}$, the lower bound α_{12} is too strong, and the temporal relation R_{12} is inconsistent with the groundings of e_1 and e_2. In general, we define the predicate *consistent* for e_1 and e_2 in $\mathcal{G}$ as:

$$\begin{aligned} consistent(e_1, e_2) \Leftrightarrow & \alpha_{12} \leq be^{\preccurlyeq}(E_1, E_2) \vee \beta_{12} \leq bb^{\preccurlyeq}(E_1, E_2) \\ & \vee \gamma_{12} \leq ee^{\preccurlyeq}(E_1, E_2) \vee \delta_{12} \leq eb^{\preccurlyeq}(E_1, E_2) \end{aligned}$$

In other words, $consistent(e_1, e_2)$ expresses that the available qualitative information about events e_1 and e_2, namely $R_{12} = [\alpha_{12}, \beta_{12}, \gamma_{12}, \delta_{12}]$, does not contradict the values that can be computed from quantitative information, i.e., from the groundings E_1 and E_2. For $e_1 \in \mathcal{E} \setminus \mathcal{G}$ or $e_2 \in \mathcal{E} \setminus \mathcal{G}$, $consistent(e_1, e_2)$ always holds.

3.2 Inconsistency Repairing

During the execution of Algorithm 1, inconsistent relations may be deduced. In the following, we make the assumption that all groundings in the knowledge base

Algorithm 1. Algebraic closure algorithm

$todo \leftarrow \{(i,j,k) | 1 \leq i,j,k \leq n, i \neq j \neq k\}$
while $todo \neq \emptyset$ **do**
  select and remove a triplet (i_0, j_0, k_0) from *todo*
  if $consistent(e_{i_0}, e_{j_0})$ and $consistent(e_{j_0}, e_{k_0})$ **then**
    $R \leftarrow R_{i_0 j_0} \diamond R_{j_0 k_0}$
    if $R \cap R_{i_0 k_0} \subset R_{i_0 k_0}$ **then**
      $R_{i_0 k_0} \leftarrow R \cap R_{i_0 k_0}$
      $todo \leftarrow todo \cup \{(i_0, k_0, j) | i_0 \neq j \neq k_0\} \cup \{(j, i_0, k_0) | i_0 \neq j \neq k_0\}$
    end if
  end if
end while

are correct. This is a reasonably safe assumption because these groundings are extracted either from Wikipedia, or from a large number of webpages. Under this assumption, whenever a temporal relation is deduced that is inconsistent with the groundings in the knowledge base, we know that one or more temporal relations in the original knowledge base are too strong. This may either be because these qualitative relations were obtained by using false information, e.g., some website states that e_1 happened before e_2, while in reality e_1 happened after e_2, because of errors introduced in the information extraction phase, or because our interpretation of the natural language fragment expressing the relation is too strong, e.g., we assume that $eb^{\preccurlyeq}(e_1, e_2) = 1$ holds, while in reality we only have that $eb^{\preccurlyeq}(e_1, e_2) = 0.8$. To make an inconsistent knowledge base consistent, we revise some of these interpretations, and apply Algorithm 1 a second time. This process is repeated until all inconsistencies have been eliminated.

Let $R_{ij}^{(0)} = [\alpha_{ij}^{(0)}, \beta_{ij}^{(0)}, \gamma_{ij}^{(0)}, \delta_{ij}^{(0)}]$ be the qualitative relation between e_i and e_j in the initial knowledge base, i.e., before the execution of Algorithm 1, and let $R_{ij}^{(1)} = [\alpha_{ij}^{(1)}, \beta_{ij}^{(1)}, \gamma_{ij}^{(1)}, \delta_{ij}^{(1)}]$ be the relation that results after Algorithm 1 is completed. Assume, for example, that $e_1 \in \mathcal{G}$, $e_2 \in \mathcal{G}$, and $\alpha_{12}^{(1)}$ leads to an inconsistency, i.e., $\alpha_{12}^{(1)} > be^{\preccurlyeq}(E_1, E_2)$. During the execution of Algorithm 1, we keep track of the components of the relations $R_{ij}^{(0)}$ that are used to obtain each conclusion. In particular, we have a set V at our disposal containing those values that were used to obtain the value $\alpha_{12}^{(1)}$; assume, for example, $V = \{\alpha_{pq}^{(0)}, \delta_{qr}^{(0)}, \beta_{rs}^{(0)}, \alpha_{st}^{(0)}\}$. Most of the values v in V will also be used in other deduction chains, leading to other conclusions. Some of these conclusions will define temporal relations between ungrounded events; hence, we cannot tell whether they are correct or not. However, other conclusions will define temporal relations between grounded events; we will call these verifiable conclusions. For v in V, let $pos(v)$ be the number of correct verifiable conclusions that were obtained using v, and $neg(v)$ the number of incorrect verifiable conclusions that were obtained using v; then, $rel(v) = \frac{pos(v)}{pos(v)+neg(v)}$ can be used as an approximation of the reliability of v (provided $pos(v) + neg(v) > 0$). The knowledge base is revised by subtracting a value from each v in V that is proportional to $1 - rel(v)$:

$$v \leftarrow v - (\alpha_{12}^{(1)} - be^{\preccurlyeq}(E_1, E_2)) \frac{1 - rel(v)}{\sum_{v' \in V} 1 - rel(v')}$$

In practice, it may occur that different inconsistencies in the knowledge base require the value v to be updated in different ways. In this case, the final value for v is the minimum of all these different updates.

Finally, Algorithm 1 is executed a second time using this revised knowledge base as a starting point. If there are still inconsistencies detected, this whole process is repeated. In practice, we found that all inconsistencies are typically eliminated after one or two iterations.

4 Question Answering

The temporal questions in which we are primarily interested consist of a non–temporal main part asking for an event (e.g., *Which battles took place in Belgium*), the participant of an event (e.g., *Which countries were involved in World War II*), or a time–dependent factoid (e.g., *Who was president of the U.S.*), and a temporal restriction (e.g., *after the invasion of Normandy*). The question analysis module separates the temporal restriction from the main part using a large set of handcrafted patterns. The temporal restriction is further analysed to identify which temporal relation is expressed in it. We use standard question answering techniques to determine, from the main part of the question, the expected semantic type of the answer (e.g., person, battle,...), the question type, i.e., whether the question is asking for an event, a participant, or a time–dependent factoid, and some additional information depending on the question type (see e.g., [6]).

Standard techniques are also used to find events in the knowledge base that satisfy the non–temporal main part of the question. Checking which of these events satisfy the temporal restriction in the question typically boils down to inferring if, and to what degree, a particular qualitative temporal relation holds between these events and the events occurring in the temporal restriction of the question. To support this reasoning task efficiently, Algorithm 1 and the techniques described in Section 3.2 are applied a priori. Hence, at question–answering time R_{ij} is the strongest qualitative relation that we can infer from the available qualitative information, i.e., using groundings of events only to detect inconsistencies. However if e_1 and e_2 are grounded events, with corresponding groundings E_1 and E_2, then $(R_{i1} \diamond R_{12}^*) \diamond R_{2j}$ might be a stronger conclusion, where

$$R_{12}^* = [be^{\preccurlyeq}(E_1, E_2), bb^{\preccurlyeq}(E_1, E_2), ee^{\preccurlyeq}(E_1, E_2), eb^{\preccurlyeq}(E_1, E_2)] \quad (12)$$

In other words, we might obtain a stronger conclusion by also considering the qualitative relation R_{12}^* between e_1 and e_2, computed directly from the groundings of these events. Hence, to obtain a maximal amount of qualitative temporal information between e_i and e_j, we should calculate:

$$R = R_{ij} \cap \left(\bigcap_{(e_1, e_2) \in \mathcal{G}^2} (R_{i1} \diamond R_{12}^*) \diamond R_{2j} \right)$$

In practice, various techniques can be used to evaluate this efficiently; we omit the details here. Note that, because of space and time requirements, it would not be feasible to add the qualitative relation R^*_{12} to the knowledge base for every pair (e_1, e_2) of grounded events a priori, before the execution of Algorithm 1. Finally, if the knowledge base contains too little information to answer a particular question, we use the web to expand it with relevant information at question answering time.

Example 2. Consider the question *Which battles took place in Asia after V-J Day*, and the knowledge base, after the execution of Algorithm 1, illustrated in Figure 1(a). Assume that only *World War II* and *the Cold War* are grounded. Intuitively, the qualitative information in this knowledge base expresses that *the Battle of Chosin Reservoir* happened during *the Korean War* which happened during *the Cold War*, and that *V–J Day* happened during *World War II*. Assume that, using external knowledge, we were able to establish that *the Battle of Chosin Reservoir* is a battle that took place in Asia. As becomes clear from Figure 1(a), it is not possible to infer that this battle happened after *V–J Day* using qualitative information alone. Using the groundings of *World War II* and *the Cold War* however, we can calculate the strongest temporal relation that holds between these two events. This is illustrated in Figure 1(b). Thus we obtain that *V–J Day* and *the Battle of Chosin Reservoir* satisfy the temporal relation given by

$$\begin{aligned}([1,0,1,0] \diamond [1,0.9,1,0.7]) \diamond [1,1,0,0] &= [1,0.7,1,0.7] \diamond [1,1,0,0] \\ &= [1,0.7,0.7,0.7]\end{aligned}$$

Hence, according to our knowledge base, *the Battle of Chosin Reservoir* was after *V–J Day* at least to degree 0.7.

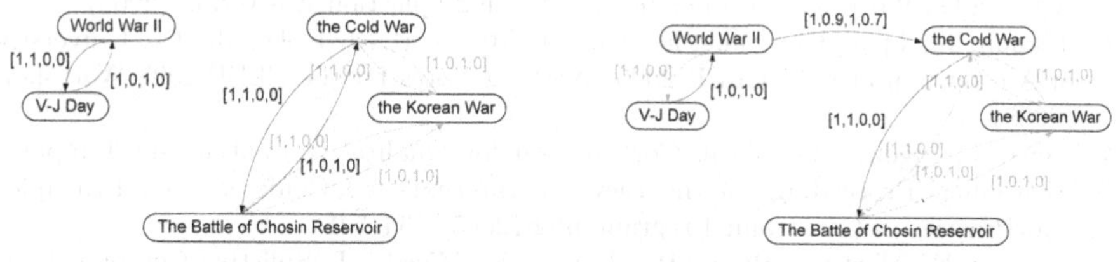

(a) Using only qualitative information

(b) Using qualitative information and groundings

Fig. 1. Verifying whether *the Battle of Chosin Reservoir* happened after *V–J Day*

5 Conclusions

We have discussed the problem of reasoning with vague and qualitative temporal information in the context of question answering. We introduced an algebra of temporal relations to express qualitative temporal information between vague events, and provided a practical characterization of weak composition. Furthermore, we introduced an algorithm to compute the algebraic closure of an initial specification, as well as a heuristic technique to eliminate inconsistencies in the knowledge base. Finally, we have shown how qualitative and quantitative temporal information can be combined to effectively support the question answering process.

Acknowledgments

The authors thank Maarten de Rijke for his useful comments on earlier versions of this draft. The first author was supported by a PhD grant from the Research Foundation – Flanders (FWO). The second author was supported by the Netherlands Organization for Scientific Research (NWO), under project number 612.066.302.

References

1. Ahn, D., Schockaert, S., De Cock, M., Kerre, E.E.: Supporting Temporal Question Answering: Strategies for Offline Data Collection. International workshop on Inference in Computational Semantics, to appear.
2. Allen, J.F.: Maintaining Knowledge about Temporal Intervals. Communications of the ACM **26** (1983) 832–843
3. Badaloni, S., Giacomin, M.: A Fuzzy Extension of Allen's Interval Algebra. Lecture Notes in Artificial Intelligence **1792** (2000) 155–165
4. Dubois, D., HadjAli, A., Prade, H.: Fuzziness and Uncertainty in Temporal Reasoning. Journal of Universal Computer Science **9** (2003) 1168–1194
5. Harabagiu, S., Bejan, C.A.: Question Answering based on Temporal Inference. AAAI-2005 Workshop on Inference for Textual Question Answering (2005)
6. Jijkoun, V., Tjong Kim Sang, E., Ahn, D., Müller, K., de Rijke, M.: The University of Amsterdam at QA@CLEF 2005. Working Notes for the CLEF 2005 Workshop (2005)
7. Renz, J., Ligozat, G.: Weak Composition for Qualitative Spatial and Temporal Reasoning. Proceedings of the Eleventh International Conference on Principles and Practice of Constraint Programming (2005) 534–548
8. Saquete, E., Martínez–Barco, P., Muñozn, R., Vicedo, J.: Splitting Complex Temporal Questions for Question Answering Systems. ACL04 (2004) 566–573
9. Schockaert, S., De Cock, M., Kerre, E.E.: Imprecise Temporal Interval Relations. Lecture Notes in Computer Science **3849** (2006) 108–113
10. Schockaert, S., De Cock, M., Kerre, E.E.: Fuzzifying Allen's Temporal Interval Relations. Submitted
11. Schockaert, S.: Construction of Membership Functions for Fuzzy Time Periods. Proceedings of the ESSLLI 2005 Student Session (2005) 297–305
12. Zadeh, L.A.: Fuzzy sets. Information and Control **8** (1965) 338–353

Analysis and Validation of Information Access Through Mono, Multidimensional and Dynamic Taxonomies

Giovanni Maria Sacco

Dipartimento di Informatica, Università di Torino,
Corso Svizzera 185, 10149 Torino, Italy
sacco@di.unito.it

Abstract. Access to complex information bases through multidimensional, dynamic taxonomies (also improperly known as faceted classification systems) is rapidly becoming pervasive in industry, especially in e-commerce. In this paper, the major shortcomings of conventional, monodimensional taxonomic approaches, such as the independence of different branches of the taxonomy and insufficient scalability, are discussed. The dynamic taxonomy approach, the first and most complete model for multidimensional taxonomic access to date, is reviewed and compared to conventional taxonomies. We analyze the reducing power of dynamic taxonomies and conventional taxonomies and report experimental results on real data, which confirm that monodimensional taxonomies are not useful for browsing/retrieval on large databases, whereas dynamic taxonomies can effectively manage very large databases and exhibit a very fast convergence.

1 Introduction

Taxonomies are a well-known approach to model complex information. A taxonomy is a hierarchy of concepts going from the most general to the most specific and naturally models IS-A relationships among concepts. An example of taxonomies is Linnaean life (botanical, animal) taxonomies. In classical taxonomies, such as Linnaeus', an item (e.g. a dog) is classified under one and only one concept. The taxonomy can be seen as an efficient encoding of properties, which concisely states the properties of an item that can be recovered by following the path from the father concept to the root concept and accumulating properties: thus, we can state that a dog is a mammalian, has a spinal cord, is an animal.

Taxonomies also organize data in such a way as to orient the search for specific items: in this case, we start from the root concept and iteratively discriminate among son concepts, in order to find the appropriate one. Each time we select a concept for further expansion we reduce the number of items that we have to consider, since the items classified under the descendants of the concepts we discarded need not be considered. Thus, taxonomies can be seen as a search device that iteratively reduces the number of documents to be manually inspected by the user. Clearly, reduction can go on only up to terminal concepts: a terminal concept is not further specializable, and therefore all the documents classified under it must be manually inspected.

H.L. Larsen et al. (Eds.): FQAS 2006, LNAI 4027, pp. 659 – 670, 2006.

Dynamic taxonomies [5, 6, 7] have been proposed as a model to describe and access large, complex information bases. From the modeling perspective, the main difference between conventional and dynamic taxonomies is that conventional taxonomies are monodimensional (i.e. an item is classified under one and only one concept), whereas dynamic taxonomies are multidimensional (i.e. an item can be classified under several different concepts at any level of abstraction). From the information access point of view, the difference between the two models is dramatic. In conventional taxonomies, the user can only iteratively expand a concept into its sons, up to the terminal level. In dynamic taxonomies, the user directly manipulates the taxonomy in order to set a focus on one or more concepts. The system is able to infer relationships between concepts and the current focus on the basis of the actual classification: related concepts are shown to the user through a reduced taxonomy, from which unrelated concepts are pruned. Concepts in the reduced taxonomy are used to effectively guide the user to reach his goal: they are all and only the concepts that can be used to set additional foci and allow further refinements even for terminal concepts.

This type of interaction implements a new paradigm of access that we call "**guided information thinning**". This paradigm can be seen as an iterative combination of exploring the information base in order to find relevant features, selecting one or more features of interest and discarding all the items that do not have these features in order to reduce the number of candidates. Subsequently, the candidates are summarized through a reduced taxonomy, from which other concepts can be selected to refine the current focus, and so on. Obviously, only a single iteration can occur in conventional taxonomies. We contend that the vast majority of user access to information benefits from this paradigm, because it is not based on precise queries (e.g. how many suppliers supply red parts…) but rather requires the identification of a set of candidate items according to specifications that are often imprecise or often not known beforehand. We further suggest that the current widespread feeling that search "does not work" is mainly due to the fact that different, ineffective paradigms (such as database queries or text retrieval) are used instead.

We want to stress here that interactive end-user access to complex information bases requires a holistic approach, in which data modeling issues are considered at least as important as human interaction ones and, in fact, data modeling and manipulation primitives can be supported only if they are easily understood by end-users. The present approach is therefore quite different in philosophy and application from most current research on ontologies and Semantic Web, which consider expressiveness and semantic richness as their main goals. Although more powerful and expressive than dynamic taxonomies, general semantic schemata are difficult to understand and manipulate by the casual user. They are better suited to programmatic access and user interaction must be mediated by specialized agents. This increases costs, time to market and decreases generality and flexibility of user access.

From this point of view, we believe that an important result for dynamic taxonomies is that a very effective and general visual exploration framework can be derived, based on conceptual machinery that is minimal and easily understood by users. In addition to the rapidly growing adoption of systems based on dynamic taxonomies by major players such as Yahoo!, Kelkoo, Bizrate, etc. starting in late 2004, Hearst et al. [2, 12] reported usability studies for systems based on dynamic taxonomies, which show a high level of user satisfaction. However, these studies do not address what we believe is the central point in using dynamic taxonomies: their quantitative information thinning effectiveness as a way of exploring, browsing and searching large information bases. The fundamental questions we are trying to answer in this paper are:

- what are the benefits of dynamic taxonomies with respect to other taxonomic approaches, as the dimension of the information base grows? and
- how many iterations are required to select a suitably small set of candidate documents?

Anticipating the results reported in the following, we feel that a much stronger case for dynamic taxonomies is given by the fact that an experiment conducted on 110,000 news articles showed that whereas the user of a naïve multidimensional taxonomy had to inspect 1242 documents on the average, the user of dynamic taxonomies needed a single interaction to reduce this quantity to 27.

2 Dynamic Taxonomies

Dynamic taxonomies are a general knowledge management model for complex, heterogeneous information bases [5, 6, 7]. It has been applied to very diverse areas, including legal databases [10], electronic commerce [9], multimedia databases [11] and medical guidelines [13]. The intension of a dynamic taxonomy is a taxonomy designed by an expert. This taxonomy is a concept hierarchy (taxonomies with multiple inheritance are supported but rarely required) going from the most general to the most specific concepts. A dynamic taxonomy does not require any other relationships in addition to subsumptions (e.g. IS-A, PART-OF relationships).

In the extension, items can be freely classified under several concepts at any level of abstraction (i.e. at any level in the conceptual tree). This multidimensional classification is a departure from the monodimensional classification scheme used in conventional taxonomies. Besides being a generalization of a monodimensional classification, a multidimensional classification models common real-life situations. First, an item is very rarely classified under a single concept. One reason is that items (especially textual items) are very often about different concepts: for example a news item on September 11th can be classified under "terrorism", "airlines", "USA", etc. Second, items to be classified usually have different features (e.g. Time, Location, etc.) or "facets", each of which can be described by an independent taxonomy.

By taking a "nominalistic" approach (concepts are defined by instances rather than by properties), a concept C is just a label that identifies all the items classified under C. Because of the subsumption relationship between a concept and its descendants, the items classified under C (items(C)) are all those items in the deep extension of C, i.e. the set of items identified by C includes all the items directly classified under C union all the items directly classified under any of C's descendants. There are two important consequences of our approach. First, since concepts identify sets of items, logical operations on concepts can be performed by the corresponding set operations on their extension. This means that the user is able to restrict the information base by combining concepts through the normal logical operations (and, or, not).

Second, dynamic taxonomies can find all the concepts related to a given concept C, which represent the conceptual summary of C. Concept relationships other than IS-A are inferred through the extension only, according to the following extensional inference rule: two concepts A and B are related iff there is at least one item *d* in the infobase which is classified at the same time under A (or under one of A's descendants) and under B (or under one of B's descendants). For example, we can infer a (unnamed) relationship between Michelangelo and Rome, if an item that is classified under Michelangelo and Rome exists in the infobase. At the same time, since Rome is a descendant of Italy, also a relationship between Michelangelo and Italy can be inferred.

The extensional inference rule can be easily extended to cover the relationship between a given concept C and a concept expressed by an arbitrary subset *S* of the universe: C is related to *S* iff there is at least one item *d* in *S* which is also in items(C). Hence, the extensional inference rule can produce conceptual summaries not only for base concepts, but also for any logical combination of concepts. In addition, dynamic taxonomies can produce summaries for sets of items produced by other retrieval methods (database queries, text retrieval queries, etc.) and therefore access through dynamic taxonomies can be easily combined with other retrieval methods.

Dynamic taxonomies can be used to browse and explore the infobase in several ways. Usually, the user is initially presented with a tree representation of the initial taxonomy for the entire infobase. Each concept label has also a count of all the items classified under it (i.e. the cardinality of items(C) for all C's). The initial user focus *F* is the universe (i.e. all the items in the infobase). In the simplest case, the user can then select a concept C in the taxonomy and **zoom** over it. The zoom operation changes the current state in two ways. First, concept C is used to refine the current focus *F*, which becomes $F \cap$items(C). Items not in the focus are discarded. Second, the tree representation of the taxonomy is modified in order to summarize the new focus. All and only the concepts related to *F* are retained and the count for each retained concept C' is updated to reflect the number of items in the focus *F* that are classified under C'. The reduced taxonomy is a conceptual summary of the set of documents identified by *F*, exactly in the same way as the original taxonomy was a conceptual summary of the universe. In fact, the term *dynamic taxonomy* is used to stress the fact that the taxonomy adapts to the current user focus.

The retrieval process can then be seen as an iterative thinning of the information base: the user selects a focus, which restricts (thins out) the information base by discarding all the items not in the current focus. Only the concepts used to classify the items in the focus (and their ancestors) are retained. These concepts, which summarize the current focus, are those and only those concepts that can be used for further refinements. From the human computer interaction point of view, the user is effectively guided to reach his goal, by a clear and consistent listing of all possible alternatives.

Techniques like the one described above are improperly referred to as faceted classification access by some researchers. It is important to note that a) a traditional faceted classification [4] is not required by dynamic taxonomies, which only require that documents be classified under at least two concepts, and that b) the concept of systematic summaries and guided searches is completely absent from traditional faceted classification theory. A taxonomic design based on facets, i.e. independent coordinates in the conceptual space, was proposed by [7] as a design guideline, but it is by no means a necessary condition nor a sufficient one. In fact, as we will show in the following, naive access based on facets does not provide sufficient convergence.

3 An Example of Interaction

The following example is taken from a collection of news articles. This and other demos are available online at [3]. In figure 1, the highest levels of the taxonomy are presented. In figure 2, the concept "Geographic Location" was expanded down to "USA": 2148 articles are classified under "USA", and the user of a conventional taxonomy would have to manually inspect these many documents since "USA" is a terminal concept no further specializable.

With a dynamic taxonomy, instead, the user can zoom on "USA" and obtain a reduced taxonomy, partially shown in figure 3 where the branch "Subjects > Society, culture and entertainment" was exploded. The reduced taxonomy describes the current set of interest (i.e. all the documents classified under USA) in the same way as the initial taxonomy described the entire information base. The term "dynamic" in dynamic taxonomies reflects the ability of the taxonomy to adapt to different foci, perspectives and interests. While the taxonomic structure is the same, all the concepts, under which no document classified under "USA" is classified, are pruned from the actual reduced taxonomy. In addition, the counters count the documents in the current set of interest that are also classified under each concept.

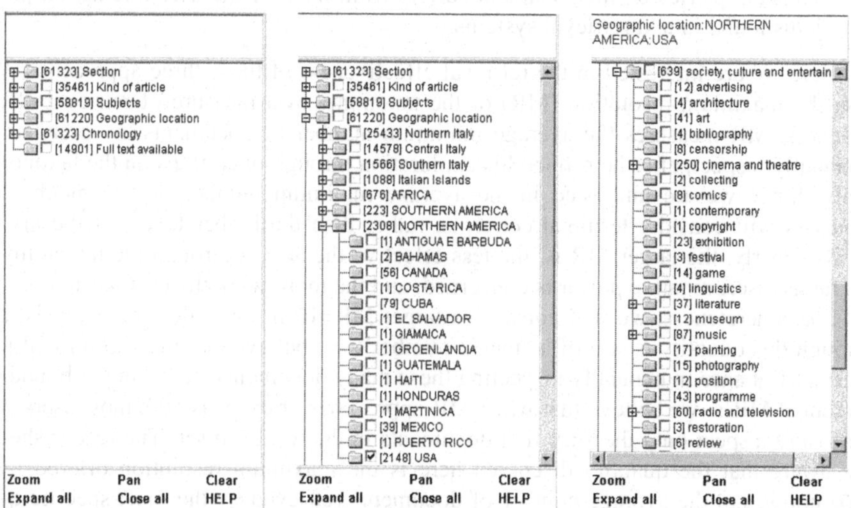

Fig. 1. Initial taxonomy

Fig. 2. Preparing to zoom on USA

Fig. 3. Taxonomic summary for the documents on USA (Subjects > Society, culture, entertainment)

We obtain a precise, systematic summary of our current focus, and the concepts displayed are those and only those concepts that can be used for additional zooms. However, a single zoom operation has already thinned the information base out in a significant way: most of the concepts reported in figure 3, in fact, identify a limited number of documents, that can be manually inspected with no need for further zooms.

4 A Comparison of Conventional and Dynamic Taxonomies

The following analysis focuses on three different approaches:

1. Conventional, monodimensional taxonomies. This is the most common browsing paradigm, and it is used, among others, by Yahoo!
2. Multidimensional taxonomies with no concept composition capabilities. This paradigm simply extends monodimensional taxonomies by allowing documents to be classified under several concepts, but retains the visual framework of conventional taxonomies, i.e. level-by-level expansion, so that concept composition is not available to end-users. This approach is used in Microsoft Knowledge Manager and in the initial version of amazon.com.
3. Multidimensional taxonomies with concept composition capabilities. This paradigm is implemented by dynamic taxonomies, and by all the systems (e.g. factiva.com) that support boolean queries on taxonomic metadata. The fundamental difference between the two approaches is that dynamic taxonomies integrate both concept composition and feedback in the same visual framework, whereas the other systems do not provide any feedback to the user who therefore has to guess which concepts to compose. In short, the latter approach is strictly equivalent to boolean queries on metadata and suffers from most of the user interaction problems found in text retrieval systems.

Here we are interested in the retrieval effectiveness of these three approaches. We use the maximum resolution (MR) of the taxonomy as a measure of retrieval effectiveness. MR measures the average minimum number of documents the user has to manually inspect, after he refined his exploration through operations on the taxonomy only. Since we are interested in the average minimum number of documents, our analysis will consider terminal concepts, rather than the higher levels of the taxonomy. Clearly, the larger MR is, the less effective the access through the taxonomy is as far as discriminative power is concerned, and the more work the user has to do.

For concreteness, we will consider a target MR=10 in the following analysis. Although this quantity is sort of a “magic number”, we believe that most users will feel perfectly at ease in manually inspecting these many documents. As an upper bound on practical MR’s, we believe that when MR approaches or exceeds 100, most users will probably inspect only the very first documents in the retrieved set. The reader should be aware that the quantity discussed here is the maximum resolution offered by a taxonomy, i.e. the average number of documents retrieved by the most specific queries on the taxonomy. The quantity of documents retrieved by the user can be considerably larger for broader queries, i.e. when the user works with concepts at high levels of abstraction in the taxonomy.

In our analysis of the maximum resolution, we will consider an information base of **D** items and a taxonomy with **T** terminal concepts and assume that items are classified under terminal concepts only. In addition, we will assume a uniform classification probability distribution and the independence of terminal concepts. These latter assumptions are used to simplify the following analysis but are acknowledged not to be realistic. For this reason, the analysis validation reported in section 6 is especially important, since it is performed on a real corpus, for which these assumptions are not verified. An analysis of the behavior of dynamic taxonomies when these assumptions are violated can also be found in [8].

4.1 Conventional Monodimensional Taxonomies

In monodimensional taxonomies no concept composition is possible, except trivial ones. If we consider two concepts C and C', C∩C'=Ø unless C' is a descendant of C, in which case, trivially, C∩C'=C'. The zoom operation on a concept C trivially preserves only the descendants and the ancestors of C.

In addition, terminal concepts cannot be further refined, and consequently the entire set of items classified under a terminal concept must be manually inspected. Therefore, under our assumptions of a uniform distribution of documents, MR=**D/T**, and consequently, our target of MR=10 requires **T=D**/10, i.e. the number of terminal concepts must be just one order of magnitude smaller than the size of the information base. This implies that very large taxonomies are required for real-life information bases and that the taxonomy must grow as the corpus grows and therefore that terminal concepts must be indefinitely specializable, which is a condition very difficult to satisfy.

4.2 Conventional Multidimensional Taxonomies with no Concept Composition Capabilities

This approach extends monodimensional taxonomies in a straightforward way, by simply allowing documents to be classified under several concepts. Although concept composition is possible in this context, it is not exploited because the same access paradigm as monodimensional taxonomies is used. In this approach, in fact, the user navigates the taxonomy tree in the same top-down way as in monodimensional taxonomies. Access through the taxonomy suffers from the same problems as in monodimensional taxonomies. The most important problem is that, once a branch of the taxonomy is chosen, subsequent refining can only involve the descendants of the selected branch. That is, all the different branches of a taxonomy are independent and all the relationships among concepts, other than the subsumptions explicitly defined in the taxonomy, are completely lost. An important consequence of this independence is that terminal concepts cannot be further refined, and consequently the entire set of items classified under a terminal concept must be manually inspected.

If we extend conventional taxonomies to a multidimensional classification, the maximum resolution becomes considerably worse. In fact, if each item is classified under j terminal concepts, the resulting MR is equal to the MR for the monodimensional classification of **jD** items, that is MR=**jD/T**. In order to reach our objective, we must have **T**=**jD**/10, which means that the required number of terminal concepts may well exceed the size of the information base when a non-trivial number of dimensions is used.

4.3 Multidimensional Taxonomies with Concept Composition Capabilities

In this approach, the composition of concepts through boolean operators (which can be translated into the corresponding set theoretic operations on the deep extension of the concepts involved [7]) is supported. It can be supported "syntactically", in the sense that the user composes a boolean query on concepts in the taxonomy, as in the current implementation of factiva.com. Alternatively, a dynamic taxonomy can be used both to compose concepts and to give the user a systematic summary of the result of such composition ([7, 2]). Such summaries include all the concepts related to the result, which can be used in further composition, and therefore guide the user to reach his goal.

In both cases, concept composition is supported. Obviously, we are concerned here with composition in ***and*** (which results in the intersection of the deep extension of the concepts involved) since it restricts the information base. As a consequence of concept composition, a terminal concept T can be composed with another concept C (possibly a terminal concept as well), so that T is further "specializable" even if it is a terminal. One of the differences between the two approaches is that in the former "syntactic" approach "T and C" can result in an empty set, whereas in dynamic taxonomies this cannot occur, by construction. In fact, the terminal concept T can be refined by a related concept C computed through extensional inference, if there is at least one document d classified under T and under C or one of C's descendants.

Since terminal concepts can be refined by other concepts and, notably, by other terminal concepts, the maximum resolution MR no longer depends on the number of terminal concepts, but rather on the most restrictive combination of terminal concepts that can be performed on the dynamic taxonomy. If we classify each item under j terminal concepts, the maximum number of terminal concepts that can be intersected is j: the intersection of more than j terminal concepts is guaranteed to produce a null result. Clearly, the result of the intersection of k ($k<j$) terminal concepts is no smaller than the intersection of j terminal concepts, and the intersection of j concepts, some of which are non-terminal, is likewise no smaller.

In order to compute the maximum resolution of a dynamic taxonomy, in which each item is classified under j terminal concepts, we will consider the two scenarios described below. In practice, real scenarios are usually a mix of the two scenarios we are considering and, quite often, the number of concepts under which an item is classified varies within the corpus.

4.3.1 Faceted Classifications

In the first scenario, each item is described by a set of j features. Each of these features is represented by an independent taxonomy. As an example, consider a digital camera that is described by features such as Price, Weight, Resolution, etc. The values of each feature can be arranged taxonomically. In this case, we assume that the set of terminal concepts in the dynamic taxonomy is partitioned into j subsets of the same size. Under this assumption, each partition has $\mathbf{T}/j$ ($\mathbf{T}/j \geq 2$) terminal concepts. Each item *d* is classified under one and only one leaf concept T in each partition. In addition, we assume that the probability of classifying *d* under T is uniform for each partition. This type of classification is similar to the faceted classification scheme proposed by Ranganathan [4].

In this case, MR can be computed as $MR=\mathbf{D}(j/\mathbf{T})^j$, $\mathbf{T} \geq 2j$. As a geometric interpretation, note that the present scenario corresponds to a j-dimensional hypercube, in which each side has $\mathbf{T}/j$ elements. By subsequent zooming, we iteratively add a dimension to the hypercube, until, after j zoom operations, we arrive at the maximal j-dimensional hypercube. Incidentally, the geometric interpretation shows that there is a strong correlation between dynamic taxonomies and OLAP techniques based on hypercubes [1], and that the browsing system of dynamic taxonomies can be useful for interactive exploration in the context of OLAP as well.

4.3.2 Unrestricted Multidimensional Classifications

In the second scenario, which commonly arises in textual applications, we have a single taxonomy (e.g. Subjects) and j terminal concepts are chosen to classify each document, the only constraint being that a specific concept C can be chosen only once. In this case, we can compute MR as a function of the number S_j of the sets generated by the intersection of j distinct terminal concepts, that is MR=j**D**/ S_j. The maximum number of different intersections S_j is equal to

$$S_j = \binom{T}{j} = \prod_{1 \le k \le j} \left(\frac{T+1-k}{k} \right)$$

which, assuming **T**>>j, can be grossly approximated by $S_j = \mathbf{T}^j$. Consequently, MR=j**D**/$\mathbf{T}^j$.

5 A Comparison

If we compare a multidimensional conventional taxonomy with a dynamic taxonomy, we find that a dynamic taxonomy has an MR that is at least $(\mathbf{T}/j)^{j-1}$ better. Furthermore, we claim that conventional taxonomies cannot meet our requirements for efficiently accessing information on large information bases. With a conventional monodimensional taxonomy, our target MR (MR≤10) requires **D=T**/10, that is that the number of terminal concepts be just one order of magnitude smaller than the size of the information base. Conventional multidimensional taxonomies have a worse MR than monodimensional taxonomies. In order to reach our objective, we must have **D**=j**T**/10, which means that the required number of terminal concepts may well exceed the size of the information base when a non-trivial number of dimensions is used.

If we consider a j-dimensional dynamic taxonomy, the situation immediately becomes manageable. In fact, we require $\mathbf{D}=10(\mathbf{T}/j)^j$ or $\mathbf{D}=10\mathbf{T}^j/j$ for scenario 1 and 2, respectively. This means that a compact taxonomy of 1,000 terminal concepts and a classification scheme in which each document is classified under 10 terminal concepts are sufficient to reach MR=10 for information bases with as many as 10^{21} (scenario 1) or 10^{30} (scenario 2) items.

Because of the high reduction factor obtained by dynamic taxonomies, zooms on less than j terminal concepts are usually sufficient. We call MR(i) the maximum resolution deriving by the intersection of i terminal concepts, i≤j: MR(i)= $j^i\mathbf{D}/\mathbf{T}^i$ in scenario 1, and MR(i)=$j\mathbf{D}/\mathbf{T}^i$ in scenario 2. The maximum information base size **D** with MR(i)=10, under the assumptions above, varies from $\mathbf{D}=10^{2i+1}$ to $\mathbf{D}=10^{3i}$ for scenario 1 and 2, respectively. This means that the composition of three concepts is sufficient for information bases with 10 million to 1 billion documents.

Finally, it could be contended that the same reducing effect of dynamic taxonomies can be achieved by a careful design of the corresponding conventional taxonomy. We could, in fact, represent as explicit concepts all the possible concept intersections and place them in the taxonomy. However, this strategy obviously results in an exponential growth of the taxonomy. Consider a faceted taxonomy on j facets and **T**/j terminals per facet: the number of different facet combinations that can be obtained at the terminal level is $(\mathbf{T}/j)^j$, an equivalent monodimensional taxonomy would require these many terminals. Assuming j=10 and **T**=1000, the equivalent monodimensional taxonomy would require 100^{10} terminals, too much to be practical.

Dynamic taxonomies can synthesize all the possible non-empty concept intersections. Although such an exhaustive synthesis would require an exponential time, concept intersections are generated on request, and in general, only an extremely small subset of all the possible intersections needs to be generated.

6 Experimental Results

In order to assess the behavior of dynamic taxonomies in the large, we worked on three different collections of documents. The first two collections include news articles from 1992 and 1993, respectively. The third collection is the union of the first two. Although the collections we consider are small when compared to those managed by web search engines, they are real-world corpora with a general focus and are sufficiently large to guarantee the statistical significance of our experiments.

The corpora are characterized by a multidimensional classification that is a mix between the two scenarios described in the previous section: in fact, each article is characterized as in Scenario 1 by the values of several independent features, such as Location, Type of Article (e.g. interview, editorial) etc. In addition, the "information content" of the article is described, as in Scenario 2, by several concepts in the Subject taxonomy.

Table 1 reports the principal statistics for the three collections. The columns *Concepts* and *Terminal concepts* count non-empty concepts only, i.e. concepts under which at least one document is classified. About 1,000 concepts were used to classify the collections. The *average concepts per document* indicates that about 11 concepts were used on the average to describe a single document. The *average document per terminal concept* measures how many documents are retrieved by simply exploding the taxonomy to a terminal concept, i.e. the MR for a conventional multidimensional taxonomy. As expected, the number of documents to be manually inspected is very large and consequently a conventional taxonomy is not useful for retrieval.

In order to assess the benefits in terms of information thinning, we have performed 10,000 random intersections of two concepts for each collection. The intersection of two concepts is the operation performed upon zooming, in the construction of the reduced tree [7]. We conservatively took the intersection of two random concepts, at any level in the tree, rather than the intersection of terminal concepts only, which is much more discriminative. For each experiment, table 2 reports the most relevant measures. At worst 491 intersections out of 1897 non-empty intersections (about 25%) resulted in sets with a size larger than 10, for which additional intersections are required. In addition, about 80% of the intersections resulted in an empty set, which indicates a quite effective pruning of concepts in the computation of reduced trees. The observed measures match our estimates and show that the deviations from uniformity and from concept independence that occur in practice do not degrade the expected performance of dynamic taxonomies in any significant way.

In conclusion, the advantages of dynamic taxonomies over conventional access methods are dramatic: whereas a conventional taxonomy would require the user to inspect result lists of several hundreds documents, a dynamic taxonomy requires only one zoom operation to produce an average result size of 13 to 27 documents.

Table 1. Collection statistics

Collection	Total docs	Size	Concepts	Terminal concepts	avg. docs per terminal	avg. concepts per doc
1992	57590	179.0Mb	1106	1021	609.41	10.80
1993	56452	180.6Mb	1109	1024	639.05	11.59
1992+1993	114042	359.6Mb	1109	1024	1246.22	11.19

Table 2. Experimental results

Collection	Avg. result size	Estimated MR(2) range	Number of nonempty sets	Avg. size of non-empty sets	nonempty sets with size >10
1992	1.87	0.6 - 6.44	1415	13.22	270
1993	2.47	0.72 – 7.23	1674	14.77	339
1992+1993	5.25	1.22 – 13.62	1897	27.68	491

7 Conclusions

We have shown that conventional taxonomies, and especially those which support a multidimensional classification, are not appropriate as a device to access non-trivial information bases. In conventional taxonomies, in fact, the only way to restrict the information base is to explode the conceptual schema to the finest specialization level (terminal concepts). We have shown, however, that if we place a reasonable bound on the number of documents to be manually inspected, the number of terminal concepts required becomes so large to be unfeasible. Simple multidimensional extensions or naïve faceted organizations make these problems even worse.

Dynamic taxonomies, on the other hand, are inherently extremely effective for reducing very large information bases. A very limited number of concept intersections is sufficient to produce result sets which are no larger than 10, on the average, even for very large information bases. We conclude that dynamic taxonomies are a requirement for effective taxonomic retrieval. If they are not used, taxonomic retrieval is impossible per se, due to the large size of result sets, and the user has to resort to other retrieval techniques (database queries, text retrieval queries, etc.) to thin information out.

References

1. Chaudhuri, S., Dayal, U. An overview of data warehousing and OLAP technology, *ACM SIGMOD Record, 26*:1 (1997)
2. Hearst, M., et al., Finding the Flow in Web Site Search, *Comm. of the ACM, 45*, 9 (2002)
3. Knowledge Processors' Universal Knowledge Processor. www.knowledgeprocessors.com
4. Ranganathan, S. R.. *The Colon Classification.* Rutgers Series on Systems for the Intellectual Organization of Information (ed. Susan Artandi). New Jersey: Rutgers University Press, Volume 4, 1965
5. Sacco, G. M., Navigating the CD-ROM, Proc. Int. Conf. Business of CD-ROM, 1987
6. Sacco, G. M., Dynamic taxonomy process for browsing and retrieving information in large heterogeneous data bases, US. Patent 6,763,349
7. Sacco, G. M., Dynamic Taxonomies: A Model for Large Information Bases. *IEEE Transactions on Knowledge and Data Engineering 12,* 2 (2000), 468-479
8. Sacco, G. M., Conventional Taxonomies vs. Dynamic Taxonomies, Univ. di Torino, Dip. di Informatica, 2/2002 (revised as Analysis and Validation of Information Access through Mono, Multidimensional and Dynamic Taxonomies, 2005)
9. Sacco, G. M., The Intelligent E-Sales Clerk: the Basic Ideas, in Krueger, H. & Rautenberg, M. (Eds.), *Proc. Interact 2003*, (2003)
10. Sacco, G. M., No (e-)Democracy without (e-)Knowledge, in M. Böhlen et al. (Eds.), TCGOV 2005, *Springer LNAI 3416*, pp. 147 – 156, (2005)
11. Sacco, G. M., Uniform access to multimedia information bases through dynamic taxonomies, in 6th IEEE International Symposium on Multimedia Software Engineering (ISMSE 2004), (2004)
12. Yee, K-P., et al., Faceted Metadata for Image Search and Browsing, *Proc. CHI 2003*, (2003)
13. Wollersheim, D., Rahayu, W. Methodology For Creating a Sample Subset of Dynamic Taxonomy to Use in Navigating Medical Text Databases, *Proc. IDEAS 2002 Conf.*, Edmonton, Canada, (2002)

The Flow Control of Audio Data Using Distributed Terminal Mixing in Multi-point Communication

Young-Mi Kim and Dae-Joon Hwang

School of Information and Communication Engineering, Sungkyunkwan University, 300 Chunchun-Dong, Jangan-Ku, Suwon-city, South-Korea, 440-746
ultraym@skku.edu, djhwang@skku.ac.kr

Abstract. This paper describes an efficient audio flow control method in the point of quantitative performance using audio-mixing, compared to existing P2P(Peer To Peer) method. In comparison with existing P2P method, using central mixing and distributed terminal mixing method, we achieved advance at the point of global network usage and each terminal's CPU load, and additionally we expect more session, more terminal can be served by same amount of network bandwidth and computers. By using P2P method in audio communication, speaker and listener must connect to each other. So it has the critical defect that as the participants grows more and more, the network bandwidth usage, each terminal's CPU load will grows rapidly. So the number of participants in same session will be extremely restricted. In comparison with P2P method, the central mixing method has the great advantage at the points of network usage and terminals CPU load. Regardless of the number of speakers and listeners, all the participants can speak and listen with all other participants by using just one stream's amount of data size and CPU load. But all the network usages and CPU loads of "Audio decompression->Buffering->Mixing->Audio Compression" are concentrated on central server. So the number of sessions and terminals can be participated in one server will be highly restricted. This study solves the problems of server's CPU load and network load by using the distributed terminal mixing method.

1 Introduction

As Internet technologies have dramatically improved and Internet services have been widely expanded and adopted in recent years, the demand for multimedia data services is much higher than ever before in our daily lives. This is remarkably true with real-time audio/video communication services, which have been deployed very much in quantity and require ensuring accurate and real-time transfer based on data loss restoration, however, considerable data volume led to too much load on networks.

In addition, the rapid advancement of computer and communication network technologies contributed to make the speed of processor as well as network much faster. However, in the other hand, there appeared more Internet-users, protocols and programs requiring considerable throughput. So there has always been and will continue to be some kind of effort to minimize required computer processing capacity and network usage in order to save costs.

H.L. Larsen et al. (Eds.): FQAS 2006, LNAI 4027, pp. 671–680, 2006.

As we do not have any specific organization responsible for controlling network resources, each network program has its own way of leveraging allocated bandwidth and servicing users. Even if some two programs' functionalities are identical, their performance and/or network bandwidth consumption may be different from each other, depending on transfer method. Especially in multi-point multimedia network programs, there are a lot of contributing factors to this kind of difference. These factors can be grouped into multimedia data compression and multimedia data transfer. Multimedia data compression has been evolved consistently. Standard organizations continue to provide CODECs with better video output and compression rate, which are being deployed to a wide variety of areas, including multimedia-enabled programs, consumer electronics, etc. The development of multimedia transfer technology which helps save network resources doesn't seem so fast as that of CODEC, however. The reason is in most cases, P2P-based approach has been deployed to multi-point area, which doesn't make full use of the opportunities for saving bandwidth. This aspect would lead to a condition where there are only several multi-point communication sessions occupying the entire network.

There is a protocol for real-time multi-point stream, called IP-multicasting.[1][6] With that protocol, we can deliver the stream to desired targets using just one transmission, but because there are not enough routers supporting IP-multicasting, in practice, we must use also another protocol with it to complete all transmission. And IP-multicasting has no gain on CPU load. And one of important defect is that it can't guarantee the delivery of data we sent. It's very difficult work to restore the lost packets to get a continuous stream in real-time in especially multi-point communication.[2]

In addition, CODEC evolvement required more CPU load. In a multi-point multimedia communication, you should transfer data to and/or receive & process data from more than one person. To process more than one stream in a single computer, it should be assumed that the computer has enough processing capacity. We cannot always make sure any user's computer would meet the requirement, however.[3][4]

Although it's not the main topic of this study, we should consider the sequence from the capturing audio signal to playing audio "analog audio signal->conversion to digital signal -> compression -> sending network packets -> receiving network packets -> decompression -> conversion from digital to analog signal -> playing with audio output device". And the compression and decompression occupy the most of load on CPU.

In this paper, we're going to focus on improvement on these issues below.

- Global network usage
- Server / terminal network usage
- Server / terminal CPU usage
- The number of sessions and terminals that can be accommodated on the same number of server and network bandwidth.

We suggested the central mixing method for reduction of global network usage and terminal's CPU load. This is the method that all the audio data must be collected in central mixing server first, and the mixing server mixes the data and sends the mixed data to each participant terminal.

But the central mixing method has the critical defect that network loads and CPU loads are centralized on server. This brought that the server can't accommodate as much sessions and terminals as the P2P method.

With supplement the central mixing method, we suggest the distributed terminal mixing method that maximizes the usage of terminals' network and CPU resources.

2 Reference Studies

Looking at the latest audio communication technologies and their more traditional counterparts, the most of multi-point audio communication use the P2P method in audio communication. Each participant sends their audio data to each other participants and each participant receives audio data from each other participants.[2][5][7] For the network data packet standardization, we uses the RTP(Real-time Transport Protocol) in packet type. [9]

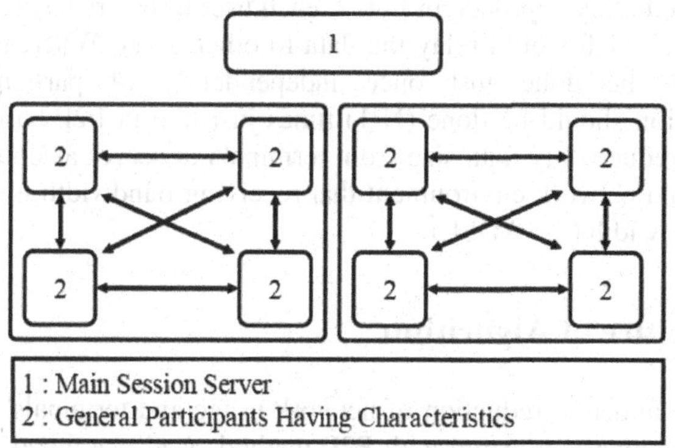

Fig. 1. P2P-based multi-point audio communication architecture

The existing P2P typed multi-point audio communication had the volume of network data increased as much as N*(N-1)*2(where 'N' is the number of participants, 2 is for listening and speaking), just as in Fig. 1. In order to listen to all speakers, the listener had to receive (N-1) data.

Not the only audio data size, the CPU load in decompressing the compressed audio data should be also considered. So with more participants, the communication data volume and CPU load from data decompression would be increased rapidly, which in turn, became one of the main reasons for placing limit on the number of simultaneous speech and its audience. Actually, in an ADSL (Asymmetric Digital Subscriber Line)-based environment, only about 4 people could speak and listen concurrently. The following figure shows the case that a session consists of 4 participants, each of whom should perform one compression and three transfers/ receives/decompressions in order to send audio data to and get the data from others. As more people participate, each terminal will experience rapid increase of network/CPU load.

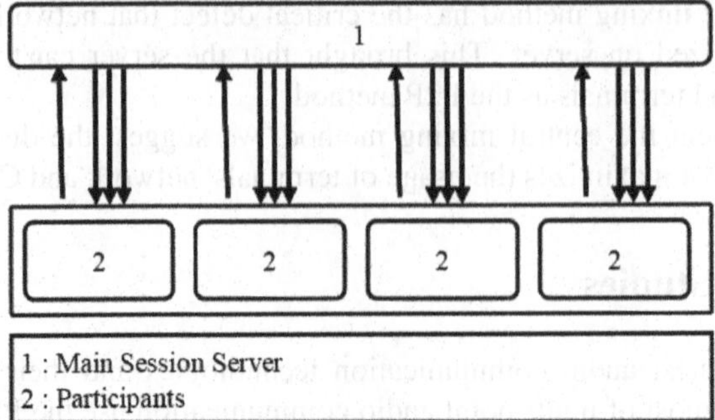

Fig. 2. Centralized relay-based multi-point audio communication architecture

In response to this problem, centralized relay (at service provider's equipments or servers) such as Fig. 2 was suggested.

In a centralized relay approach in Fig. 2, each user transfers his/her own data to the server just once, which would relay the data to other users. Whereas transfer data to the server will be done just once independently of participants, receiving and decompression should be done (N-1) times just like in P2P-based. This solution will, therefore, reduce only data size from terminals to server as compared to P2P. It is useful in such a network environment that receiving-bandwidth is much larger than the sending-bandwidth (ex: ADSL).

3 The Structure of Algorithm

In this study we aimed at reduction of network usage and terminals' CPU load, using central mixing method compared with P2P method. And we aimed at distribution of server's network and CPU load, for the same amount of servers to accommodate as more sessions and terminals as possible.

In this study, the base of idea is the audio's key characteristics that many audio streams can be mixed into the stream equivalent to just one stream in size. In real life, when various sounds are audible, we can just hear some loudest sounds. This is

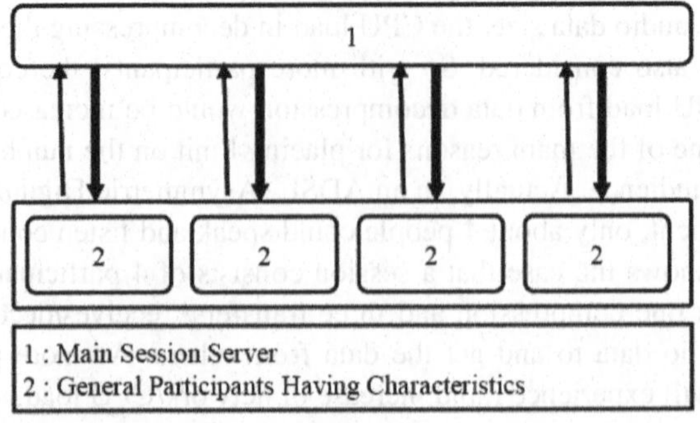

Fig. 3. Centralized mixing-based multi-point audio communication architecture

because the sounds having different frequency counterbalance each other. With other media such as video, text, we can't see these mixing effects.

In a centralized audio mixing approach in Fig. 3, along with outgoing network data size at terminals shown in Fig. 2, incoming network data size and CPU load during decompression can be reduced. Each terminal compresses its own audio data and sends it to the server, which in turn, decompresses all data and mixes them. The size of mixed data will be of only one audio stream. Mixed data will be compressed and distributed to each terminal, which in turn, receives just one stream, decompresses it and sends the decompressed data to audio output, in order to listen to all the other participants' audio.

Irrespective of the number of participants, by sending and receiving just one stream size data, all the participants can speak to all the participants and can listen to all the other participants' audio. This is the remarkable advantage compared with P2P or central relay method.

However, with this approach, when many session being is created (a session means a communication group), the main server had to get lots of network load and processing load caused by decompression, mixing and compression. Because of this, the cost of load balancing and network maintenance will rise very rapidly, according to the number of sessions and terminals. So it didn't seem to be so feasible for multi-user configuration. As CPU load from audio compression/decompression is considerably heavy, server load balancing cost may be much higher than the network cost.

In this paper, we suggest the distributed terminal mixing method to minimize processing time and network loads on servers in central mixing method, and to minimizing processing time and network loads on terminals in P2P method.

In this paper, we're providing a scenario where each session has its own mixing agent responsible for processing and transferring the session's audio data, and there is an audio data relay server which helps network transfer in case network capacity is not enough.

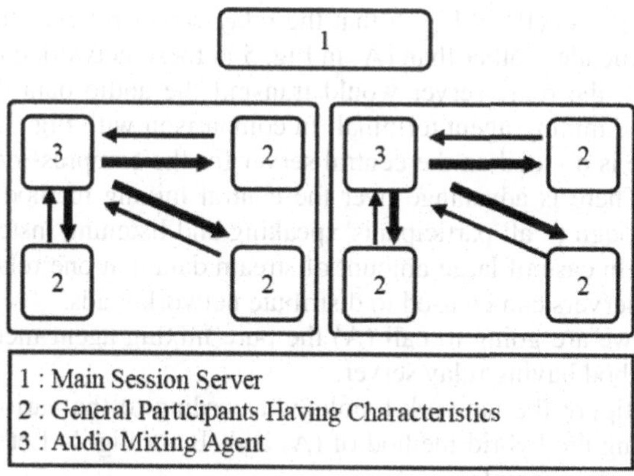

Fig. 4. Distributed terminal mixing audio communication architecture

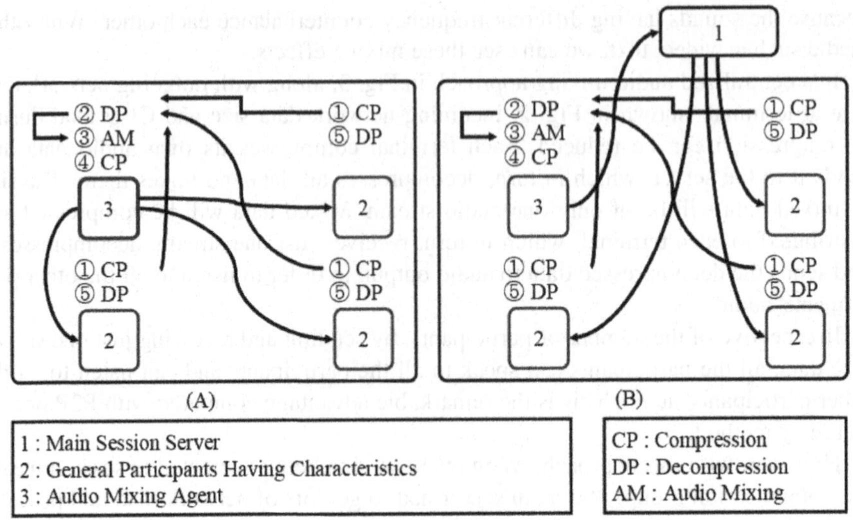

Fig. 5. Two detailed algorithms for the distributed terminal mixing method

The advanced architecture provided here is shown in Fig. 4. (A) and (B) in Fig. 5 represent the two data processing / transfer algorithms for implementing Fig. 4.

In (A) in Fig. 5, a mixing agent terminal, one of the participants takes the role of the main server in centralized mixing method. The mixing server does nothing on the audio data. The normal participants (counterpart of the mixing agent terminal) send their compressed audio data to the mixing agent terminal. And the mixing agent terminal receives all other participants' stream and stores them into each stream buffer. And then, it extracts some audio samples in each time slot, and mixes it into one stream. And the mixing agent terminal sends the mixed stream to all other participants. Other participants receive the stream, and decompress it and output to the audio device. Normal ADSL has a wide download network bandwidth relative to upload network bandwidth. So (B) in Fig. 5 that the relay server relieves the network transmission is recommended rather than (A) in Fig. 5 in these network environment.

In this method, the relay server would transmit the audio data that is mixed and compressed by the mixing agent terminal. In comparison with Fig. 3, the central mixing method, there is no load on the central server for the compression and mixing and decompression. There is advantage over the central mixing method in that only one stream can be enough to all participants' speaking and listening instead of all the participants' stream. In case of large amount of stream data that one relay server can't afford, more relay servers can be used to distribute network loads.

In the Fig. 5, we are going to call (A) the pure mixing agent method, and (B) the mixing agent method having relay server.

We can reconfigure the network topology according to the various situations and conditions by using the hybrid method of (A) and (B) in Fig. 5. Let's take a look into some useful topology example.

The first example is this. The mixing agent terminal processes all the participants' stream until its capability of CPU and network come to a limit. After the limit, central mixing-relay server would process the next participants joining same session. This is reasonably nice for distribution of CPU and network load besides the simplicity in implementation.

So the agent should have enough CPU and network capacity to process all the session data on each terminal.

The mixing agent from (B) in Fig. 5 collects data from participants, mixes and compresses the data, transferring it to the relay server.

If you want for the servers not to be used for mixing or relaying, you can distribute CPU and network load by constructing the tree transfer topology. When the mixing agent terminal comes to a limit in CPU's processing power or network bandwidth, it selects another mixing agent terminal among its children terminal, and then makes it process the some of terminals. The children mixing agent terminal sends its mixed data to there parent mixing agent terminal. In sending audio data mixed, the same topology can be used. For the better quality of distribution, different topology between the upstream and downstream is recommended. This type of transfer topology has a week point in reconstruction of tree when one of mixing agent terminals leaves the session. A good reconstructing algorithm must be accompanied not to degrade audio stream quality. But this is a good adaptation at the point of view of saving maintenance cost.

By adjusting the (A) and (B) in Fig. 5, we can make many useful topologies according to the environment.

The (A) algorithm in Fig. 5 is used In the data for comparison in [Table 1].

Table 1. The numeric comparison between flow control method

<table>
<tr><td colspan="6">• In a N-concurrent user configuration (all can speak and listen)
• The Network Usage Unit: Amount of one stream
• CPU load type: Compression, Decompression, Audio Mixing
• S: Sending , R:Receiving, C:Compression, D:Decompression</td></tr>
<tr><td rowspan="2">Criteria</td><td rowspan="2">P2P Method</td><td rowspan="2">Central Relay Method</td><td rowspan="2">Central Mixing Method</td><td colspan="2">Distributed Terminal Mixing Method</td></tr>
<tr><td>Ordinary Participant</td><td>Mixing Agent</td></tr>
<tr><td>Network Usage Per Participant</td><td>S(N-1)
R(N-1)</td><td>S(1)
R(N-1)</td><td>S(1)
R(1)</td><td>S(1)
R(1)</td><td>S(N-1)
R(N-1)</td></tr>
<tr><td>Network Usage In Server</td><td>0</td><td>S(N*(N-1))
R(N)</td><td>S(N)
R(N)</td><td colspan="2">0</td></tr>
<tr><td>The number of Comp. /Decompression Per Participant (CPU load)</td><td>C(1)
D(N-1)</td><td>C(1)
D(N-1)</td><td>C(1)
D(1)</td><td>C(1)
D(1)</td><td>C(1)
D(N-1)</td></tr>
<tr><td>The number of Comp./Decomp. In Server(CPU load)</td><td>0</td><td>0</td><td>C(1)
D(N)</td><td colspan="2">0</td></tr>
<tr><td>The number of Audio Mixing Per Participant (CPU load)</td><td>1</td><td>1</td><td>0</td><td>0</td><td>1</td></tr>
<tr><td>The number of Audio Mixing In Server (CPU load)</td><td>0</td><td>0</td><td>1</td><td colspan="2">0</td></tr>
<tr><td>Global Network Usage</td><td>N(N-1)</td><td>N*N</td><td>N*2</td><td colspan="2">(N-1)*2</td></tr>
</table>

Seeing the above table, the global network usage in the central mixing method and the distributed terminal mixing method is much less than the P2P method as the N is growing. At the point of view of the global network usage, the distributed terminal mixing method has same amount of network usage, N*2 to central mixing method. But at the point of view of server, because the distributed terminal mixing method does not use server's network, it is far better at the point of view of maintenance cost than the central mixing method.

Taking the account of the CPU load, in P2P method, all participant terminals compresses one time, and decompress N-1 times. In central mixing method, all participant terminals compress and decompress just one time to speak to all participants and to listen to all participants. In distributed terminal mixing method, the ordinary participant terminals compress and decompress once just like central mixing method except that the mixing agent terminal decompresses N-1 times and compress once. Although the central mixing method is better than the distributed terminal mixing method in this respect, the latter is far better than the former in respect to CPU load on server.

The comparison of network usage data gotten from simulation is shown in Fig. 6

All nodes can listen and speak simultaneously. We used 44.1 khz, 16 bits, stereo samples, bitrate of 128 kbps in the simulation. In network, TCP is used. As it shows in Fig. 6, as the number of nodes increase, the distributed missing method is far better than others.

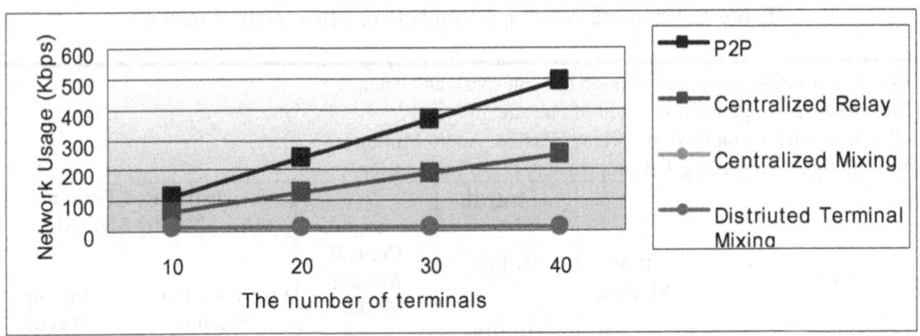

Fig. 6. The network usage for one normal participant

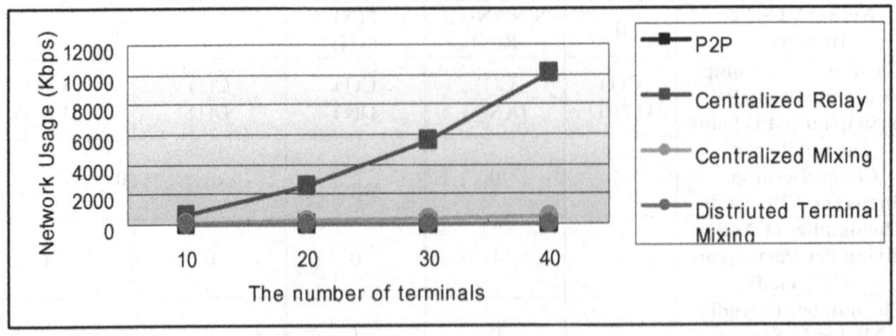

Fig. 7. The network usage in server

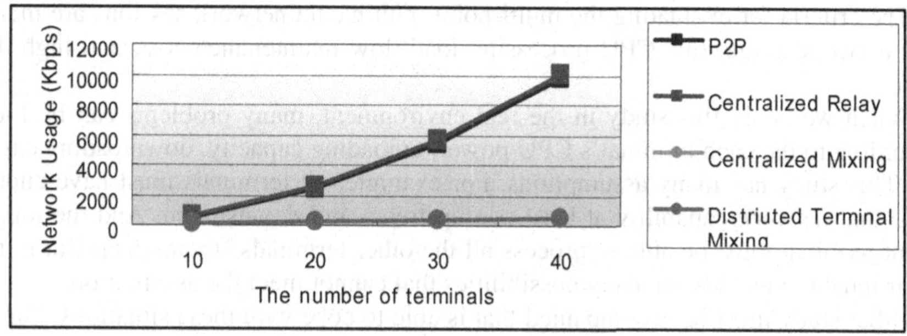

Fig. 8. The global network usage

Fig. 6 shows the network usage for one normal participant according to the number of terminals. In this figure, the centralized mixing method and the distributed terminal mixing method have the same values. And they have always the same value of 2 stream's bandwidth, regardless of the number of terminals.

Fig. 7 shows the network usage in server according to the number of terminals. In this figure, the P2P method and the distributed terminal mixing method have the value of 0 in all cases. This is because in these methods, there is no intervention of server to the communication.

Fig.8 shows the global network usage value, the sum of all terminals' network usage and server's network usage. In this figure, we could see that the network usage increases by geometric progression by the number of terminals, in P2P method and the centralized relay method. But in the centralized mixing method and distributed terminal mixing method, the network usage increases in proportion to the number of terminals. At the point of view of only global network usage, the distributed terminal mixing method is the best method.

In this study, we use some method to select a mixing agent. The first case is that the president takes the responsibility of the mixing agent. In that case there is assumption that the terminal CPU and network is good enough to process the job. And the next case is that we select the mixing agent by measuring and comparing the CPU and network resources of all terminals. In this case, too many changes of topology by using dynamic selection of the mixing agent terminal will result to degradation of audio stream quality. It's recommended not to change the topology too frequently.

4 Conclusion and Further Studies

In this paper, in order to solve the problem of P2P based multi-point audio communication we suggested two major methods. The one is the central mixing method that uses audio's special characteristic that mixing multiple streams makes only one stream. And the other is the distributed terminal mixing method that makes some of the terminals share the CPU and network load of server. We suggested also some adaptations of the two methods. In addition to solve the problem of the existing P2P method, this is far advanced audio flow control method in respect to minimizing maintenance cost.

The criteria for evaluating the multi-point multimedia network sessions are mainly low network usage, low CPU processing load, low maintenance cost, and high data quality.

When we apply this study in the real environment, many problems can be found according to the each terminal's CPU power, uploading capacity, downloading capacity. This study has many assumptions. For example, all terminals must have enough CPU and network capability at least one upstream and downstream. And the mixing agent terminal must be able to process all the other terminals stream data. But in real environment, there are so many possibilities that cannot meet the assumption.

Other study must be accompanied that is able to cope with these situations. For example, network topology must be changed dynamically according to the all situations without user's intervening. And it must be done without the degradation of the stream quality. Although the topology must not be so frequently changed, in case of the blocking of stream it must be changed rapidly. This study doesn't mention the methodology about dynamic topology. This touched just a possibility that dynamic topology can be constructed according to the server and the terminals' CPU and network capabilities.

References

[1] SE. Dering, "Host Extensions for IP Mlticasting", *RFC 1112, Stanford University* , Aug. 1989

[2] A.Oram, "Peer-To-Peer", *O'Reilly*, Mar. 2001

[3] S.G. Lee, "The Study On RMTL(Reliable Multipoint Transport Layer) in IP-multicasting environment", *SungKyunKwan Uni*,, Oct. 1997

[4] Y.S. So, C.Y.Choi, "The Multi-source media streaming capable of distribution the contents in P2P network", *Korea Information Communication Society,* 2004

[5] Tsutomu Kawai, Joutarou Akiyama, Minoru Okada, "Point-to-Multipoint Communication Protocol PTMP and Evaluation of Its Performance", Jan. 1998

[6] H.R. Kim, K.S. Song, J.S. Jeon, "Implementation of Multicast protocl and management of resource for the multi-point multimedia", *Korea Industrial Engineering So-ciety,* 1998

[7] W. Simpson, "The Point-to-Point Protocol (PPP) for the Transmission of Multi-protocol Datagrams over Point-to-Point Links", *RFC 1331*, May. 1992.

[8] H. Schulzrinne, S. Casner, R. Frederick, V. Jacobson, RTP: "A Transport Protocol for Real-Time Applications". RFC 1889, *Audio-Video Transport Working Group*. Jan. 1996.

[9] Endeavors Tech., "Introducing Peer-To-Peer", *White Paper, Endeavors Technology Inc.*, 2002

[10] Y. Kim and Y. Eom, "An Efficient Peer Connection Scheme for Pure P2P Network Environment", *Korea Information Science Society*, Feb. 2004.

Three-Dimensional Representation of Conceptual Fuzzy Relations

Jose A. Olivas and Samuel Rios

Dept. of Information Technologies and Systems
University of Castilla-La Mancha
Paseo de la Universidad 4,
13071, Ciudad Real, Spain
Joseangel.olivas@uclm.es,
i92riros@uco.es

Abstract. In this work, T-DiCoR is presented (Three **Di**mensional **Co**nceptual **R**epresentation) as a tool for representing the fuzzy relations among the most representative concepts of a domain. Using this tool in a Metasearcher, the user may observe what other concepts are related to the searched concept, and what the connection forces are (fuzzy relations between concepts). This knowledge can be useful for making new queries with words conceptually related in a specific domain with the original ones.

1 Introduction

Nowadays, the task of recovering information of big data sources, especially the Web, has great relevancy to many users of different areas and of the whole world. The search engines play a determinant role in this task, but increasingly, the users need help to centre the search on their aims.

In this work a tool is presented that can be useful to centre the search, since it allows showing the relations among the most relevant concepts of a certain domain. This allows the user to refine his queries, verifying what concepts are the most relevant in the domain and with which ones and how they are related.

The presented tool T-DiCoR (Three Dimensional Conceptual Representation) shows the user a three-dimensional form, a graph with the form of molecule, where the nodes are the most relevant concepts of a domain and the edges show the forces (fuzzy) that join them. These edges will be represented in different colours and thicknesses according to the intensity of the relation between the concepts. The user can change the view of the graph using the mouse.

It is very important to know how to get the input matrix that represents the fuzzy relations between the concepts. It is done with a fuzzy aggregation of different values from different sources (as is shown in point 2). In point 3 the T-DiCoR tool and the algorithms used are described. A complete example is explained in section 4, and the paper finishes with some conclusions and future trends.

H.L. Larsen et al. (Eds.): FQAS 2006, LNAI 4027, pp. 681 – 690, 2006.

2 The Input Matrix

The input matrix contains the fuzzy relations among the 20 most important concepts of a specific domain. The weight values came from the aggregation of several different sources:

2.1 Contextual, Linguistic and Ontology Relations (FIS-CRM vectors)

FIS-CRM [1] is a model for representing the concepts contained in any kind of document. It can be considered an extension of the vector space model (VSM). Its main characteristic is that it is fed on the information stored in a fuzzy synonym dictionary and various fuzzy thematic ontologies. The dictionary stores the synonymy degree between every pair of recognized synonyms. Each ontology stores the generality degree between every word and its more general words. The way of calculating this value is the one proposed by Widyantoro & Yen in 2001 [2].

The key of this model is first to construct the base vectors of the documents considering the number of occurrences of the terms (what we call VSM vectors) and afterwards to readjust the vector weights in order to represent concept occurrences, using for this purpose the information stored in the dictionary and the ontologies.

The readjustment process involves sharing the occurrences of a concept among the synonyms which converge in the concept and give a weight to the words that represent a more general concept than the ones contained.

2.2 Causal Relations

To detect the causal relationships that exist in a collection of documents, a starting point could be to detect conditional phrases. Nevertheless, this is not an easy task. Descartes could not have possibly imagined that to propose his famous phrase "I think, therefore I am", would have given birth to so many conjectures and interpretations for centuries after. In reality, what did he want to say, "First I think and after I am a person, or As I am capable of thought, I am a person".

To sum up, even on this occasion the intention of Descartes seems clear when he expressed his maxim, it is not easy to interpret and format the information expressed in natural language, especially when it involves complex sentences with complicated turns.

With the aim of detecting conditional phrases, we have developed a basic system [3] of detecting structures and a classification of sentences that allows us to locate, in terms of basic components (verb tenses, adverbs, linguistic turns, etc.), certain causal forms.

To make the grammatical analysis, we have observed on the one hand, that we can separate certain causal relationships based on the verb form used, while on the other hand we can separate others based on the adverbs used in the sentences. Both analyses give rise to some causal rules that we will use afterwards to make an automatic extraction of knowledge. In the same way, every structure is subdivided into two structures which correspond to the antecedent and consequence of the causal relationship, and a parameter that measures the degree of certainty, conjecture, or compliance of the said causal relationship. In other words, it is not the same to form a sentence such as: “If I win the lottery, I will buy a car”, in which there is no doubt that if the antecedent comes true the consequence will come true, as to form the sentence “If we had bought a ticket in Segovia, we could have won the lottery” which leaves many more doubts and conjectures, in which you cannot be sure that the completion of the antecedent guarantees the consequences.

2.3 Aggregation of Fuzzy Values

The aggregation for constructing the input matrix is still an open problem. Nowadays it is done using standard OWA operators [4] or more sophisticated ones, such as the ones presented by Castro and Trillas [5], for example:
Arithmetic Weighted Generalized Mean: $m(A, B)(x) = \sup_a A(a) \wedge B((x-(1- p)a)/p)$, $p \in [0, 1]$
Geometric Weighted Generalized Mean: $m(A, B)(x) = \sup_a A(a) \wedge B((x/a^{(1-p)})^{1-p}$, $p \in [0, 1]$, or
Fuzzy Weighted Generalized Mean: $m(A, B)(x) = p\, A(x) + (1-p)\, B(x)$, $p \in [0, 1]$.

3 T-DiCoR

T-DiCoR (Three Dimensional Conceptual Representation) is designed to show the user a three-dimensional graph with the form of molecule, where the nodes are the most relevant concepts of a domain (up to a maximum of 20, for visualization reasons) and the edges are the forces (fuzzy) that join them (a concept will take 7 relations as a maximum, for the same reason). These edges will be represented in different colours (from the coldest up to the hottest) and thickness according to the intensity of the relation between two concepts. The user can rotate the graph using the mouse. The user can also choose one or more concepts to see them separately (with their relations).

3.1 Used Technology

The tool has been developed with Microsoft Visual Studio 2005 (V. 8.0.50727.42) in C# language.

3.2 Transformation: Fuzzy Conceptual Matrix to Fuzzy Conceptual Graph

The Conceptual Matrix is characterized for being square and triangular, in which every row represents the conceptual relations that every term has with the others. Due to this, the matrix only contains floating point numerical values, there must exist another vector that contains the list of ordered terms so that the relative position with the above mentioned vector coincides with the position inside the matrix.

The matrix will transform into a graph in which every node will represent a term and every edge will represent the existing relation between two concepts. The steps that the algorithm will follow are the following:

Being that:

F: the data file that contains the terms and the relations.
t: a term.
M: the matrix.
f: a row of the matrix.
c: a column of the matrix.
L: list of terms.
G (V, E): the graph where V are the nodes and E the edges.

Transformation Matrix-Graph (Matrix M, Graph G):

1.-To read the data file and extract the list L of terms and the matrix M of information.
2.-For each t ∈ L
  2.1. To insert a node v in V
3.-For each f ∈ M
  3.1.-For each c ∈ M when c> f
    3.1.1. To create an edge from the term [row] up to the term [column]

3.3 Representation of the Fuzzy Conceptual Graph

3D Model

The graph was designed in a 3D model due to the fact that this model facilitates the visualization of a graph that will be complex enough.

Chemical Molecule

The 3D representation is based on a model used in another tool that visualizes chemical molecules, adapting it to our needs [6]. The particularity of this visor is that it allowed rotating the molecule on itself using the mouse.

Really, the representation is in 2 dimensions and the nodes are shown in the position of their coordinates XY, but to simulate a 3 dimensional space, when we rotate the graph with a single drag-and-drop with the mouse left button, the tool uses a mathematical model that in addition to re-calculate the positions XY, it also calculate the Z coordinate of all the nodes. When it re-draws the nodes in their new positions, the edges are easy to draw.

The mathematical model that simulates the graph rotation is based on the calculation of the positions by matrices, but it could be summarized as follows:

1. First, we have to calculate the rotation angles for the two dimensions of the representation:

$$X_{angle} = \left(prev_y - y\right)\left(\frac{360}{width}\right) \quad (1)$$

$$Y_{angle} = \left(x - prev_x\right)\left(\frac{360}{height}\right) \quad (2)$$

Being that:

$prev_x/prev_y$: Previous mouse 'x' and 'y' coordinates, that is, the coordinates that we obtain when the user clicks on the graph drawing.

x/y: Actual mouse 'x' and 'y' coordinates.

width/height: Dimensions of the representation zone.

2. Then, when we have obtained the angles, the next step is to calculate the new positions of all the graph nodes as follows:
   a. We could transform the 'y' and 'z' coordinates of the nodes position with the 'Xangle':

$$\begin{aligned} ct &= \cos(Xangle) \\ st &= \sin(Xangle) \\ \\ n_y &= n_y \cdot ct + n_z \cdot st \\ n_z &= n_z \cdot ct - n_y \cdot st \end{aligned} \tag{3}$$

   The node position vector is:

$$N = (n_x, n_y, n_z)$$

   b. And the 'Yangle' could transform the 'x' and 'z' coordinates:

$$\begin{aligned} ct &= \cos(Yangle) \\ st &= \sin(Yangle) \\ \\ n_x &= n_x \cdot ct + n_z \cdot st \\ n_z &= n_z \cdot ct - n_x \cdot st \end{aligned} \tag{4}$$

   The node position vector is:

$$N = (n_x, n_y, n_z)$$

In conclusion, each node final position will be calculate using the (3) and (4) formulas.

Positioning Nodes. Fruchterman – Reingold Algorithm

Once the graph is generated, the only thing that we must still do is to redistribute the nodes of the same one so that its representation is the clearest possible (that is to say, avoiding crossings of edges and that the nodes stay closer to one another). For this, the algorithm of Fruchterman - Reingold [7] is used, it is a model based on the tracing of graphs directed by forces.

The method that it uses is based on the Eades' *spring embedder* [7], which can be briefly explained by saying that the nodes of the graph are like positive charges that are repelled, and the edges that join them are like springs that exercise a force of attraction between them (Hooke's physical law).

The algorithm of Fruchterman - Reingold is implemented as follows:

Notation:

$$G = (V, E)$$

$$p_v = (x_v, y_v, z_v)$$

$$\overrightarrow{p_u p_v} = \frac{p_u - p_v}{\|p_u - p_v\|_2} \tag{5}$$

$$d_{uv} = \left\|\overrightarrow{p_u - p_v}\right\| = \|p_u - p_v\|_2 \tag{6}$$

Repulsive force between nodes:

$$k = C\sqrt{\frac{a}{|V|}} \tag{7}$$

$$f_r(u,v) = \frac{k^2}{d_{uv}} \overrightarrow{p_v p_u} \tag{8}$$

Where:

C: experimental constant

a: area of the surface where the graph is going to be represented

|V |: number of nodes of the graph

Attractive force of the edge:

$$f_a(u,v) = \frac{d_{uv}{}^2}{k} \overrightarrow{p_v p_u} \tag{9}$$

Total force on a node:

$$f(u,v) = \sum_{(u,v)\in E} f_a(u,v) + \sum_{v\in V, u\neq v} f_r(u,v) \tag{10}$$

Algorithm:

FR (Graph G)

1. Assign an initial temperature ($t = t_0$)
2. Randomly assign a position to every node v of G
3. Repeat M times:

   3.1.-For every $v \in V$

   3.1.1. Calculate $f(v)$ (according to the previous formula)

   3.2.-For each p_v

   3.2.1. $p_v = p_v + \frac{f(v)}{\|f(v)\|} \min(\|f(v)\|, t)$ (11)

   3.2.2. Control that p_v does not stay out of the area of drawing

   3.2.3. t = cool (t)

Painting the Edges According to Their Weights

The last important aspect to consider is the weight of the relations between terms. The idea of painting the edges with a specific thickness and colour is used to represent the degree of relation that the connected terms have. So, a small weight will be represented by a thin line and a cold colour such as the green. Nevertheless, a strong relation will be represented by a thick red line. The intermediate relations will be represented with thicknesses and colours spread between both ends.

4 An Example

An example of the tool is presented. The domain used is "My home". A set of documents of the field were retrieved, and the 20 most relevant concepts were: *Home, place, domicile, abode, habitation, dwelling house, house, household, legal residence, base, property, space, family, ménage, position, situation, placement, stance, emplacement* and *location*. Then, the fuzzy relations matrix is the one that it is shown in table 1.

Table 1. Input matrix for the domain "My home"

	1	2	3	4	5	6	7	8	9	10	11	12	13	14	15	16	17	18	19	20
1 home		.66	.83	.44	.36	.78	.86	.88												
2 place			.53		.32		.68				.94	.91				.76				
3 domicile									.96	.52				.46				.38		
4 abode					.32		.41		.95	.65		.58								
5 habitation											.55									
6 dwelling house																				
7 house											.65	.62		.54						
8 household																				
9 legal residence											.78									.62
10 base															.74	.71	.56		.92	
11 property																				
12 space														.89				.64		.51
13 family														.79						
14 menage																.94				
15 position																			.74	.75
16 situation																	.81			.88
17 placement																			.99	
18 stance																				
19 emplacement																				.92
20 location																				

Table 1 shows the fuzzy relations between concepts, extracted from the aggregation of the fuzzy values of its linguistic, contextual, ontological and causal relations among the concepts.

Figure1 shows the tool interface and the graph generated to visualize in 3D all the relations of the input matrix. It can be observed that 20 concepts could be the limit for a correct visualization of all concepts and relations.

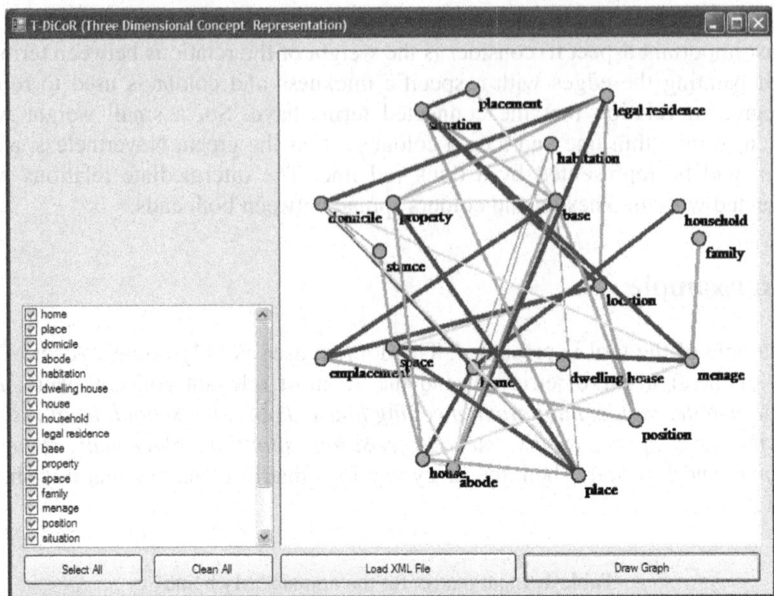

Fig. 1. Graph among all the concepts

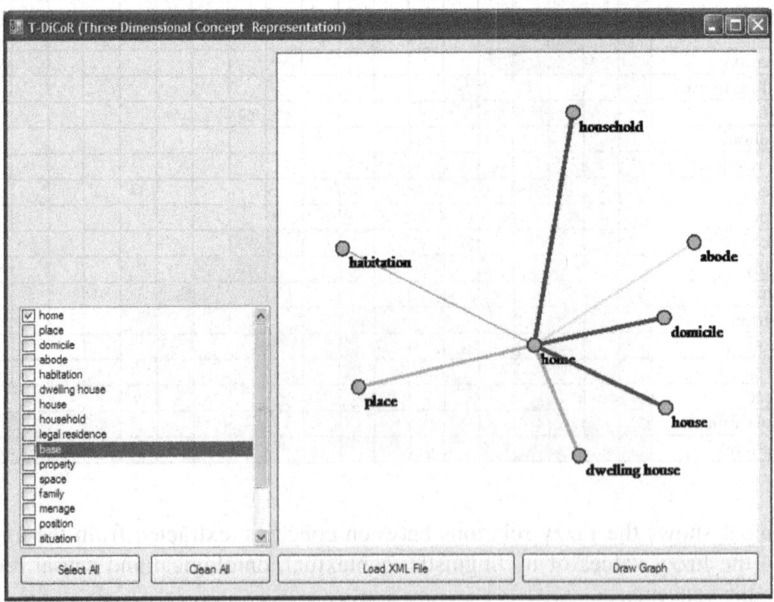

Fig. 2. Graph related to the concept "home"

Figures 2 and 3 depict the detailed relations of the concept "home", the concepts "home" and "base", and the concepts "home", "base" and "position" (figure 3).

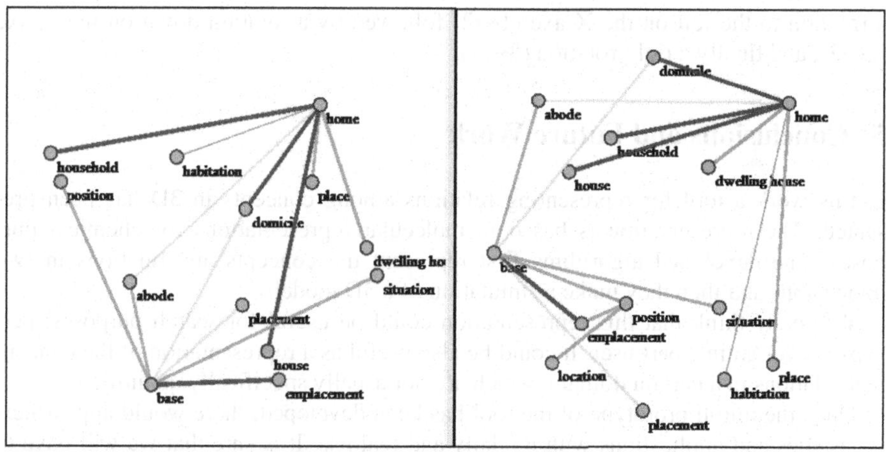

Fig. 3. Graphs related to the relations between "home" and "base" and to the relations between "home", "base" and "position"

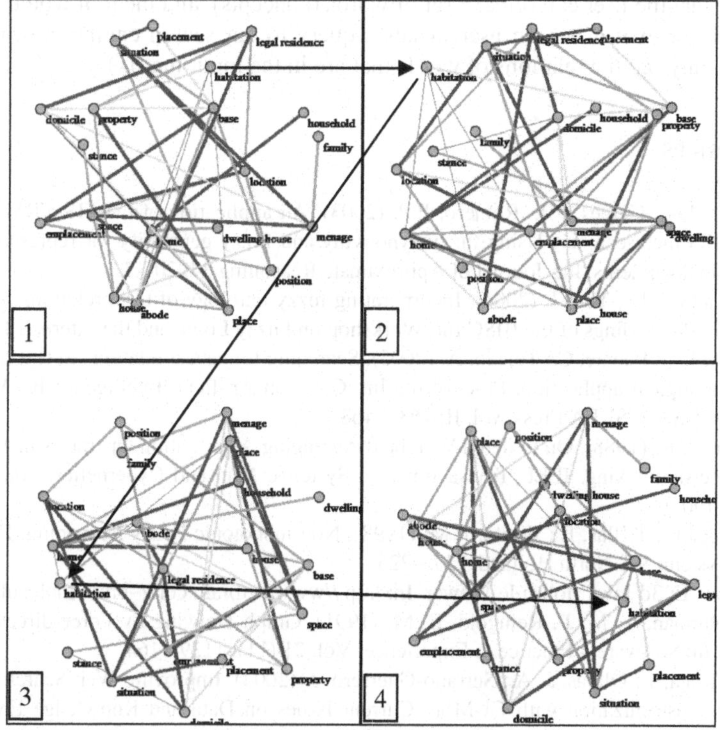

Fig. 4. Example of a 3D movement

In figure 4, a mouse 3D movement done by the user can be observed. Since it is difficult to represent 3D movements in a static 2D figure, the movements in figure 4 can be followed focusing our point of view in the concept "habitation". First, there is a rotation to the left on the X axe (1→2) followed by a rotation down on the Y axe (2→3), and finally a right rotation (3→4).

5 Conclusions and Future Work

In this work a tool for representing relations among concepts in 3D has been presented. The representation is based in molecular representations for chemical purposes. The developed algorithms first represent the concepts and relations in two dimensions and then they make a simulation of a 3D model.

We really think that this representation could be useful for search purposes, perhaps not for an inexpert user. It could be also useful as a representation of the conceptual relations in a certain domain, which are not usually specifically quantified.

Once the initial prototype of the tool has been developed, there would appear new necessities and applications with its daily and real use. It is sure that we will have to work in the integration of T-DiCoR in the framework that our team had been developing (tools such as FISS [1] or GUMSe [8]). For example, to define the XML formats of the interchange documents will be necessary. Another interesting improvement could be that the user can select a set of words (concepts), and the tool would generate the graph (or even when an user makes a query to our search engine, nowadays the user can only see the relations of words that are in the input matrix).

References

1. Olivas, J.A., Garcés, P.J., Romero, F.P. (2003). An application of the FIS-CRM model to the FISS metasearcher: Using fuzzy synonymy and fuzzy generality for representing concepts in documents, Int. Journal of Approximate Reasoning 34, 201-219.
2. Widyantoro, D., Yen, J. (2001). Incorporating fuzzy ontology of term relations in a search engine, Proceedings of the BISC Int. Workshop on Fuzzy Logic and the Internet, 155-160.
3. Olivas, J.A.; Puente, C.; Tejado, A. (2005). Searching for causal relations in text documents for ontological application. Proc. of the Int. Conf. on Artificial Intelligence IC-AI'05, Las Vegas, USA, CSREA Press, vol. II. 463 – 468.
4. Yager, R. R. (1988). On Ordered Weighted Averaging Aggregation Operators in Multicriteria Decisionmaking. IEEE Transactions on Systems, Man and Cybernetics, vol. 18, nº 1, 183 - 190.
5. Castro, J.L.; Trillas, E.; Zurita, J. M. (1998). Non-monotonic Fuzzy Reasoning. Fuzzy Sets and Systems 94, North Holland, 217 - 225.
6. Harlow, E: 3d Java Molecule Viewer. In: http://www.netbrain.com/~brain/molecule/, 1999.
7. Fruchterman, T. M. J., Reingold, E. M. (1991). Graph Drawing by Force-directed Placement. In: Software – Practice & Experience, Vol. 21 (11): 1129-1164.
8. de la Mata, J.; Olivas, J. A.; Serrano-Guerrero, J. (2004). Improving Web Search by Using Query Customization with GUMSe, Current Issues on Data and Knowledge Engineering EUROFUSE'04, Warsaw, Poland, 325 – 333.

Fuzzy Ontologies for the Semantic Web

Elie Sanchez[1] and Takahiro Yamanoi[2]

[1] Université de la Méditerranée, LIF – Biomathématiques et Informatique Médicale
Faculté de Médecine, 13385 Marseille Cedex 5, France
elie.sanchez@medecine.univ-mrs.fr

[2] Hokkai Gakuen University, Division of Electronics and Information Engineering
Faculty of Engineering, Sapporo 064-0926, Japan
yamanoi@eli.hokkai-s-u.ac.jp

Abstract. It is presented several connections between Fuzzy Logic, the Semantic Web, and its components (Ontologies, Description Logics). It is then introduced and illustrated by an example ("Ontology of Art") a Fuzzy Ontology structure, Lexicon and Knowledge Base.

1 Introduction: Fuzzy Logic, Semantic Web and Ontologies

The field of Fuzzy Logic has been maturing for forty years. These years have witnessed a tremendous growth in the number and variety of applications, with a real-world impact across a wide variety of domains with humanlike behavior and reasoning. Fuzzy logic is now confronted with a new challenge, namely the vision of the Semantic Web. During recent years, important initiatives have led to reports of connections between Fuzzy Logic and the Internet [11,12]. Scattered papers were published on Fuzzy Logic and the Semantic Web, and a special session was organized during the previous IPMU conference [8]. Then, the first workshop on Fuzzy Logic and the Semantic Web (FLSW) [5] at Marseille was attended by European experts in the field. During BISC-SE 2005 at Berkeley, a panel [4, pp.27-30] discussed recent advances in these combined fields. A recently published volume [13] has shown the positive role Fuzzy Logic, and more generally Soft Computing, can play in the development of the Semantic Web. Finally, the Second Workshop on Fuzzy Logic and the Semantic Web (FLSW-II) will take place during IPMU 2006 at Paris. These are healthy symptoms that indicate, as we believe, that in the coming years, the Semantic Web will be a major field of applications of Fuzzy Logic.

The Semantic Web allows relational knowledge to be embedded as metadata in web pages enabling machines to use ontologies and inference rules in retrieving and manipulating data. *Ontologies* are a key component of the Semantic Web. There are several ways to describe the meaning of concepts (or classes of individuals or categories or types) and relationships between them. Ontologies facilitate a machine processable representation of information. They bridge an effective communication gap between users and machines.

There are many (descriptive) definitions of ontologies, depending also on communities. Basically, they are executable, formal conceptualizations with shared agreement

H.L. Larsen et al. (Eds.): FQAS 2006, LNAI 4027, pp. 691 – 699, 2006.

between members of a community of interest. They can be viewed as "collections of statements written in a language such as RDF that define the relations between concepts and specify logical rules for reasoning about them. Computers *can understand* the meaning of semantic data on a web page by following links to specified ontologies" [3].

The most typical kind of ontology has a *taxonomy* and a *set of inference rules.* Note that besides the Semantic Web, ontologies have been studied in various domains, for ex. in knowledge engineering, natural language processing, knowledge management, information retrieval, digital libraries, electronic commerce, etc.

There are several types of ontologies, and one may consider, among others:

- *Upper-level (or generic or reference) ontologies.* They describe general concepts, like structure, space, time, state, substance, which are independent of a particular domain.
- *Domain ontologies.* They cover concepts in particular domains and in a *specific way* (for ex. human anatomy or E. coli) or in a *general way* (for ex. organs or gene function). They are the most common and agreed-upon types of ontologies.
- *Task (or application) ontologies.* They express conceptualizations relative to task models (for ex. reasoning processes for medical diagnosis).

Note that in biology, most ontologies are formed by a mixture of these three types.

The construction of an ontology implies the parallel construction of a vocabulary for it. As T. Gruber pointed out in [6], "pragmatically, a common ontology defines the vocabulary with which queries and assertions are exchanged among agents." But most of the information which relates to world knowledge is ill-structured, uncertain and imprecise. What is then needed is a collection of tools drawn from fuzzy logic, for example Zadeh's *PNL* (Precisiated Natural Language) [19,20]. Usually in the Semantic Web, knowledge is assumed to be crisply defined and no uncertainty or imprecision is allowed in the description of objects. The Semantic Web, as presented under *W3C* recommendations [17], deals with hard semantics in the description and manipulation of crisp data, like in "the Huveaune is a river." RDF based languages do not have the ability to represent soft semantics as in "the Huveaune is a *very_small* river." To process this type of information, fuzzy logic concepts and techniques are needed: "the Huveaune is a *very_small* river" can be translated into "length(Huveaune) is *very_ small.*" It can then be encoded in RDF format with a triple

< Huveaune , length , very_small >,

where the term "very_small" is assumed to be the label of a fuzzy set *[note: the Huveaune is a 51 km long river that flows into the Mediterranean sea at Marseille].* It can be considered as a typed literal and an XML schema [18] can be defined to describe its membership function.

2 Fuzzy Ontologies

There has been different approaches to characterize or define *fuzzy ontologies*. In [16] the query refinement *PASS* System (Personalized Abstract Search Services) uses a fuzzy ontology of term associations to suggest alternative queries for searching for abstracts of research papers. The ontology is automatically generated. It provides information on sets of terms with *broader* and *narrower* semantic meaning.

The following chapters of [13], that we are going to survey, report an overview and recent advances on fuzzy ontologies. Our approach on Fuzzy Ontologies and related structures will be presented in section 4.

In *"On the Expressiveness of the Languages for the Semantic Web - Making a Case for 'A Little More'"*, Ch. Thomas and A. Sheth introduce the need for fuzzy-probabilistic formalisms on the Semantic Web, in particular within OWL. In *"Fuzzy ontologies for information retrieval on the WWW"*, D. Parry uses fuzzy ontologies, and presents a broad survey of relevant techniques, leading up to the notions of fuzzy search and fuzzy ontologies.

The second section, "Fuzzy description logics for ontology construction," deals with fuzzy description logics in theoretical aspects and applications. In *"A Fuzzy Description Logic for the Semantic Web"*, U. Straccia describes a fuzzy version of SHOIN(D), the corresponding Description Logic of the ontology description language OWL DL. He shows that its representation and reasoning capabilities go clearly beyond classical SHOIN(D). In *"What does mathematical fuzzy logic offer to description logic ?"*, Petr Hajek proposes a fuzzy description logic based on fuzzy predicate logic, to deal with vague (imprecise) concepts. In *"Possibilistic uncertainty and fuzzy features in description logic. A preliminary discussion"*, D. Dubois, J. Mengin, and H. Prade introduce another approach by injecting fuzzy features in Description Logics, this time based on fuzzy and possibilistic logic. In *"Uncertainty and Description Logic Programs over Lattices"*, U. Straccia presents a Description Logic framework for the management of uncertain information. In this approach, sentences are certain to some degree, where certainty values are taken from a certainty lattice. Finally, in the last chapter of this section, *"Fuzzy Quantification in Fuzzy Description Logics"*, D. Sanchez and A. Tettamanzi, introduce reasoning procedures for a fuzzy description logic with fuzzy quantifiers.

In *"Bottom-up Extraction and Maintenance of Ontology-based Metadata"*, P. Ceravolo, A. Corallo, E. Damiani, G. Elia, M. Viviani and A. Zilli, present an approach to build fuzzy ontologies in a bottom-up fashion, by clustering documents, based on a fuzzy representation of XML documents structure and content.

In *"A fuzzy logic approach to information retrieval using an ontology-based representation of documents"*, M. Baziz, M. Boughanem, G. Pasi and H. Prade, work on Information Retrieval using fuzzy ontologies. In *"Towards a Semantic Portal for Oncology using a Description Logic with Fuzzy Concrete Domains"*, M. d'Aquin, J. Lieber and A. Napoli, present a work on encoding medical guidelines in fuzzy description logics and using that for a portal. The three systems that are presented are fully implemented within the KASIMIR oncology project. In *"Fuzzy Relational Oncological Model in Information Search Systems"*, R. Pereira, I. Ricarte and F. Gomide, introduce another approach to Information Retrieval using fuzzy ontologies encoded by fuzzy relations.

Finally, in *"Evolving Ontologies for Intelligent Decision Support"*, P. Gottgtroy, N. Kasabov and S. MacDonell, integrate soft computing techniques and ontology engineering. They investigate the rather different topic of evolving ontologies, presenting biomedical case studies.

3 Fuzzy Logic and Description Logics

Description Logics (DLs) [1] are a logical reconstruction of frame-based knowledge representation languages, that can be used to represent the knowledge of an application domain in a structured and formally well-understood way. For ex., here are some simple assertions:

"Human $\sqsubseteq$ Mammal"

"Woman $\sqcap$ Parent $\equiv$ Mother"

"(Human$\sqcap\neg$Male)$\sqcap\exists$married.Biologist$\sqcap$($\geq$3hasChild)$\sqcap\forall$hasChild.student" (denotes "a woman who is married to a biologist and has at least three children, all of whom are students.")

They are considered as a good compromise between expressive power and computational complexity. DLs are essentially the theoretical counterpart of the Web Ontology Language OWL DL [7], the state of the art language to specify ontologies. DLs can be used to define, integrate and maintain ontologies (see [2].) But these DLs embodied in Semantic Web languages do not allow a treatment of uncertainty and imprecision encountered in real-world applications. To this end, DLs have been extended with fuzzy capabilities, yielding *FDLs* (Fuzzy Description Logics) in which concepts are interpreted as fuzzy sets. In [14] U. Straccia has extended the DL $\mathcal{ALC}$, a significant representative of DLs. For example a *concept* C of the language $\mathcal{ALC}$ has an *interpretation* I, which is a pair I = ($\Delta^I, \cdot^I$) consisting of a *domain* Δ^I and an *interpretation function* $\cdot^I$. In FDL, a concept C is interpreted as a fuzzy set and a statement like "a is C" has a truth-value in [0,1]. In this case, $\cdot^I$ is an *interpretation function* mapping C into a membership function C^I, $C^I : \Delta^I \rightarrow [0,1]$. Acting on concepts, the crisp operations of conjunction, disjunction, negation and quantification are naturally extended to their fuzzy counterparts [14]. Here are some examples of assertions, involving fuzzy sets [15]:

"YoungPerson = Person$\sqcap\exists$age.Young", where *Young* is the label of a fuzzy set;

"SportsCar = Car$\sqcap\exists$speed.very(High)", where *very* is a concept modifier and *High* is a fuzzy concrete predicate over the domain of speed expressed in km/h.

4 Fuzzy Ontology Structure, Lexicon and Knowledge Base

The following developments are an extension of work on crisp ontologies [10]. Now a *fuzzy ontology structure* and other associated structures will be introduced: *lexicon* and *knowledge base.*

Basically, a fuzzy ontology structure can be defined as consisting of concepts, of fuzzy relations among concepts, of a concept hierarchy or taxonomy, of non-hierarchical associative relationships and of a set of ontology axioms, expressed in an appropriate logical language.

Then, a lexicon for a fuzzy ontology will consist of lexical entries for concepts (knowledge about them can be given by fuzzy attributes, with context-dependent

values), of lexical entries for fuzzy relations, coupled with weights expressing the strength of associations, and of reference functions linking lexical entries to concepts or relations they refer to.
So, a Fuzzy Ontology structure can now be defined as follows.

Definition 1. A *Fuzzy Ontology structure* is a quintuple

$$O := (C, R, T, A, X),$$

where

- C is a set of *(fuzzy) concepts* (or *classes* — cf. in OWL — of individuals, or *categories*, or *types*), for ex.: Mountain, Patient, Cell, Diabetes, Pneumonia, Fracture of neck of femur, etc. Concepts can be *primitive concepts* or *defined from other concepts*, for ex.: "*Prokaryotic cells* are cells that do not have a nucleus." Note the fuzziness, and vagueness, that can be inherent in the definition of concepts. For ex. a *hill* is "a landform that extends less than 600 metres above the surrounding terrain (the Encyclopædia Britannica requires a prominence of 2,000 feet — 610 m — for a *mountain*) and that is smaller than a mountain." Many hills are higher than 600 metres, but hills are generally smaller (note that in the definition of a *mountain,* one has: a *mountain* is generally much higher and steeper than a *hill*, but there is considerable overlap ...)."
- R is set of *(fuzzy) relations* (or *roles*, or *slots*) in C x C, for ex.: "the concept *Nucleus* has a *part-of* relationship with the concept *Cell*" or "a *Very Tall* person is *Tall*."
- T is a relation in C x C, called *Taxonomy* (or *concept hierarchy*). It organizes concepts into sub-(super-)concept tree structures, most commonly in *Specialisation* relationships (for ex. "an *enzyme* is_a *protein*" or "*cancer* is_a *disease*") or in *Mereological* (or *Partonomic*) relationships (for ex. $T(C_1, C_2)$ means that C_1 is a subconcept of C_2, like in "*eukaryotic cells* are *cells* that have a nucleus").
- A is a set of non-taxonomic (fuzzy) *Associative* relationships that relate concepts across tree structures, for ex.:
  - *Naming* relationships, describing the names of concepts
  - *Locating* relationships, describing the relative location of concepts
  - *Functional* relationships, describing the functions (or properties) of concepts
- X is a set of *Ontology Axioms* (or *rules*), expressed in an appropriate logical language, for ex. asserting class subsumption, equivalence, more generally to (fuzzily) constrain the possible values of concepts or instances (for "*instances,*" see below).

Now, a *lexicon* is a list of words in a language, a *vocabulary*, including some knowledge of how each word is used. Each word, or group of words, in a lexicon is described in a *lexical entry*. So, a lexicon can be viewed as an index that maps a written form of a word to information about that word. Let us now define a lexicon associated with a fuzzy ontology structure.

Definition 2. A *Lexicon* for the fuzzy ontology structure O := (C, R, T, A, X) is a quadruple

$$L := (L^C, L^R, F, G)$$

consisting of:

- a set L^C of lexical entries for concepts; knowledge about them is given by (fuzzy) attributes, with context-dependent values
- a set L^R of lexical entries for (fuzzy) relations, from C to C, coupled with weights in [0,1] expressing the strength of associations
- two *reference functions* F and G ($F : L^C \rightarrow 2^C$ and $G : L^R \rightarrow 2^R$) that link lexical entries of L^C, resp. of L^R, to the set of concepts, resp. of relations, they refer to.

Because an ontology is a conceptualization of a domain, it is not supposed to contain instances, hence the following definition.

Definition 3. A *Fuzzy Knowledge Base* structure is a couple

$$KB = (O, I)$$

where O := (C, R, T, A, X) is a Fuzzy Ontology structure and I is a set of *Instances* (or *Individuals*) associated with the ontology, i.e. 'objects' represented by a concept. For ex.: *Haptoglobin* is an instance of the concept *Protein*, or in *"Carol has Diabetes"*, *"Carol"* is an instance/individual and *"Diabetes"* is a concept/class.

Illustrative Example

(Fuzzy) Ontology Structure (see figure 1): Ontology of Art

$C = \{C_1,C_2,C_3,...,C_{24}\}$

$R = \{r_1,r_2,r_3,...,r_9\}$

$T(C_2,C_1)$, $T(C_3,C_1)$,...., $T(C_6,C_1)$, $T(C_{15},C_{16})$

$r_1(C_4,C_7)$, $r_1(C_4,C_8)$, $r_1(C_4,C_9)$

$r_2(C_4,C_{10})$, $r_2(C_4,C_{11})$, $r_2(C_4,C_{12})$

$r_3(C_4,C_{13})$

$r_4(C_4,C_{14})$, $r_4(C_{13},C_{14})$

$r_5(C_5,C_{15})$

$r_6(C_4,C_{17})$, $r_6(C_4,C_{18})$, $r_6(C_4,C_{19})$, $r_6(C_5,C_{17})$, $r_6(C_5,C_{18})$, $r_6(C_5,C_{19})$

$r_7(C_{19},C_{20})$

$r_8(C_5,C_{21})$, $r_8(C_5,C_{22})$, $r_8(C_5,C_{23})$

$r_9(C_{23},C_{24})$

Lexicon (see figures 2 and 3)

L^C = {artist, musician, singer, painter, sculptor, dancer, ..., marble, region}

L^R = {paints, uses, is_influenced_by,…, creates, comes_from}

F(artist) = $\{C_1\}$, F(musician) = $\{C_2\}$, F(singer) = $\{C_3\}$, F(painter) = $\{C_4,C_{13}\}$, …, F(region) = $\{C_{24}\}$

$T(C_2,C_1)$ = is_a, $T(C_3,C_1)$ = is_a, ..., $T(C_{15},C_{16})$ = is_a

G(paints) = $\{r_1\}$, G(uses) = $\{r_2, r_8\}$, G(creates) = $\{r_5\}$,…, G(comes_from) = $\{r_9\}$.

Relations in R (r_i's) can be associated with weights, expressing the strength of relations, or linguistic quantifiers. For ex. “a painter (C_4) paints (r_1) *mostly* still life (C_9)” or “he prefers using (r_2) water colors (C_{10}), with a *weight of preference* $w_{4;10}$ in [0,1]” or “he is influenced_by (r_3) a *famous* painter (C_{13}), with weight $w_{4;13}$.”

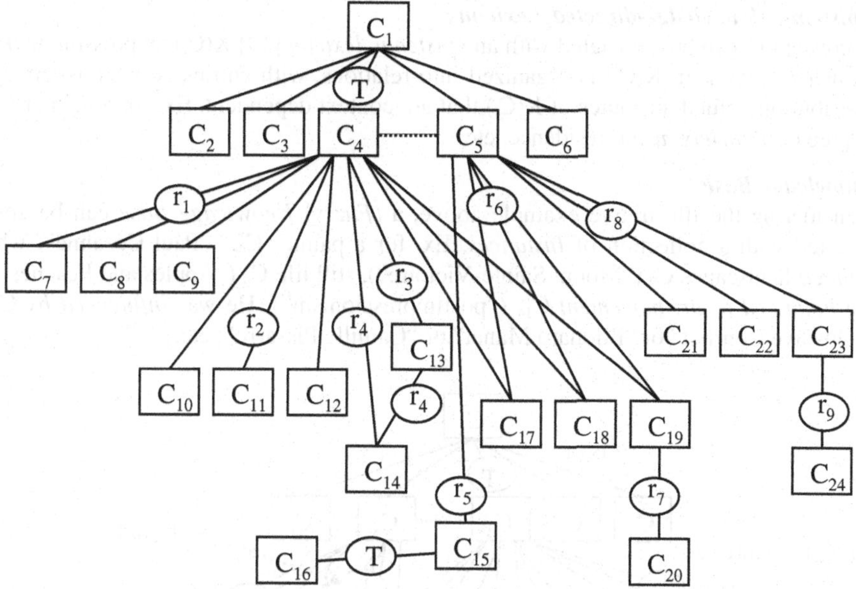

Fig. 1. Ontology of Art

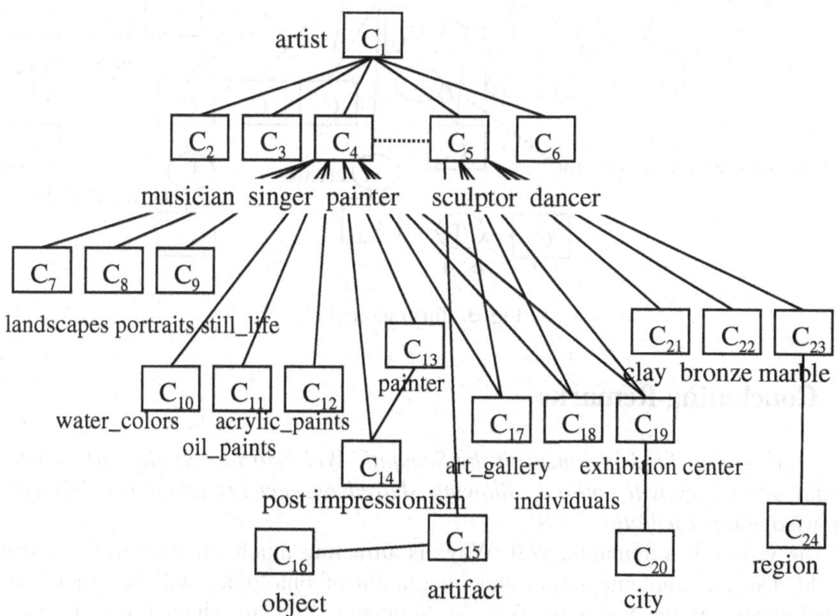

Fig. 2. Illustration of L^c

Epistemic (knowledge-directed)Lexicons

A concept C_i can be associated with an *epistemic lexicon* [19] $K(C_i)$, expressing *world knowledge* about it. $K(C_i)$ is organized into relations, with entries defined as (fuzzy) distribution-valued attributes of $K(C_i)$ that are context dependent. Ex. for a painter C_4: degree of *notoriety*, *usual* residence, etc.

Knowledge Base

Considering the illustrative example above, a *(Fuzzy) Knowledge Base* can be constructed with a collection of *Instances.* Ex. for a painter C_4: "Paul Cézanne", who *painted* landscapes C_7 ("Mount Sainte-Victoire"), still life C_9 ("Apples and Peaches"). He *belonged to art movement* C_{14} ("postimpressionism"). He was *influenced by* C_{14} ("Gustave Courbet" or "Edouard Manet" or "Camille Pissarro", etc.).

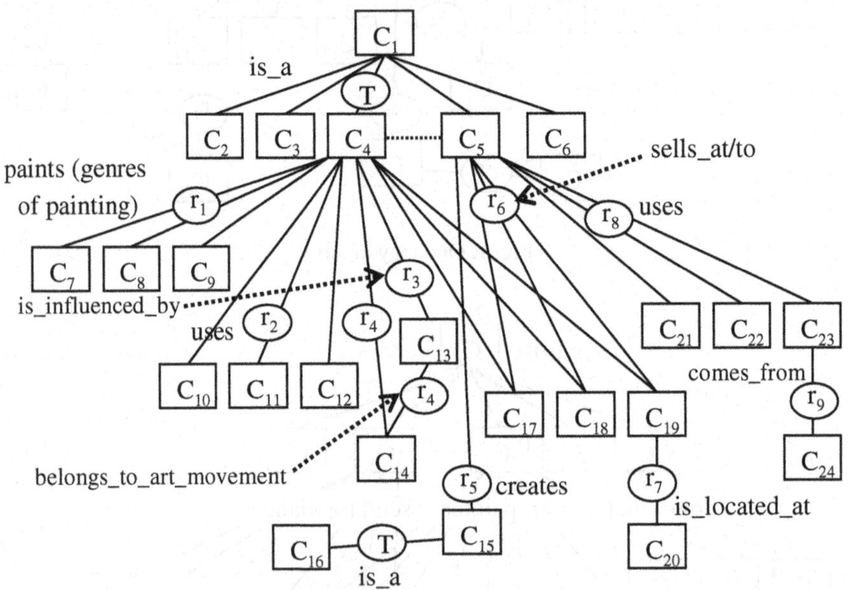

Fig. 3. Illustration of L^R

5 Concluding Remarks

"The success of the deployment of the Semantic Web will largely depend on whether useful ontologies will emerge, allowing shared agreements about vocabularies for knowledge representation." [9]

The vision of a Semantic Web Wave is attracting much attention in the scientific world. Design, implementation and integration of ontologies will be crucial in the development of the Semantic Web. A Semantic Web, in which Fuzzy Logic, and more generally Soft Computing, will certainly have a positive role to play.

It is expected that the structures that have been introduced in this paper around the notion of Fuzzy Ontology will enrich the ingredients that will contribute to the real success of the Semantic Web.

References

1. F. Baader, D. Calvanese, D. McGuinness, D. Nardi, P. Patel-Schneider, "The Description Logics Handbook: Theory, Implementation and Applications", Cambridge university Press (2003).
2. F. Baader, I. Horrocks, U. Sattler, "Description Logics as Ontology Languages for the Semantic Web", in D. Hutter, W. Stephan (Eds.), Festschrift in honor of Jörg Siekmann. Lecture Notes in Artificial Intelligence, Springer-Verlag (2003).
3. T. Berners-Lee, J. Hendler, O. Lassila, "The Semantic Web", *Scientific American*, May 2001.
4. BISC-SE 2005, BISC Special Event in Honor of Prof. Lotfi A. Zadeh, "Forging New Frontiers", Proceedings: M. Nikravesh (Ed.), Memo No. UCB/ERL M05/31, Nov. 2, 2005.
5. "Fuzzy Logic and the Semantic Web" Workshop, Extended abstracts available at: http://www.lif.univ-mrs.fr/FLSW , Marseille, France, 2005.
6. T. R. Gruber, "Toward principles for the design of ontologies used for knowledge sharing". Originally in N. Guarino and R. Poli (Eds.), *Int. Workshop on Formal Ontology*, Padova, Italy (1993). Published in Int. J. of Human-Computer Studies, Vol.43, Issue 5-6 (1995) 907-928.
7. I. Horrocks, P.F. Patel-Schneider, F. van Harmelen, "From SHIQ and RDF to OWL: the making of a Web Ontology Language", *J. of Web Semantics* 1, 1 (2003) 7-26.
8. IPMU 2004, Special Session "Fuzzy Logic in the Semantic Web: a New Challenge", Proc. pp.1017-1038, IPMU04@dipmat.unipg.it, Perugia, Italy, 2004.
9. O. Lassila and D. L. McGuinness: " The Role of Frame-Based Representation on the Semantic Web ", Knowledge Systems Laboratory Report KSL-01-02, Stanford University (2001).
10. A. Maedche, "Ontology Learning for the Semantic Web", Kluwer Academic Publishers (2002).
11. "New directions in Enhancing the Power of the Internet" (Proceedings UCB/ERL, Berkeley, Memo N° M01/28, August 2001) and "Enhancing the Power of the Internet", M. Nikravesh, B. Azvine, R. Yager and L.A. Zadeh (Eds.), Springer Verlag, 2004.
12. NAFIPS-FLINT 2002 Int. conf., IEEE SMC Proceedings 02TH8622, New-Orleans, 2002.
13. E. Sanchez (Editor), "Fuzzy logic and the Semantic Web", Elsevier (2006).
14. U. Straccia, "Reasoning with Fuzzy Description Logics", *J. of Artificial Intelligence Research* 14 (2001) 137-166.
15. U. Straccia, "A Fuzzy Description Logic for the Semantic Web", in E. Sanchez (Ed.), "Fuzzy logic and the Semantic Web", Elsevier (2006) 73-90.
16. D. H. Widyantoro, J. Yen, "Incorporating Fuzzy Ontology of Term Relations in a Search Engine", *2001 BISC Int. Workshop on Fuzzy Logic and the Internet,* Proceedings (2001) 155-160.
17. www.w3.org
18. www.w3.org/XML/Schema
19. L. A. Zadeh, "Web Intelligence and Fuzzy Logic – The concept of Web IQ (WIQ)", Invited talk at the 2003 IEEE/WIC Int. Conference on Web Intelligence (WI 2003), Halifax, Canada, available at: www.comp.hkbu.edu.hk/IAT03/InvitedTalk1.htm
20. L.A. Zadeh, "From Search Engines to Question-Answering Systems — The Problems of World Knowledge, Relevance, Deduction and Precisiation", in E. Sanchez (Ed.), "Fuzzy logic and the Semantic Web", Elsevier (2006) 163-210.

Flexible Intensional Query-Answering for RDF Peer-to-Peer Systems

Zoran Majkić

University of Maryland, College Park, USA
zoran@cs.umd.edu

Abstract. We consider the Peer-To-Peer (P2P) database systems with RDF ontologies and with the semantic characterization of P2P mappings based on logical views over local peer's ontology. Such kind of virtual-predicate based mappings needs an embedding of RDF ontologies into a predicate first-order logic, or at some of its sublanguages as, for example, logic programs for deductive databases. We consider a peer as a *local* epistemic logic system with its own belief based on RDF tuples, independent from other peers and their own beliefs. This motivates the need of a semantic characterization of P2P mappings based not on the extension but on the *meaning* of concepts used in the mappings, that is, based on intensional logic. We show that it adequately models robust weakly-coupled framework of RDF ontologies and supports decidable query answering for the union of conjunctive queries.

1 Introduction

The notion of ontology has become widespread in fields such as intelligent information integration, cooperative information systems, information retrieval, electronic commerce and knowledge management. Using ontologies, semantic annotations on Web resources will allow structural and semantic definitions of documents, providing completely new possibilities: Intelligent search instead of keyword matching, query answering instead of information retrieval, document exchange between departments via ontology mappings, and *definition of views* on documents. The Semantic Web is a proposal to build an infrastructure of machine-readable semantics for the data on the Web.

RDF [1] follows the W3C design principles of interoperability, extensibility, evolution and decentralization. Particularly, the RDF model was designed with the following goals: simple data model and extensible URI-based vocabulary allowing anyone to make statements about any resource.

Data integration in RDF - Motivation
The new P2P data integration systems in Semantic Web [2] needs rich ontologies for the peer databases and efficient query-answering algorithms for expressive SQL-like query languages. So, the mapping between peer databases has to be based on the *views* (expressed by such SQL-like query languages), defined over peer ontologies, as in other cases of data integration systems [3, 4, 5, 6].

Thus, our attempt is to extend database technology of data integration based on rich ontologies and view-based P2P mappings also for semantic for the data on the Web

H.L. Larsen et al. (Eds.): FQAS 2006, LNAI 4027, pp. 700–712, 2006.

expressed in the RDF syntax: principal motivation is that RDF is a reality in Web applications, so that P2P integration of RDF ontologies is necessarily very important issue.

Data integration in RDF - open problems and actual challenges

All such actual systems of view-based data integration systems, are based on some sublanguage of the FOL (First Order Logic), and also their query-rewriting algorithms are sound and complete w.r.t. the FOL semantics, differently from RDF. In fact, RDF semantics are given in terms of a non-standard model theory. This needs a bridge between RDFS and FOL theory. The embedding presented in this paper can be used to efficiently answer conjunctive queries in heterogeneous P2P settings.

Basically, RDF defines a data model for describing machine-understandable information on the Web. The basic data model consists of three object types: Resources, Properties and Statements. The modeling primitives of RDF are very basic: actually they correspond to binary predicates (RDF-properties) of ground terms (source and value), where, however the predicates may be used as terms so that RDF can not be embedded into the first order logic (FOL), which can be serious drawback in order to be fully integrated into the current logic based frameworks with *extensional equational* theory. Such problem will be explored in more details in the following (the use of *intensional* FOL [7] needs much more investigation). The RDF Schema (RDFS) [8] enriches RDF by giving an externally specified semantics to specific resources, e.g., to rdfs:subclassOf, to rdfs:Class, etc.. It is only because of this external semantics that RDFS is useful. RDFS is recognizable as an *ontology* representation language: it talks about classes and RDF-properties (binary relations), range and domain constraints (on RDF-properties), and subclass and subproperty (subsumption) relations.

So, all attempts to integrate RDFS into some more expressive FOL sublanguage with a built-in *extensional* equality theory (as OWL, largely based on Description Logic, or other interesting languages as Logic Programming, Deductive databases, or Modal Logic languages (e.g., epistemic logic), etc..) are unsuccessful [9, 10].

The difficulty comes from the fact that all FOL sublanguages have the model theory in which individuals are interpreted as *elements* of some domain, classes are interpreted as subsets of the domain, and RDF-properties are interpreted as binary relations on the domain; the semantics of RDFS, on the other hand, is given by a non-standard model theory, where individuals, classes and RDF-properties are *all* elements in the domain, RDF-property elements have extension which are binary relations on the domain, and class extensions are only implicitly defined by the rdf:type property.

A very big number of Web applications is based on simple data structures which actually do not need reification capability of RDFS, so that is really interesting to consider some FOL extensions of RDFS. Because of that we prefer to use directly logic expressions and logic connectives of FOL in a particular subset of RDFS language, which can be naturally embedded into decidable FOL sublanguages.

Data integration in RDF - Main contributions

1. We define the RDF sublanguage which can be embedded in the decidable FOL.
2. We extend the original syntax of such RDF sublanguge, which has only conjunction operator, by defining negation, disjunction and implication algebraic operators. Such

language can be used in order to define richer RDF ontologies, and to give them the expressive power of FOL data integration systems.
3. We define the intensional semantics for P2P database mappings between RDF ontologies, with query-answering systems based on intensionally equivalent views of database peers (see the Appendix for more details).

The plan of this work is the following: After a brief resume in Section 2 of the First-order logic stratification of the RDFS non-standard models, in Section 3 we will present a particular sublanguage of RDFS which can be embedded in any FOL sublanguage. Based on this embedding, in Section 4 we will define the syntax and semantics for P2P database system based on RDFS ontologies and we will show how the intensional equivalence of RDF-views defined over different peers can be used in a query answering to conjunctive RDF queries.

2 First-Order Logic for RDFS Ontology

As we pointed in the introduction, the RDFS has non-standard models, which makes some elements in the model to have dual roles in the RDFS ontology specification. A class in programming languages is regarded as a set, and an instance of the class is a member of the set. The fact that in RDFS the class rdfs:Class is an instance of itself, is a source of Russell paradox (when considering the set of all sets that are not members of themselves). Russell resolved this non-well founded set problem by introducing a kind of stratification (layers), and this approach is technically developed in [11]. We will briefly reassume this approach as follows:

We eliminate dual roles (that is a polymorphism) by a kind of Typed logic [12], defining the universe of discourse in different (and disjoint) strata (layers), each of a particular *type*, with a vocabulary $V = V_0 \bigcup V_1 \bigcup V_2 \bigcup ..$, where $V_i,\ 0 \leq i$ are mutually disjoint sets of URIrefs (typed-URIrefs), with a total-domain $D = D_0 \bigcup D_1 \bigcup D_2 \bigcup ..$, where each $D_i,\ 0 \leq i$ is the domain in layer i, and we define modeling primitives explicitly for each layer R_i, C_i, P_i which are interpreted as the set of all elements, all classes, and all RDF-properties respectively in layer i.

The interpretation for this layered RDFS is a mapping $IE : V \rightarrow D$ such that $IE = I_0 + I_1 + ..$ disjoint sum of typed interpretations $I_i : V_i \rightarrow D_i$, such that:

1. Layer 0, of type D_0: Every individual name $x \in V_0$ is mapped to an object in the domain D_0. This domain of constants D_0 corresponds to the standard domain definition in a FOL.
2. The domains in higher layers $i \geq 1$, of higher types, are defined recursively by $D_i = \mathcal{P}(D_{i-1}) \bigcup \mathcal{P}(D_{i-1} \times D_{i-1})$, where $\mathcal{P}(A)$ denotes the power set (set of all subsets) of the set A, and $\times$ is a Cartesian product for sets. That is, the domain D_i is equal to the union of the set of all classes and the set of all RDF-properties in layer i, such that:

- each class primitive $c_i \in V_i$ is interpreted as set of elements in layer $i-1$, that is $IE(c_i) \in \mathcal{P}(D_{i-1})$;
- each RDF-property primitive $p_i \in V_i$ is interpreted as set of pairs of elements (binary relation) in layer $i-1$, that is $IE(p_i) \in \mathcal{P}(D_{i-1} \times D_{i-1})$.

Thus, the above interpretation IE of this layered RDFS can be embedded into the following three-level FOL interpretation for RDF databases:

1. The level 0, of the type $T = D_0$, consists of the FOL domain for constants, and names in V_0, can be considered as *constant symbols* in FOL. Thus, an interpretation IE (that is, I_0) assigns values from D_0 to these constants as in FOL.
2. The level 1 (*Ontological* level), of the type $T_1 = (D_0 \Rightarrow \mathbf{2}) + (D_0 \times D_0 \Rightarrow \mathbf{2})$ (that is, $T_1 = \mathbf{2}^{D_0} + \mathbf{2}^{D_0 \times D_0}$), where the type $A \Rightarrow B$ denotes the set of all functions from A to B, $+$ denotes the set disjunctive union, $\times$ Cartesian product, and $\mathbf{2} = \{0, 1\}$ (truth values), consists of the FOL unary predicates with attribute variable over a domain D_0 (for RDF classes) and binary predicates (for RDF-properties) in V_1. Thus, an interpretation IE (that is, I_1) assigns set of constants from a domain D_0 (that is, a characteristic function from D_0 to $\mathbf{2}$) to unary predicates in V_1, and set of pairs of constants to binary predicates in V_1.
3. The level 2 (*Metalanguage* FOL level), of the type $T_2 = ((D_0 \Rightarrow \mathbf{2}) \Rightarrow \mathbf{2}) + ((D_0 \times D_0 \Rightarrow \mathbf{2}) \Rightarrow \mathbf{2})$, consists of meta concepts in FOL which correspond to RDFS concepts as rdf:Class, rdfs:Property, etc.., which are not used in the specification language for RDF ontologies.

In this way we obtained a kind of monomorphic type logic, where each constant (name) in the vocabulary V has a unique interpretation, for example, it is an instance (type T_0) or a class (type T_1), but can not be both of them as in polymorphic case used in a full RDF. The specification language for RDF ontologies is composed by only primitives in the first two layers, and as consequence this subset of RDF ontologies can be embedded into (decidable) FOL sublanguages with unary (for RDF classes) and binary (for RDF-properties) predicates only. We will denote such layered RDFS ontologies by FOL-RDF ontologies, and we introduce the Herbrand semantics for them:

Definition 1. *Let $IE : V \rightarrow D$ be an RDF interpretation of FOL-RDF ontology $\mathcal{O}$. We define the following transformation of $\mathcal{O}$ into the predicate logic theory $\mathcal{L}_P$, as follows:*

1. The set D_0 will be the domain and V_0 the set S of all constant symbols in $\mathcal{L}_P$.
2. The set of all class primitives $c \in V_1$ will be the set A of attribute variables over a domain D_0 in $\mathcal{L}_P$.
3. The set of all RDF-property primitives $p \in V_1$ will be the set of binary predicates.

Then, $I : H_B \rightarrow \mathbf{2}$ is the Herbrand interpretation for this logic theory $\mathcal{L}_P$, where $H_B = \{p(a, b) \mid p \in P$, and $a, b \in D_0\}$ is its Herbrand base and $\mathbf{2} = \{0, 1\}$ the set of logic values (false and true respectively), such that $I(p(a, b)) = 1$ iff $(a, b) \in IE(p)$.

3 FOL-RDFS Ontology

The approach to use conventional first order logic (FOL) as the semantic underpinning for RDF has many advantages: FOL is well established and well understood. There is a family of languages based on various FOL subsets offering different tradeoffs with respect to expressive power, complexity and computability, and the direct mapping of such languages into subset of FOL provides semantic interpretability also. This approach is not directly compatible with full RDFS, but it is compatible with the following simplified version of RDFS:

In what follows we will adopt the approach used in [11] but not constrained only to Description Logic. Instead of that we will consider this RDF sublanguage as Herbrand semantic bases for a world-based introduction of probabilistic information into RDF theory.

We will consider an RDF-ontology as finite set of triples $< r, p, v >$, where r is a *resource* name (for class, an instance or a value), p is a *property* (InstanceOf or Property in RDF, or Subclass or Property in RDFS), and v is a value (which could also be a resource name). We denote by $\mathcal{T}$ the set of all triples which satisfy such requirements.

Throughout the rest of this paper we will assume that $\mathcal{R}$ is a fixed set of resource names, P is a fixed set of property names and $dom(p)$ is a fixed set of values associated with any property name $p \in P$. An RDF-ontology can be seen as an ontology graph. It can be converted in the following logic program (clauses):

Definition 2 (Logic embedding of RDF-ontology). *We define the logic embedding as a mapping $\mathcal{E} : \mathcal{T} \rightarrow \mathcal{L}$, where $\mathcal{L}$ is FOL with a domain D, such that for any triple $< r, p, v > \in \mathcal{T}$ holds:*

1. Case when $p = Subclass$: $\mathcal{E}(< r, Subclass, v >) = r'(x) \leftarrow v'(x)$
where r', v' are unary predicates for the subject and object of a triple respectively, and x is a variable over a domain D.
2. Case when $p = InstanceOf$: $\mathcal{E}(< r, InstanceOf, v >) = r'(v) \leftarrow$
where r' is an unary predicate for the resource of the RDF triple.
3. Case when $p \notin \{InstanceOf, Subclass\}$:
$\mathcal{E}(< r, p, v >) = (r'(x) \wedge v'(y)) \leftarrow p'(x, y),$ *if r, v are classes;*
$= r'(x) \leftarrow p'(x, v),$ *if r is a class and v is an instance or value;*
$= v'(y) \leftarrow p'(r, y),$ *if v is a class and r is an instance or value;*
$= p'(r, v) \leftarrow,$ *if r and v are instances or values;*

where, in the right side of equation, p' is a binary predicate assigned by this embedding to the property name p, and r', v' are unary predicates assigned to the subject and the object classes of a triple.

Given an RDF-ontology $\mathcal{O} \subset \mathcal{T}$, we denote by $\mathcal{E}(\mathcal{O})$ its logic ontology obtained by this embedding, that is, $\mathcal{E}(\mathcal{O}) = \{\mathcal{E}(< r, p, v >) \mid < r, p, v > \in \mathcal{O}\}$. Let H be a Herbrand model of this logic programs obtained from an RDF-ontology.
We define the RDF-model $\mathcal{M}(\mathcal{O})$ of an RDF-ontology $\mathcal{O}$ recursively for any triple $< r, p, v > \in \mathcal{O}$, and for the following cases (a, b are elements of a domain D):
1. r, v are classes: $< a, p, b > \in \mathcal{M}(\mathcal{O})$ if $p'(a, b), r'(a), v'(b) \in H$
2. r is a class and v is an instance or value: $< a, p, v > \in \mathcal{M}(\mathcal{O})$ if $p'(a, v), r'(a) \in H$
3. v is a class and r is an instance or value: $< r, p, b > \in \mathcal{M}(\mathcal{O})$ if $p'(r, b), v'(b) \in H$
4. r, v are instances or values: $< r, p, v > \in \mathcal{M}(\mathcal{O})$; in this case $p'(r, v) \in H$ also.
Thus, all triples in the RDF-model of an ontology $\mathcal{O}$ are ground triples.

Notice that if $\mathcal{M}(\mathcal{O})$ is an RDF-model of an ontology $\mathcal{O}$, then, for any ground RDF triple $< r, p, v >$ holds that $\mathcal{E}(< r, p, v >)$ is true iff (if and only if) $< r, p, v > \in \mathcal{M}(\mathcal{O})$.

Definition 3. *(Negation) We define the negation algebraic operation $\sim$ for extended algebraic RDF-ontology language by*
$\mathcal{E}(\sim< r,p,v >) = \neg\mathcal{E}(< r,p,v >)$, *for any* $< r,p,v > \in \mathcal{M}(\mathcal{O})$,
where $\neg$ is the logic negation. The triples or their negations will be called RDF-literals.

Notice that for any ground RDF triple $< r,p,v >$ holds: $\mathcal{E}(\sim< r,p,v >)$ is true iff $< r,p,v > \notin \mathcal{M}(\mathcal{O})$. It is reasonable to use negation $\sim$ in order to specify complex terms for RDF ontologies. It is kind of explicit constraint. For example, when we introduce the ground literal term $\sim< r,p,v >$ in an ontology specification, we specify that the triple $< r,p,v >$ *cannot* be part of any RDF-model of such ontology (like the specification of explicit negative information in a *logic* ontology language).

Currently only algebraic operation $\curlywedge$ for conjunction of atomic terms (RDF triples) is defined for RDF-ontologies: its semantics corresponds to the semantics of the symbol 'comma' used to specify the set of triples of a RDF-ontology. Now we will extend this simple algebra for triples $(\mathcal{T}, \curlywedge)$ by other RDF connectives: $\sim$ for negation, $\curlyvee$ for disjunction, and $\hookrightarrow$ for implication. We use different symbols from standard *logic* connectives in order to make clear this difference: these connectives for extended RDF ontologies are algebraic *constructors*; by using them we are able to specify complex RDF *structures*, not to write logic formulae (with variables) or logic statements.

Definition 4. *Let $(\mathcal{L}, \wedge, \neg, \vee, \Rightarrow)$ be the algebra for a predicate-based logic language $\mathcal{L}$, where $\wedge, \neg, \vee, \Rightarrow$ are classical logic operators for conjunction, negation, disjunction and material implication respectively. Then, the semantics for the algebraic operators of the extended RDF-algebra $(\mathcal{T}, \curlywedge, \sim, \curlyvee, \hookrightarrow)$ is defined by the following homomorphism, which extends the embedding mapping, $\mathcal{E} : (\mathcal{T}, \curlywedge, \sim, \curlyvee, \hookrightarrow) \rightarrow (\mathcal{L}, \wedge, \neg, \vee, \Rightarrow)$, such that for any two triples $< r,p,v >, < r',p',v' > \in \mathcal{T}$ hold*
1.$\mathcal{E}(< r,p,v > \curlywedge < r',p',v' >) = \mathcal{E}(< r,p,v >) \wedge \mathcal{E}(< r',p',v' >)$,
2.$\mathcal{E}(< r,p,v > \curlyvee < r',p',v' >) = \mathcal{E}(< r,p,v >) \vee \mathcal{E}(< r',p',v' >)$,
3.$\mathcal{E}(< r,p,v > \hookrightarrow < r',p',v' >) = \mathcal{E}(< r,p,v >) \Rightarrow \mathcal{E}(< r',p',v' >)$,

Such connectives are extended to all RDF-expressions which can be obtained from this algebra $(\mathcal{T}, \curlywedge, \sim, \curlyvee, \hookrightarrow)$, in standard way, so that any extended RDF-ontology $\mathcal{O}$ can be specified as one RDF-expression. Let H be a Herbrand model of a logic theory $\mathcal{E}(\mathcal{O})$, then the model $\mathcal{M}(\mathcal{O})$ of this extended RDF-ontology can be defined in the same way as in Definition 1.

It is easy to verify that RDF-disjunction and RDF-implication can be defined by RDF-conjunction and RDF-negation, (hold De Morgan laws), as for connectives in classical logic. Any extended RDF-ontology can be specified as a single RDF-expression of the algebra $(\mathcal{T}, \curlywedge, \sim, \curlyvee, \hookrightarrow)$; for the standard RDF-ontology (set of triples) such expression is just the conjunction of all triples in that set. Notice that the operators of the RDF-algebra are somewhat weaker than the correspondent operators of logic: for example, while logic conjunction $\wedge$ is the cartesian product (with left and right projections), the correspondent 'comma' operator $\curlywedge$ in RDF is tensorial (commutative and associative) operator *without* projections.

In this extended language for RDF ontologies we are able to specify constraints, as for instance, in an RDF-ontology $\mathcal{O}$ a ground expression $< r,p,v > \curlyvee < r',p',v' >$ means that in each model $\mathcal{M}(\mathcal{O})$ must hold that $< r,p,v > \in \mathcal{M}(\mathcal{O})$ or $< r',p',v' > \in$

$\mathcal{M}(\mathcal{O})$; or, for instance, the ground expression $< r, p, v > \hookrightarrow < r', p', v' >$ means that in each model $\mathcal{M}(\mathcal{O})$ if $< r, p, v > \in \mathcal{M}(\mathcal{O})$ than also $< r', p', v' > \in \mathcal{M}(\mathcal{O})$.
In what follows we will consider only the sublanguage of this extended RDF language for conjunctive-with-negation ontologies, composed by RDF-literals and conjunctive connective: any such RDF-ontology is just a conjunctive expression of RDF-literals, but we will often forgot the conjunction and see such RDF-ontology as a *set* of RDF-literals.

4 P2P Database System Based on RDF Ontologies

The Peer-to-Peer (P2P) database systems offer an alternative to traditional client-server systems for some application domains. A P2P system has no centralized schema and no central administration. Instead, each peer is an autonomous information system, and information integration is achieved by establishing P2P mappings among various peers. Queries are posed to one peer, and the role of query processing is to exploit both the data that are internal to the peer, and the mappings with other peers in the system.

In what follows we consider an RDF ontology as a basic data strata of a peer database. In order to define the logical views over such RDF ontologies we will use the logic theory $\mathcal{E}(\mathcal{O})$ obtained by embedding this RDF-ontology $\mathcal{O}$ into FOL (in the case of standard RDF syntax, without negation, we obtain a definite logic program (DATALOG)).

It has become customary to define the notion of RDF programming via a long list of triples (binary RDF-properties) which resource must posses. In relational language instead data are conceptually grouped around n-ary predicates with a set of attributes which together describe different properties attributed to such logical concept.

The implementation of views are an established technology for both relational and object-oriented databases. They are mainly used to provide data customization, that is, the adaptation of content to meet the demands of specific applications and users, so that they present the key technology for integrating heterogeneous and distributed systems. The simple idea is to see a view $\varphi(x_1, ..., x_n)$ over an RDF-ontology, expressed as a formula in some query language for RDF databases (for example, as a SELECT-FROM-WHERE structure in [13, 14], as n-ary relation-in-intension (intensional name) whose extension in the actual world (a possible world corresponds to the possible RDF database extension) is equal to its query answer.

Example 1. (from [15]) To find all (sculpture, museum) pairs, in an RDF peer database, where the sculpture was created by Rodin, the museum houses the given sculpture, and the museum Web site was not modified since Jan 1, 2001, we can define the following query: $rdql - query =: \;\; SELECT\ ?sculpture, ?museum$
$WHERE\ (?sculptor, < ns1 : lname >, "Rodin"),$
$(?sculptor, < ns1 : creates >, ?sculpture),$
$(?sculpture, < ns1 : exhibited >, ?museum),$
$(?museum, < ns1 : last - modified >, ?date),$
$AND\ \ ?date\ \ <\ \ 2001\ -\ 01\ -\ 01\ \ USING\ \ ns1\ \ FOR\ \ <\ \ http\ \ :$
$//www.icom.com/schema1 >$
and the correspondent view, by:

$\varphi(x_1, x_2) = CREATEVIEW\ view - name\ AS\ rdql - query,$
where $\varphi(x_1, x_2)$ is a virtual predicate, obtained by the following FOL translation (Def.1):
$\varphi(x_1, x_2) \leftarrow lname(y, "Rodin") \wedge creates(y, x_1) \wedge exhibited(x_1, x_2)$
$\wedge\ last - modified(x_2, z) \wedge z < 2001 - 01 - 01,$
where x_1, x_2 are free variables for `sculpture` and `museum` respectively. □

The peer database in this framework is just the logic theory, defined as union of the RDF-ontology FOL-embedding $\mathcal{E}(\mathcal{O})$ and a number of views defined over it (they constitute a virtual user-type interface). Such embedding of an RDF-ontology, together with its view-extension can be used as mean for intensional mapping with other peer databases in a Web P2P networks. There are the following nice properties for this peer database RDF-ontology framework:

1. The FOL embedding of standard RDF-ontology together with views corresponds to the definite logic program, thus the database model of such RDF peer database has a *unique* Herbrand model, differently from standard Data Integration Systems (DIS) with *relational* schema ontology, which usually suffer incomplete information and very high number of Herbrand models (possible completions of this withdraw): so, the query answering from peer databases with RDF-ontology is very efficient (polynomial complexity).
2. The defined views can be materialized and there are efficient algorithms [15] for maintenance of RDF views when a new RDF triples are inserted in a peer database, when some of them are deleted, or modified.
3. From the theoretical point of view, the possibility to transform original RDF based peer database into the less expressive, but *decidable*, FOL sublanguages, is important if we want to add also integrity constraints over a peer database ontology (for example, in the simplest case, the key constraints over a view). In that case we are able to parse the original RDF structures into a deductive predicate-based database. In such way we are able to enrich the expressive power of standard relational DIS .

Let P_i and P_j be the two different peer databases, denominated by 'Peter' and 'John' respectively, and $q_1(\mathbf{x})$, $q_2(\mathbf{x})$ be the concepts of "the Italian art in the 15'th century" with attributes in $\mathbf{x}$, written in local languages of P_i and P_j respectively. We will consider the *intensional* semantics for peer mappings [16, 17, 6], expressed by the *intensional equivalence* $q_i \approx q_j$, where each peer is completely independent entity with its own epistemic state, which has not to be directly, externally, changed by the mutable knowledge of other independent peers, needs other approach to the mapping between their local knowledge based on the *meaning* of the mapped concepts.

First requirement is that the knowledge of other peers can not be directly transferred into the local knowledge of a given peer. The second is that, during the life time of a P2P system, any local change of knowledge must be independent of the beliefs that can have other peers: thus, we have not to constrain the *extension* of knowledge which may have different peers about the same type of real-world concept.

Informally, if we pose query to 'John', 'John' can answer only for a part of knowledge that it really has about Italian art, and not for a knowledge that 'Peter' has. Thus, when somebody (call him 'query-agent') ask 'John' about the Italian art in the 15'th century, 'John' is able to respond only by the facts known by himself (i.e., *known* answers), and eventually indicate to query-agent that for such question, probably, also 'Peter' is able to give some answer. Thus, it is the task of the *query-agent* to reformulate the request (w.r.t. the local language of 'Peter') to 'Peter' in order to obtain some other *possible* answers.

We can paraphrase this by the kind of *belief-sentence*-mapping '*John believes that also Peter knows something about Italian art in the 15'th century*'. Such belief-sentence has *referential* (i.e., extensional) *opacity*. In this case we do not specify that the knowledge of 'John' is included in the knowledge of 'Peter' (or viceversa) for the concept 'Italian art in the 15'th century', but only that this concept, $q_1(\mathbf{x})$, for 'John' (expressed in a language of 'John') *implicitly corresponds* to the 'equivalent' concept, $q_2(\mathbf{x})$, for 'Peter' (expressed in a language of 'Peter'). We will briefly define this equivalence(see [18] for more information):

Tarski's elaboration of a semantics for formal languages, Kripke's invention of a possible-world semantics in connection with modal logic and Montague's semantics for Intensional logic provided powerful tools by means of which natural languages could be analyzed rigorously. In what follows we will use one simplified modal logic framework (we will not consider the time as one independent parameter as in Montague's original work [19]) with a model $\mathcal{M} = (\mathcal{W}, \mathcal{R}, S, V)$, where $\mathcal{W}$ is the set of possible worlds, $\mathcal{R}$ is the accessibility relation between worlds ($\mathcal{R} \subseteq \mathcal{W} \times \mathcal{W}$), S is a non-empty domain of individuals, while V is a function defined for the following two cases:

1. $V : \mathcal{W} \times F \rightarrow \bigcup_{n<\omega} S^{S^n}$, with F a set of functional symbols of the language, such that for any world $w \in \mathcal{W}$ and a functional symbol $f \in F$, we obtain a function $V(w, f) : S^{arity(f)} \rightarrow S$.
2. $V : \mathcal{W} \times P \rightarrow \bigcup_{n<\omega} \mathbf{2}^{S^n}$, with P a set of predicate symbols of the language and $\mathbf{2} = \{t, f\}$ is the set of truth values (true and false, respectively), such that for any world $w \in \mathcal{W}$ and a predicate symbol $p \in P$, we obtain a function $V(w, p) : S^{arity(p)} \rightarrow \mathbf{2}$, which defines the extension $[p] = \{\mathbf{a} | \mathbf{a} \in S^{arity(p)}$ and $V(w, p)(\mathbf{a}) = t\}$ of this predicate p in the world w.

The extension of an expression α, w.r.t. a model $\mathcal{M}$, a world $w \in \mathcal{W}$ and assignment g is denoted by $[\alpha]^{\mathcal{M},w,g}$. Thus, if $c \in F \bigcup P$ then for a given world $w \in \mathcal{W}$ and the assignment function for variables g, $[c]^{\mathcal{M},w,g} = V(w, c)$, that is, for any set of terms $t_1, .., t_n$, where n is the arity of c, we have $[c(t_1, .., t_n)]^{\mathcal{M},w,g} = V(w, c)([t_1]^{\mathcal{M},w,g}, .., [t_n]^{\mathcal{M},w,g})$; with terms defined by:

- All variables $v \in Var$ and the constants $d \in S$ are terms; If $f \in F$ is a function symbol of arity n, and $t_1, .., t_n$ are terms, then a functional form $f(t_1, .., t_n,)$ is a term. For any formula A, $\mathcal{M} \vDash_{w,g} A \equiv ([A]^{\mathcal{M},w,g} = t)$, means 'A is true in the world w of a model $\mathcal{M}$ for assignment g'.

Montague defined the *intension* of an expression α as follows:
$[\alpha]_{in}^{\mathcal{M},g} =_{def} \{w \mapsto [\alpha]^{\mathcal{M},w,g} \mid w \in \mathcal{W}\}$,
i.e., as graph of the function $[\alpha]_{in}^{\mathcal{M},g} : \mathcal{W} \rightarrow \bigcup_{w \in \mathcal{W}} [\alpha]^{\mathcal{M},w,g}$.

One thing that should be immediately clear is that intensions are more general that extensions: if the intension of an expression is given, one can determine its extension with respect to a particular world but not viceversa, i.e., $[\alpha]^{\mathcal{M},w,g} = [\alpha]_{in}^{\mathcal{M},g}(w)$.

In particular, if c is a non-logical constant (individual constant or predicate symbol), the definition of the extension of c is, $[c]^{\mathcal{M},w,g} =_{def} V(w,c)$. Hence, the intensions of the non-logical constants are the following functions: $[c]_{in}^{\mathcal{M},g} : \mathcal{W} \rightarrow \bigcup_{w\in\mathcal{W}} V(w,c)$.

Definition 5. *Any two expressions, α, β, are intensionally equivalent, respectively denoted by $\alpha \approx \beta$, if and only if $lub^{\mathcal{M},g}(\alpha) = lub^{\mathcal{M},g}(\beta)$, where for a given expression δ, its lub (Least Upper Bound) is defined by: $lub^{\mathcal{M},g}(\delta) =_{def} \bigcup_{w\in\mathcal{W}}[\delta]_{in}^{\mathcal{M},g}(w)$.*

This definitions of intensional equivalence given in [18], based on Montague's possible world semantics, have the *higher-order logic* language syntax. But it has no consequence for the logic theory of P2P system, which remain embedded into a *decidable first-order* logic sublanguage. The reason is that in our framework we do not use modal formulae nor we need the deductive capabilities able to deduce which concepts are intensionally equivalent: the intensional equivalence of views of RDF-ontologies are established by the developer of the peer's RDF-ontology (who *believes* that they are intensionally equivalent). Only what the system is interested is to compute the *extension* of these views (intensional-in-relations) in the *actual* world.

P2P network definition: In order to be able to communicate with other peer P_j in the network $\mathcal{N}$, each peer P_i has also an export-interface module $\mathcal{M}^{ij}$ composed by groups of ordered pairs of intensionally-equivalent logical views, denoted by $q_i \approx q_j$.

Definition 6. *The P2P network system $\mathcal{N}$ is composed by $2 \leq N$ independent peers. Each peer module P_i, based on the RDF-ontolgy $\mathcal{O}_i$, is defined as follows:*
$P_i := \langle \mathcal{O}_i, \mathcal{M}_i \rangle$, where $\mathcal{M}_i =< \mathcal{M}^{i1}, ..., \mathcal{M}^{iN} >$ is an interface tuple with $\mathcal{M}^{ij}$, $1 \leq j \leq N$ a (possibly empty) interface to other peer P_j in the network, defined as a group of query-connections, denoted by $(q_{1k}^{ij}, q_{2k}^{ij})$ where q_{1k}^{ij} is a conjunctive query defined over $\mathcal{O}_i$, while q_{2k}^{ij} is a conjunctive query defined over the ontology $\mathcal{O}_j$ of the connected peer P_j : $\mathcal{M}^{ij} = \{(q_{1k}^{ij}, q_{2k}^{ij}) \mid q_{1k}^{ij} \approx q_{2k}^{ij}, \text{ and } 1 \leq k \leq \mid ij \mid\}$ where $\mid ij \mid$ denotes the total number of query-connections of the peer P_i toward P_j.

Intuitively, when a user defines a query over a virtual schema of the peer P_i, the intensionally equivalent concepts between this peer and other peers will be used in order to obtain answers from other peers also. They will be the "bridge" which a query agent can use to rewrite the original user query over a peer P_i into *intensionally-equivalent* query over other peer P_j which has different (and independent) RDF-ontology from the peer P_i. The answers of other peers will be epistemically considered as *possible* answers because they are based on the *belief* which has the peer P_i about the knowledge of a peer P_j: this belief is formally represented by supposition that the pair of queries $(q_{1k}^{ij}, q_{2k}^{ij}) \in \mathcal{M}^{ij}$ is intensionally-equivalent.

Query answering in RDF based P2P system

The fundamental question is how to use these intensional equivalences of views in order to be able to compute the query answer in the *actual* world. Intuitively, we would like to use the *substitutive feature* of intensionally equivalent concepts during query-rewriting of the original user query over all other peers in a P2P network. The following holds:

Proposition 1. *[18] Let consider the class of peers with integrity constraints which does not contain negative clauses of the form $\neg A_1 \vee ... \vee \neg A_m,\ m \geq 2$. Then, the intensional equivalence is preserved by conjunction logic operation, that is,*
if $\varphi \equiv (b_1 \wedge ... \wedge b_k),\ k \geq 1,$ *and* $b_i \approx c_i,\ 1 \leq i \leq k,$ *then* $\varphi \approx \psi$
where $\equiv$ *is a logic equivalence and* $\psi \equiv (c_1 \wedge .... \wedge c_k)$.

Thus, in the case of the RDF-ontology of a peer database, together with views, the following corollary holds:

Corollary 1. *For peer databases with an RDF-ontology the intensional equivalence is preserved by conjunction logic operation, that is,*
if $\varphi \equiv (b_1 \wedge ... \wedge b_k),\ k \geq 1,$ *and* $b_i \approx c_i,\ 1 \leq i \leq k,$ *then* $\varphi \approx \psi$
where $\equiv$ *is a logic equivalence and* $\psi \equiv (c_1 \wedge .... \wedge c_k)$.

This Corollary is very important in order to define the semantics for conjunctive-query answering in P2P database systems: each original user query φ, which can be defined over a set of views $b_i,\ 1 \leq i \leq k$ of an actual peer, can be rewritten to the query ψ over other peer which has the correspondent set of intensionally equivalent views $c_i,\ 1 \leq i \leq k$ w.r.t. the views of the first peer (the *substitutivity* requirement for intensionally equivalent queries).

There is a number of different *context-dependent* scenarios for query-answering with intensional semantics, as in human society: for example

- the *confidential* scenario where an interviewer can interview a single person at time (we will denominate it as a *pure* P2P context), or
-*conference* scenario where an interviewer can interact with a number of people at time and possibly integrate partial knowledge of them in order to obtain the answer.

Example 2. Let us consider the simplest scenario: the *pure* P2P context.

Informally, given a conjunctive query $\varphi(x_1, .., x_n)$ over a peer P_i with RDF-ontology, the answer to this query of the whole P2P system, w.r.t. *intensional semantics* is the union of known answers from this peer, and (known) answers of all other peers which have intensionally equivalent to $\varphi(x_1, .., x_n)$ virtual predicates. This paradigm corresponds to the query-answering in a society of individuals: given a question $\varphi(x_1, .., x_n)$ to some person P_i , and its beliefs about the knowledge of other people in this society, the interviewer can obtain the answer from P_i and from other people who know something about the same concept $\varphi(x_1, .., x_n)$.

5 Conclusion

We have presented a formal framework for representing interschema knowledge in Peer-to-peer database systems based on intensional equivalence between concepts of peers with RDF-ontology. Such interschema mappings is not invasive w.r.t. the local epistemic knowledge of any single peer: each database-peer with a proper RDF-ontology, and the number of *intensional views* defined by RDF queries, is completely free to change its local RDF structure (insert, delete and modification of RDF triples). It does not import the extensional knowledge from other peer-databases of a P2P information system, but specify only which part of its own knowledge have the same meaning as some knowledge (intensional views) of other actors.

We consider only RDF ontologies which can be embedded in the FOL (with built-in extensional equality theory of predicates and functions), for which the resulting logic theory corresponds to definite logic programs with a *unique* Herbrand model of a peer database: so, the query answering for such peer is very efficient and suitable for intensive Web information retrieval.

The intensional views (RDF queries) over peers present the key technology for integrating heterogeneous and distributed systems, facilitating interoperability by hiding the foibles of each information component and gluing individual components together to form an integrated P2P application system. The epistemic independence of such peers is a guarantee for development of very robust P2P database systems.

For any given conjunctive RDF query submitted by a query agent to a particular peer database, the query-agent obtains as answer the set of *certain* (known) answers from this interrogated peer, and the set of *possible* answers from other peers which are able to define the intensionally equivalent virtual concepts to the original user query. This query answering is *context sensitive*, and can be modeled for different context scenarios of P2P systems.

We believe that the intensional mapping semantics for peer databases with RDF ontologies, presented in this paper, constitutes a sound basis for studying the various issues related to interschema knowledge representation and reasoning, especially for P2P database systems in Web environment, where peers can be considered as complex database agents.

References

1. O.Lassila and R.R.Swick, "Resource descrition framework (RDF): Model and syntax specification," *World Wide Web Consortium, http://www.w3.org/TR/REC-rdf-syntax*, 1999.
2. T.Berners-Lee, J.Hendlar, and O.Lassila, "The semantic web," *Scientific American*, vol. 279, 2001.
3. A.Levy, A.Mendelzon, and Y.Sagiv, "Answering queries using views," *Proc. 14th ACM Symp. on Principles of Database Systems*, pp. 95–104, 1995.
4. K.Aberer, M.Punceva, M.Hauswirth, and R.Schmidt, "Improving data access in P2P systems," *IEEE Internet Computing*, 2002.
5. D.Calvanese, G. De Giacomo, M.Lenzerini, and R.Rosati, "Logical foundations of Peer-to-Peer data integration," *PODS 2004, June 14-16, Paris, France*, 2004.
6. Z.Majkić, "Weakly-coupled ontology integration of P2P database systems," *1st Int. Workshop on Peer-to-Peer Knowledge Management (P2PKM), August 22, Boston, USA*, 2004.
7. G.Bealer, "Theories of properties, relations, and propositions," *The Journal of Philosophy*, vol. 76, pp. 634–648, 1979.
8. D.Brickley and R.Guha, "Resource descrition framework (RDF) schema specification 1.0," *World Wide Web Consortium, http://www.w3.org/TR/2000/CR-rdf-schema-20000327*, 2000.

9. P.F.Patel-Schneider and D.Fensel, "Layering the semantic Web: Problems and directions," *In 2002 Interantional Sematic Web Conference*, 2002.
10. I.Horrocks and P.F.Patel-Schneider, "Three thesis of representation in the semantic web," *In Proc. of the 12th International World Wide Web Conference (WWW2003)*, pp. 39–47, 2003.
11. J.Z.Pan and I.Horrocks, "RDFS(FA): A DL-ised sub-language of RDFS," *In Proc. of the 2003 Description Logic Workshop, (DL 2003), vol. 81 of CEUR*, pp. 95–102, 2003.
12. S.Lappin, C.Fox, and C.Pollard, "First-order, curry-typed logic for natural language semantics," *In Proc. of the Workshop on Natuaral Language Understanding and Logic Programming, Copenhagen, Denmark*, pp. 175–192, 2002.
13. Hewlett-Packard, "RDQL-RDFdata query language," *http://www.hpl.hp.com/semweb/rdql.html.*
14. S.Alexaki, V.Christophides, D.Plexousakis, M.Scholl, G.Karvounarakis, A.Magnaraki, and K.Tolle, "Quering the semantic web with RQL," *Computer Networks and ISDN Systems Journal*, vol. 42.
15. Y.Deng, E.Hung, and V.S.Subrahmanian, "Maintaining RDF views," *Tech. Rep. CS-TR-4612 (UMIACS-TR-2004-54)*, 2004.
16. Z.Majkić, "Weakly-coupled P2P system with a network repository," *6th Workshop on Distributed Data and Structures (WDAS'04), July 5-7, Lausanne, Switzerland*, 2004.
17. Z.Majkić, "Massive parallelism for query answering in weakly integrated P2P systems," *Workshop GLOBE 04, August 30-September 3,Zaragoza, Spain*, 2004.
18. Z. Majkić, "Intensional logic and epistemic independency of intelligent database agents," *2nd International Workshop on Philosophy and Informatics (WSPI 2005), April 10-13, Kaiserslautern, Germany*, 2005.
19. R.Montague, "Universal grammar," *Theoria*, vol. 36, pp. 373–398, 1970.

Author Index

Lecture Notes in Artificial Intelligence (LNAI)

Vol. 4027: H. Legind Larsen, G. Pasi, D. Ortiz-Arroyo, T. Andreasen, H. Christiansen, (Eds.), Flexible Query Answering Systems. XVIII, 714 pages. 2006.

Vol. 3978: B. Hnich, M. Carlsson, F. Fages, F. Rossi (Eds.), Recent Advances in Constraints. VIII, 179 pages. 2006.

Vol. 3960: R. Vieira, P. Quaresma, M.d.G.V. Nunes, N.J. Mamede, C. Oliveira, M.C. Dias (Eds.), Computational Processing of the Portuguese Language. XII, 274 pages. 2006.

Vol. 3955: G. Antoniou, G. Potamias, C. Spyropoulos, D. Plexousakis (Eds.), Advances in Artificial Intelligence. XVII, 611 pages. 2006.

Vol. 3946: T.R. Roth-Berghofer, S. Schulz, D.B. Leake (Eds.), Modeling and Retrieval of Context. XI, 149 pages. 2006.

Vol. 3944: J. Quiñonero-Candela, I. Dagan, B. Magnini, F. d'Alché-Buc (Eds.), Machine Learning Challenges. XIII, 462 pages. 2006.

Vol. 3930: D.S. Yeung, Z.-Q. Liu, X.-Z. Wang, H. Yan (Eds.), Advances in Machine Learning and Cybernetics. XXI, 1110 pages. 2006.

Vol. 3918: W.K. Ng, M. Kitsuregawa, J. Li, K. Chang (Eds.), Advances in Knowledge Discovery and Data Mining. XXIV, 879 pages. 2006.

Vol. 3910: S.A. Brueckner, G.D.M. Serugendo, D. Hales, F. Zambonelli (Eds.), Engineering Self-Organising Systems. XII, 245 pages. 2006.

Vol. 3904: M. Baldoni, U. Endriss, A. Omicini, P. Torroni (Eds.), Declarative Agent Languages and Technologies III. XII, 245 pages. 2006.

Vol. 3900: F. Toni, P. Torroni (Eds.), Computational Logic in Multi-Agent Systems. XVII, 427 pages. 2006.

Vol. 3899: S. Frintrop, VOCUS: A Visual Attention System for Object Detection and Goal-Directed Search. XIV, 216 pages. 2006.

Vol. 3898: K. Tuyls, P.J. 't Hoen, K. Verbeeck, S. Sen (Eds.), Learning and Adaption in Multi-Agent Systems. X, 217 pages. 2006.

Vol. 3891: J.S. Sichman, L. Antunes (Eds.), Multi-Agent-Based Simulation VI. X, 191 pages. 2006.

Vol. 3890: S.G. Thompson, R. Ghanea-Hercock (Eds.), Defence Applications of Multi-Agent Systems. XII, 141 pages. 2006.

Vol. 3885: V. Torra, Y. Narukawa, A. Valls, J. Domingo-Ferrer (Eds.), Modeling Decisions for Artificial Intelligence. XII, 374 pages. 2006.

Vol. 3881: S. Gibet, N. Courty, J.-F. Kamp (Eds.), Gesture in Human-Computer Interaction and Simulation. XIII, 344 pages. 2006.

Vol. 3874: R. Missaoui, J. Schmidt (Eds.), Formal Concept Analysis. X, 309 pages. 2006.

Vol. 3873: L. Maicher, J. Park (Eds.), Charting the Topic Maps Research and Applications Landscape. VIII, 281 pages. 2006.

Vol. 3863: M. Kohlhase (Ed.), Mathematical Knowledge Management. XI, 405 pages. 2006.

Vol. 3862: R.H. Bordini, M. Dastani, J. Dix, A.E.F. Seghrouchni (Eds.), Programming Multi-Agent Systems. XIV, 267 pages. 2006.

Vol. 3849: I. Bloch, A. Petrosino, A.G.B. Tettamanzi (Eds.), Fuzzy Logic and Applications. XIV, 438 pages. 2006.

Vol. 3848: J.-F. Boulicaut, L. De Raedt, H. Mannila (Eds.), Constraint-Based Mining and Inductive Databases. X, 401 pages. 2006.

Vol. 3847: K.P. Jantke, A. Lunzer, N. Spyratos, Y. Tanaka (Eds.), Federation over the Web. X, 215 pages. 2006.

Vol. 3835: G. Sutcliffe, A. Voronkov (Eds.), Logic for Programming, Artificial Intelligence, and Reasoning. XIV, 744 pages. 2005.

Vol. 3830: D. Weyns, H. V.D. Parunak, F. Michel (Eds.), Environments for Multi-Agent Systems II. VIII, 291 pages. 2006.

Vol. 3817: M. Faundez-Zanuy, L. Janer, A. Esposito, A. Satue-Villar, J. Roure, V. Espinosa-Duro (Eds.), Nonlinear Analyses and Algorithms for Speech Processing. XII, 380 pages. 2006.

Vol. 3814: M. Maybury, O. Stock, W. Wahlster (Eds.), Intelligent Technologies for Interactive Entertainment. XV, 342 pages. 2005.

Vol. 3809: S. Zhang, R. Jarvis (Eds.), AI 2005: Advances in Artificial Intelligence. XXVII, 1344 pages. 2005.

Vol. 3808: C. Bento, A. Cardoso, G. Dias (Eds.), Progress in Artificial Intelligence. XVIII, 704 pages. 2005.

Vol. 3802: Y. Hao, J. Liu, Y.-P. Wang, Y.-m. Cheung, H. Yin, L. Jiao, J. Ma, Y.-C. Jiao (Eds.), Computational Intelligence and Security, Part II. XLII, 1166 pages. 2005.

Vol. 3801: Y. Hao, J. Liu, Y.-P. Wang, Y.-m. Cheung, H. Yin, L. Jiao, J. Ma, Y.-C. Jiao (Eds.), Computational Intelligence and Security, Part I. XLI, 1122 pages. 2005.

Vol. 3789: A. Gelbukh, Á. de Albornoz, H. Terashima-Marín (Eds.), MICAI 2005: Advances in Artificial Intelligence. XXVI, 1198 pages. 2005.

Vol. 3782: K.-D. Althoff, A. Dengel, R. Bergmann, M. Nick, T.R. Roth-Berghofer (Eds.), Professional Knowledge Management. XXIII, 739 pages. 2005.

Vol. 3763: H. Hong, D. Wang (Eds.), Automated Deduction in Geometry. X, 213 pages. 2006.

Vol. 3755: G.J. Williams, S.J. Simoff (Eds.), Data Mining. XI, 331 pages. 2006.

Vol. 3735: A. Hoffmann, H. Motoda, T. Scheffer (Eds.), Discovery Science. XVI, 400 pages. 2005.

Vol. 3734: S. Jain, H.U. Simon, E. Tomita (Eds.), Algorithmic Learning Theory. XII, 490 pages. 2005.

Vol. 3721: A.M. Jorge, L. Torgo, P.B. Brazdil, R. Camacho, J. Gama (Eds.), Knowledge Discovery in Databases: PKDD 2005. XXIII, 719 pages. 2005.

Vol. 3720: J. Gama, R. Camacho, P.B. Brazdil, A.M. Jorge, L. Torgo (Eds.), Machine Learning: ECML 2005. XXIII, 769 pages. 2005.

Vol. 3717: B. Gramlich (Ed.), Frontiers of Combining Systems. X, 321 pages. 2005.

Vol. 3702: B. Beckert (Ed.), Automated Reasoning with Analytic Tableaux and Related Methods. XIII, 343 pages. 2005.

Vol. 3698: U. Furbach (Ed.), KI 2005: Advances in Artificial Intelligence. XIII, 409 pages. 2005.

Vol. 3690: M. Pěchouček, P. Petta, L.Z. Varga (Eds.), Multi-Agent Systems and Applications IV. XVII, 667 pages. 2005.

Vol. 3684: R. Khosla, R.J. Howlett, L.C. Jain (Eds.), Knowledge-Based Intelligent Information and Engineering Systems, Part IV. LXXIX, 933 pages. 2005.

Vol. 3683: R. Khosla, R.J. Howlett, L.C. Jain (Eds.), Knowledge-Based Intelligent Information and Engineering Systems, Part III. LXXX, 1397 pages. 2005.

Vol. 3682: R. Khosla, R.J. Howlett, L.C. Jain (Eds.), Knowledge-Based Intelligent Information and Engineering Systems, Part II. LXXIX, 1371 pages. 2005.

Vol. 3681: R. Khosla, R.J. Howlett, L.C. Jain (Eds.), Knowledge-Based Intelligent Information and Engineering Systems, Part I. LXXX, 1319 pages. 2005.

Vol. 3673: S. Bandini, S. Manzoni (Eds.), AI*IA 2005: Advances in Artificial Intelligence. XIV, 614 pages. 2005.

Vol. 3662: C. Baral, G. Greco, N. Leone, G. Terracina (Eds.), Logic Programming and Nonmonotonic Reasoning. XIII, 454 pages. 2005.

Vol. 3661: T. Panayiotopoulos, J. Gratch, R. Aylett, D. Ballin, P. Olivier, T. Rist (Eds.), Intelligent Virtual Agents. XIII, 506 pages. 2005.

Vol. 3658: V. Matoušek, P. Mautner, T. Pavelka (Eds.), Text, Speech and Dialogue. XV, 460 pages. 2005.

Vol. 3651: R. Dale, K.-F. Wong, J. Su, O.Y. Kwong (Eds.), Natural Language Processing – IJCNLP 2005. XXI, 1031 pages. 2005.

Vol. 3642: D. Ślęzak, J. Yao, J.F. Peters, W. Ziarko, X. Hu (Eds.), Rough Sets, Fuzzy Sets, Data Mining, and Granular Computing, Part II. XXIII, 738 pages. 2005.

Vol. 3641: D. Ślęzak, G. Wang, M. Szczuka, I. Düntsch, Y. Yao (Eds.), Rough Sets, Fuzzy Sets, Data Mining, and Granular Computing, Part I. XXIV, 742 pages. 2005.

Vol. 3635: J.R. Winkler, M. Niranjan, N.D. Lawrence (Eds.), Deterministic and Statistical Methods in Machine Learning. VIII, 341 pages. 2005.

Vol. 3632: R. Nieuwenhuis (Ed.), Automated Deduction – CADE-20. XIII, 459 pages. 2005.

Vol. 3630: M.S. Capcarrère, A.A. Freitas, P.J. Bentley, C.G. Johnson, J. Timmis (Eds.), Advances in Artificial Life. XIX, 949 pages. 2005.

Vol. 3626: B. Ganter, G. Stumme, R. Wille (Eds.), Formal Concept Analysis. X, 349 pages. 2005.

Vol. 3625: S. Kramer, B. Pfahringer (Eds.), Inductive Logic Programming. XIII, 427 pages. 2005.

Vol. 3620: H. Muñoz-Ávila, F. Ricci (Eds.), Case-Based Reasoning Research and Development. XV, 654 pages. 2005.

Vol. 3614: L. Wang, Y. Jin (Eds.), Fuzzy Systems and Knowledge Discovery, Part II. XLI, 1314 pages. 2005.

Vol. 3613: L. Wang, Y. Jin (Eds.), Fuzzy Systems and Knowledge Discovery, Part I. XLI, 1334 pages. 2005.

Vol. 3607: J.-D. Zucker, L. Saitta (Eds.), Abstraction, Reformulation and Approximation. XII, 376 pages. 2005.

Vol. 3601: G. Moro, S. Bergamaschi, K. Aberer (Eds.), Agents and Peer-to-Peer Computing. XII, 245 pages. 2005.

Vol. 3600: F. Wiedijk (Ed.), The Seventeen Provers of the World. XVI, 159 pages. 2006.

Vol. 3596: F. Dau, M.-L. Mugnier, G. Stumme (Eds.), Conceptual Structures: Common Semantics for Sharing Knowledge. XI, 467 pages. 2005.

Vol. 3593: V. Mařík, R. W. Brennan, M. Pěchouček (Eds.), Holonic and Multi-Agent Systems for Manufacturing. XI, 269 pages. 2005.

Vol. 3587: P. Perner, A. Imiya (Eds.), Machine Learning and Data Mining in Pattern Recognition. XVII, 695 pages. 2005.

Vol. 3584: X. Li, S. Wang, Z.Y. Dong (Eds.), Advanced Data Mining and Applications. XIX, 835 pages. 2005.

Vol. 3581: S. Miksch, J. Hunter, E.T. Keravnou (Eds.), Artificial Intelligence in Medicine. XVII, 547 pages. 2005.

Vol. 3577: R. Falcone, S. Barber, J. Sabater-Mir, M.P. Singh (Eds.), Trusting Agents for Trusting Electronic Societies. VIII, 235 pages. 2005.

Vol. 3575: S. Wermter, G. Palm, M. Elshaw (Eds.), Biomimetic Neural Learning for Intelligent Robots. IX, 383 pages. 2005.

Vol. 3571: L. Godo (Ed.), Symbolic and Quantitative Approaches to Reasoning with Uncertainty. XVI, 1028 pages. 2005.

Vol. 3559: P. Auer, R. Meir (Eds.), Learning Theory. XI, 692 pages. 2005.

Vol. 3558: V. Torra, Y. Narukawa, S. Miyamoto (Eds.), Modeling Decisions for Artificial Intelligence. XII, 470 pages. 2005.

Vol. 3554: A.K. Dey, B. Kokinov, D.B. Leake, R. Turner (Eds.), Modeling and Using Context. XIV, 572 pages. 2005.

Vol. 3550: T. Eymann, F. Klügl, W. Lamersdorf, M. Klusch, M.N. Huhns (Eds.), Multiagent System Technologies. XI, 246 pages. 2005.

Vol. 3539: K. Morik, J.-F. Boulicaut, A. Siebes (Eds.), Local Pattern Detection. XI, 233 pages. 2005.

Vol. 3538: L. Ardissono, P. Brna, A. Mitrović (Eds.), User Modeling 2005. XVI, 533 pages. 2005.